DEVELOPMENTAL ISSUES IN THE CLINICAL TREATMENT OF CHILDREN

Edited by

Wendy K. Silverman
Florida International University

Thomas H. Ollendick
Virginia Polytechnic Institute and State University

Allyn and Bacon
Boston   London   Toronto   Sydney   Tokyo   Singapore

Editor-in-Chief, Social Sciences and Education: Sean W. Wakely
Series Editorial Assistant: Susan Hutchinson
Manufacturing Buyer: Suzanne Lareau
Editorial-Production Services: Omegatype Typography, Inc.
Electronic Composition: Omegatype Typography, Inc.

Copyright © 1999 by Allyn & Bacon
A Viacom Company
160 Gould Street
Needham Heights, MA 02494

Internet: www.abacon.com

Library of Congress Cataloging-in-Publication Data

Developmental issues in the clinical treatment of children / edited by
 Wendy K. Silverman and Thomas H. Ollendick.
     p.   cm.
   Includes bibliographical references and index.
   ISBN 0-205-17001-3
   1. Child psychopathology.   2. Child psychology.   3. Child
 psychotherapy.   I. Silverman, Wendy K.   II. Ollendick, Thomas H.
 RJ499.D4823   1999
 618.92′89—dc21   98-20824
                                                    CIP

Printed in the United States of America

10 9 8 7 6 5 4 3 2 1   02 01 00 99 98

In loving memory of my mother, Gloria
WKS

And to my father, Fritz
THO

CONTENTS

PREFACE

This book is directed to advanced graduate students in psychology, clinical and developmental researchers, practitioners, and other professionals (e.g., school counselors, family therapists) who are interested in, and who work with, children and families. This is not a volume, however, in clinical child psychology; nor is it a volume in developmental psychology or in developmental psychopathology. It is also not a volume that focuses on one particular child disorder (e.g., conduct disorder) or on one particular context (e.g., the family).

If the book is not a volume in any of these areas, then what is it? The book is all of these things! That is, the book is an interface of all of these areas. It is an interface of clinical child psychology, developmental psychology, developmental psychopathology, specific child disorders, and contextual issues attendant to these fields of study.

We believe it is important to interface these areas because, although these areas (and literatures) have historically been "separate," in recent years these areas have become even more detached and isolated from each other. These areas have become so disjoined that keeping up with each is now virtually impossible, for clinicians and researchers alike. As a consequence, although much progress has been made in recent years in furthering our knowledge base about children and adolescents and their problems, as well as about prevention and treatment, we believe that to move forward even more in knowledge development, it is important to bring these areas (and literatures) together in a systematic way.

Hence, the main goal of this volume is to bring these areas together to build upon the current knowledge base about children and adolescents, child and adolescent problems, and child and adolescent treatment. This goal is accomplished by having each chapter in the volume cut across the literature of the various areas (e.g., clinical child psychology, developmental psychology, developmental psychopathology) and present a consolidated and integrative picture of this literature. In addition, each chapter provides detailed, practical information that will prove useful to students, practitioners, and researchers.

Part 1 addresses developmental clinical issues in working with youth, including issues pertinent to theory, classification, assessment, and intervention. In the chapters in the second part, each of the main developmental phases of childhood is covered (i.e., infancy, the preschool years, middle childhood, and adolescence). Part 3 summarizes key contextual influences on children and adolescents and their development, namely, the family, school, peers, religion, social class, ethnicity and culture, and sexual orientation. In Part 4, developmental issues in child psychopathology (internalizing problems, externalizing problems, mental retardation, and pervasive developmental disorders) are covered. Part 5 covers in even greater detail and depth the contextual influence of the family, reviewing the most common family forms and structures in which children live. These include children of divorce, stepfamilies and blended families, adoption, children of parents with particular problems (i.e., depression, alcohol problems, and chronic medical illness), and children from abusive families. In the final section of the book, Part 6, issues in treatment evaluation (process and outcome) and ethics and the law are presented.

In summary, this book represents an important step in bridging the various contexts and disciplines. The chapters contained also will, hopefully, set the stage for improved clinical research and practice with youth and their families for the future. This book was the product of the efforts of many people. We first would like to thank the fine contributions of the chapter authors. It was truly an honor to work with such an outstanding group of scholars. In addition, we want to express our recognition and appreciation of the apprehension that was felt among many of the authors when they first received our invitation to participate in this project. For example, many of the clinical child psychologists cautioned us that they were not developmental psychologists, and many of the developmental psychologists cautioned us that they were not clinical child psychologists! In our view, each contributor successfully met the challenge of linking the various literatures and showing how these diverse areas of child study can be integrated in a way that provides for a full and comprehensive view about children and adolescents and their problems as well as about prevention and treatment intervention efforts. For the contributors' hard work in analyzing and synthesizing these literatures, we thank them.

We also would like to thank the staff of Allyn and Bacon, for their patience and encouragement throughout the various phases of this project, as well as the many colleagues and students who provided us with many worthwhile ideas and assistance. We wish to thank the following reviewers of the manuscript for their helpful comments and suggestions: Marilyn T. Erickson, Virginia Commonwealth University; Christopher A. Kearney, University of Nevada, Las Vegas; and Brian Rabian, University of Southern Mississippi. Finally, Wendy Silverman would like to thank her husband, Efraim Ben-Zadok, and her two children, Daniel and Rachel, and Tom Ollendick would like to thank his wife, Mary Catherine, and his two daughters, Laurie Kristine and Kathleen Marie, for demonstrating during this project what they have always demonstrated in the past—patience and support. Without our families, this book would have remained "another good idea," rather than a completed project.

CONTRIBUTORS

Thomas M. Achenbach, Ph.D., is professor of psychiatry and psychology, and director of the Center for Children, Youth, and Families at the University of Vermont. He was a postdoctoral fellow at the Yale Child Study Center, was on the Yale faculty, and was a research psychologist at the National Institute of Mental Health (NIMH). He has been a fellow at the University of Heidelberg, Germany, and at Jean Piaget's Centre d'Epistemologie Genetique in Geneva, Chair of the American Psychological Association's Task Force on Classification of Children's Behavior, and a member of the American Psychiatric Association's Advisory Committee on DSM-IIIR.

Edward R. Anderson, Ph.D., is a faculty research associate at the Prevention Research Center and adjunct assistant professor, Department of Psychology, Arizona State University. His research interests include family process in remarried families, adolescent development, sibling relationships, and longitudinal research methodology.

Sandra T. Azar, Ph.D., is associate professor and director of the clinical psychology training program at the Frances L. Hiatt School of Psychology at Clark University. She has published extensively on cognitive theory, research, and treatment in child abuse.

Sharon L. Bober, Ph.D., is a clinical fellow in the Department of Psychiatry at Harvard Medical School. Her primary areas of interest include motivation, social support, and both family and individual adjustment to illness. Dr. Bober also has conducted research that involves developing and evaluating an intervention that helps mothers with breast cancer address related parenting concerns.

Lisa Ann Boyum, Ph.D., is a clinical psychologist and assistant faculty member in the Pediatric Behavioral Health Division at National Jewish Medical and Research Center and an assistant professor in the Department of Psychiatry at the University of Colorado Health Sciences Center in Denver.

Lisa M. Brown is a graduate student in clinical child psychology at Ohio State University. Her research is focused on information processing biases in childhood anxiety and their relationship to broader dimensions of temperament.

Ronald T. Brown, Ph.D., is associate professor of psychiatry and pediatrics at the Emory University School of Medicine. Collectively, he and the co-authors on the chapter in this book have authored approximately 200 articles in the areas of pediatric and clinical child psychology.

Tom W. Cadwallader is a graduate student in development psychology at University of North Carolina–Chapel Hill. He has a B.A. from San Diego State, an M.A. from UNC–Chapel Hill, and 20 years' experience as a criminal investigator. His research interest is the development of aggressive and antisocial behavior, with an emphasis on peer influences.

Robert B. Cairns, Ph.D., is a Cary C. Boshamer professor of psychology at University of North Carolina–Chapel Hill, Director of the Center for Developmental Science, and Director of the Carolina Consortium of Human Development. His research focuses primarily on developmental behavior genetics, childhood aggression, and the sociogenesis of self-concepts.

Domini R. Castellino received her B.A. from Pennsylvania State University and is currently pursuing a Ph.D. at Michigan State University. Her current affiliation is the Center for Developmental Science at the University of North Carolina–Chapel Hill. Her research interests include maternal employment, maternal role satisfaction, and marital quality as they influence adolescent development and parent–child relationships.

Giuseppe Costantino, Ph.D., is the clinical director of the Sunset Park Mental Health Center of Lutheran Medical Center, a large community mental health center delivering culturally competent mental health services. In addition, he is Adjunct Professor of Psychology at St. John's University; and Senior Research Associate with the Department of Social Services, Fordham University. Dr. Costantino is the author and developer of TEMAS, a multicultural thematic apperception test, and of the Cuento and Hero/Heroine Modeling Therapies for Hispanic children and adolescents. Those clinical research programs have been developed in collaboration with Dr. Robert Malgady. In addition, Dr. Costantino is the recipient of several grants from the National Institute of Mental Health. He has published more than 50 articles and several book chapters on culturally sensitive treatment and assessment of minority individuals. He is consulting editor of *Journal of Personality Assessment, Hispanic Journal of Behavioral Science,* and *Revista Iberoamericana de Psicologia.*

Eric L. Daleiden, Ph.D., is currently assistant professor of psychology at the University of Tulsa. His primary research interests concern developmental and information processing features of childhood anxiety.

Jack Demick, Ph.D., is currently professor in and chair of the Department of Psychology at Suffolk University in Boston. He previously held teaching appointments at Clark and Harvard Universities. His research interests include both cognitive development (e.g., cognitive style, environmental cognition) and social development (e.g., adaptation to adoption) across the life span. His is also editor of the *Journal of Adult Development.*

Lisa M. Diamond is a Ph.D. candidate in the Department of Human Development at Cornell University where she conducts research on the friendships, romantic relationships, and sexual identity development of adolescent and young adult women.

V. Mark Durand, Ph.D., is professor and chair of the Department of Psychology at the University of Albany. He has contributed research in the area of self-injurious and disruptive behavior in persons with severe disabilities, including autism. He has published in various journals, is the author of several books, and has co-authored a textbook with Dr. David Barlow entitled *Abnormal psychology: An integrative approach.*

Tiffany M. Field, Ph.D., is Director and Founder of the Touch Research Institute at the University of Miami School of Medicine in Miami and Nova Southeastern University in Ft. Lauderdale, FL. She is also Dean of the Family, School and Wellness Center at Nova Southeastern University. She conducts research and is author of over 300 journal papers.

Frank D. Fincham received his Ph.D. in 1980 at Oxford University, where he was a Rhodes Scholar. Since then he has been a professor in the United States and Great Britain, teaching in a variety of areas in psychology. He is currently at the University of Wales. He was recently listed among the top twenty-five psychologists in the world (*APS Observer,* 1996) and is the recipient of the President's Award from the British Psychological Society for "distinguished contributions to psychological knowledge." He is a practicing clinical psychologist and serves on editorial boards of numerous professional journals in clinical, social, and family psychology.

Gordon E. Finley, Ph.D., professor of psychology at Florida International University, received a B.A. in sociology and anthropology from Antioch College and a Ph.D. in social relations from Harvard University. His earlier research emphasized cross-cultural life-span development in Latin America. Current interests include adoption, adoptive fatherhood, and parental age.

Jack W. Finney, Ph.D., is professor and chair of the Department of Psychology at Virginia Polytechnic and State University. His research has focused on improving children's health status by changing risk factors that threaten health and encouraging protective factors that maintain or enhance health outcomes. His interests include adherence to medical regimens, injury control, and adjustment to chronic illnesses.

Celia B. Fisher, Ph.D., is professor and former director of the doctoral specialization in Applied Developmental Psychology at Fordham University. She is Chair of the American Psychological Association's Ethics Code Revision Task Force and former chair of the Society for Research in Child Development (SRCD) Ethics Committee and the New York State Board for Psychology.

Myrna L. Friedlander, Ph.D., is a professor in the Department of Counseling Psychology, University of Albany. Her research on the process of change in individual and family therapy has appeared in numerous journals. An American Psychological Association Fellow, she has served as clinician, supervisor, and consultant in independent practice and in various hospitals and community agencies.

Sherryl H. Goodman, Ph.D., is a professor in both the departments of psychology and psychiatry and behavioral sciences at Emory University in Atlanta, Georgia. She has been funded since 1981 for research on risk for the development of psychiatric disorders and adjustment problems in children with schizophrenic or depressed mothers.

Ian H. Gotlib, Ph.D., is professor of psychology at Stanford University. In his research, Dr. Gotlib examines the effects of depression on marital and family functioning, the emotional and behavioral functioning of children of depressed mothers, depression in adolescents, and information-processing approaches to the study of the cognitive functioning of depressed persons.

Lori Isman Greene is a doctoral candidate in the Clinical Psychology Training Program at Fordham University. She completed her undergraduate studies at Cornell University's College of Human Ecology in 1992, her master's and doctoral studies at Fordham University, and her clinical internship at the New York Hospital-Cornell Medical Center.

Shannon M. Greene, Ph.D., is a National Institute of Mental Health Postdoctoral Fellow in the Program for Prevention Research at Arizona State University. Her research involves observational studies focusing on microsocial interactions for non-normative family transitions, chronic illness, and psychopathology.

John H. Grych, Ph.D., is an assistant professor of psychology at Marquette University who has published theoretical and empirical papers on the relationship between marital discord, divorce, and children's adjustment. With Frank Fincham he developed one of the dominant conceptual models guiding the study of the effects of interparental conflict on children. He is on the editorial board of the *Journal of Family Psychology* and serves as editorial consultant for other professional journals dedicated to the study of children and families.

Michi Hatashita-Wong, M.A., is a doctoral candidate in clinical psychology at Fordham University.

John M. Hintze, Ph.D., is assistant professor of educational psychology at the University of Massachusetts at Amherst, School Psychology Program. His current research interests include alternative assessment and service delivery practices with a focus on the use of behavioral and social–cognitive strategies in schools.

James H. Johnson, Ph.D., is currently professor of clinical and health psychology at the University of Florida–Gainesville. He is past president of the American Psychological Association's Section on Clinical Child Psychology and a past associate editor of the *Journal of Clinical Child Psychology.* He has over seventy-five publications dealing with a wide range of child-related topics. He is the author of *Life Events as Stressors in Childhood and Adolescence* (Sage, 1986), senior author (with W. Rasbury and L. Siegel) of *Approaches to Child Treatment: Introduction to Theory, Research and Practice* (2nd ed., Allyn & Bacon, 1997), and editor (with J. Goldman) of *Developmental Assessment in Clinical Psychology: A Handbook* (Pergamon, 1991).

Charlotte Johnston, Ph.D., is associate professor in the clinical training program, Department of Psychology, University of British Columbia. She has published numerous articles concerning parent–child interactions in families of children with externalizing disorders. Her most recent work focuses on parent attributions in families of children with attention-deficit hyperactivity disorder.

Annette M. La Greca, Ph.D., is a professor of psychology and pediatrics at the University of Miami where she directs graduate programs in clinical child and pediatric health. Dr. La Greca edited the *Journal of Pediatric Psychology* (1993–1997) and received the 1997 Distinguished Research Award from the Society of Pediatric Psychology. Her primary areas of research interest are the role of peer relations in emotional development, children's social anxiety, and children's and adolescents' adjustment to chronic disease (diabetes).

Richard M. Lerner, Ph.D., is the Anita L. Brennan Professor of Education at Boston College and the director of the Boston College Center for Child, Family, and Community Partnerships. He is the editor of the new journal, *Applied Developmental Science.*

Scott Liepack received his master's degree in clinical child psychology from the University of Miami in 1994 and is currently working to complete the requirements for his Ph.D. He has been involved in developing, implementing, conducting, and evaluating research with young children. His particular areas of interest are in the incorporation of bio-ecological and constructivist theory in the provision of services for young children and their families. He is also interested in the development of data-analytic techniques, such as neural networks and fuzzy logic, to adequately evaluate change within a bio-ecological framework.

Joseph L. Mahoney is an NICHD predoctoral trainee at the Center for Developmental Science, University of North Carolina–Chapel Hill. His research interests include the development and prevention of antisocial behavior patterns, and person-oriented methods for studying development.

Robert G. Malgady, Ph.D., is professor of quantitative studies at New York University and senior research associate in the Department of Public Health at Cornell University Medical College. He has authored four books on Hispanic mental health and over sixty-five journal articles and book chapters. He is an American Psychological Association Fellow and has served on editorial boards of the *Journal of Educational Psychology, Psychological Assessment,* and *Professional Psychology.* He also serves on review committees for the National Institute of Mental Health (NIMH) and the National Institute on Drug Abuse (NIDA).

Eileen Mapstone is a doctoral student in psychology at the University of Albany. Her research interests include sleep disorders in children with disabilities, using functional communication training with deaf–blind students, and exploring the impact of different mood states on challenging behaviors.

Johnny L. Matson, Ph.D., is professor of psychology and director of the clinical psychology Ph.D. program at Louisiana State University. He has served on the faculties of Northern Illinois University and the University of Pittsburgh. He is author of over 325 publications, including 26 books with a primary emphasis on children and adults with developmental disabilities.

Katherine M. Miller, Ph.D., completed a predoctoral internship at the University of Maryland School of Medicine and is presently completing a postdoctoral fellowship in pediatric psychology at Nemours Children's Clinic in Jacksonville. Her research and clinical interests focus on understanding the relationship between children's physical health and their emotional and behavioral functioning in an effort to promote the positive adjustment of children with medical or physical problems and their families.

Jeneva L. Ohan received a B.Sc. from McMaster University and is currently a graduate student in clinical psychology at the University of British Columbia. She is presently researching reasons for adherence to medication among adolescents with attention-deficit hyperactivity disorder and the causal attributions children and adolescents make for their behavior.

Thomas H. Ollendick, Ph.D., is professor of psychology and director of Training Clinics at Virginia Polytechnic Institute and State University. He has authored numerous papers and chapters on assessment and treatment of childhood disorders and is co-author or co-editor of several books. He is past president of American Psychological Association's Section on Clinical Child Psychology and currently serves as editor of its *Journal of Clinical Child Psychology.* He is also past president of the Association for Advancement of Behavior Therapy and currently serves as its International Associates Chair.

Ross D. Parke, Ph.D., is currently professor of psychology and director of the Center for Family Studies at the University of California at Riverside. He has held positions at the University of Wisconsin, the University of Illinois, and the Fels Research Institute. His research focuses on the father's role in family systems, the impact of families on children's social adaptation to peers, and the effect of economic stress on

Latino families. His most recent book, *Fatherhood,* was published by Harvard University Press in 1996.

Robert C. Pianta, Ph.D., is professor of clinical and school psychology in the Curry School of Education of the University of Virginia. He is the principal investigator on a National Institute of Child Health and Development study of early child care, co-director of the Kindergarten Transitions Strand of the National Center for Early Development and Learning, and co-director of the Child-Parent Attachment Project. His research and applied interests combine developmental, clinical child, and school psychology with a particular emphasis on the role of child–adult relationships in the regulation of development in high-risk children.

Mitchell J. Prinstein received his Ph.D. in clinical child psychology at the University of Miami. He completed his internship at Brown University and was awarded a National Institute of Health training grant for postdoctoral study there. Dr. Prinstein is the chair of the American Psychological Association of Graduate Students (1996–1999). His research interests include family influences on children's peer relations in normal and psychiatric inpatient populations and children's coping with traumatic stressors.

Ritch C. Savin-Williams, Ph.D., is professor of clinical and developmental psychology in the Department of Human Development at Cornell University. Recent books include *Gay and Lesbian Youth: Expressions of Identity* (1990), *The Lives of Lesbians, Gays, and Bisexuals: Children to Adults* (1996), and *...and then I became gay: Young Men's Stories* (1998). He is currently writing a book on the relations sexual-minority youth have with their families.

Edward S. Shapiro, Ph.D., has been professor and coordinator of the School Psychology Program at Lehigh University since 1980. He was editor of *School Psychology Review,* official journal of the National Association of School Psychologists, and has numerous publications in the areas of curriculum-based assessment, behavioral assessment, behavioral interventions, and self-management strategies for classroom behavior change.

Lisa B. Sheeber, Ph.D., is an early career scientist at the Oregon Research Institute in Eugene, Oregon. She has been actively involved in the development of interventions to help parents deal with children displaying difficult temperament characteristics. A major focus of her current research relates to family factors as contributors to adolescent depression.

Stephen R. Shirk, Ph.D., is associate professor of psychology and director of the Child Study Center at the University of Denver. He edited *Cognitive Development and Child Psychotherapy* and recently co-authored *Change Processes in Child Psychotherapy.* His current research focuses on interpersonal processes in child treatment and childhood depression.

Wendy K. Silverman, Ph.D., is professor of psychology and director of the Child and Family Psychosocial Research Center at Florida International University, Miami. Her research interests are primarily in the areas of childhood anxiety disorders, particularly their assessment and treatment. She has received several grants from the National Institute of Mental Health to design and evaluate psychosocial interventions for anxiety disorders in children. She is also author (with William M. Kurtines) of *Anxiety and Phobic Disorders: A Pragmatic Approach* (Plenum Press) and currently serves as Associate Editor of *Journal of Clinical Child Psychology.*

Susan J. Simonian, Ph.D., is assistant professor of psychology at the College of Charleston. Collectively, she and the co-authors on the chapter in this book have authored approximately 200 articles in the areas of pediatric and clinical child psychology.

Brandi B. Smiroldo, M.A., is a doctoral student at Louisiana State University. Her research interests include dual diagnosis, behavioral treatment of individuals with developmental disabilities, functional analytic approaches to treatment, and staff training issues.

Kenneth J. Tarnowski, Ph.D., is professor of psychology at Florida Gulf Coast University (formerly University of South Florida at Fort Myers). Collectively, he and his co-authors on the chapter in this book have authored approximately 200 articles in the areas of pediatric and clinical child psychology.

Jonathan G. Tubman is associate professor of psychology at Florida International University. He received his Ph.D. in human development and family studies in 1990 from Pennsylvania State University. He received postdoctoral training at the Research Institute on Addictions in Buffalo, New York, before joining the faculty at Florida International University in 1993. His current research interests focus on intrapersonal and interpersonal factors that initiate and maintain problem behaviors and emotional problems among adolescents. In addition, his recent publications have investigated individual and contextual factors associated with health risk behaviors among substance-abusing adolescents.

Michael W. Vasey, Ph.D., is currently associate professor of psychology at Ohio State University. His research is focused on cognitive and emotional factors in childhood anxiety, with particular emphasis on information-processing biases and deficits in emotion regulation skills.

Francisco A. Villarruel, Ph.D., is assistant professor in the Department of Family and Child Ecology and adjunct professor in the Department of Counseling, Educational Psychology, and Special Education at Michigan State University. His research interests include Latino child and family issues and the use of computer technologies with children and adults in home and community settings.

Seymour Wapner is chair of the executive committee of the Heinz Werner Institute for Developmental Analysis, Frances L. Hiatt School of Psychology, Clark University. His programmatic research in perception, development, and environmental psychology has been informed by and instrumental in the development of the sensory–tonic field theory of perception and of the holistic, developmental systems-oriented theory.

Vanessa Robin Weersing received her M.A. from University of California Los Angeles (UCLA) where she is currently working on her doctorate. Her research examines mediators and moderators of child and adolescent treatment effectiveness, with particular interest in therapy process and cognitive development.

John R. Weisz, Ph.D., is professor of psychology at University of California Los Angeles (UCLA). He has held faculty positions at Cornell, University of North Carolina-Chapel Hill, and UCLA. His research focuses on child and adolescent psychopathology and treatment, with an additional emphasis on culture.

M. Gawain Wells, Ph.D., is associate professor of psychology at Brigham Young University. His research interests include psychotherapy research with children as well as the development of religious commitment in children and adolescents.

Michael Windle, Ph.D., is professor of psychology and director of the doctoral program in developmental psychology at the University of Alabama at Birmingham. Dr. Windle also is associate editor of *Alcoholism: Clinical and Experimental Research* and is on the editorial boards of *Developmental Psychology* and *Journal of Studies on Alcohol.*

Hongling Xie is currently a Ph.D. student in developmental psychology and a predoctoral fellow in the Center for Developmental Science at University of North Carolina–Chapel Hill. Her research is focused on exploring the role of peer social networks in human development, especially the development of aggressive behavior, and on identifying resilient and vulnerable developmental trajectories.

PART 1

CONCEPTUAL ISSUES

In this first section, the authors examine a host of issues related to the integration of developmental theory and the practice of clinical child psychology. These four chapters serve as the foundation for those that follow.

In Chapter 1, the basic tenets of developmental theory are explicated and its broad implications for the conceptualization of disorder, including classification, assessment, and treatment, are explored. Basically, the developmental approach espoused in this chapter is a holistic, systems-oriented one. It emphasizes the transactions (experiences and actions) of the child with all aspects of his or her environment. It does not ignore biological features of the growing child, however. Stated most simply, biological functioning (e.g., breathing, eating), psychological functioning (e.g., thinking, feeling), and sociocultural functioning (e.g., mores and customs) are all hypothesized to be interrelated in a contingency fashion such that, for example, functioning at the sociocultural level requires functioning at the psychological and biological levels and psychological functioning, in turn, requires biological functioning. The levels differ qualitatively; moreover, functioning at one level is not reducible to functioning at the prior, less complex level because it is posited that higher level functioning does not substitute for, but rather integrates and trans-

forms, lower level functioning. Taken together, the notions proposed in this chapter have direct implications for the practice and science of clinical child psychology. Namely, elaborated views of child, of environment, and of child-in-environment relations are necessary for characterizing the functioning of the child in his or her everyday world, and in the ways we conceptualize, assess, and treat the myriad of "child" behavior problems.

In the chapter that follows, the implications of a developmental approach for the classification of child behavior disorders is examined in-depth. A comprehensive understanding of classification issues requires an in-depth analysis of the forms that psychopathology may assume across development. Some problems may be homotypic (i.e., the same) across long periods of development, whereas others are heterotypic (i.e. they undergo phenotypic changes from one developmental period to another). Of course, as noted by the authors, patterns of problems and their intensity also may vary systematically across situations and interaction partners, including parents, teachers, siblings, and peers. Thus, taxonomic constructs that aggregate findings across situations, times, sources of data, and developmental periods are needed. The strengths and limitations of extant classifications models are addressed in this chapter and new and exciting models—models that are both developmentally and contextually sensitive—are suggested.

In the third chapter in this opening section, issues associated with the "developmental assessment" of diverse child behavior problems are explored in more depth. Stated succinctly, albeit with some circularity, developmental assessment can be characterized as a process through which clinical information is obtained to provide answers to developmentally related questions. For example, the focus may be on identifying the presence or absence of specific developmentally related difficulties (e.g., separation concerns, learning difficulties, and attempts to establish individuation and autonomy), on determining the precise nature and the severity of those difficulties, on delineating factors that have contributed to and/or serve to maintain such problems, and on obtaining information relevant to the development of appropriate strategies. Given this general mission, it should come as no surprise that developmental assessment is a complex and multifaceted endeavor that entails considerable knowledge and judgment on the part of the clinician. Nonetheless, much is already known and this chapter provides rich guidelines on how to proceed with an informed and developmentally sensitive assessment approach. It also provides suggestions for future research in this most important facet of the science and practice of clinical child psychology.

In the final chapter in this section, issues associated with development and therapy are examined in some detail. Given the protean nature of development, this is a task that is complex and necessarily incomplete at this stage of our knowledge. Much remains to be learned. Nonetheless, four basic developmental principles serve to highlight the many issues addressed in this chapter. First, development involves a series of reorganizations in the child's cognitive, social and emotional capacities (i.e., development involves not only incremental changes in capacities, but also qualitative changes in behavioral organization). Second, development is characterized by the principle of "equifinality" (the notion that multiple pathways or processes may lead to similar outcomes). Third, development entails adaptation to a series of stage-salient or age-related challenges such as the establishment of early affectional bonds or adjustments to various situations (thus reflecting a developmental dialectic between the child's emerging capacities and psychosocial demands). And fourth, child and adolescent development does not occur in a vacuum; rather, it is embedded in a complex system of social contexts. These four developmental principles are then used to examine four common myths in child therapy: namely, the developmental uniformity myth, the developmental invariance myth, the developmental consistency myth, and the myth of individual development. A developmental model of therapy is articulated and challenges to the profession are presented.

Thus, in this opening of foundational chapters, the stage is set for the work that follows. Throughout the remainder of this book, the issues raised in these chapters will be revisited in varying form and substance, and the discerning reader will no doubt want to consult these chapters periodically for reference.

CHAPTER 1

DEVELOPMENTAL THEORY

Seymour Wapner
Jack Demick

Researchers have long posited numerous theoretical approaches to both abnormal psychology and developmental psychopathology. Some of these approaches have been explicit (e.g., Freudian theory), while others have been relatively more implicit (e.g., genetics); some have conceptualized psychopathology as a function of characteristics of the person (e.g., Freudian theory, genetics), while others have considered psychopathology as a function of the environmental context (e.g., family systems theory, sociological theory); and still others have contained a clear focus on development (e.g., cognitive–developmental theory), while others (e.g., learning theory) have been relatively adevelopmental insofar as they do not postulate a directional endpoint for development. While scientists and practitioners alike are generally aware that theories differ on a variety of dimensions, there has been relatively little systematic examination of the underlying theoretical assumptions that have bearing on conceptual issues such as world view, unit of analysis,

endpoint of development, characteristic methodologies, and paradigmatic problems. Indeed, there are even some researchers and mental health professionals who carry out their occupational activities without considering their underlying theoretical assumptions.

OVERVIEW OF PERSPECTIVES

Just as there are different perspectives for analyzing developmental aspects of psychopathology, there are different perspectives for categorizing models of developmental psychopathology (e.g., Achenbach, 1990; also Achenbach, Chapter 2 in this volume; Lewis, 1990). Consider, for example, the approach taken by Lewis (1990), who has focused on the relationship between the child and the environment. In doing so, he has elaborated three models of development that are relevant for understanding the "etiology of psychopathology." These include trait (largely ignoring environmental factors), environmental (environmental factors play a critical causal role), and interactional (both the child and the environment determine the course of development, e.g., as obtains in the goodness of fit and transformational paradigms) models.

An article closely related to this chapter was presented by S. Wapner at the Korchin Memorial Symposium in Rome (May 29–30, 1992) and is published in Italian (Wapner, 1995).

Our own perspective—the holistic, developmental systems-oriented approach[1]—partly falls into the last category because of its emphasis on the transactions (experience and action) of the person with all aspects of his or her environment. However, our emphasis is also on the organismic as well as on the transactional features of human functioning. Accordingly, we have chosen to make overt the underlying theoretical assumptions that have bearing on the problem, theory, and method of child and adolescent treatment by presenting a comparative analysis of major theories related to development organized around the levels of integration concept (e.g., Feibelman, 1954; Herrick, 1949; Novikoff, 1945a, 1945b; Schneirla, 1949) that has figured prominently in our approach for some time now.

Stated most simply, biological functioning (e.g., breathing), psychological functioning (e.g., thinking), and sociocultural functioning (e.g., living by a moral code) are related in a contingency fashion. Functioning at the sociocultural level requires functioning at the psychological and biological levels and psychological functioning requires biological functioning. The levels differ qualitatively, and functioning at one level is not reducible to functioning at the prior, less complex level because we assume that higher level functioning does not substitute for, but rather integrates and transforms lower level functioning (see Wapner & Demick, 1990, 1991b; Werner, 1957a).

Using this concept, we have categorized in Table 1.1 the major, representative theories as those that primarily treat human functioning at the *biological level* (viz., genetic, neurological–neurochemical, and ethological–attachment theories), the *psychological level* (viz., Freudian/neo-Freudian, learning–social learning, and cognitive–developmental theories), or the *sociocultural level* (viz., Soviet development theory, family systems theories, and sociological theories more generally). Because our holistic, developmental, systems-oriented approach is biopsychosocial in nature, that is, encompassing all three levels of integration, the table treats it separately for purposes of comparison. More specifically, there are striking differences between our approach and the other representative approaches.

Most notably, there are major differences with respect to underlying world view/philosophical underpinnings; unit of analysis; concepts of person, of environment, and of development; principles and endpoints of development; adaptation; individual differences; examples of paradigmatic problems; preferred method of research; assumptions underlying modes of generalization; goal of empirical information; and concepts of assessment, of psychopathology, and of treatment. In keeping with Table 1.1, we will first discuss general differences among the approaches. The remainder of the paper will then focus on differences between the majority of approaches and our own related to the specific areas of clinical child psychology, namely, assessment, psychopathology, and treatment.

World View/Philosophical Underpinnings

There is a major difference between the underlying "world view" (Altman & Rogoff, 1987) or "world hypothesis" (Pepper, 1961) of our approach and those of the others. For example, theories that treat the biological and psychological levels would predominantly be termed *interactional* or *mechanistic,* emphasizing a sensorial analysis of the effects of isolated independent variables within the organism (e.g., serotonin levels) and/or the environment (e.g., patterns of reinforcement) on dependent variables (e.g., psychological functioning of the child). In contrast, our approach, which adopts elements of both organismic (organicist) and transactional (contextual) world views, treats the person-in-environment system as a holistic entity in its physical–interpersonal–sociocultural contexts. While ecological/attachment theory and cognitive–developmental theory share aspects of our underlying world view (e.g., organicism, constructivism), our approach is also related to sociocultural theories, specifically, Soviet and family systems theories in which the unit of analysis is the person-in-society and the person-in-family, respectively.

Unit of Analysis (Holism)

In line with this conceptualization, our unit of analysis is the person-in-environment system. This system is assumed to operate as a unified whole (holism) so that a disturbance of any part (i.e., of person, of environment, of any transaction, of means, and of ends) affects the system as a whole at all three levels of organization. Such a disturbance to the person-in-environment system, which is presumed to be operating in a dynamic equilibrium, may make for qualitative (regressive) changes in relations among system components that are linked to the developmental status of the system; under various conditions, reestablishment of a new dynamic equilibrium occurs in terms of a progressive developmental sequence (see later discussion).

Concepts of Person

There are also striking differences between the concepts of person in our approach versus the approaches of others. Specifically, the other theories conceptualize the person in terms of part-processes, for example, as a collection of biological–psychological qualities (e.g., mental retardation, stage of psychosexual development) in biological and some psychological (e.g., Freudian and cognitive-developmental) theories

TABLE 1.1 Perspectives in Clinical Child Psychology

CATEGORY OF COMPARISON	BIOLOGICAL LEVEL	PSYCHOLOGICAL LEVEL	SOCIOCULTURAL LEVEL	HOLISTIC, DEVELOPMENTAL, SYSTEMS PERSPECTIVE
World view	Genetic Theory (G): Mechanistic Neurological–Neurochemical Theory (N): Mechanistic Ethological–Attachment Theory (A): Organismic	Freudian/neo-Freudian theory (F): Mechanistic and organismic Learning–social learning theory (L): Mechanistic Cognitive–developmental theory (C): Organismic and contextual	Soviet theory (S): Organismic and transactional (dialectical) Family systems theory (FS): Organismic and transactional Sociological theory (SOC): Mechanistic	Organismic/transactional (organicist/contextual)
Philosophical underpinnings	G & N & A: Biological determinism	F: Biological determinism L: Environmental determinism C: Constructivism (interactionism)	S & FS & SOC: Environmental determinism	Constructivism (interpretationism)
Unit of analysis	G & N: Person A: Mother–child dyad	F & L & C: Person	S & FS & SOC: Person in the context of other (S)	Person-in-environment as holistic entity
Concept of person	G & N & A: Biological–psychological qualities (e.g., mental retardation, attachment)	F & C: Biological–psychological qualities (e.g., stage of psychosexual development, cognitive–developmental status) L: Psychological qualities (e.g., traits)	S & FS & SOC: Psychological (e.g., cognitive–developmental status, behavior, mental status)	Defined with respect to levels of integration: Physical/biological psychological (cognition, affect, values) and sociocultural (e.g., rules) mutually defining aspects of person (e.g., roles)
Concept of environment	G & N: Physical environment as separate underlying entity A: Physical and "social" environment as separate underlying entities	F & L & C: Physical and "social" environment as separate underlying entities	S & FS & SOC: Physical and "social" environment as separate underlying entities	Defined with respect to levels of integration: Physical (things), interpersonal (people) and sociocultural (rules, mores, customs) as mutually defining aspects of environment
Concept of development	G & N & A: Physical development	F and C: Physical and cognitive development L: Behavior change but no unidirectional development	S: Cognitive and social development FS & SOC: Social development	Mode of analysis of person-in-environment, contextual functioning across the life span; in addition to ontogenesis, concerned with microgenesis, phylogenesis, etc.
Principles of development	G & N: Genetic structure that provides a potential for development (genotype) that may vary with environmental circumstances (phenotype) A: Imprinting and critical periods	F: Continuity, resolution of conflict as basis of change, invariant nature of stages L: Reinforcement, modeling C: Directedness, equilibration of assimilation and accommodation, unilinearity, discontinuity	S: Social determination of development, mechanism of change (contradictions), interiorization and zone of proximal development; nonuniversality FS: Homeostasis SOC: Social determination of development; nonuniversality	Underlying regulatory mechanisms, homeostasis, works in accord with orthogenetic principle (globality, differentiation, hierarchic integration, and others, e.g., law of *pars pro toto*)

Continued

Table 1.1 continued

CATEGORY OF COMPARISON	BIOLOGICAL LEVEL	PSYCHOLOGICAL LEVEL	SOCIOCULTURAL LEVEL	HOLISTIC, DEVELOPMENTAL, SYSTEMS PERSPECTIVE
Endpoints of development	G & N: Genetically mature organism A: Stable attachment status	F: Final stage of psychosexual (Freud), psychosocial (Erikson), or ego (e.g., Hartmann) development L: Change only; no specified endpoint C: Final stage of cognitive (Piaget), moral (Kohlberg), or ego (Loevinger) development	S: Person's lifelong mastering of historically determined material conditions of society FS: Optimal self and family functioning SOC: Optimal relations with society	Long-range ideal of developmental person-in-environment system state (differentiation and hierarchic integration of structure and function) characterized by optimal self-world relation (e.g., microgenetic, mobility, freedom, self-mastery)
Adaptation	G & N & A: Adaptation of person	F & L & C: Adaptation of person (e.g., assimilation and accommodation)	S & SOC: Adaptation of person to society FS: Adaptation of person to family	Congruent person-in-environment system state: Optimal relations between person and environment
Individual differences	Interpreted as a source of error	Manifest in different psychopathological states (e.g., schizophrenia, antisocial personality)	Interpreted as a source of error	Differential developmental psychology complementary to general developmental psychology
Examples of paradigmatic problems	G: Concordance rates of isolated traits N: Brain injury, neurotransmitters, and depression A: Relations between attachment in childhood and adulthood	F: Adult behavior & its relation to resolution of conflict in childhood (e.g., conversion hysteria, character traits); persistence in normal adulthood of earlier modes of functioning (e.g., slips of tongue, humor, dreams) L: Changing behavior through learning C: Attainment of object permanence, symbolic functioning, independent thought; personality, moral, and social development	S: Social nature of thought and language (e.g., zone of proximal development); impact of sociocultural historic change on psychological processes FS: Resolving conflict and improving communication among family members SOC: Effects of society (e.g., media, family values) on the individual	Critical person-in-environment transitions (with perturbation induces at any level of organization of person and/or environment), e.g., transition from home to nursery school
Preferred method of research	G & N: Experimental method A: Naturalistic observational and experimental methods	F: Case history method, psychoanalysis, dream analysis L: Naturalistic observational and experimental methods C: Clinical method	S: Natural experiments FS: Naturalistic observational and interview methods SOC: Naturalistic observational and interview methods	Methodological flexibility depending on level of organization and nature of problem under scrutiny; draws from experimental, naturalistic observational, and phenomenological methods

	G & N & A	F, L, C	S, FS, SOC	
Assumption underlying mode of generalization	G & N & A: Nomothetic (generalization from representative sample)	F: Idiographic (sample as prototype) L: Nomothetic C: Idiographic and nomothetic	S: Nomothetic FS: Idiographic SOC: Idiographic	Nomothetic and idiographic: Generalizational from representative sample as well as sample as prototype
Goal of empirical information	G & N & A: Formal theory development and general laws	F: Formal theory development, diagnosis, and treatment L: Formal theory development, treatment	S: Formal theory development, praxis FS: Formal theory development, diagnosis, and treatment	Formal theory development; qualitative understanding of context-specific psychological events; praxis
Concept of psychodiagnosis and assessment	G: Assessment of genetic status N: Blood levels, CAT & PET scans, MRI, neuropsychological tests A: Assessment of attachment status (Strange Situation Test)	F: Diagnoses based on psychological tests L: Behavioral rating scales without focus on diagnosis C: Assessment of cognitive–developmental status	S: Discrepancy from social context FS: Structural (e.g., boundaries), and functional (e.g., alliances) assessment of family system SOC: Relation of community to individual	Analysis of process as opposed to achievement
Concept of psychopathology	G & N: Nativistic, dependent on nature of organism A: Insecure, avoidant, and ambivalent attachments	F: Fixation(s) at particular stage(s) L: Maladaptive behavior(s) C: Cognitive disequilibrium and cognitive errors	S: Opposition between child's present means and demands of society FS: Family dysfunction SOC: "Psychopathological" communities and societies	Degree of self–world differentiation
Concept of treatment	G: Genetic counseling N: Cognitive retraining A: Psychotherapy	F: Psychoanalysis, psychodynamic psychotherapy L: Behavioral, cognitive–behavioral therapies C: Educationally oriented interventions	S: Activity directed by social relationships (educationally oriented interventions) FS: Family therapy SOC: Grass roots initiatives, community psychology, and prevention	Multiple means to foster optimal degree of self–world differentiation; flexibility, stability, and integration of person-in-environment system(s)

or as a collection of psychological qualities (e.g., traits, cognitive-developmental status) in sociocultural and some psychological (e.g., learning) theories. In contrast, we define the person with respect to levels of integration and so assume that the person (child) is comprised of mutually defining physical–biological (e.g., health), intrapersonal–psychological (e.g., self-esteem), and sociocultural (e.g., role as child, student, family member) aspects. Moreover, we do not focus on the person per se but rather consider the person and the environment as parts of a relational whole.

Concepts of Environment

Analogous to our conceptualization of person, we assume that the environment is comprised of mutually defining physical (e.g., natural and built objects), interpersonal (e.g., father, mother, friend), and sociocultural (e.g., rules and mores of the home, school, country, and other cultural contexts—cf. Harkness & Super, 1990; Chapter 14 in this volume) aspects. This implies that these aspects must always be treated relationally as parts of one whole. Thus, for us, environmental context is built into, and is an essential part of, the unit of analysis, namely, the person-in-environment system state. This stands in marked contrast to the other theories that treat either the physical environment (e.g., genetic and neurological theories) or the social environment as separate underlying entities.

Concepts, Principles, and Endpoints of Development

There is a striking difference between our conceptualization of development and the others. As is typical in the field, most theories are limited to ontogenesis or child development. We, on the other hand, view development more broadly as a mode of analysis of diverse aspects of person-in-environment functioning. This mode of analysis encompasses not only ontogenesis, but also microgenesis (e.g., development of an idea or percept), pathogenesis (e.g., development of neuro- and psychopathology), phylogenesis (development of a species), and ethnogenesis (development of a culture). Such a difference in viewing development is clearly linked to other differences in developmental concepts (e.g., in the variety of perspectives delineated in Table 1.1).

Specifically, we assume that the person-in-environment system develops toward an ideal endpoint as defined by the orthogenetic principle that specifies development as a change from a dedifferentiated to a differentiated and hierarchically integrated system in terms of its parts, its means, and its ends. Optimal development entails a differentiated and hierarchi-

cally integrated person-in-environment system with the capacity for flexibility, freedom, and self-mastery as well as the capacity to shift from one mode of person-in-environment relationship to another as required by long- and short-term goals, by the demands of the situation, and by the instrumentalities available (e.g., Kaplan, 1966, 1967; Wapner, 1977, 1980, 1987; Wapner & Werner, 1957; Werner, 1957a, 1957b; Werner & Kaplan, 1956, 1963).

The orthogenetic principle has also been specified with respect to a number of polarities, which at one extreme represent developmentally less advanced and at the other more advanced functioning (cf. Kaplan, 1966; Werner, 1957a). These polarities, relevant to child development, are as follows:

1. *Interfused to subordinated.* In the former, ends or goals are not sharply differentiated and, in the latter, functions are differentiated and hierarchized with drives and momentary states subordinated to more long-term goals. For example, for the less developmentally advanced child, watching television is not differentiated from the need to complete a homework assignment (i.e., each is viewed as a short-term goal); in contrast, the more developmentally advanced child differentiates and subordinates the short-term goal (television watching) to the long-term goal (doing well in school).

2. *Syncretic to discrete.* Syncretic refers to the merging of several mental phenomena whereas discrete refers to functions, acts, and meanings that represent something specific and unambiguous. Syncretic thinking is represented, for example, by the younger (preoperational) child's (as well as the schizophrenic's) lack of differentiation between inner and outer experience (i.e., lack of separation of one's own feelings from that of others out-there); in contrast, discrete is exemplified by the older (concrete operational) child's capacity for accurately distinguishing between one's own feelings and those of others out-there.

3. *Diffuse to articulate.* Diffuse represents a relatively uniform, homogeneous structure with little differentiation of parts whereas articulate refers to a structure in which differentiated parts make up the whole. For example, diffuse is a structure represented by the law of *pars pro toto* (i.e., the part has the quality of the whole) as is the case of the autistic child's displeasure at variation from some routine set of behaviors; articulate is represented by experience in which distinguishable parts make up the whole, each contributing to and yet being distinguishable from the whole.

4. *Rigid to flexible.* Rigid refers to behavior that is fixed and not readily changeable whereas flexible refers to behavior that is readily changeable or plastic. Rigid is exemplified by the compulsive child's perseveration, ceremoniousness, unchangeability, and routine behavior; flexible implies the capacity to change depending on the context and particular requirements of a given situation.

5. *Labile to stable.* Finally, labile refers to the fluidity and inconsistency that goes along with unchangeability whereas stable refers to the consistency or unambiguity that occurs with fixed properties. For example, lability is evident in the young child's rapidly changing, fluid, inconsistent behavior, by stimulus bounded shifts of attention, and by the use of words with many meanings; in contrast, stability is represented by thinking that permits precise definition of terms, ideas, and events.

Adaptation

In contrast to the other approaches that conceptualize adaptation as either the general adaptation level (Helson, 1948) of the person (i.e., biological and psychological theories) or adaptation of the individual to a particular sociocultural context such as society or the family (i.e., sociocultural theories), we conceptualize adaptation as consisting of optimal relations between the person (child) and his or her environment. Such relations may be achieved in several ways: The child may conform to the environment (e.g., Puerto Rican migrant adolescents to the United States may adopt the dress and customs of American adolescents); the environment may conform to the child (e.g., American schools may provide lessons in both Spanish and English for Puerto Rican adolescents); or the person and the environment may mutually conform to one another (e.g., attempts may be made both at home and at school to integrate the two cultures; cf. Malgady, Rogler, & Costantino, 1990).

Individual Differences

There is also a major difference between our approach and the others in the concept of individual differences. That is, the other approaches either interpret individual differences as a source of error (viz., biological and sociocultural theories) or as manifest in different psychopathological states (viz., psychological theories). In contrast, we see individual differences as contributing to a differential developmental psychology that is complementary to a general developmental psychology (e.g., see Wapner & Demick, 1991a, on the role of field dependence–independence cognitive style across the life span).

For example, our developmental analysis of individual differences utilizing the orthogenetic principle can be applied to a broad variety of content areas and modes of coping. Least developmentally advanced is (1) the *dedifferentiated* person-in-environment system state (e.g., child

immediately, unequivocally, and unquestioningly goes along with parents' wishes). Next are (2) the *differentiated and isolated* person-in-environment system state (e.g., withdrawal and removal of self from desires of parents and others); (3) the *differentiated and in conflict* state (e.g., the child maintains conflict relations between his or her own desires and those of parents or teacher); and (4) the *differentiated and hierarchically integrated* person-in-environment system state (e.g., where a distinction is made by the child between short- and long-term goals with the capacity to subordinate the former if requested by his or her parent) (cf. Apter, 1976; Wapner, 1987).

Problem Formulation, Methodology, and Related Issues

Finally, there are also vast differences among the theories with respect to problem formulation and methodology. For example, using a constructivist underpinning, we are concerned with describing the relations both among and within the parts (person, environment) that make up the integrated whole (person-in-environment system) as well as with specifying the conditions that make for changes in the organization of these relations. Thus, our approach is wedded to the complementarity of explication (description) and causal explanation (conditions under which cause-effect relations occur) rather than, as in the majority of other approaches, being restricted to one or the other (cf. Friedlander, 1992, Chapter 27 in this volume; Weisz, Chapter 28 in this volume; Weisz, Weiss, & Donenberg, 1992). This impacts our choice of paradigmatic problems (e.g., critical person-in-environment transitions induced by perturbations at *all* levels of integration) as well as our preferred method of research (i.e., flexible drawing from both quantitative and qualitative methodologies depending on the level of integration and nature of the problem under scrutiny).

Because the features of a theoretical approach to developmental psychopathology shape the nature of assessment, the characterization of psychopathology, and modes of treatment, the above issues will now be briefly treated both with respect to traditional perspectives as well as to our own perspective. More specifically, these applications will examine both general and specific processes evident in a number of person-in-environment relations that differ with respect to the unit of analysis (e.g., mother-child dyad, adopted child-family system, adolescent-sociocultural context). Where available, research conducted from our own perspective will be briefly reviewed; mention will also be made of the work of the contributors to this volume and of some open, relevant research problems.

ASSESSMENT

Mainstream clinical assessment differs from our approach to assessment. Traditionally, clinical assessment techniques have been classified in terms of the specific problem area with which they are most concerned (e.g., cognitive–neuro-psychological assessment, intellectual assessment, speech–language assessment, personality–projective assessment). In contrast, our approach to assessment is more general and is based on theoretical notions that cut across diverse areas of functioning. Thus, we shall briefly present an overview of representative traditional assessment techniques and then provide a description of techniques generated from our holistic, developmental, systems-oriented approach. With respect to the latter, we will identify techniques already employed as well as some that can be readily adapted from research previously conducted.

Traditional Approaches

The central features of traditional assessment techniques in clinical child psychology have been summarized effectively by Johnson and Goldman (1990); also Johnson & Sheeber, Chapter 3 in this volume. These features include the following. First, developmental assessment is multipurpose: It may be used for screening both individuals or groups (e.g., school readiness skills) and/or for making individual treatment recommendations (e.g., clinical cases in which developmental problems are paramount such as pervasive developmental disorders or attention-deficit disorders; cf. Durand & Crimmins, 1987; Fee, Matson, Moore, & Benavidez, 1993). Second, and most relevant here, developmental assessment can involve obtaining measures of child functioning in multiple domains. Third, data in a given developmental assessment are usually obtained from various sources (e.g., child, parents, teachers). Table 1.2 briefly specifies these domains and sources of data with respect to means of assessment; person(s) to which assessment is applicable; relevant findings and/or research; and source (a more complete presentation is given in Chapter 3 by Johnson & Sheeber).

As can be gleaned from Table 1.2, the unit of analysis for those interested in developmental assessment has ranged from the individual child (e.g., as obtains in most traditional child assessment techniques; cf. Johnson & Goldman, 1990) or the individual parent (see Azar, 1986, 1991; also see Azar & Siegel, 1990, regarding distorted cognitions and skill deficits in parents) to the parent–child dyad (e.g., see Azar, 1986, 1991 and Azar & Siegel, 1990, on lowered levels of parent–child interaction within abusive families; cf.

Holman & Stokols, 1994; Gotlib & Goodman, Chapter 23 in this volume). Although such conceptualization has acknowledged *the role* of child characteristics and environmental variables *as important contributors* to the child's behavior, these variables have usually been examined as separate, though interactive, underlying entities.

This stands in marked contrast to more recent approaches in the field of psychology—such as our own—that adopt a transactional perspective whereby the person and the environment mutually define one another (cf. Sameroff, 1975). For example, while traditional approaches often neglect sociocultural factors associated with the child and his or her family (e.g., socioeconomic status of the child and the culture), environmental context for us is built into, and an essential part of, the unit of analysis (cf. Tarnowski & Blechman, 1991, on socioeconomic status and Wells, Chapter 12, on religion). These and other assumptions as related to our conceptualization of developmental assessment are presented below.

The Holistic, Developmental, Systems-Oriented Perspective

There are a number of factors that guide our modes of assessment. First, with respect to classification, we have generally followed our basic assumption that the person-in-environment is the unit to be analyzed and that transactions with the environment include both *action* and *experience.* Experience with physical, interpersonal, and sociocultural objects (things and people) is assumed to take place in terms of cognitive processes ("objects" as known through sensorimotor, perceptual, and conceptual processes), affective processes (involved in feeling and emotional tone), and valuative processes (involving comparisons with personal and collective standards). Thus, we would most generally organize the content of psychological tests as those that deal with the psychological part-processes of cognition, affect, valuation, action, and planning.

Further, the general theoretical and methodological notions that guide our analysis of psychological tests across diverse areas of functioning have included the distinctions between *process and achievement;* and between *structural and dynamic analyses.* With respect to the former, Werner (1937) stressed that the final solution to a problem may be arrived at through diverse processes reflecting different activities of various structures in the central nervous system. For example, although two children may obtain the same IQ scores on a standardized intelligence test (e.g., WISC-III), the underlying processes that they have utilized to obtain their final answers most probably reflect different patterns of

TABLE 1.2 Some Examples of Traditional Child Assessment Techniques (Johnson & Goldman, 1990)

SPHERE OF FUNCTIONING	MEANS OF ASSESSMENT	SUBJECT APPLICABILITY	RELEVANT FINDINGS AND/OR RESEARCH	SOURCE
Motor skills	Bayley Scales of Infant Development	Normal and impaired infants and young children	Provides Infant Behavior Record for rating behavioral responses; in addition to Mental Developmental Index (MDI), generates Psychomotor Development Index (PDI)	Bayley (1969); Field (1987)
Cognition	WPSSI-R, WISC-III, WAIS-R	Normal and psychopathological infants, children and adolescent (3 wks.–23 yrs.)	Provide numerical indices of cognitive development (e.g., verbal & performance measures) usually with $M = 100$	Cattell (1960); Kaufman & Kaufman (1983); McCarthy (1972); Thorndike, Hagen, & Sattler (1986); Uzgiris & Hunt (1975); Wechsler (1989)
Language	Auditory Discrimination Test, Illinois Test of Psycholinguistic Ability	Normal and impaired children and adolescents	Assess receptive and expressive language, including syntax, morphology, semantics, pragmatics, speech fluency, and voice	Kirk, McCarthy, & Kirk (1968); Parks (1985); Wepman (1958)
Social and adaptive behavior	Vineland Adaptive Behavior Scales	Normal and impaired children, adolescents and adults	Measure degree to which individual functions independently satisfy cultural requirements for personal and social responsibilities	Doll (1935, 1965); Sparrow, Balla, & Cicchetti (1984)
Personality	TAT, Rorschach	Normal and impaired children, adolescents and adults	Measure personality functioning including self-concept, self-esteem, defense mechanisms, and object relations	McClelland (1975); Murray (1943); Rorschach (1921)
Temperament and behavioral style	Questionnaires, interviews, field observations	Infancy through adulthood (data collected from child and parents)	Measure child's style of responding to environment including activity level, mood, adaptability, and predictability; can also assess match/mismatch between child and parent(s)	Chess & Thomas (1986); Thomas & Chess (1977)
Home environment	Home Inventory, Parenting Stress Index	Infancy through adulthood (data collected from child and parents)	Assesses risk factors such as malnutrition and exposure to toxins; also considers stimulation, parental disciplinary practices, and parent–child interaction	Abidin (1983); Bloom (1964); Hunt (1961); Laing & Sines (1982)

cognitive assets and liabilities. Thus, our approach to *all* psychological tests has advocated the use of process analyses to complement the more achievement-oriented measures that are customarily employed (e.g., see E. Kaplan, 1983, on a process approach to neuropsychological assessment).

The other theoretical idea permeating our treatment of assessment concerns structural and dynamic analyses of the person-in-environment system. From our perspective, the organism (child) and the environment (physical, psychological, and sociocultural aspects) are viewed as structural components. Drawing on Werner's (1957a) theme of self–world differentiation, *structural (or part–whole) analyses* focus on the characteristic structure of person-in-environment systems with an eye toward discerning whether the parts (e.g., focal child and mother) are more or less differentiated and/or integrated with one another in specifiable ways (e.g., see Ainsworth, Blehar, Waters, & Wall, 1978, on attachment patterns). We also assume that *dynamic (or means–ends) analyses* are complementary aspects of a formal description of the person-in-environment system. Focusing on the dynamics of a system entails a determination of the means (e.g., temper tantrums vs. rational discussion) by which a goal (e.g., ice cream cone) is achieved.

In contrast to other perspectives, for us, cognition, for example, encompasses sensorimotor action, perception, and conception (e.g., Wapner, 1969; Werner, 1957a). Sensorimotor acts are transactions whereby the person acts on objects (things and people) in the environment (e.g., grasping a rattle, walking, playing tennis). Perceptual processes are those involved in organizing and making sense of incoming sensory information. In this regard, Werner (1957a) distinguished between geometric-technical perception (objects perceived in terms of objective, measurable properties such as shape, length, and hue) and physiognomic perception (objects perceived in terms of dynamic and expressive qualities such as the perception of a chair as inviting). Conceptual (symbolic) processes include thinking, memory, problem solving, imagination, symbolization, and language.

While Piaget (1960) has spoken of unilinear stages of cognitive development, the position taken here—in line with Werner (1957a)—is that cognitive development (sensorimotor action, perception, conception) may proceed along many separate lines (multilinear). Further, it is assumed that microgenetic mobility is an endpoint of development insofar as a developmentally mature individual can utilize both primitive and advanced forms of cognition depending on the demands of the situation.

The general approach of the holistic, developmental, systems-oriented approach to assessment may be described more specifically with respect to the following domains or spheres of functioning:

1. *Cognition.* Including sensorimotor action; perceptual orientation in space; perceptual organization encompassing part–whole relations and sequential organization; conceptual representation entailing gestural representation, spatial representation, and relations among self, object, and body experience; and modes of cognitive organization consisting of sensorimotor, perceptual, and conceptual organization, vicariousness, and role-taking ability
2. *Affect and values.* Including psychological distance from others and from places; cherished possessions; and multiple worlds of home and play

3. *Action.* Including levels of action and relations between experience and action
4. *Planning.* Including relations to experience and action.

For purposes of comparison, Table 1.3 delineates and specifies these spheres of functioning with respect to research conducted from our own perspective. Further, careful examination of this table will show how the broad variety of tasks employed complement traditional child assessment techniques and has relevance to assessing the clinical status of the child. For example, *egocentricity* and *stimulus boundedness* (cf. Strauss & Werner, 1942; Werner & Strauss, 1939, 1941; Werner & Weir, 1956) can be assessed by techniques drawn from research on perceptual orientation in space; formal, organizational analyses of the Rorschach can shed light on the developmental status of the child; the capacity to handle aspects of serial organization touches on a critical feature of everyday life; and the variety of features of spatial representation (e.g., drawing sketch maps of a newly entered environment, drawings of self–object relations) and conceptual representation as well as the sampling of modes of cognitive organization, affective/valuative experience, and relations between experience and action and between planning and action, are of marked value in complementing existent clinical techniques. By means of the methodologies described here, our approach will hopefully serve to advance understanding of the general functioning of normal and disordered child populations as well as their relations to the people who are significant in their lives.

PSYCHOPATHOLOGY

Traditional Approaches

As indicated by reexamination of Table 1.1, the various theoretical orientations lead to conceptualizing psychopathology (and specific psychopathologies) in alternative manners. For example, proponents of biological theories for the most part conceptualize psychopathology as an entity caused by aberrant somatic or bodily processes (e.g., medical or disease model; cf. Achenbach, 1990, 1992). Those adopting psychological theories instead view psychopathology as the result of some malfunction at the psychological level of the individual. For example, those with a psychoanalytic (psychodynamic) orientation conceptualize psychopathology as resulting from problems (e.g., fixations) in psychosexual development; learning theories argue that psychopathology (abnormal behavior) is learned in much the same way as other human behavior. Finally, those adhering to sociocultural perspectives typically conceptualize psychopathology

TABLE 1.3 Some Assessment Techniques Linked to Research Relevant to or Drawn from the Holistic, Developmental, Systems-Oriented Perspective

SPHERE OF FUNCTIONING	MEANS OF ASSESSMENT	SUBJECT APPLICABILITY	RELEVANT FINDINGS AND/OR RESEARCH	SOURCE
Cognition Sensorimotor action	Umwelt Assessment Scale including: Swiss cheese board (assesses stepping; attention); slidesphere (integrating physical events); symbolic play	Autistic, developmentally and emotionally impaired children	Procedures focus on *process analysis* that aids in treatment/therapy; tasks represent developmental ordering of child's abilities with sensorimotor action underpinning other cognitive processes.	Miller & Eller-Miller (1989); Werner (1957a)
Perceptual orientation in space	Object and body perception assessed by perception of verticality and body location when tilted 30°	7 year olds to adulthood and old age; mentally retarded individuals, schizophrenics	When body is tilted 30°, relative to adults, children: 1. more *egocentrically* experience a luminous rod in a darkroom as vertical; 2. exhibit *stimulus boundedness* insofar as the starting position of the rod has greater potency; 3. *egocentrically* underestimate their body tilt. Schizophrenics and older adults function like children.	Comalli, Wapner, & Werner (1959); Guyette, Wapner, Werner, & Davidson (1964); Liebert, Wapner, & Werner (1957); Wapner (1964, 1968); Wapner & Werner (1957)
	Other dimensions of space: up-down; left-right; near-far	Children; schizophrenics, manic–depressives	For children and schizophrenics, apparent eye level is located above, whereas in normal adults it is located below physical eye level. For patients in the manic phase of manic–depressive psychosis, apparent eye level is up relative to those in the depressed phase. Following success, apparent eye level lowers.	Krus, Wapner, & Freeman (1958); Rosenblatt (1966); Wapner (1966); Wapner & Werner (1965); Wapner, Werner, & Krus (1957)
Perceptual organization: Part–whole relations	Rorschach (developmental scoring)	Children; adults; schizophrenics	Children, schizophrenics, and normals with brief exposure provide vague, diffuse, global, whole responses whereas normal adult responses are characterized by an integration of parts.	Dandonoli, Demick, & Wapner (1990); Exner (1978); Friedman (1952); Hemmendinger (1951); Rapaport (1951); Siegel (1951); Werner (1957b)
Sequential organization	A. Place-name learning	Children	On learning a sequential sequence of flashing lights, there was evidence of ontogenetic changes in efficiency (trials; time) and mnemonic devices varying from lesser to higher developmental status (e.g., unit designating; ordering).	Wapner & Rand (1967)
	B. Stroop Color Word Test	Normal individuals through life cycle	To assess capacity to maintain a set while carrying out a task in the face of intrusions, subjects read 100 items on Cards A (color words); B (name color patches); and C (color words printed in different inks). In addition to traditional scoring (errors and total time) that shows striking differences between cards and between ages, two classes of measures—identification and capacity to organize serially in a smooth unbroken manner—also reveal age differences.	Demick, Salas-Passeri, & Wapner (1986); Golden (1978); Koerber & Demick (1991); Ligon (1932); Rand, Wapner, Werner, & McFarland (1963); Stroop (1935); Toshima, Demick, Miyatani, Ishii, & Wapner (1996)

continued

13

Table 1.3 continued

SPHERE OF FUNCTIONING	MEANS OF ASSESSMENT	SUBJECT APPLICABILITY	RELEVANT FINDINGS AND/OR RESEARCH	SOURCE
Conceptual representation	A. Gestural representation of absent implement	Beginning at 4 yrs. through old age	The task "Show me how to brush your teeth with a toothbrush" revealed responses at 4 levels that comprise a developmental progression: *deictic behavior* (e.g., pointing); *body part as object* (e.g., index finger as brush); *holding without extent* (e.g., holding brush too close to teeth); and *holding with extent* (e.g., holding brush at a short distance from teeth).	E. Kaplan (1968, 1983, 1988); Goodglass & Kaplan (1963)
	B. Spatial representation; micro-genetic development	Beginning at 4 yrs. through old age; schizophrenics, antisocial personalities	Development of cognitive organization of a new, physical place is linked to "anchor points"; over time, sketch maps become increasingly differentiated and integrated; evidence of *pars pro toto* (neighborhood stands for entire city).	Demick & Wapner (1980); Demick, Hoffman, & Wapner (1985); Schouela, Steinberg, Leveton, & Wapner (1980); Wapner, Kaplan, & Ciottone (1981)
	C. Relations between self and object	Normal and disabled populations from 6 yrs. through old age	Disabled children read material psychologically distanced from them with fewer errors than material set in the here-and-now. Developmental assessment of drawings (person looking for penny) revealed: youngest children depict self or penny in grass; older children depict looking at object but no relationship between them; oldest children and adults exhibit representation of searching (e.g., searchlight to find penny).	Nair (1961); Rand & Wapner (1970)
	D. Body experience including sensorimotor, perceptual, and conceptual aspects	Normal and disordered child and adult populations	By asking subjects to indicate, with outstretched fingers and eyes closed, the width of one's head, it was found that: children overestimate head width and this overestimation decreases with age; schizophrenics and those under LSD-25 overestimate their apparent head width. With stress of relocation, schizophrenic members of a psychiatric community increase overestimation and antisocial personalities decrease overestimation, immediately preceding and following the move.	Demick & Wapner (1987); Demick, Ishii, & Inoue (1995); DesLauriers (1962); Fisher (1986); Fisher & Cleveland (1958); Head (1920); Merlean-Ponty (1962); Piaget (1952); Schilder (1935); Wapner & Werner (1965)
Modes of cognitive organization	A. Place name task (Sensorimotor and perceptual vs. conceptual organization)	Normal, hyperactive, and hypoactive children	A higher proportion of less developmentally advanced subjects (hyperactives as well as 8 year olds) indicated the stimulus in terms of "place" (sensorimotor and perceptual organization) whereas the more developmentally advanced subjects (hypoactives as well as 12 year olds) indicated the stimulus in terms of "name" (conceptual organization); relative to inexperienced pediatricians, experienced ones used more modes in evaluating a febrile infant.	Crain & Crain (1987); Rand & Wapner (1970)
	B. Vicariousness	Hyperactive and hypoactive children; impulsive and assaultive persons	Relative to hypoactive children, hyperactive children showed significantly fewer human movement responses on the Rorschach; motorically inhibited groups and patients who verbally threatened but never carried out an assault produced more developmentally advanced responses on the Rorschach than assaultive individuals.	Kruger (1956); Krus, Werner, & Wapner (1953); Misch (1954)
	C. Thematic Apperception Test (TAT)	Normal and disordered child populations	Developmental measures of role-taking ability were developed from multiple stories given for each TAT card from the perspective of each character depicted on standard TAT cards.	Feffer (1959, 1967)

Affective–valuative experience	A. Psychological Distance Map (PDM)	Normal, developmentally, and emotionally impaired people from childhood to old age; schizophrenics, antisocial personalities	On the PDM for "people" and "places," subjects indicate psychological closeness to others (in places) in terms of how close or far circle placement is to a centered circle labelled "me." Findings indicated that relative to other children, kindergartners included fewer people and places; and adolescents more often associated places with people.	Demick & Wapner (1980), Wapner (1971, 1977); Wapner, Demick, & Mutch-Jones (1990)
	B. Cherished possessions	Normal, developmentally, and emotionally impaired people from childhood to old age	In response to "What is your favorite object?" and a series of specific questions, the *nature, meaning,* and *function* of cherished possessions with children from 6 to 8 years indicated: (1) younger children were egocentric in relation to their possessions whereas older children stressed social relationships; (2) females favored items to be contemplated whereas males favored action items; and (3) possessions that were meaningful for the "enjoyment" they provided decreased after 7 years of age for females, but persisted in males throughout the ages studied.	Dyl & Wapner (1996); Rubinstein (1987); Wapner, Demick, & Redondo (1991); Winnicott (1958)
	C. Multiple Worlds Questionnaire	All ages of the normal population	Assesses the nature of the relationship among a person's experiential worlds, e.g., for use in assessing the linkages among the child's and the adolescent's worlds of experience (friends, recreation, family, school, community, etc.).	Hornstein & Wapner (1984, 1985)
Action	Levels of action	All ages; pathological individuals	Actions in terms of levels: (1) sensorimotor action (involves tactile manipulation and movement of body parts and the body itself); (2) movement of the body through space; (3) differentiation of the body from objects out-there; (4) use of body parts in space (e.g., deiction); and (5) use of body parts to represent expressive function.	E. Kaplan (1983); Wapner (1987)
Relations between experience and action	General factors and precipitating events	Childhood through old age; pathological individuals	Relations between "wanting to do something" and "doing it," *general factors* and *precipitating events or triggers* that underpin the taking of action are assessed. For example, how does a child's experience in the home context get translated into action in the school context? Can child violence be understood in terms of general factors and triggers so that intervention programs might be tailored for specific individuals?	Clark (1995); Demick, Inoue, Wapner, Ishii, Minami, Nishiyama, & Yamamoto (1992); Raeff (1990); Raeff & Wapner (1993); Rioux & Wapner (1986); Tirelli & Wapner (1992); Wapner, Demick, Inoue, Ishii, & Yamamoto (1986)
Planning	Handling problem situations	Childhood through old age	Planning is used in the sense of plotting a future course of action that moves the person-in-environment system from some initial state of functioning to some desired end state. Formulating a plan involves a set of acts that are preparatory for carrying out a more complex set of concrete actions. Significance of consonance or dissonance between "what we want to do or plan to do" and "what we actually in fact do" is also assessed.	Neuhaus (1988); Wapner & Cirillo (1973)

15

as a joint function of the individual and his or her environment (e.g., family, community, society).

While the above may appear intuitively obvious, there have been recent attempts to integrate classic theories of psychopathology with more developmentally oriented theories. Two notable attempts at such integration are represented by recent developments in contemporary psychoanalytic theory and in the emerging subfield of developmental psychopathology. Let us briefly consider each of these.

Contemporary Psychoanalytic Theory

Historically, the various schools of psychoanalysis have each utilized selected developmental principles as part of their body of thought (e.g., Hartmann, 1950; Rapaport, 1960). The most general propositions of psychoanalytic developmental psychology have included the following notions: (1) behavior is determined by both intrinsic maturational factors (e.g., instinctual drives) and the structures restraining them; (2) the process of development involves a sequence of discontinuous, qualitatively distinct stages; (3) the interaction of instinctual drives with experience can be traced by changes in cathexes, modes, and objects; and (4) there is a progression of thought from primary process forms (e.g., dreams, slips of the tongue) to the dominance of secondary process forms (e.g., rational forms of adult thought).

Further, there are within psychoanalysis striking differences in conceptualizations of development. As Wapner (1995) has written:

> While Rapaport's (1960) representation is linked to basic drives characteristic of Freud's psychosexual stages, Erikson's (1963, 1980) stages are psychosocially or interpersonally grounded. Similarly, Mahler, Pine, and Bergman's (1975) theory is also psychosocially-oriented with a focus on separation (emergence from fusion with mother) and individuation (child's assumption of his or her own individual characteristics) in early childhood. Kohut's (1971, 1977) focus, on the other hand, is on intersubjectivity and how the self develops in the context of an intersubjective system involving another person (e.g., parent–child, patient–therapist). Stern (1985) has integrated developmental psychology with Kohut's self psychology and has postulated four developmental stages in the early growth of the self, viz., emergent self, core self, subjective self, and verbal self.

In each of these modern psychoanalytic models, psychopathology has been conceptualized as developmentally ordered with severe forms of psychopathology linked to earlier developmental stages. For example, in Mahler, Pine, and Bergman's (1975) approach, psychotic conditions are linked to pre-individuation disturbances. In Ko-

hut's (1971, 1977) system, severe psychopathology is thought to be associated with the failure of an adequate structurization of the self and with persistence of early modes of bonding beyond their age appropriate era. (pp. 3–4 of English translation)

As these examples indicate, not only have these modern psychoanalytic theories incorporated developmental principles, but the emphasis on developmental consideration in psychoanalysis and the impact of developmental research on this school of thought has contributed "to a revolution in contemporary psychoanalytic theory" (Leichtman, 1990, p. 915).

Developmental Psychopathology

A second striking example of the integration of developmental and psychopathological considerations is evident in the relatively recent emergence of the field of developmental psychopathology. Wapner (1995) has written about this field:

> As noted by Cicchetti (1984), its roots may be found in neurophysiology, physiological psychology, developmental neurobiology, the work of Hartmann (1950), Anthony (1956), and Wolff (1960) among others, and its "coming of age" is marked by the publication of a special issue of *Child Development* (1984, *55,* No. 1). Stressing the interdisciplinary aspect of the field, Rolf and Read (1984) define it as "...the study of abnormal behavior within a context of measuring the effects of genetic, ontogenetic, biochemical, affective, social, or any other ongoing influence on behavior" (p. 9). Sroufe and Rutter (1984) describe the focus of developmental psychopathology as "...the ontogenetic process whereby early patterns of individual adaptation evolve to later patterns of adaptation. The aim is to understand the origins and course of disordered behavior..." (p. 27). Kazdin (1989) more generally characterizes it as "...the study of clinical dysfunction in the context of maturational and developmental processes," and points to its rapid growth in diagnosis, assessment, and treatment of childhood disorders. This growth has been a function of a variety of contextual forces, including setting priorities at research institutions, promoting forums for interdisciplinary communication, promoting national research networks, providing new publication outlets, and fostering research training....
>
> In the developmental perspective Sroufe and Rutter (1984) present, they stress that the course of each individual's development is coherent and lawful, and at the same time, point to the complexities of predicting adult behavior from childhood behavior. They characterize the links between early adaptation and later disorders in terms of such salient developmental issues as fixation of effective attachment relations, mastery of the object world, flexible self-controls, social understanding, formal operations, loyal friendships, and so forth.

Garber (1984) focuses on the theme that the absence of a developmental perspective has inhibited the advancement of knowledge in the field of developmental psychopathology. As she sees it, the issues for such a perspective concern (1) the relationship between childhood and adult disorders and (2) the definition and classification of normality and deviance. With respect to the former, there are such problems as the questionable similarity between child and adult psychiatric illnesses, differences in child's intellectual and emotional capacities at different ages, lack of continuity of neurotic as compared with psychotic disturbances. Garber (1984) thereby concludes that childhood psychopathology be diagnosed independently of its relationship to adult psychopathology. As to the second issue, definition and classification should take into account: age and sex trends; levels of functioning and the progression of development; developmental tasks (here, object permanence, differentiation of self, time perspective, moral development, delay of gratification, autonomy, peer relations); and such parameters of deviance as intensity, frequency and duration.

Despite the vigorous growth of the developmental psychopathology field, Kazdin (1989) concludes that "Additional research is needed that draws on and integrates conceptual and empirical work from developmental psychology" (p. 180). It may be that a systematic elaboration and development of Werner's organismic-developmental perspective could serve such a role.

Werner (1959) himself rejected any dichotomy between the approach of the developmental psychologist and the clinician; he suggested that general psychology become developmentally rather than agenetically oriented, more organismically than elementaristically oriented, more field-oriented than oriented toward studying the person in isolation; he suggested that psychologists accept the need to "probe" rather than "prove"; he believed that clinical practice could serve as a laboratory for further theoretical and empirical study. (pp. 3–4 of English translation)

These two theoretical attempts at the integration of clinical and developmental psychology clearly speak to differences among perspectives in conceptualizations of person, of environment, and of development. These differences are sharpened in the context of recent theorizing about general psychological models. Following a brief presentation of Lewis's (1990) characterization of these models, we will then discuss our own formulation of psychopathology.

Models Characterized by the Role of Person and of Environment

As already noted, Lewis (1990) has described three developmental models of psychopathology—trait, status, or medical model; environmental model; and interactional model—all presumed to be prototypic of different views of development. The *trait model* employs the notion that traits are tendencies to respond in a particular manner that is not easily

changed or affected by commerce with the world of others. Such traits are regarded by some as based on an unchangeable genetic structure (e.g., Kallman, 1946) and by others as developing at an early age (e.g., mother–child attachment; see Ainsworth, 1973; Bowlby, 1969) and having long-term impact on social–emotional and health status. It is of interest that though traits may be regarded as characteristic of the person, Mischel (1965), for example, has shown that they may be linked to the specific situation.

The *environmental model* assumes that behavior is a function of the environment. It is recognized that the environmental effects may be of diverse origin, including the nature of the physical environment (e.g., living and playing space for children with and without homes; cf. Aptekar, 1994), the social environment (e.g., abuse of the young child by mother or father; cf. Pianta & Nimetz, 1992), and the sociocultural context including the immediate context as well as the culture (e.g., consider Harkness & Super's, 1990, extensive treatment of the role of culture in psychopathology). As noted by Lewis (1990), although the environmental model touches on the notion of critical period (i.e., environmental influences are more or less potent at different periods of time or stages in child development) so that child status begins to enter in this way, the position of the environmental theorist is largely restricted to the powerful influence of the environment.

Lewis (1990) has largely put the *interactional model* in the same class as the transactional model. Although it is true that both models are concerned with the person and the environment playing a role, an important distinction must be made between them. The interactional views treat unidirectional effects of both person and environmental variables existing independently; for example, some theorists focus on child development as a function of the physical environment (Wohlwill, 1973; Wohlwill & Heft, 1987). The critical point is that transactionalism considers the person and the environment as parts of a whole (cf. Sameroff, 1975; Wapner, 1995). One cannot, so to speak, deal with one aspect of the whole without treating the other (cf. Dewey & Bentley, 1949; Lewin, 1936). Altman and Rogoff (1987) have characterized transactionalism as follows: "Relations among the aspects of the whole are not conceived of as involving mutual influences of antecedent-consequent causation. Instead, the different aspects of wholes co-exist as intrinsic and inseparable qualities of the whole" (p. 25).

Further, Lewis (1990) has illustrated what he terms the interactional model with the goodness of fit model and his transformational model. The former is the model proposed by Thomas and Chess (1977) and Lerner (1984) that speaks to the discord that obtains when there is a *mismatch* (leading to psychopathology) between the child's characteristics and demands and/or characteristics of the parents. Lewis's (1990) own model, described as transformational, approaches transactional insofar as "it is a circular pattern of child causes affecting the environment and the environmental causes affecting the child" (p. 25).

The Holistic, Developmental, Systems-Oriented Perspective

In contrast to all other perspectives, our contribution to the conceptualization of psychopathology and related phenomena to date revolves largely around two central themes: (1) self–object differentiation (Werner, 1957a) and (2) critical person-in-environment transitions across the life span (e.g., Wapner, 1997; Wapner & Demick, 1998). Each will be discussed in turn. Finally, reference will be made to some of our earlier cited assessment studies that also have relevance to our conceptualization of psychopathology.

Self–Object Differentiation

The critical dimension of self–object (things and people) differentiation in psychopathology has been developed in both the contexts of Werner and Kaplan's (1963) work on symbolic formation and Wapner and Werner's (1957) work on perceptual development. With respect to the former, we refer to the classic volume, *Symbol Formation* (Werner & Kaplan, 1963). As part of the overall treatment of representational development, it has considered the ontogenesis of this representative function in terms of the following operations: "(1) the formation of objects of contemplation; (2) the denotation of objects, that is, reference; and (3) the depiction of objects" (p. 66). Further, the authors have described and evaluated a number of concepts (e.g., primitivity, formal parallelism, polarities, multiple modes of functioning, levels of organization) that bear on the application of the comparative–developmental approach to psychopathology. Given "the assumption that pathology entails some degree of 'primitivization of mentality,' it expects to find, in pathological individuals, a *dedifferentiation* and *disintegration* of functioning" (Kaplan, 1966, p. 665).

Specifically, Kaplan (1966) has offered definitions of symbolization ("representation, in a relatively circumscribed medium, of some organismic experience that would otherwise be ineffable and incogitable") and language ("a socially shared instrumentality") that are distinguished from speech. Thus, affective, lucid, practical representation and dialectical uses of language have been distinguished, and symbolization and language usage in psychopathology

elaborated, in a variety of examples from schizophrenia and related disorders.

To illustrate, consider Werner and Kaplan's (1963) analysis of the components that constitute symbol situations: *addressor* (one who uses symbols to communicate); *addressee* (one who is addressed); *referent* (object or event that the addressor calls to the addressee's attention); *context* (situation in which communication takes places); and *medium* (means for representing referents). In general, Kaplan (1966) has noted that in schizophrenics these aspects of the symbol situation are less differentiated and articulated than in normals. For example, there may be fusion between the patient (as addressor) and addressee; fusion and ambivalence with regard to the other; an egocentric–affective posture; relations to objects defined affectively and asocially; obliviousness to the scene; communal symbol system apprehended affectively–mythopoetically; personal meanings penetrating conventional symbols; transformation of gestures; symbol–realism; and neologisms (cf. Arieti, 1967).

In line with these notions, E. Kaplan (1952) found that, relative to speech directed toward others (*outer speech*), speech directed toward self (*inner speech*) is more abbreviated, holophrastic, personal, and differentiated with articulated subject matter. Slepian (1959) found that schizophrenics exhibited egocentricity and failure to respond to task demands as evidenced by a lack of differentiation of means (internal vs. external speech) appropriate to the required end, namely, object description through communication with self versus with another person. In a task involving interpersonal communication (i.e., subjects had to relate a story to another person who disagreed with their account), Mirin (1955) found that schizophrenics could not adopt a hypothetical attitude, could not maintain a stable orientation to the task, and could not differentiate between speech used for self versus for others. Finally, employing Werner and E. Kaplan's (1950) Word Context Test (the task is to define the meaning of an artificial word from its use in the context of six sentences), Baker (1953) found that relative to normals, schizophrenics were less able to differentiate between sound pattern and meaning as well as word and sentence and showed greater concreteness and semantic instability.

The comparative aspect of both the original theory and our elaborated approach has suggested that there may be formal similarity (though not identical underlying process) between schizophrenics and young children as well as between schizophrenics and other psychopathological groups (e.g., autistic children). In fact, Zigler and Glick (1986)—using a perspective consonant with our own—have more recently attempted to examine all (childhood and adult) psychopathologies from a developmental perspective, which makes for a comprehensive developmental ordering of various psychopathological states. Although recent research (e.g., Rogers & Kegan, 1990) has attempted to cast doubt on this possibility, the implications of the above research for the conceptualization and treatment of childhood psychopathologies should not be underestimated.

A second line of empirical research demonstrating the importance of considering the dimension of self–other differentiation for the understanding of psychopathology grew out of Wapner and Werner's (1957) initial research program on perceptual development more generally. For example, Comalli, Wapner, and Werner (1959), Wapner (1968), and Wapner and Werner (1965) found less differentiation between self and object (evidenced by closeness of alignment of a luminous rod with tilted body) or greater egocentricity in children and older adults than in young and middle-aged adults. Carini (1965) obtained parallel findings with several subgroups of schizophrenics: A catatonic group showed the most extreme dedifferentiation between self and object, less for paranoid schizophrenics, and least for normal adults. Guyette, Wapner, Werner, and Davidson (1964) assessed perception of verticality in mentally retarded males between the ages of 13 and 21 years; they found that the compensatory developmental change in effect of body tilt that occurs during development (toward less egocentricity) was less in this group relative to normals.

Studies of other dimensions of space have also revealed linkages to psychopathology. Consider the up–down dimension as measured by the position in space perceived to be located at eye level. For children and schizophrenics, apparent eye level is located above its physical position whereas in normal adults it is located below physical eye level (Wapner, 1966; Wapner & Werner, 1965). However, of interest is another relationship linked to manic–depressive psychosis: Rosenblatt (1966) found that patients in the manic phase of manic–depressive psychosis adjusted an indicator of apparent eye level up relative to patients in the depressed phase who adjusted it significantly lower. Relevant here is also a study conducted by Wapner, Werner, and Krus (1957) that showed that following an experience of success, apparent eye level rises and, following an experience of failure, apparent eye level is lowered. These studies are complemented by others dealing with the effects of exciting versus tranquilizing drugs in which apparent eye level is significantly higher under the former than the latter condition (Krus, Wapner, & Freeman, 1958; also see Glick, 1964, and Barton, 1964, for discussion of the left–right dimension of space).

In a related vein, though using a different methodology, Nair (1961) studied children with a severe reading disability. She assumed that reading disability is a manifestation of the lack of distance between the reader and the referential world (i.e., the reader and the referents and the symbols and their referents). There was significant evidence that the reading skills of these children was improved when stories were psychologically distanced (e.g., stories about two young boys having a bloody fight with knives presented in past tense and in a setting of long ago, viz., the Middle Ages) and physically distanced (e.g., projected on a screen instead of in a book). Thus, the manifestation of reading disability assessed was "a function of inadequate separation between self and world, i.e., a disruption in the subject–symbol–referent relationship" (p. 11) and could be improved by distancing the nature of the reading material.

In a more recent study on the effects of environmental relocation on members of a psychiatric therapeutic community, Demick and Wapner (1980) found that: (1) with respect to self experience, schizophrenics exhibited increased diffuseness, and antisocial personalities heightened awareness, of body boundaries on two test occasions closest to the move (2 to 3 days before and after relative to 3 to 4 weeks before and after), while staff showed no such differential changes; (2) with respect to environmental experience, schizophrenics' descriptions of various locations became less accurate and detailed closer to the relocation; and (3) with respect to the experience of self–environment relations, schizophrenics rated their relationships with others as less intense and permanent, and antisocial personalities rated their relationships as more intense, on the occasions closest to the move, while staff showed no such changes. These data have led to the following developmental conceptualization of psychopathology and hospitalization outcome.

Whereas schizophrenics typically exhibit a lack of differentiation between self and world with an egocentric focusing on self, antisocial personalities reveal rigid, differentiated boundaries between self and environment with an overfocusing on environment at the expense of self. Further, the stress of relocation exacerbates the symptomatology and fosters developmental regression by creating greater rigidity of the figure–ground relationship typical of the particular pathology. Such conceptualization is consistent with that of researchers who have conceptualized aspects of childhood psychopathology as consisting of internalizing disorders or overcontrolled behaviors such as anxiety and depression (e.g., King, Ollendick, & Gullone, 1991; Silverman & Kearney, 1991; Silverman & Ollendick, Chapter 16 in this volume) and externalizing disorders or undercontrolled behaviors such as attention-deficit hyperactivity disorder and conduct disorder (e.g., Richters, Chapter 17 in this volume; Richters & Cicchetti, 1993).

Further, our previous conceptualization is applicable not only to individual psychopathology but also to family systems. For example, in their study of the effects of open versus closed adoption (communication vs. no communication between biological and adoptive parents), Demick and Wapner (1988) have suggested that the family patterns generated by the different adoption practices may be developmentally ordered with respect to self–world relationships. Adoptive families characterized by a total separation between the adoptee and his or her family of origin (as is usually the case in traditional closed adoption) may be conceptualized as exhibiting one of the following: a *dedifferentiated self–world relationship* (all family members consciously or unconsciously deny that the child has been adopted); a *differentiated and isolated self–world relationship* (adoptive parents shelter the adoptee so that he or she will not learn about the biological parents from others and/or will not have to deal with the stigma of being adopted); or a *differentiated and in conflict self-world relationship* (the family worries that the adoptee may fantasize that the biological parents would treat him or her differently and/or may threaten to leave the adoptive family to find the "real parents" when of age).

In contrast, the adoptive family that is characterized by less absolute separation between the adoptee and his or her family of origin (as is the case in open adoption) may be conceptualized as exhibiting a *differentiated and integrated self–world relationship* (the adoptee may be better able to integrate the various aspects of his or her dual identities, possibly mitigating potential problems with identity and self-esteem; similarly, the adoptive parents may be better able to integrate the different aspects of the adoptee's identity so as to avoid blaming "bad blood in the background" for any of their difficulties). In this way, relative to those families who have practiced closed adoption, those who have practiced open adoption may be more developmentally advanced insofar as: (1) the structure of the family system may be better integrated and (2) the identities of the biological and adoptive families may be better integrated within the adoptee. Our ongoing data collection (Demick, 1993; Silverstein & Demick, 1994) has begun to support such conceptualization for all forms of open adoption except that of continuing open adoption (ongoing contact between biological and adoptive families over the course of the child's development; cf. Finley, Chapter 22 in this volume).

The above research has suggested that there may be value in conceptualizing the child-in-environment system as the unit of analysis in clinical child psychology. This conceptualization has applicability to both individual and systemic functioning. Further, the crucial dimension of self–other differentiation has shown itself to have heuristic potential for the study of both child development and psychopathology.

Critical Person-In-Environment Transitions across the Life Span

The study of critical person-in-environment transitions, a paradigmatic problem for the last two decades, also derives from the transactional, holistic, developmental, systems-oriented assumptions underlying our approach. Here, a critical transition has been conceptualized as initiated by a potent perturbation to any part of the person-in-environment system at any level of organization. That is, perturbations may be initiated at the *biological–physical* (e.g., onset of juvenile rheumatoid arthritis; cf. Finney & Miller, Chapter 26 in this volume), *psychological–intrapersonal* (e.g., changes in self-esteem on entering adolescence; cf. Lerner, Villarruel, & Castellino, Chapter 8 in this volume), or *sociocultural* (e.g., transition to a new sex role orientation; cf. Savin-Williams & Diamond, Chapter 15 in this volume) level of the *person* and/or at the *physical* (e.g., moving into a stepparent's home; cf. Anderson & Greene, Chapter 21 in this volume), *interpersonal* (e.g., loss of friendship; cf. Farmer & Cairns, 1991, and La Greca & Prinstein, Chapter 11 in this volume), or *sociocultural* (e.g., transition to high school; cf. Hintze & Shapiro, Chapter 10 in this volume) level of the *environment*. While our research has focused on various critical life transitions in the life cycle from infancy to old age, most relevant here are those studies that have treated the child's transition to nursery school (e.g., Ciottone, Demick, Pacheco, Quirk, & Wapner, 1980; Ellefsen, 1987) and the adolescent's transition to college (e.g., Lauderback, Demick, & Wapner, 1987; Schouela, Steinberg, Leveton, & Wapner, 1980).

From these and related studies, we have noted that expertise in development is required for clinicians to intervene effectively in all crises related to various critical transitions in the life cycle. For example, the clinician might benefit from considering the following: the person-in-environment system as the unit of analysis (e.g., the child in the contexts of family, school, peers, culture, and/or society; cf. Grych & Fincham, 1992); the ways in which a particular transition impacts all levels of the system (e.g., with entry into nursery school, a child's body experience as well as self-experience may be affected); the individual's cognitive, affective, and valuative status during various life transitions (e.g., the child's cognition may become compromised by affect when changing schools; cf. Cairns & Cairns, 1992); the nature of the skills available and the adaptation required during various transitions (e.g., a child having been involved in previous physical relocations may find it easier to move than a child who have never relocated before); and the ways in which an individual's multiple worlds become reorganized following a transition (e.g., a child's parent might go back to school when the child enters kindergarten; cf. Barth & Parke, 1993).

Such notions put our work in tune with recent volumes in clinical psychology (e.g., Kendall & Norton-Ford, 1982; Schlossberg, 1990) as well as provide practical suggestions for crisis intervention with children. In all instances of critical transitions, the clinician should note whether there is progression, regression, or stasis of the child-in-environment system as defined by the orthogenetic principle. Here, the main task then becomes defining and introducing conditions to foster optimal, more advanced person-in-environment functioning, which touches on the larger issue of treatment.

TREATMENT

Traditional Approaches

Similar to the manner in which they conceptualize psychopathology, proponents of the major theoretical orientations in Table 1.1 also have alternative views of treatment and therapy. On the most general level, those adhering to biological theories have typically advocated for some form of *biological* treatment (e.g., pharmacotherapy, electroconvulsive shock therapy); those with *psychological* theories have generally argued in favor of some form of individual therapy related to their theoretical orientation (e.g., insight therapy for psychoanalytic theorists, cognitive–behavioral therapies for cognitive and/or learning theorists); finally, those with *sociocultural* orientations have argued for group, couples, and/or family therapy as well as for more grassroots initiatives as exemplified by the subfield of community psychology (see Demick & Andreoletti, 1995). Further, based on research with depressed adults (e.g., Weisman, Klerman, Prusoff, Sholomskas, & Padian, 1981), there is a growing sentiment among mental health professionals that various therapies may complement one another so that simultaneous intervention at all levels of functioning may be most efficacious. This *biopsychosocial* notion is very clearly related to the holistic focus of our approach, which will be discussed below.

The Holistic, Developmental, Systems-Oriented Perspective

The manner in which some aspects of our perspective penetrate treatment approaches may be illustrated with reference to specific work in four areas, namely, schizophrenia, family therapy, family practice, and health education. Each will be discussed in turn. Implications of these approaches for the specific treatment of children will be highlighted when appropriate.

Schizophrenia

Relevant work on the treatment of schizophrenia, which introduces notions resonant with organismic–developmental systems conceptualization, has been conducted for some time now. For example, over three decades ago, Des Lauriers (1962) posited the notions that for the schizophrenic patient there is a

> gap between undifferentiated ego and surrounding realities that the discovery of his bodily boundaries serves as a beginning to his separation and differentiation from everything that is not within these boundaries. The therapist's role then is to strengthen such a separation and differentiation by strongly asserting himself as the first clear-cut reality separated and different from the reality of the patient and yet related to him. Physical contacts are important here.... The activity of the therapist, constantly stimulating the patient through the boundaries of his body, elicits motor responses from the patient which bring to his awareness the closeness or distance of his body from that of the therapist. (pp. 141–142)

This procedure, coupled with others, such as the therapist making clear that his or her thoughts belong to him or her and are not or do not have to be the same as those of the patient, lead to clear awareness of spatial relationships, a feeling of permanence and continuity, stability of objects, and the further development of relationships with things and with other people.

It is of significance that this analysis is underpinned by the well-known belief that a critical feature in development is the differentiation between self and world. As described earlier, there is evidence that dedifferentiation of these entities are characteristic of young children, older adults, schizophrenics, people under conditions of stress, and individuals under the influence of LSD-25. Thus, treatment approaches aimed at sharpening the boundary between self and world that have been utilized with schizophrenics appear equally applicable for use in clinical child psychology, particularly for disordered children with boundary problems (e.g., those exhibiting acting out behavior, autism, etc.). Caution should be taken, however, in introducing physical interaction between therapist and child since such interaction more generally has become an ethical issue in the practice of psychotherapy (see Fisher, 1993, and chapter 29).

More recently, Watkins (1986) has focused on the child in such activities as imaginal play, dialogues, and daydreaming. These activities have been conceptualized as involving imaginal dialogues that are important in normal development as well as in psychopathological conditions involving hallucinations (e.g., schizophrenia). That is, such dialogues have usually been conceptualized as involving an inability to discriminate between a percept and a centrally aroused thought that becomes void and externalized. Unlike most other approaches, Watkins' approach to therapy has not been to obliterate imaginal dialogues but rather to differentiate, articulate, coordinate, and integrate them with the dynamic nature of the child's thought.

Family Therapy

Melito (1985, 1988) has employed some aspects of our perspective with respect to the problem of adaptation in family systems. In particular, he has employed the orthogenetic principle as a standard for assessing whether family change (e.g., transition to parenthood) involves transactions characterized as developmental progression, regression, or stasis. For him, adaptability has been linked to greater differentiation and hierarchic integration of family members, especially as evidenced by the degree to which the system is flexible and stable.

In considering issues of treatment, Melito has employed the idea of regulation and operation as two forms of equilibratory mechanisms. Regulation involves displacement of equilibrium to some new behavior. A more advanced level of self-regulation, operational functioning, involves coordination of action into a unified whole to avoid or eliminate previous errors. In common parlance, he has raised the question of "how can the therapist work to help move a family to the level of adaptability corresponding to operational functioning?" Such techniques as video playback, role reversals, and sculpting may help family members become sensitive to their own modes of operation, to take the perspective of others, and to see how they fit within the family system as a whole.

Because adaptation of the family system has been linked to its overall organization, the system with greater adaptability (i.e., greater flexibility and stability) is more differentiated and hierarchically integrated. This state of organization implies that there is an integration of tendencies to change and tendencies to maintain sameness. Melito has quoted Werner (1957b) as follows:

> Increasing subject–object differentiation involves the corollary that the organism becomes increasingly less dominated by the immediate concrete situation.... A consequence of this freedom is the clearer understanding of goals, the possibility of employing substitutive means and alternative ends. There is hence a greater capacity for delay and planned action. The person is better able to exercise choice and willfully rearrange a situation.... This freedom from domination of the immediate situation also permits a more accurate assessment of others. (p. 127)

According to Melito (1988), there must be differentiation "from one's interpersonal context, a state which may perhaps be facilitated by the techniques mentioned but probably not brought about without additional and more arduous procedures" (p. 98). For example, with respect to differentiation, Melito has considered structural techniques that focus on fostering appropriate boundaries among family members. Additional methods for fostering integration have included structural techniques that make for use of and respect for family authority as well as methods that emphasize loyalty to and the values of the family.

Family Practice

Bibace and Walsh (1979a, 1979b), who were also the first in the literature to coin the term *clinical–developmental psychology,* have applied a variant of Wernerian theory to describe potential patterns of collaboration between clinical–developmental psychologists and family physicians. Compatible with many of the assumptions inherent within our own elaborated approach, their specific suggestions for collaboration include helping the family physician: (1) to differentiate between the form versus content, or structure versus function, of a patient's communications to the physician and vice versa; (2) to conceptualize development as extending across the life span (generalist orientation) rather than being restricted to one age group (specialist orientation); and (3) to consider, in a more holistic manner, not only the biological but also the psychological and sociocultural aspects of behavior in both sickness and health (e.g., see Bibace & Walsh, 1979b, on children's conceptions of health and illness). In particular, this last focus has direct implications for clinical child psychology.

Health Education

Related to the above work on family practice, Quirk and his associates (e.g., Clark, 1995; Quirk & Wapner, 1995; Quirk & Young, 1990; Quirk, Letendre, Ciottone, & Lingly, 1989; Wapner, 1994) have applied some of the assumptions of our elaborated approach to the more general field of health education. Specifically, employing the assumptions concerning the person-in-environment as the unit of analysis, holism and levels of integration, teleological directedness, development and optimal functioning, and experience and action, these researchers have discussed ways to promote and achieve optimal functioning through (1) disease prevention and (2) cooperation in following a treatment regime for an existing illness. Prevention has largely been illustrated with respect to smoking cessation, human immunodeficiency virus (HIV), and prognosis after hip fracture and compliance with treatment by reference to juvenile rheumatoid arthritis.

Consider the problem of HIV prevention, especially in adolescence. Specifically, these researchers have applied our self-world relationship categories to modes of sexual transaction with others. Least developmentally advanced is the *dedifferentiated* person-in-environment system state (e.g., transactions characterized by going along with the immediate situation such as the desire for sexual gratification and the availability of a partner). Next are the *differentiated and isolated* person-in-environment system state (e.g., rigid abstinence from sexual activity as well as from interpersonal contexts and transactions that could lead to sexual activity) and the *differentiated and in conflict* person-in-environment system state (e.g., willingness to use condoms but embarrassed and in conflict about purchasing them, unable to subordinate short-term to long-term goals and indulging in sexual activity without protection). At the most advanced, optimally functioning level is the *differentiated and hierarchically integrated* person-in-environment system state where short-term goals are subordinated to long-terms goals (e.g., the short-term goal of desire for sexual activity is subordinated to the long-term goal of maintaining health by avoiding the possibility of HIV transmission).

Further, employing our conceptualization of the relationship between experience and action (i.e., general factors and specific triggers) as relevant for HIV prevention, these researchers (Quirk & Wapner, 1991) have suggested that

the closer or more immediate the experience (e.g., through direct transactions with a relative or friends who has AIDS), the more salient the impact, thus the greater the value placed upon optimal functioning and the greater the likelihood of carrying out the health related action (e.g., using condoms to prevent HIV transmission). Conversely, the more remote the experience (e.g., general information about AIDS), the less salient the impact, thus the lesser the value placed upon the action and the less the likelihood of carrying it out (p. 208).

In line with this, Clark and others (Clark, 1995; Clark, Wapner, & Quirk, 1995) have utilized three interventions varying in psychological distance from the perceived threat of acquiring HIV/AIDS (information about HIV/AIDS; information and behavioral accounts; information and individually tailored imagery exercises) to reduce sexually risky behavior in women. They found that relative to the other two conditions, the intervention condition providing lesser psychological distance (i.e., imagery exercises in which the participant was guided through one of her own past experiences of not protecting herself, was asked to picture herself with AIDS, and was requested to picture how she could

avoid not protecting herself in the future) was associated with significantly safer sex practices. As an aside, it is noteworthy that while prevention of disease in this case was fostered by *less* psychological distance from the perceived threat, *greater* self-world distancing (Nair, 1961) was utilized in helping learning disabled children to improve their reading.

These researchers also have theorized that our conceptualization of self-world relationships may be equally useful for describing patterns of families in which a child must comply with medical treatment. Such conceptualization appears equally relevant to all aspects of clinical child psychology and, in particular, to the child and/or family's compliance with psychological treatment as well.

While there are clearly other examples of research programs either directly from or consonant with our elaborated perspective that have implications for the treatment of children and their families (e.g., see previous discussions of Demick & Wapner, 1988, on adoption, and Miller & Eller-Miller, 1992, on disordered children; Nair, 1961, on children with reading disabilities; cf. Santostefano, 1978, on cognitive control therapy with children), it should also be noted that other developmental approaches to treatment (e.g., see Ivey, 1986, and Shirk, 1988 and Chapter 4 in this volume, on developmental therapy and Arbuthnot, 1984, on the use of the "just community" concept with delinquent adolescents) are in existence and flourishing. Though generated from alternative developmental perspectives (e.g., Kohlberg, 1984; Piaget, 1960), they agree with our belief in an underlying set of general assumptions that are summarized below.

SUMMARY AND CONCLUSIONS

Developmental approaches to the clinical treatment of children and adolescents—of which our own holistic, developmental, systems-oriented approach is one exemplar—typically share a set of general underlying assumptions. These assumptions include the concepts of holism; psychological directedness (active structuring of behavior); multiple modes and goals; stages of development (with psychopathology often conceptualized as developmentally ordered with severe forms of psychopathology linked to earlier developmental stages); mobility of behavioral functions and of developmental stages (progression, regression, or stasis); long-range and short-range motivating forces and regulating structures; and reciprocal relations of adaptive processes.

Further, developmental conceptualization (particularly our own) has implications for the study of individuality, which is of central significance for clinical psychology. Werner (1957a, 1957b) highlighted a number of aspects of this problem, namely, the overall maturity status of the individual or his or her level of operation under optimal conditions, the use of microgenetic techniques that study the developmental unfolding of a percept, the way in which the person is structured into spheres of operation differing with respect to developmental level and, finally, the rigidity/flexibility of the individual to operate at different levels depending on the requirements of the situation.

Taken together, these notions all have direct implications for clinical child psychology. In particular, elaborated views of person, of environment, and of person-in-environment relations are necessary for adequately characterizing the functioning of the child in his or her every day world in all of its physical, intrapersonal/interpersonal, and sociocultural complexity. Such a description, if complemented by an elaborated view of development, has the potential to lead toward a unified theory-driven science of clinical child psychology.

NOTES

1. The perspective utilized here—a variation of Werner's (1957a) original conception later recast as the organismic-developmental perspective (Werner, 1957b; Werner & Kaplan, 1956, 1963)—systematically builds on: Werner & Kaplan's (1963) now classic work on *Symbol Formation:* Werner & Wapner's (1949, 1952) sensory–tonic field theory of perception (see Wapner, Cirillo, & Baker, 1969, 1971); the writings of colleagues and students of Werner who applied his approach to a variety of subject matters in psychology (cf. Barten & Franklin, 1978; Kaplan & Wapner, 1964; Wapner & Kaplan, 1983); Kaplan's efforts to integrate the approach of Kenneth Burke with organismic–developmental conceptualization in a perspective that Kaplan (1983) characterized as "genetic dramatism"; and on Wapner's recent work in environmental psychology with colleagues and students (e.g., Kaplan, Wapner, & Cohen, 1976; Wapner, 1977, 1980, 1981, 1987; Wapner & Demick, 1990, 1998).

REFERENCES

Abidin, R. R. (1983). *Parenting stress index.* Charlottesville, VA: Pediatric Psychology Press.

Achenbach, T. M. (1990). What is "developmental" about developmental psychopathology? In J. Rolf, A. Masten, D. Cicchetti, K. Nuechterlein, & S. Weintraub (Eds.), *Risk and protective factors in the development of psychopathology* (pp. 29–48). New York: Cambridge University Press.

Achenbach, T. M. (1992). Developmental psychopathology. In M. H. Bornstein & M. E. Lamb (Eds.), *Developmental psychology: An advanced textbook* (pp. 629–675). Hillsdale, NJ: Erlbaum.

Agli, S., Raeff, C., & Wapner, S. (1992, April). *Cessation of alcohol consumption among college women.* Paper presented at the annual meeting of the Eastern Psychological Association, Boston.

Ainsworth, M. D. (1973). The development of infant-mother attachment. In B. M. Caldwell & H. N. Ricciuti (Eds.), *Review of child development research* (Vol. 3; pp. 1–95). Chicago: University of Chicago Press.

Ainsworth, M. D., Blehar, M., Waters, E., & Wall, S. (1978). *Patterns of attachment.* Hillsdale, NJ: Erlbaum.

Altman, I., & Rogoff, B. (1987). World views in psychology: Trait, interactional, organismic and transactional perspectives. In D. Stokols & I. Altman (Eds.), *Handbook of environmental psychology* (pp. 7–40). New York: Wiley.

Anthony, E. J. (1956). The significance of Jean Piaget for child psychiatry. *British Journal of Medical Psychology, 29,* 20–34.

Aptekar, L. (1994). Research on street children: Some conceptual and methodological issues. *Newsletter of the International Society for the Study of Behavioural Development, 1,* 1–2.

Apter, D. (1976). *Modes of coping with conflict in the presently inhabited environment as a function of variation in plans to move to a new environment.* Unpublished master's thesis, Clark University, Worcester, MA.

Arbuthnot, J. (1984). Moral reasoning development programs in prison: Cognitive-developmental and critical reasoning approaches. *Journal of Moral Education, 13,* 112–123.

Azar, S. T. (1986). A framework for understanding child maltreatment: An integration of cognitive behavioural and developmental perspectives. *Canadian Journal of Behavioural Science, 18,* 340–355.

Azar, S. T. (1991). Models of child abuse: A metatheoretical analysis. *Criminal Justice and Behavior, 18,* 30–46.

Azar, S. T., & Siegel, B. R. (1990). Behavioral treatment of child abuse: A developmental perspective. *Behavior Modification, 14*(3), 279–300.

Baker, R. W. (1953). *The acquisition of verbal concepts in schizophrenia: A developmental approach to the study of disturbed language behavior.* Doctoral dissertation, Clark University, Microfilm No. AAG005835.

Barten, S. S., & Franklin, M. (1978). *Developmental processes: Heinz Werner's selected writings.* New York: International Universities Press.

Barth, J. M., & Parke, R. D. (1993). Parent-child relationship influences on children's transition to school. *Merrill-Palmer Quarterly, 39,* 173–195.

Barton, M. I. (1964). *Aspects of object and body perception in hemiplegics: An organismic-developmental approach.* Doctoral dissertation, Clark University, Microfilm No. AAG6413153.

Bayley, N. (1969). *Bayley scales of infant development.* New York: Psychological Corporation.

Bibace, R., & Walsh, M. E. (1979a). Clinical developmental psychologists in family practice settings. *Professional Psychology, 10,* 441–450.

Bibace, R., & Walsh, M. E. (1979b). Developmental psychology and health. In G. C. Stone, F. Cohen, & N. Adler (Eds.), *Health psychology* (pp. 285–301). San Francisco: Jossey-Bass.

Bloom, B. (1964). *Stability and change in human characteristics.* New York: Wiley.

Bowlby, J. (Ed.). (1969). *Attachment and loss* (Vol. 1). New York: Basic Books.

Cairns, R. B., & Cairns, B. D. (1992). The sociogenesis of aggressive and antisocial behaviors. In J. McCord (Ed.), *Facts, frameworks, and forecasts: Advances in criminology theory* (Vol. 1, pp. 157–191). New Brunswick, NJ: Transaction Publishers.

Carini, L. P. (1965). *An experimental investigation of perceptual behavior in schizophrenics.* Doctoral dissertation, Clark University, Microfilm No. 13009.

Cattell, P. (1960). *Cattell infant intelligence scale.* Cleveland, OH: Psychological Corporation.

Chess, S., & Thomas, A. (1986). *Temperament and clinical practice.* New York: Guilford Press.

Cicchetti, D. (1984). The emergence of developmental psychology. *Child Development, 55,* 1–7.

Ciottone, R., Demick, J., Pacheco, A., Quirk, M., & Wapner, S. (1980, November). *Children's transition from home to nursery school: The integration of two cultures.* Paper presented at the annual meeting of the American Association of Psychiatric Services for Children, New Orleans, LA.

Clark, E. F. (1995). *Women's self-reported experience and action in relation to protection against sexual transmission of HIV: A randomized case comparison study of three interventions.* Unpublished Ph.D. dissertation, Clark University, Worcester, MA, Microfilm No. AAG9625335.

Clark, E. F., Wapner, S., & Quirk, M. (1995, August). *Interventions in protecting women against sexual transmission of HIV.* Paper presented at the annual meeting of the American Psychological Association, New York.

Comalli, P. E., Wapner, S., & Werner, H. (1959). Effect of enhancement of head boundary on head size and shape. *Perceptual and Motor Skills, 8,* 319–325.

Crain, W., & Crain, E. F. (1987). Can humanistic psychology contribute to our understanding of medical problem-solving? *Psychological Reports, 61,* 779–788.

Dandonoli, P., Demick, J., & Wapner, S. (1990). Physical arrangement and age as determinants of environmental representation. *Children's Environments Quarterly, 7,* 28–38.

Demick, J. (1993). Adaptation of marital couples to open versus closed adoption: A preliminary investigation. In J. Demick, K. Bursik, & R. DiBiase (Eds.), *Parental development* (pp. 175–201). Hillsdale, NJ: Erlbaum.

Demick, J., & Andreoletti, C. (1995). Some relations between environmental and clinical psychology. *Environment and Behavior, 27*(1), 56–72.

Demick, J., Hoffman, A., & Wapner, S. (1985). Residential context and environmental change as determinants of urban experience. *Children's Environments Quarterly, 2,* 44–54.

Demick, J., Inoue, W., Wapner, S., Ishii, S., Minami, H., Nishiyama, S., & Yamamoto, T. (1992). Cultural differences in impact of governmental legislation: Automobile safety belt usage. *Journal of Cross-Cultural Psychology, 23,* 468–487.

Demick, J., Ishii, S., & Inoue, W. (1995, August). *Body and self experience: Japan versus USA.* Paper presented at Fourth Japan–US Seminar on Environment-Behavior Relations, Clark University, Worcester, MA.

Demick, J., Salas-Passeri, J., & Wapner, S. (1986, April). *Age differences among preschoolers in processes underlying sequential activity.* Paper presented at the annual meeting of the Eastern Psychological Association, New York.

Demick, J., & Wapner, S. (1980). Effects of environmental relocation on members of a psychiatric therapeutic community. *Journal of Abnormal Psychology, 89,* 444–452.

Demick, J., & Wapner, S. (1987, November). *A holistic, developmental approach to body experience.* Paper presented at Body Experience and Literature: An Interdisciplinary Conference, SUNY-Buffalo, Buffalo, NY.

Demick, J., & Wapner, S. (1988). Open and closed adoption: A developmental conceptualization. *Family Process, 27,* 229–249.

Des Lauriers, A. (1962). *The experience of reality in childhood schizophrenia.* New York: International Universities Press.

Dewey, J., & Bentley, A. F. (1949). *Knowing and the known.* Boston: Beacon Press.

Doll, E. A. (1935). A genetic scale of social maturity. *American Journal of Orthopsychiatry, 5,* 180–188.

Doll, E. A. (1965). *The Vineland Social Maturity Scale.* Circle Pines, MN: American Guidance Service.

Durand, V. M., & Crimmins, D. B. (1987). Assessment and treatment of psychotic speech in an autistic child. *Journal of Autism and Developmental Disorders, 17,* 17–25.

Dyl, J., & Wapner, S. (1996). Age and gender differences in the nature, meaning, and function of cherished possessions for children and adolescents. *Journal of Experimental Child Psychology, 62,* 340–377.

Ellefsen, K. F. (1987). *Entry into nursery school: Children's transactions as a function of experience and age.* Unpublished master's thesis, Clark University, Worcester, MA.

Erikson, E. H. (1963). *Childhood and society* (Rev. ed.). New York: W. W. Norton.

Erikson, E. H. (1980). *Identity and the life cycle.* New York: W. W. Norton. (Original work published 1959)

Exner, J. E. (1978). *The Rorschach: A comprehensive system. Vol. 2: Current research and advanced interpretation.* New York: Wiley.

Farmer, T. W., & Cairns, R. B. (1991). Social networks and social status in emotionally disturbed children. *Behavioral Disorders, 16,* 288–298.

Fee, V. E., Matson, J. L., Moore, L. A., & Benavidez, D. A. (1993). The differential validity of hyperactivity/attention deficits and conduct problems among mentally retarded children. *Journal of Abnormal Child Psychology, 21,* 1–12.

Feffer, M. (1959). The cognitive implications of role-taking behavior. *Journal of Personality, 27,* 152–168.

Feffer, M. (1967). Symptom expression as a form of primitive decentering. *Psychological Review, 74,* 16–28.

Feibelman, J. K. (1954). Theory of integrative levels. *British Journal of Philosophy of Science, 5,* 59–66.

Field, T. (1987). Affective and interactive disturbances in infants. In J. D. Osofsky (Ed.), *Handbook of infant development* (2nd ed., pp. 972–1005). New York: Wiley.

Fisher, C. B. (1993). Joining science and application: Ethical challenges for researchers and practitioners. *Professional Psychology: Research and Practice, 24,* 378–381.

Fisher, S. (1986). *Development and structure of the body image.* Hillsdale, NJ: Erlbaum.

Fisher, S., & Cleveland, S. E. (1958). *Body image and personality.* Princeton, NJ: Van Nostrand.

Friedlander, M. L. (1992). Psychotherapeutic processes: About the art, about the science. *Journal of Counseling and Development, 70,* 740–741.

Friedman, H. (1952). Perceptual regression in schizophrenia: An hypothesis suggested by the use of the Rorschach test. *Journal of Genetic Psychology, 81,* 63–98.

Garber, J. (1984). Classification of childhood psychopathology: A developmental perspective. *Child Development, 55,* 30–48.

Glick, J. (1964). *An experimental analysis of subject–object relationships in perception.* Doctoral dissertation, Clark University, Microfilm No. AAG6413160.

Golden, C. J. (1978). *Stroop color and word test: A manual for clinical and experimental uses.* Chicago: Stoelting.

Goldman, A. E. (1953). Studies in vicariousness: Degree of motor activity and the autokinetic phenomenon. *American Journal of Psychology, 66,* 613–617.

Goodglass, H., & Kaplan, E. (1963). Disturbance of gesture and pantomime in aphasia. *Brain, 86,* 703–720.

Grych, J. H., & Fincham, F. D. (1992). Interventions for children of divorce: Toward greater integration of research and action. *Psychological Bulletin, 111,* 434–454.

Guyette, A., Wapner, S., Werner, H., & Davidson, J. (1964). Some aspects of space perception in mental retardates. *American Journal of Mental Deficiency, 69,* 90–100.

Harkness, S., & Super, C. M. (1990). Culture and psychopathology. In M. Lewis & S. M. Miller (Eds.), *Handbook of developmental psychopathology* (pp. 41–52). New York: Plenum Press.

Hartmann, H. (1950). Psychoanalysis and developmental psychology. *Psychoanalytic Study of the Child* (Vol. 5, pp. 7–17). New York: International Universities Press.

Head, H. (1920). *Studies in neurology* (Vol. 2). London: Oxford University Press.

Helson, H. (1948). Adaptation level as basis for a quantitative theory of frame of reference. *Psychological Review, 55,* 297–313.

Hemmendinger, L. (1951). *A genetic study of structural aspects of perception as reflected in Rorschach responses.* Unpublished doctoral dissertation, Clark University, Worcester, MA, Microfilm No. AAG0274469.

Herrick, C. J. (1949). A biological survey of integrative levels. In R. W. Sellars, V. J. McGill, & M. Farber (Eds.), *Philosophy for the future* (pp. 222–242). New York: Macmillan.

Holman, E. A., & Stokols, D. (1994). The environmental psychology of child sexual abuse. *Journal of Environmental Psychology, 14,* 237–252.

Hornstein, G., & Wapner, S. (1984). The experience of the retiree's social network during the transition to retirement. In C. M. Aanstoos (Ed.), *Exploring the lived world: Readings in phenomenological psychology* (pp. 119–136). Carrollton: West Georgia College Press.

Hornstein, G., & Wapner, S. (1985). Modes of experiencing and adapting to retirement. *International Journal on Aging and Human Development, 21,* 291–313.

Hunt, J. (1961). *Intelligence and experience.* New York: Ronald Press.

Hurwitz, I. (1954). *A developmental study of the relationships between motor activity and perceptual processes as measured by the Rorschach test.* Doctoral dissertation, Clark University, Microfilm No. AAG0009011.

Ivey, A. E. (1986). *Developmental therapy.* San Francisco: Jossey-Bass.

Johnson, J. H., & Goldman, J. (1990). *Developmental assessment in clinical child psychology: A handbook.* New York: Pergamon Press.

Kallman, F. J. (1946). The genetic theory of schizophrenia: An analysis of 691 schizophrenic twin index families. *American Journal of Psychiatry, 103,* 309–322.

Kaplan, B. (1966). The study of language in psychiatry. In S. Arieti (Ed.), *American handbook of psychiatry* (Vol. 3, pp. 659–668). New York: Basic Books.

Kaplan, B. (1967). Meditations on genesis. *Human Development, 10,* 65–87.

Kaplan, B. (1983). Genetic-dramatism: Old wine in new bottles. In S. Wapner & B. Kaplan (Eds.), *Toward a holistic developmental psychology* (pp. 53–74). Hillsdale, NJ: Erlbaum.

Kaplan, B., & Wapner, S. (1964). *Heinz Werner, 1890–1964: Papers in memoriam.* Worcester, MA: Clark University Press.

Kaplan, B., Wapner, S., & Cohen, S. B. (1976). Exploratory applications of the organismic-developmental approach to man-in-environment transactions. In S. Wapner, S. B. Cohen, & B. Kaplan (Eds.), *Experiencing the environment* (pp. 207–233). New York: Plenum Press.

Kaplan, E. (1952). *An experimental study on inner speech as contrasted with external speech.* Unpublished master's thesis, Clark University, Worcester, MA.

Kaplan, E. (1968). *Gestural representation of implement usage: An organismic-developmental study.* Unpublished doctoral dissertation, Clark University, Worcester, MA. Microfilm No. AAG6817231.

Kaplan, E. (1980). Changes in cognitive style with aging. In L. K. Obler & M. L. Albert (Eds.), *Language and communication in the elderly* (pp. 121–132). Lexington, MA: D.C. Heath.

Kaplan, E. (1983). Process and achievement revisited. In S. Wapner & B. Kaplan (Eds.), *Toward a holistic developmental psychology* (pp. 143–156). Hillsdale, NJ: Erlbaum.

Kaplan, E. (1988). A process approach to neuropsychological assessment. In T. Boll & B. K. Bryant (Eds.), *Clinical neuropsychology and brain function: Research, measurement, and practice* (pp. 125–167). Washington, DC: American Psychological Association.

Kaufman, A. S., & Kaufman, N. L. (1983). *K-ABC: Kaufman assessment battery for children.* Circle Pines, MN: American Guidance Service.

Kazdin, A. E. (1989). Developmental psychopathology: Current research, issues, and directions. *American Psychologist, 44,* 180–187.

Kendall, P. C., & Norton-Ford, J. D. (1982). *Coping with life transitions.* New York: Wiley.

King, N. J., Ollendick, T. H., & Gullone, E. (1991). Negative affectivity in children and adolescents: Relations between anxiety and depression. *Clinical Psychology Review, 14,* 441–459.

Kirk, S., McCarthy, J., & Kirk, W. (1968). *The Illinois test of psycholinguistic abilities.* Urbana: University of Illinois Press.

Koerber, H., & Demick, J. (1991, April). *Relations among cognitive style and reading readiness in preschoolers.* Paper presented at the annual meeting of the Eastern Psychological Association, New York.

Kohlberg, L. (1984). *The psychology of moral development: The nature and validity of moral stages.* San Francisco: Harper & Row.

Kohut, H. (1971). *The analysis of the self.* New York: International Universities Press.

Kohut, H. (1977). *The restoration of the self.* New York: International Universities Press.

Kruger, A. (1956). *Direct and substitute modes of tension-reduction in terms of developmental level: An experimental analysis by means of the Rorschach test.* Unpublished doctoral dissertation, Clark University, Worcester, MA, Microfilm No. AAG009013.

Krus, D. M., Wapner, S., & Freeman, H. (1958). Effects of reserpine and iponiazid (marsilid) on space localization. *AMA Archives of Neurology and Psychiatry, 80,* 768–770.

Krus, D. M., Werner, H., & Wapner, S. (1953). Studies in vicariousness: Motor activity and perceived movement. *American Journal of Psychology, 66,* 613–617.

Laing, J., & Sines, J. (1982). The home environment questionnaire: An instrument for assessing several behaviorally relevant dimensions of children's environments. *Journal of Pediatric Psychology, 4,* 425–449.

Lauderback, A., Demick, J., & Wapner, S. (1987, April). *Planning and coping with conflict: Transfer versus nontransfer college students.* Paper presented at the annual meeting of the Eastern Psychological Association, Arlington, VA.

Leichtman, M. (1990). Developmental psychology and psychoanalysis: I. The context for a revolution in psychoanalysis. *Journal of the American Psychoanalytic Association, 38,* 915–950.

Lerner, R. M. (1984). *On the nature of human plasticity.* New York: Cambridge University Press.

Lewin, K. (1936). *Principles of topological psychology.* New York: McGraw-Hill.

Lewis, M. (1990). Models of developmental psychopathology. In M. Lewis & S. M. Miller (Eds.), *Handbook of developmental psychopathology* (pp. 15–27). New York: Plenum Press.

Liebert, R. S., Werner, H., & Wapner, S. (1958). Studies in the effect of lysergic acid diethylamide (LSD-25): Self- and object-size perception in schizophrenic and normal adults. *AMA Archives of Neurology and Psychiatry, 79,* 580–584.

Ligon, E. M. (1932). A genetic study of color naming and word reading. *American Journal of Psychology, 44,* 103–121.

Mahler, M. S., Pine, F., & Bergman, A. (1975). *The psychological birth of the human infant.* New York: Basic Books.

Malgadi, R. J., Rogler, L. H., & Costantino, G. (1990). Hero heroine modeling for Puerto Rican adolescents: A preventative mental health intervention. *Journal of Consulting and Clinical Psychology, 58,* 469–474.

McCarthy, D. (1972). *Manual for the McCarthy Scales of Children's Abilities.* New York: Psychological Corporation.

McClelland, D. C. (1975). *Power: The inner experience.* New York: Irvington.

Melito, R. (1985). Adaptation in family systems: A developmental perspective. *Family Process, 24,* 89–100.

Melito, R. (1988). Combining individual psychodynamics with structural family therapy. *Journal of Marital and Family Therapy, 14,* 29–43.

Merleau-Ponty, M. (1958). *Phenomenology of perception.* London: Routledge & Kegan Paul.

Miller, A., & Eller-Miller, E. (1989). *From ritual to repertoire: A cognitive developmental systems approach to behavior-disordered children.* New York: Wiley.

Mirin, B. (1955). A study of the formal aspects of schizophrenic verbal communication. *Genetic Psychology Monographs, 52*(2), 149–190.

Misch, R. B. (1954). *The relationship of motoric inhibition to developmental level and ideational functioning: An analysis by means of the Rorschach test.* Doctoral dissertation, Clark University, Microfilm No. AAG0009016

Mischel, W. (1965). *Personality assessment.* New York: Wiley.

Murray, H. A. (1943). *The thematic apperception test: Manual.* Cambridge, MA: Harvard University Press.

Nair, P. J. (1961). *Distancing: The application of a developmental construct to learning disability.* Doctoral dissertation, Clark University, Microfilm No. AAG6105008.

Neuhaus, E. C. (1988). *A developmental approach to children's planning.* Doctoral dissertation, Clark University, Microfilm No. AAG8825801.

Novikoff, A. (1945a). The concept of integrative levels and biology. *Science, 101,* 209–215.

Novikoff, A. (1945b). Continuity and discontinuity in evolution. *Science, 102,* 405–406.

Parks, J. (1985). *Naturally occurring adult language strategies that effectively elicit language from reticent children.* Unpublished master's thesis, University of Texas at Austin.

Pepper, S. C. (1961). *World hypotheses.* Berkeley, CA: University of California Press.

Piaget, J. (1952). *The origins of intelligence in children.* New York: International Universities Press.

Piaget, J. (1960). *The child's conception of the world.* Totowa, NJ: Littlefield, Adams.

Pianta, R. C., & Nimetz, S. L. (1992). Development of young children in stressful contexts: Theory, assessment, and prevention. In M. Gettinger, S. N. Elliott, & T. R. Kratochwill (Eds.), *Preschool and early childhood treatment directions: Advances in school psychology* (pp. 151–185). Hillsdale, NJ: Erlbaum.

Quirk, M., Letendre, A., Ciottone, R., & Lingly, J. (1989). Anxiety in patients undergoing MRI imaging. *Radiology, 170,* 463–466.

Quirk, M., & Wapner, S. (1991). Notes on an organismic-developmental, systems perspective for health education. *Health Education Research: Theory and Practice, 6,* 203–210.

Quirk, M., & Wapner, S. (1995). Environmental psychology and health. *Environment and Behavior, 27,* 90–99.

Quirk, M., & Young, M. (1990). The impact of JRA on adolescents and their families: Current research and implications for future studies. *Arthritis Care and Research, 3,* 107–114.

Raeff, C. (1990). *General factors and precipitating events influencing action: Initiation of a weight loss regimen.* Unpublished master's thesis, Clark University, Worcester, MA.

Raeff, C., & Wapner, S. (1993). *General factors and precipitating events influencing action: Initiation of a weight loss regimen.* Unpublished manuscript, Clark University, Worcester, MA.

Rand, G., & Wapner, S. (1970). Graphic representations of a motivated act: An ontogenetic study. *NAEA Studies in Art Education, 12,* 25–30.

Rand, G., Wapner, S., Werner, H., & McFarland, J. H. (1963). Age differences in performance on the Stroop color-word test. *Journal of Personality, 31,* 534–558.

Rapaport, D. (1960). Psychoanalysis as a developmental psychology. In B. Kaplan & S. Wapner (Eds.), *Perspectives in psychological theory* (pp. 209–255). New York: International Universities Press.

Richters, J. E. & Cicchetti, D. (1993). Toward a developmental perspective on conduct disorder. *Development and Psychopathology, 5,* 1–4.

Rioux, S., & Wapner, S. (1986). Commitment to use of automobile seat belts: An experiential analysis. *Journal of Environmental Psychology, 6,* 189–204.

Rogers, L., & Kegan, R. (1990). "Mental growth" and "mental health" as distinct concepts in the study of developmental psychopathology: Theory, research, and clinical implications. In H. Rosen & D. Keating (Eds.), *Constructivist approaches to psychopathology* (pp. 103–147). Hillsdale, NJ: Erlbaum.

Rolf, J., & Read, P. B. (1984). Programs advancing developmental psychopathology. *Child Development, 55,* 8–16.

Rorschach, H. (1921). *Psychodiagnostik.* Bern, Switzerland: Bircher.

Rosenblatt, B. P. (1966). *The influence of affective states upon the body image and upon the perceptual organization of external space.* Doctoral dissertation, Clark University, Microfilm No. AAG0018088.

Rubinstein, R. L. (1987). The significance of personal objects to older people. *Journal of Aging Studies, 1,* 225–238.

Sameroff, A. (1975). Transactional models in early social relations. *Human Development, 18,* 65–79.

Santostefano, S. (1978). *A biodevelopmental approach to clinical child psychology: Cognitive controls and cognitive control therapy.* New York: Wiley.

Schilder, P. (1935). *The image and appearance of the human body.* London: Kegan, Trench, Turbner.

Schlossberg, N. (1984). *Counseling adults in transition: Linking practice with theory.* New York: Springer.

Schneirla, T. C. (1949). Levels in the psychological capacity of animals. In R. W. Sellars, V. J. McGill, & M. Farber (Eds.), *Philosophy for the future* (pp. 243–286). New York: Macmillan.

Schouela, D. A., Steinberg, L. M., Leveton, L. B., & Wapner, S. (1980). Development of the cognitive organization of an environment. *Canadian Journal of Behavioural Science, 12,* 1–16.

Shirk, S. R. (Ed.). (1988). *Cognitive development and child psychotherapy.* New York: Plenum Press.

Siegel, E. L. (1950). *Genetic parallels of perceptual structurization in paranoid schizophrenia.* Unpublished doctoral dissertation, Clark University, Worcester, MA, Microfilm No. AAG0274470.

Silverman, W. K., & Kearney, C. A. (1991). The nature and treatment of childhood anxiety. *Educational Psychology Review, 3,* 335–342.

Silverstein, D., & Demick, J. (1994). Toward an organizational relational model of open adoption. *Family Process, 33*(2), 111–124.

Slepian, H. J. (1959). *A developmental study of inner versus external speech in normals and schizophrenics.* Doctoral dissertation, Clark University, Microfilm No. 59–06194.

Sparrow, S. S., Balla, D. A., & Cicchetti, D. V. (1984). *The Vineland Adaptive Behavior Scales I. A revision of the Vineland Social Maturity Scale by Edgar A. Doll, survey form.* Circle Pines, MN: American Guidance Service.

Sroufe, L. A., & Rutter, M. (1984). The domain of developmental psychopathology. *Child Development, 55,* 17–29.

Stern, D. N. (1985). *The interpersonal world of the infant: A view from psychoanalysis and developmental psychology.* New York: Basic Books.

Strauss, A. A., & Werner, H. (1942). Disorders of conceptual thinking in the brain-injured child. *Journal of Nervous and Mental Disorders, 2,* 153–172.

Stroop, J. R. (1935). Studies of interference in serial verbal reactions. *Journal of Experimental Psychology, 18,* 643–661.

Tarnowski, K. T., & Blechman, E. A. (1991). Introduction to the special section: Disadvantaged children and families. *Journal of Clinical Child Psychology, 20,* 338–339.

Thomas, A., & Chess, S. (1977). *Temperament and development.* New York: Brunner/Mazel.

Thorndike, R. L., Hagen, E. P., & Sattler, J. M. (1986). *Stanford-Binet Intelligence Scale* (4th ed.). Chicago: Riverside.

Tirelli, L., & Wapner, S. (1992). *Desistance from and attempts to stop smoking.* Unpublished manuscript, Clark University, Worcester, MA.

Toshima, T., Demick, J., Miyatani, M., Ishii, S., & Wapner, S. (1996). Cross-cultural differences in processes underlying sequential cognitive activity. *Japanese Psychological Research, 38,* 90–96.

Uzgiris, I. C., & Hunt, J. McV. (1975). *Assessment in infancy.* Chicago: University of Illinois Press.

Wapner, S. (1964). An organismic-developmental approach to the study of perceptual and other cognitive operations. In C. Scheerer (Ed.), *Cognition: theory, research, promise.* New York: Harper & Row.

Wapner, S. (1966, May). *Perceived "body: object" relations.* Paper presented at the colloquium on perception and personality at the

University of Cincinnati Department of Psychology and Psychiatry and the Veterans Administration Hospital, Cincinnati, OH.

Wapner, S. (1968). Age changes in perception of verticality and of the longitudinal body axis under body tilt. *Journal of Experimental Child Psychology, 6,* 543–555.

Wapner, S. (1969). Organismic-developmental theory: Some applications to cognition. In J. Langer, P. H. Mussen, & M. Covington (Eds.), *Trends and issues in developmental psychology* (pp. 38–67). New York: Holt, Rinehart & Winston.

Wapner, S. (1971, April). *Toward a theoretical approach and development of man-environment systems.* Paper presented at the Howard University colloquium, Washington, DC.

Wapner, S. (1977). Environmental transition: A research paradigm deriving from the organismic-developmental systems approach. In L. van Ryzin (Ed.), *Proceedings of the Wisconsin Conference on Research Methods in Behavior-Environment Studies* (pp. 1–9). Madison: University of Wisconsin Press.

Wapner, S. (1980). Toward an analysis of transactions of persons-in-a-high speed society. In *Reports on man and a high speed society: The IATSS Symposium on Traffic Science* (pp. 35–43). Tokyo: IATSS.

Wapner, S. (1981). Transactions of persons-in-environments: Some critical transitions. *Journal of Environmental Psychology, 1,* 233–239.

Wapner, S. (1987). A holistic, developmental, systems-oriented environmental psychology: Some beginnings. In D. Stokols & I. Altman (Eds.), *Handbook of environmental psychology* (pp. 1433–1465). New York: Wiley.

Wapner, S. (1994). AIDS: The holistic, developmental, systems-oriented approach. *The General Psychologist, 30,* 95–99.

Wapner, S. (1995). Psicologia clinica e psicologia dell-eta evolutiva: un approccio olistico, evolutive, ad orientamento sistemico. *Psicologia Clinica, 1* (Gennaio-Aprile), 38–82. (Available in English: "Developmental and clinical psychology: A holistic, developmental, systems-oriented approach.")

Wapner, S., & Cirillo, L. (1973). *Development of planning.* Public Health Service Grant Application, Clark University, Worcester, MA.

Wapner, S., Cirillo, L., & Baker, A. H. (1969). Sensori-tonic theory: Toward a reformulation. *Archivio di Psicologia Neurolgia e Psichiatria, 301,* 493–512.

Wapner, S., Cirillo, L., & Baker, A. H. (1971). Some aspects of the development of space perception. In J. P. Hill (Ed.), *Minnesota symposia on child psychology* (Vol. 5, pp. 162–204). Minneapolis: University of Minnesota Press.

Wapner, S., & Demick, J. (1990). Development of experience and action: Levels of integration in human functioning. In G. Greenberg & E. Tobach (Eds.), *Theories of the evolution of knowing: The T. C. Schneirla conference series* (Vol. 4; pp. 47–68). Hillsdale, NJ: Erlbaum.

Wapner, S., & Demick, J. (Eds.). (1991a). *Field dependence-independence: Cognitive style across the life span.* Hillsdale, NJ: Erlbaum.

Wapner, S., & Demick, J. (1991b). Some relations between developmental and environmental psychology: An organismic-developmental systems perspective. In R. M. Downs, L. S. Liben, & D. S. Palermo (Eds.), *Visions of aesthetics, the environment and development: The legacy of Joachim F. Wohlwill* (pp. 181–211). Hillsdale, NJ: Erlbaum.

Wapner, S., & Demick, J. (1998) Developmental analysis: A holistic developmental, systems-oriented perspective. In R. M. Lerner (Ed.), *Theoretical models of human developmental, vol.4: Handbook of child psychology* (5th ed., pp. 761–805). New York: Wiley.

Wapner, S., & Demick, J. (1992). The organismic-developmental, systems approach to the study of critical person-in-environment transitions through the life span. In T. Yamamoto & S. Wapner (Eds.), *Developmental psychology of life transitions* (pp. 243–265). Tokyo: Kyodo Shuppan.

Wapner, S., Demick, J., Inoue, W., Ishii, S., & Yamamoto, T. (1986). Relations between experience and action: Automobile seat belt usage in Japan and the United States. In W. H. Ittelson, M. Asai, & M. Carr (Eds.), *Proceedings of the 2nd USA-Japan seminar on environment and behavior* (pp. 279–295). Tucson: University of Arizona Press.

Wapner, S., Demick, J., & Mutch-Jones, K. (1990, March). *Children's experience of people and places.* Paper presented at the annual meeting of the Eastern Psychological Association, Philadelphia.

Wapner, S., Demick, J., & Redondo, J. P. (1990). Cherished possessions and adaptation of older people to nursing homes. *International Journal on Aging and Human Development, 31,* 299–315.

Wapner, S., & Kaplan, B. (Eds.). (1983). *Toward a holistic developmental psychology.* Hillsdale, NJ: Erlbaum.

Wapner, S., Kaplan, B., & Ciottone, R. (1981). Self-world relationships in critical environment transitions: Childhood and beyond. In L. Liben, A. Patterson, & N. Newcombe (Eds.), *Spatial representation and behavior across the life span* (pp. 251–282). New York: Academic Press.

Wapner, S., & Rand, G. (1967). Age changes in verbal satiation. *Psychonomic Science, 9,* 467–468.

Wapner, S., & Werner, H. (1957). *Perceptual development.* Worcester, MA: Clark University Press.

Wapner, S., & Werner, H. (1965). An experimental approach to body perception from the organismic–developmental point of view. In S. Wapner & H. Werner (Eds.), *The body percept* (pp. 9–25). New York: Random House.

Wapner, S., Werner, H., & Krus, D. M. (1957). Studies in physiognomic perception: IV. Effect of muscular involvement on the properties of objects. *Journal of Psychology, 44,* 129–132.

Watkins, M. (1986). *Invisible guests: The development of imaginal dialogues.* Hillsdale, NJ: Analytic Press.

Wechsler, D. (1989). *Manual for the Wechsler preschool and primary scale of intelligence-revised.* New York: Psychological Corporation.

Weissman, M. M., Klerman, G. L., Prusoff, B. A., Sholomskas, D., & Padian, N. (1981). Depressed outpatients: Results one year after treatment with drugs and/or interpersonal psychotherapy. *Archives of General Psychiatry, 38,* 51–56.

Weisz, J. R., Weiss, B., & Donenberg, G. R. (1992). The lab versus the clinic: Effects of child and adolescent psychotherapy. *American Psychologist, 47,* 1578–1585.

Wepman, J. (1958). *Auditory discrimination test.* Chicago: Language Research Associates.

Werner, H. (1937). Process and achievement: A basic problem in education and developmental psychology. *Harvard Educational Review, 7,* 353–368.

Werner, H. (1957a). *Comparative psychology of mental development* (3rd ed.). New York: International Universities Press. (Original work published 1940)

Werner, H. (1957b). The concept of development from a comparative and organismic point of view. In D. Harris (Ed.), *The concept of development* (pp. 125–148). Minneapolis: University of Minnesota Press.

Werner, H. (1959). Significance of general experimental psychology for the understanding of abnormal behavior and its correction or prevention. In T. Dembo & G. Leviton (Eds.), *The relationship between rehabilitation and psychology* (pp. 62–75). Washington, DC: U.S. Department of Health, Education and Welfare, Office of Vocational Rehabilitation.

Werner, H., & Kaplan, B. (1956). The developmental approach to cognition: Its relevance to the psychological interpretation of anthropological and ethnolinguistic data. *American Anthropologist, 58,* 866–880.

Werner, H., & Kaplan, B. (1963). *Symbol formation.* New York: Wiley.

Werner, H., & Kaplan, E. (1950). Development of word meaning through verbal context: An experimental study. *Journal of Psychology, 29,* 251–257.

Werner, H., & Strauss, A. A. (1939). Types of visuo-motor activity in relation to low and high performance ages. *Proceedings of the American Association of Mental Deficiency, 44,* 163–168.

Werner, H., & Strauss, A. A. (1941). Pathology of figure-background relation in the child. *Journal of Abnormal and Social Psychology, 36,* 236–248.

Werner, H., & Wapner, S. (1949). Sensory-tonic field theory of perception. *Journal of Personality, 18,* 88–107.

Werner, H., & Wapner, S. (1952). Toward a general theory of perception. *Psychological Review, 59,* 324–338.

Werner, H., & Weir, A. (1956). The figure-ground syndrome in the brain-injured child. *International Record of Medicine and General Practice Clinics, 169,* 362–367.

Winnicott, D. (1958). *Through pediatrics to psychoanalysis.* New York: Basic Books.

Wohlwill, J. F. (1973). The environment is not in the head. In W. F. G. Preiser (Ed.), *Environmental Design Research Association Symposia and Workshops* (Vol. 2, pp. 166–181). Stroudsberg, PA: Bowden, Hutchinson & Ross.

Wohlwill, J. F., & Heft, H. (1987). The physical environment and the development of the child. In D. Stokols & I. Altman (Eds.), *Handbook of environmental psychology* (pp. 281–328). New York: Wiley.

Wolff, P. H. (1960). The developmental psychologies of Jean Piaget and psychoanalysis. *Psychological Issues, 2*(1), (Monograph 5). New York: International Universities Press.

Zigler, E. F., & Glick, M. (1986). *A developmental approach to adult psychopathology.* New York: Wiley.

CHAPTER 2

DEVELOPMENTAL TAXONOMY

Thomas M. Achenbach

In seeking to treat behavioral and emotional problems, we must first ask, "What is to be treated?" This question raises the following additional questions: What evidence indicates that something is wrong? If something is wrong, what is it? What outcome is to be sought?

The answers to all these questions depend on taxonomy—that is, our systems for distinguishing among different patterns of problems. The answers also depend on developmental considerations, such as the following: What is normal versus abnormal for the developmental level of the individuals who are to be treated? How can the individuals' future development be facilitated?

If we already had complete knowledge of disorders, how best to treat them, and how they relate to development, there might be little need for this chapter. However, because the developmental study of psychopathology is relatively new, a great deal remains to be learned. To optimize treatment, we therefore need to approach psychopathology with an open mind, prepared to search out new knowledge that will enable us to enlarge our understanding of the disorders and thereby to improve our ways of treating them.

Between infancy and adulthood, humans undergo massive changes in physique, abilities, behavior, emotions, and social status. (For brevity, this entire period will be referred to as "childhood.") These changes greatly complicate the task of distinguishing between the normal and abnormal. They also complicate the task of distinguishing between different kinds of abnormality, which may involve different patterns of problems, etiologies, degrees of impairment, courses, appropriate treatments, and outcomes. In addition to massive developmental changes, behaviors and emotions change from moment to moment, from context to context, and from one interaction partner to another. Because behaviors and emotions change so much, judgments of abnormality cannot be based on snapshots of static conditions. Instead, judgments of abnormality must be based on assessment procedures and taxonomic constructs that aggregate data across situations, time, and developmental periods.

All humans display maladaptive behavior and emotions from time to time. Many of the behaviors and emotions for which children are referred to mental health practitioners are manifested by most children in some degree at some time in their lives. With the exception of such rare and extreme conditions as autism, most behavioral and emotional problems for which help is sought are not intrinsically pathological. Instead, they are considered pathological because they interfere with adaptive development and/or because they are quantitatively deviant from normative expectations for an individual's age. Quantitative aspects of deviance include the sheer number of different problems, their frequency, intensity, effects on other people, and pervasiveness.

To take account of situational and developmental changes and the quantitative nature of most behavioral/emotional problems, we need assessment and taxonomic models that are sensitive both to quantitative variations and to underlying continuities in psychopathology.

MAPPING IMPORTANT ASPECTS OF DEVELOPMENT

To cope with the diverse challenges of understanding psychopathology in relation to development, it is essential to have a clear picture of the typical course of development. A comprehensive picture requires maps of various aspects of development, such as physical, linguistic, cognitive, behavioral, and emotional. Physical development has been well mapped in terms of norms for maturational sequences, height, weight, and various motor skills. Linguistic development has been mapped in terms of phonology, vocabulary, pragmatics, and syntactics (Gleason, 1993).

Mapping Cognitive Development

Cognitive development has been persuasively mapped by Piaget (1983). Although there are efforts to revise and qualify Piaget's developmental map (e.g., Siegler, 1991), it still provides powerful guidance to the main cognitive processes and sequences that occur between birth and maturity.

Cognitive development is mapped in a different way by standardized tests that provide developmental norms for accomplishments ranging from the sensory–motor responses found at the early levels of the Bayley (1993) Scales, to the rudimentary verbal and problem-solving skills found on the McCarthy (1972) Scales, and the progressively more abstract tasks found on the Kaufman Assessment Battery for Children (Kaufman & Kaufman, 1983), the Wechsler (1991) Intelligence Scale for Children, and the Wechsler (1981) Adult Intelligence Scale.

Some may regard Piaget's developmental map as more "theory driven" than the maps provided by standardized ability tests. However, a great deal of empirical research by Piaget, his collaborators, and many others contributed to the actual content of his developmental map. The empirical findings also stimulated many conceptual extensions and revisions of Piaget's theory and developmental map. In fact, Piaget argued for a continual interplay between data and concepts in both science and ontogeny. He maintained that

the genetically transmitted aspects of our physical and cognitive equipment shape the ways in which we assimilate input, but also that the development of our genetically transmitted equipment is shaped by the input to which it must accommodate. Researchers must thus be sensitive to the canalizing effects of both their own mental structures and of the structures of the human organisms that they study. Researchers must also be sensitive to the specific phenomena that are to be mapped.

DEVELOPMENTAL MAPPING OF PSYCHOPATHOLOGY

When we turn from mapping physical, linguistic, and cognitive development to the developmental mapping of psychopathology, we must make decisions about the phenomena to be mapped, the conceptual strategies to be employed, and the methodology for operationally defining the phenomena in conceptually useful ways.

A comprehensive understanding of psychopathology from infancy to adulthood requires an understanding of the pervasive developmental changes that occur during that period. Unlike maps of physical, linguistic, and cognitive development, however, psychopathology may not be mappable in terms of developmental progressions that follow the same general course across all humans. Instead, the developmental mapping of psychopathology involves meshing multiple maps that may share certain common developmental reference points but that lead to and from different destinations. For the sake of contrast, mapping one aspect of development, such as cognitive development, is analogous to mapping all the roads from New York City to Boston. There are a great many interconnecting roads, but we can discern routes that will take us from one city to the other.

In the developmental mapping of psychopathology, by contrast, we need to conceptualize numerous possible starting points, way stations, and endpoints, each with a variety of possible interconnecting routes of varying importance. Although physical, linguistic, and cognitive aspects of development provide reference points against which to map psychopathology, most forms of child psychopathology are not coherent, self-evident entities like the cities of New York and Boston. Instead, we are faced with streams of behavior and emotions from which we must derive configurations that may be useful for distinguishing phenomena that are pathologically detrimental to development versus phenomena that are within the normal range of functioning.

In terms of our map metaphor, it is as if we start with a map that shows no cities but only a tangle of roads running in many directions. The roads represent behavioral and emotional pathways. A key task of a developmental approach to taxonomy is to detect coherent configurations of intersecting roads that can help us distinguish normal from developmentally detrimental functioning and also to distinguish among different kinds of detrimental functioning. The end product of developmental taxonomy can be thought of as a map that shows many municipalities, some of which are very distinct and far from one another, such as San Francisco and Detroit. Other municipalities are contiguous and hard to distinguish from one another, such as Minneapolis and St. Paul. Some municipalities may be very small, whereas others are much larger. Over the temporal course of development, certain municipalities may serve as gateways to others. Some of the others may become permanent destinations from which there are few departures, as exemplified by antisocial personality disorders, which seldom seem to remit. To date, efforts at developmentally mapping psychopathology have taken several different directions, as outlined in the following sections.

Psychoanalytic Efforts

The most influential early effort to map the development of psychopathology was via psychoanalytic theory. The initial data base consisted largely of the free associations of adult analytic patients from which Sigmund Freud (1905, 1940) constructed his theory of the stages of psychosexual development. Anna Freud (1965) later applied the theory more directly to children by proposing a Developmental Profile for mapping psychopathology in terms of stages of instinctual drives, defense mechanisms, conflicts, ego differentiation, and personality structure.

The main taxonomic implication of the Developmental Profile was that disorders could be diagnostically classified in terms of instinctual drives, ego and superego development, regressions, fixation points, and conflicts (A. Freud, 1965). Illustrations have been published to show how the Profile might look for a particular child (Yorke, 1980), but no specific assessment procedures nor data have been published. The Developmental Profile has thus remained at the level of a theoretical proposal, with no published research on its reliability, validity, or utility.

Nosological Efforts

Since the late nineteenth century (Kraepelin, 1883), major adult psychopathology has been classified according to categories modeled on classifications of physical diseases. Known as *nosologies,* these classifications of diseases use a variety of conceptual principles and types of data for defining their categories. Some categories are defined primarily by pathogens that are known to cause particular diseases, such as diphtheria and tuberculosis. Other categories are defined in terms of descriptive characteristics of particular conditions, such as types of bone fractures, with the specific causes being of less relevance. Still other categories, such as tumors of unknown etiology, are provisionally defined in terms of descriptive characteristics, pending discovery of etiologies that are then likely to become key defining criteria.

The nosological approach was successful in mapping major domains of adult psychopathology in terms of categories such as schizophrenia, manic–depressive disorders, unipolar affective disorders, anxiety disorders, and character disorders. These categories became the main foci for research, training, communication, and reimbursement relating to adult psychopathology. However, official nosologies provided little differentiation for childhood disorders or for developmental sequences of psychopathology.

The GAP Nosology

Dissatisfied with the neglect of children in the official nosology, the Group for the Advancement of Psychiatry ("GAP," 1966) proposed a nosology for childhood disorders. Intending to incorporate developmental considerations, the GAP included a category of normal responses to stresses that are typical of particular developmental periods. An example was the separation anxiety that 6-month-old babies show whenever their mothers or primary caretakers leave.

Although the GAP nosology was intended to define disorders operationally, no assessment operations were actually specified. Furthermore, some of the categories were defined in terms of psychoanalytic inferences analogous to those required for Anna Freud's (1965) Developmental Profile. Unlike the Developmental Profile, however, the GAP nosology was tested for reliability. In one study, Freeman (1971) found 59 percent agreement (uncorrected for chance) between diagnosticians' applications of a few broad diagnostic categories to case histories. In a second study of diagnoses made from case histories, 40 percent agreement was found for broad diagnostic categories and 23 percent for more specific diagnoses, both uncorrected for chance (Beitchman, Dielman, Landis, Benson, & Kemp, 1978). These findings indicated that the GAP nosology was quite unreliable even when all the diagnosticians were exposed to the same information via case histories.

The DSM Nosology

In the United States, the dominant nosology for psychopathology is the *Diagnostic and Statistical Manual* (DSM) published by the American Psychiatric Association (APA). Until the 1968 edition of the DSM (DSM-II, APA, 1968), the only categories specific to childhood disorders were Adjustment Reaction of Childhood and Schizophrenic

Reaction, Childhood Type. DSM-II added several new categories of childhood disorders, which later underwent major changes in the third edition (DSM-III), the third edition-revised (DSM-III-R), and the fourth edition (DSM-IV; APA, 1980, 1987, 1994).

DSM-III represented a major advance over previous editions of the DSM in that it provided explicit criteria for deciding whether individuals qualified for each diagnosis. The criteria for some categories of major adult disorders, such as schizophrenia, were based on research diagnostic criteria that had been developed by researchers who wanted to discriminate more reliably between different kinds of psychopathology. RDC indeed contributed to making the diagnostic process more testable and reliable. However, agreement among various sets of RDC was mediocre, even for major adult disorders such as schizophrenia (e.g., Overall & Hollister, 1979). Furthermore, no RDC had been developed for the DSM-III's categories of childhood disorders, several of which were introduced for the first time in DSM-III and had no previous history of research or clinical usage. It should therefore not be surprising that the diagnostic reliability of the DSM-III childhood disorders was considerably lower than the reliability of adult disorders, as found in the DSM-III field trials (APA, 1980) and several other studies (Mattison, Cantwell, Russell & Will, 1979; Mezzich, Mezzich, & Coffman, 1985; Strober, Green, & Carlson, 1981; Werry, Methven, Fitzpatrick, & Dixon, 1983).

Regarding developmental mapping, the DSM makes a general distinction between "disorders usually first evident in infancy, childhood, or adolescence," and all other disorders. However, there is little other mapping of nosological categories in relation to development. Furthermore, the criteria for most disorders are identical regardless of the age or other characteristics of the individuals to be classified. Thus, for example, children of all ages and both sexes must meet the same criteria to qualify for a diagnosis of Attention-Deficit Hyperactivity Disorder (ADHD), Conduct Disorder (CD), or Major Depressive Disorder (MDD).

Empirically Based Efforts

The psychoanalytic and nosological efforts both started with conceptual models derived from adult psychopathology. The psychoanalytic model originated with a developmental theory constructed from inferences based on the free associations of adult analytic patients. The nosological model, by contrast, originated with the application of medical disease concepts to the classification of major adult psychopathology, such as schizophrenia and bipolar disorders. Both models were extrapolated downward to children without the benefit of direct taxonomic research on representative samples of children.

In contrast to the psychoanalytic and nosological efforts, empirically based efforts have derived taxonomies of psychopathology from data on actual samples of children. This entails devising standardized procedures for assessing behavioral and emotional problems, applying these procedures to large samples of children, performing statistical analyses to identify sets of co-occurring problems, and deriving taxonomic constructs that can then guide further research, theory, and services. The following sections outline developmental implications of empirical findings at the level of specific problems, variations among data sources, the derivation of syndromes of co-occurring problems, scores on empirically based syndromes, and predictive relations between syndromes assessed at different ages.

Standardized Assessment of Specific Problems

An initial step in empirically based efforts is to apply standardized procedures to the assessment of behavioral and emotional problems in large samples of children. To obtain data that are appropriate for taxonomies of psychopathology, it is important to employ samples of children whose problem rates are high enough to yield well-differentiated patterns of psychopathology. However, it is also important to obtain data on large representative samples of relatively normal children in order to compare the rates of particular problems in normal versus deviant children. If we assess only deviant children, we might erroneously assume that some problems are pathognomonic when they are actually no more common among deviant than normal children. On the other hand, if we assess only normal children, we would not be able to distinguish among patterns of deviance that involve low prevalence problems.

Because the prevalence of particular problems may differ for males versus females as well as for referred versus nonreferred children, the empirically based approach also documents developmental trends separately for each sex. This may reveal differences that argue for sex-specific taxonomic criteria at particular ages, rather than criteria that are identical for both sexes at all ages.

As an example, the graph at the left side of Figure 2.1 shows that, according to parents' reports for a national sample, the percentage of nonreferred boys who tease a lot increases with age, but the percentage of referred and nonreferred girls who tease a lot decreased after age 11. Among referred boys, however, there was a big increase in teasing at ages 8 and 9, when the difference in rates for referred versus nonreferred boys became considerably larger

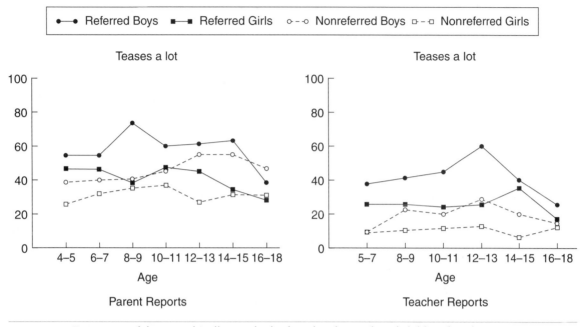

FIGURE 2.1   Percentage of demographically matched referred and nonreferred children for whom parents or teachers endorsed the item "Teases a lot" (from Achenbach, 1991b, 1991c)

than at any other age. By ages 16 to 18, teasing was actually reported for somewhat fewer referred than nonreferred boys.

Variations among Data Sources

Prevalence rates for particular problems may vary not only with the age, sex, and clinical status of the children, but also with the source of data. For example, the graph at the right side of Figure 2.1 shows that teachers reported an especially high peak in teasing by boys at ages 12 and 13, when the biggest difference between referred and nonreferred boys occurred. The factors that affect actual teasing, as well as adults' awareness of it, may differ between the home and school. Different pictures of particular problems may also be obtained from children's self-ratings, clinical interviews, and direct observations in natural settings.

   Meta-analyses of many studies have revealed statistically significant but modest correlations between reports of children's problems obtained from different sources (Achenbach, McConaughy, & Howell, 1987). Although many of the studies supported the reliability and validity of the reports from different sources, the low agreement among sources indicates that no single source can be substituted for all others. Instead, both the cross-situational variance in children's

functioning and the variance associated with informant and method differences inevitably limit the degree of agreement that can be attained. Because different sources may validly contribute important, yet different, assessment data, the empirically based approach employs data from multiple sources both in deriving taxonomic constructs and in assessing individual children. Although this complicates taxonomic and assessment tasks, it broadens the data base and avoids the distortions that may arise from any single source, any single method, or a fixed criterion that is uniformly applied to all sources of data.

Derivation of Syndromes

The metaphor of a map was used earlier to illuminate a key task of developmental taxonomy. Like a map displaying a tangle of roads with no cities, data on individual behavioral and emotional problems would become much more useful if we could parse the undifferentiated tangle into coherent configurations.

   The task of detecting configurations of behavioral and emotional problems has been addressed by performing factor analyses and principal components analyses of the correlations among scores on large sets of problem items (e.g.,

Achenbach, 1966; Goyette, Conners, & Ulrich, 1978; Miller, 1967; Quay, 1964). Although the rating instruments, items, informants, samples, and specific analytic methods differed among these studies, there was considerable convergence among the sets of co-occurring problems that were found (reviewed by Achenbach, 1985, and Quay, 1986). These sets of co-occurring problems can be viewed as syndromes in the sense of "a set of concurrent things" (Gove 1971, p. 2320), without any assumptions about why particular problems tend to co-occur. The reasons for the co-occurrence of particular problems may range from genetic to environmental influences and various combinations of determinants.

Following the "first generation" exploratory studies, a "second generation" study was done to test syndromes hypothesized on the basis of the first generation findings (Achenbach, Conners, Quay, Verhulst, & Howell, 1989). In this second generation study, a lengthy rating instrument—the ACQ Behavior Checklist—was completed by parents of 4,481 children referred to eighteen mental health services distributed throughout the United States. The ACQ was specifically designed to test replication of syndromes hypothesized from the first generation studies. Data were also obtained on the Child Behavior Checklist (CBCL; Achenbach, 1991b) for 2,300 American children and 1,913 Dutch children referred for mental health services. Several of the hypothesized syndromes were replicated in both the ACQ and CBCL analyses for both sexes in multiple age ranges. Other syndromes were replicated for only one sex or limited ages.

The second generation study of parents' ratings supported several syndromes that had been identified in varying forms by previous first generation exploratory studies. To derive taxonomic constructs that reflect the perspectives of multiple informants, a "third generation" effort was undertaken (Achenbach, 1991a). Problem scores were obtained for large samples of referred children via the CBCL, the Teacher's Report Form (TRF; Achenbach, 1991c), and the Youth Self-Report (YSR; Achenbach, 1991d). These instruments have 89 parallel problem items, plus items that are specific to each type of informant. Separate principal components/varimax analyses of each sex within particular age ranges were used to identify syndromes that were similar for both sexes and different ages on each instrument. The syndromes thus identified from the individual instruments were compared to identify those that had counterparts across at least two of the three instruments (CBCL, TRF, YSR). Problem items that were included in versions of a syndrome for at least two of the three instruments were used to form a *cross-informant syndrome construct.* That is, the common items were used to represent a *hypothetical construct* (or, in statistical terms, a *latent variable*) inferred to underlie the sets of items found to co-occur in parent, teacher, and self-ratings.

As an example, a syndrome designated as Aggressive Behavior was identified in parent, teacher, and self-ratings of both sexes within all age ranges. On all three instruments, the Aggressive Behavior syndrome included items such as Argues a lot; Gets in many fights; Physically attacks people; and Threatens people. However, on the version derived from teachers' ratings, it also included several items that were specific to the TRF, such as Defiant, talks back to staff; Disturbs other pupils; and Disrupts class discipline.

Syndrome Scale Scores

The scales that are used to score children for each syndrome construct include the items specific to each instrument, in addition to the items that define the construct across all three instruments. For example, the TRF scale for scoring the Aggressive Behavior syndrome includes Defiant, talks back to staff, Disturbs other pupils, and Disrupts class discipline, even though these items are not rated by parents on the CBCL or by youths on the YSR.

The operational definitions of the syndromes thus differ somewhat among raters in terms of some variations in the specific items and also in terms of item wording (e.g., first person on the YSR, third person on the CBCL and TRF). In addition, there are differences in the raters' perspectives and in the contexts in which they know the subjects' behavior. To take account of these differences, as well as differences associated with the age and sex of the subjects, norms for the syndrome scales have been derived separately for each type of informant rating children of each sex within particular age ranges. The norms provide T scores that enable users to compare a subject's score on a particular syndrome with the scores of a national sample of nonreferred peers of the same age range and sex, as rated by the same type of informant. Even though parents and teachers may tend to score particular classes of subjects (e.g., adolescent boys) differently on the average, the informant-specific norms enable users to determine whether particular parents and teachers agree in scoring the same subjects in the normal, borderline, or clinical range.

Figure 2.2 depicts mean raw scores for the Aggressive Behavior syndrome obtained from parents' CBCL ratings (left graph) and teachers' TRF ratings (right graph). As the graphs indicate, teachers' ratings showed larger differences between boys and girls in both nonreferred normative samples (open circles and squares) and clinically referred samples (filled circles and squares) than did parents' ratings. However, because boys are compared with separate norms for each type of rater, the teachers' general tendency to report proportionally more aggressive behavior for boys does not affect decisions about how aggressive a particular boy is in terms of ratings by his parents versus his teachers.

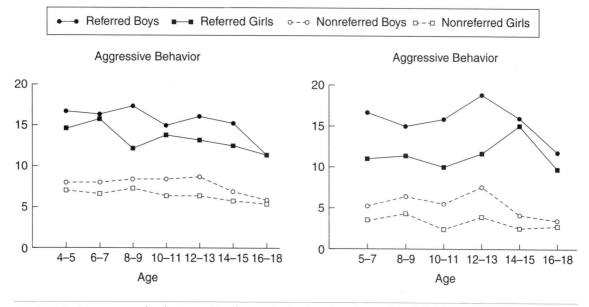

FIGURE 2.2 Mean scores for demographically matched referred and nonreferred children on the Aggressive Behavior syndrome scale scored from parent and teacher ratings (from Achenbach, 1991b, 1991c)

Predictive Relations between Syndromes

Our map metaphor was used to make the point that a primary task of taxonomy is to identify coherent configurations on which research, theory, and services can focus. The empirically based approach has done this by deriving syndromes through factor analysis and principal component analysis of the correlations among problem items rated by different types of informants.

Longitudinal research is necessary when we wish to move from the cross-sectional mapping of configurations to mapping developmental relations between configurations. The empirically based approach has generated a variety of research on the ability of syndrome scores to predict developmentally later variables, such as suicidal behavior, referral for mental health and special education services, substance abuse, trouble with the law, and long-term outcomes of mental health services (Achenbach, Howell, McConaughy, & Stanger, 1995b; Stanger, Achenbach, & McConaughy, 1993; Stanger, MacDonald, McConaughy, & Achenbach, 1995; Verhulst, Koot, & van der Ende, 1994).

The empirically based approach also facilitates research on developmental relations between the syndromes themselves. This has been done by testing the prediction of developmentally later syndrome scores from earlier syndrome scores (Achenbach, Howell, McConaughy, & Stanger, 1995a). Because syndrome scores may not be the only rele-

vant predictors, many other child, family, and intervening variables, such as stressful experiences, have been tested in the predictive models. In addition, the outcome syndromes have included some that have been identified for young adults which differ from those that have been identified for children and adolescents (Achenbach, Howell, McConaughy, & Stanger, 1995c). The inclusion of multiple early syndromes as candidate predictors of multiple later syndromes enables us to identify patterns of problems that remain relatively stable across development versus patterns that change across development. Patterns that remain stable are called *homotypic,* whereas those that develop into other patterns are called *heterotypic* (Kagan, 1969).

As an example, the previously described methodology for deriving syndromes for children also has been applied to parent and self-ratings of young adults on the Young Adult Behavior Checklist (YABCL) and the Young Adult Self-Report (YASR; Achenbach, 1997). Some of the syndromes found for young adults are quite similar to those found for children and adolescents. These include syndromes designated as Anxious/Depressed, Withdrawn, Somatic Complaints, and Delinquent Behavior. In addition, a young adult syndrome designated as Aggressive Behavior comprises many of the same behaviors that are included in the pre-adult Aggressive Behavior syndrome, such as Argues a lot; Gets in many fights; Physically attacks people; and Threatens people. However, an additional syndrome found for adults comprises another set of behaviors that are included in the pre-adult Aggressive Behavior syndrome but not in the young adult Aggressive Behavior syndrome. Designated originally as "Shows Off" (now called "Intrusive"), the adult syndrome includes items such as Showing off (the highest loading item); Bragging; Demands attention; Talks too much; Teases a lot; and Unusually loud. It thus appears that these obnoxious but not overtly aggressive behaviors become separated from overtly aggressive behaviors in young adulthood. In fact, path analyses have shown that adolescent scores on the Aggressive Behavior syndrome are strong predictors of the young adult Shows Off syndrome.

Figure 2.3 depicts the significant predictive paths for the young adult Shows Off and Aggressive Behavior syndromes that were obtained in a national sample that was assessed in 1986, 1989, and 1992. The candidate predictors from 1986 and 1989 included scores on eight empirically based syndromes, family variables such as socioeconomic status, marital status of the subjects' parents, mental health services received by family members, the number of related and unrelated adults in the home, and stressful experiences that affected the subjects between the 1986 and 1989 assessments and between the 1989 and 1992 assessments.

To detect possible sex differences, the actual distributions of scores on each syndrome were computed separately for each sex. Thus, rather than using a single fixed cutpoint for defining deviance in both males and females, as done in the DSM, scores for males were compared with scores for other males, and likewise for females. Consequently, the significant predictive paths could capture developmental relations among particular syndromes from one age to another for each sex, even though the absolute magnitude of the syndrome scores might differ for males versus females.

As Figure 2.3 shows, 1989 scores on the Aggressive Behavior syndrome were strong and specific predictors of both the Aggressive Behavior and Shows Off syndrome among young adults of both sexes. In fact, the 1989 Aggressive Behavior syndrome was the only significant predictor of the Shows Off syndrome among males, accounting for 30 percent of the variance in 1992 scores for Shows Off, a large effect by Cohen's (1988) standards for regression analyses. The predictive relations were more complex for the adult Aggressive Behavior syndrome among males and for both adult syndromes among females, although the adolescent Aggressive Behavior syndrome was the strongest predictor for both syndromes in both sexes. These results indicate a form of heterotopy in the developmental course of the Aggressive Behavior syndrome. That is, some aggressive adolescents remain overtly aggressive in young adulthood, whereas others become less aggressive but remain socially obnoxious.

A form of heterotypy was also found in the adult outcome of the child/adolescent Attention Problems syndrome. Among young adults, the cross-sectional taxonomic analyses yielded a syndrome designated as Irresponsible (now designated as "Attention Problems"; Achenbach, 1997), which included many problems of the child/adolescent Attention Problems syndrome. Unlike the child/adolescent Attention Problems syndrome, however, the Irresponsible syndrome did not include items indicative of overactivity but it did include Irresponsible behavior (the highest loading item); Fails to finish things; Lacks initiative; Has trouble making decisions; and Too dependent. The strongest predictor of adult scores on the Irresponsible syndrome were pre-adult scores on the Attention Problems syndrome (Achenbach et al., 1995c). The Irresponsible syndrome thus appears to be a heterotypic adult successor of the Attention Problems syndrome.

In path analyses done separately for males and females, it was found that the pre-adult Attention Problems syndrome accounted for more variance in the adult Irresponsible syndrome among females than males (16% vs. 6%). This was consistent with the finding that more variance in adolescent Attention Problems was accounted for by childhood Attention Problems scores among females than males (21% vs. 13%). In addition, early scores on the Attention Problems syndrome predicted a greater variety of later problems among females than males in both adolescence and young adulthood (Achenbach et al., 1995a, c).

Even though many fewer females than males meet DSM criteria for ADHD, the empirically based approach suggests that females who score higher than other females on the empirically based Attention Problems syndrome are at high risk for a variety of problems in subsequent developmental periods. Studies that have deliberately sought out females with attention problems have also found high rates of other kinds of dysfunction (Biederman et al., 1994; Ernst et al., 1994).

Accelerated Longitudinal Analyses

The quantitative scores on an empirically based syndrome measure a child's standing on that syndrome relative to the standing of peers of the same age and sex. Because children can be repeatedly scored via the same procedures at successive ages, the developmental course of syndrome scores can be analyzed both within and between cohorts. This opens the door to using accelerated longitudinal strategies for the developmental study of taxonomy.

Accelerated longitudinal strategies have long been discussed by developmentalists as means for using data from relatively short-term longitudinal assessments to study

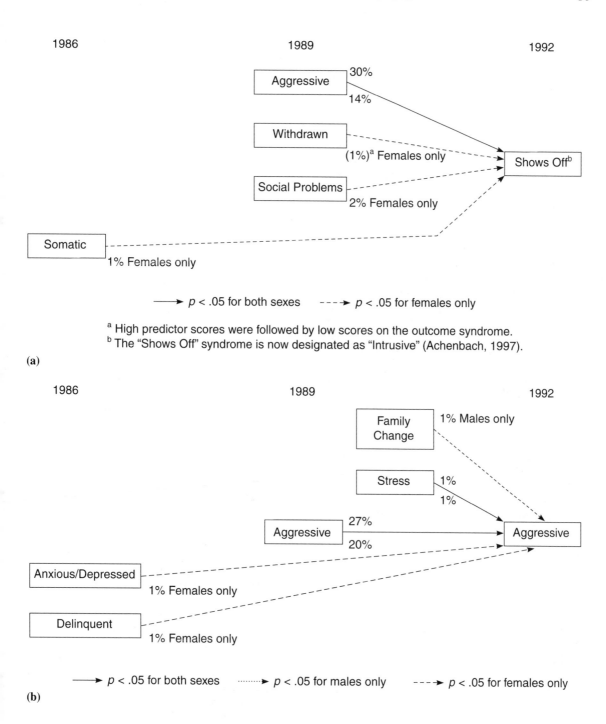

FIGURE 2.3   Direct predictive paths that were significant ($p < .05$) in ≥ 2 out of 3 combinations of parent, self, and combined parent/self ratings on syndromes in a national sample assessed at ages 13–16 (1986), 16–19 (1989), and 19–22 (1992) (Figure for the Aggressive syndrome is from Achenbach et al., 1995c.)

longer periods of development (e.g., Bell, 1953). These strategies involve assessing multiple birth cohorts via the same standardized procedures on several occasions. Individual subjects from a younger birth cohort are then selected for matching to subjects from an older birth cohort on the basis of their similarities in scores on the assessment procedures and in demographic characteristics. The aim is to link similar individuals from different birth cohorts so that the outcome scores obtained by individuals in the older cohorts can be used to estimate the scores that would have been obtained by their matched partners from younger cohorts, if the younger partners had been studied long enough to reach those outcome ages.

As an example, suppose that one birth cohort was assessed at ages 4, 6, 8, 10, and 12 years. A second cohort, 2 years older than the first, was assessed in the same years, but at ages 6, 8, 10, 12, and 14. Subjects who were age 4 when first assessed would then be individually matched on the basis of their age 6 scores to subjects in the older cohort on the basis of *their* age 6 scores and demographic characteristics. If the accelerated longitudinal strategy works, it should be possible to use the scores obtained by the older subjects at age 14 to estimate the scores that would have been obtained by their matched partners from the younger cohort, if the younger cohort had actually been assessed at age 14.

In what are perhaps the first applications of this strategy to the developmental study of psychopathology, CBCL scores were analyzed from seven birth cohorts of Dutch children who were assessed at five two-year intervals (Stanger, Achenbach, & Verhulst, 1994, 1997). The seven cohorts of children ranged from ages 4 to 10 at the first assessment and 12 to 18 at the final assessment. The findings revealed that CBCL scores initially obtained by younger cohorts correlated with scores obtained years later by their matched older partners about as well as the younger subjects' scores correlated with their own later scores. This was true for all three scales that were analyzed, including scales for total problems and for syndromes designated as Aggressive Behavior and Delinquent Behavior.

To answer a specific question of developmental taxonomy, the longitudinal correlations of scores on the Aggressive Behavior syndrome were compared with those on the Delinquent Behavior syndrome, which comprises such problems as lying or cheating, stealing, and truancy. Both the within-cohort correlations (i.e., correlations between subjects' early scores and their own later scores) and the between-cohort correlations (i.e., correlations between subjects' early scores and their matched partners' later scores) were significantly higher over all measurement intervals for the Aggressive syndrome than for the Delinquent syndrome.

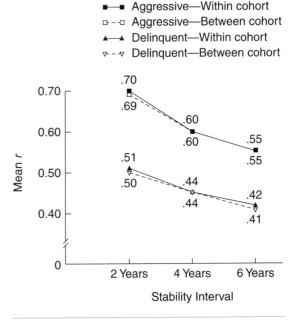

FIGURE 2.4 Mean predictive correlations computed within cohorts (same subject at each assessment) and between cohorts (different subject from first to later assessment) in accelerated longitudinal analyses of a Dutch general population sample scored on the Child Behavior Checklist (data from Stanger, Achenbach, & Verhulst, 1997)

As illustrated in Figure 2.4, the within-cohort and between-cohort correlations for Aggressive Behavior ranged from about .70 over 2-year intervals down to .55 over 6-year intervals. The corresponding correlations for Delinquent Behavior ranged from about .51 over 2-year intervals to about .42 over 6-year intervals. Both kinds of behavior are included in the DSM-IV criteria for Conduct Disorder, but Aggressive Behavior is considerably more stable over multiple developmental periods than is delinquent behavior. Other research has also revealed higher heritability and stronger biological correlates for the Aggressive Behavior syndrome than the Delinquent Behavior syndrome (e.g., Birmaher et al., 1990; Edelbrock, Rende, Plomin, & Thompson, 1995; Gabel, Stadler, Bjorn, & Shindledecker, 1993; van den Oord, Boomsma, & Verhulst, 1995). Collectively, these findings indicate that Aggressive Behavior and Delinquent Behavior are worth separating into different taxonomic constructs that are apt to have different determinants, developmental courses, and responsiveness to various treatments.

SUMMARY AND CONCLUSIONS

Effective treatment of children requires a clear picture of what is to be treated. To obtain a clear picture of what is to be treated, we need to distinguish the normal range of functioning from problems that will impair adaptive development. To tailor treatments effectively to the needs of individual children and their families, we must distinguish among different patterns of problems in ways that enable us to apply knowledge gained from previous cases to new cases that manifest similar patterns. These are tasks for taxonomy, that is, systems for grouping individuals and problems on the basis of their distinguishing features.

Constructing taxonomic systems for childhood disorders is greatly complicated by the rapid developmental changes in behavior, emotions, cognition, physique, and social status that occur from infancy to adulthood. Behavior that may be within the normal range at one age may be maladaptively deviant at other ages. Some problems may be homotypic across long periods of development, whereas others are heterotypic, that is, they undergo phenotypic changes from one developmental period to another.

Patterns of problems and their intensity may vary not only across development but also across situations and interaction partners, such as parents, teachers, siblings, and peers. This further complicates the task of developing useful foci for treatment and research. Because behaviors and emotions change so much, psychopathology cannot be understood in terms of static snapshots. Instead, we need assessment procedures and taxonomic constructs that aggregate data across situations, times, sources of data, and developmental periods.

Some aspects of normal development, including physical, linguistic, and cognitive development, have been well mapped. The developmental mapping of psychopathology, however, presents special challenges that can be visualized in terms of a map of crosscutting roads, with no nodal entities such as cities. A key task of a developmental approach to taxonomy is therefore to detect coherent configurations that can help us distinguish normal from developmentally detrimental functioning and also to distinguish among different kinds of detrimental functioning.

Psychoanalytic efforts to map the development of psychopathology have been applied to children in terms of Anna Freud's (1965) Developmental Profile. The Profile consists of an outline for classifying disorders according to inferences about instinctual drives, ego and superego development, regressions, fixation points, and conflicts. Except for case illustrations, the Profile has remained at the level of a theoretical proposal that lacks data to support its reliability, validity, and utility.

Nosological efforts to map the development of psychopathology have included a proposal by the Group for the Advancement of Psychiatry (GAP, 1966) that drew heavily on psychoanalytic inferences, but that also was subjected to tests of reliability. The GAP nosology emphasized the importance of distinguishing normal responses to stress from pathological conditions, but its reliability was found to be mediocre.

The DSM-III (APA, 1980) introduced numerous diagnostic categories designated as "disorders usually first evident in infancy, childhood, or adolescence." These disorders were defined in terms of explicit criteria modeled on research diagnostic criteria that had been developed for adult disorders. Because the criteria for most of these disorders are identical for all ages and both sexes, they fail to allow for possible developmental variations in the prevalence, patterning, and pathognomicity of particular problems.

Empirically based efforts have derived taxonomies from data on actual samples of children. These efforts employ standardized assessment of problems, multivariate statistical analyses to derive syndromes of co-occurring problems, formation of taxonomic constructs on the basis of syndrome patterns derived from multiple sources, and norming of syndrome scales via large representative samples.

Applications of the empirically based approach to young adult problems have yielded some syndromes that are similar to those found in the pre-adult years and some that are different. Longitudinal studies have revealed predictive relations from pre-adult to adult syndromes that are as strong as the predictive relations found in childhood and adolescence. Some of the predictive relations are homotypic, whereas others are heterotypic. The pre-adult Aggressive Behavior syndrome strongly predicted an adult version of the Aggressive Behavior syndrome. In addition, the pre-adult Aggressive Behavior syndrome also predicted an adult syndrome designated as Shows Off (now called "Intrusive"), which comprises obnoxious but not overtly aggressive behavior. Analogously, the pre-adult Attention Problems syndrome predicted a young adult syndrome designated as Irresponsible (now called "Attention Problems"), which includes attention problems and a variety of feckless behaviors. But it does not include the overactivity that is in the pre-adult syndrome and in diagnostic criteria for ADHD, which is strongly associated with the Attention Problems syndrome in childhood (Chen, Faraone, Biederman, & Tsuang, 1994).

The quantitative scoring of empirically based syndromes facilitates accelerated longitudinal analyses of the developmental course of psychopathology. These analyses have revealed differences between the developmental stability of overtly aggressive versus more covertly delinquent behaviors that argue for a taxonomic distinction between them, rather than combining them, as is done in the DSM criteria for conduct disorder.

Developmental research on taxonomy and other aspects of psychopathology has increased markedly in recent years. However, much remains to be learned about how to improve treatment in relation to both normal and abnormal development.

REFERENCES

Achenbach, T. M. (1966). The classification of children's psychiatric symptoms: A factor-analytic study. *Psychological Monographs, 80*(No. 615).

Achenbach, T. M. (1985). *Assessment and taxonomy of child and adolescent psychopathology.* Newbury Park, CA: Sage.

Achenbach, T. M. (1991a). *Integrative guide for the 1991 CBCL/4-18, YSR, and TRF profiles.* Burlington: University of Vermont Department of Psychiatry.

Achenbach, T. M. (1991b). *Manual for the Child Behavior Checklist/4-18 and 1991 Profile.* Burlington: University of Vermont Department of Psychiatry.

Achenbach, T. M. (1991c). *Manual for the Teacher's Report Form and 1991 Profile.* Burlington: University of Vermont Department of Psychiatry.

Achenbach, T. M. (1991d). *Manual for the Youth Self-Report and 1991 Profile.* Burlington: University of Vermont Department of Psychiatry.

Achenbach, T. M. (1997). *Manual for the Young Adult Self-Report and Young Adult Behavior Checklist.* Burlington: University of Vermont Department of Psychiatry.

Achenbach, T. M., Conners, C. K., Quay, H. C., Verhulst, F. C., & Howell, C. T. (1989). Replication of empirically derived syndromes as a basis for taxonomy of child/adolescent psychopathology. *Journal of Abnormal Child Psychology, 17,* 299–323.

Achenbach, T. M., Howell, C. T., McConaughy, S. H., & Stanger, C. (1995a). Six-year predictors of problems in a national sample of children and youth: I. Cross-informant syndromes. *Journal of the American Academy of Child and Adolescent Psychiatry, 34,* 336–347.

Achenbach, T. M., Howell, C. T., McConaughy, S. H., & Stanger, C. (1995b). Six-year predictors of problems in a national sample of children and youth: II. Signs of disturbance. *Journal of the American Academy of Child and Adolescent Psychiatry, 34,* 488–498.

Achenbach, T. M., Howell, C. T., McConaughy, S. H., & Stanger, C. (1995c). Six-year predictors of problems in a national sample: III. Transitions to young adult syndromes. *Journal of the American Academy of Child and Adolescent Psychiatry, 34,* 658–669.

Achenbach, T. M., McConaughy, S. H., & Howell, C. T. (1987). Child/adolescent behavioral and emotional problems: Implications of cross-informant correlations for situational specificity. *Psychological Bulletin, 101,* 213–232.

American Psychiatric Association. (1952, 1968, 1980, 1987, 1994). *Diagnostic and statistical manual of mental disorders* (1st ed., 2nd ed., 3rd ed., 3rd rev. ed., 4th ed.). Washington, DC: Author.

Bayley, N. (1993). *Bayley Scales of Infant Development* (2nd ed.). New York: Psychological Corporation.

Beitchman, J. H., Dielman, T. E., Landis, J. R., Benson, R. M., & Kemp, P. L. (1978). Reliability of the Group for the Advancement of Psychiatry diagnostic categories in child psychiatry. *Archives of General Psychiatry, 35,* 1461–1466.

Bell, R. Q. (1953). Convergence: An accelerated longitudinal approach. *Child Development, 24,* 145–152.

Biederman, J., Faraone, S. V., Spencer, T., Wilens, T., Mick, E., & Ley, K. A. (1994). Gender differences in a sample of adults with Attention Deficit Hyperactivity Disorder. *Psychiatry Research, 53,* 13–29.

Birmaher, B., Stanley, M., Greenhill, L., Twomey, J., Gavrilescu, A., & Rabinovich, H. (1990). Platelet imipramine binding in children and adolescents with impulsive behavior. *Journal of the American Academy of Child and Adolescent Psychiatry, 29,* 914–918.

Chen, W. J., Faraone, S. V., Biederman, J., & Tsuang, M. T. (1994). Diagnostic accuracy of the Child Behavior Checklist scales for Attention-Deficit Hyperactivity Disorder: A receiver-operating characteristic analysis. *Journal of Consulting and Clinical Psychology, 62,* 1017–1025.

Cohen, J. (1988). *Statistical power analysis for the behavioral sciences* (2nd ed.). New York: Academic Press.

Edelbrock, C., Rende, R., Plomin, R., & Thompson, L. A. (1995). A twin study of competence and problem behavior in childhood and early adolescence. *Journal of Child Psychology and Psychiatry, 5,* 775–785.

Ernst, M., Liebenauer, L. L., King, A. C., Fitzgerald, G. A., Cohen, R. M., & Zametkin, A. J. (1994). Reduced brain metabolism in hyperactive girls. *Journal of the American Academy of Child and Adolescent Psychiatry, 33,* 858–868.

Freeman, M. (1971). A reliability study of psychiatric diagnosis in childhood and adolescence. *Journal of Child Psychology and Psychiatry, 12,* 43–54.

Freud, A. (1965). *Normality and pathology in childhood.* New York: International Universities Press.

Freud, S. (1940). *An outline of psychoanalysis.* New York: W. W. Norton.

Freud, S. (1905/1953). Three essays on the theory of sexuality. In *Standard edition of the complete psychological works of Sigmund Freud* (Vol. 7). London: Hogarth Press.

Gabel, S., Stadler, J., Bjorn, J., & Shindledecker, R. (1993). Dopamine-beta-hydroxylase in behaviorally disturbed youth. Relationship between teacher and parent ratings. *Biological Psychiatry, 34,* 434–442.

Gleason, J. B. (Ed.). (1993). *The development of language* (3rd ed.). New York: Macmillan.

Gove, P. (Ed.). (1971). *Webster's third new international dictionary of the English language.* Springfield, MA: Merriam.

Goyette, C. H., Conners, C. K., & Ulrich, R. F. (1978). Normative data on revised Conners Parent and Teacher Rating Scales. *Journal of Abnormal Child Psychology, 6,* 221–236.

Group for the Advancement of Psychiatry. (1966). *Psychopathological disorders in childhood: Theoretical considerations and a proposed classification.* GAP Report No. 62.

Kagan, J. (1969). The three faces of continuity in human development. In D. A. Goslin (Ed.), *Handbook of socialization theory and research* (pp. 983–1002). Chicago: Rand McNally.

Kaufman, A. S., & Kaufman, N. L. (1983). *Kaufman Assessment Battery for Children.* Circle Pines, MN: American Guidance Service.

Kraepelin, E. (1883). *Compendium der Psychiatrie* (1st ed.). Leipzig, Germany: Abel.

Mattison, R., Cantwell, D. P., Russell, A. T., & Will, L. (1979). A comparison of DSM-II and DSM-III in the diagnosis of childhood psychiatric disorders. *Archives of General Psychiatry, 36,* 1217–1222.

McCarthy, D. (1972). *McCarthy Scales of Children's Abilities.* New York: Psychological Corporation.

Mezzich, A. C., Mezzich, J. E., & Coffman, G. A. (1985). Reliability of DSM-III vs. DSM-II in child psychopathology. *Journal of the American Academy of Child Psychiatry, 24,* 273–280.

Overall, J. E., & Hollister, L. E. (1979). Comparative evaluation of research diagnostic criteria for schizophrenia. *Archives of General Psychiatry, 36,* 1198–1205.

Piaget, J. (1983). Piaget's theory. In W. Kessen (Ed.) & P. H. Mussen (Series Ed.), *Handbook of child psychology: Vol. 1. History, theory, and methods* (4th ed., pp. 103–128). New York: Wiley.

Quay, H. C. (1964). Personality dimensions in delinquent males as inferred from the factor analysis of behavior ratings. *Journal of Research in Crime and Delinquency, 1,* 33–37.

Quay, H. C. (1986). Classification. In H. C. Quay & J. S. Werry (Eds.), *Psychopathological disorders of childhood* (3rd ed., pp. 1–42). New York: Wiley.

Siegler, R. S. (1991). *Children's thinking* (2nd ed.). Englewood Cliffs, NJ: Prentice Hall.

Stanger, C., Achenbach, T. M., & McConaughy, S. H. (1993). Three-year course of behavioral/emotional problems in a national sample of 4- to 16-year-olds: 3. Predictors of signs of disturbance. *Journal of Consulting and Clinical Psychology, 61,* 839–848.

Stanger, C., Achenbach, T. M., & Verhulst, F. C. (1994). Accelerating longitudinal research on child psychopathology: A practical example. *Psychological Assessment, 6,* 102–107.

Stanger, C., Achenbach, T. M., & Verhulst, F. C. (1997). Accelerated longitudinal comparisons of aggressive versus delinquent syndromes. *Development and Psychopathology, 9,* 43–58.

Strober, M., Green, J., & Carlson, G. (1981). The reliability of psychiatric diagnosis in hospitalized adolescents: Interater agreement using the DSM-III. *Archives of General Psychiatry, 38,* 141–145.

Van den Oord, E. J., Boomsma, D. I., & Verhulst, F. C. (1994). A study of problem behaviors in 10- to 15-year-old biologically related and unrelated international adoptees. *Behavioral Genetics, 24,* 193–205.

Verhulst, F. C., Koot, H. M., & van der Ende, J. (1994). Differential predictive value of parents' and teachers' reports of children's problem behaviors: A longitudinal study. *Journal of Abnormal Child Psychology, 22,* 531–546.

Wechsler, D. C. (1981). *Wechsler Adult Intelligence Scale—Revised.* New York: Psychological Corporation.

Wechsler, D. C. (1991). *Wechsler Intelligence Scale for Children—Third edition.* San Antonio, TX: Psychological Corporation.

Werry, J. S., Methven, R. J., Fitzpatrick, J., & Dixon, H. (1983). The interrater reliability of DSM-III in children. *Journal of Abnormal Child Psychology, 11,* 341–354.

Yorke, C. (1980). The contributions of the Diagnostic Profile and the assessment of developmental lines to child psychiatry. *Psychiatric Clinics of North America, 3,* 593–603.

CHAPTER 3

DEVELOPMENTAL ASSESSMENT

James H. Johnson
Lisa B. Sheeber

Developmental assessment is best characterized as a process through which relevant clinical information is obtained to provide answers to developmentally related questions. The focus of assessment may be on determining the presence or absence of specific developmentally related difficulties, on determining the precise nature and the severity of those difficulties that are found, on delineating factors that have contributed to and/or maintain such problems, and on obtaining information relevant to the development of appropriate intervention strategies.

Considering this very general characterization, it should be obvious that developmental assessment is a complex and multifaceted endeavor that can have different foci and involve an assessment of the child's functioning at different levels, in multiple areas, and from multiple perspectives. Thus, in some instances, assessment may simply involve screening to determine whether the child is functioning normally or shows evidence of developmental delay or the presence of emotional or behavioral problems. In other instances, assessment may be designed to provide a detailed and in-depth assessment of the child's functioning in some specific area (e.g., cognitive development) or across multiple areas. In still other instances, the focus may be on documenting changes over time, as in the case of a child undergoing treatment for a brain tumor who is assessed on multiple occasions to determine whether changes in functioning have resulted from radiation therapy. Repeated assessments can likewise be of value in tracking gains that may be made by developmentally delayed children involved in ongoing intervention programs.

Although the term *developmental assessment* is probably most commonly associated with the assessment of younger children and the assessment of variables such as the child's level of cognitive, motor, language, and social development, the term also can apply to the assessment of older children and adolescents and to the assessment of behavioral and emotional problems, if assessment findings are considered in light of ongoing developmental processes. Considering relevant personality characteristics and child psychopathology within the context of developmental assessment is clearly pertinent because psychological problems of childhood often occur secondary to developmental difficulties, and the presence of certain forms of child psychopathology may contribute to or otherwise be correlated with delayed developmental progression.

Portions of the present chapter draw on a previous discussion of issues in developmental assessment by Johnson and Goldman (1993).

The importance of considering developmental factors in the assessment of child psychopathology was suggested by Wenar (1982) who argued cogently that all child psychopathology should be viewed as "normal development gone awry" (p. 198). From this perspective, child behaviors are considered pathological only if they represent a departure from normal developmental processes.

Wenar cited a number of developmental criteria that can be used in judging whether behaviors are normal or pathological. Two of these relate to whether the behavior in question represents fixations or regressions in behavior. Here, fixations refer to behaviors that continue beyond the age where they are considered developmentally appropriate. Wetting the bed, for example, might be considered quite normal for a 3 year old but abnormal for a child of 7. Regression refers to a child having initially achieved an appropriate level of development in some area, only to revert back to behaviors characteristic of an earlier age. Staying with the problem of bedwetting, the child who was toilet trained at age 4, but starts wetting the bed again at age 6, would be seen as having regressed and as displaying evidence of psychopathology.

Psychopathology also may be suggested by the failure of the child to display behaviors that are expected at a given age. Not displaying communicative speech at age 3 or 4 would be an example. Likewise, deviant development might be suggested by an exaggeration of otherwise normal behaviors. Mild fears and aggressive behaviors are quite common in young normal children and in this mild form are not usually viewed as deviant. On the other hand, extreme fears and violent displays of aggression would be seen as pathological because the exaggerated nature of these responses are inconsistent with what is expected developmentally. Sometimes, on rare occasions, a child's behavior may be judged abnormal because it is qualitatively different from behavior normally seen at any developmental level. Here, Wenar cited, as examples, the failure of certain children to engage in exploratory behaviors and the negative response of some children to environmental stimulation. Such responses are to be contrasted with the tendency of normal children to engage in environmental exploration and to seek out sources of stimulation. With knowledge of normal child development, including information concerning the frequency of occurrence of various child behaviors at various age levels, it should be possible to use developmentally based criteria to make reasonable judgments regarding the degree to which child behaviors are normal or deviant in nature.

Considering the very general definition of developmental assessment presented here, it could be argued that *all* assessment approaches with children and adolescents are (or should be) developmental assessments, because all aspects of the child's functioning can be influenced by, and should be viewed within, the context of ongoing developmental processes. The nature of developmental assessment is defined not so much in terms of whether the focus is on cognitive development, motor development, or on the behavioral and emotional problems of children, but rather in terms of the degree to which developmental factors are taken into account in the choice of assessment procedures, the range of variables assessed, in the conceptualization of assessment findings, and in designing intervention strategies based on assessment data.

In this chapter we attempt to highlight those issues that are of relevance for clinicians involved in the developmental assessment of children. Although page limitations preclude an in-depth coverage of specific assessment methods, an attempt is made to provide the reader with a general conceptual framework for assessment and with at least an overview of more well-known measures and approaches that have been found useful in working with children and adolescents from a developmental perspective.

CONCEPTUAL ISSUES
IN DEVELOPMENTAL ASSESSMENT

Obtaining assessment data through the use of even the most well-developed test instruments is likely to be of little value unless the assessment data are processed in a manner that leads the clinician to a reasonably accurate view of the patient's strengths, difficulties, and an understanding of the patient's problem areas. Thus, the conceptual activities of the clinician are central to the assessment process. Indeed, it is the clinician's ability to see meaningful consistencies in the data derived from multiple sources and methods, to resolve and accurately explain contradictory findings, and to integrate assessment findings in a way that allows for a meaningful description of the patient and his or her difficulties that separates the clinician from the technician. Given this situation, it would seem useful at this point to comment, at least briefly, on a general framework that can help the clinician approach the often difficult process of dealing with the complexities inherent in the data derived from developmental assessment.

A Scientist–Practitioner Approach to Assessment

For many years clinical psychologists have been trained in a manner consistent with the scientist–practitioner model (Shakow, 1969). Within this model, training emphasizes developing knowledge of basic psychological principles and of scientific methodology while, at the same time, fostering the development of those clinical skills necessary for the psychologist to function in the applied clinical arena.

Although advocates of scientist–practitioner training often highlight the need to train psychologists who can engage in both research and applied clinical activities, providing training for these dual professional roles is only one aspect of the scientist–practitioner model. It also perhaps is not the most important aspect of the model. Indeed, it might be argued that the essence of training in the scientist–practitioner model is the fostering of a scientific hypothesis–testing approach to clinical work that can be applied at the level of the individual clinical case. Such an approach has much to offer the clinician involved in the developmental assessment of children. The focus of this model is on generating clinical hypotheses that guide the process of assessment and that lead to a reliable, valid, and clinically relevant portrayal of the child's current level of functioning with implications for intervention.

Processing Assessment Findings: A Hypothesis-Generation/ Hypothesis-Testing Approach

The scientist–practitioner approach to assessment begins with developing initial hypotheses that are supported, rejected, revised, or expanded in light of new bits of data that accumulate throughout the evaluation. The development of clinical hypotheses can begin at the earliest stages of assessment. Indeed, preliminary hypotheses are often generated from referral information prior to the child being seen. For example, information indicating that the child to be assessed is the offspring of a cocaine-abusing mother may lead to one set of preliminary hypotheses concerning the nature and severity of the problems the child may display. These hypotheses may be quite different from those generated in a case in which the referral was prompted by parental concern over the child's extreme levels of social aloofness and repetitive, stereotyped behaviors (possibly suggestive of autism). These early hypotheses may result in the clinician focusing on different types of information during the clinical interview and perhaps choosing very different types of assessment tools.

As assessment often begins with a parental interview, the clinician may early on obtain historical data as well as information regarding major problem areas and factors that may possibly contribute to the child's difficulties. Information derived from the interview may or may not provide support for earlier hypotheses based on referral information alone and may result in the development of new or revised hypotheses that serve to guide the selection of test measures and other aspects of the assessment process. Sometimes the clinician may be led to develop competing hypotheses to be tested. This may result in the selection of assessment procedures that yield data allowing a choice between them. For example, in the case of a child who is described as noncompliant it is possible that this noncompliance simply reflects oppositional–defiant behavior. It might also be that the behavior results from the parents' use of commands that are too complex and imprecise and/or that the child has a receptive language deficit or limited cognitive abilities that make it difficult to comprehend what he or she is being asked (or told). This sort of situation might necessitate that the clinician assess the child's level of intellectual functioning and receptive language abilities, observe parental communication patterns, and obtain detailed information on instances of oppositional behavior and factors in the child's environment that might elicit or maintain noncompliant behavior. Given these data, the clinician may be in a position to choose between rival hypotheses.

Hypotheses derived from the initial referral, the interview, and specific test findings can be evaluated in light of the total range of clinical information obtained. Thus, support for a diagnosis of mental retardation, tentatively suggested by a parent's retrospective report that the child was delayed in meeting certain developmental milestones, may or may not be supported by subsequent observations of the child's behavior and assessments of the child's cognitive functioning and adaptive behavior. Findings from an assessment of cognitive functioning that causes the clinician to tentatively hypothesize the presence of significant developmental delay, may or may not be supported by parent and teacher report data or by behavioral observations of the child; lowered test scores, for example, might best be accounted for in terms of the child's oppositional behavior during testing and/or significant attentional deficits that contribute to lowered levels of functioning in structured assessment situations. Likewise, the clinician who learns from a parental interview that a child has experienced a number of stressors in the recent past and subsequently observes the child to show many signs of anxiety in an informal clinical interview may entertain the tentative hypothesis that the child has an anxiety disorder. Given subsequent test findings from parent-report questionnaires, along with data from a structured interview with the child, which are suggestive of anxiety-related problems, the clinician may conclude that his or her initial hypothesis is well supported by the assessment data. Alternatively, given low scores on parent-report measures and the finding that few anxiety-related symptoms are reported within a structured interview format, a clinician with the same tentative hypothesis may come to view this hypothesis as having little support. In this instance, the signs of anxiety initially observed in the interview may come to be seen as situational in nature rather than reflective of significant psychopathology.

As suggested by these few examples, it is primarily through an ongoing reciprocal process of developing and testing (and perhaps revising and reevaluating) clinical hypotheses, within the context of accumulating assessment data, that the clinician is best able to develop a comprehensive picture of the child's difficulties (and strengths), factors that contribute to these problems, and insights into the nature of those intervention approaches that are most likely to be of value in dealing with them.

SELECTION OF ASSESSMENT METHODS

In light of the approach being advocated here, it should be apparent that considerable thought needs to be given to the nature of those assessment procedures used with a particular child. Given that children are referred for many reasons and that a variety of clinical hypotheses may be generated within the context of assessment, it would seem that relying on any standard battery of tests is ill-advised. Rather, the choice of specific tests and other assessment procedures (e.g., school observations, home observations) should be determined by the degree to which they can provide information relevant to the reason for referral and/or those clinically generated hypotheses that, if supported, are most likely to lead to a better understanding of possible contributors to the child's functioning and, therefore, to appropriate interventions.

Thus, selection of assessment procedures should represent an attempt to obtain *specific* information for *specific* purposes. In this regard it seems especially important that before assessment, the clinician clarify the precise nature of the referral question(s). Here, it can be noted that a referral request such as "Evaluate for ADHD as a source of school-related problems" is much more likely to result in the referral source being provided with the information he or she desires than is a request such as "Assess for emotional and behavior problems" or "Evaluate need for treatment". Though clinicians typically engage in a variety of assessment activities designed to screen for problems in certain areas, to address concerns raised by parents, and to obtain information relevant to various assessment-generated hypotheses, the careful delineation of the specific reasons for referral is essential in allowing the clinician to strike an appropriate balance between the range of domains assessed and the targeting of specific areas of concern.

In selecting assessment procedures it seems important to emphasize that, as when testing research hypotheses, data collected for clinical purposes should be obtained by measures that are both reliable and valid and of the type that pro-

vide adequate tests of those hypotheses under consideration. Such data can be obtained from a number of sources, the most obvious of which are the child's parents and the child.

The Parents as Sources of Assessment Data

One important source of assessment data is the child's parents. As we have noted, a great deal of developmentally relevant information can be obtained within the context of the parental interview. Indeed the interview is usually the starting point in the assessment process. Within the context of an interview parents can provide useful information on pregnancy and birth complications that may have contributed to the child's problems, information on childhood illnesses or injuries, as well as information on the extent to which developmental milestones (e.g., crawling, walking, saying first words, making simple sentences, becoming toilet trained) have been met. Information on school performance, peer and family relationships, and the existence and nature of any behavioral difficulties or adjustment problems also can be obtained.

In addition to information obtained through the more typical open-ended parental interview there are a variety of structured interview schedules such as the American Association on Mental Deficiency (AAMD) Adaptive Behavior Scales (Nihira, Foster, Shellhaas, & Leland, 1974) and the Vineland Social Maturity Scales (Sparrow, Balla, & Cicchetti, 1984) that are designed specifically for obtaining information on the child's level of adaptive behavior. Likewise, several structured parent interviews, designed to provide information on the presence and nature of childhood psychopathology, have also been developed for use in the clinical setting (see Hodges, 1993; Silverman, 1994).

Parents also can provide useful assessment information via parent-report questionnaires. Measures such as the Child Behavior Checklist (CBCL; Achenbach, 1991 and Chapter 2 in this volume), the Personality Inventory for Children (PIC; Wirt, Lachar, Klinedinst, & Seat, 1990), and the Parenting Stress Index (PSI; Abidin, 1990) can be used to obtain information about behavior problems (CBCL), childhood psychopathology (PIC), and sources of strain on the parent–child system (PSI). Other parent-report questionnaires, such as the Child Development Inventory (Ireton, 1993), also can be used to obtain information specifically related to the child's developmental status.

One concern that has been raised is that parents' reports of child behavior and ability may be influenced by the parents' own moods, personality characteristics, or other sources of bias. Though it is undoubtedly true that parent ratings will have a subjective element, it would be a mistake to dismiss the utility of parent reports as a component of a multisource evaluation. Parents are natural observers of child behavior and have been in a position to observe their child's behavior in far more situations than an examiner ever could. Thus, they are an invaluable source of information about behavior and development.

The Child as a Source of Assessment Data

A second and perhaps most obvious source of data is the child. Indeed, many measures of overall development, intellectual functioning, psychological adjustment, and of functioning in specific areas have been developed to assist in the direct assessment of the child. Included here are screening measures such as the Denver Developmental Screening Scale (Frankenburg, Dodds, Fandel, Kazuk, & Cohrs, 1975) and the Boyd Developmental Progress Scale (Boyd, 1984), as well as a range of other carefully developed measures of developmental and intellectual functioning. Well-known examples include the Bayley Scales of Infant Development (Bayley, 1993), the McCarthy Scales of Children's Abilities (McCarthy, 1972), the Stanford-Binet Intelligence Scale: Fourth Edition (Thorndike, Hagen, & Sattler, 1986), the Wechsler Preschool and Primary Scale of Intelligence-Revised (WPPSI-R: Wechsler, 1989), and the Wechsler Intelligence Scale for Children: Third Edition (WISC-III; Wechsler, 1991). Notable examples of child and adolescent measures of psychopathology include several child-oriented structured interview techniques (Hodges, 1993; Silverman, 1994), projective tests such as the Thematic Apperception Test (TAT) and the Rorschach (Levitt & French, 1992), and the adolescent version of the Minnesota Multiphasic Personality Inventory (MMPI-A; Butcher, Williams, Graham, Archer, Tellegen, Ben-Porath, & Kraemmer, 1992). A number of these measures are considered in more detail in the sections to follow.

In considering child assessment it must be emphasized that scores derived from specific measures, no matter how well developed, represent only a portion of the clinically relevant data available. A wealth of other information can come from observing the child as he or she deals with test items and with the demands of the testing situation. Here, the clinician can obtain important data on the degree to which the child is able to understand instructions, attend to test stimuli, and comply with the requirements of testing. The clinician also may have an opportunity to observe how the child deals with frustration, whether the child tends to give up easily or continues to give maximum effort in the face of difficulty, and whether he or she responds to encouragement and/or direct reinforcement or appears unaffected by such interventions. Information of this type is valuable,

not only in determining whether the results of testing must be qualified in some way, but also in providing data on how the child is likely to respond in similar situations that occur in the natural environment.

Other Sources of Assessment Data

It is often useful to consider sources of data other than the parent and child. In many instances, useful information can be obtained from existing medical records or from the records of other professionals with whom the child has had contact. Information provided by teachers may be especially valuable. With the exception of parents, teachers are probably in the best position to observe the child's behavior. Because teachers have contact with a large number of children, they are also in a position to comment on the extent to which the child's behavior deviates from the norm on relevant dimensions. As such, they are often able to give information that can provide the clinician with a much broader perspective on the child's functioning than would be possible if the focus is only on data obtained in the clinical setting.

TOWARD A COMPREHENSIVE DEVELOPMENTAL ASSESSMENT

As previously suggested, the goal of developmental assessment is to obtain a detailed and accurate picture of the child's functioning, his or her strengths and weaknesses, factors that contribute to difficulties, and specific targets for intervention.

Given the availability of a range of developmental assessment methods, it seems desirable that clinical data in areas of interest be obtained through the use of multiple measures. Whenever possible it seems desirable that the clinician also obtain data from multiple sources. This is because different sources tend to provide different types of data, and the data obtained from one source may be more useful than the data obtained from another source, depending on the question being asked. For example, although it may be possible to obtain useful information on the presence of childhood depression from parents who may have noted things like the child's loss of appetite and sleep difficulties (which can result from a variety of factors) the child may be in a better position to provide information on the more subjective features of depression (e.g., feelings of hopelessness). Likewise, obtaining data from multiple sources may provide useful information on the degree to which the child's problem behaviors (or deficits) are exhibited across situations or are situationally specific. In considering data derived in this manner the emphasis should be on determining those instances in which there is a convergence of findings that allow meaningful descriptive statements to be made about important aspects of the child's functioning.

A comprehensive developmental assessment should go beyond simply documenting the presence and nature of the child's difficulties. Assessment should not only focus on the nature of the child's strengths and difficulties, but also on those factors within the child, family, school, and larger environment that contribute to his or her difficulties. Such information may be essential for treatment planning.

Finally, developmental assessment is often, of necessity, an interdisciplinary enterprise. Although clinical child and pediatric psychologists are typically trained to assess variables such as cognitive and motor development, adaptive behavior, psychopathology and the like, detailed assessment of certain problems may require a referral to other professionals. Most psychologists, for example, do not have the training necessary to conduct a detailed speech and language evaluation, although they are often in an excellent position to observe behaviors that may suggest the need for an evaluation by a speech pathologist. Children with apparent receptive language problems may likewise benefit from an evaluation by an audiologist to determine the extent to which their problems relate to hearing deficits. Depending on the specific nature of the child's problems, other professionals such as pediatricians, neurologists, occupational therapists, and physical therapists also may need to be consulted.

APPROACHES TO DEVELOPMENTAL ASSESSMENT: AN OVERVIEW

Throughout this chapter we have noted that developmental assessment involves obtaining information through the use of diverse measures and approaches. In the following sections we provide an overview of some of the more widely used approaches that have been found useful in assessing children from this perspective.

Developmental Screening Measures

Denver Developmental Screening Scale

The Denver Developmental Screening Scale (DDSS) (Frankenburg & Dodds, 1967; Frankenburg et al., 1975) consists of 105 items designed to screen for developmental problems during the first five years of life. The DDSS takes only 10 to 20 minutes to administer and yields scores reflective of gross motor, fine motor–adaptive, language, and personal–social development.

Although this measure has achieved a degree of popularity, it possesses significant limitations. For example, Ireton (1990) has noted that the measure has a relatively small

number of items for assessing development at upper age levels as well as few language-related items for children age 3 to 5. Research has also suggested that the DDSS may fail to identify many children who are not retarded but who have lesser degrees of developmental delay or specific developmental disabilities. Given these limitations, the DDSS should be used with caution in making screening decisions.

Child Development Inventory

The Child Development Inventory (CDI) (Ireton, 1993) is a 270-item parent-report measure developed for use with children between the ages of 15 months and 6 years. The measure can be used for screening children suspected of developmental delay, for assessing children with known developmental disabilities, or for assessing the developmental progress of normal children (Ireton, 1993). When scored, the CDI yields age equivalents that reflect the child's level of functioning in eight domains. These include an index of general development, individual scales assessing gross motor development, fine motor development, expressive language, language comprehension, self-help skills, and social development as well as two scales that assess knowledge of letters and numbers.

In general, the CDI appears to be a reasonably valid and reliable parent-report measure that may be especially appropriate for those screening situations in which it is not possible to obtain assessment data directly from the child.

Miscellaneous Screening Measures

There are a variety of other developmental screening measures in addition to the two described above. Noteworthy are the Boyd Developmental Progress Scale as well as several measures that can be useful in screening for child psychopathology, such as the Child Behavior Checklist (CBCL; Achenbach, 1991) and the Personality Inventory for Children (PIC; Wirt et al., 1990).

The Boyd Developmental Progress Scale (Boyd, 1984) is a screening measure suitable for use with children from birth to 7 years. It consists of 150 items assessing motor skills, cognitive skills, and adaptive behavior. Included are items based on observation of the child, test items that are administered directly to the child, and items based on parent report of child behavior. Although the Boyd is easy to administer and seems to be a potentially useful screening tool, there has been little research on this instrument, leaving questions on its validity and reliability largely unanswered.

In addition to the Boyd, as noted, there are a number of brief measures that can be used to screen for emotional and behavioral problems in children and adolescents. Of note are the CBCL and the shortened version of the PIC (Wirt et al., 1990). These measures are considered in more detail in a later section that focuses on assessment of psychopathology.

Assessment of Cognitive and Motor Development

The Bayley Scales

The Bayley Scales of Infant Development (Bayley, 1993) are among the most well-developed and time-honored approaches for assessing the development of infants and young children. The currently used second edition (BSID-II) is an individually administered measure designed to assess the developmental level of children between the ages of 1 and 42 months. It consists of 288 items, graded in terms of developmental level, which tap both cognitive and motor development. An associated 30-item Behavior Rating Scale, which is completed after testing, assesses aspects of behavior that are of relevance to the testing situation (e.g., attention to tasks, cooperation, activity level).

Administering the Bayley takes about 45 minutes to 1 hour. When scored, it provides a Mental Development Index and a Psychomotor Development Index that have standard score means of 100 and a standard deviation of 15. These measures allow one to determine the degree to which a child differs from others of his or her age in terms of development and to estimate the child's current level of functioning in these areas. Scores on the Behavior Rating Scale simply provide for categorizing the child's performance as Normal, Questionable, or Nonoptimal. The BSID-II is not only useful in testing very young children, but may also be of value in assessing somewhat older but low functioning children, whose abilities lie in the 1- to 42-month range and who cannot be assessed by standard intelligence measures.

In general, the Bayley is probably the best available measure of infant development. As such, the measure has much to recommend it for the clinician who wishes to obtain information on the cognitive and motor development of infants and very young children.

McCarthy Scales of Children's Abilities

Taking up where the Bayley leaves off are the McCarthy Scales of Children's Abilities (McCarthy, 1972). This measure, which can be used with children between the ages of 2½ and 8½ years, takes about 45 minutes to an hour to administer and consists of eighteen subtests that can be scored to yield indices of development on five scales that assess verbal, perceptual–performance, quantitative, memory, and motor skills. By combining subtests for the Verbal, Perceptual–Performance, and Quantitative scales it is also possible to de-

rive a General Cognitive Index (GCI: mean = 100; Standard Deviation = 16), which provides a reliable and valid measure of cognitive functioning (Culbertson & Gyurke, 1990; Sattler, 1988). Although the GCI is similar to an IQ score in certain respects, it is not interchangeable with measures of IQ because GCI scores are generally lower than scores obtained from standard intelligence tests, particularly among gifted children, mentally retarded children, and children with learning disabilities (Culbertson & Gyurke, 1990). As a consequence, it has been recommended that the McCarthy not be used when school placement issues are in question or when school personnel desire a specific index of intellectual functioning. Culbertson and Gyurke (1990) also note that the scale fails to assess important variables such as social intelligence (e.g., social comprehension and judgment), verbal reasoning, and abstract problem-solving, which are important domains to be considered in the assessment of school-age children. The McCarthy also lacks a sufficient ceiling for children age 7 and above on many of the subtests. Such issues are not problematic with the preschool child, for which the McCarthy is more ideally suited.

Stanford-Binet Intelligence Scale: Fourth Edition (S-B IV)

The S-B IV (Thorndike, Hagen & Sattler, 1986) is a revision of the 1960 Stanford-Binet Form L-M. It differs markedly in format from earlier versions and in most respects can be thought of as a new test. Although the measure is rightly thought of as an intelligence scale (spanning the 2–23 year age range), rather than a developmental scale, it has been widely used in the assessment of young children with suspected developmental delay.

This measure is based on a three-level hierarchical model of intelligence (Thorndike, Hagen, & Sattler, 1986). At the top of this hypothesized hierarchy is a general reasoning or general intelligence factor. At the second level are other more specific intellectual factors involving crystallized abilities, fluid–analytic abilities, and short-term memory abilities. Organized under these second-level attributes are more specific factors reflective of verbal reasoning, quantitative reasoning, abstract–visual reasoning, and short-term memory abilities, each of which is assessed by three to four subtest that tap abilities specific to the area and for which subtest scores can be derived.

The S-B IV differs from Form L-M in a number of respects. Unlike the earlier version, the S-B IV can derive not only an overall index of cognitive functioning but can also assess strengths and weaknesses through analysis of the child's test profile. This measure also differs from earlier versions in that rather than using an age-scale format, a point-scale format is used by which items within each scale are graded by level of difficulty. As with the earlier edition, basal and ceiling levels of performance are assessed, although for each subscale rather than across the age range covered by the test. Both of these changes make this version of the Stanford-Binet more similar to existing Wechsler Intelligence Scales.

The Stanford-Binet has much to recommend it. It is well-standardized with good normative data. The Composite Score has been shown to have good reliability and the validity of this index has been supported by finding significant correlations between this overall index of intelligence and scores derived from the Stanford-Binet Form L-M, the Wechsler Intelligence Scale for Children-Revised (WISC-R), and the Wechsler Adult Intelligence Scale-Revised (WAIS-R). Additionally, the format that allows for a profile analysis of the individual's strengths and weaknesses adds to the usefulness of the test as a clinical diagnostic instrument.

Despite these positive attributes, there are certain issues that detract from this revision. Most noteworthy is the fact that, although composite scores from the S-B IV are generally similar to those of other IQ measures, this measure tends to yield significantly lower scores than other measures when gifted or mentally retarded individuals are assessed (Sattler, 1988). This detracts from the usefulness of the measure with those very groups that the child clinician may be most interested in assessing. Although this issue is problematic, Culbertson and Gyurke (1990) suggest that the most important limitation of this scale, when used with the very young child, is the fact that it takes a long time to administer (1 to 2 hours) and there are not enough easy items on various scales to establish a basal range when assessing mentally retarded or developmentally delayed preschoolers. Those difficulties, coupled with the fact that most referrals of preschool-age children involve questions of developmental delay, make the utility of the S-B IV for children under 4 years of age questionable (Culbertson & Gyurke, 1990).

The Wechsler Preschool and Primary Scale of Intelligence-Revised (WPPSI-R)

The WPPSI-R (Wechsler, 1989), like the Binet, represents a carefully developed test of intelligence that can be used in the assessment of young children ages 3 years through 7 years, 3 months. The expanded age range of this revised version makes the test more suitable for use with both younger and older children than the WPPSI. It is noteworthy that with the age range of the scale being expanded upward, as well as downward, the scale now overlaps approximately one year with the WISC-III, allowing the clinician a choice between the two measures. Thus, with the child in the 6 to 7 age range, who is thought to be low functioning, the clinician

might choose to use the WPPSI-R to obtain a more adequate sample of his or her abilities than might be obtained with the WISC-III (in which the child might have considerable difficulty with even easier items).

As with the original measure, the WPPSI-R provides Verbal, Performance, and Full-Scale IQ scores. Although similar in many respects to the WPPSI, approximately 50 percent of the items are new to the test. The scale also includes one subtest (object assembly) that was not a part of the original scale. As with the other Wechsler scales, the WPPSI-R appears to be well standardized, shows good test–retest reliability and adequate internal consistency, and research findings provide satisfactory support for its validity. In addition, the full color art work and more up-to-date content is likely to make the stimulus materials more appealing to children than was the original measure (Culbertson & Gyurke, 1990). Although space constraints preclude a detailed discussion of this measure, it should be noted that the WISC-III (Wechsler, 1991) is likely to be the measure of choice for assessing the intellectual functioning of older children and adolescents. This measure, which is suitable for use with children between the ages of 6 and 16 years, 11 months, is similar to the WPPSI-R in terms of providing indices of verbal, performance, and full-scale IQ and scores on both verbal and performance subscales. Like the WPPSI-R, the WISC III is well normed and is well supported by both validity and reliability findings.

Assessment of Adaptive Behavior

There are a variety of measures that provide information about the degree to which the child shows evidence of age-appropriate adaptive or social behaviors. Two screening measures (Child Development Inventory; Boyd Developmental Progress Scale) described earlier provide rough indices of the child's level of adaptive behavior, self-help, and personal–social skills. Other measures that have attempted to assess adaptive behavior in a more comprehensive manner include the AAMD Adaptive Behavior Scales and the Vineland Adaptive Behavior Scales. Although the AAMD Adaptive Behavior Scales have been widely used in the past and are of demonstrated value in assessing the level of adaptive behavior in mentally retarded and developmentally delayed children (Nihara et al., 1974), these measures have been largely replaced by the more recently published revision of the Vineland Adaptive Behavior Scales (Sparrow et al., 1984). Although we do not minimize the historical contribution of the AAMD scales as measures of adaptive behavior, we have chosen to focus on the Vineland as the most commonly used measure of adaptive behavior in the developmental assessment of children and adolescents.

The Vineland Adaptive Behavior Scales (Sparrow et al., 1984) represent a revision and elaboration on the original Vineland Social Maturity Scale (Doll, 1953), which was widely used for many years as an index of social development. There are three separate forms of the Vineland: a Survey Form, developed for diagnostic and classification purposes; an Expanded Form, for use in developing individualized educational programs; and a Classroom Edition, for obtaining school based estimates of adaptive functioning. Data for the Vineland are obtained through a semistructured interview with the primary caregiver, in the case of the Survey and Expanded Forms, or with the classroom teacher, in the case of the Classroom Edition. Although the Classroom Edition is suitable for use with school-age children, the other two forms are suitable for use with those from birth to adulthood. Each form of the Vineland assesses four dimensions of adaptive behavior (Communication, Daily Living Skills, Socialization, and Motor Skills) and yields an Adaptive Behavior Composite index as well as standard scores for each of the four domains.

By way of critique, the Vineland Adaptive Behavior Scales represent a significant elaboration and improvement on the original Vineland Social Maturity Scale. The current measure is well standardized, shows acceptable levels of reliability, and studies with the measure have provided reasonable support for its validity (Sparrow et al., 1984). Domains of adaptive functioning, assessed by this measure, represent a useful supplement to other measures of development or intellectual functioning that are commonly used in developmental assessment. Indeed, this measure would seem to have much to offer in obtaining a more comprehensive view of the child's functioning in the natural environment than would be the case with measures of cognitive and motor functioning alone.

Assessment of Child Psychopathology

As was suggested earlier, a comprehensive assessment of child psychopathology is, by its nature, always a developmental assessment in that it considers problematic child behavior within the context of relevant developmental variables. As such, the initial question in assessing child psychopathology is whether the pattern of behavioral or emotional difficulties demonstrated by a child is consistent with his or her expected developmental level.

The assessment of behavioral or emotional difficulties will certainly include a clinical interview with parents and, if the child's developmental capabilities permit, with the child. During this interview, the clinician will typically inquire as to the nature, severity, frequency, and/or duration of the behavior problem(s) as well as the degree of distress that

such problems cause the child or parent. This information is necessary both to determine whether the behaviors are more difficult or distressing than would be expected given the child's age or developmental level and to assist in planning intervention efforts. It is likely for example, that while the intervention for a 10-year-old experiencing a separation anxiety disorder might warrant a multifaceted behavioral intervention, the clinical response for a toddler demonstrating distress at separation might require little more than reassuring the parent and helping to identify ways to reduce the toddler's distress.

Parent and child interviews also can be conducted using standardized structured or semistructured diagnostic methods. Though these are less commonly used in clinical practice than in research settings, such interviews provide a mechanism of obtaining a thorough and reliable psychodiagnostic history. The Schedule for Affective Disorders and Schizophrenia for School-Age Children (K-SADS) is the most commonly used in this regard. The K-SADS is a semistructured interview that covers a broad range of psychiatric diagnoses and is available in forms for generating current (K-SADS-P; Puig-Antich & Chambers, 1987) and lifetime (K-SADS-E; Orvaschel, Puig-Antich, Chambers, Tabrizi, & Johnson, 1982) diagnoses. The parent and child are interviewed separately by the same interviewer who then integrates their reports to yield diagnoses. Though the developers provide some guidelines for integrating discrepant reports, the process relies heavily on the clinical judgment of the interviewer. The K-SADS appears to provide more reliable diagnoses for depressive and conduct disorder diagnoses than for anxiety disorders (Chambers et al., 1985). Other widely used interviews include the Child Assessment Schedule (CAS; Hodges, Kline, Stern, Cytryn, & McKnew, 1982), the Diagnostic Interview for Children and Adolescents (DICA; Herjanic, Herjanic, Brown, Wheatt, 1975), the Diagnostic Interview Schedule for Children (DISC; Costello, Edelbrock, Kalas, Kessler, & Klaric, 1984) and the Anxiety Disorders Interview Schedule for Children (Silverman & Nelles, 1988). Each of these interviews are similar in that they provide for parent and child report of symptoms and generate DSM diagnoses for a range of disorders (Hodges, 1993). Significant differences between them have to do with the method of generating diagnoses (clinical judgment vs. algorithm), treatment of parent and child report (integrated vs. separate), and the format of the interview (by diagnosis or content area). More detailed information on these approaches is provided by Hodges (1993) and Silverman (1994).

If the clinician's objective is to develop an effective intervention, diagnosis is only the beginning of the assessment. Interviews with the child and parent (as well as other caregivers) also provide essential information on the environmental factors that may elicit and maintain the specific behaviors of concern, recent stressors that may have initiated or exacerbated the difficulties, and a description of the ways in which parents and other caregivers have attempted to address the child's emotional or behavioral problems in the past. This last item may be of particular relevance to treatment planning in that it can provide the clinician with information about the parents' values and parenting styles as well as perhaps their expectations about what will and won't work as far as recommended treatments are concerned.

In addition to the interview, there are a range of parent, teacher, and child report measures available for assessing child psychopathology. Of special note is the Child Behavior Checklist (CBCL; Achenbach, 1991; see Chapter 2). The CBCL is a parent-report measure that assesses social competence and behavior problems in children between 2 and 18 years old (there is a separate form for ages 2 to 3). The profile depicts the child's behavioral pattern across a range of empirically determined syndromes that reflect both broadband (i.e., internalizing and externalizing) and narrowband (e.g., depression) syndromes. The CBCL was normed on a large, national sample, and scores provide an index of the child's behavior relative to other children of the same age and gender. A particularly attractive feature of the CBCL is the availability of similar teacher-, self-, and observer-rating forms that facilitate a multisource assessment.

The Personality Inventory for Children-Revised (PIC-R; Wirt et al., 1990) is a parent-report measure appropriate for children age 3 to 16. This revised version is comprised of 420 items that yields scores on three validity scales and twelve clinical scales. Though the clinical scales largely assess child characteristics (e.g., somatic concerns, depression, delinquency, withdrawal, anxiety, psychosis, hyperactivity, social skills), one scale assesses family relationships. In addition to obtaining scores on each of the measures based on the full complement of items, it is possible to obtain clinical scale scores on a short form of this test by scoring only 280 of the items or to obtain factor scores on four broad-band measures of psychopathology (undisciplined/poor self-control; social incompetence, internalization/somatic symptoms; cognitive development) by administering 131 of the items. As noted earlier, the shortened versions of the PIC-R may be quite appropriate for screening purposes in situations in which the clinician is conducting a developmental assessment that is focused on some other area but wishes to at least screen for adjustment problems. The PIC-R was normed on a large sample of children with separate profiles being provided for each gender. Data on the validity and reliability support its use in clinical settings (Wirt et. al., 1990).

Other measures such as the adolescent version of the Minnesota Multiphasic Personality Inventory (MMPI-A; Butcher et al., 1992) also are widely used in the assessment of psychological difficulties in older children and adolescents. This measure, which is suitable for use with adolescents between the ages of 14 and 18 years, consists of a total of 478 items and yields scores on all of the original MMPI clinical and validity scales as well as several new validity and content scales. The measure, which has been carefully normed on an adolescent population, appears to be much more suitable for use with adolescents (and possibly children as young as 12) than the MMPI-2, which is more suitable for individuals 18 years of age and older (Butcher et al., 1992).

Although not specifically a measure of child psychopathology, the Parenting Stress Index (PSI; Abidin, 1990) is a useful component of a developmental assessment. The PSI assesses stress in the parent–child relationship that exists as a function of parent and child characteristics. Child characteristics assessed here are most easily conceptualized as temperament attributes (e.g., adaptability, demandingness, mood). The parent domain includes scales tapping the marital relationship, parental depression, social isolation, perceived parenting competence, attachment, and feelings of being restricted by the parenting role. As the PSI was normed on mothers of preschool children, it is likely to be of most use with this population in assessing specific sources of strain on the parent–child relationship.

Due to space constraints, our review of measures is necessarily abbreviated. We have highlighted only a select group of broad-band, frequently used, and empirically based rating scales and measures that are likely to be useful in developmental assessments. Clinicians who are primarily interested in personality assessment of children and adolescents may also find projective techniques such as projective drawings, sentence completion tests, the Thematic Apperception Test (TAT), and the Rorschach to be of value in clinical assessment. A useful overview of these techniques is provided by Levitt and French (1992).

Additionally, a large number of parent, teacher, and child report measures as well as observational techniques have been developed to assess specific aspects of child psychopathology. Such narrow-band measures may be particularly useful in providing additional data when the nature of the behavioral or emotional concerns have been clearly delineated up front or as supplements to more broad-based instruments. Mash and Terdal (1988) provide an excellent discussion of behavioral assessment methods that is organized according to domains of psychopathology whereas Ollendick and Hersen (1984) provide a similar discussion of behavioral assessment methods arranged according to procedures or modalities.

Assessment of Temperament and Behavioral Style

A comprehensive developmental assessment should also include consideration of the child's temperament. Although definitions of temperament vary, most clinicians and researchers agree that temperament characteristics reflect relatively stable individual differences in behavioral tendencies that are at least partially biological in origin (Goldsmith et al., 1987). Variables that have commonly been included under this rubric include quality and intensity of mood, response to novelty, soothability, attention span, activity level, predictability of biological functions, and sociability (Bates, Freeland, & Lunsbury, 1979; Buss & Plomin, 1975; Rothbart & Derryberry, 1981; Thomas & Chess, 1977). These characteristics are important in that they shape the child's response to the environment and may, in turn, influence the response of important caretakers to the child.

Temperament variables may have a significant impact on the way in which deficits in development are displayed as well as on how the child copes with his or her disabilities. Chess and Thomas (1986), for example, have noted that the child's temperament makeup may be of relevance to a number of handicapping conditions (and this would appear to include developmentally related deficits). They suggest that although such conditions make life more difficult for the child, adjustment to such conditions may be more or less difficult and outcomes more or less positive depending on the child's temperament. To illustrate, they note that the child high in persistence, through continued efforts, may succeed in dealing with many of the difficulties and frustrations experienced as a result of his or her handicap, while the child lower in persistence may give up more easily and fail to accomplish many things that are within his or her range of abilities. The finding that academic performance in nonhandicapped children is associated with more positive ratings on temperament attributes such as activity, distractibility, persistence, and adaptability (see Keogh, 1989; Martin, 1989) lends support to this hypothesis. Likewise, the child characterized by predominately negative mood and high-intensity emotional responses may be more likely to respond to deficit-related frustrations with tantrums and other problem behaviors.

Such responses may be significant to the clinician both because of the difficulties they create for those interacting with the child and because they may presage or be early indicators of child psychopathology. Parents who perceive their children to have more difficult temperament characteristics, in particular, negative moods and high-intensity emotional expressions, report greater anxiety and dysphoria, less self-confidence in parenting, and greater disruption in family functioning than do parents with children who have a less difficult temperament style (Sheeber & Johnson, 1992; Stevenson-Hinde & Simpson, 1982; Thomas & Chess, 1977). Additionally, it has been suggested that temperament characteristics not normally considered difficult by parents of healthy children may be stressful for parents of children with developmental delays (Marcovitch, Goldberg, Lojkasek, & MacGregor, 1987). For example, the low level of emotional expression in infants with Down syndrome is reported to be distressing to their parents (Goldberg & Marcovich, 1989).

Moreover, as suggested earlier, difficult temperament may be associated with increased risk of child psychopathology (e.g., Bates & Bayles, 1988; Goldberg, Corter, Lojkasek, & Minde, 1990; Rende, 1993). One interpretation of this finding is that adverse temperament characteristics are, in fact, early symptoms of childhood disorder. Alternatively, as initially posited by Thomas and Chess (1977), behavioral and emotional problems may develop in part as a result of a poor fit between the child's temperament characteristics and the demands of the environment. Though the concept of "goodness of fit" has proven easier to describe than to operationalize (see Bates, 1989), it does appear that examining child temperament in the context of environmental characteristics may be important in understanding the development of behavioral disorders (Maziade, 1989; Nitz, Lerner, Lerner, & Talwar, 1988; Rende & Plomin, 1992). The goodness of fit model is particularly well suited for use in treatment planning because it encourages the use of interventions that are tailored to the child's unique characteristics. For example, one could imagine that a child who demonstrates low task persistence and intense negative responses to frustration might be less likely to tantrum or develop other oppositional behaviors if demands were carefully structured so as to ensure frequent success experiences.

Temperament characteristics may thus be most relevant to the clinician to the extent that they guide intervention efforts. Because adverse temperament characteristics such as low persistence, withdrawal from new situations, or low adaptability may hamper the child's ability to benefit maximally from intervention efforts, the clinician may need to specifically incorporate temperament information in treatment planning. For example, educational strategies for a child with mental retardation who is a persistent, adaptable, and easy-going child might include rewarding and supporting continued efforts at mastery, the use of creative and flexible teaching activities, and careful attention to ensure that this child's frustration, disappointment, or accomplishments are not missed because of their quiet expression. On the other hand, a distractible, active, unadaptable child with similar cognitive deficits might be better served by a program tailored to provide short, familiar exercises in the context of close supervision and frequent breaks. In fact, in a preliminary investigation, Orth and Martin (1994) have demonstrated that temperament style interacted with instructional method to predict the classroom performance of kindergarten children.

In line with these suggestions, it seems important that those conducting developmental assessments obtain information regarding both the nature of the child's temperament makeup and the fit between child temperament and parenting style (and other demands of the child's environment). This information can then be considered, along with other developmentally relevant data, in developing the most comprehensive view of the child and his or her needs. Though parent-report temperament questionnaires have been more widely used for research than for clinical purposes, there are several measures that may provide useful clinical information. The series of measures developed by Carey and his associates (Carey & McDevitt, 1978; Fullard, McDevitt, & Carey, 1978; Hegvick, McDevitt, & Carey, 1982; McDevitt & Carey, 1975) were developed for use in clinical settings and have been the most widely used in this regard. These measures include the Infant Temperament Questionnaire, the Toddler Temperament Scale, Behavioral Style Questionnaire (for use with 3- to 7-year-old children) and the Middle Childhood Temperament Questionnaire. Each of these scales was designed to assess the nine temperament dimensions defined in the New York Longitudinal Study (Thomas & Chess, 1977). There are a range of other measures that have primarily been used as research instruments. Of these, the Revised Dimensions of Temperament Survey (DOTS-R; Windle & Lerner, 1986) is notable in two ways. First, because it consists of items that appear to tap temperament dimensions across the age span from childhood through young adulthood, it can be used to obtain parent-report of young children's temperament as well as self-report of older children and parent temperament. Second, a companion version has been created to assess the expectational demands about temperament held by the child's significant others; that is, one can assess whether a child's temperament style is congruent with the parents' (or teachers') preferences. This measure includes seven scales that tap temperament dimensions similar to those suggested by Thomas and Chess (1977).

Additionally, as interventions for children with developmental delays will likely include a school-based component, it may be advisable to obtain a teacher rating of child temperament (McDevitt, 1988). This is particularly the case given that parent and teacher ratings of child temperament tend to be only moderately correlated (e.g., Sheeber &

Johnson, 1992; Victor, Halverson, & Wampler, 1988). Two commonly used teacher-report measures are the teacher form of the Temperament Assessment Battery (Martin, 1983) and the Teacher Temperament Questionnaire (Keogh, Pullis, & Caldwell, 1982). These measures are both revisions of the Teacher Temperament Questionnaire developed by Thomas and Chess (1977). A more detailed consideration of the range of temperament measures available and other approaches to the assessment of temperament is provided in several reviews (Rothbart & Goldsmith, 1985; Windle, 1988).

Finally, it has been suggested that temperament may be best assessed within the context of a semistructured parent interview because this format allows the clinician to follow up on parent descriptions of child behavior, respond to contradictory bits of information, and gain more clinically relevant information that can be obtained from simply administering a questionnaire (Chess & Thomas, 1986). A range of useful guidelines on structuring the parent interview so as to obtain information on child temperament characteristics and how these relate to other domains of child functioning has been provided by Chess and Thomas (1986). This point may be particularly relevant in assessing the fit between child characteristics and parenting styles. There is probably no substitute for a thorough clinical interview for obtaining information on how parents (or other care providers) make demands, structure experiences, and respond to difficult child behavior.

RELATIONSHIP OF ASSESSMENT TO INTERVENTION

Assessment and Intervention: General Issues

As has been suggested previously, developmental assessment is best viewed as a process that leads to action rather than to an end, in and of itself. It is not an endeavor designed to obtain knowledge for knowledge's sake, or simply to gain a better intellectual understanding of the child, but an approach designed to yield information that allows the psychologist and other professionals to work for the best interests of the child.

Except in those instances in which the assessment finds behaviors of concern to be the result of normal developmental processes (and even here some sort of intervention to allay the concerns of the parents may be warranted), assessment findings should generally yield recommendations for possible interventions. For this purpose, it will typically be important to identify those factors within the child, family, or elsewhere in the environment that are impeding his or her ability to successfully master age-appropriate behaviors or are contributing to psychological and behavioral difficulties. Mental retardation, neurological impairment, temperament characteristics, the residual effects of early sexual abuse, and the presence of debilitating levels of phobic anxiety might all be examples of child factors. Relevant environmental factors could include disturbed family communication patterns, faulty behavior management approaches, or the more chronic difficulties associated with poverty. Assessment of the child's developmental status also helps the clinician to determine the extent to which the child can be an active contributor to planning for, and being an active participant in, treatment. Later in the intervention process, developmental assessment can be useful for evaluating progress, rethinking intervention strategies, and engaging in continued treatment planning. It should be kept in mind that for children with serious difficulties, assessment and treatment may well be an ongoing and interactive process.

Assessment Feedback as a Starting Point for Intervention

Sharing information obtained in the course of the evaluation might be seen as the first essential step in making the transition from assessment to treatment. Although in some cases the clinician may only need to provide feedback to the family, it is often the case that information will be shared with teachers and other professionals who will be involved in the child's treatment. In fact, a feedback session may be the best opportunity to engage the family and other professionals in treatment (Gordon & Schroeder, 1990). This meeting also provides an occasion to share ideas, address questions or concerns, and develop a plan for continued collaboration.

In planning for a feedback session, it is important to keep in mind that obtaining the results of a developmental assessment may be a difficult experience for parents. Imagine, for example, the position of parents learning that their child has mental retardation. Their own emotional response to the information as well as any preconceived ideas they may have as to the nature of mental retardation may interfere with their ability to attend to and understand the findings. It is necessary, therefore, to take steps to minimize these difficulties. As in any difficult clinical situation, the evaluator must be able to communicate information in a manner that is both honest and empathic. It is important, moreover, to use language that is appropriate for a lay audience; technical terms, if needed, must be carefully defined. As mentioned above, the clinician needs to take time to elicit family members' responses and address questions; this is important not only to provide desired information but also to check on the family's understanding. Finally, it may

be useful to provide a brief written summary of assessment findings and recommendations to which parents can refer after they have left the office.

It is likely that the evaluator will also be providing a more formal, written report to teachers, pediatricians, or other professionals. The clinician should take care to target this written feedback to fit the audience. Several distinct points are at issue here. First, the language of the report should be appropriate to the training of the audience. For example, raw scores should be provided only to individuals who are trained to interpret them. Second, to protect the family's privacy, information of a sensitive nature should be shared only to the extent that it is relevant for treatment planning. That is, although the impact of marital conflict on the child's behavior would be important to convey to a social worker providing family therapy, it may not be important or appropriate to convey this information to the speech therapist. Finally, to be most helpful, treatment recommendations should be clear, specific, and tailored to the unique needs of the particular child and family.

Selection of Targets for Intervention

It should be apparent at this point that developmental assessment may lead to a range of outcomes. As noted above, one possible outcome of an assessment is the determination that a child is progressing well. In this case, providing information to the parents on the developmental achievements and behavioral difficulties to be expected at a given age may be all the intervention required. On the other hand, parents who feel ill-equipped to handle developmental challenges—be that the nighttime fears of a young child or the adolescent's striving for independence—may benefit from brief, problem-focused counseling, referral to community-based parenting support/education programs, or the recommendation of relevant books written for parents or children.

The situation is clearly more complicated when the child evidences a developmental delay or severe emotional or behavioral problems. In the case of the former, the first intervention will be to help the family understand the nature of the child's current functioning, including strengths and difficulties, as well as the developmental course that can be expected. As may be apparent from the breadth of the assessment, subsequent interventions may be myriad and should always be tailored to the unique strengths and difficulties exhibited by the child, family, and community. For example, in addition to developing effective remediation strategies, intervention may be targeted at helping the parents access community resources and become effective advocates for their child. Similarly, in the case of a child with evidence of significant psychopathology, the approach to intervention should emerge directly from assessment findings. To illustrate, although one parent with a behaviorally difficult child may benefit from learning effective behavior management strategies, another may need treatment for a depressive disorder in order to apply skills she or he already possesses. Likewise, in one instance, assessment findings may suggest that the aggressive and conduct-disordered behavior displayed by a child is likely the result of having observed others who model these types of behavior and of the child being reinforced for engaging in such behavior. In another instance, assessment may suggest that similar behaviors are likely the result of conflicts associated with the child having been subjected to ongoing sexual abuse by a close family member.

Assessment findings in the first case might lead the clinician to take a primarily behavioral approach to intervention by which the child is increasingly exposed to models of prosocial behavior and by which environmental contingencies are arranged so as to increase prosocial and decrease conduct-disordered behavior. In the second example the focus of treatment might be on helping the child resolve emotional issues related to the sexual abuse (through individual therapy) rather than focusing exclusively on problem behaviors themselves (although these might also be addressed simultaneously).

Considering other issues, it should be noted that the treatment of both cases might be influenced in various ways by assessment findings indicating that the child in question displays significant intellectual deficits. This might be especially likely in the case where treatment recommendations involve individual psychotherapy, because the ability of children to express themselves and deal with problems on a verbal level is influenced by level of cognitive functioning.

These examples serve to underline the view that approaches to intervention should be directly linked to data derived from the assessment process. Intervention efforts should be directed toward modification of those factors that are found to contribute to the child's difficulties (whether these are associated with biological factors, intrapsychic conflicts, environmental contingencies, or faulty family interaction patterns). In some cases this will result in a focus on modification of the problem behavior itself while in other instances the focus may be on factors that appear to underlie and thus indirectly contribute to the child's difficulties. From this perspective, treatment may involve a single approach that focuses on some well-delineated problem area or, alternatively, the concurrent application of several approaches that focus on multiple targets for intervention, as in the case of the child with Attention Deficit Hyperactivity Disorder who displays comorbid features of depression. Again, the approach taken should be a natural outgrowth of assessment findings. Given this position, it should also be emphasized that treatment is facilitated by a comprehensive assessment that considers the full range of factors that may contribute to the child's difficulties.

SUMMARY AND CONCLUSIONS

In this chapter we have attempted to provide an overview of the commonly used measures and approaches to developmental assessment. Herein, developmental assessment has been characterized as a complex and multifaceted endeavor that can have different foci and can involve an assessment of the child's functioning at different levels, in multiple areas, and from multiple perspectives to provide answers to developmentally related questions. It was suggested that the defining features of developmental assessment relate less to variables such as age of the child and the specific methods employed and more to the degree to which developmental factors are taken into account in the choice of assessment procedures, the range of variables assessed, the conceptualization of assessment findings, and in the planning of intervention strategies based on assessment data. It was further suggested that all assessment approaches with children and adolescents are, or should be, seen as examples of developmental assessment, given that all aspects of the child's functioning can be influenced by, and should be viewed within, the context of ongoing developmental processes.

In our discussion considerable attention was paid to the role of the clinician in processing clinical data. Highlighted in this regard was the value of a scientist–practitioner-oriented approach to assessment in which the clinician is constantly involved in developing, in testing, and perhaps in revising and retesting, relevant clinical hypotheses generated throughout the assessment process. Central to this approach to assessment is a clinician who maintains the role of information processor and active decision maker and who gives appropriate weighting to developmentally related factors because they are relevant to the nature of the assessment process and the interpretation of assessment data.

It should be obvious from the material presented in this chapter that a tremendous amount of research effort has been expended in the development and validation of the range of measures that are commonly used in the developmental assessment of children and adolescents. Additional research is still needed on many of the measures considered herein. There also is the continued need for the development of additional measures that assess various developmentally relevant domains. An additional area of special importance would seem to be research designed to study the nature of the cognitive decision-making processes engaged in by skilled clinicians as they participate in assessment-related activities. Of special relevance would be the development of cognitively based methods that may be useful in teaching individuals, such as psychology trainees, to effectively employ the type of hypothesis-generating/hypothesis-testing approach associated with a scientist–practitioner model as described. Given the usefulness of modeling in facilitating the acquisition of overt behaviors, it would seem that cognitive modeling procedures, whereby the observer can tune in to the cognitive strategies and decision-making activities of skilled clinicians, may be especially useful in helping individuals develop approaches that maximize the clinical information derived from developmental assessments.

REFERENCES

Abidin, R. R. (1990). *Parenting Stress Index: A manual.* Charlottesville, VA: Pediatric Psychology Press.

Achenbach, T. M. (1991). *Manual for the Child Behavior Checklist/4-18 and 1991 Profile.* Burlington: University of Vermont Department of Psychiatry.

Bates, J. E. (1989). Applications of temperament concepts. In G. A. Kohnstamm, J. E. Bates, & M. K. Rothbart (Eds.), *Temperament in childhood* (pp. 321–355). New York: Wiley.

Bates, J. E., Freeland, C. A., & Lounsbury, M. L. (1979). Measure of infant difficultness. *Child Development, 50,* 794–803.

Bayley, N. (1993). *Bayley Scales of Infant Development* (2nd ed.). San Antonio, TX: Psychological Corporation.

Boyd, R. D. (1984). *The Boyd Developmental Progress Scale* (Rev. ed.). Portland, OR: Morrison Center for Youth and Family Services.

Buss, A. H., & Plomin, R. (1975). *A temperament theory of personality development.* New York: Wiley.

Butcher, J. N., Williams, C. L., Graham, J. R., Archer, R. P., Tellegen, A., Ben-Porath, Y., & Kaemmer, B. (1992). *MMPI—A: Manual for administration, scoring, and interpretation.* Minneapolis: University of Minnesota Press.

Carey, W. B., & McDevitt, S. C. (1978). Revision of the Infant Temperament Questionnaire. *Pediatrics, 61,* 735–739.

Carey, W. B., & McDevitt, S. C. (Eds.). (1994). *Prevention and early intervention: Individual differences as risk factors for the mental health of children.* New York: Brunner/Mazel.

Chambers, W. J., Puig-Antich, J., Hirsch, M., Paez, P., Ambrosini, P. J., Tabrizi, M. A., & Davies, M. (1985). The assessment of affective disorders in children and adolescents by semistructured interview. *Archives of General Psychiatry, 42,* 696–702.

Chess, S., & Thomas, A. (1986). *Temperament in clinical practice.* New York: Guilford Press.

Costello, A. J., Edelbrock, C. S., Dulcan, M. K., Kalas, R., & Klaric, S. H. (1984). *Report on the NIMH Diagnostic Interview Schedule for Children (DIS-C).* Washington, DC: National Institute of Mental Health.

Culbertson, J. L., & Gyurke, J. (1990). Assessment of cognitive and motor development in infancy and childhood. In J. H. Johnson & J. Goldman (Eds.), *Developmental assessment in clinical child psychology: A handbook.* New York: Pergamon Press.

Frankenburg, W. K., & Dodds, J. B. (1967). The Denver Developmental Screening Test. *Journal of Pediatrics, 71,* 181–191.

Frankenburg, W. K., Dodds, J. B., Fandel, A. W., Kazuk, R., & Cohrs, M. (1975). *Denver Developmental Screening Scale* (Rev. ed.). Denver, CO: Denver Developmental Methods.

Fullard, W., McDevitt, S. C., & Carey, W. B. (1978). *Toddler Temperament Scale.* Philadelphia: Temple University, Department of Educational Psychology.

Goldberg, S., Corter, C., Lojkasek, M., & Minde, K. (1990). Prediction of behavior problems in 4-year-olds born prematurely. *Development and Psychopathology, 2,* 15–30.

Goldberg, S., & Marcovitch, S. (1989). Temperament in developmentally disabled children. In G. A. Kohnstamm, J. E. Bates, & M. K. Rothbart (Eds.), *Temperament in childhood* (pp. 387–403). New York: Wiley.

Goldsmith, H. H., Buss, A. H., Plomin, R., Rothbart, M. K., Thomas, A., Chess, S., Hinde, R. A., & McCall, R. B. (1987). Roundtable: What is temperament? Four approaches. *Child Development, 58,* 505–529.

Gordon, B. N., & Schroeder, C. S. (1990). Clinical practice: From assessment to intervention. In J. H. Johnson & J. Goldman (Eds.), *Developmental assessment in clinical child psychology: A handbook.* New York: Pergamon Press.

Hegvik, R. L., McDevitt, S. C., & Carey, W. B. (1982). The Middle Childhood Temperament Questionnaire. *Journal of Developmental and Behavioral Pediatrics, 3,* 197–200.

Herjanic, B., Herjanic, M., Brown, F., & Wheatt, T. (1975). Are children reliable reporters? *Journal of Abnormal Child Psychology, 3,* 41–48.

Hodges, K. (1993). Structured interviews for assessing children. *Journal of Child Psychology and Psychiatry, 34,* 49–68.

Hodges, K., Kline, J., Stern, L., Cytryn, L., & McKnew, D. (1982). The development of a child assessment interview for research and clinical use. *Journal of Abnormal Child Psychology, 10,* 173–189.

Ireton, H. (1990). Developmental screening measures. In J. H. Johnson & J. Goldman (Eds.), *Developmental assessment in clinical child psychology: A handbook.* New York: Pergamon Press.

Ireton, H. R. (1993). *Child Development Inventory.* Minneapolis, MN: Behavior Science Systems.

Johnson, J. H., & Goldman, J. (1993). Issues in clinical development assessment. In T. H. Ollendick & R. J. Prinz (Eds.), *Advances in clinical child psychology* (Vol. 15). New York: Plenum Press.

Keogh, B. K. (1989). Applying temperament research to school. In G. A. Kohnstamm, J. E. Bates, & M. K. Rothbart (Eds.), *Temperament in childhood* (pp. 437–450). New York: Wiley.

Keogh, B. K., Pullis, M. E., & Caldwell, J. (1982). A short form of the Teacher Temperament Questionnaire. *Journal of Educational Measurement, 19,* 323–329.

Levitt, E. E., & French, J. (1992). Projective testing of children. In C. E. Walker & M. C. Roberts (Eds.), *Handbook of clinical child psychology* (pp. 149–162). New York: Wiley.

Marcovitch, S., Goldberg, S., Lojkasek, M., & MacGregor, D. (1987). The concept of difficult temperament in the developmentally disabled preschool child. *Journal of Applied Developmental Psychology, 8,* 151–164.

Martin, R. P. (1983). Temperament: A review of research with implications for the school psychologist. *School Psychology Review, 12*(3), 266–274.

Martin, R. P. (1989). Activity level, distractibility, and persistence: Critical characteristics in early schooling. In G. A. Kohnstamm, J. E. Bates, & M. K. Rothbart (Eds.), *Temperament in childhood* (pp. 451–461). New York: Wiley.

Mash, E. J., & Terdal, L. G. (Eds.). (1988). *Behavioral assessment of childhood disorders* (2nd ed.). New York: Guilford Press.

Maziade, M. (1989). Should adverse temperament matter to the clinician? An empirically based answer. In G. A. Kohnstamm, J. E. Bates, & M. K. Rothbart (Eds.), *Temperament in childhood* (pp. 421–435). New York: Wiley.

McCarthy, D. A. (1972). *Manual for the McCarthy Scales of Children's Abilities.* San Antonio, TX: Psychological Corporation.

McDevitt, S. C. (1988). Assessment of temperament in developmentally disabled infants and preschoolers. In T. D. Wachs & R. Sheehan (Eds.), *Assessment of young developmentally disabled children* (pp. 255–265). New York: Plenum Press.

McDevitt, S. C., & Carey, W. B. (1975). The measurement of temperament in 3–7 year old children. *Journal of Child Psychology and Psychiatry, 19,* 245–253.

Nihira, K., Foster, R., Shellhaas, M., & Leland, H. (1974). *AAMD Adaptive Behavior Scale, 1974 Revision.* Washington, DC: American Association on Mental Deficiency.

Nitz, K., Lerner, R. M., Lerner, J. V., & Talwar, R. (1988). Parental and peer ethnotheory demands, temperament, and early adolescent adjustment. *Journal of Early Adolescence, 3,* 243–263.

Ollendick, T. H., & Hersen, M. (1984). *Child behavior assessment: Principles and procedures.* New York: Pergamon Press.

Orth, L. C., & Martin, R. P. (1994). Interactive effects of student temperament and instruction method on classroom behavior and achievement. *Journal of School Psychology, 32*(2), 149–166.

Orvaschel, H., Puig-Antich, J., Chambers, W., Tabrizi, M. A., & Johnson, R. (1982). Retrospective assessment of prepubertal major depression with the Kiddie-SADS-E. *Journal of the American Academy of Child Psychiatry, 4,* 392–397.

Puig-Antich, J., & Chambers, W. (1978). *The Schedule for Affective Disorders and Schizophrenia for School-Age Children* (Kiddie-SADS). New York: New York State Psychiatric Institute.

Rende, R. D. (1993). Longitudinal relations between temperament traits and behavioral syndromes in middle childhood. *Journal of the American Academy of Child and Adolescent Psychiatry, 32*(2), 287–290.

Rende, R. D., & Plomin, R. (1992). Relations between first grade stress, temperament, and behavior problems. *Journal of Applied Developmental Psychiatry, 13,* 435–446.

Rothbart, M. K. (1981). Measurement of temperament in infancy. *Child Development, 52,* 569–578.

Rothbart, M. K., & Derryberry, D. (1981). Development of individual differences in temperament. In M. L. Lamb & A. L. Brown (Eds.), *Advances in developmental psychology* (Vol. 1, pp. 37–86). Hillsdale, NJ: Erlbaum.

Rothbart, M. K., & Goldsmith, H. H. (1985). Three approaches to the study of infant temperament. *Developmental Review, 5,* 237–260.

Sattler, J. M. (1988). *Assessment of children* (3rd ed.). San Diego, CA: Jerome Sattler.

Shakow, D. (1969). *Clinical psychology as science and profession.* Chicago: Aldine.

Sheeber, L. B., & Johnson, J. H. (1992). Child temperament, maternal adjustment, and changes in family life style. *American Journal of Orthopsychiatry, 62*(2), 178–185.

Sheeber, L. B., & Johnson, J. H. (1994). Evaluation of a temperament-focused, parent-training program. *Journal of Clinical Child Psychology, 23*(3), 249–259.

Silverman, W. K. (1994). Structured diagnostic interviews. In T. H. Ollendick, N. J. King, & W. Yule (Eds.), *International handbook of phobic and anxiety disorders in children and adolescents* (pp. 293–315). New York: Plenum Press.

Sparrow, D., Balla, D. A., & Cicchetti, D. V. (1984). *Vineland Adaptive Behavior Scales.* Circle Pines, MN: American Guidance Service.

Stevenson-Hinde, J., & Simpson, A. E. (1982). Temperament and relationships. In *Temperamental differences in infants and young children* (Ciba Foundation Symposium No. 90, pp. 168–175). London: Pitman Books.

Thomas, A., & Chess, S. (1977). *Temperament and development.* New York: Brunner/Mazel.

Thorndike, R. L., Hagen, E. P., & Sattler, J. M. (1986). *Guide for administering and scoring the Stanford-Binet Intelligence Scale: Fourth Edition.* Chicago: Riverside Publishing.

Victor, J. B., Halverson, C. F., Jr., & Wampler, K. S. (1988). Family-school context: Parent and teacher agreement on child temperament. *Journal of Consulting and Clinical Psychology, 56*(4), 573–577.

Wechsler, D. (1989). *Manual for the Wechsler Preschool and Primary Scale of Intelligence—Revised.* New York: Psychological Corporation.

Wenar, C. (1982). Developmental psychopathology: Its nature and models. *Journal of Clinical Child Psychology, 11,* 192–201.

Wilson, R. S., & Matheny, A. P. (1983). Assessment of temperament in infant twins. *Developmental Psychology, 19,* 172–183.

Windle, M. (1988). Psychometric strategies of measures of temperament: A methodological critique. *International Journal of Behavioral Development, 11*(2), 171–201.

Windle, M., & Lerner, R. M. (1986). Reassessing the dimensions of temperamental individuality across the life span: The revised Dimensions of Temperament Survey (DOTS-R). *Journal of Adolescent Research, 1*(2), 213–230.

Wirt, R. D., Lachar, D., Klinedinst, J. K., & Seat, P. D. (1990). *Multidimensional description of child personality: A manual for the Personality Inventory for Children.* Los Angeles: Western Psychological Services.

CHAPTER 4

DEVELOPMENTAL THERAPY

Stephen R. Shirk

Over three decades have passed since Kiesler (1966) challenged some of the basic assumptions of psychotherapy research and practice by explicating a set of therapeutic myths. Among the most important were what he called the "uniformity assumption myths" of psychotherapy (Kiesler, 1966, p. 110). Common to these "myths" was the assumption of patient, therapist, and treatment homogeneity. For example, the patient uniformity assumption referred to the belief that "patients at the start of treatment are more alike than they are different" by virtue of the fact that they all have sought psychotherapy (p. 110). A corollary of this assumption is that patients who receive the "same" treatment should show uniform improvement. Given these assumptions, it makes sense that early psychotherapy researchers were preoccupied with the effectiveness of psychotherapy *in general* and that practitioners, typically trained in and strongly allied with one therapeutic orientation, often assumed that a single therapeutic method could be equally effective for a wide variety of patients.

Thirty years later it is difficult to comprehend how such basic assumptions could have held sway over psychotherapy research and practice. In the intervening years, researchers and practitioners increasingly have embraced a different set of assumptions that acknowledge the heteroge-

neity of patients, therapists, and treatments as well as the contextual dependencies of treatment processes and outcomes. This new set of assumptions is most succinctly captured by what has been called the "matrix paradigm" of psychotherapy (Stiles, Shapiro, & Elliott, 1986; p. 168). Researchers and practitioners are now challenged by the question: "*What* treatment, by *whom,* is most effective for *this* individual with *that* specific problem, and under *which* set of circumstances" (Paul, 1967, p. 111). Specificity has replaced the assumptions of uniformity.

Given this paradigmatic shift, have the myths of psychotherapy been buried as Kiesler wished in his seminal critique? Kendall (1984; Kendall, Lerner, & Craighead, 1984) was among the first to note that "child-clinical psychologists are often guilty of another uniformity myth" (p. 143). As Kendall observed (1984), it is a myth to assume that "children at various ages, but with the same behavior problems, are alike" (p. 143). "Children," like the broad category "patients," are far from homogeneous, and to ignore important developmental differences among children represents a variation of the patient uniformity myth. In turn, we should not expect uniform outcomes for treatments delivered to children who vary widely in their social, cognitive, and emotional capacities. Instead, it is likely that developmental differences will moderate the effectiveness of many child treatments (Shirk, 1988a).

Kendall's explication of the developmental uniformity myth alerts us to the possibility that some of the basic assumptions of child therapy may require revision when viewed from a developmental perspective. The purpose of this chapter is to re-examine some of the basic tenets of child therapy from a developmental point of view and to address the question, What are the implications of a developmental perspective for the conduct of therapy with children and adolescents? It is proposed that the application of a developmental perspective to child and adolescent therapy will reveal a number of "myths" that continue to guide the practice of therapy with children and adolescents.

A DEVELOPMENTAL PERSPECTIVE

Given the protean nature of the concept of development, and the multitude of developmental theories, the formulation of a developmental perspective must be, by necessity, selective. Increasingly, the investigation of child and adolescent psychopathology has been informed by a set of developmental principles and concepts (Cicchetti, 1990). The developmental perspective utilized in this analysis draws upon some of the basic developmental principles that have guided research in developmental psychopathology (Cicchetti, 1990; Masten, Best, & Garmezy, 1990; Sroufe, 1979; Sroufe & Rutter, 1984). Specifically, four basic principles will serve as the framework for this review.

First, development involves a series of reorganizations in the child's cognitive, social, and emotional capacities (Sroufe, 1979). In brief, development involves not only incremental additions in capacities, but qualitative changes in behavioral organization (Werner, 1957). Consequently, the cognitive, emotional, and social repertoires of children at different levels of development can be expected to vary significantly.

Second, development is characterized by the principle of "equifinality" (von Bertalanffy, 1968). In this context, equifinality refers to the assumption that multiple pathways or processes can lead to similar outcomes (Cicchetti, Toth, & Bush, 1988). Werner (1957) described this phenomenon in terms of the *multiformity of development,* or in his words, "The same achievement may be reached by operations genetically quite different" (p. 132). This perspective stands in sharp contrast to a conceptualization of development in which single, invariant pathways and processes are posited for particular outcomes.

Third, development entails *adaptation* to a series of stage-salient or age-related challenges such as the establishment of early affectional bonds or adjustment to the demands of

school (Cicchetti et al., 1988; Sroufe & Rutter, 1984). The dual emphasis on adaptation and challenge reflects a developmental dialectic between the child's capacities and psychosocial demands. On the one hand, this dual perspective draws attention to the evolution of *competencies* that enable the child to master developmental tasks and, on the other, it underscores the fact that the course of development is not continuous (or smooth), but involves multiple challenges that represent potential departure points from the path of normal development. Furthermore, because development entails diverse tasks or challenges, adaptation cannot be reduced to a single set of behaviors or skills. Instead, consideration must be given to the varied competencies that engender adaptive functioning across the course of development (Kohlberg, LaCrosse, & Ricks, 1972; Masten, Best, & Garmezy, 1990).

Fourth, child and adolescent development does not occur in a vacuum, but is embedded in a system of social contexts (Belsky, 1981; Bronfenbrenner, 1979). Developmental achievements are not attained in isolation, but depend on a facilitating social environment (Rogoff, 1990). Conversely, developmental casualties often reflect deficits or deviations in the social contexts, especially in the caregiving contexts, that promote healthy development (Masten et al., 1990). Within the domain of developmental psychopathology, maladaptation is a function not only of the ratio of individual vulnerabilities and competencies, but of the balance between environmental potentiating and protective factors (Cicchetti & Aber, 1986). Consequently, the unit of analysis (or the unit of intervention) cannot be restricted to the individual child but must encompass the social contexts, particularly the family context, in which the child develops.

These four basic principles, by no means exhaustive of the conceptual richness of developmental theory, will be used to frame the developmental perspective utilized in this review. It is proposed that the application of these principles will call into question some of the assumptions that guide the practice of child and adolescent therapy.

THE DEVELOPMENTAL UNIFORMITY MYTH

Some years ago, Orlinsky and Howard (1978) reminded psychotherapy researchers that psychotherapy is a form of social interaction, and though it is often imbued with unique features, therapeutic interaction can be understood in terms of processes that apply to all social interactions. Developmentalists have long recognized that the character and outcome of social interactions are, in part, a function of the cognitive, social, and emotional repertoires that the participants bring to social exchanges (Selman, 1980; Shantz, 1987). The same could be said of therapeutic interactions between children and therapists. The child's cognitive, emotional, and social capacities are not deposited at the clinic door, but enter the therapy session just as surely as the child's presenting problems. However, as Kendall (1984) has observed, child clinicians often have focused on children's presenting problems while ignoring important developmental differences in their cognitive and social capacities. This tendency is also found in child therapy research in which the impact of nondiagnostic child characteristics, including developmental level, have often been ignored (Kazdin, Bass, Ayers, & Rodgers, 1990).

Given the progressive reorganization of children's capacities, it can be expected that children, even children with the same presenting problems, will vary in terms of the cognitive, emotional, and social repertoires they bring to therapy. To ignore these differences and to treat children as a homogeneous group commits what Kendall (1984) has called the "developmental level uniformity myth" (p. 143). A variation of this myth, dubbed the "developmental continuity myth" (Shirk, 1990, p. 19), involves the unmodified "downloading" of adult treatment procedures to children. This tendency appears to be based on the assumption that the major discontinuity between adult and child therapy involves differences in language competence. The assumption, then, is that the basic processes of adult therapy can be imported to the treatment of children if one simplifies the language or changes the communicative medium (Shirk, 1990). Although such changes are often necessary to make therapy accessible to children, the simplification of vocabulary or the substitution of play for discourse often fails to address the *conceptual* demands of therapy process.

The main point is that therapeutic processes are embedded in, and at times constrained by, developmental processes (Kendall et al., 1984; Shirk, 1988a). Consequently, the child's emerging cognitive, emotional, and interpersonal capacities influence "what type of clinical interventions may be efficacious, and which may be ineffective, inefficient, or even contraindicated" (Kendall et al., 1984, p. 72). Put simply, children at different developmental levels cannot be expected to uniformly utilize or benefit from specific sets of interventions. In other words, developmental level represents a potentially important moderator of treatment utility and effectiveness. Clear examples of the intersection of developmental processes with therapeutic processes can be found in most of the major approaches to child treatment. The following represent illustrative examples.

Insight-Oriented Child Therapy

Traditional insight-oriented child therapy relies heavily on a communicative process referred to as *interpretation* (Erik-

son, 1964; Freud, 1965). Although numerous definitions of interpretation have been offered, at its core the process of interpretation involves the application of "an alternative frame of reference, or language system, to bear on a set of observations or behaviors, with the end in view of making them amenable to change" (Levy, 1963, p. 7). In the context of dynamic child therapy this process has been characterized as restructuring the child's self-understanding in a way that connects thoughts, feelings, and behaviors in new ways (Wilson, 1981). Of course, the underlying assumption is that such new understandings or insights will enable the child to alter behavior or experience different emotions.

One of the basic aims of interpretation is to highlight or clarify *causal* relations between current feelings, behaviors, and attitudes and antecedent conditions or underlying motivations (Shirk, 1988c). As Meeks (1971) notes, "In interpretation, we address ourselves to *why* the patient performs certain actions or expresses certain thoughts" (p. 116). Thus, interpretations typically involve either implicit or explicit causal communications. Close examination of typical interpretations in child therapy reveals that the causal structure of these communications varies in complexity along several dimensions (Shirk, 1988b). These include whether the causal referent is proximal or distal in time, psychological or situational in origin, and within or outside of conscious awareness. Research indicates that these dimensions of causal reasoning do not emerge uniformly, and that children at different ages vary in their capacity to make these types of causal distinctions (Leahy & Shirk, 1984). Thus, in many instances the causal structure embedded in therapists' interpretations may be far more complex than the causal reasoning of most "normal" children, not to mention disturbed children. For example, the use of interpretations that link current behavior to internal processes or past events is incongruent with the younger child's tendency to focus on situational and temporally proximal explanations for behavior. This type of discrepancy between the therapist's level of causal communication and the child's level of causal reasoning may render many interpretations incomprehensible. Furthermore, without comprehension, it is unlikely that interpretations will function to promote insight or therapeutic change.

Client-Centered Child Therapy

According to client-centered child therapists (Axline, 1947; Wright, Everett, & Roisman, 1986), emotional and behavioral problems are markers of underlying vulnerabilities in self-esteem that have resulted from inadequate support, acceptance, or love from caregivers. The aim of treatment, then, is compensatory—to enhance the child's self-worth through the provision of a warm, accepting relationship.

Embedded in the client-centered formulation is a conceptualization of self-esteem as an outgrowth of a unitary process. In brief, the development and maintenance of positive self-worth is viewed exclusively in terms of the child's experience of positive regard from others (Axline, 1947; Moustakas, 1959). In turn, this formulation leads to a single therapeutic prescription, namely, the provision of a warm, accepting relationship with a substitute caregiver. Furthermore, implicit in this view is the assumption that the provision of a warm, accepting relationship will enhance self-esteem in a uniform manner across developmental levels. This assumption appears problematic when viewed from a developmental perspective.

Although research indicates that acceptance and social support are positively related to self-worth across the life span (Harter, 1993), a substantial body of evidence reveals that perceived competence in areas of importance is also a major determinant of self-esteem (Harter, 1986). In fact, for older children and adolescents these two factors appear to operate in an additive fashion (Harter, 1993). Harter (1986) has proposed that the relative contribution of these two broad determinants of self-worth varies with one's developmental level. As she notes, positive regard may be a potent force during the early years, especially when need for adult approval is high (Harter, 1986). Moreover, because young children lack the cognitive skills to "simultaneously compare hierarchies of perceived competence and the importance of success," this determinant of self-esteem may be less influential with younger children than with older children and adolescents (Harter, 1986, p. 172). This perspective is supported by findings that indicate that children become more proficient in the use of efficacy information with increasing age (Bandura, 1981). With the acquisition of the requisite cognitive skills, perceived competence could become a more powerful determinant of self-esteem. Transposed to the therapeutic context, the impact of acceptance and positive regard on self-esteem may vary with developmental level as children become increasingly focused on their emerging competencies.

A similar point has been expressed by Pope, McHale, and Craighead (1988), who contend that adult attention and responsiveness, particularly from a therapist, may differentially affect the self-esteem of preschoolers and school-age children. Younger children may be more concerned with adult approval than with the quality of task performance, whereas older children may be more concerned with adult feedback that contributes to the development of competence than with noncontingent adult approval (Pope et al., 1988). Thus, when one adopts a developmental perspective the enhancement of self-esteem cannot be reduced to a unitary process. Approval and positive regard may be highly salient, and therapeutically efficacious, for younger children, but with increasing age therapeutic interactions that focus on building competencies or increasing self-efficacy beliefs may become more potent mechanisms of change.

Cognitive Behavioral Therapy

Based on the assumption that enduring changes in behavior are predicated on changes in cognition, cognitive–behavioral approaches rely heavily on the modification of cognitive content, structures, and processes (Kendall, 1991). Among the most prominent interventions in this tradition are training procedures aimed at establishing self-regulation through the development of self-monitoring, self-generated problem-solving strategies, and self-evaluations of outcomes (Kendall & Braswell, 1985; Lochman & Curry, 1986). Given the emphasis on promoting cognitive mediational processes, it is likely that the acquisition of these skills will depend on the child's level of cognitive development (Kendall et al., 1984). That is, the acquisition of such processes may hinge on the existence of basic cognitive structures that enable the child to integrate new cognitive skills into his or her cognitive repertoire.

In their meta-analysis of the effectiveness of cognitive–behavioral therapy, Durlak, Fuhrman, and Lampman (1991) evaluated the hypothesis that children's cognitive–developmental level would moderate treatment responsiveness. Because most studies of cognitive–behavioral therapy have not directly assessed the child's cognitive level prior to treatment, Durlak and colleagues (1991) were forced to rely on age as a proxy for developmental level. Based on Piagetian theory, effect sizes were calculated for children approximating three levels of cognitive development: preoperational (ages 5–7), concrete–operational (ages 7–11), and formal operational (ages 11–13). Consistent with the developmental moderation hypothesis, Durlak and his colleagues found that the treatment effect for the oldest group—assumed to be formal operational—was nearly twice as large as the effects obtained for the two younger, and presumably, cognitively less-advanced groups. These results suggest that troubled children who enter therapy with more advanced cognitive abilities are likely to attain greater benefit from cognitively oriented treatments than children who are less advanced. However, it should be noted that these results are based on treatment outcomes that have been aggregated across a variety of cognitive–behavioral procedures. As Durlak and colleagues (1991) note, cognitive–behavioral therapy is an "umbrella term" for a variety of treatment procedures, and because their meta-analysis did not examine the effects of developmental level by specific treatment procedures, it is not possible to determine which cognitive interventions are most strongly affected by developmental level. It should be noted, however, that a meta-analysis of one form of cognitive-behavioral therapy, self-instructional training, has revealed that effect sizes are positively related to age (Dush, Hirt, & Schroeder, 1989). Additional research is needed to determine which age-related cognitive processes moderate the impact of cognitive–behavioral interventions.

Behavioral Parent Management Training

Parent management training (PMT) is based on the assumption that child behavior problems are primarily a function of "faulty interaction between parent and child" (Miller & Prinz, 1990, p. 292). The basic rationale for this intervention is that parents lack essential child-management skills that would promote prosocial or adaptive development in their children. Thus, parent management training involves teaching parents to interact differently with their children (Kazdin, 1991). Although there are a number of variations of parent management training, Kazdin (1991) has identified several common characteristics that include the following: (1) treatment is primarily conducted with the parents with little or no direct involvement with the child, (2) treatment focuses on teaching behavioral observation skills and the application of social learning principles, for example, instruction in the use of systematic rewards and mild punishments (time-out), and (3) treatment sessions provide parents with the opportunity to implement and review the effects of behavior change programs.

There is substantial evidence that PMT produces significant improvement in functioning for families with behaviorally disordered children (Kazdin, 1987; Wells & Forehand, 1985). However, there is also evidence that relatively younger children are more likely to benefit from this form of treatment than older children (Strain, Young, & Horowitz, 1981). In fact, the majority of outcome studies have focused on the application of this method with preadolescent children (McMahon & Wells, 1989).

Forehand and Wierson (1993) have proposed that the extension of PMT to the treatment of adolescents must account for important developmental transitions that occur during early and middle adolescence. Most importantly, they suggest that the increasing press toward autonomy and independence decreases the adolescent's willingness to "accept their parents as authority figures who control all the power" (Forehand & Weirson, 1993). Similarly, Robin and Foster (1989) contend that the process of separation and individuation upsets the balance of control in the family, and that the manner in which families respond to this challenge "determines whether the normal perturbation of early adolescence is resolved or whether it escalates to clinically significant problems" (p. 8).

The developmental process of individuation carries important implications for the design and implementation of PMT for families with adolescents. With its almost exclusive focus on training parents, in contrast to treating parents *and* children, the basic framework for PMT is essentially unilateral. Parents are provided with a set of skills for modifying their own and their child's behavior. Children, in contrast, are basically respondents to this intervention. Typically, they are neither directly engaged in treatment sessions, nor are they provided with a set of skills for altering parent–child interactions. These treatment parameters are likely to conflict with and be undermined by the social developmental processes of adolescence.

The process of adolescent individuation, accompanied by the tendency for adolescents to challenge parental control, suggests that parent management must be reconceptualized in terms of mutual rather than unilateral interventions. In fact, families who remain "stuck" in a unilateral mode of discipline during the adolescent transition may be more likely to become clinical cases. The shift from a unilateral to mutual framework points to a number of basic changes in PMT with adolescents. First, interventions should focus on the development of negotiation and compromise skills (Forehand & Wierson, 1993; Robin & Foster, 1989). Second, PMT must move away from an exclusive focus on parent intervention and include the adolescent in treatment sessions. Negotiation is a reciprocal process and is likely to be most effective when both parties are trained in the requisite skills.

It should be noted that behavior therapists are beginning to address these developmental issues. For example, in their work with delinquent adolescents Patterson and his colleagues (Marlowe, Reid, Patterson, Weinrott, & Bank, 1988) have increased the involvement of adolescents in sessions, particularly around formulating behavioral contracts. Similarly, Robin and Foster (1989) have reconceptualized parent–adolescent conflict from a behavioral-systems perspective and have emphasized communication and negotiation skills with all family members. Accommodation of the developmental processes that influence parent–child interaction at different stages could enhance the effectiveness of PMT.

Summary and Clinical Implications

As these examples suggest, the design and selection of interventions for children and adolescents must consider the evolving capacities, and not just the types of problems, presented by youngsters in therapy. Developmental theory and emerging evidence indicate that the effectiveness of specific interventions will be moderated by the patient's level of development. Thus, child clinicians need to be aware of the "developmental fit" between therapeutic tasks and the emerging capacities of their patients. In brief, child therapists should be trained to conduct developmental task analyses of psychosocial interventions to maximize the likelihood that treatment processes are compatible with the child's developmental level (Shirk & Phillips, 1991).

Furthermore, for certain interventions to be effective it may be necessary to begin treatment by promoting the development of capacities that will enable the child to utilize specific treatment procedures. For example, cognitive interventions that rely on monitoring internal processes, such as self-talk, might be enhanced for younger children by training perspective-taking skills during the initial phase of treatment. The acquisition of such capacities could increase children's ability to observe their own behavior and internal states (Selman, 1980), thereby increasing their responsiveness to traditional cognitive–behavioral procedures. Thus, it is possible that interventions could be enhanced, not only by ensuring a developmental fit with the child's capacities, but by facilitating developmental processes that underlie the use of treatment procedures.

THE DEVELOPMENTAL INVARIANCE MYTH

Although developmental theory contains numerous references to invariant developmental sequences (cf. Erikson, 1950; Freud, 1905; Kohlberg, 1969), a counterpoint to this perspective is found in Werner's (1957) description of *developmental multiformity*. Put simply, similar developmental achievements or attainments can be reached by way of different developmental pathways or processes. Within the field of developmental psychopathology there is increasing recognition that very different paths can lead to similar maladaptive outcomes (Cicchetti et al., 1988; Kazdin & Kagan, 1994). This perspective represents a significant departure from a "one size fits all" model of dysfunction in which single causal pathways and processes are posited for specific disorders (Kazdin & Kagan, 1994, p. 36).

Consider, for example, three children who share a similar maladaptive outcome, in this case, dysthymic disorder. All three present with symptoms of depressed mood, low energy, and diminished interest in previously appealing activities. The first child comes from a stable family but is harshly self-punitive when she fails to meet exceedingly high self-standards. The second is rejected by her peers at school and spends most of her afternoons alone watching television. The third was removed from her family in early childhood and has suffered through a series of failed foster home placements. Although each of these children present with the same diagnostic outcome, the pathways and corresponding developmental processes that led to this outcome are strikingly

different. Self-criticism, social isolation, and attachment disruption represent core processes, but not in equal measure for each child. At the heart of the developmental invariance myth is the assumption that there is an invariant relation between developmental outcomes and the developmental processes that produced them. The clinical translation of this assumption is that there are invariant relations between specific disorders and underlying pathogenic mechanisms. Or as Kazdin and Kagan (1994) note: "Many popular explanations of dysfunction assume a simple relation between a small number of antecedent conditions and a particular pathological outcome" (p. 36). In contrast to this perspective, developmentalists have maintained that similar manifest behaviors do not necessarily share the same substructure (Shapiro, 1995; Werner, 1957). In fact, the tendency to equate phenotype and genotype, that is, to assume that there is an invariant relationship between developmental outcome and underlying developmental process commits what Werner (1957) has called the *behavioral constancy fallacy*.

Ironically, the recognition of multiple pathways to the same maladaptive outcome has taken place during a time when diagnostic classification has divorced itself from systematic consideration of underlying pathogenic processes (Shirk & Russell, 1996). Current diagnostic systems, especially the DSMs, have emphasized classification on the basis of observable symptom clusters. Disorders, then, are largely defined in terms of patterns of overt problems with very limited reference to underlying developmental processes. Yet the recognition of multiple pathways to the same disorder mitigates against such a restrictive approach to classification. Children with phenotypically similar emotional or behavioral problems may evince different pathogenic processes as a result of markedly different developmental histories. In other words, it is a myth to assume that there is an invariant relation between manifest disorder and underlying pathogenic process.

Unfortunately, the current quest for *prescriptive treatments* (Beutler & Clarkin, 1990) for children and adolescents appears to be based on the developmental invariance myth. This approach to treatment selection is based on the assumption that "there are specific discernible and homogeneous diagnostic categories to which identified and validated treatments can be applied" (Kendall & Clarkin, 1992, p. 833). The problem with this approach, as it is currently formulated, is that homogeneity is defined principally in terms of shared diagnoses that are based on phenotypic similarities among cases. However, if one accepts the developmental principle of multiformity, then the current approach to prescriptive treatment is confronted with the problem of heterogeneity, only one step removed. Children may share the same diagnosis but not the same pathogenic process. In other words, there may be substantial within (diagnostic) group variability in the developmental histories and associated pathogenic processes that contribute to the manifest disorder. Yet, as Persons (1991) has observed, the prescriptive approach assumes that individuals with the same disorder have the disorder for the same reason. The assumption of an invariant relation between diagnosis and underlying pathogenic process is undermined by evidence of multiple developmental pathways to the same maladaptive outcome. Heterogeneity in developmental histories and pathogenic processes can be expected for children who are classified with the same disorder. Thus, for some children a prescribed treatment will address the underlying process, for others it may be irrelevant and essentially inconsequential, and still for others it may be detrimental. The fact that specific treatments often increase outcome variability among treated children may reflect unassessed heterogeneity in pathogenic processes within the same diagnostic group (Shirk & Russell, 1996).

Summary and Clinical Implications

What are the implications of the developmental invariance myth for the conduct of therapy with children and adolescents? The recognition of multiple developmental pathways and pathogenic processes creates problems for diagnostically driven models of intervention. Children, even children at the same developmental level who share the same diagnosis, are not homogeneous. The paths and processes that have produced their symptomatology are likely to be quite varied. In fact, a single causal pathway for a specific disorder is likely to be the exception rather than the rule (Kazdin & Kagan, 1994). Consequently, the design and implementation of a treatment plan must move beyond diagnosis to an assessment of the factors that contribute to the child's presenting problems. In brief, assessment and treatment must be closely linked, and assessment cannot be reduced to accurate diagnosis.

For example, given the growing recognition of multiple determinants of childhood depression, Stark and colleagues (1991) have increasingly emphasized "individual tailoring" of treatment procedures rather than the application of a standardized protocol (p. 166). Treatment procedures are selected on the basis of an assessment of the pathogenic mechanisms contributing to the child's depression (Stark et al., 1991). Such an approach to treatment embraces the principle of multiformity by acknowledging the fact that depressive symptoms may be a function of different processes in different children. Thus, for some depressed children the focus of intervention will be on social skills training, whereas

for other children who demonstrate adequate skills, treatment might be geared toward restructuring biased cognitions. As this example suggests, simply because a child is diagnosed with depression does not mean that he or she will receive social skills training even though *as a group* depressed children show social deficits (Weisz, Rudolph, Granger, & Sweeney, 1992). Individualized treatments depend on the assessment of individuals and not just on inferences from group means.

As an alternative to standardized treatments, Persons (1991) has advocated for a *case-formulation approach* to intervention. Here the therapist constructs and tests working hypotheses (case formulations) about underlying pathogenic mechanisms that contribute to a patient's presenting problems. Interventions are selected or designed on the basis of an individualized case formulation. Recently, Shirk and Russell (1996) have proposed a set of *formulation prototypes* that could guide the development of working hypotheses about pathogenic mechanisms. In addition, it is important to note that diagnosis can play a pivotal role in the construction of case formulations. Insofar as diagnoses draw attention to probabilistic relations between manifest symptoms and pathogenic mechanisms, they provide a starting point, hopefully grounded in empirical evidence, for the development of a case formulation. However, probabilistic relations should not be confused with invariant relations. The existence of multiple pathways to the same disorder requires an assessment of the pathogenic processes that are relevant for a particular case. In sum, the recognition of developmental multiformity contraindicates the standardization of treatments for many disorders and necessitates the individualization of treatments based on an assessment of underlying pathogenic mechanisms.

THE DEVELOPMENTAL CONSISTENCY MYTH

Conceptualizing development in terms of adaptation to a series of stage-salient issues or challenges draws attention to the evolution of adaptive competencies and highlights the fact that the path of development is not consistent, but involves qualitatively different tasks at different ages (Cicchetti, Toth, Bush, & Gillespie, 1988; Sroufe, 1979). The concept of developmental pathways has prompted some to redefine the aim of child therapy as returning children to a healthy developmental path (Vernberg, Routh, & Koocher, 1992). As Vernberg and colleagues (1992) note, "Instead of trying to provide a permanent cure that will protect the child from distress throughout his or her life, the therapist tries using a variety of methods to help the child regain a footing on a developmental pathway more likely to lead to adequate adaptation in subsequent periods of life" (p. 73). Implicit in this view is the assumption that developmental systems are not primarily homeostatic, but are characterized by a pattern of progressive change. "Developmental therapy," then, involves returning the child to this progressive developmental track (Vernberg et al., 1992, p. 75).

The notion of returning the child to a healthy pathway, though appealing from a developmental perspective, raises critical issues about how the process of return or restoration should be conceptualized. It is in this context that the developmental consistency myth is encountered.

When development is framed in terms of adaptation to a series of stage-salient issues or challenges, one is reminded that the path of "normal" development is neither smooth nor consistent. Consequently, the processes that return a child to a healthy pathway are not likely to be consistent *across developmental periods*. To assume that there is consistency in these processes constitutes the developmental consistency myth.

The clearest example of this type of thinking can be found in early psychoanalytic formulations. To her credit, Anna Freud (1947) was among the first to conceptualize child therapy from a developmental perspective. For Anna Freud, the aim of treatment was to restore the child to the path of normal development (cf. Sandler, Kennedy, & Tyson, 1980). However, in her conceptualization of the processes that restore "normal" development, one encounters two variations of the developmental consistency myth. The more extreme version is that restoration hinges on the resolution of a singular form of neurotic conflict, typically the Oedipal conflict. This perspective has been criticized from within the psychoanalytic tradition itself for failing to account for multiple core conflicts that arise during different developmental periods (Erikson, 1963). The less extreme version is that restoration consistently involves the resolution of internal conflicts. Research in developmental psychopathology has indicated that deviation from a healthy pathway often involves multiple individual and contextual determinants (Robbins & Rutter, 1990). Thus, it is highly unlikely that one type of therapeutic process will consistently return the child to a normal developmental pathway.

A variation on this perspective is implicit in treatment models that focus exclusively on symptom reduction as the best means to restore "normal" developmental processes. According to this perspective, maladaptive or symptomatic behavior interferes with the child's ability to engage in activities or interactions that promote healthy development. For example, hyperactive or aggressive behavior is often associated with peer rejection which, in turn, potentiates involvement in deviant groups (Ledingham, 1990). Thus, the

child not only misses opportunities for learning adaptive social behaviors, but the symptoms tend to "snowball" as the child moves onto a deviant pathway (Kagan & Kazdin, 1994). Furthermore, increasing evidence for the stability of both internalizing and externalizing behaviors (Achenbach, Howell, McConaughy, & Stanger, 1995; Verhulst & Ende, 1992) lends credence to the importance of eliminating maladaptive symptoms early in development. As Feehan, McGee, Williams, and Nada-Raja (1995) suggest, early disorders are clear predictors of later disorders, and interventions that reduce maladaptive symptoms may be the best method for preventing future mental health problems.

A major question for this approach is whether symptom reduction is sufficient for returning the child to a healthy path at different points in development. For example, symptom reduction might be adequate in early development before the deleterious effects of maladaptive behaviors begin to accumulate. Early corrective interventions increase the likelihood that children will be able to participate in contexts that promote healthy development. However, it is likely that the longer the child has been on a deviant pathway the greater the probability he or she will have accumulated deficits in adaptive capacities. That is, the longer the child's symptoms have interfered with participation in healthy developmental processes, the greater the likelihood that adaptive competencies will be delayed. Thus, the length of time a child has been on a deviant path is likely to moderate the effectiveness of symptom-focused approaches.

A related concern is that symptom reduction, for example, through pharmacological or targeted behavioral interventions, may not be sufficient to "*keep* the child on the path of healthy development" (emphasis mine). For example, Puig-Antich and colleagues (1985) have contended that treating only the affective disorder is not sufficient for many children with major depression. Despite changes in depressive symptoms, some children continue to evince interpersonal deficits that interfere with normal social interaction and potentially make them vulnerable to recurrent depressive episodes (Puig-Antich, Lukens, Davies, Goetz, Brennan-Quattrock, & Todak, 1985). Such findings suggest that targeted symptom reduction may not produce lasting results across different types of disorders.

In fact, a variation of the developmental consistency myth involves the belief that symptom reduction or, for that matter, any single form of intervention, will consistently return children with different *classes* of disorders to a healthy developmental pathway. Evidence is beginning to accumulate that different types of childhood disorders involve distinctive developmental trajectories (Cicchetti et al., 1988; Kohlberg et al., 1972; Ledingham, 1990). For example, some childhood disorders can be characterized as essentially chronic, such as autism or dyslexia, whereas others, such as major depression or bulimia, show a remitting/relapsing pattern. In fact, within some classes of disorders, such as disruptive behavior disorders, there appear to be different developmental courses (Loeber et al., 1993). Consequently, interventions aimed at "returning the child to a healthy pathway" must account for developmental variations in the trajectories of different classes of disorders. For example, in the case of remitting/relapsing types of disorders a major aim of intervention must be on promoting the development of competencies that enable children to *stay* on a healthy developmental path.

Many interventions aimed at returning children to healthy pathways focus on the development of adaptive competencies (Strayhorn, 1988). The emphasis on facilitating competencies is highly congruent with a developmental perspective on treatment. That is, a developmental perspective provides an antidote to the clinical preoccupation with symptoms and problems by emphasizing the importance of emerging competencies for adaptive functioning.

Research on risk and resilience has uncovered a number of factors that might be targeted for returning the child to a healthy pathway. This research indicates that children who experience high levels of risk or adversity "fare better or *recover more successfully*" when they (1) receive stable care or maintain a relationship with a competent adult, (2) have good problem-solving skills, (3) are engaging to other people, and (4) have an area of competence that is valued by society (Masten et al., 1990, p. 438, italics added). Thus, interventions aimed at restoring healthy development could focus on promoting interpersonal and problem-solving skills and could facilitate the development of specific strengths in areas such as athletics, academics, or the arts. Such an approach would emphasize "building on strengths" as much as remediating weaknesses.

Based on the risk and resiliency literature it is tempting to advocate for the promotion of a core set of competencies as the "royal road" to healthy development. However, such a prescription would again embrace the developmental consistency myth. Although this approach incorporates the developmental emphasis on adaptive competencies, it fails to acknowledge variability in the issues or challenges presented at different points in development. As Waters and Sroufe (1983) have maintained, a developmental conceptualization of competence necessitates consideration of the stage-salient issues encountered at different ages. Because these issues or challenges are not consistent across the course of development, many critical competencies tend to be age-specific. Consequently, interventions aimed at promoting competence must be coordinated with the varied psychosocial de-

mands of different developmental periods. For example, skills that enhance group entry might be especially important for preschoolers and young school-age children for whom the expansion of social relations, especially peer relations, represents a salient developmental task. For older children, who are faced with the demands of school performance, the enhancement of academic skills or interventions aimed at efficacy beliefs could be emphasized. In each case, specific competencies are targeted based on their relevance to stage-salient developmental tasks.

Summary and Clinical Implications

The basic tenet of "developmental psychotherapy" is that the goal of treatment is to return children to healthy developmental pathways (Vernberg et al., 1992). Although this approach is based on developmental assumptions, recognition of multiple pathways and variations in stage-salient tasks requires a developmental conceptualization of the processes of restoration or return. Just as no single form of therapy is likely to be equally effective across different disorders, the processes involved in restoration or return are likely to be diverse and developmentally specific. Effective strategies for returning children to healthy pathways must account for stage-salient developmental issues, variations in the developmental trajectories of different disorders, and the duration a child has been on a deviant developmental path. Failure to consider these developmental differences amounts to endorsing the developmental consistency myth.

A developmental perspective highlights the role of emerging competencies in adaptive functioning and redistributes attention to children's strengths as well as to their weaknesses. Thus, it is proposed that a second tenet of developmental psychotherapy is that treatments aimed at returning children to healthy pathways must consider the competencies required to master stage-salient developmental challenges.

THE MYTH OF INDIVIDUAL DEVELOPMENT

Historically, maturational models of development with their emphasis on the unfolding of individual capacities have given way to interactive models that emphasize the interplay between biological givens and the formative influence of social experience (Sroufe, 1979). One of the best examples of this perspective is found in attachment theory (Bowlby, 1980). Here the child's biologically given behavior of proximity-seeking interacts with variations in caregiver responsiveness to produce individual differences in social development (Sroufe, 1979). This perspective is concisely summarized in Winnicott's (1965) assertion that there is no such thing as a baby, implying that the emergence of individual developmental potential depends on a facilitating social environment.

A substantial body of evidence has accumulated over several decades, which indicates that the quality of child adjustment is closely associated with the nature of parental care (Baumrind, 1978; Maccoby & Martin, 1983; Schaefer, 1959). One of the most consistent findings to emerge from this vast literature is that high levels of parental warmth combined with consistent levels of behavioral control are predictive of adaptive child outcomes. More recently, attachment researchers have demonstrated that the quality of early parent–infant relationships is predictive of variations in children's mastery of stage-salient developmental issues (Sroufe, 1979; Waters & Sroufe, 1983).

Conversely, a growing body of clinical evidence indicates that child maladjustment is linked with problematic parental care. For example, research on disruptive behavior disorders shows that factors that interfere with adequate parenting, such as parental maladjustment, substance abuse, and marital conflict, are related to the development of disruptive behavior problems (Frick, 1994; Patterson, 1982). Furthermore, longitudinal studies of risk and resilience reveal that many of the lasting effects of early adversity can be attributed to "severe interference with the protective processes embedded in the caregiving system" (Masten et al., 1990, p. 438).

Taken together these results indicate that the character of individual development is closely linked to the quality of parental care. Others have expanded on this perspective and have emphasized the "embedded" nature of development by noting that the proximal developmental context of the parent–child relationship is nested inside other influential social contexts, such as the extended family, neighborhood, or community (Belsky, 1984; Bronfenbrenner, 1979).

Thus, a developmental perspective draws attention to the psychosocial contexts, especially the caregiving contexts, that support or obstruct the child's development. Interventions that focus exclusively on the treatment of individual children are based on a decontextualized model of development or what might be called the *myth of individual development*. A developmentally informed approach to child therapy would broaden the unit of analysis—and intervention—to include the social contexts, especially the caregiving relationships, that facilitate or impede the child's development.

Child Therapy in Context

Many traditional forms of child therapy, particularly psychodynamic and play therapy approaches, emphasize individual treatment of the symptomatic child. Although the treatment procedures prescribed by these approaches differ in important ways, they appear to share a critical assumption about the temporal relationship between symptoms of maladjustment and their precipitating conditions. In brief, the factors that contribute to maladjustment are often located in the child's past. A typical formulation, then, is that the child's current problems reflect difficulties in early relationships. For example, enduring deficits in a child's self-esteem might be traced to a history of parental unresponsiveness (Wright et al., 1986). In turn, treatment is viewed as filling the gaps created during early development, for example, through the provision of a supportive relationship. Given this prototypical formulation, the contribution of the child's current relationships, including ongoing relationships with caregivers, is often neglected. Instead, the child is viewed as the repository of inadequate early care and treatment tends to emphasize correcting *internalized* problems or conflicts.

It is important to note that traditional child therapists are not the only clinicians who succumb to this type of thinking. As Braswell (1991) has observed, cognitive–behavioral therapists typically encourage parental involvement, but "the literature indicates that explicitly involving parents in the treatment process has been the exception rather than the rule" (p. 316). Again, the neglect of parents in the treatment process appears to stem from the basic formulation underlying many cognitive–behavioral treatments. In brief, the skill-deficit formulation emphasizes developmental problems in the acquisition of functional capacities such as social problem-solving, coping, and self-monitoring skills. In turn, treatments such as self-instructional training aim at remediating developmental deficits. Although these deficits are typically conceptualized in terms of early social learning processes, that is, caregivers are often implicated in the etiology of skill deficits, the current contribution of the child's caregivers and other significant figures such as peers is often neglected by cognitive behaviorists (Braswell, 1991). As Braswell (1991) points out, problems with the generalization and maintenance of cognitive strategies can be attributed to the failure to involve key figures who may support or undermine what the child has learned in individual therapy. Although individual skill training is essential for improved functioning, successful transfer of newly acquired skills requires attention to the current social contexts in which these skills might be utilized. In essence, cognitive behaviorists must not forget their behavioral legacy with its focus on the environmental determinants of child maladjustment (Braswell, 1991).

However, even behavioral child treatments have not been immune to the problem of decontextualization. One of the most widely practiced and effective behavioral interventions, parent management training (PMT), is based on the premise that ineffective parenting is a major contributor to child maladjustment (Kazdin, 1991). Interventions are directly aimed at the modification of the caregiving system through the teaching of appropriate child management skills. Thus, parent involvement is an essential feature of PMT. However, there is growing recognition that families characterized by multiple risk factors such as marital dysfunction, social isolation, and parental psychopathology show fewer treatment gains and are less likely to maintain gains (Kazdin, 1991). The problem, it seems, is that PMT has focused on teaching parenting skills in isolation from the contextual determinants of parenting (Griest & Forehand, 1982; Miller & Prinz, 1990).

Belsky (1984) has proposed that effective parenting cannot be reduced to a single set of skills, but is influenced by multiple determinants including the parents' own developmental history, their marital relationship, their work relations, and their network of support. The exclusive focus on individual parent attributes (i.e., their behavior management skills) represents a variation on the individual development myth. That is, individual behavior, in this case, problematic parenting behavior, is lifted from the broader developmental context that supports or undermines effective functioning.

It is important to note that behavior therapists are beginning to address this problem by devising "enhanced" interventions that emphasize the broader social context in which the family functions (Miller & Prinz, 1990). To date, the most inclusive approach has been developed by Henggeler and colleagues (Henggeler & Borduin, 1990; Henggeler, Rodick, Borduin, Hanson, Watson, & Urey, 1986). Consistent with the ecological-developmental perspective (Bronfenbrenner, 1979), this approach includes interventions at multiple levels including the individual, the family, the extrafamilial system, and the community–cultural system. Initial evaluations of the effectiveness of family–ecological treatment have been promising and suggest that this comprehensive approach may maximize generalization of treatment gains (Miller & Prinz, 1990).

Summary and Clinical Implications

Developmental theory and research underscore the fact that healthy child development depends on a facilitating social environment. Developmental casualties often reflect deficits or deviations in the caregiving contexts that support children's growth. Consequently, a developmentally–informed approach to child therapy must encompass the social contexts, especially the caregiving contexts, that sustain or obstruct the child's development. Failure to account for developmental context in devising interventions perpetuates the myth of individual development.

Despite the developmental foundation for a contextual approach, research supporting the effectiveness of inclusive forms of intervention is rather sparse. Meta-analyses have not revealed significantly larger effect sizes for treatments that include parents (Casey & Berman, 1985) or whole families (Hazelrigg, Cooper, & Borduin, 1987) compared to traditional forms of child psychotherapy. However, given the limited number of controlled outcome studies, and their mixed methodological quality, "the relative efficacy of child treatments as a function of the extent to which they involve family participation, regardless of theoretical orientation, has not been examined" (Fauber & Long, 1991, p. 814). Evaluations of interventions that target multiple developmental contexts, though promising, are even more limited. Thus, the contextual prescription derived from developmental theory and research awaits empirical support.

SUMMARY AND CONCLUSIONS

In his critique of the prevailing psychotherapy paradigm of his day, Kiesler (1966) hoped to bury what he called the myths of psychotherapy. There is no doubt that psychotherapy theory and research have undergone a paradigmatic shift during the intervening years. The assumptions of uniformity have gradually been replaced by an emphasis on specificity of treatments, patients, and outcomes. This basic shift increasingly guides prescriptions for the conduct of child and adolescent therapy. Nevertheless, a developmental perspective on child treatment reveals a number of other "myths" embedded in this field. In order to overcome the myths of uniformity, invariance, consistency, and individual development, several corrective prescriptions, derived from developmental theory and research, must be applied to the conduct of child and adolescent therapy.

First, given substantial developmental variability in children's cognitive, social, and emotional capacities, child clinicians must conduct developmental task analyses of the treatment procedures they plan to utilize. Treatment processes that are incompatible with the developmental capacities of child and adolescent patients cannot be expected to be beneficial. Second, lack of invariant relations between manifest symptomatology and underlying pathogenic processes mitigates against standardized treatments based on phenotypic similarities among child patients. Given the existence of multiple developmental pathways to the same disorder, selection or design of treatments must be based on an individual assessment of the pathogenic processes contributing to the child's presenting problems. Third, a developmental perspective draws attention to the role of age-related competencies in adaptive functioning and serves as an antidote to the clinical preoccupation with symptoms and problems. A developmentally informed approach to child treatment emphasizes the building of competencies that are relevant to mastering stage-salient developmental issues. And finally, given that development does not occur in social isolation, but depends on a facilitating social environment, interventions must address not only the deficits, distortions, and conflicts presented by the individual child, but also the system of relationships that support or obstruct the child's progressive development. A developmentally informed child therapy goes beyond individual treatment and includes interventions into the systems that promote or maintain healthy development. In summary, lack of adherence to these developmental prescriptions could perpetuate the myths of child therapy.

REFERENCES

Achenbach, T., Howell, C. T., McConaughy, S., & Stanger, C. (1995). Six-year predictions of problems in a National Sample: III. Transitions to young adult syndromes. *Journal of the American Academy of Child and Adolescent Psychiatry, 34,* 958–968.

Axline, V. (1947). *Play therapy.* Boston: Houghton Mifflin.

Bandura, A. (1981). Self-referent thought: A developmental analysis of self-efficacy. In J. Flavell & L. Ross (Eds.), *Social cognitive development* (pp. 200–239). Cambridge, MA: Cambridge University Press.

Baumrind, D. (1978). Parental disciplinary patterns and social competence in children. *Youth and Society, 9,* 239–276.

Belsky, J. (1984). The determinants of parenting: A process model. *Child Development, 55,* 83–96.

Bertalanffy, L. von (1968). *General system theory.* New York: Braziller.

Bowlby, J. (1980). Attachment and loss. In *Vol. 3: Loss, sadness, and depression.* New York: Basic Books.

Braswell, L. (1991). Involving parents in cognitive-behavioral therapy with children and adolescents. In P. Kendall (Ed.), *Child and adolescent therapy: Cognitive-behavioral procedures.* New York: Guilford Press.

Bronfenbrenner, U. (1979). *The ecology of human development.* Cambridge, MA: Harvard University Press.

Casey, R. J., & Berman, J. (1985). The outcome of psychotherapy with children. *Psychological Bulletin, 98,* 388–400.

Cicchetti, D. (1990). An historical perspective on the discipline of developmental psychopathology. In J. Rolf, A. Masten, D. Cicchetti, K. Nuechterlein, & S. Weintraub (Eds.), *Risk and protective factors in developmental psychopathology* (pp. 2–28). New York: Cambridge University Press.

Cicchetti, D., Toth, S., & Bush, M. (1988). Developmental psychopathology and incompetence in childhood: Suggestions for intervention. In B. Lahey & A. Kazdin (Eds.), *Advances in clinical child psychology* (Vol. 11, pp. 1–71). New York: Plenum Press.

Cicchetti, D., Toth, S., Bush, M., & Gillespie, J. (1988). Stage-salient issues: A transactional model of intervention. In E. Nannis & P. Cowen (Eds.), *New directions in child development* (Vol. 39, pp. 123–145). San Francisco: Jossey-Bass.

Durlak, J., Fuhrman, T., & Lampman, C. (1991). Effectiveness of cognitive-behavioral therapy for maladapting: A meta-analysis. *Psychological Bulletin, 110,* 204–214.

Dush, D., Hirt, M., & Schroeder, H. (1989). Self-statement modification in the treatment of child behavior disorders: A meta-analysis. *Psychological Bulletin, 106,* 97–106.

Erikson, E. (1963). *Childhood and society.* New York: W. W. Norton.

Erikson, E. (1964). Clinical observations of play disruption in young children. In M. Haworth (Ed.), *Child psychotherapy* (pp. 264–276). New York: Basic Books.

Fauber, R., & Long, N. (1991). Children in context: The role of the family in child psychotherapy. *Journal of Consulting and Clinical Psychology, 59,* 813–820.

Feehan, M., McGee, R., Williams, S., & Nada-Raja, S. (1995). Models of adolescent psychopathology: Childhood risk and the transition to adulthood. *Journal of the American Academy of Child and Adolescent Psychiatry, 34,* 670–684.

Forehand, R., & Wierson, M. (1993). The role of developmental factors in planning behavioral interventions for children: Disruptive behavior as an example. *Behavior Therapy, 24,* 117–141.

Freud, A. (1946). *The psychoanalytical treatment of children.* New York: International Universities Press.

Freud, A. (1965). *Normality and pathology in childhood: Assessments of development.* New York: International Universities Press.

Freud, S. (1905). *Three essays on the theory of sexuality.* London: Avon Library.

Frick, P. (1994). Family dysfunction and disruptive behavior disorders: A review of recent empirical findings. In T. Ollendick & R. Prinz (Eds.), *Advances in clinical child psychology* (Vol. 16, pp. 203–226). New York: Plenum Press.

Greist, D., & Forehand, R. (1982). How can I get any parent training done with all these other problems going on? The role of family variables in child behavior therapy. *Child and Family Behavior Therapy, 4,* 73–80.

Harter, S. (1986). Processes underlying the construction, maintenance, and enhancement of the self-concept in children. In J. Suls & A. Greenwald (Eds.), *Psychological perspectives on the self* (Vol. 3, pp. 137–181). Hillsdale, NJ: Erlbaum.

Harter, S. (1993). Causes and consequences of low self-esteem in children and adolescents. In R. Baumeister (Ed.), *Self-esteem: The puzzle of low self-regard* (pp. 87–116). New York: Plenum Press.

Hazelrigg, M., Cooper, H., & Borduin, C. (1987). Evaluating the effectiveness of family therapies: An integrative review and analysis. *Psychological Bulletin, 101,* 428–442.

Henggeler, S., & Borduin, C. (1990). *Family therapy and beyond: A multisystemic approach to treating behavior problems of children and adolescents.* Pacific Grove, CA: Brooks/Cole.

Henggeler, S., Rodick, J., Borduin, C., Hanson, C., Watson, S., & Urey, J. (1986). Multisystemic treatment of juvenile offenders: Effects on adolescent behavior and family interaction. *Developmental Psychology, 22,* 132–141.

Kazdin, A. (1987). Treatment of anti-social behavior in children: Current status and future directions. *Psychological Bulletin, 102,* 187–203.

Kazdin, A. E. (1991). Effectiveness of psychotherapy with children and adolescents. *Journal of Consulting and Clinical Psychology, 59,* 785–789.

Kazdin, A., & Kagan, J. (1994). Models of dysfunction in developmental psychopathology. *Clinical Psychology: Science and Practice, 1,* 35–52.

Kendall, P. C. (1984). Social cognition and problem solving: A developmental and child-clinical interface. In B. Coholson & T. Rosenthal (Eds), *Applications of Cognitive-Developmental Theory* (pp. 115–148). New York: Academic Press.

Kendall, P. (1991). Guiding theory for therapy with children and adolescents. In P. Kendall (Ed.), *Child and adolescent therapy: Cognitive-behavioral procedures* (pp. 4–24). New York: Guilford Press.

Kendall, P., & Braswell, L. (1985). *Cognitive-behavioral therapy for impulsive children.* New York: Guilford Press.

Kendall, P., & Clarkin, J. (1992). Introduction to special section: Comorbidity and treatment implications. *Journal of Consulting and Clinical Psychology, 60,* 833–834.

Kendall, P., Lerner, R. M., & Craighead, W. E. (1984). Human development and intervention in child psychopathology. *Child Development, 55,* 71–82, 777–784.

Kiesler, D. (1966). Some myths of psychotherapy research and a search for a paradigm. *Psychological Bulletin, 65,* 110–136.

Kohlberg, L. (1969). Stage and sequence: A cognitive-developmental approach to socialization. In D. Goslin (Ed.), *Handbook of socialization theory and research* (pp. 347–480). Chicago: Rand McNally.

Kohlberg, L., LaCrosse, J., & Ricks, D. (1972). The predictability of adult mental health from childhood behavior. In B. J. Wolman (Ed.), *Manual of child psychopathology* (pp. 1217–1283). New York: McGraw-Hill.

Leahy, R., & Shirk, S. (1984). The development of social cognition: Children's conceptions of personality. In G. Whitehurst (Ed.), *Annals of child development, 1* (pp. 175–200). Greenwich, CT: JAI Press.

Ledingham, J. (1990). Recent developments in high risk research. In B. Lahey & A. Kazdin (Eds.), *Advances in clinical child psychology* (Vol. 3, pp. 91–138). New York: Plenum Press.

Levy, D. (1963). *Psychological interpretation.* New York: Holt, Rinehart, & Winston.

Lochman, J., & Curry, J. (1986). Effects of social problem-solving training and self-instructional training with aggressive boys. *Journal of Clinical Child Psychology, 15,* 159–164.

Loeber, R. (1990). Development and risk factors of juvenile antisocial behavior and delinquency. *Clinical Psychology Review, 10,* 1–42.

Maccoby, E., & Martin, J. (1983). Socialization in the context of the family: Parent-child interaction. In E. M. Hetherington (Ed.), *Handbook of child psychology: Vol. 4. Socialization, personality, and social development* (pp. 1–101). New York: Wiley.

Marlowe, H., Reid, J., Patterson, G., Weinrott, M., & Bank, L. (1988). A comparative evaluation of parent training for families of chronic delinquents. Cited in R. McMahon & K. Wells (1989). Conduct disorders. In E. Mash & R. Barkley (Eds.), *Treatment of childhood disorders* (pp. 73–132). New York: Guilford Press.

Masten, A. S., Best, K., & Garmezy, N. (1991). Resilience and development: Contributions from the study of children who overcome adversity. *Development and Psychopathology, 2,* 425–444.

Meeks, J. (1971). *The fragile alliance.* New York: Krieger.

Miller, G., & Prinz, R. (1990). Enhancement of social learning family interventions for childhood conduct disorders. *Psychological Bulletin, 108,* 291–307.

Moustakas, C. (1959). *Children in play therapy.* New York: McGraw-Hill.

Orlinsky, D., & Howard, K. (1978). The relation of process to outcome in psychotherapy. In S. Garfield & A. Bergin (Eds.), *Handbook of psychotherapy and behavior change* (pp. 283–329). New York: Wiley.

Patterson, G. (1982). *Coercive family process.* Eugene, OR: Castalia Publishing.

Paul, G. (1967). Strategy of outcome research in psychotherapy. *Journal of Consulting Psychology, 31,* 109–118.

Persons, J. (1991). Psychotherapy outcome studies do not accurately represent current models of psychotherapy. *American Psychologist, 46,* 99–106.

Pope, A., McHale, S., & Craighead, W. E. (1988). *Self-esteem enhancement with children and adolescents.* Boston: Allyn and Bacon.

Puig-Antich, J., Lukens, E., Davies, M., Goetz, D., Brennan-Quattrock, J., & Todak, G. (1985). Psychosocial functioning in prepubertal major depressive disorders. *Archives of General Psychiatry, 42,* 511–517.

Robin, A., & Foster, S. L. (1989). *Negotiating parent-adolescent conflict.* New York: Guilford Press.

Robbins, L., & Rutter, M. (1990). *Straight and devious pathways from childhood to adulthood.* Cambridge, MA: Cambridge University Press.

Rogott, B. (1990). *Apprenticeship in thinking: Cognitive development in social context.* New York: Oxford University Press.

Sandler, J., Kennedy, H., & Tyson, R. L. (1980). *The techniques of child psychoanalysis—Discussions with Anna Freud.* Cambridge, MA: Harvard University Press.

Schaefer, E. (1959). A circumplex model for maternal behavior. *Journal of Abnormal and Social Psychology, 59,* 226–235.

Selman, R. (1980). *The growth of interpersonal understanding: Developmental and clinical analyses.* New York: Academic Press.

Shantz, C. (1987). Conflicts between children. *Child Development, 58,* 283–305.

Shapiro, T. (1995). Developmental issues in psychotherapy research. *Journal of Abnormal Child Psychology, 23,* 31–44.

Shirk, S. (Ed.). (1988a). *Cognitive development and child psychotherapy.* New York: Plenum Press.

Shirk, S. R. (1988b). Causal reasoning and children's comprehension of therapeutic interpretations. In S. Shirk (Ed.), *Cognitive development and child psychotherapy* (pp. 53–90). New York: Plenum Press.

Shirk, S. (1990). Cognitive processes in child psychotherapy: Where are the developmental limits? In J. de Wit, W. Slot, H. van Leeuwen, & M. Terwogt (Eds.), *Developmental psychopathology and clinical practice* (pp. 19–31). Amsterdam: Acco.

Shirk, S., & Phillips, J. (1991). Child therapy training: Closing gaps with research and practice. *Journal of Consulting and Clinical Psychology, 159,* 766–776.

Shirk, S., & Russell, R. L., (1996). *Change Processes in child psychotherapy: Revitalizing treatment and research.* New York: Guilford Press.

Sroufe, A. (1979). The coherence of individual development: Early care, attachment, and subsequent developmental issues. *American Psychologist, 34,* 834–841.

Sroufe, A., & Rutter, M. (1984). The domain of developmental psychopathology. *Child Development, 55,* 17–29.

Stark, K., Rouse, L., & Livingston, R. (1991). Treatment of depression during childhood and adolescence: Cognitive-behavioral procedures for the individual and the family. In P. Kendall (Ed.), *Child and adolescent therapy: Cognitive-behavioral procedures* (pp. 165–208). New York: Guilford Press.

Stiles, W., Shapiro, D., & Elliott, R. (1986). Are all psychotherapies equivalent? *American Psychologist, 41,* 165–180.

Strain, P., Young, C., & Horowitz, J. (1981). Generalized behavior change during oppositional child training: An examination of child and family demographic variables. *Behavior Modification, 5,* 15–26.

Strayhorn, J. (1988). *The competent child: An approach to psychotherapy and preventive mental health.* New York: Guilford Press.

Verhulst, F., & Ende, J. (1992). Six-year developmental course of internalizing and externalizing problem behaviors. *Journal of the American Academy of Child and Adolescent Psychiatry, 31,* 924–931.

Vernberg, E., Routh, D., & Koocher, G. (1992). The future of psychotherapy with children: Developmental psychotherapy. *Psychotherapy, 29,* 72–80.

Waters, E., & Sroufe, A. (1983). Social competence as a developmental construct. *Developmental Review, 3,* 79–97.

Weisz, J., Rudolph, K. D., Granger, D., & Sweeney, L. (1992). Cognition, competence, and coping in child and adolescent depression: Research findings, developmental concerns, therapeutic implications. *Development and Psychopathology, 4,* 627–653.

Wells, K., & Forehand, R. (1985). Conduct and oppositional disorders. In P. Bornstein & A. Kazdin (Eds.), *Handbook of clinical behavior therapy with children* (pp. 218–265). Homewood, IL: Dorsey.

Werner, H. (1957). The concept of development from a comparative and organismic point of view. In D. Harris (Ed.), *The concept of development* (pp. 125–148). Minneapolis, MN: University of Minnesota Press.

Wilson, S. (1981). A Piagetian-based analysis of insight and the interpretive process. *American Journal of Orthopsychiatry, 51,* 626–631.

Winnicott, D. (1965). *The maturational process and the facilitating environment.* New York, NY: International Universities Press.

Wright, L., Everett, F., & Roisman, L. (1986). *Experiential therapy with children.* Baltimore, MD: Johns Hopkins University Press.

PART 2

ISSUES ACROSS DEVELOPMENT

In this section the tasks of development in infancy, early childhood, middle childhood, and adolescence are examined and their clinical implications explored. As such, these chapters present important stage-salient or age-appropriate issues that serve to inform the practice of clinical child psychology across development.

The first chapter (Chapter 5) covers the period of infancy. The chapter begins by noting the controversies surrounding the "discontinuity" versus "continuity" of this period, and then devotes attention to two of the most common problems in infancy—colic and sleep disturbances. Difficulties involved in defining these problems are discussed as are etiological influences. The chapter further summarizes promising interventions for these problems. Perhaps most fascinating are the positive effects reported for massage therapy. Undoubtedly, researchers and clinicians will find this discussion about the benefits of massage therapy for these common problems of infants to be "stimulating."

In Chapter 6, the period of life that is marked roughly by the end of toddlerhood and the early grades of schooling is addressed. This period is one of remarkable transformation, and it is also a period that is linked to many problems that present in clinical settings. The chapter is divided into four

major sections. In the first, the developmental–organizational perspective discussed in earlier chapters is reviewed briefly. In the second, key developmental themes in early childhood are discussed, including varying tasks of adaptation. In the third section, developmental processes and the mechanisms/structures responsible for regulatory action during this period are detailed. The processes that account for developmental transformations are highlighted because they link normal and abnormal behavior and form the basis for understanding the development of clinical behavior problems in early childhood. In the fourth and fifth sections, implications for assessment and treatment are addressed. All in all, this chapter is an indispensable aid to understanding early childhood and to designing effective assessment and intervention strategies.

In the chapter that follows, Chapter 7, issues related to middle childhood and their implications for assessment and treatment are examined. The chapter presents the developmental framework that guided the authors' systematic research on two of the main problem domains that occur with relatively high frequency in middle childhood and that are the main foci of the chapter: aggressive behaviors and isolation as well as rejection and poor peer relations. Specifically, the chapter highlights several phenomena that seem especially relevant for understanding psychopathology and change during this period. The first is that interactional adaptations observed in infancy or the juvenile period are poorly correlated with adult social interactions. The second is that behavioral characteristics most closely linked to the regulation of hormonal and neurobiological states tend to show the most enduring effects of early and youthful experience. The third is that events that are required for the establishment of an interaction pattern are not necessarily required for its maintenance or change. The chapter also provides additional insights that serve to highlight the dynamic, holistic, and integrative perspective of development, including the development of psychopathology in middle childhood.

In chapter 8, the period of adolescence is addressed. Adolescence, as noted by the authors of this engaging chapter, can be defined as the period within the life span when most of the person's biological, psychological, and social characteristics are changing from what is typically viewed as "child-like" to what is considered "adult-like." For the adolescent, this period is frequently a dramatic challenge, one requiring adjustment to changes in the self, in the family, and in the peer group. Fortunately, most adolescents meet these challenges and remain unscathed. For others, however, the challenges are not easily nor readily met and the authors explore a diversity of interventions for adolescents that take into consideration the developmental contexts in which their behavior occurs. For example, the authors assert that interventions should be aimed at changing the developmental system within which the adolescent is embedded, rather than at changing the adolescent alone. Such speculations demand that we reexamine our basic hypotheses about adolescent deviance and that we develop innovative interventions. It also demands that we examine sociopolitical policies that result in such negative outcomes for our youth.

Collectively, these four chapters serve to remind us that not all children are alike (the developmental uniformity myth) and that many of the problems we encounter in clinical settings are deeply embedded in contextual forces oftentimes ignored by us in our everyday clinical practice. They also serve to indicate that we must move beyond the comfort of our offices and extend our reach to the settings that serve to inculcate and perpetuate many of the problems that we see "in" our children and adolescents. Contexts that nurture many of these problems are examined in the section that follows.

CHAPTER 5

INFANCY

Tiffany M. Field
Scott Liepack

A number of clinical problems have been studied during infancy primarily because they hold risks for developmental delays. Infants are considered at risk if they experience an undesirable prenatal or birth condition or if they are exposed to an early postnatal environment that might contribute to early interaction problems and developmental delays. Undesirable prenatal conditions include maternal disease and the use of drugs, alcohol, or tobacco. Problems at birth that might lead to difficulties include premature or postmature delivery, low birth weight, and the presence of congenital anomalies such as Down syndrome, craniofacial defects, deafness, blindness, and autism. Chronic diseases such as cancer, cystic fibrosis, and asthma can also have their onset in infancy, and accidents such as burns present a threat to early development. In addition, postnatal environments that include a mother who is a low-income teenager, or who is

neglectful or abusive, or who experiences postpartum depression might contribute to infants' developmental delays.

Most infants, however, experience none of the above problems. In contrast, all infants experience frustrations associated with developmental milestones such as learning to sit, crawl, walk, and talk. Emotional trauma is also associated with stages of development, such as stranger fear that happens around 9 months and separation anxiety that typically occurs at around 1 year. Increasing numbers of infants are experiencing early separations to attend infant day care and the frustrations of peer conflicts as well as separation anxiety when they leave or are left by their young parents. The end of infancy is most particularly marked by moves toward autonomy, more typically called "the terrible twos."

Any of these problems at any of these stages can become exaggerated and present a clinical or pediatric problem. The primary concern, of course, is that these early problems may become predictors of later development. Sigmund Freud and John B. Watson, as well as other developmental psychologists, assumed that experiences beginning in infancy were critical for later development (Freud, 1949; Watson, 1928). Freud asserted that trauma during a particular stage of

This research was supported by an NIMH Research Scientist Award (#MH00331) and an NIMH Research Grant (#MH46586) to Tiffany Field.

infancy would cause a fixation, for example, at the oral or anal stage, precluding development to the next stage and affecting some personality characteristic such as temperament. Freud considered these effects reversible through therapy involving free association and dream analysis. Watson similarly believed that infants subjected to early conditioning experiences would carry the effects of these experiences throughout life. He similarly considered early experiences reversible through counter-conditioning techniques.

At first glance, retrospective reconstruction of events tends to confirm a largely linear developmental model such as Watson's or Freud's. For example, many cerebral palsy and mentally retarded infants are found to have been subjected to a variety of adverse perinatal conditions, such as lack of oxygen. However, most studies suggest that infants who have experienced perinatal complications do not develop cerebral palsy or mental retardation. An additional criticism of Freud in the psychoanalytical tradition is that the infant does not appear to pass through oral or anal stages, so it is not clear how fixation could occur (Stern, 1985).

For many developmental psychologists, the failure to find continuity has given rise to theories that propose that infancy is discontinuous with later developmental stages and, therefore, is a less critical stage of development than previously thought. As Kagan and others have suggested, the developmental course of individual infants may not be linear or even unidirectional. Given the multitude of interactional events that occur, there is little reason to expect to make precise predictions from the earliest period (Kagan, Kearsley & Zelazo, 1978). Lipsitt, however, has pointed out that this need not mean that there is little or no continuity between earlier conditions or experiences and later events (Lipsitt, 1988). He presents two caveats: First the overpowering or reversing effects of later experiences on a seemingly preset condition do not diminish the importance of the earlier condition. Second, noncontinuities can be examples of continuities not yet sufficiently investigated.

The most important clinical problem in infancy is that infants cannot verbally communicate their problems. Hence, the term *infancy,* meaning "without language." Darwin trusted that the infants' facial expressions reflected their states of mind. He said: "In order to acquire as good a foundation as possible, and to ascertain, independently of common opinion, how far particular movements or the features and gestures are really expressive of certain states of mind, I have found the following means the most serviceable. In the first place, to observe infants, for they exhibit many emotions, as Sir C. Bell remarks, with extraordinary force. Whereas, in afterlife, some of our expressions cease to have the pure and simple force from which they sprang in infancy" (Darwin, 1965, p. 147).

Although infants have other ways of communicating their pain, problems, and dislikes, those ways are a problem, because they are disturbing communications such as fussing and crying. Fussiness and crying are not easy to tolerate by most adults, which probably explains why the most popular presenting problem for pediatric clinicians is excessive irritability. This is particularly true when it is concentrated at one developmental stage, as in infant colic. Although the colic ends almost abruptly at 3 months, fits of irritability and excessive crying have been known to continue, punctuating every frustrating developmental milestone from sitting to crawling to walking to virtually any stage of learning that poses frustration.

The second most common clinical complaint during infancy is the related problem of sleeplessness, often following periods of excessive irritability and perhaps also caused by the frustrations surrounding developmental milestones and learning new skills, much as adults experience sleeplessness during the stressful periods of final exams and career changes. This chapter is focused on these two common clinical problems in infancy, colic and sleep disturbance, as well as on some effective therapeutic approaches for these problems.

COLIC

Colic is one of the most common problems in infancy, the reported incidence ranging from 10 to 35 percent (Keefe, 1988). Researchers disagree about the definition and clinical criteria for colic, which invariably presents a confused or incomplete picture to parents (Carey, 1984; Lester, Boukydis, Garcia-Coll, & Hole, 1990). This confusion has resulted in two seemingly opposite reactions, the physician's reaction that "colic does not exist" and the researcher's reaction that "more literature is needed." The latter response is apparent in the plethora of review papers devoted to the subject (Barr, 1993; Gurry, 1994; Miller & Barr, 1991; St. James-Roberts, 1991; Treem, 1994).

The word "colic" is derived from the Greek word *kolikos,* the adjective of *kolon,* meaning the large intestine. Colic also goes by the label *infantile colic* and *paroxysmal fussing.* Colic has been described as intermittent and unexplained crying during the first 3 months of life by infants who are otherwise well fed and healthy (Schmitt, 1986). Colic usually starts during the second or third week of life and spontaneously disappears at around 3 months (Keefe, 1988). The crying is generally intense and typically lasts from 30 minutes to 2 hours, often occurring in the late afternoon or evening followed by difficulty falling asleep (Carey, 1984). The crying may also occur intermittently and last for several hours at any time of day or night, although the crying episodes tend to recur at the same time of day (Schmitt, 1981).

The most widely accepted definition of colic is probably that of Wessel (Wessel, Cobb, Jackson et al., 1954): 3 or more hours of crying for 3 or more days per week for 3 or more weeks. Other clinicians have accepted the Brazelton definition of colic as the mean crying times of 1.75 hours per day at 2 weeks, 2.75 hours per day at 6 weeks, and 1 hour per day at 12 weeks (Brazelton, 1962). In those data, infant fussing was most frequent from 6 to 11 P.M. at 3 weeks and 3 P.M. to midnight at 6 weeks. Still another definition was provided by Carey (1984): Full force crying for at least 3 hours per day, for 4 or more days per week.

According to Lester and colleagues' (1990) review of the literature, colic begins with a sudden onset of crying. The cry is often high pitched and accompanied by facial grimacing, suggesting that the infant is experiencing severe pain. The crying is accompanied by increased motor activity, flexion of the elbows, clenched fists, hypertonicity, knees drawn up or legs stiffly extended, and tense and distended abdomen. The infant's eyes are either tightly closed or wide open, the back is arched, the feet are often cold, bowel sounds can be heard, infants may hold their breath for brief periods of time, and they may resist soothing. Thus, the four salient signs are sudden onset, high-pitched pain cry, hypertonia, and inconsolability (Lester et al., 1990).

Recent studies have conducted acoustic analyses of cries from colic and noncolic infants (Fuller, Keefe & Curtin, 1994). The cries of the colic infants were higher in jitter, proportion of noise, and tenseness than the cries of control infants. These acoustic characteristics suggest an increase in stress arousal, which thus supports the thesis of a state regulation disorder.

In general, the literature seems to suggest that: (1) the assessment of complaints about crying and colic present particular diagnostic problems; (2) the crying brought as a complaint seldom indicates disease; (3) once clinical disease has been ruled out, the clinical meanings of normality and abnormality no longer apply; (4) at that point, one should not try to determine a cutoff point for abnormal crying, because (a) it is unhelpful clinically, and (b) it is not likely that any specific amount of crying is normal or abnormal, independent of context; (5) as a possible alternative, it is proposed that we think of the behavior as not a symptom of something the infant "has" but as something the infant "does." This behavior may have consequences that are functional or dysfunctional for the infant, the caregiver, or the infant–caregiver interaction.

If this argument has merit, it may have some interesting and important implications for the way we think about, treat, and investigate developmental and behavioral problems including (but not limited to) infant crying and colic. First, what holds true for crying and colic may also hold for bedwetting and enuresis, overactivity and attention-deficit hyperactivity disorder, and abdominal pain and recurrent abdominal pain syndrome, to name just a few. As a brief test of their applicability, one might ask how often organic disease is found in these entities, or how often patients are investigated and treated because an arbitrary amount of these behaviors is taken to be "excessive" or abnormal (Barr, 1993).

Etiology

Several factors may be involved in infant colic including biological factors such as central nervous system maturation, temperament and sleep state organization as well as environmental factors such as parent–infant interactions. Biological factors include hypertonicity, gastrointestinal and allergic factors, and an immature central nervous system. Environmental factors would include, for example, overstimulation by parents.

Although gastrointestinal factors have typically been described for colic, serial radiographs by Harley (1969) suggest a normal amount of gas in the gastrointestinal tracts of colic infants. Excessive abdominal gas was observed after crying, suggesting that abdominal distention resulted from, rather than caused, crying.

Other biological explanations that have been advanced include the following: (1) hypocontractility of the gallbladder, indicating abnormal biliary tract physiology (Lehtonen, Svedstrom, & Korvenranta, 1994); (2) a difference in bacterial cellular fatty-acid profiles that could either contribute to the cause of colic or be secondary to the colic (Lehtonen, Korvenranta, & Eerola 1994); and (3) the hypothesis of Weissbluth and Weissbluth (1992) that in the evening, peak serotonin concentration causes intestinal cramps associated with colic because serotonin increases intestinal smooth muscle contractions. Melatonin has the opposite effect of relaxing intestinal smooth muscles. Both serotonin and melatonin exhibit a circadian rhythm with peak concentrations in the evening. However, serotonin intestinal contractions are unopposed by melatonin during the first 3 months because only serotonin circadian rhythms are present at birth. Melatonin circadian rhythms appear at 3 months of age. The cramps of colic frequently disappear at 3 months of age (Weissbluth & Weissbluth, 1992).

Breast milk, cow's milk, and soy milk have also been implicated in colic. Digestion of milk and soy proteins produces excessive intestinal gas and peristalsis, which can result in colic (Adams & Davidson, 1987). However, colic occurs as commonly in breast-fed as in formula-fed infants. The similar prevalence of colic in infants fed mother's milk (20%), formula (19%), and formula supplemented mother's milk (21%) suggests that colic is not associated with dietary protein intolerance (Thomas, McGilligan, Eisenberg, Lieberman, & Rissman, 1987). Taubman (1988) came to a similar conclusion after studying the elimination of cow's milk or soy milk proteins. Although dietary changes were beneficial, he concluded that colic is not caused by milk protein allergy. Another study examined the influence of cow's milk and found no relation between cow's milk and colic (Carey, 1990; Lothe, Lindberg, & Jakobsson, 1990).

Indications that colic has a physiological base are the frequency of colic in our culture, and in diverse groups, its apparent familial predisposition, its delayed onset in premature infants, and its spontaneous resolution around 3 months (Paradise, 1966; Schmitt, 1986). Colic may also relate to maturational growth in sensory systems at a time when stimulus barriers are not adequate (Keefe, 1988). Decreased crying with increasing age may relate to the developing inhibition of excessive arousal (Parmelee, 1977). The underlying mechanism may be an imbalance in the sympathetic and parasympathetic nervous systems (Lester et al., 1990). Elevated sympathetic activity may trigger the high-pitched pain cry. Reduced vagal activity during sympathetic arousal could lead to the simultaneous changes in gastrointestinal activity and the pain cry during colic episodes (Lester et al., 1990). The "smart" vagus branch of the vagal complex (Porges, 1995) stimulates the larynx, determining the acoustic characteristics of the cry (Lester & Boukydis, 1991), and the vegetative branch of the vagus, which normally stimulates gastric motility and the release of food absorption hormones, would be interrupted by sympathetic dominance (or a state of high arousal) (Uvnas-Moberg, Widstrom, Marchine, & Windberg, 1987).

Reduced parasympathetic activity (inhibition) might also explain the infants' inability to be soothed (Lester & Boukydis, 1991). Infants with colic are noted to have more frequent wakings (Weissbluth, Davis, & Poncher, 1984), and sleep duration at 4 and 5 months (after the colic had ended) was shorter for infants with colic than for infants without colic. These infants also were more likely to have difficult temperaments (Weissbluth, Christoffel, & Davis, 1984). Recent data, however, call these findings into question (Lehtonen, Korhonen, & Korvenranta, 1994). These authors from Finland reported that although mothers regarded their colicky infants as more active and less persistent, the Toddler Temperament Scale yielded no differences in any area of temperament. In addition, no differences were found between the two groups on sleeping patterns.

Other cultures have also reported minimal differences between fussy and nonfussy infants. In a Korean study (Lee, 1994) there was no definite clustering of crying during the evening hours. The most common responses of mothers towards their infants' crying were making feeding contact and the least common response was no response. Compared with Western studies, the duration of crying of Korean infants was shorter and the time of holding and/or close contact with mothers was longer, and colic was rare.

In a comprehensive study on environmental factors (Paradise, 1966) that included familial incidence of colic, education, socioeconomic status, occupation, and intelligence and Minnesota Multiphasic Personality Inventory scores of the mother as well as birth order, only familial incidence was correlated with infant colic. In contrast, a more recent study reported that mothers of infants with colic had multidimensional psychological distress. They reported more bodily dysfunction, fears, disordered thinking, depression, anxiety, fatigue, hostility, and impulsive thoughts and actions and stronger feelings of inadequacy (Pinyerd, 1992).

Feeding patterns have been implicated as a potential contributor to colic. Moreover, Barr and Elias (1988), for example, reported that infant crying did not differ whether the infants required bottle feeding or continuous breast-feeding at 4 months. However, there was a difference at 2 months, suggesting that short intervals between feedings were related to decreased crying. Carrying has also been related to colic. In a study by Barr and his colleagues (Hunziker & Barr, 1986), mothers carrying their infants eliminated the crying peak at 6 weeks, and the crying and fussing that tended to occur in the early evenings decreased. In a more recent study, Barr (1990) reported a 43 percent reduction in cry/fuss behavior and a 54 percent reduction in evening cry/fuss behavior at 6 weeks following increased carrying. This was a decrease in duration of the crying bouts, but not in their frequency. Cross-cultural comparisons of crying, such as the comparison between the Kung infants in Africa and American infants, also suggest that crying can be decreased by carrying.

Overstimulation also apparently contributes to colic (Keefe, 1988) inasmuch as infants who are hospitalized for colic show a significant decrease in crying once they are hospitalized (Carey, 1984). Other potentially noxious factors include excessive noise, bright lights, and irritating blankets or clothing. The spontaneous remission that occurs around 3 months may happen because infants can now use gaze aversion, thumb sucking, turning over, reaching, and grasping to avoid or remove noxious stimuli (Schmitt, 1986).

In the interim, parents' use of sleep/wake and basic rest/activity schedules, including feeding, bathing, and sleeping routines, may be very effective. In addition, supplemental tactile stimulation such as massaging the infant, vestibular stimulation such as rocking or swinging, and auditory stimulation such as classical music or white noise, that is, types of stimulation that may be calming or may reduce arousal, may also be successful parenting strategies (Keefe, 1988).

Colic is considered a significant clinical problem because of its very disruptive effects on parents. Mothers of colicky infants have been described as having less adequate marital adjustment, poorer parent–child relationships, and a greater sense of inadequacy as women (Geertsma & Hymans, 1989). Wessel and colleagues (1954) have noted tension in entire families of colicky babies. They defined family tension as emotional turmoil both before and after the weeks the infant was fussy. In families with high tension, 72 percent of infants had colic versus 26 percent in tension-free families. It is not clear whether parental anxiety was a factor that led to the excessive crying or a response to it. However, parental anxiety in itself may contribute to inappropriate handling of infants (Carey, 1984).

Parents have even cited excessive crying as the reason for child abuse. For example, Mortimer & Bradstock (1985) found that over half the mothers of colicky infants reported that their infants' crying made them feel like battering their child, and 20 percent reported hitting and shaking the baby in response to the crying. That is perhaps not surprising since mothers of colicky infants perceive their infants' cry as significantly *more aversive* than the cries of non-colicky infants and perceive their infants as having more difficult temperaments (Lester et al., 1990). Abusive mothers in general show more autonomic arousal and have more negative perceptions of crying babies (Boykydis & Burgess, 1982; Frodi, 1989).

Interventions

The more standardized interventions have ranged from drugs to parent counseling. To determine the efficacy of simethicone in the treatment of colic, a randomized, double-blind, placebo-controlled design was used in three general pediatric practices (Metcalf, Irons, Sher, & Young, 1994). Eighty-three infants between 2 and 8 weeks of age with infant colic were treated with simethicone and placebo in a double-blind crossover fashion. A total of 166 treatment periods, ranging from 3 to 10 days, were evaluated. Compared to baseline symptoms, improvement in symptoms was reported in 54 percent of the treatment periods, worsening was reported in 22 percent, and, in 24 percent there was no change. The likelihood of the treatment period being rated as showing improvement, worsening, or no change was the same whether the infant was receiving placebo or simethicone. Twenty-eight percent of the infants responded only to simethicone, 37 percent only to placebo, and 20 percent responded to both. No statistically significant differences

were noted among these three groups of responders. No difference could be shown even when infants with "gas-related symptoms" (by parental report) were separated out as a group. Although simethicone was no more effective than placebo in the treatment of infantile colic, both produced perceived improvements in symptoms.

To determine the efficacy of behavioral management counseling in the treatment of persistent excessive infant crying (>3 hours per day), two treatment groups and one no treatment control group were set up (Wolke, Gray & Meyer, 1994). Treatments were carried out sequentially by the same counselors. The counseling was done by telephone by volunteers (mothers) of CRY-SIS, a national support group for the parents of crying infants. A sequential sample of twenty-seven mother–infant pairs received Treatment One (Tr1, empathy: talking through the problem), twenty-one received Treatment Two (Tr2, behavioral management: specific care-taking suggestions) and forty-four received no treatment (C, controls). Infants were 1 to 5 months of age. Mother–infant pairs had a pretreatment baseline assessment and a posttreatment follow-up (3 months after baseline) using 1-week diaries. Total fuss/cry duration was reduced significantly more in the behavioral management group (by 51%) than in the empathy group (37%) or the control group (35%). This was mainly due to significantly reduced evening fussing/crying in Tr2 (67%) compared with Tr1 (45%) and C (42%). No differences in total number of fuss/cry bouts/day were found. However, the number of fuss/cry bouts was reduced significantly more in the evening in Tr2 (by 55%) than in Tr1 (27%) and C (32%). Behavioral management mothers evaluated the same counselors as more sympathetic, knowledgeable, and understanding. Tr2 was also perceived by mothers to have helped them more in reducing the crying problem, coping with the infant, and improving the relationship with their infant than did those in Tr1. No effects of treatment were noted for infants with difficult temperaments. Behavioral management was more effective in reducing fussing/crying than spending time with the mother talking through the problem or just waiting for spontaneous remission. Thus treatment by suitably but briefly trained lay counselors is an inexpensive and successful treatment option.

Summary

The etiology of colic is not fully known. However, soothing techniques can reduce irritable crying associated with colic. Clinicians should inform parents about the multiple factors that influence colic and the interventions that have been effective with colicky infants.

SLEEP DISTURBANCES

Sleeplessness, in the form of difficulty falling asleep and/or nighttime waking, is another very common pediatric problem presented by infants and toddlers and affecting some 15 to 35% (Holliday et al., 1987; Richman, 1981). Sleep problems as early as infancy may reflect a complex pattern of interactions including physiological factors, temperamental features of the infants, and parents' responses to difficult sleep patterns (Ferber, 1985). In recent years the rates of sleep disorders have supposedly increased, possibly because parents are less tolerant or more worried about sleep disturbance and its disruptiveness to the working family, or possibly due to the more sophisticated methods of monitoring sleep and knowledge about the development of sleep patterns.

Various methods have been developed to study infant sleep including facial muscle activity (EMG), EEG, heart rate, and respiration. In addition, diaries are frequently kept by parents to record information on duration of sleep, crying, and other activities. The data collected by these methods suggest that newborn infants have shorter sleep cycles (90 minutes and 50 minutes) and more active or REM sleep (60% of infants' sleep time). The disproportionate amount of REM sleep is thought to provide the brain stimulation for normal maturation (Deneberg & Thoman, 1981). Another way in which adult and neonatal sleep differ is that adult sleep can be easily classified into four stages of sleep, while newborn sleep is generally categorized as quiet or indeterminate (i.e., not easily coded sleep) (Anders & Weinstein, 1972).

Studies tracking the development of sleep over infancy suggest that the infants' wakeful time gradually increases from an average of 8 hours at birth to 12 hours at 6 months with a reduction in REM sleep but continuity of non-REM sleep. By the time the infant is 3 months old, sleep occurs predominantly during the nighttime hours with the infant tending to remain awake during the latter afternoon and early evening hours. By 6 months the time awake has increased from a mean of 2 hours at 3 months to about 3½ hours, and the longest waking period is about one-third of the total awake time. Although a diurnal sleep–wake pattern is established by this time and the infant is capable of sustaining sleep during the nighttime hours, many infants continue to wake during the night (Anders et al., 1983). Also at this time the amount of time the infant takes to fall asleep increases, and parents begin to establish bedtime routines and the use of blankies and other self-comforting objects to facilitate earlier sleeping. Despite these rituals, approximately 60 percent of 2 month olds and about the same percentage of 9 month olds reportedly are still remaining awake (Edwards & Christophersen, 1994).

Once infants are put to bed, there is a large variation in the amount of time required for sleep onset depending on age. For example, 2 month olds are thought to require approximately 28 minutes and 9 month olds only 6 minutes (Anders, 1979). The infants' total sleep time also becomes a fairly stable pattern early in life with the total sleep at 13 weeks being similar to that at 26 weeks and 52 weeks. Night wakings are thought to occur in approximately 29 percent of infants during the third month, approximately 17 percent by the sixth month, and 10 percent during the first year (Moore & Ucko, 1957). Once asleep, newborns typically sleep approximately 17 hours per day (including naps) and by the sixth month they are sleeping only about 14 hours (including naps); this remains consistent across the first 2 years.

Etiology

Certainly individual differences in these patterns as well as individual differences in temperament may contribute to sleep disturbance differences including irritability, restlessness, and activity levels (Richman, 1981). Other temperamental features reported for sleep disturbances include low sensory thresholds (Carey, 1974), difficulty establishing regular routines, and reluctance to move from one activity to another (Richman, 1981). Given that infants who are stimulated less seem to organize their sleep states sooner (Salaarulo, Fagioli & Salomon, 1980), it may be that overstimulation by parents is disruptive to infant sleep.

As in colic, the underlying mechanism may be an imbalance in the sympathetic and parasympathetic nervous systems. Elevated sympathetic activity could prevent or disrupt sleep, or reduced parasympathetic activity might also explain the infants' sleep disturbance. Unlike colic, very little research has been conducted on the etiology of infants' sleep disturbances. One reason may be that infant sleep is difficult to study because of the first nap effect (Sostek & Anders, 1975). Infants' sleep is disturbed simply by being observed or by having EEG monitoring during sleep. In contrast, many intervention studies have been conducted with infants experiencing sleep disturbances. These studies have been driven by questions of etiology, for example, reducing parental stimulation to assess the parental overstimulation question and, in turn, the intervention studies have helped inform the question of etiology.

For example, in one study a 10 percent prevalence of sleep problems was noted in children over 1 year (Minde, 1988). Some children appeared to have parents who overresponded to their children or did not set routines and limits. Other children seemed to have biological vulnerabilities such as perinatal insult, early feeding difficulties, colic, or a "difficult temperament." Approximately 55 percent of those children also showed other signs of behavioral disorders.

Interventions

A study on healthy infants suggests that most children need something to help them fall asleep (Wolf & Lozoff, 1989). In the Wolff and Lozoff (1989) study, regular use of a transitional object such as a blanket or toy was described for 44 percent of the children, bedtime thumbsucking for 22 percent, and both for 14 percent, leaving only 20 percent of the children who fell asleep without assistance.

Parents have been noted to try a number of comforting techniques to induce sleep in young infants including swaddling, rocking, and sound. In an early study, Brackbill (1973) studied young infants' responses to these comforting strategies and found that a combination of rhythmic modalities (e.g., sound and rocking) was more effective than providing one without the other. Others have noted that swaddling is the most effective method and suggested that restricted movement by swaddling helps sustain the infants' sleep (Chisholm & Richards, 1978). Others have advocated letting the child cry (Schmitt, 1981) or taking the child into the parents' bed (Bax, 1980; Sears, 1985) or supplying toys (Jolly, 1985).

The use of objects for comforting has been relatively effective whether the child has a blanket to rub, something furry to hold on to, or sucks on a pacifier (Thelen, 1979). In addition, infants have been noted to use their own bodies to self-comfort including sucking on hands, rocking, or head banging in a rhythmic way (Sallustro & Atwell, 1978).

Several more formal procedures have been tried in studies giving parents instructions. These have mostly involved having the parents find a consistent sleeping place, a regular bedtime, and a bedtime ritual. In one study parents were asked to try a quiet play routine before bed. They were asked to use soothing and relaxing techniques such as massage, stroking and pleasant music when the child was being put to bed, and they were asked to refrain from using a light, changing diapers, and talking during their nighttime interactions (Bidder et al., 1986). The majority of infants showed improvement during the first few weeks of treatment. In another study several interventions were used including eliminating inappropriate nighttime feeding, setting a consistent sleep/wake schedule, and teaching the infants to fall asleep without external help (Schaefer, 1987). Marked improvement was shown for 81 percent of the infants.

Christophersen and his colleagues (Edwards & Christophersen, 1994), in a recent review on sleep disturbances, noted that several investigators have concluded that whenever parents are present at the time of sleep onset, there are more frequent night wakings. Adair and colleagues (1991), for example, reported 40 percent versus 22 percent night wakings when parents were present at bedtime. In another study, Adair and colleagues (1992) gave an intervention group instructions to establish a bedtime routine including putting the infant in the crib partially awake so the infant would learn to go to sleep without adult assistance. There was also a control group who followed their normal routine. Parental presence at bedtime occurred less often in the intervention group (21% vs. 33%), and the intervention infants experienced 36 percent less nighttime awakenings. In another recent study (Pinilla & Birch, 1993), parents were taught to breastfeed their newborns between 10 P.M. and midnight and to refrain from holding, rocking, or nursing their infants to sleep in order to accentuate the difference between night and day, and they were further instructed not to pick the infant up until the infant was "really complaining." Mothers were also discouraged from leaving their infants alone crying but were asked to provide alternative interventions such as reswaddling, patting, diapering, or walking in lieu of feeding. By 2 months of age, 100 percent of the infants in the treatment group were sleeping through the night (midnight through 5 A.M.) compared to 23 percent of the control group.

Another study of this kind was conducted in Australia (Leeson, Barbour, Romaniuk & Warr, 1994). Torrens House provided a short residential program for families with a baby (8 to 12 months of age) identified by parents as having a sleep problem such as waking frequently at night and being difficult to settle. The program involved the promotion of infant self-settling by the use of a controlled crying technique, together with wrapping, cessation of night feeds, and establishment of a daytime routine. Twenty families (with 23 babies) were followed through the program and for 3 months afterwards. There were significant decreases in the number of times the babies awakened, the number of night feeds, and the length of time awake at night at 1 month follow-up, with a reduction in depressive symptomatology of the parents and a perceived improvement in their infants' behavior. Twenty of the 23 babies were sleeping well at the 3 month follow-up.

Interventions of this kind might be most effective if started very early in development or even before the infant is born, for example, during birthing classes, as was done by Wolfson and colleagues (Wolfson, Lacks, & Futterman, 1992). First-time parent couples from childbirth classes were randomly assigned to a four-session training group ($N = 29$) or a control group ($N = 31$). Members of the training group were taught behavioral strategies to promote healthy, self-sufficient sleep patterns in their infants, whereas the control group received the same amount of personal contact without the behavioral training. Six sleep variables were derived from a daily infant sleep diary completed by parents at two time points. Results showed that at age 6 to 9 weeks, infants in the training group displayed significantly better sleeping patterns than did control infants. Training-group parents awakened and responded less often to infant signaling and reported greater parental competence. By contrast, control group parents indicated increased stress over time.

Another suggestion provided by Edwards and Christophersen (1994) involved teaching the infants self-quieting skills during the day. As these authors suggested, ignoring children when they are put to bed usually works relatively quickly, but the parents are typically distressed. They suggested that the infants might learn self-quieting skills both during the day and at naptime or bedtime, such as using time-out. Time-out can first be used during the day so that the parents can learn the "ignoring" procedures without having them be so stressful at bedtime.

For night wakings similar procedures have been recommended. Pritchard and Appleton (1988), for example, requested that parents check the child once upon awakening and at 20-minute intervals thereafter. They noted improvements in the average number of nights, and times each night, that the children awakened. In a similar study on fifty sleep-disturbed infants, Sadeh (1990) asked the parents to check the child every 5 minutes on settling and awakening, to restore his or her sleeping position, tell the child goodnight and leave the room. In the second group the parents were instructed to sleep in the child's room for a week without having any interaction or involvement with the child during the night, even if the child awakened. After the end of this period the parents resumed sleeping in a separate room. As the authors reported, on both parent-report and activity measures, both groups showed a significant increase in the percent time spent asleep during the night and a significant decrease in the number of night wakings. Interestingly, they also reported an increase in active (REM) sleep, which they suggested probably indicated "less vulnerability to awakening."

Because several authors have questioned whether these various procedures are harmful, two studies empirically addressed that question (France, 1992; Sanders et al., 1984). In one study, increases were noted in "security and likeability" and decreases in emotionality and tension in the infants who were in the treatment groups were noted (France, 1992). Similarly, no deleterious effects were found in the study by Sanders and colleagues (1984).

We recently used massage therapy with infants of depressed mothers to enhance their sleep (Field, Grizzle, Scafidi, Abrams, & Richardson, 1995). Forty full-term 1- to 3-month-old infants born to depressed adolescent mothers who were of low socioeconomic status and single parents were given 15 minutes of either massage ($N = 20$) or rock-

ing by an infant nursery teacher just before bedtime for 2 days per week for a 6-week period. The infants who experienced massage therapy, compared to infants in the rocking control group, spent more time in active alert and active awake states during the day, and they cried less and had lower salivary cortisol levels, suggesting lower stress. The infants who had massage therapy spent less time in an active awake state after the session than those in the rocking control group, suggesting that massage may be more effective than rocking for inducing sleep. Over the 6-week period the massage therapy infants gained more weight; showed greater improvement on emotionality, sociability and, soothability temperament dimensions; and had greater decreases in urinary stress catecholamines/hormones (norepinephrine, epinephrine, cortisol).

In many instances, several behavioral strategies are tried before resorting to pharmacological approaches. However, at least one group has reported that medical practitioners usually manage pediatric sleep disturbances by prescribing sedative medications (Werry & Carlielle, 1983). Although sedatives have been widely used and reputedly have been effective for night wakings (Lask, 1977; Valman, 1981), there have been very few control studies on their effectiveness with infants. Exceptions are a study by Richman (1985) who used a sedative (30–60 mg in an increasing dose depending on response) in infants between the ages of 12 and 24 months. The sedative medication was given in a randomized sequence with each child serving as his own control, receiving the sedative during one time period and the placebo during another time period. The authors noted that there were significant changes in the scores on the sleep behavior scale, but these were limited in their extent and were also temporary inasmuch as the infants had returned to baseline levels at the 6-month follow-up period.

Using a larger average dose and longer duration of administration (the sedative at 45–90 mg) and using the double-blind crossover design for 4 weeks, Simonoff and Stores (1987) also found that night wakings decreased, although they were not eliminated and there was no effect of the medication at 1-month follow-up. These results generally support claims that have been made by others that medication is not effective with infant sleep disturbances in the long run (Jones & Verduyn, 1983; Richman, 1985; Seymour, 1987). As these authors have concluded, the effectiveness of medications is restricted to short-term relief.

SUMMARY AND CONCLUSIONS

Sleeplessness continues to be a difficult pediatric problem and one that is not only disruptive to infant sleep but to parent sleep as well. These, in turn, may lead to other problems such as irritability in both infants and parents and ultimately to illness due to sleep deprivation. Fortunately, several rather simple parent interventions such as reducing stimulation and establishing a bedtime routine appear to be effective.

Fussiness and crying are not easy to tolerate by most adults, which probably explains why the most popular presenting problem for pediatric clinicians is excessive irritability. This is particularly true when it is concentrated at one developmental stage, as in infant colic. Colic is one of the most common problems in infancy, with the reported incidence ranging from 10 to 35 percent (Keefe, 1988). Researchers disagree about the definition and clinical criteria for colic. Several factors may be involved in infant colic, including biological factors such as hypertonicity, gastrointestinal and allergic factors, an immature central nervous system, temperament, and sleep state organization as well as environmental factors such as parent–infant interactions and overstimulation by parents. Standardized interventions have ranged from drugs to parent counseling.

Sleeplessness, in the form of difficulty falling asleep and/or nighttime waking, is another very common pediatric problem presented by infants and toddlers and affecting some 15 to 35 percent. Sleep problems as early as infancy may reflect a complex pattern of interactions including physiological factors, temperamental features of the infants, and parents' responses to difficult sleep patterns.

Studies on healthy infants suggest that most children need something to help them fall asleep. Parents have been noted to try a number of comforting techniques to induce sleep in young infants, including swaddling, rocking, and sound. Several more formal procedures have been tried in studies that provide parents with instructions. These have mostly involved having the parents find a consistent sleeping place, a regular bedtime, and a bedtime ritual. Several investigators have concluded that whenever parents are present at the time of sleep onset, there are more frequent night wakings. Although sedatives have been widely used and reputedly have been effective for night wakings, there have been very few control studies on their effectiveness with infants.

We recently used massage therapy and rocking with infants to enhance their sleep. After the massage versus the rocking sessions, the infants spent less time in an active awake state, suggesting that massage may be more effective than rocking for inducing sleep.

Irritability and sleep problems affect many infants and, because they are disruptive, they affect many parents and families as well. Because both colic and sleep disturbances are typically more responsive to behavior management techniques than they are to medications, clinical, developmental and pediatric psychologists are perhaps more qualified than

pediatricians to manage these problems. Unfortunately, however, parents typically take their infants' problems to pediatricians. In addition to psychologists researching these problems and interventions, they need to educate parents and pediatricians about the data.

REFERENCES

Adair, R., Bauchner, H., Philipp, B., Levenson, S., & Zuckerman, B. (1991). Night waking during infancy: Role of parental presence at bedtime. *Pediatrics, 87*, 500–504.

Adair, R., Zuckerman, B., Bauchner, H., Philipp, B., & Levenson, S. (1992). Reducing night waking in infancy: A primary care intervention. *Pediatrics, 89*, 585–588.

Adams, L., & Davidson, M. (1987). Present concepts of infant colic. *Pediatric Annals, 16*, 817–820.

Anders, T. F. (1979). Night waking in infants during the first year of life. *Pediatrics, 63*, 860–864.

Anders, T. F., , & Sostek, A. (1983). A longitudinal study of nighttime sleep-wake patterns in infants from birth to one year. In J. D. Call, E. Galenson, & R. L. Tyson (Eds.), *Frontiers of infant psychiatry* (pp. 150–166). New York: Basic Books.

Anders, T. F., & Weinstein, P. (1972). Sleep and its disorders in infants and children. *Pediatrics, 50*, 312–324.

Barr, R. G. (1990). The "colic" enigma: Prolonged episodes of a normal predisposition to cry. *Infant Mental Health Journal, 11*, 340–348.

Barr, R. G. (1993). Normality: A clinically useless concept. The case of infant crying and colic. *Journal of Developmental & Behavioral Pediatrics, 14*, 264–270.

Barr, R. G., & Elias, M. F. (1988). Nursing interval and maternal responsivity: Effect on early infant crying. *Pediatrics, 81*, 529–536.

Bax, M. C. O. (1980). Sleep disturbance in the young child. *British Medical Journal, 1*, 1177–1179.

Bidder, R. T., Gray, O. P., Howells, P. M., & Eaton, M. P. (1986). Sleep problems in preschool children: Community clinics. *Child: Care, Health and Development, 12*, 325–337.

Boukydis, C. F. Z., & Burgess, R. L. (1982). Adult physiological response to infant cries: Effects of temperament of infant, parental status and gender. *Child Development, 53*, 1291–1298.

Brackbill, Y. (1973). Continuous stimulation reduces arousal level: Stability of the effects over time. *Child Development, 44*, 43–46.

Brazelton, T. B. (1962). Crying in infancy. *Pediatrics, 29*, 579–588.

Carey, W. B. (1974). Night waking and temperament in infancy. *Journal of Pediatrics, 84*, 756–758.

Carey, W. B. (1984). "Colic"—primary excessive crying as infant-environment interaction. *Pediatric Clinics of North America, 31*, 993–1005.

Carey, W. B. (1990). Infantile colic: A pediatric practitioner-researcher's point of view. *Infant Mental Health Journal, 11*, 334–339.

Chisholm, J. S., & Richards, M. P. M. (1978). Swaddling, cradleboards and the development of children. *Early Human Development, 2*, 255–275.

Darwin, C. (1965). *The expression of the emotions in man and animal.* Chicago: University of Chicago Press.

Denenberg, V. H., & Thoman, E. G. (1981). Evidence for a functional role for active (REM) sleep in infancy. *Sleep, 4,* 185–191.

Edwards, K. J., & Christophersen, E. R. (1994). Treating common sleep problems of young children. *Journal of Developmental & Behavioral Pediatrics, 15,* 207–213.

Ferber, R. (1985). *Solve your child's sleep problems.* New York: Simon & Schuster.

Field, T., Grizzle, N., Scafidi, F., Abrams, S., & Richardson, S. (1996). Massage therapy for infants of depressed mothers. *Infant Behavior & Development, 19,* 107–112.

France, K. G. (1992). Behavior characteristics and security in sleep disturbed infants treated with extinction. *Journal of Pediatric Psychology, 17,* 467–475.

Freud, S. (1949). *An outline of psychoanalysis.* New York: Norton.

Frodi, A. M. (1989). Contribution of infant characteristics to child abuse. *American Journal of Mental Deficiency, 85,* 341–349.

Fuller, B. F., Keefe, M. R., & Curtin, M.. (1994). Acoustic analysis of cries from "normal" and "irritable" infants. *Western Journal of Nursing Research, 16,* 243–251.

Geertsma, M. A., & Hymans, J. S. (1989). Colic—a pain syndrome of infancy? *Pediatric Clinics of North America, 36,* 905–919.

Gurry, D. (1994). Infantile colic. *Australian Family Physician, 23,* 337–340.

Harley, L. M. (1969). Fussing and crying in young infants. *Clinical Pediatrics, 8,* 138–141.

Holliday, J., Sibbald, B., & Tooley, M. (1987). Sleep problems in two-year-olds. *Family Practice, 4,* 32–35.

Hunziker, U. A., & Barr, R. G. (1986). Increased carrying reduces infant crying: A randomized controlled trial. *Pediatrics, 77,* 641–647.

Jolly, H. (1985). *Book of child care* (3rd ed.). London: George Allen & Unwin.

Jones, D. P. H., & Verduyn, C. M. (1983). Behavioural management of sleep problems. *Archives of Diseases in Childhood, 58,* 442–444.

Kagan, J., Kearsley, R. B., & Zelazo, P. R. (1978). *Infancy: Its place in human development.* Cambridge, MA: Harvard University Press.

Keefe, M. R. (1988). Irritable infant syndrome: Theoretical perspectives and practice implications. *Advances in Nursing Science, 10,* 70–78.

Lask, B. (1977). Emotional and behaviour problems in childhood. Part 2. Sleep and feeding disorders. *Midwife, Health Visitor and Community Nurse, 13,* 384–389.

Lee, K. (1994). The crying pattern of Korean infants and related factors. *Developmental Medicine & Child Neurology, 36,* 601–607.

Leeson, R. Barbour, J., Romaniuk, D., & Warr, R. (1994). Management of infant sleep problems in a residential unit. *Child: Care, Health & Development, 20,* 89–100.

Lehtonen, L., Korhonen, T., & Korvenranta, H. (1994). Temperament and sleeping patterns in colicky infants during the first year of life. *Journal of Developmental & Behavioral Pediatrics, 15,* 416–420.

Lehtonen, L., Korvenranta, H., & Eerola, E. (1994). Intestinal microflora in colicky and noncolicky infants: Bacterial cultures and gas-liquid chromatography. *Journal of Pediatric Gastroenterology & Nutrition, 19,* 310–314.

Lehtonen, L., Svedstrom, E., & Korvenranta, H. (1994). Gallbladder hypocontractility in infantile colic. *Acta Paediatrica Scandinavica , 83,* 1174–1177.

Lester, B. M., & Boukydis, C. F. Z. (1991). No language but a cry. In H. Papousek (Ed.), *Origin and development of non-verbal communication.* New York: Cambridge University Press.

Lester, B. M., Boukydis, C. F. Z., Garcia-Coll, C. T., & Hole, W. T. (1990). Colic for developmentalists. *Infant Mental Health Journal, 11,* 321–333.

Lipsitt, L. P. (1988). Stress in infancy. In N. Garmezy and M. Rutter, (Eds.), *Stress, coping and development in children.* Baltimore: Johns Hopkins University Press.

Lothe, L., Lindberg, T., & Jakobsson, I. (1990). Macromolecular absorption in infants with infantile colic. *Acta Paediatrica Scandinavica, 79,* 417–421.

Metcalf, T. J., Irons, T. G., Sher, L. D., & Young, P. C. (1994). Simethicone in the treatment of infant colic. A randomized, placebo-controlled, multicenter trial. *Pediatrics, 94,* 29–34.

Miller, A. R., & Barr, R. G. (1991). Infantile colic. Is it a gut issue? *Pediatric Clinics of North America, 38,* 1407–1423.

Moore, T., & Ucko, L. E. (1957). Night waking in early infancy. *Archives of Diseases in Childhood, 32,* 333–342.

Mortimer, P., & Bradstock, A. S. (1985). Infant care: Frustration and despair. *Community Outlook, 8,* 19–22.

Paradise, J. L. (1966). Maternal and other factors in the etiology of infantile colic. *Journal of the American Medical Association, 197,* 123–131.

Parmelee, A. H. (1977). Remarks on receiving the C. Anderson Aldrich award. *Pediatrics, 59,* 389–395.

Pinilla, T., & Birch, L. L. (1993). Help me make it through the night: Behavioral entrainment of breast-fed infants' sleep patterns. *Pediatrics, 91,* 436–444.

Pinyerd, B. J. (1992). Infant colic and maternal mental health: Nursing research and practice concerns. *Issues in Comprehensive Pediatric Nursing, 15,* 155–167.

Porges, S. W. (1995). Orienting in a defensive world: Mammalian modifications of our evolutionary heritage. A Polyvagal theory. *Psychophysiology, 32,* 301–318.

Pritchard, A., & Appleton, P. (1988). Management of sleep problems in pre-school children. *Early Child Development and Care, 34,* 227–240.

Richman, N. A. (1981). A community survey of characteristics of one-to-two-year-olds with sleep disruptions. *Journal of the American Academy of Child Psychiatry, 20,* 281–291.

Richman, N. A. (1985). A double-blind drug trial of treatment in young children with waking problems. *Journal of Child Psychology & Psychiatry, 26,* 591–598.

Sadeh, A. (1990). Actigraphic home monitoring of sleep-disturbed infants: Comparison to controls and assessment of intervention. In J. Horne (Ed.), *Sleep: Proceedings of the 10th European Congress on Sleep Research* (pp. 469–470). Bochum, Germany: Pontenagel Press.

Sallustro, F., & Atwell, C. W. (1978). Body rocking, head banging and head rolling in normal children. *Journal of Pediatrics, 93,* 704–708.

Salzarulo, P., Fagioli, I., & Salomon, F. (1980). Maturation of sleep patterns in infants under continuous nutrition from birth. *Acta Chirurgica Scandinavica, 498,* 78–82.

Sanders, M. R., Bor, B., & Dadds, M. (1984). Modifying bedtime disruptions in children using stimulus control and contingency management techniques. *Behavioural Psychotherapy, 12,* 130–141.

Schaefer, C. E. (1987). The efficacy of a multimodal treatment programme for infant night waking [Abstract]. *Sleep Research, 16,* 422.

Schmitt, B. D. (1981). Infants who do not sleep through the night. *Journal of Developmental & Behavioral Pediatrics, 2,* 20–23.

Schmitt, B. D. (1986). The prevention of sleep problems and colic. *Pediatric Clinics of North America, 33,* 763–774.

Sears, W. (1985). *Night-time parenting: How to get your baby and child to sleep.* Franklin Park, IL: La Leche League International.

Seymour, F. W. (1987). Parent management of sleep difficulties in young children. *Behaviour Change, 4,* 39–48.

Simonoff, E. A., & Stores, G. (1987). Controlled trial of trimeprazine tartrate for night waking. *Archives of Disease in Childhood, 62,* 253–257.

Sostek, A. M., & Anders, T. S. (1975). Effects of varying laboratory conditions on behavioral-state organization of 2- and 8-week-old infants. *Child Development, 46,* 871–878.

St. James-Roberts, I. (1991). Persistent infant crying. *Archives of Disease in Childhood, 66,* 653–655.

Stern, D. N. (1985). *The interpersonal world of the infant.* New York: Basic Books.

Taubman, B. (1988). Parental counseling compared with the elimination of cow's milk or soy milk protein for the treatment of infant colic syndrome: A randomized trial. *Pediatrics, 81,* 756–761.

Thelen, E. (1979). Rhythmical stereotypes in normal human infants. *Animal Behaviour, 27,* 699–715.

Thomas, D., McGilligan, K., Eisenberg, L., Lieberman, H., & Rissman, E. (1987). Infantile colic and type of milk feeding. *American Journal of Diseases of Children, 141,* 451–453.

Treem, W. R. (1994). Infant colic. A pediatric gastro-enterologist's perspective. *Pediatric Clinics of North America, 41,* 1121–1138.

Uvnas-Moberg, K., Widstrom, A. M., Marchine, G., & Windberg, J. (1987). Release of GI hormone in mothers and infants by sensory stimulation. *Acta Paediatrica Scandinavia, 76,* 851–860.

Valman, H. B. (1981). Sleep problems. *British Medical Journal, 283,* 422–423.

Watson, J. B. (1928). *Psychological care of infant and child.* New York: W. W. Norton.

Weissbluth, M., Christoffel, K. K., & Davis, T. (1984). Treatment of infantile colic with dicyclomine hydrochloride. *Journal of Pediatrics, 104,* 951–955.

Weissbluth, M., Davis, T., & Poncher, J. (1984). Night waking in 4- to 8-month-old infants. *Journal of Pediatrics, 104,* 477–480.

Weissbluth, L., & Weissbluth, M. (1992). Infant colic: The effect of serotonin and melatonin circadian rhythms on the intestinal smooth muscle. *Medical Hypotheses, 39,* 164–167.

Werry, J. S., & Carlielle, J. (1983). The nuclear family, suburban neurosis, and iatrogenesis in Auckland mothers of young children. *Journal of the American Academy of Child Psychiatry, 22,* 172–179.

Wessel, M. A., Cobb, J. C., & Jackson, E. G. (1954). Paroxysmal fussing in infancy, sometimes called 'colic.' *Pediatrics, 14,* 421–424.

Wolff, A. W., & Lozoff, B. (1989). Object attachment, thumb sucking, and the passage to sleep. *Journal of the American Academy of Child & Adolescent Psychiatry, 28,* 287–292.

Wolfson, A., Lacks, P., & Futterman, A. (1992). Effects of parent training on infant sleeping patterns. Parents' stress, and perceived parental competence. *Journal of Consulting & Clinical Psychology, 60,* 41–48.

Wolke, D., Gray, P., & Meyer, R. (1994). Excessive infant crying: A controlled study of mothers helping mothers. *Pediatrics, 94,* 322–332.

CHAPTER 6

EARLY CHILDHOOD

Robert C. Pianta

The period of life that is marked roughly by the end of tod-dlerhood and the early grades of schooling is one of remark-able transformation. It is also a period with links to many forms of behavioral and developmental problems that sur-face in clinical settings, in this and in subsequent periods (Campbell, 1990; Greenberg, Kusche, & Speltz, 1991).

The child's competencies advance on numerous fronts. Communication changes from one-word and gestural forms to the use of print and symbols in complex arrangements having subtle meanings. Motor development reorganizes fairly isolated skills into coordinated units of throwing and catching, hopscotch, and handwriting. The toddler who was frustrated by alternatives, ambiguity, and delay shows rea-soning and problem-solving skills requiring planning and symbolic mediation. Physical contact with familiar caregiv-ers gives way to a social world in which peers have increas-ing dominance, rule structures for group relations are processed and examined, and symbolic exchanges replace touch. The sense of self, once largely physical in nature,

grows to encompass aspects of competence and mastery, self-evaluation, attributions, and social exchange. Finally, emotions, once used reflexively and regulated by caregivers, come under the influence of regulatory processes internal to the child. In short, this period embodies basic principles of development—continuity and coherence in the face of dra-matic change and reorganization.

The changes in, and coherence of, individual identity during the early childhood period have great psychological significance for many of the clinical syndromes of child-hood. Adequate clinical practice with these syndromes is de-pendent on an understanding of the processes that regulate development during the early childhood epoch. Linking clin-ical practice in early childhood with developmental theory requires a common language for describing (normal) devel-opmental processes, deviations from those processes (abnor-mal), and treatment and assessment methods targeted toward those deviations (clinical practice). Optimally, such descrip-tions have the child at center stage. This differs from most current approaches to early childhood problems, which more frequently have notions of "disorder" at center stage. Child-focused and disorder-focused research and theory parallel the distinction between normal and abnormal development

This chapter was prepared with partial support from NICHD R01 HD26911 and NIDRR H133G20188.

and can lead to two different endpoints for clinical practice. It is one of the goals of the interdisciplinary science of developmental psychopathology to identify concepts, terms, and descriptions that provide continuity between considerations of normal and abnormal development (Cicchetti, 1994; Sroufe 1989a), thereby breaking down barriers between theory and treatment of disorder and knowledge and practice concerning normative developmental change.

This chapter is focused on processes common to normal and abnormal development in the period of early childhood. A central question in clinical psychology is the differentiation between normal and abnormal (or "cases"). In early childhood this is made more difficult because the immaturity of the organism, and the high degree to which the child's competencies are influenced by contextual forces, make subthreshold symptomatic behavior (e.g., bedwetting, noncompliance, anxiety) quite common in the population (e.g., MacFarlane, Allen & Honzik, 1954; Richman, Stevenson, & Graham, 1982). It is assumed that most forms (and cases) of "abnormal" development seen in clinical and school settings in early childhood have their roots in normative developmental processes. This means that early childhood disorders are not the product of development that is regulated by mechanisms different than those for normal development. Furthermore, the key to distinguishing clinical "caseness" from normative behavior lies in identifying the organization and function of normative processes in a given subject. This dialectic between normal and abnormal is evident even for disorders as extreme as autism and pervasive developmental disorder, in which, despite well-documented deficits in joint-attention and social communication processes (Mundy & Hogan, 1994), functional child–parent attachment processes have been shown to exist (Capps, Sigman, & Mundy, 1994; Rogers, Ozonoff, & Maslin-Cole, 1993). This kind of knowledge simply would not exist without a perspective that assumed continuity between normal and abnormal.

The chapter is divided into four major sections. In the first section, the developmental–organizational framework is described briefly, with emphasis given to the systems theory concepts that are used throughout the remaining sections. The second section describes key developmental themes in early childhood. The third section focuses on developmental processes and the mechanisms and structures responsible for regulatory action during the early childhood period. I emphasize the processes that account for developmental transformations in part because they link normal and abnormal and form the basis for understanding the *development* of clinical syndromes in early childhood. Applications to assessment and treatment practice will be outlined in a final section.

THE NEED FOR AN ORGANIZATIONAL–DEVELOPMENTAL SYSTEMS FRAMEWORK

An example may help clarify the need for a developmental psychopathology perspective. The October 1993 issue of the journal *Exceptional Children* published a special issue on attention-deficit hyperactivity disorder (ADHD) in children. ADHD receives a great deal of attention from parents, educators, mental health professionals, and physicians because it is considered to be a frequent and problematic condition for children and families (Campbell, 1990; Kazdin, 1992; McBurnett, Lahey, & Pfiffner, 1993). In fact, attention, activity, and disruptive behavior comprise a constellation of symptoms that is the single most frequent cause for referral for behavioral and mental health services in early childhood (Greenberg et al., 1991; Richman et al., 1982).

In this special issue, several papers addressed the possible causes of ADHD. Findings were summarized suggesting that neurochemical or neuroanatomical factors are a cause of these behavioral symptoms (Dykman & Ackerman, 1993; Riccio, Hynd, Cohen, & Gonzalez, 1993). A neurochemical or physiological explanation for ADHD is frequently used to support the use of stimulant medication for treatment of this problem, and response to stimulant medication has been viewed as confirmation of the neurological basis of the disorder (Swanson et al., 1993). Together, the findings reported in this special issue reinforce the notion that children with self-regulatory problems are a distinct group, and that the processes governing their behavior somehow differ from those governing the behavior of children who are not members of this group.

These conclusions regarding childhood behavior disorders are common. Notions of what constitutes "normal and abnormal" are typically drawn from adult-oriented definitions (e.g., see *DSM-IV* definitions for depression) and considerable research effort and debate are focused on drawing lines to distinguish normal and abnormal. This debate can reify the apparent differences in question and lead to a different set of explanatory constructs used to describe normal and abnormal populations. Cross-sectional and retrospective research frequently is the basis for developing theories of etiology. Treatment approaches are informed not by knowledge of developmental mechanisms but by short-term symptom reduction.

In the case of the ADHD special issue, *development* of attention, or the *developmental processes regulating motor and attention behaviors* were not a focus, especially of the articles on etiology (Riccio et al., 1993). The integration of biological, psychological, and social mechanisms are often not discussed when the focus is on distinguishing normal and abnormal (Reid, Maag, & Vasa, 1994). Consequently, treatment approaches (e.g., stimulant medication for ADHD) are not informed by knowledge of how developmental mechanisms regulate change in target behaviors (e.g., attention) but on how to make "abnormal" attention and activity indistinguishable from normal: i.e., how to close the symptom gap between groups of children. In this way, two languages describe two different "types" of children, with intervention focused on making one group look like the other.

Sroufe (1989a; b) and others (Cicchetti, 1994) argue that little progress will be made relative to understanding the development of abnormal behavioral patterns unless we consider both normal and abnormal together and how the developmental processes underlying both states are fundamentally similar (and when they differ) and what factors alter pathways from normal to disordered trajectories. Knowledge about "disorders" remains unintegrated with knowledge about the children who develop and "have" these disorders, in part as a function of the lack of a common discourse.

Applications of Systems Theory to Early Childhood Disorders

Conceptualizations of developmental processes have come to rely on systems theory as a means of generating explanatory constructs and mechanisms (e.g., Cicchetti, Ackerman, & Izard, 1994; Fox, 1994; Sameroff, 1989). The developmental psychopathology perspective (Cicchetti, 1994) emphasizes molar units (such as relationships or neural networks), global processes such as adaptation, and networked, organized activity of interlocking systems. In this way, systems theory provides a language with which to engage in discourse on the activity of complex organisms and the principles that govern their behavior (Ford & Ford, 1987; Sameroff, 1983, 1989).

Systems approaches have been used before in explanations of clinical phenomena, most frequently in reference to families (Marvin & Stewart, 1990; Reiss, 1989). Interpreting the behavior of individuals in the context of role(s) and function(s) in interpersonal systems and social groups is not new to most clinicians (Walsh, 1982). Systems constructs deal with questions on (1) the appropriate unit of analysis, (2) the notion of relationships or networks, (3) activity (behavior) and its regulation, and (4) change. Yet systems theory has not yet penetrated theory on the development of childhood disorders (Sameroff, 1989).

Holism

Developing children are systems composed of many interrelated parts and processes. These processes and parts—

intelligence, social competence, aggressive behavior, time on task, learning style, brain morphology, and concentration of neurochemicals and their metabolites—*by themselves* do not describe the child. The holistic emphasis of systems theory implies methods of inquiry that focus "upward" through the different levels of analysis that might be used to inquire about or explain behavior. Although typical clinical assessment and treatment tools focus downward—reducing complex behavior into component parts—systems-informed approaches explain behavior in terms of larger units. As Sameroff (1989) notes, "individuals are not seen as integrated systems of biological, psychological, and social functioning, but rather divided into a biological and behavioral self" (p. 19). In practice, this leads to addressing problems of attention or externalizing behavior by examining the social correlates and functions that organize the behavior in question.

Distributed Properties of Units in Networks

Children, as systems, are in dynamic interchange with contexts, exchanging information, material, energy, and activity (Ford & Ford, 1987). Many theories of development posit in fact that the interchanges that take place early in life have particular importance (Bornstein, 1989). The child, as a distinct entity, has quite permeable boundaries, and properties that appear to belong or "reside" in the child, in fact, are distributed across the child and the systems with which the child exchanges information (Hofer, 1994; Resnick, 1994). With respect to behavioral and emotional problems in early childhood, the role of social context in organizing, causing, sustaining, and giving meaning to child behaviors has been the subject of much attention, and research confirms the distributed nature of child competence (e.g., Campbell, 1990; Greenberg et al., 1991; Patterson, DeBaryshe, & Ramsey, 1989). Campbell's work on hard-to-manage preschoolers clearly demonstrates that behavioral disruption is embedded within an organized constellation of family factors, parenting behaviors, life stress, and child characteristics that may be causal and maintaining influences (e.g., Campbell, 1994; Campbell, March, Pierce, Ewing, & Szumowski, 1991).

Context cannot be separated from child adaptation. In this way, adaptation is *distributed* (Resnick, 1994).

> Under normal circumstances, mental activity involves social coordination with others. What makes an individual competent is not just what he or she knows but also how his or her knowledge fits with that of others with whom activity must be coordinated . . . activity is shared with tools . . . and with physical material. Thus there is a distribution of cognitive work not only among people but also between people and tools. . . . The tools embody a portion of the intelligence that is needed to accomplish a particular task. (p. 476)

Similarly, attention, emotion, social behavior, social cognition, peer relations, and self-control are distributed across the child, the situation(s) in which the challenge occurs, and the relation of the child to the challenge and the situation(s). All aspects of this distributed network must be observed before adaptation can be understood and described. This view suggests that child psychopathology is not a property of the child per se, but is more properly located in the network in which the processes and behaviors that define it are distributed. To the extent that the early childhood period is one in which development is particularly sensitive to context, pathology is even more likely to be distributed in nature (Bornstein, 1989; Campbell, 1992).

Activity and the Regulation of Activity

Children and the contexts in which they develop are complex systems, the interactions of which can be thought of in terms of *co-action* (Gottlieb, 1991). Co-action refers to the premise that activity of a given system (e.g. the brain, or the classroom) relies on and affects the activity of other systems. The networked nature of systems allows for regulation of activity. Behavior of one unit is regulated by relations within the system(s) in which that unit is embedded. In this way, co-action is nonrandom, patterned and, to some extent, predictable. Developmental change follows as a consequence of regulated co-activity (Ford & Ford, 1987; Sameroff, 1983).

In this view the child is inherently active: constructing meaning, adapting, seeking challenges, practicing emergent capacities. Activity is a bias built into development as a consequence of evolutionary pressure (Breger, 1974), and this bias creates endless opportunities for transformation and change. Motivation, or the "desire" to change, is derived from the co-action of systems. This notion of change and activity as a property of the developing system itself opens the way for developmental views of treatment (Cicchetti & Toth, 1992) in which intervention is seen as the intentional structuring or harnessing of developmental activity or the skilled use of context to developmental advantage (Lieberman, 1994).

A Theory of Change

Any theory of development or of intervention must account for behavioral change. For child–clinical interventions, the predominant model of change has been described by behavioral psychology's principles and by principles of physiology and brain chemistry (Swanson et al., 1993). Discussions of early childhood have also relied on maturationist views and stage theories to describe change (Walsh, 1991). These models have limited usefulness in describing *systems change,* thereby contributing to the gap between normal and abnormal

in treatment of childhood behavioral and emotional problems (Ford & Lerner, 1992).

Change occurs when systems reorganize and transform. The interactions of units within a system, the influence or introduction of new units and subsystems, and external demands create pressures on a system to adapt. A system may change through processes of differentiation and integration. Differentiation refers to the creation of separate subunits that take on different roles in order for the system as a whole to function with respect to a given challenge. But for the system as whole to maintain its integrity and identity, differentiated subunits must also be integrated with one another. Differentiation and integration allow systems to behave efficiently. Theories of adaptation to trauma, and the dissociative processes involved in maladaptation, focus attention on the role of differentiation as adaptive (to promote survival of the organism) and maladaptive, if differentiated units are not integrated, as in dissociation (Fisher & Ayoub, 1994; Putnam, 1994).

Therapeutic interventions frequently focus on different means by which differentiated behavioral or mental structures can be integrated with other functional systems involving the child's behavior (e.g., Lieberman, 1992). Change, in this view, is not solely a function of adding new behaviors to an existing repertoire, reaching a new stage, or maturing physiology, but is found in the reorganization of relations among units within a system. Change is indexed by level of organization (simple to complex, differentiated vs. undifferentiated, integrated vs. non-integrated) not by discrete behaviors, stages, or maturity (Greenspan & Greenspan, 1991).

Organisms also must maintain continuity in the face of change agents (internal and external). *Self-stabilization* refers to the gyroscopic property of complex systems in which the system can respond to minor perturbations or demands. The system responds by rearranging internal dynamics or relations and adapts to pressure without altering its basic structure or identity. Self-stabilization preserves identity in the face of pressure to change and ensures that major change, or reorganization, occurs at a slow, regulated, pace. If it were not for self-stabilization, the behavior of systems would be unpredictable and unstable. Many of the indices of development in early childhood are self-regulatory behaviors that serve this self-stabilization function (Kopp & Wyer, 1994).

Self-reorganization refers to the response of a complex system to a more constant or intense pressure. Small calibrations of the self-stabilizing type are inadequate for the system to function with respect to this new challenge and the system must re-organize. In re-organizing, the system changes fundamental aspects of its functioning in relation to pressures to change. For example, in language development, as children acquire more words they begin to re-organize their use of words and how they communicate—the function of language changes.

Behaviorally oriented views of clinical problems and their treatment tend to describe change in terms of accumulation of fairly discrete units governed by processes of reinforcement and association. These concepts break down fairly rapidly in the face of the task of describing the complexity of developmental change, the interrelations among developmental domains, and the discontinuities present in the organism over time (see earlier discussion). Viewed from a developmental systems perspective, therapeutic change, or change that is the result of some intentional action, involves processes that are more dynamic and probabilistic than those described in most theories of psychotherapy.

What Is a Healthy System?

Within clinical child psychology many different methods are used for scaling the health of children. These include methods of assessment such as behavior checklists, diagnostic systems, and certain treatment protocols. Most of these rely on documentation of discrete behaviors or symptoms, with relatively little attention to molar constructs (such as organization or adaptation) or contextual influences. From a developmental systems and organizational perspective, the health of a system (child, home, etc.) can be described in terms of global properties involved in the regulation of system activity (Sroufe & Rutter, 1984).

The capacity of a system to *adapt* is the main "developmental" task of systems. Adaptation refers to the system's capacity to mobilize resources to achieve a "fit" with respect to a certain internal or external demand. Greenspan (1989) refers to the child's capacities and skills that can be mobilized to adapt as the *modes of adaptation*. For example, the infant has very few modes within her behavioral repertoire to use in the service of adaptation; she can cry or smile. For the 4 year old, language, cognitive delay strategies, symbolic expression in play, and direct discharge of feelings are all available for use.

According to Greenspan, the developing system is also oriented (or biased) to accomplish certain "tasks" in order to achieve fit—these are the *goals of adaptation*. The infant has fairly reflexive, homeostatic interactions around feeding, sleeping, and needing stimulation, in which the goal is some degree of regulation of physical tension and arousal. The 4 year old's interactions with its context are organized around elaboration of a symbol system, mastery of the object world in increasingly complex ways, and regulation of behavior in peer context, all of which involve complex, multipurpose relationships with context. As development proceeds, modes and goals become increasingly differentiated

and organized. For Greenspan (1989), the level of organization of modes and goals is a marker of healthy adaptation.

A *flexible* system is able to respond to a wide range of contextual conditions and internal pressures because functions are differentiated and integrated via feedback loops (Ford & Lerner, 1992). Demands are responded to by the coordinated activity of several subsystems. Coordinated activity involves feedback loops. If feedback is not prompt and accurate, then the activity of the system is delayed, distorted, or compromised. Feedback tends to be very slow in overly differentiated systems and distorted when systems lack regular linkages or communication between subsystems. These properties of feedback are related to child behavioral and emotional problems when they affect the regulation of child–caregiver dyadic systems, family systems (Marvin & Stewart, 1990), or self-regulatory systems (Kopp & Wyer, 1994; Thompson, 1994). Variation in nature and function of feedback and regulation is apparent in development of conduct and externalizing problems. Coercion is a regulatory style evident between parents and child in early phases of conduct disorder (Patterson et al., 1989), and the combination of maternal control and negativity has been related to disruptive behavior in early childhood (Campbell, 1992).

The value of systems theory concepts is in mobilizing attention to overarching processes that account for both normal and abnormal development. These concepts are not intended to replace or discount concepts that describe disorder or account for change within other paradigms, but to organize those competing concepts into an explanatory system that allows researchers and clinicians the opportunity to speak the same language. It focuses attention on new and different units of analysis in the evaluation of problems and offers different views on the mechanisms of change.

KEY DEVELOPMENTAL THEMES IN EARLY CHILDHOOD

This section describes the course of development in the early years, emphasizing organization and context (Greenspan & Greenspan, 1991; Sroufe, 1989a; 1989b; & Rutter, 1984). Central to this perspective is that as development proceeds, the child *as a developing system* is faced with adaptational challenges of increasing complexity that are both a product of his or her own behavior and the response of his or her context to the perceived level of adaptation (Ford & Lerner, 1992; Greenspan, 1989; Sroufe, 1989a, 1989b). Greenspan and Greenspan (1991) describe multiple changes in level of organization in the preschool and early childhood years. In their view, the child–context systems increase in level of organization from primarily reflexive and simple engagement to intentional, reciprocal, and symbolic relations. Co-action between child and context give rise to increasingly diverse and complex modes and goals of adaptation. These modes and goals, increasingly complex and differentiated over time, are themes that frame the specific components of adaptation at a given developmental phase or period (Greenspan, 1989; Sroufe & Rutter, 1984).

Prior history and current circumstances influence the quality of the child's adaptation with respect to these themes. Over developmental time, patterns of adaptation to earlier developmental challenges are organized within adaptation to subsequent challenges; early adaptation lays the foundation for subsequent competence.

Adaptation occurs in a relational context. It is embedded in relationships—with parents, peers, teachers (and the wider social context). Context plays a central role in providing the conditions for adaptation at a given period or in a particular situation (Ford & Lerner, 1992). Everyone has noticed the difference in the functional capacity of a preschooler under circumstances of differing structure and support. When called upon to leave a favorite activity, given ample warning, a soothing tone of voice, and statements reflecting his or her feelings, the 4 year old might comply willingly and shortly thereafter describe feeling states connected to his or her behavior. However, if approached by an irritated, hurried adult, the child is more likely to tantrum and stubbornly refuse to comply, using behaviors, not words to express himself or herself.

Consideration of context also challenges notions of the quality of adaptation, and what is considered adaptive and maladaptive. Because children (like other systems) are active in achieving fit with their environments, all aspects of their response are in some way adaptive. Yet behavioral patterns (such as emotion regulation) that develop with the goal of achieving fit in one environment (e.g., a maltreating parent or dangerous neighborhood) may be maladaptive in another environment (Miller & Moore, 1989). For this reason, it is critical that quality of adaptation be viewed through the lens of developmental history and current circumstances (Bowlby, 1968; Thompson, 1991).

Although it is the subject of another chapter (see Field, Chapter 5), themes involving infancy are mentioned here because many clinical problems seen in early childhood involve some failure of adaptation with respect to these themes. These themes are drawn from work by Greenspan (1989), Sroufe (1989a, 1989b), and others (e.g., Greenberg et al., 1991).

Regulation and Modulation of Arousal

The first theme involves regulation and modulation of physiological arousal and joint attention. The infant (and caregiver) must tolerate increasingly complex physical and social stimulation and maintain an organized state in the face of this increasing arousal. This organized state leads to periods of joint attention and mutuality—the basis of exploration of the object and the interpersonal world. Cycles of sleep and alertness, feeding, interest, and arousal all begin to become organized very early on within this period. The immature status of the newborn predisposes the child to require caregiver interactions to help maintain organization in the face of cyclic variations (Hofer, 1994; Sander, 1975). The competent infant adapts to routines set by caregivers and, with caregivers, establishes regular rhythms of feeding, activity and alertness, and sleep. High affordance contexts ensure the maintenance of smooth, regular, predictable routines and practices that are contingent upon infant cues. In the context of interaction, the infant and caregiver mesh behaviors to establish these routines that form the basis of self and relationships (Sroufe, 1989b). Over time, these patterns broaden to include interactive play and form a relational matrix that organizes the infant in the face of increasingly complex stimulation.

The less competent forms of adaption at this stage: the tendency toward over-arousal and under-arousal, the infant who shows little or no predictability in terms of routines, who shows little interest in interactions, or who is so difficult to settle and soothe that caregivers become increasingly stressed and unpredictable, are linked with patterns of incompetent adaptation later in development: insecure attachment, poor exploration, and inadequate self-regulation (Greenspan, 1989) Likewise, highly stressful environments, intrusive caregiving interactions, overstimulating and understimulating environments, and maltreatment contribute to infant and relational maladaptation via disordered interactions stemming from the caregiving environment (Cohn, Campbell, Matias, & Hopkins, 1990; Egeland, Pianta, & O'Brien, 1993; Field, 1991).

This early phase of development has marked consequences for early childhood psychopathology. Difficulties in establishing shared attention and engagement predict problems in behavioral and emotional regulation in early childhood (Egeland et al., 1993) and early experiences of maltreatment have consequences for maladaptation in preschool and through the early school years (Cummings, Hennessy, Rabideau, & Cicchetti, 1994; Dodge, Pettit, & Bates, 1994). In this way, deviance or distortions in the caregiving regulatory system (Hofer, 1994) early in infancy are frequently stable and shape the emergent self-regulatory capacities of the child.

Effective Attachment Relationship

A major theme for the second 6 months of life and throughout the early childhood period is the formation and maintenance of an effective attachment relationship. In nearly every theoretical consideration of early development, an effective attachment develops as a consequence of early patterns of interaction, affords the child a sense of security in the context of a relationship, and provides a basis for exploration of the object and interpersonal world. Adult responsiveness, emotional availability, and an effective signaling system all play important roles in regulating experience in relation to this theme (Ainsworth, Blehar, Waters, & Wall, 1978) as does the caregiver's previous attachment experiences and self-regulation of attention and emotion (Fonagy, Steele, & Steele, 1991; Main & Hesse, 1990; Zeanah, Benoit, Barton, Regan, Hirschberg, & Lipsitt, 1993).

Ineffective attachment relationships reflect one of three ways of regulating arousal through contact with the caregiver (Cassidy, 1994). (1) Avoidant—The child avoids the caregiver in situations of distress because she or he has learned that the caregiver is unlikely to be available and will reject the child's bids for comfort. (2) Ambivalent—The child amplifies his or her distress in an attempt to always keep the caregiver close. This strategy of attachment regulation is consistent with a caregiving pattern of inconsistency—at times available and at time hostile and punitive; leaving the child in uncertainty regarding the caregiver's availability, hence the "need" to always stay close. (3) Disorganized—A mixture of approach and avoidance behaviors in situations in which the child needs comfort or support. In this pattern the child simultaneously emits both approach and avoidance behaviors, behaving in a style that appears confused and disorganized. The disorganized pattern of behavior is consistent with caregiving styles that are frightening to the child, as in cases in which the child has been maltreated (Carlson, Cicchetti, Barnett, & Braunwald, 1989) and in which the caregiver is made anxious by the child's expressed desire for closeness (Main & Hesse, 1990).

In many theories of development, attachment is accorded special significance. It is the first emotional, intimate relationship in which the child is involved, and patterns of emotion regulation, attention to emotion, and strategies for behavioral regulation are developed in this context (Cassidy, 1994). To the extent that attachment behaviors (proximity-seeking under threat) and secure base behaviors (exploration in presence of caregiver) have a strong evolutionary function, then development has a bias toward attachment, affiliation, and social and emotional engagement with a caregiver (Breger, 1974).

The child develops an internal "model" of his or her attachment relationship with caregiver(s) that contains beliefs about the self as worthy of care (the roots of self-esteem)

and beliefs about providers of care that are the roots of security and exploration (Blatt, 1995; Bowlby, 1968). Children classified as insecurely attached to their primary caregivers perform more poorly on measures of language development, emergent literacy and reading, cognitive development and play, and social interaction with peers and other adults (Bus & van Izjendoorn, 1993; Erickson, Sroufe, & Egeland, 1985; Sroufe, 1983, 1989a, 1989b). Internal models of self and other are carried forward and predict behavior in several relationship contexts (Elicker, Englund, & Sroufe, 1992). The mechanisms accounting for these relations are thought to involve a number of self and dyadic regulatory processes. Insecure attachment strategies involve executive cognitive functions such as selective attention and working memory such that emotion and social interaction concerning attachment-related needs and interactions shape patterns of internal processing that subsequently bias later processing and behavior (Main & Hesse, 1990). Sroufe (1989b) emphasizes dyadic regulation in attachment relationships as the core mechanism for development of the self, whereby the level of organization present in interaction is the level of organization internalized as the early self.

Greenberg, Speltz, and deKleyn (1993) describe three ways in which attachment can be linked to psychopathology (disruptive behavior) in early childhood. As noted earlier, attachment is linked with the information-processing aspect of affective–cognitive structures for the regulation of emotion, beliefs about the self, and expectations about the behavior of others (Dodge & Garber, 1991). Symptomatic markers can also be seen in observable patterns of attachment behaviors. That is, some of the behavior patterns that distinguish attachment classifications (whining, crying, clinging, tantrums) are symptoms of certain behavior disorders (e.g., oppositional defiant disorder) in early childhood and may serve as a substrate for coercive family processes that mediate the development of later conduct problems (Patterson et al., 1989). Finally, attachment affects the child's motivation to explore and thereby expand the self and associated skills and competencies. In sum, the early child–caregiver relationship provides a context for the development of a close, intimate, emotion-laden relationship that helps shape later development in many domains.

Attachment relationships do not exist only between mothers and children, nor are children limited to only one such relationship (Pianta, 1992). Instead, the centrality of attachment is, in part, a consequence of the developing child being an *open system*. Evolution, for a variety of selective purposes, requires considerable regulatory input to the child in the preschool years in the context of a relationship with a caregiver (Hofer, 1994).

Effective Self-Reliance

During the second year of life and continuing throughout early childhood, effective self-reliance or autonomy (object mastery, active problem solving, motivation) becomes increasingly important. In contrast to the concept of independence, the concept of self-reliance recognizes the relational base of the preschooler's efforts to meet the increasing demands of the object and interpersonal world. Effective self-reliance emphasizes that the child enthusiastically engages problems in the world, persists in using his or her own efforts to address the problem, and before giving up or frustrating, signals for resources from others, and uses those resources to solve the problem. Confidence in self and other are hallmarks of competent adaptation.

Part and parcel of this competent exploration and mastery of the object world is the provision of a secure base for exploration. Building on the effective attachment relationship developed within infancy, the caregiver–preschooler dyad now reorganizes within it the child's advancing motor, cognitive, and communicative skills to support exploratory forays. Now the caregiver provides regulatory actions (comfort, information) at a distance while the child displays strivings for autonomy and relentless practicing of emerging capacities (Breger, 1974; Crittenden, 1992). These strivings create new challenges and rewards to child–caregiver interaction—on the one hand they afford some relief from some physical aspects of caregiving, while on the other they elicit new feelings in the caregiver (anxiety over control) and child limit-testing as a challenge to the relationship.

Greenspan and Greenspan (1991) and Kopp and Wyer (1994) suggest that intentional, nonverbal communication involving gestures and behaviors (body posture, intentional movements, facial expressions) are a core process in regulation of self-reliance and attendant experiences. How the child maintains homeostatic relations with the world while at the same time exploring it requires a more advanced level of communication and organization than the simple reflexive loops characteristic of infancy and early toddlerhood. In Greenspan's view, preverbal processes provide this function. Verbal processes enhance preverbal processes but do not supplant them, nor are verbal processes yet linked to basic homeostatic and regulatory function in toddlerhood, in large part because they are unstable and organized at a more advanced level. Thus the toddler and preschooler acquires a sense of self as effective largely as a function of preverbal interactions with the social and object world (Kopp & Wyer, 1994).

Self-reliance in the early childhood period is not equivalent to notions of independence that involve the child's solo behavior. Instead, self-reliance refers to the child's motivation to explore, persistence in the face of frustration, and effective use of adults as resources. In the preschool period, the relational context remains a core aspect of the self, but its importance recedes somewhat in comparison to previous periods when the self was equivalent to the relational context (Kopp & Wyer, 1994; Sander, 1975). Self-reliance, like most other personality and behavioral constructs in early childhood, is distributed across child and context.

Self-reliance stands on its own, separate from its roots in attachment and as a distinct aspect of early childhood development because of the emergence of the self as a distinct entity in the preschool period and onward (Sroufe 1989a, 1989b). Self-reliance will play a prominent role in the child's capacity to adapt to the challenges of preschool and school settings; aspects of social interaction with peers, response to instruction, and motivation to perform in academic tasks will all be organized, in part, on how early patterns of self-reliance were acquired and expressed.

Environmental and Personal Resources

An expanded ability to organize and coordinate environmental and personal resources builds upon attachment and early self-reliant strivings as demands on the child become increasingly complex. In Greenspan's model (Greenspan & Greenspan, 1991), creating internal images and sharing them with others through symbols and mental representations is a core process. This integrated, organized, and intentional use of language, cognition, and interactions for the purposes of self-regulation is the hallmark of development in early childhood (Crittenden, 1992; Greenspan, 1989; Kopp & Wyer, 1994; Thompson, 1994) and is a central factor in a wide variety of internalizing and externalizing symptoms (e.g., Berlin et al., 1995; Greenberg et al., 1991; Stewart & Rubin, 1995).

Unlike the toddler and preschooler, whose systems of self and social engagement are organized preverbally, in preschool and throughout early childhood words and symbolic actions (play) are used intentionally to communicate goals, desires, expectations, and to organize and share meanings. This more advanced level of organization is easily observable in preschoolers and is core to processes of emotion regulation. Thus, behavioral and emotional flexibility, and an increasing capacity to modulate arousal using relational and self-resources, emerge as signs of competent adaptation in this and in future periods. A key feature of competent adaptation at this level, noted primarily by Greenspan (1989), is the development of an emerging *representational capacity.* Greenspan calls attention to the use of symbols, gesture, and beginning language to mediate child–context interactions.

Symbols and words are purposive; words and sentences are substituted for behavior in the expression of emotion, intent, needs, comfort, or goals. Bowlby also discusses this as a phase in which a goal corrected partnership emerges. The child and parent (adult) negotiate contact using symbols; goals and plans mesh (Bowlby, 1968; Crittenden, 1992). The emergence of a representational capacity is a fundamental shift in development in which experience is no longer coded only directly in behavior, but indirectly in symbols (Kopp & Wyer, 1994), making possible a range of new self-regulatory capacities.

The capacity to represent experience symbolically alters the way in which the child's relationship with the world is organized. For example, the attachment behavior system reorganizes in the preschool period (Cassidy, 1994; Cassidy & Marvin, 1989; Crittenden, 1992). The emphasis of the attachment relationship shifts in the preschool years from a focus on caregiving and protection to joint negotiation, expectations, and the formation of a goal-corrected partnership. Cicchetti, Cummings, Greenberg, and Marvin (1990) note changes in the spatial, temporal, and relationship contexts in which the attachment system operates and that perceptual, cognitive–representational, and communicative abilities change the form of relational behaviors that serve attachment functions. The attachment relationship integrates with other developmental functions (e.g., problem solving, communication), while retaining its protective function, and organizes within it the expanding capacity of the child for abstract representation and use of symbols. The attachment behavior system becomes organized within affiliative relations (intimate and more distal), exploration of the object world, and regulation of fear and anxiety (Sroufe, 1989).

The emergence of representation introduces new capacities into many behavioral domains and, provides the foundation for sophisticated language, reading, self-control mechanisms, new levels of cognitive processing, friendships (perspective-taking and other forms of social cognition), and other higher-order functions. In addition, representation and associated capacities force a more complex reorganization of the self and the child's relationship with the world.

This period of emergent representational capacity is a critical period for context, and problems in development in the preschool period frequently can be traced to contextual affordances for representation. Many children develop problems related to this phase of development, both as a function of maladaptation with respect to previous developmental themes and because of the challenges of the present period.

Greenberg, Kusche, and Speltz (1991) have written extensively on children who show impulse-control problems in the preschool and early school years, relating problems in impulse control to the regulation of the child–caregiver system in interactions around attachment and exchange of symbols. In their studies of children referred for mental health services because of disruptive behavior, caregivers were more coercive, less able to follow their child's lead in play, gave more commands, were less responsive to the child's cues, and showed fewer expressions of positive affect. The controlling, coercive, negative, power-oriented aspects of the environment associated with behavioral and emotional problems in early childhood are indicators of contexts that lack representational capacity (Campbell, 1992; Campbell et al., 1991; Patterson et al., 1989).

Effective Peer Relations

From the preschool years onward, effective peer relations are a central issue of concern. Peers are sources of challenges and resources, and the child must learn to integrate affiliative peer systems with competition, mastery, and increasingly abstract and representational forms of information exchange (Dodge et al., 1994). Parker and Asher (1987) helped establish the importance of peer relations for later development in a comprehensive review of peer relations studies, concluding that the quality of peer relations is a major indicator of developmental competence in social and emotional development and a critical indicator of mental health and general adaptation.

Peer relations are clearly linked with the child's early relationship history with parents, caregivers, and other family members as well as neurobiological regulatory processes that predispose the child toward high or low interactivity (Rubin, Coplan, Fox, & Calkins, 1995). This nesting of earlier forms and processes of adaptation within adaptation to later developmental themes is a major premise of the developmental–organizational approach. Sroufe (1983) provides a strikingly clear example of how early forms of adaptation become layered within peer relations in the preschool and early school context. Following a sample of high-risk children from birth through the preschool years, this study demonstrates the high degree of continuity between early patterns of adaptation and competence in preschool. Children with histories of secure attachment tended to become friends with one another. They related better to teachers, were rated by teachers as the most competent, and were well-suited to activities that went on in a school setting: They were rated by teachers to be attentive, flexible, sociable, compliant, self-reliant, and persistent. By contrast, children with histories of insecure attachment were much more poorly adapted. Children classified as showing avoidant attachment in infancy were rated by teachers as aggressive, noncompliant, inattentive, and tended toward a bullying style of peer relations, especially if paired with another child with a history of insecurity.

Maladaptation in peer relations is seen consistently for children with histories of anxious–ambivalent attachment. These children report considerably more loneliness than their avoidant or securely attached counterparts (Berlin et al., in press). They process social information in ways that are biased toward victimization of the self and toward involvement with aggressive, victimizing peers (Dodge, 1991). Unlike the more aggressive behavior seen with children who have histories of avoidance, children with histories of ambivalent attachment alienate both peers and teachers. This pattern is consistent with Rubin's findings (Rubin et al., 1995) that these children are poor emotion regulators and low on social interaction and initiation. They are highly reactive in peer settings and ultimately excluded from the benefits of peer relations. In the Sroufe (1983) follow-up of the Minnesota high-risk sample, children with a history of ambivalent attachment were very poorly adapted to the demands of the preschool: They were whiny, petulant, dependent, and generally lacked resilience or persistence. In peer relations they were typically victimized, especially if paired with a child with a history of avoidance. Erickson, Sroufe, and Egeland (1985), using a larger sample than Sroufe (1983), showed that children with anxious resistant attachment histories were less agentic, assertive, and confident than their peers and had poor social skills relative to children with secure histories.

A history of avoidant attachment is associated with a variety of behavior problems and signs of maladaptation in preschool (Erickson et al., 1985; Greenberg et al., 1991; Sroufe, 1983). In the Sroufe (1983) study, these children were rated by observers as more dependent on teachers and less socially skilled than secure peers and expressed more negative emotion than either of the other two attachment groups. Children classified as avoidant were rated by their preschool teachers as more withdrawn, exhibitionistic, and impulsive, and less persistent than the other two groups and as more hostile than the children with histories of resistance. The avoidant children received the highest total score on the index of behavior problems. The interactive style of children with avoidant histories is not unlike that described by Rubin and colleagues (1995) for children who are poor self-regulators but highly sociable; these children tend to show externalizing behaviors with peers and more aggression, hostility, and disruption than their regulated counterparts.

Adaptation in the peer context is viewed as a core component of the quality of adaption in early childhood. By the end of this period children are expected to have stable, fairly close friendships or "chums," and peer relations become the focus for self-regulatory skills either mastered (or not) in the context of family and child–caregiver relationships (Elicker et al., 1992). Failure in peer relations is frequently an indicator for referral for mental health problems both because it is

a salient feature of adaptation at that time and because it is a strong predictor of later disorder (Kazdin, 1992; Loeber, 1990).

The Reorganized Child

Toward the end of early childhood, formation of a stable sense of self, effective self-control, and symbolic exchange expand rapidly and consolidate within reorganized child and child–context systems. These are key elements of adaptation in cognitive and academic achievement, cooperation in social groups, and the beginnings of a sense of identity. It is at this phase, marking the end of early childhood, that self-regulation is a hallmark of competence and a nearly universal expectation. Failure in self-regulation describes a large number of childhood symptoms in this phase because it is expected that the child has by now "passed through" the phases in which self-regulation has emerged, or developed (Kopp & Wyer, 1994).

Greenspan suggests that by the late preschool and elementary school ages, children's adaptation is a function of fairly sophisticated representational processes. Children intentionally manipulate language, symbols, and internal representations (images, etc.) in the service of self-control, peer interaction, conflict resolution, goal attainment, problem solving, and mastery of the information world. The matrix of increasingly complex internal representations is mirrored by a more complex external world and accompanied, hopefully, by equally complex capacities to operate on those internal representations. At the end of early childhood, children learn roles and practice them internally and behaviorally, trying on new parts of their identity. They use internal images and selective attention to maintain goal-directed behavior in the face of frustration, that is, to delay gratification and control impulses.

As was the case for peer relations, the use of symbolic exchange to self-regulate behavior and activity in early childhood is directly traced to early experiences in relationships. Representational capacity, language, meta-cognition, and problem solving all have been linked to the quality of early relationships (Greenberg et al., 1991). Crittenden (1992) suggests that secure attachment allows children to regulate their feelings in the context of safe, supportive adults, and thereby down-regulate anxiety, allowing for creativity, problem solving, and experience of mastery. On the other hand, children with avoidant attachments must develop emotion regulation strategies that are prematurely autonomous; through their own efforts they work to minimize anxiety, reducing their attention and motivation to expand true self-regulatory skills. These children do not learn to moderate emotion through mediated processing, but instead to defend and shut it out. Thus, self-regulatory skills that enhance peer relations and expanding capacity to mediate experience are not acquired. Likewise, the children with resistant or ambivalent attachment relations remain under the regulatory influence of parents for too long, never acquiring the minimal skills necessary to assume responsibility for regulating their emotional and social experiences, so their adaptation in peer contexts, often requiring fairly advanced skills, is poor.

Like previous phases of adaptation, context plays a considerable role in the extent to which representational capacity is extended and organized within middle childhood and is used in the service of competent adaptation to issues of self-control and identity. Availability of appropriate role models is one important feature of context—adult and older peer models play an increasingly important role in the regulation of children's behavior through middle childhood. Furthermore, learning tasks must also be available in ways that are linked to the ways in which the child has come to make meaning of the world—again in connection with role models and in connection to real-world problem solving (Resnick, 1994).

These themes mark the changing landscape of development across the early childhood period. Like the introductory paragraph to this chapter, they describe *what* it is that changes during this period and the ways in which the child is different at the beginning and end of this period. The systemic nature of the child, and child–context relationships, should be evident. Social behavior and emotion play a central role in this model. Social interaction is the means by which many feedback functions occur and provides the points of contact between the child and contextual systems. Through these interactions with context, development occurs.

Role of Context in Child Adaptation

It is important to reiterate the distributed nature of development during early childhood (and other periods). The child's competence and adaptation with respect to the themes described are largely a function of the affordance value of context. It is unlikely, for example, for a young preschooler to become an effective explorer of the social or object world when his or her caregiver requires the child's attention to the caregiver's own emotional needs. Likewise, it is difficult even for the most well-tuned physiology to regulate itself in the context of home environments that are unpredictable or violent (e.g., Cummings, Hennessy, Rabideau, & Cicchetti, 1994).

For preschoolers and children in the primary grades (and later grades for many high-risk children), one cannot underestimate the extent to which relationships with people and environments support or inhibit progress through the devel-

opmental themes described earlier. In a larger sense, the distributed nature of competence means that children are only as competent as their context affords them the opportunity to be. In short, their competence is a property of these systems. One of the biggest errors that clinicians can make when working with children in the early childhood period is to assume competence is a property of the child and fail to make the necessary observations of the child in context.

A developmental perspective suggests that periods of heightened sensitivity to certain environmental stressors may occur. It could be argued that the preschool period is one of increased sensitivity relative to other developmental phases, especially with respect to the development of externalizing forms of psychopathology (Loeber, 1990), largely because of the role that family and relationship processes play in the formation of the child's underlying capacities for self-regulation. The rapid growth in skills closely tied to social and emotional adjustment (peer relations, emotion regulation, social cognition, etc.) suggest that this period may be a sensitive period (Bornstein, 1989) in the development of a range of emotional and behavior problems. Evidence from studies of brain function and plasticity confirms this notion of developmental sensitivity during early childhood (Cicchetti and Tucker, 1995). Furthermore, context plays a critical role in the development of these processes during this period and so is implicated in the notion of early childhood as a sensitive period in which development is particularly open to contextual influences. Developmental trajectories established in this phase have consequences for years to come (Sroufe, 1989a).

Finally, context is not equivalent to the relationship between the child and the caregiver, to the interactions between the child and the caregiver, or to the family system. For example, behavioral and emotional problems in early childhood and later periods are related to poverty, neighborhood violence, and overcrowding, in some cases independent of the quality of attachment (Huston, 1991; Masten, 1992; Radke-Yarrow, McCann, DeMulder, Belmont, Martinez, & Richardson, 1995). Although many of the effects of distal contextual forces are transmitted to the child via the parent–child relationship, it would be a mistake to overlook their own independent influences.

The Organizational Lens

Developmental change takes place as a function of coordinated action among systems—systems internal to the child, child–caregiver, and child–peer dyadic systems as well as larger group-level systems associated with family and social context (day care, school) influences. The tasks described by developmental theorists refer, in many ways, to the level of complexity at which these systems are organized (Greenspan, 1989). Viewing child–context as a system, each developmental theme in early childhood is fundamentally a challenge to the child–context system to reorganize itself into a more sophisticated form. The child–context system in infancy is a reflexive system with fairly rigid or fixed responses. The child–context system in the preschool period contains multiple means of interacting (behavior, symbols), with internal feedback loops (memory, beliefs, attributions, expectations) and capacity for decision making that enable it to be a much more flexible system, capable of tolerating considerable challenges (e.g., strong feelings) while maintaining identity and organization.

In this way development in early childhood is marked not only by changes within a particular domain (e.g., cognitive or motor development) but in the progress to more complex, sophisticated systems that regulate adaptation. Running though the key developmental themes just discussed are processes and mechanisms that account for the emerging competencies or higher levels of organization that were described. These include emotion regulation, symbolic representation and use, experience of self as competent and effective, and involvement in affiliative relationships. The increased organization, intentionality, functionality, and complexity of these processes mark the difference between "infancy" and "middle childhood." In so doing these provide a developmentally informed window on continuities and discontinuities between "normal" and "abnormal" in early childhood.

DEVELOPMENTAL PROCESSES AND MECHANISMS

The discussion of developmental themes in early childhood highlights the centrality of emotion in shaping the nature of child–context interactions and the form that adaptation will take. The development of emotion-regulation processes in the context of child–caregiver dyadic relationships accounts for considerable individual variation in early childhood.

Emotion Regulation

The development of capacities related to the understanding, expression, and regulation of emotion is a major current running through the developmental themes of early childhood (Thompson, 1994). Deficits in these skills or capacities are viewed as central to the most common behavior problems in children—externalizing and overactive behaviors that are disruptive to adults and other children (Greenberg et al., 1991). Better understanding of emotion regulation and component subprocesses allows one to then better understand

the developmental mechanisms behind clinical symptomatology in early childhood.

Cicchetti, Ackerman, and Izard (1995) note the recent emphasis on emotions as constituting their own developmental system, the central function of which is to motivate and organize adaptive behavior. Like most developmental systems, the emotions system is itself organized with associated systems of cognition, language, physiology, and neural processes. The relation of cognition and emotion is considered of paramount importance in many theories of emotional development and emotion regulation and appears prominently in many theories of psychopathology and in approaches to intervention with childhood disorders (Diaz & Berk, 1995). Cognition also is considered to play a prominent role in the regulation of emotion. Furthermore, the relation of cognition and emotion, considered to be fairly independent early in life, proceeds with rapid pace throughout the period of early childhood (Thompson, 1994).

The importance of emotion regulation for adaptation and psychopathology in early and middle childhood is underscored by several investigators' work. Thompson notes that problems in the management of emotions play a key role in social dysfunction, including the reading of social cues, differentiation of cue salience, interpretation of cues, and evaluation of response alternatives. Likewise, Cole and colleagues (Cole, Michel, & Teti, 1994) suggest that emotion dysregulation is part and parcel of definition, etiology, and treatment of certain forms of psychopathology in early childhood. Regulation of the emotions of anger, sadness, and anxiety are core aspects of the behavioral signs of a number of childhood disorders. For these reasons then, the process of emotion regulation—what it is and how it develops—figures centrally in any discussion of early childhood clinical issues.

Emotion regulation has been defined as "the extrinsic and intrinsic processes responsible for monitoring, evaluating, and modifying emotional reactions, especially their intensive and temporal features...necessary both to provide flexibility to the behavioral processes that emotions help to motivate and direct, and also to enable organisms to respond quickly and efficiently to changes in their environments by maintaining internal arousal within performance-enhancing limits" (Thompson, 1991, p. 271). The child is capable of using internal representations and their manipulation to tolerate arousal states and events and to respond with behaviors appropriate to the situation and its demands.

Thompson (1994) suggests that neurophysiological processes, attention, interpretation of emotion-related events, encoding of internal emotion cues, access to coping resources, regulation of emotional demands of certain settings, and the selection of adapting response alternatives are all regulated by emotion-regulation processes. Note the similarity of many of these processes to features of clinical intervention with children. Cicchetti and colleagues (1995) specify three component regulatory processes: those that address specific emotions (e.g. arousal, anger modulation), those that target emotion–cognition links, and those that regulate emotion–action links.

Regulatory processes that target specific emotions influence emotional intensity, including those that deal with the causes of individual emotions and those that concern emotional output and expression. With respect to causes of emotions, regulatory processes are involved in neural, physiological, and cognitive inputs to the emotion system. Cicchetti and colleagues (1995) suggest that at a minimum there is evidence for some form of gating mechanisms that reduce arousal and shut down perseverative mechanisms, such as crying in infancy. Attachment-related behavior is one means of regulating the intensity of anxiety in early childhood (Cassidy, 1994; Crittenden, 1992).

Cognitive processes are frequently introduced as central to control systems that operate to modulate the expression of emotions or the output of the emotions system. As noted earlier, the development of emotion–cognition links is a fundamental theme in the preschool period. Virtually nonexistent prior to the early childhood period, emotion–cognition links are functionally operative by the beginning of the middle childhood period. This progression reflects the extent to which the expression of emotion moves from distinctly reflexive and physical to sophisticated cognitive–affective blends (Cicchetti et al., 1995). These blends play a role in the links between internalizing and externalizing pathology in early childhood and social information processing packages. Dodge (1991) has identified attributional biases regulating aggressive behavior while Garber and colleagues (Garber, Braafladt, & Zeman, 1991) focus on cognitive–affective blends in childhood depression. Subcomponents of cognitive–affective blends include affective labeling, understanding differential emotions, and clarity of emotional expression (Greenberg et al., 1991; Thompson, 1994).

Greenberg and colleagues (1991, 1993) outline three phases in the development of emotion regulation in their affect behavior cognition model. Early in development, emotion is expressed behaviorally by the child and regulated by the caregiver. This phase is critical for establishing the acceptability of emotion expression by the child, for establishing a regulated emotional experience for the child (by the caregiver), and for forming early routines in which the caregiver-as-regulator can be integrated into the child's emotion expression and management system. The caregiver provides comfort for arousing experiences, then provides labels for the child's affective states. These labels, at first nonsymbolic, and then symbolic, form the basis for emerging links between cognition, language, and emotion.

The subprocesses of emotion regulation are also interrelated. General emotion tone and the capacity to shut down or regulate specific positive and negative emotions affect the understanding and labeling of emotion. Cognitive–affective blends, in turn, feed back to regulate emotional output and to provide input to the processes that link emotion and behavior and that play a large role in early childhood competence (Rubin et al., 1995).

The third set of emotion-regulation processes described by Cicchetti and colleagues (1995) involve the coordination of emotion and action. They note that although the primary function of the emotions systems may be to motivate behavior, behavior must be directed toward adaptive goals and organized within the larger social context. Internal behaviors for coping with arousal and emotions can also be the target of these emotion–action regulations. Problems associated with regulation of emotion–action links in the preschool period are well documented, both with respect to social interactions with adults and in the peer group. Children who have difficulties inhibiting arousal and aggression are more frequently referred for problems with externalizing symptomatology, referred for special education, and are more frequently rejected and excluded in the peer group (Greenberg et al., 1993; Rubin et al., 1995). Furthermore, children who are inhibited and withdrawn overregulate emotion and emotion–action links. They are frequently viewed as anxious and depressed and fail to benefit from the peer group because of their low initiation and interaction frequencies.

The particulars of control mechanisms surrounding the regulation of emotion–action links, like other aspects of emotion regulation, are not well understood (Cicchetti et al, 1995). This is problematic for clinical applications, given that a large portion of clinical referrals involve these very processes. Although developmental theories of emotion regulation posit that emotion–action links emerge from a matrix of subprocesses involving direct action on emotional input and output as well as cognitive–affective links, most interventions designed to improve emotion–action links or emotion–cognition links involve direct instruction in some of these skills (Diaz & Berk, 1995). The failure of these skills to generalize beyond the treatment room or the immediate situation points out the large difference between a skill or capacity that emerges as a function of development and one that emerges as a function of instruction or intervention.

The relational context is involved in very basic emotion-regulation processes (Cohn & Tronick, 1988). The attachment behavior system can be viewed, in large part, as a system for regulating emotions aroused by separation from the caregiver or a threat (Cassidy, 1994). Secure attachment reflects a relational state in which emotions are acknowledged by the child's consciousness, communicated to the caregiver, who then brings the child's emotional experience within tolerable levels through actions designed to acknowledge the child's experience and operate on it. The child thus learns to identify and tolerate emotion.

If a caregiver is unavailable, avoidant strategies are used by the child to downregulate emotions associated with separation. In this case, the child develops hypermature mechanisms for the internal gating of negative emotion, shutting down or minimizing the extent to which emotions reach conscious experience. Over the long term, this selective bias of emotion-related attention and cognition has consequences for development of empathy, perspective-taking, and the development of necessary links between emotion and behavior that will help the child to be regulated in social interactions.

In the case of ambivalent-resistant attachment, emotions are not regulated by the child but in fact are frequently amplified by the child in the process of "handing over" regulatory duties to the parent. This strategy serves to keep the unpredictable parent close during separations (ensuring survival) but fails to allow the child to acquire the means of tolerating emotion. Instead the child fails to acquire any gating mechanisms.

In sum, emotion regulation is central to any description of adjustment or adaptation in the early childhood period and nearly isomorphic to a clinician's working definitions of psychopathology. Emotion regulation is a global developmental process that bridges the normal and abnormal. Think for a moment about how these aspects of emotion regulation are linked with our very definitions of what differentiates normal and abnormal: that is, access to a full range of emotions, modulation of intensity and duration of emotion, fluid, smooth shifts of emotion, conformity with cultural display rules, verbal regulation of emotion processes, and the management of emotions about emotions (Cole et al., 1994). These aspects of emotion regulation account for a great deal of individual variability on childhood adjustment and can be the focus of developmentally oriented nosology, assessment, and treatment during this period.

Child–Caregiver Dyadic Relationships

Processes for behavioral and psychological development in infancy and early childhood are regulated in large part by relationships (and interactions) between the child and the child's caregiver(s). According to Thompson (1994), the parents' regulatory role involves the production of emotion, intervention to relieve distress, selective attention and reinforcement of certain emotional experiences, interpretation of emotion and emotion cues, and direct instruction in strategies for self-regulation.

But parents' regulatory role is not only involved with emotion. Parents are also involved in the management and regulation of the child's behavioral repertoire (which includes emotion regulation skills). Motor activity and motor control, and social behaviors involving conformity to accepted rules for greeting, interaction, and communication, are all under the regulatory influence of the caregiving system (Kopp & Wyer, 1994). Even aspects of physiological activity in early childhood are under the regulatory influence of parenting. Using animal models, Hofer (1994) demonstrates the importance of caregivers' interactions for regulation of basic physiological systems, including temperature, sleep, and activity. These findings illustrate the importance of child–caregiver dyadic relationship systems for the development of young children.

Earlier it was emphasized that child psychopathology (or competence) is a distributed property of the child–context system. Psychological processes that are typically viewed as properties of the child (e.g., cognition, emotion regulation) are in fact organized within a larger system involving contextual influences. No context (or system) has been as widely linked to child psychopathology, especially in the early childhood years, than the dyadic child–caregiver relationship system. A PsychLit search using the search keys "parent–child interaction" and "behavior problems" yielded more than 100 published references reporting relations between these two constructs in early childhood (Pianta & Ferguson, unpublished manuscript). These findings support the notion that in early childhood some of what are viewed as disorders located within children may in fact be disorders located in relationships (Anders, 1989) and perhaps larger systems.

Figure 6.1 represents a model of dyadic systems, in particular the parent–child system. This model will be discussed in some detail, in part because of the prominence of this system for the development and description of emotional and behavior problems and, likewise because of the role it plays in the regulation of key developmental processes.

First, it should be noted that the child–caregiver relationship is what can be termed an *asymmetric relationship*. That is, the child is the less mature system or organism, and for evolutionary reasons, this less mature organism is tethered to a more mature organism that is responsible for its survival and developmental fitness. In this way, some influences between the child and the caregiver are biased toward unidirectionality from caregiver to child (recognizing certain child influences). Such an arrangement makes good evolutionary sense when the less mature organism is not capable

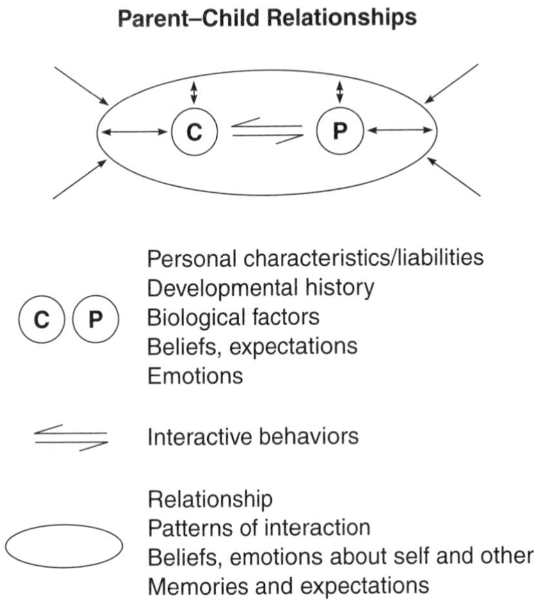

Parent–Child Relationships

FIGURE 6.1 A model of dyadic parent–child relationship systems

of surviving to reproductive age on its own (Bowlby, 1968; Breger, 1974).

In the model presented in Figure 6.1, the child and parent are represented as distinct. Their interactions are reflected in the arrows that are directed toward each other. However, as Hinde (1987) and others note, interactions are not equivalent to a relationship. Therefore, the relationship between child and parent is depicted as an oval encompassing the child, the parent, and their interactions with one another. At the organizational level, relationships are not simply the sum of the individual interactions of individuals, or their individual properties, but have their own identity apart from the features of interactions or individuals (Sroufe, 1989a, 1989b). Relationships have a history, a memory; they are patterns of interactions, expectations, beliefs, and affects organized at a level more abstract than observable behaviors. That is why when one wants to observe properties of a relationship, they must be observed over time, over situations, and from multiple windows.

The model also includes the influences of individuals on the relationship—that is, the developmental history of each individual constrains or shapes the interactions and the relationship formed on the basis of these interaction (Zeanah et al., 1993). For example, the attachment history of adults influences the quality of attachment of their child in infancy

(Fonagy et al., 1991). Processes involving the adult's selective attention, emotion management, belief systems, and interpretive biases all exert pressure on interactions between parent and child and constrain the behaviors of the caregiver. Other less mutable features of individuals such as temperament and gender constrain relationships from within. Likewise, characteristic of systems external to the child–caregiver relationship also exert influence on it and shape interactions. Cultures exert influences through what Sameroff (1989) terms the "developmental agenda" by prescribing timetables for weaning, expectations about child-rearing, and discipline practices.

Arguably, the period of early childhood is a *sensitive period* for the influences of the dyadic child–caregiver system (Bornstein, 1989). Many basic internal regulatory mechanisms are either nonexistent or influenced by caregiver interactions (Hofer, 1994; Sander, 1975). The level of organization of this child–caregiver system during this period will bias later development, particularly for the types of regulatory processes that have been the focus of much of this chapter (Thompson, 1994). Sensitivity to input from child–caregiver relationships and interactions is heightened in the infancy–early childhood period. By the end of this period, the role of the child–caregiver system both as an input to developing self-regulatory systems and as a means of maintaining organism organization and homeostasis diminishes somewhat as responsibility for these processes of adaptation is transferred gradually to the developing child.

For these reasons the child–caregiver dyadic system figures prominently in *developmentally oriented* theories of psychopathology (Sroufe, 1989) and is considered increasingly important in assessment and intervention (Lieberman, 1992) practices with children. Results for recent applications of developmentally based interventions using lessons and techniques based on this theory have shown great promise for enhancing self-control and adaptation to school in young children with disruptive behavior problems (Greenberg, Kusche, Cook, & Quamma, 1995; Lieberman 1992). As our knowledge of the function of the child–caregiver relationship expands and differentiates with respect to developmental processes in early childhood, it is likely to acquire greater prominence in clinical practice with children well into middle childhood.

For these reasons many developmental psychopathologists have suggested that psychological or psychiatric disorder is best represented, in early childhood, by the concept of a relationship disorder (e.g., Anders, 1989). The construct of relationship disorder recognizes that the core processes underlying behavioral and emotional symptoms are distributed as properties of the child–caregiver dyad (or in other influential relationships). Taken seriously, the construct of relationship disorder radically alters beliefs about the nature of the disorder, its identification, and its treatment. It is toward these implications that the chapter now turns.

DISORDER, ASSESSMENT, AND TREATMENT IN THE EARLY CHILDHOOD YEARS

It has been suggested that emotion-regulation processes and asymmetric, dyadic systems between children and caregivers are keys to development of emotional and behavior disorders in early childhood and link normal and abnormal development in this period. Systems theory concepts such as holism, distribution, co-action, self-stabilization, and self-reorganization are helpful in describing these developmental processes and mechanisms and for linking clinical applications to developmental theory. This section describes clinical applications of the developmental and organizational perspective in the early childhood years.

Disorder

Several investigators have called attention to the differences between symptoms, syndromes, and disorders in childhood psychopathology (e.g., Cantwell, 1983). Symptoms, the behavioral manifestation of mental functioning, are often loosely organized into collections or groups that are characterized as syndromes (Achenbach & McConaughy, 1987). Disorders refer to collections of symptoms that have a characteristic etiology, clinical presentation, and treatment, with treatment based on knowledge of etiological processes. Most of what are called childhood psychopathological disorders are in fact syndromes.

To the extent that developmental pathways have been identified in prospective studies, child–parent relationships frequently are identified as predictors and correlates of early childhood symptoms and syndromes (e.g., Campbell, 1992; Greenberg et al., 1991; Sroufe, 1989a, 1989b). Common (and successful) treatment regimens for the period of early childhood frequently involve rearranging dyadic caregiving interactions or family interactions (e.g., Barkley, 1987; Kazdin, 1992; Patterson et al., 1989). Because relationships play such a key role in etiology and treatment of behavioral maladaptation on early childhood, maladaptation may be best conceived of as distributed across (or *located* in) these relationship processes.

Several authors have suggested relationship system constructs that may be applied to the conceptualization of disorder as a relationship level entity (Anders, 1989; Sroufe, 1989). These include characteristics of the boundary delineating the individuals within the relationship, features of the regulatory activity of the relationship (overregulated or underregulated; rigid or flexible), and affective quality. Each of these constructs is holistic; they do not reflect the activity of one member of the relationship, nor do they depend upon single, discrete behaviors as markers.

How the relationship identifies, maintains, and recognizes boundaries between caregiver and child (as distinct entities) is certainly one aspect of relationship functioning with relevance for nosology. Gender boundary dissolution (Sroufe, Jacobvitz, Mangelsdorf, DeAngelo, & Ward, 1985) and inadequate control mechanisms (Campbell, 1994) are examples of boundary-level problems. Anders (1989) identifies overregulation, underregulation, and chaotic regulation as indicative of relationship pathology.

Several relationship subprocesses are involved in regulating behavior. These include how tolerances are set for the child's behavior, child characteristics such as temperament, caregiver regulatory behaviors, feedback mechanisms between caregiver and child, and the number and nature of communicative channels between child and caregiver. These subprocesses operate to regulate child experience and development in many functional domains—emotion, motor activity, communication, learning, and exploration.

Tolerances that trigger regulatory actions by the parent are influenced by parents' developmental history (Fonagy et al., 1991; Zeanah et al., 1993) and culture (Super & Harkness, 1986). Expectations for child behavior are set as a function of the parent's own experience and acquired knowledge and influence interaction with the child on an ongoing basis (Sameroff, 1989). Likewise, characteristics of the child play a role in setting tolerances, and the child also actively emits behavior intended to regulate the parent. Feedback mechanisms operate to exchange information between partners regarding the effects of the other's behavior. To the extent that feedback processes are biased or distorted, child (or adult) cues cannot be responded to, and homeostatic processes become more complex and less functional (Cassidy, 1994). Mutuality, reciprocity, attunement, and synchrony are all constructs that reflect the contingent and sensitive nature of feedback and regulatory actions. Finally, as noted by Greenspan, early in development, regulation takes place largely through communication channels involving touch and nonsymbolic actions. Eventually symbols replace actions and regulation is more flexibly adaptive to a range of circumstances. To the extent that communicative channels are distorted and oversensitive or undersensitive, regulation will be impaired (Greenspan, 1989).

These relationship-level constructs provide a different lens for describing pathology in early childhood. They are developmentally informed and therefore contribute to understanding the links between normal and abnormal in ways that traditional adult-oriented or individual-oriented constructs do not.

Assessment

There are several implications of the developmental–organizational lens for assessment in early childhood. First, developmental–organizational constructs broaden the focus of most assessments of young children. Instead of independent views of the child within different domains (e.g., language skills, cognitive skills, motor skills), they focus on the functional integration or organizational level of the child's capacities in key developmental themes. These themes provide the context for observational assessment and can also be used as interpretive frames for standardized test data (Greenspan & Greenspan, 1991).

Developmentally informed assessment in early childhood also focuses on emotion regulation and its subprocesses and the regulatory activity of child–caregiver relationships. Assessment data from observation of functional behavior patterns in naturalistic settings can link description of child problems (nosology) with treatments.

Treatment

To the extent that the languages of (1) development, (2) mental health problems (e.g., nosology), (3) assessment methods, and (4) treatment methods share a common set of constructs and language, treatment will be integrated with knowledge of development and change. Currently each of these tasks involves different concepts and constructs. The case for common constructs, informed by a developmental–organizational lens, has been made. The biggest contribution of the developmental–organizational lens to treatment is the theory of how change occurs. Fundamental to this contribution is the recognition that development is change. Thus the more known about development, the more that is known about change. Consequently, therapy can be the strategic and intentional use of developmental processes toward enhancing the adaptation of the child (or family).

A wide range of therapeutic strategies for young children already integrate developmental constructs and processes. Most focus on relationship-level processes or on parent skills in the context of relationship processes (e.g., Barkley, 1987; Lieberman, 1992). Most place heavy emphasis on using child-centered playtime as a foundation for intervention. These sessions alter parents' representations of the child, "loosen" rigid tolerances and beliefs, and introduce new elements into child–parent interaction patterns based on more accurate reading of child cues and sensitive responsivity. Child adaptation improves as a consequence of the reorganization of the child–parent relationship. These principles of systems change evident in parent–child relationship treatment are also evident in individual therapy for the child during which the therapist can control input to the child and regulatory processes involved in the parent–child relationship.

In this way, both therapeutic change and developmental change are described by common constructs: co-activity, differentiation, integration, and homeostasis; self-stabilization; and self-reorganization. Context plays the central role in inducing change. To the extent that multiple, co-acting regulatory systems are brought "on line" to make consistent challenges (and supports) to the child or child–parent relationship, then change is more likely. The network of interventions then involve targeting boundaries, tolerances, regulatory behaviors, feedback mechanisms, and communicative channels across parent–child, child–peer, and school system contexts.

SUMMARY AND CONCLUSIONS

The developmental–organizational lens provides a common discourse for development, psychopathology, assessment, and treatment methods in early childhood. The regulation of emotion and the increasingly representational and symbolic nature of the child's relationship with the world is a core process linking normal and abnormal development during this period. These core processes of emotion regulation and representation are regulated in large part by the relationship between the child and caregivers. Thus the developmental–organizational approach provides an integrative frame for clinical and basic research in early childhood.

REFERENCES

Achenbach, T. M., & McConaughy, S. H. (1987). *Empirically based assessment of child and adolescent psychopathology.* Newbury Park, CA: Sage.

Ainsworth, M. D., Blehar, M. C., Waters, E., & Wall, D. (1978). *Patterns of attachment: A psychological study of the strange situation.* Hillsdale, NJ: Erlbaum.

Anders, T. F. (1989). Clinical syndromes, relationship disturbances, and their assessment. In A. Sameroff and R. Emde (Eds.), *Relationship disturbances in early childhood* (pp. 125–144). New York: Basic Books.

Barkley, R. (1987). *Defiant children: A clinician's manual for parent training.* New York: Guilford Press.

Berlin, L., Cassidy, J., & Belsky, J. (1995). Loneliness in young children and infant mother attachment. *Merrill Palmer Quarterly, 41,* 91–103.

Blatt, S. J. (1995). Representational structures in psychopathology. In D. Cicchetti and S. Toth (Eds.), *Emotion, cognition, and representation: Rochester Symposium on Developmental Psycho-*

pathology (Vol. 6, pp. 1–34). Rochester, NY: University of Rochester Press.

Bornstein, M. (1989). Sensitive periods in development: Structural characteristics and causal interpretations. *Psychological Bulletin, 105,* 179–197.

Bowlby, J. (1968). *Attachment and loss, vol. 1: Attachment.* New York: Basic Books.

Breger, L. (1974). *From instinct to identity.* Englewood Cliffs, NJ: Prentice-Hall.

Bus, A. G., & van Ijzendoorn, M. H. (1988). Mother-child interactions, attachment, and emergent literacy: A cross-sectional study. *Child Development, 59,* 1262–1273.

Campbell, S. B. (1990). *Behavior problems in preschool children.* New York: Guilford Press.

Campbell, S. B. (1994). Hard-to-manage preschool boys: Externalizing behavior, social competence, and family context at two-year follow-up. *Journal of Abnormal Child Psychology, 22,* 147–166.

Campbell, S. B., March, C. L., Pierce, E., Ewing, L. J., & Szumowski, E. K. (1991). Hard-to-manage preschool boys: Family context and stability of externalizing behavior. *Journal of Abnormal Child Psychology, 19,* 301–318.

Cantwell, D. P. (1983). Depression in childhood: Clinical picture and diagnostic criteria.. In D. P. Cantwell and G. A. Carlson (Eds.), *Affective disorders in childhood and adolescence* (pp. 3–18). New York: Spectrum.

Capps, L., Mundy, P., & Sigman, M. (1994). Attachment security in children with autism. *Development and Psychopathology, 6,* 149–261.

Carlson, V., Cicchetti, D., Barnett, D., & Braunwald, K. (1989). Disorganized/disoriented attachment relationships in maltreated infants. *Developmental Psychology, 25,* 525–531.

Cassidy, J. (1994). Emotion regulation: Influences of attachment relationships. In N. A. Fox (Ed.), *The development of emotion regulation: Biological and behavioral considerations. Monographs of the Society for Research in Child Development, 59* (Serial No. 240), 228–249.

Cassidy, J., & Marvin, R. S. (1989). *Attachment organization in three- and four-year-olds: Coding guidelines.* Unpublished manuscript, University of Virginia.

Cicchetti, D., Ackerman, B. P., & Izard, C. (1995). Emotions and emotion regulation in developmental psychopathology. *Development and Psychopathology, 7,* 1–10.

Cicchetti, D., Cummings, M., Greenberg, M., & Marvin, R. S. (1990). An organization perspective on attachment beyond infancy. In M. Greenberg, D. Cicchetti, & M. Cummings (Eds.), *Attachment in the preschool years* (pp. 3–50). Chicago: University of Chicago Press.

Cicchetti, D., & Toth, S. (1992). The role of developmental theory in prevention and intervention. *Development and Psychopathology, 4,* 489–493.

Cicchetti, D., & Tucker, D. (1994). Development and self-regulatory structures of the mind. *Development and Psychopathology, 6,* 533–550.

Cohn, J. F., Campbell, S., Matias, R., & Hopkins, J. (1990). Face-to-face interactions of postpartum depressed and non-depressed mother-infant pairs. *Developmental Psychology, 26,* 15–23.

Cole, P. M., Michel, M. K., & Teti, L. O. (1994). The development of emotion regulation and dysregulation: A clinical perspective. In N. A. Fox (Ed.), *The development of emotion regulation: Biological and behavioral considerations. Monographs of the Society for Research in Child Development, 59* (Serial No. 240), 73–102.

Crittenden, P. (1992). Quality of attachment in the preschool years. *Development and Psychopathology, 4,* 209–241.

Cummings, E. M., Hennessy, K., Rabideau, G., & Cicchetti, D. (1994). Responses of physically abused boys to interadult anger involving their mothers. *Development and Psychopathology, 6,* 31–42.

Diaz, R. M., & Berk, L. E. (1995). A Vygotskian critique of self-instructional training. *Development and Psychopathology, 7,* 369–392.

Dodge, K. (1991). Emotion and social information processing. In J. Garber & K. Dodge (Eds.), *The development of emotion regulation and dysregulation* (pp. 159–181). New York: Cambridge University Press.

Dodge, K., Pettit, G., & Bates, J. (1994). Effects of maltreatment on the development of peer relations. *Development and Psychopathology, 6,* 43–57.

Dykman, R. A., & Ackerman, P. T. (1993). Behavioral subtypes of attention deficit disorder. *Exceptional Children, 60,* 132–142.

Egeland, B., Pianta, R. C., & O'Brien, M. (1993). Maternal intrusiveness in infancy and child maladaptation in early school years. *Development and Psychopathology, 5,* 359–370.

Elicker, J., Egeland, B., & Sroufe, L. A. (1992). Predicting peer competence and peer relationships in childhood from early parent-child relationships. In R. Parke & G. Ladd (Eds.), *Family-peers relationships: Modes of linkage* (pp. 77–106). Hillsdale, NJ: Erlbaum.

Erickson, M. F., Sroufe, L. A., & Egeland, B. (1985). The relationship between quality of attachment and behavior problems in preschool in a high-risk sample. In I. Bretherton & E. Waters (Eds.), *Growing points of attachment: Theory and research. Monographs for the Society of Research in Child Development, 50* (1–2, Serial No. 209).

Field, T. (1989). Maternal depression effects on infant interaction and attachment behavior. In D. Cicchetti & S. Toth (Eds.), *Developmental perspectives on depression: Rochester Symposium on Developmental Psychopathology* (Vol. 1, pp. 139–163). Rochester, NY: University of Rochester Press.

Fisher, K. W., & Ayoub, C. (1994). Affective splitting and dissociation in normal and maltreated children: Developmental pathways for self in relationships. In D. Cicchetti and S. Toth (Eds.), *Disorders and dysfunctions of the self: Rochester Symposium on Developmental Psychopathology* (Vol. 5, pp. 149–222). Rochester, NY: University of Rochester Press.

Fonagy, P., Steele, H., & Steele, M. (1991). Maternal representations of attachment during pregnancy predict the organization of mother-infant attachment at one year of age. *Child Development, 62,* 891–905.

Ford, D. H., & Ford, M. E. (1987). *Humans as self-constructing living systems.* Hillsdale, NJ: Erlbaum.

Ford, D. H., & Lerner, R. M. (1992). *Developmental systems theory: An integrative approach.* Newbury Park, CA: Sage.

Fox, N. A. (1994). *The development of emotion regulation: Biological and behavioral considerations. Monographs of the Society for Research in Child Development, 59* (Serial No. 240).

Garber, J., Braafladt, N., & Zeman, J. (1991). The regulation of sad affect: An information processing perspective. In J. Garber & K. Dodge (Eds.), *The development of emotion regulation and dysregulation* (pp. 208–240). New York: Cambridge University Press.

Gottlieb, G. (1991). Experimental canalization of behavioral development: Theory. *Developmental Psychology, 27,* 4–13.

Greenberg, M. T., Cicchetti, D., & Cummings, M. (1990). *Attachment in the preschool years.* Chicago: University of Chicago Press.

Greenberg, M. T., Kusche, C. A., Cook, E. T., & Quamma, J. P. (1995). Promoting emotional competence in school-aged children: The effects of the PATHS curriculum. *Development and Psychopathology, 7,* 117–136.

Greenberg, M. T., Kusche, C. A., & Speltz, M. (1991). Emotional regulation, self-control, and psychopathology: The role of relationships in early childhood. In D. Cicchetti & S. Toth (Eds.), *Rochester Symposium on Developmental Psychopathology* (pp. 21–55). Hillsdale, NJ: Erlbaum.

Greenberg, M. T., Speltz, M. L., & DeKlyen, M. (1993). The role of attachment in the early development of disruptive behavior disorders. *Development and Psychopathology, 5,* 191–213.

Greenspan, S. I. (1989). *Development of the ego.* Madison, CT: International Universities Press.

Greenspan, S. I., & Greenspan, N. (1991). *Clinical interview of the child* (2nd ed.). Madison, CT: International Universities Press.

Hinde, R. (1987). *Individuals, relationships, and culture.* New York: Cambridge University Press.

Hofer, M. A. (1994). Hidden regulators in attachment, separation, and loss. In N. A. Fox (Ed.), *The development of emotion regulation: Biological and behavioral considerations. Monographs of the Society for Research in Child Development, 59* (Serial No. 240) 192–207.

Huston, A. C. (1991). Children in poverty: Developmental and policy issues. In A. C. Huston (Ed.), *Children in poverty: Child development and public policy* (pp. 1–22). New York: Cambridge University Press.

Kazdin, A. E. (1992). Child and adolescent dysfunction and paths toward maladjustment: Targets for intervention. *Clinical Psychology Review, 12,* 795–817.

Kopp, C., & Wyer, N. (1994). Self-regulation in normal and atypical development. In D. Cicchetti & S. Toth (Eds.), *Disorders and dysfunctions of the self: Rochester Symposium on Developmental Psychopathology* (Vol. 5, pp. 31–56). Rochester, NY: University of Rochester Press.

Lieberman, A. F. (1992). Infant-parent psychotherapy with toddlers. *Development and Psychopathology, 4,* 559–574.

Loeber, R. (1990). Development and risk factors of juvenile antisocial behavior and delinquency. *Clinical Psychology Review, 10,* 1–41.

MacFarlane, J. W., Allen, L., & Honzik, M. P. (1954). *A developmental study of the behavior problems of normal children between 21 months and 14 years.* Berkeley: University of California Press.

Main, M., & Hesse E. (1990). Is fear the link between infant disorganized attachment status and maternal unresolved loss? In M.

Greenberg, D. Cicchetti, & M. Cummings (Eds.), *Attachment in the preschool years* (pp. 161–182). Chicago: University of Chicago Press.

Marvin, R. S., & Stewart, R. (1990). A family systems framework for the study of attachment. In M. Greenberg, D. Cicchetti, & M. Cummings (Eds.), *Attachment in the preschool years* (pp. 51–86). Chicago: University of Chicago Press.

Masten, A. S. (1992). Homeless children in the United States: Mark of a nation at risk. *Current Directions in Psychological Science, 1,* 41–44.

McBurnett, K., Lahey, B., & Pfiffner, L. (1993). Diagnosis of attention deficit disorders in DSM-IV: Scientific basis and implications for education. *Exceptional Children, 60,* 108–117.

Miller, P. J., & Moore, B. B. (1989). Narrative conjunction of caregiver and child: A comparative perspective on socialization through stories. *Ethos, 17,* 428–449.

Mundy, P., & Hogan, A. (1994). Intersubjectivity, joint attention, and autistic developmental pathology. In D. Cicchetti & S. Toth (Eds.), *Disorders and dysfunctions of the self: Rochester Symposium on Developmental Psychopathology* (Vol. 5, pp. 1–30). Rochester, NY: University of Rochester Press.

Parker, J. G., & Asher, S. R. (1987). Peer relations and later peer adjustment: Are lower-accepted children "at risk"? *Psychological Bulletin, 102,* 357–389.

Patterson, G. R., DeBaryshe, B. D., & Ramsey, E. (1989). A developmental perspective on antisocial behavior. *American Psychologist, 44,* 329–335.

Pianta, R. C. (1992). *Beyond the parent: The role of other adults in children's lives. New Directions in Child Development, Vol. 57.* San Francisco: Jossey-Bass.

Pianta, R. C., & Ferguson, J. *Prediction of behavior problems in children from mother-child interaction.* Unpublished manuscript, University of Virginia.

Putnam, F. (1994). Dissociation and disturbances of self. In D. Cicchetti & S. Toth (Eds.), *Disorders and dysfunctions of the self: Rochester Symposium on Developmental Psychopathology* (Vol. 5, pp. 251–266). Rochester, NY: University of Rochester Press.

Radke-Yarrow, M., McCann, K., DeMulder, E., Belmont, B., Martinez, P., & Richardson, D. T. (1995). Attachment in the context of high-risk conditions. *Development and Psychopathology, 7,* 247–265.

Reid, J. B. (1994). Prevention of conduct problems before and after school entry: Relating interventions to developmental findings. *Development and Psychopathology, 5,* 243–262.

Reid, R., Maag, J. W., & Vasa, S. F. (1994). Attention Deficit Hyperactivity Disorder as a disability category: A critique. *Exceptional Children, 60,* 198–214.

Reiss, D. (1989). The represented and practicing family: Contrasting visions of family continuity. In A. Sameroff & R. Emde (Eds.), *Relationship disturbances in early childhood* (pp. 191–220). New York: Basic Books.

Resnick, L. B. (1994). Situated rationalism: Biological and social preparation for learning. In L. Hirschfield & S. Gelman (Eds.), *Mapping the mind: Domain specificity in cognition and culture* (pp. 474–493). Cambridge, England: Cambridge University Press.

Riccio, C. A., Hynd, G. W., Cohen, M. J., & Gonzalez, J. J. (1993). Neurological basis of attention deficit hyperactivity disorder. *Exceptional Children, 60,* 118–124.

Richman, N., Stevenson, J., & Graham, P. J. (1982). *Preschool to school: A behavioral study.* London: Academic Press.

Rogers, S. J., Ozonoff, S., & Maslin-Cole, C. (1993). Developmental aspects of attachment behavior in young children with pervasive developmental disorders. *Journal of the American Academy of Child and Adolescent Psychiatry, 32,* 1274–1282.

Rubin, K., Coplan, R. J., Fox, N. A., & Calkins, S. D. (1995). Emotionality, emotion regulation, and preschoolers' social adaptation. *Development and Psychopathology, 7,* 49–62.

Sameroff, A. J. (1983). Developmental systems: Context and evolution. In P. Mussen (Ed.), *Handbook of child psychology: Vol. 1. History, theory and methods* (pp. 237–294). New York: Wiley.

Sameroff, A. J. (1989). Principles of development and psychopathology. In A. Sameroff & R. Emde (Eds.), *Relationship disturbances in early childhood* (pp. 17–32). New York: Basic Books.

Sander, L. (1975). Infant and caretaking environment: Investigation and conceptualization of adaptive behavior in a system of increasing complexity. In E. J. Anthony (Ed.), *Explorations in child psychiatry* (pp. 129–166). New York: Plenum Press.

Sroufe, L. A. (1983). Infant-caregiver attachment and patterns of adaptation in preschool: The roots of maladaptation and competence. In M. Perlmutter (Ed.), *The Minnesota Symposium on Child Psychology* (Vol. 16) Hillsdale, NJ: Erlbaum.

Sroufe, L. A. (1989a). Pathways to adaptation and maladaptation: Psychopathology as developmental deviation. In D. Cicchetti (Ed.), *Emergence of a discipline: Rochester Symposium on Developmental Psychopathology* (pp. 13–40). Hillsdale, NJ: Erlbaum.

Sroufe, L. A. (1989b). Relationships and relationship disturbances. In A. Sameroff & R. Emde (Eds.), *Relationship disturbances in early childhood* (pp. 97–124). New York: Basic Books.

Sroufe, L. A., & Fleeson, J. (1986). Attachment and the construction of relationships. In W. Hartup & Z. Rubin (Eds.), *Relationships and development.* Hillsdale, NJ: Erlbaum.

Sroufe, L. A., Jacobvitz, D., Mangelsdorf, S., DeAngelo, E., & Ward, M. J. (1985). Generational boundary dissolution between mothers and their preschool children: A relationship systems approach. *Child Development, 56,* 317–325.

Sroufe, L. A., & Rutter, M. (1984). The domain of developmental psychopathology. *Child Development, 55,* 17–29.

Stewart, S., & Rubin, K. (1995) The social-problem solving skills of anxious-withdrawn children. *Development and Psychopathology, 7,* 323–336.

Super, C., & Harkness, S. (1986). The developmental niche: A conceptualization at the interface of child and culture. *International Journal of Behavioral Development, 9,* 545–569.

Swanson, J. M., et al. (1993). Effect of stimulant medication on children with attention deficit disorder: A "review of reviews." *Exceptional Children, 60,* 154–162.

Thompson, R. A. (1991). Emotional regulation and emotional development. *Educational Psychology Review, 3,* 269–307.

Thompson, R. A. (1994). Emotion regulation: A theme in search of definition. In N. A. Fox (Ed.), *The development of emotion regulation: Biological and behavioral considerations. Monographs of the Society for Research in Child Development, 59* (Serial No. 240), 25–52.

Walsh, D. J. (1991). Reconstructing the discourse on developmental appropriateness: A developmental perspective. *Early Education and Development, 2,* 109–119.

Walsh, F. (1982). *Normal family processes.* New York: Guilford Press.

Zeanah, C. H., Benoit, D., Barton, M., Regan, C., Hirschberg, L., & Lipsitt, L. (1993). Representations of attachment in mothers and their one-year-old infants. *Journal of the American Academy of Child and Adolescent Psychiatry, 32,* 278–286.

CHAPTER 7

MIDDLE CHILDHOOD

Robert B. Cairns
Joseph L. Mahoney
Hongling Xie
Tom W. Cadwallader

It has been broadly assumed that a straight line can be drawn between emotional–behavioral problems in childhood and psychopathological disorders in adulthood. Most investigators in modern developmental psychopathology and psychiatry—but not all—have adopted this assumption in one form or another. The belief resonates, as well, with common sense and popular beliefs about the formative role of early social and family experience for young children. The continuity assumption is broadly accepted, but is it accurate? The question must be raised because the results of recent longitudinal studies on this matter have yielded mixed results. While some middle childhood problems have been moderately linked to adult disorders, others have weak or nonidentifiable linkages.

In this chapter we examine the development and continuity of middle childhood behavior disorders from the perspective afforded by recent longitudinal studies. We begin with an overview of the developmental framework that guided the studies and that has been corrected by their results. We then focus on the longitudinal study of problem domains that occur with some frequency in middle childhood: aggressive behaviors, peer neglect, and social isolation.

A CENTURY OF CONTROVERSY AND A DESIGN DILEMMA

When the discipline was still in its infancy, William James (1890, Vol. I) observed the following:

> However closely psychical changes may conform to law, it is safe to say that individual histories and biographies will never be written in advance no matter how "evolved" psychology will become. (pp. 576–577)

In a similar vein, James Mark Baldwin (1897) observed that "Personality is after all an ever changing thing" (p. 30). James and Baldwin argued that focus upon early individual experiences and characteristics could tell only part of the story. The early effects upon children or attitudes of parents in early childhood were open to modification with changing situations, changing characteristics of the child, and changing characteristics of the parents. Unfortunately, these propositions were offered with virtually no systematic empirical evidence; they represented the reflections of astute observers of human behavior, coupled with the commonsense assumption that behaviors are necessarily linked to situations in which individuals live and adapt.

At about the same time, J. Breuer and S. Freud (1895/ 1936) offered a drastically different hypothesis on continuity. In their preliminary statement of psychoanalysis, early experiences were seen as formative, critical and, for certain key characteristics, irreversible. This position on the fundamental importance of early experience for understanding later problems and dispositions was adopted by theorists as diverse as John B. Watson (1926) in the formulation of behaviorism and Konrad Lorenz (1937) in the establishment of classical ethology. In the modern era, John Bowlby (1952, 1973) and Mary D. Ainsworth (1972) argued persuasively for the compelling importance of the mother–infant attachment as a critical period in early development.

There are modern proponents of the James–Baldwin proposition as well, researchers who have proposed that behavior patterns are open to modification in the years of childhood and adolescence (e.g., Bandura, 1973; Cairns, 1979; Hunt, 1961; Kagan, 1997; Magnusson, 1985). The contemporary view of developmental accommodation has focused upon (1) the conditions and outcomes that are susceptible either to change or continuity, and (2) the interwoven mechanisms of maturation and social learning in children, families, and social networks that lead to stability or modification.

Why has this key question on the nature of developmental continuity and change remained unresolved after a century of research? One reason seems to be that the issue has overwhelmed the capabilities of the young science and the methods that it had available. New research strategies, measures, and analyses have had to be developed that were appropriate for the challenge of studying persons over time. The procedure employed in the classical methods of the "new psychology" were simply not appropriate for studying persons over time in the natural settings of lives.

Over the years, it became generally accepted that the appropriate design for studying continuity—or change— would require the investigator to track individuals over a significant portion of their lives in the concrete circumstances in which they live. Moreover, this class of research design—longitudinal—would be most informative when observations are reasonably closely spaced observations across childhood and adolescence. The measures should include assessments not only of the individual but of their social and physical surrounds as well. On this score, Jessor, Donovan, and Costa (1991) have observed:

> Understanding the integrity of the life course, tracing its continuity over large segments of time, distinguishing what is ephemeral from what is lasting, grasping the role that the past plays in shaping the future—all these, and more, are issues that yield only to research that is longitudinal or developmental in design. (p. 3)

But special problems have arisen trying to implement longitudinal designs for the study of developmental psychopathology. One limitation is the costs incurred. Serious forms of adult psychopathology are infrequent, and a very large number of individuals must be followed from childhood to maturity in order to identify an adequate sample of children who will encounter serious disorders as adults. Even when such longitudinal investigations qualify on the basis of numbers—say, 500 persons or more—they tend to be compromised by features of their design or assessment. Beyond extraordinary costs in funds and time, other difficulties include the possible confounding produced by repeated assessments of the same individuals, biased attrition in that the most vulnerable people drop out of the research, the unknown events that occur between observations and must be somehow recovered, and the problem of data tyranny and becoming overwhelmed by massive amounts of information.

Although measures in social science age slowly, they are not timeless. Every two decades or so, measures of choice tend to become outdated, and measures taken at the beginning of a study tend to become displaced by new ones. For example, the self-report survey methodology employed in longitudinal studies launched in the 1960s is now suspect, and in the 1990s, the preferred assessment battery shifted to multiple-agent, multiple-method measures. Such time limitations on measure utility create a basic dilemma for researchers who aspire to study individuals over a 20-, 30-, or 40-year span. The investigators inevitably grow old, and the measures they originally employed become outdated.

Given these limitations of prospective longitudinal designs, various alternatives have been explored for gaining the same information more efficiently and effectively. Three of the main alternatives are (1) retrospection, (2) backward tracking of clinical cases, and (3) animal developmental investigations. We examine briefly the strengths and weaknesses of each of these designs for the study of developmental psychopathology.

Retrospective recall—asking persons about their past, including the events that occurred and their attitudes—is efficient and provides the individual's own account of perceived causes. But it also invites subjective, constructive errors. Given the chance, most people construct accounts of the past that are consistent with their current circumstances (Ceci, 1995; Radke-Yarrow, Campbell, & Burton, 1968; Ross & Buehler, 1994; Rutter et al., 1998).

A second alternative—the use of clinical records that permit both the forward and backward tracking of cases from adulthood to middle childhood—has been used productively by Robins (1986) and others. One advantage of the use of record data is that a significant number of serious problems of middle childhood psychopathology can be identified from the onset, a state of affairs that precludes the sampling of hundreds or thousands of participants in order to identify a small number of index cases. Moreover, the use of objective records minimizes exclusive reliance upon the recall and recollections of participants, which invite multiple risks in interpretation.

However, the archival use of clinical records is not without pitfalls. First, the design invites the fortuitous identification of linkages between adult psychopathology and high rates of negative childhood events (e.g., exposure to violence or physical punishment, mild head injuries). Second, there is a serious problem of sampling bias. For example, special control samples are required to identify cases that escaped the clinical sampling procedure (i.e., children who were abused or maladjusted but who did not appear in clinics at childhood nor in residential institutions at adulthood).

Finally, developmental studies in animals provide a third approach to the analysis of continuity and change. Given relatively short intervals from birth to maturity, openness to manipulation, and the complexity of social behaviors, nonhuman mammals from mice to monkeys can be employed in longitudinal study. They can be prospectively tracked over their entire life span with efficiency and economy. Some of our basic information on developmental psychopathology was initially identified in ontogenetic studies of monkeys (e.g., Harlow, 1958), dogs (Scott & Fuller, 1965), and mice (Cairns, 1973).

Comparative investigations have identified three phenomena that seem especially relevant for understanding psychopathology continuity and change:

1. *Interactional adaptations observed in infancy or the juvenile period are poorly correlated with adult social interactions.* This empirical generalization has emerged in the wake of the reexamination of the "critical period" and "sensitive period" proposals. In contrast with the classical proposal of the irreversibility of the effects of early social exposure (i.e., "imprinting" in birds; "attachment" in mammals), systematic studies indicate that considerable modification in social preferences occurs throughout the life course, depending on the contexts in which development occurs. Similarly, aggressive behaviors have proved to be specific to contexts and others, and they have proved to be modifiable over the course of development. When continuities occur, they typically are mediated by continuities in the social context and social interaction milieu. Change—or continuity—is influenced both by events in the individual and events in the social context.

2. *Behavioral characteristics most closely linked to the regulation of hormonal and neurobiological states tend to show the most enduring effects of early and youthful experi-*
ence. These include, for example, links between early isolation or "handling" to startle reactivity in adulthood, or the early manipulation of steroid hormones to sexual and aggressive patterns at maturity. Conversely, early social learning experiences in the formation of interactions tend to lose their distinctive identity by virtue of being merged with, or canceled out by, subsequent learning experiences. These findings suggest that some effects of early stress or early hormonal manipulation are mediated directly by enduring changes in neurobiological organization, not by social learning.

3. *Events that are required for the establishment of an interaction pattern are not necessarily required for its maintenance or change.* Consolidation refers to the process whereby interchanges become more tightly organized with each recurrence. Once an interchange pattern has become consolidated in context, it becomes increasingly resistant to change and can be elicited even in the absence of conditions originally required for its establishment. For example, male mice that were tested for aggressive behavior and then castrated tended to persist in fighting. However, males that were castrated before maturity typically did not attack other males. Miczek and Grossman (1972) conclude that learning processes maintain aggressive behavior in the absence of the neurological conditions that were initially required for establishment.

Animal behavior investigations—no matter how careful and exhaustive—cannot substitute for the direct longitudinal investigations of human beings. Though they cannot stand alone, comparative data may be coupled with information from longitudinal and retrospective human studies to help construct a coherent framework for understanding both continuity and change.

TOWARD A DEVELOPMENTAL PERSPECTIVE ON PSYCHOPATHOLOGY

Given the gradual accumulation of information from longitudinal and quasi-longitudinal research designs, various proposals have been recently offered on developmental psychopathology (e.g., Angold & Costello, 1996; Bergman & Magnusson, 1997; Sroufe & Rutter, 1984). Although there are large differences among these proposals—reflecting in part the aims and backgrounds of those who offered them—they seem to share certain premises on the dynamic, reciprocal, and holistic nature of psychological development. These proposals are worth considering here to appreciate the range of issues involved in understanding middle childhood and the problems that emerge during this period of development.

In an attempt to identify similarities across recent developmental statements, Magnusson and Cairns (1996) abstracted seven assumptions on the nature of development:

1. An individual develops and functions psychologically as an integrated organism. Maturational, experiential, and cultural contributions are fused in ontogeny. Single aspects do not develop and function in isolation, and they should not be divorced from the totality in analysis.
2. An individual develops and functions in a dynamic, continuous, and reciprocal process of interaction with his or her environment, including relations with other individuals, groups, and the subculture.
3. Individual functioning depends upon and influences the reciprocal interaction among subsystems within the individual; namely, the organization of interactional perceptual–cognitive, emotional, physiological, morphological, perceptual, and neurobiological factors over time.
4. Novel patterns of individual functioning arise during individual ontogeny.
5. Differences in the rate of development may produce major differences in the organization and configuration of psychological functions. The developmental rate of individual components may be accelerated or delayed relative to other features.
6. Patterns of psychological functioning develop like dynamic systems in that they can be extremely sensitive to the conditions under which they are formed. The emergence of psychological patterns thus cannot be accounted for solely in terms of the hierarchical organization of more elementary systems, nor can they be reduced to simpler experiential antecedents or more elementary biological units.
7. Conservation in development is supported by constraints from without and from within, as well as by the correlated action of external and internal forces. The upshot is that social and cognitive organization in development tends to be continuous and conservative despite continuous change. (pp. 12–19)

The dynamic, holistic, and integrative perspective of development leads to a new examination of old problems, including the twin issues of continuity and change. Hence, longitudinal studies have been challenged to clarify processes that contribute to change, reversal, and continuity in development, whether development is viewed as normal or psychopathological. A correlated task is to establish ontogenetic periods of onset and organization and to identify windows of change. This requires, among other things, plotting individual pathways over time and describing the nature of integration across levels of analysis.

The issues and their proposed resolution have been in the field for a surprisingly long time. Some years ago, Cairns (1979) wrote:

> The problem for developmental models is to explain continuity, not change, since ontogeny necessarily involves modification. Developmental orientations have investigated maturational, interactional, and societal–generational sources of change. None of these domains can be expected to remain constant throughout the life of the individual, and changes in one domain can trigger changes in

another. . . . Even if the social–cultural context remains relatively unchanged over a generation, an individual child's status in the society surely will not remain unchanged over ontogeny. Given the dynamic nature of social development, the challenge is to explain why continuities occur, not why changes are observed.

How, then, do individual consistencies arise in social development? Five factors that support continuity of social behavior over development have been identified.

1. *Social network.* In the light of the importance of reciprocal controls on the social actions of the child, reliable predictions to other settings and later developmental states require information about the social networks in which the child will participate and their relations to the present one. If all other factors are equal, similarities in the child's social actions from one point in time to a future time should be the greatest when the social systems are similar over the two times. Conversely, drastic changes in the social adaptation requirements should produce concomitant changes in the child's social behavior. Consistencies in social settings promote consistencies in social behaviors.
2. *Evocation.* The child is not a passive agent in the process. Individual children may evoke common responses across time by virtue of their stimulus properties (sex or gender role, size age, race) or by virtue of their social actions. Obviously, some stimulus properties are likely to remain constant over time and across settings; others are likely to change. Sex classification, say, is in most cases highly stable while physical characteristics, such as height and weight, are likely to change over the course of development. Similarly, the social patterns of children can evoke common responses. The loud assertive child can re-create for himself similar environments and reactions across several different contexts and time intervals.
3. *Choices.* The child may also behave in ways that help to promote continuity in social settings and relationships by virtue of his choices and preferences. Although attachment is considered the prototype of the child's attempt to preserve the familiar and avoid the unfamiliar, a comparable process can occur throughout development in the maintenance of friendships and the choice of activities. Once the choices are made, reciprocal processes permit the child to adapt to the demands of the new relationship and situation. Obviously, not all choices preserve continuity. Some, as in the case of religious conversion, marriage, or joining a political movement, can produce radical changes.
4. *Biological constraints* and *maturation.* At each developmental stage (and for some characteristics, across developmental stages), the child is predisposed to perform particular social acts by virtue of biological constraints. These constraints include those of a basic physiological nature (including endocrine gland and neural activity) that may support differences in activity levels, reactivity, and other "emotional" or temperament differences. They also include biological differences related to motor, cognitive, linguistic, and perceptual capabilities. Hence similarities in a child's

interactions across two or more time intervals may arise simply because the child is not competent to make different responses, or because the perceptual–cognitive discriminations necessary for formulating new responses are not yet in the repertory.

5. *Consolidation.* Children (and older persons as well) tend to repeat a social act or pattern if the conditions for its prior elicitation recur, and social sequences become consolidated by virtue of their repeated occurrence. Once consolidated, social interchanges will be elicited by fewer cues than were originally required for establishment and hence will be more readily generalized to new settings and maintained in old ones. Such consolidation also provides a major experiential basis for the maintenance of individual differences, and thereby constitutes a major mechanism for social continuity (Cairns, 1979, pp. 375–378).

Despite the formidable barriers to longitudinal investigation, the developmental disciplines have produced in the past 20 years an unprecedented body of information on the ontogeny of middle childhood aggressive behaviors and their sequelae. These hard-won data, obtained from different laboratories, countries, measures, and theoretical perspectives, provide the empirical substructure for a developmental orientation.

LONGITUDINAL FINDINGS ON THE CONTINUITY AND CHANGE IN AGGRESSION

We begin with the examination of a classical issue—that of individual difference prediction of aggressive behavior—and then examine some conditions for continuity and change.

Can We Predict Aggressive Behavior from Middle Childhood to Maturity?

Twenty years ago, Olweus (1979) published an influential review of longitudinal studies that focused upon the developmental stability of aggressive behavior. In his overview, Olweus concluded that measures of aggressive behavior were about as stable over development as measures of intelligence. The evidence was mostly from males, but the implication was that a similar pattern would hold for females. This review was particularly important at the time because it was one of the first demonstrations that social development could be viewed as likely to follow certain laws or principles as cognitive development or otherwise more "fundamental" behavior systems.

The longitudinal research completed over the past two decades permits a critical evaluation of Olweus's assertion. Different research teams throughout the world have now reported evidence relevant to the issue. The groups have been

directed by Pulkinnen (1982) in Finland, Magnusson (1988) in Sweden, Farrington and West (1990) in England, Patterson (Patterson, Reid, & Dishion, 1992) in Oregon, Eron and Huesmann (1987) in New York, Huizinga and Elliot (Elliot, Huizinga, & Menard, 1989) in the National Youth Study, Werner (Werner & Smith, 1992) in Hawaii, Block (1971) in California, and Masten (Masten & Braswell, 1991) in Minnesota, among others.

The Carolina Longitudinal Study (CLS), a project that we began in 1981, provides findings that pertain to risk and resilience in childhood and adolescence. Our goal was to track the pathways of risk and resilience from middle childhood to early maturity in a representative population of rural and suburban youth. The investigation involved 695 children in two grade-school cohorts (Cairns & Cairns, 1994). At the beginning of the study, the two samples of children were enrolled in the fourth and seventh grades of public schools in counties that had been designated as suburban or rural in the 1980 census. The 220 subjects of Cohort I were a mean 10.3 years of age, and the 475 subjects of Cohort II were a mean of 13.3 years of age.

In annual assessments from grade 4 to grade 12, we followed these young people individually, viewing them through the eyes of their peers, their teachers, their parents, and their grandparents. We used multiple methods and multiple agents in the assessment of aggressive behaviors, including direct observations, teacher and self-ratings, and self and peer reports of conflicts. Assessments of criminal behavior, teenage parenthood, and school dropout were completed, including post-high school assessments at 20 years and 24 years of age. Twenty five percent of the original subjects were African American and the remainder were white. The sample mirrors the proportion of minority children in the counties that were sampled. Virtually the full range of familial occupational levels was represented, and the socioeconomic range was from 11 to 88 on the Duncan–Featherman scale.

Embedded within the total sample was a subgroup of 40 children who were identified at the outset as being at extremely high risk for violent behavior. A comparison group of 40 children was individually matched to the high-risk subjects with respect to gender, race, classroom attended, physical size, and neighborhood residence. Children were seen individually on an annual basis through the end of high school, regardless of whether they had changed residence or dropped out of school. The longitudinal tracking in this study has been exhaustive over the several years of the investigation, with 100 percent of the original subjects located and 98 percent interviewed at the end of high school.

Our own findings on the issue of developmental stability of aggressive behavior are informative because they both illustrate the issue and clarify the limitations. Given the two sources of ratings—the self and others—there are two potential trajectories of individual-difference stability.

Teacher Ratings

The median 1-year stability correlation for the aggressive factor was moderate but highly significant (r = .48, p < .0001). This figure was obtained by computing all of the 1-year stabilities (4th–5th grade, 5th–6th grade, and on), then computing the median. Two surprising features of these results concern the limited extent to which they conform to the empirical generalizations on stability. First, the median 8-year stability correlation (r = .38, p < .001) was not unlike the median 1-year stability correlation, suggesting only modest decay over time. The 1-year stability was the same for boys and girls, though the 8-year stability was somewhat higher for boys (r = .44) than girls (r = .38). Second, there does not appear to be much gain in the stability of teacher ratings as a function of age at first assessment. On both counts, the matrices of stability correlations for aggression are remarkably similar for boys and girls.

These results on the stability of teacher ratings are especially striking because the present design was biased against finding stability for evaluations in ratings by multiple "others." The students were assigned to new classes each year.

Self-Ratings

How well do self-ratings perform in terms of year-to-year and long-term stability? On a priori grounds, it would seem for three reasons that self-ratings should be more stable than teacher ratings. First, while the same individual is involved in the self-ratings each year, different persons are involved in the outside-the-self assessments over time. Second is an unlikely, although possible, methodological confounding of memory and recall of one's self-evaluations from year to year. Third, children should know themselves better than does anyone else. On this score, teachers and researchers widely vary in the length and situation of their knowledge of individual children. On intuitive grounds, any one of these three factors should heighten self-stability. Intuition is half-right.

It was hardly surprising to find that the median 1-year stabilities of the self-ratings of aggression were high and positive. The median 1-year stability for self-ratings of aggression was r = .53. What was surprising—given the fact that the self (the participant) generated these ratings—was the sharp decay in long-term self-stability. On this score, the stability of the self-ratings was barely above chance after 9 years (r = .16 overall, and r = .18 for females and r = .14 for males). In addition, there is a reasonable indication in the

data that the older the participants at the time of first self-ratings, the higher the stability. Both of these self-stability findings for aggression are in accord with the two empirical generalizations on intelligence and nonbehavioral domains.

Recall the Olweus speculation that aggressive behavior was virtually as stable as intelligence. Do our findings support or refute that claim? The problem in evaluating this assertion is that the assessments of intelligence and aggression differ markedly in measurement properties and goals.[1] In general, tests of intelligence have superior psychometric properties, hence bias the procedures toward higher levels of stability. To create a level playing field, it would be desirable to assess the two factors by the same method. In the present work, it is possible to directly evaluate the proposition by the same method (i.e., teacher and self-ratings of academic competence and of aggressive behavior). Although such a comparison has some limitations, it provides a good approximation of the stability of two characteristics when the methods are roughly similar. The remarkable finding is that the two characteristics yielded parallel stability curves, with the self-ratings of academic competence decaying more rapidly than the "other" ratings.

Are the self-ratings and other ratings measuring the same characteristic from different perspectives? Or have the different perspectives identified qualitatively different characteristics? With regard to this question, it may be noted that the self-ratings and other ratings of aggressive behavior were only modestly correlated, regardless of the cohort studied (r = .21–.32 for girls and r = .28–.34 for boys). Although these correspondence correlations are statistically reliable, they suggest that there is a problem with assuming that the two kinds of assessments are measuring the same thing. It looks as if the constructions of the self are qualitatively different from the judgments of other persons outside the self.

Have Olweus's (1979) generalizations on the stability of aggression held up? Yes and no. Yes, in that correlations between the same measures are consistently significant over periods of 5 to 10 years, from childhood to adolescence and early maturity. This is a nontrivial accomplishment for the science. No, in that the magnitude of individual difference predictions in aggressive behavior do not rival the stability of intelligence measures. Moreover, the modest levels of the correlations observed from childhood to maturity do not support the proposition that there exist robust individual difference predictions. One of the problems is that variable-to-variable analyses leave out contextual information which, in a developmental framework, is the key to whether or not stability is observed. The characteristic is analyzed as if it were an independent component, divorced from the person and his or her environmental circumstances.

Does Aggression Increase or Decrease over Time?

One of the conundrums of the aggression literature concerns the shape of the developmental trajectory of aggressive behaviors. Does aggression increase, decrease, or remain the same over development? The question arises because evidence has been reported for all three possibilities. Paradoxically, empirical support may be claimed for each of the three seemingly contradictory answers. On the possible increase, there is a sharp rise in arrests for assaults and violent crimes from 10 years through 19 years, with a gradual drop-off through later maturity (Cairns & Cairns, 1994; Crime in the United States, 1995). Eron, Huesmann, Brice, Fischer, and Mermelstein (1983, also Huesmann, Lagerspetz, & Eron, 1985) show a developmental increase in peer nominations for aggression. Further, Ferguson and Rule (1980) have identified the rise of a brutality norm in adolescence (i.e., acceptability of physical aggression). With regard to a developmental decrease, Loeber (1982) has indicated that most longitudinal studies of children typically show decrements in ratings of aggressive behavior as they enter adolescence. Consistent with this report, longitudinal assessments by teacher ratings and self-ratings show a consistent drop in the frequency of aggressive expression from early childhood through late adolescence (Cairns & Cairns, 1994).

Why the diversity of findings? The answer is that the confusion has arisen because researchers have used the same term—aggression—to refer to quite different operations. Once these operations are distinguished, the data are quite lawful and consistent.

Consider first the assertion that aggressive and violent behaviors increase from middle childhood to adolescence. The primary evidence for this generalization comes from reports of arrests for violence and the incidence of interpersonal acts that lead to serious injury and hospitalization. According to successive years of reports of national arrest data in the Department of Justice publication, *Crime in the United States,* the initial rise in arrests for assaultive and violent behaviors begins at age 10 to 12 (1992). For males, there is a dramatic increase in the incidence of arrests for crimes of violence from 11 to 18 years of age. The drop-off in violence arrests and victimization begins in the twenties and decreases steadily until senescence, or old age. For females, there is a rise in female arrests for violence at adolescence, but the increase is modest compared to males. These national statistics have yielded the same curves each year since the age by sex breakdown was first reported in the U.S. Department of Justice's *Uniform Crime Reports* in the 1970s. These phenomena are wholly consistent with the proposition that key events in the organization of violent behavior occur during late childhood and early adolescence for many youth (Cairns & Cairns, 1994; Loeber & Hay, 1997). By organization of violent behavior, we refer to the time in development when individuals ordinarily gain the capability and motivation to intentionally inflict by their own actions serious and permanent physical injuries to another person.

Other regional and national data—including murder and victimization information—yield parallel outcomes. In this regard, Wolfgang and colleagues (1972) show the age-related rise over adolescence in both index and non-index crimes in their study of a 1945 birth cohort of Philadelphia boys. In this monograph, Wolfgang and colleagues (1972) conclude that "both whites and nonwhites commit a greater number of violent crimes as they age, although the rate of increase is greater for nonwhites" (p. 251). Tracy and co-workers (1990) reported a follow-up study by this research team using a Philadelphia birth cohort born 13 years later. Comparisons between the two cohorts showed that there was increasing occurrence of serious crimes (i.e., weighted for seriousness) as a function of age, with the median asymptote occurring at 16 years. There was, in addition, a marked cohort difference in the occurrence of serious offenses at all age levels. Philadelphia boys born in 1958 were much more likely to be arrested for serious crimes than boys born in 1945. More broadly, Hirschi and Gottfriedson (1983) have employed national, cross-national, and historical data sets to demonstrate the ubiquity of the age-delinquency function. Although the asymptote of the curve has shifted over time and context, its basic configuration has remained constant.

Is adolescence a bloody battleground that gains its distinction in the life span as a special period of violence, with increasingly severe levels of violence from late childhood through late adolescence? If the criminological, injury, and suicide statistics are taken as criteria, the answer is yes. But a different picture is obtained when psychological and interpersonal measures are employed. In general, the picture is one of decreasing rather than increasing rates of aggression. In self-evaluations of aggressive behavior (e.g., fighting, arguing) from large representative populations, individuals show a strong, replicable, and significant tendency to see themselves as becoming *less aggressive* in the years from middle childhood to adolescence and early adulthood. This trend holds for both males and females. The same effects are observed regardless of whether self or teacher ratings are employed.

Return to the primary question for this section: Does aggression increase or decrease with development? The "arrest for violence" measure presupposes that the aggressive actions have produced serious outcomes for the victim. Hence the criminological measure has a built-in severity criterion; it calls for absolute (i.e., age-independent) judgments by courts of injury or harm to the victim, rather than relative (i.e., age-dependent) judgments of severity by the self or others. With age and maturation, the consequences of aggressive acts can become increasingly severe.

Simply stated, the stakes of aggression get higher with age. Older youth gain access to lethal weapons, they form gangs, and there is age-related increase in the capability to produce harm by brute force, particularly for males. Because the risks associated with any given conflict become higher, there could be increasing selectivity in whom one confronts, and when. Consider, for example, the possibility that access to lethal weapons is a factor in the increased positive relation noted to exist between the intensity of aggressive acts and age. In this regard, the mortality rate for unintentional or "accidental" firearm deaths is highest among 15- to 19-year-old youth, and firearms are involved in the majority of teenage suicides and homicides (Fingerhut & Kleinman, 1989).

Because the mortality rates for males significantly exceed females in all accidents involving firearms, we were curious as to how this pattern emerged in a general population. In the Carolina Longitudinal Study investigation, we were surprised at the number of participants who lived in households in which firearms were accessible to them. Depending on whether the respondent was male or female, firearms were available in 65 to 84 percent of the households. Over half of these suburban and rural subjects claimed firearm ownership themselves. How did the boys get the guns in the first place? Of those boys who claimed gun ownership, the age of first gun ownership was 12.5 years of age. The primary giver was the father or some other male relative. Mothers rarely were identified as the agent who gave the child the firearm (Cairns & Cairns, 1994). In contrast, few girls claimed gun ownership of any kind (9%), and they tended to be vague about the nature of the weapons that were available in the home (Sadowski, Cairns, & Earp, 1989).

Configurations of Antecedents, Consequents, and Trajectories

Perhaps the most important contemporary advance in modern longitudinal study has been the discovery that developmental variables derive their meaning in combination rather than in isolation. In a contemporary developmental framework, the researcher's goal shifts from the identification of distinctive variance associated with a specific variable to the identification of patterns of influence and outcomes. This chapter is not the place to recap the several issues involved in the analytic shift from variables to persons, patterns, and configurations. Besides, that task was confronted elsewhere (see Bergman, 1998; Cairns & Rodkin, 1998; Magnusson, 1995, 1998). Here we examine how this shift in goals has permitted the organization of findings that otherwise seem to compete.

Virtually all longitudinal studies that have been completed have identified a configuration of children who are at high risk for psychopathological disorders (Cairns, Cairns, & Neckerman, 1989; Magnusson, 1988; Pulkinnen, 1988). Two distinguishing features of children in such multiple-risk configurations are (1) high levels of aggressive behavior and (2) school failure and low levels of academic achievement. Longitudinal follow-up studies of children characterized by such configurations show they are at risk for a wide range of subsequent problems, typically those classified as "externalizing disorders."

Aggression and low academic competence have been salient distinguishing properties of multiple-risk configuration. It is of interest that other aspects of children have been represented less consistently. That is, children in these high-risk configurations have been seen as slightly less popular than classmates, but they are as likely as peers to have reciprocal friendships and to be nuclear members in the social network of the school. Similarly, self-evaluations of members of the high-risk configuration are somewhat below those of classmates, but they not markedly different. Moreover, the self-evaluations are not as low as the evaluations assigned to them by teachers and peers.

As we have observed elsewhere, social support from friendship and social networks is not necessarily protective of problems during middle childhood (Cairns, Cairns, Neckerman, Gest, & Gariépy, 1988). The reciprocal friendships of aggressive children may promote antisocial behaviors because of the propensity for these children to affiliate with others who are like themselves. Although there is considerable fluidity in friendships and social networks, in both aggressive and nonaggressive children, the new friends tend to resemble the old (Neckerman, 1996). There is consistency in social influence despite changing faces. To the extent that these social influences have been incorporated into longitudinal equations, they have helped sharpen predictions and suggested reasons for change and "turning points" in development.

Configuration analysis of longitudinal data yields two other findings that deserve special attention. First is the importance of interactions among variables. For example, extreme unpopularity or social isolation, when it appears as a distinguishing characteristic of a configuration and is not associated with other problems, does not emerge as predictive of negative externalizing outcomes. Similarly, low socioeco-nomic status, taken alone, is not particularly predictive when it occurs independently of other features of a risk profile.

Second, the configurations indicate that there remains ample opportunity in development for change for good or for ill. A significant proportion of the protected or nonrisk configurations develop problems in the course of develop-ment, and a significant proportion of the high-risk subjects reach tolerable levels of adolescent and adult adaptation. All this is to say that development remains a probabilistic affair, even though the field has been successful in estimating the probabilities with increasing precision.

The broader problem is whether measures of childhood aggression obtained during middle childhood can predict problems of real-life adaptations in adolescence and adult-hood, including antisocial and deviant sequelae of criminal arrests, violent activity, or suicide. In this regard, longitudi-nal samples permit us to compute the developmental proba-bilities on whether a person judged to be at high risk for problems of aggression in middle childhood would subse-quently encounter serious problems of social adaptation in late adolescence and adulthood (e.g., arrest for violence, early school dropout, hard drug addiction, teen parenthood, residential treatment for an emotional disorder). Using these criteria for psychopathology in young adulthood, we compared the approximately one-half of the childhood-designated high-risk males and females qualified for serious problems. By contrast, roughly one-fifth (20%) of the indi-vidually matched controls encountered parallel problems of adult adaptation. Extreme aggression in middle childhood—or its absence—provides statistically significant but proba-bilistic predictions.

Peer Social Networks and the Development of Aggression

The current empirical literature has demonstrated that affilia-tion with delinquent peers is closely related to adolescents' aggressive behavior (e.g., Cairns, Cairns, Neckerman, Gest, & Gariépy, 1988), delinquency (e.g., Clarke-McClean, 1996; Elliot, Huizinga, & Menard, 1989; Giordano et al., 1986), school dropout (Cairns, Cairns, & Neckerman, 1989), teenage parenthood (Cairns & Cairns, 1994), and substance abuse (e.g., Dishion, Reid, & Patterson, 1988). Not only in adoles-cence do peer social networks play a supportive role in the de-velopment of aggression, it is also true for middle childhood. Analyses of peer social networks of children and adolescents indicated that group members are similar in the levels of ag-gression (e.g. Cairns & Cairns, 1994); aggressive children tend to hang around with other aggressive children. This find-ing has been replicated in both cross-context and cross-cultural studies (e.g., Gaines, Cairns & Cairns, 1994; Leung, 1996; Sun, 1995). Besides aggression, members of the same peer group resemble each other on multiple behavioral dimen-sions, such as popularity, academic competence, athletic abil-ity (Leung, 1996; Neckerman, 1992; Xie, Cairns, & Cairns, 1997). The strong evidence of "homophily" (i.e., similarity among group members) may reflect both the opportunities af-forded in the community and school and the continuing im-pact of common background and value structures.

Other evidence also supports the proposition that recip-rocal relationships in dyads and in groups play a significant role in aggressive behaviors of both middle childhood and adolescence. In suburban and rural American schools, there is no difference among highly aggressive children and ado-lescents in terms of whether they are nuclear members of social groups, nor in whether they have reciprocal friend-ships (Cairns et al., 1988). In some inner-city schools highly aggressive boys even have higher centrality in the peer so-cial networks than less aggressive boys (Xie, Cairns, & Cairns, 1997). Large differences appear, however, in the kinds of friends they have.

The current literature suggests that the supportive role that peer social networks play in the development of aggres-sion may differ across gender. In comparisons of male groups to female groups, there is a modest yet consistent gender difference in group size. Boys tend to form slightly larger groups than girls (e.g., Eder & Hallinan, 1978; Lager-spetz, Björkqvist, & Peltonen, 1988). In terms of group ho-mophily, girls within a group tended to share a broader web of similarities than did boys (e.g., Neckerman, 1992; Xie et al., 1997). These results support the proposal that girls form more cohesive, exclusive groups relative to those of boys. Gender difference also exists in the type of behavior that is associated with centrality in the social networks. In an inner-city sample, it was reported that high social network central-ity in girls was associated with high levels of popularity; however, high social network centrality in boys was associ-ated with high levels of aggressive behavior (Xie et al., 1997). All together, these findings suggest that peer social networks may play a more supportive role in the develop-ment of aggressive patterns in males than in females.

Gender Difference in Aggressive Development

Beginning in late childhood and early adolescence (10–13 years of age), there is an accentuation of gender differ-ences. The onset of puberty and romantic and sexual inter-ests in adolescence is associated with a fresh social role differentiation. This accentuation of gender differences has two profound consequences for aggressive expression. For females, there is the rapid development of adult-like non-confrontational aggressive strategies of anger expression that may coexist with the direct confrontational actions of childhood. For males, there is an inevitable increase in the intensity of confrontations due, in part, to gender-relative differences in masculine role, sexual dimorphism, and weapon availability.

At approximately 10 to 11 years of age, girls begin to employ nonconfrontational strategies in aggressive expression to supplement the confrontational acts of childhood (Cairns et al., 1989). In adolescence, this takes the form of social aggression—including rumor spreading, social ostracism, and group alienation. These "indirect" forms of aggression are themselves correlated and serve as nonconfrontational forms of attack. Indirect or social aggression has some remarkable advantages over confrontational attacks by reducing the likelihood of immediate escalation and overt physical violence. The victim may not be able to distinguish between friend or enemy, given that the originators of the attacks are concealed by the fabric of the social framework.

The findings indicate that these "hidden" techniques rapidly become a preferred strategy for aggressive expression in mid-adolescence and later, particularly among girls. From the fourth grade to the tenth grade, the percentage of female-to-female conflicts involving themes of alienation, ostracism, or character defamation rises from 14 percent to 56 percent.

Although nonconfrontational strategies become increasingly dominant in female conflicts, it would be inaccurate to indicate that adolescent females lose the capability to produce serious harm and damage. Confrontational and nonconfrontational strategies seem to coexist for girls throughout adolescence.

What about males during early and mid-adolescence? One remarkable feature of male–male aggressive expression in this age range is the failure to develop and employ nonconfrontational strategies. They persist in the strategy of childhood, but with new and more powerful physical resources for creating injury and maiming. With this quantitative shift in intensity, there is a qualitative shift in consequences. The "aggression" of middle childhood becomes the "violence" of adolescence and adulthood.

Relative to girls, boys in the middle childhood and early adolescent period seem "socially retarded" in the use of indirect forms of aggressive expression. They rarely report the use of nonconfrontational strategies in their conflicts with other boys or girls. Factor analytic analyses have indicated that the gender difference in strategies was not present at 10 years of age, but it was clearly present by 13 years of age and beyond.

One consequence of the failure to shift to nonconfrontational strategies is that males in this age range become more vulnerable to assaults and escalation in the intensity of fights. For adolescent males, this means that a mere insult or being "dissed" can escalate to physical assaults or to life-threatening conflicts involving lethal weapons.

THE SEQUELAE OF PEER NEGLECT AND SOCIAL ISOLATION

Modern statements on social learning theory and emotional development tend to converge in interesting ways with basic psychoanalytic propositions. Accordingly, deficits in information processing that were established in early familial dynamics are assumed to give rise to faulty attributions and a fundamental lack of social skills in children. The aggressive behavior that is observed reflects deficits in information processing and social skills. Alternatively, other social–cognitive deficits—such as low levels of self esteem or failures of feelings of self efficacy—may give rise to both aggression and other failures of social adaptation. These proposals are closely linked to propositions that implicate low levels of self-regulation of emotions and impulses. Again, such deficits are typically tracked to the problems in early family relationships and, in many cases, to problematic attachment patterns.

Theorists have long recognized positive peer relationships as an important factor in childhood adjustment (Baldwin, 1897; Piaget, 1926; Youniss, 1980). Sociometric status is a prevailing measure of peer relationships, particularly among boys in school (Coie & Dodge, 1983; Coie, Dodge & Coppotelli, 1982; Kupersmidt & Coie, 1990; Parker & Asher, 1987; 1993). Sociometric status relies on peer nominations to determine the child's standing in one of several categories: popular, average, neglected, controversial, and rejected. Typically, children are asked to list peers they like most, and peers they like least. Standardized scores determine popular (highly liked), average, neglected (infrequent nomination), controversial (both highly liked and disliked), and rejected (highly disliked) status. Behavioral measures, including teacher measures, interviews, and parent and teacher ratings on the Child Behavior Checklist (CBCL; Achenbach & Edelbrook, 1983) provide outcome assessments to evaluate the effects of assignment to a status category over time.

Based on those assessments, aggression and peer rejection during middle childhood have emerged as mutually and separately linked to negative outcomes (Coie, Terry, Lenox, Lochman, & Hyman, 1995.) This has lead to a concentration on aggression and rejected status as predictors in middle childhood for deviant outcomes in adolescence (Coie, Lochman, Terry, & Hyman, 1992; Lochman & Wayland, 1994). Investigators have suggested that the level of adolescent deviance is mediated by chronicity of aggressiveness and rejected status. Moffit (1993) proposed a "dual pathway" model that distinguishes children who are aggressive and rejected in early and middle childhood from those whose deviant behavior appears to bloom later in adolescence (see also Patterson, DeBaryshe, & Ramsey, 1989). According to this model, early deviance is more likely to result in a lifelong pattern of antisocial conduct. Both chronicity and recency of rejected status have been shown to influence deviant behavioral patterns. Males appear to be more negatively influenced by chronic peer rejection than females, although both sexes demonstrate heightened acting-out behaviors (DeRosier, Kupersmidt, & Patterson, 1994).

By contrast, findings from Cairns and Cairns (1994) indicate that the magnitude of aggressiveness, as assessed by teacher ratings, decreases across adolescence for both risk and nonrisk groups. Other findings indicate that rejected status is not necessarily stable over time. Although there is evidence that reputational bias and other dynamics tend to maintain peer rejection, Coie and Dodge (1983) found that half of the rejected children in their sample did not retain that status over a 5-year period.

WHOSE INFORMATION PROCESSING IS BIASED: AGGRESSIVE OR NONAGGRESSIVE CHILDREN?

From an information-processing perspective, rejected status and acting-out behavior can be viewed as the product of attributional bias (Dodge, 1980). Aggressive, rejected boys are considered to misperceive or misunderstand the behavioral intentions of others (or fail to attend to relevant cues) and to incorrectly ascribe hostile or negative intentions to ambiguous acts (Crick & Dodge, 1994; Dodge, 1980; Dodge & Tomlin, 1987; Sancilio, Plumert, & Hartup, 1989).

In the typical research paradigm employed to assess the presence of an attributional bias, children are shown a series of vignettes in which the intent of the actor has been defined as either hostile, nonhostile, or ambiguous. The children are then probed on their perceptions about the intent of the actor. Highly aggressive boys frequently identify "ambiguous" situations and actions to have hostile intent. As a result, these children are seen as likely to overreact to harmless or unintentionally negative stimuli. This "biased information processing" sets the stage for an escalating relation between aggressive and reactive behaviors, leading to peer rejection and further entrenchment of biases toward hostile attribution. Although the usual focus of these studies is on dyadic relationships, group influences have been recognized as contextually important in mediating this escalation of aggressive behavior (DeRosier, Cillessen, Coie, & Dodge, 1994).

This set of proposals has had a strong impact on theoretical conceptions of aggressive development. It marries central propositions from social psychology on attributional biases with dyadic analyses of the evolution of negative, escalating interactions. Moreover, it seems to be backed up by a large body of empirical literature that demonstrates that aggressive youth are more likely than nonaggressive ones to report higher levels of aggression in pictorial displays, vignettes, and other settings. These propositions have been extended to incorporate concepts from the cognitive developmental literature, including the role of "knowledge structures" and internal memory representations of past experience (Dodge, 1993).

Although the propositions are persuasive, and cognitive constructions and interpretations clearly play a role in children's aggressive behaviors, there are two central questions that can be raised about the proposal. Specifically:

1. Whose social perceptions are biased, those of aggressive or nonaggressive children? This question is raised because early studies of the attributions of highly aggressive adolescents suggest that these youth are *more* accurate than nonaggressive youth in describing conflicts, deviance, and violence. The problem here is that there may be biases in social perception, but the biases are those found in "normal" or "nonaggressive" children. Aggressive encounters, whether in reality or in fiction, can inspire apprehension, fear, and, in extreme cases, avoidant anxiety in most persons. Accordingly, there may be a general bias in perception and communication to overlook, avoid, or misperceive situations that are, in fact, characterized by threat or hostility. Such a bias would be consistent with the "Pollyanna hypothesis" of Boucher and Osgood (1969) that these investigators found in their cross-national analyses a preponderance of adjectives relative to negative ones. It is also consistent with the robust finding that in social interchanges the ratio of positive to negative interactions is 5:1 to 10:1. Moreover, direct observations of middle childhood boys and girls indicates that the preferred strategy in potential conflicts has been to ignore insults and negative actions.

Although this shift in focus—from the biased perceptions of aggressive children to the biased perceptions of nonaggressive children—may seem modest, it speaks to a broader issue of where the deficits reside and how intervention should proceed. Perhaps some social perception "deficits" are productive and adaptive in that it is functional to overlook or not even recognize challenges and insults. Such attributions may be akin to the positive biases of many self-perceptions, by which children typically view themselves as being more competent, friendly, and intelligent than they are viewed by other persons (e.g., Leung, 1996).

2. Social attributional accounts of aggressive behavior tend to decontextualize the phenomena. The decontextualization is invited by the theoretical focus on within-individual processes. Aggressive instigation is seen as being controlled primarily by intra-organism processes—perceptions, attributions, knowledge, and memory representation—and the answers to the main questions of aggressive development will be found by careful examination of the child's cognitive structures and the historical events that contributed to the formation of those structures. The inherently interpersonal phenomena of aggressive exchanges are thus reduced to intrapersonal mechanisms.

In addition, methods that have been adopted for the study of attributional biases may also contribute to decontextualization. Typically the assessments are made of the individual's response to pictorial, verbal, or symbolic stimuli, including vignettes, videos, or cartoons. This paradigm greatly facilities the analysis and presentation of data and provides focus on the individual's interpretation of decontextualized events. However, the assessment procedures remove children and their actions from the concrete realities of their own lives and interactions. The attributional assessments are inevitably linked to the children's cognitive space.

Rejection and Popularity

Another link between group and dyadic processes has been clarified through exploration of the relations between popularity and friendship. Bukowski, Pizzamiglio, Newcomb, and Hoza (1996) point out that popularity is essentially unilateral, in that it is a measure of how well the group likes or dislikes an individual. Friendship, on the other hand, is a reciprocated mutual relationship. These are overlapping constructs, joined by measures of likability. These researchers find support for the idea that popularity is an "affordance" for friendship and is antecedent to friendship. Popularity is one of multiple factors that leads to friendship, but being popular does not guarantee having friends. Furthermore, current research indicates that friendship becomes increasingly complex and less a function of mutual liking as children leave middle childhood and enter adolescence (Bukowski et al., 1996).

Parker and Asher (1993) demonstrated that having a friend, friendship quality, and group acceptance have separate effects on feelings of loneliness. Among subgroups of rejected children, aggressive children reported less loneliness and social dissatisfaction than children who were identified as withdrawn (Parker & Asher, 1993). In fact, children who were identified as rejected by sociometric measures may have had just as many friends as their non-rejected peers, and those groups of friends were situated in positions of power within intergroup networks (Cairns & Cairns, 1994; Cairns, Cairns, Neckerman, Gest, & Gariépy, 1988).

Just as rejection does not necessarily imply a lack of friends or social standing, so may neglected status correspond to certain positive outcomes. Neglected children, neither liked nor disliked, have significantly positive academic profiles. In comparison to average status children, neglected children have been shown to be academically motivated, more self-regulated in learning, and more prosocial and compliant (Wentzel & Asher, 1995).

More generally, classifications such as "rejected" or "neglected" reflect time-bound and situation-bound outcomes of peer surveys of classroom popularity. It is a big leap to assign causal significance to such categories without inquiring why a child may be nominated as a friend or foe. For example, the above findings suggest that some "neglected" children may be adept at avoiding contact and conflicts. Likewise, some "rejected" children may be victims, but other may be bullies or both bullies and victims. Moreover, being "disliked" by a majority of peers can reflect temporary states (e.g., being new to the classroom) or enduring ones (e.g., being poor, being a different race). Similarly, the sociometric category "controversial" refers to children who receive high numbers of best-liked *and* least-liked peer nominations. These children are "controversial" only for the classification system, not for individuals or the peer network. The classification problem arises because the same child may be liked by many peers and disliked or feared by several others.

Why is a child liked or disliked by classroom peers? Aggression clearly plays a role (Coie & Dodge, 1983), but there appears to be a number of other factors. In this regard, only modest attention has been given to the roles that teachers play in influencing who is liked, disliked, or ignored in the classroom. Teachers can directly affect how children are viewed by their classmates through the teacher's ridicule, humiliation, and inattention of individuals or, conversely, by rewards, recognition, and praise. The multiple processes whereby children gain or lose esteem in the eyes of peers—and possibly in their own eyes—constitute a productive area for further research.

IMPLICATIONS FOR PREVENTION AND CLINICAL INTERVENTION

It is a happy finding that at least half of the persons who demonstrate high-risk aggressive profiles in childhood do not manifest disorders later in life. Development proceeds in the face of multiple inter-related constraints. The correlated nature of these constraints imposes limits on the trajectories by which development proceeds, but the correlations are not perfect. At every point opportunity for behavioral reorganization and change is present—developmental trajectories are never frozen in time. Indeed, one feature of an interdependent, correlated system is that fundamental, lasting change in a salient aspect of that system can potentially realign other system components. This potential for reorganization of life trajectories prevents us from predicting individual outcome with certainty.

To be sure, the linkages between earlier patterns of adaptation and resulting outcomes may not be simple or direct (Sroufe & Rutter, 1984). Single antecedents can lead to multiple and diverse outcomes and multiple antecedents can result in the identical outcome (Kellam & Reebok, 1992). However, there is likely to exist an underlying coherence in adaptive functioning over ontogeny such that early behavior patterns and subsequent adjustment are lawfully related (Sroufe, 1979). Accordingly, the identification of person-oriented configurations early on can be useful in understanding the developmental course of the disorder.

Once the relation between specific configuration profiles and various mental disorders and outcomes is understood, follow-up assessments may identify "turning points" in the lives of individuals who appeared to be at high risk (Pickles & Rutter, 1991). For example, using a person analysis strategy, Mahoney and Cairns (1996) found that high-risk children who participated in one extracurricular activity in secondary school were far less likely to drop out of high school than high-risk individuals with no extracurricular involvement (5 vs. 55% dropout rates, respectively). When these children participated in more than one activity none of them dropped out. Moreover, the associated reduction in rates of early school dropout were most marked for students at the highest risk, a finding that was uncovered by person analysis.

The preceding discussion suggests three nonobvious implications for prevention.

1. The likelihood of subsequent disorders in childhood may be reduced by capitalizing on the child's inherent behavioral bias toward health and adaptation. Specifically, the context in which development occurs serves to determine what behavior patterns are adaptive and successful among children. Providing an opportunity and rewards for children to become individually engaged and successful in conventional activities and structures may provide a safety net for many children. This net should apply especially to children who are at risk (i.e., children whose familial resources are poor, whose school competencies are modest, and/or whose social behaviors are problematic). It is not merely skill mastery and personal efficacy that may be achieved through such engagement. In addition, it opens the possibility for realignment of peer relationships and relationships with teachers and other persons who can serve to provide guidance and support. At a concrete level, this refers to the importance of, for example, involvement in school extracurricular activities

and involvement by mentors who are committed to individual children.

2. The efficacy of any prevention or intervention program is likely to have differential influence, depending on the individual's configuration of internal and external characteristics. Attention should be given to the linkages between constraining factors such as maturational timing, social networks and peer status, school engagement, and family socioeconomic conditions. To the extent that prevention or interventions are focused on single behaviors divorced from developmental contexts in which they occur, they may produce only short-lived changes.

3. Consistent with James's (1890) proposal, biographies cannot be written in advance, and developmental trajectories do not appear to be fixed, either by genes or by early experience. Despite multiple constraints in development, reorganization can and does occur, but it is likely that all points in development are not equally vulnerable to modification. It is easier to prevent the organization of a behavior system than it is to change it, once organized. Substance use that begins at adolescence, for example, is more readily prevented than changed. Accordingly, middle and late childhood may be particularly important as entry points for the prevention or amelioration of serious problems of living that have their onset in early and mid-adolescence.

SUMMARY AND CONCLUSIONS

Significant advances have been achieved over the past two decades in defining the empirical links between childhood adaptation and later psychopathology. Recent long-term longitudinal studies have helped clarify the essential questions of continuity, change, and prevention. Furthermore, the basic empirical generalizations derived from these longitudinal investigations are basically congruent with the empirical generalizations that have been repeatedly demonstrated in comparative investigations.

Some of the generalizations on continuity are negative. For example, social interactions observed in infancy provide, at best, low levels of accuracy in the longterm prediction of behavior problems in adolescence and adulthood. Other generalizations are positive. By middle childhood, the predictive equations to adolescent and adult psychopathology are robust, though far from perfect. Certain behavioral measures—particularly those that involve aggressive interchanges—have been linked to a wide band of problematic adaptations in adolescence and adulthood.

Much of this chapter has been concerned with three questions implicated by these empirical generalizations, namely,

1. What underlies the predictive linkage between childhood aggressive measures and subsequent psychopathology?
2. What accounts for the change and variability over time, including the bias toward resilience and adaptation?
3. How can recent research findings be systematically employed to reduce the occurrence of subsequent problems?

To summarize findings relevant to the first question, the predictive validity of childhood measures of aggression seems to depend upon the configurations in which they occur. In the absence of other problem adaptations in childhood, aggression taken alone is not a robust predictor of subsequent problems of adaptation. This outcome is consistent with an emergent body of evidence that suggests that developmental adaptations are appropriately viewed in context. A similar conclusion holds for other single variable measures, including the popularity–unpopularity index of sociometric status. Predictions become more stable when there are correlated constraints on adaptation; that is, when aggression and rejection occur as part of a package of multiple problems.

In addition, the continuity of problems from childhood through adolescence reflects, in part, the social context in which development occurs. Bidirectional constraints exist in childhood and adolescent development whereby temperamental, cognitive, and interactional characteristics of the individual become correlated with similar characteristics of peer groups. Internal configurations are correlated with social networks. Both selection and socialization processes have been implicated in this correlation, such that intimate peer interactions both attract and shape a child's attitudes, values, and behaviors. Furthermore, social networks are essential for the deployment of indirect or "social aggression" strategies in late childhood. These strategies of social ostracization, gossip, and defamation are remarkably versatile tools for interpersonal injury and control. They appear to be used so broadly that they are normative for girls in adolescence. Unlike direct, confrontational aggression, they appear to be poorly linked to subsequent psychopathology.

The answer to the second question—why there is developmental resilience—must be more speculative. In general, measures of childhood problems over-predict subsequent adolescent and adult psychopathology. Virtually all longitudinal investigations find fewer instances of subsequent problems than would be expected from the childhood assessments (e.g., Cairns & Cairns, 1994; Magnusson, 1988; Werner & Smith, 1986). Why the overprediction? While at least part of the problem lies in the assessment strategies employed, it may be speculated that the more basic problem is that the discipline has failed to consider the essential human bias toward health and adaptation. As the contexts shift over development, so should basic patterns of social adaptation. Each major developmental transition—adolescence, young adulthood, marriage, parenthood, working—affords an opportunity for change and sometimes demands it. Failures of prediction cannot be blamed simply on our assessment instruments; they may reflect, as well, the positive dynamics and changing contingencies of human development.

Propositions relevant to the third question, regarding prevention and change, were covered in the last part of this chapter. It seems reasonable to propose that prevention and intervention programs should capitalize on the inherent human bias toward health and adaptation. In this process, developmental time can be either an enemy or ally. Time may be seen as an enemy because adolescent problem behaviors become increasingly difficult to address once they have become organized and consolidated. But time can also be viewed as an ally, because an understanding of time-based processes potentially provides directions on when to begin and how long to persist in an intervention program. On this count, middle and late childhood seem to be especially important stages to engage children in school if they have not already become engaged or if they have experienced repeated failures. As may be expected by the integrated nature of social regulation, multiple strategies have proved to be effective in enhancing engagement and reducing school problem behaviors among high-risk children (e.g., success in extracurricular activities and successful mentoring); however, patterns of development and adaptation are inherently progressive and dynamic, and they can rarely be altered by single event "turning points." Accordingly, the long-term success of prevention and intervention programs depends on the extent to which they are maintained from childhood through adolescence.

NOTES

1. Intelligence measures usually involve assessments of an individual's optimal performance under standard conditions; aggressive assessments usually involve judgments of an individual's typical performance in the natural circumstances of her or his life.

REFERENCES

Achenbach, T. M., & Edelbrock. (1983). *Manual for the Child Behavior Checklist and Revised Child Behavior Profile.* Burlington: University of Vermont Press.

Ainsworth, M. D. S. (1972). Attachment and dependency: A comparison. In J. L. Gewirtz (Ed.), *Attachment and dependency.* New York: Wiley.

Angold, A., & Costello, J. (1996). Toward establishing an empirical basis for the diagnosis of oppositional defiant disorder. *Journal of the American Academy of Child and Adolescent Psychiatry, 35,* 1205–1212.

Baldwin, J. M. (1897). *Social and ethical interpretations in mental development: A study in social psychology.* New York: Macmillan.

Bandura, A. (1973). *Aggression: A social learning analysis.* Englewood Cliffs, NJ: Prentice-Hall.

Bergman, L. (1998). A pattern-oriented approach to studying individual development: Snapshots and processes. In R. B. Cairns, L. Bergman, & J. Kagan (Eds.), *Methods and models for studying the individual* (pp. 83–122). Thousand Oaks, CA: Sage.

Bergman, L. R., & Magnusson, D. (1997). A person-oriented approach in research on developmental psychopathology. *Development & Psychopathology, 9,* 291–319.

Block, J. (1971). *Lives through time.* Berkeley, CA: Bancroft Books.

Boucher, J., & Osgood, C. E. (1969). The Pollyanna hypothesis. *Journal of Verbal Learning and Verbal Behavior, 8,* 1–8.

Bowlby, J. (1952). *Maternal care and mental health* (2nd ed.). Geneva, Switzerland: World Health Organization.

Bowlby, J. (1973). *Attachment and loss. Vol. 2: Separation.* New York: Basic Books.

Breuer. J., & Frued. S. (1936). *Studies in hysteria.* New York: Nervous and Mental Disease Publishing Co. (Originally published in 1895. Translated by A. A. Brill)

Bukowski, W. M., Pizzamiglio, M. T., Newcomb, A. F., & Hoza, B. (1996). Popularity as an affordance for friendship: The link between group and dyadic experience. *Social Development, 5,* 189–202.

Cairns, R. B. (1973). Fighting and punishment from a developmental perspective. In J. K. Coles & D. D. Jensen (Eds.), *Nebraska Symposium on Motivation* (pp. 159–124). Lincoln: University of Nebraska Press.

Cairns, R. B. (1979). *Social development: The origins and plasticity of interchanges.* San Francisco: Freeman.

Cairns, R. B., & Cairns, B. D. (1994). *Lifelines and risks: Pathways of youth in our time.* New York: Cambridge University Press.

Cairns, R. B., Cairns, B. D., & Neckerman, H. J. (1989). Early school dropout: Configurations and determinants. *Child Development, 60,* 1437–1452.

Cairns, R. B., Cairns, B. D., Neckerman, H. J., Ferguson, L. L., & Gariépy, J. L. (1989). Growth and aggression: I. Childhood to early adolescence. *Developmental Psychology, 25,* 320–330.

Cairns, R. B., Cairns, B. D., Neckerman, J. J., Gest, S., & Gariépy, J-L. (1988). Social networks and aggressive behavior: Peer support or peer rejection? *Developmental Psychology, 24,* 815–823.

Cairns, R. B., & Rodkin, P. C. (1998). Phenomena regained: From configurations to pathways in longitudinal research. In R. B. Cairns, L. Bergman, & J. Kagan (Eds.), *Methods and models for studying the individual* (pp. 245–266). Thousand Oaks, CA: Sage.

Ceci, S. J. (1995). Cognitive and social factors in children's testimony. In B. D. Sales and G. R. VandenBos (Eds.), *Psychology in litigation and legislation: Master lectures in psychology.* (pp. 15–54). Washington, DC: American Psychological Association.

Clarke-McLean, J. G. (1996). Social networks among incarcerated juvenile offenders. *Social Development, 5,* 203–217.

Coie, J. D., & Dodge, K. A. (1983). Continuities and changes in children's social status: A five-year longitudinal study. *Merrill-Palmer Quarterly, 29,* 261–282.

Coie, J. D., Dodge, K. A., & Coppotelli, H. (1982). Dimensions and types of social status: A cross-age perspective. *Developmental Psychology, 18,* 557–570.

Coie, J. D., Lochman, J. E., Terry, R., & Hyman, C. (1992). Predicting early adolescent disorder from childhood aggression and peer rejection. *Journal of Consulting and Clinical Psychology, 60,* 783–792.

Coie, J. D., Terry, R., Lenox, K. F., Lochman, J. E., & Hyman, C. (1995). Childhood peer rejection and aggression as predictors of stable patterns of adolescent disorder. *Development and Psychopathology, 7,* 697–713.

Crick, N. R., & Dodge, K. A. (1994). A review and reformulation of social information-processing mechanisms in chidren's social adjustment. *Psychological Bulletin, 115,* 74–101.

Crime in the U.S. (1992). *Uniform crime reports.* Washington, DC: U.S. Department of Justice, Federal Bureau of Investigation.

Crime in the U.S. (1995). *Uniform crime reports.* Washington, DC: U.S. Department of Justice, Federal Bureau of Investigation.

DeRosier, M. E., Cillessen, A. H. N., Coie, J. D., & Dodge, K. A. (1994). Group social context and children's aggressive behavior. *Child Development, 65,* 1068–1079.

DeRosier, M. E., Kupersmidt, J. B., & Patterson, C. J. (1994). Children's academic and behavioral adjustment as a function of the chronicity and proximity of peer rejection. *Child Development, 65,* 1799–1813.

Dishion, T. J., Reid, J. B., & Patterson, G. R. (1988). Empirical guidelines for a family intervention for adolescent drug use. *Journal of Chemical Dependency Treatment, 1,* 181–216.

Dodge, K. A. (1980). Social cognition and children's aggressive behavior. *Child Development, 51,* 162–170.

Dodge, K. A. (1993). Social–cognitive mechanisms in the development of conduct disorder and depression. *Annual Review of Psychology, 44,* 559–584.

Dodge, K. A., & Tomlin, A. (1987). Cue utilization as a mechanism of attributional bias in aggressive children. *Social Cognition, 5,* 280–300.

Eder, D., & Hallinan, M. T. (1978). Sex differences in children's friendships. *American Sociological Review, 43,* 237–250.

Elliott, D. S., Huizinga, D., & Menard, S. (1989). *Multiple problem youth: Delinquency, substance use, and mental health problems.* New York: Springer-Verlag.

Eron, L., & Huesmann, L. R. (1987). The control of aggressive behavior by changes in attitudes, values, and the conditions of learning. In R. J. Blanchard & C. Blanchard (Eds.), *Advances in the study of aggression* (Vol. 2, pp. 139–171). New York: Academic Press.

Eron, L., Huesmann, L. R., Brice, P., Fischer, P., & Mermelstein, R. (1983). Age trends in the development of aggression, sex typing, and related television habits. *Developmental Psychology, 19,* 71–77.

Farrington, D. P., & West, D. J. (1990). The Cambridge study in delinquent development: A long-term follow-up of 411 London males. In H. J. Kerner and G. Kaiser (Eds.), *Criminality: Personality, behavior, and life history.* Berlin, Germany: Springer-Verlag.

Ferguson, T. J., & Rule, B. G. (1980). Effects of inferential set, outcome severity, and basis of responsibility on children's evaluation of aggressive acts. *Developmental Psychology, 16,* 141–146.

Fingerhut, L. A., & Kleinman, J. C. (1989). Mortality among children and youth. *American Journal of Public Health, 79,* 899–901.

Gaines, K. R. E., Cairns, R. B., & Cairns, B. D. (1994, March). *Social networks and risk for school dropout.* Paper presented at the Society for Research in Adolescence, San Diego, CA.

Giordano, P. C., Cernkovich, S. A., & Pugh, M. D. (1986). Friendship and delinquency. *American Journal of Sociology, 91,* 1170–1201.

Harlow, H. F. (1958). The nature of love. *American Psychologist, 13,* 673–685.

Hirschi, T., & Gottfredson, M. (1983). Age and explanation of crime. *American Journal of Sociology, 89,* 552–584.

Hunt, J. McV. (1961). *Intelligence and experience.* New York: Ronald Press.

Huesmann, L. R., Lagerspetz, K., & Eron, L. D. (1984). Intervening variables in the TV violence-aggression relation: Evidence from two countries. *Developmental Psychology, 20,* 746–775.

James, W. (1890). *The principles of psychology* (Vol. 1). New York: Macmillan.

Jessor, R., Donovan, J. E., & Costa, F. M. (1991). *Beyond adolescence: Problem behavior and young adult development.* New York: Cambridge University Press.

Kagan, J. (1997). Temperament and the reactions to unfamiliarity. *Child Development, 68,* 139–143.

Kellam, S. G., & Rebok, G. W. (1992). Building developmental and etiological theory through epidemiologically based preventive intervention trials. In J. McCord and R. E. Tremblay (Eds.), *Preventing antisocial behavior: Interventions from birth through adolescence* (pp. 162–195). New York: Guilford Press.

Kupersmidt, J. B., & Coie, J. D. (1990). Preadolescent peer status, aggression, and school adjustment as predictors of externalizing problems in adolescence. *Child Development, 61,* 1350–1362.

Lagerspetz, K. M. J., Björkqvist, K., & Peltonen, T. (1988). Is indirect aggression typical of females? Gender differences in aggressiveness in 11- to 12-year-old children. *Aggressive Behavior, 14,* 403–414.

Leung, M.-C. (1996). Social networks and self enhancement in Chinese children: A comparison of self reports and peer reports of group membership. *Social Development, 5,* 146–157.

Lochman, J. E., & Wayland, K. K. (1994). Aggression, social acceptance, and race as predictors of negative adolescent outcomes. *Journal of the American Academy of Child and Adolescent Psychiatry, 33,* 1026–1035.

Loeber, R. (1982). The stability of antisocial and delinquent child behavior: A review. *Child Development, 53,* 1431–1446.

Loeber, R., & Hay, D. (1997). Key issues in the development of aggression and violence from childhood to early adulthood. *Annual Review of Psychology, 48,* 371–410.

Lorenz, K. Z. (1937). The companion in the bird's world. *Auk, 54,* 245–273.

Magnusson, D. (1985). Implications of an interactional paradigm for research on human development. *International Journal of Behavioral Development, 8,* 115–137.

Magnusson, D. (1988). *Individual development from an interactional perspective: A longitudinal study.* Hillsdale, NJ: Erlbaum.

Magnusson, D. (1995). Individual development: A holistic integrated model. In P. Moen, G. H. Elder, Jr., and K. Lücher (Eds.), *Examining lives in context: Perspectives on the ecology of human development* (pp. 19–60). Washington, DC: American Psychological Association.

Magnusson, D. (1998). The logic and implications of a person-oriented approach. In R. B. Cairns, L. Bergman, & J. Kagan (Eds.), *Methods and models for studying the individual* (pp. 33–64). Thousand Oaks, CA: Sage.

Magnusson, D., & Cairns, R. B. (1996). Developmental science: Principles and illustrations. In R. B. Cairns, G. H. Elder, Jr., & J. Costello (Eds.), *Developmental science.* New York: Cambridge University Press.

Mahoney, J. L., & Cairns, R. B. (1996). Do extracurricular activities protect against early school dropout? *Developmental Psychology, 33,* 241–253.

Masten, A. S., & Braswell, L. (1991). Developmental psychopathology: An integrative framework for understanding behavior problems in children and adolescents. In P. R. Martin (Ed.), *Handbook of behavior therapy and psychological science: An integrative approach* (pp. 35–56). New York: Pergamon Press.

Miczek, K. A., and Grossman, S. P. (1972). Effects of spatial lesions on inter- and intraspecies aggression in rats. *Journal of Comparative and Physiological Psychology, 79,* 37–45.

Moffitt, T. E. (1993). Adolescence-limited and life-course-persistant antisocial behavior: A developmental taxonomy. *Psychological Review, 100,* 674–701.

Neckerman, H. J. (1992). *A longitudinal investigation of the stability and fluidity of social networks and peer relationships of children and adolescents.* Unpublished doctoral dissertation. University of North Carolina at Chapel Hill.

Neckerman, H. J. (1996). The stability of social groups in childhood and adolescence. *Social Development, 5,* 131–145.

Olweus, D. (1979). Stability of aggressive reaction patterns in males: A review. *Psychological Bulletin, 86,* 852–875.

Paris, S. G., & Cairns, R. B. (1972). An experimental and ethological analysis of social reinforcement with retarded children. *Child Development, 43,* 717–729.

Parker, J. G., & Asher, S. R. (1987). Peer relations and later personal adjustment: Are low accepted children at risk? *Psychological Bulletin, 102,* 537–589.

Parker, J. G., & Asher, S. R. (1993). Friendship and friendship quality in middle childhood: Links with peer group acceptance and feelings of loneliness and social dissatisfaction. *Developmental Psychology, 29,* 611–621.

Patterson, G. R., DeBaryshe, B. D., & Ramsey, E. (1989). A developmental perspective on antisocial behavior. *American Psychologist, 44,* 329–335.

Patterson, G. R., Reid, J. B., and Dishion, T. J. (1992). *Antisocial boys.* Eugene, OR: Castalia Publishing.

Piaget, J. (1926). *The language and thought of the child.* New York: Harcourt Brace. (Original work published 1923)

Pickles, A., & Rutter, M. (1991). Statistical and conceptual models of "turning points" in developmental process. In D. Magnusson, L. R. Bergman, G. Rudinger, and B. Törestad (Eds.), *Problems and methods in longitudinal research* (pp. 323–336). Cambridge, England: Cambridge University Press.

Pulkkinen, L. (1982). Self-control and continuity from childhood to late adolescence. In P. B. Baltes & O. G. Brim, Jr. (Eds.), *Lifespan development and behavior* (Vol. 4, pp. 64–105). New York: Academic Press.

Pulkkinen, L. (1988). Delinquent development: Theoretical and empirical considerations. In M. Rutter (Ed.), *Studies of psychosocial risk: The power of longitudinal data* (pp. 184–199). Cambridge, England: Cambridge University Press.

Radke-Yarrow, M. R., Campbell, J. D., & Burton, R. V. (1968). *Child rearing: An inquiry in research and methods.* San Francisco: Jossey-Bass.

Robins, L. N. (1986). The consequences of conduct disorder in girls. In D. Olweus, J. Block, & M. Radke-Yarrow (Eds.), *Development of antisocial and prosocial behavior: Research, theories, and issues* (pp. 385–414). New York: Academic Press.

Ross, M., & Buehler, R. (1994). Creative remembering, In U. Neisser & R. Fivush (Eds.) *The remembering self: Construction and accuracy in the self-narrative. Emory symposia in cognition, 6* (pp. 205–235). New York: Cambridge University Press.

Rutter, M., Manghan, B., Pickles, A., & Simonoff, E. (1998). Retrospective recall recalled. In R. B. Cairns, L. R. Bergman, & J. Kagan (Eds.), *Methods and models for studying the individual* (pp. 219–242). Thousand Oaks, CA: Sage.

Sadowski, L. S., Cairns, R. B., & Earp, J. A. (1989). Firearm ownership among nonurban adolescents. *American Journal of Diseases of Children, 143,* 1410–1413.

Sancilio, M. F. M., Plumert, J. M., & Hartup, W. W. (1989). Friendship and aggressiveness as determinants of conflict outcomes in middle childhood. *Developmental Psychology, 25,* 812–819.

Scott, J. P., & Fuller, J. L. (1965). *Genetics and the social behavior of the dog.* Chicago: University of Chicago Press.

Sroufe, L. A., & Rutter, M. (1984). The domain of developmental psychopathology. *Child Development, 55,* 17–29.

Sroufe, L. A. (1979). The coherence of individual development: Early care, attachment, and subsequent developmental issues. *American Psychologist, 34,* 834–841.

Sun, S. L. (1995). *The development of social networks of Chinese children in Taiwan.* Poster presented at the biennial meeting of Society for Research in Child Development, Indianapolis, IN.

Tracy, P. E., Wolfgang, M. E., & Figlio, R. M. (1990). *Delinquency careers in two birth cohorts.* New York: Plenum Press.

Watson, J. B. (1926). What the nursery has to say about instincts. In C. Murchison (Ed.), *Psychologies of 1925.* Worcester, MA.: Clark University Press.

Wentzel, K. R., & Asher, S. R. (1995). The academic lives of neglected, rejected, popular and controversial children. *Child Development, 66,* 754–763.

Werner, E. E., & Smith, R. S. (1986). *Kuai's children come of age.* Honolulu: University of Hawaii Press.

Wolfgang, M. E., Figlio, R. M., & Sellin, T. (1972). *Delinquency in a birth cohort.* Chicago: University of Chicago Press.

Xie, H., Cairns, R. B., & Cairns, B. D. (1997). *Social networks among inner-city children: The centrality of aggressive boys and popular girls.* Unpublished manuscript, University of North Carolina, Chapel Hill.

Youniss, J. (1980). *Parents and peers in social development.* Chicago: University of Chicago Press.

CHAPTER 8

ADOLESCENCE

Richard M. Lerner
Francisco A. Villarruel
Domini R. Castellino

Adolescence has been described as a phase of life beginning in biology and ending in society (Petersen, 1988). Indeed, adolescence may be defined as the period within the life span when most of a person's biological, psychological, and social characteristics are changing from what is typically considered child-like to what is considered adult-like (Lerner & Spanier, 1980). For the adolescent, this period is a dramatic challenge, one requiring adjustment to changes in the self, in the family, and in the peer group. In contemporary American society, adolescents typically experience institutional changes as well. Among young adolescents, there is a change in school setting, typically involving a transition from elementary school to either junior high school or middle school; and in late adolescence in America there is a transition from high school to either the world of work or to college.

Understandably, then, for both adolescents and their parents, adolescence is a time of excitement and of anxiety; of happiness and of troubles; of discovery and of bewilderment; and of breaks with the past and yet of continuations of child-like behavior. Adolescence is a period about which much has been written but, until relatively recently, little has been known. In short, adolescence can be a confusing time—for the adolescent experiencing this phase of life, for the parents who are nurturing the adolescent during his or her progression through this period, and for the adults charged with enhancing the development of youth during this period of life.

The feelings and events pertinent to parents' reactions to their adolescent children are well known to parents, to teachers, and to many writers who have romanticized or dramatized the adolescent experience in novels, short stories, or news articles. Indeed, it is commonplace to survey a newsstand and to find a magazine article describing the "stormy years" of adolescence, the new crazes or fads of youth, or the "explosion" of problems with teenagers (e.g., crime or sexuality).

Until the last 20 to 25 years, when medical, biological, and social scientists began to study intensively the adolescent period, there was relatively little sound scientific information available to verify or refute the romantic, literary characteristics of adolescence. Today, however, such information does exist, and it is not consistent with the idea that early adolescence is a necessarily stormy and stressful period (Feldman & Elliott, 1990; Lerner, 1988, 1993b, 1995; Lerner, Petersen, & Brooks-Gunn, 1991; Lerner & Villarruel, 1994; Petersen, 1988).

KEY FEATURES OF ADOLESCENT DEVELOPMENT

Today, there is an increasingly more voluminous and sophisticated scientific literature about adolescence. This literature allows several generalizations to be made about this period of life.

Multiple Levels of Context Are Influential during Adolescence

There are ubiquitous individual differences in adolescent development, and they involve connections among biological, psychological, and societal factors—and *not* one of these influences (e.g., biology) act either alone or as the "prime mover" of change (Brooks-Gunn & Petersen, 1983; Lerner, 1987, 1993b, 1995; Lerner & Foch, 1987; Lerner & Villarruel, 1994; Petersen, 1988).

Adolescence is a period of extremely rapid transitions in such characteristics as height, weight, and body proportions. Indeed, except for infancy, no other period of the life cycle involves such rapid changes. Moreover, hormonal changes are part of the development of early adolescence. Nevertheless, hormones are not primarily responsible for the psychological or social developments during this period (Finkelstein, 1993; Petersen & Taylor, 1980). In fact, the quality and timing of hormonal or other biological changes influence and are influenced by psychological, social, cultural, and historical factors (Elder, 1980; Gottlieb, 1992; Magnusson, 1988; Stattin & Magnusson, 1990; Tanner, 1991).

Good examples of the integrated, multilevel changes in adolescence arise in regard to cognitive development during this period (Graber & Petersen, 1991). Global and pervasive effects of puberty on cognitive development do not seem to exist. When biological effects are found they interact with contextual and experiential factors (Stattin & Magnusson, 1990). Accordingly, there is no evidence for general cognitive disruption over adolescence. Indeed, cognitive abilities increase over this period. Moreover, pubertal timing is not predictive of gender differences on such tasks as spatial cognition. Girls' earlier maturation does not result in general sex differences in cognition (Graber & Petersen, 1991).

Changing Relations between Adolescents and Their Contexts Produce Development

The period of adolescence is one of continual change and transition between individuals and their contexts (Lerner, 1987, 1995). These changing relations constitute the basic process of development in adolescence; they underlie both positive and negative outcomes during this period (Lerner, 1984, 1993a, 1993b, 1995).

Accordingly, when the multiple biological, psychological and sociocultural changes of adolescence occur simultaneously (e.g., when menarche occurs at the same time as a school transition), there is a greater risk of problems occurring in a youth's development (Simmons & Blyth, 1987). Indeed, in adolescence bad decisions (e.g., involving school, grades, sex, and drugs) have more negative consequences than in childhood (Dryfoos, 1990), and the adolescent is more "responsible" for those consequences than in childhood (Petersen, 1988); that is, the adolescent is more often involved than are younger individuals in making the behavioral and contextual choices (e.g., engaging in drug use with a particular peer group) associated with involvement in problem behaviors.

Nevertheless, most developmental trajectories across this period involve good adjustment on the part of the adolescent. Indeed, for most youth there is a continuation of positive parent–child relationships (Guerney & Arthur, 1984). Simply, young adolescents are strongly tied to the family (e.g., Offer, 1969).

Thus, adolescence is a good time to do intervention involving the family. For instance, whereas minor parent-child conflicts (e.g., regarding chores and privileges) are normative in adolescence, major conflicts are less frequent; thus, when major conflicts occur often in a family, parents should be concerned. However, the continued salience of the family in the adolescent period makes such conflicts an appropriate intervention target.

Individual Differences— Diversity—Characterize Adolescence

There are multiple pathways through adolescence (Offer, 1969). Inter-individual (between-person) and intra-individual (within-person) differences in development are the "rule" in this period of life. Accordingly, there is diversity between and within all ethnic, racial, or cultural minority groups. Therefore, generalizations that confound class, race, and/or ethnicity are not useful (Lerner, 1991).

Unfortunately, however, there is a major limitation in the status of the contemporary scientific literature about adolescent development. Despite the value of the extant knowledge base about development in adolescence, most studies in the literature have involved the study of European American, middle-class samples (e.g., Fisher & Brennan, 1992; Graham, 1992; Lerner, 1995). There are, of course, some prominent, high-quality investigations that either have studied samples other than European-American middle-class ones (e.g., Brookins, 1991; Reid, 1991; Spencer 1990, 1991; Spencer & Dornbusch, 1990; Spencer & Markstrom-Adams, 1990) or have studied adolescents from national or cultural settings other than American ones (e.g., Magnusson, 1988; Mead, 1928, 1930, 1935; Silbereisen, 1991; Stattin & Magnusson, 1990; Whiting & Whiting, 1991).

In regard to policies and programs, then, any intervention must be tailored to the specific target population and, in particular, to a group's developmental and environmental circumstances (Lerner, 1995; Lerner & Miller, 1993; Lerner & Villarruel, 1994). However, because adolescents are so different from each other, one cannot expect any single policy or intervention to reach *all* of a given target population or to influence everyone in the same way.

Furthermore, *normal* adolescent development involves variability within the person as well as between people. Temperamental characteristics involving mood and activity level are good examples (Lerner & Lerner, 1983). There are differences among adolescents in such characteristics. In addition, a given adolescent may change over the course of his or her life in the quality of the temperament he or she manifests (Chess & Thomas, 1984).

Implications of the Features of Adolescent Development for Research and Application

The breadth and depth of high-quality scientific information currently and increasingly available about development in adolescence underscores the diversity and dynamics of this period of life. Theoretical interest in studying dynamic person–context relations is a key reason that the changes of this period have garnered increasing scientific attention (Lerner, 1987, 1993a, 1993b).

This burgeoning scientific activity devoted to adolescence has occurred synergistically with the recognition within society of the special developmental challenges of this period, for example, those involving pubertal change and the emergence of reproductive capacity, and the development of a self-definition and of roles that will allow youth to become productive and healthy adult members of society. In addition, there has been a recognition in society, emerging in concert with the growing scientific data base, that the individual differences that occur in adolescent development, and the problems youth encounter in meeting the stressors of this period, represent a special intellectual and professional challenge. For those who wish not only to understand the nature of adolescence, but who desire as well to apply this knowledge to enhance the lives of adolescents and thereby help secure an optimal future for the invaluable human capital represented by a nation's youth, a synthesis of research, policy, and intervention must exist.

Research must be conducted with an appreciation of individual differences in adolescent development, differences that arise as a consequence of people's diverse development in distinct families, communities, and sociocultural settings (Lerner, 1993b, 1995; Lerner & Miller, 1993; Lerner & Villarruel, 1994). In turn, policies and programs must be similarly attuned to the diversity of people and context to maximize the chances of meeting the specific needs of particular groups of youth (Lerner, Terry, McKinney, & Abrams, 1994).

Such programs and policies must be derived appropriately from research predicated on integrative, multidisciplinary models of human development (Ford & Lerner, 1992). As will be explained below, developmental contextualism is based on such a model (Lerner, 1986, 1991, 1992, 1995). Here, however, it is important to note that the evaluation of applications of developmental theory should provide both societally important information about the success of endeavors aimed at youth enhancement *and* theoretically invaluable data about the validity of the synthetic, multilevel processes presumed to characterize human development (Lerner, 1986, 1988, 1989, 1991). The need for this dual outcome of the application of theory-based scholarship, that is, of applied developmental science (Fisher et al., 1993; Fisher & Lerner, 1994), is brought to the fore by a discussion of the several major problems besetting American adolescents.

CONTEMPORARY CRISES OF ADOLESCENT BEHAVIOR AND DEVELOPMENT

Across the communities of our nation, youth are dying—from violence, from drug and alcohol use and abuse, from unsafe sex, from poor nutrition, and from the sequelae of persistent and pervasive poverty (Dryfoos, 1990; Hamburg, 1992; Huston, 1991; Lerner, 1993a, 1993b, 1995; McKinney, Abrams, Terry, & Lerner, 1994; Schorr, 1988; Wilson, 1987). And if our youth are not dying, their life chances are being squandered—by school failure, underachievement, and dropout; by crime; by teenage pregnancy and parenting; by lack of job preparedness; by prolonged welfare dependency; by challenges to their health (e.g., lack of immunizations, inadequate screening for disabilities, insufficient prenatal care, and lack of sufficient infant and childhood medical services); and by the feelings of despair and hopelessness that pervade the lives of children whose parents have lived in poverty and who see themselves as having little opportunity to do better, that is, to have a life marked by societal respect, achievement, and opportunity (Dryfoos, 1990, 1994, 1995; Huston, 1991; Huston, McLoyd, & Coll, 1994).

There are numerous manifestations of the severity and breadth of the problems besetting our nation's youth, families, and communities. To illustrate, consider the four major categories of risk behaviors in late childhood and adolescence: (1) drug and alcohol use and abuse, (2) unsafe sex, teenage pregnancy, and teenage parenting, (3) school underachievement, school failure, and dropout, and (4) delinquency, crime, and violence (Dryfoos, 1990). Clearly, participation in any one of these behaviors would diminish a youth's life chances. Indeed, engagement in some of these behaviors would eliminate the young person's chances of even having a life. Such risks to the life chances of America's children and adolescents are occurring, unfortunately, at historically unprecedented levels.

Today, in America, there are approximately 28 million children and adolescents between the ages of 10 and 17 years. About 50 percent of these youth engage in *two or more* of the above-noted categories of risk behaviors (Dryfoos, 1990)! Moreover, 10 percent of our nation's youth engage in *all* of the four categories of risk behaviors (Dryfoos, 1990).

These data indicate that risk behaviors are highly interrelated in children and adolescents. Half of our nation's youth are at least at moderate risk as a consequence of engaging in two or more risk behaviors. And one American youth in every ten is at very high risk as a consequence of "doing it all," of engaging in behaviors associated with every category of risk behavior.

To illustrate some of the instances of adolescents' engagement in these risk behaviors, we note that adolescents commit a disproportionately large share of the crime in the United States and are also victims of an especially large share of the crimes committed. For instance, youth, aged 13 to 21 years, accounted for 35.5 percent of all nontraffic related arrests in the United States during the mid-1980s, although this age group represented only 14.3 percent of the population during this period (Kennedy, 1991).

Juvenile delinquency is defined as the violation of a law committed by a person prior to his or her eighteenth birthday, a violation that would have been a crime if committed by an adult. In turn, a *status offense* is a violation of the law that involves a behavior that would not have been illegal if engaged in by an adult. Some of the problems of adolescence that are classified as delinquent because, for instance, they involve a status offense, really signify more of an issue of poor social relationships than of criminality. For example, running away from home technically is considered a delinquent act, but it is really more than that. Between 750,000 and one million American adolescents run away from home each year (Adams, 1991). Home environments that involve rejection, neglect, disinterest, hostile control, parent–child conflict, inadequate supervision, and lack of family organization are associated with adolescents' running away (Adams, 1991). Thus, running away is a sign of a youth's inability to tolerate the social setting in which he or she resides. Leaving home may also be a way of telling parents

that the home situation has become seriously negative, or it may be a way of indicating that one needs and wants help.

Other problematic behaviors also remain on the borderlines between status offenses, social relationship issues, and actual illegality. Problems of teenage sexuality—unsafe sex, pregnancy, and childbearing—pertain both to status offenses and social relationships. In turn, issues of tobacco, alcohol, and drug use cross the borderlines between status offenses and illegality.

In regard to teenage sexuality, adolescents are not contraceptively protected when they begin sexual activity, and a large proportion are inadequately protected throughout adolescence. To illustrate, about two-thirds of sexually active American adolescent females either use no contraceptives at all or use only nonbarrier methods, such as withdrawal (Boyer & Hein, 1991). As a result of such practices, there are hundreds of thousands of cases of *sexually transmitted diseases* (STDs) and of pregnancies among adolescents each year in the United States.

Individuals aged between 15 and 19 years account for 25 percent of the STD cases reported annually (Boyer & Hein, 1991). Some instances of STDs may be life threatening, if not lethal. For instance, as of 1990, although adolescents 13 to 19 years of age accounted for only 1 percent of the cases of AIDS in the United States, current data indicate that this rate is doubling each year (Boyer & Hein, 1991). Moreover, among adolescents considered at risk for sexually transmitted diseases, for example, adolescent runaways or youth attending an STD clinic, positive results of serum tests for the AIDS virus (i.e., the HIV virus) were 6.4 percent and 2.2 percent, respectively (Rotheram-Borus & Koopman, 1991).

In regard to pregnancy, adolescent females who become pregnant have four options: They may marry, have an abortion, give birth to the child (as a single mother) and keep him or her, or give birth to the child and give it up for adoption. Between 1960 and 1975 the number of births to American adolescent mothers increased by 50 percent (Coates & Van Widenfelt, 1991). Today, about 1 million American adolescents a year (about 11% of the adolescent population) become pregnant, and about 9 percent of these youth will have at least one live birth (Coates & Van Widenfelt, 1991). By the age of 18 years, 25 percent of American females have been pregnant at least once. In 1987 almost 500,000 babies were born to adolescents while, in turn, about 44 percent of pregnant adolescents opted to have an abortion. Of the adolescents who became mothers during 1987, about two-thirds were unmarried (Coates & Van Widenfelt, 1991). About 40,000 babies are born each year in the United States to unwed mothers less than 15 years of age.

There are racial differences among adolescents in pregnancy and birth rates (Jenkins & Westney, 1991). Among unwed African American females, aged 15 to 19, the pregnancy rate in the United States in the mid-1980s was 86.4 per 1,000; the corresponding rate for European American unwed females of this age group was only 18.5 per 1,000 (Taylor-Gibbs, 1991). During this period the birth rate for African American adolescents was 18.6 percent, whereas the corresponding rate for European-American adolescents was 9.3 percent (Coates & Van Widenfelt, 1991).

Of course, adolescent males are involved in pregnancy and childbirth. Between 30 to 40 percent of adolescent mothers have been impregnated by males who have not yet reached their twentieth birthday (Elster, 1991). About 15 percent of all African American males have, by age 19 years, fathered a child; corresponding rates among similarly aged Latino and European American males are 11 percent and 6.5 percent, respectively (Elster, 1991).

In regard to drugs, illicit use has been decreasing among American youth. At the end of the 1970s, 60 percent of high school seniors reported having used marijuana; by the end of the 1980s the corresponding percentage was 44 percent (Kandel, 1991). However, 51 percent of American high school seniors have tried at least one illicit drug (Kandel, 1991). Moreover, almost all American high school seniors—92 percent—report some experience with alcohol (Rauch & Huba, 1991), and 19 percent of the group report smoking cigarettes daily (Rauch & Huba, 1991). However, 66 percent have had at least some experience with cigarettes (Kandel, 1991).

Tobacco, alcohol, and drug use is initiated in early adolescence (Perry, 1991). Parents and teachers may model such behaviors to adolescents. If parents or teachers smoke, the probability of an adolescent doing so is increased significantly (Perry, 1991). Moreover, many "early users" of tobacco, alcohol, and drugs eventually develop habits of regular use. For example, 10 percent of American sixth graders have initiated alcohol use (Johnston, O'Mally, & Bachman, 1989). In turn, by the end of high school more than one-third of seniors report that they use alcohol at least daily (Johnston et al., 1989).

Thus, there is a high proportion of adolescents for whom early use leads to continued adult use. Nevertheless, for many adolescents there is only brief experimentation with such substances. Indeed, most adolescents recognize the dangers of drug, alcohol, and tobacco use, and it is still the case that for most youth problems of addiction do not arise.

Unfortunately, as noted above, given the proportion of adolescents who are involved in this and other risk behaviors, and the absolute number of youth that these proportions involve, we may not be sanguine about this conclusion. Moreover, temporal trends in adolescents' involvement in risk behaviors exacerbates the nature of the crisis confronting youth.

Temporal Trends in the Risk Behaviors Engaged in by American Youth

The above-noted data regarding the prevalence of risk behaviors indicate that the current status of American youth is exceedingly problematic. Indeed, these data suggest that nothing short of a "generational time bomb" (Lerner, 1993a) is confronting American society. With so many of our nation's youth beset with so many instances of behavioral risk, America is on the verge of shortly losing much of its next generation, that is, the human capital upon which the future of our nation relies (Hamburg, 1992; Lerner, 1993a, 1993b). Moreover, the "fuse" on the time bomb appears to be growing appreciably shorter: Several sources of data indicate that many of the key problems of American youth are increasing at relatively rapid rates.

For instance, information from the 1993 *Kids Count Data Book,* published by the Center for the Study of Social Policy, indicates that between 1985 and 1992 many of the above-noted problems of children and youth grew substantially worse. For instance, the rate of violent deaths of 15 to 19 year olds increased by 13 percent; whereas for European American youth this increased rate was 10 percent, for African American 15- to 19-year-olds it was 78 percent. In addition, the percentage of youth graduating from high school decreased by 4 percent; the percentage of all births that were to single teenagers increased by 16 percent (and involved a 26 percent increase among European American youth and no increase among African American teenagers); the arrest rate among 10- to 17-year-olds increased by 48 percent (with European Americans increasing by 58 percent and African Americans by 29 percent); and the number of children in single parent families increased by 9 percent (with the corresponding rates for European American and for African American children increasing by 9 percent and by 6 percent, respectively).

These latter changes in family structure are associated with both poverty and with the interrelation of risk behaviors among children and adolescents. Indeed, youth poverty exacerbates the risk behaviors of adolescents, and poverty is a growing problem for America's youth (Lerner, 1993a). By the end of the 1980s approximately 20 percent of America's children and adolescents were poor (Huston, 1991).

As a means to summarize the costs—not only to youth but to all of America as well—of pervasive youth poverty, we note Hamburg's (1992) view:

> Not only are many more children growing up in poverty than was the case a decade or two ago, but many more are mired in persistent, intractable poverty with no realistic hope of escape. They are profoundly lacking in constructively oriented social-support networks to promote their

education and health. They have very few models of competence. They are bereft of visible economic opportunity. The fate of these young people is not merely a tragedy for them, but for the entire nation: A growing fraction of our potential work force consists of seriously disadvantaged people who will have little if any prospect of acquiring the necessary competence to revitalize the economy. If we cannot bring ourselves to feel compassion for these young people on a personal level, we must at least recognize that our economy and our society will suffer along with them. Their loss is our loss. (p. 10)

Addressing the Crisis of America's Youth through an Integrative Theory of Human Development

Given the number of youth that are at such profound levels of risk, we are faced as a society with a crisis so broad that the entire fabric of American society is in serious jeopardy (Hamburg, 1992; Lerner, 1995). Simply, America is wasting its most precious resource—the human capital represented by its youth (Hamburg, 1992; Lerner, 1993a, 1993b, 1995; Lerner & Miller, 1993). And this destruction of human capital is a problem that cuts across race, ethnicity, gender, and rural or urban environments (Center for the Study of Social Policy, 1992, 1993; Simons et al., 1991). Accordingly, all Americans, including all of our children and adolescents, are now and for the foreseeable future confronted by this crisis of youth development. Of course, the pervasiveness of this crisis does not diminish the need to prioritize our efforts. In fact, results of evaluation studies of preventive interventions indicate that great success can occur with programs directed to youth and families most in need (Dryfoos, 1990, 1994, 1995; Hamburg, 1992; Schorr, 1988). Nevertheless, the breadth of the problems affecting our nation's youth requires that we see the issues we face as pertaining to all of us and not to only a segment or a subgroup of America.

Yet, despite the magnitude of this crisis confronting all the youth of our nation, it is still the case that the preponderant majority of child and adolescent development research does not focus on the behavioral risks confronting the diverse youth of America; as a consequence, there are also relatively few developmental studies of youth poverty and its sequelae. In fact, most studies published in the leading scientific journals in child development focus on investigations of European American, middle-class children (Fisher & Brennan, 1992; Graham, 1992). Moreover, most of these studies appraise children in laboratory settings, as compared to "real-life" (i.e., ecologically valid; Bronfenbrenner, 1977, 1979) ones and do not address topics that are relevant to developing, delivering, or sustaining programs preventing either risk be-

haviors and/or the sequelae of persistent and pervasive poverty (Fisher & Brennan, 1992; Graham, 1992; McKinney et al., 1994; McLoyd, 1994).

As such, there is a considerable substantive distance between the work of many of America's child and adolescent developmentalists and the problems facing the youth of America (Graham, 1992; McLoyd, 1994). A similar gap exists between, on the one hand, those who seek to develop policies and programs that will help youth lead better lives within their families and communities and, on the other, the scientists who can provide the intellectual base upon which to build these endeavors.

A theory of human development called *developmental contextualism* (Lerner, 1986, 1991, 1995; Lerner & Kauffman, 1985; Lerner & Miller, 1993; Miller & Lerner, 1994) embeds the study of children in the actual families, neighborhoods, and communities within which they live their lives. Moreover, the model—when fully implemented—synthesizes research with policy and program design, delivery, and evaluation and involves both multiprofessional collaboration and full partnership with the communities within which science and service are being conducted (Lerner & Miller, 1993). In other words, the people that science is intended to serve are full collaborators in the process of research and outreach.

This theory may be of use in narrowing the above-noted gaps between research and the practical needs of our nation's diverse youth and families. As such, we first provide some background to this perspective, and then describe the model's synthetic approach to research and application.

DEVELOPMENTAL CONTEXTUALISM: AN OVERVIEW

Termed *developmental contextualism*, the theoretical perspective we employ views the basic process of human development as involving changing *relations* between developing individuals and their complex (i.e., multilevel) context. Because the contextual levels within which human development occurs are integrated, or "fused" (Tobach & Greenberg, 1984), and include history (Elder, 1980; Tobach, 1981), both the context of humans and person–context relations involve temporality (Dixon & Lerner, 1992).

Thus, in developmental contextualism the development of youth is seen as occurring in relation to the specific features of their actual, "ecologically valid" context, that is, their specific family, neighborhood, society, culture, physical environments, and even the particular point in history within which they live (Lerner, 1986, 1991, 1992, 1994, 1995; McKinney et al., 1994). Moreover, because developmental contextualism sees human development as occurring within a systematically changing and complex (multilevel) system (Ford & Lerner, 1992), youth as much influence their contexts—for example, adolescents as much affect their parents—as their contexts (their parents) influence them (Lerner, 1982; Lerner & Busch-Rossnagel, 1981).

Developmental contextualism leads, then, to descriptions of both the problems and the potentials for healthy development that are associated with these bidirectional relationships between youth and their contexts (Lerner, 1994). Moreover, to explain development one must also turn to the system of relations between youth and their contexts. And to test these explanations, one must change something about the actual context within which youth live. These changes constitute both "experimental" manipulations designed to test theoretical ideas about the variables that influence the course of human development *and* interventions aimed at changing for the better the life paths of children and youth (Lerner, 1995; Lerner & Miller, 1993). Depending on the level of organization involved in these contextual manipulations/interventions, we can label them as either policies or programs (Lerner, Miller et al., 1994).

Thus, when we evaluate the efficacy of these interventions, we are learning something about the adequacy of particular policies and programs to bring about desired changes among adolescents *and* we are learning something very basic about how human development occurs through changing relations between the developing person and his or her actual context (Lerner, 1991, 1994, 1995). In other words, within developmental contextualism there is a synthesis of "basic" theory-testing research and "applied" scholarship (or "outreach") associated with program and policy design, delivery, and evaluation (Lerner, 1995; Lerner & Miller, 1993). Building on the seminal work of Dryfoos (1990, 1994), Schorr (1988), and Hamburg (1992), we use developmental contextualism to discuss both the features of successful prevention and development-enhancing programs for youth and the principles that seem to be key in the design and implementation of such programs.

USING DEVELOPMENTAL CONTEXTUALISM AS A FRAMEWORK FOR PREVENTIVE AND ENHANCEMENT INTERVENTIONS

Dryfoos (1990) has discussed the contrasting sets of individual and contextual factors that are associated with the actualization of risk behaviors in adolescence—that is, with substance use and abuse; with unsafe sex, adolescent pregnancy, and childbearing; with school failure and dropping out; and with crime and delinquency—*or* with the prevention of these risk behaviors, respectively. Dryfoos finds that there are six common characteristics that are involved in the occurrence of one or more of these risk behaviors during adolescence. She identifies three individual and three contextual factors:

1. *Age.* The earlier the initiation of any of the risk behaviors of adolescence, the more likely it is that the youth will engage in the behavior to a great extent and that he or she will suffer negative consequences.

2. *Expectations for education and school grades.* All risk behaviors are associated with the adolescent's sense of self, especially insofar as self-perceived academic competence is concerned. Youth who do not expect to do well in school, and who in fact do not do well, are at risk for all the problem behaviors studied by Dryfoos (1990).

3. *General behavior.* Inappropriate behaviors and inadequate conduct (e.g., acting out, truancy, and conduct disorders) are related to the appearance of risk behaviors.

4. *Peer influences.* As noted by Stattin and Magnusson (1990), an individual's likelihood of engaging in problem behaviors is not due just to individual factors (such as early pubertal maturation). Contextual factors, for instance, the nature of the peer group within which the youth is embedded, also are involved. Similarly, Dryfoos (1990) found that having peers who engage in risk behaviors and having a low resistance to joining the peers in risk behaviors contribute to the adolescent showing such risk behaviors as well.

5. *Parental influences.* Particular styles of parenting, that is, authoritarian or permissive styles, as compared to an authoritative one (Baumrind, 1971), place a youth at risk for problem behaviors. Similarly, if parents do not monitor their children, or do not supervise, guide, or communicate with them effectively, there is a strong likelihood that an at-risk status will be actualized. In addition, if adolescents are not positively affectively tied to their parents, ties that have been noted as being *normative* during this period (e.g., Douvan & Adelson, 1966), risk behaviors are also likely to occur.

6. *Neighborhood influences.* The community context also plays a role in the actualization of risk. A neighborhood characterized by poverty, or by urban, high-density living, is involved with risk actualization. Not surprisingly, race and minority status are also associated with higher likelihoods of risk behaviors, since particular groups (African Americans and Latinos) are likely to be the people living in such communities in the United States.

Thus, in accordance with developmental contextualism, there are multiple features of person and context that should be combined to design and deliver a successful program to prevent the actualization of risk in adolescence. Key principles involved more specifically in the design of such programs are presented next.

Key Principles for the Design of Successful Prevention Programs

Development in relation to the system of person–context relations as depicted within the framework of developmental contextualism provides the basis of both the genesis of problems of adolescence *and* of pathways resilient to the occurrence of these problems. Thus, this developmental system has to be engaged in any comprehensive solution to the problems of youth development (Ford & Lerner, 1992; Lerner, 1994). As such, and as Dryfoos (1990) points out, *there is no one solution to a problem of adolescence.* The developmental system may be, and for comprehensive and integrated solutions, must be, engaged at any of the levels of organization represented in the developmental contextual view of human development, that is, levels ranging from the biological/ physiological, through the psychological, interpersonal/ familial, social network/community, and institutional/societal, to the cultural, physical ecological, and historical (Lerner, 1986, 1991, 1994). Thus, for any particular problem of youth behavior and development, for example, for youth violence, solutions may be sought by, for instance, entering the system at the level of the individual, of his or her family, of the community, or of the societal–cultural context (e.g., through working to affect social policies) (Mincy, 1994; Pittman & Zeldin, 1994).

A second reason why it is important to recognize the potential for multiple solutions to a problem is that *high-risk behaviors are interrelated.* As noted by Dryfoos (1990), 10 percent of all 10- to 17-year-olds in America engage in behaviors associated with all four major categories of high-risk behaviors (i.e., unsafe sex, school failure, substance abuse, and delinquency and crime).

The interrelation, and systemic bases, of high-risk behaviors means, then, that no one type of program is likely to be of sufficient scope to adequately address all the interconnected facets of a problem. Instead, as Dryfoos (1990) notes, *a package of services is needed within each community.* However, because of the systemic interconnections of the problems this package is to address, program comprehensiveness, in and of itself, will not be adequate. Rather, an integration of services is required.

Moreover, because of the systemic nature of the problems of children and youth, the integrated services that are provided to address these problems should be directed at this system and not solely at the individuals within it. In other words, the relations—among individuals, institutions, and

levels of the context—provide both the bases of, and potential sources of change in, the problems of youth. As such, *interventions should be aimed at changing the developmental system, within which people are embedded, rather than at changing individuals* (Dryfoos, 1990).

Moreover, because of the systemic nature of youth problems and of their potential solutions, *the timing of interventions is critical* (Dryfoos, 1990; Lerner, 1984). That is, across life the developmental system not only becomes more organized, but this organization involves, in a sense, over-organization; in other words, redundant, as well as alternative, portions of the system function to support developmental functioning (Hebb, 1949; Schneirla, 1957; see Chapter 1). For example, problem behaviors in adolescence may involve emotional shortcomings on the part of a youth (e.g., low self-esteem) *and* poor childrearing skills on the part of his or her parents *and* negative appraisals about, and loss of hope for, the youth by school personnel *and* a peer group that promotes norm-breaking or even illegal behavior. Each part of this system may reinforce, support, or maintain the adolescent's problem behaviors. Accordingly, problems of behavior and development, once embedded in this redundantly organized system, are more difficult to alter than is the case if the same problems were embedded in the system at an earlier portion of its development (Clarke & Clarke, 1976; Ford & Lerner, 1992; Lerner, 1984).

It is the case that the developmental system remains open to intervention across the life span of individuals; that is, there is relative "plasticity" in human behavior and development through life (Lerner, 1984). Nevertheless, the above-noted developmental changes that occur in the organization of a system over the course of life mean that to effect a given change in behavior or development, those interventions occurring later in life require greater effort and require involvement of greater portions of the system than is the case in earlier potions of the life span (Baltes & Baltes, 1980; Clarke & Clarke, 1976; Ford & Lerner, 1992; Lerner, 1984).

Accordingly, preventive interventions are more economical—in terms of time, scope, and other resources—than are ameliorative interventions. An excellent illustration of this point is provided by Hamburg (1992). Young, pregnant adolescents have a higher probability than do postadolescent females of giving birth to a high-risk baby, for example, a low-birth-weight and/or premature baby. Hamburg (1992) notes that the total cost of good prenatal care for a pregnant adolescent would be much less than $1,000. However, the intensive care that would be needed to keep a low-birth-weight or premature baby alive would be at least $1,000 a day for many weeks or months. Often, the initial hospital cost of such care is $400,000 (Hamburg, 1992). Thus, preventive prenatal care for pregnant adolescents would not only save a lot of money but would eliminate also the sequelae of emotional, behavioral, social, and physical problems—for both mother and infant—associated with the birth of a high-risk baby. Yet most pregnant adolescents, especially those under 15 years of age, receive either no prenatal care or inadequate degrees of care (Hamburg, 1992). Moreover, about 50 percent of pregnant adolescent African Americans do not receive prenatal care or they receive care only in the last 3 months of pregnancy (Hamburg, 1992). Furthermore, poor, inner city, and isolated rural youth are among those most likely to have no or inadequate prenatal care (Hamburg, 1992).

Thus, as illustrated by the information Hamburg (1992) presents about the economic and human benefits of preventing high-risk births through prenatal care, preventive interventions—although insufficiently used—seem most efficacious in the promotion of healthy youth and family development. That is, although the relative plasticity of human behavior and development across the life span means that there is always some probability that the intervention can be successful, the nature of the developmental system indicates that prevention has the best likelihood of effecting desired changes.

Of course, a system that remains open to changes for the better also remains open to changes for the worse. Accordingly, "one shot" interventions into human behavior and development are unlikely to effect enduring changes. Instead, interventions must be designed to be longitudinal in scope (Lerner & Ryff, 1978) or, as both Dryfoos (1990) and Hamburg (1992) note, continuity of programming must be maintained across development. Programs, conceived of as life-span "convoys of social support" (Kahn & Antonucci, 1980), should be implemented to protect and enhance the positive effects of preventive interventions.

Clearly such continuity of effort is expensive. However, a commitment to life span programming must be coupled with a commitment to discontinue programs that have proven to be ineffective (Dryfoos, 1990). Accountability is a necessary feature of professionally responsible, ethical, and humane programs (cf. Hamburg, 1992). Of course, making decisions about continuing or discontinuing programs requires that appropriate evaluation information exists. Moreover, such decisions should also mean that the community involved in choices about youth programs—a community that, we believe, must include youth themselves—has the vision, commitment, and political will and ability to pursue only those actions that, based on community values and evaluation evidence, will promote positive youth development.

SUMMARY AND CONCLUSIONS

The "glass" of adolescence is both half-full and half-empty. The moderate or greater levels of risk—of engaging in un-healthy, unproductive, and even life-threatening behaviors—confronting at least half of our nation's youth, arise because of an unfortunate confluence of sets of individual and contextual factors. In turn, however, individual and contextual levels may be used integratively to design and deliver programs preventing risk actualization among adolescents.

Adolescence is, then, a double-edged sword. It is a period during which myriad social problems may exist. Yet the scientific evidence indicates that individual differences are prominent throughout adolescence, and conditions either exist or can be created to allow most youth to pass through this period with few, if any, devastating scars. There is great resiliency among youth (Werner & Smith, 1982), and for most adolescents the period is or can be one of favorable physical and mental health. Most youth can successfully meet the challenges of this transition period; they can integrate in a coherent way the biological, cognitive, emotional, and social changes they are experiencing, and they can form a useful (if sometimes provisional) self-definition. This sense of self, or identity, will allow youth to make decisions and commitments—first to educational paths and then to careers and to other people. These decisions and commitments can eventuate in the adoption of social roles (e.g., worker, spouse, and parent) that will keep society moving forward effectively into the future.

One may conclude that, insofar as one limits one's generalizations to the samples studied within the contemporary scientific literature, youth have or can be given the personal, emotional, and social context resources necessary to meet successfully the biological, psychological, and social challenges of this period of life. They can leave the period of adolescence with a developmentally new, but nevertheless useful, sense of themselves. Parents, educators, health care professionals, and other caregivers can be confident, then, that if a social context attuned to the developmental changes and individuality of youth is present, healthy and successful people will emerge from the period of adolescence.

Ultimately, we must all continue to educate ourselves about the best means available to promote enhanced life chances among *all* of our youth, but especially those whose potentials for positive contributions to our nation are most in danger of being wasted (Lerner, 1993a, 1995). The collaborative expertise of the "research" and "application" communities can provide much of this information, especially if it is obtained in partnership with strong, empowered communities. Policies promoting such coalitions will be an integral component of a national youth development policy aimed at creating caring communities that have the capacity to nurture the healthy development of our children and youth.

There is no time to lose in the development of such policies. America as we know it—and, even more, as we believe it can be—will be lost unless we act now. All the strengths and assets of our universities, of all of our institutions, and of all of our people must be marshaled for this effort.

The agenda is clear and the means to achieve it appear available. We need only the will. And this motivation will be able to be readily evoked when Americans recognize the validity of the point made by Marian Wright Edelman (1992), president of the Children's Defense Fund, that:

> in the waning years of the twentieth century, doing what is right for children and doing what is necessary to save our national economic skin have converged (p. 93).

Let us work together to save our save our youth, to save our families and communities, and—superordinately—to save America.

REFERENCES

Adams, G. R. (1991). Runaways, negative consequences for. In R. M. Lerner, A. C. Petersen, & J. Brooks-Gunn (Eds.), *Encyclopedia of adolescence* (pp. 947–950). New York: Garland.

Baltes, P. B., & Baltes, M. M. (1980). Plasticity and variability in psychological aging: Methodological and theoretical issues. In G. E. Gurski (Ed.), *Determining the effects of aging on the central nervous system* (pp. 41–66). Berlin, Germany: Schering.

Baumrind, D. (1971). Current patterns of parental authority. *Developmental Psychology Monographs, 4* (1, Pt. 2).

Boyer, C. B., & Hein, K. (1991). Sexually transmitted diseases in adolescence. In R. M. Lerner, A. C. Petersen, & J. Brooks-Gunn (Eds.), *Encyclopedia of adolescence* (pp. 1028–1041). New York: Garland.

Bronfenbrenner, U. (1977). Toward an experimental ecology of human development. *American Psychologist, 32,* 513–531.

Bronfenbrenner, U. (1979). *The ecology of human development.* Cambridge, MA: Harvard University Press.

Brookins, G. K. (1991). Socialization of African-American adolescents. In R. M. Lerner, A. C. Petersen, & J. Brooks-Gunn (Eds.), *Encyclopedia of adolescence* (pp. 1072–1076). New York: Garland.

Brooks-Gunn, J., & Petersen, A. C. (1983). *Girls at puberty: Biological and psychosocial perspectives.* New York: Plenum Press.

Chess, S., & Thomas, A. (1984). *The origins and evolution of behavior disorders: Infancy to early adult life.* New York: Brunner/Mazel.

Clarke, A. M., & Clarke, A. D. B. (Eds.). (1976). *Early experience: Myth and evidence.* New York: Free Press.

Coates, D. L., & Van Widenfelt, B. (1991). Pregnancy in adolescence. In R. M. Lerner, A. C. Petersen, & J. Brooks-Gunn (Eds.), *Encyclopedia of adolescence* (pp. 794–802). New York: Garland.

Dixon, R. A., & Lerner, R. M. (1992). A history of systems in developmental psychology. In M. H. Bornstein & M. E. Lamb (Eds.), *Developmental psychology: An advanced textbook* (3rd ed., pp. 3–58). Hillsdale, NJ: Erlbaum.

Douvan, E., & Adelson, J. (1966). *The adolescent experience.* New York: Wiley.

Dryfoos, J. G. (1990). *Adolescents at risk: Prevalence and prevention.* New York: Oxford University Press.

Dryfoos, J. G. (1994). *Full service schools: A revolution in health and social services for children, youth and families.* San Francisco: Jossey-Bass.

Dryfoos, J. G. (1995). Full service schools: Revolution or fad? *Journal of Research on Adolescence, 5,* 147–172.

Edelman, M. W. (1992). *The measure of our success: A letter to my children and yours.* Boston: Beacon Press.

Elder, G. H., Jr. (1980). Adolescence in historical perspective. In J. Adelson (Ed.), *Handbook of adolescent psychology* (pp. 3–46). New York: Wiley.

Elster, A. B. (1991). Fathers, teenage. In R. M. Lerner, A. C. Petersen, & J. Brooks-Gunn (Eds.), *Encyclopedia of adolescence* (pp. 360–364). New York: Garland.

Feldman, S., & Elliott, G. (Eds.). (1990). *At the threshold: The developing adolescent.* Cambridge, MA: Harvard University Press.

Finkelstein, J. W. (1993). Familial influences on adolescent health. In R. M. Lerner (Ed.), *Early adolescence: Perspectives on research, policy and intervention* (pp. 111–126). Hillsdale, NJ: Erlbaum.

Fisher, C. B., & Brennan, M. (1992). Application and ethics in developmental psychology. In D. L. Featherman, R. M. Lerner, & M. Perlmutter (Eds.), *Life-span development and behavior* (Vol. 2, pp. 189–219). Hillsdale, NJ: Erlbaum.

Fisher, C. B., & Lerner, R. M. (1994). Foundations of applied developmental psychology. In C. B. Fisher & R. M. Lerner (Eds.), *Applied developmental psychology* (pp. 3–20). New York: McGraw-Hill.

Fisher, C. B., Murray, J. P., Dill, J. R., Hagen, J. W., Hogan, M. J., Lerner, R. M., Rebok, G. W., Sigel, I., Sostek, A. M., Smyer, M. A., Spencer, M. B., & Wilcox, B. (1993). The national conference on graduate education in the applications of developmental science across the life span. *Journal of Applied Developmental Psychology, 14,* 1–10.

Ford, D. L., & Lerner, R. M. (1992). *Developmental systems theory: An integrative approach.* Newbury Park, CA: Sage.

Gottlieb, G. (1992). *Individual development and evolution: The genesis of novel behavior.* New York: Oxford.

Graber, J. A., & Petersen, A. C. (1991). Cognitive changes at adolescence: Biological perspectives. In K. R. Gibson & A. C. Petersen (Eds.), *Brain maturation and cognitive development: Comparative and cross-cultural perspectives* (pp. 253–279). New York: Aldine de Gruyter.

Graham, S. (1992). "Most of the subjects were white and middle class": Trends in published research on African Americans in selected APA journals, 1970–1989. *American Psychologist, 5,* 629–639.

Guerney, L., & Arthur, J. (1984). Adolescent social relationships. In R. M. Lerner & N. L. Galambos (Eds.), *Experiencing adolescence: A sourcebook for parents, teachers, and teens* (pp. 87–118). New York: Garland.

Hamburg, D. A. (1992). *Today's children: Creating a future for a generation in crisis.* New York: Time Books.

Hebb, D. O. (1949). *The organization of behavior.* New York: Wiley.

Huston, A. C. (Ed.). (1991). *Children in poverty: Child development and public policy.* Cambridge, England: Cambridge University Press.

Huston, A. C., McLoyd, V. C., & Coll, C. G. (1994). Children and poverty: Issues in contemporary research. *Child Development, 65,* 275–282.

Jenkins, R. R., & Westney, O. E. (1991). Sexual behavior in black adolescents, imitation of. In R. M. Lerner, A. C. Petersen, & J. Brooks-Gunn (Eds.), *Encyclopedia of adolescence* (pp. 262–267). New York: Garland.

Johnston, L. D., O'Mally, P. M., & Bachman, J. G. (1989). *Drug use, drinking, and smoking: National survey results from high school, college, and young adult populations.* Rockville, MD: U.S. Department of Health.

Kahn, R. L., & Antonucci, T. C. (1980). Convoys over the life course: Attachment, roles, and social support. In P. B. Baltes & O. G. Brim, Jr. (Eds.), *Life-span development and behavior* (Vol. 3). Hillsdale, NJ: Erlbaum.

Kandel, D. (1991). Drug use, epidemiology and developmental stages of involvement. In R. M. Lerner, A. C. Petersen, & J. Brooks-Gunn (Eds.), *Encyclopedia of adolescence* (pp. 262–267). New York: Garland.

Kennedy, R. E. (1991). Delinquency. In R. M. Lerner, A. C. Petersen, & J. Brooks-Gunn (Eds.), *Encyclopedia of adolescence* (pp. 199–206). New York: Garland.

Lerner, J. V., & Lerner, R. M. (1983). Temperament and adaptation across life: Theoretical and empirical issues. In P. B. Baltes & O. G. Brim, Jr. (Eds.), *Life-span development and behavior* (Vol. 5, pp. 197–230). New York: Academic Press.

Lerner, R. M. (1982). Children and adolescents as producers of their own development. *Developmental Review, 2,* 342–370.

Lerner, R. M. (1984). *On the nature of human plasticity.* New York: Cambridge University Press.

Lerner, R. M. (1986). *Concepts and theories of human development* (2nd ed.). New York: Random House.

Lerner, R. M. (1987). A life-span perspective for early adolescence. In R. M. Lerner & T. T. Foch (Eds.), *Biological-psychosocial interactions in early adolescence* (pp. 9–34). Hillsdale, NJ: Erlbaum.

Lerner, R. M. (1988). Early adolescent transitions: The lore and laws of adolescence. In M. D. Levine & E. R. McArarney (Eds.), *Early adolescent transitions* (pp. 1–21). Lexington, MA: D. C. Heath.

Lerner, R. M. (1989). Developmental contextualism and the life-span view of person-context interaction. In M. Bornstein & J. S. Bruner (Eds.), *Interaction in human development* (pp. 217–239). Hillsdale, NJ: Erlbaum.

Lerner, R. M. (1991). Changing organism-context relations as the basic process of development: A developmental-contextual perspective. *Developmental Psychology, 27,* 27–32.

Lerner, R. M. (1992). *Final solutions: Biology, prejudice, and genocide.* University Park: Penn State Press.

Lerner, R. M. (1993a). Investment in youth: The role of home economics in enhancing the life chances of America's children. *AHEA Monograph Series, 1,* 5–34.

Lerner, R. M. (1993b). Early adolescence: Toward an agenda for the integration of research, policy, and intervention. In R. M. Lerner (Ed.), *Early adolescence: Perspectives on research, policy, and intervention* (pp. 1–13). Hillsdale, NJ: Erlbaum.

Lerner, R. M. (1994). Schools and adolescents. In P. C. McKenry & S. M. Gavazzi (Eds.), *Visions 2010: Families and adolescents* (pp. 14–15, 42–43). Minneapolis, MN: National Council on Family Relations.

Lerner, R. M. (1995). *America's youth in crisis: Challenges and options for programs and policies.* Thousand Oaks, CA: Sage.

Lerner, R. M., & Busch-Rossnagel, N. A. (Eds.). (1981). *Individuals as producers of their development: A life-span perspective.* New York: Academic Press.

Lerner, R. M., & Foch, T. T. (Eds.). (1987). *Biological-psychosocial interactions in early adolescence.* Hillsdale, NJ: Erlbaum.

Lerner, R. M., & Kauffman, M. B. (1985). The concept of development in contextualism. *Developmental Review, 5,* 309–333.

Lerner, R. M., & Miller, J. R. (1993). Integrating human development research and intervention for America's children: The Michigan State University model. *Journal of Applied Developmental Psychology, 14,* 347–364.

Lerner, R. M., Petersen, A. C., & Brooks-Gunn J. (Eds.). (1991). *Encyclopedia of adolescence.* New York: Garland.

Lerner, R. M., & Ryff, C. D. (1978). Implementation of the life-span view of human development: The sample case of attachment. In P. B. Baltes (Ed.), *Life-span development and behavior* (pp. 1–44). New York: Academic Press.

Lerner, R. M., & Spanier, G. B. (1980). A dynamic interactional view of child and family development. In R. M. Lerner & G. B. Spanier (Eds.), *Child influences on marital and family interaction: A life-span perspective* (pp. 1–20). New York: Academic Press.

Lerner, R. M., & Villarruel, F. A. (1994). Adolescence. In T. Husen & N. Postlethwaite (Eds.), *International encyclopedia of education* (2nd ed., pp. 83–89). Oxford, England: Pergamon Press.

Magnusson, D. (1988). Individual development from an interactional perspective. In D. Magnusson (Ed.), *Paths through life* (Vol. 1, pp. 3–31). Hillsdale, NJ: Erlbaum.

McKinney, M., Abrams, L. A., Terry, P. A., & Lerner, R. M. (1994). Child development research and the poor children of America: A call for a developmental contextual approach to research and outreach. *Family and Consumer Sciences Research Journal, 23,* 26–42.

McLoyd, V. C. (1994). Research in the service of poor and ethnic/racial minority children: A moral imperative. *Family and Consumer Sciences Research Journal, 23,* 56–66.

Mead, M. (1928). *Coming of age in Samoa: A psychological study of primitive youth for western civilization.* New York: Morrow.

Mead, M. (1930). *Growing up in New Guinea.* New York: Morrow.

Mead, M. (1935). *Sex and temperament in three primitive societies.* New York: Morrow.

Miller, J. R., & Lerner, R. M. (1994). Integrating research and outreach: Developmental contextualism and the human ecological perspective. *Home Economics Forum, 7,* 21–28.

Mincy, R. B. (Ed.). (1994). *Nurturing young black males: Challenges to agencies, programs, and social policy.* Washington, DC: Urban Institute Press.

Offer, D. (1969). *The psychological world of the teen-ager.* New York: Basic Books.

Perry, C. L. (1991). Smoking and drug prevention with early adolescents, programs for. In R. M. Lerner, A. C. Petersen, & J.

Brooks-Gunn (Eds.), *Encyclopedia of adolescence* (pp. 1049–1053). New York: Garland.

Petersen, A. C. (1988). Adolescent development. In M. R. Rosenzweig (Ed.), *Annual review of psychology* (pp. 583–607). Palo Alto, CA: Annual Reviews, Inc.

Petersen, A. C., & Taylor, B. (1980). The biological approach to adolescence: Biological change and psychological adaptation. In J. Adelson (Ed.), *Handbook of adolescent psychology* (pp. 117–155). New York: Wiley.

Pittman, K. J., & Zeldin, S. (1994). From deterrence to development: Shifting the focus of youth programs for African-American males. In R. B. Mincy (Ed.), *Nurturing young black males: Challenges to agencies, programs, and social policy* (pp. 165–186). Washington, DC: Urban Institute Press.

Rauch, J. M., & Huba, G. J. (1991). Drug use, adolescent. In R. M. Lerner, A. C. Petersen, & J. Brooks-Gunn (Eds.), *Encyclopedia of adolescence* (pp. 256–261). New York: Garland.

Reid, P. T. (1991). Black female adolescents, socialization of. In R. M. Lerner, A. C. Petersen, & J. Brooks-Gunn (Eds.), *Encyclopedia of adolescence* (pp. 85–87). New York: Garland.

Rotheram-Borus, M. J., & Koopman, C. (1991). Safer sex and adolescence. In R. M. Lerner, A. C. Petersen, & J. Brooks-Gunn (Eds.), *Encyclopedia of adolescence* (pp. 951–960). New York: Garland.

Schneirla, T. C. (1957). The concept of development in comparative psychology. In D. B. Harris (Ed.), *The concept of development* (pp. 78–108). Minneapolis: University of Minnesota Press.

Schorr, L. B. (1988). *Within our reach: Breaking the cycle of disadvantage.* New York: Doubleday.

Schorr, L. B. (1991). Effective programs for children growing up in concentrated poverty. In A. C. Huston (Ed.), *Children in poverty: Child development and public policy* (pp. 260–281). Cambridge, MA: Cambridge University Press.

Silbereisen, R. (1991). Adolescent behavior in context: Comparative analyses of beliefs, daily contexts, and substance use in West Berlin and Warsaw. In D. L. Featherman, R. M. Lerner, & M. Perlmutter (Eds.), *Life-span development and behavior* (Vol. 11). Hillsdale, NJ: Erlbaum.

Simmons, R. G., & Blyth, D. A. (1987). *Moving into adolescence: The impact of pubertal change and school context.* Hawthorne, NJ: Aldine.

Simons, J. M., Finlay, B., & Yang, A. (1991). *The adolescent and young adult fact book.* Washington, DC: Children's Defense Fund.

Spencer, H. (1990). *The principles of sociobiology.* New York: D. Appleton & Co.

Spencer, M. B. (1991). Identity, minority development of. In R. M. Lerner, A. C. Petersen, & J. Brooks-Gunn (Eds.), *Encyclopedia of adolescence* (pp. 111–130). New York: Garland.

Spencer, M. B., & Dornbusch, S. (1990). Challenges in studying minority adolescents. In S. Feldman & G. Elliott (Eds.), *At the threshold: The developing adolescent.* Cambridge, MA: Harvard University Press.

Spencer, M. B., & Markstrom-Adams, C. (1990). Identity process among racial and ethnic minority children in America. *Child Development, 61,* 290–310.

Stattin, H., & Magnusson, D. (1990). *Pubertal maturation in female development.* Hillsdale, NJ: Erlbaum.

Tanner, J. (1991). Menarche, secular trend in age of. In R. M. Lerner, A. C. Petersen, & J. Brooks-Gunn (Eds.), *Encyclopedia of adolescence* (pp. 637–641). New York: Garland.

Taylor-Gibbs, J. (1991). Black adolescents at-risk: Approaches to prevention. In R. M. Lerner, A. C. Petersen, & J. Brooks-Gunn (Eds.), *Encyclopedia of adolescence* (pp. 73–78). New York: Garland.

Tobach, E. (1981). Evolutionary aspects of the activity of the organism and its development. In R. M. Lerner & N. A. Busch-Rossnagel (Eds.), *Individuals as producers of their development: A life-span perspective* (pp. 37–68). New York: Academic Press.

Tobach, E., & Greenberg, G. (1984). The significance of T. C. Schneirla's contribution to the concept of levels of integration. In G. Greenberg & E. Tobach (Eds.), *Behavioral evolution and integrative levels* (pp. 1–7). Hillsdale, NJ: Erlbaum.

Werner, E. E., & Smith, R. S. (1982). *Vulnerable but invincible.* New York: McGraw-Hill.

Whiting, B. B., & Whiting, J. W. M. (1991). Preindustrial world, adolescence in. In R. M. Lerner, A. C. Petersen, & J. Brooks-Gunn (Eds.), *Encyclopedia of adolescence* (pp. 814–829). New York: Garland.

Wilson, W. J. (1987). *The truly disadvantaged: The inner city, the underclass, and public policy.* Chicago: University of Chicago Press.

PART 3

CONTEXTUAL INFLUENCES

No child is an island. For both the good and the bad, no child can grow up untouched or unscathed by his or her surrounding world. There are a multitude of events and a multitude of people (and a multitude of factors associated with these events and people) that the child comes into contact with during the course of his or her development. These interact with one another, as well with other experiences, to lead to diverse outcomes. This notion of diversity in process and outcome is one of the main themes of this book, and this theme is apparent as well in the chapters that are contained in this section.

In accord with this theme, it is helpful to review once again the principles of equifinality and multifinality. Equifinality refers to the notion that in an open system, which is one in which there is maintenance in change, dynamic order of processes, organization, and so forth, the same end state may be reached from different initial conditions and through different processes (Cicchetti & Rogosch, 1996). Multifinality refers to the notion that a particular adverse event should not necessarily be seen as leading to the same outcome in every individual (Cicchetti & Rogosch, 1996).

In this section of the book the concepts of equifinality and multifinality are illustrated by the myriad of *contextual* influences that impact on the child and his or her development. These include the most important people in the child's life (e.g., family members, peers), the most important places (e.g., school), and the most important factors associated with each (i.e., religion, social class, ethnicity, and sexuality). Although these contextual influences are each covered separately in the subsequent chapters for purposes of discussion, these contexts are embedded and mutually interrelated. In keeping with equifinality and multifinality we see from these chapters how various contexts may lead to similar outcomes (equifinality), or how the same context may lead to diverse outcomes (multifinality). In addition to discussing the ways in which each of these contexts influence development and the emergence of child clinical problems, the chapters in this section discuss the ways in which each of these contexts may be "used" for designing effective prevention, intervention, and treatment programs.

The section begins with the primary social context wherein most children are embedded, namely, the family. Using a tripartite model of family influence, Chapter 9 summarizes the literature on family influence and development as it relates to parent–child relationships (with a focus on emotion skills and cognitive representations of social interactions as mediators of social competence), the parent as a teacher of social skills, and the parent as a provider of opportunity for developing social competence. One important area of developmental psychopathology, namely family factors that influence and maintain conduct-disordered behavior, is used for purposes of illustration. Also discussed are the ways in which the family can be targeted in intervention programs through the use of marital therapy, family therapy, parent training in discipline and behavior management, and connections to the community to enhance social support. All in all, this chapter raises issues pertinent to understanding children and families. It provides an important base for the chapters that follow in Part 5 of the book, which is devoted entirely to this most critical of contexts—the family.

Chapter 10 focuses on the place—outside of the home—that is paramount in children's lives, namely, the school setting. The chapter summarizes those key domains of childhood development that play especially important roles in the interaction between child and school. This includes a summary of theory and research on achievement-related constructs, particularly those related to problem-solving abilities and the development of achievement related beliefs. The chapter also summarizes theory and research on the school's influence on socially related constructs, particularly those related to social competence and social skills. Illustrative school-based intervention programs that have been found to be effective in enhancing children's social behaviors also are described. This chapter should be essential reading to anyone who works with children, because it underscores the point that working exclusively in our clinic office or research laboratory is insufficient. That is, the chapter drives home the point that to fully address the needs of children we need to extend our efforts into children's school settings.

Chapter 11 focuses on the peer group, presenting an overview of the developmental literature on children's peer relationships and friendships. This chapter provides many examples of the important role that children's peer relationships and friendships play in children's development and how problems in these areas are linked to problems in other domains. The chapter further shows how many psychosocial intervention strategies emphasize increased direct intervention with children within their peer context through the use of such strategies as the improvement of children's social skills, the reduction of behavior problems that interfere with peer relationships, and the enhancement of peer networks, social contacts, and friendships. The description of how to intervene with children's peer relationships is well worth integrating into everyday clinical practice and well worth considering in future research.

In Chapter 12 the focus is on the context of religion. Unlike the contexts of family, peer group, and school, this is a context that has been rarely studied and written about by researchers and theorists in the child area. What is known is covered in this chapter, with some extrapolation made downwards from the adult literature. Three main issues that are covered include developmental issues in children's religious growth, the role of religion in children's lives, and how religion may be used (and not used) in the clinical treatment of children, including directly intervening with children and working with religious parents. This chapter will undoubtedly make us all aware of a contextual influence that might be either subtle or readily apparent in our work with children and families. This chapter makes clear that the role of religion in children's (and parents') lives oftentimes needs attention, and even oftentimes needs to be embraced, if our work is to be effective. This chapter should serve as an important springboard from which to pursue intriguing clinical and research ideas.

Chapter 13 provides an overview of developmental considerations in the context of social class. Although economic resources have long been recognized as important influences on children's development, only fairly recently have such contextual factors been studied using rigorous experimental procedures. The chapter begins with a discussion of the complexities involved in studying and understanding these contextual factors, first presenting the issues and intricacies involved in defining social class. Next, a review of the research studies that have documented the effects of social class on children's well-being, particularly on child health and developmental and psychological outcomes, is presented. An overview of some of the most promising family, school-based, and community intervention programs for disadvantaged children is presented next, followed by a discussion of the impediments that affect treatment and the outlook for enhanced service delivery to children of disadvantaged social class. All in all, the issues raised in this chapter have important implications, not only because they inform research and practice, but also because they have the potential to inform policy. Within this frame, this chapter is all the more important.

Chapter 14 focuses on the contextual issues involved in working with ethnic minority children, using examples drawn from a research program that has been concerned with the development, implementation, and evaluation of culturally sensitive interventions for Hispanic youth. Based on conceptualizations in the narrative process and rooted in social learning theory principles (i.e., modeling), the chapter summarizes how culturally sensitive narrative therapy for Hispanic youth has been used in light of developmental considerations (i.e., folktale, pictorial, and biography therapeutic modalities). The research and intervention program described in this chapter is of clear importance in multicultural settings, a context that has increasingly become a part of the larger reality of the clinical practitioner and researcher as our society has itself increasingly become more culturally diverse and pluralistic.

In the final chapter, Chapter 15, another contextual influence that also might be either subtle or apparent, but nevertheless, oftentimes requires our attention, is children's sexual orientation. A "differential developmental trajectory" approach is first presented, which emphasizes the diversity among nonheterosexuals in addition to their relevant differences from heterosexuals. Following this, the chapter presents an overview of current theory and research pertinent to understanding the distinctive developmental process of sexual minority youth, highlighting the clinical implications of this work. The material contained in this chapter provides an insightful and up-to-date view of how to think about and how to intervene with sexual minority adolescents and should prove useful to clinicians and researchers.

In summary, the chapters in this section of the book make clear the complexities involved in development and child clinical problems. In addition, as a whole, the chapters demonstrate that in designing effective prevention, intervention, and treatment programs it is necessary to consider the "big picture" and to think about the myriad influences that impact the child and, as necessary, to "use them" to improve children's and families' lives.

REFERENCES

Cicchetti D., & Rogosch, F. A. (1996). Equifinality and multifinality in developmental psychopathology. *Development and Psychopathology, 8,* 597–600.

CHAPTER 9

FAMILY

Lisa Ann Boyum
Ross D. Parke

Families influence children's development across a multitude of domains, including cognitive and academic skills, speech and language, play and behavioral skills, social competence, emotional expressiveness, and morality. Recently, attention has turned to the role of the family in the development of children's psychopathology. The goal of this chapter is to review the recent research examining the relationship between family influences on children's social and emotional development and children's social outcomes with peers, and to demonstrate connections between family factors, social competence, and psychopathology in youth. Social competence is considered to be a marker of healthy psychosocial adjustment, and deficits in social competence and social skills are related to poor developmental outcomes. We have chosen to focus on the familial antecedents and consequences of social competence to provide a basis for comparison between the range of developmental outcomes and clinical indicators. We will be making the assumption that environmental effects on development are best represented as a continuum rather than as a discrete process. If that assumption is correct, then it will be important to look at nonclinical populations to ask what factors produce outcome variations in normal development, and to use those prototypic findings to better understand the processes at work in the development of psychopathology in children and adolescents.

First we review the developmental literature on family influences on social competence, using the three-mode model of family influence articulated by Parke and his colleagues (e.g., Parke, Burks, Carson, Neville, & Boyum, 1994). Next, for illustrative purposes, we examine an area of developmental psychopathology that has been correlated with family factors: specifically family factors that influence and maintain conduct-disordered behavior. Recommendations are made for developmentally based clinical intervention with families. The reader is referred to the chapters contained in the next section for further detailed discussions about how different types of family factors (such as parental depression) may influence the development of children and adolescents, including the development of clinical problems.

Several general assumptions are implicit in the literature that is reviewed and in the conclusions drawn from our review. First, families are conceptualized as a social system and interrelationships among multiple subsystems need to be considered, including the parent–child dyad, the marital relationship, and sibling relationships (e.g., Minuchin, 1985). Second, although family research has traditionally focused on studying the impact of dyadic, face-to-face interactions between family members (e.g., parent–child interactions), recent family research has begun to shift focus to studying the impact of child witnessing of family interactions (e.g., mother-father conflicts) (Cummings & Davies, 1994). Third, families are viewed as being embedded in a set of external social systems, including extended family networks, neighborhoods, schools, and communities, which influence family functioning and children's social adaptation (Bronfenbrenner, 1989). Family management of children's interactions with the larger social and physical environment is viewed as a powerful tool for influencing children's development (Ladd, LeSieur, & Profilet, 1993; Parke & Bhavnagri, 1989). Fourth, a life course view of development suggests that children's development cannot be understood without the recognition of shifts in adult development (Baltes, 1987; Parke, 1988). Fifth, a life course developmental perspective reminds us that different behavioral contexts yield potentially different developmental patterns due to secular changes in family structure (e.g., single parent and stepfamilies), in family–work linkages, in child care, and in governmental policies (e.g., Elder, Modell, & Parke, 1993). Finally, despite the recent emphasis on the role of genetics in the development of psychopathology, it is known that in even the most biologically based disorders (e.g., bipolar affective disorder, schizophrenia), the proportion of the variance accounted for in the expression of these disorders is probably no greater than 50 percent. This leaves a large portion of behavioral expression unexplained and invites a closer look at the environmental contributions to the development of dysfunctional behavior.

A significant way in which families influence children's course of development is by their impact on children's social relationships and social competence. Problematic peer relationships have been identified as signs and symptoms of psychopathology as well as precursors of psychopathology. Children's and adolescents' social skills and social success with peers outside of the home have been shown to relate to cognitive skills and academic performance (Ladd, 1990; Rubin, 1985) and mental health and personal adjustment in childhood, adolescence and early adulthood (Coie, Lochman, Terry, & Hyman, 1992; Ollendick, Weist, Borden, & Greene, 1992; Roff & Wirt, 1984). Problematic peer relationships have been shown to predict to such extreme outcomes as school dropout, criminality, and psychopathology (Parker & Asher, 1987; Rubin & Ross, 1988). Social acceptance and good social skills can therefore be used as a marker of good adjustment and mental health.

Particular interest has been shown in the ways that families influence the acceptance or rejection of children by their peers. Research in the area of social competence has primarily focused on children's development of specific knowledge and behavioral skills (e.g., Asher & Renshaw, 1981; Putallaz, 1987), or on the development of cognitive expectations about social relationships in the context of the family environment (e.g., Pettit, Dodge, & Brown, 1988), and the impact of these developing skills and expectations on children's social competence. Families also facilitate the development of children's social relationships by providing social opportunities and monitoring, supervising, or facilitating the child's interactions with peers (e.g., Bhavnagri & Parke, 1991). In addition, an emerging literature on family emotion skills and emotional expressiveness provides an additional link between family and extrafamilial social systems (e.g., Boyum & Parke, 1995).

Families influence children's social and emotional development through a combination of direct and indirect methods. Direct methods represent deliberate efforts to instruct the child in appropriate behaviors and to impart specific knowledge that it is believed will be useful to the child in extrafamilial social contexts. Direct effects include provision of advice, support or directions, specific strategies, coaching, supervision, and social opportunities. Indirect methods of influence are those that arise out of everyday interactions between the child and the family and may or may not be intended to educate, but that may be seen as ways in which familial styles or patterns of interaction are transmitted. In other words, the parents' goal is not explicitly to modify or enhance the child's relationships with others. Indirect effects include interpersonal interaction styles, childrearing practices, use of emotion cues, and physical expressions of inner experiences. In reality, many situations afford both direct and indirect opportunities for social learning, and it may not always be possible to completely separate the two.

A TRIPARTITE MODEL OF FAMILY INFLUENCE

In the following section, we review the literature on family influences on development as it relates to (1) indirect effects of parent–child relationships, with a focus on emotion skills and cognitive representations of social interactions as mediators of social competence, (2) direct effects of the parent as a teacher of social skills, and (3) direct and indirect effects of the parent as a provider of opportunity for developing social competence.

Parent–Child Social Interactions

During face-to-face interaction in everyday encounters, children learn, rehearse, and refine social skills that are important ingredients of social competence. Studies of parental discipline and parent–child interaction in nondisciplinary contexts provide a clear profile of the connections between parental behavior and children's social adjustment. In this section we review this research as well as examine recent work that may account in part for the links between parent–child interaction and child outcomes.

Specifically, the role of cognitive representations (e.g., attributions, expected consequences) and affect management skills (e.g., encoding/decoding skills, family expressiveness) as mediators between the family context and children's social relationships is examined.

Discipline

Parental disciplinary strategies have been explored in terms of the association with the quality of children's peer relationships. Drawing on previous models of parenting, Maccoby and Martin (1983) classified parenting styles of interaction and discipline along the dimensions of warmth and control. The four parenting styles resulting from the intersection of these two dimensions (i.e., authoritarian, authoritative, indulgent, and indifferent–uninvolved) have been shown to relate to the quality of children's peer relations. Authoritarian and power-assertive styles of parenting tend to be associated with aggression or withdrawal in children's peer interactions (e.g., Patterson, 1982). Lax monitoring of children's activities, a characteristic of indifferent or uninvolved parenting, predicts to delinquent peer activities in children and adolescents (e.g., Dishion, 1990; Patterson & Stouthamer-Loeber, 1984), and possible increased aggression (Attili, 1989). In contrast, authoritative parenting, a combination of warmth and moderate control, is highly associated with children's prosocial behavior (e.g., Attili, 1989) and higher levels of social responsibility and independence (e.g., Baumrind, 1971).

Recent observational studies of parent–child interaction in play or teaching contexts confirm the earlier studies of disciplinary tactics. Parents who are responsive, warm, and engaging are more likely to have socially competent children (Putallaz, 1987). High levels of positive synchrony and low levels of nonsynchrony in patterns of mother–child interactions are related to school adjustment (Harrist, Pettit, Dodge, & Bates, 1994). In contrast, parents who are hostile and overcontrolling have children who experience more difficulty with age-mates (Barth & Parke, 1993; MacDonald & Parke, 1984), in both the preschool period (MacDonald, 1987) and middle childhood (Dishion, 1990).

Mediating Processes

In this section, we consider two sets of processes that are acquired in the course of parent–child interchanges that, in turn, serve as mediators between familial and peer contexts: cognitive representations and affect management skills.

Cognitive Representations

It is assumed that children develop mental representations about social interactions that guide their social behaviors. Within the attachment tradition (Bretherton & Waters, 1985), the notion of the "internal working model" posits that children develop expectations about relationships based upon qualities of the parent–child relationship (such as warmth, predictability, consistency, and responsiveness), seeking out and responding to new individuals and groups in ways that reinforce prior beliefs about relationships. Alternatively, the social interaction tradition (e.g., Baldwin, 1992) has been guided by the assumption that the child develops cognitive maps or scripts through their interactions with parents, which serve as a model for future social interactions.

Parke and O'Neil (1997) suggest that cognitive models of relationships may be transmitted across generations, serving as mediators between the family context and children's social relationships. Links have been established between parent and child cognitions on social relationships and social problem solving. For example, Burks and Parke (1996) found evidence for similarities between children and their mothers, and Spitzer and Parke (1994) for similarities between children and both parents, in their goals, attributions, strategies, and expected consequences when responding to a series of social vignettes. Children nominated as aggressive by their peers were more likely to have mothers who were low in their use of prosocial strategies. Children rated by teachers as high on measures of aggression, avoidance, and being disliked, and low on prosocial behaviors, had fathers who endorsed more confrontational or instrumental problem-solving strategies. Popular children, as rated by their peers, were more likely to have mothers who provided specific, skilled advice. Similarly, children nominated by peers and teachers as less aggressive and more liked had fathers who relied more on relational goals. Rubin, Mills, and Rose-Krasnor (1989) also found links between maternal beliefs and preschool children's problem-solving behavior in the classroom. Mothers who more highly valued social skills, including making friends, sharing, and being leaders, and those who viewed social behavior as more controllable, had children who were more prosocial and more competent social problem solvers.

Several studies provide support for the hypothesis that children of differing social statuses vary in terms of their cognitive models of social relationships. Pettit, Dodge, and Brown (1988) found that mothers' attributional biases concerning their children's behaviors, specifically the extent to which they interpreted an ambiguous provocation as hostile or benign, and their endorsement of aggression as a solution to interpersonal problems, were both related to children's interpersonal problem-solving skills. These skills, in turn, were associated with the children's social competence with school peers. MacKinnon-Lewis and colleagues (1994) found that mother–son hostile attributions were significantly related to the coerciveness of their interactions, and maternal attributions were related to reports of children's aggression in the classroom.

In summary, these studies suggest that cognitive models of relationships may be transmitted across generations and may serve as mediators between family and peer contexts.

Affect Management Skills

The family provides the first setting for learning about affective communication. As the child moves beyond the confines of the family, he or she will encounter others who communicate in ways that differ from those at home. It is to the child's advantage to have a wide repertoire of skills with which to meet the world. The following studies have demonstrated connections between family affective skills and children's social competence with peers.

Encoding/Decoding Skills. Mothers who are good encoders of affect, that is, who accurately produce and communicate affect, have children who are good at decoding, or recognizing, emotional expression. Mothers whose affect is less clearly produced have children who decode less well (Daly, Abramovitch, & Pliner, 1980). Studies by Beitel and Parke (1985) and Field and Walden (1982) both found positive relationships between children's decoding abilities and peer outcomes.

In a posed encoding study by Carson and Parke (1998), no sociometric differences were found in the ability of the mothers to identify their preschool children's expressions. However, videotapes of the children's expressions were later shown to non-family adult raters, and their accuracy in recognition of the children's expressions was found to correlate positively with the child's sociometric status (Carson & Parke, 1998). Children's ability to encode and decode emotional signals, skills related to successful peer interactions, may be at least partially acquired through affect-arousing physical play. Burks and colleagues (1987) found that the length of time spent by parent–child dyads in "play bouts" (defined as time elapsed between initiation and termination of an interaction) correlated positively with children's ability to decode facial expressions of both parents. Length of the play bouts also correlated positively with recognition of the child's posed expressions by nonfamily raters.

Family Emotional Expressiveness. Family emotional expressiveness has been suggested as an important mediator between family and peer systems because of its linkages to variations in encoding and decoding skills of children and adults. Expressiveness is a broader concept than encoding–decoding and refers to the norms and expectations about emotion use that are communicated in the family context, such as when, where, and with whom to use different types of emotion; appropriate levels of intensity to be displayed with different emotions; and appropriate frequency of use.

Several studies have found cross-generational links in emotional expressiveness, with most reporting similarities between mothers' and children's levels of expressiveness (e.g., Denham, 1993; Eisenberg et al., 1992), with some exceptions (Halberstadt, Fox, & Jones, 1993). Halberstadt (1986) found that adult subjects who reported high levels of emotional expressiveness in their families of origin were better encoders of affect, while those from less expressive families were better judges, or decoders, of affect. Recent studies by Cassidy, Parke, Butkovsky, and Braungart (1992) and Boyum and Parke (1995) have found that highly expressive parents had children who were higher in peer ratings of social acceptance.

Boyum and Parke (1995) also found connections between self-reported intensity and clarity of parent expressiveness and children's social competence. Intensity of parents' positive affect was positively correlated with sociometric ratings by peers and prosocial ratings by teachers. Clarity of both positive and negative parental emotion was also positively associated with peer sociometric ratings. These results are similar to those in the encoding-decoding literature, suggesting that children whose parents are better senders of affect, that is, they encode affect more clearly, are better liked by their peers. Mothers reporting high intensity of negative affect had children who were rated by their teachers as being higher in aggression, while mothers and fathers who were high in clarity of negative expression had children who were rated as lower in aggression and higher in prosocial behavior. Intense negative expressiveness may be more often associated with anger, which is often noninteractive, noninstructive, and does not give others the opportunity to respond effectively. In contrast, clarity of negative affect may provide a model of more precise and perhaps more modulated negative affect, giving the child the opportunity to learn to regulate negative affect. This is consistent with findings that parental acceptance and assistance with negative affect, especially by fathers, is associated with less aggression and more prosocial behavior in children (Gottman, Katz, & Hooven, 1996; Roberts, 1994). Family affect exchanges are also predictive of peer sociometric ratings and teacher ratings of specific classroom behaviors (Boyum & Parke, 1995). Low-level negative maternal affect toward sons was positively related to boys' social status with peers and prosocial ratings by teachers. Both father-to-child and mother-to-son anger, a more intense form of negative affect, had the opposite effect and was related to lower sociometric status. Popular and prosocial girls received more happy affect from fathers and observed more happy affect from father to mother.

In summary, a variety of affective skills, including the ability to accurately encode and decode emotion signals, may be acquired in the context of familial interactions and thus impact children's social competence outside of the home.

Beyond the Parent–Child Dyad: The Impact of Marital Conflict on Children's Adjustment

Children's experiences in families extend beyond direct interactions with their parents. As family systems theorists (e.g., Minuchin, 1985) suggest, other family subsystems, such as the marital dyad, have both direct and indirect influences on children's adjustment. By direct influence, we mean that children are directly affected by witnessing marital interaction (e.g., by becoming anxious), while they are influenced indirectly when marital conflict modifies parent–child interaction patterns (e.g., when a distressed parent takes out anger on the child or withdraws from family interactions).

Marital distress may be one of the best familial predictors of childhood problems (e.g., Katz & Gottman, 1993). High levels of parental conflict have been associated with behavior problems in children of intact marriages (e.g., Peterson & Zill, 1986), and of divorced couples (e.g., Hetherington, Cox, & Cox, 1982). Negativity in marriages is associated with many poor child outcomes, including insecure attachment, poor social competence, poor academic performance, depression, withdrawal and aggression, and delinquency (see Katz & Gottman, 1994, for a review). Katz and Gottman (1994) propose that child outcomes are related to parents' emotional and conflict resolution styles in managing disagreements. Cummings and colleagues (e.g., Cummings & Davies, 1994) have explored children's reactions to witnessing anger between adults and have found distress to be the most common reaction. In addition, increased displays of physical aggression in younger children have been found, with more verbal aggression found in older children.

In summary, this area of inquiry is emerging as a promising direction for uncovering familial antecedents of childhood adjustment. Although controversy continues to exist on the pathways by which marital conflict exerts its effect on children, the importance of marital conflict on children's development is not in dispute.

Parent as Direct Teacher

Parents may also have explicit goals to educate, coach, or advise their children on appropriate ways to initiate and maintain social relationships. Results of recent studies suggest that children's needs for parental intervention change with age, and that strategies effective at one age may be less effective, or even detrimental, at later ages. With increasing age, management styles shift from direct involvement, supervision of activities, and specific advice-giving to less obtrusive consultation or advice.

Giving advice appears to be a common, naturally occurring activity between mothers and preschool children. In a recent study by Laird, Pettit, Mize, Brown, and Lindsey (1994), about half of the mothers reported engaging in frequent conversation about peer relationships with their children. Even after controlling for amount of conversation, advice-giving was found to relate to both peer and teacher ratings of children's social competence. Bhavnagri and Parke (1985) found that the social competence of 2-year-old children was greater during periods of maternal supervision. The children demonstrated more cooperation and turn-taking, and longer play bouts with peers, when assisted by an adult than when playing without parental supervision. A similar study (Bhavnagri & Parke, 1991) found that both mothers and fathers were effective facilitators of children's social play with peers. The effects of this assistance were found to be greater for younger children (2 to 3½ years of age) than for older children (3½ to 6 years of age), demonstrating developmental changes in social skills and needs over a relatively brief time span. Parents are more likely to intervene during peer conflicts—events that tax children's developing social skills—which generally leads to positive outcomes such as increased sharing of toys and materials (Lollis & Ross, 1987).

The quality of parental intervention is related to child behaviors. Finnie and Russell (1988) observed mothers of 4- and 5-year-old children who varied by sociometric status. Mothers were observed when assisting their child in joining with two other children who were playing together. More skillful entry strategies (such as verbal coaching and positive discipline) were used by mothers of sociometrically well-accepted children, while less effective strategies (such as avoidance, talking with only one child, and power-assertive discipline) were employed by mothers of low-accepted children. It is unclear whether these maternal behaviors contributed to the children's sociometric status, or whether mothers were acting in response to existing child behaviors. In a study of third-grade children and their mothers (Cohen, 1989), children whose mothers were overly involved or interfering were found to be socially withdrawn. Children whose mothers were supportive without interference had more positive social behaviors. Cohen cautions that the direction of effects is unknown, as child skills may lead to varying responses in the mother, but suggests that children's efforts to develop their own social strategies may be inhibited by high levels of parental control.

Several studies suggest that parents' ability to discuss emotions with their children is related to children's awareness and understanding of others' emotions (e.g., Denham, Cook, & Zoller, 1992; Dunn & Brown, 1994). Denham and her colleagues have examined the ways in which parents directly instruct their children about emotion concepts. For example, Denham (1995) observed preschool children and their mothers as they looked at a wordless picture book together. Mothers used more frequent emotion language than children, and their questioning techniques, guiding language, and explanations were effective in stimulating emotion language in the children. Mothers who used a teaching tactic of questioning without accompanying socialization language had children who showed greater emotion knowledge, leading Denham to suggest that questioning may prompt children to access and process their ideas about emotion. Mothers who pinpointed the meaning of emotion concepts and did not excessively repeat the child's utterances had children who showed more happiness while children with mothers who used more socializing language without supporting explanations showed more fear responses in preschool.

In summary, direct advice-giving and teaching are common activities in families of young children and are linked to children's peer competence. Children's needs from parents change over time, and the effective parent will have to provide support that is appropriate to those needs.

Parent as Provider of Opportunity

In addition to influencing children's social relationships in direct ways, parents influence development of children's social relationships by monitoring social activities and supervising choice of social settings, activities, and friends. On a broad level, this includes choice of neighborhood and school system, selection of day care or preschool facilities, and availability of child-centered activities, such as clubs and sports (Rubin & Sloman, 1984). Bhavnagri and Parke (1991) found that children's use of neighborhood varies with age, with younger children (ages 2 to 3 ½ years old) being permitted less unsupervised access to neighborhood facilities and playmates than older children (3 ½ to 6 years old). Bryant (1985) found that accessibility to neighborhood resources is a correlate of social–emotional functioning. Children with less access to parks and schoolyards and fewer opportunities to play with other children report less large-group play and fewer friends than children in higher density neighborhoods with more facilities (Medrich, Roizen, Rubin, & Buckley, 1982).

Children whose parents arrange peer contacts have a larger range of playmates and more frequently meet with play companions outside of school than children whose parents are less active in facilitating peer contacts (Ladd & Golter, 1988). Boys with parents who initiated peer contacts for them were better liked and less rejected by classmates when they entered kindergarten. There is an overall increase with age in participation in sponsored organizations with structured activities, with participation greatest among preadolescent children (Bryant, 1985). Participation in formally-sponsored organizations with unstructured activities was associated with greater skill in social perspective-taking for 10-year-old children, but not for 7 year olds.

Adolescents who are monitored by their parents exhibit less antisocial behavior. Monitoring has referred to a composite measure that indexes how well parents track their children's whereabouts, the kinds of companions they keep, or the types of activities in which they engage. Steinberg (1986) found that children in grades 6 to 9, especially girls, who are on their own after school are more susceptible to peer pressure to engage in antisocial activity (e.g., vandalism, cheating, stealing) than are adult-supervised adolescents. He notes that this supervision need not be face-to-face, and that adolescents who are "distally monitored" (i.e., through telephone calls, agreed-upon schedules, or being in their own homes) are less susceptible to peer pressure than adolescents who are "hanging out" and not at home. In addition, use of authoritative parenting practices decreases adolescents' susceptibility to peer pressure in the absence of monitoring. The type of parental monitoring changes developmentally, with younger children more likely to receive direct supervision, while distal supervision is more common for adolescents.

To summarize, parents function as managers of children's social environments by initiating, arranging, and monitoring their contacts with peers. Although some understanding of the effects of these strategies is becoming evident, less is known about the determinants of individual differences in parents' use of these strategies.

Integration of Findings

Families have been shown to influence children's social competence and their acceptance or rejection by the peer group in three major ways. First, they affect the child through face-to-face interactions with the child and other family members. Socially accepted children have parents whose disciplinary styles are warm, responsive, engaging, appropriately controlling, and synchronous with the child's needs. Their parents demonstrate prosocial strategies, value relational goals, and view social relationships as controllable. These parents demonstrate clear and frequent emotions, with fewer displays of intense negative emotion than parents of less accepted children, and they expose their children to fewer demonstrations of hostile marital conflict. Second, families provide children with direct social information. Socially accepted children have parents who provide coaching and supervision, offer specific and useful advice without interference, and discuss emotional experiences with the child. Third, families provide social opportunity and supervision. Socially accepted children have parents who facilitate contacts with other children, engage their children in organized social activities, and monitor their children's friends and whereabouts.

APPLICATIONS TO CONDUCT DISORDER

In the next section, we apply our three-mode model of family influence to one important area of childhood psychopathology, conduct disorder, and assess the value of prior work with nonclinical populations to understanding children with more severe adjustment difficulties. Dodge (1990) has previously shown the utility of applying this model to the study of developmental psychopathology.

Conduct Disorder

Conduct disorder in children and adolescents is related to a broad range of adjustment problems including poor peer relations, low academic achievement, substance use, and low self-esteem. Defined as "a repetitive and persistent pattern of behavior in which the basic rights of others or major age-appropriate societal norms or rules are violated" (American Psychiatric Association, 1994, p. 85), conduct disorder represents an extreme example of externalized behavior. Further detailed discussion about externalizing behavior problems, particularly conduct disorder, is found in Chapter 17; see Chapter 7 for discussion of the development of aggression in middle childhood.

There are several types of maladaptive parental behaviors that are likely contributors to the development of conduct disorder, including decreased frequency of positive affect, more frequent and hostile negative affect, increased marital hostility, reciprocal negativity, and ineffective discipline. Although determinants of one type of child outcome over another are not clear, they may be due in part to particular biological predispositions (e.g., temperament), environmental conditions (e.g., major family disruptions), and differential cultural influences on boys and girls.

Approximately one-third of children with either a diagnosis of depression or conduct disorder will in fact meet the criteria for both (Capaldi, 1991), with estimates of co-occurrence ranging from 16 to 46 percent. The wide range may reflect the effects of subject age and the length of time during which the symptoms were measured. Dishion (1987), in a study of longitudinal data, showed that 10-year-old boys classified as rejected and isolated by peers were rated a year later by parents and teachers as being at significant risk for depression. Patterson and Stoolmiller (1991) found significant path coefficients from peer relations to dysphoric mood for three samples of boys at risk for antisocial behavior. The study by Kovacs and colleagues (1988) found that co-morbid conduct disorder did not affect symptom presentation, was not differentially related to type of depression, was not significantly different for boys and girls, and was unrelated to demographic factors.

Most studies of conduct disorder have focused on boys, due to the preponderance of males with the diagnosis. More recently, there has been speculation that girls may be showing increasing rates of conduct disorder, or at least are being recognized as demonstrating such traits (Cairns & Cairns, 1994). It is possible that similar symptoms in girls have been labeled differently, or that supervising adults are quicker to respond to demonstrations of "unfeminine" behavior than they might be to boys' inappropriate behaviors. At any rate, boys are much more likely to be diagnosed with conduct disorder while girls are more likely to be diagnosed with affective disorders and certain types of personality disorder.

Capaldi (1991) found that early adolescent boys with both conduct problems and depressed mood showed worse adjustment than boys with a single diagnosis. Patterson and Capaldi (1990), in a study of fourth-grade boys, found support for a mediational model of boys' depression, in that the depressive effect of poor academic achievement was mediated through its disrupting effect on peer relations. These authors conclude that children's antisocial behaviors precede depression by leading to social rejection and academic failure, and thereby increasing the child's vulnerability to depressed mood. However, at least one other study has suggested that depression may precede aggression (Puig-Antich, 1982). It may be likely that familial factors influence development of affective and behavioral patterns that are related to both types of disorders, but which may be enacted either in a primarily internalizing or primarily externalizing manner.

Family Interactions

A meta-analysis by Loeber and Stouthamer-Loeber (1986) identified four categories of family influence on the development of conduct disorder: demographic factors (e.g., socioeconomic status, family size), parental characteristics (e.g., criminality), parental management techniques (e.g., lack of supervision, strict discipline), and family climate (e.g., rejection).

Parental childrearing practices were found to be consistent and important predictors of later antisocial behaviors, particularly levels of parental involvement, discipline, monitoring, attachment, and rejection (Dishion, Patterson, Stoolmiller, & Skinner, 1991; Loeber & Stouthamer-Loeber, 1986). Parenting variables had a direct effect even when controlling for other predictors of delinquency, while other variables appear to be mediated through parenting.

In a study by Fendrich, Warner, and Weissman (1990), family risk factors including marital discord, parent–child conflict, affectionless control, low family cohesion, and parental divorce were associated with higher rates of major depression, conduct disorder and any other psychiatric diagnosis in children. When the children were grouped by the diagnostic status of their parents, the risk factors were associated with increased depression and other diagnoses for children of nondepressed parents, while depression was the most important factor in predicting depression, anxiety, and other diagnoses for children of depressed parents. However, family risk factors were consistently the primary risk for conduct disorder whether or not the parents were depressed.

Parental Caregiving. Rothbaum and Weisz (1994), in a meta-analysis of the literature, found the broader construct of "acceptance-responsiveness" to better capture the qualities related to caregiving and externalizing behaviors, as opposed to single parenting behaviors. They found negative associations between caregiving variables including approval, guidance, motivational strategies, synchrony, and lack of aversive control, and child externalizing behavior. They also discussed a shift from conduct-disordered children's autonomy-seeking motives to more hostile motives during the time between preschool and middle childhood and suggested that the hostility may be more strongly associated with the activating effects of negative caregiving. Father involvement in caregiving appeared to be a protective factor for boys. In her meta-analysis of sex differences in children's response for divorce, Zaslow (1989) found that boys did not demonstrate more externalizing behaviors than girls following divorce when there was a stepfather or when the biological father had custody.

Reciprocity. In order to experimentally separate effects of child behaviors from parent behaviors, Anderson, Lytton, and Romney (1986) observed conduct-disordered and normal boys (ages 6–12) and their mothers interact in related and unrelated pairs during structured and unstructured tasks. Neither set of mothers differed significantly from each other in levels of positive and negative behaviors or in commands, but all mothers addressed more negative responses and commands to the problem boys. They concluded that the negative interactions of mothers and conduct-disordered boys are driven mainly by the boys. Rothbaum and Weisz (1994) came to the opposite conclusion. They found that associations between quality of caregiving and child externalizing behaviors increased over time. Their depiction of a "cumulative-reciprocity model" suggests that although studying older boys at single points in time may identify the child as the problem, their externalizing behaviors in fact represent a product which has been mutually constructed over time.

Discipline/Coercion. The most influential theory of how families contribute to the development of antisocial behavior is that of Patterson (1982). His coercion model proposed that parents of delinquent children reinforce the child's coercive behaviors (such as noncompliance, temper tantrums, yelling, whining, arguing, and hitting) by providing reinforcing contingencies that function as escape conditioning or negative reinforcement for the delinquent behavior. Less skilled parents are inadvertently rewarding antisocial behaviors and failing to provide effective punishments for them. The overall effect, then, is that the boys become deficient in the types of social skills that are necessary for acceptance by the nondeviant peer group. Subsequent studies (e.g., Dishion, Patterson, Stoolmiller, & Skinner, 1991) have confirmed that there are high levels of coercion in these families and poor discipline (e.g., low anger control, high inconsistency, permissiveness, low use of reasoning, and nagging) to be significant predictors of later involvement with deviant peers.

Patterson, Capaldi, and Bank (1991) identified a key requirement for family training in antisocial behavior: that the child live in a coercive family. They suggested that all members of families with an antisocial member will be more coercive than like members of normal families, in that coercion is a necessary adaptive strategy. This social interaction perspective suggests that families characterized by high levels of coercive exchanges create a homogeneous environment that is shared by both parents and siblings. They emphasize the central roles of both the family and the peer group in maintaining the performance of both prosocial and deviant child behaviors.

In addition, because research on depressed parents shows that such parents tend to avoid punishment and discipline and rely on less effortful discipline strategies such as coercion or withdrawal with their children, Patterson's research might suggest that there is a high occurrence of depression, or of other psychopathology, in parents of conduct-disordered children, which leads to similar parental behaviors. Such parents may model coercive behaviors for the child or may withdraw effort from difficult interactions and thus reinforce negative behaviors. In addition, Stoolmiller (1994) suggests that temperamental differences may influence ways in which different children react to a coercive environment, for example, increasing the likelihood that a child will tend to withdraw or counterattack (act out).

Nonsynchronous Behaviors. In a longitudinal study, Bank, Patterson, and Reid (1993) examined the behavioral exchanges between delinquent adolescent boys and their siblings and parents. They identified "start-up" behaviors (neutral or positive behaviors followed by negative behaviors), "synchronicity" (negative behavior followed by another negative behavior), and "backoff" behaviors (a negative behavior followed by a neutral or positive behavior), as well as reinforcement for coercive behaviors, as primary family factors supporting delinquent behaviors. All categories of psychopathology on a symptom checklist were predicted by startup and synchronicity with siblings. Juvenile crime was predicted by coercive behavior on the part of mothers and boys' startup behaviors with their mothers, while adult arrests were predicted by synchronous negative behaviors with siblings during middle childhood. Hostility toward women was predicted by startup and synchronicity behaviors with siblings. The researchers suggest that unsupervised siblings have limitless opportunities to practice negative behavioral interaction patterns, resulting in ingrained disdain and disrespect for their victims. They note that less skilled parents do not supervise and discipline problem children in capable ways, thus increasing the likelihood that they will victimize siblings at high rates and quickly perfect their antisocial behaviors. In summary, the Patterson work clearly suggests that family interaction patterns are potent contributors to the emergence of antisocial behaviors.

Cognitive Models of Conduct Disorder. Some theorists have proposed information-processing models for the development of conduct disorder. According to this view, as a consequence of family interaction patterns some children develop maladaptive strategies for processing social information. For example, antisocial children develop hostile attribution biases that lead them to interpret ambiguous social cues as aggressive overtures (Dodge et al., 1986). Although this perspective has received considerable support (see Crick & Dodge, 1994), the role of family in the emergence of social information–processing deficits is less well explored. Recent work by MacKinnon-Lewis and colleagues (1994), which found similarities in the hostile attributional biases of mothers and their sons, suggests this as a promising avenue for future research in the effort to understand potential cognitive mediators of family interaction and the development of conduct-disordered behaviors.

Summary. In addition to the problems with affective communication and caregiving that were described in the preceding section and that are hypothesized to underlie parent–

child interactions in at least some families of conduct-disordered children, these families show consistent patterns of their own. They tend to be differentiated by higher levels of disapproval, aversive control strategies, and nonsynchronous communications. Families of conduct-disordered children are characterized by high levels of coercion, which is rewarded and reinforced by other family members, ineffective punishment techniques, and expectations of hostile interactions with others. By middle childhood there appears to be a shift in power, in which the child is driving his or her interactions with others, both at home and away.

Parent of Conduct-Disordered Child as Direct Instructor

Parents may contribute to the development of conduct problems in their children not only as an interactive partner, but as a direct instructor, coach, or teacher. In comparison with parents of normal children, parents of conduct-disordered children were less effective teachers. They were more directive and used more low-level cognitive strategies in teaching their children (Gauvain & DeMent, 1991). As shown previously in research with normal samples, the strategies are unlikely to be very effective and may relate to less effective social skills as well. More work is clearly needed to more fully establish the role of parent as "teacher" in the development of conduct problems in children.

Parent of Conduct-Disordered Child as Provider of Opportunity

To understand the development of anti-social behavior, the family must be viewed as a social system in which not only the interrelationships among family members are recognized, but also the role of the family as a buffer or gatekeeper of outside influences. Next we turn to the role of the parent as manager of the child's social contacts.

Monitoring. As children move into preadolescence and adolescence, and the peer influence begins to supplant that of the family, parental monitoring of social behaviors becomes particularly crucial. Association with peers in places without adult supervision or structure makes children more susceptible to peer pressures to engage in problem behaviors (Steinberg, 1986).

Parents of delinquent and antisocial children engage in less monitoring and supervision of their children's activities, especially in regard to evening time, than parents of nondelinquent children (e.g., Patterson & Stouthamer-Loeber, 1984). Monitoring behaviors include adequacy of tracking and supervision, appropriate communication with children about what they are doing, expectations of child accountability, and amount of time spent with the child. Among boys in grades 7 and 10, Patterson and Stouthamer-Loeber (1984) found significant relationships between lack of parental monitoring and court-reported delinquency, attacks against property, delinquent lifestyle, rule-breaking outside the home, and antisocial disposition (e.g., fighting with peers, talking back to teachers, breaking school rules). Stoolmiller (1994) found that increases in "unsupervised wandering" (unmonitored) behaviors are closely linked with delinquent peer association and antisocial behavior for boys in late childhood through early adolescence. Unsupervised wandering was also found to be a key predictor of onset of arrest, and the timing of the wandering spurt coincided with a substantial increase in the probability of first arrest (Patterson, 1996). Because children who are loosely monitored are having less interaction with their parents, receiving less direct instruction from their parents, and obtaining less assistance in connecting with appropriate social opportunities, they may also be missing out on the development of alternative social skills.

Deviant Peer Group. Patterson, DeBarshyshe, and Ramsey (1989) have described a developmental sequence in the formation of conduct disorder that flows from early experiences in the family. Poor parental discipline and lack of monitoring results in children who are aggressive and socially unskilled. When these unskilled children enter school, they are rejected by their peer group and they experience academic failure. In late childhood and adolescence, these children seek out deviant peers who, in turn, provide further training in antisocial behavior and opportunities for delinquent activities. Patterson and Bank (1989) have provided support for this sequence, but make a distinction between "early starter" and "late starter" groups of conduct-disordered boys and the differential role of the delinquent peer group (Patterson, Capaldi, & Bank, 1991). Early starters are primed by the family environment for antisocial behaviors, through deficits in discipline, modeling, attachment processes, and so forth. This training takes place approximately between the ages of 4 and 9, before the primacy of the peer group, resulting in significant deficits in social skills by mid to late adolescence. Early starter boys are identified as problematic across settings and are often engaged in serious offenses before adolescence. They may form the core of the alternative delinquent peer group and are likely to develop serious and persistent antisocial behavior (see also Campbell, Pierce, & Ewing, 1995, for stability of early-identified hard-to-manage children).

In contrast, late starters are not identified as problem children before adolescence, usually beginning their offending at age 15 or later. They are at least somewhat proficient in peer relations and academic skills in the early grades. The process for these boys generally begins in early adolescence

with a major family stressor (e.g., divorce, unemployment, major illness, transition to adolescence) that disrupts fragile family management skills, decreases parental supervision, and creates an opportunity to become involved in and influenced by the deviant peer group. Thus, the delinquent peer group may have more of an influence on late-starting delinquents. Clearly, developmental timing of earlier experience makes an important difference in determining whether childhood aggression results in serious conduct disorder.

Summary. Antisocial behavior may follow a developmental trajectory that reflects the interaction of individual child characteristics and family influences. The family may have differing effects on the development of antisocial behaviors depending on the initial level of family competencies and on the timing of, and response to, stressful family events. Parents essentially provide their conduct-disordered children with opportunity to act in a delinquent manner. This lack of monitoring is related to a variety of antisocial behaviors and is a key predictor of juvenile arrests. In addition, children who are unmonitored are missing out on opportunities to learn appropriate social behaviors.

Integration of Findings

Social relationships of the conduct-disordered child are affected by multiple family influences. First, the increased level of intense negative emotion and ineffective discipline in families has been associated with poor child outcomes, including increased rates of physical and verbal aggression and peer rejection, all characteristics of conduct-disordered children. Second, though few direct links have been established to parental instruction, parents of conduct-disordered children have been shown to use less effective teaching strategies overall. Also, increased rates of criminality in these families suggest that there may be modeling and perhaps even coaching of antisocial behaviors in some families. Third, tacit parental approval of a negative peer group through lack of monitoring, as well as the inability to coach or structure children's peer relationships when the parent is not present, reduces the child's success in learning to cope with the more sophisticated demands of a more skilled peer group. As Fendrich, Warner, and Weissman (1990) concluded, family risk factors appear to go beyond parental diagnosis in predicting child outcomes for conduct disorder.

The issue of sex differences begs consideration. What factors set in motion the coercive cycle leading to conduct disorder for so many boys and so few girls? In young children, there appear to be few sex differences in the clinical diagnosis of depression, and recent studies suggest that very young boys and girls do not differ in the rates of antisocial behaviors (Eddy, Leve, & Fagot, 1996); however, by adolescence there is a clear and significant gender polarization. Presumably these conduct-disordered boys have sisters who are growing up in the same household and yet are not developing antisocial behavior at nearly the same rates as their brothers. Maternal factors are shown to be stronger predictors of boys' antisocial behaviors in nonclinic samples, while paternal factors (primarily aggression and abuse) are factors in clinic-referred samples (Rothbaum & Weisz, 1994). As noted earlier, the presence of a supportive father can offset otherwise risky family effects. Factors such as gender identification and sex role development, as well as biological, temperamental, or hormonal differences, may also play a part. As we have noted throughout, the absence of fathers in developmental and clinical research populations leaves many questions unanswered in regard to their effects on children's outcomes.

SUMMARY AND CONCLUSIONS

In the course of this chapter, we have looked to the issue of peer competence as a way to track the effects of family influences on children's development. We have shown that there is a continuum of social acceptance and rejection that is consistently associated with familial patterns of caretaking and disciplinary behavior, affect use, cognitive representations about relationships, direct teaching and coaching strategies, and supervision and monitoring. We have attempted to sort through the extensive literatures on childhood conduct disorder, as a prevalent example of an externalizing pathology, to identify similarities and connections between normal developmental pathways and extreme clinical outcomes in the ways in which families shape their children's abilities to move successfully beyond the boundaries of the home. We have shown that deficits in social competence may lead to increased pathology because the child is increasingly limited to interactions with similarly unskilled peers or isolated on the fringe of activity where their opportunities again are limited.

Applications to Clinical Intervention

This chapter highlights the importance of assessing and treating mental health needs of the child or adolescent in the broader context of the family system. The family has been shown to influence the development of social and emotional skills and the quality of social relationships and personal perceptions of self-adequacy and acceptance in ways that are appropriate to the focus of treatment interventions.

First, it is recommended that an assessment of the child include an assessment of the parents in terms of disciplinary techniques and ability to monitor the child, parents' marital or dating relationships, family social support systems, and parents' mental health history. Appropriate referrals should be made for the parents, such as parent training in discipline and behavior management, marital therapy, and connections to the community to increase social support. Parental psychopathology, (e.g., affective disorders), should further be considered as an especially urgent concern in light of the many ways in which it can disrupt parenting skills, marital relationships, and overall child adjustment. The degree and chronicity of the parents' problems will determine appropriate levels of intervention. For example, limited episodes of disruption in a parent with otherwise good underlying skills may require referrals for time-limited medication and individual or marital therapy. More chronic problems, particularly those with associated characterological features and generally poor parenting skills, may require a more extensive set of referrals, including medication and ongoing individual or group treatment, training in basic parenting skills, assistance with monitoring children or enrolling them in structured day care or other activities, and enlisting more intensive social supports.

Parent training will be especially important for addressing externalizing behaviors. A number of studies (e.g., Dishion, Patterson, & Kavenagh, 1991) have demonstrated the effectiveness of parent training programs in long-term reduction of conduct problems in children. These programs have focused on teaching parents effective discipline skills (i.e., non coercive discipline, increased use of positive support) and problem-solving skills and on motivating the parents to supervise and monitor their children's activities. As Stoolmiller (1994) has observed, because most serious misconduct is committed outside of the presence of adults, increased monitoring by parents or other adults can reduce the opportunity to commit these acts as well as reduce the reinforcement that is received for those acts from the delinquent peer group. As might be expected, the younger the child, the stronger the effect of such parenting interventions.

Family approaches to therapy have been shown to be effective for improving family communication and providing in vivo rehearsal of appropriate limit setting, disciplinary techniques, and interpersonal behaviors. Family therapy can also be an effective setting in which to assess and intervene with family emotional communications. Such interventions might include working with families on clear expression of feelings that matches verbalizations and physical behaviors, providing practice in identifying others' expressions, modeling and managing appropriate levels of emotional intensity, and shifting the ratio of positive and negative expressions of emotion.

Prevention and intervention with children and adolescents also needs to occur within the broader social context surrounding the child. This is particularly true for those youth who have reduced access to appropriate peer groups and organized activities, whether for reasons of geographic isolation, personal handicap, or parental limitations. With the passing of the neighborhood school concept, as schools are forced to cut back on youth programs (e.g., sports, music, interest clubs), and as parents' availability to facilitate peer contacts is impacted by work or other demands, community groups and churches and even local businesses need to be encouraged and expected to take a bigger role in providing the social experiences necessary for healthy social and emotional development. This includes organized activities with developmentally appropriate levels of structure; active monitoring of children's whereabouts and behaviors; appropriate modeling of affect, behavioral attributions, and problem-solving skills; and interactive play that includes both children and adults.

Recommendations for Continuing Research

Our review suggests the utility of expanding our views of the ways in which families contribute to the development of children's psychopathology. First, in addition to the traditional emphasis on face-to-face interaction, more attention to witnessing marital conflict is clearly warranted. Similarly, attention to the roles of parents as teachers, coaches, and managers of their children's environment is necessary if we are to appreciate the diverse pathways through which families influence their children and adolescents. Although we have discussed different aspects of our model as separate influences, it is clear that these parental strategies often operate together (e.g., parental discipline and monitoring) in producing various child outcomes.

Second, the issue of direction of effects remains unresolved. While it is assumed that families influence their offspring's subsequent adjustment, it is clear that children shape parental behavior as well (Lytton, 1990). It is likely that both directions of influence are operative, and the task is to delineate how the relative balance changes across age and setting. Third, more developmental analysis of these issues is needed. Little is understood, for example, of the significance of early infancy or childhood onset of disorders as opposed to adolescent onset, or of the short-term and long-term effects of family influences on these differing trajectories. Do the relative roles of family and outside social networks differ for these two groups? Clearly, treatment programs should be sensitive to these differences in developmental history. Closely related is the role of families in the emergence of major gender differences in the expression of psychopathology at later points in development. What are the familial con-

ditions that lead to greater rates of conduct disorder in boys than in girls, despite the high degree of overlap in early family conditions for the two genders? Fourth, more research is needed on single-parent families, because children in these families may be at particular risk for later problems (McLanahan & Sandefur, 1994).

Fifth, the maternal bias of the literature needs to be corrected by a further focus on the father's role in the development of clinical problems in children and adolescents (Phares, 1996). For example, do fathers and mothers play different roles in the emergence of internalizing versus externalizing behaviors? Sixth, families can serve as a protective resource in the prevention of serious disorders in children and youth. More attention to the role of families as a protection and buffer during development would help increase our understanding of dysfunctional families, but would also point to new strategies for strengthening families. In addition, more attention needs to be given to variations across ethnic and racial groups, both in terms of the role of the family in the emergence of childhood difficulties and in the development of more culturally sensitive intervention and treatment strategies. Finally, the relative role of families and other socializing influences, such as peers, continues to be a major concern, especially in the ways in which these influences change across development. Of particular importance is the protective role that families can play in helping children resist deviant peer influences.

In conclusion, by increasing our understanding of the role of the family in the development of childhood and adolescent disorders, we will be in a better position to design effective prevention, intervention, and treatment programs for these children.

REFERENCES

American Psychiatric Association. (1994). *Diagnostic and Statistical Manual of Mental Disorders* (4th ed.). Washington, DC: Author.

Anderson, K. E., Lytton, H., & Romney, D. M. (1986). Mothers' interactions with normal and conduct-disordered boys: Who affects whom? *Developmental Psychology, 22,* 604–609.

Asher, S. R., & Renshaw, P. D. (1981). Children without friends: Social knowledge and social skills training. In S. R. Asher & J. M. Gottman (Eds.), *The development of children's friendships* (pp. 273–296). New York: Cambridge University Press.

Attili, G. (1989). Social competence versus emotional security: The link between home relationships and behavior problems at school. In B. H. Schneider, G. Attili, J. Nadel, & R. P. Weissberg (Eds.), *Social competence in developmental perspective* (pp. 293–311). Dordrecht, Netherlands: Kluwer.

Baldwin, M. J. (1992). Relational schema and the processing of information. *Psychological Review, 112,* 461–484.

Baltes, P. (1987). Theoretical propositions of life span developmental psychology: On the dynamics between growth and decline. *Developmental Psychology, 23,* 611–626.

Bank, L., Patterson, G. R., & Reid, J. B. (1996). Negative sibling interaction patterns as predictors of later adjustment problems in adolescent and young adult males. In G. H. Brody (Ed.), *Advances in applied developmental psychology: Sibling relationships.* Norwood, NJ: Ablex.

Barth, J., & Parke, R. D. (1993). Parent-child relationship influence on children's transition to school. *Merrill-Palmer Quarterly, 39,* 173–195.

Baumrind, D., (1971). Current patterns of parental authority. *Developmental Psychology Monograph, 4* (1, Pt. 2).

Beitel, A., & Parke, R. D. (1985). *Relationships between preschoolers' sociometric status and emotional decoding ability.* Unpublished manuscript, University of Illinois, Urbana.

Bhavnagri, N., & Parke, R. D. (1985, April). *Parents as facilitators of preschool children's social relationships.* Paper presented at the biennial meeting of the Society for Research on Child Development, Toronto, Canada.

Bhavnagri, N., & Parke, R. D. (1991). Parents as direct facilitators of children's peer relationships: Effects of age of child and sex of parent. *Journal of Social and Personal Relationships, 8,* 423–440.

Boyum, L. A., & Parke, R. D. (1995). The role of family emotional expressiveness in the development of children's social competence. *Journal of Marriage and the Family, 57,* 593–608.

Bretherton, I., & Waters, E. (Eds.). (1985). Growing points in attachment theory and research. *Monographs of the Society for Research in Child Development, 50* (1–2, Serial No. 209).

Bronfenbrenner, U. (1989). Ecological systems theory. In R. Vasta (Ed.), *Annals of child development* (Vol. 6, pp. 187–250). Greenwich, CT: JAI Press.

Bryant, B. K. (1985). The neighborhood walk: Source of support in middle childhood. *Monographs of the Society for Research in Child Development, 50* (3, Serial No. 210).

Burks, V. M., Carson, J. L., & Parke, R. D. (1987). *Parent–child interactional styles of popular and rejected children.* Unpublished manuscript, University of Illinois, Urbana.

Burks, V. M., & Parke, R. D. (1996). Parent and child representations of social relationships: Linkages between family and peers. *Merrill-Palmer Quarterly, 42,* 358–378.

Cairns, R., & Cairns, B. (1994). *Lifelines and risks.* New York: Cambridge University Press.

Campbell, S. B., Pierce, E. W., & Ewing, L. J. (1995, March). *Hard-to-manage preschool children in middle childhood: Family predictors of continuing externalizing problems.* Paper presented at the biennial meeting of the Society for Research in Child Development, Indianapolis, IN.

Capaldi, D. M. (1991). Co-occurrence of conduct problems and depressive symptoms in early adolescent boys: I. Familial factors and general adjustment at grade 6. *Development and Psychopathology, 3,* 277–300.

Carson, J. L., & Parke, R. D. (1996). Reciprocal negative affect in parent–child interactions and children's peer competency. *Child Development, 67,* 2217–2226.

Carson, J. L., & Parke, R. D. (1998). *Peer acceptance and the quality of children's production of facial displays of emotion with parents.* Unpublished manuscript, University of San Francisco, CA.

Cassidy, J., Parke, R. D., Butkovsky, L., & Braungart, J. M. (1992). Family-peer connections: The roles of emotional expressiveness within the family and children's understanding of emotions. *Child Development, 63,* 603–618.

Cohen, J. S. (1989). *Maternal involvement in children's peer relationships during middle childhood.* Unpublished doctoral dissertation, University of Waterloo, Waterloo, Ontario, Canada.

Coie, J. D., Lochman, J. E., Terry, R., & Hyman, C. (1992). Predicting early adolescent disorder from childhood aggression and peer rejection. *Journal of Consulting and Clinical Psychology, 60,* 783–792.

Crick, N. R., & Dodge, K. A. (1994). A review and reformulation of social information-processing mechanisms in children's social adjustment. *Psychological Bulletin, 115,* 74–101.

Cummings, E. M., & Davies, P. T. (1994). *Child and marital conflict: The impact of family dispute and resolution.* New York: Guilford Press.

Daly, E. M., Abramovitch, R., & Pliner, P. (1980). The relationship between mothers' encoding and their children's decoding of facial expression of emotion. *Merrill-Palmer Quarterly, 26,* 25–33.

Denham, S. (1993). Maternal emotional responsiveness to toddlers' social-emotional functioning. *Journal of Child Psychology and Psychiatry, 34,* 715–728.

Denham, S. A. (1995). *Mother–child dialogue about emotions and preschoolers' emotional competence.* Paper presented at the biennial meeting of the Society for Research on Child Development, Indianapolis, IN.

Denham, S. A., Cook, M., & Zoller, D. (1992). Baby looks very sad: Implications of conversations about feelings between mother and preschooler. *British Journal of Developmental Psychology, 10,* 301–315.

Dishion, T. J. (1987). *A developmental model for peer relations: Middle childhood correlates and one-year sequelae.* Unpublished doctoral dissertation, University of Oregon, Department of Psychology, Eugene.

Dishion, T. (1990). The family ecology of boys' peer relations in middle childhood. *Child Development, 61,* 874–892.

Dishion, T. J., Patterson, G. R., & Kavenagh, K. A. (1991). An experimental test of the coercion model: Linking theory, measurement and intervention. In J. McCord & R. Trembley (Eds.), *The interaction of theory and practice: Experimental studies of intervention* (pp. 253–281). New York: Guilford Press.

Dishion, T. J., Patterson, G. R., Stoolmiller, M., & Skinner, M. L. (1991). Family, school, and behavioral antecedents to early adolescent involvement with antisocial peers. *Developmental Psychology, 27,* 172–180.

Dodge, K. A. (1990). Developmental psychopathology in children of depressed mothers. *Developmental Psychology, 26,* 3–6.

Dodge, K. A., Pettit, G. S., McClaskey, C. L., & Brown, M. M. (1986). Social competence in children. *Monographs of the Society for Research in Child Development, 51,* (Serial No. 213), 1–85.

Dunn, J., & Brown, J. (1994). Affect expression in the family, children's understanding of emotions and their interactions with others. *Merrill-Palmer Quarterly, 40,* 120–137.

Eddy, J. M., Leve, L. D., & Fagot, B. I. (1996). *Sex differences in antisocial behavior: Myths, methods, and models.* Unpublished manuscript, University of Oregon, Eugene.

Eisenberg, N., Fabes, R. A., Carlo, G., Troyer, D., Speer, A. L., Karbon, M., & Switzer, G. (1992). The relations of maternal practices and characteristics to children's vicarious emotional responsiveness. *Child Development, 63,* 583–602.

Elder, G., Modell, J., & Parke, R. D. (Eds.). (1993). *Children in time and place.* New York: Cambridge University Press.

Fendrich, M., Warner, V., & Weissman, M. M. (1990). Family risk factors, parental depression, and psychopathology in offspring. *Developmental Psychology, 26,* 40–50.

Field, T. M., & Walden, T. A. (1982). Production and discrimination of facial expressions by preschool children. *Child Development, 53,* 1299–1300.

Finnie, V., & Russell, A. (1988). Preschool children's social status and their mothers' behavior and knowledge in the supervisory role. *Developmental Psychology, 24,* 789–801.

Gauvain, M., & DeMent, T. (1991). The role of shared social history in parent–child cognitive activity. *Newsletter of the Laboratory of Comparative Human Cognition, 13,* 58–66.

Gold, M. (1963). *Status forces in delinquent boys.* Ann Arbor: University of Michigan Press.

Gottman, J. M., Katz, L. F., & Hooven, C. (1996). *Meta-emotion: How families communicate emotionally.* Hillsdale, NJ: Erlbaum.

Halberstadt, A. G. (1986). Family socialization of emotional expression and nonverbal communication styles and skills. *Journal of Personality and Social Psychology, 51,* 827 836.

Halberstadt, A. G., Fox, N. A., & Jones, N. A. (1993). Do expressive mothers have expressive children? The role of socialization in children's affect expression. *Social Development, 2,* 48–65.

Harrist, A. W., Pettit, G. S., Dodge, K. A., & Bates, J. E. (1994). Dyadic synchrony in mother-child interactions: Relations with children's subsequent kindergarten adjustment. *Family Relations, 43,* 417–424.

Hetherington, E. M., Cox, M., & Cox, R. (1982). Effects of divorce on parents and children. In M. Lamb (Ed.), *Nontraditional families* (pp. 233–288). Hillsdale, NJ: Erlbaum.

Katz, L. F., & Gottman, J. M. (1993). Patterns of marital conflict predict children's internalizing and externalizing behaviors. *Developmental Psychology, 29,* 940–950.

Katz, L. F., & Gottman, J. M. (1994). Patterns of marital interaction and children's emotional development. In R. D. Parke & S. G. Kellam (Eds.), *Exploring family relationships with other social contexts* (pp. 49–74). Hillsdale, NJ: Erlbaum.

Kovacs, M., Paulauskas, S., Gatsonis, C., & Richards, C. (1988). Depressive disorders in childhood: III. A longitudinal study of comorbidity with and risk for conduct disorders. *Journal of Affective Disorders, 15,* 205–217.

Ladd, G. W. (1990). Having friends, keeping friends, making friends, and being liked by peers in the classroom: Predictors of children's early school adjustment. *Child Development, 61,* 1081–1100.

Ladd, G. W., & Golter, B. S. (1988). Parents' management of preschoolers' peer relations: Is it related to children's social competence? *Developmental Psychology, 24,* 109–117.

Ladd, G. W., LeSieur, K., & Profilet, S. M. (1993). Direct parental influences on young children's peer relations. In S. Duck (Ed.), *Learning about relationships* (Vol. 2). London: Sage.

Laird, R. D., Pettit, G. S., Mize, J., Brown, E. G., & Lindsey, E. (1994). Mother-child conversations about peers—contributions to competence. *Family Relations, 43,* 425–432.

Loeber, R., & Stouthamer-Loeber, M. (1986). Family factors as correlates and predictors of juvenile conduct problems and delinquency. In M. Tonry & N. Morris (Eds.), *Crime and justice: An annual review of research,* (Vol. 7). Chicago: University of Chicago Press.

Lollis, S., & Ross, H. (1987, April). *Mothers' interventions in toddler-peer conflicts.* Paper presented at the biennial meeting of the Society for Research in Child Development, Baltimore.

Lytton, H. (1990). Child and parent effects in boys' conduct disorder: A reinterpretation. *Developmental Psychology, 26,* 683–697.

Maccoby, E. E., & Martin, J. A. (1983). Socialization in the context of the family: Parent child interaction. In P. Mussen (Series Ed.) & E. M. Hetherington (Vol. Ed.), *Handbook of child psychology: Vol. 4. Socialization, personality, and social development* (4th ed., pp. 1–102). New York: Wiley.

MacDonald, K. (1987). Parent-child physical play with rejected, neglected and popular boys. *Developmental Psychology, 23,* 705–711.

MacDonald, K., & Parke, R. D. (1984). Bridging the gap: Parent-child play interaction and peer interactive competence. *Child Development, 55,* 1265–1277.

MacKinnon-Lewis, C., Volling, B. L., Lamb, M. E., Dechman, K., Rabiner, D., & Curtner, M. E. (1994). A cross-contextual analysis of boys' social competence: From family to school. *Developmental Psychology, 30,* 325–333.

McLanahan, S., & Sandefur, G. (1994). *Growing up with a single parent.* Cambridge, MA: Harvard University Press.

Medrich, E. A., Roizen, J. A., Rubin, V., & Buckley, S. (1982). *The serious business of growing up: A study of children's lives outside school.* Berkeley: University of California Press.

Minuchin, P. (1985). Families and individual development: Provocations from the field of family therapy. *Child Development, 56,* 289–302.

Ollendick, T. H., Weist, M. D., Borden, M. C., & Greene, R. W. (1992). Sociometric status and academic, behavioral, and psychological adjustment: A five-year longitudinal study. *Journal of Consulting and Clinical Psychology, 60,* 80–87.

Parke, R. D. (1988). Families in life-span perspective: A multi-level developmental approach. In E. M. Hetherington, R. M. Lerner, & M. Perlmutter (Eds.), *Child development in life span perspective* (pp. 159–190). Hillsdale, NJ: Erlbaum.

Parke, R. D., & Bhavnagri, N. (1989). Parents as managers of children's peer relationships. In D. Belle (Ed.), *Children's social networks and social supports* (pp. 241–259). New York: Wiley.

Parke, R. D., Burks, V. M., Carson, J. L., Neville, B., & Boyum, L. A. (1994). Family-peer relationships: A tripartite model. In R. D. Parke & S. G. Kellem (Eds.), *Exploring family relation-*

ships with other social contexts (pp. 115–146). Hillsdale, NJ: Erlbaum.

Parke, R. D., & O'Neil, R. (1997). The influence of significant others on learning about relationships. In S. W. Duck (Ed.), *Handbook of personal relationships* (2nd ed., pp. 29–59). New York: Wiley.

Parker, J. G., & Asher, S. R. (1987). Peer relations and later personal adjustment: Are low-accepted children "at-risk"? *Psychological Bulletin, 102,* 357–359.

Patterson, G. R. (1982). *A social learning appproach to family intervention. III. Coercive family process.* Eugene, OR: Castalia Publishing.

Patterson, G. R. (1996). Some characteristics of a developmental theory for early-onset delinquency. In M. L. Lenzenweger & J. J. Haugaard (Eds.), *Frontiers of developmental psychopathology* (pp. 81–124). New York: Oxford University Press.

Patterson, G. R., & Capaldi, D. M. (1990). A mediational model for boys' depressed mood. In J. E. Rolf, A. S. Masten, D. Cicchetti, K. H. Neuchterlain, & S. Weintraub (Eds.), *Risk and protective factors in the development of psychopathology* (pp. 141–163). New York: Cambridge University Press.

Patterson, G. R., Capaldi, D., & Bank, L. (1991). An early starter model for predicting delinquency. In D. J. Pepler and K. H. Rubin (Eds.), *The development and treatment of childhood aggression* (pp. 139–168). Hillsdale, NJ: Erlbaum.

Patterson, G. R., DeBarshyshe, B., & Ramsey, R. (1989). A developmental perspective in antisocial behavior. *American Psychologist, 44,* 329–335.

Patterson G. R., & Stoolmiller, M. (1991). Replications of a dual failure model for boys' depressed mood. *Journal of Consulting and Clinical Psychology, 59,* 491–498.

Patterson, G. R., & Stouthamer-Loeber, M. (1984). The correlation of family management practices and delinquency. *Child Development, 55,* 1299–1306.

Peterson, J. L., & Zill, N. (1986). Marital disruption, parent–child relationships, and behavior problems in children. *Journal of Marriage and the Family, 48,* 295–307.

Pettit, G. S., Dodge, K. A., & Brown, M. M. (1988). Early family experience, social problem solving patterns, and children's social competence. *Child Development, 59,* 107–120.

Phares, V. (1996). *Fathers and developmental psychopathology.* New York: Wiley.

Puig-Antich, J. (1982). Major depression and conduct disorder in prepuberty. *Journal of the American Academy of Child Psychiatry, 21,* 118–128.

Putallaz, M. (1987). Maternal behavior and sociometric status. *Child Development, 58,* 324–340.

Roberts, W. (1994). *The socialization of emotional expression: Relations with competence in preschool.* Paper presented at the meetings of the Canadian Psychological Association, Penticton, British Columbia.

Roff, J. D., & Wirt, R. D. (1984). Childhood social adjustment, adolescent status, and young adult mental health. *American Journal of Orthopsychiatry, 54,* 595–602.

Rothbaum, F., & Weisz, J. R. (1994). Parental caregiving and child externalizing behavior in no-clinical samples: A meta-analysis. *Psychological Bulletin, 116,* 55–74.

Rubin, K. H. (1985). Socially withdrawn children: An at-risk population? In B. H. Schneider, K. H. Rubin, & J. E. Ledingham (Eds.), *Children's peer relations: Issues in assessment and intervention* (pp. 125–140). New York: Springer-Verlag.

Rubin, K. H., Mills, R. S. L., & Rose-Krasnor, L. (1989). Maternal beliefs and children's social competence. In B. Schneider, J. Nadel, G. Attili, & R. Weissberg (Eds.), *Social competence in developmental perspective* (pp. 313–331). Amsterdam: Klewer Academic Publishers.

Rubin, K. H., & Ross, H. S. (1988). Toward the study of social competence, social status, and social relations. In C. Howes (Ed.), *Peer interaction in young children. Monographs of the Society for Research in Child Development, 53* (1, Serial No. 217).

Rubin, Z., & Sloman, J. (1984). How parents influence their children's friendships. In M. Lewis (Ed.), *Beyond the dyad* (pp. 223–250). New York: Plenum Press.

Spitzer, S., & Parke, R. D. (1994). *Family cognitive representations of social behavior and children's social competence.* Paper presented at the annual meeting of the American Psychological Society, Washington, DC.

Steinberg, L. (1986). Latchkey children and susceptibility to peer pressure: An ecological analysis. *Developmental Psychology, 22,* 433–439.

Stoolmiller, M. (1994). Antisocial behavior, delinquent peer association, and unsupervised wandering for boys: Growth and change from childhood to early adolescence. *Multivariate Behavioral Research, 29,* 263–288.

Zaslow, M. J. (1989). Sex differences in children's response to parental divorce: Samples, variables, ages and sources. *American Journal of Orthopsychiatry, 59,* 118–141.

CHAPTER 10

SCHOOL

John M. Hintze
Edward S. Shapiro

Perhaps more than any institution besides family, the influence of school on children's development remains tantamount. As one of the major forces in socializing expectations and values associated with achievement in many domains, school experiences have a substantial impact on development across the lifespan.

Schooling influences are strong, due to experiences not afforded elsewhere. It is in school where children have the opportunity to interact with a large group of same-aged peers, are presented with formal instruction and curriculum, and where performance is both publicly and privately evaluated. Nowhere else is competence and performance so steadily stressed across a variety of domains. Although to some degree school mediates the effects of family, its unique characteristics give it special importance in the children's development (Stipek, 1992).

This chapter focuses on domains of development in which school plays a critical role. Although an all-inclusive chapter of this nature could include countless topics, an attempt was made to summarize domains of childhood development that play especially important roles in the interaction between the child and school. The first section focuses on theory and research on achievement-related constructs, par-

ticularly those related to problem-solving abilities and the development of achievement-related beliefs. How children problem solve and how problem solving is taught is especially relevant given current cognitive views of learning and a revitalization of the importance between curriculum and instruction. An associated but often overlooked topic on children's beliefs about their competencies is also presented. "What am I good at?" "Will I succeed?" "How can we as professionals help instill competency beliefs in our children?" are judgements that influence the domains of achievement that children pursue in school and throughout their lives. How this naturally develops and how school can help modify these beliefs are presented.

The second section discusses socially related constructs with a particular emphasis on the development of social skills and competence. Long considered the obligation of parents, schools are becoming increasingly responsible for the development of social behavior of youth. Indeed, the prognosis for children with social deficits later in life has been shown to be quite poor. An awareness of these issues from a developmental and intervention perspective is of paramount importance for those working with children and youth in the schools.

ACHIEVEMENT-RELATED CONSTRUCTS

Development of Problem-Solving Abilities

Although the biological correlates of intelligence continue to be greatly debated (cf. Brody, 1992), there is a growing recognition that changes in learning and problem-solving abilities are affected by the interaction of a range of situations in which children successfully execute problem-solving processes (Ellis & Siegler, 1994). These changes in large part result from specific experiences faced by children as they go to school and are required to interact with an ever-growing range of people and demands. Schooling influences the types of problems presented (e.g., curriculum and instruction—reading, writing, mathematics, science, social studies, etc.), the basic skills children have available for solving problems (e.g., fluency and comprehension of reading, mathematical calculations, written expression, etc.), and relevant knowledge that children apply to solve problems in specific domains (Ellis & Siegler, 1994).

The development of problem-solving strategies follows conspicuously different courses, depending on whether children have had extensive experience with the task or not. In particular, on tasks in which children have little experience, behavior is often governed by the use of a single strategy to solve problems. Such *domain-general strategies* can be applied to a variety of problems, independent of content. However, as is true of other domain-general procedures, their flexibility is also their weakness. In contrast, on tasks in which children have considerable experience, behavior is often governed by the use of multiple unique strategies. Unique or *domain-specific strategies* have a more strategic quality than do generalized strategies. That is, they do not apply to all similar situations in a domain but only to a specified goal under specified conditions (Gagné, Yekovich, & Yekovich, 1993).

Natural Development of Problem-Solving Abilities

Just how do children make the transition from domain-general to domain-specific strategies? Evidence suggests that the transition may be part natural development. For example, in a series of studies, Siegler and colleagues (Richards & Siegler, 1981; Siegler, 1976, 1978) empirically demonstrated the transition from domain-general strategies to domain-specific strategies across the early years of childhood. Using a balance scale with pegs spaced at regular intervals along each end of the arm, children were asked to predict which side of the balance scale would go down depending on the number of metal disks placed on each side, and on which pegs the disks were placed (either nearer or farther away from the fulcrum).

Results indicated that children rely on domain-general strategies in the preschool period. When asked to predict which side of the balance scale would go down, 3 year olds tended to guess or switch frequently among alternative approaches. By their fourth year, children evidenced more refined domain-general strategies by predicting that the side that had more metal disks would go down. If each side had an equal number, however, their responses were random (rather than predicting that the scale would remain balanced). This problem was resolved by the fifth year whereby children began to refine their strategies by predicting that whatever side had more weight would go down, and that when the weights were equal, the scale would balance. By age 8 or 9, most children adopted domain-specific strategies that took into account not just the amount of weight on each side but also the distance of the weight from the fulcrum.

Evidence for domain-specific strategies was further demonstrated by observing that some children employed strategies that considered the distance from the fulcrum only when the amount of weight on each side was equal; while others used a more sophisticated strategy that considered both weight and distance, regardless of whether the weight on the two sides were equal. However, children who applied this domain-specific strategy still could not solve problems in which one side had more weight and the other side had its weight farther from the fulcrum (e.g., 3 weights on the fourth peg to the left of the fulcrum versus 6 weights on the second peg to the right of the fulcrum). Finally, consistent solutions to these problems emerge in mid to late adolescence when children understand that the relative torques on the two sides is what determines which side will go down.

Although by no means exhaustive, these series of studies (Richards & Siegler, 1981; Siegler, 1976, 1978) provide an excellent example of what many consider to be the constructivistic and structuralistic development of problem solving. That is, children "come to know what they know," moving from general to specific strategies, by way of a process that involves actively constructing and working with materials in their environment and subsequently arranging their knowledge by similar or underlying organizational properties. Such models suggest that problem solving and cognitive development proceed through a series of stages, where a stage is a period of time in which a child's thinking and behavior in a variety of situations reflect a particular type of underlying logical structure (Tharinger & Lambert, 1990). Similar developmental accounts have also been noted in areas of logical classification (e.g., additive classification, hierarchical classification, multiplicative classification); numerical processes (e.g., ordering, one-to-one correspondence, conservation of quantity, transitivity, ratio, and proportion); orientation in space (e.g., reproduction of geometrical figures, locating objects in space, subdivision of objects in space); chance and probability (e.g., use of proportions for quantification and, permutations) and measurement (e.g., measurement and conservation of length, weight, area and volume, and time) (Copeland, 1988; Ginsburg & Opper, 1979; Wadsworth, 1978).

Development of Problem-Solving Abilities within the Context of School

Advances and broadening perspectives in recent years have given rise to the belief that knowledge and problem solving are not separable from the actions or the culture in which those actions occur; positions that are consistent with Soviet thought regarding psychological analyses of activity and thought (e.g.,Vygotsky, 1962; Vygotsky, 1978; Wertsch, 1985). Teachers often assist children in thinking about problems they are confronting (e.g., how to solve a puzzle, how many more days until their birthday, etc.). What goes on in these interactions is thinking, thinking that involves both the teacher and the student. The child could not work through many problems without assistance, but with teacher support makes adequate progress. Years of participating in such interactions lead to internalization by the child of the types of actions once carried out between the child and the teacher. That is, thought processes that were once interpersonal become intrapersonal (Pressley & McCormick, 1995).

The process or mechanism through which these interactions develop has been referred to as *apprenticeship models* or *situated cognition* (Brown, Collins, & Duguid, 1989). When children learn how to read, write, and problem solve in school, their understanding of reading, writing, and problem solving are largely tied to the schooling environments. According to Vygotsky (1962, 1978) cognitive development moves forward largely because the child is in a social world that provides assistance when the child needs it and can benefit from it. Critical developmental interactions occur with tasks in between two extremes—tasks that the child can not do independently, but can do with some assistance (e.g., from a teacher, parent, or peer). The responsive social world provides assistance with tasks within this continuum, or on tasks that are within the child's *zone of proximal development,* that is, behaviors beyond the child's autonomous functioning but within reach with assistance. Children learn how to perform tasks within their zone by interacting with more competent and responsive others who provide hints, prompts, and assistance to the child on an as needed basis (Pressley & McCormick, 1995). Such guided practice helps facilitate problem solving and eventually enables the child to internalize the steps and ultimately perform the task without assistance.

Implicit within situated cognition or the apprenticeship model are a number of processes that facilitate the development of autonomous problem solving. According to Collins, Brown, and Newman (1989) six interactional components are involved between teacher and student: (1) modeling, (2) coaching, (3) scaffolding, (4) articulation, (5) reflection, and (6) exploration. During the first step, the teacher demonstrates how to do tasks that are important and explains the subtleties of the specific task(s). The teacher makes obvious to the children his or her actions, often calling attention to overt behaviors that would normally be carried out automatically or covertly. During this stage students have the opportunity to observe the behavior(s) and hear a detailed rationale by an expert as to why the actions were taken. Second, during coaching, students have an opportunity to problem solve and work with the task directly while the teacher offers clues, performance feedback, and suggestions or guidance. If difficulties arise, the teacher may offer additional modeling or explanation. Coaching may occur at any time during the apprenticeship period. Third, the teacher employs scaffolding by which support and guidance are slowly faded until the student can perform the task independently. Scaffolding requires great diagnostic skills on the part of the teacher who must determine both when the child needs help and subsequently appropriate redirection. To efficiently do this, teachers must be well versed with the many different types of errors that children may exhibit and how to handle such errors. To effectively do this, teachers must evaluate the demands of the task and learner characteristics such that an appropriate match is made between child and task. As such, it is imperative that the teacher have a thorough understanding of individual differences as they relate to zones of proximal development. Fourth, during articulation, the teacher asks the children to explain what they are doing. Thus, the teacher may ask a child to explain how she or he went about solving a problem and why the particular solution method was used over alternative methods. Next, children are asked to reflect and evaluate or compare their solution with that of the teacher or even their peers. For example, reflection may occur when a third-grade student evaluates a writing sample or math problem individually with the teacher or makes some formative comparisons with the work of their fellow students. Evaluating how one is doing with the long-term goal of improving one's skills is an important component of the apprenticeship model of problem solving. Finally, children are encouraged to explore new ways of problem solving on their own. Although prior steps are important in the development of problem-solving skills, the ultimate goal is to have children self-regulate their strategies such that reliance on an "expert" or teacher diminishes over time. Good teachers teach children how to explore and encourage them to do so.

Relationship of Problem Solving to Psychopathology

Research on problem solving has found that the ability to produce problem solutions may be related to poor adjustment, including both internalizing and externalizing behavior problems (Baum, 1989; March, 1995; Stark, 1990). For example, several researchers have hypothesized that the interpersonal difficulties of children who exhibit antisocial and conduct disorders may be due to differences in their interpretation of social stimuli, particularly the tendency to attribute hostile intentions to others (Baum, 1989). Children who exhibit antisocial and conduct disorders often show a problem-solving response bias in which they interpret ambiguous interpersonal stimuli as being hostile (Dodge, Price, Bachorowski, & Newman, 1990; Dodge & Somberg, 1987). This problem-solving bias may result in and justify aggressive responses to the misperceived hostile stimulus. Children who exhibit antisocial and conduct disorders have also been shown to have difficulties generating multiple and/or prosocial problem solutions (Short & Shapiro, 1993). Such children tend to be limited and inflexible in solution generation, resulting in a narrow repertoire for responding to conflict situations (Spivack, Platt, & Shure, 1976).

Aggressive boys also present perceptual biases in their own and others' problem-solving abilities with regard to the level of aggression demonstrated in interpersonal interactions. More often than not, aggressive children underestimate their own aggression and overestimate the aggressive behavior of their nonaggressive peers (Lochman, 1987). Milich and Dodge (1984) examined problem-solving deficits in boys with one or a combination of externalizing disorders. Overall, boys who exhibited one or more externalizing disorders were more likely than normal controls to interpret hostile intent in the actions of others and choose aggressive response alternatives, and they attended to fewer interpersonal cues before making an attributional decision. Children with attention-deficit hyperactivity disorder (ADHD) have been shown to be poorer in complex problem solving strategies and organizational skills and to apply less efficient strategies in approaching learning tasks (Barkley, 1990). Difficulties in problem solving often arise when these children must apply executive strategies in approaching a task. Although children with ADHD do not have significant memory problems in general, their problem-solving strategies are often impulsive, poorly organized, and relatively inefficient (Zentall, 1988).

Children with internalizing disorders have also been shown to demonstrate faulty problem-solving processes.

For example, children with anxiety disorders often possess a problem-solving style that increases rather than decreases uncertainty and unpredictability in conditions of perceived threat (Silverman & Ginsburg, 1995). Excess coping and problem-solving strategies in children with anxiety are often unmodulated and interfere with the ability to manage anxiety (Kendall & Chansky, 1991). Although children with anxiety disorders appear to possess a reservoir of coping and problem-solving strategies, their inability to selectively attend to those that are most salient often leads to maladaptive outcomes. Furthermore, difficulty concentrating, indecisiveness, and problem solving has been reported in children with depression (Stark, 1990). Difficulties solving problems and making decisions can further exacerbate feelings of hopelessness and negative self-evaluations, two of the most commonly reported symptoms of children with depression.

Treatment Applications of Problem-Solving within the Context of School

Reciprocal Teaching

Peer-mediated models of problem solving have provided powerful perspectives on instructional delivery models within schools. One method known as *reciprocal teaching* developed by Palincsar and colleagues (Palincsar, 1986; Palincsar & Brown, 1988; Palincsar, Brown, & Martin, 1987) is based on the use of metacognitive instructional techniques. As described by Palincsar (1986), reciprocal teaching involves the use of dialogue between teachers (or peers) and students for the purpose of jointly constructing meaning from text. Based largely on strategy instruction, reciprocal teaching is characterized by the use of summarizing, question generating, clarifying, and predicting to solve problems and increasing comprehension. As an example of reciprocal teaching, children with their teacher begin each session by reviewing the strategies that they are learning, emphasizing their important features and the context within which the strategies are useful. New content for the day is presented and children are encouraged to make use of the background information they have on the topic at hand to make predictions about what they will learn in the text and to indicate what they would like to learn about the topic. Children then review the material silently followed by a teacher summary and an invitation for elaboration by the students. This leads to group clarification of relevant issues, themes, and so forth, and ends with predictions for material that they have not yet reviewed. During initial training the teacher is principally responsible for initiating and maintaining the dialogue. Over time this responsibility is transferred to the children while the teacher provides more specific feedback and coaching on the use of the specific strategies. A characteristic of successful metacognitive strategy instruction is the gradual transfer of control of the strategy from the teacher to the students. This type of guided, interactive instruction has been called *scaffolded instruction,* a metaphor suggested by the fact thata scaffold is a support system that is temporary and adjustable (Palincsar, 1986).

The bulk of the research on reciprocal teaching has been conducted with junior high-aged students. In the initial research, teachers worked with groups of approximately five students (Brown & Palincsar, 1982; Palincsar & Brown, 1984). The groups read expository passages from basal readers written at the seventh-grade level. Reciprocal teaching was employed for 20 consecutive school days. Transcripts taken from the groups indicated substantial changes in the dialogue that occurred during the 20-day period. Students became increasingly sophisticated in their ability to employ the strategies independently of the teacher. Progress was also indicated on daily measures of reading comprehension. Each day, following reciprocal teaching, students read silently a 450-word passage and answered 10 comprehension questions from memory. All but one of the 27 student participants achieved criterion performance of 70 percent accuracy for 4 out of 5 consecutive days. Furthermore, assessment of reading comprehension conducted in social studies and science suggested that students' improvement generalized to these settings as well. Students who, prior to the initiation of the study, ranked below the twentieth percentile on comprehension relative to their peers, placed at the fiftieth percentile or higher following the reciprocal teaching problem-solving model.

In slightly different application, same age tutor–tutee dyads engaged in reciprocal teaching instructional procedures. Following 10 days of reciprocal teaching instruction, tutor–tutee pairs began working together, independent of teacher instruction. The results indicated that the use of reciprocal teaching from a peer-tutoring perspective was successful. In fact, the gains indicated by the tutees on comprehension assessments were comparable to those made by students working with teachers. In addition, the amount of student engagement was quite high during tutoring sessions, a variable that has been found to be a strong predictor of achievement.

Cooperative Learning

In a somewhat more prescriptive and task-focused model of problem solving, Slavin and associates (Slavin, 1985; Slavin, 1987; Slavin, Madden, & Leavey, 1984; Slavin & Oickle, 1981; Slavin, Stevens, & Madden, 1988) have developed a model of problem solving entitled *cooperative learning* that blends the developmental theories of Piaget and Vygotsky with theories of motivation. The fundamental

assumption of cooperative learning from a developmental perspective is that interaction among children around appropriate tasks increases their mastery of critical concepts or skills. However, in addition to this developmental focus, cooperative learning is also concerned with the reward or goal structures under which children operate (Slavin, 1985).

From the developmental perspective, the effect of cooperative learning on student achievement is largely or entirely due to the use of cooperative task structures (Slavin, 1985). In this view, the opportunity for students to discuss, to argue, to present and hear one anothers' viewpoints is the critical element of academic growth. In contrast, the motivational perspective on cooperative learning emphasizes the cooperative reward structure as a critical element, maintaining that children problem solve and increase their achievement because of cooperative reward structures, which in turn create peer norms and sanctions supporting individual efforts toward the solution of problems (Slavin, 1985).

As an example, Stevens, Slavin, and Farnish (1991) compared the effects of cooperative learning to typical basal instruction on reading comprehension strategies and identification of main ideas in text. A total of 468 third- and fourth-grade children in four elementary schools were randomly assigned by class to either treatment (i.e., cooperative learning) or control (i.e., typical basal instruction) conditions. In the cooperative learning condition, following an introduction by the teacher to new material, students were divided into four- or five-member groups for team practice. Depending on the content, students' activities included practice exercises, drilling each other on vocabulary words, discussing comprehension questions through consensus, and so forth. Individual assessments were conducted during the cooperative groups and were scored by team members. Problem solving incorrect responses was done by individual team members. At the end of each session all groups received public team recognition. Children in the control groups received typical teacher-led basal reading instruction (e.g., teacher introduces new vocabulary words, listens as children read in a round-robin format, asks comprehension questions, monitors individual skill worksheets). Results indicated that children in the cooperative learning groups used significantly more inference questions to problem solve and comprehend the main idea of what was read than did children in the typical teacher-led basal reading condition. When compared to typical teacher-led instruction, cooperative learning evidenced an effect size of +.82. This study provided evidence of the strong effect that cooperative learning formats can have on the problem-solving and the metacognitive strategies of children.

Although this serves as only one example, Slavin (1983) in a comprehensive review of the research identified forty-six studies that used cooperative learning to improve prob-lem solving and academic achievement. The identified stud-ies represented children across nearly all grades (i.e., second through twelfth), in urban and suburban settings in four countries, and across diverse subject areas such as mathematics, language arts, social studies, science, and for-eign language. Overall, the findings of the forty-six studies were fairly consistent in showing significantly greater gains in problem solving and achievement for cooperative learn-ing formats as compared to control conditions. Twenty-nine of the studies (63%) found such effects, and in only two (4%) did control students achieve significantly more than experimental students.

The efficacy of such alternative teaching efforts on problem-solving and achievement has been further illustrated by instructional models such as cooperative learning (e.g., Johnson & Johnson, 1977); reciprocal peer tutoring (e.g., Fantuzzo, Polite, Grayson, 1990; Fantuzzo, Riggio, Connelly, & Dimeff, 1989); classwide peer tutoring (e.g., Greenwood, Delquadri, & Hall, 1984; Greenwood, Terry, Arrega-Mayer, & Finney, 1992; Hall, Delquadri, Greenwood, & Thurston, 1982); and direct instruction (e.g., Rosenshine, 1979; Rosen-shine & Stevens, 1984). Although procedural uniqueness is evident in how instruction is provided, conceptually each ar-rangement highlights the importance of constructs such as modeling good problem-solving strategies, providing an ap-propriate match between child variables and task demands, evaluation, and reinforcement and the subsequent positive ef-fects on problem-solving and achievement.

Development of Achievement-Related Beliefs

Natural Development of Academic Competence and Beliefs

In school and other contexts that involve performance and competition, children formulate a set of interrelated beliefs about their competencies. In any particular situation, chil-dren make judgements about what causes success and fail-ure and how likely their effort is to lead to success and to be rewarded (Stipek, 1992). Systematic age differences have important implications for how children behave in school and in achievement settings, which in turn influence chil-dren's perceptions of school experiences.

Children's perceptions of achievement-related compe-tence becomes increasingly differentiated with age. Thus, for example, academic ability becomes conceptually differ-entiated from social competence (Stipek & Daniels, 1990; Yussen & Kane, 1985); from work habits and effort (Blu-menfeld, Pintrich, Meece, & Wessels, 1982; Stipek & Tan-

natt, 1984); and competence ratings in different academic domains (Marsh, Barnes, Cairns, & Tidman, 1984).

Studies in pre- and early-elementary school suggest that children focus on effort expended (Harter & Pike, 1984), per-sonal mastery (Blumenfeld, Pintrich, & Hamilton, 1986; Sti-pek, 1981), and social reinforcement (Spear & Armstrong, 1978) in their ability assessments. For example, preschool through second-grade children explain high self-perceptions of academic competence by citing habitual engagement in activities that foster skill development (e.g., "I practice a lot"). Thus, effort is an isolated construct that explains most if not all of a child's academic competence. If a child in the early years of schooling performs well academically, it is likely that she or he will attribute academic competence to the level of effort expended. Furthermore, younger children of-ten cite mastery as evidence of their competence, but unlike older children tend not to accept nonmastery as evidence of incompetence (Stipek, 1992). Younger children may at-tribute nonmastery to a lack of effort rather than ability con-structs, while older children may conjecture that nonmastery is evidence of incompetence and lack of ability.

The way that children process social feedback also changes with age. Children's interpretations of teacher feedback is related to developmental changes in their under-standing that success on easy tasks requires less ability than success on difficult tasks and that, given equal outcomes, ef-fort and ability are inversely related (Stipek, 1992). Both young and older children understand that teachers praise success and express displeasure for failure when they per-ceive that a child has exerted high or low effort, respectively (Harari & Covington, 1981). Only older children, however, infer low ability when success on an easy task requires high effort (and therefore praise) or when failure on an easy task is not attributed to low effort (and therefore is not responded to with displeasure) (Stipek, 1992). Children apparently be-come increasingly attentive to the context in which feed-back is given (e.g., difficulty of the task, effort expended, and whether other children are praised) and to teachers' re-sponses (praise or displeasure) to their performance.

Development of Academic Competence and Self-Efficacy within the Context of School

Self-efficacy theory postulates that people acquire informa-tion to appraise efficacy from their performance accom-plishments, vicarious experiences, forms of persuasion, and physiological indexes (Bandura, 1977, 1986). As such, a child's own performances can offer reliable guides for him-self or herself to assess their own efficacy. Success raises ef-ficacy and failure lowers it. However, once a strong sense of efficacy is developed, a failure is likely to have much less

impact (Bandura, 1986). Children who meet the task demands of school successfully are more likely to perceive
themselves as competent in the same or similar situations in
the future. Furthermore, once a sense of competence is
formed, episodic bouts with failure are less likely to substantially impact the child's sense of competence.

Self-efficacy is developed by children in a variety of ways.
First, children have shown to be quite adept at acquiring information and knowledge through the observation of others.
Similar others offer the best basis for comparison (Schunk,
1989). Observing similar peers perform a task communicates
to the child that he or she is also capable of accomplishing it.
Information acquired vicariously typically has a weaker effect on self-efficacy than performance-based information.
For this reason, vicarious increases in efficacy can be negated
by subsequent failures (Schunk, 1991). Second, children can
be influenced by the persuasory information that they possess
the capabilities to perform a task (e.g., "You can do this").
Positive persuasory feedback enhances self-efficacy; however, this increase will be temporary if subsequent efforts turn
out poorly. Third, children also derive efficacy information
from physiological indices (e.g., heart rate and sweating). For
example, bodily symptoms signaling anxiety might be interpreted to indicate a lack of skills to a child (Schunk, 1991).
Finally, information acquired from these sources does not automatically influence efficacy; rather, it is cognitively ap-
praised (Bandura, 1986). Efficacy appraisal is an inferential
process in which persons weigh and combine the contributions of such personal and situational factors as their perceived ability, the difficulty of the task, amount of effort
expended, amount of external assistance received, number
and pattern of successes and failures, their perceived similarity to models, and persuader credibility (Schunk, 1989).

Development of Academic Competence
and Self-Efficacy within the Context of School

The operation of self-efficacy in a model of academic competence had been proposed by Schunk (1984, 1985) and incorporates elements of social learning theory, attribution
theory, and instructional psychology. As a precursor, children enter into learning situations with different aptitudes
and prior experiences for subject matter. Aptitudes include
general abilities, skills, strategies, interests, attitudes, and
personality characteristics (Cronbach & Snow, 1977). Educational experiences derive from prior schools attended, interactions with teachers, time spent in different subjects,
and so forth. Nonetheless, these two factors are not independent. Observed outcomes for any child is a result of the dynamic interplay between aptitude for a given content area

and a child's subsequent experiences with the content. Aptitudes and prior experiences will affect childrens' initial
beliefs about their capabilities for learning. Indeed, children
who previously have performed well in a subject area ought
to believe that they are capable of learning a new task in that
area, whereas children who have experienced difficulties
may doubt their capabilities (Schunk, 1989).

Although self-efficacy is influenced by aptitudes and prior
experiences, it is not merely a reflection of them. Collins
(1982) administered standardized tests to children and identified those with high, average, and low mathematical ability.
Within each ability level, children were also identified as exhibiting high and low mathematical self-efficacy. Children
were then given problems to solve and the opportunity to rework those that they missed. Results indicated that prior
mathematical ability was positively related to competence
and performance; however, regardless of ability level, children with higher self-efficacy solved more problems correctly
and chose to rework more of the problems that they missed.

Although entry characteristics such as aptitude and prior
experience explain part of a child's academic competence,
efficacy cues also affect children's beliefs about academic
competence. *Efficacy cues* signal to children how well they
are learning. Children in turn use the cues to appraise their
own self-efficacy for continued learning. Self-efficacy then
affects both motivational and skill acquisition properties of
academic competence (Schunk, 1989).

The actual cognitive processes involved in appraising
self-efficacy may be very similar to how children cognitively process instructional information. Winne (1985) suggests that efficacy expectations are represented in memory
as a series of "if–then" statements, much like that of declar-
ative and procedural knowledge (Gagné, Yekovich, & Yekovich, 1993). In appraising academic self-efficacy, children
attend to cues while they are engaged with a task, evaluate
their performance, and then form beliefs about their competence that are compatible with preexisting efficacy representations (Schunk, 1989). When disparity exists between a
child's current self-evaluation and preexisting self-efficacy
representations, the latter is apt to change. For this reason,
performance outcomes and self-evaluation are important
cues that children use for appraising academic self-efficacy
and competence. Successes generally raise, and failures generally lower, self-efficacy; however, after many successes an
occasional failure is likely to have little impact, as would one
success after many failures. Even in earlier stages of learning in which failure is commonplace, the belief that
progress is being made will promote academic self-efficacy.
Problems arise, however, when children perceive that their
progress is slow or that their skills have stabilized at low lev-

els (Schunk, 1985). Finally, evaluations or attributions associated with achievement are critical in academic self-efficacy. As previously noted, children in earlier stages of development view effort as the prime cause of achievement outcomes, but as they gain experience and develop, a distinct conception of ability emerges (Nicholls, 1978). Over time, ability attributions become increasingly important influences on expectations, while the role of effort declines in importance (Harari & Covington, 1981).

Nonetheless, the task of creating environments conducive to learning rests heavily on the talents and self-efficacy of teachers. Evidence indicates that classroom atmospheres are partly determined by teachers' beliefs in their instructional efficacy (Bandura, 1993). Gibson and Dembo (1984) found that teachers who have a high sense of instructional efficacy devote more classroom time to academic learning, provide students who have difficulty learning with the help they need to succeed, and praise them for their accomplishments. In contrast, teachers who have a low sense of instructional efficacy spend more time on nonacademic tasks, are less persistent with children who required modifications in instructional delivery, and are typically more punitive when children fail. Teachers who believe strongly in their teaching efficacy create mastery experiences for their students, while those with self-doubt towards their teaching are less likely to foster academic self-efficacy in their students.

In addition, from an instructional delivery perspective, Brophy (1983) has shown that the manner in which a teacher begins a lesson can have an impact on student self-efficacy. A teacher who provides no introduction and moves directly into a task may have little or negative effect on the academic belief system of a group of children. In contrast, beginning a lesson with positive expectations by asserting that children will enjoy the task and do well on it provides a markedly different learning atmosphere. To the extent that children view the teacher as a credible judge of their abilities, instructional delivery that clearly specifies the expectations for performance can have a profound impact on academic self-efficacy.

Modeling outcomes and outcome procedures by teachers is another way in which academic self-efficacy is enhanced within the classroom (Bandura, 1986). Observing a superior model, such as a teacher, succeed using a strategy that students believe they can apply themselves helps to increase the probability that children will be successful. The manner in which teachers set goals and reward performance can also have important consequences on academic self-efficacy. Goals that incorporate specific performance standards are more likely to raise learning efficacy because progress towards an explicit goal is easier to gauge. Setting the difficulty of a goal just beyond that which a child can comfortably mas-

ter ensures that the child witnesses progress towards the ultimate goal without becoming frustrated. Finally, goals that are proximally distant in time result in greater motivation than more distant goals as children can once again monitor their own progress towards the ultimate goal (Bandura, 1986; Locke, Shaw, Saari, & Latham, 1981).

Similarly, reinforcement constitutes an important influence on children's task performance (Bijou, 1993). Reinforcement is likely to enhance academic self-efficacy when it is tied to children's actual accomplishments. Providing contingencies for rewards can instill a sense of self-efficacy for learning (Schunk, 1985). As children then work at a task and note their progress, this sense of efficacy is validated. Receipt of the reward further validates self-efficacy, because it is tied directly to progress. When rewards are not tied to actual performance, they may convey negative efficacy information as children may infer that they are not expected to learn much because they do not possess the requisite capability (Schunk, 1989).

Relationship between Academic Self-Efficacy, Achievement, and Psychopathology

To date, research on the causal ordering of the relationship between academic beliefs and self-efficacy and achievement has been equivocal. Although Marsh (1990) has reported that academic beliefs and self-efficacy lead to improved or impaired academic achievement, other studies (e.g., Calsyn & Kenny, 1977) have concluded that prior achievement (e.g., either positive or negative) is more important in forming subsequent academic beliefs. Still others have stressed the degree to which the relation between academic self-efficacy and achievement is reciprocal and that this relation may change direction at any one time during a child's or student's development (Wigfield & Karpathian, 1991).

Nonetheless, regardless of the orientation to which one ascribes, there is an undeniable link between academic and school failure and later adjustment from a life span perspective. Children who present with low academic performance and self-efficacy are more likely to exhibit antisocial (Bale, 1981), delinquent (Frick, Lahey, Christ, Loeber, & Green, 1991; Tremblay et al, 1992), or disruptive classroom behaviors (Finn, 1988; Rincker, 1990; Walker, Stieber, & Ramsey, 1990, 1991).

Treatment Applications of Academic Beliefs and Self-Efficacy within the Context of School

The belief that one possesses the capability to perform given activities has shown to be an accurate predictor of academic performance. Perceived self-efficacy affects behavioral functioning by influencing children's choice of activities, effort expenditure, and persistence in the face of difficulties. Children who have a strong sense of efficacy in a given subject matter generally exhibit strong achievement strivings. In contrast, children who perceive themselves as inefficacious tend to shun achievement tasks or engage in them halfheartedly and give up readily in the fact of obstacles.

Schunk (1981) examined the effect of attribution training and modeling on the academic achievement and self-efficacy of children who displayed repeated failure in the area of arithmetic. Fifty-six children ranging in age from 9 years 2 months to 11 years 3 months, with a mean of 9 years 10 months, participated and received either standard didactic instruction or a cognitive-modeling treatment in arithmetic. Cognitive modeling involved observing an adult solve arithmetic problems while verbalizing aloud the solution strategies used to arrive at correct answers. For half of the children in each treatment condition, attribution training was also provided. As such, the teacher attributed children's successes to high effort and difficulties to low effort on the average of once every 5 to 6 minutes while the children were working on arithmetic problems. The remaining children received competency training without causal attribution for their performances. Arithmetic skill, persistence, and self-efficacy were measured before and after treatment. Results indicated that children with higher percepts of self-efficacy subsequently persisted longer and achieved more success on arithmetic tasks than their less efficacious and persistent counterparts. Furthermore, those children who received attribution statements from the teacher judged themselves to be more competent in arithmetic than did children who did not receive attribution statements. On a cautionary note, however, the use of effort attribution statements with children whose performances reflect basic skill deficiencies bears warning. Teachers who mistakenly attribute children's failure to insufficient effort, especially after children have worked hard at problems, might demoralize children who lack the requisite skills to succeed. For this reason, effort attributions and corrective feedback need to be specific to the conditions under which they occur. Nonetheless, this study provided support for the idea that children's self-perceptions of capabilities have a substantial effect on their subsequent academic achievement.

In a follow-up study, Schunk (1982) assessed the effects of providing past (e.g., "You've been working very hard") versus future (e.g., "You need to work harder") oriented attributional statements on the academic achievement of forty children age 7 to 11. Results indicated that children who had received "past" attributional statements judged their arithmetic efficacy to be significantly higher than children who

received either "future" attributional statements or controls. Furthermore, children who received attributional statements in the "past" format completed 30 to 35 percent more arithmetic work than did their "future" or control counterparts. Regression analysis indicated that self-efficacy accounted for the largest portion of total variation in achievement besides that which could be credited to the natural improvement of skills over time. More so than persistence, believing that one was capable and competent in an assigned area leads to more skillful performance. Moreover, self-efficacy is strengthened by feedback related to what a child *has* done in the past that was appropriate, rather than what the child *should* do in the future that they have neglected to do in the past. Past performance feedback provides authentic information for judging personal capabilities based on success. Imploring that a child "try harder" may actually undermine self-efficacy because the child may perceive this as a sign that he or she lacks ability. This study supported the notion that children's perceptions of their capabilities have important effects on their subsequent achievement.

Lastly, Schunk and Hanson (1985) investigated how children's self-efficacy and achievement were influenced by observing peer models learning a cognitive skill. A total of seventy-two children ages 8 to 11 who exhibited math difficulties viewed videotapes of an adult teacher providing subtraction operations to a child model of the same sex and age as themselves, followed by the model solving problems; viewed videotapes that portrayed only the teacher providing instruction; or did not view videotapes at all. Results indicated that self-efficacious beliefs were positively related to posttest skill and performance in arithmetic. Students who observed child models reported higher levels of self-efficacy than children who viewed a teacher model only or control. Viewing models that exhibit similar abilities, traits, and so forth, and watching them succeed, strengthens the belief of an observer that "if she or he can do it, so can I."

Taken in total, what these series of studies exemplify is the role that self-efficacy and self-perceptions have in relation to achievement. Children who have a low sense of efficacy in a given domain evidence low aspirations and weak commitment to the goals that they choose to pursue. They maintain a self-diagnostic focus rather than concentrate on how to perform successfully. When faced with difficult tasks, they dwell on their personal deficiencies, on the obstacles that they will encounter, and so forth. Because they diagnose insufficient performance as deficient aptitude, it does not require much failure for them to lose faith in their capabilities (Bandura, 1993).

On the other hand, a strong sense of self-efficacy enhances personal accomplishment. Children with high self-efficacy approach difficult tasks as challenges to be mastered rather than as threats to be avoided. Efficacious children set challenging goals for themselves and maintain a strong commitment to them. When failure is met, academically self-efficacious children increase their effort, fill gaps in knowledge, and learn the skills that will foster success. Once formed, self-efficacy beliefs contribute significantly to the level and quality of academic functioning (Bandura, 1993).

SOCIALLY RELATED CONSTRUCTS

The Development of Prosocial Behavior

Many studies have demonstrated that young children show lower levels of prosocial behavior and that these behaviors increase during early and middle elementary-school years (Radke-Yarrow, Zahn-Waxler, & Chapman, 1983). For example, older preschool children tend to show more prosocial behavior than younger preschool children in response to negative emotions simulated by an unfamiliar adult (Denham & Couchard, 1991). In children ranging in age from late preschool to early adolescence, older children were more likely than younger children to provide verbal comfort or physical help to a crying infant and to help an injured adult or an animal in distress (Chapman, Zahn-Waxler, Cooperman, & Iannotti, 1987; Zahn-Waxler, Friedman, & Cummings, 1983).

Social Competence

Social competence is a complex, multidimensional construct, consisting of a variety of behavioral and cognitive variables, as well as aspects of emotional adjustment useful and necessary to developing adequate social relations and obtaining desirable social outcomes (Merrell, 1994). Gresham (1986) conceptualized the broad domain of social competence as being comprised of three subdomains: (1) adaptive behavior, (2) social skills, and (3) peer relations. Based largely on Leland's (1978) views, adaptive behavior is subdivided into areas related to independent functioning (i.e., ability of an individual to accomplish critical survival skills expected by society as a function of chronological age); personal responsibility (i.e., reflecting the individual's decision-making and choice ability); and social responsibility (i.e., individual's levels of social conformity, social adjustment, and emotional maturity). Unlike other definitions, Gresham's (1986) places a heavy emphasis on the role of personal and social responsibility. Social skills on the other hand, include interpersonal behaviors (e.g., accepting authority, conversation skills, cooperative behaviors, play behaviors), self-related behaviors (e.g., expressing feelings, ethical behavior, positive attitude toward self), and task-related behaviors (e.g., attending behavior, completing tasks, following directions, independent work). Finally, peer rela-

tions refer to the result or product of a child's social skills. Peer relations as a by-product of adaptive behavior and social skills is extremely important given its high correspondence with peer acceptance and rejection.

Social Competence within the Context of School

A growing body of literature in the fields of child development, education, and psychology collectively points to the conclusion that the development of adequate social skills and peer relationships during childhood has important and far reaching ramifications (Merrell, 1994). The development of appropriate social skills during childhood is an extremely important precursor to adequate peer relationships (Asher & Taylor, 1981). There is also evidence that childhood social skills and consequent peer relationships have a significant impact on academic success during the school years (Walker & Hops, 1976).

Given that adequate social skills and peer relations are important foundations for various types of success in life, it is not surprising that inadequate development in these areas can lead to a variety of deleterious or negative outcomes. A classic and frequently cited investigation by Cowen, Pederson, Babigian, Izzo, and Trost (1983) involving an 11- to 13-year follow-up study of third-grade students has provided convincing evidence that early peer relationship problems are strong predictors of mental health problems later in life. Other frequently cited studies have suggested that inadequate social skills and poor peer relations during childhood may lead to a variety of other problems later in life, such as juvenile delinquency, dropping out of school, conduct-related discharges from military service, chronic unemployment and underemployment, and psychiatric hospitalizations (Loeber, 1985; Parker & Asher, 1987; Roff, 1963; Roff & Sells, 1968; Roff, Sells, & Golden, 1972).

Treatment Applications of Social Competence and Skills within the Context of School

As is readily apparent, social skills and peer acceptance are extremely important for school-age children and youth. For these reasons, social skills training has become a major treatment effort for children who are deficient in these areas.

For example, Lewis and Sugai (1993) altered environmental contingencies in combination with the Procedures for Establishing Effective Relationship Skills (PEERS) program (Hops et al., 1978) in an attempt to promote the maintenance of treatment effects. Three socially withdrawn children (two girls, one boy) were selected for treatment on the basis of teacher nominations and low frequency of interaction with peers during observation in free-play settings. Functional analyses were conducted for each child and contextual interventions developed to decrease withdrawn behavior. Each child's teacher was trained to implement both PEERS procedures (i.e., social skills training, joint-task activities, group contingencies, and self-management) and contextual interventions. A multiple baseline across subjects design was employed to ascertain treatment-related changes in daily observations of social behavior during recess. The combination of PEERS and individualized classroom interventions led to immediate and significant increases in the rates of peer interactions for all three subjects. Further, these changes in the frequency of social behavior were maintained at 1- and 2-month follow-up periods.

In a related study, Paine and colleagues (1982) used the PEERS program with nine elementary school children who exhibited low rates of interaction with their peers. In addition, each day before recess, the target child and a classmate met with the trainer to practice the skills and train sufficient exemplars. As such, each dyad role-played a variety of social situations for each target skill (e.g., initiating interactions, responding to the initiation of others, etc.). Results of the study indicated that repeated application of social skill training combined with a multiple exemplar strategy resulted in consistent increases in social interaction rates for eight of the nine participants. One notable observation was the fact that some children had previously gone through the PEERS program. For these children effects were even stronger. Because of this, it appears that social skills training may need to be conducted for periods of up to 2 months before children incorporate the skills into their behavior repertoire.

Finally, Walker and colleagues (1983b) systematically investigated the use of the ACCEPTS (A Curriculum for Children's Effective Peer and Teacher Skills; Walker et al., 1983a) curriculum with twenty-eight children in the first through sixth grades. Participants were randomly assigned to one of three groups: ACCEPTS curriculum alone ($n = 8$), ACCEPTS curriculum plus contingency management ($n = 10$), and no-treatment control ($n = 10$). The ACCEPTS procedures included coaching, modeling, and behavioral rehearsal of specific social skills (e.g., taking turns talking, etc.) in the context of small group instruction. Group sessions were conducted for 45 minutes per day over a period of 4 to 7 weeks. Children in the ACCEPTS plus contingency management group received the same intervention as the ACCEPTS alone group, except that their behavior was also monitored in natural settings (e.g., classroom or playground). Specifically, an adult prompted and reinforced the exhibition of social skills targeted by the ACCEPTS curriculum. Results showed that the children in the ACCEPTS treatment groups exhibited a greater quantity and quality of social skills in the context of the behavioral role-plays than the no-treatment controls. A similar pattern was found for direct observations of classroom on-task behavior as well as for the frequency of inappropriate interactions on the playground. The two treatment groups were more attentive to classroom instruction and less likely to engage in inappropriate interactions than members of the control group. No differences were found, however, between the two treatment groups.

Social skills are the tools with which positive and rewarding relationships are built and negative and deleterious relationships are modified or eliminated. Some children, however, lack the necessary tools to build, maintain, or terminate interpersonal relationships in a socially acceptable manner. As a microcosm of society, the school is a place where children spend 6 hours per day, 5 days per week, and at least 180 days per year. At a minimum, children spend approximately 5,400 hours per year in school and are exposed to numerous social interactions. Although most social skills instruction in school can be characterized as informal, there is a growing awareness of the importance of directly teaching social skills as part of the school's curriculum given our current knowledge regarding the long-term adjustment of children exhibiting social skill and performance deficits.

SUMMARY AND CONCLUSIONS

Although far from exhaustive, the current chapter has elucidated the importance of some commonly overlooked concepts that have far reaching implications for children as they develop in school and potentially throughout their lifespan. Formal recognition of issues such as problem solving, academic self-efficacy, and social skill development are critical to successful outcomes for schools and the children that they serve. Difficulties in problem solving, low academic self-efficacy and competence, poorly developed social skills, and combinations thereof, portend substantial difficulties for children not only during the school-age years but later on into adulthood. As is readily apparent, the demands of school and the child's cognitive, affective, academic, and social repertoire interact with each other in a dynamic and reciprocal fashion and bear ramifications not only for the child but for the school ecology as well. Undoubtedly, children who are healthy, have high self-esteem and efficacy, adroit social skills, and are intelligent and good problem solvers are at a distinct advantage as they enter the classroom. Because of these attributes, such children are more likely to engage in behaviors while in school that bring about social acceptability from peers and adults, self-esteem, critical thinking skills, and achievement.

This perspective on the child's reciprocal interaction with the social ecology of the school is entirely consistent with research (Hess & Holloway, 1984). Additionally, and perhaps more importantly from the perspective of schools, the same coercive process found in families of males who exhibit antisocial behavior (Patterson, Reid, & Dishion, 1992) can also be found sometimes in schools. Among their interactions with peers, teachers, and administrators, children with problematic development in areas of social skills, cognitive problem solving, and academic self-efficacy are highly susceptible to negative reinforcement exchanges. As such, educators (like parents) and classroom peers (like siblings) can become entangled in escalating contests of aversiveness in which the individual whose behavior causes greater discomfort is the winner and is negatively reinforced for his or her actions in the future. Such interaction patterns place students at an increased risk for truancy, delinquency, and a host of psychopathological disorders. Although schools can be the great equalizer for shaping and providing opportunities for the development of cognitive, affective, and social skills, they can also serve as an inauspicious venue through which adjustment difficulties are maintained and reinforced.

From a developmental and psychopathological perspective, the constructs discussed have shown considerable stability over time and can be quite resistant to intervention attempts. This may be particularly true when interventions are not implemented until behaviors reach an intensity serious enough to call attention to the child. Unfortunately, clinical history is replete with ill-fated attempts at remediating severe learning disabilities, conduct disorders, aggression, severe anxiety, depression, and the like. A combination of serious and long-standing behavioral difficulties, resistance to treatment, and late intervention increases the probability of costly and negative outcomes for children, schools, communities, and society. To counteract these difficulties what is sorely needed are primary prevention efforts to lower their incidence rather than treat occurring episodes of the problem. As such, schools (i.e., teachers, administrators, counselors, school psychologists, etc.) must make conscious efforts toward facilitating the development of effective problem solving, a belief system that embraces the value of learning, and impresses upon children the significance of social behavior and citizenship.

REFERENCES

Asher, S. R., & Taylor, A. R. (1981). The social outcomes of mainstreaming: Sociometric assessment and beyond. *Exceptional Children Quarterly, 1,* 13–30.

Bale, P. (1981). Behaviour problems and their relationship to reading difficulty. *Journal of Research in Reading, 3,* 123–135.

Bandura, A. (1965). Influence of models' reinforcement contingencies on the acquisition of imitative responses. *Journal of Personality and Social Psychology, 1,* 589–595.

Bandura, A. (1977). Self-efficacy: Toward a unifying theory of behavioral change. *Psychological Review, 84,* 191–215.

Bandura, A. (1986). *Social foundations of thought and action: A social cognitive theory.* Englewood Cliffs, NJ: Prentice-Hall.

Bandura, A. (1993). Perceived self-efficacy in cognitive development and functioning. *Educational Psychologist, 28,* 117–148.

Barkley, R. A. (Ed.). (1990). *Attention deficit hyperactivity disorder: A handbook for diagnosis and treatment.* New York: Guilford Press.

Baum, C. G. (1989). Conduct disorders. In T. H. Ollendick & M. Hersen (Eds.), *Handbook of child psychopathology* (2nd ed., pp. 171–196). New York: Plenum Press.

Bijou, S. W. (1993). *Behavior analysis of child development.* Reno, NV: Context Press.

Blumenfeld, P., Pintrich, P., & Hamilton, V. (1986). Children's concepts of ability, effort, and conduct. *American Educational Research Journal, 23,* 95–104.

Blumenfeld, P., Pintrich, P., Meece, J., & Wessels, K. (1982). The formation and role of self-perceptions of ability in elementary classrooms. *Elementary School Journal, 82,* 401–420.

Bornstein, M., & Lamb, M. E. (Eds.). (1992). *Developmental psychology: An advanced textbook* (3rd ed.). Hillsdale, NJ: Erlbaum.

Brody, N. (1992). *Intelligence* (2nd ed.). New York: Academic Press.

Brophy, J. (1983). Conceptualizing student motivation. *Educational Psychologist, 18,* 200–215.

Brown, A. L., & Palincsar, A. S. (1982). Inducing strategic learning from text by means of informed, self-control training. *Topics in Learning and Learning Disabilities, 2,* 1–17.

Brown, A. L., & Palincsar, A. S. (1989). Guided, cooperative learning and individual knowledge acquisition. In L. B. Resnick (Ed.), *Knowing, learning, and instruction: Essays in honor of Robert Glaser* (pp. 393–451). Hillsdale, NJ: Erlbaum.

Brown, J. S., Collins, A., & Duguid, P. (1989). Situated cognition and the culture of learning. *Educational Researcher, 18,* 32–42.

Calsyn, R., & Kenny, D. (1977). Self-concept of ability and perceived evaluations by others: Cause or effect of academic achievement? *Journal of Educational Psychology, 69,* 136–145.

Chapman, M., Zahn-Waxler, C., Cooperman, G., & Iannotti, R. (1987). Empathy and responsibility in the motivation of children's helping. *Developmental Psychology, 23,* 140–145.

Collins, A., Brown, J. S., & Newman, S. E. (1989). Cognitive apprenticeship: Teaching the crafts of reading, writing, and mathematics. In L. B. Resnick (Ed.), *Knowing, learning, and instruction: Essays in honor of Robert Glaser* (pp. 453–494). Hillsdale, NJ: Erlbaum.

Collins, J. (1982, March). *Self-efficacy and ability in achievement behavior.* Paper presented at the meeting of the American Educational Research Association, New York.

Copeland, R. (1988). *Piagetian activities: A diagnostic and developmental approach.* Eau Claire, WI: Thinking Publications.

Cowen, E. L., Pederson, A., Babigian, H., Izzo, L. D., & Trost, M. A. (1973). Long-term follow-up of early detected vulnerable children. *Journal of Consulting and Clinical Psychology, 41,* 438–446.

Cronbach, L. J., & Snow, R. E. (1977). *Aptitudes and instructional methods.* New York: Irvington.

Denham, S. A., & Couchard, E. A. (1991). Social-emotional predictors of preschoolers' responses to adult negative emotion.

Journal of Child Psychology and Psychiatry and Allied Disciplines, 32, 595–608.

Dodge, K. A., Price, J. M., Bachorowski, J., & Newman, J. P. (1990). Hostile attributional biases in severely aggressive adolescents. *Journal of Abnormal Psychology, 99,* 385–392.

Dodge, K. A., & Somberg, D. R. (1987). Hostile attributional biases among aggressive boys are exacerbated under conditions of threats to the self. *Child Development, 53,* 213–224.

Ellis, S., & Siegler, R. S. (1994). Development of problem solving. In R. J. Sternberg (Ed.), *Thinking and problem solving: Handbook of perception and cognition* (2nd ed., pp. 334–368). New York: Academic Press.

Fantuzzo, J. W., Polite, K., & Grayson, N. (1990). An evaluation of reciprocal peer tutoring across elementary school settings. *Journal of School Psychology, 28,* 309–323.

Fantuzzo, J. W., Riggio, R. E., Connelly, S., & Dimeff, L. A. (1989). Effects of reciprocal peer tutoring on academic achievement and psychological adjustment: A component analysis. *Journal of Educational Psychology, 81,* 173–177.

Finn, J. D. (1988). School performance of adolescents in juvenile court. *Urban Education, 23,* 150–161.

Frick, P. J., Lahey, B. B., Christ, M. A. G., Loeber, R., & Green, S. (1991). History of childhood behavior problems in biological relatives of boys with attention-deficit hyperactivity disorder and conduct disorder. *Journal of Clinical Child Psychology, 20,* 445–451.

Gagné, E. D., Yekovich, C. W., & Yekovich, F. R. (1993). *The cognitive psychology of school learning* (2nd ed.). New York: HarperCollins.

Gibson, S., & Dembo, M. H. (1984). Teacher efficacy: A construct validation. *Journal of Educational Psychology, 76,* 569–582.

Ginsburg, H., & Opper, S. (1979). *Piaget's theory of intellectual development* (2nd ed.). Old Tappan, NJ: Prentice-Hall.

Greenwood, C. R., Delquadri, J. C., & Hall, R. V. (1984). Opportunity to respond and student academic performance. In W. L. Heward, T. E. Heron, D. S. Hill, & J. Trap-Porter (Eds.), *Focus on behavior analysis in education* (pp. 58–88). Columbus, OH: Merrill.

Greenwood, C. R., Terry, B., Arrega-Mayer, C., & Finney, R. (1992). The classwide peer tutoring program: Implementation factors moderating students' achievement. *Journal of Applied Behavior Analysis, 25,* 101–116.

Gresham, F. M. (1986). Conceptual issues in the assessment of social competence in children. In P. Strain, M. Guralnick, & H. Walker (Eds.), *Children's social behavior: Development, assessment, and modification* (pp. 143–179). New York: Academic Press.

Hall, R. V., Delquadri, J., Greenwood, C. R., & Thurston, L. (1982). The importance of opportunity to respond in children's academic success. In E. B. Edgar, N. G. Haring, J. R. Jenkins, & C. G. Pious (Eds.), *Mentally handicapped children: Education and training* (pp. 107–140). Baltimore: University Park Press.

Harari, O., & Covington, M. (1981). Reactions to achievement from a teacher and a student perspective: A developmental analysis. *American Educational Research Journal, 18,* 15–28.

Harter, S., & Pike, R. (1984). The pictorial scale of perceived competence and social acceptance for young children. *Child Development, 55,* 1969–1982.

Hess, R. D., & Holloway, S. D. (1984). Family and school as educational institutions. In R. D. Parke (Ed.), *Review of child development research* (Vol. 7). Chicago: University of Chicago Press.

Hops, H., Guild, J. J., Fleischman, D. H., Paine, S. C., Street, A., Walker, H. M., & Greenwood, C. R. (1978). *PEERS (Procedures for Establishing Effective Relationship Skills): Manual for consultants.* Unpublished manuscript, University of Oregon, Center at Oregon for Behavioral Education of the Handicapped, Eugene.

Johnson, D. W., & Johnson, R. T. (1977). Instructional goal structure: Cooperative, competitive, or individualistic. *Review of Educational Research, 44,* 213–240.

Kendall, P. C., & Chansky, T. E. (1991). Considering cognition in anxiety-disordered children. *Journal of Anxiety Disorders, 5,* 167–185.

Lewis, J. T., & Sugai, G. (1993). Teaching communicative alternatives to socially withdrawn behavior: An investigation in maintaining treatment effects. *Journal of Behavior Education, 3,* 61–75.

Lochman, J. E. (1987). Self- and peer perceptions and attributional biases of aggressive and nonaggressive boys in dyadic interactions. *Journal of Consulting and Clinical Psychology, 55,* 404–410.

Locke, E. A., Shaw, K. N., Saari, L. M., & Latham, G. P. (1981). Goal setting and task performance: 1969–1980. *Psychological Bulletin, 90,* 125–152.

Loeber, R. (1985). Patterns of development of antisocial child behavior. *Annals of Child Development, 2,* 77–116.

Marsh, H. W. (1990). Causal ordering of academic self-concept and academic achievement: A multiwave, longitudinal panel analysis. *Journal of Educational Psychology, 82,* 646–656.

Marsh, H. W., Barnes, J., Cairns, L., & Tidmann, M. (1984). Self-description questionnaire: Age and sex effects in the structure and level of self-concept for preadolescent children. *Journal of Educational Psychology, 76,* 940–956.

Merrell, K. W. (1994). *Assessment of behavioral, social & emotional problems.* New York: Longman.

Milach, R., & Dodge, K. A. (1984). Social information processing in child psychiatric populations. *Journal of Abnormal Child Psychology, 12,* 471–490.

Nicholls, J. G. (1978). The development of the concepts of effort and ability, perception of academic attainment, and the understanding that difficult tasks require more ability. *Child Development, 49,* 800–814.

Ormrod, J. E. (1995). *Human learning.* Englewood Cliffs, NJ: Merrill.

Paine, S. C., Hops, H., Walker, H. M., Greenwood, C. R., Fleischman, D. H., & Guild, J. J. (1982). Repeated treatment effects: A study of maintaining behavior change in socially withdrawn children. *Behavior Modification, 6,* 171–199.

Palincsar, A. S. (1986). Metacognitive strategy instruction. *Exceptional Children, 53,* 118–124.

Palincsar, A. S., & Brown, A. L. (1984). Reciprocal teaching of comprehension-fostering and monitoring activities. *Cognition and Instruction, 1,* 117–175.

Palincsar, A. S., & Brown, A. L. (1988). Teaching and practicing thinking skills to promote comprehension in the context of group problem solving. *Remedial and Special Education, 9,* 53–59.

Palincsar, A. S., Brown, A. L., & Martin, S. M. (1987). Peer interaction in reading comprehension instruction. *Educational Psychologist, 22,* 231–253.

Parker, J. G., & Asher, S. R. (1987). Peer relations and later personal development: Are low-accepted children "at-risk"? *Psychological Bulletin, 102,* 357–389.

Patterson, G. R., Reid, J. B., & Dishion, T. J. (1992). *Antisocial boys.* Eugene, OR: Castalia Publishing.

Pressley, M., & McCormick, C. B. (1995). *Cognition, teaching, & assessment.* New York: HarperCollins.

Radke-Yarrow, M., Zahn-Waxler, C., & Chapman, M. (1983). Children's prosocial dispositions and behavior. In P. H. Mussen & E. M. Hetherington (Eds.), *Handbook of child psychology: Socialization, personality, and social development* (Vol. 4, pp. 469–545). New York: Wiley.

Richards, D. D., & Siegler, R. (1981). Very young children's acquisition of systematic problem-solving strategies. *Child Development, 52,* 1318–1321.

Rincker, J. L. (1990). Academic and intellectual characteristics of adolescent juvenile offenders. *Journal of Correctional Education, 41,* 124–131.

Roff, M. (1963). Childhood social interactions and young adult psychosis. *Journal of Clinical Psychology, 19,* 152–157.

Roff, M., & Sells, S. (1968). Juvenile delinquency in relation to peer acceptance-rejection and sociometric status. *Psychology in the Schools, 5,* 3–18.

Roff, M., Sells, B., & Golden, M. (1972). *Social adjustment and personality development in children.* Minneapolis: University of Minnesota Press.

Rosenshine, B. V. (1979). Content, time, and direct instruction. In P. L. Peterson & H. J. Walberg (Eds.), *Research on teaching: Concepts, findings, and implications* (pp. 28–56). Berkeley, CA: McCutchan.

Rosenshine, B. V., & Stevens, R. (1984). Classroom instruction in reading. In P. D. Pearson, R. Barr, M. L. Kamil, & P. Mosenthal (Eds.), *Handbook of reading research* (pp. 745–798). New York: Longman.

Schunk, D. H. (1981). Modeling and attributional effects on children's achievement: A self-efficacy analysis. *Journal of Educational Psychology, 73,* 93–105.

Schunk, D. H. (1982). Effects of effort attributional feedback on children's perceived self-efficacy and achievement. *Journal of Educational Psychology, 74,* 548–556.

Schunk, D. H. (1984). Self-efficacy perspective on achievement behavior. *Educational Psychologist, 19,* 48–58.

Schunk, D. H. (1985). Self-efficacy and classroom learning. *Psychology in the Schools, 22,* 208–223.

Schunk, D. H. (1989). Self-efficacy and cognitive skill learning. In C. Ames & R. Ames (Eds.), *Research on motivation in education: Vol. 3. Goals and cognitions* (pp. 13–44). San Diego, CA: Academic Press.

Schunk, D. H. (1991). Self-efficacy and academic motivation. *Educational Psychologist, 26,* 207–231.

Short, R. J., & Shapiro, S. K. (1993). Conduct disorders: A framework for understanding and intervention in schools and communities. *School Psychology Review, 22,* 362–375.

Siegler, R. S. (1976). Three aspects of cognitive development. *Cognitive Psychology, 8,* 481–520.

Siegler, R. S. (1978). The origins of scientific reasoning. In R. S. Siegler (Ed.), *Children's thinking: What develops?* Hillsdale, NJ: Erlbaum.

Silverman, W. K., & Ginsburg, G. (1995). Specific phobias and generalized anxiety disorder. In J. S. March (Ed.), *Anxiety disorders in children and adolescents* (pp. 151–180). New York: Guilford Press.

Slavin, R. E. (1983). When does cooperative learning increase student achievement? *Psychological Bulletin, 94,* 429–445.

Slavin, R. E. (1985). Team-assisted individualization: Combining cooperative learning and individualized instruction in mathematics. In R. E. Slavin, S. Sharan, S. Kagan, R. H. Lazarowitz, C. Webb, & R. Schmuck (Eds.), *Learning to cooperate, cooperating to learn* (pp. 177–210). New York: Plenum Press.

Slavin, R. E. (1987). Developmental and motivational perspectives on cooperative learning: A reconciliation. *Child Development, 58,* 1161–1167.

Slavin, R. E., Madden, N. A., & Leavey, M. (1984). Effects of cooperative learning and individualized instruction on mainstreamed students. *Exceptional Children, 50,* 434–443.

Slavin, R. E., & Oickle, E. (1981). Effects of cooperative learning teams on student achievement and race relations: Treatment by race interactions. *Sociology of Education, 54,* 174–180.

Slavin, R., Sharan, S., Kagan, S., Lazarowitz, R. H., Webb, C., & Schmuck, R. (Eds.). (1985). *Learning to cooperate, cooperating to learn.* New York: Plenum Press.

Slavin, R. E., Stevens, R. J., & Madden, N. A. (1988). Accommodating student diversity in reading and writing instruction: A cooperative learning approach. *Remedial and Special Education, 9,* 60–66.

Spear, P., & Armstrong, S. (1978). Effects of performance expectancies created by peer comparisons as related to social reinforcement, task difficulty, and age of the child. *Journal of Experimental and Child Psychology, 25,* 254–266.

Spivack, G., Platt, J. J., & Shure, M. B. (1976). *The problem-solving approach to adjustment.* San Francisco: Jossey-Bass.

Stark, K. D. (1990). *Childhood depression: School-based intervention.* New York: Guilford Press.

Stevens, R. J., Slaving, R. J., & Farnish, A. M. (1991). The effects of cooperative learning and direct instruction in reading comprehension strategies and main idea identification. *Journal of Educational Psychology, 81,* 8–16.

Stipek, D. (1981). Children's perceptions of their own and their classmates' ability. *Journal of Educational Psychology, 73,* 404–410.

Stipek,. D. (1992). The child at school. In M. H. Bornstein & M. E. Lamb (Eds.), *Developmental psychology: An advanced textbook* (3rd ed., pp. 579–628). Hillsdale, NJ: Erlbaum.

Stipek, D., & Daniels, D. (1990). Children's use of dispositional attributions in predicting the performance and behavior of classmates. *Journal of Applied Developmental Psychology, 11,* 13–28.

Stipek, D., & Tannatt, L. (1984). Children's judgements of their own and their peers' academic competence. *Journal of Educational Psychology, 76,* 75–84.

Tharinger, D. J., & Lambert, N. M. (1990). The contributions of developmental psychology to school psychology. In T. B. Gutkin & C. R. Reynolds (Eds.), *The handbook of school psychology* (2nd ed., pp. 74–103). New York: Wiley.

Tremblay, R. E., Masse, B., Perron, D., Leblanc, M., Schwartzman, A. E., & Ledingham, J. E. (1992). Early disruptive behavior, poor school achievement, delinquent, and delinquent personality: Longitudinal analyses. *Journal of Consulting and Clinical Psychology, 60,* 1–10.

Vygotsky, L. S. (1962). *Thought and language.* Cambridge, MA: MIT Press.

Vygotsky, L. S. (1978). *Mind in society: The development of higher psychological processes.* Cambridge, MA: Harvard University Press.

Wadsworth, B. J. (1978). *Piaget for the classroom teacher.* New York: Longman.

Walker, H. M., & Hops, H. (1976). Increasing academic achievement by reinforcing direct academic performance and/or facilitating nonacademic responses. *Journal of Educational Psychology, 68,* 218–225.

Walker, H. M., McConnell, S. R., Holmes, D., Todis, B., Walker, J. L., & Golden, H. (1983a). *The Walker social skills curriculum: The ACCEPTS program.* Austin, TX: Pro Ed.

Walker, H. M., McConnell, S. R., Walker, J. L., Clarke, J. Y., Todis, B., Cohen, G., & Rankin, R. (1983b). Initial analysis of the ACCEPTS curriculum: Efficacy of instructional and behavior management procedures for improving the social adjustment of handicapped children. *Analysis and Intervention in Developmental Disabilities, 3,* 105–177.

Walker, H. M., Stieber, S., & Ramsey, E. (1990). Middle school behavioral profiles of antisocial and at-risk control boys: Descriptive and predictive outcomes. *Exceptionality: A Research Journal, 1,* 61–77.

Walker, H. M., Stieber, S., & Ramsey, E. (1991). Longitudinal prediction of the school achievement, adjustment, and delinquency of antisocial versus at-risk boys. *Remedial and Special Education, 12,* 43–51.

Wertsch, J. V. (1985). *Vygotsky and the social formation of mind.* Cambridge, MA: Harvard University Press.

Wigfield, A., & Karpathian, M. (1991). Who am I and what can I do: Children's self-concepts and motivation. *Educational Psychologist, 26,* 233–261.

Winne, P. H. (1985). Cognitive processing in the classroom. In T. Husen & T. N. Postlethwaite (Eds.), *The international encyclopedia of education* (Vol. 2, pp. 795–808). Oxford, England: Pergamon Press.

Yussen, S., & Kane, P. (1985). Children's conception of intelligence. In S. R. Yussen (Ed.), *The growth of reflection in children* (pp. 207–241). Orlando, FL: Academic Press.

Zahn-Waxler, C., Freidman, S. L., & Cummings, E. M. (1983). Children's emotions and behaviors in response to infants' cries. *Child Development, 54,* 1522–1528.

Zentall, S. S. (1988). Production deficiencies in elicited language but not in the spontaneous verbalizations of hyperactive children. *Journal of Abnormal Child Psychology, 16,* 657–673.

CHAPTER 11

PEER GROUP

Annette M. La Greca
Mitchell J. Prinstein

Peer relations play an extremely important role in children's social and emotional development. From early childhood on, children spend a considerable amount of time with peers (Ellis, Rogoff, & Cromer, 1981). Prior to the school years, children interact with peers in child care settings, playgroups, or preschool programs. By ages 6 to 7 years, children spend most of their daytime hours in school or in play settings with classmates and friends; this trend continues, and accelerates, through adolescence. It is in the context of these peer interactions that children learn how to share and take turns, how to interact with others on an equal basis, and how to place others' concerns before their own. Indeed, volumes have been written about the developmentally unique and essential social behaviors that develop in the context of children's peer interactions (Asher & Coie, 1990; Hartup, 1983, 1996; Newcomb, Bukowski & Pattee, 1993).

Children's peer relations also contribute to emotional adjustment in important ways. Abundant evidence sug-

gests that children who experience interpersonal difficulties with peers during the elementary school years are at substantial risk for later emotional problems (Kupersmidt & Coie, 1990; Parker & Asher, 1987). During middle childhood, for example, children who are disliked or ignored by their classmates often display high rates of internalizing difficulties, such as depression, anxiety, and loneliness (Asher & Wheeler, 1985; La Greca & Stone, 1993; Strauss, Lahey, Frick, Frame, & Hynd, 1988). Moreover, over time, problematic peer relations may contribute to serious mental health and academic adjustment problems. Investigators have found that elementary school children who are actively rejected by their classmates display more mental health problems during late adolescence and early adulthood than their more accepted peers (Cowen, Pederson, Babigian, Izzo, & Trost, 1973). Also, fifth and sixth grade children who are not well liked drop out of high school at much higher rates than their more well-accepted classmates (Barclay, 1966; Gronlund & Holmlund, 1958; Kupersmidt & Coie, 1990). Findings such as these underscore the critical role of peer relations in social and emotional adjustment.

Preparation of this manuscript was supported by a grant from the National Institute of Mental Health (RO1-MH48028).

From a clinical perspective, it is essential for professionals to attend to children's peer relations for several reasons. First, peer relationship problems occur at high rates among clinically referred children and may be a major factor contributing to the overall clinical picture of the child. Children are rarely referred for treatment because parents or teachers are concerned about their peer status. Most commonly, children are referred for conduct problems, attention deficits, depression and mood disorders, adjustment problems, and anxiety disorders (Kazdin, Siegel, & Bass, 1990). However, it is noteworthy that deficient or problematic peer relations are a prominent feature of all these childhood disorders (American Psychiatric Association, 1994; also see Dodge, 1989). Because most children seen in clinical settings have concurrent social problems, an assessment of children's peer relations and friendships should be an essential part of any comprehensive psychological evaluation.

Second, peer relations are often disrupted during major life crises and transitions. Children may be seen in clinical settings for problems that arise as a result of major life stressors (e.g., parental divorce, serious illness or death in the family, catastrophic natural disasters). In these instances, it is also critical to consider the child's peer relations. Peers represent a significant source of emotional support that can help to buffer the negative impact of stressors, such as parental conflict (Sandler, Wolchik, & Braver, 1985; Wasserstein & La Greca, 1996), recovering from a natural disaster (La Greca, Silverman, Vernberg, & Prinstein, 1996), or entering a new school (Felner, Ginter, & Primavera, 1982; Simmons, Carlton-Ford, & Blythe, 1987). When family relocation occurs, as in the case of a divorce or a disaster, this may precipitate a major disruption of a child's peer relations and friendships. Under these circumstances, children may need special assistance in developing new peer relationships and friendship ties.

Finally, even when peer relationships are not problematic, they may serve as an important source of emotional support for children who are otherwise experiencing considerable personal or family stress. Friendships and peer relationships may represent an area of strength that the clinician can build upon in developing an effective treatment plan for a child.

With these concerns in mind, the present chapter is organized around two major themes: a general overview of the developmental literature on children's peer relationships and friendships and the clinical implications of this body of research. Because of the tremendous changes in the importance and salient features of children's peer relationships across development, clinical implications are presented separately for each developmental stage. It is our intent that the information presented herein will help professionals become better informed as to how to integrate this important aspect of children's functioning into their everyday clinical practice.

INFANT AND TODDLER YEARS

The Development of Peer Relationships and Related Social Skills

Although it is true that children have far fewer opportunities to interact with peers during infancy and toddlerhood than in later years, during the first 2 years of life children begin to establish contact with peers, develop rudiments of play behavior, and establish playmate preferences (Hartup, 1983). Interestingly, some research suggests that infants' and toddlers' peer relationships are important and necessary for adaptive social development (Gunnar, Senior, & Hartup, 1984) and are even predictive of future academic success and emotional well-being (Field, 1994).

Within the first year of life, infants can receive considerable exposure to peers. This is especially true with the growing use of day care settings in the past decade (Erwin, 1993). Some research has demonstrated that infants prefer peer interactions to activities that focus on toys, adults, or their surroundings (Becker, 1977). However, dyadic infant interactions still represent a minority of a child's social exchanges during the first 12 months of life.

The beginning rudiments of important social skills can be observed in infant–infant exchanges. At approximately 2 months, infants' peer interactions include mostly mutual eye contact; between 6 and 12 months of age, smiling and touching can also be observed between peers (Vandell, Wilson, & Buchanan, 1980). In some situations, peer interactions can occur quite frequently. Research has suggested that children are likely to initiate some type of social interaction every 1 to 2 minutes (Eckerman, Whatley, & McGhee, 1979) and to respond to peers' initiations up to 40 percent of the time (Becker, 1977).

Despite these findings, however, infants' social actions are often isolated and limited. In other words, infants can appear to be interacting "accidentally," perhaps without a true intent to communicate. This may be why infant–infant contacts are most frequent in "intense" circumstances, for instance, when infants are placed within extremely close proximity (e.g., in the same crib) and the opportunity for happenstance touching or eye contact can occur (Eckerman, Whatley, & Kutz, 1975). Additionally, although infants are able to initiate a social interaction, and this may be reciprocated with a response, the ability of infants to advance a social interaction beyond this sequence is not yet developed by 12 months of age (Hartup, 1983).

By the second year of life, toddlers' peer interactions increase in frequency. Play bouts are likely to be longer, involve more reciprocal turn-taking, and appear more complex (Eckerman et al., 1975; Mueller & Brenner, 1977). For instance, children display a wider variety of affective states during peer play (e.g., by smiling, laughing), although this remains quite limited (Ross & Goldman, 1977). Also, 2 year olds' interactions can include problem solving, expressions of empathy, and conflict regulation (Brownell & Brown, 1992).

Toddlers may also develop the ability to form relationships with peers by 2 years of age. Rubenstein and Howes (1976) demonstrated that among 18-month-old children the length of interaction between long-acquainted peers was greater than between unacquainted peers, suggesting that children form relationships with their peers that influences their social behavior. Over an extended period of time, 2 to 3 year olds can form relationships in which they consistently initiate and maintain interactions with select peers and exhibit negative behavior (e.g., aggression, sadness) in their friends' absence (Whaley & Rubenstein, 1994). Also, toddlers seem to prefer contacts with peers to contact with adults. When both mothers and peers were present, young children's interactions with peers exceeded their interactions with the mother (Rubenstein & Howes, 1976). By the preschool years, this trend towards a preference for social interaction with peers, rather than adults, becomes more well defined.

Within the first 2 years of life, toddlers also begin to develop peer preferences within groups of peers and to alter their social behavior according to these preferences (Lee, 1973). In one often-cited study by Lee (1973), 9 month olds appeared to prefer social interactions with peers who displayed positive social responses (e.g., smiling) than with peers who exhibited negative social behavior (e.g., grabbing a toy). Other research suggests that as a group toddlers prefer to play with sociable peers, as opposed to withdrawn ones (Brown & Brownell, 1990). Such studies suggest that the development of social skills and peer preferences begin within the first 2 years of life.

Clinical Implications of Peer Relations Research for Infants and Toddlers

Infants and toddlers are rarely seen for "peer problems." At this point, however, it is extremely important for parents and caretakers to provide appropriate exposure to peers and settings for peer interactions. Because parents are often the only resource for the management of infants' and toddlers' peer activities, it is recommended that parents take an active role in initiating peer interactions for their children. For instance, parents can arrange for their children to attend play groups with same-aged peers. Parents may also seek neighborhood settings (e.g., parks, community centers) in which interaction with other children is possible.

Children who are enrolled in child care have many more opportunities to interact with similar-aged peers. However, although the number of parents who enroll their children in child care may be increasing, parents vary on their reasons for utilizing child care, and this may influence their selection of programs (Bhavnagri & Parke, 1991). Parents who place a high priority on their children's socialization, for instance, may select child care environments that foster children's relationships with each other. Such environments can be important for the development of children's social skills and the formation of friendships. Studies by Field (1994) and others (e.g., Whaley & Rubenstein, 1994) document some of the social advantages of early child care. For example, even at this early stage of development, peer preferences are evident, and may represent early signs of friendship formation. Providing opportunities for children to interact in a supervised child care setting also may go a long way toward eventually helping children to cultivate and develop friendships (Howes, 1988).

Overall, although no evidence exists to suggest that one method of peer exposure is more advantageous than another for infants' and toddlers' social development, there appears to be consensus that early peer exposure in any form can be an important aspect of children's healthy peer relations, relationship formation, and subsequent successful transition into formal schooling (Ladd, Profilet, & Hart, 1992). In some cases, however, children may evidence difficulties adjusting to the social setting (e.g., children who bite or hit others). In such cases, distraction or simple time-out procedures may be useful in reducing inappropriate play. Also, providing interesting materials for children (e.g., balls, etc.) and structured activities (e.g., turn-taking games) may stimulate fun interactions and potentially may help to establish appropriate social behavior. It is possible that early identification of and intervention with problematic behaviors may be especially important for children's later social development.

Parents may also play a role in children's social development by modeling social interaction skills. Through parents' own play interactions with their infant or toddler (e.g., peek-a-boo, patty-cake) parents teach children skills in mutual eye contact, turn-taking, mutual responsiveness, and expression of positive affect (Whaley & Rubenstein, 1994). Whaley (1990) suggests that these parent–child interactions may also teach children the necessary imitation skills that children use to develop social behavior in the presence of same-aged peers.

THE PRESCHOOL YEARS

By the preschool years (ages 3 to 5), children dramatically increase the frequency of their peer interactions. This is primarily due to children's attendance in nursery or preschool programs in which multiple opportunities to interact and form relationships with peers are present (Hartup, 1983). By and large, it is in these contexts that preschoolers' peer relations have been studied.

Overall, the preschool period is a time when children begin to develop and refine their social skills while in an environment where they can get practice through increased exposure to peers. Children begin to exhibit more sophisticated play behavior, social language, and also form clear playmate preferences based on children's personal and behavioral characteristics. Children also form more mutual friendships during preschool. These areas will be discussed in more detail below.

Peer Interactions and Social Behaviors

Although preschool settings may facilitate peer interactions, preschoolers' increased contact with peers is not solely a function of the amount of time spent in school settings. Ellis and colleagues (1981), for instance, observed children of different ages and their playmates in a middle-class neighborhood throughout a summer. While infants and toddlers were more likely to be in the company of adults (55% of the time) rather than peers (29% of the time), preschoolers showed a clear preference for peer companionship (49% of the time), as compared to adult companionship (25% of the time), when both adults and peers were present. This shift towards increased social contacts with peers and decreased social contacts with adults begins during the preschool years and continues throughout childhood and adolescence (Ellis, Rogoff, & Cromer, 1981).

In addition to increased social contacts with peers, there is evidence that preschoolers have developed more sophisticated skills in interacting with peers. For instance, in a play group of same-aged children, preschoolers are likely to interact with peers whereas infants in this situation are likely to engage in solitary play (Mueller & Brenner, 1977). Older preschoolers, as compared with younger preschoolers and toddlers, are also more likely to communicate verbally with their peers (Mueller, 1972). And, as children get older, peers' responses to these verbal prompts also increase. In general, the increased frequency of peer interactions among preschoolers sets the stage for children to develop more sophisticated social skills and form more substantial peer relationships. In this regard, opportunities for peer interactions represent a necessary first step in social development.

More striking than the increased frequency of peer interactions among preschoolers, however, is the heightened sophistication and complexity that characterizes preschoolers' peer relationships. By preschool age, children display a variety of play skills, maintain reciprocal play interactions and conversations with peers, form clear playmate preferences, and develop elementary friendships.

Between the ages of 3 and 5 years, children interact with their peers primarily through various forms of play, and their play behaviors develop substantially. For example, the frequency of *rough and tumble play* and *aggressive play* increases during the preschool years (Hartup, 1983). By the third year of life, most children have also developed the cognitive representational skills necessary to engage in *symbolic or pretend play* (Fein, 1981). This is an important milestone in the development of peer relations, as prior to this age, children often engage in solitary play or play that excludes the participation of peers (Stone & La Greca, 1986). Pretend play becomes more complex with increasing age. Early pretend play can reflect children's egocentrism, manifested by a poor ability to share another's perspective during play (Piaget, 1926). For instance, young preschoolers may form self-referenced roles during play and enact them independent of their playmates' ideas. By the end of the preschool years, however, children can adopt different roles for themselves and for playmates that are better integrated (Fein, 1981). This more advanced type of pretend play is related to positive social behavior in children (Fein, 1981).

In preschool settings, children also advance their social skills through more complex verbal exchanges. Mueller (1972) observed the verbal behavior of 3- to 5-year-old dyads during a normal bout of play. Contrary to predictions of egocentric, self-directed verbal exchanges between the children, the results suggested that preschool children were likely to speak frequently to each other, respond to verbal initiations, and maintain a reciprocal verbal interaction. Specifically, children were likely to address each other at an average rate of six to seven utterances each minute. The vast majority (i.e., 94%) of these verbalizations were rated as intentional attempts to communicate with a playmate, rather than self-narration of behavior. In addition, 85 percent of these verbal initiations were met with a verbal or behavioral (i.e., facial) response from the playmate (Mueller, 1972). There were no apparent age differences in the use of these verbal communication skills; many of these skills were evident in 3 year olds as well as 5 year olds.

Preschoolers develop clear playmate preferences and are able to rate their peers as potential playmates based on demographic and behavioral characteristics. For instance, on average, girls are more likely to play with girls, and boys with boys (Leiter, 1977). In addition, children who initiate social interactions are regarded positively by peers, whereas children who exhibit aggressive behavior towards peers are regarded negatively (Ladd & Mars, 1986; Leiter, 1977).

One factor that emerges as a consistent predictor of likability among preschoolers is shyness. Rubin (1982) has confirmed that shy or withdrawn children are less likely to initiate interactions with children, respond to others' initiations, or receive initiations from others as frequently as other children. Shy preschoolers engage in less mature forms of peer play and are more likely than other children to use egocentric speech (Rubin, 1985). In addition, shyness in preschoolers is associated with poorer ability at social problem-solving tasks (Rubin, 1985). Perhaps as a consequence of these behavioral differences, shyness is associated with social withdrawal among preschool-age peers. This is especially important because social withdrawal, which may be manifested as solitary or "onlooker" play, is a consistent and strong predictor of lower peer acceptance scores and higher peer rejection (Ladd, Price, & Hart, 1990). Perhaps this is why interventions with preschool-age children strongly focus on increasing children's exposure and opportunities to interact with peers.

Another factor that is predictive of peer difficulties is aggression. Aggressive preschoolers engage in more rough play then their peers, start fights more frequently with other children, and are more disruptive in group or classroom settings. Not surprisingly, therefore, children's aggression is strongly and consistently predictive of lower levels of peer acceptance and higher levels of peer rejection concurrently and over time (Coie, Dodge, & Kupersmidt, 1990; Ladd et al., 1992). Conversely, preschool-age children who are rejected by peers are also observed to display more hostile, hyperactive, and disruptive and aggressive behavior with their peers (Coie et al., 1990).

Peer Friendships

Also important during the preschool years are children's developing abilities to form friendships. Research has demonstrated that children between 3 and 5 years old can identify reciprocal friendships in which two children name each other as best friends (Gershman & Hayes, 1983). The reliability and stability of these friendships, however, is still in question. While some investigations have suggested that preschoolers' friendships are strongly influenced by recent behavior and thus are subject to change (e.g., Selman & Selman, 1979), other research has produced evidence that preschool children nominate friends with moderate stability over a period of several months (e.g., Asher, Singleton, Tinsley, & Hymel, 1979; Gershman & Hayes, 1983). Additionally, preschoolers' friendships are marked by differences in social behavior. For

instance, children are likely to engage in positive social behaviors more often with friends than with nonfriends (Masters & Furman, 1981) and are more likely to play with friends than with nonfriends (Gershman & Hayes, 1983).

It is important that preschoolers begin to develop relationships with their peers. Investigations have demonstrated that successful preschool friendships are not only the product of appropriate social skills and peer acceptance, but are also related to continued improvement in these domains (Howes, 1983; Ladd et al., 1990).

Clinical Implications of Peer Relations Research for Preschool Children

Although few preschool children may be referred for peer relationship difficulties, clinicians may wish to take a preventive stance and encourage developmentally appropriate peer relationships and friendships. Specifically, interventions with preschool-age children can address several relevant goals: improving preschoolers' interactions among groups of peers, cultivating friendships among preschool aged children, and/or encouraging appropriate social behaviors in children. Social interventions during the preschool years could potentially reduce children's risk for developing maladaptive social behavior patterns that may become increasingly problematic in future years.

Because parents and teachers play an extremely important role in the management of preschoolers' social activities, it is advisable for clinicians to work with these adults in designing interventions. Indeed, recent investigations confirm the linkages between parents' behavior and children's social functioning (e.g., Ladd, Profilet, & Hart, 1992; Putallaz, 1987). The following discussion includes suggestions for improving preschoolers' relationships with peers, developing and maintaining friendships, and encouraging the development of socially appropriate behavior.

Improving Preschoolers' Interactions with Peers

Preschoolers' peer interactions can be most effectively addressed via classroom interventions that include children and their peers. One useful strategy for increasing sociability between preschool children is through systematic prompting and reinforcement of an isolated child to interact in peer-initiated activities. This approach has been shown to be especially effective for children with learning disabilities, mental retardation, or behavior disorders, and who are also experiencing peer difficulties (Strain & Fox, 1981). Similarly, teachers may use prompting and reinforcement of an isolated child's peers to increase peers' interaction with a specific child.

Teachers may also improve preschoolers' sociability by staging an environment that promotes peer interaction. For example, introducing toys and games that involve numerous children has been shown to be effective for reducing some children's social isolation (Strain & Fox, 1981). Teachers may also promote activities that require groups of children to take an active role together (e.g., play-acting, team games). When these types of activities precede a free-play period, notable increases in peer contact during free-play have been observed (Strain & Wiegerink, 1976).

Another approach to increasing preschoolers' social interactions is one that focuses on peers as the agents of change. For instance, peers may model specific social behaviors and teach socially isolated peers how to interact more effectively. Some research has documented that isolated children display increases in prosocial behavior and initiation of peer interactions after being taught to observe and imitate a more socially competent peer (Apolloni & Cooke, 1978). When such behaviors are reinforced by teachers, investigations have demonstrated a spillover effect, in which other socially isolated children also benefit from witnessing the reinforced successes of their classmate (Strain, Shores, & Kerr, 1976).

Developing Friendships

When it comes to the formation and maintenance of preschool-age children's friendships, parents play an integral role. Clinicians should encourage parents to be active in this area, both by placing children in environments that may maximize children's opportunities to meet peers and by assisting children in initiating play contacts.

Parents facilitate their children's friendships through formal and informal means (Ladd et al., 1992). Informally, parents' selection of a neighborhood to live in can be important in creating opportunities for peer friendships. Neighborhoods that have a dense population of young children and that offer a variety of children's "meeting areas" (e.g., parks, schoolyards) can provide opportunities for children to meet and get to know one another on a daily basis. Parents can also increase their children's social opportunities by enrolling them in preschool programs or arranging children's play groups. Investigations have demonstrated that child care has a positive effect on socialization (e.g., Field, 1994); in addition, preschool children in day care have been observed to develop relationships with peers that lasted up to 2 years (Howes, 1988). Others have found that play group involvement has a positive effect on preschoolers' adjustment to kindergarten and on their adaptive social behavior as rated by kindergarten teachers (Ladd, Hart, Wadsworth, & Golter, 1988). As another suggestion, parents can in-

crease children's opportunities for peer interactions by their participation in community-based settings, such as parks, playgrounds, or a community pool.

Aside from these informal avenues, parents may also influence children's friendship development in more formal ways by helping preschoolers to initiate social contacts with their peers. At younger ages (2 to 3½ years), parents typically initiate and arrange social activities for their children (Bhavnagri & Parke, 1991), whereas older children (3½ to 6 years) may begin to initiate social contacts on their own, but may need parents to coach them and arrange for transportation (Bhavnagri & Parke, 1991).

Encouraging Socially Appropriate Behaviors

Helping preschool age children to develop appropriate social skills will not only increase the likelihood that they will be successful in their peer interactions, but may also prevent social difficulties down the road. Indeed, teaching children adaptive social behaviors (e.g., sharing, turn-taking, cooperative play) has long been recognized as an important clinical intervention.

Although social skills training programs have been most widely used with older children (see the section of this chapter on Middle Childhood for more details), instruction plus positive reinforcement appear to be effective tools for improving young children's social skills (Dodge, 1989; Furman, 1980). Specifically, teachers or parents can be encouraged to target adaptive social behaviors (e.g., sharing, responding positively to peers), to train or instruct the child in these behaviors, and then to administer reinforcement following the presence of these behaviors in a real peer context. In terms of reinforcement strategies, preschoolers respond best to low incentive, tangible rewards (e.g., small quantities of candy, stickers) and to social praise (Furman, 1980).

One promising approach discussed by McGinnis and Goldstein (1990) involves a four-step intervention for preschoolers' social skills training. Here, children are first exposed to examples of role models who demonstrate the use of appropriate social skills. Second, children are asked to role-play these new social behaviors in a safe environment in which negative evaluation is kept at a minimum. As a third step, role-playing is followed by performance feedback, during which preschoolers receive predominantly positive reinforcement (e.g., praise) for behavior that closely emulates the model. Finally, efforts are made to increase the likelihood that new skills will be generalized outside of the training environment, such as by keeping the training sessions as "real" as possible, providing continued reinforcement for children as they attempt new skills in a real setting, and tapering off training sessions gradually, rather than abruptly ending the social skills program.

In addition to structured skills training programs, parents can play an important role in social skills development by monitoring their children's social activities and coaching them when they need assistance. By monitoring social activities parents are able to remain aware of their children's peer relationships and to provide help or assistance when problems arise (Ladd & Golter, 1988). For instance, parents may be present for their children's peer activities and assist in their children's handling of conflict in unobtrusive ways. Parents may also serve as models for preschoolers' social skills; this idea has been supported by recent investigations (Putallaz, 1987).

It is also important to note that certain parent behaviors may be detrimental to children's social skill development. Parents who supervise their children's activities too closely, such as by joining their play or by resolving rather than assisting their children during conflicts with peers, may inhibit the development of these social skills in their children. Thus, parents may help their children's social skills best by providing appropriate models and "lessons," while allowing their children to practice these skills on their own.

MIDDLE CHILDHOOD

Children's peer relations have been most widely studied during the elementary school years (ages 6 to 12). During this developmental period, children typically spend the school day in self-contained classrooms with a set group of classmates, although some youngsters may interact with peers in special educational settings (e.g., resource services for learning disabled youth, enhancement activities for gifted children). After school hours and on weekends, many children are involved in organized activities with peers (e.g., sports teams, dance, scouts, etc.) as well as in unstructured play activities with friends and neighborhood youth. In this social context, two aspects of children's peer relations become highly salient—their *peer status* (or degree of acceptance from the peer group) and their close *friendships.*

Peer acceptance refers to the extent to which a child is liked or accepted by the peer group (i.e., classmates). In contrast, peer friendships refer to close, supportive ties with one or more peers, and these friendships may occur within or outside the classroom (Furman & Robbins, 1985). Furman and Robbins (1985) emphasize that friendships and acquaintanceships serve different emotional needs; friendships provide children with a sense of intimacy, companionship, and self-esteem, whereas group acceptance may provide children with a sense of belonging or social inclusion. Thus, peer acceptance and peer friendships are related, but are distinct

constructs. Both are critical for a child's emotional health and psychological adjustment.

Peer Acceptance and Social Status

Children's social status is composed of two separate dimensions: *acceptance* and *rejection* (Coie, Dodge, & Coppotelli, 1982; Coie, Dodge, & Kupersmidt, 1990; Dodge, Coie, & Brakke, 1982; Newcomb et al., 1993). Peer acceptance (or "peer liking") reflects the extent to which a child is liked by classmates or the larger peer group. Peer rejection (or "peer disliking") reflects the extent to which a child is actively disliked by his or her peers. By examining children's relative standing on the dimensions of peer liking and disliking, various social status classifications have been identified, each with associated characteristics (see Figure 11.1).

Popular children are those who are very well liked (i.e., *high* on peer liking) and who have very few, if any, enemies or detractors (i.e., *low* on peer disliking). These children tend to excel in social relations and display positive interaction skills with peers (e.g., Coie et al., 1982; Coie et al., 1990; Dodge et al., 1982; Hartup, 1983). In a comprehensive review of the social status literature, Coie and colleagues (1990) suggested that the basis for popular children's high levels of acceptance from peers are their positive social skills and personal competencies, such as being helpful and considerate, following rules, and demonstrating good athletic and academic abilities.

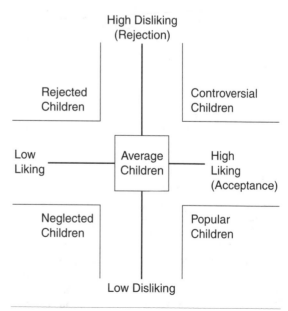

FIGURE 11.1 Children's social status groups

In contrast, children who are actively *rejected* by peers (i.e., those who are highly disliked and who lack friends or supporters) appear to have the most interpersonal, emotional, and academic difficulties. Rejected children often demonstrate aggressive, disruptive, or inattentive behaviors in addition to low levels of positive social skills such as cooperation, friendliness, and leadership (Coie & Dodge, 1988; Coie et al., 1982; Dodge et al., 1982; see Coie et al., 1990). Furthermore, rejected children often display academic problems (Green, Forehand, Beck, & Vosk, 1980; Stone & La Greca, 1990) and report feelings of depression, loneliness, and social anxiety (Asher & Wheeler, 1985; La Greca & Stone, 1993). In short, children who are rejected by peers may display a host of internalizing and externalizing behavior problems, as well as poor school achievement. In many respects, they are the polar opposite of popular youth (Newcomb et al., 1993).

Children who are *neglected* by peers have often been defined as "social isolates" (i.e., low on peer liking *and* disliking); they go unnoticed by their peers. Neglected children do not typically demonstrate behavior problems, but have been distinguished from more socially accepted peers by their low rates of social interaction (Coie & Dodge, 1988; Dodge et al., 1982) and high levels of social anxiety and social avoidance (La Greca, Dandes, Wick, Shaw, & Stone, 1988; La Greca & Stone, 1993). In comparison to their classmates, neglected children display low levels of aggressive, disruptive behaviors as well as low levels of social interaction and positive social skills (Newcomb et al., 1993). Although they are not as overtly problematic as rejected youth, neglected children may have difficulty developing supportive friendship ties, given their low sociability and low rates of social interactions with peers.

One additional social status group of note is *controversial* children; these youngsters have lots of friends *and* enemies among their peers (i.e., highly liked and disliked). Because they are usually few in number, however, little research has been directed specifically at controversial youth. Existing evidence suggests that these youngsters are highly visible, even leaders, yet may also be aggressive (e.g., Coie et al., 1982; Coie et al., 1990; Dodge et al., 1982). Unlike rejected children, controversial youth often display positive qualities (e.g., sociability, academic competencies) that help to balance their assertive and aggressive behaviors with peers (Newcomb et al., 1993).

Not all children can be classified into one of the above social status groups. Studies typically find that approximately 50 percent of the children fall within the "average" range (i.e., near the mean on liking and disliking) or cannot be classified at all (i.e., "other" social status). Such children often provide a "normal comparison" group for the more extreme social status classifications described above; they do not appear to be at risk for social or emotional difficulties.

To some extent, the above characterizations belie the heterogeneity *within* the social status groups. Studies suggest that only about 50 percent of rejected children are aggressive (e.g., French, 1988; Pope, Bierman, & Mumma, 1991). The remainder are likely to be rejected for other reasons, such as poor academic skills, physical handicaps, or an unattractive physical appearance. For example, children with poor academic achievement, including those with learning disabilities, tend to be more rejected and less accepted than their normally achieving classmates (Bryan, 1974, 1976; Green et al., 1980; Stone & La Greca, 1990). Neglected children are also likely to be a heterogeneous group; some may be disinterested in peer interactions, while others may desire to be a part of the larger peer group but may be too inhibited or anxious to actively take part in social activities (La Greca & Stone, 1993; Newcomb et al., 1993).

Regardless of the specific pathway by which children come to be rejected by peers, it is apparent that these children are at risk for current and future psychological difficulties. Of all the social status groups, peer rejection appears to be the most stable over time and the most resistant to change (Coie & Dodge, 1983). Once children develop a negative reputation among their classmates, it becomes exceedingly difficult to develop new friendship ties in the classroom (Ladd, 1983). In addition, peers interpret rejected children's behaviors in ways that continue to promote a negative bias; for example, peers are less likely to give rejected children the "benefit of the doubt" when their behavior could potentially be either benign or aggressive (Hymel, 1986). Not surprisingly, then, being rejected by one's peer group represents a significant source of stress for a child (Coie, 1990). Moreover, as Newcomb and colleagues (1993) suggest, "the aggression, withdrawal, and social deficits of rejected children represent potential antecedents for psychological disturbance" (p. 121).

Following from the above, when evaluating a child's peer relations in clinical settings, perhaps the first question to ask is, "How is this child viewed by peers and classmates?" Children who are actively disliked or rejected may need help developing better peer relations; often specific interventions will be needed to increase these children's positive interaction skills and to modify the aversive or annoying behaviors (or other personal characteristics) that contribute to peers' dislike (see La Greca, 1993). On the other hand, children who are neglected, socially isolated, or who lack friends and playmates may need assistance in developing friendship ties.

Children's Friendships

Although peer group acceptance is important, the ability to form and maintain satisfying and supportive dyadic friendships also represents a critical social adaptation task (Parker & Asher, 1993a). Much of children's social lives revolve around dyadic or small group interactions with their same-age friends (Parker & Asher, 1993b).

Both theoretical writings and empirical studies point to the importance of children's friendships for social and emotional development. According to Sullivan's interpersonal theory (1953), "true" friendships emerge in preadolescence, in response to children's needs for intimacy (see Buhrmester & Furman, 1986; Parker & Asher, 1993b). During middle childhood and adolescence, close friendships are considered to be a major factor contributing to youngsters' social competence (e.g., social perspective-taking, altruistic behavior) and self-esteem. In contrast, failure to establish close friendships at this time is believed to lead to feelings of loneliness and social isolation.

As suggested by recent reviews (Bukowski & Hoza, 1989; Hartup, 1996; Parker & Asher, 1993b), there are at least three key elements of children's friendships: the extent of a child's *participation* in friendships, the *quality* of the friendships, and the *types of children* that comprise a child's close friends. Greater emphasis in the research literature has been placed on the first two of these elements.

Friendship Participation

Friendship participation is often defined as having at least one mutual friendship with another child (Parker & Asher, 1993b). During the elementary school years, a variety of factors contribute to children's friendship selection. One major factor is social proximity; that is, children are likely to choose peers from their classroom, scouts group, or immediate neighborhood as friends (Hartop, 1983). Beyond proximity, however, other considerations come into play. Children choose as friends others who are similar to themselves (e.g., same age, same gender), who share common interests (e.g., play sports, listen to music), and who are fun to be with (Hartup, 1996; Parker & Asher, 1993b).

Little normative data are available on children's friendship participation. However, existing findings suggest that most children do have close friends in school. For example, in a study of third to fifth grade children ($n = 881$) (Parker & 1993a), 78 percent had at least one reciprocal "best friend" in the classroom,[1] and 55 percent of the children had a "very best friend." Girls were more likely to have a best friend than boys (82% vs. 74%, respectively); girls also had significantly more best friends than boys ($M = 1.54$ for girls; 1.35 for boys).

Also of interest was the linkage between children's peer acceptance and their participation in best friendships. Based on sociometric ratings, children were classified as "low accepted" (17%), "average accepted" (67.5%), or "high accepted" (14.5%). Low-accepted children were less likely to have a best friend (45%) than average (82%) or high accepted (94%) children; similarly, 29 percent of the low-accepted, 58 percent of the average-accepted, and 70 percent of the high-accepted children had *very* best friends. Of further note, low-accepted boys fared the worst, in that only 19 percent had a very best friend, in comparison to almost 40 percent of the low-accepted girls. These data underscore the heightened social vulnerability of low accepted (i.e., rejected and neglected) youth; they lack the acceptance of their peer group *and* they are less likely than other students to have a mutual best friend.

Studies of friendless children have confirmed some of the predictions derived from Sullivan's (1953) theory about the unique and developmentally important functions of close friendships (see Parker & Asher, 1993b, for a review). For example, Mannarino (1976, 1978) found that boys and girls who had friends displayed greater altruism than friendless children. Regardless of how well accepted they are by the larger peer group, friendless children have also been found to report significantly more loneliness and social dissatisfaction than children who have close friends (Parker & 1993a). Thus, children who have at least one close mutual friendship appear to fare better emotionally than those who lack such personal ties.

Friendship Quality

In addition to friendship participation, it is critical to consider the quality of children's friendships. Studies with children and adolescents reveal that peers are significant providers of emotional support (e.g., caring, intimacy, validation), second only to the emotional support received from parents. Furthermore, peers serve as children's primary source of companionship (Berndt, 1989; Cauce, Reid, Landesman, & Gonzales, 1990; Furman & Buhrmester, 1985; Reid, Landesman, Treder, & Jaccard, 1989).

Peer friendships vary tremendously in terms of the amount and type of support they provide, the degree to which conflict is present, and their level of reciprocity, among other dimensions (Parker & Asher, 1993b). Indeed, several investigators have begun to evaluate the qualitative aspects of children's friendships, although the specific qualities examined have varied across studies.

Several investigators have observed friendship qualities to vary as a function of age and gender. For example, Sharabany and associates (1981) studied close friendships in a large sample of children and adolescents (5th to 11th grades). Eight friendship qualities were examined: frankness and spontaneity, sensitivity, attachment, exclusiveness, giving help and sharing, receiving help, trust and loyalty, and common activities. Age and gender differences were explored, as well as differences between same- and cross-sex friends. In terms of same-sex friendships, findings revealed that several friendship qualities (sharing common activities, receiving help, and trust and sharing) did not vary with age, although frankness and sensitivity did show age-related increases. In addition, girls reported more giving and sharing, trust, and attachment in their same-sex friendships than did boys. Not surprisingly, Sharabany and colleagues also found that differences between same- and opposite-sex friendships were greatest for the younger children (i.e., elementary school aged); fewer differences were apparent for adolescents. Intimacy and support from cross-sex friends showed a steady increase with age; in addition, adolescent girls generally rated their cross-sex friendships as more intimate than did boys.

In another study, Furman and Buhrmester (1985) examined six qualitative aspects of fifth and sixth grader's personal relationships with friends, parents, and others in their social networks: degree of reliable alliance, enhancement of worth, instrumental help, level of companionship, level of affection, and amount of intimate disclosure. Children also rated the amount of conflict in and their degree of satisfaction with their personal relationships. Girls reported more intimate disclosure, greater enhancement of worth, and more affection in their friendships than boys. However, boys and girls did not report differences on the other friendship qualities, or on the amount of conflict in or perceived satisfaction with their friendships.

Work by Berndt and colleagues (Berndt, 1986; Berndt, Hawkins, & Hoyle, 1986; Berndt & Perry, 1986) has confirmed and extended earlier findings regarding age and gender. Of additional interest, Berndt and colleagues (1986), who followed youngsters' friendships over the course of a school year, found that friendships that had dissolved over the year had lower levels of contact and intimacy early on. In other respects, the friendships that eventually dissolved were not qualitatively different from those that continued. These data provide an intriguing glimpse of friendship processes in children.

Building on this earlier foundation, current efforts to understand qualitative aspects of children's friendships have incorporated both positive and negative qualities into the assessment of children's friendships and have gone beyond documenting age and gender differences in children's friendships. Most recently, Parker and Asher (1989, 1993) developed the Friendship Quality Questionnaire to assess six qualitatively distinct aspects of children's friendships: validation and caring, intimate exchange, help and guidance, companionship and recreation, conflict resolution, and conflict and betrayal. The first three qualities bear close resemblance to what others have described as aspects of "emotional support" (Cauce et al., 1990; Harter, 1985).

Consonant with prior research, girls reported higher levels of friendship quality for all of the dimensions assessed, with the exception of conflict and betrayal, which was infrequently reported for both boys and girls (see Parker & Asher, 1993b). Of greater interest was the fact that across the two studies the close friendships of low-accepted children were found to be more problematic than those of average- or high-accepted youngsters. Low-accepted children reported less validation and caring, less help and guidance, less intimate disclosure, and more difficulty resolving conflict in their friendships than other children. This suggests that low-accepted children receive substantially less emotional support from their close friends than do other children. On the other hand, the friendships of low-accepted children did not differ substantially from their peers' in terms of companionship and recreation, or conflict. In other words, all groups of children reported spending considerable amounts of time with their close friends and reported some conflict in these relationships, although the low-accepted youth had greater difficulties *resolving* conflict when it occurred. One other difference was that low-accepted children reported greater concerns than others on friendship items that pertained to betrayal (e.g., "I can think of many times when *my friend* has said mean things about me to other kids.").

In summary, research on the close friendships of elementary school-age children indicate that the qualitative features of these relationships vary as a function of gender and social status. Girls often report more intimate and supportive relationships with their friends than do boys. This most likely reflects the different types of activities that characterize children's play groups; for example, during the elementary school years, boys tend to associate with peers in large groups that are often centered on sports and outdoor games, whereas girls are more likely to be involved in dyads or small groups and to spend greater time in conversation and quiet activities (e.g., Lever, 1976; Thorne, 1986). In addition, the friendships of low-accepted children are more problematic and less supportive than those of more accepted youth.

With these findings in mind, it becomes apparent that the number and quality of children's close friendships are important clinical concerns. Professionals should consider whether a child has close friends and companions, both inside and outside of the classroom, and attempt to understand the *qualitative* features of these relationships. Developing more positive, supportive friendship ties may be an important goal for intervention.

Types of Friends

In addition to considering what a child's friendships are like, we also need to ask, "What are the child's *friends* like?" Substantial folk wisdom recognizes the importance and influence of one's associates: "You can judge a person by the company he or she keeps," or, "Birds of a feather flock together." Indeed, the identity of a child's friends may be more important for emotional development than merely whether or not the child has friends (Hartup, 1996).

The tendency for a person to associate with others who are similar on various attributes has been defined as *homophily* (Kandel, 1978a). Two distinct processes contribute to homophily: selection and socialization. *Selection* refers to the notion that youngsters seek out friends who are similar to themselves, whereas *socialization* refers to the tendency for friends to shape and reinforce similar attitudes and behaviors in each other (Cohen, 1977; Hogue & Steinberg, 1995; Kandel, 1978a). Indeed, associations with deviant peers have been well documented as a factor that contributes to antisocial behaviors among preadolescent and adolescent boys, presumably through the processes of selection and socialization (Cairns, Cairns, Neckerman, Gest, & Gariepy, 1988; Dishion, Patterson, Stoolmiller, & Skinner, 1991). With the exception of boys' aggressive behavior, however, most of the research on homophily has been conducted with adolescents (e.g., Brown, Clasen, & Eicher, 1986; Kandel, 1978a, 1978b).

Research on children's friendships has focused instead on child characteristics (e.g., age, gender, level of peer acceptance) and their association to the number and quality of friendships; much less attention has been paid to the *types of peers* children select as friends. However, some indirect evidence suggests that socially competent, well-adjusted children are likely to have friends with similar qualities and, conversely, that children with behavior and academic difficulties are likely to have friends with similar problems. For example, in Parker and Asher's studies of children's friendships (1989, 1993), low-accepted children were disproportionately more likely to have friends who were low accepted and less likely to have high-accepted friends. Conversely, high-accepted children were much more likely to have high-accepted peers as friends and less likely to be friends with low-accepted children. When this information is considered in the context of the substantial research on the social and behavioral characteristics of low- and high-accepted children (Coie et al., 1990), it becomes apparent that many low-accepted children, who may already display academic,

social, and behavior problems, are likely to be friends with other problematic children.

Consistent with this perspective, Vuchinich, Bank, and Patterson (1992) examined linkages between peer relations and antisocial behavior in a 2-year longitudinal study of preadolescent boys. They found that boys' antisocial behavior had a strong, negative effect on peer relations, although the reverse was not true (i.e., being unpopular did not lead to antisocial behavior). In attempting to understand the contribution of peers to the stability of antisocial behavior, these authors speculated that peer rejection may represent a child's initial step toward involvement in antisocial peer groups because individuals who are rejected by peers tend to drift toward association with each other and, thus, form groups that promote antisocial behaviors (Dishion et al., 1991). These observations fit with findings from Cairns and associates (1988), who found that highly aggressive children often choose to associate with other highly aggressive youth.

It is also likely that children with internalizing problems (e.g., anxiety, depression, social withdrawal) associate with others who share these same characteristics, although, to our knowledge, this has not been investigated with preadolescent children. Among 14 to 18 year olds, evidence suggests that adolescents tend to choose friends who possess similar levels of internal distress (Hogue & Steinberg, 1995).

In summary, although this area of research in still in its early stages, evidence is accumulating to suggest that children *choose* friends with whom they share similar behavioral characteristics and are *influenced* by their friends to behave in certain ways. Peer homophily is most clearly apparent with respect to boys' aggressive behaviors, but is also likely to be a factor in other areas, such as internalizing problems and academic achievement. Thus, in clinical settings it will be of critical importance to consider what a child's friends are like. Efforts to reduce a child's aggressive or anxious behaviors, for example, may be undermined by close associates who share those same behavioral characteristics and who reinforce and encourage undesirable behaviors in the child.

Clinical Implications of Peer Relations Literature

During the middle childhood years, an assessment of peer relationships and friendships should be an essential component of any comprehensive child evaluation. As noted earlier, most professionals will encounter children with substantial social dysfunction in their clinical practice, even if it is not articulated as part of the referral problem. For this reason, most clinicians will want to "screen" children for social dysfunction early in the assessment process. When social problems are evident, a more detailed assessment of social functioning should be pursued, and some form of social intervention should be considered as part of the overall treatment plan.

Even when social dysfunction is not a part of the overall clinical picture, peer relationships are important to consider clinically, as they may represent an important area of strength for a particular child. If this is the case, clinicians may wish to bolster and support these peer relationships as a means of helping a child cope with other ongoing stressors in his or her life.

Evaluating Children's Social Competence

Following from the review of children's peer relationships (above), in most clinical situations it will be important to gain some understanding of (1) how the child is viewed by peers, (2) how the child feels about peer interactions, (3) what the child's friends and friendships are like, and (4) what a child's interpersonal skills are like.

First, some assessment of *peers' acceptance/rejection of the child* may be useful to understand how the child is viewed by peers and to identify peers who are receptive to the child. Peer nominations represent the most widely accepted method for evaluating children's peer acceptance. Typically, youngsters nominate the three classmates they "like the most" and the three they "like the least" and these nominations are used to classify children into one of the five social status groups (Coie et al., 1982; Landau & Milich, 1990). Although peer ratings are sensitive and ecologically valid, such ratings are difficult to obtain in clinical settings. However, teachers' and parents' reports of peer acceptance and rejection may be useful when peer ratings are not available. In particular, teachers may be able to pinpoint children who are popular or rejected, although they may be less aware of children who are ignored or neglected by classmates.

Second, it is critical to obtain a picture of the *child's current friendships* and social contacts, as well as the *child's feelings about friendships and peer relationships*. Specifically, in gathering information, clinicians should attempt to understand (1) whether the child's friends reciprocate the friendship, (2) what the child's friends are like (i.e., personal characteristics and behaviors), and (3) what the qualitative features of the friendships are (e.g., supportive, caring, conflictual). These issues can be directly addressed in an interview with the child and the parents. In addition, several child self-reports are available that may supplement clinical interviews, such as the Friendship Questionnaire (Bierman & McCauley, 1987) or the Friendship Quality Questionnaire (Parker & 1993a) (see Table 11.1). These measures may enable the clinician to pinpoint why a partic-

ular child has difficulty keeping friends; this in turn may translate into specific intervention goals.

Third, children's feelings of loneliness, social anxiety, or lack of support from friends and classmates may help to identify children who are distressed by their current social situation. Improvements in subjective feelings of distress may also help to monitor a child's progress through treatment. Several scales useful for this purpose are the Social Anxiety Scale for Children-Revised, the Loneliness Scale, and the Social Support Scale for Children and Adolescents (see Table 11.1).

Fourth, when peer relationship problems are evident, the clinician will need to continue the assessment process in greater detail, and gather information on the child's *positive social skills*. Behavioral observations may be especially useful in this regard (see La Greca & Stark, 1986; Michelson, Sugai, Wood, & Kazdin, 1983). However, observations are time-consuming to gather and difficult to obtain for older children. Thus, other assessment methods have also gained favor in clinical settings. For example, several rating scales have been designed to assess children's social skills, such as the Social Skills Rating System and the Matson Evaluation of Social Skills in Youth (see Table 11.1.)

Finally, in addition to these areas, assessments should focus on obtaining a good picture of the child's (1) behavior problems (i.e., presence of internalizing or externalizing problems), (2) cognitive skills and academic achievement, and (3) physical characteristics (i.e., physical appearance, handicaps) to determine the extent to which these areas of functioning contribute to peer relationship difficulties.

Strategies for Clinical Intervention

When conducting social interventions, the clinician must keep in mind the intervention's primary *objectives or goals*. For children who are rejected by their classmates, an important intervention goal may be to increase peer acceptance; this means that the intervention will need to involve classmates and teachers. On the other hand, for children who have few or no friends, a major goal of intervention would be to increase peer contacts and friendships, and this may be done inside and/or outside the classroom setting. Moreover, because many children have multiple problems (peer rejection, few friends, few positive social skills, presence of intrusive behaviors), interventions that incorporate multiple strategies and goals may be required (see Bierman, Miller, & Stabb, 1987; La Greca & Fetter, 1995; La Greca, Stone, & Noriega-Garcia, 1989; Vaughn, McIntosh, Spencer-Rowe, 1991). Table 11.2 lists some potential intervention approaches as a function of the types of social problems children display. Several of these approaches are next discussed.

TABLE 11.1 Selected Measures of Children's and Adolescents' Social Competence

INSTRUMENT	ASSESSES	FORMAT AND AGES	RELIABILITY	COMMENTS
I. Affective Reactions (all child report)				
Loneliness Scale (see Asher et al., 1984; Asher et al., 1990)	Feelings of social dissatisfaction and loneliness	24 items; 5-point scale K–8th grade	Internal consistency: K–1st grade: .79; .90 or higher with older children	Rejected children and those with few friends report more loneliness than accepted youth.
Social Anxiety Scale for Children-Revised (SASC-R) (La Greca & Stone, 1993) (Adolescent version: La Greca & Lopez, 1998)	Fear of evaluation from peers (FNE); social avoidance and distress in general (SAD-G) and in new situations (SAD-N)	22 items; 5-point scale Children: 1st–6th grade Teens: 7th–12th grade	Internal consistency .69 to .86 across scales; .76 to .91 for adolescents	Girls report more FNE than boys; neglected and neglected youth report elevations on FNE; neglected also elevated on SAD scales; high Social Anxiety linked with less support from friends.
Self-Perception Profile for Children (SPPC) (Harter, 1988) (Adolescent version available from author)	Perceptions of competence: Social Acceptance, Physical Appearance, Behavioral Conduct, Athletic Competence, Scholastic Competence, Global Self-Worth.	36-item, forced choice rating format Ages: 7–16 years	Internal consistency: .71 to .86 across subscales	Social acceptance scores are related to peer popularity.
Social Support Scale for Children and Adolescents (SSSC) (Harter, 1985)	Perceptions of support from Classmates, Parents, Close friends, Teachers	24-item; forced choice rating format Ages: 7–16 years	Internal consistency .72 to .88 across scales for elementary school through middle school	Classmate support related to social acceptance; friend support related to ability to disclose thoughts and feelings to friends; girls have more friend support.
Survey of Children's Social Support (Dubow & Ullman, 1989)	Appraisals of support from Family, Teachers, Peers	31 items; 5-point rating format Grades: 3–5	Internal consistency of .88; range of .78 to .83 across subscales	Girls list more support providers; friend support related to less loneliness, higher peer-rated preference, and higher perceived social acceptance.
II. Friendships and Friendship Quality (all child report)				
Friendship Questionnaire (Bierman & McCauley, 1987)	Positive Interactions (PI), Negative Interactions (NI), and Extensiveness of Peer Network (EPN)	32 items, 5-point rating format plus 8 questions; Ages: 8–13 years	Internal consistency: .80 for PI, .82 for NI, .72 for EPN.	Emotionally disturbed children report less PI and EPN, and more NI, than nondisturbed youth; rejected children report more NI than accepted youth; older children's ratings more related to peer status than younger children's.
Friendship Quality Questionnaire (Parker & Asher, 1993).	Intimate exchange, Help and guidance, Conflict resolution, Validation/caring, etc.	40 items, 5-point rating scale; Ages: 7–12 years	Internal consistency: .73 to .80 across subscales	Girls have higher quality friendships than boys; low-accepted children have lower quality friendships and less conflict resolution.

Continued

Table 11.1 continued

INSTRUMENT	ASSESSES	FORMAT AND AGES	RELIABILITY	COMMENTS
III. *Social–Interpersonal Skills*				
Social Skills Rating System SSRT (Gresham & Elliott, 1992)	Parent (P), teacher (T), and student (S) ratings for social skills, behavior, and academic skills	50 to 54 items, 3-point rating scale Grades: K–6; adolescent version as well	Internal consistency: generally above .75	Greater support for utility of scale with preadolescents; assesses broader constructs than social skills, specific scales depend on child's age.
Matson Evaluation of Social Skills for Youngsters (Matson et al., 1983)	Inappropriate assertiveness/ impulsiveness; Appropriate social skills (5 factors)	Parent/teacher, 64 items; Self-report, 62 items; 5-point scale Ages: 4–18 years	Adequate internal consistency	Greater support for the utility of the scale with preadolescents than adolescents.
Teenage Inventory of Social Skills (TISS; Inderbitzen & Foster, 1992)	Positive (P) scale; Negative (N) scale.	20 Positive and 20 Negative items; 6-point rating scale Adolescents	Internal consistency: .88 for P and N scales	Promising inventory for identifying adolescents' peer relations difficulties and designing social interventions.
Measure of Adolescent Social Competence (MASC; Cavell & Kelley, 1992)	Three subscales: Peer, Family, and School	50 items; Multiple choice questionnaire Grades: 6–12	Internal consistency: .87 for total; subscales range from .65 to .78	MASC scores correlate with self-reports of friendship quality and self-worth; older adolescents have higher MASC scores.
IV. *Peer Evaluations*				
Pupil Evaluation Inventory (PEI; Pekarik et al., 1976)	Peer, teacher, or self-ratings: Aggression, Withdrawal, Likability	35 behavioral items; peers or teacher indicate which children match the descriptors Grades: 1–9	Split half reliability: $r > .70$ for all subscales	Best used with teachers and peers; lower Likability scores obtained with middle school youth.
Adjustment Scale for Sociometric Evaluation of Secondary-School Students (ASSESS; Prinz et al., 1978)	Five subscales: Withdrawal, Anxiety, Aggression–Disruptiveness, Social Competence, and Academic Difficulty	Extension of PEI; 45 items High school students	Internal consistency of subscales range from .82 to .94	Higher Social Competence and lower Academic Difficulty scores were found for older versus younger adolescents; gender differences were minimal.

184

TABLE 11.2 Summary of Social Intervention Strategies

TYPE OF SOCIAL PROBLEM	POTENTIAL INTERVENTION STRATEGY
Few Peer Contacts/Opportunities	Extracurricular activities that involve peers (e.g., scouts, sports activities); Develop other opportunities for peer contacts
Low Levels of Positive Social Skills	Social Skills Training
Low Levels of Peer Acceptance/High Levels of Rejection	Work with classmates to modify perceptions of child; Develop peer-pairing or buddy system in school
Few Friendships	Develop peer buddy in school; Cooperative play and work activities in school or clinic; Develop social contacts outside the school setting
Subjective Distress from Negative Peer Contacts	Find positive peer contacts; Teach positive reframing; "Inoculate" against occasional rejection
High Levels of Intrusive Behaviors (e.g., inattention, aggression)	Contingency management; Incentives for reducing aversive behavior
Presence of Internalizing Problems (e.g., anxiety, social withdrawal)	Gradual exposure to peers; Anxiety-Reduction procedures
"Problematic" Child Characteristics (e.g., learning problems, obesity)	Modify peers' perceptions; Modify the child characteristics (e.g., educational interventions)

Social skills training. Social skills training (SST) programs typically teach or reward positive interaction skills that are important for successful peer relations (see Table 11.3). The most common approach to SST involves the combination of *modeling* of appropriate social behavior, *coaching* or instruction in how to behave with peers, *behavioral rehearsal* of social skills, usually through role-plays or actual social interactions, *corrective feedback,* and *reinforcement* of appropriate social skills. SST has been used with rejected and low-accepted elementary school students (Bierman & Furman, 1984; Gresham & Nagle, 1980; La Greca & Santogrossi, 1980; Oden & Asher, 1977), with learning disabled youth (Hazel, Schumaker, Sherman, & Sheldon, 1982; La Greca & Mesibov, 1979, 1981; Vaughn et al., 1991), and with behaviorally disordered children (Bornstein, Bellack, & Hersen, 1980; Kolko, Loar, & Sturnick, 1990). Applications of SST for individual children (Bierman et al., 1987; La Greca et al., 1989; Oden & Asher, 1977) as well as for small groups (La Greca & Mesibov, 1981; La Greca & Santogrossi, 1980) can be found.

Prior to beginning SST, the clinician must first identify the specific social skills to be taught or emphasized; these may be based on one child's needs or the collective needs of group members. Once the skills for training have been identified, a standard format is used. First, the desired social behavior is described, discussed, and modeled. It is essential that children understand what is expected and the social contexts that are appropriate and inappropriate for the behavior (e.g., talking with others on the playground, but not during class). In a group, children may provide examples of how the skills can be used. Second, children are provided with opportunities to practice the skills (Behavioral Rehearsal)—either with the clinician or with other children if a group format is used. Ideas for role-plays and practice may come from social situations generated by children or suggested by the therapist. Third, the practice is critiqued by the clinician or, for group interventions, by the other group members (Coaching/Feedback). This includes pointing out the good aspects of the behavior as well as areas for improvement. Practice is provided until children master the skills. To make the training fun and rewarding, generous use of praise and/or contingent reinforcement for appropriate social skills is important (see Cartledge & Milburn, 1980; La Greca et al., 1989). Finally, once skills have been practiced sufficiently, opportunities to use the skills in naturalistic settings should be provided. This might entail specific assignments to use the skills with classmates or neighborhood children. Parents and teachers can be useful partners in helping children identify receptive peers and implementing their homework (e.g., inviting peers to play at home; sitting with a classmate during lunch) (La Greca, 1993). At each meeting, assignments should be reviewed and discussed, with appropriate feedback and reinforcement provided.

The above description provides a brief overview to SST. Additional details are contained in treatment studies and

TABLE 11.3   Positive Interpersonal Skills that Contribute to Children's Social Interactions with Peers

SKILL AREA	SOME KEY COMPONENTS
Enjoyment of Interactions	Smiling Laughing
Joining Others	Stand near others; smile Ask to join; fit in with ongoing activity Acknowledge others when they join you Handling refusals (e.g., Don't get mad)
Extending Invitations	Ask other person to do something; be specific Accept invitations in a positive way Handling refusals (e.g., Ask for another day)
Conversation Skills	Ask conversational questions Talk/share information about self Keeping a conversation going Taking turns in conversation Topics for conversation
Sharing/Cooperation	Taking turns in peer activities Following the game rules Being a "good sport" (good winner or loser)
Complimenting/Giving Positive Feedback	Looking at the person, smiling Making positive statements Accepting compliments from others positively
Conflict Resolution	Compromising Sharing Handling name-calling and teasing

Adapted from La Greca & Mesibov, 1979; Vaughn & La Greca, 1993

reviews (Bierman & Furman, 1984; Bierman et al., 1987; La Greca & Santogrossi, 1980; Ladd, 1985; Vaughn & La Greca, 1993) as well as treatment manuals (Jackson, Jackson, & Monroe, 1983; La Greca, 1981; McGinnis & Goldstein, 1984).

Most SST programs have focused on skills considered to be important for initiating and maintaining peer interactions. However, it should be possible to adapt the SST content to include specific friendship skills, such as conflict resolution, help and guidance, and intimate exchange.

Reducing concomitant behavior problems. A second key strategy for improving children's social functioning involves reducing the types of behavior problems that interfere with peer relationships. In most clinical settings, a child will be referred for behavior problems (e.g. anxiety, aggressive behavior) rather than social difficulties. In such cases, the clinician will want to treat the referred behavior problems, but additionally assess the child's peer relations and

social skills and include social interventions in the overall treatment plan.

Socially rejected children often behave aggressively towards peers. Bierman (1989; Bierman et al., 1987) advocates two strategies for reducing children's negative behaviors: (1) contingency management to consequate the negative behaviors of target children and (2) teaching peers to ignore the negative behaviors of the target child. For example, response cost (punishment) procedures can be used to reduce the aggressive behaviors of rejected children who participate in social skills training (Bierman et al., 1987). In clinical settings, professionals should be prepared to use contingency management during individual or group SST (e.g., La Greca et al., 1989). Teaching parents and teachers skills for behavior management would also be advisable. Although training classmates to ignore negative behaviors in the target child has proved to be another useful strategy in the classroom (Bierman, 1989), this strategy may be difficult to implement in a clinical setting.

For children who have internalizing problems (i.e., anxiety, social withdrawal) that interfere with peer relations, social skills treatment may help by providing gradual exposure to peers in social settings. In addition, contingent reinforcement for social engagement may be useful. For example, Kirby and Toler (1970) identified children with low levels of social interaction, who were then instructed by their teachers to distribute candy to the other children in the classroom—a task that required them to ask others for their preferences. After completing the task, children received praise, money, and candy (i.e., reinforcements) from their teachers. Following the task, these children engaged in increased interactions with peers during free-play, perhaps due to the combination of reinforcement, exposure to peers, and reinforcement from peers (Kirby & Toler, 1970). Thus, for children who are anxious or avoidant with peers, gradual exposure in the clinic and in planned activities outside the clinic, with associated reinforcement for social engagement, may facilitate their social skills treatment (also see Ginsburg, Silverman, & Kurtines, 1995).

Strategies for enhancing peer networks, social contacts, and friendships. To improve a child's peer *interactions,* it is critical to consider *both* sides of the interaction equation—that is, both the child and his or her peers (La Greca, 1993). Social interventions that incorporate elements of the child's social environment have a greater impact on the child's peer acceptance and help to maintain treatment gains. In fact, SST interventions that included (nonproblem) classmates in the treatment program have been more successful than those that did not (e.g., Bierman & Furman, 1984; Oden & Asher, 1977; Vaughn & Lancelotta, 1991).

Two ways of increasing a child's peer contacts within the school setting are through peer-pairing and cooperative peer activities (see La Greca, 1993). Both activities help nonproblem peers to get to know the target child and thus may help the target child gain entry into peer networks that might otherwise exclude the child. Furthermore, nonproblem peers may serve as role models for social skills and positive interaction behaviors and may potentially become friends with the target child.

Peer-pairing involves matching a child with social difficulties with another child who has good social skills and is accepted by others. These pairs can work together on social skills, friendship-making, or cooperative learning tasks (Bierman & Furman, 1984; Oden & Asher, 1977; Vaughn & Lancelotta, 1991). When a child is seen in a clinical setting, peer-pairing might be accomplished by working with classroom teachers. For example, teachers could help to identify a "peer buddy" or socially skilled classmate who could be as-signed to work with the target child on classroom projects and activities. Parents may also be helpful in identifying appropriate neighborhood children who could be invited to participate in play or other fun activities with their child.

In addition to peer-pairing, classroom-based cooperative activities have been developed to enhance children's peer networks in the classroom. Cooperative activities involve children in games or tasks that have a shared goal and that promote cooperation and interdependence (Furman & Gavin, 1989). Typically, children from the same classroom (or children who are seen in a clinical setting), who are not mutual friends or enemies, work together on a nonacademic activity for which there is a group goal. Cooperative interaction tasks have a positive impact on children's liking for one another, even when the target child was initially disliked by peers (Furman & Gavin, 1989; Price & Dodge, 1989). This may be because the helping and sharing behaviors displayed during group activities disconfirm peers' negative impressions of disliked children (Price & Dodge, 1989) or because peers are provided with an opportunity to discover ways in which the target child is like them (Vaughn et al., 1991).

A supportive environment, such as the one created through cooperative peer activities, may also foster friendships. Following cooperative tasks, children report feeling more friendly towards others in their group and feeling that peers care more about them (Furman & Gavin, 1989).

In treatment settings, cooperative group activities can be established in a clinic through structured group activities. In addition, teachers may be excellent consultants, because they may be able to identify school activities in which target children can work or play cooperatively with peers. As noted earlier, parents may also be helpful in supporting extracurricular activities, such as scouts, sports, and so on, that bring children together in a cooperative manner (La Greca, 1993).

Despite the appeal of peer-pairing and cooperative peer interactions as an intervention strategy, there is good reason to believe that this approach will work best when combined with SST and/or contingency management. Although cooperative peer interactions may have a positive effect on children's peer acceptance and friendships, children with poor peer relations may still require specific SST to ensure that they have the requisite social behaviors to participate in cooperative peer activities and interact appropriately with others (Price & Dodge, 1989). In fact, Bierman and Furman (1984) found that peer involvement increased the frequency of low-accepted children's peer interactions and increased their peer acceptance, but these positive gains were *only* maintained at follow-up when cooperative tasks were combined with specific training in social skills.

In summary, because many children display a variety of social difficulties, interventions need to be multifaceted. Some combination of creating opportunities for peer interactions and friendships, promoting positive social and friendship skills, and reducing competing negative or intrusive behaviors will be critical. Although some of this may be accomplished outside the school setting, given the extensive amount of time children spend in school with the same peer group, strategies that involve teachers (or counselors) and classmates may enhance an intervention's effectiveness.

ADOLESCENCE

During the adolescent years, peer relations take on increasing prominence, importance, and complexity. Most adolescents have a rich network of peer relations that includes their best friends, other close friends, larger friendship groups or cliques, social crowds, and even romantic relationships (Furman, 1989; Urberg, Degirmencioglu, Tolson, & Halliday-Scher, 1995).

In trying to understand the various facets of adolescents' peer relations, and their impact on social–emotional development and adjustment, it will be useful to describe these relationships in terms of their level of interaction. *Crowds* are reputation-based peer groups—that is, a large collective of similarly stereotyped individuals who may or may not spend much time together; *cliques* typically are a small number of adolescents who spend time together; and *dyads* refer to pairs of friends or romantic partners (Brown, 1989, pp. 189–190). In keeping with the information provided on the peer relations of younger children, in the sections that follow we first discuss adolescents' larger social networks before focusing on adolescent friendships.

Adolescents' General Peer Relationships

Peer Groups or Crowds

To the extent that crowds reflect adolescents' peer status and reputation, they are a developmental outgrowth of the social status groups observed in the classroom settings of younger children. A particular crowd affiliation reflects the primary attitudes or behaviors by which an adolescent is known to his or her peers (Brown, 1989).

The specific types of crowds adolescents identify appear to vary with age, with some changes occurring between middle school and high school (O'Brien & Bierman, 1987); crowds also vary with the particular school or neighborhood setting (Brown, 1989). In spite of these shifts, remarkable cross-setting consistencies have been observed. The most commonly mentioned crowds include populars (or elites),

brains, jocks, druggies or burnouts, loners, nonconformists, or special interest groups (e.g., drama, dance, band) (Brown & Clausen, 1986; Mosbach & Leventhal, 1988; Urberg, 1992). Some adolescents identify with more than one group (i.e., hybrids), and many do not identify with any particular group or may consider themselves to be "normals" or "average."

Peer crowds vary in obvious and not-so-obvious ways. For instance, "brains" typically are smart, do well in school, and value academic activities; however, they also tend to be low in their levels of sexual activity, smoking, and alcohol and drug use (e.g., Prinstein, La Greca, & Fetter, 1996; Mosbach & Leventhal, 1988). "Jocks" typically are involved in athletic activities or competitive sports but, relative to "average" adolescents, jocks are less likely to smoke or use drugs, and more likely to be sexually active. Thus, if an adolescent identifies with a particular crowd, this may provide some information about the adolescent's behavior and reputation.

The relative status of crowds can vary from school to school. In one recent study of high school students (Prinstein et al., 1996), "populars" and "jocks" represented the most liked groups, with "brains" and "nonconformists" in the middle range, and "burnouts" among the least liked. Brown (1989) has hypothesized that the status of crowds may vary as a function of the community's value system; for example, jocks may enjoy higher status in schools that have active community involvement in athletic competitions than in schools where mostly a small network of friends and family members attend athletic events.

Although little research has addressed the question of the stability of peer crowds in adolescence, Brown (1989) suggests that shifts in crowd allegiance are probably not very common, in large part because of the reputation-based nature of crowds. Generally speaking, adolescents are "selected" to be part of a crowd based on their personality or behavior. As with elementary school children, peer-based reputations may be slow or difficult to change. Shifts in crowd membership may also be difficult because of the "status hierarchy" of crowds; when shifts occur, they most likely occur between crowds with adjacent or similar positions in the status hierarchy (Brown, 1989). As with preadolescents, it may be very difficult, if not impossible, to move from a low-status group like the burnouts or druggies, to a high-status crowd, such as the populars or jocks.

Some of the foundations for adolescents' crowd affiliation may begin in the preadolescent or early adolescent years. For example, Prinstein and colleagues (1996) found that adolescents' *initial* identification with a particular crowd varied; most adolescents who identify themselves as "brains" reported being a part of this crowd since elementary school and most "burnouts" or "druggies" reported being a part of this crowd since middle school. In contrast, most "jocks" and "populars" reported that their crowd affiliation began during high school.

From a developmental perspective, the significance of crowds is that they contribute to adolescents' reputation and identity; they provide a sense of belonging. In addition, crowd membership may determine the pool of individuals from which adolescents meet and select friends. Finally, although close friends may have more influence than crowds (Urberg, 1992), crowd affiliation may also influence behavior, in that an adolescent who wishes to be a part of a particular crowd may feel compelled to maintain behaviors that are compatible with the crowd's reputation. For example, youngsters who are part of the "burnout" or "druggie" crowd, may feel compelled to smoke, drink alcohol, or engage in risky behaviors in order to "fit in" with others. Moreover, if the crowd is an especially low-status one, as may be the case with burnouts, the adolescent's options for becoming part of another crowd may be fairly limited, further enhancing the crowd's influence.

From a clinical perspective, little is known about the psychological or emotional correlates of various crowd affiliations among adolescents or whether, for example, adolescents who are not a part of a crowd feel left out, lonely, or isolated. It does seem apparent, however, that much can be learned about an adolescent's attitudes towards school, substance use, and the general peer culture by understanding the particular crowd with which he or she identifies.

Peer Rejection Experiences

In sharp contrast to the extensive literature on peer rejection among preadolescents, there is a paucity of data available on peer rejection among adolescents, even though this appears to be a critical concern for adolescents as well. During adolescence, being a part of the peer group and fitting in with one's peers becomes a major priority for most youngsters (Bowker, Sippola, & Bukowski, 1996). In this context, when peer rejection does occur, it may be particularly salient and stressful. Several recent studies of early adolescents suggest that this is indeed the case. For example, Bowker and colleagues (1996) found that peer rejection experiences accounted for more than 50 percent of the "peer-related hassles" reported by seventh graders.

In one of the few studies of adolescent peer rejection, Parkhurst and Asher (1992) identified behavior patterns and emotional responses associated with peer rejection among seventh and eighth graders, using peer nomination procedures similar to those used with preadolescents. Compared with average youth, rejected students were more likely to be viewed by peers as lacking cooperativeness and trustworthiness and as unable to take teasing. Rejected students also re-

ported significantly more loneliness than popular students. In addition, two subgroups of rejected adolescents were examined: rejected–aggressive (i.e., those who "start fights") and rejected–submissive (i.e., those who are "easy to push around"). The rejected–submissive students were more lonely than a matched group of average students, although rejected–aggressive students did not report elevated loneliness levels. Also of interest, the rejected–submissive adolescents reported significantly more interpersonal concerns about being rejected or humiliated by peers in school than did average students, whereas rejected–aggressive youth did not report any more interpersonal concerns than other adolescents. These findings suggest that some adolescents may be "victimized" and pushed around by peers in school and that this type of peer rejection is associated with considerable subjective distress.

Another approach to understanding peer rejection in adolescence is through studies of aversive exchanges among peers. Vernberg and associates (1995) surveyed 130 middle school students, and found that 73 percent of them reported at least one aversive exchange (i.e., teased, hit, threatened, or excluded) during the prior 3 months. A substantial proportion of the adolescents did not talk to anyone about these events, and when they did, they were significantly more likely to disclose this information to an age-mate (friend, classmate, or sibling) than to an adult (parent or teacher). This suggests that parents and other concerned adults may be completely unaware of these aversive exchanges. Furthermore, adolescents who reported more frequent occurrences of verbal and physical harassment or peer exclusion reported greater loneliness, especially if they did not talk to anyone else about these events.

Several prospective studies further indicate that aversive exchanges with peers during early adolescence lead to feelings of internal distress. Vernberg (1990) found that rejection experiences in the fall of the school year predicted greater depressive symptomatology and lower perceived social acceptance 6 months later. In a subsequent investigation (Vernberg et al., 1992), peer rejection experiences in the beginning of the school year predicted adolescents' social anxiety later in the year. Complementary to this work are large-scale longitudinal investigations of bullying among Scandinavian youth (Olweus, 1993), which find that adolescents who are bullied frequently during early adolescence are more likely to report low self-esteem and symptoms of anxiety as adults.

One particular subgroup of adolescents who appear to be at very high risk for verbal and physical harassment from peers are lesbian, gay, and bisexual youth. Existing evidence suggests that verbal and physical harassment and abuse is a frequent and significant source of stress to these youth and is associated with a host of negative outcomes, including school-related problems, substance abuse, and suicide (Savin-Williams, 1994; see also chapter 15, this volume).

In summary, although peer rejection and rejection experiences (i.e., harassment, exclusion) have not received much empirical attention, they appear to be common occurrences and represent a significant source of subjective distress for many adolescents. Because adolescents are not likely to talk about aversive peer exchanges with other adults, they may go undetected and underreported.

Adolescents' Friendships

Peer friendships are especially salient during the early adolescent years. By their own account, adolescents spend more time talking to peers than in any other activity; they also describe themselves as happiest when talking to peers (Berndt, 1982, p. 1448).

Adolescents' interactions with friends take place primarily in the context of dyadic interactions (friendship pairs, romantic partners) or in cliques. Cliques are friendship-based groupings that can vary in size (usually from 5 to 8 members), density (the degree to which each person regards others in the clique as friends), and their degree of "tightness" (extent to which they are closed or open to outsiders) (Brown, 1989; Urberg et al., 1995). Cliques constitute the primary base for adolescents' interactions with peers (Brown, 1989). They typically contain specific dyadic friendship pairings as well. Developmental trends indicated that the percentage of students who participate in cliques peaks in middle school, and then decreases in high school (Crockett, Losoff, & Peterson, 1984; Shrum & Check, 1987), although some studies have not obtained such age-related changes (e.g., Urberg et al., 1995). It does seem to be the case, however, that adolescents' best friends are likely to participate in the same clique or group (Urberg et al., 1995). Over time, cliques may be replaced by adolescents' interactions within dyads or smaller friendship-based groups.

Ethnic minority status appears to have implications for adolescents' participation in cliques. According to Urberg and associates (1995), within-school minorities (either whites or African Americans) were less likely to be members of cliques and were more likely to be "unconnected."

In general, greater attention in the research literature has been devoted to understanding adolescents' dyadic friendships and intimate relationships than to the study of cliques, perhaps due to the difficulty of identifying and defining a clique (e.g., some cliques may be no more than a loose association of dyadic friendships). For whatever reason, most of the work on adolescents' friendships has focused on the

qualitative features of these relationships and to some extent on the characteristics of adolescents's friends. These areas are summarized below.

Features of Adolescents' Friendships: Friendship Quality

Many of the qualities observed in preadolescents' friendships (companionship, tangible aid, validation and caring, and trust) are important for adolescents as well (Berndt, 1982). In addition, however, one of the defining features of adolescents' friendships is their degree of intimacy. *Intimacy* refers to the sharing of personal, private thoughts and feelings with friends, as well as to the knowledge of intimate details about one's friends. Compared to the middle childhood years, close friendships become significantly more intimate during early adolescence (12–16 years), and this upward trend continues through late adolescence (Berndt, 1982). Increasing levels of intimacy are evident in the friendships of boys and girls and are apparent for both same-sex and cross-sex friendships (Berndt, 1982).

Significant gender differences in adolescents' friendships have been observed. Adolescent girls report having more friends than boys and are more likely than boys to have a mutual best friend (Urberg et al., 1995). Adolescent girls also report higher levels of intimacy in their friendships than do boys (Berndt, 1982). Girls' higher levels of intimacy in their close relationships may reflect their apparent preference for "exclusive" relationships (Elder & Hallinan, 1978; Waldrop & Halverson, 1975); boys appear to be more flexible and open in their friendship choices (Urberg et al., 1995). Others have observed that adolescent girls have more closed peer groups and are less willing to let other peers join ongoing interactions than seems to be the case for boys (Urberg et al., 1995).

The psychological benefits of having an intimate friendship during adolescence (enhances self-esteem, reduces fears and anxieties) have been discussed by a number of theorists (e.g., Sullivan, 1953); however, empirical findings are relatively scant. Thus far, it does appear that friendship quality is linked with adolescents' psychological adaptation and that greater closeness with a best friend may protect adolescents from developing negative self-perceptions following peer rejection (Vernberg, 1990).

Other research on the qualitative dimensions of adolescents' friendships reveals that support from close friends is positively associated with school involvement and achievement (Berndt & Keefe, 1992; Cauce, 1986), with self-esteem and psychosocial adjustment (e.g., Buhrmester, 1990; Compas, Slavin, Wagner, & Cannatta, 1986; Perry, 1987), and with peer popularity (Cauce, 1986). In addition, adolescents (especially girls) with supportive and intimate close friendships report less social anxiety than those with less positive friendships (La Greca & Lopez, 1998).

Characteristics of Adolescents' Friends

An important determinant of adolescents' friendships is similarity or homophily, that is, youngsters are likely to select as friends others who share similar attributes and characteristics and are influenced by the behaviors and attitudes of the friends they choose. Although youngsters of all ages are more likely to chose friends who are similar in age, sex, and race, studies additionally reveal that similarities in specific interests, school attitudes and achievement, orientation to the contemporary peer culture, and substance use are important factors in adolescents' friendship choices (Berndt, 1982; Brown, 1989; Hartup, 1996). This friendship similarity is likely the result of greater interpersonal attraction among similar adolescents, as well as a function of proximity, in that adolescents have greater opportunities to meet and get to know peers from the same schools, academic classes, or neighborhoods (Hartup, 1996). Once friendships are established, mutual socialization may further enhance the similarities between friends (Hartup, 1996; Kandel, 1978a).

However, unlike preadolescents who typically choose same-sex peers for friends, cross-sex friendship choices become increasingly common during the adolescent years (Bukowski, Gauze, Hoza, & Newcomb, 1993; Elder & Hallinan, 1978; Schneider, Weiner, & Murphy, 1994). During early adolescence, cross-gender friendships may be a sign of low social competence (Bukowski et al., 1993); however, during mid to late adolescence, cross-gender friendships are more common (Degirmencioglu & Urberg, 1996) and their presence is not associated with social dysfunction (Kuttler, La Greca, & Prinstein, 1998). In fact, adolescents with cross-gender friendships appear to be better integrated into the peer network at school (Degirmencioglu & Urberg, 1996).

Clinical Implications of Peer Relations Research for Adolescents

In most clinical situations it will be essential to gain some understanding of adolescents' friendships and general peer relations. As with younger children, the general strategy of "screening," followed by more in-depth evaluation as needed, may be useful. In terms of assessment, many of the measures and strategies described in the chapter section on Middle Childhood will be useful for adolescents as well (see Table 11.1). However, as a rule, teachers will be less useful informants for adolescents (Loeber, Green, & Lahey, 1990); in fact, with adolescents, most of the assessment and intervention will focus on the adolescent and family.

In general, it will be useful to assess the following areas: (a) the general peer group or crowd with which the adolescent affiliates, (b) the adolescent's feelings about peer interactions, (c) what the teen's friends and friendships are like, (d) what kind of interpersonal skills the adolescent has, and (e) the occurrence of any aversive experiences with peers. Since several of these issues have already been discussed in the section on Middle Childhood, here we will highlight issues that are especially salient for adolescents.

The sections that follow also present ideas for social interventions. The ideas are intended to supplement those previously discussed in this chapter as well as other published resources on adolescent social intervention (Hansen, Watson-Perczel, & Christopher, 1989; Inderbitzen, 1994).

Peer Group Affiliation

Because of the linkage between adolescents' peer group affiliations and their attitudes towards school, substance use, and the general peer culture, it is advisable to ask adolescents about these affiliations. Specifically, one could ask an adolescent to identify the peer groups in their school, and to indicate how these peer groups are generally viewed and with which group (or groups) the adolescent identifies (see Mosbach & Leventhal, 1988). It would also be of interest to know whether or not any of the adolescent's closest friends are a part of the same peer group. This information may provide an important context for understanding the adolescent's behavior and attitudes and social pressures to behave or act in a certain way (e.g., "brains" may feel substantial pressures to perform well in school). It may also indicate, to some extent, the broader social networks that the adolescent has available for developing further social contacts and friendships.

Clinically, little is known about methods or strategies for "changing" an adolescent's peer reputation or even whether this would be an important or desirable goal. Adolescents typically have a much wider circle of peers available to them as potential friends and associates than do elementary school children (who are often restricted, at least during the school day, to a rather small circle of classmates for much of their social interactions). Adolescents change classes and classmates throughout the school day and may be involved with different peers through after-school activities, sports, interest-oriented clubs, or part-time jobs. This broader peer network may provide greater opportunities for findings others who are "like them" and for developing friendships.

Friends and Friendship Quality

Clinicians should actively discuss friendships with the adolescent and, if necessary, engage parents in the process of facilitating their youngsters' friendships. In terms of potential strategies for improving friendship quality (e.g., sharing, confiding, conflict resolution), the social skills training model (described in the Middle Childhood section) could be adapted to focus on friendship skills. Clinicians could work with adolescents to identify problematic friendship skills (e.g., resolving arguments, talking about feelings) and improve these skills using the strategies of modeling, coaching, rehearsal, and practice. Using group-based treatments, or even on occasion including the adolescent's friends in a treatment session, might also prove useful for practicing and facilitating better friendship skills.

With adolescents' increasing age and autonomy, parents have less opportunity to control their youngster's peer networks, so it may be more difficult for a parent to directly influence friendship choices. Nevertheless, clinicians may advise parents that they can be influential by remaining involved and interested in their youngster's social life (Brown, Hamm, & Meyerson, 1996). For example, parents should be knowledgeable about their child's friends, and "monitor" their teen's social interactions (by showing an interest in their friends, getting to know their friends when they are in their home, asking questions about social activities, and staying informed). Parents may also be encouraged to get to know their youngster's friends, such as by including them in family outings and activities. When a youngster chooses friends who are "inappropriate" (e.g., engage in antisocial behaviors, use drugs, etc.), parents should actively discourage these relationships and try to redirect their child to more appropriate friendship choices. By choosing "quality friends," the adolescent is also more likely to have quality friendships.

Parents also play a role in facilitating adolescents' friendship quality during transition periods. For example, in a study of adolescents following relocation to a new community, Vernberg and associates (1993) found that several aspects of parental behavior facilitated greater companionship and intimacy in their adolescents' friendships. The "friendship facilitation strategies" took the form of "enabling proximity" (e.g., driving the teen to a friend's house, allowing friends to sleep over), "meeting other parents" (e.g., getting to know the parents of a friend), "talking to the adolescent" (e.g., talking about life and friends, pointing out qualities to look for in a friend), and "encouraging activity" (e.g., encouraging the teen to make a team at school or to make more effort to get together with friends). Of these four strategy types, "enabling proximity" was the most influential.

Rejection Experiences/Aversive Exchanges

As indicated earlier, evidence suggests that negative exchanges with peers (e.g., being bullied, threatened, or teased in a mean way; being excluded from peer activities) represent a significant source of stress for adolescents and may contribute to feelings of subjective distress (i.e., anxiety, loneliness, depression). Yet, a substantial number of adolescents do not discuss these events with anyone, and when they do, adults are much less likely to be consulted than other agemates.

Clinically, this suggests that parents and teachers may be completely unaware of aversive exchanges among adolescents. Thus, it may be advisable to ask adolescents directly about these kinds of events. Further, it may be appropriate to help adolescents identify someone whom they can talk to when such events occur. Vernberg and colleagues (1995) found that adolescents who were able *to disclose* such events to a peer or adult were significantly less lonely and displayed less subjective distress. Aside from disclosure, in some instances, recruiting the assistance of adults (e.g., teachers, school personnel) may be appropriate to reduce harassment and abuse in the school setting.

SUMMARY AND CONCLUSIONS

As indicated throughout this chapter, from early childhood on, peer relationships play an extremely important role in youngsters' social and emotional development. In the context of peer interactions, children learn appropriate social skills that contribute to their social adaptation throughout childhood and adolescence. Furthermore, when interpersonal difficulties with peers are evident, they are typically associated with a host of emotional and adjustment problems.

Because peer relationship problems occur at high rates among clinically referred children, an assessment of the child's peer relationships and friendships should comprise an essential part of any comprehensive psychological evaluation, and social interventions should be considered as part of the overall treatment plan for many clinically referred youth. Moreover, efforts to build and strengthen children's peer relationships and friendships are essential from a preventive standpoint. Good quality friendships, in particular, provide an important source of emotional support for children who are otherwise experiencing considerable personal or family distress and may help youngsters to better negotiate major life crises and transitions.

In working with children and adolescents, professionals should be mindful of the developmental context within which peer relationships occur. Although positive interactions with peers are important from early childhood on, the impact of the peer group does not become a salient issue until middle childhood. Then, during the adolescent years, youngsters' friendships take on increasing importance, especially in terms of their closeness and intimacy. These developmental shifts gradually prepare children and adolescents for the more mature and challenging interpersonal relationships of adulthood. In tandem with these changes, social intervention strategies increasingly emphasize working directly with youngsters within their peer context. In addition, the roles that parents and teachers play gradually alter, as they become less "directive" and more "facilitative" of youngsters' peer relations.

With these critical considerations in mind, we hope that the ideas and suggestions represented in this chapter will enable professionals to take a very serious look at children's social functioning and to assess and intervene with youngsters' peer relationships on a routine basis. In our view it is essential that professionals become better informed as to how to integrate this important aspect of children's functioning into their everyday clinical practice.

NOTES

1. To meet the criterion for having a "best friend," at least one of the child's three nominees for "best friend" had to also nominate the child as a best friend. To meet the criterion for having a "very best friend," the child's *single* best friend among the three nominees had to also nominate the child as a best friend.

REFERENCES

American Psychiatric Association. (1994). *Diagnostic and statistical manual of mental disorders* (4th ed.). Washington, DC: Author.

Apolloni, T., & Cooke, T. P. (1978). Integrated programming at the infant, toddler, and preschool levels. In M. Guralnick (Ed.), *Early intervention and the integration of the handicapped and nonhandicapped children* (pp. 147–165). Baltimore: University Park Press.

Asher, S. R., & Coie, J. D. (Eds.). (1990). *Peer rejection in childhood.* New York: Cambridge University Press.

Asher, S. R., Hymel, S., & Renshaw, P. D. (1984). Loneliness in children. *Child Development, 55,* 1456–1464.

Asher, S. R., Parkhurst, J. T., Hymel, S., & Williams, G. A. (1990). Peer rejection and loneliness in childhood. In S. R. Asher & J. D. Coie (Eds.), *Peer rejection in childhood* (pp. 253–273). Cambridge, England: Cambridge University Press.

Asher, S. R., Singleton, L. C., Tinsley, B. R., & Hymel, S. (1979). A reliable sociometric measure for preschool children. *Developmental Psychology, 15,* 443–444.

Asher, S. R., & Wheeler, V. A. (1985). Children's loneliness: A comparison of rejected and neglected peer status. *Journal of Consulting and Clinical Psychology, 53,* 500–505.

Barclay, J. R. (1966). Sociometric choices and teacher ratings as predictors of school dropout. *Journal of Social Psychology, 4,* 40–45.

Becker, J. (1977). A learning analysis of the development of peer oriented behavior in nine-month-olds. *Developmental Psychology, 13,* 481–491.

Berndt, T. J. (1982). The features and effects of friendship in early adolescence. *Child Development, 53,* 1447–1460.

Berndt, T. J. (1986). Children's comments about their friendships. In M. Perlmutter (Ed.), *Minnesota symposium on child psychology: Vol. 18, Cognitive perspectives on children's social and emotional development* (pp. 189–212). Hillsdale, NJ: Erlbaum.

Berndt, T. J. (1989). Obtaining support from friends during childhood and adolescence. In D. Belle (Ed.), *Children's social networks and social supports* (pp. 308–331). New York: Wiley.

Berndt, T. J., Hawkins, J. A., & Hoyle, S. G. (1986). Changes in friendship during a school year: Effects on children's and adolescents' impressions of friendship and sharing with friends. *Child Development, 57,* 1284–1297.

Berndt, T. J., & Keefe, K. (1992). Friends' influence on adolescents' perceptions of themselves in school. In D. H. Schunk & J. L. Meece (Eds.), *Students' perceptions in the classroom* (pp. 51–73). Hillsdale, NJ: Erlbaum.

Berndt, T. J., & Perry, T. B. (1986). Children's perceptions of friendships as supportive relationships. *Developmental Psychology, 22,* 640–648.

Bhavnagri, N., & Parke, R. D. (1991). Parents as direct facilitators of children's peer relationships: Effects of age of child and sex of parent. *Journal of Social and Personal Relationships, 8,* 423–440.

Bierman, K. L. (1989). Improving the peer relationships of rejected children. In B. B. Lahey & A. E. Kazdin (Eds.), *Advances in clinical child psychology* (Vol. 12, pp. 53–84). New York: Plenum Press.

Bierman, K. L., & Furman, W. (1984). The effects of social skills training and peer involvement on the social adjustment of preadolescents. *Child Development, 55,* 151–162.

Bierman, K. L., & McCauley, E. (1987). Children's description of their peer interactions: Useful information for clinical child assessment. *Journal of Clinical Child Psychology, 16,* 9–18.

Bierman, K. L., Miller, C. L., & Stabb, S. D. (1987). Improving the social behavior and peer acceptance of rejected boys: Effects of social skills training with instructions and prohibitions. *Journal of Consulting and Clinical Psychology, 55,* 194–200.

Bornstein, M., Bellack, A. S., & Hersen, M. (1980). Social skills training for highly aggressive children. *Behavior Modification, 4,* 173–186.

Bowker, A., Sippola, L. K., & Bukowski, W. (1996, March). *Coping with daily hassles in the peer group during early adolescence.* Paper presented at the biennial meeting of the Society for Research in Adolescence, Boston.

Brown, B. B. (1989). The role of peer groups in adolescents' adjustment to secondary school. In T. J. Berndt and G. W. Ladd (Eds.), *Peer relationships in child development* (pp. 188–215). New York: Wiley.

Brown, B. B., & Clausen, D. R. (1986, March). *Developmental changes in adolescents' conceptions of peer groups.* Paper presented at the biennial meeting of the Society for Research in Adolescence, Madison, WI.

Brown, B., Clausen, D., & Eicher, S. (1986). Perceptions of peer pressure, peer conformity dispositions, and self-reported behavior among adolescents. *Developmental Psychology, 22,* 521–530.

Brown, B. B., Hamm, J. V., & Meyerson, P. (1996, March). *Encouragement, empowerment, detachment: Ethnic differences in approaches to parental involvement with peer relationships.* Paper presented at the biennial meeting of the Society for Research in Adolescence, Boston.

Brown, E., & Brownell, C. (1990). *Individual differences in toddlers' interactional styles: Profiles and peer responses.* Paper presented at the International Conference on Infant Studies, Montreal, Canada.

Brownell, C. A., & Brown, E. (1992). Peers and play in infants and toddlers. In V. B. Van Hasselt & M. Hersen (Eds.), *Handbook of social development: A lifespan perspective* (pp. 183–200). New York: Plenum Press.

Bryan, T. H. (1974). Peer popularity of learning disabled children. *Journal of Learning Disabilities, 7,* 261–268.

Bryan, T. H. (1976). Peer popularity of learning disabled children: A replication. *Journal of Learning Disabilities, 9,* 307–311.

Buhrmester, D. (1990). Intimacy of friendship, interpersonal competence, and adjustment during preadolescence and adolescence. *Child Development, 61,* 1101–1111.

Buhrmester, D., & Furman, W. (1986). The changing function of friends in childhood: A neo-Sullivan perspective. In V. J. Derlega & B. A. Winstead (Eds.), *Friendship and social interaction* (pp. 41–62). New York: Springer-Verlag.

Bukowski, W. M., Gauze, C., Hoza, B., & Newcomb, A. F. (1993). Differences and consistency between same-sex and other-sex peer relationships during early adolescence. *Developmental Psychology, 29,* 255–263.

Bukowski, W. M., & Hoza, B. (1989). Popularity and friendship: Issue in theory, measurement, and outcome. In T. J. Berndt & G. W. Ladd (Eds.), *Peer relationships in child development* (pp. 15–45). New York: Wiley.

Cairns, R. B., Cairns, B. D., Neckerman, H. J., Gest, S. D., & Gariepy, J. (1988). Social networks and aggressive behavior: Peer support or peer rejection? *Developmental Psychology, 24,* 815–823.

Cartledge, G., & Milburn, J. F. (Eds.). (1980). *Teaching social skills to children.* New York: Pergamon Press.

Cauce, A. M. (1986). Social networks and social competence: Exploring the effects of early adolescent friendships. *American Journal of Community Psychology, 14,* 607–628.

Cauce, A. M., Reid, M., Landesman, S., & Gonzales, N. (1990). Social support in young children: Measurement, structure, and behavioral impact. In B. R. Sarason, I. G. Sarason, & G. R. Pierce (Eds.), *Social support: An interactional view* (pp. 64–94). New York: Wiley.

Cavell, T. A., & Kelley, M. L. (1992). The measure of adolescent social performance: Development and initial validation. *Journal of Clinical Child Psychology, 21,* 107–114.

Cohen, J. (1977). Sources of peer group homogeneity. *Sociology of Education, 50,* 227–241.

Coie, J. D. (1990). Toward a theory of peer rejection. In S. R. Asher & J. D. Coie (Eds.), *Peer rejection in childhood* (pp. 365–401). Cambridge, MA: Cambridge University Press.

Coie, J. D., & Dodge, K. A. (1983). Continuities and changes in children's social status: A five-year longitudinal study. *Merrill-Palmer Quarterly, 29,* 261–282.

Coie, J. D., & Dodge, K. A. (1988). Multiple sources of data on social behavior and social status in the school: A cross-age comparison. *Child Development, 59,* 815–829.

Coie, J. D., Dodge K. A., & Coppotelli, H. (1982). Dimensions and types of social status: A cross-age perspective. *Developmental Psychology, 18,* 557–570.

Coie, J. D., Dodge K. A., & Kupersmidt, J. B. (1990). Peer group behavior and social status. In S. R. Asher & J. D. Coie (Eds.), *Peer rejection in childhood* (pp. 17–59). Cambridge, MA: Cambridge University Press.

Coie, J. D., & Kupersmidt, J. B. (1983). A behavioral analysis of emerging social status in boys' groups. *Child Development, 54,* 1400–1416.

Compas, B. E., Slavin, L. A., Wagner, B. A., & Cannatta, K. (1986). Relationship of life events and social support with psychological dysfunction among adolescents. *Journal of Youth and Adolescence, 15,* 205–221.

Cowen, E. L., Pederson, A., Babigian, H., Izzo, L. D., & Trost, M. A. (1973). Long-term follow-up of early detected vulnerable children. *Journal of Consulting and Clinical Psychology, 41,* 438–446.

Crockett, L., Losoff, M., & Petersen, A. C. (1984). Perceptions of the peer group and friendship in early adolescence. *Journal of Early Adolescence, 4,* 155–181.

Degirmencioglu, S. M., & Urberg, K. A. (1996, March). *Cross-gender friendships in adolescence: Who chooses the "other"?* Paper presented at the biennial meeting of the Society for Research in Adolescence, Boston.

Dishion, T. J., Patterson, G. R., Stoolmiller, M., & Skinner, M. S. (1991). Family, school, and behavioral antecedents to early adolescent involvement with antisocial peers. *Developmental Psychology, 27,* 171–180.

Dodge, K. A. (1989). Problems in social relationships. In E. J. Mash & R. A. Barkley (Eds.), *Treatment of childhood disorders* (pp. 222–244). New York: Guilford Press.

Dodge, K. A., Coie, J., & Brakke, N. (1982). Behavioral patterns of socially rejected and neglected pre-adolescents: The roles of social approach and aggression. *Journal of Abnormal Child Psychology, 10,* 389–409.

Eckerman, C., Whatley, J., & Kutz, S. (1975). Growth of social play with peers in the second year of life. *Developmental Psychology, 11,* 42–49.

Eckerman, C., Whatley, J., & McGhee, L. (1979). Approaching and contacting the object another manipulates: A social skill of the 1-year-old. *Developmental Psychology, 15,* 585–593.

Elder, D., & Hallinan, M. (1978). Sex differences in children's friendships. *American Sociological Review, 43,* 237–250.

Ellis, S., Rogoff, B., & Cromer, C. C. (1981). Age segregation in children's social interactions. *Developmental Psychology, 17,* 399–407.

Erwin, P. (1993). *Friendship and peer relations in children.* Chichester, England: Wiley.

Fein, G. G. (1981). Pretend play in childhood: An integrative review. *Child Development, 52,* 1095–1118.

Felner, R., Ginter, M., & Primavera, J. (1982). Primary prevention during school transition: Social support and environmental structure. *American Journal of Community Psychology, 10,* 227–290.

Field, T. M. (1994). Infant day care facilities and later social behavior and school performance. In H. Goelman & E. V. Jacobs (Eds.), *Children's play in child care settings* (pp. 69–84). Albany: State University of New York Press.

French, D. C. (1988). Heterogeneity of peer rejected boys: Aggressive and non-aggressive subtypes. *Child Development, 59,* 976–985.

Furman, W. (1980). Promoting social development: Developmental implications for treatment. In B. B. Lahey & A. E. Kazdin (Eds.), *Advances in clinical child psychology* (Vol. 3, pp. 1–40). New York: Plenum Press.

Furman, W. (1989). The development of children's social networks. In D. Belle (Ed.), *Children's social networks and social supports* (pp. 151–172). New York: Academic Press.

Furman, W., & Buhrmester, D. (1985). Children's perceptions of the personal relationships in their social networks. *Developmental Psychology, 21,* 1016–1024.

Furman, W., & Gavin, L. A. (1989). Peers' influence on adjustment and development: A view from the intervention literature. In T. J. Berndt & G. W. Ladd (Eds.), *Peer relationships in child development* (pp. 319–340). New York: Wiley.

Furman, W., & Robbins, P. (1985). What's the point?: Issues in the selection of treatment objectives. In B. H. Schneider, K. H. Rubin, & J. E. Ledingham (Eds.), *Children's peer relations: Issues in assessment and intervention* (pp. 41–56). New York: Springer-Verlag.

Gersham, E. S., & Hayes, D. S. (1983). Differential stability of reciprocal friendships and unilateral relationships among preschool children. *Merrill-Palmer Quarterly, 29,* 169–177.

Ginsburg, G. S., Silverman, W. K., & Kurtines, W. M. (1995). Cognitive-behavioral group therapy. In A. R. Eisen, C. Kearney, & C. E. Schaefer (Eds.), *Clinical handbook of anxiety disorders in children and adolescents* (pp. 521–549). Northvale, NJ: Jason Aronson.

Green, K. D., Forehand, R., Beck, S. J., & Vosk, B. (1980). An assessment of the relationship among measures of children's social competence and children's academic achievement. *Child Development, 51,* 1149–1156.

Gresham, F. M., & Elliot, S. N. (1992). *Social skills rating system.* Circle Pines, MN: American Guidance Service.

Gresham, F. M., & Nagle, R. J. (1980). Social skills training with children: Responsiveness to modeling and coaching as a function of peer orientation. *Journal of Consulting and Clinical Psychology, 84,* 718–729.

Gronlund, N. E., & Holmlund, W. S. (1958). The value of elementary school sociometric status scores for predicting pupils' adjustment in high school. *Educational Administration and Supervision, 44,* 225–260.

Gunnar, M., Senior, K., & Hartup, W. (1984). Peer presence and the exploratory behavior of 18-and 30-month-olds. *Child Development, 55,* 1103–1109.

Hansen, D. J., Watson-Perczel, M., & Christopher, J. S. (1989). Clinical issues in social skills training with adolescents. *Clinical Psychology Review, 9,* 365–391.

Harter, S. (1985). *Manual for the Social Support Scale for Children and Adolescents.* Denver, CO: Department of Psychology, University of Denver Press.

Hartup, W. W. (1983). Peer relations. In P. H. Mussen (Series Ed.) & E. M. Hetherington (Vol. Ed.), *Handbook of child psychology: Vol. 4. Socialization, personality, and social development* (4th ed., pp. 103–196). New York: Wiley.

Hartup, W. W. (1996). The company they keep: Friendships and their developmental significance. *Child Development, 67,* 1–13.

Hazel, J. S., Schumaker, J. B., Sherman, J. A., & Sheldon, J. (1982). Applications of a group training program in social skills and problem solving to learning disabled and non-learning disabled youth. *Learning Disabilities Quarterly, 5,* 398–408.

Hogue, A., & Steinberg, L. (1995). Homophily of internalized distress in adolescent peer groups. *Developmental Psychology, 31,* 897–906.

Hops, H., & Greenwood, C. R. (1988). Social skill deficits. In E. J. Mash & L. G. Terdal (Eds.), *Behavioral assessment of childhood disorders* (2nd ed., pp. 263–314). New York: Guilford Press.

Howes, C. (1983). Patterns of friendship. *Child Development, 54,* 1041–1053.

Howes, C. (1988). Peer interaction of young children. *Monographs of the Society for Research in Child Development, 53* (1, Serial No. 217).

Hymel, S. (1986). Interpretations of peer behavior: Affective bias in childhood and adolescence. *Child Development, 57,* 431–445.

Inderbitzen, H. M. (1994). Adolescent peer social competence: A critical review of assessment methodologies and instruments. In T. H. Ollendick and R. J. Prinz (Eds.), *Advances in clinical child psychology* (Vol. 16, pp. 227–259). New York: Plenum Press.

Inderbitzen, H. M., & Foster, S. L. (1992). Teenage Inventory of Social Skills: Development, reliability and validity. *Psychological Assessment: A Journal of Consulting and Clinical Psychology, 4,* 451–459.

Jackson, N. F., Jackson, D. A., & Monroe, C. (1983). *Getting along with others: Teaching social effectiveness to children.* Champaign, IL: Research Press.

Kandel, D. (1978a). Homophily, selection, and socialization in adolescent friendships. *American Journal of Sociology, 84,* 427–436.

Kandel, D. (1978b). Similarity in real-life adolescent friendship pairs. *Journal of Personality and Social Psychology, 36,* 306–312.

Kazdin, A. E., Siegel, T. C., & Bass, D. (1990). Drawing on clinical practice to inform research on child and adolescent psychotherapy: Survey of practitioners. *Professional Psychology: Research and Practice, 21,* 189–198.

Kirby, F. D., & Toler, H. C. (1970). Modification of preschool isolate behavior: A case study. *Journal of Applied Behavior Analysis, 3,* 309–314.

Kolko, D. J., Loar, L. L., & Sturnick, D. (1990). Inpatient social-cognitive skills training groups with conduct disorders and attention deficit disordered children. *Journal of Child Psychology and Psychiatry and Allied Disciplines, 31,* 737–748.

Kupersmidt, J. B., & Coie, J. D. (1990). Preadolescent peer status, aggression, and school adjustment as predictors of externalizing problems in adolescence. *Child Development, 61,* 1350–1362.

Kuttler, A. H., La Greca, A. M., & Prinstein, M. J. (1998). *Adolescents' close friends: Same- versus cross-sex friendships.* Paper submitted for publication.

Ladd, G. W. (1983). Social networks of popular, average, and rejected children in school settings. *Merrill-Palmer Quarterly, 29,* 283–307.

Ladd, G. W. (1985). Documenting the effects of social skills training with children: Process and outcome assessment. In B. H. Schneider, K. H. Rubin, & J. E. Ledingham (Eds.), *Children's peer relations: Issues in assessment and intervention* (pp. 243–271). New York: Wiley.

Ladd, G. W., & Golter, B. S. (1988). Parents' management of preschoolers' peer relations: Is it related to children's social competence? *Developmental Psychology, 24,* 109–117.

Ladd, G. W., Hart, C. H., Wadsworth, E. M., & Golter, B. S. (1988). Preschoolers' peer network in nonschool settings: Relationship to family characteristics and school adjustment. In S. Salzinger, J. Antrobus, & M. Hammer (Eds.), *Social networks of children, adolescents, and college students* (pp. 61–92). Hillsdale, NJ: Erlbaum.

Ladd, G. W., & Mars, K. T. (1986). Reliability and validity of preschoolers' perception of peer behavior. *Journal of Clinical Child Psychology, 15,* 16–25.

Ladd, G. W., Price, J. M., & Hart, C. H. (1990). Preschoolers' behavioral orientations and patterns of peer contact: Predictive of peers status? In S. R. Asher & J. D. Coie (Eds.), *Peer rejection in childhood* (pp. 90–115). New York: Cambridge University Press.

Ladd, G. W., Profilet, S. M., & Hart, C. H. (1992). Parents' management of children's peer relations: Facilitating and supervising children's activities in the peer culture. In R. D. Parke & G. W. Ladd (Eds.), *Family-peer relationships. Modes of linkage* (pp. 215–254). Hillsdale, NJ: Erlbaum.

La Greca, A. M. (1981). Social skills training with elementary school students: A skills training manual. *JSAS Catalogue of Selected Documents in Psychology, #2194.*

La Greca, A. M. (1993). Children's social skills training: Where do we go from here? *Journal of Clinical Child Psychology, 22,* 288–298.

La Greca, A. M., Dandes, S., Wick, P., Shaw, K., & Stone, W. (1988). The development of the Social Anxiety Scale for Children (SASC): Reliability and concurrent validity. *Journal of Clinical Child Psychology, 17,* 84–91.

La Greca, A. M., & Fetter, M. (1995). Peer relations. In A. R. Eisen, C. A. Kearney, & C. E. Schaefer (Eds.), *Handbook of anxiety disorders in children* (pp. 82–130). Northvale, NJ: Jason Aronson.

La Greca, A. M., & Lopez, N. (1998). Social anxiety among adolescents: Linkages with peer relations and friendships. *Journal of Abnormal Child Psychology, 26,* 83–94.

La Greca, A. M., & Mesibov, G. B. (1979). Social skills intervention with learning disabled children: Selecting skills and implementing training. *Journal of Clinical Child Psychology, 8,* 234–241.

La Greca, A. M., & Mesibov, G. B. (1981). Facilitating interpersonal functioning with peers in learning disabled children. *Journal of Learning Disabilities, 14,* 197–199, 238.

La Greca, A. M., & Santogrossi, D. A. (1980). Social-skills training: A behavioral group approach. *Journal of Consulting and Clinical Psychology, 48,* 220–228.

La Greca, A. M., Silverman, W. K., Vernberg, E. M., & Prinstein, M. J. (1996). Posttraumatic stress symptoms in children after Hurricane Andrew: A prospective study. *Journal of Consulting and Clinical Psychology, 64,* 712–723.

La Greca, A. M., & Stark, P. (1986). Naturalistic observations of children's social behavior. In P. Strain, M. Guralnick, & H. Walker (Eds.),*Children's social behavior: Development, assessment, and modification* (pp. 181–213). New York: Academic Press.

La Greca, A. M., & Stone, W. L. (1993). The Social Anxiety Scale for Children-Revised: Factor structure and concurrent validity. *Journal of Clinical Child Psychology, 22,* 17–27.

La Greca, A. M., Stone, W. L., & Noriega-Garcia, A. (1989). Social skills intervention: A case of a learning disabled boy. In M. C. Roberts & C. E. Walker (Eds.), *Case studies in clinical child/pediatric psychology* (pp. 139–160). New York: Guilford Press.

Landau, S., & Milich, R. (1990). Assessment of children's social status and peer relations. In A. M. La Greca (Ed.), *Through the eyes of the child: Obtaining self-reports from children and adolescents* (pp. 259–291). Boston: Allyn and Bacon.

Lee, L. (1973). *Social encounters of infants: The beginnings of popularity.* Paper presented at the International Society for the Study of Behavioral Development, Ann Arbor, MI.

Leiter, M. P. (1977). A study of reciprocity in preschool play groups. *Child Development, 48,* 1288–1295.

Lever, J. (1976). Sex differences in the games children play. *Social Problems, 23,* 478–487.

Loeber, R., Green, S. M., & Lahey, B. B. (1990). Mental health professionals' perceptions of the utility of children, parents, and teachers as informants on childhood psychopathology. *Journal of Clinical Child Psychology, 19,* 136–143.

Mannarino, A. P. (1976). Friendship patterns and altruistic behavior in preadolescent males. *Developmental Psychology, 12,* 555–556.

Mannarino, A. P. (1978). Friendship patterns and self-concept in preadolescent males. *Journal of Genetic Psychology, 133,* 105–110.

Masten, A. S., Morrison, P., & Pelligrini, D. (1985). A revised class play method of peer assessment. *Developmental Psychology, 21,* 523–533.

Masters, J. C., & Furman, W. (1981). Popularity, individual friendship selection and specific interaction among children. *Developmental Psychology, 17,* 344–350.

Matson, J. L., Rotatori, A. F., & Helsel, W. J. (1983). Development of a rating scale to measure social skills in children: The Matson Evaluation of Social Skills with Youngsters (MESSY). *Behaviour Research and Therapy, 21,* 335–340.

McGinnis, E., & Goldstein, A. P. (1984). *Skill-streaming the elementary school child: A guide for teaching prosocial skills.* Champaign, IL: Research Press.

McGinnis, E., & Goldstein, A. P. (1990). *Skill-streaming in early childhood: Teaching prosocial skills to the preschool and kindergarten child.* Champaign, IL: Research Press.

Michelson, L., Sugai, D. P., Wood, R. P., and Kazdin, A. E. (1983). *Social skills assessment and training with children: An empirically based handbook.* New York: Plenum Press.

Mosbach, P., & Leventhal, H. (1988). Peer group identity and smoking: Implications for intervention. *Journal of Abnormal Psychology, 97,* 238–245.

Mueller, E. (1972). The maintenance of verbal exchanges between young children. *Child Development, 43,* 930–938.

Mueller, E., & Brenner, J. (1977). The origins of social skills and interaction among playgroup toddlers. *Child Development, 48,* 854–861.

Newcomb, A. F., Bukowski, W. M., & Pattee, L. (1993). Children's peer relations: A meta-analytic review of popular, rejected, neglected, controversial and average sociometric status. *Psychological Bulletin, 113,* 99–128.

O'Brien, S. F., & Bierman, K. L. (1987, April). *Conceptions and perceived influence of peer groups: Interviews with preadolescents and adolescents.* Paper presented at the biennial meeting of the Society for Research in Child Development, Boston.

Oden, S., & Asher, S. R. (1977). Coaching children in social skills for friendship making. *Child Development, 48,* 495–506.

Olweus, D. (1993). *Bullying at school: What we know and what we can do.* Oxford, England: Blackwell.

Parker, J. G., & Asher, S. R. (1987). Peer relations and later personal adjustment: Are low-accepted children at risk? *Psychological Bulletin, 102,* 357–389.

Parker, J. G., & Asher, S. R. (1989, April). Peer relations and social adjustment: Are friendship and group acceptance distinct domains? In W. M. Bukowski (Chair), *Properties, processes, and effects of friendship during childhood and adolescence.* Symposium presented at the biennial meeting of the Society for Research in Child Development, Kansas City, MO.

Parker, J. G., & Asher, S. R. (1993a). Friendship and friendship quality in middle childhood: Links with peer group acceptance and feelings of loneliness and social dissatisfaction. *Developmental Psychology, 29,* 611–621.

Parker, J. G., & Asher, S. R. (1993b). Beyond group acceptance: Friendship and friendship quality as distinct dimensions of peer adjustment. In W. H. Jones & D. Perlman (Eds.), *Advances in personal relationships* (Vol. 4, pp. 261–294). London: Kingsley.

Parkhurst, J. T., & Asher, S. R. (1992). Peer rejection in middle childhood: Subgroup differences in behavior, loneliness, and interpersonal concerns. *Developmental Psychology, 28,* 231–241.

Pekarik, E. G., Prinz, R. J., Liebert, D. E., Weintraub, S., & Neale, J. M. (1976). The Pupil Evaluation Inventory: A sociometric technique for assessing children's social behavior. *Journal of Abnormal Child Psychology, 4,* 83–97.

Piaget, J. (1926). *The language and thought of the child.* New York: Harcourt & Brace.

Pope, A. W., Bierman, K. L., & Mumma, G. H. (1991). Aggression, hyperactivity, and inattention-immaturity: Behavior dimensions associated with peer rejection in elementary school boys. *Developmental Psychology, 27,* 663–671.

Price, J. M., & Dodge, K. A. (1989). Peers' contributions to children's social maladjustment: Description and intervention. In T. J. Berndt & G. W. Ladd (Eds.), *Peer relationships in child development* (pp. 341–370). New York: Wiley.

Prinstein, M. J., Fetter, M. D., & La Greca, A. M. (1996, March). *Can you judge adolescents by the company they keep?: Peer group membership, substance use, and risk-taking behavior.* Paper presented at the biennial meeting of the Society for Research in Adolescence, Boston.

Prinz, R. J., Swan, G., Liebert, D. E., Weintraub, S., & Neale. J. M. (1978). ASSESS: Adjustment Scales for Sociometric Evaluation of Secondary School Students. *Journal of Abnormal Child Psychology, 6,* 493–501.

Putallaz, M. (1987). Maternal behavior and children's sociometric status. *Child Development, 58,* 324–340.

Reid, M., Landesman, S., Treder, R., & Jaccard, J. (1989). "My family and friends." 6 to 12 year old children's perceptions of social support. *Child Development, 60,* 896–910.

Ross, H., & Goldman, B. (1977). Establishing new social relations in infancy. In T. Alloway & P. Pliner (Eds.), *Advances in communication and affect* (Vol. 3, pp. 61–79). New York: Plenum Press.

Rubenstein, J., & Howes, V. (1976). The effects of peers on toddler interaction with mother and toys. *Child Development, 47,* 597–605.

Rubin, K. H. (1982). Non-social play in preschoolers: Necessary evil? *Child Development, 53,* 651–657.

Rubin, K. H. (1985). Socially withdrawn children: An "at risk" population? In B. H. Schneider, K. H. Rubin, & J. E. Ledingham (Eds.), *Children's peer relations: Issues in assessment, and intervention* (pp. 125–139). New York: Springer-Verlag.

Sandler, I. N., Wolchik, S., & Braver, S. (1985). Social support and children of divorce. In I. G. Sarason & B. R. Sarason (Eds.), *Social support: Theory, research, and applications* (pp. 371–390). Boston: Martinus Nijhoff.

Savin-Williams, R. C. (1994). Verbal and physical abuse as stressors in the lives of lesbian, gay male, and bisexual youths: Associations with school problems, running away, substance abuse, prostitution, and suicide. *Journal of Consulting and Clinical Psychology, 62,* 261–269.

Schneider, B. H., Weiner, J., & Murphy, K. (1994). Children's friendships: The giant step beyond peer acceptance. *Journal of Social and Personal Relationships, 11,* 323–340.

Selman, R. L., & Selman, A. P. (1979). Children's ideas about friendship: A new theory. *Psychology Today, 13,* 71–114.

Sharabany, R., Gershoni, R., & Hofman, J. (1981). Girlfriends, boyfriends: Age and sex differences in intimate friendship. *Developmental Psychology, 17,* 800–808.

Shrum, W., & Check, N. (1987). Social structure during the school years: Onset of the degrouping process. *American Sociological Review, 52,* 218–223.

Simmons, R., Carlton-Ford, S., & Blythe, D. (1987). Predicting how a child will cope with the transition to junior high school. In R. M. Lerner & T. T. Foch (Eds.), *Biological-psycho-social interactions in early adolescence* (pp. 325–375). Hillsdale, NJ: Erlbaum.

Stone, W. L., & La Greca, A. M. (1986). The development of social skills in children. In E. Schopler & G. B. Mesibov (Eds.), *Social behavior in autism* (pp. 35–60). New York: Plenum Press.

Stone, W. L., & La Greca, A. M. (1990). The social status of children with learning disabilities: A reexamination. *Journal of Learning Disabilities, 23,* 32–37.

Strain, P. S., & Fox, J. J. (1981). Peers as behavior change agents for withdrawn classmates. In B. B. Lahey & A. E. Kazdin (Eds.), *Advances in clinical child psychology* (Vol. 4, pp. 167–198). New York: Plenum Press.

Strain, P. S., Shores, R. E., & Kerr, M. M. (1976). An experimental analysis of "spillover" effects on the social interaction of behaviorally handicapped preschool children. *Journal of Applied Behavioral Analysis, 10,* 31–40.

Strain, P. S., & Wiegerink, R. (1976). The social play of two behaviorally disordered preschool children during four activities: A multiple baseline study. *Journal of Abnormal Child Psychology, 3,* 61–69.

Strauss, C. C., Lahey, B. B., Frick, P., Frame, C. L., & Hynd, G. (1988). Peer social status of children with anxiety disorders. *Journal of Consulting and Clinical Psychology, 56,* 137–141.

Sullivan, H. S. (1953). *The interpersonal theory of psychiatry.* New York: W. W. Norton.

Thorne, B. (1986). Girls and boys together...but mostly apart: Gender arrangements in elementary schools. In W. W. Hartup & Z. Rubin (Eds.), *Relationships and development* (pp. 167–184). Hillsdale, NJ: Erlbaum.

Urberg, K. A. (1992). Locus of peer influence: Social crowd and best friend. *Journal of Youth and Adolescence, 21,* 439–450.

Urberg, K. A., Degirmencioglu, S. M., Tolson, J. M., & Halliday-Scher, K. (1995). The structure of adolescent peer networks. *Developmental Psychology, 31,* 540–554.

Vandell, D., Wilson, K., & Buchanan, N. (1980). Peer interaction in the first year of life: Its structure, content, and sensitivity to toys. *Child Development, 51,* 481–488.

Vaughn, S., & La Greca, A. M. (1993). Social skills training: Why, who, what, and how? In W. N. Bender (Ed.), *Learning disabilities: Best practice for professionals* (pp. 251–271). Boston: Andover Medical Publishers.

Vaughn, S., & Lancelotta, G. (1991). Teaching interpersonal social skills to low accepted students: Peer-pairing versus no peer-pairing. *Journal of School Psychology, 28,* 181–188.

Vaughn, S., McIntosh, R., & Spencer-Rowe, J. (1991). Peer rejection is a stubborn thing: Increasing peer acceptance of rejected students with learning disabilities. *Learning Disabilities Research, 6,* 83–88.

Vernberg, E. M. (1990). Psychological adjustment and experiences with peers during early adolescence: Reciprocal, incidental, or unidirectional relationships? *Journal of Abnormal Child Psychology, 18,* 187–198.

Vernberg, E. M., Abwender, D. A., Ewell, K. K., & Beery, S. H. (1992). Social anxiety and peer relationships in early adolescence: A prospective analysis. *Journal of Clinical Child Psychology, 21,* 189–196.

Vernberg, E. M., Beery, S. H., Ewell, K. K., & Abwender, D. A. (1993). Parents' use of friendships facilitation strategies and the formation of friendships in early adolescence: A prospective study. *Journal of Family Psychology, 7,* 356–369.

Vernberg, E. M., Ewell, K. K., Beery, S. H., Freeman, C. M., & Abwender, D. A. (1995). Aversive exchanges with peers during early adolescence: Is disclosure helpful? *Child Psychiatry and Human Development, 26,* 43–59.

Vuchinich, S., Bank, L., & Patterson, G. R. (1992). Parenting, peers, and the stability of antisocial behavior in preadolescent boys. *Developmental Psychology, 28,* 510–521.

Waldrop, M. F., & Halverson, C. F. (1975). Intensive and extensive peer behavior: Longitudinal and cross-sectional analyses. *Child Development, 46,* 19–26.

Wasserstein, S., & La Greca, A. M. (1996). Can peer support buffer against behavioral consequences of parental discord? *Journal of Clinical Child Psychology, 25,* 177–182.

Whaley, K. L. (1990). The emergence of social play in infancy: A proposed developmental sequence of infant-adult social play. *Early Childhood Research Quarterly, 5,* 347–358.

Whaley, K. L., & Rubenstein, T. S. (1994). How toddlers "do" friendship: A descriptive analysis of naturally occurring friendships in a group child care setting. *Journal of Social and Personal Relationships, 11,* 383–400.

CHAPTER 12

RELIGION

M. Gawain Wells

That religious training or experience is a salient context for children and adolescents in America is unassailable. Indeed, while the figures may be lower among children today, 97 percent of clinical psychologists who returned surveys by Shafranske and Malony (1990) reported that they themselves as children were raised in a particular religion. It is equally clear that religion is a controversial issue in the profession. On the one hand, APA Division 36 exists as a forum to address the interests of psychologists concerned about religion, several journals are devoted to the topic, and there is a resurgence of interest in its clinical applications (e.g., Bergin, 1980; Bergin & Jensen, 1990). On the other hand, Jones's (1994) recent call for religion to "participate as an active partner with psychology as a science and as an applied professional discipline" (p. 184) was met with comments that ranged from applause to warning that such a rapprochement was impossible (see Aguinis & Aguinis, 1995; Cox, 1995; Hosmand, 1995; Ward, 1995; Weiss, 1995). Interestingly and perhaps prototypically, Jones's (1995) response to the comments suggested that he was now disquieted and that he had been misunderstood even by those who had applauded his call, evidencing the controversy of the topic even among those in favor of religion's place in psychology. Although it may necessarily be true that science and religion are mutu-

ally distinct realms of inquiry (Ward, 1995), religious beliefs and training are an integral part of a majority of children's lives and even that of their therapists (Bergin & Jensen, 1990; Shafranske & Malony, 1990). The child's early learning about family and community in such practices as prayer and religious ritual observances, as well as one's responsibilities to others that are such a central ingredient in religious teachings, make the context of religion an important formative influence. Thus, the consideration of religion as a developmental issue for clinical child psychologists in this text is richly deserved.

Three caveats should be considered at the outset of this chapter. First, the context of *religion* is something of a portmanteau concept; like a large traveling bag it carries several possible meanings even in the literature we will examine. What does it mean, for instance, when children ask, "What religion are you?" Consider how an adult might respond to the question from three separate levels. At the broadest, the answer may be synonymous with no more than identification with a cultural tradition and its history ("Well, I was raised Catholic..."). At another, somewhat more personal level the question may be directed at religious activity or practice ("...but I don't go to church anymore"). And at the most personal level, the question speaks to faith or commitment ("I still believe in God, though"). We will see in the first section that the several authors focus on different aspects of the concept. Indeed, the levels just described parallel somewhat Elkind's (1978) description of children's developmental levels of understanding. However, the overall thrust for the later sections of the chapter is toward the clinician's understanding of the interface of the client's developmental level with his or her personal religious beliefs.

Second, although there is useful developmental literature to be examined, my best search efforts have yielded nothing published in the clinical child psychology literature. Moreover, the subject is virtually absent even from developmental texts. A casual perusal of the texts in my own library yielded no mention of religion from ten different texts on clinical child psychology, none in eleven of thirteen general developmental texts, and none in two parenting texts. However, three of four adolescent development texts contained a page each describing the general distancing from religion that occurs in adolescence. Lehr and Spilka (1989), in their survey of introductory psychology texts over three decades, have documented more thoroughly the scarce page space given to research on religion in psychology.

Thus, like other areas of clinical child psychology, perhaps the only available approach presently is to extrapolate downwards from the adult literature where possible. The obvious caution, of course, is the concern for solipsism which is the *raison d'etre* for this volume. Children are not like adults; indeed, in some ways they are not like each other at different ages, as will be indicated in the chapter.

Second, it is important in any text such as this to be evenhanded. It is not my intention to trivialize religion, considering it simply as another example of cultural diversity that should be respected or tolerated, although some useful analogues will be considered. Nor is it simply a tool for fashioning useful interventions. The inquiry of science by definition must focus on the observable and replicable. The bulk of this chapter must necessarily focus on the scientist's understanding of the child and the clinician's developing accurate and meaningful interventions. That which is not discussed in any depth here is the other half of the equation in which religion is concerned—God's side. Does God exist? Does He hear and answer prayers? Is there a benevolent, caring entity that does indeed provide security in loneliness, comfort in fear and bereavement, and guidance in moments of trial? As a believer in God, I would answer these questions affirmatively. As Ochberg (1991) has noted:

Long before psychology and psychiatry were invented, before medicine was a science, there were healers who treated the sick and the wounded . . . invariably, there was a sacred, ritual dimension to the treatment. The medicine-man invoked spiritual assistance. Sacrifices were required to the gods. Prayers were said, individually, and collectively. There is abundant evidence that healing was facilitated. The power of prayer in surviving captivity and torture is well known (Fly, 1973; Jackson, 1973), although the mechanism of action is subject to debate. (p. 9)

On the other hand, it is equally clear that like any other position of influence, the concepts of religion may be used malevolently. Parents or others who emphasize guilt and shame may find religious teachings a readily available weapon as a means of behavioral control. Similarly, the elements of power or the attribution of sin in religious concepts continue to provide excuses for disturbed behavior of horrendous proportions, as witnessed by the Jonestown massacres. An early review notes: "the authors find evidence that religion has many relationships to mental disorder. It attracts, reduces, increases, and heals mental disorder. It can serve as a haven in a psychological storm by providing an outlet for abnormality; it can serve as an educative means for conventionalizing the deviant and helping him find social acceptance" (Spilke & Werme, 1971, p. 462).

The chapter is organized into three sections. The first provides an overview of the developmental issues in children's religious growth. In other words, the section attempts to answer the question: In the general case, how do children at different ages differ in their understanding of and response to religion? The second section considers the roles that religion may play in the lives of children and adolescents, both generally and clinically. The final section comprises a discussion of how religion may be used *and* perhaps should not be used to influence the clinical treatment of children and adolescents. It is divided into two parts: Intervening directly with children, and considerations in working with religious parents, inasmuch as much of the work of the psychologist must take place through the parents to the child.

RELIGIOUS DEVELOPMENT IN CHILDREN

This section reviews the literature on religious development in children, particularly the work of David Elkind (1978, 1981, 1982) on Piagetian/cognitive stages in children's understanding of prayer and institutional identification, James Fowler (1981, 1991) on faith development, Fritz Oser's (1991) descriptions of religious thinking, and Kalevi Tamminnen's (1991) studies of religious development among Finnish children and youth. As will be seen, children do experience a developmental process in the incorporation of religious knowledge and belief, a process described by three of the authors which parallels the Piagetian cognitive constructivist perspective. By contrast, Tamminen focused on the pivotal influence of children's attitudes toward religion and their reports of religious experiences as well as changing perceptions of God's nearness and influence over time. His work is unique among the group for its empirical–descriptive nature.

Most of the research focuses on children from ages 5 to 7 and up into late adolescence. Yet the writers in the field often preface their work with the mention of the fundamental importance of children's very early years in their experiences of trust—or "faith"—in their parents, hopefully creating a sense of security about life. As their language and thinking develop, they learn the language of the family, begin to see the world through their parents' eyes, as it were, and likely first hear about God. They observe their parents' attitudes about God and religious practices, and they are often involved with their family church group before being exposed even to school. If their parents view the "world" as espousing values significantly at variance with their own, the children will have been both protected from and warned against those influences. Thus, early internalization processes impact children well before the ages from which most empirical work is done. Kirkpatrick (1992), for instance, has suggested that the degree and quality of their attachment relationship to the parents may affect their feeling for God as an attachment figure. And Vergote and Tamayo (1981) have shown that children's images of God have grown from parental images of both the mother and father. As summarized by Hyde, "The image of God is thus seen to develop in early childhood from children's perceptions of their parents—what they are and what ideally they should be. Punitive or loving images of God are closely related to parental attitudes" (1990, p. 96).

David Elkind

The work of David Elkind provides two major thrusts of interest: developmental considerations that derive from Piagetian theory (Elkind, 1981, 1982), and his specific research in developmental stages in the understanding of prayer and institutional religion (Elkind, 1978).

Elkind has noted the very important role of internalization, the means by which children acquire their values and morals, indeed, their Weltanschauung or world view. He has suggested that the process entails more than just learning, memorizing, or imitating models; that which is acquired by internalization is similar to the acquisition of conservation, which when obtained, is incorporated much more deeply within children's cognitive substructures. Piaget (1950)

termed this process *operative learning* whereby children "reflectively abstract" (Piaget, 1971) or operate on experiences to cognitively abstract rules and transformations that have wide-ranging applications. For Elkind, children also abstract from the attitudes and behaviors of parents or others, but only others with whom they are attached. It is as though the child were saying: "This is what I have learned about life and myself from hundreds of small moments of observing my parents, the way they talk and think and act towards others and towards me." Moral and religious beliefs, then, become the understanding of one's responsibilities to others and to God through years of active constructions of events with parents. These beliefs are both persistent and pervasive in the child's interpretations of experience. As active constructions, however, interpretations are liable to change over time if and as the child experiences events that may disconfirm or disequilibrate the existing abstractions. Thus, as we shall see, children come to interpret God as being less intimately involved with their lives over time as they experience what seem to be unheard prayers or observe tragedies that should have had God's intervention but did not.

Elkind (1978) employed a semiclinical method much like that of Piaget to study both the development of religious knowledge and prayer in children. He suggested that religious development occurs through two paths which, though separate, interact to influence one another: *institutional religion,* which encompasses formal religious instruction, rituals, and observances presented to the child, and *spontaneous religion,* the child's feelings, concepts, and attitudes that arise from his or her interpretation of institutional religion.

Elkind's interviews of several hundred children of different ages from Protestant, Catholic, and Jewish families found three identifiable stages of development involved in their understanding of religious–denominational identity and prayer. Children interviewed at ages 5 to 7 evidenced a global, undifferentiated pattern that Elkind called Stage 1. Corresponding to preoperational thought, children recognized and identified their associated denominational terms such as Protestant or Catholic or Jewish with a concept of God and recognized that not all people were a part of the denomination. However, the possibility of belonging to both a religious denomination and a nationality group was generally unrecognized. Thus, Catholics are Catholics because "God makes them that way," but one cannot be a Catholic and an American at the same time. Similarly, at this stage prayer was often described as a formularized activity in which God was associated with a loving old man with a white beard who protected people and gave children things they asked for. Children seemed to view prayer as though it were a physical substance that somehow was carried to

Heaven. Like many other dimly understood but completely accepted activities (e.g., you push a button and a light comes on, we always wash our hands after going to the bathroom, and so on), children at this age may pray with total belief in its efficacy, or they may pray without any clear idea of doing more than imitating the activity.

Children in Stage 2 understanding (corresponding to the concrete operational stage), usually ages 7 to 9, had advanced considerably from those in Stage 1, primarily because they had learned to discriminate religious actions as concrete signs that differentiate religious denominations. At this point they had grasped the concept of multiple group membership, that people can be Protestant and American at the same time. The key to understanding this concrete differentiated stage was their awareness of actions as the discriminator, not beliefs; in other words, they had more accurately discriminated what people do who belong to a particular denomination. Similarly, when asked about prayer, children at this stage described the activity of prayer, *what one does* when one prays, but generally overlooked the thoughts and feelings behind the prayer.

Beginning at ages 10 to 12 and increasingly thereafter, children began evidencing more abstract, differentiated religious reasoning. When describing religious identity and prayer, children now used words such as belief, understanding, or inner feelings. They were apparently distinguishing between what one thinks and what one says and does. This Stage 3 reasoning, for Elkind, was characterized by the ability for *reflection*. Religious identity and denomination identity were determined by inner belief. Prayer had become a private experience, a personal conversation with God, and an experience that was much more affect-laden than that of younger children. Elkind further observed that these older children were more likely to pray spontaneously, particularly when experiencing negative feelings such as being upset, lonely, or worried. They also were more likely to volunteer that prayer activity made them feel better, and helped them to relax and feel comforted.

Summary

Elkind's research suggests that children's religious development coincides with cognitive development. Comparable to Piaget's constructivism arguments, the individual child's religious reasoning and belief depends upon both exposure to religious experiences and his or her interpretations thereof, which are influenced in some measure by the child's parents' responses to the experiences. A clinician's application of Elkind's work would suggest some normative developmental levels, but with the clinician's awareness of individual interpretations. Perhaps Elkind's central thrust for parents or clinicians is to remind them that adults are likely to think that youngsters are like them in their thoughts but different in their feelings. His work suggests that the reverse is true. Most children before age 11 or 12 do not understand religion the way adults do, applying their own meanings to religious issues.

A brief example of what Elkind calls *adult egocentrism* (what I have called solipsism) may serve to illustrate the importance of the clinician's careful effort to understand the child, religiously or otherwise. Elkind (1976) observed that the idea of sharing is a value strongly held by American parents and that preschool children appear to be particularly uninclined to share possessions. The adult solipsistic conclusion is that preschool children are stingy. The problem, he notes, is that in the preschool child's level of egocentrism, use means possession or entitlement. To the child, if she or he lets another child use the toy, it now belongs to that child and it may not be returned. Elkind suggests that the solution—the therapeutic intervention—is to label the toy, because putting the child's name on the toy confers entitlement beyond use. The toy remains the child's now, even when another child is playing with it, because the child's name is on it.

Applying Elkind's work clinically, at Stage 1 the therapist might expect that younger children live in an assumptive world in which *magic* works, even though they cannot explain it. The individual child's concept of God and prayer at this age may well be highly idiosyncratic but meaningful and comforting or, alternatively, confusing and tension-producing, depending on their experience with their parents. Kirkpatrick and Shaver (1990) have noted the correlation between children's attachment relationships to their parents and their "attachment" to God.

With Stage 2 children, the clinician might observe that children now know how "to do" religion, but perhaps be less able "to reflect upon or understand" religion. The social, religious community elements are likely to be strong, and the child may take identity in belonging and being "competent" in doing what his or her church group does. The converse side, then, may be that children of this age can be remarkably intolerant of those who do not belong or who violate the rules, his or her own spiritual teachings notwithstanding.

For Stage 3 children and adolescents, the clinician may expect a more thorough and comprehensive, adult-like understanding of institutional religion coupled with their highly personal (spontaneous) religious questioning and strivings. The degree to which parents or the therapist understands the adolescent's religious belief depends a great deal on his or her willingness to communicate that belief. As will be described, adolescence is often a time of crisis for religious commitment, coinciding with separation–individuation issues with parents, the ability for true but still egocentric self-consciousness, and a host of other concerns.

James Fowler

Fowler's (1991, 1981) research and theorizing on the development of stages of faith were derived primarily from in-depth interviews. Like Elkind, he associated his stages with the cognitive–developmental frameworks of Piaget and Kohlberg, paralleling the form of logic and moral reasoning with the several stages of faith.

Faith, Fowler suggested, is a process of making meaning out of life, one in which people create loyalties and commitments to what he called *centers of value*. People focus their lives on persons, causes, or ideals that are at the "center" of what they value, which may be God or religious beliefs, but which may be devotion to family or financial success or some charismatic personality. In that sense, he suggested, faith may not always be religious, but does have the motive power in one's life to order priorities and to call forth one's devotion to that value. In addition to the trust one may have in the object of faith, the process creates for the person a "mastery story" that guides a person in choices and predicates the interpretation of events in life.

Fowler found evidence for the existence of seven stages of faith in people from ages 4 to 84. I focus only on the first four stages that are germane to children and adolescents. They are: (1) primal faith, occurring in infancy; (2) intuitive–projective faith, emerging in early childhood; (3) mythic–literal faith, manifested in the elementary school years primarily, but present in some adolescents as well; and (4) synthetic–conventional faith, beginning usually in adolescence and continuing for some as their faith position in adulthood.

Primal Faith

Like Erik Erikson's (1950) earliest psychosocial crisis of trust versus mistrust, Fowler suggested that primal faith is a prelanguage disposition, a faith in one's caretakers. It is, for him, a mutuality, an interplay between the infant and adults which, when well established, helps the infant tolerate the anxieties of separation. The regular interchanges of care and enjoyment of one another are the first basic rituals that form primal faith. This faith is faith in the continuity, predictability, and abiding care of one's parents. Although not determining later faith, it is the foundation upon which more advanced faith developments is begun.

Intuitive–Projective Faith

The acquisition of language and the accompanying ability for imagination marks the beginnings of intuitive–projective faith. Although logical thinking is not yet present, the child can use stories and symbols to create images that may be long-lasting, including images of God. As might be expected, the representations of God are deeply affected by the child's experiences with parents. These abilities intertwine with an emerging sense of standards and morality. In addition, it creates within the child the struggle for balance between the exercise of self-will and the demand for conformity and obedience. Thus, the stage is intuitive in the sense that the child has begun the course of trying to make sense of words, actions, and demands of others, especially parents. It is projective in that the child transfers or projects those understandings onto both the image of God and his or her beliefs about the self in relationship to others.

Mythic–Literal Faith

The cognitive advances of concrete operations herald the opportunity for the child to develop continuity, a considerably more consistent (but still incomplete) view of life in the context of the family's belief system. Now the child has the ability (and feels the internal demand) to connect the narrative pieces of his or her life into a more explicit mastery story. Like the Eriksonian crisis of industry versus inferiority, the child can become "competent" in understanding, remembering, and acting out the literal beliefs of the family's religious heritage. Literality is a very important element in the child's acceptance of the family's religious faith. Indeed, this stage may be the last time during development when the child is not assailed by the doubts of conflicting points of view from others. Adults may settle upon a mythic–literal faith, but it is usually a choice made in the midst of the press of other, often conflicting, faith alternatives.

Synthetic–Conventional Faith

In early adolescence the emergence of formal operational thought permits the child to move to true self-consciousness. Recall that Elkind suggested that a hallmark of this stage was the ability for reflection. As the adolescent engages in that part of "choosing the self" that forms one's religious identity, he or she strives to fashion a world view with a set of beliefs, values, and commitments. Moreover, according to Fowler, there is a hunger ingredient in the striving for identity that seeks connectedness with other people. In other words, adolescents are not just looking at themselves; they examine themselves in the light of relationships with others. Fowler finds that many adolescents express that hunger for connectedness by seeking a relationship with God. It is important to note, as suggested in the title of this stage, that the theme is usually one of rapprochement with externally declared values—from parents, churches, or other belief groups. In spite of the common wisdom of the adolescent becoming more individualistic (at least in the United States), Fowler's research suggested that individuated faith was not likely to appear until young adulthood.

Summary

Fowler's work yields a general theoretical position as a backdrop to understand individual children. His description of the several stages suggest the critical importance of parental and other cultural influences. The structure of the stages are clearly dependent upon the child's attachment relationships to parents and his or her desire to identify with social groups. In its more general thrust, traditional developmental themes are observable—trusting relationships with parents, transference relationships of the preschooler to adult caretakers, and the Eriksonian "industrious" school-age child.

Fritz Oser

Like Elkind and Fowler, Oser (Oser, 1991; Oser & Reich, 1990) utilized the analysis of semiclinical interviews to extract seven bipolar dimensions that people must resolve when attempting to make religious judgments or interpretations in their lives. He defined religious judgment as "reasoning that relates reality as experienced to something beyond reality and that serves to provide meaning and direction beyond learned content" (Oser, 1991, p. 6). An example might be how people reconcile the events of a tragedy as they attempt to make sense of the phenomena, knowing that their interpretation of meaning might or might not exist. How much does God or an Ultimate Being control the accidents or tragedies of life? Is God less involved in everyday life, and chance essentially rules? To what degree can people affect events by pleasing or displeasing God in their activities? Or, is the Ultimate Being a more impersonal influence, less related or unconcerned about the mundane circumstances of people's lives?

From the bipolar dimensions, Oser constructed religious dilemmas and probe questions to elicit and then classify individuals' religious judgments from ages 7 to 75. He described five levels or stages of religious judgments that represented these attempts to balance different value elements against each other. Again, I focus on only those germane to children and adolescents.

At Stage 1, children viewed God or the Ultimate Being as all-powerful and very directly involved in the events of the world. Generally imagined anthropomorphically, the Ultimate Being must be obeyed without hesitation. Disobedience brings punishments in an immediate way, such as an accident or illness, and the child does not see himself or herself as having influence with God. Although 40 percent of the 8 to 9 year olds evidenced Stage 1 judgment, by age 11 to 12 the percentage had dropped to 10 percent and continued to decline. None of Oser's participants exhibited Stage 1 reasoning by age 17.

At Stage 2, the Ultimate Being is seen as somewhat less imperious and dangerous, as more loving and ameliorable by the child's good efforts, and not so immediately and concretely responsive. Now the child's loving God is evidenced by good works, and God's love is demonstrated by the individual's healthy and successful life. Like Kohlberg's Stage 3 of moral reasoning, the child assumes that being good guarantees receiving good. Approximately 55 percent of the 8 to 9-year-old children demonstrated Stage 2 judgment. At ages 11 to 12 the percentage was even higher, approximately 65 percent, followed by a return to 55 percent at 14 to 15 and a rapid decline to 15 percent by ages 17 to 18.

Stage 3 religious judgment continues a movement apparently away from the Ultimate Being's immanence towards transcendence and a corresponding sense of one's autonomy or responsibility. Now God is seen as apart from or above the world and less involved in the details of human existence. Oser noted that the reasoning of this stage may well also coincide with the adolescent's developmental need for autonomy and resistance to external control. Moreover, it is a time of considerable increase in atheistic attitudes. Adolescent disillusionment with God's apparent inactivity in tolerating injustice and misery is convincing evidence for many that God must not exist or must be less personal than before imagined. Among a minority of adolescents the issue of immanence versus transcendence is answered in the opposite direction by cult religions wherein they apparently abandon autonomy in favor of serving God with single-minded fervor. In his validation study, Oser found a steady and rapid increase in Stage 3 reasoning, from zero percent in 8- to 9-year-olds, to 25 percent at ages 11 to 12, to 35 percent at ages 14 to 15, and 75 percent by ages 17–18.

Stage 4 religious judgment is seldom seen in children and adolescents (approximately 4% in 14 to 15 year olds and 15% in 17 to 18). At this stage individuals who continue to interpret events religiously have a strong sense of their own autonomy, but recognize that they enjoy such freedom and meaningfulness in life through the existence and influence of the Ultimate Being or God. They find evidence of an underlying divine plan in life that gives meaning to both life's joys and sorrows.

Summary

Oser's stages appear to describe a religious judgment trajectory that roughly moves from dependence and belief in the immanence of God's power towards autonomous responsibility for decisions and God's more distant, transcendent influence. Foreshadowing an important theme later in the chapter, Oser has attempted to observe people in the process of meaning-making, somewhat like Fowler's mastery story. Oser's descriptions may be particularly relevant to a clinician's understanding a child's interpretation of his or her relationship to God in the face of tragic events. Psychologists have long been concerned about how children mourn the death of a loved one. Ingredients in the early stages Oser has portrayed are evidences for the oft-observed belief in school-age children that they are responsible for their parent's death. Thus, if I were a child in Stage 1 or 2 reasoning and I believe that God punishes bad deeds, the death of a parent certainly hurts bad enough to feel like a punishment. Ergo, if I am being punished, I must have done something wrong to cause this hurt.

Kalevi Tamminen

While each of the authors reviewed thus far has focused on the essentially cognitive elements of religious development, Kalevi Tamminen's (1991) work is an empirical–descriptive report on a set of studies of Finnish youth from age 7 to 20 that considered several different dimensions of religiousness, particularly the affective elements of youth's religious experience. Tamminen suggested that the study of religiousness needed to take into account one's dependency on or commitment to God or deity, and that different levels of commitment would, therefore, differentially affect many elements of the individual's life. It should be noted that religious training is an integral part of Finnish education, with 95 percent of the students being Lutheran, and, therefore, significantly different from public education in the United States.

Tamminen classified the pupils into one of four groups according to their level of commitment: (1) *the believers,* who had internalized religion and expressed deep commitments; (2) *the positives,* who were conventionally active in their religion but without deep commitment, religion apparently viewed as an acceptable role one performs; (3) *the neutrals,* whose attitudes suggested that religion was acceptable but not central to their lives; and (4) *the negatives,* who were critical or negative about religion. He found clear sex differences across ages; girls were consistently more positive and committed religiously than boys. Especially striking was the greater percentage of boys negative toward religion as compared to girls. By mid-adolescence twice as many boys as girls were critical towards religion. Not surprisingly, the percentage of *the believers* declined in a nearly linear fashion until by ages 17 to 20, only 17 percent of the girls and 6 percent of the boys were strongly committed (down from 55% of girls and 27% of boys at age 9 to 10).

(Tamminen did recognize, however, that *believing* at age 18 is of qualitatively different significance than at age 10.) Tamminen divided the age groups into four arbitrary groupings for comparison: (1) age group 7 to 11, representing late childhood; (2) age group 11 to 13, preadolescence (which in America might be called early adolescence); (3) age group 13 to 15, representing the age of puberty; and (4) age group 15 to 20, representing what he called adolescence proper.

Age Group 7 to 11. Children at this age reported experiencing more events that they considered religious than students of any other age group. While a minority said they had never experienced a time when they felt God's influence, the majority reported that they had at some time sensed God being close. Those situations were most likely to be in times when they were alone at night or times of difficulty or fear. At this age, the children generally accepted the Bible as true and had no doubts about the existence of God. Although they understood that God rewarded and punished good and bad behaviors, their image of God was of a benevolent, loving individual who cared about them and provided security. Prayer was very important to them and, illustrating their concreteness, it was important to many of them to even fold their hands during prayer.

Age Group 11 to 13. Although there was no appreciable change in beliefs in God at this age, children at this age appeared to be more hesitant to express awareness of God's presence. Indeed, the entire age group could be typified by a measure of reserve or doubt—they had some uncertainty about the truth of the Bible, God seemed more distant, and answers to prayers were not expected with such literalness as among the younger group.

Age Group 13 to 15. Tamminen noted that this age is known as the religious "crisis" phase. A considerably larger percentage of children expressed either lack of interest or negative feelings about religion than earlier groups. For a small minority, it was a time of personalizing religion. Half of the children in this age group stated that they had never experienced God's closeness. Those who did were likely to have experienced God's influence at times of the death of someone close or under situations of danger. Doubts about God's existence had increased markedly, and the Bible was believed literally by only a small percentage.

Age Group 15 to 20. The hallmark of later adolescence appeared to be clarification and stabilization. Although there were many who reported feeling God's influence, there was a general sense of God being more distant than earlier in childhood. Moreover, a sizable percentage reported seldom considering God in their lives. Only a third continued to pray. For those who did, they anticipated God's answer to prayers to come indirectly.

Summary. Tamminen questioned children and adolescents directly to learn about the affective elements of their religious experiences rather than focusing on the cognitive elements of religious development. His empirical conclusions corroborated some of the motifs described by the authors who have been considered here. In addition, Tamminen's work contributed other valuable findings, such as the overall greater religious commitment of girls than boys and the circumstances in which the nearness of God was likely to be felt by children. For the clinician, Tamminen's work emphasized the importance of understanding the individual child's affect towards religion. A believing stance versus a more neutral or even negative position would predicate the degree to which a clinician would consider employing religious constructs or interventions with an individual client. Given that rapport entails "joining" or "aligning" with a client, the religious "register" may be central to younger children's lives and yet much more sensitive an issue for work with some adolescents.

The Role of Religion in the Lives of Children

It goes without saying that the observations described above characterize children and adolescents who have been raised with religious training. Parents' continuing identification with religious culture, their activity, and personal level of commitment will have significant effects upon their children. This section surveys several topics that speak to individual differences in religious belief among young people, including secularization and family and church group variables.

Tamminen's work in Finland illustrated the normative developmental movement for many adolescents away from religious commitment. However, this century has seen an erosion of religious belief and practice across all ages and in many parts of the world. In many of the countries of Europe, including England, less than 10 percent of the affiliated members attend church, and the numbers of people who declare no religious affiliation has risen dramatically (Cox, 1982). McAllister (1988) suggested that modernization has brought changes in the social climate that mitigate against young parents participating in religious activities to set an example for their children. Survey studies have highlighted the decline of religious involvement among adolescents. Yankelovich (1974) found that although belief in God remained high, percentages of adolescents reporting that religion was a "very important personal value" steadily declined in the sixties and seventies. Similarly, Johnston, Bachman,

and O'Malley (1986) found that approximately 35 percent of high school seniors reported weekly attendance at religious services; another 30 percent reported that religion was "very important to them," even though they did not worship regularly; and about 10 percent of high school seniors reported no religious preference at all. The remaining 25 percent reported having a religious preference but did not feel that religion was important to them (Johnston, Bachman, & O'Malley, 1986). On the other hand, however, Norback (1980) reported a return to fundamentalist religious involvement among some adolescents, including both so-called cult religions as well as mainstream church activity.

Other investigations have noted factors that deleteriously affect religiousness, particularly in the adolescent crisis years. A study of Mormon adolescents (Cornwall, 1987) found that external friendships were sufficiently powerful as to either strengthen or weaken religious belief. Potvin and Lee (1982) pointed to ages 15 and 16 as a pivotal time among North American adolescents for both peer influence and the establishment of an individual philosophical world view that could potentially conflict with religious identity.

As expected, parental childrearing attitudes and religious values have a strong influence on adolescent religious attitudes. Hoge and Petrillo (1978) cited studies showing that parental religious practices, particularly that of the father, were strongly associated with adolescent religiousness. The childrearing elements of high mother control, good communication, and strong emotional support were related to greater religiousness among children and adolescents. Similarly, Hyde (1990) reviewed evidence that a good relationship with a trusted adult in the church community greatly strengthened a commitment to religious belief and practice but the perception of adults as hypocritical was most damaging. He also noted that although most children regarded worship as uninteresting and boring, those regularly involved in church activity were most likely to continue or return to the habit of church attendance when free to abandon it. A set of sociology of religion studies conducted by Weigert and Thomas (1970, 1974, 1979) among Catholic adolescents from American, European, and Hispanic cultures found that parental support was the strongest predictor of continuing religiousness, particularly when combined with cultural expectations.

A Swedish psychologist, Nils Holm (1991), citing the work of Hjalmar Sunden, proposed that parents' style of transmitting their religious beliefs had predictable effects upon their children's faith. He distinguished between three categories of religious tradition bearers: *Unconfident transmitters* of tradition were parents who themselves had ambivalent religious feelings. When their children asked questions about God, he suggested that these parents were unable to

pass along the ideas and teachings wholeheartedly and usually also communicated their doubts or their anger about the
religion as well. *Confident transmitters,* on the other hand,
were parents harmoniously committed to their beliefs. Holm
suggested that their comfort with their beliefs were more apt
to allow the children to grow in the tradition at their own
pace. A third group were described as *overconfident transmitters* of religious tradition. These people, according to
Holm, demanded intense religious obedience and were
likely to be intolerant of any doubt or hesitation on the part of
their children. Holm's research indicated that many of the
children of the overconfident transmitters rejected the family
religious traditions because they were, in essence, saying,
"Dad or Mom, if your faith makes you so harsh and demanding, I want nothing to do with it."

RELIGION IN THE CLINICAL TREATMENT OF CHILDREN

Thus far, the text of this chapter has focused on a description
of the context of religion in the lives of children and adolescents. I turn now to its applications for the clinician. As
mentioned above, the absence of literature in clinical child
psychology must force us to extrapolate from adult literature, albeit cautiously. Two recent survey studies (Kazdin,
Siegel, & Bass, 1990; Shafranske & Malony, 1990) may be
useful to inform us in a general way. The first queries practitioners who work extensively with children and adolescents to ascertain the nature of their practices and clinically
relevant treatment research. From it we may ask, How
might the current nature of child clinical practice help us
consider the utility of religious issues with particular ages
and diagnostic groups? The second study is a survey of clinicians' personal religiousness and spirituality as well as
their use of religious interventions in psychotherapy. The
findings speak to the experience of clinicians about the spiritual or religious practices that they choose to employ in
treatment *and* practices which, among those surveyed, generally go beyond ethical appropriateness.

The survey of child and adolescent psychotherapy practice by Kazdin, Siegel, and Bass (1990) provides a schematic
by which to tentatively delineate the ways in which religious
issues may enter into the treatment of child internalizing and
externalizing problems. From a sample of 1,162 psychologists and psychiatrists who spent a mean of 20 hours per
week providing direct care for clinical child problems, the
authors queried several pertinent practice characteristics. In
brief, the five most frequent diagnostic categories seen by the
respondents were Conduct/Oppositional Disorder, Attention-
Deficit Hyperactivity Disorder, Depression/Mood Disorder,

Adjustment Disorder, and Anxiety Disorder. Similarly, when
describing more general problem areas without regard to diagnosis, the highest percentage cases seen were emotional
(internalizing) problems, behavioral problems at home and at
school, parent–child problems, and learning problems. Parents were included as a part of treatment in most cases (approximately 78 percent with children, and 61 percent with
adolescents). Moreover, parental and family characteristics
such as parental cooperation, parental involvement in treatment, stable home life, and absence of parental clinical dysfunction were considered as very important to treatment
outcome.

Given the above data, we might ask: How might religious
issues enter into treatment, and where might religious interventions be salient in clinical child treatment? Much depends,
of course, upon the individual and family religious context;
however, we might hypothesize that therapeutic religious interventions directly applied to children expressing externalizing disorders such as Conduct Disorder or Attention-Deficit
Hyperactivity Disorder may well be counterproductive.
When the quintessential issues are obedience and conformity, any added emphasis of authority that has no here-and-
now power leverage would be useless at best. If a power
conflict develops, each party to the conflict is gradually
more and more likely to gravitate to using as a weapon the
values that mean most to the other. Parents ground the 16
year old from the car and his or her friends. The 16 year old
in the religious family boycotts church.

It is within the spectrum of internalizing disorders and
adjustment disorders that we might hypothesize the most
likely utility for religious interventions. Among adults, a
small research literature has found religious beliefs and practices to be a frequent coping mechanism for people dealing
with stressful negative events (Bulman & Wortman, 1977;
Koenig, George, & Siegler, 1988; McCrae, 1984). Spinetta
(1982) similarly found that religious belief was an important
source of support for parents during the time of treatment of
their child for cancer.

Pargament and his colleagues (Pargament, 1990; Pargament et al. 1990; Pargament, Kennell, Hathaway, Grevengoed, Newman, & Jones, 1988) have investigated the
efficacy of religion, finding that, in the words of Talcott Parsons, "Religion has its greatest relevance to the points of
maximum strain and tension in human life as well as positive
affirmations of faith in life, often in the face of these strains"
(in Fichter, 1981, p. 21). Thus, Jenkins and Pargament
(1988) reported that religiously committed cancer patients
were described as being less upset, possessing greater self-
esteem and happiness, and rating themselves as experiencing
less pain than their less religious counterparts. Pargament

and colleagues (1990) found evidence that religious beliefs may be particularly worthwhile when people are coping with difficult situations that cannot be personally controlled. Positive beliefs in a just, loving, and merciful God helped believers view themselves in their difficult circumstance as being in a supportive relationship with God rather than being alone. The authors noted that involvement with religious rituals provided an active coping response to threats about which nothing else could be done. In agreement with religious theorists, they concluded that "religion provides a unique framework for coming to grips with the *limits* of personal knowledge, control, and resources in coping,…limits that may be more apparent in the face of serious negative events" (p. 818).

More tangential corroboration comes from work with children. Diane Komp (1993), a pediatric oncologist, has written poignantly of the importance of prayer and religious faith for children with cancer, both as a source of hope and one of acceptance. Stern, Canda, and Doershuk (1992) interviewed the families of adolescent cystic fibrosis patients. Among the nonmedical treatments employed by the families, 57 percent utilized at least one form of religious intervention, such as group prayer. Of the many possible nonmedical remedies, prayer and meditation were seen most often as beneficial (94% and 92%, respectively). Koocher and Gudas (1992) opined that younger children experiencing the death of a family member may benefit from involvement in religious and family funerary rituals, but only if the activities are well explained and conducted in the context of family support. If not handled thoughtfully, being pressured to comply with adult expectations in funerary situations may be a source of trauma for the child.

From the second survey mentioned above, Shafranske and Malony (1990) sent questionnaires to 1,000 clinical psychologists, of whom 41 percent responded. The authors found that less religiously oriented clinicians were less likely to respond to the questionnaire, creating a positive skew towards more religiously oriented clinicians. However, even if one were to take the most conservative interpretation that all the nonresponders were uninterested and uninvolved in religion, the results demonstrate that nearly 30 percent (70% of those who responded) of clinical psychologists remain personally identified with religion to some degree.

Of more importance is what clinical psychologists who responded can tell us about their experience in integrating religious issues in psychotherapy. Seventy-four percent felt that religious–spiritual considerations are relevant issues for psychotherapy, 60 percent found that clients use religious language to describe their experiences, and approximately one-half of the therapists indicated that at least one in six of their clients present religious concerns as a focus in treatment. While two-thirds of the group felt that psychologists are generally unprepared to assist clients in their spiritual development, approximately one-third saw themselves as competent to counsel clients in religious–spiritual matters.

In spite of majority assent to the relevance of religious issues in psychotherapy, the clinicians were more tentative about the use of spiritual interventions. Although most clinicians believed that knowledge of the client's religious background was appropriate and 59 percent felt that the clinician's use of religious language and concepts were acceptable, 55 percent were opposed to the use of scriptures and religious texts in therapy and 68 percent considered praying with a client inappropriate. The trend of responses suggested that as interventions became more explicitly religious, fewer therapists agreed to its appropriateness. It is important to add that clinicians' personal experiences with religion was correlated with their opinions about the acceptability of religious interventions. That is, the more negatively an individual subject viewed her or his own religious experience, the more likely she or he was to consider religious intervention unacceptable, and vice versa. Parenthetically, in the present atmosphere of concern for respect for diversity it is disturbing that apparently 27 percent of the respondents agreed that it would be appropriate for a psychologist to recommend to a client to leave his or her religion if the therapist determined that such a decision would be psychologically helpful.

In summary, Shafranske and Malony's survey suggests that although both religious commitment and opinions about religion's involvement in psychotherapy vary considerably, it is a relevant consideration for many practitioners. Perhaps more importantly, the survey informs us that religious–spiritual issues are relevant considerations for many clients. And in a general way, the survey tells us that (1) most therapists find that understanding a client's religious background is helpful; (2) a client's religious language and concepts in therapy worthwhile; but that (3) fewer practitioners are positive about using more explicitly religious activities within the therapy hour.

In the context of Shafranske and Malony's findings, I propose that religious issues be considered a valuable and integral part of the clinical child psychologist's work *when it is a valuable and integral part of the client's life and when the clinician is knowledgeable and comfortable with that domain of discourse.* In the generic case, perhaps the sine qua non of psychotherapy is that the clinician/therapist truly understand the client. Although the concept of rapport entails an affective "warmth response" as well, the synonym of *helping alliance* (Luborsky, 1984) underscores the importance of understanding metaphorically where the client "is." As Jerome Frank (1987) has suggested, all psychotherapies traffic in meanings. Human thinking, feeling, and behavior depend on a person's "assumptions about reality, that is, the meanings that he or she attributes to events and experiences, rather than their objective properties" (p. 294). The therapeutic relationship is, then, defined by the clinician's ability to persuade the client that the therapist understands him or her—even in behaviorally oriented treatments in which the importance of the relationship is more implicit. Frank suggests that therapeutic interpretations may be likened to a process of hermeneutics, wherein the client and therapist are making meaning of the events of the client's life together: "The power of an interpretation to carry conviction to the patient depends on many factors, among them its ability to make sense out of the material the patient has offered, the terms in which the interpretation is expressed, the patient's confidence in the therapist, and, perhaps most important, its fruitfulness—the beneficial consequences of the interpretation for the patient's ability to function and sense of well-being" (p. 297). It is as though the therapist discovers the structure and language of the client's Weltanschauung or world view and then employs that understanding in the verbal interactions. Even in play therapy with children where the language is metaphorical, the therapist can communicate understanding inside the metaphor.

Recent developments in the theory of psychotherapy have suggested the power of narrative in the lives of people (e.g., Bruner, 1986, 1990; Sarbin, 1986; Schafer, 1981; Spence, 1984). According to the constructivist theories of both philosophers and psychologists, humans create their own meanings of reality, particularly in regard to their understanding of themselves. Having constructed a reality, individuals then interpret and respond to the events of their lives within that construction. Recall that Fowler (1981) suggested one of the elements of faith was the active construction on the part of the individual of his or her mastery story or narrative of life which made sense to the individual in terms of helping him or her to make meaning out of his or her life. The mastery story entails the values that give the individual hope and courage to continue in the face of difficulty. In that light, psychological symptoms may be seen as evidence of disrupted or shattered narratives in which hope has been lost because the story's assumptions have been violated. Psychotherapy becomes a process of narrative repair. Inasmuch as religious constructions may be the framework upon which the narrative is built, the therapist, by accurately understanding the child's constructions, can present interventions that align themselves within the child's existing constructions. We frequently speak of such a process in psychotherapy as *reframing*.

For example, a young father experienced a major depression following the death of his infant son. Through the course of the baby's hospitalization, the father remained at the hospital, convinced that if he had enough faith, the baby would recover. When, after 24 days, the child died, the father imputed its death to his lack of faith and lack of worthiness to be the recipient of such a blessing. In his eyes, the father construed the event as a continuing proof of his own inadequacy and, in moments of self-hatred, saw himself as responsible for the child's death. The therapist observed that a psychological challenge to the client's guilt and self-blame was perceived by the client as an attack on his religious beliefs. In a poignant moment that proved to be pivotal in the client's treatment, the therapist moved inside the client's belief system to suggest that he had attempted to have such faith in himself that God would have to grant him the miracle. The clinician suggested that all of us are so fallible as to make it difficult to have great faith in ourselves. Was not the concept rather that he have faith in God, in His love and understanding, and that the outcome of the child's illness would, in God's wisdom, be in the best interests of the child?

Similarly, Keith-Lucas (1992) offered case vignettes of children and adolescents in residential treatment which illustrate sensitively how religion may be integral to a child's therapeutic growth. His vignettes also serve as a reminder of how religion may be employed in damaging ways. Contrary to my suggestion of religion's inapplicability to children with conduct disorders generally, he described Connie, a 15 year old who was "foul-mouthed, openly scornful of religion, blatantly adolescent, and believed to be sexually active" (p. 65). In a long conversation with her during a time of uncertainty, he suggested that she knew what she wanted to be, but wondered if she were strong enough to do it. She looked puzzled for about 30 seconds. Then, with a little smile: 'I don't think I could do it alone. But maybe God and I could do it together'" (p. 66). The author suggested that Connie's change would not have occurred if he had specifically discussed religion with her; indeed, he believed that Connie's experience with organized religion was one in which adults used it as a weapon to enforce demands: "But when Connie was pushed to the wall, when I challenged her ability to be what she had decided to be, when she felt weak and in need of support she turned to God, much more sincerely than if I had made the suggestion that she pray to Him" (p. 67).

Keith-Lucas' (1992) description of 9-year-old Marian is also instructive on the abuses of religion. Apparently someone had used fear in religion, threatening her with Hell, in an ill-advised attempt to make her a "good child." The result was paralyzing, making Marian believe that she was irretrievably bad. A pivotal therapeutic moment for her came when her psychologist responded to her claim of hopeless badness, by admitting that she was indeed a difficult girl, but that the staff would continue to love her anyway, in spite of anything that she did. Then he added, "If we're like that, what do you think God might be like?" (p. 68).

It is important, too, to briefly consider parents' religious beliefs in the treatment of children. Child therapy also often involves working with the parents as well: In operantly focused treatments, the therapist will usually see the child but will work primarily with parents; family therapy by definition involves parents directly; and therapists may teach parents to utilize a form of play therapy (VanFleet, 1994). Even in more insight or cognitively oriented therapies used with older children and adolescents, therapists, with the permission or presence of the child, often keep the parents generally informed of the progress of treatment. Recall that Kazdin and colleagues (1990) found that 77 percent of therapists routinely included parents in their treatment and that parental support was crucial to the positive outcome of clinical child treatment.

It need hardly be said that establishing a helping alliance with parents is as essential as with the child or adolescent. Yet, in that context, working with religious parents may be particularly delicate and not unlike the challenge of establishing rapport with clients of minority culture. Gibbs (1985) observed among African American clients that their sensitivity to the possibility of racism led them to be suspicious of the interpersonal process between themselves and their therapists more acutely and longer than typical middle-class clients. They are, therefore, initially more aloof and often proceed to "check out" the therapist's empathy for their value positions, which may mitigate their expectations for positive treatment. Equally importantly, Jenkins (1997) suggested that there is great variability in minority cultures. The therapist who would genuinely attempt to understand the client must "locate" the client's position individually within her or his larger minority culture. The application to the context of religion is transparent as regards religious parents and children of religious parents. The therapist cannot assume to have located the child's religious frame by inference from her or his parents.

In a similar vein Worthington (1988) has written about the match between therapists' values and religious clients' values, proposing that each individual in the relationship has a "zone of toleration" for differences in values. When the values of the client and the therapist are widely discrepant, the likelihood of a disrupted therapeutic relationship is greater than when their values are shared. Furthermore, he suggests that people who are experiencing either chronic difficulty or intense current psychological pain will have a constricted zone of tolerance, and, therefore, will be sensitive to perceptions of value differences. Ambivalent about seeking help from a "secular" professional in the first place, and fear-

ful in their pain that no one can help, Worthington suggested that highly religious clients are particularly prone to viewing psychotherapy as a mistake and terminating prematurely. Thus, for instance, one psychologist found that parents from a fundamental conservative religious background were surprisingly opposed to their daughter receiving assertiveness training: The concept violated their literal religious ethic of obedience.

SUMMARY AND CONCLUSIONS

The context of religion in clinical psychology is still in its nascence. There may be several reasons for this observation, such as the suggested incompatibility of science and religion's epistemological foundations (Ward, 1995), antireligious sentiment among some psychologists (e.g., Bergin, 1980; Lehr & Spilka, 1989), and perhaps the complexity of finding shared meanings in the language of the therapist and client. However, it is clear that the context deserves both research attention and much more clinical consideration. Jenkins and Pargament's (1988) findings on the beneficial influence of religious faith in coping with cancer are illustrative.

In the domain of clinical child psychology, the task for the therapist is even more complex and yet may be more important. First, Worthington's (1988) descriptions of wary religious clients suggest that clinicians must approach religious parents with an express desire to understand and respect the family's values to even have the opportunity to work with their children. Second, adults generally have more intellectual and social resources at hand with which to deal with difficulties than do children. On the other hand, they also are likely to have much longer histories of shattered hopes, stresses, and doubts about their own efficacy. For the child, religious faith may be an integral element of his or her more limited life space. Yet the conceptual form of that faith may vary with the developmental stage of the child. In the hands of a sensitive *and* knowledgeable clinician, using a child's religious beliefs may be a valuable, perhaps even sacred, tool to help him or her make sense out of difficult situations and to find hope for a fulfilling future.

REFERENCES

Aguinis, H., & Aguinis, M. (1995). Integrating psychological science and religion. *American Psychologist, 50,* 541.

Bergin, A. E. (1980). Psychotherapy and religious values. *Journal of Consulting and Clinical Psychology, 48,* 95–105.

Bergin, A. E. (1991). Values and religious issues in psychotherapy and mental health. *American Psychologist, 46,* 394–403.

Bulman, J., & Wortman, C. (1977). Attributions of blame and coping in the "real world": Severe accident victims react to their lot. *Journal of Personality and Social Psychology, 35,* 351–363.

Cornwall, M. (1987). The social bases of religion: A study of factors influencing religious belief and commitment. *Review of Religious Research, 29,* 44–56.

Cox, B. L. (1995). Belief versus faith. *American Psychologist, 50,* 541.

Cox, J. (1982). *The English church in secular society: Lambeth, 1870–1930.* New York: Oxford University Press.

Elkind, D. (1976). Cognitive development and psychopathology: Observations on egocentrism and ego defense. In E. Schopler & R. J. Reichler (Eds.), *Psychopathology and child development* (pp. 167–183). New York: Plenum Press.

Elkind, D. (1978). *The child's reality: Three developmental themes.* Hillsdale, NJ: Erlbaum.

Elkind, D. (1981). Child development research and early childhood education: Where do we stand today? *Young Children, 36,* 2–9.

Elkind, D. (1982). Piagetian psychology and the practice of child psychiatry. *Journal of the American Academy of Child Psychiatry, 21,* 435–445.

Erikson, E. (1950). *Childhood and society.* New York: W. W. Norton.

Fichter, J. H. (1981). *Religion and pain: The spiritual dimensions of health care.* New York: Crossroad.

Fly, C. L. (1973). *No hope but God.* New York: Hawthorne.

Fowler, J. W. (1981). *Stages of faith: The psychology of human development and quest for meaning.* San Francisco: Harper & Row.

Fowler, J. W. (1991). Stages in faith consciousness. In F. K. Oser & W. G. Scarlett (Eds.), *Religious development in childhood and adolescence* (pp. 27–45). San Francisco: Jossey-Bass.

Frank, J. D. (1982). Therapeutic components shared by all psychotherapies. In J. H. Harvey & M. M. Parks (Eds.), *Psychotherapy research and behavior change* (pp. 5–38). Washington, DC: American Psychological Association.

Frank, J. D. (1987). Psychotherapy, rhetoric, and hermeneutics: Implications for practice and research. *Psychotherapy, 24,* 293–302.

Greenberg, D., & Witztum, E. (1991). Problems in the treatment of religious patients. *American Journal of Psychotherapy, 4,* 554–565.

Hoge, D. R., & Petrillo, G. H. (1978). Determinants of church participation and attitudes among high school youth. *Journal for the Scientific Study of Religion, 17,* 359–379.

Holm, N. (1991). Tradition, upbringing, experience: A research program for the psychology of religion. In Malony, H. N. (Ed.), *Psychology of religion: Personalities, problems, possibilities* (pp. 223–230). Grand Rapids, MI: Baker Book House.

Hoshmand, L. T. (1995). Psychology's ethics of belief. *American Psychologist, 50,* 540–541.

Hyde, K. E. (1990). *Religion in childhood and adolescence: A comprehensive review of the research.* Birmingham, AL: Religious Education Press.

Jackson, S. G. (1973). *Surviving the long night.* New York: Vanguard.

Jenkins, A. (1997). The empathic context in psychotherapy with people of color. In A. C. Bohart & L. S. Greenberg (Eds.), *Empathy reconsidered: New directions in psychotherapy* (pp. 321–341). Washington, DC: American Psychological Association.

Jenkins, R., & Pargament, K. I. (1988). Cognitive appraisals in cancer patients. *Social Science and Medicine, 26,* 625–633.

Johnston, L. S., Bachman, J. G., & O'Malley, P. M. (1986). *Monitoring the future: Questionnaire responses from the nation's high school seniors: 1985.* Ann Arbor, MI: Survey Research Center, Institute for Social Research, University of Michigan.

Jones, S. L. (1994). A constructive relationship for religion with the science and profession of psychology: Perhaps the boldest model yet. *American Psychologist, 49,* 184–199.

Jones, S. L. (1995). Psychology and religion. *American Psychologist, 50,* 545.

Kazdin, A. E., Siegel, T. C., & Bass, D. (1990). Drawing on clinical practice to inform research on child and adolescent psychotherapy: Survey of practioners. *Professional Psychology: Research and Practice, 21,* 189–198.

Keith-Lucas, A. (1992). Encounters with children: Children and religion. *Residential Treatment for Children and Youth, 10,* 65–73.

Kirkpatrick, L. A. (1992). An attachment-theory approach to the psychology of religion. *The International Journal for the Psychology of Religion, 2,* 3–28.

Kirkpatrick, L. A., & Shaver, P. R. (1990). Attachment theory and religion: Childhood attachments, religious beliefs, and conversation. *Journal for the Scientific Study of Religion, 29,* 315–334.

Koenig, H., George, L., & Siegler, J. (1988). The use of religion and other emotion-regulating coping strategies among older adults. *Gerontologist, 28,* 303–310.

Komp, D. M. (1993). *A child shall lead them: Lessons in hope from children with cancer.* Grand Rapids, MI: Zondervan Publishing House.

Koocher, G. P., & Gudas, L. J. (1992). Grief and loss in childhood. In C. E. Walker & M. C. Roberts (Eds.), *Handbook of clinical child psychology* (pp. 1025–1034). New York: John Wiley & Sons.

Lehr, E., & Spilka, B. (1989). Religion in the introductory psychology textbook: A comparison of three decades. *Journal for the Scientific Study of Religion, 28,* 366–371.

Luborsky, L. (1984). *Principles of psychoanalytic psychotherapy: A manual for supportive–expressive treatment.* New York: Basic Books.

McAllister, I. (1988). Religious change and secularization: the transmission of religious values in Australia. *Sociological Analysis, 3,* 249–263.

McCrae, R. R. (1984). Situational determinants of coping responses: Loss, threat, and challenge. *Journal of Personality and Social Psychology, 46,* 919–928.

Mussen, P. H., Conger, J. J., Kagan, J., & Huston, A. C. (1990). *Child development and personality* (7th ed.). New York: Harper & Row.

Norback, C. (Ed.). (1980). *The complete book of American surveys.* New York: New American Library.

Ochberg, F. (1991). Post-traumatic therapy. *Psychotherapy, 28,* 5–15.

Oser, F. K. (1991). The development of religious judgment. In F. K. Oser & W. G. Scarlett (Eds.), *Religious development in childhood and adolescence* (pp. 5–25). San Francisco, CA: Jossey-Bass.

Oser, F. K., & Reich, K. H. (1990). Moral judgment, religious judgment, world view, and logical thought: A review of their relationship. *British Journal of Religious Education, 12,* 94–101.

Pargament, K. I. (1990). God help me. Toward a theoretical framework of coping for the psychology of religion. *Research in the Social Scientific Study of Religion, 2,* 195–224.

Pargament, K. I., Ensing, D. S., Falgout, K., Olsen, H., Reilly, B., Van Haitsma, K., & Warren, R. (1990). God help me: Religious coping efforts as predictors of the outcomes to significant negative life events. *American Journal of Community Psychology, 18,* 793–824.

Pargament, K. I., Kennell, J., Hathaway, W., Grevengoed, N., Newman, J., & Jones, W. (1988). Religion and the problem solving process: Three styles of coping. *Journal for the Scientific Study of Religion, 27,* 90–104.

Piaget, J. (1950). *Play, dreams, and imitation in childhood.* New York: W. W. Norton.

Piaget, J. (1971). *Mental imagery in the child—A study of mental imaginal representation.* New York: Basic Books.

Potvin, R. H., & Lee, C. F. (1982). Adolescent religion: A developmental approach. *Sociological Analysis, 43,* 131–144.

Santrock, J. W. (1993). *Adolescence: An introduction* (5th ed.). Madison, WI: Brown & Benchmark.

Shafranske, E. P., & Malony, H. N. (1990). Clinical psychologists' religious and spiritual orientations and their practice of psychotherapy. *Psychotherapy, 27,* 72–78.

Spilka, B., Hood, R. W., Jr., & Gorsuch, R. L. (1985). *The psychology of religion: An empirical approach.* Englewood Cliffs, NJ: Prentice-Hall.

Spilka, B., & Werme, P. H. (1972). Religion and disorder: A research perspective. In M. P. Strommen (Ed.), *Research on religious development, a comprehensive handbook* (pp. 461–481). New York: Hawthorne.

Spinetta, J. J. (1982). Psychosocial issues in childhood cancer: How the professional can help. In M. Wolraich & D. K. Routh (Eds.), *Advances in developmental and behavioral pediatrics* (pp. 51–72). Greenwich, CN: JAI Press, Inc.

Steinberg, L. (1993). *Adolescence.* (3rd ed.). New York: McGraw-Hill.

Stern, R. C., Canda, E. R., & Doershuk, C. F. (1992). Use of nonmedical treatment by cystic fibrosis patients. *Journal of Adolescent Health, 13,* 612–615.

Tamminen, K. (1991). *Religious development in children and youth: An empirical study.* Helsinki, Finland: Suomalinen Tiedeakatemia.

VanFleet, R. (1994). *Filial therapy: Strengthening parent–child relationships through play.* Sarasota, FL: Professional Resource Press.

Vergote, A., & Tamayo, A. (1981). *The parental figures and the representation of God.* The Hague, Netherlands: Moulton.

Vygotsky, L. S. (1962). *Thought and language.* New York: Wiley.

Ward, L. C. (1995). Religion and science are mutually exclusive. *American Psychologist, 50,* 542.

Weigert, A. J., & Thomas, D. L. (1970). Secularization: a cross-cultural study of Catholic adolescents. *Social Forces, 49,* 28–35.

Weigert, A. J., & Thomas, D. L. (1970). Secularization and religiosity: A cross-cultural analysis of Catholic adolescents. *Sociometry, 33,* 305–326.

Weigert, A. J., & Thomas, D. L. (1974). Secularization and religiosity: A cross-national analysis of Catholic adolescents in five societies. *Sociological Analysis, 35,* 1–23.

Weigert, A. J., & Thomas, D. L. (1979). Family socialization and adolescent conformity and religiosity: An extension to Germany and Spain. *Journal of Comparative Family Studies, 10,* 371–383.

Weiss, A. S. (1995). Can religion be used as a science in psychotherapy? *American Psychologist, 50,* 543.

Worthington, E. L. (1988). Understanding the values of religious clients: A model and its application to counseling. *Journal of Counseling Psychology, 2,* 166–174.

Yankelovich, D. (1974). *The new morality: A profile of American youth in the 1970s.* New York: McGraw-Hill.

CHAPTER 13

SOCIAL CLASS

Kenneth J. Tarnowski
Ronald T. Brown
Susan J. Simonian

Social class, often considered simply as a univariate index of relative social standing, is a complex multivariate construct that has broad general implications for family well-being and the developmental trajectories of children and adolescents. Indeed, the pervasive impact of social class can be observed in the context of a variety of domains of child and adolescent functioning including cognitive, sociemotional, physical, and behavioral adjustment. It is the intent of the present chapter to provide an overview of developmental considerations in the context of social class with emphasis on how this set of contextual variables is related to specific parent, child, and adolescent outcomes.

The literature on social class is voluminous and diverse and is found in a variety of sources outside that of the typical domain that we consider "psychological" in nature. Specifically, data from sociology, pediatrics, economics, education, social policy, and international studies are of direct relevance. Because of the breadth and complexity of the issues involved, the presentation will necessarily focus on a subset of central topics.

We begin by presenting an overview of considerations involved in defining social class. Although this topic may appear straightforward, it is not as there are many ways in which "social class" has been operationalized. To a large ex-

tent, we will focus our discussion on a particular social class stratum (lower socioeconomic status [SES] families alternatively called disadvantaged families). This latter emphasis was chosen for several important reasons among which include: (1) the increasing prevalence of such families in the United States over the past 25 years, and (2) the burgeoning literature attesting to the deleterious effects (developmental, biological, and psychopathological) associated with specific forms of disadvantage. The second section of the chapter reviews a subset of studies that document the effects of SES on specific indices of parent and child well-being with a focus on child health and developmental and psychological outcomes. The third section outlines basic mental health considerations, and selected examples of intervention efforts are presented. Finally, impediments to effective treatment are highlighted and prospects for enhanced service access and care discussed.

DEFINITIONAL ISSUES

Entwisle and Astone (1994) outline several trends related to efforts to better define social class and race and ethnicity variables. First, they note that although traditional large scale efforts (e.g., U.S. Census) have traditionally tabulated data by age and gender, the introduction of other background variables including education, income, and ethnicity are more recent developments. Second is the increasing diversity of the U.S. population. They cite the well-know projection that by the middle of the next century the majority of the population will be comprised of nonwhite individuals. Third, they cite the relevance of social constructs such as gender, race, and SES for understanding specific developmental and social processes such as birth weight, school achievement, family structure, behavioral adjustment, mortality, and physical and psychiatric morbidity.

Concerning the measurement of SES, Entwisle and Astone (1994) note that it is often difficult to identify the individual in the household who has the most influence in overall family economic functioning. Differences between families and households can obscure important income data, as can lack of acknowledgment of resources outside the household, allocation of resources within households, and household division of labor. They note that traditional attempts to define social class rely on composite measures of characteristics of the householder and include education, occupation, and labor status. The advantages of such approaches are that they avoid direct reliance on income reporting. It is well-known that the latter data can be difficult to obtain or may be considered suspect due to subject nonresponse (approximately 15%) or inaccuracies. However, there are problems with occupational indicators including the fact that women often are employed in high-prestige occupations that are associated with low wages. Entwisle and Astone argue that this leaves occupational status as a less valid indicator of financial status for women than for males. They also note that in the case of stepfamilies, children may be more impacted by the status of the biological father as opposed to the breadwinner of the family with which they live. Finally, assumptions about occupational status indicators may be most suspect when used in the context of studies and interventions involving minority racial and ethnic groups and other high-risk subpopulations.

Based on a conceptual scheme proposed by Coleman (1988), Entwisle and Astone (1994) note that children and adolescents have potential access to three types of capital: financial, human, and social. The first is a traditional index of yearly income. The second has to do with the notion that youth may have access to nonmaterial resources related to parental education. More highly educated parents may be better equipped to assist children with academic functioning and instill higher educational aspirations. The third aspect of this model is based on the fact that children's interactions with broader society will be, in large part, determined by the characteristics of their parents' social networks. Collection of data related to the first two dimensions is straightforward. Concerning social capital, this is a composite of the number of birth parents, stepparents, and grandparents in the household.

Although generally opposed to utilizing parental occupation status to measure SES, Entwisle and Astone propose that there may be justification for the collection of such data. They recommend that single-item occupational indicators be avoided. The Alphabetical Index of Occupation and Industries (U.S. Bureau of the Census, 1992a) and the Classified Index of Occupation and Industries (U.S. Bureau of the Census, 1992b) are the recommended sources for such occupational coding. To determine SES, Entwisle and Astone recommended the use of the Nakao and Treas (1992) indices. The interested reader is referred to the Entwisle and Astone (1994) guidelines for complete information about establishing SES and related classifications. However, it should be noted that some investigators do not completely agree with this approach and have suggested variants that researchers and interventionists should consider (see Hauser, 1994).

As is apparent, past conceptualizations of "social class" have often equated this concept with family background. Often, social class is operationalized in terms of the occupational and educational status of the parents or head of household. According to Duncan (1991), there are several limitations inherent in this approach: (1) it promotes the often-held belief that social class is a "fixed" variable that is persistent and does not change over the course of development, (2) data indicate that although occupational status and educational attainment provide useful information about families, it is economic status (that is income per se) that appears to be the most critical determinant of the resources available to parents and thus children, and (3) reviews of longitudinal data indicate that the economic resources available to children are volatile. Importantly, income has been repeatedly found to exert significant effects on parent, family, and child well-being after the effects of other covariates such as parental occupational status and ethnicity have been controlled (Huston, 1991). Given these data, we will limit the remainder of our discussion to that segment of the SES strata that has the most limited economic resources, namely that of families living in poverty (alternatively labeled disadvantaged children and families) (Tarnowski, 1991; Tarnowski & Blechman, 1991; Tarnowski & Rohrbeck, 1993).

Disadvantage

A large and growing segment of the U.S. population is comprised of disadvantaged children. Recent census data indicate that 20 percent of the nation's children and adolescents are living in poverty (U.S. Bureau of the Census, 1989). Although poverty is often persistent, more children are affected by intermittent poverty. Data indicate that approximately 50 percent of U.S. youth live in a vulnerable economic condition at least once during the course of their development (Duncan & Rodgers, 1988).

From the government's perspective, disadvantage is typically defined by family income that falls below a specified cutoff criterion. Such cutoffs are periodically adjusted for inflation and the current cutoff for a family of four is $12,092. It is also clear that economic disadvantage is relative and that one need acknowledge that the median family income in 1987 was $36,800 (Bane & Ellwood, 1989). The poverty cutoff was originally based on the estimated expenses of basic food supplies multiplied times three. A number of criticisms of such a cutoff criterion has been noted. Specifically, it has been argued that such a cutoff overestimates disadvantage because it only reflects cash income. Other criticisms focus on the fact that the index may underestimate disadvantage because it fails to reflect variability in family income below the specified cutoff. Although economic cutoffs have been the most frequently used criteria, there remain obvious limitations associated with their use. Mincy, Sawhill, and Wolf (1990) note that family income does not inform us of the reasons for, duration, or social context of family economic disadvantage. Mincy and colleagues (1990) and Bane and Ellwood (1989) present several options in this regard, noting the biases and limitations associated with persistence-based, behavior-based, and location-based indices. For a detailed review, the interested reader should consult these sources directly. Given that economic thresholds have been the most frequently employed defining criteria, these criteria will be used to operationalize disadvantage for the purpose of the present chapter.

Demographic Considerations

Who are the disadvantaged in the United States? Where do they reside? What are the characteristics of disadvantaged youth? Considerable effort has been devoted to answering these and related questions. Unfortunately, much of the information relevant to these issues appears in diverse and unpublished sources. Recently, the National Center for Children in Poverty (NCCP) has established a compendium of statistical information on disadvantaged children and families. The organization of the statistics presented below is based on Tarnowski and Rohrbeck (1993) and are gleaned from NCCP resources (Klerman,1991; NCCP, 1990).

Concerning geographic location, impoverished economic status is most prevalent in the South where 26 percent of youth are affected (West, 22%; Midwest, 20%; and Northeast, 18%). Although the South has the largest number of disadvantaged youth, poverty rates have increased

most precipitously outside of this area since 1975. For young children, poverty disproportionately affects those in central cities (31%) (suburban, 13%; rural, 28%). A recent disturbing trend concerns the number of children living in concentrated areas of poverty (defined as areas in which greater than 20% of the population are adversely affected). Between 1975 and 1987, the percentage of children residing in such areas in central cities rose from 54 to 61 percent. Although media attention is often directed to documenting the plight of disadvantaged families residing in the inner city, such an exclusive focus would be inappropriate from an intervention and policy perspective as such efforts would not address the concerns of the majority of children who are affected. It is noteworthy that in 1980 only approximately 9 percent of children resided in central cities with poverty rates greater than 40 percent (Bane & Ellwood, 1989).

Using pretax income as the defining criterion, there were 33 million individuals living in poverty in 1987. Of these individuals, 13 million were children and adolescents less than 18 years of age, and 5 million were young children less than 6 years of age. Using an expanded definition of disadvantage (income between 100–150% of federal cutoff), an additional 2.7 million youth were considered to be living in economically impoverished households.

In 1987, poverty affected 23 percent of children under 6 years of age and 19 percent of youth 6 to 16 years of age. NCCP data indicate that in 1987 the percentage of children living in poverty varied markedly by race (42% Caucasian, 32% African American, 21% Hispanic). It is well-known that although more Caucasian children are disadvantaged, minority youth are disproportionately affected (in 1987, 48%, 42%, and 29% of African American, Hispanic, and other minority groups, respectively).

Factors Contributing to Economic Status

In general, pathways to poverty are complex and multidetermined. Although limited, our understanding of the familial, educational, employment, and income variables associated with disadvantage has increased over the past decade. Importantly, recent research has moved to emphasize the concept of multiplicative risks concerning the effects of specific SES correlates on the developmental trajectory of children and adolescents.

Data abstracted from recent NCCP (1990) analyses indicate the following: (1) the poverty rate is five times greater for children in single-parent families compared to those in married-couple families; (2) the number of disadvantaged children residing with single mothers appears to be increasing; (3) the declining value of father's earnings is contributing to the number of affected children; (4) minority children are 1.5 times more likely than Caucasian youth to be disadvantaged; (5) African American youth are disproportionately represented in mother-only families (74% of all poor African American children under age 6 live in such family environments); (6) an increase in the number of women giving birth outside of marriage (children in such circumstance have the highest risk of persistent poverty); (7) there has been a marked increase in the number of teenagers giving birth outside of marriage; and (8) parents in poverty have a greater number of children than do parents who are not similarly disadvantaged.

Concerning educational and employment variables: (1) expectedly, higher levels of educational attainment are associated with decreased disadvantage for all racial and ethnic groups; (2) in 1987, more than 50 percent of children less than 6 years of age resided in family environments where at least one parent had finished high school; (3) skills needed to generate income above the poverty level are not necessarily ensured by a high school education (e.g., more than 50% of new employment opportunities between 1984 and the year 2000 will demand postsecondary education); (4) a large proportion (41%) of young (< 6 years of age) disadvantaged children reside with parents who are employed on a full- or part-time basis; and (5) regardless of whether they reside with one or both parents, children residing with employed mothers evidence decreased poverty risk.

Concerning income: (1) approximately one-third of disadvantaged families rely entirely on public assistance, (2) the vast majority (90%) of the Aid to Families with Dependent Children (AFDC) goes to mother-only families with minimal support directed to poor intact families; (3) poor mothers are less likely than nonpoor father-absent families to receive paternal financial support; (4) in 1987, minimum wage employment only generated income that was 77 and 60 percent of the poverty line for a family of three and four, respectively; (5) minimum wage comprises a progressively smaller portion of the resources needed to maintain oneself above the poverty line; (6) since 1973 there has been a decline in real family income; and (7) tax law modifications (1986 Federal Tax Reform) have decreased the tax burden of disadvantaged families; however, tax credits (e.g., Dependent Care Tax Credit) are typically not available to impoverished families.

In summary, a diversity of factors are related to SES. The data underscore the heterogeneity of impoverished families and reveal the fallacious logic behind the simplistic, yet commonly held, notion that if the poor were working they would no longer be poor. The collective demographic and economic data indicate that numerous factors are at work on multiple levels that challenge and undermine families' efforts to modify their disadvantaged status.

A few additional points deserve mention. They include issues related to the persistence of disadvantage, income volatility, divorce, and the impact of adolescent parenting. It is often assumed that poverty is recalcitrant to change and that those affected by economic hardship will continue to do so when followed across time. Although this is true for many individuals, we need to take a close look at persistence data particularly as they relate to children and adolescents. Data reported by Bane and Ellwood (1986) indicated that approximately one-third of children experience poverty for at least 1 year. However, only about 5 percent live in impoverished conditions for two-thirds of childhood. Thus, in examining the effects of SES on specific developmental processes and developmental psychopathology, it is critical to attempt to determine whether one is studying transient or persistent poverty status.

Duncan and Rogers (1988) noted marked racial differences in their persistence data. Less than one in seven African American children lived above the poverty line for a 15-year period, and more than 25 percent were disadvantaged for two-thirds of the 15-year developmental period. Importantly, African American youth accounted for approximately 90 percent of all children who were poor during at least 10 of the preceding 15 years.

It is clear that disadvantage can be acute or chronic. However, studies of income volatility (Duncan & Rogers, 1988) have noted that a large percentage (27%) of young children (less than 5 years of age) resided in families subjected to large (50% decrements) income fluctuations. Data linking such negative large income changes to mental health are presented in Perline, Liberman, Menaghan, and Mullan (1986). However, for our purposes, a central cause of such volatility that often invokes persistent negative changes in family status is that of divorce. As noted by Duncan (1991), for women and children, income drops by about 40 percent following divorce.

Unfortunately, as noted by Duncan (1991), although studies (to be presented in the next section) have examined the correlates and effects of the persistently disadvantaged, no studies have been conducted linking income volatility and latter childhood developmental outcomes.

Finally, a subset of data on single parenthood is relevant to some of the persistence statistics cited above. Specifically, Bane and Ellwood (1983) reported that the length of time children spend in poverty was about 7 years if the family was headed by a single mother versus 4.6 years in intact families. This difference was even more pronounced for African American children: 12 years for single mother families versus 6 years for intact families. An additional note here concerns adolescent parents. Moore (1978) noted that more than 50 percent of AFDC payments in 1975 went to households where the mother gave birth before the age of 20. Because adolescent mothers complete less schooling, tend to have more children, and have relatively low employment rates, this group is at particular risk for persistence of economic hardship (Hayes, 1987; Klerman, 1991).

With this as background, we now turn to an overview of the health risks and the developmental and psychological outcomes (both child and parent) associated with disadvantage.

HEALTH CONSEQUENCES ASSOCIATED WITH SOCIAL CLASS

Relative to their peers who are more advantaged, children who are disadvantaged are more likely to become victims of infant mortality and those who survive are more apt to suffer from poor health. There are a multitude of familial factors that contribute to the poor health of these children, including specific demographic characteristics (i.e., lack of education), insufficient financial resources that are necessary to promote good health care and to satisfy other basic needs, time constraints, unhealthy life styles, and underuse of personal health services (Klerman, 1991; Tarnowski & Rohrbeck, 1993). Each of these health-related factors significantly impacts children's development.

Infant Mortality

At the beginning of this decade, the infant mortality rate in the United States was estimated to be 9 deaths per 1,000 live births (National Center for Health Statistics, 1991). Despite the wealth of resources in this country, this rate exceeds that of Japan and a number of European countries. Risk factors that predict high infant mortality include poor parental education, maternal age of less than 20 years, and low SES status (Klerman, 1991). The most frequent direct causes of infant mortality include low birth weight (less than 2,500 grams), congenital anomalies, respiratory distress syndrome, and sudden infant death syndrome (SIDS) (National Center for Health Statistics, 1991). During the neonatal period, factors associated with subsequent infant mortality include poor maternal health during pregnancy, labor, and/or delivery, while environmental factors have been posited to be strongly linked to postneonatal deaths (Klerman, 1991). The majority of infant deaths occur prior to the twenty-eighth day of life while the remainder transpire after the first month through the end of the first year (postneonatal period) (Klerman, 1991).

Intrauterine Growth Retardation, Prematurity, and Low Birth Weight

Low birth weight most frequently results from intrauterine growth retardation and/or prematurity, and such children are at particular risk for a multitude of health problems.

The variables related to low-birth-weight babies include low maternal weight gain during pregnancy due to poor nutrition, infections during pregnancy, specific obstetrical complications including high blood pressure and preeclampsia, smoking, abuse of drug substances, and poor access to, as well as poor utilization of, prenatal care programs (Institute of Medicine Committee to Study Outreach for Prenatal Care, 1988).

Relative to their normal-birth-weight peers, low-birth-weight children are more likely to be hospitalized in neonatal intensive care units and rehospitalized during their first 12 months of life. Further, these children are more prone to experience respiratory tract difficulties and to sustain developmental and learning handicaps (McCormick, 1985). In addition to physical problems, many of these infants have been found to manifest delayed physical, cognitive, and social development during childhood (Parker, Greer, & Zuckerman, 1988). Moreover, Liaw and Brooks-Gunn (1994) demonstrated an inverse linear relationship between the frequency of risk factors and the level of intellectual functioning among children who were classified as low birth weight as neonates. Thus, the frequency of risk factors was demonstrated in this study to be more predictive of intelligence rather than the existence of any specific risk factor.

The Institute of Medicine has concluded that low SES is clearly associated with an increased frequency of low-birth-weight and preterm deliveries (prior to 37 weeks of gestation). In fact, there are data to indicate that disadvantaged pregnant women are three times more likely to receive poor obstetrical care relative to their more advantaged counterparts. The conclusion reached by most experts in the field is that low-birth-weight infants result from a multitude of factors, all of which are associated with poverty (Klerman, 1991). For example, Binsacca and associates (Binsacca, Ellis, Martin, & Pettiti, 1987) have provided important data that indicate that women who experienced financial difficulties during their pregnancies were at increased risk for delivering a low-birth-weight infant even when other factors were controlled for statistically. Similarly, Lieberman and colleagues (Lieberman, Ryan, Monson, & Schoenbaum, 1987) found that the presence of one or more indices of low SES, including being a recipient of welfare, not having graduated from high school, single marital status, and being less than 20 years of age, represents a strong risk factor for a preterm birth.

Thus, there is a consensus in the literature that there are numerous adverse sequelae for low-birth-weight infants who are born to disadvantaged parents. Specific maternal risk factors such as low prepregnancy weight and age have been found to be directly associated with preterm births as have important additional mediating factors such as social class. All of these variables may be useful in predicting gestational duration due to their influence on prenatal care.

Childhood Health Problems: Acute and Chronic

The relationship between children's health and family income continues to affect the child well into late adolescence (Adams & Benson, 1990). Disadvantaged children are at significant risks due to lack of preventative health care interventions that have been demonstrated to prevent the incidence of many childhood diseases. For example, many health problems among disadvantaged youth have been shown to be directly related to the failure to immunize for specific infectious diseases (Centers for Disease Control, 1990). Because the immunization status of disadvantaged children is less adequate relative to their more advantaged peers, there is a higher occurrence of measles and other childhood communicable diseases for which vaccines are available. In addition, children from lower SES groups are more likely to incur developmental delays, learning disabilities, and psychiatric disorders (Klerman, 1991; Zill & Schoenborn, 1990).

Poorer children are at higher risk for rheumatic fever, hemophilium influenza, meningitis, gastroenteritis, and parasitic diseases (Klerman, 1991). There also is a higher prevalence of anemia as well as growth retardation among disadvantaged children relative to their more advantaged peers. Both anemia and growth retardation have been demonstrated to produce delays in the development of children's cognitive skills. Further, these delays have been linked to poor nutrition which, in turn, is a function of inadequate maternal education and young maternal age. As corroborated by other investigations, the aforementioned maternal factors are shared characteristics of low SES mothers (Kramer, 1987; Yip, Binkin, Fleshood, & Townbridge, 1987).

Vision and hearing problems also are more frequent among low SES children due to restricted access to primary care (Egbuonu & Starfield, 1982). For example, disadvantaged children are more likely to suffer from hearing losses due to untreated ear infections (Klerman, 1991). These hearing problems commonly affect communication skills. Similarly, poor vision may impede classroom learning and ultimately impact academic achievement. In addition, the dental hygiene of disadvantaged children is often deficient because they are less apt to have access to fluoride supple-

ments and prophylactic dental care (Pinkham, Casamassimo, & Levy, 1988). Moreover, this deficiency commonly results in a higher frequency of dental problems that often go untreated.

Finally, the prevalence of pediatric AIDS is significantly higher among disadvantaged children due to the greater frequency of drug abuse among poorer mothers during their pregnancies relative to more advantaged women. In fact, disadvantaged children account for approximately 80 percent of the incidence of AIDS in children who are under the age of five years (Tarnowski & Rohrbeck, 1993).

Not surprisingly, due to substandard living conditions that include peeling paint in older rundown homes, disadvantaged children are more frequently exposed to lead poisoning than are their more advantaged peers. Lead poisoning has been found to be inversely related to income, with blood lead levels increasing as family income decreases (Klerman, 1991; Needleman, Schell, Leviton, & Allred, 1990). The developmental sequelae of lead poisoning are significant. The impressive body of research in this area points to enduring cognitive and physical problems during childhood as the result of exposure to lead (Klerman, 1991; Needleman et al., 1990).

In summary, the aforementioned children's health problems are strongly associated with poverty, and most often have their origins in the poor education of their caretakers, as well as in growing up in homes that have failed to provide adequately for their physical and emotional needs (Werner, Bierman, & French, 1971). These health problems significantly impact the children's physical, cognitive, emotional, and social development (Klerman, 1991). Specifically, a number of experts (Dougherty, Saxe, Ross, & Silverman, 1987; Klerman, 1991) have argued that health problems, including physical handicaps, have a serious negative impact on the development of socialization skills in disadvantaged children. For example, children with chronic illnesses are often isolated from their peers, thus potentially diminishing their social competencies, while children with visible physical handicaps may even be rejected by some of their peers (Klerman, 1991).

Teratogenic Influences

Prenatal drug and alcohol exposure have been associated with social class and have been demonstrated to impact significantly on the children's physical, cognitive, and social–emotional development. Alcohol is one potent teratogen that has been definitively related to dysmorphology, growth retardation, and neurological damage in the children who are born to the women who abuse this substance during their pregnancies (Abel, 1984; Streissguth, Landesman-Dwyer, Martin, & Smith, 1980; Streissguth, Barr, Sampson, Darby, & Martin,

1989). Brown and associates (Brown et al., 1991; Coles et al., 1991) conducted a longitudinal investigation of a group of disadvantaged African American children who were exposed prenatally to alcohol and compared these children to a control group having no prenatal alcohol exposure. Those children who had been exposed to alcohol prenatally were found to have smaller head circumferences and to evidence a higher frequency of alcohol-related birth defects relative to the control group. Moreover, at the age of 5 years, the children who had been exposed were found to perform more poorly in the areas of intellectual functioning and academic readiness skills. In addition, these children evidenced deficits in their capacity to sustain attention and were rated by teachers as exhibiting internalizing and externalizing behavioral problems, even when the current use of alcohol by their caretakers was controlled for statistically. Thus, the use of alcohol by women during their pregnancies has adverse physical, cognitive, and behavioral consequences that may endure throughout the life span. The original cohort gain was evaluated at the age of 8 years (Brown et al., 1993). Findings were that the children who were exposed to alcohol throughout pregnancy suffered from more internalizing and externalizing behavior problems and fared more poorly academically than their nonexposed peers. This longitudinal investigation has been continued to study these children into adolescence and early adulthood. Thus, the teratogenicity of alcohol has far-reaching developmental effects into the elementary years and possibly into adolescence and even adulthood.

The corpus of findings on the teratogenic effects of alcohol soon led to the investigation of the effects on the developing neonate of other drug substances including heroin, cocaine, and phencyclidine. The results of these early studies generally suggested significant teratogenic effects such as growth retardation and congenital and neurobehavioral abnormalities (Chasnoff, Burns, Schnoll, Hatcher, & Burns, 1983; Chasnoff, Burns, Schnoll, & Burns, 1985), while the more recent investigations have consistently found few differences between the drug exposed and non-exposed children (Chasnoff, Griffith, Freier, & Murray, 1992; Hans, 1992; Zuckerman & Frank, 1992). Clearly, one of the difficulties in investigating the effects of various teratogens in children who are disadvantaged is found in efforts to differentiate the consequences of in utero exposure to various substances from the environmental effects of poverty (Bernstein & Hans, 1994).

Injuries

Rates of injuries are the highest among economically disadvantaged youth (Tarnowski & Rohrbeck, 1993) and account for approximately 15 percent of the deaths of children who are less than 15 years of age (Rivara & Mueller, 1987). Sameroff and colleagues (Sameroff, Seifer, Barocas, Zax, & Greenspan, 1987) have indicated that disadvantaged parents are less likely than advantaged caretakers to engage in injury prevention activities. For example, due to a characteristic level of low education, caretakers of disadvantaged children are less apt to use infant car seats or seat belts for their children and are less inclined to employ burn safety techniques (Sameroff, Seifer, Barocas, Zax, & Greenspan, 1987).

PSYCHOLOGICAL CORRELATES

Issues Pertaining to Developmental Psychopathology

The association between poverty and psychiatric disturbances is one of the best documented relationships in psychiatric epidemiology (Belle, 1990). There is nearly a 150 percent increase in the prevalence of psychopathology for the disadvantaged relative to higher SES groups (Neugebauer, Dohrenwend, & Dohrenwend, 1980), and the influence of poverty on psychiatric status seems to be nonspecific, that is, disadvantaged individuals seem to be at greater risk for all psychiatric disorders. Thus, the mental health of parents is an important ingredient in predicting children's adjustment, particularly for disadvantaged youth.

Of particular relevance to disadvantaged children is the literature pertaining to depression and poverty (McLoyd & Wilson, 1991). There is a significant association between socioeconomic stressors and psychological adjustment and adaptation (McLoyd, 1990), and poverty serves to diminish the individual's capacity to cope with new problems and stressors thereby producing adjustment problems. Moreover, there is a corpus of findings to suggest that psychological distress in adults coupled with the few utilitarian resources available to these individuals results in a number of symptoms related to distress including depression, anxiety, and somatic complaints.

Paralleling the literature on the relationship of SES and mental health problems are those studies pertaining to depressed mothers. This research has generally suggested that the parenting behaviors of depressed mothers are characterized by unresponsiveness, emotional unavailability, and hostile coerciveness of their children (Gotlib & Goodman, Chapter 25 in this volume; McLoyd & Wilson, 1991). For example, when interacting with their children, depressed mothers have been demonstrated to be more critical, less active and spontaneous, and to demonstrate less positive affect than their nondepressed counterparts (Downey & Coyne, 1990). Thus, when managing their children, these mothers are more apt to initiate demands, or attempt to enforce unilateral obedience when their children are noncompliant to their requests (Kochanska, Kucynski, Radke-Yarrow, & Walsh, 1987). In fact, the more severe the depression in the mother, the more negative the perception of the child (Forehand, McCombs, & Brody, 1985), and the greater probability of both verbal and physical abuse (McLoyd & Wilson, 1991). In support of this notion, Zelkowitz (1982) found that disadvantaged mothers who reported depression and anxiety were more likely to expect immediate compliance from their children even though these mothers, in comparison to mothers who reported generally adequate adjustment, were less apt to follow through on consequences for noncompliance.

Taken together with the data from the developmental psychopathology literature underscoring the role of maternal distress, particularly depression, in the psychological adjustment of their children (Downey & Coyne, 1990; Gelfand & Teti, 1990; Lee & Gotlib, 1989; Merikangus et al., 1990), the relationship between distress or depression in mothers and psychopathology in their children is quite clear. This association becomes particular strong in families struggling with economic disadvantage, especially when the higher prevalence of depression among the disadvantaged coupled with less education and other risk factors that place these mothers at greater jeopardy for poorer parenting is taken into account. The result of this constellation of psychopathology in mothers coupled with children being reared in an environment characterized by poverty interact synergistically to impede development. Particularly during the early years, these children are deprived of both cognitive and affective dimensions that are essential to development. Thus, poverty appears to be a significant mediating factor of distress and psychiatric disorders, including depression in mothers and adjustment difficulties in their offspring.

In a similar investigation, Dodge and colleagues (Dodge, Pettit, & Bates, 1994) studied specific processes in socialization that accounted for the relationship between SES and later child behavior problems. Findings from their longitudinal investigation indicated that SES in preschool predicted through the third grade both teacher-rated externalizing behavioral problems and aggression as rated by peers. SES was negatively associated with harsh discipline, lack of maternal warmth, exposure to aggressive adult models, family life stressors, mother's lack of social support, peer group instability, and a lack of intellectual stimulation. These aforementioned socialization processes predicted externalizing behavioral problems as rated by teachers and peer-nominated aggression and were found to account for over one-half of the effect of SES on externalizing behavior and aggression. Thus, the findings lend support to the notion that maternal adjustment difficulties are predictive of

children's behavioral problems as rated by teachers and peers. Moreover, the data are important because they underscore the increased risk of adjustment difficulties that are associated with being disadvantaged and the particular socialization experiences of these children that place them at risk for symptoms of psychopathology.

Although much of the research has focused on the psychiatric status of mothers, there is an emerging literature that examines the effect of financial stressors on family systems and the psychosocial adjustment of children. In a recent longitudinal investigation of nearly 400 youth and their families who were challenged by economic decline in the Midwest, Conger, Ge, Elder, Lorenz, and Simons (1994) proposed a family conflict model relating economic distress to adolescent internalizing and externalizing symptoms of behavior. Findings were that economic stressors experienced by the parents of these adolescents increased parental dysphoria and marital conflict, as well as conflicts between the parents and their teenagers. Higher levels of spouse irritability coupled with conflicts about money matters were significantly associated with parental hostility toward their children and adolescents. Consistent with the proposed model, the hostile and coercive exchanges between the youth and their families increased the likelihood of emotional and behavioral problems in the adolescents. This investigation by Conger and colleagues (1994) is important because it further supports the influence of financial stressors on the eventual adjustment of children and adolescents. Moreover, the study is important because it presents a family system's perspective in underscoring the role of poverty, stress, and behavioral adjustment in children and adolescents.

Thus, disadvantaged status clearly places children at greater risk for the developmental psychopathology. Much of the research has focused primarily on maternal influences on children's adjustment, although more recent research has begun to direct its efforts on the role of the family and parental interactions that are characteristic of the disadvantaged and which may influence child adjustment. Clearly, there are a dearth of studies examining paternal influences on children's adjustment and this is certainly true across all social classes. Those programs of research involving fathers are likely to prove more challenging for investigators as families headed by nonmarried women have increased significantly over the years, and there is a high incidence of single mothers in impoverished families (McLoyd & Wilson, 1991).

Child Abuse and Neglect

Although poverty is not directly causal in child abuse and neglect, there has been a repeated association between child abuse and neglect and social class (Gelles, 1992; National Research Council, 1993). Poverty has been demonstrated to be intertwined with several factors associated with child abuse and neglect. These factors include unrealistic expectations on appropriate developmental behavior of children, limited knowledge and education, and generally low intellectual functioning (see Azar & Bober, Chapter 23 in this volume; Azar & Wolfe, 1989), all of which are variables that are associated with low SES. Often the abuse is a result of frustration and poor management and is not necessarily maliciously intended (Azar & Wolfe, 1989).

Coulton, Korbin, Su, and Chow (1995) evaluated administrative data for 177 urban census tracts and found child maltreatment to be associated with economic and familial resources, residential instability, household and age structure, and the geographic proximity of neighborhoods to concentrated poverty. Findings also indicated that the children who are at greatest risk for maltreatment reside in neighborhoods characterized by poverty, crowded living conditions, population turnover, and single-parent families headed by females.

Thus, child abuse and neglect are negative sequelae of children being reared in poverty. There is a preponderance of evidence to suggest that parents at risk for abuse and neglect of their children have limited knowledge about appropriate developmental norms and are also limited in education. These findings have important implications for secondary prevention programs. Based on this evidence, it would follow that intervention programs that would prove most effective are those that focus on educating at-risk caretakers on appropriate developmental expectations and management strategies that are consistent with their children's level of development.

Social Support

One potential mediator of familial adjustment and ultimately child mental health is the extent to which social support is available to disadvantaged children and their families (Afflek, Tennen, & Rowe, 1991; Dunst, Trivette, & Deal, 1988; Green, 1993). As Dodge and colleagues (1994) point out, parenting in the disadvantaged environment can be a very isolating experience, particularly without encouragement and feedback from others. For example, poor social support has been found to be associated with maladaptive parenting (Dumas, 1986) and increased conduct problems among disadvantaged children. Dodge and colleagues (1994) have found that social support, in part, mediated the effects of SES on children's behavioral adjustment. In their review of the social support literature and the adjustment of disadvantaged

school children, McLoyd and Wilson (1991) reviewed the compelling evidence on the association between psychological adjustment in children and their families and social support. In essence, social support tends to provide a buffering effect between stressful life events and experiences including poverty and psychological adjustment in families and children (Sandler, Miller, Short, & Wolchik, 1989). For example, in an investigation of lower-class African American adolescents, Cauce (1986) found that perceived emotional support from friends and the number of reciprocated best friends significantly predicted competence at school as well as self-competence for these adolescents. Although not all studies have provided unequivocal support for the association of social support and psychological adjustment in children and their families (for review see McLoyd & Wilson, 1991), the potential influence of perceived social support on the adaptation of disadvantaged families and the successful development of the children within these families is an important variable that affects development. Clearly, intervention programs that test the efficacy of social support for the purpose of providing empirical validation for the correlational studies that relate social support to children's adjustment are needed. Thus, studies that investigate intervention strategies for providing social support networks to children and their families will be an important step in this program of research.

SELECTED INTERVENTIONS

The increase in children and families living in poverty since the 1970s can be linked to a number of economic, family, and government sources (Huston, 1991). It has been proposed that the effects of poverty must be examined within a broad social context (Bronfenbrenner, 1979). The literature is replete with examples of the overwhelming effects of poverty on the physical and psychological development and mental health of children. The enormity of the problems faced by disadvantaged children and families, and the global economic and social costs of poverty, underscore the need for appropriate and effective intervention programs. However, traditional treatment modalities (i.e., those utilized by more advantaged children and families) are often too inaccessible, restrictive, expensive, and fragmented to meet the needs of disadvantaged families (Tarnowski & Rohrbeck, 1993). If interventions programs are to successfully address the antecedent risk factors and adverse outcomes of low social class, they must be specifically designed to meet the diverse, multifaceted, and complex needs of this population.

Schorr (1991) argued that successful programs for high-risk, disadvantaged children share the following characteristics: (1) they view the child within the context of the family network, and the family in the context of its broader environment; (2) they are multigenerational; (3) services are comprehensive and diverse; (4) services are integrated and provided by a single agency (i.e., minimization of outside referrals); (5) services and program personnel are flexible and provide high-intensity services in a collaborative relationship with caregivers; (6) provision of service is characterized by mutual trust, caring, and respect; (7) program personnel are highly skilled; and (8) program professionals shed traditional role constraints and reduce program obstacles (e.g., fixed appointments, geographic constraints, etc.).

Tarnowski and Rohrbeck (1993), in their review of community-based interventions for disadvantaged children, concluded that most of the empirical investigations involving disadvantaged subjects were not studies of intervention programs. Furthermore, the efficacy of many community-based intervention programs supported by government organizations (e.g., the National Council of Community Mental Health Centers, National Institute of Mental Health, etc.) remains at issue due to the lack of rigorous scientific methodology employed in outcome studies, that is, lack of control groups and random assignment. The following section focuses on an overview of some of the most recent promising family support, school-based, and community intervention programs for disadvantaged children.

Family Support Programs

Family based programs can be divided into those focusing on parent support and education and those targeting family preservation. Family support programs often involve some form of structured parent education. However, conventional parent training programs are largely irrelevant and ineffective for seriously disadvantaged and insular families (Dumas & Wahler, 1983). Blechman (1984) suggested that "self-sufficiency training" may be more germane to the needs of disadvantaged mothers. Similarly, Schorr (1991) stated that disadvantaged mothers need direct support for their needs (e.g., depression, economic stress, substance abuse) before they can provide an adequate environment for their children. Although controlled investigations of family support programs are limited due to a number of methodological and practical limitations, the data generally indicate that family support programs for disadvantaged families result in improvements in parental competence and amelioration of parenting stress (Telleen, Herzog, & Kilbane, 1989), decreases in child behavior problems (Halvorson, 1992), and reductions in out-of-home placements (Waite, 1988).

Many successful family support programs include multiple intervention strategies. For example, Project SHaRE

(Source of Help Received and Exchanged; Dunst et al., 1988) provides a wide range of services to families with disabled, handicapped, and developmentally at-risk children. The primary focus of the program is to build and maintain social support networks. The foundation of services is based on reciprocal obligation of all program participants. Through this barter system, individuals learn to help and support each other. Outcome of a multimethod evaluation of the program (Dunst, Trivette, Gordon, & Pletcher, 1989) indicated that participating families were able to identify and meet their own needs, as well as to improve personal and family functioning, to expand social networks, and to access available resources.

The Houston Parent–Child Development Center Program targeted disadvantaged, minority children and their families. The goal of this 2-year program was to improve children's social and intellectual competence and school performance through culturally sensitive, multifaceted early intervention. Services included home visits and family workshops that focused on personal and parenting competence, access to community-based resources, and child care education. A nursery school was provided for all program children when they were two years of age, that is, during the second year of the program. Relative to a control group, children participating in this intervention program demonstrated reductions in behavior problems and improvements in school performance at the 5- to 8-year follow-up. Despite significant subject attrition (50%), results of the program appear to be promising. This program is exemplary due not only to positive behavioral outcomes, but also because of its emphasis on cultural variables that may impact treatment (e.g., language barriers). Future efforts need to examine the role of cultural variables in treatment planning and outcome (e.g., program completion).

Family preservation services represent a second main focus in family support programs. Although rigorous scientific investigations are generally lacking, home-based services (Hinckley & Ellis, 1985) and therapeutic foster homes appear to be a viable intervention for dysfunctional, multiproblem, disadvantaged families. Many of these programs are modeled after the Homebuilders, Inc. program (Kinney, Madsen, Fleming, & Haapala, 1977). The goal of the Homebuilders program is to prevent out-of-home placement for family members through a brief (i.e., 4 to 6 weeks) crisis intervention approach. Intensive in-home and community-based services are provided 24 hours a day by trained workers with limited case loads. Treatment focuses on the amelioration of the current crisis and prevention of future problems through skills training. Components of intervention include communication skills training, assertion training, and networking of families with available community resources. After the initial crisis intervention, families are referred for outpatient treatment or other case management services. Although most of the measures of program effectiveness are based on self-report data from family members or therapists, the program boasts a success rate ranging from 70 to 90 percent (Hinckley & Ellis, 1985). Program participants report improved communication, decreased family violence, decreased symptoms of mental illness, and high social validity. However, the success of the program may diminish as follow-up time increases.

Interventions based on the Homebuilders program have been implemented in a number of states and have targeted a variety of high-risk populations, including neglected and abused children (Nelson, 1991), emotionally disturbed children (Hinckley & Ellis, 1985), and juvenile offenders (Haapala & Kinney, 1988; Henggeler, Melton, & Smith, 1992). Most of these programs are based on principles of the social-learning theory and incorporate a wide array of crisis prevention and intervention-based strategies. Despite a number of difficulties in evaluating these programs, recent attempts have been made to document the effectiveness of family preservation services. For example, Feldman (1991) evaluated the efficacy of five New Jersey-based family preservation programs. Families who participated in intensive family preservation services were compared to control families that received traditional community services. Although there were differences in out-of-home placement rates between treatment and control families at the 9-month follow-up, these differences diminished by the 1-year follow-up.

The results of other controlled investigations of family preservation programs are more promising. Schwartz, AuClaire, and Harris (1991) found reductions in out-of-home placements at 12- and 16-month follow-ups for families that received family preservation services (56%) versus traditional community services (91%). In an earlier study, Auclaire and Schwartz (1986) found that it was not necessarily the frequency of child placements that were impacted by family preservation treatment, but rather the duration of the out-of-home placements. Family preservation intervention resulted in shorter out-of-home placements.

Therapeutic foster care programs are an alternative to more costly and restrictive residential placements. Although many states advocate the use of therapeutic foster care for dysfunctional youth and families, the efficacy of structured foster parent training, including the effects of these programs on child development and controlled investigations of outcome, is limited. One exception is the PRYDE program, a behaviorally based treatment program that utilizes well-trained foster care providers as agents of behavior change (Hawkins, Meadowcroft, Trout, & Luster, 1985). Foster parents are provided with training in behavior modification techniques, stress management, communication skills, and first aid. Initial training is supplemented by monthly in-service training. Foster parents are responsible for monitoring and recording relevant target child behaviors and are held accountable for the treatment program. Follow-up data at 1 and 2 years postdischarge indicated that more than 70 percent of PRYDE children were still living in less restrictive environments. Furthermore, 70 percent of those children and adolescents were either full-time students or employed (Jones, 1989). Further long-term outcome studies of the PRYDE and other therapeutic foster care programs are warranted. In addition, it remains unclear as to the type of children and socioeconomic groups that may benefit most from this approach.

Although the data generally support the promise of these, and similar, family support programs, Illback (1994) maintains that family support and education programs rarely address all of the diverse developmental and social needs of disadvantaged children and families. In addition, these programs are often difficult to implement. Merely increasing the availability of services does not always result in improved program access, largely due to the lack of coordination among service components (Illback, 1994). Further data are needed on the short- and long-term effectiveness of these programs for disadvantaged youth and need to include a more explicit focus on developmental impact.

Dunst, Trivette, and Thompson (1990) suggested that the effectiveness of family support programs needs to be viewed in terms of positive, demonstrable, and broad-based measures (i.e., improved family function, and utilization of available resources) rather than unidimensional change, that is, absence of problems.

School-Based Programs

A number of intervention programs for disadvantaged children offer a range of academic and nonacademic services in the school setting. The school setting is an important site for service delivery for two reasons. First, schools are a primary agent of socialization. Second, and perhaps most importantly, schools represent the one institution with which all children and families have contact (Illback, 1994). A number of programs (e.g., Head Start) have documented that disadvantaged children evidence developmental, intellectual, and academic gains relative to control children as a result of participation in high-quality early educational intervention. However, data are equivocal concerning the long-term maintenance of these effects.

The Carolina Abecedarian Project (Ramey & Campbell, 1993) was designed to increase the intellectual competence and academic achievement of disadvantaged children. In the initial phases of the program, parents and children were provided with an integrated network of early childhood education, pediatric care, and family support services. The second phase of intervention began when the children entered kindergarten and continued for 3 years. In this phase, parents were given structured, systematic support in assisting their children's educational activities. One hundred eleven high-risk children were randomly assigned to either the treatment (the Abecedarian Project) or control group. Children were re-randomized before entry into kindergarten. Therefore, half of each preschool group received the school-age intervention program. Children were evaluated both at the completion of phase one (3 years of age) and phase two (8 years of age). Data revealed that the preschool intervention program significantly enhanced performance on standardized IQ measures. Although both intervention and control group children evidenced some decrease in IQ from infancy to age 8, the decline was more significant in the control versus intervention group. Importantly, educational intervention that began during the primary grades did not result in the same increase in IQ performance. In terms of academic achievement, performance tended to increase as a function of the amount of intervention, with children in the preschool intervention plus secondary intervention group achieving at or above the national average in reading and mathematics. In addition, grade-retention rates were inversely related to the amount of intervention received. Children who participated in both forms of intervention evidenced a retention rate similar to that for the local population. The results of the Abecedarian experiment suggest that disadvantaged children require intensive and long-term educational intervention to reach their potential.

Ramey and Campbell (1993) compared the results of the Abecedarian project to other well-designed early educational interventions, including the Perry Preschool Project (Schweinhart & Weikart, 1989) and the Milwaukee Project (Garber, 1988). The Perry Preschool Project was based on the Head Start Model and targeted 128 inner-city, low-income African American 3 and 4 year olds with pretest IQs between 70 and 90. One-half of the children attended a preschool program for 2 ½ hours per day for 7 months each year. Teachers made weekly home visits focusing on family education enrichment. The Milwaukee Project compared the effects of intensive early educational intervention (i.e., beginning in infancy) in seventeen disadvantaged children versus eighteen untreated control group children. Mothers of children admitted to the program were required to have IQs of 75 points or less. In addition to educational intervention for children, mothers participated in a family education and employment training program. Significant differences

between the experimental and control group children were reported in evaluations of both of these programs. Children who participated in programs that began in infancy scored significantly higher on measures of IQ than children who began intervention at age 3. Gains in IQ were best maintained in children who began intervention in infancy. Children who participated in the Milwaukee studies evidenced greater gains in IQ than children in either the Perry Preschool or Abecedarian Project. Martin, Ramey, and Ramey (1990) suggested that these differences may be due to the restricted range of IQ in mothers in the Milwaukee sample (i.e., IQs 75 points or lower). These data indicate that impoverished children of low-IQ mothers may particularly benefit from high-quality, intensive early intervention.

A recent area of concern focuses on the need for major reforms in the design and implementation of primary educational programs for disadvantaged children. Levin (1993) maintains that our current system of education ensures the failure of disadvantaged children by reducing expectations for their learning, stigmatizing them as inferior students, and isolating them from mainstream instruction. He asserts that for educational programs to be effective for disadvantaged children, they must involve parents, utilize community resources, and involve teachers in the design of the program.

A model of this type of innovative program is the Accelerated Schools Program at Stanford University. The goal of the program is to accelerate the progress of at-risk students so that they perform at grade level by the completion of sixth grade. Curriculum and instructional decisions are made on an on-site basis and are under the direct control of the instructional staff. The staff work cooperatively with parents and administrators in guiding program planning. The curriculum is heavily language-based and critical thinking is emphasized. Parents play an important role in supporting the program in the home setting (e.g., encouraging children to read on a daily basis, checking for completion of homework, etc.). In addition, parents participate on program steering committees and task forces. The Accelerated School Program site has not completed the full transformation from a conventional school to an accelerated program (estimated to take approximately 6 years). However, preliminary data indicate an increase in parent participation (e.g., increased attendance at back-to-school night and teacher conferences), reductions in student discipline problems, and improved student attendance. There is evidence of improved performance on standardized achievement tests and reduced grade retention as well.

Other innovative school programs such as Higher Order Thinking Skills (HOTS; Pogrow, 1990) and the Reading Recovery Program (Clay, 1987) have demonstrated equally promising results. Proposals for innovations such as the

School of the Future (Holzman, 1992) include the coordination and delivery through the school system of multiple components of health, psychological and developmental, family preservation, and education services for disadvantaged families.

School districts have established after-school programs to offer disadvantaged students a variety of educational and developmentally stimulating recreational opportunities. Studies of low-income children participating in academically oriented after-school programs (Mayesky, 1980; Sheley, 1984) have demonstrated improvements in grades and achievement test scores. Posner and Lowe Vandell (1994) investigated four types of after-school care: (1) formal after-school programs, (2) maternal care, (3) informal adult supervision, and (4) self-care. Relative to the other forms of after-school care, attendance at a formal after-school program was associated with superior academic subject and conduct grades, higher teacher ratings of work habits, positive peer relations, and emotional adjustment. Furthermore, data indicated that disadvantaged children in formal after-school programs were exposed to more learning opportunities and structured activities with adults and peers than children in other forms of care. Structured after-school programs are likely to be one way to address the developmental needs of low-income children living in urban high-risk environments.

Community-Based Interventions

Early, quality child care is essential to the social–emotional and cognitive development of children. The impact of such care is likely most pronounced in disadvantaged children. Huston (1991) maintains that early, high-quality child care is a central feature of all social programs for children, particularly children from single-parent families living in poverty. Although child care programs should be considered a form of early education, a majority of these programs are delivered in the community setting and are therefore discussed in this section.

Day care has been hypothesized to be a protective environmental factor for low-income children. For example, O'Brien, Caughy, DiPietro, and Strobino (1994) found that participation in early day care was associated with the development of mathematics and reading recognition skills in children from impoverished environments. However, this study focused only on high quality day care. The majority of studies documenting positive outcomes for low-income children enrolled in early child care programs have focused explicitly on programs designed to provide high-intensity, compensatory, early intervention. Few data are available on the effects of enrollment in "ordinary" day care on disadvantaged children. Phillips, Voran, Kisker, Howes, and White-

book (1994) examined the differences in quality of day care across income groups by analyzing data from a nationally representative survey of child care centers. Quality of center care was determined by examining multiple variables including classroom size, child–staff ratios, level of education of teachers and staff, teacher participation in in-service training, annual teacher turnover rate, percentage of budget spent on personnel costs, teacher benefits, teachers' hourly wage, and specialized training for teachers. Results indicated that centers that served predominantly high-income children provided the best quality of care. The quality of care in centers that served predominantly low-income children, although generally adequate, was highly variable. Many of the classrooms in low-income centers did not meet recommended child–staff ratios and group sizes. In addition, although the centers serving low-income children did not differ in quality from high-income centers on many indices, teachers in the low-income centers were observed to have interactions with children that were characterized as detached and harsh. Interestingly, centers that served children from predominantly middle-income families tended to provide the poorest overall quality of care. Phillips and colleagues (1994) explained that the curvilinear relationship between center quality and family income may be related to the fact that middle-income families lack both the financial resources to pay for high-quality care and the access to government assistance that allows for participation in subsidized intervention programs. Although low-income centers appeared to offer "adequate" overall care, one must not overlook the fact that disadvantaged children are at high risk for a number of developmental and behavioral problems. Therefore, the issue is whether "adequate care" is sufficient to meet the special needs of this population.

In 1984 the National Institute of Mental Health sponsored the Child and Adolescent Service System Program initiative to encourage states to provide coordinated, comprehensive services for severely emotionally disturbed children (Day & Roberts, 1991). In response, a number of statewide and regional initiatives has been developed to support community-based programs targeting the reduction of out-of-home placements and the efficient, cost-effective integration of services between community agencies.

Heflinger and colleagues (1991) described a longitudinal study of the Fort Bragg Community Health Project in North Carolina. The goal of this program was to increase service coordination and improve access to community-based resources. Data indicated that the Fort Bragg Project resulted in a reduced number of disadvantaged children being placed in inpatient and residential treatment settings (Bickman, 1993). In addition, parents in the program were more satisfied and confident about treatment efficacy than parents in the control group (Behar, 1992). Analysis of program cost-effectiveness indicated that the cost per client in the Fort Brag project was 51 percent lower than in nonprogram comparison sites (Behar, 1992).

Kentucky's Interagency Mobilization for Progress in Adolescent and Children's Treatment (IMPACT; Kentucky Cabinet for Human Resources, 1990) program represents another attempt to streamline community service for disadvantaged families. In general, the program "emphasizes collaboration among social service, education, mental health, and juvenile justice systems through state, regional, and local interagency councils" (Illback, 1993, p. 418). Parent involvement and comprehensive case management are integral components of the program. Compared to placement histories prior to program involvement, children in the IMPACT program exhibited a decrease in out-of-home placements. In addition, 1-year follow-up data indicated lower parental ratings of child behavior problems in program children. Program parents perceived the support services network to be efficient and helpful. The annual cost of serving emotionally disturbed children was reduced relative to the year prior to program involvement. This likely was due to the reduction in more expensive, restrictive inpatient placements (Illback, 1993).

SUMMARY AND CONCLUSIONS

We have moved from an overview of definitional issues related to social class, to a review of epidemiological data on disadvantaged children with emphasis on the health and psychological consequences associated with economic impoverishment, to a more specific discussion of community prevention and intervention efforts. Specifically, we have observed that economic hardship erodes parental psychological and utilitarian resources that, in turn, undermine effective parenting and positive child adjustment (McLoyd, 1990). In addition, we have seen that adults are adversely affected by such contextual variables.

Only recently have researchers begun to devote much needed attention to evaluating the psychological impact of poverty and associated environmental stressors on parents and children. Fortunately, we have begun to establish an empirical developmental and intervention database and are gaining a more comprehensive understanding of how families are affected by economic hardship. Although the relationship between economic resources and the mental health status of parents and children has been recognized for some time, only recently have the effects of such contextual factors on child behavior, development, and health become the focus for methodologically rigorous study. Although long

overdue, these developments have far outstripped advances in the development and refinement of culturally sensitive and cost-effective intervention methods.

Huston, McLoyd, and Garcia Coll (1994) have argued that despite a long history of scientific interest in intervention programs, research has fallen short in adequately defining the essential components of effective interventions for the array of developmental, cognitive, and behavioral difficulties experienced by disadvantaged children. Although the present review of the literature suggests that a number of approaches successfully address some of the needs of disadvantaged children, a long-term, comprehensive, integrated model of intervention is generally lacking. In general, intervention programs continue to focus on change at the individual level, rather than on the broader social and political climate that fosters poverty.

Illback (1994) has stressed the need for an integrated services movement with the goal of creating a comprehensive and coordinated system of care for disadvantaged children and families. In contrast to the existing uncoordinated system, an integrated service approach would involve a collaborative effort on the part of government, service providers, state and local agencies, school districts, and families. An integrated program network would likely remove some of the impediments to effective treatment of disadvantaged families (e.g, geographic location of a single service site, standardized vs. individualized intervention protocols). Pooling state and community resources may help reduce the costs of providing a long-term, broad-based intervention program. Preliminary studies of integrated program networks such as the Fort Bragg and IMPACT projects have documented the short-term cost-effectiveness of this approach. The long-term benefits from this investment in the health, development, and care of children in poverty include breaking the cycle of intergenerational poverty and improving the likelihood that these children will lead productive adult lives.

Although a focus on contextual factors invokes the need for sweeping social policy changes, it is also evident that clinicians will need to expand their roles to provide a better mix of concrete clinical and supportive services (Halpern, 1990). It is worth emphasizing that although we have attempted to present general statistical data that characterize the status of disadvantaged children and families (e.g., income, access to health care, physical and psychological morbidity, etc.), individual families and children reflect a unique constellation of strengths and weaknesses. Effective clinical services mandate that these unique risks and resources be thoroughly assessed. Furthermore, one need acknowledge the fact that there is a continuum of need among disadvantaged families. Because of the heterogeneity of children and families, it is unlikely that a single social initiative will prove of value to all families. Finally, it should be noted that although one can easily feel overwhelmed by the quantity and severity of the difficulties that beset a particular family, not all problems require direct intervention. Schorr (1988) provides a detailed discussion of the interrelatedness of several problems and notes that positive collateral changes are often observed in the context of interventions that target only a subset of risk variables or conditions.

Clearly, many of the concerns outlined here require immediate attention. Substantive gains have been made concerning the development of intervention strategies. Unfortunately, what remains unclear at present are the sources of funding that will be required for many of these efforts.

REFERENCES

Abel, E. L. (1984). *Fetal alcohol syndrome and fetal alcohol effects.* New York: Plenum Press.

Adams, P. F., & Benson, V. (1990). Current estimates from the National Health Interview Survey, 1989. *Vital and health statistics,* Series 10, No. 176. (DHHS Publication No. PHS 90–1504). Hyattsville, MD: National Center for Health Statistics.

Afflek, G., Tennen, H., & Rowe, J. (1991). *Infants in crisis: How parents cope with newborn intensive care and its aftermath.* New York: Springer-Verlag.

Auclaire, P., & Schwartz, I. (1986). *An evaluation of the effectiveness of intensive home-based services as an alternative to placement of adolescents and their families.* Minneapolis: Hennepin County Services Department and the University of Minnesota, Hubert H. Humphrey Institute of Public Affairs.

Azar, S. T., & Wolfe, D. A. (1989). Child abuse and neglect. In E. J. Mash & R. A. Barkley (Eds.), *Treatment of childhood disorders* (pp. 451–459). New York: Guilford Press.

Bane, M. J., & Ellwood, D. T. (1989). One fifth of the nation's children: Why are they poor? *Science, 245,* 1047–1053.

Behar, L. (1992). *Fort Bragg child and adolescent mental health demonstration project.* Raleigh: North Carolina Division of Mental Health, Developmental Disabilities, and Substance Abuse Services, Child and Family Services Branch.

Belle, D. (1990). Poverty and women's mental health. *American Psychologist, 45,* 385–389.

Bernstein, V. J., & Hans, S. L. (1994). Predicting the developmental outcome of two-year-old children born exposed to methadone: Impact of social-environmental risk factors. *Journal of Clinical Child Psychology, 23,* 349–359.

Bickman, L. (1993). *The evaluation of the Fort Bragg demonstration project.* Nashville, TN: Vanderbilt University, Center for Mental Health Policy.

Binsacca, D. B., Ellis, J., Martin, D. G., & Petitti, D. B. (1987). Factors associated with low birthweight in an inner-city population: The role of financial problems. *American Journal of Public Health, 77,* 505–506.

Blechman, E. A. (1984). Competent parents, competent children: Behavioral objectives of parent training. In R. F. Dangel & R. A. Polster (Eds.), *Parent training: Foundations of research and practice* (pp. 34–63). New York: Guilford Press.

Bronfenbrenner, U. (1979). *The ecology of human development: Experiments by nature and design.* Cambridge, MA: Harvard University Press.

Brown, R. T., Coles, C. D., Smith, I. E., Platzman, K., Silverstein, J., Erickson, S., & Falek, A. (1991). Effects of prenatal alcohol exposure at school age: II. Behavior and medicine. *Neurotoxicology and Teratology, 13,* 369–376.

Campbell, F. A., & Ramey, C. T. (1994). Effects of early intervention on intellectual and academic achievement: A follow-up study of children from low-income families. *Child Development, 65,* 684–698.

Cauce, A. M. (1986). Social networks and social competence: Exploring the effects of early adolescent friendships. *American Journal of Community Psychology, 14,* 609–628.

Chasnoff, I. J., Burns, W. J., Hatcher, R. P., & Burns, K. A. (1983). Phencyclidine: Effects on the fetus and neonate. *Developmental Pharmacology and Therapeutics, 6,* 404–408.

Chasnoff, I. J., Burns, W. J., Schnoll, S. H., & Burns, K. A. (1985). Cocaine use in pregnancy. *New England Journal of Medicine, 313,* 666–669.

Chasnoff, I. J., Griffith, D. R., Freier, C., & Murray, J. (1992). Cocaine/polydrug use in pregnancy: Two-year follow-up. *Pediatrics, 89,* 284–289.

Clay, M. (1987). Implementing reading recovery: Systematic adaptations to an educational innovation. *New Zealand Journal of Educational Studies, 22,* 35–58.

Coleman, J. S. (1988). Social capital in the creation of human capital. *American Journal of Sociology, 94* (Suppl.), S95–S120.

Coles, C. D., Brown, R. T., Smith, I. E., Platzman, K. A., Erickson, S., & Falek, A. (1991). Effects of prenatal alcohol exposure: I. Physical and cognitive development. *Neurotoxicology and Teratology, 13,* 357–367.

Conger, R. D., Ge, X., Elder, G. H., Jr., Lorenz, F. O., & Simons, R. L. (1994). Economic stress, coercive family process, and developmental problems of adolescents. *Child Development, 65,* 541–561.

Coulton, C. J., Korbin, J. E., Su, M., & Chow, J. (1995). Community level factors and child maltreatment rates. *Child Development, 66,* 1262–1276.

Day, C., & Roberts, M. C. (1991). Activities of the child and adolescent service system program for improving mental health services for children and families. *Journal of Clinical Child Psychology, 20,* 340–350.

Dodge, K. A., Pettit, G. S., & Bates, J. E. (1994). Socialization mediators of the relation between socioeconomic status and child conduct problems. *Child Development, 65,* 649–665.

Dougherty, D. H., Saxe, L. M., Cross, T. L., & Silverman, N. (1987). *Children's mental health: Problems and services.* Durham, NC: Duke University Press.

Downey, G., & Coyne, J. (1990). Children of depressed parents: An integrative review. *Psychological Bulletin, 108,* 50–76.

Dumas, J. E. (1986). Indirect influence of maternal social contacts on mother-child interactions: A setting event analysis. *Journal of Abnormal Child Psychology, 14,* 205–216.

Dumas, J. E., & Wahler, R. G. (1983). Predictors of treatment outcome in parent training: Mother insularity and socioeconomic disadvantage. *Behavioral Assessment, 4,* 301–313.

Duncan, G. J. (1991). The economic environment of childhood. In A. C. Huston (Ed.), *Children in poverty: Child development and public policy* (pp. 23–50). New York: Cambridge University Press.

Duncan, G. J., & Rodgers, W. L. (1988). Longitudinal aspects of childhood poverty. *Journal of Marriage and the Family, 50,* 1007–1021.

Dunst, C., Trivette, C., & Deal, A. (1988). *Enabling and empowering families.* Cambridge, MA: Brookline Books.

Dunst, C. J., Trivette, C. M., Gordon, N. J., & Pletcher, L. L. (1989). Building and mobilizing informal support networks. In G. H. Singer & L. K. Irvin (Eds.), *Support for caregiving families: Enabling positive adaptation to disability* (pp. 121–142). Baltimore: Brookes.

Egbuonu, L., & Starfield, B. (1982). Child health and social status. *Pediatrics, 69,* 550–557.

Entwisle, D. R., & Astone, N. M. (1994). Some practical guidelines for measuring youth's race/ethnicity and socioeconomic status. *Child Development, 65,* 1521–1540.

Feldman, L. H. (1991). Evaluating the impact of intensive family preservation services in New Jersey. In K. Wells & D. E. Biegel (Eds.), *Family preservation services: Research and evaluation* (pp. 47–71). Newbury Park, CA: Sage.

Forehand, R., McCombs, A., & Brody, G. H. (1987). The relationship between parental depressive mood states and child functioning. *Advances in Behaviour Research & Therapy, 9,* 1–20.

Garber, H. L. (1988). *The Milwaukee Project: Preventing mental retardation in children at risk.* Washington, DC: American Association on Mental Retardation.

Gelfand, D., & Teti, D. (1990). The effects of maternal depression on children. *Clinical Psychology Review, 10,* 329–353.

Gelles, R. J. (1992). Poverty and violence towards children. *American Behavioral Scientist, 35,* 258–274.

Green, G. (1993). Social support and HIV. *AIDS Care, 5,* 221–228.

Haapala, D. A., & Kinney, J. M. (1988). Avoiding out-of-home placement of high-risk status offenders through the use of intensive home-based family preservation services. *Criminal Justice and Behavior, 15,* 334–348.

Halpern, R. (1990). Poverty and early childhood parenting: Towards a framework for intervention. *American Journal of Orthopsychiatry, 60,* 6–18.

Halvorson, V. M. (1992). A home-based family intervention program. *Hospital and Community Psychiatry, 43,* 395–397.

Hans, S. L. (1992). Maternal opioid drug use and child development. In I. S. Zagon & T. A. Slotkin (Eds.), *Maternal substance abuse and the developing nervous system* (pp. 177–213). New York: Academic Press.

Hauser, R. M. (1994). Measuring socioeconomic status in studies of child development. *Child Development, 65,* 1541–1545.

Hawkins, R. P., Meadowcroft, P., Trout, B., & Luster, W. C. (1985). Foster family-based treatment. *Journal of Clinical Child Psychology, 14,* 220–228.

Hayes, C. D. (1987). *Risking the future: Adolescent sexuality, pregnancy, and childbearing.* Washington, DC: National Academy Press.

Heflinger, C. A., Bickman, L. B., Lane, T., Keeton, W. P., Hodges, V. K., & Behar, L. B. (1991). The Fort Bragg child and adolescent demonstration: Implementing and evaluating a continuum of care. In A. Algarin & R. M. Friedman (Eds.), *A system of care for children's mental health: Expanding the research base* (pp. 83–96). Tampa: Florida Mental Health Institute.

Henggeler, S. W., Melton, G. B., & Smith, L. A. (1992). Family preservation using multisystemic therapy: An effective alternative to incarcerating serious juvenile offenders. *Journal of Consulting and Clinical Psychology, 60,* 953–961.

Hinckley, E., & Ellis, G. (1985). An effective alternative to residential placement: Home-based services. *Journal of Clinical Child Psychology, 14,* 209–213.

Holtzman, W. H. (Ed.). (1992). *School of the future.* Austin, TX: American Psychological Association and Hogg Foundation for Mental Health.

Huston, A. C. (1991). *Children in poverty: Child development and public policy.* New York: Cambridge University Press.

Huston, A. C., McLoyd, V. C., & Garcia Coll, C. (1994). Children and poverty: Issues in contemporary research. *Child Development, 65,* 275–282.

Illback, R. J. (1993). *Evaluation of the Kentucky IMPACT program for children and youth with severe emotional disabilities: Year two.* Frankfort: Kentucky Division of Mental Health, Children and Youth Services Branch.

Illback, R. J. (1994). Poverty and the crisis in children's services: The need for services integration. *Journal of Clinical Child Psychology, 23,* 413–424.

Institute of Medicine Committee to Study Outreach for Prenatal Care. (1988). *Prenatal care: Reaching mothers, reaching infants.* Washington, DC: National Academy Press.

Jones, R. (1989). Evaluating therapeutic foster care. In P. Meadowcroft & B. Trout (Eds.), *Troubled youths in treatment homes: A handbook of therapeutic foster care* (pp. 219–246). Washington, DC: Child Welfare League of America.

Kinney, J. M., Madsen, B., Fleming, T., & Haapala, D. (1977). Homebuilders: Keeping families together. *Journal of Consulting and Clinical Psychology, 45,* 667–673.

Klerman, L. V. (1991). The health of poor children: Problems and programs. In A. C. Huston (Ed.), *Children in poverty: Child development and public policy* (pp. 136–157). New York: Cambridge University Press.

Kochanska, G., Kuczynski, L., Radke-Yarrow, M., & Walsh, J. D. (1987). Resolutions of control episodes between well and affectively ill mothers and their young child. *Journal of Abnormal Child Psychology, 15,* 441–456.

Kramer, M. S. (1987). Intrauterine growth and gestational duration determinants. *Pediatrics, 80,* 502–511.

Lee, C. M., & Gotlib, I. (1989). Maternal depression and child adjustment: A longitudinal analysis. *Journal of Abnormal Psychology, 98,* 78–85.

Levin, H. M. (1993). Educational acceleration for at-risk students. In A. C. Huston (Ed.), *Children in poverty: Child development and public policy* (pp. 223–239). New York: Cambridge University Press.

Liaw, F., & Brooks-Gunn, J. (1994). Cumulative familial risks and low-birthweight children's cognitive and behavioral development. *Journal of Clinical Child Psychology, 23,* 360–372.

Lieberman, E., Ryan, K. J., Monson, R. R., & Schoenbaum, S. C. (1987). Risk factors accounting for racial differences in the rate of premature birth. *New England Journal of Medicine, 317,* 743–748.

Martin, S. L., Ramey, C. T., & Ramey S. L. (1990). The prevention of intellectual impairment in children of impoverished families: Findings of a randomized trial of educational daycare. *American Journal of Public Health, 80,* 844–847.

Mayesky, M. E. (1980). A study of academic effectiveness in a public school daycare program. *Phi Delta Kappan, 62,* 284–285.

McCormick, M. C. (1985). The contribution of low birth weight to infant mortality and childhood morbidity. *New England Journal of Medicine, 312,* 82–90.

McLoyd, V. C. (1990). The impact of economic hardship on black families and children: Psychological distress, parenting, and socioemotional development. *Child Development, 61,* 311–346.

McLoyd, V. C., & Wilson, L. (1991). The strain of living poor: Parenting, social support, and child mental health. In A. C. Huston (Ed.), *Children in poverty: Child development and public policy* (pp. 105–135). New York: Cambridge University Press.

Merikangus, K., Weissman, M., & Prusoff, B. (1990). Psychopathology in offspring of patients with affective disorders. In G. Keiter (Ed.), *Depression and families: Impact and treatment* (pp. 87–100). Washington, DC: American Psychiatric Press.

Mincy, R. B., Sawhill, I. V., & Wolf, D. A. (1990). The underclass: Definition and measurement. *Science, 248,* 450–453.

Moore, K. A. (1978). Teenage childbirth and welfare dependency. *Family Planning Perspectives, 10,* 233–235.

Nakao, K., & Treas, J. (1992). *The 1989 Socioeconomic Index of Occupations: Construction from the 1989 Occupational Prestige Scores* (General Social Survey Methodological Rep. No. 74). Chicago: University of Chicago, National Opinion Research Center.

National Center for Children in Poverty. (1990). *Five million children: A statistical profile of our poorest citizens.* New York: Columbia University Press.

National Center for Health Statistics. (1991). Births, marriages, divorces, and deaths for 1990. *Monthly Vital Statistics Report,* Vol. 39, No. 12, Suppl. (DHHS Publication No. PHS 91–1120). Hyattsville, MD: Public Health Service.

National Research Council. (1993). *Understanding child abuse and neglect.* Washington, DC: National Academy Press.

Needleman, H. L., Schell, A., Bellinger, D., Leviton, A., & Allred, E. N. (1990). The long-term effects of low doses of lead in childhood. *New England Journal of Medicine, 322,* 83–88.

Nelson, K. E. (1991). Populations and outcomes in five family preservation programs. In K. Wells & D. E. Biegel (Eds.), *Family preservation services: Research and evaluation* (pp. 72–91). Newbury Park, CA: Sage.

Neugebauer, D. D., Dohrenwend, B. P., & Dohrenwend, B. S. (1980). The formulation of hypotheses about the true prevalence of functional psychiatric disorders among adults in the United States. In B. P. Dohrenwend, B. S. Dohrenwend, M. S. Gould, B. Link, R. Neugebauer, & R. Wunsch-Hitzig (Eds.), *Mental illness in the United States* (pp. 45–94). New York: Praeger.

O'Brien Caughy, M., DiPietro, J. A., & Strobino, D. M. (1994). Day-care participation as a protective factor in the cognitive development of low-income children. *Child Development, 65,* 457–471.

Parker, S., Greer, S., & Zuckerman, B. (1988). Double jeopardy: The impact of poverty on early child development. In B. Zuckerman, M. Weitzman, & J. Alpert (Eds.), Children at risk. *Pediatric Clinics of North America, 35,* pp. 1227–1240.

Perlin, L. I., Liberman, M. A., Menaghan, E. F., & Mullan, J. (1981). The stress process. *Journal of Health and Social Behavior, 22,* 337–356.

Phillips, D. A., Voran, M., Kisker, E., Howes, C., & Whitebook, M. (1994). Child care for children in poverty: Opportunity or inequity? *Child Development, 65,* 472–492.

Pinkham, J. R., Casamassimo, P. S., & Levy, S. M. (1988). Dentistry and the children of poverty. *Journal of Dentistry for Children, 55,* 17–24.

Pogrow, S. (1990). Challenging at-risk students: Findings from the HOTS program. *Phi Delta Kappan, 71,* 389–397.

Posner, J. K., & Lowe Vandell, D. L. (1994). Low-income children's after-school care: Are there beneficial effects of after-school programs? *Child Development, 65,* 440–456.

Ramey, C. T., & Campbell, F. A. (1993). In A. C. Huston (Ed.), *Children in poverty: Child development and public policy* (pp. 191–221). New York: Cambridge University Press.

Rivara, F. P., & Mueller, B. A. (1987). The epidemiology and causes of childhood injuries. *Journal of Social Issues, 43,* 13–32.

Sameroff, A. J., Seifer, R., Barocas, R., Zax, M., & Greenspan, S. (1987). Intelligence quotient scores of 4-year-old children: Social-environmental risk factors. *Pediatrics, 79,* 343–350.

Sandler, I., Miller, P., Short, J., & Wolchik, S. (1989). Social support as a protective factor for children in stress. In D. Belle (Ed.), *Children's social networks and social supports* (pp. 277–307). New York: Wiley.

Schorr, L. B. (1988). *Within our reach: Breaking the cycle of disadvantage.* New York: Anchor.

Schorr, L. B. (1991). Effective programs for children in poverty. In A. C. Huston (Ed.), *Children in poverty: Child development and public policy* (pp. 261–281). New York: Cambridge University Press.

Schwartz, I. M., AuClaire, P., & Harris, L. J. (1991). Family preservation services as an alternative to out-of-home placement of adolescents: The Hennipin County experience. In K. Wells & D. E. Biegel (Eds.), *Family preservation services: Research and evaluation* (pp. 33–46). Newbury Park, CA: Sage.

Schweinhart, L. J., & Weikart, D. P. (1989). The High/Scope Perry Preschool Study: Implications for early childhood care and education. *Prevention in Human Services, 7,* 109–132.

Sheley, J. (1984). Evaluation of the centralized structured after-school tutorial. *Journal of Educational Research, 77,* 213–217.

Streissguth, A. P., Barr, H. M., Sampson, P. D., Darby, B. L., & Martin, D.C. (1989). I.Q. at age 4 in relation to maternal alcohol use and smoking during pregnancy. *Developmental Psychology, 25,* 3–11.

Streissguth, A. P., Landesman-Dwyer, S., Martin, J. C., & Smith, D. W. (1980). Teratogenic effects of alcohol in humans and animals. *Science, 209,* 353–361.

Tarnowski, K. J. (1991). Disadvantaged children and families in pediatric primary care settings: I. Broadening the scope of integrated mental health service. *Journal of Clinical Child Psychology, 20,* 351–359.

Tarnowski, K. J., & Blechman, E. (1991). Introduction to the Special Section: Disadvantaged children and families. *Journal of Clinical Child Psychology, 20,* 338–339.

Tarnowski, K. J., & Rohrbeck, C. A. (1993). Disadvantaged children and families. In T. H. Ollendick & R. J. Prinz (Eds.), *Advances in clinical child psychology* (Vol. 15, pp. 41–79). New York: Plenum Press.

Telleen, S., Herzog, A., & Kilbane, T. L. (1989). Impact of a family support program on mothers' social support and parenting stress. *American Journal of Orthopsychiatry, 59,* 410–419.

U.S. Bureau of the Census. (1992a). *Alphabetic Index of Occupations and Industries.* Washington, DC: Author.

U.S. Bureau of the Census. (1992b). *Dictionary of Occupational Titles.* Washington, DC: Author.

Waite, S. (1988). Real help for families in trouble: Evaluation of a family support program. *Journal of Child Care, 3,* 47–54.

Werner, E. E., Bierman, J. M.,& French, F. E. (1971). *The children of Kauai: A longitudinal study from the prenatal period to age ten.* Honolulu: University of Hawaii Press.

Yip, R., Binkin, N.J., Fleshood, L., & Trowbridge, F. L. (1987). Declining prevalence of anemia among low-income children in the United States. *Journal of the American Medical Association, 258,* 1619–1623.

Zelkowitz, P. (1982). Parenting philosophies and practices. In D. Belle (Ed.), *Lives in stress: Women and depression* (pp. 154–162). Beverly Hills, CA: Sage.

Zill, N., & Schoenborn, C. A. (1990). *Health of our nation's children: Developmental, learning, and emotional problems, United States, 1988. Advance Data* (No. 190). Hyattsville, MD: National Center for Health Statistics.

Zuckerman, B., & Frank, D. (1992). "Crack kids": Not broken. *Pediatrics, 89,* 337–339.

CHAPTER 14

ETHNICITY AND CULTURE: HISPANIC YOUTH

Robert G. Malgady
Giuseppe Costantino

The need for mental health services addressing the special problems of ethnic minority adults and youngsters is a widely acknowledged issue in the minority mental health literature (e.g., Rogler, Malgady, & Rodriguez, 1989). At the root of this issue, the cultural distance experienced by minority clients when seeking mainstream mental health services has prompted efforts to increase the sensitivity of services to their ethnic identity and cultural values. Indeed, mental health services have become more culturally sensitive in several ways: by matching clients with therapists of the same ethnicity, by matching the theoretical orientation of therapy to clients' cultural values, and by introducing ethnic and cultural considerations directly into the therapeutic process (Rogler, Malgady, Costantino, & Blumenthal, 1987, 1993). Yet there is limited empirical evidence that such efforts, which are largely limited to adults, result in

less premature treatment dropout, increased participation, and more effective treatment outcomes (Sue, Fujino, Hu, Tackeuchi, & Zane, 1991). This chapter describes a program of culturally sensitive treatment outcome research on developmental experimental mental health interventions for Hispanic children and adolescents. A more detailed description of the most recently developed treatment modality is provided in the appendix to this chapter. These studies were preventive interventions developed on the basis of narrative therapy using cultural role modeling (varying the narrative modality by age cohort) to impact on high-risk indicators such as anxiety symptomatology, acting-out behavior, and poor ethnic and self-concept (e.g., Costantino, Malgady, & Rogler, 1986, 1994; Malgady, Rogler, & Costantino, 1990).

PSYCHIATRIC EPIDEMIOLOGY OF HISPANIC YOUTH

In 1993 there were nearly 23 million Hispanics living in the United States, representing an increase of over 50 percent between the 1980 and 1990 censuses (U.S. Bureau of the Census, 1994). This is a growth rate more than seven times

Robert G. Malgady, Program in Quantitative Studies, New York University. The research reported in this chapter was supported by the National Institute of Mental Health, Services Research Branch (Grant Nos. RO1-MH33711-01-06 and R01-MH30569-15-16) and the William T. Grant Foundation (Grant No. 83-0868).

that of any other ethnic population, attributable to high birth rates, youthful age distribution, and high levels of immigration. These figures do not include an estimated 5 percent of the Hispanic population missed by the 1990 census (U.S. Bureau of the Census, 1991), an estimated 2.5 million undocumented Hispanic immigrants (Warren, 1994), and the more than 3.5 million population of the Commonwealth of Puerto Rico.

Epidemiological studies of psychiatric prevalence rates and symptomatology have, for the most part, neglected the rapidly growing population of Hispanic children and adolescents. In New York City, for example, the Hispanic population is a youthful one, with 32 percent of Puerto Ricans and Dominicans under age 18 compared to 16 percent of the non-Hispanic white population. From 1980 to 1990 the largest population growth rate (67%) was among "other" Hispanics (i.e., not Mexican, Puerto Rican, or Cuban), largely Salvadorans and Dominicans (U.S. Bureau of the Census, 1994). The New York region is the major settlement area of Puerto Ricans (50%), Dominicans (78%), and South Americans (Ecuadorans, 62%; Colombians, 43%). More Hispanics reside in New York City than in any other city in the United States, representing nearly one-quarter of the city's population (New York City Department of City Planning, 1997). During a 3-year period from 1990 to 1993, more than 120,000 immigrants entered New York City schools, with the largest group being from the Dominican Republic and accounting for about 20 percent of this increase (New York City Board of Education, Division of Public Affairs, 1993). There are vast patterns of socioeconomic, family structure, and cultural similarities and differences among these Hispanic groups (Malgady, 1994).

Some early studies have reported findings of lower self-esteem among Hispanic children compared to African American and non-Hispanic white children (Anderson & Johnson, 1971; Fisher, 1974), while others reported more behavioral problems among Hispanic children and adolescents compared to non-Hispanic whites (e.g., Langner, Gersfen, & Eisenberg, 1974). More recently, Canino, Gould, Prupis, and Schafer (1986) found that Hispanic children and adolescents disclosed more depression and anxiety symptoms than did those of African American descent. However, the literature on depression is equivocal with some studies reporting more severe depressive symptoms among Hispanic youth relative to other ethnic groups (e.g., Emslie, Weinberg, Rush, Adams, & Reintelmann, 1990), and others not (e.g., Garrison, Jackson, Marsteller, McKeon, & Addy, 1990). Roberts (1992) reported that Hispanic adolescents express somatic complaints more prominently than do whites and blacks.

According to some estimates (Aspira, 1983; Canino, Earley, & Rogler, 1980), Hispanic youngsters exhibit the highest high-school dropout rate of all ethnic groups and alarming rates of referral for problems such as social and emotional disorientation, conduct and anxiety disorders, adjustment reactions with anxiety features, and low self-esteem. Estimates of Puerto Rican dropout rates have ranged to as high as 60 percent, and comparative data indicate that New York City rates are "as bad or worse" than the national average (National Puerto Rican Forum, 1980). Studying prevalence and risk factors among a multinational group of Hispanic early adolescents, Vega, Zimmerman, Warheit, Apospori, and Gil (1993) found a high prevalence of drug use. One study, with therapeutic implications, indicated that adherence to more traditional Hispanic cultural values was associated with lower risk of drug use among Hispanic youth (Pumariega et al., 1992).

Related to school dropout and substance use, Hispanic youth are the most rapidly increasing incarcerated population in the United States (Martinez, 1987). According to the New York State Office of Mental Health (1994), among the primary DSM-III-R (*Diagnostic and Statistical Manual of Mental Disorders,* third edition-revised; American Psychiatric Association, 1987) diagnoses of nearly 8,000 Hispanic children and adolescents enrolled in community-based services, the rate of disruptive behavior disorders (46.9%) eclipses all others. Furthermore, these disorders are nearly equally distributed between conduct and oppositional defiant disorders.

Rogler, Malgady, and Rodriquez (1989) have indicated that Hispanic families present a profile of demographic characteristics, such as low socioeconomic status (SES), ethnic minority status, and a high rate of single-parent households, that are associated with increased risk of mental disorder. The fragmented picture that emerges from the scattered research efforts suggests that such risk factors are associated with lower ethnic and self-esteem, and possibly increased anxiety, depression, and comorbid substance use. The undeniable result, however, is an alarmingly high rate of high school dropouts and disruptive behavior disorders.

In 1978 the Special Populations Sub-Task Panel on the Mental Health of Hispanic Americans reported to the President's Commission on Mental Health that Hispanic youngsters are at especially high risk of mental disorder, but that mental health research had contributed little to the resolution of the problem. Today, two decades later, neglect of the special mental health needs of Hispanic children and adolescents persists, and there remains a need to develop and evaluate effective psychotherapeutic modalities for Hispanic youth (Rogler et al., 1989). Cross, Bazron, Dennis, and Isaacs (1989) have estimated that by the year 2000 about 40 percent of the clients in the mental health delivery system will be members of ethnic minority groups. Vargas and Willis (1994) lamented the paucity of research and theoretically driven descriptions of culturally sensitive interventions that are in sharp contrast to the growing mental health needs of ethnic minority populations.

THE MEANING OF CULTURAL SENSITIVITY

Despite considerable attention to problems attending the delivery of mental health services to Hispanics, such as underutilization of services (Rodriguez, 1987), premature dropout rates from psychotherapy (Sue et al., 1991), and allegations of ineffective treatment modalities (Padilla, Ruiz, & Alvarez, 1975; Rogler et al., 1987, 1993), there has been little research evaluating the effectiveness of psychotherapy for Hispanics and even less attention to outcomes of services for Hispanic children and adolescents.

The more general literature on Hispanics, largely focused on Mexican American adults, implicates cultural distance between the typically low SES, Spanish-dominant Hispanic client and the middle-class, English-speaking non-Hispanic therapist as the root of psychotherapeutic calamity. The recognition of cultural conflict not only between the client and therapist, but also between Hispanic cultural values and the orientations embodied by mainstream health care services, has prompted considerations of cultural "sensitivity" (Rogler et al., 1987, 1993) or cultural "responsiveness" (Sue, 1988) in the provision of mental health services. A common definition of ethnicity and culture embraced by many psychologists—though not by modern anthropologists—is that of Triandis (1972), who distinguishes common heritage or ethnicity from the qualities of an ethnic group's shared experience (i.e., culture), which consist of values, social norms, and communication patterns.

Based on a review of the Hispanic mental health literature, Rogler and colleagues (1987, 1993) identified three approaches to the delivery of culturally sensitive services. The first approach seeks to increase the accessibility of treatments for Hispanics by narrowing the gap between the client's and professional's cultures, while accommodating what often may be a culturally patterned lay referral system. Such efforts, which reportedly result in increased service utilization, involve recruiting bilingual and bicultural staff, coordinating service networks with the Hispanic community, and creating a therapeutic atmosphere in which Hispanic cultural values are accepted (e.g., Acosta & Cristo, 1981; Scott & Delgado, 1979; Trevino, Bruhn, & Bunce, 1979; Sue et al.,1991).

Once services are utilized, the second approach involves selection of a treatment modality that is congruent with the Hispanic client's perceived cultural values. Ruiz (1981), for example, has recommended screening Hispanic clients according to their level of acculturation and then assigning acculturated clients to mainstream treatment modalities and less acculturated clients to special culturally sensitive interventions. Whether such efforts to increase the sensitivity of interventions to the Hispanic client's cultural orientation affect treatment outcomes, however, is a question that remains unanswered.

The third approach to cultural sensitivity introduces the client's cultural values directly into the therapeutic modality. Two premises have guided this approach. One is that the client's value structure should be matched by a similar set of therapeutic assumptions, such as focusing on Cubans' strong sense of familism to treat intergenerational and acculturative conflict with family therapy (Szapocznik, Kurtines, & Santisteban, 1994). The other does not simply reproduce a culturally congruent ambiance, but establishes therapeutic goals that integrate conflicting cultural values and behavioral norms. For example, Costantino, Malgady, and Rogler (1986) introduced Puerto Rican folktales (adapted to reflect Anglo cultural values and settings) into a therapeutic modality to treat young, high-risk children; Malgady, Costantino, and Rogler (1990) based a modeling therapy modality on heroic Puerto Rican biographies with older adolescents; Costantino, Malgady, and Rogler (1994) used a narrative therapy model with young adolescents. In other words, the bicultural approach shapes behavior by bridging cultural conflict.

DEVELOPMENTAL MODALITIES OF CULTURAL INTERVENTION

The majority of programmatic, culturally sensitive treatment outcome research efforts for Hispanic youth have been conceptualized, in the broadest sense, in the narrative process and rooted in social learning theory principles (modeling). The specific treatment modalities within narrative modeling interventions have varied depending upon developmental considerations.

Narrative psychotherapy is rapidly gaining acceptance as a culturally sensitive treatment modality (Howard, 1991). Cognitive psychologists such as Bruner (1986) and Mair (1988) have affirmed that identity development occurs as a result of life-story construction. Howard (1991) conceptualizes psychopathology as an incoherent story with an incorrect ending; psychotherapy presents a coherent story with a correct ending. Further, he describes the technique of storytelling as the most adept process in understanding culturally diverse individuals and in conducting cross-cultural psychotherapy.

Cuento Therapy

In an initial study of bicultural intervention with young children (5 to 8 years old), Costantino, Malgady, and Rogler

(1986) developed a storytelling modality using Puerto Rican *cuentos* or folktales as a modeling therapy. In this approach, the characters in folktales were posed as therapeutic peer models conveying the theme or moral of the stories. The nature of such stories motivates young children's attention to the models, which is critical to the first stage of the modeling process. Second, the models were adapted to present attitudes, values, and behaviors that reflect adaptive responses to the designated targets of therapeutic intervention, such as acting out, anxiety symptoms, and impoverished self-concept. The folktales were adapted to bridge both Puerto Rican and Anglo cultural values and settings. Reinforcement of children's imitation of the models through active therapeutic role-playing facilitated social learning of adaptive responses which were targeted in the stories' themes. In this manner, the modality was rooted in the children's own cultural heritage, presented in a format with which they could readily identify and imitate, and therapeutically aimed to impact on adjustment to mainstream cultural demands.

The intervention was conducted with children of mixed gender who were accompanied by their mothers in small group sessions led by bilingual Puerto Rican therapists. Because of the children's young age, it was thought that both the presence and interactive engagement of their mothers in the therapeutic process would enhance treatment effectiveness. In addition, because the mother was still the children's primary agent of socialization at this age, it was also thought that she would be the most effective dispenser of reinforcement. Therefore, mothers were trained for their role in the therapeutic process and on how to provide (upon the therapist's cue) verbal reinforcement of their child.

This was considered a preventive intervention because the children were screened for presenting emotional and behavior problems in school and at home and did not satisfy diagnostic criteria for DSM-III-R disorders. In addition, their uniformly low SES and high rate of single-parent household composition also characterized these children as representing a high-risk population.

The effectiveness of the bicultural folktale modality was determined by a comparison with three other groups: (1) a second folktale condition in which the same stories were not adapted to bridge cultural conflict, (2) a mainstream (art/play) intervention, and (3) a nonintervention control group. Results indicated that the bicultural folktale intervention led to the greatest improvement in social judgment and reduction in anxiety symptomatology; this persisted at a 1-year follow-up. Interaction effects also were evident, revealing that the bicultural folktale intervention was most effective with younger children (5 and 6 year olds). Further analysis of the treatment process indicated that when interviews were conducted with

the 7- and 8-year-old children, they found some of the *cuentos* to be too childish. This developmental consideration prompted the development of another narrative modeling modality that was appropriate for older children and adolescents.

Hero/Heroine Therapy

The second modeling intervention appropriate for older youth was based on "heroic" adult role models (Malgady, Rogler, & Costantino, 1990). A major consideration in developing this modality was the frequency of single-parent households, typically headed by young mothers. This suggests that Puerto Rican adolescents often lack appropriate adult role models with whom they can identify and, therefore, adaptive values and behaviors to imitate during the critical adolescent years. National figures indicate that 41 percent of Hispanic households are headed by females (U.S. Bureau of the Census, 1991); estimates specific to Puerto Ricans in New York City are somewhat higher (44%, according to Mann & Salvo, 1985); and among the sample of research participants drawn from New York City public schools in Hispanic communities the rates of female-headed households exceeded 60 percent. Consequently, Puerto Rican adolescents appeared to be suitable candidates for a modeling therapy that fulfills their developmental need for adaptive role models in a culturally sensitive way.

This narrative modeling modality was based on stories of heroic Puerto Ricans in an effort to bridge the bicultural, intergenerational, and identity conflicts faced by Puerto Rican adolescents. The modality, which was implemented with 12- to 14-year-old adolescents, sought to enhance the relevance of therapy for adolescents by exposing them to successful male and female adult models in their own culture, by fostering ethnic pride and identity as a Puerto Rican, and by modeling achievement-oriented behavior and adaptive coping with the stress common to life in the urban Hispanic community. The content of the biographies embodied themes of cultural conflict and adaptive coping with stress. This intervention was also considered preventive because although the adolescents were screened for behavior problems in school, they did not meet DSM-III-R diagnostic criteria.

Given that the research participants were adolescents, parents were not included in the therapeutic process as they were in the cuento therapy modality because it was thought that doing so would reduce self-disclosure. Moreover, same-gender therapy groups were formed, led as in the cuento modality by bilingual and bicultural therapists, because pilot work had indicated that there were significantly more behavioral management problems (with boy–girl disruptiveness) in a mixed-gender context.

Contrary to social-learning principles, models presented in the intervention were not restricted to the same gender of the research participants. This point of departure was pursued for two reasons. First of all, the content of the biographies was very gender-distinct. There was a large pool of male heroic candidates to draw from in Puerto Rican history, representing a wide diversity of occupations or fields of achievement and spanning the history of the Island. Female characters in Puerto Rican history tended to be more contemporary and less variable in endeavors. Second, there was a concern that parents consenting for their children's participation might view the protocols as sexist.

Treatment outcomes were assessed relative to an attention-control group participating in a school-based dropout prevention program. Evaluation of treatment effectiveness revealed that the culturally sensitive modeling intervention generally decreased anxiety symptomatology and increased ethnic identity. However, treatment interacted with household composition and participants' gender. Consistent with the intention of the intervention, the role models promoted greater ethnic identity in the absence of a male adult in the adolescents' households—but only among male adolescents. Female adolescents had stronger Puerto Rican identities than males regardless of treatment, possibly because of stable maternal identification. Similarly, the role models promoted greater self-esteem among male and female adolescents from female-headed households; however, although females from intact families felt "more Puerto Rican," their self-image diminished in the process. The role models presented in treatment may have been perceived as idealized and aroused conflict concerning their real parents, such that parental identification led to lower self-esteem. This process may have operated only among females because the female role models presented in treatment often represented untraditional female sex roles.

Interviews with research participants provided information consistent with this interpretation of developmental interaction effects. Male adolescents in father-absent households often related strong feelings of identification with male models. Regardless of their family context, males tended to prefer sports figures and had little appreciation of achievements in the political arena or on the part of female role models. Female adolescents seemed to have a very different perspective and were often dismayed by the altruistic and patriotic acts of some role models that disrupted family harmony. Although a research panel selecting the role models judged these stories to be among the most heroic, adolescent females were disturbed by themes of family separation (e.g., a painter leaving his family to study in Spain; a political party leader sending his family away while struggling for

independence). The interactions impacting on treatment outcomes call attention to the importance of being mindful of an adolescent's social context when considering the mental health value of culturally sensitive interventions. This implicates the need to investigate both the integrity and quality of intrafamilial relations as potential mediators or moderators of treatment outcomes.

Another informative observation concerns the decision to present both male and female role models to adolescents regardless of their own gender, contrary to the social-learning principle, which suggests that same-gender modeling is most effective. The initial rationale was that there are prominent qualitative differences in the biographies of heroic male and female characters that might bias the intervention across genders. However, in retrospect, both the findings and the interviews with participants suggest that in future studies the treatment protocols should include same-gender models and that the narrative therapy should be conducted in separate sex groups.

Storytelling Therapy

The third intervention developed in this program of treatment outcome research was also a narrative modality with older children and young adolescents, ages 9 to 11, including a more ethnically and culturally diverse group consisting of Puerto Ricans, Dominicans, and a small group of Central and South Americans (Costantino, Malgady, & Rogler, 1994). The participants were screened for DSM-III-R symptomatology; the most symptomatic were included in the study (though none reached caseness). The most prevalent symptoms were those associated with conduct, anxiety, and phobic disorders.

The intervention consisted of a storytelling modality based on pictorial stimuli depicting Hispanic cultural elements (e.g., traditional foods, games, gender roles), family scenes, and neighborhoods (e.g., bodegas) in urban settings. The pictures were selected from the stimulus cards of the "Tell-Me-A-Story" (TEMAS) thematic apperception test (Costantino, Malgady, & Rogler, 1988). They portrayed multiracial Hispanic characters interacting in a variety of home, city, and school settings. The therapy sessions were conducted in three phases. In the first, group members collaborated to develop a composite story about a particular picture, identifying the characters, setting, what is happening, and the resolution of the plot. In the second phase, group members shared their personal experiences as related to the composite story, and the therapist verbally reinforced those themes in their personal narratives that were adaptive. Maladaptive themes were also discussed in the group so that alternative, more adaptive resolutions of interpersonal conflict could be determined. This phase engaged the youths in self-disclosure of personal conflict in their lives and how they coped, seeking to reinforce and internalize adaptive models of coping with stress. In the third phase, participants dramatized the composite story by performing the roles of the characters in the pictures. Verbally supportive reinforcement of imitative target behaviors was administered by the therapist and by peers. The psychodrama was videotaped and played back for critical review and discussion of appropriate behavior. The narrative intervention was compared to an attention-control group who engaged in discussion sessions with a psychoeducational purpose.

Because the age range of research participants corresponded to preadolescence and early adolescence, parents did not participate in the therapeutic process and small, same-gender therapy groups were formed as in the hero/heroine modality. However, because of the results of the later study, the main character presented in the stimulus pictures was of the same gender as the therapy group members.

Results indicated that although there was no effect on depression symptoms, there was significant reduction of conduct disorder and phobic symptoms. Once again, there were interactions involving the age factor (but not gender) such that treatment effects were enhanced among the younger adolescents.

SUMMARY AND CONCLUSIONS

The introduction of cultural sensitivity into the treatment process is a promising approach to impacting on the special mental health needs of Hispanic adolescents. The special developmental considerations that were introduced into therapy protocols as a function of participants' age and gender are summarized in Table 14.1. Clearly, however, further research is needed to determine how culturally sensitive services can be implemented more effectively given that dynamic processes may intervene to enhance or impugn their effectiveness. A major objective of such research should be to investigate the dynamic interplay between a culturally sensitive modeling intervention and the familial context of male and female Hispanic youngsters to make gender-specific and family-specific refinements in treatment protocols.

The bulk of the research literature on Hispanic mental health reflects an emphasis on Mexican Americans, while the remaining research on Hispanics involves scattered studies mostly concentrating on Puerto Ricans in New York City or Cuban Americans in Miami. Only a small fraction of all this research, as noted earlier, has been devoted to children or adolescents. Part of the reason for this neglect is the wide

TABLE 14.1 Summary of Developmental Considerations in Culturally Sensitive Narrative Therapy for Hispanic Youth

PARTICIPANT AGE GROUP	THERAPY MODALITY	DEVELOPMENTAL CONSIDERATIONS
5–8	Folktale	Verbal fairy tale/fantasy Parent present in therapy Mixed gender groups
9–11	Pictorial	Composite storytelling Parent not present in therapy Same gender groups Same gender stimuli
12–14	Biography	Group discussion Parent not present in therapy Same gender groups Same gender stimuli

geographic disparity of the major Hispanic groups across the country; however, the New York metropolitan area has distinctive enclaves of the several Hispanic subcultures distributed throughout its five boroughs and northern New Jersey. Preventive intervention research has been previously limited to Puerto Ricans and although classified as "high-risk," the children and adolescents did not represent clinical (DSM-III-R) groups. Nonetheless, modeling principles are logically generalizable to other Hispanic nationalities and to the more severely dysfunctional. Therefore, future research should extend narrative role modeling therapy with Dominican and Central/South American adolescents and African American and non-Hispanic white comparison groups with DSM-IV diagnoses of disruptive behavior disorders.

Perhaps the most fundamental question to face in culturally sensitive psychotherapy research is whether the attenuation of cultural distance is consequential to treatment outcome (Malgady, 1994). In a review of two decades of cross-cultural psychotherapy research on ethnic minority populations, Sue (1988) identified two competing conclusions pertinent to this fundamental question. The first is that ethnic or cultural mismatch decreases the likelihood of favorable treatment outcomes; the second is that cultural differences are, for the most part, irrelevant to treatment outcomes. Sue (1988; Sue & Zane, 1987) has proposed an interesting hypothesis that synthesizes these apparently contradictory conclusions. This hypothesis is that cultural factors may have a "distal" rather than "proximal" effect on treatment outcomes. Consideration of a client's culture in treatment planning may not necessarily have a direct link to outcome, but may enhance the process of therapy, which in turn is more directly linked to outcome. This reasoning calls attention to the need for process-oriented research on culturally sensitive treatment outcomes. Process research is needed to determine the extent to which treatment outcomes are a direct or indirect function of culture introduced into the modality and the extent to which outcomes are a result of mediating responses to culture.

A related but unexamined question is whether culture-specific interventions enhance treatment outcomes in the cultural target group more than in other ethnic or cultural groups. For example, an intervention based on Hispanic role models who are black may produce similar treatment outcomes among non-Hispanic African Americans. Given that the role models were often of low SES, similar effects might be found with low SES non-Hispanic whites. Thus, similar to the refined questions that can be posed about whether culture's effects are direct or indirect through intervening processes, the decomposition of a therapeutic role model's salient features (e.g., culture, race, gender) also need to be experimentally investigated. These are some of the issues that future research should begin to investigate.

REFERENCES

Acosta, F., & Cristo, M. (1981). Development of a bilingual interpreter program: An alternative model for Spanish-speaking services. *Professional Psychology, 12,* 474–482.

American Psychiatric Association. (1987). *Diagnostic and statistical manual of mental disorders* (3rd ed., rev.). Washington, DC: Author.

Anderson, J. C., & Johnson, W. H. (1971). Stability and change among three generations of Mexican-Americans: Factors affecting achievement. *American Educational Journal, 8,* 285–307.

ASPIRA (1983). *Racial and ethnic high school dropout rate in New York City.* New York: Author, Career Education Program.

Bruner, J. (1986). *Actual minds, possible worlds.* Cambridge, MA: Harvard University Press.

Canino, I., Earley, B., & Rogler, L. H. (1980). *The Puerto Rican child in New York: Stress and mental health.* (Mon. #4), New York: Fordham University, Hispanic Research Center.

Costantino, G., Malgady, R. G., & Rogler, L. H. (1986). Cuento therapy: A culturally sensitive modality for Puerto Rican children. *Journal of Consulting and Clinical Psychology, 54,* 739–746.

Costantino, G., Malgady, R. G., & Rogler, L. H. (1988). *The TEMAS thematic apperception test: Technical manual.* Los Angeles: Western Psychological Services.

Costantino, G., Malgady, R. G., & Rogler, L. H. (1994). Storytelling-through-pictures: Culturally sensitive psychotherapy for Hispanic children and adolescents. *Journal of Clinical Child Psychology, 23,* 13–20.

Cross, T. L., Bazron, B., Dennis, K. W., & Isaacs, M. R. (1989). *Towards a culturally competent system of care.* Washington, DC: CAASP Technical Assistance Center, Georgetown University.

Emslie, G. J., Weinberg, W. A., Rush, A. J., Adams, R. M., & Rintelmann, J. W. (1990). Depressive symptoms by self-report in adolescence. *Journal of Child Neurology, 5,* 114–121.

Fisher, R. I. (1974). A study of non-intellectual attributes of children in a first grade bilingual–bicultural program. *Journal of Educational Research, 67,* 323–328.

Garrison, C., Jackson, K., Marsteller, F., McKeown, R., & Addy, C. (1990). A longitudinal study of depressive symptomatology in young adolescents. *Journal of the American Academy of Child Adolescent Psychiatry, 29,* 581–585.

Howard, G. S. (1991). Culture tales: A narrative approach to thinking, cross-cultural psychology, and psychotherapy. *American Psychologist, 46,* 187–197.

Langner, T., Gersfen, J., & Eisenberg, J. (1974). Approaches to measurement and definition in the epidemiology of behavior disorders: Ethnic background and child behavior. *International Journal of Health Services, 4,* 483–501.

Mair, M. (1989). *Between psychology and psychotherapy.* London: Routledge.

Malgady, R. G. (1994). Hispanic diversity and the need for culturally sensitive mental health services. In R. G. Malgady & O. Rodriguez (Eds.), *Theoretical and conceptual issues in Hispanic mental health.* Melbourne, FL: Krieger.

Malgady, R. G., Rogler, L. H., & Costantino, G. (1990). Hero/heroine modeling for Puerto Rican adolescents: A preventive mental health intervention. *Journal of Consulting and Clinical Psychology, 58,* 469–474.

Mann, E. S., & Salvo, J. J. (1985). Characteristics of new Hispanic immigrants to New York City: A comparison of Puerto Rican and non-Puerto Rican Hispanics. *Research Bulletin* (Hispanic Research Center, Fordham University), *8,* Nos. 1–2.

Martinez, O. (1987). Minority youth and crime. *Crime and Delinquency, 33,* 325–328.

National Puerto Rican Forum (1980). *The next step towards equality.* New York: Author.

New York City Board of Education. (1997). *Immigrant enrollment in the public schools.* New York: Division of Public Affairs.

New York City Department of City Planning. (1992). Demographic profiles: A profile of New York City's Community Districts from the 1980 & 1990 Censuses of Population and Housing. No. 92-32. New York: Author.

New York State Office of Mental Health (1994). *Primary diagnoses of all children in CDF database.* Albany, NY: Author.

Padilla, A. M., Ruiz, R. A., & Alvarez, R. (1975). Community mental health services for Spanish-speaking/surnamed population. *American Psychologist, 30,* 892–905.

Pumariega, A. J., Swanson, J. W., Holzer, C. E., Linskey, A. O., & Qintero-Salinas, R. (1992). Cultural context and substance abuse in Hispanic adolescents. *Journal of Child and Family Studies, 1,* 75–92.

Roberts, R. R. (1992). Manifestation of depressive symptoms among adolescents. *Journal of Nervous and Mental Disease, 180,* 627–633.

Rodriguez, O. (1987). *Hispanics and human services: Help-seeking in the inner city* (Monograph No. 14). New York: Hispanic Research Center, Fordham University.

Rogler, L. H., Malgady, R. G., Costantino, G., & Blumenthal, R. (1987). What does culturally sensitive mental health services mean? The case of Hispanics. *American Psychologist, 42,* 565–570.

Rogler, L. H., Malgady, R. G., Costantino, G., & Blumenthal, R. (1993). What do culturally sensitive mental health services mean? In G. G. Ramos (Ed.), *Ethnocultural issues in social work practice.* Needham Heights, MA: Ginn.

Rogler, L. H., Malgady, R. G., & Rodriguez, O. (1989). *Hispanics and mental health: A framework for research.* Melbourne, FL: Krieger.

Ruiz, R. (1981). Cultural and historical perspectives in counseling Hispanics. In D. Sue (Ed.), *Counseling the culturally different* (pp. 186–215). New York: Wiley.

Scott, J., & Delgado, M. (1979). Planning mental health programs for Hispanic communities. *Social Casework, 60,* 451–455.

Special Populations Sub-Task Panel of Mental Health of Hispanic Americans. (1978). Report to the President's commission on mental health. Los Angeles: University of California, Spanish-Speaking Mental Health Research Center.

Sue, S. (1988). Psychotherapeutic services for ethnic minorities. *American Psychologist, 43,* 301–308.

Sue, S., Fujino, D.C., Hu, L. T., Tackeuchi, D. T., & Zane, N. W. S. (1991). Community mental health services for ethnic minority groups: A test of the cultural responsiveness hypothesis. *Journal of Consulting and Clinical Psychology, 59,* 533–540.

Sue S., & Zane, N. (1987). The role of culture and cultural techniques in psychotherapy: A critique and reformulation. *American Psychologist, 42,* 37–45.

Szapocznik, J., Kurtines, W., & Santisteban, D. A. (1994). The interplay of advances among theory, research and application in family interventions for Hispanic behavior-problem youth. In R. G. Malgady & O. Rodriguez (Eds.), *Theoretical and conceptual issues in Hispanic mental health.* Melbourne, FL: Krieger.

Trevino, F., Bruhn, J., & Bunce, H. (1979). Utilization of community mental health services in a Texas-Mexican border city. *Social Science and Medicine, 13,* 331–334.

Triandis, H. C. (1972). *The analysis of subjective culture.* New York: Wiley.

United States Bureau of the Census. (1991). 1990 Census of Population and Housing, Summary Tape File 1A, Data User Services Division, Washington, DC, September.

United States Bureau of the Census. (1994). Current Population Reports, Population Characteristics, March. Vargas, L. A., & Willis, D. J. (1994). Introduction to the special section: New directions in the treatment and assessment of ethnic minority children and adolescents. *Journal of Clinical Child Psychology, 23,* 2–4.

Vega, W. A., Zimmerman, R. S., Warheit, G. J., Apospori, E., & Gil, A. G. (1993). Risk factors for early adolescent drug use in four ethnic and racial groups. *American Journal of Public Health, 83,* 185–189.

Warren, R. (1994). *Estimates of the unauthorized immigrant population residing in the United States, by country of origin and state of residence.* Paper presented at California Immigration 1994 conference, Immigration and Naturalization Service, Statistics Division, Los Angeles, CA.

APPENDIX

STORYTELLING THERAPY PROTOCOL

The theory behind and description of narrative role modeling therapy are described in more detail elsewhere (see Costantino et al., 1994; Malgady, et al. 1990); here, I present a brief overview of the process. According to principles of social-learning theory, the fundamental idea behind role modeling therapy is that in order to imitate the target behavior, the observer must first pay attention to the model. Hence, the cultural familiarity of the models is expected to increase attention to the model's target behaviors and, therefore, the probability of imitation. Second, as imitative behavior is repeatedly followed by positive reinforcement, the acquired behaviors become psychologically internalized. In the absence of the model, verbal labeling of imitative behavior, followed by reinforcement, facilitates acquisition. Within this theoretical framework, characters in the narratives can be therapeutically presented as symbolic models of adaptive emotional and behavioral functioning with the various Hispanic cultural settings in which the adolescents live. The stories motivate attention processes by presenting culturally familiar characters of the same ethnicity as the adolescents by modeling beliefs, values, and behaviors with which they can identify, and by modeling functional relationships with peers and authority figures. This is particularly appropriate for adolescents diagnosed with disruptive behavior disorders.

The intervention protocols are implemented with small groups of up to six participants, proceeding in three stages: constructing the narrative, relating the narrative to personal experiences, and role-playing.

In the first stage, the narrative is constructed collectively by the group members. The stimulus for constructing the narrative is a picture from the TEMAS ("Tell-Me-A-Story") thematic technique for assessment of cognitive, affective, and behavioral functioning (Costantino, et al., 1988). The TEMAS consists of twenty-three chromatic pictures depicting either minority (African American and Hispanic) or non-minority (white) characters interacting in familiar settings, such as school, street, home. Intrafamilial scenes are de-

picted, as well as peer relationships, among boys and girls. The pictures portray a bipolar situation (e.g., complying with a parental request vs. continued playing with peers; helping an elderly person carry groceries vs. molesting an elderly person). Ten TEMAS pictures are used, one to be used in each therapy session. The Hispanic and African American participants construct narratives from the minority TEMAS pictures, whereas the non-Hispanic white participants construct narratives from the parallel nonminority TEMAS pictures. The ten pictures selected have been previously validated as evoking themes of interpersonal relationships, aggression, delay of gratification, and moral judgment, all of which are related to DSM-IV criteria for disruptive behavior disorders.

The group participants are prompted by the therapist to tell a story about the pictures, identifying the characters, the setting, what has happened leading up to the present scene, what is presently happening, and how the story will end. The therapist guides a structured discussion of the main themes of the story, stimulating the participants to identify good and bad behavior, issues, and consequences of the actions. Positive verbal and emotional reinforcement is administered to encourage cooperation.

In the second stage, discussion turns to relating the elements identified in the stories to the participants' lives and the consequences of their own behavior. The behavior of group members is carefully monitored and shaped: evidence of imitative approximations to target behaviors are positively reinforced, while disruptive behaviors are discouraged.

In the third stage, the group members enact a semi-structured, open-ended role-playing scenario related to the elements of the biography. Group members portray various roles and reinforcement of behavior occurs spontaneously. The role-playing skit is videotaped and then played back for group discussion. Therapists/group leaders and the participants fill out evaluation forms at the conclusion of each session. Attendance at sessions is motivated by monetary compensation after fixed intervals. The outline below is an example of the structure of the therapy protocols.

Outline of Narrative Role-Modeling Sessions

1.0 Create Composite Group Narrative (15–20 minutes)

   1.1 Therapist brings group to order.

   1.2 Group members take turns creating a story about the picture presented.

   1.3 Therapist highlights important issues.

   1.4 Therapist uses structured questioning to promote attention/identification (e.g., What was the main character's concern? What were his or her feelings? What were his or her obstacles? What did he or she do to overcome them?).

2.0 Similar Personal Experiences (20–30 minutes)

   2.1 Introductory question: Did any of you have (or know of person with) a similar experience? Discuss responses.

   2.2 Identify people who were emotionally supportive during this experience.

   2.3 Comparison of personal stories with the narrative (e.g., The main character faced poverty. What are you doing about this problem?).

   2.4 Identify positive and negative ideas, behaviors, and consequences.

   2.5 Therapist reinforcement of behaviors.

3.0 Role-Playing (15–20 minutes)

   3.1 Present semistructured scenario, characters, and dilemma, and solicit volunteers for roles.

   3.2 Enact a story spontaneously about the given narrative, achieving a resolution of the dilemma.

   3.3 Characters are administered appropriate rewards.

   3.4 Review and discuss videotape (reinforcement).

   3.5 Provide summary evaluation of session.

CHAPTER 15

SEXUAL ORIENTATION

Ritch C. Savin-Williams
Lisa M. Diamond

Very little is known about gay, lesbian, and bisexual children and adolescents, in large part because North American cultural mythology denies nonheterosexual orientations to children and adolescents. Further contributing to our ignorance is the hesitancy of child and adolescent researchers to become involved in a topic that has been historically stigmatized. In fact, until recently, professional conferences, journals, and books have been reluctant to include symposia, articles, and monographs on children and adolescents with same-sex attractions. Although researchers have begun to acknowledge the existence of these individuals, the limited research on their experiences conveys the view that sexual orientation has little or no impact on the developmental processes of children and adolescents with same-sex attractions—a view we contest.

Methodologically, a dearth of reliable early indicators of sexual orientation in childhood has also been an obstacle. Consequently, researchers have had to rely on retrospective data from adults to glean information about the experiences and developmental processes of sexual-minority (a term we use to refer to those who do not consider themselves to be a

part of mainstream heterosexuality) youth, resulting in a developmental psychology of the "remembered past" (Boxer & Cohler, 1989). Furthermore, in their search for events, characteristics, or experiences that distinguish sexual-minority children, researchers have tended to simplistically document the apparent differences between nonheterosexual individuals and their heterosexual counterparts at the expense of identifying features accounting for diversity *within* lesbian, gay, and bisexual populations across time.

In this chapter we first outline a "differential developmental trajectory" approach to the study of developmental processes among sexual-minority individuals. This approach emphasizes the diversity among nonheterosexuals in addition to their relevant differences from heterosexuals. We then review that which is known about the distinctive developmental processes of sexual-minority children and adolescents and highlight the clinical implications of this growing body of knowledge.

TWO DEVELOPMENTAL POSITIONS

The very assertion that sexual orientation is an important context for child and adolescent development assumes that

We are deeply indebted to the editorial assistance and ideas of Kenneth M. Cohen.

gay, lesbian, and bisexual individuals have meaningfully different life courses than heterosexual individuals. The converse, ignoring the topic, may very well indicate the belief that basic development processes do not differ between heterosexual and sexual-minority individuals. In either case, both assumptions mask an enormous number of complex and controversial issues. For example, where do these differences come from, when do they appear, how long do they last, and, perhaps most importantly, of what significance are they? In what ways are sexual minorities *indistinguishable* from heterosexuals, and how might we interpret these similarities? Would the differences cease to exist in a culture that did not stigmatize same-sex attractions or would the similarities cease to exist in a "lesbian nation" or a separatist gay culture?

In the literature, two theoretical stances have addressed these issues. With regard to their developmental trajectories, lesbians, gay men, and bisexuals are:

1. similar to everyone else except in the objects of their sexual attractions *or*
2. unique because of their same-sex attractions.

If similar, then the debate centers on the degree and manner in which same-sex attractions affect development; thus, interpopulation differences would seldom be addressed. If unique, then the debate hinges on whether same-sex attractions promote unique developmental trajectories or whether developmental uniqueness precedes same-sex attractions. These two alternatives are often articulated in the following manner:

2.a. Culture gives no choice. Because of their same-sex attractions, lesbians, bisexuals, and gays are treated differently by both the near and far culture, ultimately leading to unique developmental trajectories. This is the cultural reductionism that often characterizes pure social constructionist positions.

2.b. Biology gives no choice. Because of their genetics, hormones, and/or neuroanatomical structures, gay men, lesbians, and bisexuals have unique developmental trajectories, regardless of cultural context. This is the biological reductionism that often characterizes pure essentialist positions.

We do not advocate either the pure sameness or uniqueness position and we do not give credence to the pure essentialist or pure social constructionist perspectives articulated above, primarily because we find little scientific merit in their positions on the developmental histories of bisexuals, lesbians, or gay men. Rather, we propose a "differential developmental trajectories" perspective.

DIFFERENTIAL DEVELOPMENTAL TRAJECTORIES

The argument that the salient similarities and differences between and within heterosexual and nonheterosexual populations have an exclusively biological or an exclusively social origin implicitly denies the most basic thesis of developmental psychology:

$$B = f (P \times E)$$

That is, behavior is a function of the interaction between the person and the environment. Those who deny any role for biology affirm a scientifically untenable tabula rasa view of human development, while those who assume that a socioculturally moderated phenomenon is inherently variable, under the individual's control, or somehow not as "real" or important as a biologically moderated phenomenon, affirm a similarly untenable biological determinism. It is impossible to talk about the significance of sexual orientation as a context for development without reference to *both* the chemistry, physiology, and neuroanatomy of the individual *and* the cultural norms stigmatizing same-sex attractions and pairings in our society. The similarities and differences between gay, lesbian, and bisexual individuals and heterosexuals have both biological and social origins, and regardless of the precise balance of these origins, patterns of similarity and difference exert a distinct and important developmental press on gay, lesbian, and bisexual individuals at multiple points along the life course.

Even if a single, perfectly predictive "cause" of sexual orientation were identified, this finding would leave unexplained the vast diversity among sexual-minority individuals. Indeed, many researchers now argue that different causes of sexual orientation may operate for different individuals (Bailey, 1996; Garnets & Kimmel, 1993). For example, prenatal hormones may be instrumental in the development of individuals who display childhood gender-atypical behavior (Meyer-Bahlburg, 1993) while gender-typical lesbian, gay, and bisexual individuals may be influenced primarily by psychosocial factors (Bell, Weinberg, & Hammersmith, 1981). Or, the sex of a person may be the critical factor. In a recent survey (Lever, 1994), nine of ten gay and bisexual men reported that they believed that they were born with their sexual orientation; women, however, tend to grant a role for choice and circumstance regarding their sexual self-identification (Esterberg, 1997; Golden, 1996). Thus not only is sexual orientation multiply determined, but the precise mix of biological, cultural, social, and psychosocial factors responsible for sexual orientation may vary across different individuals (Richardson, 1987).

Most importantly, however, knowing about the origins of sexual orientation may not necessarily tell us much about the outcomes of sexual orientation in different times and places, for different sexes and ethnic groups, and in different cultural and historic circumstances. Some researchers have argued that developmental outcomes deserve more scientific attention than origins (Boxer & Cohler, 1989). Debate also centers on whether explorations into etiology are at all useful for a developmental psychology of sexual orientation. We advocate a middle position that places the experiences of gay, lesbian, and bisexual individuals at the center of developmental psychology. Regardless of researchers' conclusions about the value of investigations into etiology, questions such as "how did I get this way" are immensely important to many sexual-minority youths and their families. Both those who experience their sexuality as essential and those who experience their sexuality as having been shaped by choice and circumstance deserve study.

The experiences of sexual minority youths who are progressing through sexual self-identification at increasingly early ages and who, if asked, eagerly tell researchers about their lives indicate that gay men and women and bisexuals are, in fact, *both* the same as everyone else *and* unique as a subgroup within the population. For example, some gay, lesbian, and bisexual individuals may indeed have sex-atypical brain structures and functioning; however, in many other areas of anatomy they are indistinguishable from heterosexuals. Regarding psychosocial domains, gay, bisexual, and lesbian adolescents face unique stresses not encountered by their heterosexual peers because they are growing up in a culture that presumes and prescribes exclusive heterosexuality. Undeniably, however, these adolescents face many of the same issues that confront their heterosexual counterparts, such as establishing a personal identity, resolving issues of autonomy and separation, and experiencing new sexual desires.

Bell and Weinberg's (1978) resolution to this web of similarities and differences was to argue persuasively for the concept of *homosexualities.* They provided data from adult lifestyle patterns that refuted the myth of a homogeneous gay/lesbian population. This was a start in the right direction. Our position is that researchers have been too intent on examining characteristics thought to distinguish "homosexual" from "heterosexual" samples and too lax in examining variations in origins, developmental processes, and outcomes within the diverse gay, lesbian, and bisexual populations. Thus, the task of developmental research is to investigate general characteristics of sexual-minority individuals *and* intrapopulation similarities and differences throughout the life course. Viewing development from a differential trajectories perspective heightens the focus on diversity within sexual-minority populations and is, we believe, the most scientifically sound approach to understanding the lives of lesbian, gay, and bisexual individuals.

CHILDHOOD ISSUES OF SEXUAL ORIENTATION

Orientation and Identity

To discuss sexual orientation as a context for development, the distinction between sexual orientation and sexual identity must be elaborated. A same-sex sexual orientation is a "consistent pattern of sexual arousal toward persons of the same gender encompassing fantasy, conscious attractions, emotional and romantic feelings, and sexual behaviors" (Remafedi, 1987, p. 331). Sexual identity refers to "organized sets of self-perceptions and attached feelings that an individual holds about self with regard to some social category" (Cass, 1984, p. 110). The contrast between these two constructs is often conceptualized as a distinction between an ever-present, invariant biological and psychological truth (sexual orientation) and a historic and culturally located social construction (sexual identity).

Although this distinction oversimplifies both constructs, it is useful in clarifying developmental issues for youths with same-sex attractions. For example, the differentiation between orientation and identity stipulates that an individual with a gay, bisexual, or lesbian sexual orientation need not claim or acknowledge a comparable sexual identity. A teenage boy may view his frequent sexual activity with other boys as "just sex" and continue to defensively think of himself as heterosexual (Savin-Williams & Rodriguez, 1993). Thus, while he appears to have a bisexual or gay sexual orientation, he has a heterosexual sexual identity. A bisexual-by-orientation adolescent girl may discover little support for this sexual orientation and thus identify as lesbian within the context of a lesbian community.

For adolescents with same-sex attractions, the most pressing developmental tasks concern the identity processes of self-recognition and self-labeling. Youths must first determine whether their same-sex attractions indicate a nonheterosexual orientation and then decide whether to forge ahead with the adoption of a gay, lesbian, or bisexual identity or attempt to preserve a heterosexual sexual identity. Once sexual-minority identity development has begun, developmental tasks shift to incorporate issues of disclosure. Who can and cannot be told? Who might ease the process and who might hinder it? How does one manage a stigmatized identity in mainstream society, among peers, and within the family?

Feelings of Differentness

The first manifestation of sexual orientation for many youths is a vague but pervasive sense that one is "different" from others (Bell et al., 1981; Isay, 1989; Newman & Muzzonigro, 1993; Savin-Williams, 1998a; Troiden, 1979). This sense is present in some rudimentary form for many years before the ability to reflect and label sexual feelings and attractions; for some, this sense comprises one of their earliest memories (Herdt & Boxer, 1993; Savin-Williams, 1998a). The existence of these early feelings implies that these children have an awareness both of a normative standard of behavior and a belief that they violate this standard. Behaviors or ideations that violate traditional norms of gendered behavior have been indexed by a variety of terms. Here, we collectively refer to these phenomena as *gender atypicality*.

Initially, feeling different is not explicitly linked with same-sex attractions but with gender atypicality. Troiden (1989) noted:

> It is not surprising that "prehomosexuals" used gender metaphors, rather than sexual metaphors, to interpret and explain their childhood feelings of difference.... [C]hildren do not appear to define their sexual experimentation in heterosexual or homosexual terms. The socially created categories of homosexual, heterosexual, and bisexual hold little or no significance for them. (p. 52)

Children do not wonder "why am I gay" but "why am I different?" These feelings often eventuate in feelings of marginality, alienation, and isolation from family, peers, and the larger society.

The basis for these feelings is difficult to discern because "pre-homosexual" children have never been asked to reflect on these issues. Retrospective data from adolescents and young adults indicate four sources: a strongly felt desire to engage in play activities and to possess gender-atypical or gender-neutral interests or traits; an early, pervasive, and emotional captivation with same-sex peers or adults that feels passionate, exotic, exciting, and mysterious; a disinterest or even revulsion in the activities and characteristics of one's sex; and a vague sense that although one does not desire intimate relations with the opposite sex, one is not sure what he or she *does* want (Bailey & Zucker, 1995; Savin-Williams, 1998a; Troiden, 1989).

Some youths act on their erotic attractions prior to pubertal onset and engage in childhood same-sex activities. These "sex play" encounters are rarely experienced as indicative of sexual identity. At the same time, early same-sex activities may not be as capricious for sexual-minority youths as they are for heterosexual youths who engage in sex play primarily for curiosity or sexual release.

Because most studies on the development of sexual orientation have focused on males, it is impossible to know whether feelings of "differentness" are as common among girls. Western culture socializes girls to believe that women do not generally enjoy or desire sex as often and as powerfully as men do, and this may inhibit women's experiences of their own sexuality (Blackwood, 1985; Faraday, 1981; Palladino & Stephenson, 1990). This could also affect a young lesbian's feelings of differentness: A girl who does not feel attracted to boys may simply attribute this to the fact that girls are not supposed to be very interested in sex. This provides a partial explanation for the fact that girls who *do* view themselves as "sexually different" label these feelings as lesbian considerably later than their male counterparts (Bell et al., 1981; Califia, 1979; Troiden, 1988). Finally, it bears noting that not all gay, lesbian, or bisexual individuals recall feeling different while growing up; also, some heterosexuals have such memories during their childhood. Examinations of sexual-minority development must take this aspect of diversity into account.

Gender Atypicality

Feeling different is one thing; acting and appearing different is quite another. The question of whether gay men are disproportionately feminine and lesbians, masculine has been at different times ubiquitous, redundant, or taboo. Although gender atypicality among children has been studied by sex researchers as a unique developmental phenomenon (Money, 1988), it is also a possible childhood correlate of adult sexual orientation (Bailey, 1996; Bailey & Zucker, 1995). In fact, it is one of the best predictors, along with adolescent same-sex sexual activity, of adult homosexuality (Bell et al., 1981).

Characteristics studied include both observable behaviors such as participation in "rough-and-tumble" play, athletic activities, play with sex-typed toys, and cross-dressing, as well as stated interests such as wishing to be the opposite sex and preference for male or female friends (for a review of studies using these measures, see Bailey and Zucker, 1995). The research findings from prospective studies using these variables (Green, 1987; Zuger, 1984) are fairly straightforward: The number of extremely feminine boys who eventually profess a same-sex sexual orientation is significantly higher than expected by chance. However, it appears likely, although unconfirmed, that the proportion of gender-atypical boys in the population remains below the proportion of gay men (Bailey, 1996). Thus, while a majority of extremely feminine boys eventually adopt a gay identity in adulthood, an unknown number of adult gay men were not particularly feminine during their childhood.

Although the small number of studies on gender-atypical girls parallels the findings on boys, the effect is less consistent and less robust (Bailey & Zucker, 1995; Bell et al., 1981; Grellert, Newcomb, & Bentler, 1982). For example, although Phillips and Over (1995) reported that lesbian women recalled more gender-atypical behavior in childhood than both bisexual and heterosexual women, there was considerable overlap among groups. Some lesbians recalled typically feminine childhoods while some heterosexual women reported having been tomboys. A recent study of female sexual-minority youth found no relationship between reports of childhood gender atypicality and/or feelings of differentness and adult same-sex attractions (Diamond, 1998).

Further complicating this picture is the finding that many youths who exhibited gender-atypical behavior in childhood ceased to exhibit this behavior in adulthood. This is because many youths who were feminine boys or masculine girls defeminized or demasculinized during adolescence (Harry, 1983; Whitam, 1977). LeVay (1993) suggested that such changes may have both biological and social origins: Pubertal increases in androgens and estrogens may stimulate the development of "dormant" gender-typical traits, while societal pressures may compel adolescents to conform more closely to gender-based norms as they approach adulthood.

To further understand the relationship between early gender atypicality and later sexual orientation, these and other conditions must be investigated. In addition, more research remains to be carried out with girls. Although the small number of studies on masculine girls parallel the findings on boys, the effect is of a smaller magnitude (Bailey, 1996; Bell et al., 1981; Grellert, Newcomb, & Bentler, 1982).

However, it is important to acknowledge that in the current political climate, such research is controversial. Powerfully negative stereotypes of gay men and lesbians as highly gender atypical exist in many if not most cultures, and the psychological research on gender atypicality among children has been interpreted by some individuals as reinforcing the very stereotypes that gay men and women have been attempting to dismantle. In light of this debate, it is crucially important to highlight the following point: Neither the proponents nor the detractors of this research should make the mistake of assuming that sexual orientation and gender atypicality are the *same phenomenon* or that they should be taken as generalizable indicators of each other. These studies are not "about" gay men; they are "about" extremely feminine boys. The fact that such boys disproportionately adopt same-sex sexual orientations does not make the findings generalizable to the many gay men, lesbians, and bisexuals who either are not gender atypical in childhood or adolescence or not to clinically relevant degrees.

Until more is known about the relationship between gender atypicality and sexual orientation, the two are most appropriately viewed as parallel developments that may, but need not, intersect in the life course of a particular individual (Carter & McCloskey, 1984; Damon, 1979; Lamb & Roopnarine, 1979). Clearly, when these phenomena intersect, important developmental consequences occur that deserve serious attention. For example, regardless of the reasons why a girl may be gender atypical, the same girl may strategically mobilize masculine and feminine attributes for different reasons at different points during her life course. Some young gay men exaggerate their masculinity to avoid stigmatization; others do so as a mark of difference that divides them from their heterosexual counterparts and symbolically unites them with their sexual-minority peers. Finally, some adolescents may experiment with gender simply because they have the opportunity. Garnets and Kimmel (1993) noted that such individuals are often "encouraged or permitted by their deviance from accepted norms to explore androgynous gender role behavior, independence, self-reliance, and educational and occupational options" (p. 7). Gender atypicality, then, may be far more than a surface phenomenon of appearance and behavior; it may have a significant developmental role in the process whereby individuals move from acknowledging same-sex attractions to negotiating and embracing a gay, lesbian, or bisexual identity.

Gender and Cultural Differences

The existing research suggests that explicit gender atypicality has fewer detrimental consequences for women than for men (Fagot, 1977; Harry, 1983; O'Heron, 1990; Sears, 1989). This may reflect both the rigidity of the Western male role and Western cultural misogyny. In his review of the research on childhood gender atypicality and its relationship to sexual orientation, Bailey (1996) speculated that there are probably far more female tomboys than feminine boys, and thus there must necessarily exist a large proportion of female tomboys who develop a heterosexual orientation. Before making broad conclusions about possible biological causes of this sex difference, it is important to note that in Western culture behaviors that cause a girl to be labeled "tomboy" by her parents or peers are those that are most esteemed in society: physical prowess, assertiveness, confidence, and athleticism, among others (Feinman, 1981). Perhaps it is "only natural" that young girls would experiment with these traits until they receive the societal message that "girls do not behave this way." To draw a sharp contrast, one might imagine the peers of a feminine boy asking, "Why would anyone want to be a girl?" In fact, parents of feminine boys answer this rhetorical question with a suspicion of same-sex desires more frequently than do the parents of masculine girls (Ant-hill, 1987; Block, 1983; Bolton & MacEachron, 1988).

Thus, in a society that values masculine over feminine traits, gender-atypical boys are problematized far more consistently and fervently than gender-atypical girls. Fagot (1977) found that girls who exhibited moderate cross-sex behavior were treated no differently than gender-typical girls, while moderate cross-sex behavior in boys led to peer rejection. This further implies that gender-atypical boys may be made aware of their "difference" at earlier ages than girls, resulting in distinctive psychological trajectories. Clearly, researchers must remain mindful of the differential social responses that accrue to gender-atypical behavior among boys and girls when attempting to draw causal inferences and identify predictors.

Limited research has also addressed whether gender atypicality is more or less prevalent in particular ethnic cultures. Ethnic communities vary in their expectations on appropriate masculine and feminine behaviors and roles for their children. For example, "etiqueta," the proper sex role for Latina girls, prescribes patience, nurturance, passivity, and subservience. Girls are showpieces to be adorned; they are virginal, docile, and faithful. Given this traditional view, few are concerned that Latina girls will become lesbian, in large part because they are not considered overtly sexual. Lesbians are thought to be outsiders who embrace masculine ways by being headstrong and independent (Hidalgo & Hidalgo-Christensen, 1976/1977; Ramos, 1994; Romo-Carmona, 1994).

A traditional virtue common in Latino communities stipulates that boys should appear defiantly heterosexual—embracing and enacting the social construct of "machismo." They are expected to personify traditional masculine traits such as courage, aggressiveness, power, and invulnerability (Carrier, 1989; Parker, 1989). Male homosexuality is equated with effeminacy and assumption of the passive role in sexual relations (Magana & Carrier, 1991). Thus, Carrier (1989) suggested that Mexican boys who exhibit feminine behavior and who have same-sex attractions more easily self-identify as gay in adulthood. A Mexican (Magana & Carrier, 1991) or Cuban (Young, 1981) boy who assumes the inserter role in anal intercourse but embraces traditional masculine behavior may rationalize that he is a heterosexual who occasionally enjoys sex with other boys. Because a masculine youth will seldom be considered gay by his culture, he may experience a much more difficult time accepting and embracing this identity.

Within Asian communities, a discrepancy between behavior sanctioned in the "homeland" and its subsequent interpretation following immigration to the United States is not uncommon among first and second generation Asian communities. For example, in Vietnam homosexuality is equated with femininity and a half-male, half-female status. Nonetheless, some adolescent boys engage in same-sex behavior such as mutual masturbation and fellatio. Close physical contact, holding hands, and sleeping in the same bed are "normal" behaviors among boys that suggest little about future sexual identification (Carrier, Nguyen, & Su, 1992). In North America, however, a "masculine" Vietnamese adolescent male who engages in these same-sex activities would raise considerable concern among peers and family.

Regardless of ethnic heritage and sexual orientation, the pressures to conform to traditional definitions of gender can undermine the psychological integrity and identity formation of any child or adolescent. If the individual is trying to integrate a sexual identity with an existing ethnic identity, the maturation of a healthy self-concept can be considerably complicated.

Thinking about Difference

In reviewing research on childhood gender atypicality, it is important to remember that researchers know far more about gender-atypical children than about gay, lesbian, and bisexual children. Because of the constraints of retrospective data, reliable generalizations about such children and their developmental experiences are very limited. Again, the diversity of lesbian, gay, and bisexual experiences must be emphasized. Although many gender-atypical children become gay, lesbian, or bisexual, many gender-normative children develop into lesbian, gay, or bisexual adults. A developmental psychology that can only describe one type of developmental trajectory into gay, lesbian, or bisexual adulthood is unacceptable, misleading, and ultimately uninformative.

ADOLESCENT ISSUES OF SEXUAL ORIENTATION

The vast majority of theory and research on adolescent developmental issues with clinical implications for sexual-minority populations has been based on coming-out models. These theoretical models, frequently referenced in the developmental and clinical literature (e.g., Cass, 1979, 1984; Coleman, 1981/1982; Troiden, 1979, 1989), characterize the life histories of nonheterosexual individuals in terms of the stages by which they move from first awareness of homo-erotic interests to an integration and perhaps celebration of that status.[1] Coming-out models are so pervasive in their scholarly and popular appeal and so convincing in their logic that seemingly the only topic worthy of discussion is which model best describes the lives of preadult lesbians, gays, and bisexuals. However, coming-out models may thwart an understanding of the diversity of those very lives if individuals whose trajectories violate these models are ignored and if alternative developmental processes experienced by sexual-minority adolescents are never investigated.

Coming-Out Models

Coming-out models suggest that pregay individuals move through a number of "ideal-typical" stages (Troiden, 1979) en route to mature, nonheterosexual adulthood. These structural models are cast in a somewhat orderly series of stages based on a particular theoretical understanding of human development, including analytic, cognitive, symbolic inter-action, and social-learning perspectives. With few exceptions, their empirical base is extraordinarily weak, in large part because they are top-down models and because few researchers have been willing to investigate the methodological complexities of assessing these models.

Sophie (1985/1986) delineated four stages of identity development that characterize most coming-out models:

1. First awareness or an initial cognitive and emotional realization that one is "different," a feeling of alienation from oneself and others, and some awareness that homosexuality is the relevant issue.
2. Testing and exploration that precede acceptance of one's homosexuality and initial but limited contact with gay and lesbian individuals or communities.
3. Identity acceptance with disclosure to heterosexuals, a preference for social interactions with other gays and lesbians, and a negative identity that gives way to a positive identity.
4. Identity integration in which the self is viewed as gay or lesbian with accompanying anger and pride, publicly coming-out to many others, and identity stability with an unwillingness to change.

Such models have been useful in describing the broad outlines by which *some* sexual minorities progress from an assumed heterosexual adolescence to a lesbian, gay, or bisexual adulthood. However, provisions for alternative pathways that allow other sexual minorities to achieve the final endpoint of self-labeling and full disclosure are seldom ac-knowledged or discussed. For example, some individuals report that they never experienced a series of discrete events constituting a "coming-out process." Rather, their sexual identity development was a gradual, progressive, and continuous endeavor with some discontinuities—"a series of realignments in perception, evaluation, and commitment" (Davies, 1992, p. 75). Others deny that a coming-out process characterized their adolescence because they were never in doubt about their identity; in a sense, they had always been "out" to themselves, if not to others. Still others forgo the adoption of a stable sexual identity altogether, instead acknowledging the ever-present possibility of change in the quality and quantity of their sexual and emotional attractions to men and women (Diamond, 1998).

Furthermore, these models often fail to incorporate the experiences of women, bisexuals, people of color, and those from various social classes, religious groups, and regional areas. This homogenization of developmental processes across populations is, in our view, a serious deficit. For example, Golden (1996) argued that women's sexual orientation may not be definitively established by adolescence or stable throughout the life course. This may account for the finding that some women undergo changes in sexual identity over time that are completely unpredicted by traditional coming-out models; others complete stages in the "wrong" order (Sophie, 1985/1986). Diamond (1998) found that nearly one third of young sexual-minority women began questioning their sexuality *before* experiencing same-sex attractions, directly contradicting the basic sequence of events outlined in most coming-out models. Thus, caution is advised regarding any attempt to apply the general conclusions of this research to particular individuals without careful examination of characteristics of the research subjects.

We prefer to avoid the term "coming-out" because its vague, generalized usage blurs rather than sharpens an understanding of the diverse ways in which sexual-minority individuals of different ages, sexes, ethnicities, and social backgrounds manage the processes of sexual identity development. In its stead we emphasize two processes that occupy a central role in the experiences of many sexual minorities—sexual questioning and disclosure to others. Unlike traditional coming-out models, we do not presume that these processes occur in a particular order, although the first usually precedes the second. Nor do we presume that they constitute discrete, finite events that lead inexorably to the adoption of a stable nonheterosexual identity. Contrary to the assumptions inherent in most coming-out models, we maintain that individuals may initiate sexual questioning and/or disclosure to others at any age, may revisit these processes multiple times over the life course, and may terminate them without adopting a gay, lesbian, or bisexual identity.

Sexual Questioning

Sexual questioning encompasses a series of internal processes by which individuals assess, recognize, and interpret features of their subjective experience that violate heterosexual norms. As noted earlier, sexual questioning often begins with an early sense of being different from others and of strongly felt attractions to the same sex, whether emotional or sexual in nature. Some youths progress to the point of labeling these same-sex desires as membership in a socially defined, sexual identity category, such as lesbian, gay, or bisexual—and others do not.

Although the process of sexual questioning may begin during childhood, for many youths the growing realization that one is not heterosexual increases exponentially after pubertal onset (Coleman, 1981/1982; Remafedi, 1987; Troiden, 1979). It is as if puberty gives sexual meaning and (sometimes) unwanted clarity to heretofore poorly understood feelings and attractions. Perhaps the dramatic increase in hormonal production sexualizes a youth's cognitions, affects, and behaviors as well as her or his physical appearance. In addition, because a youth now looks, acts, thinks, and emotes sexuality, others understand and interact with her or him in a sexual manner. It is at this point that socially defined sexual identity labels become cognitively important in the sexual questioning process. Adoption of a sexual identity label often gives concrete meaning to formerly vague and misunderstood feelings and affords a context in which future thoughts, emotions, and experiences can be understood.

Facilitative factors may ease or speed the transition from an assumed heterosexual identity to a gay, lesbian, or bisexual identity. For example, because European American culture presupposes a linkage between gender-atypical characteristics and sexual orientation, those who exhibited gender atypicality in childhood, same-sex arousal and behavior during adolescence, and an absence of heterosexual experiences may most easily come to adopt a sexual-minority identity (Harry, 1982; Troiden, 1989). By contrast and implication, teenagers who are gender congruent in their behavior, lack same-sex encounters, and have had heterosexual experiences should have the most difficult time self-labeling as gay, lesbian, or bisexual. Internalization of cultural values and beliefs about homosexuality may also lead some youths to postpone completion of the self-labeling process for several years, decades, or a lifetime. This may prove particularly salient in certain income and ethnic groups. Among ethnic youths, personal identity often intersects with culture, class, and gender-specific reference group identities (Cross, 1991).

In integrating sexual and ethnic/class identity, ethnic minority adolescents must negotiate a formidable task not present among many majority youths (Icard, 1986; Tremble, Schneider, & Appathurai, 1989).

Perhaps because of the recent visibility of gay, lesbian, and bisexual issues and individuals in the media, current cohorts of sexual-minority youths are questioning and labeling their sexual orientation at increasingly younger ages (Herdt & Boxer, 1993; Savin-Williams, 1990, 1998a). This public focus may eventually render needless the most rigid defenses of homoerotically inclined adolescents who deny or ignore their same-sex attractions altogether. However, it is important to note that although the adoption of a gay, lesbian, or bisexual identity label constitutes a positive, psychologically healthy resolution of the sexual questioning process for most youths with same-sex attractions (Savin-Williams, 1990), this is not the only alternative. Some youths openly reject heterosexual labels *without* embracing a gay, lesbian, or bisexual label, particularly those who experience attractions for both sexes. The scant research that has been conducted on these youths suggests that although they may face difficult pressures from friends, family members, and romantic partners to "pick" an identity, they often feel as comfortable and happy with their sexuality as youths who identify as gay, lesbian, or bisexual, choosing to remain open to all relationship possibilities (Diamond, 1997)

Future research is clearly necessary to examine the similarities and differences between these youths and those who adopt lesbian, gay, or bisexual identity labels. In the meantime, however, researchers and clinicians should take care not to conflate the rejection of an identity label with the denial of one's subjective sexual feelings. Although the latter may prove maladaptive in the long run, the former may not.

Disclosure to Others

Another unique developmental process that many lesbian, bisexual, and gay individuals face is disclosure of information about their same-sex attractions, sexual experiences, or sexual identity to others. Disclosure may occur prior to sexual questioning, in the midst of sexual questioning, or (most usually) after a gay, bisexual, or lesbian self-identification has been at least tentatively adopted. Final disclosure may never be achieved because there is always someone new to tell, although individuals are often defined as "totally out" when they no longer care who knows about their sexual orientation.

The process of disclosing to others can be arduous and protracted. Many youths choose to conceal their same-sex attractions from others because they more strongly fear negative reprisals than anticipate the long-term positive, healthy consequences of disclosure to others. Many who recognize their same-sex attractions keep them secretive because they fear the unknown; wish not to hurt or disappoint a loved one, or want to avoid being rejected, verbally harassed, or physically abused by parents and peers (Savin-Williams, 1994). Some choose to compartmentalize their lives by developing two distinct groups of friends: those who know and those who do not (Davies, 1992).

When inquiring about disclosure, it is critical to distinguish among who is told earliest, who is most difficult to disclose to, and who is most important to tell. It is also critical to determine *what* information is disclosed. Although some youths may announce that they are lesbian, bisexual, or gay, others may simply reveal that they have same-sex attractions, or that they once engaged in same-sex sexual activity. For some youths, the process of discussing their feelings is a key component of the sexual questioning process, and thus they may not have reached any solid conclusions about their sexual identity by the time they begin disclosing to others.

Youths usually reveal their same-sex-attractions first to close friends who are likely to understand and offer support (Herdt & Boxer, 1993; Savin-Williams, 1990, 1998a). Because parents are often most difficult to tell, youths may delay disclosing to parents until they feel absolutely certain about adopting a gay, lesbian, or bisexual identity, often waiting until they are involved in a serious same-sex relationship. Perhaps no single event evokes more fear and anxiety than disclosure to parents. Notwithstanding, many youths report never fully feeling comfortable or "out" until they disclose their sexual orientation to parents (D'Augelli, 1991; Savin-Williams, 1996, 1998b).

Ethnic minority youths have many of the same difficulties as do majority youths in disclosing a nonheterosexual sexual identity to their families. However, cultural issues frequently complicate the process, as Morales (1983) noted in his discussion of the constellation of the traditional ethnic family:

> The ethnic family support system resembles more of a tribe with multiple family groups rather than a nuclear family structure consisting solely of parents and children. For the ethnic person the family constitutes a symbol of their basic roots and the focal point of their ethnic identity. (p. 9)

These youths may thus feel that they can never publicly disclose same-sex attractions for fear of humiliating that which is most important in their life—the close-knit family that extends beyond immediate members to include multiple generations. They must contend with maintaining family honor, fulfilling expectations of marriage, and satisfying cultural

definitions of masculinity and femininity. Thus, a wall of silence is likely to form around an ethnic family with a lesbian, gay, or bisexual child. Even if a youth advances to the point of self-recognition of sexual status, the inhibitions against stating this publicly may lead him or her to significantly delay self-disclosure or completely forgo disclosure to parents (Chan, 1989, 1995; Wooden, Kawasaki, & Mayeda, 1983; Hidalgo & Hidalgo-Christensen, 1976/1977).

Gender Differences in Sexual Identity Development

The literature on gay, lesbian, and bisexual identity development recounts a diverse array of gender differences. The process of lesbian identity development is frequently triggered by nonsexual cues and events (Blumstein & Schwartz, 1990; Cass, 1990). For many women, a lesbian or bisexual identity is bound not only in same-sex desires, but also in ideology, reference groups, and a rejection of, or commitment to, particular roles (Cooper, 1990; Silber, 1990). Same-sex erotic attraction is a necessary, but not sufficient condition for the formation of a lesbian or bisexual identity (Nichols, 1990), and sexual behavior may have a similar status. Women are less likely than men to adopt a same-sex identity on the basis of one or two same-sex sexual experiences (Blumstein & Schwartz, 1993; deMonteflores & Schultz, 1978), and many self-identified lesbians continue to engage in (albeit infrequent) sexual contact with men (Chapman & Brannock, 1987; Diamond, 1998; Rust, 1992).

Clearly, the process of developing a sexual identity congruent with sexual orientation is not identical for women and men. Moreover, gender differences may extend to the level of sexual orientation itself. As noted previously, research suggests that while men define their sexuality as essential in nature, women are more likely to experience their sexuality as fluid and variable over the life course (Esterberg, 1994, 1997; Golden, 1996; Lever, 1994; Rust, 1992, 1993; Whisman, 1993). Models of sexual development positing sexual orientation as definitively established during adolescence and undergoing little subsequent change do not characterize most women. These observations may provide a partial explanation for the fact that women label their feelings as lesbian considerably later than their male counterparts (Bell et al., 1981; Califia, 1979; Troiden. 1988). First, women do not organize their sexuality solely around physical cues; second, these cues themselves may be conflicting. Women may therefore require interpersonal contexts (e.g., a community of women) in which to make sense of their sexual feelings and to transform them from "orientation" to "identity."

This interpretation is supported by the fact that women do not necessarily interpret sexual flexibility as bisexuality.

Some women who engage in sexual relationships with both women and men alternate between heterosexual and lesbian identifications according to the gender of their current partner and identify as bisexual during the periods between partners (Blumstein & Schwartz, 1976; Diamond, 1997). Thus, although sexuality may remain fluid over the life course, discrete moments of sexual attraction and behavior become concretized into identity through the context in which they occur.

Finally, studies have consistently reported that lesbians disclose their sexual identity at a slightly older age than do gay males. Several reasons for this robust gender gap have been suggested. Women may take longer to connect "feeling different" with their same-sex erotic feelings and behaviors because physical affection between women is socially acceptable in Western culture; greater sexual fluidity among women may render bisexuality a more prevalent option for women than for men (Golden, 1996), prolonging the disclosure process; and lesbian identity "may be more contingent upon the complete understanding of the internal, private aspects of sexual identity rather than the public, social aspects," while young gay men may disclose earlier in order to use social and sexual arenas to "work through" their sexual identity (Dubé, Giovanni, & Willemsen, 1995, p. 10). Thus, lesbians may be more likely than gay men to integrate their sexual identity with other aspects of personal identity before disclosing this intimacy to others. Consistent with this view, in a study by Schafer, lesbians were more likely than gay men to disclose their sexual identity within an affectionate, romantic relationship with another woman (Schafer, 1976); to be discriminating in their disclosure, divulging first to close friends before family and the general public; to believe that they had a choice in their sexual identity; and, once fully disclosed, to feel most comfortable with their sexual identity (Savin-Williams, 1990).

Conclusion

Although we have emphasized the distinction between privately questioning one's sexual identity and disclosing same-sex attractions to others, these processes are not completely independent. Instead, they exist in a dialectic relationship, as noted by Davies (1992): "Coming out to others constantly redefines one's notion of self and the development of a self-identity drives the process of disclosure" (p. 76). Not only do individuals who engage in sexual questioning often feel compelled to discuss their concerns with supportive friends, but any report that it was the process of discussing "the hypothetical possibility" of same-sex relationships with a friend or a lover that prompted them to actively question their sexual identity (Diamond, 1997).

Although coming-out models posit a sequential relationship between self-labeling and disclosure to others, in reality some youths recognize their nonheterosexual identity and never disclose to others. They may acknowledge to themselves their homoerotic desires but never disclose this information because they feel they must maintain a particular social class status, because they grew up within a culturally repressive context (e.g., rural Midwest); or because they have committed themselves to a religiously celibate life. Some, perhaps many, adolescents resolve to conceal their homoerotic affections as a final solution to their "homosexual crisis." This may be a short-term resolution, "until I get to college," or a life-long pattern.

The reverse, disclosure to others of same-sex attractions without experiencing the self as having a gay, bisexual, or lesbian identity, is exemplified by adolescents who are known or highly suspected of being gay or lesbian before they arrive at that same realization. Such adolescents may engage in same-sex encounters, thus revealing their sexual orientation to sexual partners, while denying to themselves that their behavior implicates a nonheterosexual identity. A particular case is the African American or Latino male youth who, for cultural reasons, does not construe same-sex behavior as meaningful to his self-identification because he maintains the "active" role in sexual encounters (Manalansan, 1996). Thus, youths may indirectly or nonverbally disclose their homosexuality or bisexuality to another but never arrive at that same conclusion.

CLINICAL CONCERNS

The processes of self-recognition, labeling, and disclosure have the potential to affect many dimensions of adolescents' life, including emotional and psychological well-being, self-concept, personal identity, and interpersonal relationships. Although most youths successfully navigate these identity terrains to become healthy, well-functioning adults, it is not always an easy travail. Some attempt suicide and others are left with permanent physical, emotional, cognitive, and social scars. The effects of peer and adult harassment and abuse that lead sexual-minority youths to run away from home, abuse drugs and alcohol, engage in criminal behavior, become sex workers, or kill themselves have been reviewed elsewhere (Savin-Williams, 1994). The focus here is on the normative concerns that clinicians and other mental health professionals will likely face in their clinical practice. These are situations in which they have opportunities to help bisexual, lesbian, and gay youths shift from a developmental trajectory of instability, fear, and anxiety to one of stability, growth, and health.

At the outset it must be noted that a unique dilemma faced by clinicians and other health care professions in offering counseling or therapeutic assistance to bisexual, gay, and lesbian adolescents is that such youths seldom come for help when they most need it. They cannot solicit or accept help for a problem they claim does not exist. They may also fear disclosure, humiliation, and discrimination (Gonsiorek, 1996). When these youths present for therapy, clinicians can best help if they are prepared with knowledge and understanding.

Feeling Different and Self-Labeling

Of issue here are the difficulties youths face in labeling their attractions and identity as lesbian, gay, or bisexual *before* disclosing this information to others. Whether real or imagined, these difficulties negatively affect youths and their development. For example, a feeling of being alone, deserted, or in a "vacuum" characterizes the childhood of many youths who eventually identify as bisexual, gay, or lesbian. Such youths feel that they belong nowhere and have no base of support. These feelings may have profound repercussions for the balance of self-acceptance and self-rejection that evolves during adolescence.

Given that contact with other gay, lesbian, and bisexual individuals can often assuage feelings of loneliness, youths raised in small, rural towns in which there is little exposure to and acceptance of diversity have limited access to supportive resources, which exacerbates their feelings of isolation (D'Augelli & Hart, 1987; Sears, 1991). Small town youths may fear detection, verbal and physical assault, or communitywide ostracism on discovery of a same-sex relationship.

The task of reconciling the cultural condemnation of homosexuality with one's own homoerotic attractions poses a formidable developmental challenge. At a time when most youths are gradually building self-esteem and establishing personal identity, lesbian, gay and bisexual youths are often struggling with their homoerotic attractions, causing delay in achieving a positive identity. A recent survey of high school students gave substance to the perception of sexual-minority adolescents who feel that they are among the most hated in society: Prejudice against sexual minorities was reported to be twice as frequent as that against ethnic minorities (High Achieving Students, 1994). To hide their sexual orientation in response to these threats results in strained and dishonest interactions with friends, parents, teachers, and others, which may ultimately undermine the development of a positive self-image.

Disclosure to Others

Disclosure of sexual identity to others poses a number of developmental and clinical hurdles. Rotheram-Borus, Rosario,

and Koopman (1991) reported that sexual-minority youths felt most vulnerable and out of control when they "came out" to others, had their sexuality discovered by others, or were ridiculed because of their sexual orientation. It is a risky venture, and adolescents may have legitimate concerns about their physical and psychological safety if their sexual orientation were to be known. At the same time, disclosure may result in a greater sense of freedom and being oneself, of not living a lie, and of experiencing genuine acceptance (Fitzpatrick, 1983).

This conflict between the possible benefits and drawbacks of disclosure is especially pronounced when youths consider disclosing to their families (Savin-Williams, 1996, 1998b). Not infrequently, gay, lesbian, and bisexual youths disclose their sexual orientation to family members while still living at home. This contrasts sharply with earlier generations of gay, lesbian, and bisexual individuals, many of whom remained closeted until they moved out of the household, when "parental responses could be held at a distance" (D'Augelli & Hershberger, 1993, p. 443). Clearly, adolescents who disclose their sexual identity to parents while still living at home must cope with parental responses more frequently, more immediately, and for longer periods of time than those who do not, thus placing them at greater risk for the negative outcomes associated with stigmatization such as decreased self-esteem, running away from home, substance abuse, and suicide (Savin-Williams, 1994).

At the same time, these adolescents are generally assumed to experience the diverse array of positive mental health outcomes that are associated with disclosure, including identity synthesis and integration (Cass, 1979; Coleman, 1981/1982), healthy psychological adjustment (Gonsiorek & Rudolph, 1991), decreased feelings of loneliness and guilt (Dank, 1973), and higher self-esteem (Savin-Williams, 1990). Disclosure to parents in particular reduces the stress that accrues to adolescents who are actively hiding their sexual orientation (Cohen & Savin-Williams, 1996).

Because both positive and negative effects of early disclosure have been reported, clinicians and other service providers should not make blanket recommendations to youths on whether to disclose to parents. Instead, they should consider family characteristics shown to correlate with positive and negative responses and attempt to make important distinctions between families to whom adolescents should disclose (to experience positive outcomes associated with disclosure) and families to whom adolescents should not disclose, at least not until the adolescent moves out of the home (to avoid the potentially debilitating experience of rejection). Unfortunately, little research addresses family characteristics that influence parental response to adolescent disclosure. Nothing is known, for example, about the role of family structure in this process: Adolescents living with both biological (or adoptive) parents may have more positive disclosure experiences than adolescents living with single parents or blended families because of the lower levels of interpersonal support available to single parents and the higher levels of stress that may accrue to blended families.

Single parents, however, may be less likely to hold rigid beliefs concerning the importance of a traditional family structure and may therefore be less likely to reject their sexual-minority child on this basis. Newman and Muzzonigro (1993) found that family traditionality, a compound variable subsuming the importance of religion, an emphasis on marriage and having children, and the use of a non-English language in the home, predicted negative parental responses to adolescent disclosure of sexual orientation in a diverse sample of gay male adolescents. This point assumes further importance when one considers the fact that negative parental responses impair adolescent development more strongly than positive or neutral responses foster it through openness (Kahn, 1991). For this reason, it may be more important and particularly efficacious for clinicians to steer adolescents away from strongly negative experiences than to optimize the timing and context of their disclosure to parents.

Although family structure and family traditionality are important areas for examination in this context, it bears repeated emphasis that not nearly enough is known about the manner in which various family characteristics interact to prefigure parental responses to adolescent disclosure. For example, although family traditionality as a whole predicts negative responses, there have been conflicting findings on the effect of family religiosity on parental responses to disclosure (Cohen & Savin-Williams, 1996). Although strict religious dogmas generally condemn homosexuality, these same dogmas may simultaneously emphasize the fundamental importance of family unity, a theme which may moderate the impact of traditionality. For example, Tremble and colleagues (1989) found that parents from Asian, Portuguese, Greek, Italian, and Indo-Pakistani cultural backgrounds who adjusted best to their offspring's homosexuality maintained, "You are my child and I love you no matter what" (p. 259). Thus, family themes, structure, and traditionality are important characteristics for clinicians to consider when faced with the task of guiding adolescents through the difficult decision of whether and when to disclose their sexual orientation to the family.

Defenses against External and Internalized Homophobia

Psychological defenses are frequently used by lesbian, gay, and bisexual youths to reduce the intrapsychic ambivalence that results when confronted with their homoerotic desires. One frequent defense is *repression* of same-sex desires. Eventually, of course, the impulses must emerge, eliciting panic or causing a major disruption of established coping strategies (Malyon, 1981). With this defense youths have little opportunity to integrate same-sex desires with their identity.

A second defense is *denial*. Tripp (1975) suggested that gay males who yield to their need for homoerotic stimulation often use denial by assuming the masculine role during sex, claiming innocence because of drunkenness or drugs, or excusing it as simply a "special friendship." In its more extreme forms, denial may result in attempts to alter sexual orientation through conversion or reparative therapy offered by therapists or religious personnel. In desperation youths may pray, date the other sex, or deny that they are sexual beings. Some may consciously choose to remain celibate, while others may unconsciously redirect their energies toward intellectual, work, or athletic pursuits. For most, these defenses prove unsuccessful and ultimately counterproductive. They may result in a temporary developmental moratorium and truncated identity formation. They may also lead to distinct underachievment or overachievment in school, unhappy interpersonal relationships with family and friends, and chronic psychological disequilibrium.

Another defense is to acknowledge same-sex attractions but to *dismiss their significance:* "It's just a phase that I'll outgrow," "I've heard all guys/girls do it once," or "It was just curiosity" (Savin-Williams & Rodriguez, 1993). Adolescents may *rationalize* or attempt to find an "acceptable" reason for their behavior, such as "I only did it because I was lonely," "It was just a means to earn money," or they engaged in the act solely for sexual gratification, rather than for a "love" of the same gender. This allows them to maintain, "I may have homosexual sex, but I'm not a homosexual."

However, the fact that many sexual-minority adolescents dismiss the significance of their sexual attractions or sexual experiences does not mean that these attractions and experiences always constitute unambiguous markers of an underlying same-sex sexual orientation. Many adolescents experiment with sexual contact or have fleeting sexual desires that are unrelated to their underlying sexual predisposition. In a national representative sample of American adults, 9 percent of men reported having engaged in some form of same-sex sexual contact since puberty, but nearly half of these men never engaged in this contact again (Laumann, Gagnon, Michael, & Michaels, 1994). In their efforts to affirm the identities of sexual-minority youth, clinicians must be careful not to over-interpret experiences of same-sex sexual activity or ideation.

Laumann and colleagues' (1994) data show that women's rates of same-sex sexual contact do not show the same drop in adulthood, suggesting that women's same-sex sexual contact is less likely to occur in the context of adolescent experimentation. However, a number of heterosexual women report experiencing strong *emotional* feelings for same-sex friends that, although passionate and intense, may be unrelated to sexual interest and sexual orientation (Diamond, Savin-Williams, & Dubé, in press). Such relationships have long been documented in the historical literature, particularly among adolescent and college-age women (Faderman, 1981; Sahli, 1979). Again, clinicians should take care not to presume that any woman engaged in such friendships is "really" a lesbian or bisexual. Although such passionate friendships are often catalysts for sexual questioning among lesbian and bisexual women, their occurrence among heterosexual women should give us pause when attempting to interpret their significance. As with sexual experimentation, the most important task for clinicians is to avoid imposing *any* sexual identity on youths—heterosexual or sexual-minority—but to provide youths with information, support, acceptance, and safety they need to explore and resolve these issues for themselves.

Youths who conclude that they *are,* in fact, gay, lesbian, or bisexual frequently attempt to *pass* as heterosexual in order to avoid stigmatization (Dank, 1971; Martin, 1982). Sears (1991) reported that two-thirds of his sample of lesbian and gay youths from the South used this strategy; few openly objected to gay-related jokes by peers and almost 90 percent dated opposite-sex peers. In another study, 85 percent of adolescents pretended to be heterosexual some of the time (Newman & Muzzonigro, 1993). To facilitate passing, D'Augelli (1991) found that many gay college students changed the pronoun of their dating partner and/or pretended to date women. Partners or lovers were introduced as friends and most avoided discussing their personal lives with others. Passing, however, has its consequences, including feelings of depression, awkwardness, and shame in interpersonal relations. If healthy personality development requires significant and substantial self-disclosure to others, then to forego this by passing engenders feelings of hypocrisy and self-alienation (Martin, 1982).

Identity Management: Special Concerns of Ethnic Minority Youths

The complex network of situations in which ethnic minority lesbian, bisexual, and gay youths find themselves creates dual identities, multiple roles, and emotional conflicts (Greene, 1994). Management of these within a society dominated by affluent white Christian men can tax even the strongest of these youths. They face a daily struggle among who they are, who they want to be, and who others presume or wish them to be, problematizing the route toward a healthy and positive sexual identity.

Ideally these adolescents should have the opportunity to acquire unique information and social support from both lesbian/gay/bisexual communities and their particular ethnic community. The former can provide affirmation of sexuality and sexual identity, a place in which to relax and discuss openly same-sex relationships, and information about activities and organizations that provide services to other sexual-minority individuals. The latter can support and affirm cultural identification, offer a deep sense of heritage and values, and foster a unique and rich sense of self (Morales, 1983). Furthermore, ethnic minority youths who have mastered the skills of integrating and managing their ethnic minority status may be better prepared to integrate and manage their sexual-minority status.

Youths, however, who embrace both their ethnic and sexual identities may feel that neither identity is capable of validating the values, behaviors, and self-concepts invoked by the other. As a result, they may feel forced to choose a primary and exclusionary identification or to alternate identifications depending on changing contexts and varying opportunities for social support. For example, Tremble and colleagues (1989) noted that openly gay, bisexual, and lesbian youths often "excluded themselves from cultural activities in order to avoid shaming the family in front of friends" (p. 261). A gay Chinese adolescent best summarized the feelings of many ethnic sexual-minority youths: "I am a double minority. Caucasian gays don't like gay Chinese, and the Chinese don't like the gays. It would be easier to be white. It would be easier to be straight. It's hard to be both" (p. 263).

These experiences may expose youths to inordinate pain, as Morales noted (1983), "To live as a minority within a minority leads to heightened feelings of isolation, depression and anger centered around the fear of being separated from all support systems including the family" (p. 2). These effects may be moderated by both the recent cultural shifts in some ethnic communities toward a more liberal attitude about sexual orientation and the traditional heightened valuation of family unity that characterizes many ethnic minority families. These factors can make a tremendous difference for youths striving to accept homoerotic attractions without rejecting their family and ethnic community. Youths who experience stress as a result of living with a family that disapproves of, but basically tolerates, their sexual identity should be distinguished from those that are flatly rejected. The latter adolescents likely face a greater risk of seriously impaired mental health than the former. Again, clinicians may be able to help youths avoid the most negative outcomes by becoming familiar with the special characteristics of ethnic minority families that are associated with differential responses to adolescent disclosure of sexual orientation.

Overall, the most readily available and perhaps most effective remedy for the special stressors facing ethnic and sexual-minority youths is access to ethnic gay/lesbian/bisexual communities, an increasing number of which have developed in large urban areas or sponsor national publications, conferences, and activities. These communities provide access to role models who have accomplished that which youths may have always thought impossible: the successful and fulfilling management of a sexual- and ethnic minority identity. Just as contact with other gay, lesbian, and bisexual individuals facilitates development of a positive gay identity (Savin-Williams, 1990, 1998a), contact with gay, lesbian, and bisexual *ethnic minorities* may be the single most important factor in promoting positive developmental outcomes among ethnic sexual-minority youths.

Conclusion

These guidelines highlight some of the issues clinicians and service providers face in aiding gay, lesbian, and bisexual youths as they work toward self-acceptance and positive self-esteem. Because the size and diversity of the contemporary cohort of gay, lesbian, and bisexual youth are historically unprecedented, many clinicians lack experience with this population. Although we have outlined some of their primary normative concerns, the diversity of this population merits further emphasis. Not all sexual-minority youths experience a clear linear pattern of developmental tasks and crises beginning with feelings of differentness and moving toward self-recognition and full disclosure. As society's treatment of sexual-minority populations continues to change, "normative" developmental trajectories will remain in flux. For this reason, gaining familiarity with the general characteristics of sexual-minority youths and their unique stressors and struggles while remaining mindful of their diverse experiences and developmental trajectories allows clinicians to make a distinct improvement in the quality of care available to these adolescents.

Finally, it must be emphasized that in spite of their status as sexual minorities, the most pressing clinical concerns for many such youths may *not* be their sexual identity. Similar to all adolescents, they may struggle with finding and keeping satisfying relationships, with school and career success, with alcohol and drugs, and with keeping parents at a safe but appropriate distance. Although the stress of managing a stigmatized sexual identity may "raise the stakes" of these struggles, it is important for clinicians to remember that sex-

ual identity concerns may not be the overriding preoccupation of a sexual-minority youth who presents for treatment.

SUMMARY AND CONCLUSIONS

The developmental processes discussed in this chapter are not universal or fixed events but are subject to considerable variation. Some individuals report that they always knew that they were gay, lesbian, or bisexual and thus have no memory of a coming-out process, while others first become aware of same-sex attractions in early adulthood. Individual differences also exist in the timing and sequencing of many of the developmental processes noted in this chapter, including the ages at which developmental milestones are achieved and the ordering of the alleged universal stages of disclosure. It is in response to this pervasive variability that we propose a differential developmental trajectory perspective when considering sexual orientation as a context for child and adolescent development. Understanding that there is no one way to be gay enhances an appreciation of the general conditions as well as the specific experiences traversed by lesbian, gay, and bisexual youths.

Troiden (1989) cataloged various "facilitating factors" theorized to ease gay, bisexual, or lesbian identity development: education, supportive friends and family, early self-recognition, same-sex sexual experience, lack of heterosexual sexual experience, and sex atypicality. Although few of these have been systematically investigated, research has demonstrated that self-labeling and disclosure are occurring earlier with each new cohort of gay, bisexual, and lesbian youth, especially in urban, media-saturated, and collegiate communities. It is no longer extremely rare for the disclosure process to begin shortly after pubertal onset and to be essentially completed—out to friends, family, and the public—by the end of adolescence. These youths may very well need and demand the assistance of mental health professionals to help them defuse the impact of social stigmatization and to learn coping skills and self-acceptance strategies. The increasing availability of knowledge and resources about gay, lesbian, and bisexual individuals has served a facilitative role for these youths, but this information also needs to be known by clinicians.

Future clinical research should address a central but unexamined set of questions: Is there a developmentally optimal time to self-identify and disclose to others? If so, does it depend on cultural, historic, and familial circumstances or on existing psychological characteristics of the individual? At the moment, it appears that self-labeling at a relatively early age, but revealing that identity only to select and supportive others, is best. Youths in this circumstance avoid the vulnerability and negative repercussions of being widely known as gay or lesbian in traditionally stigmatizing junior and senior high school settings. They take their time, disclosing their sexual identity to "safe" persons who are willing and able to provide social and psychological support. In the process they learn crisis competence and develop self-respect and ego integrity that prepare them to face the cruelty of a homophobic society (Coleman, 1981/1982; Malyon, 1981). However, as noted above, cultural and historic factors moderate the importance of this particular timing; as more resources and clinicians become available, even earlier disclosure may prove both manageable and optimal for individuals who are in the most facilitative and supportive circumstances.

As cultural understanding and acceptance of sexual-minority individuals grow, the identity development processes of gay, lesbian, and bisexual individuals may well increasingly resemble that of heterosexual youths as they manage self, family, peers, and culture. Although sexual-minority individuals will always face unique stressors and challenges, we hope and expect that families, service providers, and clinicians will use developmental knowledge to foster a supportive, nurturing, and facilitative environment for identity development and self-expression among future cohorts of sexual-minority youths.

NOTES

1. Note the omission of bisexual development. Coming out stage models do not explain the processes that bisexuals encounter in moving from a heterosexual to a bisexual identity.

REFERENCES

Anthill, J. K. (1987). Parents' beliefs and values about sex roles, sex differences, and sexuality: Their sources and implications. In P. Shaver & C. Hendrick (Eds.), *Review of personality and social psychology: Sex and gender (Vol. 7)*. Newbury Park, CA: Sage.

Bailey, J. M. (1996). Gender identity. In R. C. Savin-Williams & K. M. Cohen (Eds.), *The lives of lesbians, gays, and bisexuals: Children to adults* (pp. 71–93). Fort Worth, TX: Harcourt Brace.

Bailey, J. M., & Zucker, K. J. (1995). Childhood sex-typed behavior and sexual orientation: A conceptual analysis and quantitative review. *Developmental Psychology, 31,* 43–55.

Bell, A. P., & Weinberg, M. S. (1978). *Homosexualities: A study of diversity among men and women*. Bloomington, IN: Indiana University Press.

Bell, A. P., Weinberg, M. S., & Hammersmith, S. K. (1981). *Sexual preference: Its development in men and women*. Bloomington, IN: Indiana University Press.

Blackwood, E. (1985). Breaking the mirror: The construction of lesbianism and the anthropological discourse on homosexuality. *Journal of Homosexuality, 11,* 1–17.

Block, J. H. (1983). Differential premises arising from differential socialization of the sexes: Some conjectures. *Child Development, 54,* 1335–1354.

Blumstein, P., & Schwartz, P. (1976). Bisexuality in men. *Urban Life, 5,* 339–358.

Blumstein, P., & Schwartz, P. (1990). Intimate relationships and the creation of sexuality. In D. P. McWhirter, S. A. Sanders, & J. M. Reinisch (Eds.), *Homosexuality/heterosexuality: Concepts of sexual orientation* (pp. 307–320). New York: Oxford University Press.

Blumstein, P., & Schwartz, P. (1993). Bisexuality: Some social psychological issues. In L. D. Garnets & D. C. Kimmel (Eds.), *Psychological perspectives on lesbian and gay male experiences* (pp. 168–183). New York: Columbia University Press.

Bolton, F. G., & MacEachron, A. (1988). Adolescent male sexuality: A developmental perspective. *Journal of Adolescent Research, 3,* 259–273.

Boxer, A., & Cohler, B. (1989). The life course of gay and lesbian youth: An immodest proposal for the study of lives. *Journal of Homosexuality, 17,* 317–355.

Califia, P. (1979). Lesbian sexuality. *Journal of Homosexuality, 4,* 255–266.

Carrier, J. M. (1989). Gay liberation and coming out in Mexico. *Journal of Homosexuality, 17,* 225–252.

Carrier, J. M., Nguyen, B., & Su, S. (1992). Vietnamese American sexual behaviors and HIV infection. *The Journal of Sex Research, 29,* 547–560.

Carter, D. B., & McCloskey, L. A. (1984). Peers and the maintenance of sex-typed behavior: The development of children's conceptions of cross-gender behavior in their peers. *Social Cognition, 2,* 294–314.

Cass, V. (1979). Homosexual identity formation: A theoretical model. *Journal of Homosexuality, 4,* 219–235.

Cass, V. (1984). Homosexual identity: A concept in need of a definition. *Journal of Homosexuality, 9,* 105–126.

Cass, V. (1990). The implications of homosexual identity formation for the Kinsey model and scale of sexual preference. In D. P. McWhirter, S. A. Sanders, & J. M. Reinisch (Eds.), *Homosexuality/ heterosexuality: Concepts of sexual orientation* (pp. 239–266). New York: Oxford University Press.

Chan, C. S. (1989). Issues of identity development among Asian American lesbians and gay men. *Journal of Counseling and Development, 68,* 16–20.

Chan, C. S. (1995). Issues of sexual identity in an ethnic minority: The case of Chinese American lesbians, gay men, and bisexual people. In A. R. D'Augelli & C. J. Patterson (Eds.). *Lesbian, gay, and bisexual identities over the lifespan: Psychological perspectives* (pp. 87–101). New York: Oxford University Press.

Chapman, B. E., & Brannock, J. C. (1987). Proposed models of lesbian identity development: An empirical examination. *Journal of Homosexuality, 14,* 69–80.

Cohen, K. M., & Savin-Williams, R. C. (1996). Developmental perspectives on coming out to self and others. In R. C. Savin-Williams & K. M. Cohen (Eds.), *The lives of lesbians, gays, and bisexuals: Children to adults* (pp. 113–151). Fort Worth, TX: Harcourt Brace.

Coleman, E. (1981/1982). Developmental stages of the coming out process. *Journal of Homosexuality, 7,* 31–43.

Cooper, M. (1990). Rejecting "femininity": Some research notes on gender identity development in lesbians. *Deviant Behavior, 11,* 371–380.

Cross, W. E. (1991). *Shades of Black: Diversity in African-American identity.* Philadelphia: Temple University Press.

D'Augelli, A. R. (1991). Gay men in college: Identity processes and adaptations. *Journal of College Student Development, 32,* 140–146.

D'Augelli, A. R., & Hart, M. M. (1987). Gay women, men, and families in rural settings: Toward the development of helping communities. *American Journal of Community Psychology, 15,* 79–93.

D'Augelli, A. R., & Hershberger, S. L. (1993). Lesbian, gay, and bisexual youth in community settings: Personal challenges and mental health problems. *American Journal of Community Psychology, 21,* 421–448.

Damon, W. (1979). *The social world of the child.* San Francisco: Jossey-Bass.

Dank, B. M. (1971). Coming out in the gay world. *Psychiatry, 34,* 180–197.

Dank, B. M. (1973). The homosexual. In D. Spiegel & P. Keith-Spiegel (Eds.), *Outsiders, USA* (pp. 269–297). San Francisco: Rinehart & Winston.

Davies, P. (1992). The role of disclosure in coming out among gay men. In K. Plummer (Ed.), *Modern homosexualities: Fragments of lesbian and gay experience* (pp. 75–83). London: Routledge & Kegan Paul.

deMonteflores, C., & Schultz, S. (1978). Coming out: Similarities and differences for lesbians and gay men. *Journal of Social Issues, 34,* 59–72.

Diamond, L. M. (1997, August). *Sexual questioning and young women's development.* Paper presented at the annual meeting of the American Psychological Association, Chicago, IL.

Diamond, L. M. (1998). The development of sexual orientation among adolescent and young adult women. *Developmental Psychology, 34.*

Diamond, L. M., Savin-Williams, R. C., & Dubé, E. M. (in press). Sex, dating, passionate friendships, and romance: Intimate peer relations among lesbian, gay, and bisexual adolescents. In W. Furman, C. Feiring, & B. B. Brown (Eds.), *Contemporary perspectives on adolescent romantic relationship.* New York: Cambridge University Press.

Dubé, E., Giovanni, C., & Willemsen, E. (1995, August). *"Coming out": Social influences and self-perceptions.* Paper presented at the Western Psychological Association Annual Meeting, Los Angeles, CA.

Esterberg, K. G. (1994). Being a lesbian and being in love: Constructing identities through relationships. *Journal of Gay and Lesbian Social Services, 1,* 57–82.

Esterberg, K. G. (1997). *Lesbian and bisexual identities: Constructing communities, constructing selves.* Philadelphia: Temple University Press.

Faderman, L. (1981). *Surpassing the love of men.* New York: William Morrow.

Fagot, B. I. (1977). Consequences of moderate cross-gender behavior in preschool children. *Child Development, 48,* 902–907.

Faraday, A. (1981). Liberating lesbian research. In K. Plummer (Ed.), *The making of the modern homosexual* (pp. 112–129). London: Hutchinson.

Feinman, S. (1981). Why is cross-sex-role behavior more approved for girls than for boys? A status characteristic approach. *Sex Roles, 7,* 289–299.

Fitzpatrick, G. (1983). Self-disclosure of lesbianism as related to self-actualization and self-stigmatization. *Dissertation Abstracts International, 43,* 4143b.

Garnets, L. D., & Kimmel, D. C. (1993). Lesbian and gay male dimensions in the psychological study of human diversity. In L. D. Garnets & D. C. Kimmel (Eds.), *Psychological perspectives on lesbian and gay male experiences* (pp. 1–51). New York: Columbia University Press.

Golden, C. (1996). What's in a name? Sexual self-identification among women. In R. C. Savin-Williams & K. M. Cohen (Eds.), *The lives of lesbians, gays, and bisexuals: Children to adults* (pp. 229–249). Fort Worth, TX: Harcourt Brace.

Gonsiorek, J. C. (1996). Mental health and sexual orientation. In R. C. Savin-Williams & K. M. Cohen (Eds.), *The lives of lesbians, gays, and bisexuals: Children to adults* (pp. 462–478). Fort Worth, TX: Harcourt Brace.

Gonsiorek, J. C., & Rudolph, J. R. (1991). Homosexual identity: Coming out and other developmental events. In J. C. Gonsiorek & J. D. Weinrich (Eds.), *Homosexuality: Research implications for public policy* (pp. 161–176). Newbury Park, CA: Sage.

Green, R. (1987). *The "sissy boy syndrome" and the development of homosexuality.* New Haven, CT: Yale University Press.

Greene, B. (1994). Ethnic minority lesbians and gay men: Mental health and treatment issues. *Journal of Consulting and Clinical Psychology, 62,* 243–251.

Grellert, E. A., Newcomb, M. D., & Bentler, P. M. (1982). Childhood play activities of male and female homosexuals and heterosexuals. *Archives of Sexual Behavior, 11,* 451–478.

Harry, J. (1982). *Gay children grown up.* New York: Praeger.

Harry, J. (1983). Defeminization and adult psychological well-being among male homosexuals. *Archives of Sexual Behavior, 12,* 1–19.

Herdt, G., & Boxer, A. (1993). *Children of Horizons: How gay and lesbian teens are leading a new way out of the closet.* Boston: Beacon Press.

Hidalgo, H. A., & Hidalgo-Christensen, E. H. (1976/1977). The Puerto Rican lesbian and the Puerto Rican community. *Journal of Homosexuality, 2,* 109–121.

High achieving students see much prejudice. (1994, November 25). *Washington Blade,* p. 16.

Icard, L. (1986). Black gay men and conflicting social identities: Sexual orientation versus racial identity. *Journal of Social Work and Human Sexuality, 4,* 83–93.

Isay, R. A. (1989). *Being homosexual: Gay men and their development.* New York: Farrar Straus Grove.

Kahn, M. J. (1991). Factors affecting the coming out process for lesbians. *Journal of Homosexuality, 21,* 47–70.

Lamb, M. E., & Roopnarine, J. (1979). Peer influences on sex-role development in preschoolers. *Child Development, 50,* 1219–1222.

Laumann, E. O., Gagnon, J. H., Michael, R. T., & Michaels, F. (1994). *The social organization of sexuality: Sexual practices in the United States.* Chicago: University of Chicago Press.

LeVay, S. (1993). *The sexual brain.* Cambridge, MA: MIT Press.

Lever, J. (1994, August 23). Sexual revelations. *The Advocate,* pp. 17–24.

Magana, J. R., & Carrier, J. M. (1991). Mexican and Mexican American male sexual behavior and spread of AIDS in California. *The Journal of Sex Research, 28,* 425–441.

Malyon, A. K. (1981). The homosexual adolescent: Developmental issues and social bias. *Child Welfare, 60,* 321–330.

Manalansan, M. F. (1996). Double minorities: Latino, Black, and Asian men who have sex with men. In R. C. Savin-Williams & K. M. Cohen (Eds.), *The lives of lesbians, gays, and bisexuals: Children to adults* (pp. 393–415). Fort Worth, TX: Harcourt Brace.

Martin, A. D. (1982). Learning to hide: The socialization of the gay adolescent. *Adolescent Psychiatry, 10,* 52–65.

Meyer-Bahlburg, H. F. L. (1993). Psychobiologic research on homosexuality. *Sexual and Gender Identity Disorders, 2,* 489–500.

Money, J. (1988). *Gay, straight, and in-between: The sexology of erotic orientation.* New York: Oxford University Press.

Morales, E. S. (1983, August). *Third world gays and lesbians: A process of multiple identities.* Paper presented at the 91st Annual Convention of the American Psychological Association, Anaheim, CA.

Newman, B. S., & Muzzonigro, P. G. (1993). The effects of traditional family values on the coming out process of gay male adolescents. *Adolescence, 28,* 213–226.

Nichols, M. (1990). Lesbian relationships: Implications for the study of sexuality and gender. In J. C. Gonsiorek & J. D. Weinrich (Eds.), *Homosexuality: Research implications for public policy* (pp. 350–364). Newbury Park, CA: Sage.

O'Heron, C. A. (1990). Stereotypic and nonstereotypic sex role trait and behavior orientations, gender identity, and psychological adjustment. *Journal of Personality and Social Psychology, 58,* 134–143.

Palladino, D., & Stephenson, Y. (1990). Perceptions of the sexual self: Their impact on relationships between lesbian and heterosexual women. *Women and Therapy, 9,* 231–253.

Parker, R. (1989). Youth, identity, and homosexuality: The changing shape of sexual life in contemporary Brazil. *Journal of Homosexuality, 17,* 269–289.

Phillips, G. & Over, R. (1995). Differences between heterosexual, bisexual, and lesbian women in recalled childhood experiences. *Archives of Sexual Behavior, 24,* 1–20.

Ramos, J. (Ed.) (1994). *Companeras: Latina lesbians.* New York: Routledge.

Remafedi, G. (1987). Adolescent homosexuality: Psychosocial and medical implications. *Pediatrics, 79,* 331–337.

Richardson, D. (1987). Recent challenges to traditional assumptions about homosexuality: Some implications for practice. *Journal of Homosexuality, 13,* 1–12.

Romo-Carmona, M. (1994). Introduction. In J. Ramos (Ed.), *Companeras: Latina lesbians* (pp. xx–xxix). New York: Routledge.

Rotheram-Borus, M. J., Rosario, M., & Koopman, C. (1991). Minority youths at high risk: Gay males and runaways. In M. E. Colten & S. Gore (Eds.), *Adolescent stress: Causes and consequences* (pp. 181–200). New York: Aldine DeGruyter.

Rust, P. (1992). The politics of sexual identity: Sexual attraction and behavior among lesbian and bisexual women. *Social Problems, 39,* 366–386.

Rust, P. (1993). Coming out in the age of social constructionism: Sexual identity formation among lesbians and bisexual women. *Gender and Society, 7,* 50–77.

Sahli, N. (1979). Smashing: Women's relationships before the fall. *Chrysalis, 8,* 17–27.

Savin-Williams, R. C. (1990). *Gay and lesbian youth: Expressions of identity.* New York: Hemisphere.

Savin-Williams, R. C. (1994). Verbal and physical abuse as stressors in the lives of lesbian, gay male, and bisexual youths: Associations with school problems, running away, substance abuse, prostitution, and suicide. *Journal of Consulting and Clinical Psychology, 62,* 261–269.

Savin-Williams, R. C. (1996). Self-labeling and disclosure among gay, lesbian, and bisexual youths. In J. Laird & R. J. Green (Eds.), *Lesbians and gays in couples and families: A handbook for therapists.* San Francisco: Jossey-Bass.

Savin-Williams, R. C. (1998a). *"...and then I became gay:" Young men's stories.* New York: Routledge.

Savin-Williams, R. C. (1998b). The disclosure of same-sex attractions by lesbian, gay, and bisexual youths to their families. *Journal of Research on Adolescence, 8,* 49–68.

Savin-Williams, R. C., & Rodriguez, R. G. (1993). A developmental, clinical perspective on lesbian, gay males, and bisexual youths. In T. P. Gullotta, G. R. Adams, & R. Montemayor (Eds.), *Adolescent sexuality* (pp. 77–101). Newbury Park, CA: Sage.

Schafer, S. (1976). Sexual and social problems of lesbians. *The Journal of Sex Research, 12,* 50–69.

Sears, J. T. (1989). The impact of gender and race on growing up lesbian and gay in the South. *National Women's Studies Association Journal, 1,* 422–457.

Sears, J. T. (1991). *Growing up gay in the South: Race, gender, and journeys of the spirit.* New York: Harrington Park Press.

Silber, L. J. (1990). Negotiating sexual identity: Non-lesbians in a lesbian feminist community. *The Journal of Sex Research, 27,* 131–139.

Sophie, J. (1985/1986). A critical examination of stage theories of lesbian identity development. *Journal of Homosexuality, 12,* 39–51.

Tremble, B., Schneider, M., & Appathurai, C. (1989). Growing up gay or lesbian in a multicultural context. *Journal of Homosexuality, 17,* 253–267.

Tripp, C. A. (1975). *The homosexual matrix.* New York: McGraw-Hill.

Troiden, R. R. (1988). *Gay and lesbian identity: A sociological analysis.* Six Hills, NY: General Hall.

Troiden, R. R. (1979). Becoming homosexual: A model of gay identity acquisition. *Psychiatry, 42,* 362–373.

Troiden, R. R. (1989). The formation of homosexual identities. *Journal of Homosexuality, 17,* 43–73.

Whisman, V. (1993). Identity crisis: Who is a lesbian anyway? In A. Stein (Ed.), *Sisters, sexperts, queers: Beyond the lesbian nation* (pp. 47–60). New York: Penguin.

Whitam, F. L. (1977). Childhood indicators of male homosexuality. *Archives of Sexual Behavior, 6,* 89–96.

Wooden, W. S., Kawasaki, H., & Mayeda, R. (1983). Lifestyles and identity maintenance among gay Japanese-American males. *Alternative Lifestyles, 5,* 236–243.

Young, A. (1981). *Gays under the Cuban revolution.* San Francisco: Grey Fox Press.

Zuger, B. (1984). Early effeminate behavior in boys: Outcome and significance for homosexuality. *Journal of Nervous and Mental Disease, 172,* 90–97.

PART 4

CHILDHOOD DISORDERS

It is now widely recognized that a comprehensive view of childhood disorders must involve a careful consideration of development. Indeed, the issue of development is important to consider with respect to *all* facets of child psychopathology, including its classification assessment, and treatment, as well as to theories about its etiology and maintenance.

This section covers the four main classes of disorders that clinicians and researchers encounter in their work with children, namely, internalizing, externalizing, intellectual, and pervasive developmental disorders, and presents what is known about each of them within the context of development. The first chapter, Chapter 16, on internalizing disorders presents an overview of developmental factors in childhood depression and anxiety. This opening chapter highlights, once again, one of the main themes of this book, including the one that is particularly salient for this section. Namely, that progress in understanding children and their problems, and progress in developing effective prevention, intervention, and treatment programs lies not in using simple main effect models but in using complex, integrative models that make use of multiple etiological pathways (i.e., multifinality and equifinality). A similar theme emerges in Chapter 17 on externalizing disorders (attention-deficit hy-

peractivity disorder, oppositional defiant disorder and conduct disorder). Specifically, the chapter contains a description of the developmental trajectories of these disorders, and summarizes prominent issues arising from a developmental psychopathology perspective, including heterotypic continuity (e.g., are the temper tantrums of the preschooler the age-appropriate demonstration of the same disorder that appears as bullying in the school-age child's bullying?) and the need for developmentally sensitive treatment. No doubt, the discerning reader will recognize these issues from their reading of earlier chapters, thereby underscoring the importance of these issues in understanding children, their problems, and effective means for prevention and intervention efforts.

In Chapter 18, the intellectual disorder, mental retardation is discussed. Problems in defining mental retardation are summarized, followed by a discussion of the developmental difference issues involved with the types of delays observed in children with mental retardation including motor, speech, and other developmental milestones. Behavior problem areas, such as memory, impulse control speech, self-help skills, and social skills, are summarized as are ways to treat these problem areas.

The final chapter in this section, Chapter 19, is on pervasive developmental disorders. After describing the four disorders that are subsumed under this broad category (i.e., autistic disorder, Rett's disorder, Asperger's disorder, and childhood disintegrative disorder), the chapter focuses on developmental theory and treatment with respect to autistic disorder—the pervasive developmental disorder that has attracted the most amount of research attention. The chapter shows how work in the areas of language, behavior problems, and early intervention have been found to be useful for helping children who suffer from autism. The chapter underscores how progress in this area will require an integration of the biological aspects of this disorder with the psychological (e.g., cognitive, social, behavioral) factors.

Collectively, the chapters in this section are rich with cutting-edge information about childhood disorders and development. As such, they will prove to be invaluable resources for students, researchers, and clinicians.

CHAPTER 16

INTERNALIZING DISORDERS

Eric L. Daleiden
Michael W. Vasey
Lisa M. Brown

Over the past decade there has been a dramatic upsurge of interest in children's internalizing disorders, reflecting changing views on their prevalence, seriousness, and persistence (see Ollendick & King, 1994). The primary aim of this chapter is to provide a guide to this rapidly expanding literature. The internalizing domain is comprised of a wide range of symptoms and syndromes that includes anxiety, fear, somatic complaints, shyness, social withdrawal, low self-esteem, sadness, and depression (Achenbach, 1991; Ollendick & King, 1994). Unfortunately, because space limitations make it impossible to address more than a subset of these, our discussion is focused on the syndromes of depression and anxiety because they have received the most attention in this domain and each is associated with multiple disorders as defined by the *Diagnostic and Statistical Manual* (DSM-IV) of the American Psychiatric Association (APA, 1994). Although much of the literature concerning these disorders is adevelopmental, consideration of developmental factors is increasing and it is on the implications of such factors for the description, etiology, and treatment of such disorders that this chapter is focused.

Given the substantial correlation between the syndromes of anxiety and depression in childhood (Achenbach, 1991;

Brady & Kendall, 1992), one might expect their respective literatures to share much in common. Surprisingly, they are largely distinct, especially with regard to developmental issues. Such issues are now commonly considered in increasingly complex models by childhood depression researchers (cf. Cicchetti, Rogosch, & Toth, 1994; Weisz, Rudolph, Granger, & Sweeney, 1992). In contrast, although the number of articles considering developmental issues in childhood anxiety is growing (e.g., Costanzo, Miller-Johnson, & Wencel, 1995; Nelles & Barlow, 1988; Vasey, 1993), integrative developmental models of childhood anxiety are only beginning to be offered (e.g., Kagan, 1994), perhaps due to the comparative youth of the childhood anxiety literature. Given this state of affairs, one goal of this chapter is to encourage further consideration of developmental issues in childhood anxiety by illustrating approaches used to study such issues in childhood depression.

MANIFESTATIONS OF INTERNALIZING DISORDERS ACROSS DEVELOPMENT

The need to define disorders within the normal developmental context is a central tenet of the developmental psychopathology perspective (Masten & Braswell, 1991). The process of validating such constructs must address several developmental issues including whether the disorder exhibits continuity across development and whether such continuity should be expected at the level of specific behaviors or broader patterns of adaptation to age-specific or stage-specific developmental tasks (Garber & Strassberg, 1991). In accord with such questions, our discussion focuses on evidence for developmental continuity and variation in these disorders and the most appropriate level at which to examine developmental continuity in the internalizing disorders.

The existence and definition of depressive disorders in childhood have been the subjects of considerable controversy (e.g., Lefkowitz & Burton, 1978). However, a clear consensus now exists that major depressive disorder and dysthymia are present in childhood and that the core symptoms closely parallel adult depression (Angold, 1993). This consensus is reflected in DSM-IV (APA, 1994) by the use of the same diagnostic criteria for children and adults. Implicit in this approach is the assumption that depression is the same coherent phenomenon at each stage of development. Thus, cross-sectional evidence of coherent symptom clustering is a necessary condition for preliminary validation of this construct. Indeed, evidence suggests that depressed mood, anhedonia, and cognitive symptoms such as guilt and worthlessness correlate in similar ways across the age range (Angold, 1993). However, consensus is growing that some symptoms of depression may be unique to childhood. DSM-IV notes that somatic complaints, irritability, and social withdrawal may be more common in children than problems like psychomotor retardation, hypersomnia, or delusions, which tend to increase during adolescence (APA, 1994). Other studies indicate that additional symptoms of depression in childhood include school refusal, headaches, and abdominal pain (Garber, Zeman, & Walker, 1990; Pearce, 1978; Weinberg, Rutman, Sullivan, Penick, & Dietz, 1973). Unfortunately, despite acknowledgment of developmental symptom variation, only irritability is specifically included as a diagnostic criterion for childhood depression in DSM-IV.

Central to the developmental psychopathology perspective is the expectation that continuity at the level of molecular behaviors is unlikely (e.g., Cicchetti & Schneider-Rosen, 1986). Indeed, Garber and Strassberg (1991) stated that "we should expect age-related differences in the clinical manifestations of the symptoms because developmental advances in cognitive structures and functions especially will influence the manner in which children experience, interpret, and express emotions and other behavioral symptoms at different ages" (p. 229). Adopting the DSM-IV's distinction between core and associated symptoms of a disorder, Garber and Strassberg (1991) identified four possible solutions to the

question of developmental continuity and discontinuity: (1) all symptoms are the same across development; (2) core symptoms are the same but associated symptoms vary; (3) core symptoms are the same at a molar but not molecular level; or (4) core symptoms of the disorder are somewhat different across development. Accordingly, theorists have questioned the wisdom of limiting the definition of childhood internalizing disorders to the features of the adult form of the disorder (e.g., Angold, 1993). Garber and Strassberg (1991) have further cautioned that assuming isomorphism in the symptoms of a disorder across the age span may focus attention too narrowly on those children who meet adult criteria "while missing a potentially larger group of children who display developmental variants of the symptomatology" (p. 229).

The importance of considering developmental continuity in nosological decisions is further highlighted by recent changes to the DSM-IV classification of anxiety disorders. With respect to anxiety, the DSM-IV is more adevelopmental than its predecessors. This is evident in the removal of avoidant disorder and overanxious disorder (OAD) from the DSM-IV, such that avoidant disorder was subsumed under social phobia and OAD was subsumed under generalized anxiety disorder (GAD). These decisions seem to reflect the view that there is continuity across ages in the central features of these anxiety disorders. However, the extant data remain ambiguous regarding this issue. For example, Francis, Last, and Strauss (1992) found that although children with avoidant disorder and social phobia did not differ in terms of gender, race, or comorbid diagnoses, children with pure avoidant disorder were significantly younger than those with pure social phobia or comorbid avoidant disorder and social phobia. Moreover, several other studies have indicated that social phobia is characterized by onset during early adolescence (Giaconia et al., 1994) whereas avoidant disorder occurs primarily in childhood (Cantwell & Baker, 1987). Francis and colleagues (1992) noted that differences in the age of onset of these disorders parallel a normal developmental progression in which fear of strangers emerges before fear of negative social evaluation. In the absence of prospective longitudinal data, two explanations for these age differences are equally compelling. First, avoidant disorder and social phobia may be distinct disorders characterized by different phobic objects (i.e., unfamiliar people in the case of avoidant disorder and social evaluation in the case of social phobia). In this case, age differences may appear simply because the cognitive skills necessary to support avoidant disorder emerge at a younger age than those underlying social phobia. Second, avoidant disorder and social phobia may represent different developmental manifestations of the same basic phenomenon, such that the expression of this underlying pathology evolves from avoidant disorder to social phobia with the emergence of new developmental capacities in early adolescence.

With respect to OAD and GAD, the few extant studies generally fail to support the continuity of these constructs. Specifically, prospective data indicate that OAD generally remits within 2 years, and retrospective data suggest that only one-fifth of adults with GAD report an age of onset in childhood or adolescence. Based on such findings, Werry (1991) concluded, "It is not impossible that OAD and GAD could be separated by a latent period, but this issue of continuity or similarity cannot be settled on the sparse data available" (p. 539). Given the unanswered questions on the equivalence of OAD and avoidant disorder to GAD and social phobia respectively, it would seem prudent for researchers to continue to collect diagnostic information pertinent to the deleted DSM-III-R categories as well as to those from DSM-IV. Only in this way can these important questions be adequately answered.

Early studies of the predictive validity of internalizing disorders primarily suggested that such problems were often transitory (see Kohlberg, LaCrosse, & Ricks, 1972; Rutter & Garmezy, 1983). However, these studies also showed that a substantial minority of children with "neurotic" symptoms were likely to continue to display such problems later in childhood or adulthood. The question of the most appropriate analytical level for examining continuity is central to the interpretation of such data. Childhood problems are likely to persist or predict later maladaptation to the extent that they interfere with adaptation to normal developmental challenges (Kohlberg et al., 1972; Masten & Braswell, 1991). Thus, the predictive value of disorders such as major depressive disorder, separation anxiety disorder (SAD), or social phobia should be far greater than that of single emotional symptoms, such as dysphoria or anxiety, because significant interference with children's adaptive functioning is necessary for diagnosing such disorders. Indeed, those few early studies that looked at more adaptationally significant internalizing problems (e.g., school phobia) showed more persistence in negative outcomes (e.g., Waldron, 1976).

Recent prospective and retrospective studies of both depressive and anxiety syndromes suggest that both carry moderate to serious risk for persistence or recurrence (see Ollendick & King, 1994). For example, Costello and Angold (1994) reviewed five epidemiological studies in which diagnostic information was obtained over periods of 2 to 5 years and concluded that there is a "moderate level of continuity beyond what might be expected by chance alone" (p. 116). Moreover, in an epidemiological study of first grade children, Ialongo, Edelsohn, Werthamer-Larsson, Crockett, and Kellam (1994) found that self-reported anxiety was relatively

stable over a 4-month period and that severity of anxiety significantly predicted academic functioning 4 months later. Similarly, these researchers (Ialongo, Werthamer-Larsson, Crockett, & Kellam, 1993) reported that depressive symptoms in the first grade had significant predictive value for depression and adaptive functioning in the fifth grade.

In sum, current consensus accepts a view that the child and adult forms of internalizing disorders are developmentally continuous phenomena. This perspective is largely based on cross-sectional evidence of coherent symptom clustering. Although such studies support this view, careful consideration of molecular isomorphism and adaptational significance emphasizes the need to examine diverse sources of evidence in pursuing the construct validational process beyond isolated, cross-sectional data. The validation of developmental disorder constructs requires longitudinal evidence that similar (although potentially multiple) etiological pathways are associated with the disorder, that children with disorders are as at risk as adults, and that other childhood problems are not linked to the disorder at later developmental levels. Thus, consideration of the continuity and discontinuity of internalizing disorders across developmental levels provides an essential perspective in the validation of these constructs.

PREVALENCE OF INTERNALIZING DISORDERS ACROSS DEVELOPMENT

Although there is some variability in specific estimates, the best evidence to date suggests that the prevalence of depression triples from childhood to adolescence. For example, Kashani, Orvaschel, Rosenberg, and Reid (1989) found that child-reported depressive disorders occurred in 1.5 percent of 8 year olds, 1.5 percent of 12 year olds, and 5.7 percent of 17 year olds. The prevalence of several anxiety disorders follows a trajectory parallel to that of depression. For example, Kashani and Orvaschel (1990) found that the percentage of children meeting criteria for OAD rose from 11.4 percent to 17.1 percent in a sample of 12 to 17 year olds. Obsessive-compulsive disorder and panic disorder also appear to increase from childhood through adolescence (Albano, Chorpita, & Barlow, 1996; Ollendick, Mattis, & King, 1994). However, other anxiety disorders such as SAD seem to decrease in prevalence as children mature (Cohen et al., 1993; Kashani & Orvaschel, 1990; Kashani et al., 1989).

The relatively low prevalence of major depressive disorder in young children is consistent with the notion that a level of cognitive development sufficient to support a generalized sense of helplessness and hopelessness is necessary to maintain depressive disorders (Rutter, 1989). Similarly, anxiety theorists speculate that the increasing prevalence of

OAD among older children is consistent with their development of the cognitive skills necessary to support generalized worry (Ollendick & King, 1994; Vasey, 1993). Also, the increasing prevalence of panic disorder among adolescents supports the necessity of formal operational cognitive abilities in supporting the catastrophic cognitions considered necessary to this disorder's development (Nelles & Barlow, 1988). Although such suggestions are intriguing, they remain speculative because such age effects leave open the possibility that many aspects of development may account for the findings (Rutter, 1989). Future studies need to examine the importance of differences in the hypothesized developing skill (e.g., formal reasoning skills) within a narrow age range to test such hypotheses (Rutter, 1989).

In a related vein, age-related decreases in specific anxiety disorders such as SAD, coupled with increases in generalized anxiety disorders such as OAD, have led a number of theorists to speculate that as children's cognitive capacities mature, specific anxiety disorders such as SAD may evolve into more generalized anxiety disorders (see Albano et al., 1996; Vasey, 1993). However, such assertions must be tempered by longitudinal findings suggesting that different risk factors predict SAD and OAD (Costello & Angold, 1994). Only longitudinal studies following the natural history of these anxiety disorders in children can rigorously test predictions about the evolution of one disorder into another.

In addition to age differences, studies have documented consistent age by gender interactions in the prevalence of several internalizing disorders. For example, evidence suggests that prepubertal males experience depression at similar rates or even more frequently than prepubertal females (e.g., Anderson, Williams, McGee, & Silva, 1987; McGee & Williams, 1988). However, as children enter adolescence, this gender ratio changes so that girls who are depressed substantially outnumber the boys (e.g., Giaconia et al., 1994; Kashani et al., 1987; Lewinsohn et al., 1993). The gender distribution of OAD appears to follow a similar pattern (Bowen, Offord & Boyle, 1990; Cohen et al., 1993). Despite this similarity between depression and OAD, gender differences in the prevalence of other anxiety disorders deviate from this pattern. For example, Cohen and colleagues (1993) found that girls experienced more SAD than boys across ages, and Kashani and colleagues (1989) found that SAD decreased with age for both genders. With respect to childhood obsessive-compulsive disorder, Albano and coworkers (1996) reported that males predominate in younger samples, but that relatively equal gender ratios are evident in samples of older children. Such age-related changes in gender ratio represent a central phenomena of the internalizing disorders that must be considered in any theory of such disorders. This issue is addressed in greater depth in the section on etiology.

Developmental consistency and variation in the prevalence of disorders may play an important role in validating disorder constructs, exploring multiple etiological pathways, and identifying the operation of specific developmental factors. For example, the discriminant validity of disorder categories is supported to the extent that different disorders are associated with divergent prevalence patterns across age and gender. Also, as previously noted, evidence that one disorder decreases as another increases highlights the need to test hypotheses about the transformation of one internalizing disorder into another. Similarly, age-related changes in the prevalence of disorders may suggest an increase in the occurrence of causal factors or may suggest the emergence of a new etiological pathway. For example, Angold (1993) suggested that the higher prevalence of depression in prepubertal boys may indicate that depression in boys is part of a developmental pathway leading to some other problem such as alcoholism. Finally, to the extent that prevalence rates follow a predictable course, researchers need to question what changed developmentally to promote prevalence shifts during that particular period of the life span.

As with prevalence data, the investigation of psychiatric comorbidity provides information about the construct validity and multiple etiological pathways of internalizing disorders. Studies of internalizing disorders suggest that comorbidity with other internalizing disorders as well as externalizing disorders is quite common (Hammen & Compas, 1994; Nottelmann & Jensen, 1995; Russo & Beidel, 1994). The comorbidity between anxiety and depression has received particular attention because the developmental pathways may differ for children suffering from mixed and pure forms of these disorders (Angold, 1993; Ollendick & King, 1994). Extant studies (for reviews see Kendall, Kortlander, Chansky, & Brady, 1992; Ollendick & King, 1994) suggest that the prevalence of comorbid anxiety and depression ranges from 15 to 60 percent and the overlap appears to be greatest among more disturbed children (i.e., estimates decrease from inpatient to outpatient to community to pediatric primary care patient samples). Further, children who are comorbid for anxiety and depression tend to be older (e.g., King, Ollendick, & Gullone, 1991) and more symptomatic (Anderson et al., 1987) than depressed-only or anxious-only children. Also, anxiety symptoms tend to predate the depression symptoms in comorbid children, and children with anxiety disorders report fewer depressive symptoms while children with depressive disorders do not report fewer anxiety symptoms (Kovacs, Gatsonis, Paulauskas, & Richards, 1989; Last, Perrin, Hersen, & Kazdin, 1992; Strauss, Last, Hersen, & Kazdin, 1988).

Theorists have offered several explanations to account for the high level of comorbidity in internalizing problems, including inadequate construct validity of nosological categories and a unitary notion of negative affectivity. For example, Watson and Clark (1984) suggested that both anxiety and depression share high levels of negative affectivity, which may contribute to comorbid diagnoses (see also King et al., 1991). Nottelman and Jensen (1995) described several developmental considerations that may account for comorbidity in children. First, they suggested that psychopathology in younger children may be less differentiated and specific than in adolescents, making the appearance of comorbidity common in younger children. However, evidence that children comorbid for anxiety and depression tend to be older than children with pure forms of these disorders seems to contradict this hypothesis. Second, the manifestation of a given disorder may change developmentally, so it is possible that the earlier and the later expressions of the disorder could co-occur during transition periods. Finally, a given disorder may interfere with acquisition of later skills, resulting in the development of another disorder. Adopting a developmental perspective may help address such issues as whether high levels of comorbidity result from imprecise diagnostic criteria or whether comorbidity stems from interference with competence and thus contributes to the emergence of additional disorders.

DEVELOPMENTAL ISSUES IN THE ETIOLOGY AND MAINTENANCE OF CHILDREN'S INTERNALIZING DISORDERS

Initially, theories of the etiology and maintenance of internalizing problems were simple downward extensions of adult theories that gave little consideration to issues of development. This has changed dramatically in the case of depression and similar changes are beginning to appear in the childhood anxiety literature. In considering the development and maintenance of children's internalizing problems, it is important to distinguish between predisposing, precipitating, and maintaining factors. Predisposing factors are those that place children at increased risk for that subsequent onset of psychological disorder. Precipitating factors are proximal stressors that promote the onset of disorder at a given point. Maintaining factors contribute to the persistence of a disorder once it has emerged. Careful consideration of these distinctions greatly enhances the clarity of developmental models due to the potential for a single variable to play multiple etiological roles (e.g., family conflict may be a predisposing, precipitating, and/or maintaining factor for depression), for diverse variables to play similar etiological roles (e.g., family conflict, academic failure, and low assertiveness may all predispose a child to develop de-

pression), and for children's developmental level to influence the etiological role of a variable (e.g., low assertiveness may predispose adolescents to depression, but may be irrelevant for grade schoolers). Similarly, important differences in the predisposing, precipitating, and maintaining factors of internalizing disorders may depend on a disorder's age of onset or the age of the child in question.

An excellent model for considering such issues can be found in Nolen-Hoeksema and Girgus's (1994) discussion of the gender shift in the prevalence of depression from childhood to adolescence. These authors considered three developmental models that are differentiated based on consistency and variation in the causal roles of predisposing and precipitating factors across ages. Their first model holds that the factors causing depression are similar for both boys and girls, but that the prevalence of such factors increases more for girls than for boys in adolescence. Model two suggests that causal factors differ for boys and girls and that the factors causing depression in females become more common in adolescence than the factors causing depression in males. Finally, model three asserts that the predisposing factors for depression are more common in girls than boys even in childhood, but that depression is more frequently precipitated in adolescent girls than boys because of the increased prevalence of relevant stressors for girls. Based on their review, Nolen-Hoeksema and Girgus concluded that model three has received the best empirical support.

These models go far in transcending simple main effects models (e.g., negative cognitions cause depression), but they do not exhaustively represent the complex interactive effects and potentially multiple etiological pathways to the formation of internalizing disorders. Each model assumes that the factors causing depression are largely the same for children and adolescents although the prevalence of these may differ across development levels. This is consistent with the common view that there is continuity, at either a molar or molecular level, in the etiology and maintenance of depression between childhood and adulthood (Angold, 1993). However, we must consider additional models that allow for changes in the form or function of causal factors from childhood to adolescence. From this perspective, a fourth model could postulate that the factors causing depression in childhood are not necessarily the same as those causing depression in adolescence. An example of model four is a psychoanalytic view (Rie, 1966) that children's superegos are not sufficiently developed to support the guilt necessary for true depression. Similarly, Harter (1986) argues that children younger than 8 years of age lack the kind of stable, global self-concept that supports depression. Thus, to the extent that younger children get depressed, it is presumably a different phenomenon, due to different causes than those seen among older children and adolescents. Additionally, a fifth model may allow for the possibility that the same factors are operative during childhood and adolescence but begin to influence depression in new and more complex ways in early adolescence. Numerous interactional and transactional models of the etiology of depression in childhood are available (e.g., Cicchetti et al., 1994; Cole & Turner, 1993). Movement toward such models is also apparent in the childhood anxiety literature (e.g., Nelles & Barlow, 1988; Vasey, 1993) but to a much lesser extent.

One approach to conceptualizing changes in the function of etiological factors is to distinguish between mediational and moderational models. In mediational models, the etiology of a disorder proceeds along a pathway where one factor contributes to another factor which in turn causes a subsequent disorder. Moderational models hold that the causal relationship between an etiological factor and a disorder varies depending on a child's status with respect to some third variable. Cole and Turner (1993) provide an excellent discussion of the mediational and moderational roles of attributional style as they influence the relationship between negative life events and depression. The mediational model suggests that the experience of negative life events contributes to the development of a negative attributional style which in turn causes depression. However, attributional style may moderate the relationship between negative life events and depression such that the experience of negative life events causes depression in those children with a negative attributional style, but the experience of negative life events may be unrelated to depression in children without a negative attributional style.

Despite the fact that mediational and moderational models of adult depression postulate that a critical negative cognitive style is acquired sometime in childhood, only a small number of studies have examined when these cognitions develop and when they begin to mediate or moderate the effects of negative life events on depression. Cole and Turner (1993) suggested that cognitive mediational models may better fit childhood depression because children are in the process of acquiring the negative cognitive style elements through negative experiences and feedback. Thus, if they only develop the cognitive elements following negative experiences, those elements cannot serve to moderate the effects of negative events and feedback on depression. To test this prediction, Cole and Turner (1993) examined the relations among cognitive style, life events, peer-rated competence, and depression in a cross section of 356 fourth, sixth, and eighth graders. They found that cognitive style mediated the relation between negative peer evaluations and depression almost completely and partially mediated the

relationship between negative events and depression. In contrast, moderational models received little support. However, when Turner and Cole (1994) examined these relations within specific content domains (i.e., the interaction of recent academic failures with cognitive style regarding academic performance), they found a significant cognitive style by life events interaction in the academic and social domains for eighth, but not fourth or sixth, graders. Among children with a negative cognitive style, negative life events predicted depression, but no relationship between life events and depression was apparent in children without a negative cognitive style. Thus, cognitive style seems to become a moderator of children's depressive response to negative life events as age increases, with this moderating capacity established by the eighth grade.

Although Turner and Cole's (1994) study was cross-sectional, at least one longitudinal study paints a similar picture. Nolen-Hoeksema and colleagues (1992) examined the relations among attributional style, life events, and depression by assessing children every 6 months over a 5-year period beginning in the third and fourth grades. They found that the correlation between attributional style for negative events and depression increased until the fifth or sixth grade and then stabilized, whereas the relation between attributional style for positive events and depression did not increase until the eighth grade. Thus, there appear to be changes in the relations between cognitive style and depression during the middle school years. Throughout the study period, life events significantly predicted depression during both short- (i.e., 6-month intervals) and long-term (i.e., more than one year) periods. However, cognitive style did not significantly predict either short-term or long-term depression until the latter years of the study (i.e., after sixth grade). More importantly, the cognitive style by life events interaction only contributed significant unique variance during the middle school years.

In sum, findings suggest that during the early school years, children's cognitive style is still under development and does not predict depression (Nolen-Hoeksema et al., 1992). Instead, negative life events predict depression with cognitive style mediating this relationship (Cole & Turner, 1993). In their summary, Nolen-Hoeksema and colleagues (1992) write that "Early in childhood, major negative life events are more important to the development of depression than explanatory style; later in childhood, explanatory style predicts depression, and negative life events predict when depression will occur in the presence of a pessimistic explanatory style" (p. 418). In other words, negative life events may predispose young children to depression or precipitate a depressive episode, whereas negative life events precipitate depressive episodes in those older children predisposed to depression by a negative cognitive style. Similarly, variables other than attributional style may shift from a mediational to a moderational role. For example, in a cross-sectional study of 8 to 12 year olds, Goodman, Gravitt, and Kaslow (1995) found that the correlation between negative life events and depression varied depending on the effectiveness of children's problem solving such that average and effective problem solvers showed little depression regardless of negative life events but ineffective problem solvers reported dramatically more symptoms of depression as the impact of their negative life events increased.

Developmental models of childhood anxiety remain in their theoretical infancy compared to those of childhood depression. This deficiency may be due in part to a lack of even adevelopmental models of childhood anxiety. For the most part, extant theories of anxiety are downward extensions of adult models. Although such extensions provide an excellent starting point (e.g., Kendall & Ronan, 1990), they have historically given little consideration to developmental factors (Krohne, 1992). Nevertheless, adevelopmental theories can play an essential role in elucidating the factors contributing to the formation and maintenance of anxiety in general. The identification of such factors may serve as a basis to which developmental theory can be applied to generate predictions about the etiological roles of such factors during different phases of the life span (e.g., Vasey, 1993). This interplay between basic theories of psychopathology and child development is readily apparent in recent discussions of the developmental psychopathology of anxiety. Specifically, in recent years, basic theories of the psychopathology have elaborated the role of cognitive factors in anxiety (e.g., Kendall & Ronan, 1990; Mathews, 1990), and accordingly, developmental discussions have tended to focus on cognition (e.g., Nelles & Barlow, 1988; Vasey, 1993). Although discussion of such isolated factors is a start, there remains a need for integrative developmental models of childhood anxiety similar to recent theories of depression (e.g., Cicchetti et al., 1994).

In a discussion of panic disorder, Nelles and Barlow (1988) were among the first to consider the implications of childrens' developing cognitive abilities for childhood anxiety. Specifically, they argued that children are unlikely to develop panic disorder prior to adolescence because they lack the cognitive abilities required to support the catastrophic misinterpretations of bodily symptoms necessary to produce the disorder. In their review of children's illness conceptions, Nelles and Barlow (1988) noted that children move from external to internal conceptions and that children in middle childhood lack the ability to make attributions to internal causes. Based on their review, they argued that children may have panic attacks and exhibit hyperventilation syndrome, but because cognitive limitations prevent children from misattributing these symptoms as signals to impending death, children do not develop panic disorders. This conclusion has proved controversial and several issues merit further consideration. First, even if children do not develop panic disorder, this may have little to do with their level of cognitive development or their illness concepts. As Rutter (1989) noted, age is a nonspecific variable that leaves unclear the specific physical, psychological, or social contextual developmental changes that are responsible for age-related differences. At present, it appears that although age differences exist in the prevalence of panic disorder, physical developmental factors may generate this effect more than cognitive developmental level. For example, evidence that pubertal status is related to increased prevalence of panic attacks, especially in females, led Hayward and colleagues (1992) to suggest that this increase may be linked to biological changes. Further, developmental research over the past few decades has consistently demonstrated that children are cognitively more adept than many early theorists thought. For example, many Piagetian notions about limitations in causal reasoning greatly underestimate children's actual abilities, particularly in domains with which children are highly familiar (e.g., Bjorklund, 1989). Thus, although children may display limited abilities in unfamiliar laboratory tasks, they may be quite proficient when reasoning about common experiences, such as emotions or physical symptoms.

A recent study by Mattis and Ollendick (1997) illustrates domain-specific proficiency in the context of children's reasoning about panic disorder. In an investigation of third, sixth, and ninth grade children's conceptions of the causes of physical (e.g., colds, heart attacks) and psychological (e.g., panic attacks) illness symptoms, they found that children of all ages had more internal conceptions of the cause of panic symptoms than the other illness symptoms. Moreover, there were no age differences in the internal–external nature of children's attributions regarding panic symptoms. Regardless of age, panic symptoms were attributed to internal and noncatastrophic causes more often than were symptoms of physical illness. Finally, an internal attributional style and greater anxiety sensitivity predicted the likelihood with which children made internal, catastrophic attributions. Based on this evidence that even third-grade children are able to formulate catastrophic attributions regarding the cause of panic symptoms, Mattis and Ollendick challenge the conclusion of Nelles and Barlow (1988). Indeed, Ollendick and colleagues (1994) argued that although panic disorder is less common in children than adolescents, children do experience panic attacks, develop panic disorder, and report both the physical and cognitive symptoms of that disorder.

Although integrative models of the development of childhood anxiety disorders are largely absent, recent research on behaviorally inhibited children offers a valuable heuristic model. Kagan (1994) reviewed evidence that some infants inherit a high level of biological reactivity and commonly respond to unfamiliar events with excessive motor activity and crying. Kagan suggests that as this predisposition interacts with social experience, the majority of such children will respond to novelty by freezing, fretting, and withdrawing and thus may be classified as behaviorally inhibited. As these children mature, their social environment assumes increasing importance, such that environmental factors (e.g., parent behaviors that encourage children's behavioral approach to novelty) may moderate the ongoing expression of an inhibited behavioral style. In addition to such environmental factors, Kagan argues that once inhibited children become self-aware, some deliberately try not to be afraid and some are successful in changing their behavioral style. Thus, in essence, Kagan has proposed a performance model of childhood anxiety similar to that of Patterson's model of antisocial behavior (Patterson, Reid, & Dishion, 1992). Behaviorally inhibited children persist in their inhibition to the extent that such behaviors are reinforced, or at least not discouraged, and less inhibited behaviors are not taught or reinforced. In other words, behaviorally inhibited children that develop anxiety disorders may fail to master their fears rather than learn fears that are not typically acquired. Indeed, Menzies and Clarke (1995) argue that many adulthood phobias are not learned, but rather are innate fears that have not been mastered.

Kagan's (1994) model highlights the potential influence of a variety of factors. For example, biological and temperamental factors are important to the extent that they predispose children to behavioral inhibition, emotional and intrapersonal factors are important to the extent that children make efforts to regulate or are successful in regulating their emotion and behavior, and social factors, such as a child's family and peer environments, are important to the extent that they reinforce or punish behaviors and foster or impede efforts at self-change. From this perspective, temperamental differences may account for why some children have more difficulty mastering fears than others. Moreover, current concepts of emotional regulation view emotions as responses that ideally serve an adaptive function by organizing and motivating behavior, but which may instead disorganize and interfere with behavior if not adequately regulated (Fox, 1994). Anxiety disorders may be readily construed as problems of emotional dysregulation, and to the extent that emotional dysregulation interferes with adaptation to important developmental challenges, it is likely to predict future dysfunction and distress. The potential for anxiety to reciprocally interfere with children's developing competence can be thought of as analogous to Patterson's notion of "limited shopping" (e.g., Patterson et al., 1992). For example, to the extent that socially anxious children avoid social situations, their opportunities to learn necessary social skills and establish friendships will be restricted. Such restriction may subsequently promote increasing deviation from a normal developmental trajectory. In this context, it is noteworthy that the early onset of psychopathology increases children's risk of developing additional disorders (e.g., Giaconia et al., 1994).

In addition to Kagan's (1994) theory, several other theoretical perspectives highlight the importance of considering family factors in the etiology and maintenance of childhood anxiety. For example, Cassidy (1996) has argued for the importance of considering children's attachment experiences. Consistent with this assertion, many anxiety-related cognitive biases, such as an attentional bias toward threat, performance interference, and predominant selection of avoidant coping responses (e.g., Daleiden & Vasey, 1997; Vasey & Daleiden, 1996) are also characteristic of insecurely attached children (e.g., Cassidy, 1996). Other parental factors that have received discussion include inconsistent and negative parental feedback, low levels of support, high levels of restriction, low expectations regarding children's coping resources, and a lack of providing developmentally appropriate assistance to foster effective coping (e.g., Krohne, 1992; Vasey, 1993; Vasey & Daleiden, 1994). Finally, empirical studies indicate that family factors can have an immediate and direct impact on the responses of anxious children. For example, anxious children are more likely to select avoidant coping responses following brief family discussions of how to cope with anxiety-provoking situations (Barrett, Rapee, Dadds, & Ryan, 1996; Dadds, Barrett, Rapee, & Ryan, 1996).

In sum, theories of childhood anxiety disorders are lagging behind theories of depression in terms of their developmental specificity. However, recent advances in the childhood depression literature may guide future work with childhood anxiety. Further, childhood anxiety researchers have identified numerous variables in the temperamental, emotional, social, and familial domains that need to be collected into an integrative theory. Finally, Kagan's (1994) work with behaviorally inhibited children provides a basis for integrating these factors into a developmental model of childhood anxiety that may clearly draw from Patterson's theory on the development of antisocial behavior.

Developmental patterns in comorbid diagnoses may also provide important clues to the etiology of various internalizing problems, and therefore represents a substantive etiological concern. As Ollendick and King (1994) expressed, "developmental pathways and outcomes of children and adolescents with multiple concurrent disorders may differ from those with single or pure disorders" (p. 919). At a minimum, the problems of children with more than one disorder should be more likely to persist because such children typically have more severe levels of disorder that are presumably likely to produce greater interference with adaptation to developmental challenges. Further, Angold (1993) has argued that some risk factors may only be related to depression by way of a mediating condition. For example, the increased likelihood of social rejection experienced by depressed children may be partially due to the comorbid presence of conduct problems.

However, comorbidity also creates methodological snares. For example, Angold (1993) has cautioned that risk factors associated with comorbid conditions may be confused with true risks for internalizing disorder. Even more generally, a given risk factor may not be associated with the pure form of either condition but may instead serve as a risk factor for a combined form of the disorders. In other words, a failure to address psychiatric comorbidity may lead to erroneous conclusions about the developmental course of depression and anxiety. In the extreme case, the factor in question may be unrelated to depression or anxiety. In less extreme cases, the factor may be related to a disorder, but only when it co-occurs with some other condition. That is, depression or anxiety in the presence of comorbid diagnoses may follow different developmental courses than the pure forms of either disorder and the combined condition may be associated with different predisposing, precipitating, and maintaining factors. Longitudinal comparisons of comorbid children and children suffering from single disorders are needed to explore the effects of psychiatric comorbidity on children's internalizing problems.

DEVELOPMENTAL ISSUES IN THE ASSESSMENT OF CHILDREN'S INTERNALIZING DISORDERS

There are two primary questions relevant to a developmentally sensitive assessment of internalizing problems in children and adolescents. The first question is how best to gather information from children at various developmental levels and concerns the operating characteristics of various assessment methods (e.g., internal consistency, stability, validity). The second question is what phenomena ought to be measured and therefore requires specification of developmentally relevant target variables. Accordingly, this section addresses issues relevant to gathering information about childhood internalizing disorders, but space limitations preclude a review of assessment targets. In short, important assessment targets are those specific factors identified in other portions of this paper as relevant to the etiology, maintenance, and treatment of childhood internalizing disorders.

At present, it seems that the most effective approach to assessing internalizing disorders in children and adolescents is through multiple-gating procedures (Kendall, Cantwell, & Kazdin, 1989; Roberts, Lewinsohn, & Seeley, 1991). Multiple-gating refers to the use of multimethod assessments at multiple time periods. For example, multiple-gating may consist of a two-stage process by which children are first screened using brief symptom questionnaires and then those with positive screens are subsequently assessed with a structured interview. However, the decision as to what measures to use for this purpose is complicated by developmental considerations. For example, can children in the early grade school years provide reliable reports of their internal states? Do measures of young children have operating characteristics (e.g., sensitivity and specificity) similar to those for high school students so that such measures may serve as effective screens across ages? How are reports from multiple informants (e.g., parents, teachers, and peers) to be integrated into multiple-gating and does this vary depending on the age of the child being assessed? Should the same decision rules and cutoff scores be used for young children and adolescents? Several studies have provided information that may serve to guide decisions about how best to implement a multiple-gating approach in the assessment of internalizing problems in children and adolescents, but firm answers await future research.

Brief symptom questionnaires are currently the measures of choice for the first stage of multiple-gating (Kendall et al., 1989; Roberts et al., 1991). Studies indicate that numerous instruments discriminate between children suffering from internalizing problems and nonclinical control groups (see Kendall et al., 1989; Silverman & Rabian, in press). With respect to the second stage in a multiple-gating approach, structured interviews have received the most research attention. Numerous diagnostic interviews that include an assessment of internalizing disorder are available (see Silverman, 1994). In general these interviews have demonstrated adequate reliability and validity, which tends to be somewhat lower for internalizing than externalizing disorders, particularly anxiety (e.g., Hodges, McKnew, Burbach, & Roebuck, 1987).

Central to any assessment strategy is the question of which sources provide the best of information. Although the utility of children's reports about their internalizing problems has not received unanimous acceptance (e.g., Patterson & Stoolmiller, 1991), recent data support the notion that children can, at a much younger age then previously thought, provide reliable self-reports about internalizing symptoms. Specifically, as early as first grade, children can provide internally consistent and relatively stable self-reports of internalizing problems, and such reports are both concurrently and predictively related to adaptation on various developmentally salient tasks (e.g., Ialongo et al., 1993; 1994; Kellam, Rebok, Mayer, Ialongo, & Kalodner, 1994).

In addition to their self-reports, young people are observed by numerous different people on a regular basis including parents, teachers, and peers. Thus, it is important to examine potential developmental differences in the number of symptoms reported as well as the reliability of and concordance between reports from multiple informants. Evidence is growing that parental reports of externalizing disorders are more reliable than children's, but that this is not the case with respect to internalizing disorders (e.g., Kazdin, French, Unis, & Esveldt-Dawson, 1983; Silverman & Eisen, 1992). Although there is some indication that the diagnosis of internalizing disorders in younger children may be more reliable than in older children and that child reports may be more reliable than parent reports (e.g., Lavigne et al., 1994; Silverman & Eisen, 1992; Silverman & Rabian, 1995), not all studies support this conclusion (Silverman & Eisen, 1992).

Although much of this chapter has emphasized how developmental psychology can inform clinical psychology, the study of diagnostic reliability highlights the converse relationship. Specifically, the issue of base rates is of central importance to research at the clinical–developmental interface. A recent study by Lavigne and colleagues (1994) emphasizes that base rates are of particular relevance when samples are subdivided according to some developmental variable (e.g., age). These researchers examined the reliability of DSM-III-R (APA, 1987) diagnoses assigned by independent clinical judges in a sample of preschool children using two agreement statistics, Cohen's kappa and Yule's Y. When age differences (i.e., 2 to 3 vs. 4 to 5 year olds) were examined, they found that the kappa statistics declined as age increased for separation anxiety, depression, and combined emotional disorder diagnoses, but the Y statistics showed a much smaller age effect with at least moderate agreement for all diagnoses. Lavigne and colleagues suggested that because the kappa statistic is relatively sensitive to base rates whereas the Y statistic is relatively impervious to base rate variations, this age-related attenuation may be due to a reduction in base rates when the sample was divided by age. Given that the majority of extant studies have examined age as a secondary analysis, have employed kappa statistics, or have not otherwise addressed base rate fluctuations, caution is warranted in drawing conclusions.

Future studies would benefit from employing designs that control base rates across developmental groupings or from selecting various statistics that allow for an assessment of the impact of base rate variations.

In contrast to evidence indicating that diagnostic reliability of internalizing disorders decreases with increasing age, the available data suggest that the agreement between child and parent reports increases as children get older. For example, in a cross-sectional analysis of clinically referred 6 to 18 year olds, Edelbrock, Costello, Dulcan, Conover, and Kala (1986) found that child–parent agreement increased with age, particularly between the 6- to 9- and 10- to 13-year-old age groups, with smaller increases for 14- to 18-year-olds. Further, Renouf and Kovacs (1994) examined longitudinal data from 51 clinic-referred 8 to 13 year olds with a diagnosis of depression who were followed longitudinally for 4 or more years. They found that parent–child and clinician–child agreement on internal, cognitive–affective symptoms of depression significantly improved from a low of 45 percent to a high of 66 percent agreement. However, some studies have failed to replicate this age effect (e.g., Angold et al., 1987).

Several developmental factors may explain the observed age difference. Edelbrock and colleagues (1986) suggested that the increase in parent–child concordance may result from an associated age-related increase in the reliability of children's self-reports. However, as previously noted, data indicate that children's self-reports on internalizing symptoms do not appear to increase in reliability with age and, in fact, the opposite effect has frequently emerged. Also, Renouf and Kovacs (1994) hypothesized that children's advances in social–cognitive development would facilitate their ability to identify and describe their psychological states. Similarly, developmental increases in verbal abilities (e.g., increased vocabulary) may aid children in accurately communicating their experiences. However, in their study, Renouf and Kovacs (1994) found no relationship between informant agreement and measures of social–cognitive development or children's verbal abilities. Thus, at present, the available evidence suggests that adult–child agreement increases as children age, but the empirical literature has failed to support explanations of this effect.

In sum, the available data suggest that both children and parents can provide reliable information about children's internalizing difficulties. Thus, the state of the art in assessment involves the use of a multiple-gating approach with multiple measures obtained from multiple sources, including child, parent, teacher, or peer report. However, the use of multiple methods, multiple informants, and multiple assessment periods raises questions on the best way to combine data from multiple sources. Unfortunately, little research on such questions is yet available and there is virtually no research on how optimal combinatory strategies may vary across development (see Roberts, Andrews, Lewinsohn, & Hops, 1990).

DEVELOPMENTAL ISSUES IN THE PREVENTION AND TREATMENT OF CHILDREN'S INTERNALIZING PROBLEMS

The best evidence to date suggests that cognitive–behavioral treatments of internalizing disorders in children and adolescents are effective compared to no treatment control conditions (Barrett, Dadds, Rapee, & Ryan, 1996; Kendall, 1994; Weisz et al., 1992). Yet, at present, the number of available studies is small and the extant studies are largely adevelopmental. For example, Weisz and colleagues (1992) noted that none of the studies in their meta-analysis reported age effects. However, recently, age differences in treatment efficacy were examined by Barrett, Dadds, Rapee, and Ryan (1996) and Weisz and coworkers (1992). Weisz and coworkers (1992) found that 7 to 12 year olds showed less improvement on average than children 12 to 18 years of age at posttreatment and only the 12 to 18 year olds maintained treatment gains at follow-up assessment. Weisz and coworkers (1992) noted that the treatment approaches used in the studies they reviewed were downward extensions of adult therapies and heavily targeted cognitions. They also suggested that research findings on depressed children's cognitions, coping, and competence were often not integrated into the treatments. For example, younger children seem to be more susceptible to cognitive errors such as catastrophization, personalization, and attributing stable causes to events; older children experience more depressive cognitions regarding stringent standard setting, high expectations for performance, and negative self-concept; and other cognitions such as hopelessness do not appear to be associated with age (see Weisz et al., 1992). Further, studies are beginning to identify age differences in the etiological role of cognitions. For example, as discussed earlier, prior to early adolescence, negative cognitions do not appear to moderate the relationship between negative life events and depression (e.g., Nolen-Hoeksema et al., 1992; Turner & Cole, 1994). Therefore, these therapies may have been more appropriate for adolescents than children.

Regarding childhood anxiety, Barrett et al. (1996) found that a combined cognitive–behavioral therapy (CBT) and family treatment was significantly more effective than CBT alone for 7 to 10-year-old children but no differences between treatments were evident for 11 to 14 year olds. Thus, Barrett and colleagues suggested that enhancing parenting

skills is an important adjunct in the treatment of younger children, but, for older children, "individual child cognitive work and exposure to feared stimuli may be sufficient to produce improvement in anxiety problems" (p. 31). However, the rate of improvement for older children in both treatment conditions was comparable to that of younger children who received CBT alone (i.e., approximately 60% diagnosis-free) whereas 100 percent of younger children in the combined treatment group were diagnosis-free. Thus, rather than suggesting that CBT alone was sufficient for older children, this pattern suggests that enhancing parenting skills is an effective adjunct to CBT for younger anxious children, but not for older children. In other words, there was just as much room for improvement in both younger and older CBT-only groups but the family therapy component produced additional gains only among younger children. Thus, there appears to be a need to explore other adjuncts to CBT that may improve treatment efficacy for older children.

Two developmental phenomena may help to account for the fact that family therapy led to improvement in the younger but not older groups in the study done by Barrett and colleagues. Silverman and colleagues (Ginsburg, Silverman, & Kurtines, 1995; Silverman & Kurtines, 1996) conceptualized the process of change in therapy as the "transfer of control" (e.g., skills, expert knowledge, etc.) from the therapist to the child through multiple pathways (e.g., direct to child, through parent to child; through school personnel to child). Such a model may be flexibly applied to children at various developmental levels by identifying the primary pathways of social influence (e.g., parents, teachers, peers) and the salience of sources of control that are external to the child, and then appropriately distributing therapeutic efforts to various direct and indirect pathways for "transferring control" to the child. Similarly, Shapiro (1995) has argued that there is an "increasing cone" of social influence moving from the primary caretaker to the parenting dyad, to family, friends, school, teacher, employer, and so forth, as children get older. Thus, for younger children, parenting approaches may be more effective because of the relative centrality of parents in children's social environment and because parents may play a larger role as "gatekeepers" in children's exposure to other social influences. For older children and adolescents, parenting behaviors may have relatively less impact on children due to increased diffusion of social influence and the child's increased autonomy from the family environment.

Conceptualizing internalizing problems as examples of emotional dysregulation highlights the importance of the locus of emotional regulation. Because external sources of emotional regulation may be more salient for younger than older children (Thompson, 1990), building external supports into treatment may also be more important for younger than older children. Based on the assumption that the threat-relevant expectations of children should be more controllable by manipulating adult supports prior to 10 years of age, Costanzo and coworkers (1995) argued that exposure treatments for younger children should generally be effective even in the absence of treatment targeted at anxious cognitions. In older children, targeting cognition is more likely to prove necessary because "in this developmental period, the clinician is treating anticipatory internal constructions that give rise to anxiety and is less focused on external guides that compose the socialization context" (p. 93). Unfortunately, Costanzo and coworkers do not review specific studies supporting this assertion. However, this view seems generally consistent with findings that negative cognitions begin to exert a moderating influence in late childhood or early adolescence, that prior to around 8 years of age children lack stable self-concepts, and that other cognitive factors may or may not relate to anxiety or depression in the same manner among younger and older children.

In addition to age main effects in treatment efficacy, there also appear to be "age by disorder" interactions. Specifically, Barrett et al. (1996) found that the efficacy of CBT for anxiety was not related to children's age, whereas Weisz and coworkers (1992) found that the efficacy of CBTs for depression seems to increase as children enter adolescence. Thus, caution is warranted in generalizing the treatment implications of developmental factors that are observed with one internalizing disorder to the therapy of all internalizing problems. Moreover, the available data are very limited and are hindered by numerous methodological problems (e.g., the lack of clinic-referred samples in studies of depression, differing age ranges used to define groups). A particular difficulty is the issue of co-morbidity (e.g., Ollendick & King, 1994; Weisz et al., 1992). For example, whereas Barrett et al. (1996) found similar effects for CBT with younger and older children, they also found that pretreatment levels of depression predicted treatment failure. Although they did not report age differences in levels of depression, as previously noted, comorbid children tend to be older and more symptomatic than depressed-only or anxious-only children. Thus, age-related changes in comorbidity may confound examinations of age differences in treatment efficacy.

Kendall and colleagues (1992) discussed a number of treatment implications that stem from the available research on comorbid anxiety and depression. First, given data suggesting that anxiety precedes depression, these authors argue that in therapy with comorbid children, it is important to explore how the symptoms of anxiety and depression may be temporally related. However, they note that younger children's difficulties in recognizing the simultaneous experience of multiple emotions may place a developmental limit on this approach. Further, Kendall and colleagues cite a number of cognitive processes that are common to both anxiety and depression (e.g., unrealistic goal setting, negative self-evaluation, avoidance of self-reinforcement) and infer that treating such common factors may simultaneously address both anxiety and depression. They also claim that because anxiety is characterized by a future orientation and depression with a past orientation, it is important to explore events at multiple points in time with children. Finally, for comorbid children, social skills problems may be due to actual deficits, lack of motivation due to depression, avoidance due to anxiety, or some combination of these factors, so that role-play activities may be especially important in addressing the underinvolvement characteristic of depression and in promoting opportunities for anxious children to learn coping skills.

Despite evidence of age differences in treatment outcomes, studies of the relationship between specific developmental variables and treatment efficacy are virtually nonexistent (but see Weisz & Weiss, 1989, for a review suggesting a relationship between cognitive capacity and improvement in cognitive-mediated treatment). However, theorists have identified a number of developmental factors that have clear implications for the treatment of internalizing disorders in children and adolescents and have evaluated the efficacy of treatments for targeting children's competence in multiple domains.

Developmental information about the role of cognition in the etiology and maintenance of internalizing disorders has important implications for their treatment. For example, information about the developmental stage at which depression-promoting cognitions form may educate prevention and treatment initiatives so that early intervention may help children to avoid developing ingrained and stable patterns that preclude the processing of disconfirming evidence (e.g., Weisz et al., 1992). Although relatively little information is available on the efficacy of modifying cognition to prevent internalizing problems, Jaycox, Reivich, Gillham, and Seligman (1994) examined the role of attributional style in mediating prevention outcomes. These authors employed a 12-week cognitive–behavioral program to teach strategies for coping with negative life events to 10 to 13 year olds at risk for depression due to episodes of dysphoria or exposure to family conflict. Treated children showed fewer depressive symptoms at post-test and 6-month follow-up than both wait-list and nonparticipant control groups. Although children's overall attributional style was similar across groups, treated children were less likely to attribute negative events to stable, enduring causes at post-treatment and follow-up. Further, the frequency of stable attributions was related to symptom severity at both post-test and follow-up. In multiple regression analyses, attributional style, but not treatment, significantly predicted depressive symptoms, whereas treatment, but not attributional style, predicted teacher-reported classroom behavior. Thus, consistent with evidence that cognition moderates the relationship between negative life events and depression for older children, this study supports the utility of targeting a stable, negative attributional style in adolescents. However, similar studies exploring the utility of this approach with younger children, whose cognitions ought not moderate the relationship between negative life events and depression, would provide an interesting test of this developmental hypothesis.

Several studies suggest that children's academic competence is related to internalizing problems (e.g., Ialongo et al., 1993) and that interventions targeting academic achievement promote reductions in internalizing symptomatology. For example, in an evaluation of a school-based prevention program aimed at improving reading achievement, Kellam, Rebok, Mayer, Ialongo, and Kalodner (1994) found that higher achievement gains from fall to spring were associated with a disruption in the continuity of depression from fall to spring for girls. For boys, only those whose achievement improved with the intervention showed reductions in depression over first grade; boys in the control group showed similar levels of depression across first grade regardless of achievement changes. To account for this gender difference, Kellam and colleagues (1994) noted that at around 8 years of age there is a transition in children's self-understanding such that prior to age 7 children judge themselves in more absolute terms but after age 7 they compare themselves to other children. Further, this social-comparative form of self-evaluation may be necessary for attributions of helplessness that are stable and global. Therefore, they suggested that girls may have this attributional characteristic prior to first grade or at earlier ages than typically suggested, but boys may have first gained this ability through the preventive intervention. In a related vein, Weisz and coworkers (1992) note that there are developmental differences in the relationship between perceived and actual competence, such that the correlation between perceived and actual academic competence in nonpathological children increases from first or second grade to sixth grade, but that for those children who change schools around seventh grade this correlation drops again. Moreover, Cole (1990) found that not only did depressed children underestimate their academic competence compared to their peers and teachers, but also that the tendency to do so significantly predicted depression.

These data have a number of interesting developmental implications for the assessment and treatment of internalizing problems. First, these results highlight the importance of assessing children's self-perceptions of academic achievement, particularly social-comparative self-evaluative processes, as well as of obtaining measures of actual academic competence. Further, to evaluate Kellam and colleagues (1994) hypothesis, studies should examine the relationship between these processes and attributional styles. Second, these results are consistent with the recommendation that various developmental variables be considered with children at younger ages than has historically been suggested and that the role of life events (e.g., changing schools) in moderating performance on measures of developmental competence be addressed. Finally, studies examining developmental differences in the impact of life events, self-perceived competence, and actual academic competence on internalizing problems may help facilitate therapeutic decisions related to cognitive restructuring of self-perceptions or academic skills training in achieving both short-term and long-term treatment goals.

Recent conceptualizations of emotional competence (e.g., Thompson, 1990) have identified a number of specific dimensions on which emotional competence may vary developmentally (e.g., recognition of emotional facial expressions, affective perspective-taking, ability to spontaneously generate emotion concepts, etc.). Such conceptualizations allow for an increasingly fine-grained analysis of developmental delays and deviations in children's emotional regulation skills. Although studies of treatment effects with respect to these dimensions are almost nonexistent, a notable exception is a study by Greenberg, Kusche, Cook, and Quamma (1995). Greenberg and colleagues (1995) examined the effectiveness of a school-based preventive intervention at promoting emotional development in 6- to 10-year-old students. Although their prevention program was primarily designed to alter behavior and social problem-solving skills, they also examined information from an interview about various dimensions of emotional competence. Children were pretested before the start of second or third grade and were tested again 1 year later. The intervention produced significant improvements in the number of positive and negative emotion words children could generate, their ability to define complex feelings, their ability to provide examples of emotions from their own experiences, their reasoning about how others feel, their understanding that feelings could be hidden, the likelihood of reporting that feelings could be changed, and their reasoning about how feelings could change. During this 1-year period, significant developmental advances were evident for both the intervention and control groups in the number of positive and negative emotion words children could generate, children's recognition of their own emotions, and children's understanding of the simultaneity of emotions. There were no significant changes for either group in children's knowledge that all feelings are okay or their reasoning about the acceptability of feelings.

Greenberg and colleagues (1995) also examined treatment effects with respect to the teacher-reported CBCL internalizing scale. When children were trichotomized on this variable, treated children in the low internalizing group showed the greatest improvement in providing examples of emotions from their own experience, whereas children with high scores in the control group showed the greatest decrement in this skill. Treated children in the high internalizing group showed the greatest improvements in the likelihood of reporting that feelings could change and reasoning about how they could change, whereas control children in the high internalizing group displayed significant declines in these skills. Taken together, these results support the efficacy of this program for improving emotional competence, particularly in changing the trajectory of emotional development in children with internalizing problems. Yet there seemed to be a fairly specific relationship between the areas the program emphasized and the changes that children displayed (e.g., fluency and comfort in discussing feeling, efficacy beliefs), and the program seemed to have less effect on metacognitive skills (e.g., understanding and reasoning about emotions). Further, this study did not examine interactions between emotional developmental gains and improvements in behavioral problems or social problem-solving skills.

The limited data available on the role of emotional competence in treating internalizing problems with children and adolescents precludes making specific recommendations at this time. However, based on research suggesting that the use of emotion-focused coping strategies increases with age, but that no age trend is apparent for problem-focused strategies, Weisz and coworkers (1992) suggest that emotion-focused strategies may be difficult (i.e., abstract or subtle) for younger children to assimilate into their coping repertoire. Therefore, they conclude that training young children to use emotion-focused coping may be counterproductive. Further, the recent theoretical advances in the area of emotional competence point in many interesting directions for future research to explore. It is recommended that future studies include a multimethod assessment of a variety of specific emotional competence variables. Finally, although studies need to examine the impact of interventions that modify emotional developmental factors, there also remains a need for much basic research in the emotional competence domain. Recent increases in research in this domain is likely to generate a number of exciting advances in the coming years.

A recent meta-analysis of social competence training for 3 to 15-year-old children by Beelman, Pfingsten, and Losel (1994) provides an excellent summary of work in this area. Beelman and colleagues (1994) describe four primary categories of training programs that have been examined, including social skills approaches that assume that children lack necessary behavioral skills for effective social interaction; social problem-solving approaches that focus on competencies in means–end thinking, generating alternative solutions, and consequential thinking; social perspective programs that address children's ability to perceive and interact from another persons perspective; and self-control training that emphasizes children's abilities to evaluate their own behavior prior to action. However, the authors note that in recent years there has been a trend toward the development of multimodal programs that employ several of these approaches. Overall, the results of Beelman and colleagues (1994) suggest that social competence training is an effective short-term intervention for children, particularly in groups of younger and at-risk children. Moreover, with respect to internalizing problems, improvements were evident for both specific skills and more global social adjustment. Finally, monomodal behavioral skills training produced the strongest effect among children with internalizing problems and is therefore recommended.

Of particular interest is Beelman and colleagues' (1994) finding that monomodal programs were more effective for younger children than for older children, and that multimodal programs were more effective for older than for younger children. Given this difference, future studies should examine if this effect also holds specifically for internalizing problems. Beelman and colleagues (1994) speculate that the differences shown between age groups may be due to younger children being overtaxed by complex, multimodal programs. Specifically, they argue that the inclusion of cognitive, behavioral, and social problem-solving components may diffuse the focus of therapy for young children. Therefore, therapy using simple circumscribed programs that maintain a discrete focus may be preferable for younger children.

In sum, empirical studies have begun to identify effective treatments that target children's cognitive, academic, emotional, and social competence. However, only limited empirical data is available on the developmental variations in the efficacy of these strategies in general and for internalizing disorders in particular. In addition to the issue of treatment efficacy, theorists have speculated about developmental implications for a number of other therapeutic decisions. For example, Kovacs and Lohr (1995) argue that cognitive, social, and emotional development can limit the content of topics covered, strategies used, the duration of treatment, and approaches to fostering the therapeutic alliance (e.g., giving overt gifts and actions). Similarly, Shapiro (1995) argues for considering developmental changes in human relationships in determining how close the therapeutic relationship can be (e.g., distant vs. aloof, authoritarian vs. collaborative), how best to modify the alliance as the child develops and how large a role verbal communication can play in therapy.

SUMMARY AND CONCLUSIONS

Several themes have consistently emerged in our review of developmental factors in childhood internalizing disorders. First, the literature on developmental factors in childhood depression is more advanced than the childhood anxiety literature. Although several integrative developmental models of childhood depression highlighting multiple etiological pathways are available, similar theories of childhood anxiety are lacking. Moreover, theorists have only recently begun to move beyond simple main effect models to consider the complex transactional pathways to internalizing disorders. Measuring specific developmental variables rather than vague indicators of development such as age is also essential. Chronological age is not the equivalent of developmental stage and potential discrepancies may be highly pronounced in clinical populations because a child's psychopathology may interfere with development in numerous ways (e.g., Kovacs & Lohr, 1995; Rutter, 1989). Finally, future research needs to address many of the methodological limitations of the extant data. In particular, longitudinal studies using multiple assessment methods with multiple information sources that clearly address the impact of psychiatric comorbidity are necessary to rigorously test developmental hypotheses.

REFERENCES

Achenbach, T. M., (1991). *Manual for the Child Behavior Checklist/4–18 and 1991 Profile.* Burlington, VT: Department of Psychiatry, University of Vermont.

Albano, A. M., Chorpita, B. F., & Barlow, D. H. (1996). Anxiety disorders in children and adolescents. In E. J. Mash & R. A. Barkley (Eds.), *Child psychopathology.* New York: Guilford Press.

American Psychiatric Association (1987). *Diagnostic and statistical manual of mental disorders* (3rd ed., Rev.). Washington, DC: Author.

American Psychiatric Association. (1994). *Diagnostic and statistical manual of mental disorders* (4th ed.). Washington, DC: Author.

Anderson, J. C., Williams, S., McGee, R., & Silva, P. A. (1987). DSM-III disorders in preadolescent children: Prevalence in a large sample from the general population. *Archives of General Psychiatry, 44,* 69–76.

Angold, A. (1993). Why do we not know the cause of depression in children? In D. F. Hay & A. Angold (Eds.), *Precursors and causes in development and psychopathology* (pp. 265–293). Chichester, England: Wiley.

Angold, A., Weissman, M. M., John, K., Merikangas, K. R., Prusoff, B. A. Wickramaratne, P., Gammon, G. D., & Warner, V. (1987). Parent and child reports of depressive symptoms in children at low and high risk of depression. *Journal of Child Psychology and Psychiatry, 28,* 901–915.

Barrett, P. M., Dadds, M. R., Rapee, R. M., & Ryan, S. M. (1996). Family intervention for childhood anxiety: A controlled trial. *Journal of Consulting and Clinical Psychology, 64,* 333–342.

Barrett, P. M., Rapee, R. M., Dadds, M. R., & Ryan, S. M. (1996). Family enhancement of cognitive style in anxious and aggressive children: Threat bias and the FEAR effect. *Journal of Abnormal Child Psychology, 24,* 187–203.

Beelmann, A., Pfingsten, U., & Losel, F. (1994). Effects of training social competence in children: A meta-analysis of recent evaluation studies. *Journal of Clinical Child Psychology, 24,* 260–271.

Bjorklund, D. F. (1989). *Children's thinking: Developmental function and individual differences.* Pacific Grove, CA: Brooks/Cole.

Bowen, R. C., Offord, D. R., & Boyle, M. H. (1990). The prevalence of overanxious disorder and separation anxiety disorder: Results from the Ontario child health study. *Journal of the American Academy of Child and Adolescent Psychiatry, 29,* 753–758.

Brady, E. U., & Kendall, P. C. (1992). Comorbidity of anxiety and depression in children and adolescents. *Psychological Bulletin, 111,* 244–255.

Cantwell, D. P., & Baker, L. (1987). The prevalence of anxiety in children with communication disorders. *Journal of Anxiety Disorders, 1,* 239–248.

Carlson, G. A., Kashani, J. H., de Fatima Thomas, M., Vaidya, A., & Daniel, A. E. (1987). Comparison of two structured interviews on a psychiatrically hospitalized population of children. *Journal of the American Academy of Child and Adolescent Psychiatry, 26,* 645–648.

Cassidy, J. (1996). Attachment and generalized anxiety disorder. In D. Cicchetti & S. Toth (Eds.), *Rochester symposium on developmental psychopathology: Vol. 6.: Emotion, cognition, and representation.* Rochester, NY: University of Rochester Press.

Cicchetti, D. A., Rogosch, F. A., & Toth, S. L. (1994). A development psychopathology perspective on depression in children and adolescents. In W. R. Reynolds & H. F. Johnston (Eds.), *Handbook of depression in children and adolescents* (pp. 123–141). New York: Plenum Press.

Cicchetti, D., & Schneider-Rosen, K. (1986). An organizational approach to childhood depression. In M. Rutter, C. Izard, & P. Read (Eds.), *Depression in young people: Developmental and clinical perspectives* (pp. 71–134). New York: Guilford Press.

Cohen, P., Cohen, J., Kasen, S., Velez, C. N., Hartmark, C., Johnson, J., Rojas, M., Brook, J., & Streuning, E. L. (1993). An epidemiological study of disorders in late childhood and adolescence: I. Age- and gender-specific prevalence. *Journal of Child Psychology and Psychiatry and Allied Disciplines, 34,* 851–867.

Cole, D. A. (1990). The relation of social and academic competence to depressive symptoms in childhood. *Journal of Abnormal Psychology, 99,* 422–429.

Cole, D. A., & Turner, J. E. (1993). Models of cognitive mediation and moderation in childhood depression. *Journal of Abnormal Psychology, 102,* 271–281.

Costanzo, P., Miller-Johnson, S., & Wencel, H. (1995). Social development. In J. S. March (Ed.), *Anxiety disorders in children and adolescents* (pp. 82–108). New York: Guilford Press.

Costello, E. J., & Angold, A. (1994). Epidemiology. In J. S. March (Ed.), *Anxiety disorders in children and adolescents* (pp. 109–124). New York: Guilford Press.

Costello, E. J., Stouthamer-Loeber, M., & DeRosier, M. (1993). *Continuity and change in psychopathology from childhood to adolescence.* Paper presented at the Annual Meeting of the Society for Research in Child and Adolescent Psychopathology, Sante Fe, NM.

Dadds, M. R., Barrett, P. M., Rapee, R. M., & Ryan, S. (1996). Family process and child psychopathology: An observational analysis of the FEAR effect. *Journal of Abnormal Child Psychology, 24,* 715–734.

Daleiden, E. L., & Vasey, M. W. (1997). An information-processing perspective on childhood anxiety. *Clinical Psychology Review, 17,* 407–429.

Edelbrock, C., Costello, A. J., Dulcan, M. K., Conover, N. C., & Kala, R. (1986). Parent-child agreement on child psychiatric symptoms assessed via structured interview. *Journal of Child Psychology and Psychiatry, 27,* 181–190.

Fincham, F. D., & Cain, K. M. (1986). Learned helplessness in humans: A developmental analysis. *Developmental Review, 6,* 301–333.

Fox, N. A. (Ed.). (1994). The development of emotion regulation: Biological and behavioral considerations. *Monographs of the Society for Research in Child Development, 59* (2–3, Serial No. 240).

Francis, G., Last, C. G., & Strauss, C. C. (1992). Avoidant disorder and social phobia in children and adolescents. *Journal of the American Academy of Child and Adolescent Psychiatry, 31,* 1086–1089.

Garber, J., & Strassberg, Z. (1991). Construct validity: History and application to developmental psychopathology. In W. M. Grove & D. Cicchetti (Eds.), *Thinking clearly about psychology: Vol. 2. Personality and Psychopathology* (pp. 219–258). Minneapolis: University of Minnesota Press.

Garber, J., Zeman, J., & Walker, L. S. (1990). Recurrent abdominal pain in children: Psychiatric diagnoses and parental psychopathology. *Journal of the American Academy of Child and Adolescent Psychiatry, 29,* 648–656.

Giaconia, R. M., Reinherz, H. Z., Silverman, A. B., Pakiz, B., Frost, A. K., & Cohen, E. (1994). *Journal of the American Academy of Child and Adolescent Psychiatry, 33,* 706–717.

Ginsburg, G. S., Silverman, W. K., & Kurtines, W. M. (1995). Family involvement in treating children with phobic and anxiety disorders: A look ahead. *Clinical Psychology Review, 15,* 457–473.

Goodman, S. H., Gravitt, G. W., & Kaslow, N. J. (1995). Social problem solving: A moderator of the relation between negative life stress and depression symptoms in children. *Journal of Abnormal Child Psychology, 23,* 473–485.

Greenberg, M. T., Kusche, C. A., Cook, E. T., & Quamma, J. P. (1995). Promoting emotional competence in school-aged children: The effects of the PATHS curriculum. *Development and Psychopathology, 7,* 117–136.

Hammen, C., & Compas, B. E. (1994). Unmasking unmasked depression in children and adolescents: The problem of comorbidity. *Clinical Psychology Review, 14,* 585–603.

Harter, S. (1986). Cognitive–developmental processes in the integration of concepts about emotions and the self. *Social Cognition, 4,* 119–151.

Hayward, C., Killen, J. D., Hammer, L. D., Litt, I. F., Wilson, D. M., Simmonds, B., & Taylor, C. B. (1992). Pubertal stage and panic attack history in sixth- and seventh-grade girls. *American Journal of Psychiatry, 149,* 1239–1243.

Hill, J. P., & Lynch, M. E. (1983). The intensification of gender-related role expectations during early adolescence. In J. Brooks-Gunn & A. C. Petersen (Eds.), *Girls at puberty* (pp. 201–228). New York: Plenum Press.

Hodges, K., McKnew, D., Burbach, D. J., & Roebuck, L. (1987). Diagnostic concordance between the Child Assessment Schedule (CAS) and the Schedule for Affective Disorders and Schizophrenia for School-Age Children (K-SADS) in an outpatient sample using lay interviewers. *Journal of the American Academy of Child and Adolescent Psychiatry, 26,* 654–661.

Hymel, S., Franke, S., and Freigang, R. (1985). Peer relationships and their dysfunction: Considering the child's perspective. *Journal of Social and Clinical Psychology, 3,* 405–415.

Ialongo, N., Edelsohn, G., Werthamer-Larsson, L., Crockett, L., & Kellam, S. (1993). Are self-reported depressive symptoms in first-grade children developmentally transient phenomena? A further look. *Development and Psychopathology, 5,* 433–457.

Ialongo, N., Edelsohn, G., Werthamer-Larsson, L., Crockett, L., & Kellam, S. (1994). The significance of self-reported anxious symptoms in first-grade children. *Journal of Abnormal Child Psychology, 22,* 441–455.

Inderbitzen-Pisaruk, H., Clark, M. L., and Solano, C. H. (1992). Correlates of loneliness in midadolescence. *Journal of Youth and Adolescence, 21,* 151–167.

Jaycox, L. H., Reivich, K. J., Gillham, J., & Seligman, M. E. P. (1994). Prevention of depressive symptoms in school children. *Behaviour Research and Therapy, 32,* 801–816.

Kagan, J. (1994). On the nature of emotion. *Monographs of the Society for Research in Child Development, 59* (2–3, Serial No. 240).

Kashani, J. H., Beck, N. C., Hoeper, E. W., Fallahi, C., Corcoran, C. M., McAllister, J. A., Rosenberg, T. K., & Reid, J. C. (1987). Psychiatric disorders in a community sample of adolescents. *American Journal of Psychiatry, 144,* 584–589.

Kashani, J. H., & Orvaschel, H. (1990). A community study of anxiety in children and adolescents. *American Journal of Psychiatry, 147,* 313–318.

Kashani, J. H., Orvaschel, H., Rosenberg, T. K., & Reid, J. C. (1989). Psychopathology in a community sample of children and adolescents: A developmental perspective. *Journal of the American Academy of Child and Adolescent Psychiatry, 28,* 701–706.

Kazdin, A. E., French, N. H., Unis, A. S., & Esveldt-Dawson, K. (1983). Assessment of childhood depression: Correspondence of child and parent ratings. *Journal of the American Academy of Child Psychiatry, 22,* 157–164.

Kellam, S. G., Rebok, G. W., Mayer, L. S., Ialongo, N., & Kalodner, C. R. (1994). Depressive symptoms over first grade and their response to a developmental epidemiologically based preventive trial aimed at improving achievement. *Development and Psychopathology, 6,* 463–481.

Kendall, P. C. (1994). Treating anxiety disorders in children: Results of a randomized clinical trial. *Journal of Consulting and Clinical Psychology, 62,* 100–110.

Kendall, P. C., Cantwell, D. P., & Kazdin, A. E. (1989). Depression in children and adolescents: Assessment issues and recommendations. *Cognitive Therapy and Research, 13,* 109–146.

Kendall, P. C., Kortlander, E., Chansky, T. E., & Brady, E. U. (1992). Comorbidity of anxiety and depression in youth: Treatment implications. *Journal of Consulting and Clinical Psychology, 60,* 869–880.

Kendall, P. C., & Ronan, K. D. (1990). Assessment of children's anxieties, fears, and phobias: Cognitive–behavioral models and methods. In C. R. Reynolds & R. W. Kamphaus (Eds.), *Handbook of psychological and educational assessment of children: Vol. 2. Personality, behavior, and context* (pp. 223–244). New York: Guilford Press.

King, N. J., Ollendick, T. H., & Gullone, E. (1991). Negative affectivity in children and adolescents: Relations between anxiety and depression. *Clinical Psychology Review, 11,* 441–459.

Kohlberg, L., LaCrosse, J., & Ricks, D. (1972). The predictability of adult mental health from childhood behavior. In B. Wolman (Ed.), *Manual of child psychopathology* (pp. 1217–1284). New York: McGraw-Hill.

Kovacs, M., Gatsonis, C., Paulauskas, S., & Richards, C. (1989). Depressive disorders in childhood IV. A longitudinal study of comorbidity with and risk for anxiety disorders. *Archives of General Psychiatry, 46,* 776–782.

Kovacs, M., & Lohr, W. D. (1995). Research on psychotherapy with children and adolescents: An overview of evolving trends and current issues. *Journal of Abnormal Child Psychology, 23,* 11–30.

Krohne, H. (1992). Developmental conditions of anxiety and coping: A two-process model of child-rearing effects. In K. A. Hagtvet & T. B. Johnson (Eds.), *Advances in test anxiety research* (Vol. 7, pp. 143–155). Amsterdam: Swets & Zeitlinger.

Last, C. G., Perrin, S., Hersen, M., & Kazdin, A. E. (1992). DSM-III-R anxiety disorders in children and adolescents: Sociodemographic and clinical characteristics. *Journal of the American Academy of Child and Adolescent Psychiatry, 31,* 1070–1076.

Lavigne, J. V., Arend, R., Rosenbaum, D., Sinacore, J., Cicchetti, C., Binns, H. J., Christoffel, K. K., Hayford, J. R., & McGuire, P. (1994). Interrater reliability of the DSM-III-R with preschool children. *Journal of Abnormal Child Psychology, 22,* 679–690.

Lefkowitz, M. M., & Burton, N. (1978). Childhood depression: A critique of the concept. *Psychological Bulletin, 85,* 716–726.

Lewinsohn, P. M., Hops, H., Roberts, R. E., Seeley, J. R., & Andrews, J. A. (1993). Adolescent psychopathology: I. Prevalence and inci-dence of depression and other DSM-III-R disorders in high school students. *Journal of Abnormal Psychology, 102,* 133–144.

Masten, A. S., & Braswell, L. (1991). Developmental psychopathology: An integrative framework. In P. R. Martin (Ed.), *Handbook of behavior therapy and psychological science: An integrative approach* (pp. 35–56). New York: Pergamon Press.

Mattis, S. G., & Ollendick, T. H. (1997). Children's cognitive responses to the symptoms of panic. *Journal of Abnormal Child Psychology, 25,* 47–57.

McGee, R., & Williams, S. (1988). A longitudinal study of depression in nine-year-old children. *Journal of the American Academy of Child and Adolescent Psychiatry, 27,* 342–348.

Menzies, R. G., & Clark, J. C. (1995). The etiology of phobias: A nonassociative account. *Clinical Psychology Review, 15,* 23–48.

Nelles, W. B., & Barlow, D. H. (1988). Do children panic? *Clinical Psychology Review, 8,* 359–372.

Nolen-Hoeksema, S., & Girgus, J. S. (1994). The emergence of gender differences in depression during adolescence. *Psychological Bulletin, 115,* 424–443.

Nolen-Hoeksema, S., Girgus, J. S., & Seligman, M. E. P. (1992). Predictors and consequences of childhood depressive symptoms: A 5-year longitudinal study. *Journal of Abnormal Psychology, 101,* 405–422.

Nottelmann, E. D., & Jensen, P. S. (1995). Comorbidity of disorders in children and adolescents: Developmental perspectives. In T. H. Ollendick & R. J. Prinz (Eds.), *Advances in clinical child psychology* (Vol. 17, pp. 109–155). New York: Plenum Press.

Ollendick, T. H., & King, N. J. (1994). Diagnosis, assessment, and treatment of internalizing problems in children: The role of longitudinal data. *Journal of Consulting and Clinical Psychology, 62,* 918–927.

Ollendick, T. H., Mattis, S. G., & King, N. J. (1994). Panic in children and adolescents: A review. *Journal of Child Psychology and Psychiatry, 35,* 113–134.

Patterson, G. R., Reid, J. B., & Dishion, T. J. (1992). *Antisocial boys.* Eugene, OR: Castalia Publishing.

Patterson, G. R., & Stoolmiller, M. (1991). Replications of a dual failure model for boys' depressed mood. *Journal of Consulting and Clinical Psychology, 59,* 491–498.

Pearce, J. (1978). The recognition of depressive disorder in children. *Journal of the Royal Society of Medicine, 71,* 494–500.

Renouf, A. G., & Kovacs, M. (1994). Concordance between mothers' reports and children's self-reports of depressive symptoms: A longitudinal study. *Journal of the American Academy of Child and Adolescent Psychiatry, 33,* 208–216.

Rie, H. E. (1966). Depression in childhood: A survey of some pertinent contributions. *Journal of the American Academy of Child Psychiatry, 5,* 653–683.

Roberts, R. E., Andrews, J. A., Lewinsohn, P. M., & Hops, H. (1990). Assessment of depression in adolescents using the Center for Epidemiologic Studies Depression Scale. *Psychological Assessment: A Journal of Consulting and Clinical Psychology, 2,* 122–128.

Roberts, R. E., Lewinsohn, P. M., & Seeley, J. R. (1991). Screening for adolescent depression: A comparison of depression scales.

Journal of the American Academy of Child and Adolescent Psychiatry, 30, 58–66.

Russo, M. F., & Beidel, D. C. (1994). Comorbidity of childhood anxiety and externalizing disorders: Prevalence, associated characteristics, and validation issues. *Clinical Psychology Review, 14,* 199–221.

Rutter, M. (1989). Age as an ambiguous variable in development research: Some epidemiological considerations from developmental psychopathology. *International Journal of Behavioral Development, 12,* 1–34.

Rutter, M., & Garmezy, N. (1983). Developmental psychopathology. In E. M. Hetherington (Ed.), *Handbook of child psychology: Socialization, personality, and social development* (Vol. 4, pp. 775–911). New York: Wiley.

Saarni, C. (1990). Emotional competence: How emotions and relationships become integrated. In R. A. Thompson (Ed.), *Nebraska symposium on motivation 1988: Vol. 36. Socioemotional development* (pp. 115–182). Lincoln: University of Nebraska Press.

Shapiro, T. (1995). Developmental issues in psychotherapy research. *Journal of Abnormal Child Psychology, 23,* 31–44.

Silverman, W. K. (1994). Structured diagnostic interviews. In T. H. Ollendick, N. J. King, & W. Yule (Eds.), *International handbook of phobic and anxiety disorders in children and adolescents* (pp. 293–315). New York: Plenum Press.

Silverman, W. K., & Eisen, A. R. (1992). Age differences in the reliability of parent and child reports of child anxious symptomatology using a structured interview. *Journal of the American Academy of Child and Adolescent Psychiatry, 31,* 117–124.

Silverman, W. K., & Kurtines, W. M. (1996). Treating internalizing disorders in youth: The evolution of a psychosocial intervention model. In E. D. Hibbs & P. Jensen (Eds.), *Psychosocial treatment research of child and adolescent disorders.* Washington, DC: American Psychological Association.

Silverman, W. K., & Rabian, B. (1995). Test-retest reliability of the DSM-III-R childhood anxiety disorders symptoms using the Anxiety Disorders Interview Schedule for Children. *Journal of Anxiety Disorders, 9,* 139–150.

Silverman, W. K., & Rabian, B. (in press). Rating scales for anxiety and mood disorders. In D. Shaffer & J. Richters (Eds.), *Assessment in child psychopathology.* New York: Guilford Press.

Strauss, C. C., Last, C. G., Hersen, M., & Kazdin, A. E. (1988). Association between anxiety and depression in children and adolescents with anxiety disorders. *Journal of Abnormal Child Psychology, 16,* 57–68.

Strauss, C. C., Lease, C. A., Last, C. G., & Francis, G. (1988). Overanxious disorder: An examination of developmental differences. *Journal of Abnormal Child Psychology, 16,* 433–443.

Thompson, R. A. (1990). Emotion and self-regulation. In R. A. Thompson (Ed.), *Nebraska Symposium on Motivation 1988: Vol. 36. Socioemotional development* (pp. 367–467). Lincoln: Univerisity of Nebraska Press.

Turner, J. E., & Cole, D. A. (1994). Developmental differences in cognitive diatheses for childhood depression. *Journal of Abnormal Child Psychology, 22,* 15–32.

Vasey, M. W. (1993). Development and cognition in childhood anxiety: The example of worry. In T. Ollendick & R. Prinz (Eds.), *Advances in clinical child psychology* (Vol. 15, pp. 1–39). New York: Plenum Press.

Vasey, M. W. (1995). Social anxiety disorders. In A. R. Eisen, C. A. Kearney, & C. E. Schaefer (Eds.), *Clinical handbook of anxiety disorders in children and adolescents* (pp. 131–168). New Jersey: Jason Aronson.

Vasey, M. W., & Daleiden, E. L. (1996). Information-processing pathways to cognitive interference in childhood. In I. G. Sarason, B. R. Sarason, & G. R. Pierce (Eds.), *Cognitive interference: Theories, methods, and findings* (pp. 117–138). Hillsdale, NJ: Erlbaum.

Vernberg, E. M., Abwender, D. A., Ewell, K. K., and Beery, S. H. (1992). Social anxiety and peer relationships in early adolescence: A prospective analysis. *Journal of Clinical Child Psychology, 21,* 189–196.

Waldron, S. (1976). The significance of childhood neurosis for adult mental health: A follow-up study. *American Journal of Psychiatry, 133,* 532–538.

Watson, D., & Clark, L. A. (1984). Negative affectivity: The predisposition to experience aversive emotional states. *Psychological Bulletin, 96,* 465–490.

Weinberg, W. A., Rutman, J., Sullivan, L., Penick, E. C., & Dietz, S. G. (1973). Depression in children referred to an educational center: Diagnosis and treatment. *Journal of Pediatrics, 83,* 1065–1072.

Weisz, J. R., Rudolph, K. D., Granger, D. A., & Sweeney, L. (1992). Cognition, competence, and coping in child and adolescent depression: Research findings, developmental concerns, therapeutic implications. *Development and Psychopathology, 4,* 627–653.

Weisz, J. R., & Weiss, B. (1989). Cognitive mediators of the outcome of psychotherapy with children. In B. B. Lahey & A. E. Kazdin (Eds.), *Advances in clinical child psychology* (Vol. 12, pp. 27–51). New York: Plenum Press.

Werry, J. S. (1991). Overanxious disorder: A review of its taxonomic properties. *Journal of the American Academy of Child and Adolescent Psychiatry, 30,* 533–544.

CHAPTER 17

EXTERNALIZING DISORDERS

Charlotte Johnston
Jeneva L. Ohan

The term *externalizing disorders* reflects a linguistic combination of dimensional and categorical approaches to the classification of behavior problems in children and adolescents. From a dimensional perspective, multivariate studies of behavior problems in children have consistently revealed two broad-band factors, identified as externalizing and internalizing (Achenbach, 1991; Quay, 1986). The externalizing factor is comprised of behaviors that place the child in conflict with the environment and contrasts with the more inner-directed problems of the internalizing factor (e.g., depression, anxiety). Externalizing problems also have been referred to as undercontrolled or acting-out behaviors, and narrow-band aggregations of these behaviors, identified through factor analyses, have been described also as *antisocial behavior, delinquency, aggression,* and *hyperactivity.* Categorically, in the current editions of both the *Diagnostic and Statistical Manual of Mental Disorders* (DSM-IV;

American Psychiatric Association, 1994) and the *International Classification of Diseases* (ICD-10; World Health Organization, 1990), the disorders that encompass externalizing behaviors include attention-deficit hyperactivity disorder (ADHD), oppositional defiant disorder (ODD), and conduct disorder (CD). The clusters of behaviors comprising these three disorders are the focus of this chapter.

According to DSM-IV, the symptoms of ADHD are grouped into two clusters; inattentive (e.g., fails to give close attention to work, difficulty sustaining attention) and hyperactive-impulsive (e.g., fidgets, blurts out answers). For a diagnosis to be made, six symptoms from one or both of these clusters must be present with a severity that substantially exceeds developmental norms. Additional criteria include an age of onset before 7 years, a minimum symptom duration of 6 months, and evidence of impairment in more than one setting (e.g., home and school). There are three subtypes of ADHD, depending on the cluster(s) of symptoms for which the child meets criteria: primarily inattentive type, primarily hyperactive–impulsive type, and combined type. Using DSM-IV criteria, the gender ratio of ADHD is estimated to range from 4 to 9 boys for every girl, with more females identified in community samples than in clinic samples.

During the writing of this chapter Charlotte Johnston was supported, in part, by a grant from the National Health and Research Development Program of Health Canada. Jeneva Ohan was supported by a scholarship from the British Columbia Health Research Foundation. We thank Wendy Freeman for her comments.

ODD is defined in DSM-IV as a pattern of negative, hostile, and defiant behavior (e.g., loses temper, argues with adults) that exceeds age norms and causes impairment. At least four symptoms must be present for a minimum of 6 months. Using these criteria, the prevalence is estimated to range from 2 to 16 percent, and the disorder is more frequent among males, at least before puberty. CD is defined as a set of behaviors that violate basic rules or the rights of others (e.g., aggression, destruction of property) and a DSM-IV diagnosis requires three such behaviors within the past year and one within the past 6 months. Again, impairment is required. Two subtypes are specified; childhood-onset and adolescent-onset. Prevalence estimates vary widely and DSM-IV lists a range from 2 to 9 percent for females and 6 to 16 percent for males.

Not only are externalizing disorders prevalent and serious, but they also demonstrate considerable stability from early childhood through to adulthood (Lahey et al., 1993; Mannuzza & Klein, 1992; Robins, 1978). This stability highlights the fact that for an unfortunate number of children the externalizing disorders are not a transient developmental stage, but rather a lifetime pathway with early behavior problems culminating in later, more serious difficulties. This continuation of externalizing problems reflects the persistence of these disorders over time, as well as the fact that earlier occurring problems such as impulse control or conduct can interfere with the development of more adaptive behaviors, and thus compound and accelerate the development of later externalizing symptomatology. Given this continuity, research describing how these disorders develop and manifest over time provides an essential foundation for prevention and treatment strategies to divert children from the negative trajectories.

This chapter presents an overview of the implications of child development for understanding externalizing disorders. We begin by considering developmental issues in the definition of these disorders and review evidence suggesting that different forms of the disorders appear at different ages. Brief descriptions of the phenomenology and correlates of the externalizing disorders from infancy through to adulthood are then presented. Theoretical models describing the developmental trajectories of these disorders are also reviewed. In the next section, we discuss the need to integrate information concerning the developmental manifestations of the externalizing disorders with treatment and prevention planning. The chapter ends with a consideration of prominent issues arising from a developmental psychopathology perspective on externalizing disorders.

DEVELOPMENTAL ISSUES IN THE DEFINITION OF EXTERNALIZING DISORDERS

From both dimensional and categorical–syndromal perspectives, a division appears between behaviors that are characteristic of ADHD (e.g., inattention, hyperactivity, and impulsivity) and behaviors that are characteristic of ODD and CD (e.g., noncompliance, aggression, antisocial acts). This division is found in factor analytic studies (Achenbach, 1991; Fergusson, Horwood, & Lloyd, 1991; Quay, 1986) and comparisons of subgroups of children formed on the basis of a predominance of ADHD versus ODD/CD behaviors indicate differences in correlates such as family dysfunction, peer status, and prognosis (see Hinshaw, 1987 for a review). However, it is important to note that these distinctions and differences occur within the context of substantial intercorrelations and comorbidities among ADHD and ODD/CD behaviors or diagnoses.

Most of the research supporting the ADHD versus ODD/CD distinction has been conducted with elementary school–age children and adolescents. The distinction between these two types of problems among younger children is more questionable. Findings from Achenbach's (1991) Child Behavior Checklist (CBCL) and earlier factor analytic studies (Behar & Springfield, 1974) support the distinction between ADHD and ODD/CD among 4- to 5-year-old preschoolers. However, as with older children, preschool children who are rated as high in either the ADHD or ODD/CD domain are often rated as high in the other as well (Campbell, Breaux, Ewing, & Szumowski, 1986). In contrast to these findings with children 4 years of age or older, the version of the CBCL developed for 2 and 3 year olds shows attentional, impulsivity, and overactivity problems and aggressive, uncooperative behaviors as loading together on one factor, although this factor is distinguished from a destructive behavior factor (Achenbach & Edelbrock, 1986). Questions have also been raised on the general usefulness of diagnostic or syndromal labels at the early preschool ages (Campbell, 1990), with preference expressed for a more descriptive and clinically based approach. In sum, although a basic division between ADHD and ODD/CD types of externalizing problems is generally supported among school-age and older individuals, this distinction appears less useful earlier in development.

Beyond their separation from ADHD, the question of whether ODD and CD problems should be viewed as distinct from each other, or whether they merely reflect differences in the timing and severity of the same disorder remains the topic of considerable research attention. As outlined by Lahey and Loeber (1994), several factor analytic studies have supported the distinction between ODD/aggressive behaviors versus more serious CD behaviors/substance abuse. A recent meta-analysis of these studies by Frick and colleagues (1993) revealed not only an overt–covert dimension that distinguished overt ODD/aggressive behaviors from covert forms of CD, but also a second dimension of destructive-nondestructive that separated nondestructive ODD behaviors from aggressive behaviors and milder or intermediate CD behaviors (e.g., status violations) from the more severe CD behaviors (e.g., property violations) that appear at older ages. Using these dimensions as the basis for a cluster analysis, Frick and colleagues found evidence for four subgroups of boys: a *not deviant* group with low scores on all combinations of behaviors, an *ODD* group with ODD and aggressive behaviors, a *younger CD* group with ODD, aggressive, and milder, nonaggressive types of CD, and an *older CD* group with marked elevations on all types of behaviors, including more advanced conduct problems. Reviewing evidence from factor analytic studies, as well as data concerning the age of onset and correlates of each type of behavior, Lahey and Loeber (1994) have proposed a developmental levels model that views ODD behaviors as the most prevalent of these problems and as occurring at the earliest ages. For some children, these ODD behaviors will desist, but for others a set of intermediate CD behaviors (e.g., fighting, bullying, lying) will be added as the children age. Finally, for a minority of children, ODD and intermediate CD behaviors will maintain with age and be joined by a set of more advanced or serious CD behaviors (e.g., mugging, truancy, theft). Thus, although ODD and CD behaviors are distinguished in this model, they are viewed as disorders that are developmentally stacked. This model is discussed further in the following section, but the evidence on which it is based clearly illustrates that any distinction made between ODD and CD behaviors must be grounded in a developmental framework.

Subtypes of ADHD have also been proposed. The most recent of these subtypologies, outlined in DSM-IV, distinguishes predominantly inattentive, predominantly hyperactive–impulsive, and combined subtypes. These distinctions reflect the findings of factor analytic studies (Bauermeister, Alegria, Bird, Rubio-Stipec, & Canino, 1992; Pelham, Gnagy, Greenslade, & Milich, 1992) that find separate dimensions of hyperactive–impulsive versus inattentive behaviors among elementary school–age children. However, this distinction is less consistently found among preschool children (Achenbach & Edelbrock, 1983). There is evidence that behaviors characteristic of the hyperactive–impulsive subtype onset in the late preschool years, whereas problems of the inattentive subtype onset at the time of school entry (Hart, Lahey, Loeber, Applegate, & Frick, 1995; Loeber, Green, Lahey, Christ, & Frick, 1992). These two symptom clusters also appear to have different developmental courses, with impulsive–hyperactive problems declining between late childhood and early adolescence while problems of inattention show greater stability over this period (Hart et al., 1995). Despite the existence of distinct inattention and impulsive–hyperactive factors in multivariate studies and the evidence of different developmental paths, evidence regarding the divergent or predictive validity of the DSM-IV subtypes is not conclusive. Whether these subtypes are more appropriately viewed as developmental stages of the same underlying problem, subtypes within the larger disorder, or distinctly different disorders, is the topic of considerable debate (Barkley, 1996; Goodyear & Hynd, 1992). Although developmental perspectives on ADHD have not been frequent, evidence such as that reviewed above clearly points to the importance of considering developmental factors in future efforts at defining ADHD and its subtypes.

As a conclusion to this section on the definition of externalizing disorders, we note the danger of taking a restricted psychological or psychiatric perspective on the development of externalizing problems. The preceding review has predominantly reflected these perspectives, with externalizing behaviors seen as characteristics inherent to the child. Hinshaw and Anderson (1996) caution that these behaviors may also be viewed as sociological problems, with origins in communities of poverty, educational disadvantage, and violence. We must remain mindful of the social context within which externalizing disorders occur and combine our description of the pathways that individual children follow in developing these disorders with a recognition of the current and evolving conditions within our cultural and social institutions.

COMORBIDITY OF ADHD AND ODD/CD

In the sections that follow we review the developmental progressions of ODD/CD and ADHD behaviors. Prior to these separate considerations, it is worthwhile to note the frequent overlap among these conditions. Research in both clinical and community samples indicates that among elementary school–age children diagnosed with either ADHD or ODD/CD, a substantial number demonstrate behaviors that meet criteria for both types of externalizing disorders (Anderson, Williams, McGee, & Silva, 1987; Hinshaw, 1987). For example, it can be conservatively estimated that among children diagnosed with ADHD, between 35 and 70 percent develop ODD, and between 30 and 50 percent become co-morbid for CD (Barkley, Fischer, Edelbrock, & Smallish, 1990; Biederman, Newcorn, & Sprich, 1991; Taylor, Sandberg, Thorley, & Giles, 1991). Evidence suggests that the co-occurrence of ADHD and ODD/CD behaviors results in both greater concurrent impairment and in poorer developmental outcome than the occurrence of either disorder alone (Faraone, Biederman, Keenan, & Tsuang, 1991; Walker, Lahey, Hynd, & Frame, 1987). Although it is well established that the presence of aggressive behavior (ODD or CD), with or without ADHD, is prognostic of continued problems in a wide range of domains (Farrington & West, 1990; Loeber, 1990; McGee, Silva, & Williams, 1983), the prognosis associated with ADHD alone is less well understood. Although the outcome risk in this sole diagnosis group usually appears less than the comorbid group, several studies have suggested that ADHD alone can be associated with academic underachievement, alcohol problems, antisocial behavior, interpersonal problems, and other forms of psychological deviance during elementary school as well as during adolescence and adulthood (Farrington, Loeber, & VanKammen, 1990; Johnston, 1996a; Taylor, Chadwick, Heptinstall, & Danckaerts, 1996).

Although far from settled, current data suggest that the most common pathway for children with dual ADHD and ODD/CD diagnoses is one in which ADHD precedes oppositional or conduct problems (Hinshaw, Lahey, & Hart, 1993; Moffitt, 1990). Following a transactional perspective, the impulsivity and attentional difficulties associated with ADHD are presumed to interact with a wide range of potential familial risks (e.g., marital discord, parent psychopathology, poor parenting skills, stress, social disadvantage) to increase the likelihood of both ODD and CD as well as continued problems in academic and social realms. For example, a young child who is impulsive and overactive presents an extreme challenge to the parenting system. Any weakness in parenting (e.g., existing stress, inexperience, or parent psychopathology) interacts with this challenging child to set in motion a pattern of coercive, nonresponsive parent–child interactions. These interactions, in turn, play a role in both the onset and exacerbation of child noncompliance and defiant behavior. The impulsivity and inattention of the young ADHD child not only drive the early onset of ODD behaviors, but continue to exert an influence across the child's development, accelerating the development of more serious forms of both ADHD and ODD/CD behaviors.

OPPOSITIONAL DEFIANT AND CONDUCT DISORDERS ACROSS THE LIFE SPAN

Although ODD/CD are seldom, if ever, diagnosed in infants or toddlers, a developmental perspective would suggest that the precursors to or risk factors for these disorders may well be present during this age period. The recently developed *Diagnostic Classification: 0 to 3* (Zero to Three/National Center for Clinical Infant Program, 1994), designed to provide a classification of problems during infancy and toddlerhood, may promote greater recognition of the types of early problems that may precede ODD/CD disorders. This taxonomy is particularly commendable in its consideration of parent–infant relational factors as essential components of child problems in this young age range. This focus on parent–child interactions is also reflected in work from an attachment perspective. For example, Greenberg, Speltz, and DeKleyen (1993) argue that insecure attachments between caregiver and infant, when they occur along with other vulnerabilities such as infant neurological dysfunction or disturbances in parenting, serve as risk factors for the development of ODD/CD problems. Supporting this view, the Minnesota Mother–Child Project has followed a high-risk group of children from birth through preadolescence and has found consistent relationships between insecure attachments in infancy and later oppositional–aggressive behaviors, as well as internalizing problems, especially among boys (Elicker, Englund, & Sroufe, 1992; Urban, Carlson, Egeland, & Sroufe, 1992). Greenberg and colleagues have proposed that the link between attachment and ODD/CD problems may arise because the child develops dysfunctional internal working models of relationships (e.g., the development of a hostile attributional bias), because the behavior problems serve an attachment function (e.g., soliciting maternal attention), or because insecure attachment reduces the motivational power of social relationships for the child.

The average age for first diagnosis of ODD is around 6 years of age and for CD diagnoses at around 9 years (Hinshaw & Anderson, 1996). However, behavior that is noncompliant, oppositional, or rule-violating is often seen during the preschool years. Whether such behavior is characteristic of the normative preschool struggle for autonomy or indicative of a psychiatric disorder is a challenging question (Campbell, 1990). Developmental researchers (e.g., Crockenberg & Litman, 1990; Kuczynski & Kochanska, 1990) suggest that child noncompliance is multifaceted, with some forms of noncompliance being relatively skilled and reflecting appropriate assertions of child autonomy, with only more unskilled forms being linked to the development of behavioral problems. For example, in a sample of 5 year olds and their mothers, Kuczynski and Kochanska (1990) observed that skilled noncompliance (e.g., negotiation, assertive refusal) and unskilled noncompliance (e.g., defiance) were unrelated to each other, and it was only the unskilled forms of child noncompliance that were predictive of externalizing child behaviors. In instances in which the preschooler's opposition to parental directions reflects developmentally appropriate behavior, applying an ODD label has the potential for harm.

Despite the common occurrence and developmental appropriateness of some degree of and forms of oppositional behavior in preschoolers, there are convincing reasons to believe that identifying the extremities of this pattern may alert clinicians and researchers to present or future problems with ODD/CD. As already noted, there is a substantial stability of ODD/CD behavior over time, and this stability is particularly strong among children with an early onset of these behaviors (Loeber & Stouthammer-Loeber, 1987). For example, Lahey, Loeber, Quay, Frick, and Grimm (1992) found evidence for the onset of behavior problems in the preschool years among children aged 7 to 12 years who were clinically-referred for ODD/CD behaviors. Based on retrospective maternal reports, these children were described as having stubborn temperaments at as early as 3 years of age, and defiance and tantrums were reported by age 5.

It is important to note that the presence of stubbornness, defiance, temper tantrums, irritability, and aggression during the preschool years does not guarantee the persistence of ODD/CD behavior. In general, the number of children engaging in particular forms of oppositional or conduct behavior declines as the behaviors become more severe, with a progression from more prevalent and milder ODD behaviors to less prevalent, more severe CD problems (Lahey & Loeber, 1994). Thus, it is expected that only some preschoolers with ODD behaviors will continue on to meet ODD diagnostic criteria during the elementary school years and fewer still will meet CD criteria as children or adolescents. Supporting this developmental progression of ODD to CD, studies of elementary school–age children typically indicate that over 90 percent of children diagnosed with CD have previously been diagnosed with ODD (Hinshaw et al., 1993; Spitzer, Davies, & Barkley, 1991); however, the majority of children with ODD diagnoses do not continue on to diagnoses of CD. For example, in the Developmental Trends Study, over 60 percent of 7- to 12-year-old boys who met ODD criteria did not progress to a CD diagnosis over a 4-year period (Lahey & Loeber, 1994). Other research reviewed by Loeber (1990) indicates that compared to those who do not, children who progress from preschool oppositional behaviors to elementary school diagnoses of ODD

and who continue on to add CD behaviors to their repertoire engage in a wider variety of disruptive behaviors across a wider range of settings and are more likely to have concomitant problems with ADHD and social relationships.

During the elementary school years, ODD/CD problems can take a variety of forms, including conflicts with authority (e.g., refusal to comply with parental rules, school truancy), overt problems (e.g., aggression, bullying, fighting), and/or covert problems such as lying, stealing, and property damage (Lahey & Loeber, 1994). In addition, children diagnosed with ODD or CD frequently experience academic difficulties (although this link may be mediated by comorbid ADHD) (Frick et al., 1991; Hinshaw, 1992), internalizing disorders (Offord, Alder, & Boyle, 1986), and a host of interpersonal problems.

Almost by definition, children diagnosed with ODD/CD show significantly higher rates of parent–child conflict than nonproblem children. Social-learning and transactional perspectives on how parenting and family variables contribute to the development and exacerbation of ODD/CD behaviors emphasize the contributions of both child and family characteristics (Moffitt, 1993; Patterson, 1986). For example, Patterson's model of antisocial behavior is grounded in early parent–child interactions in which aversive attacks, exhibited by either child or parent, are occasionally reinforced by the other's withdrawal of demands. Termed *coercive interactions,* these family exchanges provide the training ground in which the child develops his repertoire of ODD/CD behaviors. Moffitt's model of early-onset ODD/CD problems adds child neurological problems (e.g., executive functioning deficits or ADHD), and family disadvantages (e.g., stress or parent psychopathology) to the early mix that sets the stage for these coercive interchanges in the parent–child system. As the child ages and moves from home to school settings, his or her existing repertoire of ODD/CD behaviors sets the stage for conflict with authority figures and peers.

Beyond family problems, peer difficulties of children with ODD/CD are also well documented (Kuperschmidt, Coie, & Dodge, 1990; Ollendick, Weist, Borden, & Greene, 1992). Aggression is a strong predictor of peer rejection (Coie & Dodge, 1983), and in a vicious cycle of causality, peer rejection serves as a predictor of further antisocial behaviors and association with deviant peers in adolescence (Bierman & Wargo, 1995; Patterson, 1986). Evidence suggests that social–cognitive mechanisms, such as a hostile attributional bias, are fundamental to many of these peer problems (Dodge, 1986). Recently, Crick and Dodge (1994) have begun to identify the influence of developmental changes, such as increases in knowledge bases and processing efficiency, on the social–cognitive problems of aggressive children. For example, with development all children are expected to become more proficient in their preferred or usual style of social information processing. Unfortunately, for aggressive children this developmental change may translate into an increasing rigidity in the use of a distorted, hostile attributional style in interpreting their peers' behaviors.

There is a rather sharp increase in the prevalence of CD problems from the elementary school age to the teen years. As summarized by Moffitt (1993), in a sample of New Zealand boys, 5 percent showed a pattern of early onset and persistent ODD/CD behaviors into adolescence. However, between the ages of 11 and 15, another 33 percent of the sample began to show CD behaviors. Thus, it was suggested that the increase in prevalence of CD among adolescents reflects the presence of two subgroups. One group is those who have followed the early-onset pathway and whose behavior problems began in early childhood (if not before). These children have a history of persistent ODD/CD behaviors of several types displayed across a number of settings. By adolescence, these young people are engaged in serious forms of misconduct, ranging from truancy, through shoplifting and other thefts, to physical violence and substance abuse. A second group of adolescents with conduct problems have been identified as late-starters or adolescent-onset (Lahey & Loeber, 1994; Moffitt, 1993). Among this group who show no history of ODD/CD problems or risk factors such as family dysfunction, poor social skills, or ADHD, the CD problems that emerge during adolescence are more likely to be nonaggressive and transitory in nature. Moffitt (1993) has proposed that the onset of CD problems in this group is related to modeling of the taking on of adult privileges and power displayed by deviant peers and may reflect an unfortunate expression of the developmentally appropriate adolescent search for independence and autonomy. In contrast to the higher prevalence of ODD/CD problems in boys compared to girls that is observed throughout childhood, at adolescence the gender ratio approaches equivalence. It is suggested that the subgroup of adolescents whose developmental history would place them in the early-starter group remains predominantly male, but that girls are more prevalent among adolescents whose CD problems are confined to this developmental period.

As adolescents move into young adulthood, some with ODD/CD problems will continue on to problems with adult antisocial behavior and psychopathy. Following the same pattern as outlined for the transition from ODD to CD behaviors, CD behaviors are found in the histories of most adults with antisocial or aggressive behaviors, but only about 25 to 40 percent of adolescents with CD go on to adult antisocial behavior (Robins, 1978). Efforts geared toward the prevention and reduction of ODD/CD problems earlier in life are judged by many to offer the only hope for reducing the current level of adult antisocial behaviors (Tolan, Guerra, & Kendall, 1995).

ATTENTION-DEFICIT HYPERACTIVITY DISORDER ACROSS THE LIFE SPAN

The onset of ADHD is typically thought to occur at about age 3 (APA, 1994; Barkley, DuPaul, & McMurray, 1990), although some mothers have traced their children's difficulties with overactivity as far back as early infancy and in utero (Shekhim, 1990). About one-third of mothers with children who have been diagnosed with ADHD retrospectively report restlessness, sleep problems, delayed speech and babbling, feeding problems, less smiling, and/or less cuddling from their children during infancy (for a review, see Weiss & Hechtman, 1993). Despite these reports of early symptoms, children with inattentive, impulsive, or overactive behavior are typically not referred to mental health professionals until the preschool or elementary school years. Developmental events that coincide with entry to preschool may account for the increased identification of ADHD during this period. For example, increased demands for following directions, ready comparisons with age-mates, and the need for the child to coordinate his or her social behavior with peers highlight the difficulties of preschool children with ADHD.

As noted previously, the first symptoms of ADHD to emerge are hyperactive–impulsive behaviors around 3 years of age, with inattentive symptoms following at 5 to 7 years of age or later (Hart et al., 1995; Loeber et al., 1992). This pattern is consistent with Barkley's (1996) recently proposed model of ADHD, which emphasizes the disorder as a deficit in inhibitory control. This deficit is present early in life and disrupts a variety of executive functions such as working memory and internalization of speech. The disruption occurs because the development of these functions relies on the ability to delay responding. Although Barkley's model has not yet received full empirical attention, it does offer a useful heuristic and is one of the first theories of ADHD to explicitly consider the role of developmental factors.

Preschoolers with ADHD are often described by parents as constantly moving, unable to complete anything, unable to play alone, and/or unresponsive to praise and punishment (Weiss & Hechtman, 1993). In the preschool classroom, these children are more likely to wander about the classroom, shift activities, and be off-task compared to their nonproblem peers (Campbell, Szumowski, Ewing, Gluck, & Breaux, 1982). For example, in a recent report of the classroom behavior of 20 preschoolers meeting DSM-III-R criteria for ADHD, Alessandri (1992) found they were less attentive, more distractible, and more restless during story time than their peers. The ADHD preschoolers were also less constructive in their play, engaged in less overall play, and played less with and around their peers during free-time.

Moving from preschool to elementary school age, there is a general decrease in the prevalence of ADHD symptoms, and only some preschoolers persist in the diagnosis. For example, Chapel, Robins, McGee, Williams, and Silva (1982) examined the continuity of hyperactivity and/or inattentiveness in a longitudinal, epidemiological study of over a thousand New Zealand children. They found that 5.5 percent of 3-year-old children could be diagnosed as hyperactive based on reports of poor concentration and/or hyperactivity from parents and a psychometrist, but that only 11 percent of these children continued to have diagnosable difficulties with attention and overactivity at age 5, and 17 percent continued to have difficulties at age 9. Preschoolers who are more likely to continue to show ADHD symptomatology upon entry into grade school are those who have exhibited hyperactive and distractible behaviors for a minimum of 1 year (Beitchman, Wekerle, & Hood, 1987). Greater maternal negativity, directiveness, and intrusiveness in parent–child interactions, along with extreme levels of child defiance, hyperactivity, and distractibility are also predictive of continuing problems with ADHD from the preschool to school years (Campbell, March, Pierce, Ewing, & Szumowski, 1991; Jacobvitz & Sroufe, 1987; Richman, Stevenson, & Graham, 1982). Finally, situationally pervasive symptoms are also predictive of persistence of ADHD diagnoses. For example, in a 3-year follow-up study, Campbell, Endman, and Bernfeld (1977) found that children who had problems with hyperactivity in both home and school settings as preschoolers were more likely to be out of their seat and off-task during elementary school than those who had problems only at home, although both groups displayed more disruptive behavior than their normal peers. In summary, findings suggest that ADHD can be identified during the preschool years, and that this diagnosis is most likely to persist into childhood when the symptoms are severe and pervasive and/or occur in the context of negative parent–child interactions.

Research with elementary school–age children diagnosed with ADHD is far more plentiful than with any other age group. Mirroring the increase in the identification of the disorder upon preschool entry, the number of referrals for ADHD also increases with entry to the primary grades (Barkley, 1990; Weiss & Hechtman, 1993). Again, this increase in identification can be linked to increased demands for attention, concentration, impulse control, and organizational skills during this time. Children are increasingly expected to adapt their behavior to the structure and routine of the classroom, to

work independently, to assume greater responsibility for self-care and home chores, and to engage in cooperative enterprises with peers. Each of these requirements will highlight the deficits experienced by the child with ADHD.

Among school-age children with ADHD, problems with inattentive symptoms often appear as daydreaming, distractibility, and an inability to concentrate on or complete tasks (Barkley et al., 1990). The hyperactive–impulsive behaviors that parents and/or teachers complain of include constant activity, impatience, low frustration tolerance, fidgeting, excessive talking, or making noises (APA, 1994; Barkley, 1996). These behaviors are not continually displayed; rather, they are sensitive to internal and external conditions. For example, under conditions of 100 percent reinforcement, children with ADHD learn much like their nonproblem peers, whereas under conditions of partial reinforcement, children with ADHD show a more pronounced difficulty with acquisition (Douglas & Parry, 1994). Other factors, such as the child's level of fatigue, the task complexity, the level of restraint required by the environment, and the presence or absence of a supervising adult, have all been found to impact the display of ADHD symptoms (see Barkley, 1996 for a review).

Behaviors that reflect the core symptoms of ADHD are not the sole problems noted during grade school, and other difficulties often arise as developmental fallout of the primary symptoms. That is, the child's inability to show age-appropriate attention and inhibition interferes with his or her acquisition of experiences and competencies in a variety of domains. By elementary school age, children with ADHD often suffer from impaired parent–child and peer relationships, negative interactions with teachers, low self-esteem, mood and anxiety disorders, and school underachievement (Biederman et al., 1991; Mash & Johnston, 1982; Pelham & Bender, 1982; Tannock, in press). Moreover, as noted above, a substantial number of these children have developed problems that are diagnostic of ODD and CD. There is some suggestion that different subtypes of ADHD may have different patterns of associated problems. For example, there is evidence for a higher comorbidity with learning problems among ADHD children who have inattentive symptoms only (Hynd et al., 1991) and a higher comorbidity with CD/ODD for ADHD children with predominantly hyperactive–impulsive symptoms (Lahey et al., 1987).

There is evidence, from both objective and subjective measures, that the core symptoms of ADHD persist into adolescence for 50 to 80 percent of children (Barkley et al., 1990; Gittelman & Mannuzza, 1985). For example, Barkley and colleagues (1990) found that over 80 percent of 123 children who had displayed significant hyperactivity levels during childhood met criteria for a diagnosis of ADHD in adolescence, based on parental reports. This should not be interpreted to mean that adolescents who meet ADHD criteria do not decline in the severity of inattentive and hyperactive symptoms, however. Results indicate that hyperactivity and inattentiveness decrease from childhood to adolescence for all children, but that adolescents with ADHD remain substantially above the mean of both age-matched and sex-matched control groups (Fischer, Barkley, Fletcher, & Smallish, 1993). Consistent with these findings, Barkley (1996) has stressed that the symptoms of ADHD are not defined by absolute deficiencies in attentiveness and behavioral control, but must be considered relative to developmentally appropriate norms.

The symptoms that adolescents with ADHD may self-report include feelings of restlessness, impulsivity, difficulty concentrating, difficulty completing tasks, irritability, and a quick temper (Gittelman & Manuzza, 1985). Although these self-reported symptoms may be useful in identifying ADHD in adolescents, they are often not the primary presenting problems at this age; rather, academic problems and antisocial behaviors may be the most prominent. Considering the developmental progression of ADHD, it is possible that these problems reflect a number of influences, including the developmental interference effects of earlier ADHD symptoms as well as a "snowballing" of social and academic problems. In addition, the developmental context of adolescence allows for the core symptoms of ADHD to have increasingly severe consequences. For example, inattentiveness may now impact driving safety and impulsive sexual behaviors may result in disease or teen pregnancy. Supporting the view that primary ADHD problems lead to the development of later difficulties in a variety of domains, Lambert (1988) reported the results of a longitudinal, epidemiological study of 240 children who met research criteria for hyperactivity and/or inattentiveness, and 127 control children. At 17 and 18 years of age, the ADHD sample displayed significantly more difficulties at school than normal controls as measured by attendance at alternative schools, dropouts from high school, and failure to continue to college. Conduct problems, which included leaving school or home, becoming an adolescent parent, and having contact with the judicial system were also significantly more prevalent in the ADHD group. Other researchers have reported similar findings (Barkley et al., 1990; Fischer et al., 1993; Weiss & Hechtman, 1993). In summary, longitudinal studies have provided evidence that for children diagnosed with ADHD, the symptoms of the disorder continue to occur at rates above those of normal peers into adolescence, and that low self-esteem, poor relationships with peers, antisocial behavior, and academic problems are also concerns for adolescents with ADHD.

Finally, within the past 5 to 10 years, there has been an increased recognition of the adult continuation and impact of ADHD. Although this area of research is limited, it is currently estimated that 20 to 50 percent of children with ADHD will have problems with ADHD symptoms as adults (Barkley, 1996; Manuzza & Klein, 1992; Weiss & Hechtman, 1993). Study of the disorder in adulthood has been plagued by diagnostic problems, particularly with regard to what symptoms best define the disorder in adulthood (Barkley, 1996; Wender, 1995). It seems that, at a minimum, more work is needed in developing age-appropriate definitions of diagnostic criteria and in gathering adult age norms for these symptoms.

DEVELOPMENTAL PERSPECTIVES ON THE TREATMENT OF ADHD AND ODD/CD

In this section we briefly review interventions for the externalizing disorders. Given the expansive nature of this literature, we have selected one example from each of three types of treatments: medication, psychosocial family-based interventions, and psychosocial child-based interventions. In addition, we discuss the growing recognition of the need for multimodal treatment and prevention programs for these disorders. This review focuses on the treatment implications of the child's developmental level and the disorder's (or disorder subtype's) typical developmental trajectory. Of the treatments that we review, some are recommended primarily for ADHD symptoms, some are used for primarily ODD/CD problems, and yet others have been used with either or both types of problems.

Medication

Consistent with views of ADHD having an underlying biological basis, the most common treatment for the disorder is pharmacological. A range of medications have been used with this population, but given space limitations and the predominant use of stimulants, we will limit our discussion to the stimulants. Literally hundreds of studies have examined the short-term efficacy of stimulant drug treatment for elementary school–age children with ADHD (Swanson, 1993), using primarily male, Caucasian participants (Spencer et al., 1996). The few studies that have been conducted with preschool-age children with ADHD have revealed mixed results, with side effects often outweighing benefits (Schleifer et al., 1975). For example, in a study of 27 preschoolers with ADHD, Barkley (1988) found evidence for medication-induced improvements in off-task behavior and mother-child interactions (e.g., decreased child noncompliance and maternal commands). However, for more than one-third of the children, the improvement was not judged sufficient to justify the continuation of medication. Research on the short-term effects of stimulant medication with elementary school–age children generally finds evidence of decreases in the core symptoms of ADHD for 70 to 90 percent of children in addition to benefits in related areas such as academic and social functioning (Campbell & Cueva, 1995; Pelham & Milich, 1991; Spencer et al., 1996). Research on children with comorbid ADHD and ODD/CD has provided evidence for medication-induced improvements in both ADHD and ODD/CD symptoms (Barkley, McMurray, Edelbrock, & Robins, 1989; Hinshaw, Heller, & McHale, 1992). Reports of the short-term efficacy of stimulant medication in improving core symptoms, academic performance, and social behavior among adolescents with ADHD also exist (Barrickman et al., 1995; Evans & Pelham, 1991; Varley, 1985). For example, Klorman, Coons, and Borgstedt (1987) found that teacher and parent ratings of inattention, hyperactivity, and noncompliance decreased for 19 adolescents with ADHD when they were taking stimulant medication compared to placebo. Few controlled studies on the use of stimulants with adults with ADHD exist, although this is a rapidly growing area of study. Although some studies report a positive response to stimulants in adults with ADHD (Spencer et al., 1995), the results both across individual clients and across research studies vary widely (Spencer et al., 1996). Issues related to the uncertainty of appropriate dose levels and diagnostic criteria for adults may explain some of these discrepancies.

Despite numerous reports attesting to medication-induced short-term improvements for both children and adolescents with ADHD, evidence that stimulant treatment in childhood appreciably improves the long-term outcome of the disorder is lacking (Hechtman, 1985; Varley, 1985). Given the marked short-term benefits of medication, this lack of long-term impact appears paradoxical. Indeed, developmental models of ADHD would seem to predict that early deficits in attention and impulse control should contribute to later problems and, as a necessary corollary, that treatments that improve symptoms at younger ages should show benefits over the course of development. Solving this intriguing paradox remains a question in the forefront of ADHD research. One possible explanation for the discrepancy is that medications are not adhered to over time. For example, researchers have found that up to 80 percent of children participating in short-term research trials with stimulant medication do not receive or take medication as stipulated by the researcher (Firestone, 1982; Johnston & Fine, 1990), and even this figure may be an underestimate considering that many children withdraw before completing medication trials (Brown, Borden, & Clingerman, 1985).

In summary, stimulant medications are a mainstay in the treatment of elementary school–age children with ADHD, and they are also beginning to demonstrate usefulness at both younger and older ages. Response to medication appears more variable at the preschool and adult ages than during childhood and adolescence. Whether this reflects a true developmental difference in the action of the medication or the limitations of diagnosis and titration at these ages is unknown.

Family-Based Psychosocial Treatments

Treatments addressing family interactions have been developed primarily with regard to ODD/CD, although they have also been applied to ADHD (particularly in instances of co-occurring ADHD and ODD/CD). These treatments reflect theoretical models that emphasize the role of parent–child interactions in the origins and exacerbation of ODD/CD behaviors. Appropriately, these programs are most commonly used with preadolescent children, the developmental stage at which family influences may be considered paramount. Although treatments based in attachment and family systems theories have been developed (Alexander & Parsons, 1982; Speltz, 1990), the best established programs are those based in social learning theory that teach behavioral management strategies to parents (Miller & Prinz, 1990). These behavioral programs have been widely validated among families of preschool and elementary school–age children (Kazdin, 1987). For example, the Forehand and McMahon (1981) program has demonstrated short-term effects in reducing aggressive and noncompliant child behavior, and evidence of generalizability across situations and to siblings. Similarly, Eyberg's Parent–Child Interaction Therapy, which teaches parents not only behavior management strategies, but also problem-solving techniques and play skills for enhancing the parent–child relationship, has demonstrated clinically significant effects and generalization (Eyberg, 1988). Perhaps most encouraging, the effects of these programs appear to generalize over time, with positive effects lasting into adolescence (Forehand & Long, 1988). Research has also addressed variables that may interfere with the effectiveness of behavioral parent training, with newer treatment models including a focus on factors such as parent cognitions, social or marital support, and therapy style (Johnston, 1996b; Patterson & Chamberlain, 1994; Webster-Stratton, 1994).

As noted above, behavioral parent training programs have also been used in the treatment of ADHD, primarily with preschool and elementary school–age children. Although data are generally supportive of the utility of these programs in the treatment of ADHD (Anastopoulos,

Barkley, & Shelton, 1996; Pisterman et al., 1989), the relative efficacy of behavioral treatments and stimulants versus combinations of these treatments is unclear (Gittelman et al., 1980; Hinshaw, Henker, & Whalen, 1984; Horn et al., 1991). Interestingly, the only treatment program that has yet to suggest any alteration of the long-term course of ADHD is the multimodal program of the Satterfields (Satterfield, Satterfield, & Cantwell, 1981), which combined medication and behavior management, both at home and school, with numerous other treatment components.

Although family influences may decrease at adolescence, research evidence supports the continued importance of family involvement in treatment at this age, at least in the area of ODD/CD (Barton, Alexander, Waldron, Turner, & Warburton, 1985; Robin & Foster, 1989). For example, in a sample of high-risk youth, Dishion and Andrews (1995) compared the effects of a behavioral parenting intervention, a teen-focused self-regulation intervention, a combined parent and teen intervention, a placebo control, and a no-treatment condition. The active treatments were all offered in group format. Results indicated immediate beneficial effects of the parenting intervention, with sustained effects at 1 year post-treatment. Interestingly, this study also suggested that the teen-focused intervention resulted in increases in ODD/CD behaviors, likely due to contagion effects in the groups of deviant youth. This study illuminates, albeit in an unplanned fashion, the importance of both family and peer influences during adolescence. Among families of adolescents with ADHD, the success of behavioral parent training is not as well demonstrated. For example, Barkley, Guevremont, Anastopoulos, and Fletcher (1992), in a sample of families of 12 to 18 year olds with ADHD (many with concurrent ODD/CD problems), found that treatments emphasizing behavior management, communication training, or family interactions revealed equal effects, and none were able to produce clinically significant change for the majority of adolescents.

In summary, behavioral parent training offers promise in altering the course of ODD/CD problems. Although most studies have focused on the preschool and elementary school ages, it is suggested that these programs remain effective during the adolescent years. Logic would suggest that interventions occurring earlier in the child's development would hold greater weight in altering the long-term course of ODD/CD than those administered later. However, this question has not yet been addressed empirically. Behavioral parent training has also demonstrated immediate benefits for children with ADHD. However, in this group, parenting interventions have yet to demonstrate long-term effects or effectiveness in families of adolescents.

Child-Based Psychosocial Treatments

Given the social interaction difficulties of children with externalizing disorders, it is not surprising that treatments have been developed to enhance the child's ability to successfully negotiate social situations with peers. For example, Kazdin and colleagues have developed a program in which aggressive children practice using problem-solving skills in a structured sequence of increasingly realistic situations. Outcome studies confirm the effectiveness of this problem-solving skills training in reducing aggressive behavior (Kazdin, Bass, Siegel, & Thomas, 1989), and this effectiveness appears enhanced if the child-focused treatment is combined with behavioral parent training (Kazdin, Siegel, & Bass, 1992). Typically, social skills or problem-solving programs are applied across the range of elementary school ages. In a review of such cognitive–behavioral treatment programs, Durlak, Furhman, and Lampman (1991) suggest greater effects with older (11 to 13 years) compared to younger (5 to 11 years) children. As would be expected, cognitive development appears to set the age parameters within which this type of treatment is most likely to yield benefits.

Cognitive–behavioral programs have also been used in the treatment of ADHD children, with a focus on both social and academic content. The results of these treatments have been consistently poor (Abikoff, 1991). Several possible reasons have been put forward to account for these treatment failures (Hinshaw, 1994). One likely explanation focuses on the possibility that children with ADHD do not lack the skills that these programs teach, but rather lack the ability to implement these skills. That is, in the heat of the moment, their poor self-regulation, impulsivity, and inattention may prevent these children from showing what they know.

Multimodal Treatments

It is evident that providing treatments for children with ODD/CD or ADHD that address one or two isolated problems for a limited period of time at one point in the child's development has limited effectiveness in altering the course of these disorders (Barkley, 1990; Kazdin, 1987). This failure of single-modality short-term treatments has combined with longitudinal research identifying multiple risk and protective factors in the development of these serious disorders to set the stage for the development of multimodal, longer-term interventions (Conduct Problems Prevention Research Group (CPPRG), 1992; Henggeler & Borduin, 1990; Richters et al., 1995).

A developmental perspective on the externalizing disorders has also encouraged researchers to identify the optimal developmental time points for initiating or refreshing interventions for these children, their parents, and their teachers. For example, the FAST (Families and Schools Together) Track Program is designed to begin intervening with children identified as high-risk based on parent and teacher reports of aggressive behavior in kindergarten (CPPRG, 1992). Based on developmental and clinical theory, the program includes behavioral parent training, home–school communication, child social skills training, academic tutoring, and classroom intervention. These multiple components are designed to be sensitive to differences in children's needs as they age and to be implemented at critical junctures when at-risk children are most vulnerable (i.e., school entry and transition to middle school). Multimodal, longer-term interventions are also currently being evaluated in the treatment of ADHD (Richters et al., 1995). Although less developmentally driven than the FAST Track Program, the Multimodal Treatment of ADHD (MTA) study examines the separate and combined effects of medication therapy and intensive psychosocial intervention (including behavioral parent training, classroom intervention, social skills training, and an intensive summer treatment experience). Treatment is offered over a 2-year period.

Although the results of the FAST Track and MTA studies are not yet available, the experimental designs and large sample sizes employed in these evaluations offer the promise of revealing not only whether these treatments are effective, but also the child, family, and treatment factors that may mediate or moderate this effectiveness. Hopefully, developmental factors will be high on the list of variables that are considered in such analyses. Certainly, previous evaluations of multimodal treatment programs, such as those of Henggeler and Borduin (1990) and Satterfield and colleagues (1981), support the value of these approaches.

ISSUES IN A DEVELOPMENTAL PERSPECTIVE ON THE EXTERNALIZING DISORDERS

Diagnostic Criteria

Integration of the research reviewed throughout this chapter is hampered by changes in diagnostic criteria across studies and time. Angold and Costello (1996) recently illustrated this problem in a study that compared DSM-III-R and DSM-IV diagnoses of ODD. Although both diagnostic criteria produced similar rates of prevalence, less than 50 percent of children were diagnosed as ODD by both diagnostic schemes. Similarly, recent work by Boyle and coworkers (1996) found dramatic differences in the prevalence, reliability, and correlates of ADHD and CD depending on how the thresholds for these disorders were defined. In conducting and evaluating studies of these disorders, particularly from a longitudinal perspective, it must be constantly borne in mind that current diagnostic categories are evolving constructs rather than final entities. Research approaches that employ multiple assessment strategies and dimensional as well as categorical approaches to the externalizing problems are the best bets for minimizing the difficulties arising from diagnostic uncertainty.

Heterotypic Continuity

Related to issues of diagnostic consistency, developmental psychopathologists face the continual challenge of distinguishing when changes in behavior over age signal a change in the underlying pathology versus when these changes reflect developmental variations of the same disorder. For example, are the temper tantrums of the preschooler the age-appropriate demonstration of the same disorder that appears as bullying in the school-age child and mugging in the adolescent, or are these behaviors symptomatic of different disorders? Numerous authors have called for researchers in this area to expect heterotypic continuity, rather than isomorphic consistency, in the disorders they study (Moffitt, 1993; Patterson, 1993). That is, from a developmental psychopathology perspective, it is expected that the behavioral topography of the externalizing disorders will change, rather than remaining invariant, across development. Interestingly, within both the ODD/CD and ADHD literatures, this issue is particularly prominent in current discussions on the expected manifestations of these problems in adulthood.

Etiological Models

Most current models of ODD/CD focus on the transactional nature of biological and environmental influences in the development of these disorders (Greenberg et al., 1993; Moffitt, 1993; Patterson, 1986). These models, while recognizing the contribution of the child's innate characteristics, do not see the unfolding of the child's behavior over time as an inevitable display of these characteristics. Rather, influences from family and social contexts are presumed to interact in an ongoing fashion with the child's nature to alter the course of behavior. In contrast, although transactional models are discussed (Hinshaw, 1994), current etiological models of ADHD tend to focus more on the biological underpinnings of this disorder (Barkley, 1996; Stevenson, 1992). Moreover, theory and research into how ADHD unfolds over time is less prevalent than in the area of ODD/CD. For example, in contrast to the long tradition of longitudinal work in ODD/CD (Lahey & Loeber, 1994; Robins, 1978), Barkley (1996) identified only four studies in North America that have followed ADHD children into early adulthood. It is hoped that greater recognition of transactional models of this disorder will be forthcoming and will spur the longitudinal research needed to shed light on the different developmental pathways that children with ADHD symptoms may follow and the risks and protective factors that influence these trajectories.

Gender

Externalizing disorders are more common in males than in females, with the possible exceptions of adolescent-onset CD and adult ADHD in which the gender ratios appear closer to equal. Although the disorders are generally more common among males, the ratio of externalizing disorder research conducted with males versus females still far outstrips the gender distributions of the disorders. Much remains to be discovered about the developmental course and outcomes of the externalizing disorders in girls and women (Zoccolillo, 1993). The need for further research in this area is highlighted by several recent pieces of evidence pointing to striking differences in how these disorders appear and change in females versus males. For example, Crick's (1995) research on relational aggression, that is, harming others by damaging their interpersonal relationships, is pointing to the increased importance and prevalence of this form of antisocial behavior among females compared to males. Similarly, Robins (1986) found that while conduct problems predict adult antisocial behavior in males, for females they hold predictive power for both antisocial behavior and internalizing problems such as depression and anxiety.

Need for Developmentally Sensitive Treatments

Unfortunately, as noted above, many of the treatments developed for the externalizing disorders are relatively adevelopmental in their approach. Greater consideration of developmental factors is needed in both the creation of treatment protocols and in the process of selecting and combining treatment components to fit individual children (Forehand & Wierson, 1993). Too often treatment choices are determined solely by the target problem, rather than by a broader consideration of the developmental context surrounding this problem. Fortunately, recent advances in the development and evaluation of programs designed to prevent the onset or continuation of ODD/CD problems reflect the increasing integration of knowledge that has accrued from developmental studies of these disorders (McMahon,

1994), and many have called for further efforts toward this integration in both ODD/CD and ADHD treatments (Hinshaw, 1994; Reid, 1993).

SUMMARY AND CONCLUSIONS

Throughout this chapter, we have reviewed evidence supporting the need for both researchers and clinicians to consider externalizing disorders within a developmental context. First, developmental factors clearly influence the assessment and diagnoses of these disorders, from the need for age-appropriate norms to issues related to the advantages and disadvantages of identifying and labeling these problems during the preschool years. Knowledge of the development courses of these disorders, and of differences in these progressions across subtypes, provides a rich supplement to assessments of current functioning. Finally, prevention and intervention efforts must occur within a context that emphasizes the child's developmental level and its continuously evolving nature.

REFERENCES

Abikoff, H. (1991). Cognitive training in ADHD children: Less to it than meets the eye. *Journal of Learning Disabilities, 24,* 205–209.

Achenbach, T. M. (1991). *Manual for the Child Behavior Checklist/4–18 and 1991 Profile.* Burlington, VT: University of Vermont Department of Psychiatry.

Achenbach, T. M., & Edelbrock, C. (1983). *Manual for the Child Behavior Checklist and Revised Child Behavior Profile.* Burlington, VT: Department of Psychiatry, University of Vermont.

Achenbach, T. M., & Edelbrock, C. (1986). *Manual for the Teacher's Report Form and Teacher Version of the Child Behavior Profile.* Burlington, VT: University of Vermont Department of Psychiatry.

Alessandri, S. M. (1992). Attention, play, and social behavior in ADHD preschoolers. *Journal of Abnormal Child Psychology, 20,* 289–302.

Alexander, J. F., & Parsons, B. V. (1982). *Functional family therapy.* Monterey, CA: Brooks/Cole.

American Psychiatric Association. (1994). *Diagnostic and statistical manual of mental disorders* (4th ed). Washington, DC: American Psychiatric Association.

Anastopoulos, A. D., Barkley, R. A., & Shelton, T. L. (1996). Family based treatment: Psychosocial intervention for children and adolescents with attention deficit hyperactivity disorder. In E. D. Hibbs & P. S. Jensen (Eds.), *Psychosocial treatments for child and adolescent disorders: Empirically based strategies for clinical practice* (pp. 267–284). Washington, DC: American Psychiatric Association.

Anderson, J. C., Williams, S., McGee, R., & Silva, P. (1987). DSM-III disorders in preadolescent children. *Archives of General Psychiatry, 44,* 69–76.

Angold, A., & Costello, J. (1996). Toward establishing an empirical basis for the diagnosis of oppositional defiant disorder. *Journal*

of the American Academy of Child and Adolescent Psychiatry,
35, 1205–1212.

Barkley, R. A. (1988). The effects of methylphenidate on the interactions of preschool ADHD children with their mothers. *Journal of the American Academy of Child and Adolescent
Psychiatry, 27,* 336–341.

Barkley, R. A. (1990). *Attention-deficit hyperactivity disorder: A
handbook for diagnosis and treatment.* New York: Guilford Press.

Barkley, R. A. (1996). Attention-deficit/hyperactivity disorder. In
E. J. Mash & R. A. Barkley (Eds.), *Child Psychopathology*
(pp. 63–107). New York: Guilford Press.

Barkley, R. A., DuPaul, G. J., & McMurray, M. B. (1990). A comprehensive evaluation of attention deficit disorder with and without hyperactivity. *Journal of Consulting and Clinical
Psychology, 58,* 775–789.

Barkley, R. A., Fischer, M., Edelbrock, C. S., & Smallish, L. (1990).
The adolescent outcome of hyperactive children diagnosed by research criteria: I. An 8-year prospective follow-up study. *Journal
of the American Academy of Child and Adolescent Psychiatry, 29,*
546–557.

Barkley, R. A., Guevremont, D. C., Anastopoulos, A. D., & Fletcher,
K. E. (1992). A comparison of three family therapy programs
for treating family conflicts in adolescents with attention-deficit
hyperactivity disorder. *Journal of Consulting and Clinical Psychology, 60,* 450–462.

Barkley, R. A., McMurray, M. B., Edelbrock, C. S., & Robins, K.
(1989). The response of aggressive and nonaggressive ADHD
children to two doses of methylphenidate. *Journal of the American Academy of Child and Adolescent Psychiatry, 28,* 873–881.

Barrickman, L. L., Perry, P. J., Allen, A. J., Kuperman, S., Arndt, S.
V., Herrmann, K. J., & Schumacher, E. (1995). Bupropion versus methylphenidate in the treatment of attention-deficit hyperactivity disorder. *Journal of the American Academy of Child and
Adolescent Psychiatry, 34,* 649–657.

Barton, C., Alexander, J. F., Waldron, H., Turner, C. W., & Warburton,
J. (1985). Generalizing treatment effects of functional family therapy: Three replications. *American Journal of Family Therapy, 13,*
16–26.

Bauermiester, J. J., Alegria, M., Bird, H., Rubio-Stipec, M., &
Canino, G. (1992). Are attentional-hyperactivity deficits unidimensional or multidimensional syndromes? Empirical findings
from a community survey. *Journal of the American Academy of
Child and Adolescent Psychiatry, 31,* 423–431.

Behar, L. B., & Springfield, S. (1974). A behavior rating scale for
the preschool child. *Developmental Psychology, 10,* 601–610.

Beitchman, J. H., Wekerle, C., & Hood, J. (1987). Diagnostic continuity from preschool to middle childhood. *Journal of the American Academy of Child and Adolescent Psychiatry, 145,* 185–190.

Biederman, J., Newcorn, J., & Sprich, S. (1991). Comorbidity of attention deficit hyperactivity disorder with conduct, depressive,
anxiety, and other disorders. *American Journal of Psychiatry, 148,*
564–577.

Bierman, K. L., & Wargo, J. B. (1995). Predicting the longitudinal
course associated with aggressive-rejected, aggressive (nonre-
jected), and rejected (nonaggressive) status. *Development and
Psychopathology, 7,* 669–682.

Boyle, M. H., Offord, D. R., Racine, Y., Szatmari, P., Fleming, J. E., &
Sanford, M. (1996). Identifying thresholds for classifying childhood psychiatric disorder: Issues and prospects. *Journal of the
American Academy of Child and Adolescent Psychiatry, 35,*
1440–1448.

Brown, R. T., Borden, K. A., & Clingerman, S. R. (1985). Adherence
to methylphenidate therapy in a pediatric population: A preliminary investigation. *Psychopharmacology Bulletin, 21,* 28–36.

Campbell, M., & Cueva, J. E. (1995). Psychopharmacology in child
and adolescent psychiatry: A review of the past seven years. Part
I. *Journal of the American Academy of Child and Adolescent
Psychiatry, 34,* 1124–1132.

Campbell, S. B. (1990). *Behavior problems in preschool children.*
New York: Guilford Press.

Campbell, S. B., Breaux, A. M., Ewing, L. J., & Szumowski, E. K.
(1986). Correlates and predictors of hyperactivity and aggression: A longitudinal study of parent-referred problem preschoolers. *Journal of Abnormal Child Psychology, 14,* 217–234.

Campbell, S. B., Endman, M., & Bernfeld, G. (1977). A three-year
follow-up of hyperactive preschoolers into elementary school.
Journal of Child Psychology and Psychiatry, 18, 238–249.

Campbell, S. B., March, C. L., Pierce, E. W., Ewing, L. J., &
Szumowski, E. K. (1991). Hard-to-manage preschool boys:
Family context and the stability of externalizing behavior. *Jour-
nal of Abnormal Child Psychology, 19,* 301–318.

Campbell, S. B., Szumowski, E. K., Ewing, L. J., Gluck, D. S., &
Breaux, A. M. (1982). A multidimensional assessment of
parent-identified behavior problem toddlers. *Journal of Abnormal Child Psychology, 10,* 569–592.

Chapel, J. L., Robins, A. J., McGee, R. O., Williams, S. M., & Silva,
P. A. (1982). A follow-up of inattentive and/or hyperactive children from birth to 7 years of age. *Journal of Operational Psychiatry, 13,* 17–26.

Coie, J. D., & Dodge, K. A. (1983). Continuities and changes in
children's social status: A five-year longitudinal study. *Merrill-
Palmer Quarterly, 29,* 261–282.

Conduct Problems Prevention Research Group. (1992). A developmental and clinical model for the prevention of conduct disorder:
The FAST Track Program. *Development and Psychopathology, 4,*
509–547.

Crick, N. R. (1995). Relational aggression: The role of intent attributions, feelings of distress, and provocation type. *Development
and Psychopathology, 7,* 313–322.

Crick, N. R., & Dodge, K. A. (1994). A review and reformulation of
social information–processing mechanisms in children's social
adjustment. *Psychological Bulletin, 115,* 74–101.

Crockenberg, S., & Litman, C. (1990). Autonomy as competence in
2-year olds: Maternal correlates of child defiance, compliance,
and self-assertion. *Developmental Psychology, 26,* 961–971.

Dishion, T. J., & Andrews, D. W. (1995). Preventing escalation in
problem behaviors with high-risk young adolescents: Immediate and 1-year outcomes. *Journal of Consulting and Clinical
Psychology, 63,* 538–548.

Dodge, K. A. (1986). A social information processing model of social
competence in children. In M. Perlmutter (Ed.), *Minnesota symposia on child psychology* (pp. 77–135). Hillsdale, NJ: Erlbaum.

Douglas, V. I., & Parry, P. A. (1994). Effects of reward and non-reward on attention and frustration in attention deficit disorder. *Journal of Abnormal Child Psychology, 22,* 281–302.

Durlak, J A., Furhman, T., & Lampman, C. (1991). Effectiveness of cognitive–behavior therapy for maladaptive children: A meta-analysis. *Psychological Bulletin, 110,* 204–214.

Elicker, J., Englund, M., & Sroufe, L. A. (1992). Predicting peer competence and peer relationships in early childhood from early parent–child relationships. In R. D. Parke & G. Ladd (Eds.), *Family-peer relationships: Modes of linkage* (pp. 77–106). Hillsdale, NJ: Erlbaum.

Evans, S. W., & Pelham, W. E. (1991). Psychostimulant effects on academic and behavioral measures for ADHD junior high school students in a lecture format classroom. *Journal of Abnormal Child Psychology, 19,* 537–551.

Eyberg, S. M. (1988). Parent-child interaction therapy: Integration of traditional and behavioral concerns. *Child and Family Behavior Therapy, 10,* 33–46.

Faraone, S. V., Biederman, J., Keenan, K., & Tsuang, M. T. (1991). Separation of DSM-III attention deficit disorder and conduct disorder: Evidence from a family genetic study of American child psychiatric patients. *Psychological Medicine, 21,* 109–121.

Farrington, D. P., Loeber, R., & VanKammen, W. B. (1990). Long-term criminal outcomes of hyperactivity–impulsivity–attention deficit and conduct problems in childhood. In L. N. Robins & M. Rutter (Eds.), *Straight and devious pathways from childhood to adulthood* (pp. 62–81). Cambridge, England: Cambridge University Press.

Farrington, D. P., & West, D. J. (1990). The Cambridge study in delinquent development: A long-term follow-up of 411 London males. In H. J. Kerner & G. Kaiser (Eds.), *Criminality, personality, behavior, and life history.* Berlin: Springer-Verlag.

Fergusson, D. M., Horwood, L. J., & Lloyd, M. (1991). Confirmatory factor models of attention deficit and conduct disorder. *Journal of Child Psychology and Psychiatry, 32,* 257–274.

Firestone, P. (1982). Factors associated with children's adherence to stimulant medication. *American Journal of Orthopsychiatry, 52,* 447–457.

Fischer, M., Barkley, R. A., Fletcher, K. E., & Smallish, L. (1993). The adolescent outcome of hyperactive children: Predictors of psychiatric, academic, social, and emotional adjustment. *Journal of the American Academy of Child and Adolescent Psychiatry, 32,* 324–332.

Forehand, R., & Long, N. (1988). Outpatient treatment of the acting-out child: Procedures, long-term follow-up data, and clinical problems. *Advances in Behaviour Research and Therapy, 10,* 129–177.

Forehand, R., & McMahon, R. J. (1981). *Helping the noncompliant child: A clinician's guide to parent training.* New York: Guilford Press.

Forehand, R., & Wierson, M. (1993). The role of developmental factors in planning behavioral interventions for children: Disruptive behavior as an example. *Behavior Therapy, 24,* 117–141.

Frick, P. J., Kamphaus, R. W., Lahey, B. B., Christ, M. A. G., Hart, E. L., & Tannenbaum, T E. (1991). Academic underachievement and the disruptive behavior disorders. *Journal of Consulting and Clinical Psychology, 59,* 289–294.

Frick, P. J., Lahey, B. B., Loeber, R., Tannenbaum, L., Van Horn, Y., Christ, M. A. G., Hart, E. A., & Hanson, K. (1993). Oppositional defiant disorder and conduct disorder: A meta-analytic review of factor analyses and cross-validation in a clinic sample. *Clinical Psychology Review, 13,* 319–340.

Gittelman, R., Abikoff, H., Pollack, E., Klein, D. G., Katz, S., & Mattes, J. (1980). A controlled trial of behavior modification and methylphenidate in hyperactive children. In C. K. Whalen & B. Henker (Eds.), *Hyperactive children: The social ecology of identification and treatment* (pp. 221–243). New York: Academic Press.

Gittelman, R., & Mannuzza, S. (1985). Diagnosing ADD-H in adolescents. *Psychopharmacology Bulletin, 21,* 237–242.

Goodyear, P., & Hynd, G. (1992). Attention-deficit disorder with (ADD/H) and without (ADD/WO) hyperactivity: Behavioral and neuropsychological differentiation. *Journal of Clinical Child Psychology, 21,* 273–305.

Greenberg, M. T., Speltz, M. L., & DeKlyen, M. (1993). The role of attachment in the early development of disruptive behavior problems. *Development and Psychopathology, 5,* 191–213.

Hart, E. L., Lahey, B. B., Loeber, R., Applegate, B., & Frick, P. J. (1995). Developmental change in attention-deficit hyperactivity disorder in boys: A four-year longitudinal study. *Journal of Abnormal Child Psychology, 23,* 729–750.

Hechtman, L. (1985). Adolescent outcome of hyperactive children treated with stimulants in childhood: A review. *Psychopharmacology Bulletin, 21,* 178–191.

Henggeler, S. W., & Borduin, C. M. (1990). *Family therapy and beyond: A multisystemic approach to treating the behavior problems of children and adolescents.* Pacific Grove, CA: Brooks/Cole.

Hinshaw, S. P. (1987). On the distinction between attentional deficits/hyperactivity and conduct problems/aggression in child psychopathology. *Psychological Bulletin, 101,* 443–464.

Hinshaw, S. P. (1992). Externalizing behavior problems and academic underachievement in childhood and adolescence: Causal relationships and underlying mechanisms. *Psychological Bulletin, 111,* 127–155.

Hinshaw, S. P. (1994). *Attention deficits and hyperactivity in children.* Thousand Oaks, CA: Sage.

Hinshaw, S. P., & Anderson, C. A. (1996). Conduct and oppositional disorders. In E. J. Mash & R. A. Barkley (Eds.), *Child psychopathology* (pp. 113–152). New York: Guilford Press.

Hinshaw, S. P., Heller, T., & McHale, J. P. (1992). Covert antisocial behavior in boys with attention-deficit hyperactivity disorder: External validation and effects of methylphenidate. *Journal of Consulting and Clinical Psychology, 60,* 274–281.

Hinshaw, S. P., Henker, B., & Whalen, C. K. (1984). Cognitive–behavioral and pharmacologic interventions for hyperactive boys: Comparative and combined effects. *Journal of Consulting and Clinical Psychology, 52,* 739–749.

Hinshaw, S. P., Lahey, B. B., & Hart, E. L. (1993). Issues of taxonomy and comorbidity in the development of conduct disorder. *Development and Psychopathology, 5,* 31–49.

Horn, W F., Ialongo, N. S., Pascoe, J. M. et al. (1991). Additive effects of psychostimulants, parent training, and self-control therapy with ADHD children. *Journal of the American Academy of Child and Adolescent Psychiatry, 30,* 233–240.

Hynd, G. W., Lorys, A. R., Semrud-Clikeman, M., Nieves, N., Huettner, M. I. S., & Lahey, B. B. (1991). Attention deficit disorder without hyperactivity (ADD/WO): A distinct behavioral and neurocognitive syndrome. *Journal of Child Neurology, 6,* 37–43.

Jacobvitz, D., & Sroufe, L. A. (1987). The early caregiver–child relationship and attention deficit disorder with hyperactivity in kindergarten: A prospective study. *Child Development, 58,* 1496–1504.

Johnston, C. (1996a). Parent characteristics and parent–child interactions in families of nonproblem children and ADHD children with higher and lower levels of oppositional-defiant disorder. *Journal of Abnormal Child Psychology 24,* 85–104.

Johnston, C. (1996b). Addressing parent cognitions in interventions with families of disruptive children. In K. S. Dobson & K. D. Craig (Eds.), *Advances in cognitive–behavioral therapy* (pp. 193–209). Thousand Oaks, CA: Sage.

Johnston, C., & Fine, S. (1993). Methods of evaluating methylphenidate in children with attention deficit hyperactivity disorder: Acceptability, satisfaction, and compliance. *Journal of Pediatric Psychology, 18,* 717–730.

Kazdin, A. E. (1987). Treatment of antisocial behavior in children: Current status and future directions. *Psychological Bulletin, 102,* 187–203.

Kazdin, A. E., Bass, D., Siegel, T., & Thomas, C. (1989). Cognitive-behavioral therapy and relationship therapy in the treatment of children referred for antisocial behavior. *Journal of Consulting and Clinical Psychology, 57,* 522–535.

Kazdin, A. E., Siegel, T. C., & Bass, D. (1992). Cognitive problem-solving skills training and parent management training in the treatment of antisocial behavior in children. *Journal of Consulting and Clinical Psychology, 60,* 733–747.

Klorman, R., Coons, H. W., & Borgstedt, A. D. (1987). Effects of methylphenidate on adolescents with a childhood history of attention deficit disorder: I. Clinical findings. *Journal of the American Academy of Child and Adolescent Psychiatry, 26,* 363–367.

Kuczynski, L., & Kochanska, G. (1990). Development of children's noncompliance strategies from toddlerhood to age 5. *Developmental Psychology, 26,* 398–408.

Kuperschmidt, J. B., Coie, J. D., & Dodge, K. A. (1990). The role of poor peer relationships in the development of disorder. In S. R. Asher & J. D. Coie (Eds.), *Peer rejection in childhood* (pp. 274–308). New York: Cambridge University Press.

Lahey, B. B., Hart, E. L., Pliszka, S., Applegate, B., & McBurnett, K. (1993). Neurophysiological correlates of conduct disorder: A rationale and review of current research. *Journal of Clinical Child Psychology, 22,* 141–153.

Lahey, B. B., & Loeber, R. (1994). Framework for a developmental model of oppositional defiant disorder and conduct disorder. In D. K. Routh (Ed.), *Disruptive behavior disorders in childhood* (pp. 139–180). New York: Plenum Press.

Lahey, B. B., Loeber, R., Quay, H. C., Frick, P. J., & Grimm, S. (1992). Oppositional defiant and conduct disorders: Issues to be resolved for DSM-IV. *Journal of the American Academy of Child and Adolescent Psychiatry, 31,* 539–546.

Lahey, B. B., Schaughency, E. A., Hynd, G. W., Carlson, C. L., & Nieves, N. (1987). Attention deficit disorder with and without hyperactivity: Comparison of behavioral characteristics of clinic-referred children. *Journal of the American Academy of Child and Adolescent Psychiatry, 26,* 718–723.

Lambert, N. M. (1988). Adolescent outcomes for hyperactive children. *American Psychologist, 43,* 786–799.

Loeber, R. (1990). Development and risk factors of juvenile antisocial behavior and delinquency. *Clinical Psychology Review, 10,* 1–41.

Loeber, R., Green, S. M., Lahey, B B., Christ, M. A. G., & Frick, P. J. (1992). Developmental sequences in the age of onset of disruptive child behaviors. *Journal of Child and Family Studies, 1,* 21–41.

Loeber, R., & Stouthammer-Loeber, M. (1987). Prediction. In H. C. Quay (Ed.), *Handbook of juvenile delinquency* (pp. 325–382). New York: Wiley.

Manuzza, S., & Klein, R. (1992). Predictors of outcome of children with attention-deficit hyperactivity disorder. In G. Weiss (Ed.), *Child and adolescent psychiatric clinics of North America: Attention-deficit hyperactivity disorder* (pp. 567–578). Philadelphia: Saunders.

Mash, E. J., & Johnston, C. (1982). A comparison of mother-child interactions of younger and older hyperactive and normal children. *Child Development, 53,* 1371–1381.

McGee, R., Silva, P. A., & Williams, S. (1983). Parents' and teachers' perceptions of behavior problems in seven year old children. *Exceptional Child, 30,* 151–161.

McMahon, R. J. (1994). Diagnosis, assessment, and treatment of externalizing problems in children: The role of longitudinal data. *Journal of Consulting and Clinical Psychology, 62,* 901–917.

Moffitt, T. E. (1990). Juvenile delinquency and attention deficit disorder: Boys' developmental trajectories from age 3 to 15. *Child Development, 61,* 893–910.

Moffitt, T. E. (1993). Adolescence-limited and life-course-persistent antisocial behavior: A developmental taxonomy. *Psychological Review, 100,* 674–701.

Offord, D. R., Adler, R. J., & Boyle, M. H. (1986). Prevalence and sociodemographic correlates of conduct disorder. *American Journal of Social Psychiatry, 4,* 272–278.

Ollendick, T. H., Weist, M. D., Borden, M. C., & Greene, R. W. (1992). Sociometric status and academic, behavioral, and psychological adjustment: A five-year longitudinal study. *Journal of Consulting and Clinical Psychology, 60,* 80–87.

Patterson, G. R. (1986). Performance models for antisocial boys. *American Psychologist, 41,* 432–444.

Patterson, G. R. (1993). Orderly change in a stable world: The antisocial trait as a chimera. *Journal of Consulting and Clinical Psychology, 61,* 911–919.

Patterson, G. R., & Chamberlain, P. (1994). A functional analysis of resistance during parent training therapy. *Clinical Psychology: Science and Practice, 1,* 53–71.

Pelham, W. E., & Bender, M. E. (1982). Peer relationships in hyperactive children: Description and treatment. In K. D. Gadow & I. Bialer (Eds.), *Advances in learning and behavioral disabilities* (Vol. 1, pp. 365–436). Greenwich, CT: JAI Press.

Pelham, W. E., Gnagy, E. M., Greenslade, K. E., & Milich, R. (1992). Teacher ratings of DSM-III-R symptoms for the disruptive behavior disorders. *Journal of the American Academy of Child and Adolescent Psychiatry, 31,* 210–218.

Pelham, W. E., & Milich, R. (1991). Measuring ADHD children's response to psychostimulant medication: Prediction and individual differences. In L. L. Greenhill & B. P. Osman (Eds.), *Ritalin: Theory and patient management* (pp. 203–221). New York: Liebert.

Pisterman, S., McGrath, P., Firestone, P., Goodman, J. T., Webster, I., & Mallory, R. (1989). Outcome of parent-mediated treatment of preschoolers with attention deficit disorder with hyperactivity. *Journal of Consulting and Clinical Psychology, 57,* 628–635.

Quay, H. C. (1986). Conduct disorders. In H. C. Quay & J. S. Werry (Eds.), *Psychopathological disorders of childhood* (3rd ed., pp. 35–72). New York: Wiley.

Reid, J. B. (1993). Prevention of conduct disorder before and after school entry: Relating interventions to developmental findings. *Development and Psychopathology, 5,* 243–262.

Richman, N., Stevenson, J., & Graham, P. (1982). *Preschool to school: A behavioral study.* New York: Academic Press.

Richters, J. E., Arnold, L. E., Jensen, P. S., Abikoff, H., Conners, C. K., Greenhill, L. L., Hechtman, L., Hinshaw, S. P., Pelham, W. E., & Swanson, J. M. (1995). NIMH collaborative multisite multimodal treatment study of children with ADHD: I. Background and rationale. *Journal of the American Academy of Child and Adolescent Psychiatry, 34,* 987–1000.

Robin, A. L., & Foster, S. L. (1989). *Negotiating parent–adolescent conflict: A behavioral-family systems approach.* New York: Guilford Press.

Robins, L. N. (1978). Sturdy childhood predictors of adult antisocial behavior: Replications from longitudinal studies. *Psychological Medicine, 8,* 611–622.

Robins, L. N. (1986). The consequences of conduct disorder in girls. In D. Olweus, J. Block, & M. Radke-Yarrow (Eds.), *The development of antisocial and prosocial behavior: Research, theories, and issues* (pp. 385–414). Orlando, FL: Academic Press.

Satterfield, J. H., Satterfield, B. T., & Cantwell, D. P. (1981). Three-year multimodality treatment of 110 hyperactive boys. *Journal of Pediatrics, 98,* 650–655.

Schliefer, M., Weiss, G., Cohen, N. J., Elman, M., Cvejic, H., & Kruger, E. (1975). Hyperactivity in preschoolers and the effect of methylphenidate. *American Journal of Orthopsychiatry, 45,* 38–50.

Shekhim, W. O. (1990). Diagnosis and treatment of attention deficit and conduct disorders in children and adolescents. In J. G. Simeon & H. B. Ferguson (Eds.), *Treatment strategies in child and adolescent psychiatry* (pp. 1–18). New York: Plenum Press.

Speltz, M. L. (1990). The treatment of preschool conduct problems. In M. T. Greenberg, D. Cicchetti, & E. Cummings (Eds.), *Attachment in the preschool years* (pp. 399–426). Chicago: University of Chicago Press.

Spencer, T., Biederman, J., Wilens, T., Harding, M., O'Donnell, D., & Griffin, S. (1996). Pharmacotherapy of attention-deficit hyperactivity disorder across the life cycle. *Journal of American Academy of Child and Adolescent Psychiatry, 35,* 409–432.

Spencer, T., Wilens, T., Biederman, J., Faraone, S. V., Ablon, S., & Lapey, K. (1995). A double-blind, crossover comparison of methylphenidate and placebo in adults with childhood-onset attention-deficit hyperactivity disorder. *Archives of General Psychiatry, 52,* 434–443.

Spitzer, R. L., Davies, M., & Barkley, R A. (1990). The DSM-III-R field trial for the disruptive behavior disorders. *Journal of the American Academy of Child and Adolescent Psychiatry, 29,* 690–697.

Stevenson, J. (1992). Evidence for a genetic etiology in hyperactivity in children. *Behavior Genetics, 22,* 337–343.

Swanson, J. M., & McBurnett, K. (1995). Stimulant medication and the treatment of children with ADHD. *Advances in Clinical Child Psychology, 17,* 265–355.

Tannock, R. (in press). Attention deficit disorders with anxiety disorders. In T. E. Brown, (Ed.), *Subtypes of attention-deficit disorders in children, adolescents, and adults.* Washington, DC: American Psychiatric Press.

Taylor, E., Chadwick, O., Heptinstall, E., & Danckaerts, M. (1996). Hyperactivity and conduct problems as risk factors for adolescent development. *Journal of the American Academy of Child and Adolescent Psychiatry, 35,* 1213–1226.

Taylor, E., Sandberg, S., Thorley, G., & Giles, S. (1991). *The epidemiology of childhood hyperactivity.* Oxford, England: Oxford University Press.

Tolan, P. H., Guerra, N. G., & Kendall, P. C. (1995). A developmental–ecological perspective on antisocial behavior in children and adolescents: Toward a unified risk and intervention framework. *Journal of Consulting and Clinical Psychology, 63,* 579–584.

Urban, J., Carlson, E., Egeland, B., & Sroufe, L. A. (1991). Patterns of individual adaptation across childhood. *Development and Psychopathology, 4,* 97–112.

Varley, C. K. (1985). A review of studies of drug treatment efficacy for attention deficit disorder with hyperactivity in adolescents. *Psychopharmacology Bulletin, 21,* 216–221.

Walker, J. L., Lahey, B. B., Hynd, G. W., & Frame, C. L. (1987). Comparison of specific patterns of antisocial behavior in children with conduct disorder with or without coexisting hyperactivity. *Journal of Consulting and Clinical Psychology, 55,* 910–913.

Webster-Stratton, C. (1994). Advancing videotape parent training: A comparison study. *Journal of Consulting and Clinical Psychology, 62,* 583–593.

Weiss, G., & Hechtman, L. T. (1993). *Hyperactive children grown up.* New York: Guilford Press.

Wender, P. (1995). *Attention-deficit hyperactivity disorder in adults.* New York: Oxford University Press.

World Health Organization. (1993). *The ICD-10 classification of mental and behavioral disorders: Diagnostic criteria for research.* Geneva, Switzerland: Author.

Zero to Three/National Center for Clinical Infant Programs. (1994). *Diagnostic classification of mental health and developmental disorders of infancy and early childhood (Diagnostic Classification: 0–3).* Washington, DC: Author.

Zoccolillo, M. (1993). Gender and the development of conduct disorder. *Development and Psychopathology, 5,* 79–89.

CHAPTER 18

INTELLECTUAL DISORDERS

Johnny L. Matson
Brandi B. Smiroldo

HISTORY AND THEORY

Developmental issues have long been recognized as a significant factor in the study of mental disorders (Matson & Mulick, 1992). The interface between developmental milestones and mental retardation is so intertwined that developmental disabilities, developmental delays, and mental retardation are often used interchangeably. Most of this focus has been on early milestones such as when the person learns to sit up, crawl, walk, eat, begin to talk, toilet independently, and engage in other significant adaptive skills. The emphasis on these developmental issues is so great that defining intelligence has added to an individual IQ test the use of a standardized adaptive behavior test such as the Vineland Social Maturity Scale or the American Association on Mental Retardation Adaptive Behavior Scale that incorporates evaluation of developmental milestones such as those noted above.

Life span development is beginning to receive some attention. However, the tradition in developmental psychology has been to focus on children, with one of the groups receiving the most attention being persons with mental retardation. This intellectually impaired group provided a model to eval-uate issues and discrepancies between normal and abnormal childhood development. Zigler (1969) asserted that cognitive development of the familially retarded is characterized by slower progression through the same sequence of cognitive stages. Also, the upper stage of cognitive development is more limited than for the normal IQ person.

Psychopathology appears to be dramatically affected by intellectual development. Persons with mental retardation from mild to profound range are much more likely to demonstrate severe behavior problems and mental illness than are persons with normal intelligence (Borthwick-Duffy, 1994; Chess, 1970; Demb, Brier, Huron, & Tomor, 1994; Iverson & Fox, 1989; Jacobson, 1990; Menolascino, 1990; Phillips & Williams, 1975; Rutter, Graham, & Yule, 1970). Along those same lines it has been demonstrated that the full range of psychopathology is evident in this group, from schizophrenia to depression to anxiety disorders (Campbell & Malone, 1991; Jakab, 1992). These problems are compounded by the accompanying physical problems that are more prevalent in persons with mental retardation. Thus, for example, children with speech and language delays are at more risk for psychopathology (Cantwell & Baker, 1977; Gualtieri, Koriath, Van Bourgondien, & Saleeb, 1983).

In addition to increased prevalence of psychopathology and behavior problems, numerous other areas of deficiency are present in individuals with mental retardation and are influenced by the developmental delays experienced by the individual. The focus of this chapter is on the relationship of developmental issues to mental retardation in general as well as to those problems often seen in individuals with mental retardation. A review of the definition of mental retardation is presented first to provide a backdrop against which the issues can be viewed.

DEFINITION OF MENTAL RETARDATION

The American Association on Mental Deficiency (AAMD) was formed in 1876. This organization has traditionally been the leader in defining the construct of mental retardation. In 1910, the AAMD used the term *feeble-minded* to refer to individuals with developmental delays (Matson & Marchetti, 1988; Scheerenberger, 1983). The term was further divided into idiots (those individuals who would not progress beyond a 2-year-old developmental level), imbeciles (those who would not progress beyond a 7-year-old developmental level), and morons (those whose developmental level would peak at 12 years old).

Traditionally the American Association on Mental Retardation (AAMR), formerly the American Association on Mental Deficiency (AAMD), has developed the most widely accepted definition of mental retardation. Although a diagnosis is currently based on test results, usually any referral is based on an *observation* by a parent, teacher, or professional that the child is functioning at a lower level than his or her same-age peers (Cleland, 1978; Coker, 1989; Jensen, 1987; Scheerenberger, 1983). In fact, testing was not used until the twentieth century. The observation usually notes some delays in developmental milestones such as speech and motor areas. Sociocultural factors also come into play in observation of deficits.

Doll in his 1936 presidential address to the AAMD defined mental retardation as social inadequacy, decreased intellect, and developmental arrestment (Matson & Marchetti, 1988; Scheerenberger, 1983). In the 1950s subgroups of individuals with mental retardation were added to the prevailing definition (Matson & Marchetti, 1988). Educable individuals were those who could attain a second to fourth grade level of functioning, while trainable individuals were those who could learn self-care skills. In addition to these two groups there were those individuals who were totally dependent on others. Despite the change in labels and reference points, these divisions are similar to the 1910 divisions in the focus on developmental expectations for each group.

Additional modifications were made to the AAMR definition in 1961 by Heber. He defined mental retardation as significant subaverage intelligence (IQ below 85) occurring in the developmental period (before age 18) and associated with deficits in adaptive behavior (Heber, 1961). Five levels were specified based on IQ scores including borderline, mild, moderate, severe, and profound. Heber's definition suggested that mental retardation was environmental and not organic because it "indicated" that IQ could be raised. This view is in contrast to much of the literature on mental retardation. Although environmental influences may affect intellectual functioning, there are numerous organic etiologies of mental retardation such as fragile X syndrome and Down syndrome (Coker, 1989). Additionally, researchers have consistently documented the stability of IQ after the age of 5 (McCall, Applebaum & Hogarty, 1973; Zigler, Balla & Hodapp, 1984). Grossman altered the Heber definition in 1983 by moving the IQ cutoff to 70 (Grossman, 1983).

The addition of adaptive behavior deficits came from the controversy and difficulties surrounding the sole use of IQ measures. However, it was not until the rulings in numerous court cases favoring the inclusion of a social competency emphasis and the passage of the Education for All Handicapped Children Act of 1975 that states began using the additional criteria (Scheerenberger, 1983). Prior to this usage, many children were being identified as mentally retarded due to low IQ scores, but had no trouble in any areas other than school performance. Mercer (1988) termed these individuals "six-hour retardates," referring to the time they spent in school.

Additionally, considerable debate over the constructs measured by intelligence tests has existed in the field of psychology since the advent of the measures (Jensen, 1987; Scheerenberger, 1983). There are numerous definitions of intelligence ranging from Galton's theory of an all-encompassing general intelligence to Spearman's two-factor theory to Thorndike's theory of numerous unrelated stimulus-response bonds (Jensen, 1987; Scheerenberger, 1983). Any definition adopted refers to an abstract construct that can only be indirectly measured. IQ testing does not appear to assess an individual's innate abilities, but rather predicts future school performance (Jensen, 1987). Although such information is useful, it brings into focus the problems of using a single IQ test score to assess for mental retardation.

Another problem related to IQ testing as the sole means of diagnosing mental retardation involves racial issues. There is a significantly greater number of minorities identified as mentally retarded, especially in the mild ranges of mental retardation (Mercer, 1988; Reschly & Ward, 1991). This discrepancy has lead to cries of cultural bias in IQ testing. Some states have outlawed the use of IQ testing as a result of this concern (Scheerenberger, 1983). To combat these problems, tests such as the SOMPA have been developed (Sattler, 1992). Although these instruments claim to be "culture-free," they have proven to be biased in the reverse direction. Thus, a resolution of this concern is not readily at hand.

The addition of adaptive behavior to combat difficulties and controversies surrounding the use of IQ tests was a step in the right direction. However, adaptive behavior is a cloudy construct. It is ill-defined and often difficult to assess (Leland, 1989). It is important to gather information through multiple methods and from sources close to the individual. In an attempt to obtain such information, instruments have been developed to assess adaptive behavior (Leland, 1989); however, problems of reliability and validity exist (Leland, 1989).

The only agreed-upon aspect of the definition of mental retardation appears to be that onset must occur before age 18. To clarify the definition and address other political and social issues surrounding a diagnosis of mental retardation, AAMR has issued a new definition (AAMR, 1992).

The New Definition of Mental Retardation

Considerable controversy currently surrounds this new definition. The resulting definition lacks empirical validation and acceptance by the American Psychological Association (APA) and the individual state governments, but does appear to be politically correct. This situation is a departure from previous years when AAMR's listing of the necessary criteria for a diagnosis was the basis for all other definitions.

This controversy over the change in criteria has particular relevance when viewing mental retardation from a life span perspective. The previous nomenclature grouped individuals by levels of functioning. Individuals with different intelligence levels have different levels of language, social, and motor skills, areas greatly impacting level of functioning (Whitman, Sciback, & Reid, 1983). These differences provide validation for the proposed groupings. Within this classification system some generalizations can be made. The new nomenclature does away with these groupings. This change is not based on recent scientific developments and ignores previous evidence that groupings are useful. Correct classification based on scientific evidence helps to delineate clearer and more homogenous groups of individuals. Thus, classification would have an impact on treatment issues. Without an adequate classification system, membership in any one group does not necessarily give the clinician useful information.

The changes in the new AAMR definition are as follows. The intelligence score cutoff is raised to 75 from a previous cutoff of 70. This change will result in an increase in the number of individuals labeled mentally retarded and will likely increase the problem of minority overrepresentation (Reschly & Ward, 1991). The new definition also subdivides adaptive behavior into ten categories and requires a deficit in at least two. There is no empirical evidence for this division nor for the contention that deficits in two areas of adaptive functioning are sufficient for a diagnosis.

The American Psychiatric Association (1994) has adopted portions of this definition for the fourth edition of the *Diagnostic and Statistical Manual of Mental Disorders* (DSM-IV), while retaining elements from the previous AAMR definition (Grossman, 1983). DSM-IV's definition involves the following criteria. First, the individual must have "significant subaverage intellectual functioning" as defined by an intelligence score of 70 or below. This intellectual functioning is usually measured by standardized intelligence tests such as the Stanford-Binet IV or the Wechsler Intelligence Scale for Children-Third Edition. The individual must also have significant deficits in adaptive functioning. DSM-IV adopts the AAMR's 1992 divisions and specifications of adaptive behavior. These deficits are typically assessed using adaptive behavior scales such as the American Association for Mental Deficiency's Adaptive Behavior Scale and the Vineland Adaptive Behavior Scale. Finally, these deficits must be present before the age of 18.

In addition to the definitions developed by the AAMR and the APA, different states may also adopt different criteria for a diagnosis. A consensus is necessary to avoid added confusion in diagnosing this disorder.

Individuals who meet criteria for a diagnosis of mental retardation are further classified by level of severity using the DSM-IV classification (APA, 1994). AAMR no longer uses severity (e.g., mild, moderate, severe, profound, and unspecified).

Despite the confusion and debate regarding diagnosis, clinicians and researchers agree that individuals diagnosed with mental retardation evince deficits and delays in numerous functioning areas. In addition to these definitions, consideration needs to be given to developmental differences issues. This approach adds additional information on specific strengths and deficits of developmentally disabled persons.

DEVELOPMENTAL CONSIDERATIONS

General Areas

There is no universally accepted definition of normal development (Hodapp, Burack & Zigler, 1990). Thus, it is often difficult to describe abnormal or delayed development. It has been documented that individuals with mental retardation differ from their "normal" peers in several areas (Coker, 1989; Hersh, Bloom, Yen, Topinka, & Weisskopf, 1988; Nidiffer & Kelly, 1983; von Wendt, Makinen, & Rantakallio, 1984). Considerable controversy exists, however, on the quality and quantity of these differences.

Some researchers suggest that there are universal sequences of development through which all individuals progress, and individuals with mental retardation simply progress at a slower rate (Hodapp, 1990). This hypothesis is a plausible explanation for several reasons. First, there are some skills that are prerequisites for other skills and must be acquired first. Also, some skills are easier than others, and it logically makes sense that these skills would be acquired earlier. However, it is also possible that uneven development may occur across various areas of development.

Although this "similar sequence" hypothesis is sometimes useful, it is far too simplistic. Some individuals with mental retardation show periods of regression, in which previously learned skills either disappear or decrease (Hodapp, 1990; Nidiffer & Kelly, 1983).

A second hypothesis is that individuals with mental retardation function at the same level as their mental-age peers (Mundy & Kasari, 1990). Research provides mixed support for this hypothesis (Groff & Linden, 1982; Spitz, 1983). Individuals with mental retardation are likely to differ from their mental-age peers, as well, because the two groups will have a different number and quality of life experiences that affect their functioning level. Additionally, individuals often show large discrepancies between functioning levels on different skills (Mundy & Kasari, 1990).

It is likely that there are quantitative and qualitative differences between individuals with and without mental retardation as well as within the mentally retarded population. There may be some universal sequences in development that apply across groups, while other areas of development are impacted by a combination of biological, social, and psychological factors. Despite the problems and uncertainties in comparing individuals with and without mental retardation across areas of development, research has consistently documented the presence of deficient areas of functioning in individuals with mental retardation including motor, speech, and developmental milestones (Coker, 1989; Matson & Marchetti, 1988; von Wendt et al., 1984). Each of these areas will be discussed briefly below.

Motor Delays

A significant number of impairments that limit or retard motor functioning have been documented in individuals with mental retardation (Cleland, 1987; Matson & Marchetti, 1988; von Wendt et al., 1984). These deficits are likely to be noticed before other deficits. Some individuals are clumsy, while others have specific deficits in fine motor skills. Typically, individuals with difficulties in this area continue to have problems into adolescence, especially those functioning in the moderate to profound range. Specific deficits or patterns of deficits have been noted in certain subgroups of individuals with mental retardation (Cicchetti & Ganiban, 1990). For example, individuals diagnosed with Down syndrome generally have trouble with the execution of voluntary motor sequences.

Speech Delays

Speech difficulties are also prevalent in the mentally retarded population, especially for those in the severe and profound levels of functioning (Cicchetti & Ganiban, 1990; Cleland, 1987; Dykens & Leckman, 1990; Whitman, Sciback & Reid, 1983). Whitman and colleagues (1983) note that 75 to 85 percent of individuals classified in the severe and profound ranges of mental retardation "could be characterized by the absence or near absence of speech" (p. 187). The early years of development are generally marked by a slow rate of progress in speech development. Deficits in speech areas are likely to be noticed at around 18 to 24 months of age (Cleland, 1987). Specific problems may arise in areas such as syntax, semantics, prosody, pragmatics, and social use of language.

As with motor delays, specific deficits have been linked to subgroups of individuals with mental retardation. Individuals with fragile X syndrome typically have problems with articulation and receptive speech (Dykens & Leckman, 1990). They may exhibit abrupt and repetitive speech, echolalia, palilalia, dysfluency, and dyspraxia. In contrast, individuals with Down syndrome typically have delays in expressive language and vocabulary development, while oftentimes having intact pragmatics (Cicchetti & Ganiban, 1990).

Delays in Developmental Milestones

Developmental milestones consist of sitting up, crawling, walking, talking, eating, and toileting independently. These skills typically occur during the early years (infancy and toddler years) of development in "normal" children (Cleland, 1987). Individuals with mental retardation will master these milestones at a slower pace than those in the general population (von Wendt et al., 1984). There will, however, be a large amount of individual variability with some individuals mastering the skills at a rate comparable to the general population and others never mastering the skills. Continence seems to be a particular problem in this population (Matson & Marchetti, 1988).

Researchers have documented differential rates of progression for developmental milestones. For example, von Wendt and colleagues (1984) investigated mastery in developmental milestones in "normal" children and those with mental retardation. They found that only 49.4 percent of individuals with mental retardation could stand by 12 months of age, compared to 82.9 percent of healthy children, even when physical handicaps were considered. Additionally, 52.3 percent of the children with handicaps had not learned to talk by 12 months of age as compared to only 23 percent of healthy children. These results provide some concrete numbers to support the contention that individuals with mental retardation master these developmental milestones at a slower rate than children without mental retardation.

Summary

Although the debate continues regarding the developmental course and progression of individuals with mental retardation, it is clear that a majority of these individuals are delayed in the development of motor, speech, and other developmental milestones. Delays in important developmental areas are likely to have an impact on or be affected by other aspects of the individual's life. The next section will discuss specific behavior problems typically present in individuals with developmental delays.

Behavior Problem Areas

In addition to general areas of delay, there is a high prevalence of behavior problems in the mentally retarded population (Bellack, Morrison, Wixted, & Mueser, 1990; Hale & Borkowski, 1991; Marchetti & Campbell, 1990). Problems may be the result of excesses or deficits in areas such as memory, impulse control, speech, self-help skills, social skills, and psychopathology.

Memory

Numerous theories exist on memory (Hale & Borkowski, 1991). A central defining feature of all theories is recall and recognition of previously presented material or the ability to learn new information. These abilities have typically been divided into two types of memory: short term (minutes or hours) or long term (days, weeks, or years).

The presence of memory deficits in individuals with mental retardation has been documented in numerous studies (Bray, Saarnio, Borges, & Hawk, 1994; Mandis, Massimino, & Mantis, 1991; Varnhagen, Das, & Varnhagen, 1987). Specific deficits vary between individuals and groups. For example, individuals with cultural–familial mental retardation

evince problems with visual and auditory short-term memory (Weisz, 1990). Other researchers suggest impairments in recognition and verbal memory for individuals with Down syndrome (Cicchetti & Ganiban, 1990; Varnhagen et al., 1987). The problems in verbal memory may contribute to poor language comprehension and production for these individuals.

Memory difficulties may be due to problems identifying items, attentional problems, or distractibility (Hale & Borkowski, 1991). The memory of individuals with mental retardation may be facilitated by allowing several presentations of material, use of external memory aids, and emphasis on their memory strengths (Bray et al., 1994; Ellis, Woodley-Zanthos, & Dulaney, 1989; McCartney, 1987; Varnhagen, Das, & Varnhagen, 1987). Ellis and colleagues (1989) noted that individuals with mental retardation perform equal to those without mental retardation on tasks involving spatial memory, while Varnhagen and colleagues (1987) found that individuals with mental retardation performed close to or equal to "normal" individuals when they were given two presentations of the material. Additionally, McCartney (1989) provides evidence that once the material is learned, individuals with mental retardation retain the information at the same level as normals.

Memory deficits are greater in individuals functioning in the severe and profound levels of mental retardation. However, specifics on such deficits are hard to determine. Individuals functioning in the lower ranges also exhibit delays in communication and language. Thus, it is harder to assess memory deficits because most tests of memory require some degree of verbal skill. The individual may remember the information presented, but without the ability to convey the memory the clinician remains unaware of it.

Impulse Control

There are a range of behavior problems present in the general population during the early years of development, including aggression, hyperactivity, and attentional difficulties (Durand, 1990). Individuals with mental retardation are more likely to evince these problems, particularly if communication and social problems are present (Durand, 1990; Whitman et al., 1983). In addition to the greater prevalence of problem behaviors seen in the general population, individuals with mental retardation also present with some problems not typically seen in the general population, such as self-injurious behavior (Durand, 1990).

Speech

Individuals with mental retardation often have speech problems, such as stuttering or elective mutism and/or delays in language acquisition. Researchers have begun to document the possibility that individuals with speech difficulties may develop aberrant behaviors to communicate their needs and desires (Carr & Durand, 1985; Carr et al., 1980; Vollmer et al., 1992; Wacker et al, 1990). Researchers have documented the maintenance of behaviors such as self-injurious behavior and aggression to communicate attention or escape and to indicate preferences, as well as the decrease of these same behaviors following functional communication training. The theory behind such research goes back to Skinner (Scheerenberger, 1983). He proposed that individuals developed communication strategies based on the effects their behavior had on others. Lack of appropriate communication skills may affect training and acquisition of other skills such as self-help and social skills, because the individual may spend most of the time engaging in maladaptive attempts at communication that are misunderstood, disruptive, and interfering.

Self-Help Skills

Self-help skills are important for any individual functioning in society. Initially the focus should be on developing basic skills such as feeding, drinking, toileting, washing, and dressing. In later years the focus is generally on those skills necessary for independent living. Individuals with mental retardation, particularly those in the lower levels of functioning, may be delayed in acquiring these skills (Matson & Marchetti, 1988; Reid, Wilson, & Faw, 1991). An additional complication to the acquisition of self-help skills is the increased rate of other health problems in this population (Matson & Marchetti, 1988). Physical impairments may make it more difficult or impossible for some individuals to acquire these skills.

In general, individuals with mental retardation master personal and domestic skills at a greater rate than community skills (Matson & Marchetti, 1988). The emphasis on personal and domestic skills in the literature may be related to this phenomenon in some way (Reid et al., 1991). This point is of particular relevance given the increasing emphasis on community placement (Gottlieb, Alter, & Gottlieb, 1991). Mastery of self-help skills is important for individuals with mental retardation for several reasons, including a greater sense of control, better health, and more independent living. The dependence and poor hygiene associated with an inability to perform self-help skills may also impact upon the social interactions and skills of these individuals.

Social Skills

Social skills are an important component of an individual's behavior and affect multiple areas of functioning (Raymond & Matson, 1989). Social skills play an important role in academic, leisure, and vocational functioning (Coe, Matson, Craigie, & Gossen, 1991; Factor & Schimoeller, 1983; Greenwood, Todd, Hops, & Walker, 1982; Kolstoe & Shafter, 1961; Wheeler, Bates, Marshall, & Miller, 1988). These problems are of particular relevance for individuals with mental retardation. Researchers have consistently demonstrated that mental retardation is associated with deficits and/or excesses in social skills (Bellack, Morrison, Wixted, & Mueser, 1990; Marchetti & Campbell, 1990).

Many factors impair the learning of appropriate social skills by individuals with mental retardation (Guralnick, 1986; Kelly, Furman, Phillips, Hathorn, & Wilson, 1979). One factor is that individuals with mental retardation may be avoided by their peers because they are socially unskilled. In fact, researchers have found that individuals functioning in the moderate to severe levels of mental retardation receive very little attention from nonhandicapped peers (Guralnick, 1986). This avoidance decreases the probability that they will learn new skills or be reinforced for any new skills they might develop.

A second obstacle to skill acquisition involves communication delays (Carr & Durand, 1985; Guralnick, 1986; Kennedy, 1988; Raymond & Matson, 1989; Wacker et al., 1990). In normal children, verbal skills become an important means of social interaction (Guralnick, 1986). However, individuals with mental retardation may experience significant delays in language development or may even be nonverbal (Whitman et al., 1983). These deficits dramatically curtail interaction with others, which not only impedes social learning but can also carry over to situations in which others are attempting to teach them independent living.

Lack of verbal skills can also result in impaired parent–child interactions (Guralnick, 1986). In dealing with a child who is socially unskilled and delayed in language acquisition, parents may misinterpret the child's behavior in a negative direction. Parents' incorrect expectations and emotional difficulties add to the problems of interacting. In an attempt to deal with the deficits and excesses present in the child's behavioral repertoire and in an effort to protect their children from negative social consequences, some parents resort to domination over their handicapped child (Guralnick, 1986). This parental dominance may continue into adulthood and can deny the individual the freedom to make choices or the opportunity to learn to do so.

Finally, social interactions may be affected by other children with whom the child associates (Guralnick, 1986; Kelly et al., 1979; Raymond & Matson, 1989). Individuals with mental retardation typically spend most of their time around other individuals with mental retardation. Thus, they lack appropriate peer models.

Psychopathology

As noted before, individuals with mental retardation are more likely to evince psychopathology than individuals in the general population. However, due to the difficulties inherent in assessing a developmentally delayed population, little is known about the exact nature and expression of psychopathology in this population. A large percentage of these individuals exhibit stereotypic movement disorder with or without self-injurious behavior (Schroeder, 1991). Beyond this readily observable category, problems arise in assessing and diagnosing psychopathology in these individuals. For individuals who are nonverbal, the clinician must rely on observable behavior in making a diagnosis. Thus, diagnosing mood and anxiety disorders that require self-report of many symptoms as well as schizophrenia (hallucinations and delusions) is difficult. Additionally, given the speech delays already present, and the prevalence of stereotypic behaviors in the general population of individuals with mental retardation, diagnosing autism is often difficult. This difficulty occurs despite the fact that the two conditions have a high rate of comorbidity.

Summary

The above discussion highlights the prevalence of multiple behavior problems in this population and the importance of identifying such problems. The presence of these maladaptive behaviors often hinders the development and exhibition of appropriate behaviors. Additionally, researchers have documented the acquisition of appropriate skills in individuals with mental retardation. Thus, early identification of problem areas and training in appropriate behaviors can help the individual live more independently and exert some control over his or her environment. The focus of the next section will be on specific treatment strategies to combat the problems noted here.

TREATMENT

Individuals with mental retardation experience significant delays across developmental areas and evince a number of problem behaviors possibly tied to these deficits. Once these problems and deficient areas have been identified, the next logical step is development of methods for teaching adaptive behaviors and decreasing maladaptive behaviors. Methods commonly and successfully employed include reinforcement methods, aversives, functional analysis, and replacement behavior technology.

Reinforcement Methods

A reinforcer is anything that increases the likelihood of the behavior it follows (Bijou, 1993; Vollmer, 1994). Rein-forcement is generally used in the treatment of skill deficits, and operant methods such as this have been used with persons who have mental retardation (Bijou, 1993; Vollmer & Iwata, 1992). These methods are generally positive and nonintrusive forms of treatment.

The efficacy of reinforcement methods has been investigated in numerous studies. Patterson and colleagues (1965) and Doubros and Daniels (1966) utilized a differential reinforcement of other behavior programs to successfully decrease hyperactive behavior in individuals with developmental delays. More recently, Vollmer and colleagues (1992) decreased self-injurious behavior and increased compliance with self-help skills in a profoundly retarded man by differentially reinforcing alternative behavior. Additionally, Ayllon and Azrin (1968) extended the reinforcement philosophy and developed the token economy system. A token economy involves presenting the individual with tokens following the appropriate behavior. The tokens can later be redeemed for reinforcing items or situations.

The appropriateness of use of these methods across functional groups within the mentally retarded population varies. Reinforcement in its most basic sense can be used with individuals functioning at all levels. However, more sophisticated techniques such as token economies must be used with higher functioning individuals with adequate receptive language skills to comprehend the relationship between the behavior, the tokens, and the acquisition of primary reinforcers.

Reinforcement methods are generally well accepted, positive forms of treatment. Increases in adaptive, more acceptable behaviors following the use of reinforcement techniques have been documented in numerous studies (Doubros & Daniels, 1966; Matson, Fee, Coe, & Smith, 1991; Patterson, Jones, Whittier, & Wright, 1965; Vollmer et al., 1992). However, when maladaptive behaviors are present, reinforcement of positive behaviors does not necessarily result in a decrease in the problem behavior (Wacker et al., 1990). In these cases, aversive methods are often used.

Aversives

In contrast to reinforcement methods, aversives are used to suppress a response (Bijou, 1993). Controversy exists on the use of such methods with developmentally disabled persons, however (Axelrod, 1990; Donnellan & LaVigna, 1990; Matson & Taras, 1989). Matson and Taras (1989) provide one review of these techniques and studies in which they were used with persons who evince developmental disabilities. In general, those who are against using aversives argue that there has been little research conducted on these procedures. They also point to negative side effects and lack of generalizability.

Despite the controversial nature of these techniques they are still used to a large degree. There are, as a result, reasons to support the use of such methods. For example, there has been a substantial amount of research on the use of aversives. This body of literature is as sound as any other research conducted in the applied behavior analysis field, and there are no data to suggest that effects are only short term or that there are negative side effects. Additionally, there are some instances in which allowing the individual to engage in a particular maladaptive behavior may be more dangerous than using the aversive procedure. Generally, these procedures should be regulated, and the choice to use any aversive procedure should be done on a case-by-case basis.

Research has documented the effectiveness of numerous aversive techniques. Wacker and colleagues (1990) and Handen and colleagues (1992) successfully instituted a time-out program to decrease maladaptive behavior in individuals with mental retardation. Fisher, Piazza, Bowman, Hagopian, and Langdon (1994) utilized several punishing procedures including contingent demands, facial screens, and water mist in treating two individuals with developmental disabilities. Self-injurious behavior significantly decreased for both individuals.

The issues presented above emphasize the importance of monitoring the use of aversive procedures while acknowledging the effectiveness of such procedures and the necessity of their use. Ideally, aversive procedures should be used in conjunction with reinforcement procedures in a training program to increase adaptive behaviors and to decrease maladaptive behaviors.

Developmental issues in the use of aversives are similar to those involved in the use of reinforcement. At the most operant level, aversive procedures may be used across functioning levels, while procedures such as response cost must be used with higher functioning individuals with adequate receptive language skills. Additionally, motor skills impact the effectiveness and/or the employment of overcorrection procedures. Individuals with poor motor skills or those who are nonambulatory may be unable to carry out an effective overcorrection procedure such as cleaning an area that was soiled. However, procedures that can be performed with physical guidance have been developed for some behaviors (e.g., stereotypes and self-injurious behavior) (Matson & Stephens, 1981).

Functional Analysis

One good by-product of the aversives debate has been the search for new and innovative ways to treat problem behaviors in a less aversive manner. To appropriately use any treatment procedure an accurate and relevant assessment must be conducted. Functional analysis provides a function-based approach to treatment that is considered positive (Carr & Durand, 1985; Carr et al., 1980; Vollmer et al., 1992; Wacker et al., 1990). As a result, it has become a very popular intervention approach. Once a maladaptive behavior is identified, an analysis of controlling variables is conducted to delineate those factors that maintain the behavior. Maintaining factors that have been empirically validated include attention, escape, tangibles, pain, and nonsocial reasons. It is generally best to conduct an analogue assessment in which certain conditions are set up to illicit the behavior. Those conditions resulting in the greatest exhibition of the problem behavior contain the maintaining factors. (For a detailed description of analogue assessment see Vollmer et al., 1992). Questionnaires and checklists have also been developed to analyze maintaining factors of aberrant behavior (Vollmer et al., 1992).

The development and use of functional analysis has allowed clinicians to directly link interventions to the results of the assessment. Interfacing assessment and treatment is important. Taking this approach provides information during assessment on areas that must be a focus of treatment, relationships between problem areas and environmental factors, and methods for evaluating treatment effectiveness.

Replacement Behavior Technology

Replacement behavior technology can be conceptualized as a direct extension of the functional analysis assessment (Bijou, 1993; Carr et al., 1980). For example, a maladaptive behavior is present (i.e., self-injurious behavior, [SIB]). A functional analysis is conducted and the SIB serves an escape function. That is, Johnny engages in SIB in situations involving task demands, and he discontinues the SIB if he is allowed to escape from that situation. Using replacement behavior technology, the clinician would attempt to teach Johnny adaptive skills that compete with the SIB and ultimately replace it. For example, Johnny might be taught to signal using a hand gesture for escape from a given situation. The signal would be reinforced by allowing Johnny to escape, while engaging in SIB would not result in escape from demands. Depending on the nature and severity of the SIB, aversives may be used to help decrease the rate of SIB.

Wacker and colleagues (1990) demonstrated the efficacy of replacement behavior training for individuals with mental retardation presenting with maladaptive behaviors. The behavior ranged from stereotypes to self-injury to aggression. Functional communication training was employed to train the participants to appropriately signal their needs and desires. Strategies were based on a functional analysis of maintaining factors. Following treatment the maladaptive behavior had decreased, and the appropriate communicative behavior occurred without prompting.

The use of replacement behavior technology necessitates a treatment focus on the information derived from the functional assessment. It is essentially a Differential Reinforcement of Incompatible Behavior (DRI) program incorporating a functional rather than an arbitrary reinforcer (Vollmer & Iwata, 1992). Providing a potent reinforcer following the replacement behavior will increase the likelihood that the individual will exhibit that behavior. Additionally, withholding this reinforcer following the maladaptive behavior will decrease the likelihood that the inappropriate behavior will be exhibited. Replacement behavior technology can be used with individuals functioning at all levels of mental retardation. For those functioning in the lower levels, more basic skills will be taught and strict operant procedures will be used. More sophisticated procedures and higher level skills can be used with higher functioning individuals.

SUMMARY AND CONCLUSIONS

The issues discussed in this chapter highlight the problems inherit in the current definition of mental retardation. A great deal of controversy exists about which definition should be followed. In addition to providing a description of individuals with mental retardation, some defining features such as delays in developmental milestones and behavior problems furnish the clinician with information to guide the treatment process. Thus, relating the diagnosis and assessment to treatment, as well as developing useful treatment strategies, are important in successfully combating the difficulties present in these individuals. Accurate and consistent use of functional analysis procedures combined with replacement behavior technology is an excellent step in this direction.

Despite current progress in the field, numerous difficulties remain. Any attempt to pinpoint specific deficits for specific groups of individuals presenting with mental retardation is hindered by the diagnostic process. Assigning a label of mild, moderate, severe, or profound to an individual only tells the clinician that overall the person functions at that level. However, some moderately mentally retarded persons may function in the moderate range in all areas, while others function in the mild range in some areas and in the profound range in other areas. Given the new specification that ten areas of adaptive functioning must be assessed, the possible combinations are endless. Thus, variations within a particular category are likely to be as great as those between categories.

Due to the difficulties mentioned above, the focus in the field of mental retardation has been on identifying individual strengths and weaknesses and on developing treatment strategies that factor in the capabilities of the individual. The diagnostic problems are compounded by the multitude of possible living arrangements and caregiver situations available to this population, as well as the greater prevalence of physical disabilities, making individualized assessment and treatment essential when working with individuals with mental retardation.

The concerns noted in this chapter exist throughout the life of the individual with mental retardation, although the specifics may vary. Specific problems associated with each stage of development are difficult to identify. However, clinicians and professionals working with this population should be cognizant of the general issues inherent in assessing and treating these individuals.

REFERENCES

American Association on Mental Retardation. (1992). *Mental retardation: Definition, classification, and systems of support.* Washington, DC: Author.

American Psychiatric Association. (1994). *Diagnostic and Statistical Manual of Mental Disorder Fourth Edition.* Washington, DC: Author.

Axelrod, S. (1990). Myths that (mis)guide our profession. In A. C. Repp & N. N. Singh (Eds.), *Perspective on the use of nonaversive and aversive interventions for persons with developmental disabilities.* Sycamore, IL: Sycamore.

Ayllon, T., & Azrin, N. (1968). *The token economy: A motivational system for therapy and rehabilitation.* New York: Appleton-Century-Crofts.

Azrin, N. H., & Armstrong, P. M. (1973). The "mini-meal": A method for teaching eating skills to the profoundly retarded. *Mental Retardation, 11,* 9–11.

Azrin, N. H., & Foxx, R. M. (1971). A rapid method of toilet training the institutionalized retarded. *Journal of Applied Behavior Analysis, 4,* 89–99.

Bellack, A. S., Morrison, R. L., Wixted, J. T., & Mueser, K. T. (1990). An analysis of social competence in schizophrenia. *British Journal of Psychiatry, 156,* 809–818.

Bensberg, G. J., Colwell, C. N., & Cassel, R. H. (1965). Teaching the profoundly retarded self-help activities by behavior shaping techniques. *American Journal of Mental Deficiency, 69,* 674–679.

Bijou, S. W. (1993). *Behavior analysis of child development.* Reno, NV: Context Press.

Borthwick-Duffy, S. (1994). Epidemiology and prevalence of psychopathology in people with mental retardation. *Journal of Consulting and Clinical Psychology, 62,* 17–27.

Bray, N. W., Saarnio, D. A., Borges, L. M., & Hawk, L. W. (1994). Intellectual and developmental differences in external memory strategies. *American Journal on Mental Retardation, 99,* 19–31.

Campbell, M., & Malone, R. P. (1991). Mental retardation and psychiatric disorders. *Hospital and Community Psychiatry, 42,* 374–379.

Cantwell, D. P., & Baker, L. (1977). Psychiatric disorders in children with speech and language retardation. *Archives of General Psychiatry, 34,* 583–591.

Carr, E. G., & Durand, V. M. (1985). Reducing behavior problems through functional communication training. *Journal of Applied Behavior Analysis, 18,* 111–126.

Carr, E. G., Newsom, C. D., & Binkoff, J. A. (1980). Escape as a factor in the aggressive behavior of two retarded children. *Journal of Applied Behavior Analysis, 13,* 101–117.

Chess, S. (1970). Emotional problems in mentally retarded children. In F. J. Menolascino (Ed.), *Psychiatric approaches to mental retardation.* New York: Basic Books.

Cicchetti, D., & Ganiban, J. (1990). The organization and coherence of developmental processes in infants and children with Down syndrome. In R. M. Hodapp, J. A. Burack & E. Zigler (Eds.), *Issues in the developmental approach to mental retardation.* Cambridge, England: Cambridge University Press.

Cleland, C. C. (1987). *Mental retardation: A developmental approach.* New Jersey: Prentice-Hall.

Coe, D. A., Matson, J. L., Craigie, C. J., & Gossen, M. A. (1991). Play skills of autistic children: Assessment and instruction. *Child and Family Behavior Therapy, 13,* 13–40.

Coker, S. B. (1989). *Developmental delay and mental retardation.* New York: PMA.

Demb, H. B., Brier, N., Huron, R., & Tomor, E. (1994). The Adolescent Behavior Checklist: Normative data and sensitivity and specificity of a screening tool for diagnosable psychiatric disorders in adolescents with mental retardation and other developmental disabilities. *Research in Developmental Disabilities, 15,* 151–165.

Donnellan, A. M., & LaVigna, G. W. (1990). Myths about punishment. In A. C. Repp & N. N. Singh (Eds.), *Perspectives on the use of nonaversive and aversive interventions for persons with developmental disabilities.* Sycamore, IL: Sycamore.

Doubros, S. G., & Daniels, G. J. (1966). An experimental approach to the reduction of overactive behavior. *Behaviour Research and Therapy, 4,* 251–258.

Durand, V. M. (1990). *Severe behavior problems: A functional communication training approach.* New York: Guilford Press.

Dykens, E., & Leckman, J. (1990). Developmental issues in fragile X syndrome. In R. M. Hodapp, J. A. Burack, & E. Zigler (Eds.), *Issues in the developmental approach to mental retardation.* Cambridge, England: Cambridge University Press.

Ellis, N. R., Woodley-Zanthos, P., & Dulaney, C. L. (1989). Memory for spatial location in children, adults, and mentally retarded persons. *American Journal on Mental Retardation, 93,* 521–527.

Factor, D. C., & Schilmoeller, G. L. (1983). Social skill training of preschool children. *Child Study Journal, 13,* 41–55.

Fiedler, C. R., & Antonak, R. F. (1991). Advocacy. In J. L. Matson & J. A. Mulick (Eds.), *Handbook of mental retardation.* New York: Pergamon Press.

Fisher, W., Piazza, C. C., Bowman, L. G., Hagopian, L. P., & Langdon, N. A. (1994). Empirically derived consequences: A data-based method for prescribing treatments for destructive behavior. *Research in Developmental Disabilities, 15,* 133–150.

Gottlieb, J., Alter, M., & Gottlieb, B. W. (1991). Mainstreaming mentally retarded children. In J. L. Matson & J. A. Mulick (Eds.), *Handbook of mental retardation.* New York: Pergamon Press.

Greenwood, C. R., Todd, N. M., Hops, H., & Walker, H. M. (1982). Behavior change targets in the assessment of socially withdrawn preschool children. *Behavioral Assessment, 4,* 273–297.

Groff, M., & Linden, K. (1982). The WISC-R factor score profiles of cultural–familial mentally retarded and nonretarded youth. *American Journal of Mental Deficiency, 87,* 147–152.

Grossman, H. J. (Ed.). (1983). *Classification in mental retardation.* Washington, DC: American Association on Mental Deficiency.

Gualtieri, C. T., Koriath, U., Van Bourgondien, M., & Saleeb, N. (1983). Language disorders in children referred for psychiatric services. *Journal of the American Academy of Child Psychiatry, 22,* 165–171.

Guralnick, M. J. (1986). *Children's social behavior: Development, assessment, and modification.* Orlando, FL: Academic Press.

Hale, C. A., & Borkowski, J. G. (1991). Attention, memory, and cognition. In J. L. Matson & J. A. Mulick (Eds.), *Handbook of mental retardation.* New York: Pergamon Press.

Handen, B. L., Parrish, J. M., McClung, T. J., Kerwin, M. E., & Evans, L. D. (1992). Using guided compliance versus time out to promote child compliance: A preliminary comparative analysis in an analogue context. *Research in Developmental Disabilities, 13,* 157–170.

Heber, R. (1961). Modification in the manual on terminology and classification in mental retardation. *American Journal of Mental Deficiency, 65,* 499–500.

Hersh, J. H., Bloom, A. S., Yen, F., Topinka, C., & Weisskopf, B. (1988). Mild intellectual deficits in a child with 49, XXXXY. *Research in Developmental Disabilities, 9,* 171–176.

Hodapp, R. M. (1990). One road or many? Issues in the similar-sequence hypothesis. In R. M. Hodapp, J. A. Burack, & E. Zigler (Eds.), *Issues in the developmental approach to mental retardation.* Cambridge, England: Cambridge University Press.

Hodapp, R. M., Burack, J. A., & Zigler, E. (1990). *Issues in the developmental approach to mental retardation.* Cambridge, England: Cambridge University Press.

Iverson, J. C., & Fox, R. A. (1989). Prevalence of psychopathology among mentally retarded adults. *Research in Developmental Disabilities, 10,* 77–83.

Jacobsen, J. W. (1990). Assessing the prevalence of psychiatric disorders in a developmentally disabled population. In E. Dibble & D. B. Gray (Eds.), *Assessment of behavior problems in persons with mental retardation living in the community.* Rockville, MD: National Institutes of Mental Health.

Jakab, I. (1992). Psychiatric disorders in mental retardation. In I. Jakab (Ed.), *Mental retardation.* New York: Karger.

Jensen, A. R. (1987). Individual differences in mental ability. In J. A. Glover & R. R. Ronning (Eds.), *Historical foundations of educational psychology.* New York: Plenum Press.

Kelly, J. A., Furman, W., Phillips, J., Hathorn, S., & Wilson, T. (1979). Teaching conversational skills to retarded adolescents. *Child Behavior Therapy, 1,* 85–97.

Kolstoe, O. P., & Shafter, A. J. (1961). Employability prediction for mentally retarded adults: A methodological note. *American Journal of Mental Deficiency, 66,* 287–289.

Kratochwill, T. R., & Bijou, S. W. (1987). The impact of behaviorism on educational psychology. In J. A. Glover & R. R. Ronning (Eds.), *Historical foundations of educational psychology.* New York: Plenum Press.

Leland, H. (1989). Adaptive behavior scales. In J. L. Matson & J. A. Mulick (Eds.), *Handbook of mental retardation.* New York: Pergamon Press.

Levitan, G. W., & Reiss, S. (1983). Generality of diagnostic overshadowing across disciplines. *Applied Research in Mental Retardation, 4,* 59–64.

Mandes, E., Massimino, C., & Mantis, C. (1991). A comparison of borderline and mild mental retardates assessed on the memory for designs and the WAIS-R. *Journal of Clinical Psychology, 47,* 562–567.

Manikam, R. (1989). Treatment overview and description of psychotherapy. In J. L. Matson (Ed.), *Chronic schizophrenia and adult autism.* New York: Springer.

Marchetti, A. G., & Campbell, V. A. (1990). Social skills. In J. L. Matson (Ed.), *Handbook of behavior modification with the mentally retarded.* New York: Pergamon Press.

Matson, J. L., & Coe, D. A. (1992). Applied behavior analysis: Its impact on the treatment of mentally retarded emotionally disturbed people. *Research in Developmental Disabilities, 13,* 171–189.

Matson, J. L., Fee, V. E., Coe, D. A., & Smith, D. (1991). A social skills program for developmentally delayed preschoolers. *Journal of Clinical Child Psychology, 20,* 428–433.

Matson, J. L., & Marchetti, A. (1988). *Developmental disabilities: A life-span perspective.* New York: Grune & Stratton.

Matson J. L., & Mulick, J. A. (1992). *Handbook of mental retardation (2nd ed.).* New York: Pergamon Press.

Matson, J. L., & Sevin, J. A. (1994). Theories of dual diagnosis in mental retardation. *Journal of Consulting and Clinical Psychology, 62,* 6–16.

Matson, J. L., & Stephens, R. M. (1981). Overcorrection treatment of stereotyped behaviors. *Behavior Modification, 5,* 491–502.

Matson, J. L., & Taras, M. (1989). A 20 year review of punishment and alternative methods to treat problem behaviors in developmentally delayed persons. *Research in Developmental Disabilities, 10,* 85–104.

McCall, R. B., Applebaum, M. I., & Hogarty, P. S. (1973). Developmental changes in mental performance. *Monographs of the Society for Research in Child Development, 38,* 1–83.

McCartney, J. R. (1987). Mentally retarded and nonretarded subjects' long term recognition memory. *American Journal on Mental Retardation, 92,* 312–317.

Menolascino, F. J. (1990). The nature and types of mental illness in the mentally retarded. In M. Lewis & S. M. Miller (Eds.), *Handbook of Developmental Psychopathology.* New York: Plenum Press.

Mercer, J. R. (1988). Ethnic differences in IQ scores: What do they mean? *Hispanic Journal of Behavioral Sciences, 10,* 199–218.

Nidiffer, F. D., & Kelly, T. E. (1983). Developmental and degenerative patterns associated with cognitive, behavioural and motor difficulties in the Sanfilippo syndrome: An epidemiological study. *Journal of Mental Deficiency Research, 27,* 185–203.

Patterson, G. R., Jones, R., Whittier, J., & Wright, M. A. (1965). A behavior modification techniques for the hyperactive child. *Behaviour Research and Therapy, 2,* 217–226.

Peterson, F. M., & Martens, B. K. (1995). A comparison of behavioral interventions reported in treatment studies and programs for adults with developmental disabilities. *Research in Developmental Disabilities, 16,* 27–42.

Phillips, I., & Williams, N. (1975). Psychopathology and mental retardation: A study of 100 mentally retarded children: I. Psychopathology. *American Journal of Psychiatry, 132,* 1265–1271.

Raymond, K. L., & Matson, J. L. (1989). Social skills in the hearing impaired. *Journal of Clinical Child Psychology, 18,* 247–258.

Reid, D. H., Wilson, P. G., & Faw, G. D. (1991). Teaching self-help skills. In J. L. Matson & J. A. Mulick (Eds.), *Handbook of mental retardation.* New York: Pergamon Press.

Reschly, D. J., & Ward, S. M. (1991). Use of adaptive behavior measures and overrepresentation of black students in programs for students with mild mental retardation. *American Journal on Mental Retardation, 96,* 257–268.

Reiss, S. (1982). Psychopathology and mental retardation: Survey of a developmental disabilities mental health program. *Mental Retardation, 20,* 128–132.

Reiss, S., Levitan, G. W., & Szyszko, J. (1982). Emotional disturbance and mental retardation: Diagnostic overshadowing. *American Journal of Mental Deficiency, 86,* 567–574.

Reiss, S., & Szyszko, J. (1983). Diagnostic overshadowing and professional experience with mentally retarded persons. *American Journal of Mental Deficiency, 87,* 396–402.

Rutter, M. I., Graham, P. J., & Yule, W. (1970). A neuropsychiatric study in childhood. *Clinics in Developmental Medicine* (Nos. 35/36, p. 175). Philadelphia: Lippincott.

Sattler, J. (1992). *Assessment of children.* San Diego: Jerome D. Sattler.

Scheerenberger, R. C. (1983). *A history of mental retardation.* Baltimore: Brookes.

Schroeder, S. (1991). Self-injury and stereotypy. In J. L. Matson and J. A. Mulick (Eds.), *Handbook of mental retardation.* New York: Pergamon Press.

Spitz, H. (1983). Critique of the developmental position in mental retardation research. *Journal of Special Education, 17,* 261–294.

Varnhagen, C. K., Das, J. P., & Varnhagen, S. (1987). Auditory and visual memory span: Cognitive processing by TMR individuals with Down syndrome and other etiologies. *American Journal on Mental Deficiency, 91,* 398–405.

Vollmer, T. R. (1994). The concept of automatic reinforcement: Implications for behavioral research in developmental disabilities. *Research in Developmental Disabilities, 15,* 187–208.

Vollmer, T. R., & Iwata, B. A. (1992). Differential reinforcement as treatment for behavior disorders: Procedural and functional variations. *Research in Developmental Disabilities, 13,* 393–418.

Vollmer, T. R., Iwata, B. A., Smith, R. G., & Rodgers, T. A. (1992). Reduction of multiple aberrant behaviors and concurrent development of self-care skills with differential reinforcement. *Research in Developmental Disabilities, 13,* 287–299.

von Wendt, L., Makinen, H., & Rantakallio, P. (1984). Psychomotor development in the first year and mental retardation—A prospective study. *Journal of Mental Deficiency Research, 28,* 219–225.

Wacker, D. P., Steege, M. W., Northup, J., Sasso, G., Berg, W., Rei- mers, T., Cooper, L., Cigrand, K., & Conn, L. (1990). A compo- nent analysis of functional communication training across three topographies of severe behavior problems. *Journal of Applied Behavior Analysis, 23,* 417–429.

Weisz, J. R. (1990). Cultural–familial mental retardation: A devel- opmental perspective on cognitive performance and "helpless" behavior. In R. M. Hodapp, J. A. Burack, & E. Zigler (Eds.), *Is- sues in the developmental approach to mental retardation.* Cam- bridge, England: Cambridge University Press.

Wheeler, J. J., Bates, P., Marshall, K. J., & Miller, S. R. (1988). Teach- ing appropriate social behaviors to a young man with moderate mental retardation in a supported competitive environment. *Edu- cation and Training in Mental Retardation, 18,* 105–116.

Whitman, T. L., Sciback, J. W., & Reid, D. H. (1983). *Behavior modification with the severely and profoundly retarded.* New York: Academic Press.

Zigler, E. (1969). Development versus difference theories of mental retardation and the problem of motivation. *American Journal of Mental Deficiency, 73,* 536–556.

Zigler, E., Balla, D., & Hodapp, R. (1984). On the definition and classification of mental retardation. *American Journal of Mental Deficiency, 89,* 215–230.

CHAPTER 19

PERVASIVE DEVELOPMENTAL DISORDERS

V. Mark Durand
Eileen Mapstone

Pervasive developmental disorders (PDDs) include four disorders (autistic disorder, Rett's disorder, Asperger's disorder, and childhood disintegrative disorder) that first make their appearance in childhood and have widespread effects on cognitive, social, emotional, and sometimes physical functioning (American Psychiatric Association, 1994). We begin the chapter by briefly describing the pervasive developmental disorders and then proceed to discuss issues related to developmental theory and treatment. All of these disorders are rare in the general population. Understandably, because of the relatively small number of persons with these disorders, there is, with one exception, little research on these disorders. The one exception is autistic disorder (or autism), which has been the focus of a great deal of empirical attention over the years. Due to the scarcity of research on the other pervasive developmental disorders, we focus the bulk of our attention on autism, describing what is known about the developmental nature of this disorder and attempts made to integrate developmental theory in its treatment.

THE PERVASIVE DEVELOPMENTAL DISORDERS

Autistic disorder, Rett's disorder, Asperger's disorder, and childhood disintegrative disorder are considered types of pervasive developmental disorders. Individuals with these disorders all experience problems with development; namely, they have trouble progressing in areas such as language, socialization, and cognition. The qualifier "pervasive" indicates that these are not relatively minor problems of development, but rather significantly affect most aspects of functioning and ultimately how these individuals will live. There is general agreement that one can reliably identify a child with a pervasive developmental disorder based on the delays observed in daily functioning (Romanczyk, Lockshin, & Navalta, 1994). What is not agreed upon so easily, however, is how this category of disorders should be divided (Waterhouse, Wing, Spitzer, & Siegel, 1992).

Most workers in this area agree that the category of autism should remain separate, a view that is based on a substantial body of research (Dawson, 1989). Yet considerable controversy exists about whether Asperger's disorder, Rett's disorder, and childhood disintegrative disorder are distinctly different disorders or, in some cases, disorders that should remain under the general heading of pervasive developmental disorders. Some maintain, for example, that these disorders—especially Asperger's disorder and autistic disorder—describe the same disorder on different points on a continuum (Rutter & Schopler, 1992). Others, however, point out that there are important differences and that these disorders should be considered distinct to help drive new research (Wing, 1981). There is also disagreement regarding the appropriateness of placing Rett's disorder—a progressive neurological disorder that affects motor as well as cognitive and social functioning—under the pervasive developmental disorder category (Gillberg, 1994; Rutter, 1994). As far as the research differentiating these disorders is concerned, Michael Rutter and Eric Schopler recently summed it up this way: "The answer is a pretty straightforward 'yes' in the case of Rett, a 'probably' in the case of disintegrative disorders, and an uncertain 'maybe' in the case of Asperger syndrome" (Rutter & Schopler, 1992; pg. 471). It should be noted that as late as 1987, in the DSM-III-R, these disorders were combined together in a category called *Pervasive Developmental Disorder Not Otherwise Specified* (or PDDNOS). With the recent introduction of DSM-IV, these disorders have been differentiated, although again, the field has not developed a consensus on this categorization.

Asperger's disorder involves a significant impairment in the ability to engage in meaningful social interaction along with restricted and repetitive stereotyped behaviors but without the severe delays in language or other cognitive skills characteristic of people with autism (APA, 1994). It was Lorna Wing in the early 1980s who recommended that Asperger's disorder be reconsidered as a separate disorder, with an emphasis on the unusual and circumscribed interests displayed by these individuals (Wing, 1981). Asperger's disorder seems to be even less frequent in the population than autism, with a prevalence rate estimated to be approximately 1 in every 10,000 births. This disorder is seen more often in boys than in girls, although accurate numbers are not yet available (Volkmar & Cohen, 1991). People with this disorder tend to have few cognitive impairments, and their IQ scores are usually within the average range.

Some evidence has been uncovered to suggest that Asperger's may be more prevalent among family members than in the general population, suggesting a possible genetic contribution (Volkmar & Cohen, 1991). In addition, recent evidence points to a possible etiological link between Asperger's disorder and bipolar affective disorder (manic depression). In a family history study, DeLong and Dwyer found that the incidence of bipolar affective disorder was higher among family members of people with Asperger's disorder than you would expect in the general population (DeLong & Dwyer, 1988).

Rett's disorder is a progressive neurological disorder that is characterized by constant hand-wringing, mental retardation, and impaired motor skills (Van Acker, 1991). These problems appear after an apparently normal start in development. This disorder was first described by Andreas Rett in 1966, but it was not until 17 years later that a published report

of this disorder among 35 girls from France, Portugal, and Sweden brought Rett's disorder to the attention of the world (Hagberg, Aicardi, Dias, & Ramos, 1983). Motor skills, such as the use of hands and walking, and cognitive skills seem to deteriorate progressively over time. However, social skills seem to develop normally from birth, then decline between the ages of 1 to 3, then partially improve after that time. Rett's disorder is also relatively rare, occurring in approximately 1 per 12,000 to 15,000 live female births. Rett's disorder is observed almost exclusively in females. To date, there have been only three cases of what appears to be Rett's disorder observed among males (Coleman, 1990; Philippart, 1990).

Childhood disintegrative disorder describes a disorder that involves severe regression in language, adaptive behavior, and motor skills after a period of normal development for approximately 2 to 4 years. Over 80 years ago, Theodor Heller reported his observations of six children who experienced severe regression, much later than is seen with Rett's, after developing normally for several years. This disorder has had a variety of names over the years, including dementia infantilis, Heller's syndrome, disintegrative psychosis, and the current, childhood disintegrative disorder. This disorder is new to DSM-IV and is probably the least understood of the disorders discussed so far. Estimates of its prevalence suggest that it is very rare, occurring once in approximately every 100,000 births (Kurita, Kita, & Miyake, 1992). It may also occur more often in boys than in girls.

Autistic disorder, or autism, is a childhood disorder that is characterized by significant impairment in social interactions, gross and significant impairment in communication, and restricted patterns of behavior, interest, and activities. Autism is also a relatively rare disorder, although the exact estimates vary. Early research placed the prevalence of this disorder at approximately 2 to 5 per 10,000 (Lotter, 1966). However, recent estimates, using more contemporary definitions of autistic disorder place the prevalence at about 2 per every 10,000 people in the population, representing the lower end of the range (Gillberg, 1984). Gender differences for autism depend on the IQ level of the person affected. More specifically, autism is more prevalent among females with IQ's under 35; while in contrast, the disorder is more prevalent among males in the higher IQ range, although it is not clear why these gender differences are present at differing IQ levels (Volkmar, Szatmari, & Sparrow, 1993). Autistic disorder appears to be a universal phenomenon, having been identified in every part of the world including Sweden (Gillberg, 1984), Japan, (Sugiyama & Abe, 1989), Russia (Lebedinskaya & Nikolskaya, 1993), and China (Chung, Luk, & Lee, 1990). The vast majority of people with autism develop the behaviors associated with this disorder before the age of 36 months (APA, 1994).

Individuals with this disorder present with a puzzling array of symptoms. Language skills are impaired and these individuals display a characteristic deficit in social skills, yet they may excel in other areas, such as in skills involving rote memory abilities. At any particular moment in time, until people with autistic disorder begin to behave in unusual ways, they often appear to have no particular problem. Their average appearance is part of the enigma of this disorder and has prompted some to suggest that these individuals were all of average or superior intelligence (Kanner, 1943). We now know, however, that people with autism fall on a continuum with regard to IQ scores. About three out of every four people with autism have some form of mental retardation. Almost half of all these individuals would fall in the severe to profound range of mental retardation (IQ less than 50), about a quarter would test in the mild to moderate range (IQ = 50–70), and the remaining people would display abilities in the borderline to average range (IQ greater than 70) (Waterhouse, Wing, & Fein, 1989).

These measures of IQ have been used to determine prognosis. In other words, the higher these children score on IQ tests, the less likely they are to need extensive support later in life. This type of heterogeneity has led some to suggest that there may be important subgroups among people with autism that represent different etiologies and developmental progressions (DeLong & Dwyer, 1988). We next turn our attention to developmental views of this most researched of the pervasive developmental disorders—autism—looking at both historical as well as contemporary theories of this enigmatic disorder.

HISTORICAL DEVELOPMENTAL VIEWS OF AUTISM

Early thinking about the etiology of autism came from Kanner's first portrait of children with autism, which included descriptions of their parents (Kanner, 1943). He noticed that all of the parents of the 11 children he studied were highly intelligent and tended to be professionals. Kanner did not automatically conclude from these observations that the parents were at fault in their children's problems. He pointed out that because the "aloneness" exhibited by these children seemed to be present from birth, their problems must be a result of some biological predisposition (Kanner, 1943). Others, however, were intrigued by the possibility of a psychological cause for autism and wrote extensively on the subject.

Probably the most famous and controversial of these theorists was Bruno Bettelheim. Bettelheim, remembering his early experiences as a Jew in a Nazi concentration camp, noted similarities between the prisoners and the children with whom he was working (Bettelheim, 1967). He believed that the observed dramatic social deficits were a result of parents' blocking these children's attempts to reach out to the world. Just as the concentration camp prisoners were prevented from having any amount of autonomy, children with autism, he said, were being frustrated by their families for attempts to gain control over their environment. This interference by their parents resulted in the withdrawal of children from contacts with the outside world.

While Bettelheim took a psychoanalytic view of what he saw as the development of autism in children, Charles Ferster explained this developmental phenomenon from a behavioral perspective (Ferster, 1961). Ferster hypothesized that by examining the early reinforcement histories between children with autistic disorder and their parents, one could observe the development of the unusual behaviors seen in autism. He theorized that parents of these children, by not attending to them, extinguished many of their early attempts at social and communicative behaviors. These children would not learn to relate to others because their parents did not encourage these behaviors. Ferster thought that factors such as parental depression, drug addiction, or illness could affect parents in such a devastating way as to result in long-term disinterest in their children.

Another developmental view of autism was proposed by two ethologists (Tinbergen & Tinbergen, 1983). Niko and Elisabeth Tinbergen, borrowing observations from the "imprinting" research, suggested that children with autism engage in unusual social reactions because of a breakdown in the normal motivational conflicts experienced by all children. According to their theory, children approach adults with a combination of social or bonding tendencies and fear of these contacts. Under normal circumstances, the timidity or fear gives way to positive social contacts. For children with autism, however, this process is not resolved in a positive way, and they fail to establish important social bonds. They theorized that this unfortunate consequence resulted from a combination of a genetic predisposition toward being overtimid and early failed attempts by parents to connect socially with the child. The Tinbergens went on to suggest that children with autism "are the victims of our modern, urbanised, crowded, rationalised and stressful environment—a 'problem environment' in which even healthy, normal parental behaviour may misfire" (Tinbergen & Tinbergen, 1972, 34). Although there are currently few who accept this view of autism, it is one of the few theories that combines both psychological and biological aspects to explain this disorder.

The psychoanalytic views of Bettelheim, the behavioral views of Ferster, and the ethological approach of the Tinbergen's are similar in many ways. From each perspective, the origins of autistic disorder were seen as arising from the failed parenting provided by mothers and fathers and the subsequent atypical social development by their children. As we will see next, there is a great deal of evidence pointing to biological influences on autistic disorder, suggesting that the *origins* of this disorder—as pointed out by Kanner—predate parental involvement. Unfortunately, the result of these previous views of autism was devastating to a generation of parents of these children, many of whom felt guilty and responsible for their child's problems (Rimland, 1994).

CONTEMPORARY DEVELOPMENTAL THEORY

In contrast to the single, unified theories offered in the past, there is no one single theory generally accepted today that adequately describes the disorder of autism (Locke, Banken, & Mahone, 1994). There are, however, several themes that run through current research in this area that are important to highlight. For example, current views of autism recognize the roles of both developmental as well as deviance models in approaching the study of autism (Volkmar, Burack, & Cohen, 1990). In other words, the pattern of development of this disorder shows signs of both developmental delay as well as unusual behavior patterns not predicted by usual delays. For example, skills such as aspects of communication can often be usefully viewed from a developmental delay model—with many of these individuals displaying typical but delayed progression of communication skills. On the other hand, the characteristic social deficits in these individuals differ markedly even from infants. This may be why—as we will see later—developmental theory has been more successful in guiding intervention efforts in the area of language and communication and less useful in improving socialization skills.

This picture is further complicated by the heterogeneous nature of the disorder itself. The concept of "equifinality" appears to be particularly appropriate for autism given that the same outcome (i.e., autism) can develop from a number of different pathogenic conditions. This has become particularly apparent with the advances in understanding the biological origins of this disorder. We next review some of the evidence for the developmental nature of autism.

Psychological Influences

Before proceeding, it is important to recall that people with autism (and the other pervasive developmental disorders) differ in significant ways from people with general developmental delays such as those with mental retardation. Rather than observing deficits in most or all areas of development, people with autism (and who do not have comorbid mental

retardation) typically show specific delays or deficits in some areas but not in others. Contemporary researchers have explored the nature of these deficits, in part, with the expectation of discovering the "primary" deficits responsible for creating the characteristic symptoms of the disorder (Fein, Pennington, Markowitz, Braverman, & Waterhouse, 1986; Goodman, 1989). We next describe the efforts to distinguish what characteristics are primary to autism from those that are outgrowths of these characteristics (i.e., "secondary" to the disorder).

A number of the abilities thought necessary for typical development of cognitive, social, and communicative skills are either missing in children with autism or develop in unusual ways (Hobson, 1989). For example, a pivotal skill for the development of a number of abilities is *imitation*, a skill that is either absent or difficult for children with autism (e.g., Lovaas, 1977). For example, Dawson and Adams (1984) observed that children with autism had more difficulty imitating actions of others such as banging a hammer and that those who were more skillful at imitating also displayed more appropriate social behavior.

Other researchers have examined the emotional expressiveness of these individuals and their ability to detect emotional responses in others, again as a possible primary deficit that could account for the unusual development of social and communicative skills. Ricks and Wing (1975), for example, found that children with autism tended to respond to emotion inducing situations (e.g., scenarios that typically elicit happiness or sadness) with a limited range of emotional expressions, and sometimes with expressions inappropriate to the situation. Some have hypothesized that people with autism have difficulties regulating their own affective states and integrating these experiences with the affective states of others (Hobson, 1989). Further, this deficit is thought to account for difficulties with social bonding and social communication.

The unusual speech evidenced by some individuals with autism—for example, the tendency to avoid first-person pronouns, such as "I" and "me," using "he" and "she" instead, has led to theories about the origins of this disorder. For instance, if you asked a child with autism, "Do you want something to drink?", he might say, "He wants something to drink" (meaning "I want something to drink"). This observation led some theorists to wonder if autism involved a lack of self-awareness (Goldfarb, 1963; Mahler, 1952). It was suggested that the withdrawal seen among people with autistic disorder was attributable to their lack of awareness that they existed. In fact, however, some people with autistic disorder do seem to have self-awareness (Dawson & McKissick, 1984; Spiker & Ricks, 1984). And this ability seems to follow a developmental progression. Just as you would find in children without a disability, those with cognitive abilities below the age of about 18 to 24 months show little or no self-recognition, while people with more advanced abilities do demonstrate self-awareness. Observations of a lack of self-concept may be attributable to the cognitive delays or deficits exhibited by some people with autism and not to the disorder of autism itself.

Research on attachment—a child's use of a parent as a source of security in the environment (Ainsworth, Blehar, Waters, & Wall, 1978)—has recently focused on children with autism. It is clear that children with autism do exhibit a form of attachment, although the quality of this relationship may differ from other children of the same age. For example, children with autism will sit near their mothers rather than strangers after being left alone for a short period of time. Although they do not make eye contact and smile at their mothers like children without autism, they still recognize the difference between their mothers and strangers and prefer to be nearer to their mothers in stressful situations (Sigman & Ungerer, 1984). Again, developmental level, rather than severity of autism, seems to predict this attachment, suggesting a developmental delay rather than a deviance explanation (Rogers, Ozonoff, & Maslin-Cole, 1993). This research points up that people with autism are not totally unaware of others as was once thought. However, for some reason we do not yet fully understand, they may not enjoy or may not have the ability to develop meaningful relationships with others.

Because of the importance placed on the socialization problems of people with autism, a recent developmental theory of this disorder has emerged, relying on the concept of Theory of Mind (Baron-Cohen, 1995). Put simply, this theory suggests that the severe social deficits observed among people with autism are a result of their inability to attribute mental states to others and themselves (Leslie, 1987). In other words, the problems these people have relating to others is a result of a cognitive deficit that prevents them from "getting inside the head" of others and explaining and predicting their behavior. This theory is controversial because it suggests that these social problems are secondary to their cognitive deficits. According to this view, their deficiency is a result of their lack of Theory of Mind, which in turn results in social problems. Although this theory is intriguing, there are some recent studies suggesting that the social problems of children with autism may occur *before* the development of the skills needed for Theory of Mind (Klin, Volkmar, & Sparrow, 1992).

Biological Influences

To fully understand the developmental nature of autism, it is essential to examine evidence for the biological bases of this disorder. Exploring the reciprocal interaction between early biological difficulties and environmental events should lead to a fuller understanding of the nature of the disorder as well as to better intervention efforts. It has been observed, for example, that a number of medical conditions have been associated with autism, including congenital rubella (German measles), hypsarhythmia, tuberous sclerosis, cytomegalovirus, and difficulties during pregnancy and labor, suggesting that autism may result from a number of different disease and biological conditions (Hunt & Dennis, 1987). For example, although a small percentage of mothers exposed to the rubella virus will have a child with autism, most of the time no autism is present. It is still not clear why these medical conditions *sometimes* result in autism, and other times do not.

It is now clear that this disorder has a genetic component (Smalley, 1991). For example, in families who have one child with autism, a 3 to 5 percent risk of another child with the disorder enlists (Falconer, 1965), a rate much higher than the general population. In one of the few twin studies, Folstein and Rutter (1977) studied eleven people with autism who had a monozygotic twin and ten people with autism who had a dizygotic twin. They found a concordance rate of 36 percent for the monozygotic twins, with four of the eleven twin pairs both having autism. In contrast, they found that none of the dizygotic twin pairs were concordant for autism. Folstein and Rutter also examined these twins for the presence of other developmental and/or cognitive problems and found that the concordance rate increased to 82 percent for the monozygotic group and to 10 percent for the dizygotic group. In other words, when they looked at developmental disorders in general, they found that if one of the monozygotic twins had autism, the other twin was highly likely to have autism or some other cognitive–developmental problem. A handful of other studies have lent support to the possible role of genetics in the etiology of autism (Ritvo, Freeman, Mason-Brothers, Mo, & Ritvo, 1985; Steffenburg et al., 1989). To date, however, the genetic mechanism (how autism is inherited) has not been clarified, although it does appear to be complex and may involve more than one gene.

Evidence that autism is associated with some form of organic or brain damage comes from a number of different areas. Prevalence data, for example, indicate that three out of every four people with autism also have some level of mental retardation (Durand & Carr, 1988). In addition, it has been estimated that between 30 and 75 percent of these people display some neurological abnormality such as abnormal posture or gait and clumsiness (Tsai & Ghaziuddin, 1992). These observations provide some suggestive evidence that autism is related to problems of an organic nature.

It was Bernard Rimland in 1964 who was among the first to provide the field of autism with a neurobiological model of this disorder. Rimland believed that autism was a cognitive disorder resulting from malfunctioning systems in the brain stem (Rimland, 1964). Subsequent research has provided very little evidence for the involvement of the brain stem in autism, but Rimland's theory inspired others to look toward the brain for explanations for the unusual behaviors observed among people with autism.

Only a handful of cases using postmortem brain examinations have been completed among people with autism. Although the initial studies indicated no specific structural differences in these individuals, more recent work has shown that damage in the cerebellum may be common. For example, Ritvo and colleagues published findings from the autopsies of four people with autism. They found that each of these individuals had abnormalities in their cerebellum; specifically, they had fewer of a particular type of cell present in this area of the brain—Purkinje cells (Ritvo et al., 1986). Although their exact function is not clearly understood, it is believed that the Purkinje cells inhibit the action of other cells and may be sensitive to GABA, a major inhibitory neurotransmitter.

Recently, researchers, using CAT (computerized axial tomography) and MRI (magnetic resonance imaging) technologies have found abnormalities in the cerebellum, more specifically, smaller cerebellar size. In one study, Courchesne and colleagues examined the brain of one 21-year-old man who had a diagnosis of autism but had no other neurological disorders and had a tested IQ score in the average range of intelligence (Courchesne, Hesselink, Jernigan, & Yeung-Courchesne, 1987). They selected someone *without* the severe cognitive deficits seen in three quarters of people with autism in order to separate out any brain damage that may have been associated with mental retardation but not necessarily with autism. The most striking finding was the abnormally small cerebellum when compared with that of a person without autism. Although this observation of cerebellar abnormality has not been found in every study using brain imaging, it appears to be one of the more reliable findings of brain involvement in autism to date (Courchesne, 1991). It may be that these findings point out an important subtype of people with autism.

An Integration

There are currently few comprehensive and generally accepted models of this disorder that take into account the biological as well as the psychosocial influences discussed. Part of the reason for this lack of integration is that considerable controversy continues to exist about the definition of autism, the nature of the brain involvement, and the importance each of the deficits plays in this disorder. For example, proponents

of the Theory of Mind model see cognitive deficits as central to the problems faced by people with this disorder. In contrast, others view problems with arousal, especially in social situations, as the root of later problems (Dawson & Lewy, 1989). In other words, neurological deficits somehow cause these individuals to be particularly sensitive to social interactions, which, in turn, makes them uncomfortable. This atypical developmental progression, in turn, results in their social withdrawal and difficulties in language development (Mundy & Sigman, 1989). It is likely that further research will uncover the biological mechanisms that ultimately lead to the early social aversion experienced by many people with autism. In addition, the psychological and social factors that very early in life interact with the biological influences, producing deficits in socialization, communication, and the unusual behaviors, will need to be outlined.

DEVELOPMENTAL PERSPECTIVES IN TREATMENT

A number of intervention issues quickly come to mind when viewing autism from a developmental perspective. For example, are all of the behavioral outcomes (e.g., language and social deficits, behavior problems) a direct function of autistic disorder or are they related to developmental delays? And are all of the outcomes related to autism inevitable? Would early intervention efforts—especially ones targeted at primary deficits—help to prevent some of the later problems? These types of questions have been the focus of some recent treatment efforts and will be outlined in this next section. It should be noted upfront, however, that most research on treatment has not incorporated a developmental perspective, and such efforts remain the exception rather than the rule in the area of autism.

Historical Views

As alluded to previously, early psychosocial interventions for autism were based on the predominant notion that the cause of this disorder lay in inadequate parenting. One outgrowth of this theory was a treatment based on establishing ego development in individuals with autism (Bettleheim, 1967). This treatment emphasis was based on the theory that parents were blocking their children's attempts to reach out to the world. Bettleheim believed that children with autism were frustrated by their families in their attempt to gain control over their environment. The ego development of the individual with autism was seen as the only way to help that person establish contact with the outer world. Unfortunately, treatments that focused solely on ego development did little to improve the lives of people with autism (Kanner & Eisenberg, 1955). This should come as no surprise in light of the more current theories of autism that recognize that autism is not the result of poor parenting.

Although Ferster (1961) also attributed autism to poor parenting style, his treatment approach was markedly different from Bettleheim's. Ferster's treatment focused on teaching very simple responses through the use of reinforcement (Ferster & DeMyer, 1961). For example, children with autism were reinforced with food when they put coins in the proper slot. Ferster's intervention efforts were based heavily on Skinner's animal learning experiments.

Ivar Lovaas, realizing the practical importance of Ferster's work, demonstrated that a child with autism could be taught to communicate through the use of reinforcers. During the mid-1960s, Lovaas and colleagues used shaping and discrimination training to teach children with autism to imitate the communication of others (Lovaas, Berberich, Perloff, & Schaeffer, 1966). Recall that this skill—imitating others—is often lacking in children with autism and that this deficit is associated with poor socialization skills (Dawson & Adams, 1984). Lovaas's procedure began by reinforcing any utterance the child made while watching the teacher. For example, the teacher might request that the child say the word "mama" and would then reinforce the child when it produced the sound of the letter "m." This procedure would continue until the child could reliably demonstrate imitation. Once the child had mastered the imitation skills, it became easier to teach the child more complex forms of language (Lovaas et al., 1966).

Current Developmental Perspectives in Treatment

Unfortunately, despite the enormous value of behavioral interventions for teaching skills such as imitation, these interventions have not proven to produce the massive changes hoped for in most people with autism. It can be argued that behavioral theory has made its contribution by defining "how" to teach and that developmental theories may provide assistance about "what" to teach people with autism and other pervasive developmental disorders (Carr, 1985; Durand, 1986). The examination of autism from a developmental perspective may provide valuable additional information that could assist the intervention strategies in this area. Several recent efforts at incorporating developmental considerations in treatment will be reviewed next.

Language and communication skills have been a primary concern for workers in the field of autism because of the marked deficits in these areas displayed by this population

(Charlop & Haymes, 1994; Prizant & Wetherby, 1989). Fortunately, the literature on normal social–communicative development is extensive and therefore is available to guide assessment and intervention efforts in cases in which development of these skills does not occur in a typical fashion (e.g., Bloom & Lahey, 1978; McLean & Snyder-McLean, 1978). One example of an area in which a developmental perspective has been applied to language is with echolalic speech.

Echolalia involves repeating all or part of the speech of others. This behavior was at one time believed to be one of the defining characteristics of autism and was included as part of the DSM-III's criteria for the disorder. However, it is clear that echolalia is part of normally developing language skills observed in most young children, and its presence in older individuals with autism is likely a sign of their language delay (Prizant & Wetherby, 1989). Recent intervention efforts have capitalized on this observation and rather than attempting to suppress echolalia have relied on it to further general language development. For example, Charlop and Milstein (1989) encouraged echolalic speech in appropriate contexts and later substituted it for functionally equivalent and more appropriate speech. This technique involves encouraging the normal developmental sequence of language progression (Charlop, 1983; Freeman, Ritvo, & Miller, 1975).

Much effort has focused on developing effective interventions for improving the communication skills of children with autism. However, as we have pointed out previously, research on the other deficit areas within autism, for example, social skills, is scarce. Some researchers have hypothesized that one can view autism from a developmental perspective only within certain deficit areas. These researchers have suggested that the language deficits observed in autism do follow a developmental pathology whereas the social skills deficits that are observed are more closely aligned with a deviance model (Mundy & Sigman, 1989). This issue becomes important in the selection of the most appropriate intervention for the various deficiencies.

Facilitated Communication

A recent intervention strategy that relates to developmental notions of language development has caused considerable controversy in the field of autism. Facilitated communication was first introduced as a new teaching technique by Rosemary Crossley from Australia (Crossley, 1988) and was later promoted in the United States by Douglas Biklen. This technique involves six basic elements (Biklen, 1990; Crossley, 1988) and includes physical support of a person's hand while he or she types out messages, initial training and introduction, maintaining focus, avoid testing for competence, generalizing, and fading. The basic premise behind facilitated communication is that people with autism have been struggling for years to communicate with others, but could not do so because of their disability. That is, they have acquired the skills essential for communication, as well as the desire to interact with others, but have been unable to communicate because of physical limitations.

How does facilitated communication as an intervention fit into a developmental view of autism? One theory is that some individuals with autism have acquired the basic skills necessary to produce expressive language. In other words, much like infants and small children, children with autism learn prerequisites to language and communication through observation. The technique of facilitated communication then serves to reinforce any communicative attempt. A problem with this theory is that children without autism do not appear to learn sophisticated reading and spelling skills without specific instruction. On the other hand, facilitated communication may make more sense from a deviance perspective. An alternative view is that the language deficits observed in autism are not the result of a developmental lag but rather a deviant developmental progression. Facilitated communication assumes that the individual with autism has acquired the skills necessary for communication but because of the deviant nature of their disability are unable to express themselves.

A growing number of research studies, however, point to problems with facilitated communication (for a review see Jacobson, Eberlin, Mulick, Schwartz, Szempruch, & Wheeler, 1994). Specifically, it appears clear that the communicative output of many individuals who have been facilitated may be unduly influenced by the person guiding their hand. Although it is apparent that facilitated communication is not a panacea for all people with autism, what is not as obvious is who may benefit the most from such an approach. Further research may help answer this question as well as help clarify the nature of the deficits that lead to the communication difficulties observed in this group.

Intervention for Behavior Problems

Traditional intervention strategies for behavior problems such as the self-injurious behavior and aggression that are often exhibited by people with autism have focused on the presentation of consequences to suppress these responses (Durand & Carr, 1989). Over the last decade, however, a developmental perspective of these behaviors has evolved and an intervention strategy has emerged based on this formulation. Specifically, some workers have begun to see some of these behaviors as early forms of communication that de-

velop in part due to the communication difficulties of persons with autism (Durand, 1986). In other words, these challenging behaviors may develop as adaptations to compensate for the relative lack of verbal communication skills exhibited by people with autism. In a series of studies, this hypothesis has been tested by teaching individuals to communicate for specific stimuli assessed to be functionally related to their behavior problems (e.g., Durand & Carr, 1991, 1992). This research has not only provided support for this view of the development of severe behavior problems in persons with autism, it has also served as an effective intervention strategy (Durand, 1990), further reinforcing the value of viewing disorders and accompanying behaviors from this perspective.

Prevention

One logical suggestion from viewing autism using a developmental perspective is to intervene as early as possible to help prevent secondary problems from developing or becoming more severe over time. Lovaas and his colleagues at UCLA have recently reported on their early intervention efforts with very young children (Lovaas, 1987). One group of children was given intensive behavioral treatment for their communication and social skills problems for 40 hours or more per week. A second group of these very young (under 3½ years of age) children with autism received less intensive behavioral treatment, averaging 10 hours or less of one-on-one treatment per week. After more than 2 years of this treatment, the children were followed up to assess their progress as they entered school. It was reported that 47 percent of the group receiving the intensive treatment (40 or more hours per week) achieved normal intellectual and educational functioning, doing well in regular first grade classes. In contrast, none of the children in the less intensive treatment group achieved this level of improvement.

The 47 percent of children who improved so dramatically tended to be those children with a higher mental age at the start of treatment. A more recent follow-up of these children who were then 11 years old indicated that these improvements were long-lasting (McEachin, Smith, & Lovaas, 1993). This series of studies has created considerable interest as well as controversy in the field, with some critics questioning the study on practical (e.g., too expensive and time-consuming to provide one-on-one therapy for 40 hours per week) as well as experimental (e.g., no proper control group) grounds (e.g., Foxx, 1993; Mundy, 1993; Schopler, Short, & Mesibov, 1989). Despite the controversy, however, the results from this study and others suggest a more optimistic attitude for early intervention with this disorder (Birnbrauer & Leach, 1993; Harris, Handleman, Gordon, Kristoff, & Fuentes, 1991).

SUMMARY AND CONCLUSIONS

Research on the nature and treatment of autism and other pervasive developmental disorders has benefited from developmental theory. Specifically, work in the areas of language, behavior problems, and early intervention have often relied on a developmental perspective and the outcomes have been useful for many individuals who experience these disorders. Future efforts in these areas will require an integration of both the biological aspects of these disorders as well as the psychological (e.g., cognitive, social, behavioral) factors. A better understanding of how these two factors interact over time to create the deficits seen in pervasive developmental disorders should in turn result in improved intervention efforts.

REFERENCES

Ainsworth, M. D. S., Blehar, M. C., Waters, E., & Wall, S. (1978). *Patterns of attachment.* Hillsdale, NJ: Erlbaum.

American Psychiatric Association (1994). *Diagnostic and statistical manual of mental disorders* (4th ed.). Washington, DC: Author.

Baron-Cohen, S. (1995). *Mindblindness: An essay on autism and theory of mind.* Cambridge, MA: MIT Press.

Bettelheim, B. (1967). *The empty fortress.* New York: Free Press.

Biklen, D. (1990). Communication unbound: Autism and praxis. *Harvard Educational Review, 60,* 291–314.

Birnbrauer, J. S., & Leach, D. J. (1993). The Murdoch early intervention program after two years. *Behaviour Change, 10,* 63–74.

Bloom, L., & Lahey, M. (1978). *Language development and language disorders.* New York: Wiley.

Carr, E. G. (1985). Behavioral approaches to language and communication. In E. Schopler & G. Mesibov (Eds.), *Communication problems in autism* (pp. 37–57). New York: Plenum Press.

Charlop, M. H. (1983). The effects of echolalia on acquisition and generalization of receptive labeling in autistic children. *Journal of Applied Behavior Analysis, 16,* 111–126.

Charlop, M. H., & Haymes, L. K. (1994). Speech and language acquisition and intervention: Behavioral approaches. In J. L. Matson (Ed.), *Autism in children and adults: Etiology, assessment, and intervention* (pp. 213–240). Pacific Grove, CA: Brooks/Cole.

Charlop, M. H., & Milstein, J. P. (1989). Teaching autistic children conversational speech using video modeling. *Journal of Applied Behavior Analysis, 22,* 275–285.

Chung, S. Y., Luk, S. L., & Lee, P. W. H. (1990). A follow-up study of infantile autism in Hong Kong. *Journal of Autism and Developmental Disorders, 20,* 221–232.

Coleman, M. (1990). Is classical Rett syndrome ever present in males? *Brain and Development, 12,* 31–32.

Courchesne, E. (1991). Neuroanatomic imaging in autism. *Pediatrics, 87,* 781–790.

Courchesne, E., Hesselink, J. R., Jernigan, T. L., & Yeung-Courchesne, R. (1987). Abnormal neuroanatomy in a nonretarded person with autism: Unusual findings with magnetic resonance imaging. *Archives of Neurology, 44,* 335–341.

Crossley, R. (1988, October). *Unexpected communication attainments by persons diagnosed as autistic and intellectually impaired.* Paper presented at the International Society for Augmentative and Alternative Communication, Los Angeles, CA.

Dawson, G. (1989). (Ed.). *Autism: Nature, diagnosis, and treatment.* New York: Guilford Press.

Dawson, G., & Adams, A. (1984). Imitation and social responsiveness in autistic children. *Journal of Abnormal Child Psychology, 12,* 209–226.

Dawson, G., & Lewy, A. (1989). Arousal, attention, and the socioemotional impairments of individuals with autism. In G. Dawson (Ed.), *Autism: Nature, diagnosis, and treatment* (pp. 49–74). New York: Guilford Press.

Dawson, G., & McKissick, F. C. (1984). Self-recognition in autistic children. *Journal of Autism and Developmental Disorders, 14,* 383–394.

DeLong, G. R., & Dwyer, J. T. (1988). Correlation of family history with specific autistic subgroups: Asperger's syndrome and bipolar affective disease. *Journal of Autism and Developmental Disorders, 18,* 593–600.

Durand, V. M. (1986). Self-injurious behavior as intentional communication. In K. D. Gadow (Ed.), *Advances in learning and behavioral disabilities* (Vol. 5, pp. 141–155). Greenwich, CN: JAI Press.

Durand, V. M. (1990). *Severe behavior problems: A functional communication training approach.* New York: Guilford Press.

Durand, V. M., & Carr, E. G. (1988). Autism. In V. B. Van Hasselt, P. S. Strain, and M. Hersen (Eds.), *Handbook of developmental and physical disabilities* (pp. 195–214). New York: Pergamon Press.

Durand, V. M., & Carr, E. G. (1989). Operant learning methods with chronic schizophrenia and autism: Aberrant behavior. In J. L. Matson (Ed.), *Chronic schizophrenia and adult autism* (pp. 231–273). New York: Springer.

Durand, V. M., & Carr, E. G. (1991). Functional communication training to reduce challenging behavior: Maintenance and application in new settings. *Journal of Applied Behavior Analysis, 24,* 251–264.

Durand, V. M., & Carr, E. G. (1992). An analysis of maintenance following functional communication training. *Journal of Applied Behavior Analysis, 25,* 777–794.

Falconer, D. S. (1965). The inheritance of liability to certain diseases, estimated from the incidence among relatives. *Annals of Human Genetics, 29,* 51–76.

Fein, D., Pennington, B., Markowitz, P., Braverman, M., & Waterhouse, L. (1986). Toward a neuro-psychological model of infantile autism: Are the social deficits primary? *Journal of the American Academy of Child Psychiatry, 25,* 198–212.

Ferster, C. B. (1961). Positive reinforcement and behavioral deficits of autistic children. *Child Development, 32,* 437–456.

Ferster, C. B., & DeMyer, M. K. (1961). The development of performances in autistic children in an automatically controlled environment. *Journal of Chronic Diseases, 13,* 312–345.

Freeman, B. J., Ritvo, E., & Miller, R. (1975). An operant procedure to teach an echolalic autistic child to answer questions appropriately. *Journal of Autism and Childhood Schizophrenia, 5,* 169–176.

Folstein, S., & Rutter, M. (1977). Genetic influences and infantile autism. *Nature, 265,* 726–728.

Foxx, R. M. (1993). Rapid effects awaiting independent replication. *American Journal on Mental Retardation, 97,* 375–376.

Gillberg, C. (1984). Infantile autism and other childhood psychoses in a Swedish urban region: Epidemiological aspects. *Journal of Child Psychology and Psychiatry, 25,* 35–43.

Gillberg, C. (1994). Debate and argument: Having Rett Syndrome in the ICD-10 PDD category does not make sense. *Journal of Child Psychology and Psychiatry and Allied Disciplines, 35,* 377–379.

Goldfarb, W. (1963). Self-awareness in schizophrenic children. *Archives of General Psychiatry, 8,* 63–76.

Goodman, R. (1989). Infantile autism: A syndrome of multiple primary deficits? *Journal of Autism and Developmental Disorders, 19,* 409–424.

Hagberg, B., Aicardi, J., Dias, K., & Ramos, O. (1983). A progressive syndrome of autism, dementia, ataxia, and loss of purposeful hand use in girls: Rett syndrome: Report of 35 cases. *Annals of Neurology, 14,* 471–479.

Harris, S. L., Handleman, J. S., Gordon, R., Kristoff, B., & Fuentes, F. (1991). Changes in cognitive and language functioning of preschool children with autism. *Journal of Autism and Developmental Disorders, 21,* 281–290.

Hobson, R. P. (1989). Beyond cognition: A theory of autism. In G. Dawson (Ed.), *Autism: Nature, diagnosis, and treatment* (pp. 22–48). New York: Guilford Press.

Hunt, A., & Dennis, J. (1987). Psychiatric disorder among children with tuberous sclerosis. *Developmental Medicine and Child Neurology, 29,* 190–198.

Jacobson, J. W., Eberlin, M., Mulick, J. A., Schwartz, A. A., Szempruch, J., & Wheeler, D. L. (1994). Autism, facilitated communication, and future directions. In J. L. Matson (Ed.), *Autism in children and adults: Etiology, assessment, and intervention* (pp. 59–83). Pacific Grove, CA: Brooks/Cole.

Kanner, L. (1943). Autistic disturbances of affective contact. *Nervous Child, 2,* 217–250.

Kanner, L., & Eisenberg, L. (1955). Notes on the follow-up studies of autistic children. In P. Hoch & J. Zubin (Eds.), *Psychopathology of childhood* (pp. 227–239). New York: Grune & Stratton.

Klin, A., Volkmar, F. R., & Sparrow, S. S. (1992). Autistic social dysfunction: Some limitations of the Theory of Mind hypothesis. *Journal of Child Psychology and Psychiatry, 33,* 861–876.

Kurita, H., Kita, M., & Miyake, Y. (1992). A comparative study of development and symptoms among disintegrative psychosis and infantile autism with and without speech loss. *Journal of Autism and Developmental Disorders, 22,* 175–188.

Lebedinskaya, K. S., & Nikolskaya, O. S. (1993). Brief report: Analysis of autism and its treatment in modern Russian defectology. *Journal of Autism and Developmental Disorders, 23,* 675–697.

Leslie, A. M. (1987). Pretense and representation: The origins of "Theory of Mind." *Psychological Review, 94,* 412–426.

Locke, B. J., Banken, J. A., & Mahone, C. H. (1994). The graying of autism: Etiology and prevalence at fifty. In J. L. Matson (Ed.), *Autism in children and adults: Etiology, assessment and intervention* (pp. 37–57). Pacific Grove, CA: Brooks/Cole.

Lotter, V. (1966). Epidemiology of autistic conditions in young children: I. Prevalence. *Social Psychiatry, 1,* 124–137.

Lovaas, O. I. (1977). *The autistic child: Language development through behavior modification.* New York: Irvington.

Lovaas, O. I. (1987). Behavioral treatment and normal educational and intellectual functioning in young autistic children. *Journal of Consulting and Clinical Psychology, 55,* 3–9.

Lovaas, O. I., Berberich, J. P., Perloff, B. F., & Schaeffer, B. (1966). Acquisition of imitative speech by schizophrenic children. *Science, 151,* 705–707.

Mahler, M. S. (1952). On child psychosis and schizophrenia: Autistic and symbiotic infantile psychosis. *Psychoanalytic Study of the Child, 7,* 286–305.

McEachin, J. J., Smith, T., & Lovaas, O. I. (1993). Long-term outcome for children with autism who received early intensive behavioral treatment. *American Journal on Mental Retardation, 97,* 359–372.

McLean, J., & Snyder-McLean, L. (1978). *A transactional approach to early language training.* Columbus, OH: Charles E. Merrill.

Mundy, P. (1993). Normal versus high-functioning status in children with autism. *American Journal on Mental Retardation, 97,* 381–384.

Mundy, P., & Sigman, M. (1989). Specifying the nature of the social impairment in autism. In G. Dawson (Ed.), *Autism: Nature, diagnosis, and treatment* (pp. 3–21). New York: Guilford Press.

Philippart, M. (1990). The Rett syndrome in males. *Brain and Development, 12,* 33–36.

Prizant, B. M., & Wetherby, A. M. (1989). Enhancing language and communication in autism: From theory to practice. In G. Dawson (Ed.), *Autism: Nature, diagnosis, and treatment* (pp. 282–309). New York: Guilford Press.

Ricks, D. M., & Wing, L. (1975). Language, communication and the use of symbols in normal and autistic children. *Journal of Autism and Childhood Schizophrenia, 5,* 191–221.

Rimland, B. (1964). *Infantile autism: The syndrome and its implications for a neural theory of behavior.* New York: Appleton-Century-Crofts.

Rimland, B. (1994). The modern history of autism: A personal perspective. In J. L. Matson (Ed.), *Autism in children and adults: Etiology, assessment and intervention* (pp. 1–11). Pacific Grove, CA: Brooks/Cole.

Ritvo, E. R., Freeman, B. J., Mason-Brothers, A., Mo, A., & Ritvo, A. M. (1985). Concordance for the syndrome of autism in 40 pairs of afflicted twins. *American Journal of Psychiatry, 142,* 74–77.

Ritvo, E. R., Freeman, B. J., Scheibel, A. B., Duong, T., Robinson, H., Guthrie, D., & Ritvo, A. (1986). Lower Purkinje cell counts in the cerebella of four autistic subjects: Initial findings of the UCLA-NSAC autopsy research report. *American Journal of Psychiatry, 143,* 826–866.

Rogers, S. J., Ozonoff, S., & Maslin-Cole, C. (1993). Developmental aspects of attachment behavior in young children with pervasive developmental disorders. *Journal of the American Academy of Child and Adolescent Psychiatry, 32,* 1274–1282.

Romanczyk, R. G., Lockshin, S. B., & Navalta, C. (1994). Autism: Differential diagnosis. In J. L. Matson (Ed.), *Autism in children and adults: Etiology, assessment and intervention* (pp. 99–125). Pacific Grove, CA: Brooks/Cole.

Rutter, M. (1994). Debate and argument: There are connections between brain and mind and it is important that Rett syndrome be classified somewhere. *Journal of Child Psychology and Psychiatry and Allied Disciplines, 35,* 379–381.

Rutter, M., & Schopler, E. (1992). Classification of pervasive developmental disorders: Some concepts and practical considerations. *Journal of Autism and Developmental Disorders, 22,* 459–482.

Schopler, E., Short, A., & Mesibov, G. (1989). Relation of behavioral treatment to "normal functioning": Comment on Lovaas. *Journal of Consulting and Clinical Psychology, 57,* 162–164.

Sigman, M., & Ungerer, J. A. (1984). Attachment behaviors in autistic children. *Journal of Autism and Developmental Disorders, 14,* 231–244.

Smalley, S. L. (1991). Genetic influences in autism. *Psychiatric Clinics of North America, 14,* 125–139.

Spiker, D., & Ricks, D. M. (1984). Visual self-recognition in autistic children: Developmental relationships. *Child Development, 55,* 214–225.

Steffenburg, S., Gillberg, C., Hellgren, L., Andersson, L., Gillberg, I. C., Jakobsson, G., & Bohman, M. (1989). A twin study of autism in Denmark, Finland, Iceland, Norway, and Sweden. *Journal of Child Psychology and Psychiatry, 30,* 405–416.

Sugiyama, T., & Abe, T. (1989). The prevalence of autism in Nagoya, Japan: A total population study. *Journal of Autism and Developmental Disorders, 19,* 87–96.

Tinbergen, E. A., & Tinbergen, N. (1972). *Early childhood autism: An ethological approach.* Berlin: Paul Parey.

Tinbergen, N., & Tinbergen, E. A. (1983). *Autistic children: New hope for a cure.* Winchester, MA: Allen & Unwin.

Tsai, L. Y., & Ghaziuddin, M. (1992). Biomedical research in autism. In D. E. Berkell (Ed.), *Autism: Identification, education, and treatment* (pp. 53–74). Hillsdale, NJ: Erlbaum.

Van Acker, R. (1991). Rett syndrome: A review of current knowledge. *Journal of Autism and Developmental Disorders, 21,* 381–406.

Volkmar, F. R., Burack, J. A., & Cohen, D. J. (1990). Deviance and developmental approaches in the study of autism. In R. M. Hodapp, J. A. Burack, & E. Zigler (Eds.), *Issues in the developmental approach to mental retardation* (pp. 246–271). Cambridge, England: Cambridge University Press.

Volkmar, F. R., & Cohen, D. J. (1991). Nonautistic pervasive developmental disorders. In R. Michels (Ed.), *Psychiatry* (pp. 201–210). Philadelphia: Lippincott.

Volkmar, F. R., Szatmari, P., & Sparrow, S. S. (1993). Sex differences in pervasive developmental disorders. *Journal of Autism and Developmental Disorders, 23,* 579–591.

Waterhouse, L., Wing, L., & Fein, D. (1989). Re-evaluating the syndrome of autism in light of empirical research. In G. Dawson (Ed.), *Autism: Nature, diagnosis and treatment* (pp. 263–281). New York: Guilford Press.

Waterhouse, L., Wing, L., Spitzer, R., & Siegel, B. (1992). Pervasive developmental disorders: From DSM-III to DSM-III-R. *Journal of Autism and Developmental Disorders, 22,* 525–549.

Wing, L. (1981). Asperger's syndrome: A clinical account. *Psychological Medicine, 11,* 115.

PART 5

CHILDREN OF SPECIAL FAMILIES

In the first chapter contained in the third section an excellent summary of the familial context is provided. That chapter makes clear the ways in which this context can exert influence on children and their behavior problems, and how the family can be targeted in intervention programs. In this section of the book the familial context is explored in even greater depth and detail. It is important to explore the familial context in greater depth and detail because of the amazing diversity that exists among families, in terms of both family structure and content. Thus, the chapters contained in this chapter basically cover the following issues: (1) the particulars of a familial context and its influence on child outcome, and (2) the implications of this particular familial context in relation to treatment intervention and prevention.

In the first two chapters of this section, two of the most prevalent family forms are covered: the single-parent family and blended families, the majority of which have come about as a result of parental divorce. The chapters examine how a developmental perspective can lead to increased understanding of the impact of divorce and parental remarriage on children. Using a developmental perspective, the chapters show how child characteristics (e.g., age, gender, temperament), child-parent relationship patterns, parents'

management of their conflict, and the changes children experience in lifestyle differ across families, and thus, account for the heterogeneity that has been found in child outcomes in these research literatures. The chapters also show how a developmental perspective is useful in terms of developing prevention intervention programs to reach children earlier, rather than later, in their developmental pathway.

Another prevalent family form is one in which a child has been adopted (i.e., the adoptive family), which is the focus of the next chapter. Because of the myths and controversies that have long characterized the adoption field (i.e., that adoption is inherently pathogenic for children and their development), the chapter begins with an evaluation of the epidemiological and clinical research literature on adopted children. The remainder of the chapter is devoted to detailing the adoptive family life-cycle focusing on developmental challenges unique to members of the adoption triangle (birthparents, adoptive parents, and adoptees) and interventions designed to meet these challenges.

The fourth chapter is devoted to children from abusive families. Here a developmental integrative framework is presented in which abuse is viewed not as a unitary event but as a series of events, any one of which may "push" children off their "normal" developmental paths. In addition, maltreatment is not viewed as occurring in a vacuum but in contexts of complexity and diversity (e.g., familial, community, and societal) all of which may lead to various outcomes. There are also variations in societal responses (e.g., foster care, court room testimony) that may influence children and their development. The implications of this type of broader, developmental perspective with respect to clinical interventions for children of abuse are discussed in the final section of the chapter.

The last three chapters in this section focus on how specific types of parental problems may influence children and their development. The first one covers children of parents with alcohol problems, the next one covers children of parents with depressive disorder, and the last one covers children of parents with medical illness. Each of these chapters does an excellent job in showing how child outcome is best characterized as heterogeneous, and (once again) how we all need to move beyond simple main effects models

when we think about intervening with these children—whether it be for clinical or research purposes.

In conclusion, the chapters contained in this section make clear that the images appearing on the television screens across America, particularly those that predominated during the 1950s and early 1960s (the "leave it to Beaver" images) are not "reality" and probably never were. The chapters also make clear, however, that just because a child does *not* grow up in a family like "Beaver" (i.e., intact, two-parent families, where both parents were physically and mentally healthy, and both knew all the ins and outs of "correct parenting"), all is not lost for the child. That is, as we learn from these chapters, child outcome is best characterized as heterogeneous, showing again the complexities involved in childhood development and how conceptualizations that involve multiple packages of influences within a developmental perspective is likely to be most fruitful in terms of facilitating the study of these diverse outcomes.

CHAPTER 20

CHILDREN OF SINGLE PARENTS AND DIVORCE

John H. Grych
Frank D. Fincham

Living in a single-parent family is becoming an increasingly common experience for children in the United States. Between 1970 and 1990 the number of single-parent families with children under the age of 18 years more than doubled, reaching 9.7 million (Kirby, 1995), and it is estimated that the majority of children born in the 1990s will experience life in a single-parent family before age 16 (Furstenberg & Cherlin, 1991). Most children in single-parent families will experience economic privation given that nine out of ten such families are headed by a female, a family form that has the highest rate of poverty across all demographic groups (Olson & Banyard, 1993). Children in single-parent families therefore may be at risk for many types of problems because of poverty (see Chapter 13). However, public debate about the growth of single-parent families has not focused on alleviating poverty but instead appears to be driven by concern about high rates of divorce (estimates vary from 50 to 66 percent,

Furstenberg, 1990) and nonmarital childbearing (approximately 25 percent of children are now born to single parents). Perhaps not surprisingly, such debate has generated more heat than light.

Cultural attitudes have been slow to adapt to the growth of the single-parent family, a family form that is still stigmatized. One possible reason for this is the uniformity myth, or the belief that all single-parent families are similar and that divorce has similar (adverse) effects on all children. This is most evident in the mass media but can also be found in the professional literature. For example, research on interventions for children of divorce rarely includes divorce-specific information in describing samples (Lee, Pichard, & Blain, 1994). Because progress requires attention to the differentiating characteristics of single-parent families, analysis of the developmental and clinical issues pertinent to all forms of single-parent families is beyond the scope of this chapter. Although single-parent families are formed through means other than divorce, most of the children living in single-parent homes have experienced a divorce (Glick, 1988), and thus we limit our analysis to this type of single-parent family.

The preparation of this manuscript was supported by a Social Science Research Fellowship from the Nuffield Foundation, a grant from the National Health Service, and a grant from the Economic and Social Research Council to Frank D. Fincham.

The goal of the chapter is to examine how a developmental perspective might increase understanding of the impact of divorce on children and enhance the quality of interventions designed to benefit such children. To provide a context for our analysis, we first offer an overview of what is known about the impact of divorce on children.

THE IMPACT OF DIVORCE ON CHILDREN

Numerous studies have investigated the well-being of children following marital disruption by comparing them to children from two-parent families. Typically, children from divorced families exhibit poorer adjustment than children from two-parent families (for reviews see Amato & Keith, 1991; Emery, 1988; Grych & Fincham, 1992a; Stevenson & Black, 1995; Zaslow, 1988, 1989). Perhaps the most robust differences occur for externalizing problems, such as aggression and conduct disorder. Differences in academic achievement are also routinely found possibly reflecting differences in classroom behavior that interferes with learning; children from divorced families are rated higher by teachers on failure anxiety, unreflectiveness, irrelevant talk, and inattention (Emery, 1988). Children from divorced families also consistently differ from those in two-parent families by exhibiting more internalizing problems, lower self-concept, and poorer interpersonal relations.

The findings reported above need to be interpreted with caution in the light of a recent meta-analysis of 92 studies involving over 13,000 children. Amato and Keith (1991) show that across studies and several outcome measures, children from divorced families are about one-fifth to one-eighth of a standard deviation below children from two-parent families, depending on the analysis conducted and measure of central tendency used. Even the largest mean effect size of −.23, which was found for externalizing problems (e.g., aggression, delinquency), indicated that the average externalizing score in divorced samples was about one-quarter of a standard deviation higher than in two-parent samples. Importantly, effect sizes tended to be smaller for methodologically more rigorous studies, more recent studies, studies using random rather than convenience samples, for higher quality or more reliable dependent measures, and when control variables (e.g., parent education, family income) were used to equate divorce and two-parent samples. Finally, this meta-analysis considered only published studies, which are more likely to contain larger effect sizes than unpublished studies.

The differences found between children who have and have not experienced marital disruption are reliable but quite small. This raises the question of whether they are clinically significant. Initial evidence in this regard is that children from divorced families evidence a higher rate of referral for mental health services than those from two-parent families (e.g., Guidubaldi et al., 1984, Kalter & Rembar, 1981; Zill, 1978). For example, in a large nationally representative sample, 13 percent of children whose parents had divorced had seen a mental health professional compared to 5.5 percent of children from intact families (Zill, 1978). In a more recent study, again using a nationally representative sample, children from divorced homes were two to three times more likely to have seen a therapist than were children living with both biological parents (Zill, Morrison & Coiro, 1993). However, referral for mental health services is an imperfect indicator of children's adjustment because it reflects many factors in addition to the child's behavior, including such things as parental characteristics (e.g., overconcern, mental health), socioeconomic status, and characteristics of the environment (e.g., availability of mental health services, community attitudes towards mental health/divorce).

Further evidence for the clinical significance of adjustment problems in some children from divorced families is provided by a small number of studies examining the severity of behavior problems reported on standardized questionnaires. For example, Hetherington and colleagues (Hetherington, Clingempeel, Anderson et al., 1992) found in a sample of adolescents who had experienced parental divorce 4 to 6 years earlier that approximately 20 percent of boys and 25 to 30 percent of girls exceeded the cutoff for clinical levels of behavior problems on the Child Behavior Checklist (Achenbach & Edelbrock, 1983), compared to approximately 10 percent of children from intact families. These data suggest that children from divorced families are at increased risk to develop clinical syndromes, but also indicate that the majority of these children do not evidence significant psychopathology.

The picture to emerge from research contrasts with that found in clinical writings. Since Bowlby (1944) noted a link between "broken homes" and delinquency, clinicians have associated divorce with severe and long-term effects on children (e.g., Gardner, 1976; Wallerstein & Kelley, 1980). Indeed, most clinicians who work with children and families can readily provide examples to illustrate the serious impact of divorce on a child. Poignant descriptions by children of the impact of their parent's divorce are consistent with clinical observations and can be found in a number of qualitative studies (e.g., Mitchell, 1985; Wallerstein & Blakeslee, 1989; Walzak & Burns, 1984).

What can one conclude about the contrasting pictures that emerge from research findings and from clinical writings? One possibility is to downplay clinical observation in favor of quantitative research because its results are more generalizable. From this perspective, parental divorce can be viewed as a stressor that has a relatively small effect on most children. However, this view does not preclude the existence of serious effects in a small minority of cases.

A second possibility is that children are seriously affected by parental divorce but that quantitative research has thus far failed to document such effects. This viewpoint receives some support from the fact that many studies on the impact of divorce in childhood have been quite weak methodologically (e.g., use of unreliable and crude measures, small unrepresentative samples, lack of appropriate comparison groups, use of a single data source for all constructs investigated; see Emery, 1988; Kurdek, 1987). Indeed, the impression that "some authors include multiple dependent variables in the hope that at least some will show significant differences" (Amato & Keith, 1991, p. 40) suggests that the documentation of any overall differences between children from divorced and two-parent families is surprising. The use of measures to examine theoretically expected differences might yield stronger findings.

A third possibility is to ask whether simple comparisons of children from divorced and two-parent families are optimal for understanding the impact of divorce on children. Divorce is part of a process of marital dissolution and family reorganization that begins prior to separation and may continue indefinitely after the final divorce decree. From this perspective it is important to conceptualize the mechanisms by which children from divorced families develop emotional and behavioral problems, a task that recently has received increased attention.

In turning to this task, it is important to address how children's age and cognitive development moderates their adaptation to divorce. Unfortunately, this remains a relatively unexplored issue in the research literature despite its theoretical importance. Theorists from diverse perspectives have proposed that younger children are at greater risk to develop adjustment problems than are older children, but with few exceptions (e.g., Kalter, 1983) these hypotheses focus on children's age only at the time of separation. Although children's reaction to parental separation clearly is influenced by their level of cognitive, emotional, and social development, a narrow focus on the event of separation fails to consider how variables that may mediate the impact of parental divorce on children's adjustment can affect their developmental pathway both prior to and following the divorce.

In the remainder of the chapter we examine developmental aspects of children's adaptation to divorce and subsequent life in a single-parent family through the lens of developmental psychopathology. We first summarize re-

search examining age-related differences in postdivorce adjustment and then address some of the developmental and clinical issues arising from parental separation and divorce.

AGE AS A MODERATOR OF CHILDREN'S ADJUSTMENT TO DIVORCE

For a variety of reasons, young children have been viewed as more vulnerable to the effects of divorce than older children or adolescents. Preadolescent children's dependency on their parents, limited coping repertoire, and lack of a supportive peer network are often offered as potential causes of this increased vulnerability. Psychoanalytic theorists view preschool children as particularly vulnerable to parental separation because it disrupts the process of identification proposed to be central for personality and gender identity development. Object relations theorists (e.g., Fraiberg, 1959) suggest that toddlers are most at risk because the loss of a parent disrupts the separation and individuation process. It also has been argued that a divorce early in life is problematic because it generally results in children spending a greater proportion of their youth in a single-parent home where parenting may be less optimal than in a two-parent family.

Given the interest in developmental aspects of divorce, it is surprising that there have been few studies directly comparing the adjustment of children experiencing divorce at different ages. Existing studies have produced inconsistent findings, with some documenting greater maladjustment in younger children (e.g., Allison & Furstenberg, 1989; Kalter & Rembar, 1981) and others failing to find a significant age effect (e.g., Guidubaldi, Perry, & Nastasi, 1987; Stolberg, Camplair, Currier, & Wells, 1987). Moreover, very few studies have examined the adjustment of infants and toddlers to divorce (for exceptions see Bretherton et al., 1995; Roseby et al., 1995; Solomon et al., 1995), and thus the implications of divorce for very young children are unknown.

Amato and Keith's (1991) meta-analysis provides a quantitative estimate of age differences in children's adjustment after divorce. They categorized children into four age groups according to their age at the time they participated in a given study and determined the effect size between divorced and intact families for each age group on a set of outcome measures. Children's age was related to effect size for four of the adjustment measures (psychological adjustment, social adjustment, mother–child relations, and father–child relations) but was not related to measures of conduct problems and academic difficulties (see Table 20.1). In general, children from divorced families who were in primary and secondary school (high school) showed larger effect sizes than children of preschool or college age, but the specific

TABLE 20.1 Association between Parental Separation and Child Outcome for Different Age Groups Reported in Amato and Keith (1991) and Allison and Furstenberg (1989)

	AMATO AND KEITH (1991, EFFECT SIZES)						
Age	Academic Achievment	Conduct	Psychological Adjustment	Self-Concept	Social Adjustment	Mother	Father
Preschool	−.17	−.25*	.06	—	.10	−.24	−.41
Primary	−.14*	−.19*	−.08*	−.02	−.20*	−.29*	−.20*
Secondary	−.17*	−.27*	−.16*	−.12*	−.05	−.14*	−.31*
College	−.24	−.07	−.02	−.09	−.04	−.05	−.18*

	ALLISON AND FURSTENBERG (1981 DATA, REGRESSION COEFFICIENTS)							
Age	Academic Difficulty		Problem Behavior		Delinquency		Distress	
	Parent	Teacher	Parent	Teacher	Parent	Child	Parent	Child
0–5	−.26*	.00	−.25*	−.31*	−.33*	.01	−.23*	−.20*
6–10	−.10	.16	−.26*	.23	−.35*	−.02	−.14	−.27*
11–16	−.07	−.13	−.11	.24	−.23*	−.26*	.05	−.13

Note: Negative values represent poorer adjustment in divorced compared to intact samples.

*$p < .05$.

Data in the top half of the table are from P. R. Amato and B. Keith. (1991). Parental Divorce and the Well-Being of Children. *Psychological Bulletin, 110,* 34. Copyright 1991 by the American Psychological Association. Data in the bottom half of the table are from P. D. Allison and F. F. Furstenberg. (1989). How Marital Dissolution Affects Children: Variations by Age and Sex, *Developmental Psychology, 25,* 545. Copyright 1989 by the American Psychological Association. Reprinted with permission.

pattern of effects differed according to the type of outcome measure assessed. Moreover, effect sizes typically were small, rarely exceeding one-fourth of a standard deviation and more often in the range of one-fifth to one-eighth of a standard deviation, suggesting that even when one age group exhibited poorer adjustment the differences between children from divorced and intact families were not great.

Although this meta-analysis has the advantage of providing a more concise estimate of age effects than a qualitative literature review, it is quite limited in its utility for understanding developmental changes in children's adaptation to divorce. Because children were categorized according to their age at the time of the study, not the age at which their parents separated, it is not clear whether the reported differences are attributable to their age at divorce, the length of time living in a divorced family, or some other factor that may have mediated their current adjustment. In addition, including studies that assess children of different ages at a single point in time confounds children's age at the time of divorce with the

amount of time elapsed since the divorce. Both represent plausible explanations for differences in the adjustment of children of different ages but cannot be distinguished in cross-sectional designs. In contrast, longitudinal studies, especially sequential designs involving children of different ages, provide a way of distinguishing the effects of children's age at divorce from the effects of spending time in a divorced family. Finally, the small number of studies included in the meta-analysis involving preschool children make the estimate of effect sizes for this group, hypothesized to be the most vulnerable, of questionable reliability and generalizability.

Allison and Furstenberg (1989) addressed the moderating effects of children's age at time of separation in a study that avoids the problems identified in the meta-analysis. Using data from a large, nationally representative sample of children (the National Survey of Children), this study assessed children's adjustment at two points in time. Children in the sample (2279 at Time 1; 1197 at Time 2, 5 years later) were classified into three groups according to their age at the time of divorce (0–5, 6–10, and 11–16 years of age) and parent, teacher, and child reports of conduct problems, psychological distress, and academic problems were obtained. Table 20.1 presents selected results from the 5-year follow-up, in which all three age groups were represented (there were no children older than 11 years at the initial assessment).

It is informative to compare the data from this study, which were not included in the meta-analysis, to the results reported by Amato and Keith (1991). Consistent with the meta-analytic results, the regression coefficients reported by Allison and Furstenberg (1989), which indicate the strength of the association between family status (divorced vs. intact) and adjustment problems, show that children from divorced families exhibited poorer adjustment on most measures at both assessment periods (whether children were from single-parent vs. remarried families did not result in significantly different findings).

The pattern of results described by Allison and Furstenburg (1989) also differed somewhat from the data reported by Amato and Keith (1989). Whereas Amato and Keith (1991) concluded that children in elementary and high school were most poorly adjusted, Allison and Furstenberg (1989) found that children who were 5 years of age or younger when their parents divorced generally exhibited the highest level of adjustment problems (larger coefficients were found for 0 to 5-year-old children than 6 to 10 year olds at both assessments). This discrepancy may be misleading for at least three reasons. First, because Amato and Keith (1991) included few studies of preschoolers in their meta-analysis, some effect sizes for this age group were not statistically significant despite being similar in magnitude to the effect sizes of older groups. Second, given the time lag that often occurs between parental separation and participation in research it is possible that many of the children in Amato and Keith's (1991) primary and secondary school groups experienced parental divorce during the preschool years, but because this information was not reported such a possibility can only be speculative. Third, even though the magnitude of the regression coefficients generally decreased across the three age groups in Allison and Furstenburg's (1989) study, this decrease was statistically significant for only one of the variables assessed, teacher reports of problem behaviors. Any conclusions from this study regarding age effects in adjustment thus should be considered tentative.

The pattern of results on particular measures of adjustment also revealed some differences across the two studies. The meta-analysis found consistently poorer academic performance in children from divorced families across ages, whereas teacher reports from the National Survey of Children did not demonstrate higher levels of academic problems for divorced children at any age, and parents viewed children from divorced families as having academic difficulties only at ages 0 to 5. A similar discrepancy occurred for conduct problems. The meta-analysis, which collapsed across different raters of adjustment, indicated that conduct problems were more common in divorced children and quite stable across age groups.

In contrast, Allison and Furstenberg (1989) found that the nature of age differences in conduct problems depended on who rated the child's behavior. Teacher reports showed a large drop in the level of problem behaviors observed (which included behaviors requiring disciplinary action as well as fighting, lying, and cheating) from the 0 to 5-year-old group to the 6 to 10 and 11 to 16 year olds. This decrease was statistically significant at the second assessment. Parent reports of delinquent and problem behavior exhibited effects of similar magnitude for 0 to 5 and 6 to 10 year olds and a small (nonsignificant) drop in the 11 to 16 year olds. Children's self-report of delinquent behavior deviated from this pattern; the only significant difference between children from intact and divorced families occurred when children were 11 to 16 years of age. Discrepancies between child and adult reports also occurred on ratings of psychological distress: Parent and teacher reports showed that the largest differences between divorced and intact families were found when children were 0 to 5 years old at the time of the divorce, whereas children's reports indicated that the greatest distress occurred when children were 6 to 10 years of age. Interpretation of these child reports are suspect, however, due to the low reliability of the self-report measures employed in the study.

Finally, it is important to note that Allison and Furstenberg (1989) were able to distinguish between effects due to children's age at separation and effects due to the length of time children lived in divorced, single-parent families. They did this by comparing the adjustment of children from divorced families at the time of initial assessment to their functioning at the time of the 5-year follow-up. If the effects attributed to children's age at the time of separation actually are due to the amount of time spent in a divorced family, then children would exhibit poorer adjustment at the second assessment. However, no evidence for this trend was found. In fact, whereas parent reports of children's functioning were fairly stable across the two assessment periods, both teacher and children's self-reports revealed lower levels of adjustment problems at the 5-year follow-up. Thus, in this sample the length of time children spent in a divorced family did not account for the age differences in adaptation.

Taken together, these studies support the hypothesis that separation and divorce have more adverse effects for preadolescent children; however, more specific conclusions regarding age and vulnerability have not been documented consistently. Moreover, the meaning and origin of these differences is not clear. In the next section, we present a framework for interpreting these age differences.

DIVORCE FROM THE PERSPECTIVE OF DEVELOPMENTAL PSYCHOPATHOLOGY

Developmental psychopathologists attempt to explain the ontogenesis of emotional and behavioral problems by describing the interplay of intrapersonal, interpersonal, and ecological influences on adjustment over time. The emphasis on describing developmental pathways has important implications for understanding the etiology, course, and treatment of psychological disturbances. Understanding factors that cause deviations from healthy functioning facilitates early identification of adjustment problems and the development of preventive interventions to avoid pathological outcomes.

Three features of the developmental psychopathology perspective are particularly pertinent for understanding developmental aspects of divorce: the application of knowledge of normal development to understanding atypical or abnormal development; the principle of hierarchic motility; and the role of risk, protective, and vulnerability factors in determining developmental outcomes (Cicchetti & Cohen, 1995). In the remainder of the chapter we describe the relevance of each principle to understanding children's adaptation to divorce and to intervention with children from divorced families.

Integrating Normal and Atypical Development

From the perspective of developmental psychopathology, behavioral and emotional disturbances are viewed as deviations from normal development, and therefore knowledge of normal developmental trajectories can provide insight into how and why deviations in development occur. This implies that understanding children's adaptation to divorce and life in a single-parent family will be facilitated by examining how normative changes in cognitive, emotional, and social development may mediate the impact of divorce-related events and how these experiences may affect children's ability to meet age-appropriate developmental challenges. The best example of this type of approach is the work on devel-

opmental changes in children's perceptions, beliefs, and understanding of divorce.

Cognitive Development and Children's Response to Divorce

The role of cognition in mediating children's response to divorce has been emphasized by clinicians and clinical researchers (e.g., Kurdek, 1986; Wallerstein, 1983). Children's understanding of the divorce and its implications for their well-being, which Wallerstein (Wallerstein & Blakesee, 1989) considers to be the first step in coping with divorce, is dependent upon their cognitive–developmental level. Although few studies have directly tested links among children's cognitive–developmental level, perceptions of their parents' divorce, and their adjustment (e.g., Kurdek & Berg, 1987), it is assumed that younger children's limited mental capacities makes divorce more confusing and difficult for them and promotes maladaptive thinking, such as self-blame, fear of abandonment, and unrealistic wishes for reunification. This is often offered as a primary reason that younger children are more vulnerable to the effects of divorce.

Kurdek (1986) proposed a scheme based on normative changes in cognitive development for understanding children's interpretation of separation and divorce. He argued that children's capacities for perspective-taking, attributional thinking, and abstract thought have particularly important implications for their adjustment to divorce. His scheme, presented in Table 20.2, indicates that 3- to 5-year-old children focus on the physical features of the situation, such as a parent moving out, and are likely to perceive the parent as leaving them, rather than the marriage. They also are likely to be confused by the seeming contradiction of a parent leaving while assuring the child that they love them and will take care of them, and to have difficulty resolving their parents' negative and positive feelings toward the other. As children get older, the tendency to interpret the separation egocentrically and concretely gives way to increasing awareness of incompatibility between the parents as the cause for the divorce, though younger children still may wonder if they added to their parents' unhappiness. Confusion and fear may be replaced by grief and anger as children try to understand the causes of the divorce. According to Kurdek (1986), the wish for reconciliation occurs at all ages but decreases as children come to understand the permanence of the situation. Children's cognitive capacities thus shape the meaning of the divorce for children and influence their affective and behavioral responses.

Although Kurdek (1986) focused on the implications of children's cognitive level for their reaction at the time of sep-

TABLE 20.2 Kurdek's Cognitive–Developmental Scheme for Children's Understanding of Divorce

AGE	CHILDREN'S PERCEPTIONS OF DIVORCE
3–5 Years	
	Define divorce in terms of parent physically moving away rather than parental incompatibility
	Perceive parent as leaving the child and family rather than the marriage
	Likely to blame self for the divorce
	Confused by parents' positive and negative feelings about each other
	Confused by nonresidential parents' assurances of love and concrete plans to move out of the house
	View parents' separation as temporary
6–8 Years	
	Divorce interpreted personally, egocentrically, and in terms of physical separation
	Increasing awareness of parent incompatibility and conflict as reasons for divorce
	Self-blame unlikely, but may worry that behavior has added to interparent distress
	Likely to blame one or the other parent for the divorce
	Wish for reconciliation but do not believe that it will occur
	View reduced conflict as beneficial outcome of divorce
9–12 Years	
	Divorce understood in psychological terms, such as parental incompatibility
	Can view divorce from each parent's perspective
	Do not believe reconciliation will occur
	Ambivalent toward both parents
	Feel angry because of loyalty conflicts
	Perceive home environment negatively
	Recognizes that one can have conflicting feelings for the same person
13–19 Years	
	Understanding of divorce increasingly abstract and differentiated
	Recognize positive and negative aspects of the divorce
	Anger due to quality of parent–child relationships, especially low levels of contact with father

L. A. Kurdek. (1986). Children's Reasoning about Parental Divorce. In R. D. Ashmore & D. M. Brodzinsky (Eds.), *Thinking about the family: Views of Parents and Children* (pp. 233–276), Hillsdale, NJ: Erlbaum. Copyright © 1986 by Lawrence Erlbaum Associates. Adapted with permission.

aration, his analysis also is relevant for understanding their adjustment in the months and years after the divorce. Children's level of cognitive sophistication will continue to influence their understanding of interparental conflict and interactions with each parent. For example, following Kurdek's scheme, 3- to 5-year-old children may tend to personalize inconsistent visitation by their nonresidential parent, perhaps viewing it as a sign that the child has done something to anger the parent or is not important to the parent. Older children may view the same event as a reflection of continuing discord between their parents or of their fathers' personality.

Clinicians have identified self-blame as a relatively common problematic belief that may lead to anxiety, sadness, and guilt (e.g., Gardner, 1976; Wallerstein & Kelly, 1980). Children below the age of 5 have been thought to be particularly likely to make this kind of attribution because of the egocentrism common at that age and a tendency to overestimate their control in situations where they have little. However, research examining this question has produced inconsistent results. Whereas some studies have found higher levels of self-blame in younger compared to older children (Neal, 1983; Wallerstein & Kelly, 1980), others indicate that self-blame is uncommon in children of any age (Kurdek,

Blisk, & Siesky, 1981; Warshak & Santrock, 1983). One reason for the discrepancy is that these studies differed in the amount of time elapsed since the divorce: those finding little evidence of self-blame occurred an average of 2 to 4½ years after the divorce, and those reporting self-blame assessed children within 18 months of the separation. It is possible that self-blame occurs shortly after the divorce as children initially seek to understand its occurrence, but dissipates with time as children gain greater understanding and recognize more properly their role in the parental separation.

This conclusion is supported by a longitudinal study assessing reports of self-blame in 6- to 12-year-old children at two points in time: when their parents had been physically separated no more than 8 months, and 1 year later (Healy, Stewart, & Copeland, 1993). At Time 1 approximately 33 percent of the children indicated that they felt that the separation could be partly their fault, but this figure dropped to 19 percent by Time 2. However, age was not correlated with self-blame. Rather, perceptions of self-blame were related to the extent to which children became involved in parental conflict or felt torn between their loyalties to each parent. The idea that perceptions of self-blame are linked to the nature of interactions in the family, and specifically the extent to which children become drawn into the parents' conflict, is supported by a study indicating that 10- to 12-year-old children living in two-parent homes were more likely to report self-blame for parental conflicts when the content involved a child-related issue (Grych & Fincham, 1993). Self-blame was correlated with greater desire to intervene in the conflict, suggesting one path by which interparental conflict can be transformed into a triadic conflict. Further, Healy and his colleagues (1993) found that self-blame was associated with lower perceived competence and greater internalizing and externalizing problems. This study suggests that self-blame may occur at the time of divorce but is quite rare 18 months later, and that 6 year olds are no more likely to make such attributions than are 12 year olds. However, self-blame is linked to adjustment problems, which may explain why clinicians have viewed it as a common problem; such maladaptive cognitions may be much more frequent in children whose problems are serious enough to be referred for mental health services.

Even if children do not blame themselves for the divorce, the attributions they make for the parental separation can have important consequences. For example, simply attributing the separation to the voluntary actions of the parents may lead the child to feel ambivalent towards one or both parents or to blame one parent for the divorce. In addition to their intrapersonal consequences relating to the child's adjustment, such attributions are also likely to have interpersonal effects

(Grych & Fincham, 1992b). However, the effect of children's attributions on their relationships with their parents has not been studied systematically.

Other cognitions that have received attention in divorce research are fear of abandonment and hope for parental reunification. Kurdek and Berg (1987) reported that preschool and elementary school–age children may be particularly likely to worry about not being taken care of because their level of cognitive development prevents them from understanding the causes of the separation. They may worry that whatever led to the divorce also could lead one or both parents to leave them. Further, Emery (1995) notes that young children's growing awareness of their parents' loss of love for each other may lead them to question whether their parents also could stop loving them as well. Typically, these children are spending less time with each parent, and parents may not be able to provide the kind of warmth and reassurance they need due to their own difficulties adapting to the separation. Thus, the fear of abandonment is based in part on children's perceptions of actual events and interactions (Emery, 1995). The fantasy that parents will remarry also appears common in childhood and most likely is based on the wish for a happy family life rather than on cognitive limitations per se. Older children are more able to recognize positive benefits of a divorce, such as reduced conflict (Kurdek, 1986), but still may long for a family situation in which they could have regular, harmonious contact with both parents.

Evidence on the implications of these thoughts for children's adjustment and on their relation to level of cognitive development is scarce. Kurdek and Berg (1983) reported that a set of "problematic" cognitions, namely self-blame, fear of abandonment, and hope of reunification, were correlated with parent and teacher ratings of children's adjustment in one study but the same cognitions were associated only with child reports of adjustment in another (Kurdek & Berg, 1987). Wolchik and her colleagues (1993) studied a sample of racially diverse, economically disadvantaged fourth through eighth grade children whose parents had been separated an average of 55 months. Over half reported having the belief that their parents would reunite one day and that they sometimes worry that they may be left alone with no one to take care of them. However, only fear of abandonment was correlated with child adjustment (in both child and parent reports). Age was not correlated with either type of thought.

The absence of an association between children's cognitions about divorce and age is surprising given age-related differences in children's cognitive capacities. However, the lack of studies including very young children, who would be most prone to distortions due to cognitive limitations, and of studies assessing children close to the time of parental separation, limit our understanding of the interplay among age, cognitive development, and child adjustment. On the other hand, the limited evidence available indicates that the fear of not being taken care of, proposed to be common in preschoolers, still exists in many older children and is linked to poorer adjustment. Parental separation may call into question children's belief that their caregivers will ensure their safety and security; alternatively, some children may never have developed a sense of security because of disruptions in the parent–child relationship, an issue discussed in more detail below (see later section on Parent–Child Relations).

Implications for intervention. The evidence that children's perceptions can mediate their adaptation to divorce indicates that interventions attempting to change their cognitions may improve their adjustment. Although there is little data on preschoolers' thinking about divorce, they in particular may benefit from interventions that clarify their thoughts and emotions about the divorce. Older children who maintain misconceptions or unrealistic fears also are likely to benefit from examination of their beliefs. For many children, this type of intervention may be less important for correcting misconceptions per se than for providing them an opportunity to express their thoughts without fear of reprisal or hurting their parents. Parents who are depleted by the strains of divorce may not be able to attend to children's concerns or may be perceived by their children as too fragile or easily upset to hear their concerns. How such problems are addressed depends on the child's age. Young children may respond best to play therapy techniques, whereas older children and adolescents can talk openly about their thoughts and feelings. Therapy involving the parent or parents may be the preferred approach even when children exhibit maladaptive thinking. For example, if fear of abandonment is a significant issue, it may be best addressed by reinforcing the security of the child's relationships with each parent rather than trying to change a child's cognitions directly.

One way to reach a larger proportion of children affected by divorce is through school-based psychoeducational groups. Several different programs now exist that present structured activities for a group of children and a therapist designed to help clarify children's perceptions and interpretations of divorce-related events, to learn coping strategies for dealing with upsetting feelings and situations, and to increase children's level of social support (for reviews see Grych & Fincham, 1992a; Lee et al., 1994). Being with a group of peers undergoing the same kinds of problems can help enhance children's self-esteem and peer relations as well as provide insights on how to cope with parental separation. For children who do not demonstrate any significant problems, this is a preventive intervention or primary prevention; for those already exhibiting problems in adaptation, it is best considered a treatment intervention or secondary prevention. Regardless of its label, at least two group programs have demonstrated their effectiveness (e.g., Pedro-Carroll & Cowen, 1985; Stolberg & Mahler, 1994). Thus far, outcome evaluations have only been reported for children in grades two through six, but it is conceivable that the group format could be adopted for younger and older children.

Timing of Divorce-Related Events

Although most attention to the links between normal development and children's adjustment to divorce has focused on children's perceptions of separation, the timing of divorce-related events and experiences vis-à-vis normal developmental changes is also relevant. For example, the toddler period is marked by increased oppositionality, which typically entails increased tension and conflict between parents and children. These normative changes may prove particularly challenging or disruptive in families in which discipline is inconsistent or where high levels of parent–child conflict already exists, circumstances that are often found in divorced families. Problems with establishing and maintaining an authoritative style of discipline have been documented for both residential and nonresidential parents (Emery, 1988), and conflict between residential mothers and their sons have been found to be quite stable over time (e.,g, Hetherington, 1988).

Adolescence, with its emphasis on increasing autonomy and revisitation of separation–individuation issues, also appears to be a time of particular difficulty for children from divorced families. Hetherington and colleagues' (1993) longitudinal study of children whose parents divorced when they were 4 years of age documents the course of this change. Two and 6 years after the divorce, boys exhibited poorer adjustment than their counterparts from intact families, but most girls in divorced families were largely indistinguishable from those in intact families. At adolescence, behavior problems tended to increase for all children, but the increases were most dramatic for children in single-parent and remarried families, especially girls. These girls now demonstrated as many externalizing, internalizing, and academic problems as boys. Single mothers, in turn, exhibited more negativity than mothers in intact or remarried families. A normative transition thus seemed to trigger an increase in adjustment difficulties in the children from divorced families. It may be that the normal distancing that occurs at adolescence is particularly difficult for girls and their mothers, who often develop very close relationships after the divorce

(Hetherington, 1993). The absence of a father who is viewed as a legitimate authority figure—stepfathers often are not—also is likely to affect parents' ability to set and enforce limits, which may be challenged frequently and heatedly by adolescents.

Implications for Intervention. As normal transitions may present particular difficulties for children and adolescents in divorced families, interventions may be particularly necessary to help families cope with these transitions. Parents may benefit from gaining greater understanding of the source of the difficulties that they are experiencing and learning new ways to adjust to the changes. Interaction with others going through similar situations may be particularly useful, and several programs for single parents have been developed that address some of these kinds of changes and how parents can cope with them (see later section on Parent–Child Relations). Family therapy addressing the unique challenges faced by members of divorced families at difficult times of transition has the additional benefit of enhancing the relationships between parents and children and helping them learn constructive ways to negotiate conflicts (see Hodges, 1991). If children are quite young, parent education or training may be the most effective method of intervention.

Hierarchic Motility

The developmental psychopathology perspective depicts development as a series of qualitative organizational changes. A competent or healthy child is one who has integrated his or her biological, cognitive, emotional, and behavioral capacities and can master the challenges of their developmental phase. The principle of hierarchic motility states that the child's quality of organization at any given time is influenced by prior levels of organization; put another way, early developmental competencies act as a foundation for later development and are hierarchically integrated into later developmental organization (Cicchetti & Cohen, 1995). Thus, areas of vulnerability and strength developed at one point influence later development even if they are not directly apparent at that later time. This promotes continuity in the quality of adaptation or competence exhibited by individuals over time. Consequently, early adaptive competence tends to foster later competence because the child has developed a set of "tools" (i.e., emotional, cognitive, and behavioral capacities) for mastering developmental challenges and opportunities.

On the other hand, adaptational difficulties early in life increase the likelihood of less competent responses to later developmental challenges because the individual has not developed the resources needed for mastering those challenges. This progression is viewed as probabilistic, not inevitable, because changes within the child or in the child's environment may enhance their ability to respond effectively to later challenges (Cicchetti & Cohen, 1995). However, the longer an individual continues along a maladaptive pathway, the more difficult it is to reclaim a normal developmental trajectory (Sroufe, 1990).

What this suggests is that parental divorce (or the experiences associated with divorce) earlier in a child's life may have a greater effect on their development because it may initiate a series of events that move the child off a normal developmental pathway. The ultimate effect of such a chain of negative experiences will depend on their nature and timing. For example, if separation results in parents being less sensitive and responsive to an infant, an insecure attachment relationship may develop. Insecurely attached children are hypothesized to develop lower self-worth and self-confidence than securely attached children and to expect more negative interactions with others (Sroufe, 1989). They would then be less prepared to successfully master later developmental tasks such as separation and individuation, establishment of peer relations, and development of academic competence.

In contrast, divorces occurring later in childhood are mapped onto a well-established developmental course. If that course was largely one of competence, children will be able to use the strengths and maturity they have developed to return more easily to healthy functioning after confronting the stresses associated with parental separation. Children who were already experiencing adaptational problems, perhaps because of chronic exposure to interparental conflict, may follow an even more maladaptive trajectory because of an inability to cope with the stresses following separation. Alternatively, if the separation leads to a reduction in interparental conflict or decreased contact with a pathological parent, the deflection in developmental trajectory may be toward greater health and competence. The impact of the separation and divorce thus depends on the child's prior developmental organization and the response of the environment.

Divorces occurring at different points in the child's life are likely to have different effects on their developmental trajectory. However, some effects may not be immediately apparent and only arise in response to particular developmental challenges or events. These "sleeper" effects have been proposed to occur when adolescents confront issues of sexuality, commitment, and marriage (Kinnaird & Gerrard, 1986; Wallerstein, 1991). Other transitions of young adulthood that involve separation from the family and the establishment of adult identity, such as educational and occupational choices, also have been proposed to cause difficulties for adolescents from divorced families (Zill et al., 1993). Using the latest data from the National Survey of Children, Zill and colleagues (1993) reported that 18- to 22-year-old children of divorce, compared to children from two-parent families, exhibited greater problems in relations with their mother (which were not present when they were 12–16 years old) and higher levels of school dropout, along with higher levels of adjustment problems. Consistent with earlier analyses of this data set, children whose parents divorced prior to age 6 showed greater problems in their relationship with their father and marginally greater difficulties with psychological adjustment and school dropout than those whose parents divorced when they were between 6 and 16 years old. It should be noted, however, that despite the higher incidence of problems 12 to 22 years later, most of the young adults were in the normal range on most measures of well-being used in the study.

Continuing problems in adjustment following a divorce may also be due to the continuation of adverse factors in the child's life. Divorce often does not end conflict and tension in the family; in fact, it may increase as parents continue to confront areas of disagreement and play out the anger and resentment built up during the marriage and the divorce. Even when effects are associated with children's age at the time of divorce, it may not be correct to infer that the child's state at the time of divorce is responsible for the effects. Adjustment problems may occur because the child continues to face difficult circumstances that make it difficult to competently resolve developmental challenges. For example, an adolescent attempting to develop a coherent identity may have particular difficulty if he or she is caught in a struggle over loyalty to his or her parents.

Implications for Intervention. The principal of hierarchic motility suggests that intervention is particularly important for divorcing families that include young children. However, because problems in functioning may not be apparent or appear significant when children are young, these children may not come to the attention of mental health professionals. It may not be until middle childhood, when problems occur in school achievement or behavior, that the need for intervention is identified.

This underscores the need to develop prevention and intervention programs that target divorcing families early in the divorce process. Such programs could take a number of forms. For example, mandated psychoeducational programs for parents filing for divorce can reach the entire population of divorcing families in a particular area. These programs may be able to raise parents' awareness of the effects of divorce on young children and help them reduce the kinds of stressors that are likely to lead to long-term problems in child adjustment (see the following section on Risk, Vulnerability, and Protection). Adapted for younger children, the group programs described earlier also have the potential to include large numbers of children in school or community settings and may help children from divorced families understand and cope with the changes in their lives. Pediatricians and divorce lawyers may be the first professionals to become aware of developmental problems during or following divorce and consequently improving their knowledge of appropriate referral situations is likely to facilitate early identification of maladjustment.

Risk, Vulnerability, and Protection

Finally, developmental psychopathologists stress the role of risk, vulnerability, and protective factors in understanding normal and deviant development. Vulnerability and protective factors make a child more or less able, respectively, to cope with stressors and challenges in their lives, but are not directly and causally related to adjustment. Risk factors, in contrast, are directly linked to adjustment. There is an attempt to understand how different domains of functioning, including genetic, biological, cognitive, emotional, environmental, and cultural, interact to increase or decrease children's exposure and vulnerability to risk situations.

Because the particular constellation of risk, vulnerability, and protective factors vary, heterogeneity in functioning is the expected outcome for children confronted with a stressor such as divorce. A range of variables, from temperament to cultural attitudes about the family, are thought to be relevant for understanding children's adjustment to divorce. By organizing these factors according to their potential role (e.g., risk vs. vulnerability factor) in a developmental process, a framework for understanding heterogeneous outcomes can be realized. Further, identification of risk, vulnerability, and protective factors provides more specific targets for intervention efforts. Prevention and treatment programs may have the largest effect on children's adjustment by reducing the impact or exposure to risk factors or by promoting the operation of protective factors. The question of what type of intervention to use for a particular family will depend on assessment of the constellation of risk and protective factors most relevant to understanding that family's functioning.

The description of risk, vulnerability, and protective factors is useful to the extent that it leads to an understanding of the process by which the probability of maladjustment is increased or decreased. These factors operate primarily through promoting or detracting from the development of competence at progressive stages of development and the consequent likelihood of an emerging pathological organization (Rutter, 1990). For example, divorce may lead to maladjustment through the process of chaining, in which the separation leads to a series of other negative experiences, such as harsh or inconsistent parental discipline (Hetherington et al., 1982) or by reducing children's exposure to growth-promoting opportunities, such as may occur if a child moves to a neighborhood with a poorer school system. Vulnerability and protective factors can mediate the impact of a risk situation in a variety of ways. For example, children's beliefs about locus of control may increase or decrease the effects of divorce-related events (Fogas et al., 1992), and their temperament may make harsh parenting more or less likely (Hetherington, 1989). Similarly, the presence of other supportive adults may help a child cope with the conflict between his or her parents or decreased time with one or both parents (Jenkins & Smith, 1990; Wolchik, et al.,1989).

Empirical research has emphasized the role of interparental conflict, disrupted parent–child relations, inconsistent or ineffective discipline practices, and the experience of negative life events in shaping children's adjustment to marital dissolution (for a review see Grych & Fincham, 1997). The same processes are linked to childhood difficulties in intact families. However, divorce can change the nature of interparental conflict, parent–child relations, and parenting styles in ways that are likely to happen much less frequently in intact families. Nonetheless, it has been argued that if parents can maintain a cooperative (or at least nonconflictual) relationship with each other, a close relationship with their child, authoritative parenting styles, and minimize the number of changes children undergo after divorce, the divorce should have little or no long-term impact on children. This does not imply that the immediate or short-term effects of the separation on children are inconsequential. On the contrary, the vast majority of children find parental separation extremely difficult and stressful and the 1 to 2 years following separation has been described as a "crisis" period during which most children (and adults) exhibit some difficulty in functioning (e.g., Hetherington, et al., 1982).

Next we turn to examine risk factors most closely associated with children's adjustment after divorce. The existence of continued interparental conflict, poor parent–child relations, and economic disadvantage each can be viewed as a risk factor that increases the likelihood that a child will exhibit maladjustment. The mechanisms by which these factors operate have only begun to be explored and little empirical work has examined developmental aspects of these risk factors. Finally, we conclude this section by discussing vulnerability and protective factors.

Interparental Conflict

The factor most closely linked to children's adjustment after divorce is interparental conflict (Amato, 1993). Numerous studies have indicated that the level of discord existing between parents before (e.g., Jenkins & Smith, 1993) and after (Johnston, Gonzalez, & Campbell., 1987) divorce is a better predictor of children's functioning than is family status. The more pertinent question is how conflict affects children and whether children's age moderates this effect.

The effect of interparental conflict on children in intact families has received more attention than conflict in divorced families. Exposure to conflict between parents is upsetting for children from toddlerhood through adolescence and is related to higher levels of internalizing and externalizing problems (for reviews see Cummings & Davies, 1994; Grych & Fincham, 1990). Although some studies have reported age-related differences in how children respond to conflict, no systematic differences between children of different ages have been found.

Rather than ending interparental conflict, divorce may exacerbate ill feelings between spouses as they attempt to work out a divorce settlement and negotiate family relationships following separation. Feelings of hurt and anger often are channeled through protracted, hostile battles over establishing and maintaining the divorce settlement. Certain aspects of conflict occurring between divorced parents tend to be particularly stressful for children. First, conflicts often revolve around child-related matters, especially child custody, support, and visitation, and this type of conflict has been shown to be more upsetting to children (Grych & Fincham, 1993) than nonchild related conflict and to be linked to child maladjustment (Camara & Resnick, 1989). Lingering anger and resentment between parents may play out in numerous ways that affect children.

The potential for a child to be drawn into an alliance with a parent becomes particularly salient when parents are actively vying for their child's affection and loyalty. This may be as blatant as one parent talking to their child about the other parents' faults and their role in the divorce, or it may be more subtle, such as using the child to find out about the other parents' activities, to send messages to him or her, or to forbid talk about the other parent. This puts the child in the untenable position of trying to remain close to two people who express anger or even hatred toward each other (Emery, 1994). Children may hear a parent deride the ex-spouse, which may elicit a desire to protect the ex-spouse;

further, because of their identification with the ex-spouse they may perceive attacks on him or her as attacks on themselves (Kalter, 1987). Even where a parent is not openly scornful of his or her ex-spouse, children's affection for the ex-spouse may be seen as disloyal, putting pressure on the child to conceal positive feelings or enjoyment experienced with the ex-spouse.

Emery (1994) points out that, even though this situation is typically viewed in terms of power ("whose side are you on"), it may reflect a struggle over intimacy issues ("who do you love more") as parents each try to maintain close relationships with their children. If each step toward one parent is viewed as a step away from the other, children risk hurting one parent at the same time they are pleasing the other (Emery, 1994). Children who perceive this kind of pressure from both parents may feel anxious, sad, or angry and may develop conflict about what they genuinely think and feel, particularly young children with limited capacity to understand multiple perspectives.

As difficult as that position is for children, it also confers a degree of power that is appealing but developmentally inappropriate (Emery, 1994). It can provide children a sense of control in a situation where they have had little, and consequently, children may actively play one parent off against the other. Children in this position may also infer that they have the ability to change things between their parents and perhaps help them reunite. This almost inevitably will result in disappointment and a sense of failure when children learn that they cannot repair the parents' marriage.

The adaptational significance of loyalty dilemmas for children was documented in a study of adolescents from divorced families (Buchanon, Maccoby, & Dornbusch, 1991). Loyalty conflicts (feeling "caught in the middle") were most likely to occur when parents were characterized as exhibiting high conflict and low cooperation. Thus, feeling "caught" between parents appears to be a result of parents pulling their children into struggles that they cannot resolve. Further, feeling caught in the middle was correlated with higher levels of depression, anxiety, and deviant behavior. In fact, being drawn into parents' continuing hostilities mediated the association between interparental conflict and child adjustment.

Whether children of a particular age are more or less likely to feel caught in the middle has not been investigated empirically. It may be that only the very youngest or most mature children can avoid being drawn into loyalty conflicts; the burden of avoiding this kind of dilemma falls on the parents and their ability to separate their parenting and ex-spousal roles. Children who want to remain close to each parent are likely to try to please them and may get pulled into uncomfortable situations in which it seems they must choose between loving their two parents. Younger children, however, may be more likely to perceive themselves as responsible for maintaining peace in the family or the happiness of their parents and thus to remain involved in triangulated relationships in an attempt to do so. Older children, in contrast, may be more likely to recognize the power of their position and have difficulty resisting the lure of such triangles.

Implications for Intervention. The significance of continuing interparental conflict for children's adjustment to divorce, and the frequency with which conflict occurs between divorcing couples, suggests that attempts to help parents learn to resolve disagreements constructively may be one of the most powerful interventions for children from divorcing families. Such efforts are not unrealistic. Court-mandated programs exist that attempt to educate parents about the effects of conflict on children and teach basic conflict resolution skills. Although this kind of program may be too brief to help couples chronically locked in conflict, the information can be helpful for raising parental awareness and improving problem solving in some couples. Moreover, it may serve as an impetus for further treatment. Therapy for divorcing or divorced couples that focuses on improving their ability to work cooperatively as coparents is a more traditional intervention that seeks to foster children's adjustment by reducing their exposure to a significant risk factor. Often unresolved issues from the marriage fuel conflicts over visitation, child support payments, and so on, and at times those issues may need to be resolved before improvements are seen in postdivorce relationships.

Divorce mediation also has the potential to reduce conflict during and after divorce. It is one of a family of alternative dispute resolution techniques designed to avoid litigation in which parents work with an impartial third party to reach mutually satisfactory agreements regarding issues such as child custody, support, and visitation. Unlike the traditional legal means for settling disputes, which is predicated on a "win-lose" philosophy, mediation is predicated on a "win-win" philosophy. By cooperating to reach settlements, it is hoped that parents learn a new means of resolving disagreements and avoid the resentment that can arise from perceived unfair treatment in the courts, which is at the root of many postdivorce disputes. Overall, spouses (particularly husbands) tend to be more satisfied with mediation than litigation (Emery, Matthews & Kitzmann, 1994), a circumstance that is also reflected in greater compliance with agreements and lower rates of relitigation following mediation (Emery, 1994). Importantly, noncustodial parents in mediation samples have been found to be more involved with their children and to show greater compliance with visitation arrangements than those who litigated (Dillon & Emery, in press; Emery et al., 1994).

Whether the beneficial effects experienced by parents in mediation lead to psychological benefits for children has received remarkably little attention. None of the available studies on this topic documents a more beneficial outcome for children of parents who mediate versus litigate on measures of psychological adjustment. However, in a 9-year follow-up of couples assigned to mediation versus litigation groups, Dillon and Emery (1996) found that litigation fathers were more likely than fathers who had experienced mediation to report that their children had behavior problems requiring treatment. No differences were found for mothers and no group differences were found for fathers or mothers in reports of general behavior problems and receipt of treatment. These results also need to be interpreted with caution owing to high attrition rate (63%) resulting in a small follow-up sample.

Parent–Child Relations

Divorce inevitably leads to the reorganization of family relationships. Although most parents now share legal custody, for most children life after divorce means living with their mother and having visitation with their father. However, many fathers decrease contact with their children over time (Seltzer, 1991). In addition, because of their own distress during and after divorce, both parents may be less sensitive to and responsive to their children's emotional needs. Children therefore often face significantly reduced time with one parent and less attention and support from both. This is likely to have a negative impact on all children, but may affect children of different ages in somewhat different ways.

For infants and toddlers, divorce may disrupt the attachment process. The development of a secure attachment is a critical developmental task in the first year of life, and results from caregiver–infant interactions in which the caregiver is attuned to the child's state and responds reliably to meet his or her needs. Although the quality of attachment between a child and caregiver typically is established by 12 months of age, significant changes in caregiver–child interactions can alter the security of attachment. Attachment theory proposes that secure attachment provides a firm foundation for children to confidently explore the world, develop a sense of autonomy, and establish healthy relationships with others. Thus, consistent with the principal of hierarchic motility, failure to establish a secure attachment relationship renders children less able to master later developmental tasks.

Despite the central role accorded to attachment by some developmental theorists and the clear implications divorce has for the development of secure attachment, there has been very little empirical research on the impact of marital dissolution and divorce on attachment quality. Several studies have shown that marital discord during the child's first year of life, and even prior to the child's birth, predicts poorer quality attachment (e.g., Howes & Markman, 1989), but no published studies have examined attachment quality in separated or divorced families. Recently, however, Solomon and her colleagues (1995) presented data to show that disorganized (Type D) attachment was more common in a sample of newly divorced couples with 12- to 20-month-old children than in a matched comparison group. This type of attachment represents the absence of a regulated, coherent response to separations. Emerging findings on long-term outcome of "D" babies suggest that they are more disordered in early childhood than babies who exhibit avoidant or ambivalent attachments (e.g., Lyons-Routh, Alpern, & Repacholi, 1993). Moreover, Solomon and colleagues reported that three factors moderated the relation between marital status and attachment. Specifically, a higher proportion of disorganized attachments was associated with high levels of conflict, low levels of communication between parents, and the mother's failure to "protect and reassure" the infant (the extent to which mothers structured visitations with fathers and actively intervened when they perceived problems occurring during visitation). Although the generalizability of results from a single study is questionable, this study suggests that the quality of the relationship between divorcing spouses affects parenting in the first years of life, with potentially significant effects on the developing child.

In middle childhood, relationships between children and their custodial parent often are tempestuous after a divorce, particularly for boys and their mothers. Hetherington and coworkers (1982) provide some of the most detailed descriptions of the course of parent–child interactions. In the first year after divorce, mothers had difficulty controlling their children, especially boys, and exhibited less affection and poorer communication. Boys tended to be more hostile and oppositional, and coercive cycles often developed in which the child and parent escalated negative behavior until one or the other relented. Girls tended to behave more positively and tended to receive more positive reinforcement and fewer commands than boys. By the second year after the divorce, mothers exhibited more nurturance and better communication, and children's behavior had improved. Whereas boys remained more negative than boys in intact families, girls often formed close relationships with their mothers. This pattern continued at an assessment 6 years after the divorce, when children were approximately age 10. At that time boys' relationships with their mothers were more conflictual than in intact families, but boys and their mothers also expressed strong positive feelings toward each other. Hetherington (1989, p. 5) describes their relationships as "intense and ambivalent." Girls tended to maintain close and relatively harmonious relationships with their mothers until adolescence.

As described earlier, adolescence appears to cause a renewal of conflict and difficulty in parent–child relationships. Hetherington (1989) reported that single-parent mothers monitored their children less than those in intact families, a variable associated with higher rates of antisocial behavior. The "distancing" between parents and children that naturally occurs during adolescence thus may be more likely to result in children from divorced families moving into delinquent peer groups or engaging in delinquent behavior.

Children's relationships with their nonresidential parent also tend to undergo change over time. Nonresidential fathers tend to gradually reduce the amount of time they spend with their children. For example, the National Survey of Children (Furstenberg & Nord, 1985) revealed that the proportion of fathers seeing their children weekly dropped from approximately 50 percent at 2 years postdivorce to 25 percent between 2 and 9 years after divorce, to 13 percent after 10 years. Despite these low levels of contact, over half of the children from divorced families interviewed for the National Survey of Children considered their fathers to be a part of their family. Nonresidential mothers tend to remain in closer contact after divorce. Kalter (1987) has argued that parents who visit infrequently or inconsistently cause continuous problems for children's self-esteem because children may question how much the parent loves them, which for young children may be understood as how worthy they are to be loved. In contrast to residential parents, who may have problems with consistent authoritative parenting, nonresidential parents are more likely to become overly permissive and fail to establish limits and consequences for child misbehavior (Emery, 1994). In addition to problems associated with such parenting styles, the inconsistency between parents' styles may cause additional confusion for young children.

Implications for Intervention. Many of the adverse effects attributed to divorce are mediated by parent–child relations, and consequently it is logical for parents to be primary targets for intervention efforts. Parent-focused interventions are particularly important for aiding the adaptation of very young children, who are most at risk for developing adjustment problems but are the least likely to be referred for clinical services. When problems arise in toddler and preschool-age children they generally can be traced to difficulties in the parent–child relationship. Ineffective discipline can lead to oppositional behavior and parent–child conflict and can be successfully treated with parent education and training in more effective disciplinary strategies. Involving both parents may be necessary in order to reduce inconsistencies between parental styles that may be contributing to behavior problems. Problems in the quality of parent–child relations, which may range from feelings of tension, anger, and resentment to the perception of a lack of closeness or warmth, may need to be addressed in dyadic therapy or individual therapy for the parent. Because of the centrality of the parent–child relationship for healthy development, parents' ability to be sensitive and responsive to their children's needs should be a primary focus of treatment. Each may be bringing qualities to the interaction that make it difficult to enjoy being together. Children who are temperamentally difficult or who express hostility and defiance elicit anger and frustration in parents, and parents who cannot modulate their responses promote cycles of coercion or avoidance. Parents who are depressed, anxious, or lacking in parenting skill or knowledge may be particularly likely to promote coercive interactions.

Parent-child relations in older children may be addressed in a variety of ways. Traditional therapy again offers the potential to focus on issues of discipline, negotiation of responsibility and family roles, autonomy, and authority. With elementary school–age children a family-oriented approach that includes the child and one or both parents is likely to be the optimal approach for addressing parent–child difficulties. A promising alternative, however, is a group program for single-parents that addresses issues and problems that commonly arise after divorce. Like the child-focused groups described above, this type of program may reach parents of children who are not yet demonstrating serious behavioral or emotional difficulties, but who are frustrated or seeking the support of others in a similar situation. Thus a parent group may operate as a preventive or early intervention for children.

One such program was developed by Wolchik and colleagues (1993). This intervention targeted several factors identified as mediators of children's adaptation to divorce: mother–child relationships, discipline, negative divorce events (including interparental conflict), contact with fathers, and support from nonparental adults. An evaluation of this 10-week group (which also included two individual sessions) involved 70 mothers of 8 to 15 year olds. It revealed positive changes in the quality of mother–child relationships for the intervention group, but little effect on interparental conflict or discipline. Children of the mothers in the intervention group also exhibited some reduction in their level of aggression but did not differ from a wait list control on self-reported anxiety, conduct disorder, or depression. Moreover, Wolchik and her colleagues found that changes in mother–child relationships mediated the impact of the group on child adjustment, supporting the importance of parent–child relations for children's adaptation to divorce.

Financial Hardship

Of the many life changes that may occur after divorce, those of greatest concern flow from increased financial hardship. Almost half of the mothers with primary placement experience a 50 percent drop in income in the year following divorce (Duncan & Hoffman, 1985); African American women and European American women whose predivorce income was below the median suffer particularly large losses. Approximately 40 percent of these women live below the poverty line after divorce. The financial situation of most mothers does not improve substantially unless they remarry. The effects on the children are varied. They may need to move to a neighborhood that is unfamiliar and less safe, they may switch to a school system that has fewer resources and provides a poorer education, they may get poorer health care, and they may have fewer opportunities to become involved in other activities that could promote competence (e.g., music lessons, summer camp).

The principle of hierarchic motility suggests that these changes may be particularly harmful for younger children. For example, children who are just entering the formal education system are likely to be affected more by poorer quality schooling because of the cumulative nature of intellectual development; developing basic skills early (e.g., in reading, writing, math) enables children to make better use of later learning opportunities. An older child moving to a school with fewer resources will be relatively less disadvantaged because their existing skills will allow them to take greater advantage of whatever opportunities are present in their new environment.

Developing friendships, a key developmental task of middle childhood, also may be disrupted by moving. The move results not only in the loss of a potentially important source of social support, but it may also affect confidence in the ability to establish friendships. This may present a particular problem in adolescence, a period when peer relationships are becoming increasingly important. Adolescents who leave an established peer group in the middle of a school year may drift toward more antisocial peers as they try to make new connections in an unfamiliar place.

Implications for Intervention. The best way to address problems arising from financial disadvantage is to prevent them from occurring. This requires changes in the legal process relating to child support and the enforcement of support orders. Support awards are often insufficient to cover the costs involved in raising children and rarely include cost-of-living increases and so the real value of payments declines over time (Duncan & Hoffman, 1985). Moreover, noncompliance with support orders is widespread, and historically there have been few consequences for men who do not reliably pay the required amounts (Weitzman, 1985). Changes have been made in the last decade to improve compliance, including self-starting enforcement strategies, garnishment of wages, and interception of state and federal income tax returns (Emery, 1988). There is some evidence that compliance with child support orders is linked to fathers' level of involvement with their children (Furstenberg et al., 1983). It may be that fathers who feel that they are an important part of their children's lives are more willing to provide financial support, and thus any attempts to strengthen fathers' relationships with their children may have economic as well as emotional advantages.

Divorce mediation, which produces higher levels of satisfaction with divorce settlements in fathers, may reduce the perception that fathers were treated unfairly and make continued involvement and financial support more likely. Other fathers may reduce their involvement because they find part-time parenting too difficult emotionally, or because they feel they have been marginalized as parents. Helping fathers, and perhaps mothers, to recognize the important place nonresidential fathers can play in their children's lives and to negotiate new relationships after divorce may help promote closer father–child relations.

Vulnerability and Protection

Thus far we have emphasized risk factors directly associated with poorer adjustment to divorce. However, a balanced understanding of children's adaptation requires attention to the variables that moderate the impact of these risk factors on children.

Vulnerability factors reduce children's capacity to cope effectively with stressful events and situations, whereas protective factors enhance their coping ability. Often vulnerability and protection represent two sides of the same coin, or opposite poles of a continuum (e.g., Rutter, 1990). For example, high intelligence may be considered a protective factor and low intelligence a vulnerability factor. Although in some situations it is preferable to identify particular constructs as either protective or vulnerability factors, in the context of divorce it makes sense to consider several variables that may increase or decrease children's resiliency in the face of stress and change depending upon at which end of the continuum a child falls.

Unfortunately, little research has focused on understanding processes that moderate the effects of the risk factors described earlier, and even less attention has been given to this issue from a developmental point of view. Using a stress and coping perspective, however, Sandler, Wolchik, and their colleagues have identified social support (Wolchik, Ruehlman, Braver, & Sandler, 1989), coping strategies (Sandler, Tein, & West, 1994), and locus of control (Fogas, Wolchik, Braver, Freedom, & Bay, 1992) as potentially important influences on children's postdivorce adaptation. Specifically, support from extended family members can buffer children against the adverse effects of stressful changes following divorce (Wolchik et al., 1989), though some studies suggest that social support has direct, rather than moderating, effects on children's postdivorce adaptation (Guidubaldi & Cleminshaw, 1983; Hetherington, 1989). Thus, the presence of supportive adults may be protective in that they can offer children reassurance, advice, and stability at a time when parents may not be able to provide the empathy and responsiveness children need. The absence of such adults leaves the child more vulnerable to the effects of disrupted parent–child relations and interparental conflict. Although support from other adults is likely to be important for children of all ages, it may be especially helpful for young children who are more dependent on their parents and less able to turn to peers for camaraderie and support (Lustig, Wolchik, & Braver, 1992).

Several studies indicate that children's coping strategies also are linked to their adjustment after divorce. Children who engage in "active" coping, which involves the use of cognitive or behavioral strategies to understand and address a problem (e.g., talking to a parent about their fears), tend to be more well-adjusted than children who use avoidance (e.g., trying not to think about a problem) as a primary coping strategy (Kliewer & Sandler, 1993; Krantz, Clark, Pruyn, & Usher, 1985; Sandler et al., 1994). Although the moderating effect of coping strategy has not yet been demonstrated consistently, coping resources become increasingly important as the level of risk or stress increases.

The efficacy of various coping strategies depends on the type of event or situation that requires a coping response. In cases in which the child has some control, active problem-focused coping (Folkman & Lazarus, 1980) is likely to be most effective because it can change the nature of the situation. In contrast, when the child does not have control (e.g., over whether parents remarry), strategies that focus on regulating the child's emotional response may be most useful. Children's use of these two broad categories of coping strategies changes with age (Compas, 1987). Emotion-focused coping strategies often depend on the child's ability to reframe the situation or see it from a different perspective, cognitive

abilities that tend to develop in middle and late childhood. For example, eighth graders tend to generate more emotion-focused strategies for coping with stressful events than sixth or seventh graders (Compas, Malcarne, & Fondacaro, 1988). Given that many divorce-related events are beyond the child's control, young children may be less able to generate effective and appropriate responses to such events. On the other hand, Sandler and colleagues (1994) found that children as young as 8 used distraction as a coping strategy (engaging in other activities rather than thinking about the problem), which in turn correlated with lower levels of depression and anxiety. This very simple strategy may be used effectively by younger children as well, although by its nature it is a short-term solution.

One type of perception relevant to coping is children's belief in their ability to exert control over a situation. Although this perception may be neither accurate nor adaptive in some situations, internal locus of control has been found to correlate with better adjustment to divorce in children from 8 to 15 years of age (Fogas, et al., 1992; Kurdek, Blisk, & Siesky, 1981). Children who can differentiate areas in which they do have some control (e.g., their interactions with their parents) from those that are beyond their control (e.g., whether their parents remarry) are likely to cope most successfully. Kurdek's model of cognitive development suggests that children below the age of 5 will overattribute control, perhaps leading to greater perceived responsibility for helping the parents work out their difficulties and to inappropriate (as well as futile) attempts to do so.

Another factor that may act as either a vulnerability or protective factor is child temperament. The only study investigating the role of temperament in children's adjustment after divorce found that it interacted with the degree of stress and support in their lives (Hetherington, 1989). Specifically, when social support was low, higher levels of stress had a more negative impact on temperamentally difficult children than those with easier temperaments. Children who are more distressed by change and prone to negative affect are more likely to contribute to difficulties in parent–child interaction; in contrast, adaptable, happy, and easily soothed children may be more able to elicit warmth and compassion from their parents.

Finally, in addition to being an index of children's adaptation, the quality of their attachment with their parents may moderate children's adjustment to divorce. Children with insecure versus secure attachment histories may respond differently to divorce-related events such as interparental conflict, a parent leaving, and decreased contact with parents, and thus attachment security may be useful for explaining why some children appear to adapt successfully while others demonstrate long-term problems. Children with secure histories may be better able to weather the changes associated with divorce because they operate from a basic position of trust, security, and confidence. In contrast, disruptions in parent–child relations may be particularly distressing for insecure children who fear the loss of important others and lack internal resources to cope with changes in their environment.

Implications for Intervention. Identification of vulnerability and protective factors is important because they can be potential targets for intervention. In fact, psychoeducational groups for children from divorced families often emphasize the development of coping skills and the provision of social support as primary goals. When risk processes like interparental conflict cannot be directly reduced, helping children to cope with them may attenuate their impact. Such groups necessarily must be sensitive to children's level of cognitive and emotional development; it would be inappropriate, for example, to teach coping skills to a 4 year old that require the cognitive sophistication of a 10 year old. The same logic applies to treatment oriented to an individual child or family. Sensitive evaluation of the child's characteristic ways of thinking and behaving can provide information about their existing strengths as well as areas of vulnerability.

Although children's temperament and attachment security may be difficult to modify, helping parents to better understand how their child responds to difficult events may interrupt negative, aversive patterns of interaction. By depersonalizing the child's response and attributing it to their disposition, parents may become less sensitive to perceiving rejection or feeling incompetent and thus better able to respond appropriately to their children's needs.

SUMMARY AND CONCLUSIONS

Although not exhaustive, the features of developmental psychopathology that we have reviewed provide a way of organizing the complicated and at times inconsistent data on children's adjustment to divorce. From the viewpoint of developmental psychopathology, the heterogeneity found in children's functioning following divorce is expected because the developmental pathway for children from divorced families is influenced by the particular constellation of circumstances and interactions experienced in the divorce process. Because children's temperament, the nature of their relationship with each parent, the parents' management of their conflict, and the changes they experience in lifestyle differ from family to family, so do children's adaptation to divorce. This perspective thus is consistent with ecological (Kurdek, 1986) and contextual

(Hetherington, 1993) models of divorce adjustment that incorporate diverse levels of influence on children's behavior.

It also has important implications for intervening with children from divorced families who are experiencing adjustment problems. Although only a small percentage of children develop clinically significant levels of adjustment problems, as a group they represent an at-risk population. Given the large number of children who experience divorce every year, traditional delivery of clinical services through outpatient mental health centers will be inadequate for meeting present and future needs. Humphreys, Fernandes, Gano-Phillips, Bhana, and Fincham (1993) therefore discuss an alternative, community-oriented approach to divorce interventions for children that involves moving from a "waiting" mode to a "seeking" mode of service delivery. Their call for greater prevention and education efforts is well founded as we now know enough about the factors that predict serious behavior problems in children from divorced families to develop interventions that address them before they develop. Of course, more traditional interventions will probably always be necessary to provide intensive treatment to children and families who experience particular difficulty adjusting to divorce, but they may best be considered backups to more widespread programs that reach children earlier in their developmental pathway. In this way, early deviations can be corrected and children can build from a position of strength, not vulnerability, and thus be more capable of coping with and mastering the challenges that occur later in development.

REFERENCES

Achenbach, T. M., & Edelbrock, C. (1983). *Manual for the Child Behavior Checklist and Revised Behavior Profile.* Burlington, VT: University Associates in Psychiatry.

Allison, P. D., & Furstenberg, F. F. (1989). How marital dissolution affects children: Variations by age and sex. *Developmental Psychology, 25,* 540–549.

Amato, P. R. (1993). Children's adjustment to divorce: Theories, hypotheses, and empirical support. *Journal of Marriage and the Family, 55,* 23–38.

Amato, P. R., & Keith, B. (1991). Consequences of parental divorce for the well-being of children: A meta-analysis. *Psychological Bulletin, 110,* 26–46.

Bowlby, J. (1944). Fourty-four juvenile thieves: Their characters and home life. *International Journal of Psycho-Analysis, 25,* 19–52.

Bretherton, I., Page, T., Halvorsen, C., Walsh, R. O. (March, 1995). *Attachment narratives of preschoolers from post-divorce families: Correlations with other relationship and personality as-*

sessments. Paper presented at the biennial meeting of the Society for Research in Child Development, Indianapolis, IN.

Buchanan, C. M., Maccoby, E. E., & Dornbush, S. M. (1991). Caught between parents: Adolescents' experience in divorced homes. *Child Development, 62,* 1008–1029.

Camara, K. A., & Resnick, G. (1989). Styles of conflict, resolution and cooperation between divorced parents: Effects on child behavior and adjustment. *American Journal of Orthopsychiatry, 59,* 560–575.

Cicchetti, D., & Cohen, D. J. (1995). Perspectives on developmental psychopathology. In D. Cicchetti & D. J. Cohen (Eds.), *Development and psychopathology: Vol. 1. Theory and methods* (pp. 3–22). New York: Wiley.

Compas, B. E. (1987). Coping with stress during childhood and adolescence. *Psychological Bulletin, 101,* 393–403.

Compas, B. E., Malcarne, V. L., & Fondacaro, K. M. (1988). Coping with stressful events in older children and adolescents. *Journal of Consulting and Clinical Psychology, 56,* 405–411.

Cummings, E. M., & Davies, P. T. (1994). *Children and marital conflict.* New York: Guilford Press.

Dillon, P. A., & Emery, R. E. (1996). Long term effects of divorce mediation in a field study of child custody dispute resolution. *American Journal of Orthopsychiatry, 66,* 131–140.

Duncan, G. J., & Hoffman, S. D. (1985). Economic consequences of marital instability. In M. David & T. Smeeding (Eds.), *Horizontal equity, uncertainty, and economic well-being* (pp. 427–469). Chicago: University of Chicago Press.

Emery, R. E. (1988). *Marriage, divorce, and children's adjustment.* Newbury Park, CA: Sage.

Emery, R. E. (1994). *Renegotiating family relationships.* New York: Guilford Press.

Emery, R. E., Matthews, S., & Kitzmann, K. M. (1994). Child custody mediation and litigation: Parents' satisfaction and functioning a year after settlement. *Journal of Consulting and Clinical Psychology, 62,* 124–129.

Fogas, S., Wolchik, S. A., Braver, S. L., Freedom, D. S., & Bay, R. (1992). Locus of control as a mediator of negative divorce-related events and adjustment problems in children. *American Journal of Orthopsychiatry, 62,* 589–598.

Folkman, S., & Lazarus, R. S. (1980). An analysis of coping in a middle-aged community sample. *Journal of Health and Social Behavior, 21,* 219–239.

Fraiberg, S. (1959). *The magic years: Understanding and handling the problems of early childhood.* New York: Scribner's.

Furstenberg, F. F. (1990). Divorce and the American family. *Annual Review of Sociology, 16,* 379–403.

Furstenberg, F. F., & Cherlin, A. J. (1991). *Divided families: What happens to children when parents part.* Cambridge, MA: Harvard University Press.

Furstenberg, F. F., & Nord, C. W. (1985). Parenting apart: Patterns of childrearing after marital disruption. *Journal of Marriage and the Family, 47,* 893–904.

Furstenberg, F. F., Peterson, J. L., Nord, C. W., & Zill, N. (1983). The life course of children of divorce: Marital disruption and parent consent. *American Sociological Review, 48,* 656–668.

Gardner, R. (1976). *The parents' book about divorce.* New York: Doubleday.

Glick, P. C. (1988). The role of divorce in the changing family structure: Trends and variations. In S. A. Wolchick & P. Karoly (Eds.), *Children of divorce: Empirical perspectives on adjustment* (pp. 3–34). New York: Gardner Press.

Grych, J. H., & Fincham, F. D. (1990). Marital conflict and children's adjustment: A cognitive–contextual framework. *Psychological Bulletin, 108,* 267–290.

Grych, J. H., & Fincham, F. D. (1992a). Interventions for children of divorce: Toward greater integration of research and action. *Psychological Bulletin, 110,* 434–454.

Grych, J. H., & Fincham, F. D. (1992b). Marital dissolution and family adjustment. In T. Orbuch (Ed.), *Close relationship loss: Theoretical perspectives* (pp. 157–173). New York: Springer.

Grych, J. H., & Fincham, F. D. (1993). Children's appraisals of marital conflict: Initial investigations of the cognitive–contextual framework. *Child Development, 64,* 215–230.

Grych, J. H., & Fincham, F. D. (1997). Children's adaptation to divorce: From description to explanation. In I. N. Sandler & S. A. Wolchik (Eds.), *Handbook of children's coping with common stressors: Linking theory, research, and interventions* (pp. 159–194). New York: Plenum Press.

Guidubaldi, J., & Cleminshaw, H. (1983, August). *Impact of family support system on children's academic and social functioning after divorce.* Paper presented at the annual meeting of the American Psychological Association, Anaheim, CA.

Guidubaldi, J., Perry, J. D., & Cleminshaw, H. K. (1984). The legacy of parental divorce. In B. B. Lahey & A. E. Kazdin (Eds.), *Advances in clinical child psychology (Vol. 7,* pp. 109–151). New York: Plenum Press.

Guidubaldi, J., Perry, J. D., & Nastasi, B. K. (1987). Assessment and intervention for children of divorce: Implications of the NASP-KSU nationwide survey. In J. Vincent (Ed.), *Advances in family intervention, assessment, and theory (Vol. 4,* pp. 33–69). Greenwich, CT: JAI Press.

Healy, J. M., Stewart, A. J., & Copeland, A. P. (1993). The role of self-blame in children's adjustment to parental separation. *Personality and Social Psychology Bulletin, 19,* 279–289.

Hetherington, E. M. (1988). Parents, children, and siblings: Six years after divorce. In R. Hinde & J. Stevenson-Hinde (Eds.), *Relationships within families* (pp. 311–331). Oxford: Clarendon Press.

Hetherington, E. M. (1989). Coping with family transitions: Winners, losers, and survivors. *Child Development, 60,* 1–14.

Hetherington, E. M. (1993). An overview of the Virginia longitudinal study of divorce and remarriage with a focus on early adolescence. *Journal of Family Psychology, 7,* 39–56.

Hetherington, E. M., Clingempeel, W. G., Anderson, E. R., Deal, J. E., Hagen, M. S., Holier, E. A., & Linder, M. S. (1992). Coping with marital transitions: A family systems perspective. With commentary by Eleanor E. Maccoby. *Monographs of the Society for Research in Child Development, 57.*

Hetherington, E. M., Cox, M., & Cox, R. (1982). Effects of divorce on parents and children In M. Lamb (Ed.), *Nontraditional families* (pp. 233–288). Hillsdale, NJ: Erlbaum.

Hodges, W. F. (1991). *Interventions for children of divorce.* New York: Wiley.

Howes, P., & Markman, H. J. (1989). Marital quality and child functioning: A longitudinal investigation. *Child Development, 60,* 1044–1051.

Humphreys, K., Fernandes, L. O., Gano-Phillips, S., Bhana, A. E., & Fincham, F. D. (1993). A community oriented approach to divorce intervention. *Family Journal, 1,* 4–12.

Jenkins, J. M., & Smith, M. A. (1990). Factors protecting children living in disharmonious homes: Maternal reports. *Journal of the American Academy of Child and Adolescent Psychiatry, 29,* 60–69.

Jenkins, J. M., & Smith, M. A. (1993). A prospective study of behavioural disturbance in children who subsequently experience parental divorce: A research note. *Journal of Divorce and Remarriage, 19,* 143–160.

Johnston, J. R., Gonzalez, R., & Campbell, L. E. (1987). Ongoing postdivorce conflict and child disturbance. *Journal of Abnormal Child Psychology, 15,* 497–509.

Kalter, N. (1987). Long-term effects of divorce on children: A developmental vulnerability model. *American Journal of Orthopsychiatry, 57,* 587–600.

Kalter, N., & Rembar, J. (1981). The significance of a child's age at the time of parental divorce. *American Journal of Orthopsychiatry, 51,* 85–100.

Kinnaird, K. L., & Gerrard, M. (1986). Premarital sexual behavior and attitudes toward marriage and divorce among young women as a function of their mothers' marital status. *Journal of Marriage and the Family, 48,* 757–765.

Kirby, J. J. (1995). Single-parent families in poverty. *Human Development and Family Life Bulletin, 1,* 1–3.

Kliewer, W., & Sandler, I. N. (1993). Social competence and coping among children of divorce. *American Journal of Orthopsychiatry, 63,* 432–440.

Krantz, S. E., Clark, J., Pruyn, J. P., & Usher, M. (1985). Cognition and adjustment among children of separated or divorced parents. *Cognitive Therapy and Research, 9,* 61–77.

Kurdek, L. A. (1986). Children's reasoning about parental divorce. In R. D. Ashmore & D. M. Brodzinsky (Eds.), *Thinking about the family: Views of parents and children* (pp. 233–276). Hillsdale, NJ: Erlbaum.

Kurdek, L. A. (1987). Children's adjustment to parental divorce: An ecological perspective. In J. P. Vincent (Ed.), *Advances in family intervention, assessment and theory (Vol 4,* pp. 1–31). Greenwich, CT: JAI Press.

Kurdek, L. A., & Berg, B. (1983). Correlates of children's adjustment to their parent's divorces. In L. A. Kurdek (Ed.), *New directions in child development: Vol 19. Children and divorce* (pp. 47–60). San Francisco: Jossey-Bass.

Kurdek, L. A., & Berg, B. (1987). Children's beliefs about parental divorce scale: Psychometric characteristics and concurrent validity. *Journal of Consulting and Clinical Psychology, 55,* 712–718.

Kurdek, L. A., Blisk, D., & Siesky, A. E. (1981). Correlates of children's long-term adjustment to their parent's divorce. *Developmental Psychology, 17,* 565–579.

Lee, C. M., Picard, M., & Blain, M. D. (1994). Methodological and substantive review of intervention outcome studies for families undergoing divorce. *Journal of Family Psychology, 8,* 3–15.

Lustig, J. C., Wolchik, S. A., & Braver, S. L. (1992). Social support in chumships and adjustment in children of divorce. *American Journal of Community Psychology, 20,* 393–399.

Lyons-Roth, K., Alpern, L., & Repacholi, B. (1993). Disorganized infant attachment classification and maternal psychosocial problems as predictors of hostile–aggressive behavior in the preschool classroom. *Child Development, 64,* 572–585.

Mitchell, A. (1985). *Children in the middle: Living through divorce.* London: Tavistock.

Neal, J. H. (1983). Children's understanding of their parents' divorce. In L. A. Kurdek (Ed.), *Children and divorce* (pp. 3–14). San Francisco: Jossey-Bass.

Olson, S. L., & Banyard, V. (1993). Stop the world so I can get off for a while: Sources of daily stress in the lives of low income single mothers of young children. *Family Relations, 42,* 50–56.

Pedro-Carroll, J. L., Cowen, E. L. (1985). The children of divorce intervention program: An investigation of the efficacy of a school-based prevention program. *Journal of Consulting and Clinical Psychology, 53,* 603–611.

Roseby, V., Johnson, J., Erdberg, P., & Bardenstein, K. (1995, March). Developmental psychopathology in high-conflict divorcing families as reflected in Rorschach Test results. Paper presented at the biennial meeting of the Society for Research in Child Development, Indianapolis, IN.

Rutter, M. (1990). Psychosocial resilience and protective mechanisms. In J. Rolf, A. S. Masten, D. Cicchetti, K. H. Nuechterlein, & S. Weintraub (Eds.), *Risk and protective factors in the development of psychopathology* (pp. 181–214). Cambridge, England: Cambridge University Press.

Sandler, I. N., Tein, J., & West, S. G. (1944). Coping, stress and the psychological symptoms of children of divorce: A cross-sectional and longitudinal study. *Child Development, 65,* 1744–1763.

Seltzer, J. A. (1991). Relationships between fathers and children who live apart: The father's role after separation. *Journal of Marriage and the Family, 53,* 663–677.

Solomon, J., & George, C. (March, 1995). The development of attachment in separated and divorced families. Paper presented at the biennial meeting of the Society for Research in Child Development, Indianapolis, IN.

Sroufe, L. A. (1989). Relationships, self, and individual adaptation. In A. J. Sameroff & R. N. Emde (Eds.), *Relationship disorders in early childhood* (pp. 70–94). New York: Basic Books.

Sroufe, L. A. (1990). Considering normal and abnormal together: The essence of developmental psychopathology. *Development and Psychopathology, 2,* 335–347.

Stevenson, M. R., & Black, K. N. (1995). *How divorce affects offspring: A research approach.* Dubuque, IA: Brown & Benchmark.

Stolberg, A. L., Camplair, C., Currier, K., & Wells, M. J. (1987). Individual familial and environmental predictors of children's post-divorce adjustment and maladjustment. *Journal of Divorce, 11,* 51–70.

Stolberg, A. L., & Mahler, J. (1994). Enhancing treatment gains in a school-based intervention for children of divorce through skill training, parental involvement, and transfer procedures. *Journal of Consulting and Clinical Psychology, 62,* 147–156.

Walzak, Y., & Burns, S. (1984). *Divorce: The child's point of view.* London: Harper & Row.

Wallerstein, J. S. (1983). Children of divorce: Stress and developmental tasks. In N. Garmezy & M. Rutter, (Eds.), *Stress, Coping, and Development in Children.* New York: McGraw-Hill.

Wallerstein, J. S. (1991). The long-term effects of divorce on children: A review. *Journal of the American Academy of Child and Adolescent Psychiatry, 30,* 349–360.

Wallerstein, J. S., & Blakeslee, S. (1989). *Second chances: Men, women, and child a decade after divorce.* New York: Ticknor & Fields.

Wallerstein, J. S., & Kelley, J. B. (1980). *Surviving the breakup: How children actually cope with divorce.* New York: Basic Books.

Warshak, R. A., & Santrock, J. W. (1983). The impact of divorce in father-custody and mother-custody homes: The child's perspective. In L. A. Kurdek (Ed.), *Children and divorce* (pp. 29–46). San Francisco: Jossey-Bass.

Weitzman, L. J. (1985). *The divorce revolution.* New York: Free Press.

Wolchik, S. A., Ramirez, R., Sandler, I. N., Fisher, J. L., Organista, P. B., Brown, C. (1993). Inner-city, poor children of divorce: Negative divorce-related events, problematic beliefs, and adjustment problems. *Journal of Divorce and Remarriage, 19,* 1–20.

Wolchik, S. A., Ruelhman, L. S., Braver, S. L., & Sandler, I. N. (1989). Social support of children of divorce: Direct and stress buffering effects. *American Journal of Community Psychology, 17,* 485–501.

Wolchik, S. A., West, S. G., Westover, S., Sandler, I. N., Martin, A., Lustig, J., Tein, J., & Fisher, J. (1993). The children of divorce parenting intervention: Outcome evaluation of an empirically-based program. *American Journal of Community Psychology, 21,* 293–331.

Zaslow, M. J. (1988). Sex differences in children's response to parental divorce: 1. Research methodology and postdivorce family form. *American Journal of Orthopsychiatry, 58,* 355–378.

Zaslow, M. J. (1989). Sex differences in children's response to parental divorce: 2. Samples, variables, ages, and sources. *American Journal of Orthopsychiatry, 59,* 118–141.

Zill, N. (1978, February). *Divorce, marital happiness, and the mental health of children: Findings from the FCD national survey of children.* Paper presented at the National Institute of Mental Health Workshop on Divorce and Children, Bethesda, MD.

Zill, N., Morrison, D. R., & Coiro, M. J. (1993). Long-term effects of parental divorce on parent–child relationships, adjustment, and achievement in young adulthood. *Journal of Family Psychology, 7,* 91–103.

CHAPTER 21

CHILDREN OF STEPPARENTS AND BLENDED FAMILIES

Edward R. Anderson
Shannon M. Greene

Parental remarriage has become an increasingly common experience in the lives of children and poses a unique array of challenges to the resulting families. In contrast to parental divorce, which involves a reduction in numbers of residential family members within a typical atmosphere of conflict and animosity, remarriage brings an addition of at least one, and perhaps several new family members, occurring against a backdrop (for the marrying partners at least) of hope and happiness. Yet there is great diversity in how stepfamilies originate, the structural organizations they adopt, and the pattern and quality of relationships that develop across time. Moreover, remarried families have developed relational patterns long before the actual legal decree.

Support for this chapter was provided by NIMH Grants #5P30MH39246-14 to support a Preventive Intervention Research Center at Arizona State University and #2T32MH18387-011 for Postdoctoral Training in Prevention Research at Arizona State University. All correspondence should be sent to Edward R. Anderson, Ph.D., Program for Prevention Research, Community Services Building, Arizona State University, P.O. Box 871108, Tempe, AZ 85287-1108. Electronic mail: erander@imap2.asu.edu

The purpose of this chapter is to provide the reader with an overview of empirical findings for children in remarried families. Toward this purpose, prevalence rates for stepfamily formation are first presented. Research relating to children's adjustment is next addressed. The context of remarriage is also explored, with a particular focus on the structural complexity of stepfamilies, as well as the myriad ways in which they arise. Additionally, relationships within stepfamilies are covered, concluding with a critique of current interventions that target stepfamilies.

Recognizing that confusion often surrounds descriptors of various family forms, we first make our terminology explicit (see Ganong & Coleman, 1994, for an excellent discussion of this issue). We use the terms *remarried family* and *stepfamily* interchangeably in reference to a marital dyad containing a custodial parent with at least one residential child not borne from the current relationship. In this sense, our use of the term remarried family indicates a residential living arrangement for at least one child in relation to a stepparent. Also, we use the terms *intact* and *nuclear* interchangeably to indicate families containing two parents with at least one residential child from their union and no children from previous relationships.

THE PREVALENCE OF REMARRIAGE

Recent U.S. estimates indicate that among households containing a married couple with children, 19 percent comprise stepfamily arrangements (Glick, 1989). About 11 percent of all minor children currently reside in stepfamilies (Bumpass, 1984; Dawson, 1991; Glick, 1980, 1984), with the most typical situation involving a stepfather and biological mother (Dawson, 1991). Even children currently within intact families are, however, at substantial risk for *eventual* entry into a stepfamily. Glick and Lin (1986) note that among first-married couples, 40 percent will divorce and remarry before their youngest child reaches age 18. Moreover, because divorces among remarriers occur somewhat more frequently and rapidly than for first-married counterparts, one in ten children will experience *two* divorces of their custodial parent before the age of 16 (Furstenberg, 1988).

These numbers underestimate *actual* rates of familial transitions, however, because de facto stepfamily arrangements have been historically excluded from consideration. De facto arrangements involve a stepfigure who cohabits with the custodial parent and residential stepchildren. Such cohabitating arrangements are an increasingly common pathway toward eventual remarriage (Cherlin, 1992). Moreover, some children may experience a number of familial transitions around these transitory living arrangements, without necessarily ever experiencing a subsequent parental remarriage (Cherlin, 1992; Ganong & Coleman, 1994; Montgomery, Anderson, Hetherington, & Clingempeel, 1992).

Despite the prevalence of de facto family arrangements, the incidence and nature of these situations remains unknown. This information would seem of critical importance, given that for many stepfamilies, de facto arrangements provide the earliest context from which daily adjustment to a potential stepparent is required. Instead, existing literature has addressed adaptation in children once a parental remarriage occurs.

CHILDREN'S ADJUSTMENT
TO PARENTAL REMARRIAGE

There is now an extensive literature documenting differences in children's adjustment between remarried and intact households. Recently, we identified eighty-two studies that report such a comparison using quantitative measures of children's psychosocial adjustment (Anderson, Greene, Nelson, & Wolchik, 1998). In addition, two meta-analyses have been conducted (Amato & Keith, 1991; Ganong & Coleman, 1993) and a third is in preparation (Anderson et al., 1998). In this section, we summarize these findings and

discuss two important moderators of these differences: source of report and time since remarriage.

Are Children in Remarried Families Different from Children in Intact Families?

Many studies find that children in remarried families experience more problems than counterparts residing in intact situations. For example, children in stepfamilies have been found to manifest more problems with anxiety, social withdrawal, self-esteem, depression, and conduct (Bowerman & Irish, 1962; Dahl, McCubbin, & Lester, 1976; Hetherington, Cox, & Cox, 1985; Kellam, Ensminger, & Turner, 1977; Lindner, Stanley Hagan, & Brown, 1992). Children in stepfamilies are also at higher risk for emergence of deviant behaviors, greater susceptibility to peer pressure, substance use, and early sexual behavior (Dornbusch et al., 1985; Flewelling & Bauman, 1990; Kinnaird & Gerrard, 1986; Needle, Su, & Doherty, 1990; Steinberg, 1987). Additionally, children in stepfamilies score lower on measures of cognitive development and intelligence and are at greater risk for school problems such as being expelled or repeating a grade (Bray, 1988; Dawson, 1991; Santrock, 1972). They are also more likely to have received prior clinical treatment for previous emotional or behavioral problems (Dawson, 1991). Such differences have been found in reports of parents, children, and teachers; with observational data; and in large, nationally representative samples.

Despite the consistency with which differences in adjustment are obtained, not all authors agree on the magnitude of these differences. The quality of these studies vary widely (Ganong & Coleman, 1984), and many reviews take a cautious tone (Coleman & Ganong, 1990; Ganong & Coleman, 1984). In their 1984 review, for example, Ganong and Coleman concluded that "there is little reported evidence that children in stepfamilies differ significantly from children in other family structures" (p. 401). The two published meta-analyses (Amato & Keith, 1991; Ganong & Coleman, 1993) found modest effect sizes, although neither of these were a comprehensive evaluation. Nevertheless, there is consistency across studies in finding that children in stepfamilies score significantly lower than children in intact families on indices of conduct disorder, social relations and peer adjustment, depression and self-esteem, and school achievement. Despite these consistent, replicable differences in the mean level of adjustment between children in stepfamilies and children in intact families, the majority of children function well and are in the normal range of adaptation. Given the substantial overlap in distributions between children in remarried and intact homes, Amato (1994) concluded that "no matter how statistically significant and widely replicated are differences in central tendency, they are not a useful basis for making individual decisions" regarding whether to remarry (p. 85). In addition, there are at least two major factors that affect the size of the differences obtained: time since remarriage and source of report.

Do the Differences That Are Found Reflect Transitory Problems?

An obvious first question to ask is whether these differences result from a temporary period of disruption associated with adjusting to new living arrangements. Hetherington (1989, 1993), for example, notes that a difficult initial period eventually gives way to improved functioning for children in stepfamilies. When children in newly remarried families who had been living with a stepfather prior to remarriage were compared to those who had no such experience, those who had cohabited showed better adjustment (Montgomery et al., 1992). Clearly, some of the differences are a consequence of living in an unsettled situation. Unfortunately, for approximately one-quarter to one-third of stepchildren, adjustment problems fail to improve with time and, in some cases, even worsening (Hetherington & Jodl, 1994).

Capaldi and Patterson (1991) argue that adjustment problems are, in part, by-products of cumulative stresses from familial transitions. In fact, some studies do show an increase in children's maladjustment with an increasing number of family transitions (Capaldi & Patterson, 1991; Kurdek, Fine, & Sinclair, 1994; Miller, 1989), even if the transition involves the noncustodial parent (Herrera & Anderson, 1989). Not all studies, however, find that remarriage increases behavior problems beyond the effects associated with parental divorce (Amato & Keith, 1991; Dawson, 1991). Thus, it is unclear how much of the observed differences are due to the legacy of parental divorce, the cumulative stress experienced by multiple transitions, temporary disruptions in living arrangements, or unique factors associated with the remarriage. Prospective studies that examine children *prior to* the onset of remarriage are clearly needed to address this issue.

Do the Differences That Are Found Reflect a Bias in the Source of Report?

It is clear from studies that the size of the differences between children in remarried and intact families depends greatly upon whom is asked. Across studies, the largest differences are usually obtained in the reports of parents rather than in the reports of children or even teachers. Moreover, it tends to be the stepparents rather than the custodial parents who report the largest differences. In a multimethod study,

Lindner and colleagues (1992) found that whereas parents in remarried families reported higher levels of problem behaviors in their children than parents in intact families, no differences were found in the reports of teachers and the children themselves. Moreover, while stepfathers reported that both boys and girls experienced adjustment problems, mothers saw only boys as exhibiting high levels of psychopathology. It is difficult, of course, to know the direction of bias. One possibility is that stepfathers may be susceptible to an overreporting bias, given less parenting experiences. Children, however, may not be accurate reporters of their own behavior, and teachers may not have access to information about behavior in other contexts. Because the study by Lindner and colleagues (1992) included multiple methods, however, an intriguing resolution to this quandary emerged from assessments of the videotaped interactions within these families. These data showed children emitting higher levels of negative behaviors toward stepfathers, as compared to counterparts interacting with their biological fathers. Thus, stepfathers may have been reporting more negative behavior in their stepchildren because they had been *exposed* to more negative behavior *from* their stepchildren. Clearly, reports of children's adjustment may reflect in part the quality of the relationship as much as an assessment of the child's well-being. In a later section, we review research on the quality of relationships that develop within stepfamilies.

Are Some Groups of Children at Greater Risk Than Others?

It is clear that not all children are equally affected by parental remarriage, and that not all stepfamilies are alike. Three areas that have been investigated include gender of the child, age of the child, and the type of stepfamily arrangement.

Are Boys and Girls Equally Affected by Parental Remarriage?

A number of studies demonstrate that boys adjust better to remarriage than girls (Brand & Clingempeel, 1987; Brand, Clingempeel, & Bowen-Woodward, 1988; Clingempeel, Brand, & Ievoli, 1984; Clingempeel, Ievoli, & Brand, 1984; Hetherington, 1988; Peterson & Zill, 1986; Pink & Wampler, 1985). Amato and Keith's (1991) meta-analysis, which compared children in remarried families to children in divorced, single-mother families, revealed no differences for girls in adjustment, but an improvement in adjustment for boys following remarriage. The most frequently given explanation for this finding is that a stepfather's presence may disrupt the close mother-daughter bond forged during time spent in a single-parent household, and boys benefit from the presence of a male adult.

As before, however, not all studies show this pattern. Some studies report no gender differences or even *greater* problems for boys than girls (Bray, 1988; Lindner et al., 1992). As we suggested above, some of this inconsistency may result from the source of the report and the confounding of measures of child adjustment with relationship quality. Thus, the available evidence provides inconsistent support for beliefs that one gender enjoys an advantage over the other. We suspect that the nature of familial relationships unfolding within the family reveals more about gender differences than do indicators of overall adjustment.

Does Age of the Child Matter?

There is some evidence that certain age groups may be more susceptible to problems in adjustment. Although far from conclusive, preadolescents and early adolescents appear to experience elevated risk for adjustment difficulties (Bray & Berger, 1993; Hetherington & Anderson, 1987; Wallerstein & Kelly, 1980). Moreover, children of these ages are also at long-term risk for minimal improvements in adjustment (Hetherington, 1993; Lindner et al., 1992).

Relative to other ages, these groups may have more adjustment problems because of the unique developmental tasks they face. These include efforts to gain autonomy, changes in familial expressions of affection, and desires for extrafamilial relationships. These tasks are at odds with goals of many newly forming stepfamilies, such as attempts to increase interdependence and build intrafamilial relationships.

This mismatch between individual and familial goals may be especially salient, given that children in divorced homes typically assume greater responsibility and autonomy at earlier ages (Anderson, Hetherington, & Clingempeel, 1989; Hetherington & Anderson, 1987). Weiss (1979) aptly terms this accelerated developmental phenomena "growing up faster." In fact, "faster" development may explain why children in stepfamilies leave home earlier than counterparts in other family structures (Goldscheider & Goldscheider, 1989; Wiser & Burch, 1989). Early adolescents are at risk of premature disengagement or distancing from their stepfamilies, which again may reflect greater levels of autonomy within these family structures (Hetherington, 1989, 1993; Stanley Hagan, Hollier, O'Connor, & Eisenberg, 1992). However, if this distancing involves alignment with prosocial peer groups, early disengagement may provide a useful strategy for attaining satisfactory adjustment and avoiding conflictual family relationships (Anderson et al., 1989; Hetherington & Anderson, 1987).

In contrast, late adolescents may experience fewer adjustment problems because social and emotional ties outside the family make the entrance of a stepparent less intrusive (Hetherington & Anderson, 1987; Hetherington, Camara, & Featherman, 1983). Additionally, younger children show more adaptation over time (Bray 1987; Hetherington, 1988, 1989, 1993), perhaps because remarriages occurring prior to adolescence demonstrate greater improvements in parenting (Hetherington & Jodl, 1994).

Regardless of age at transition, though, the onset of adolescence does create renewed conflict within remarried households (Hetherington, 1993; Wallerstein, Corbin, & Lewis, 1988). To some degree, these increases in conflict reflect normative developmental processes that occur even in intact family settings, because roles and relationships are renegotiated (Hill, Holmbeck, Marlow, Green, & Lynch, 1985a, 1985b). However, conflict within stepfamily settings may be confounded with continued demands of adjustment to a stepfamily situation (Anderson et al., 1989). Attributions for the cause of such conflicts may also differ by family type. Remarried parents are more likely than intact counterparts to blame difficulties with children on stepfamily life (Pasley, Dollahite, & Ihinger-Tallman, 1993). Thus, normative developmental issues such as parent–adolescent conflict may be mistakenly attributed to problems with adjustment to stepfamily arrangements.

Does the Type of Stepfamily Matter?

Only a few studies have examined the adjustment of children residing in different types of stepfamilies. Most of these show few differences in overall measures of children's adjustment between stepmother and stepfather households (Brand et al., 1988; Clingempeel & Segal, 1986; Coleman & Ganong, 1990; Fine, Kurdek, & Henningen, 1992; Fine, Voydanoff, & Donnelly, 1994), although there is some evidence that children living with stepfathers have better psychosocial adjustment than children living with stepmothers (Fine & Kurdek, 1992). The complexity of the family— whether half-siblings or stepsiblings are also present—is also associated with few differences in children's overall adjustment (Fine & Kurdek, 1992; Fine et al., 1994; Kurdek & Fine, 1993). More work is needed, however, before definitive conclusions can be drawn.

Summary of Findings for Children's Adjustment

In sum, a variety of outcome indicators provide evidence that children in stepfamily arrangements fare worse than counterparts in intact households. The extent of these differences depends markedly upon who is being asked to rate the child. Even when accounting for the source of assessments, though, differences are consistent enough to conclude that children in stepfamilies are at an elevated risk for maladaptive responses. Although many differences are transitory, approximately one-quarter to one-third are at risk for persistent or worsening problems (Hetherington & Jodl, 1994). Despite these differences in mean level, however, there is a great deal of variation in children's responses. Differences are moderated by gender, with some evidence indicating that boys in stepfamilies make gains relative to counterparts in divorced households. These gender differences may reflect the quality of the familial relationships that subsequently form rather than adjustment per se. Transitions into stepfamily arrangements prove most difficult for preadolescents and early adolescents, perhaps because of developmental tasks that conflict with goals of early stepfamily formation. An inability to resolve these problems may explain why only minimal improvements in adjustment are noted over time for this age group. Finally, because the study of stepfamilies is a relatively recent phenomena, little is known about how various types of stepfamilies may differ. The chapter turns next to considering the context of remarriage, including its structural complexity, pathways to remarriage, and types of relationships that form.

THE CONTEXT OF REMARRIAGE

In this next section, we discuss the complexity of stepfamily arrangements, the pathways by which stepfamilies form, and the relationships that develop within stepfamilies.

Structural Complexity

A critical aspect of remarried families involves their structural complexity. There are myriad new relationships that can develop with remarriage, and the nature of these relationships is often ambiguous. This ambiguity can be appreciated when considering the level of familial disagreement generated over a seemingly simple question, Who is in your immediate family? Furstenberg (1987), for example, notes that 15 percent of stepparents excluded their spouse's residential children from their list. For children, 31 percent excluded their residential stepparent and 41 percent excluded stepsiblings from their lists of immediate family members. Interestingly, Furstenberg finds that these exclusions were unrelated to the length of time spent living in a stepfamily.

Structural complexity within stepfamilies is demonstrated by the unique array of members they may contain. Clingempeel, Brand, and Segal (1987) identified nine different types of stepfamilies, depending on whether the

step-parent was residential, relative to the child under consideration. Others define typologies by whether the current marital union produces children (Pasley & Ihinger-Tallman, 1982) or by where children reside (see Ganong & Coleman, 1984). Because residence can vary substantially, the potential complexity of households can increase dramatically. For example, common custody arrangements allow extended visitation over holidays or summer vacations. Thus, children may temporarily join or leave an existing household. Similarly, children from the noncustodial parent's union may be moving in and out of that related household as well. Moreover, such living arrangements often change as children develop (Hetherington & Hagan, 1986).

For a visual grasp of this complexity, consider Figure 21.1, which represents the potential web of relationships within stepfamily life. Solid lines in the figure represent biological relationships; dotted lines represent relationships with half-siblings. The focus of this discussion is from the point of view of the child, shown by a circle in the "residential household." Thus, the child has a biological mother, biological siblings, and a stepfather. The child's mother and stepfather produce mutual children, and the stepfather has custody of children from a previous marriage. If we consider nonresidential arrangements, a number of possible relationships emerge: a residential biological mother and a nonresidential biological father; a residential stepfather and a nonresidential stepmother; and, an opportunity for five different types of siblings: full residential biological siblings—offspring of the previous marriage who are currently residential; residential half-siblings—the offspring of the current (re)marriage; residential stepsiblings—the offspring of the stepfather's previous marriage; nonresidential half-siblings—the offspring of the biological father's new marriage; and nonresidential stepsiblings—the offspring of the nonresidential stepmother, who become residential siblings to the child during extended visitation within that household.

In addition, there are extended family members, shown above the households, who may play important roles. Children may have two sets of living biological grandparents, and three types of stepgrandparents: the residential stepfather's parents who are the biological grandparents of the stepfather's children from the previous marriage and any half-siblings in the current marriage; the nonresidential stepmother's parents who may be involved because of new offspring in the biological father's household; and, the residential stepfather's ex-spouse's parents who may continue involvement with their biological grandchildren now residing with the target child.

Stepfamilies with this level of complexity are rare in the population. Cherlin and McCarthy (1985) report that only 6 percent of remarried couples under age 40 in 1980 had three

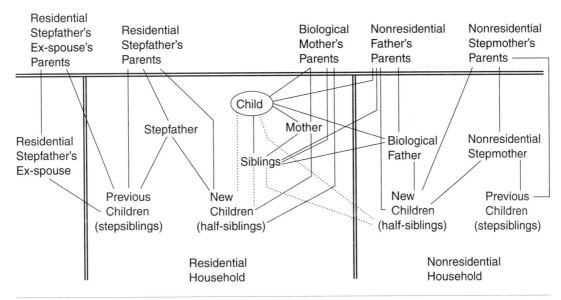

FIGURE 21.1 Potential complexity in stepfamilies. Solid lines represent biological relationships; dashed lines indicate sibling relationships less than full biological relatives.

sets of children. Nevertheless, it seems likely that most step-families will *eventually* contain more members than the most common pattern of stepfather, custodial mother, and one or more full siblings. Bumpass (1984) found that acquisition of a half-sibling occurred for one-third of those children entering a stepfamily within 4 years; two-thirds of children eventually have either a half-sibling or a stepsibling.

Some have hypothesized that more complex families have greater difficulty relative to simpler stepfamily arrangements. According to Cherlin (1978), for example, because societal norms are lacking for stepfamilies, there are more opportunities for disagreement and conflict among stepfamily members than among intact families. Thus, more complex types of stepfamilies, with presumably fewer societal guidelines to structure their interactions, should evidence greater difficulty. Empirical confirmation of this notion is, however, inconsistent. In support, Clingempeel and Brand (1985) found that marital partners in complex stepfamilies exhibited lower rates of positive nonverbal behaviors compared to simple stepmother families. Similarly, Clingempeel (1981) found that complex stepfamilies experienced greater difficulties. Yet others note no differences across stepfamily complexity (MacDonald & DeMaris, 1995). This issue of complexity within existing stepfamily relationships will be revisited in greater detail later in the chapter. First though, a discussion of how stepfamilies form is warranted.

Pathways to Remarriage

Before the Great Depression, remarriage was more likely to arise with bereaved rather than divorced individuals (Cherlin, 1992). Since then, divorce has become the most typical pathway to remarriage. Researchers have primarily focused on studying the most common family form: the remarriage of a single-parent, mother-custody divorcee. This research reveals a great deal of diversity in patterns of repartnering among divorcees. Montgomery and colleagues (1992) found, for example, that one-third of these divorcees began dating their future husbands within a year after separating, while a wait of 5 years or more characterized the dating patterns of another fifth of the sample.

Although dating patterns differ, cohabitation in de facto family arrangements has become an increasingly common vehicle toward eventual remarriage for these divorcees. Montgomery and colleagues (1992), for example, found that 17 percent of custodial mothers had begun to reside with their future spouse within a year after separating from their previous husbands. Longer delays were about as common, with 19 percent of custodial mothers beginning cohabitation at least 7 years after the original separation.

These pre-remarital repartnering patterns have important implications for future research. Bumpass and Sweet (1989) believe that rather than the date of the actual legal decree, cohabitation may comprise a more salient starting point for the study of stepfamily formation, given that it comprises the initial establishment of a joint household. The study of these living arrangements is also warranted given the theoretical belief that familial responses to the remarriage have been shaped by previous experiences with potential partners (Hetherington, 1993; Hetherington & Jodl, 1994; Hetherington, Stanley Hagan, & Anderson, 1989).

In support of this belief, Montgomery and colleagues (1992) compared family relationships among three groups: remarried families who had previously cohabited, remarried families who had never cohabited, and intact families. As compared to noncohabiting stepfamilies, cohabiting stepfamilies had lower levels of negativity for mother–child and stepfather–child relationships during the first 2 years following remarriage (length of time since remarriage was equivalent). Moreover, parent–child relationships in remarried families of prior cohabitators were similar to intact counterparts, a finding that held up across all waves of the longitudinal study.

In contrast, among noncohabitators, conflict and negativity in parent–child relationships rose in the year after the remarriage, with some declines thereafter. These findings, taken together, support the claim by Bumpass and Sweet (1989) that cohabitation is the more salient beginning for a remarried household. What remains unknown is whether cohabiting remarriers experienced more conflictual adult–child relationships earlier during the formation of the joint household.

Further support for the notion that cohabitation is the more salient marker of remarriage comes from Forgatch, Patterson, and Ray (1996), who found that externalizing behavior in sons increased among families in which mothers had begun cohabiting, compared to those who had remained single. The custodial mothers, themselves, however, reported much lower levels of stress after this pre-remarital repartnering. These authors also found evidence that effective problem-solving skill between custodial mothers and their sons prevented some adjustment problems from developing during the repartnering process.

Some authors have argued that less rapid family change should lead to greater stability (e.g., Rodgers & Conrad, 1986). Thus, the most successful remarried families should form gradually, over a longer period of time. This hypothesis has not received support, as Montgomery and colleagues (1992) noted more problem behavior in children in stepfamilies who had spent longer durations in a single-parent household. These authors offered several explanations for this contradictory finding. Single-parent families may face greater economic stress, which places additional burdens on the household. Alternately, longer periods of time in a divorced household may allow for greater stability in roles and routines, making it difficult for a new member to join. Or perhaps children with high levels of problem behavior interfere with the process of repartnering, resulting in delays to eventual remarriage. The final explanation has received recent support from the study of Forgatch and coworkers (1996).

In sum, stepfamily relationships begin to form long before the remarriage ceremony. Cohabitors may have faced difficulties in family relationships when the joint household was formed, and this event may be the more relevant marker for stepfamily formation. Little is known about this process, however, and no research to date has examined the impact of temporary dating or cohabiting relationship formations and dissolutions that may have occurred before remarriage. These likely will affect the quality of future relationships that develop with other partners. Other pathways to remarriage remain unexplored as well, such as those involving never-married parents, custodial fathers, or bereaved parents.

Relationships in Stepfamilies

Most research examining the quality of relationships that develop within stepfamilies has focused on the most common type of stepfamily: custodial mothers with children from a previous marriage and a stepfather. Less is known about relationships with stepmothers, noncustodial fathers, extended and quasi-kin, and stepsiblings. We first review literature on relationships between parents and their children, and then discuss research dealing with marital relationships, sibling relationships, and relationships with quasi-kin. When differences occur between stepfamilies and intact families, it is often tempting to depict such differences as reflecting a deficit in remarried family relationships. At this stage in the research on stepfamilies, such a depiction is premature and clearly not warranted. We are only beginning to examine the patterns of relationships that form in stepfamilies that are associated with positive outcomes for children. It is simply too early to tell which patterns of relationships are maladaptive. Given that societal norms surrounding steprelationships are ambiguous at best, different models of successful steprelationships have yet to be developed.

Parent–Child Relationships

There are clear differences between biological parent–child relationships and steprelationships. Perhaps not surprisingly, a common finding is that relationships between children and their stepparents are more disengaged than between children and their biological parents. Further, there are clear differences between residential and nonresidential relationships. Different tasks are required in negotiating day-to-day struggles *within* a household than in managing tensions and standards *between* households. Finally, from the limited longitudinal information available, parent–child relationships change over time as roles and routines become established.

Children's relationships with biological mothers. After temporary disruptions in parenting and associated increases in conflict and negativity, eventual improvements are noted in the quality of relationships between children and their remarried mothers (Bray, 1987, 1988; Bray, Berger, Silverblatt, & Hollier, 1987; Hetherington, 1988, 1989; Pink & Wampler, 1985; Stanley Hagan, et al., 1992). Remarried mothers experience improved moods, because stepfathers often provide financial and emotional support, and children typically view this enhanced maternal mood as a positive event (Hetherington, Cox, & Cox, 1982).

There is evidence that improvements in parenting occur more readily when remarriages take place prior to adolescence (Hetherington & Jodl, 1994). Stanley Hagan and colleagues (1992), for example, in a study of preadolescent and early adolescent children, reported that in the first months after remarriage, mother–child relationships were characterized by higher rates of negativity and less effective monitoring than those in nuclear families. One year after remarriage much of the negative interchanges had subsided. Even so, some parenting problems persisted for remarried mothers, as evidenced by lower scores for efforts to monitor and control children. Thus, for children entering adolescence when remarriage occurs, issues related to parental control may be more difficult to manage.

Children's relationships with stepfathers. In contrast to mother–child relationships, a different scenario arises for stepfathers. Stanley Hagan and colleagues (1992) characterized the behavior of the residential stepfather, in the first months after remarriage, as that of a "polite stranger" (p. 130). In that study, stepfathers demonstrated limited awareness of, and few efforts to control, their stepchildren's behavior, particularly for male offspring. Yet the affective quality of the relationship was relatively benign, with little evidence that stepfathers were anything more or less than "polite."

Over time, the nature of this relationship changed. Stepfathers become even less effective at controlling and monitoring the behaviors of stepchildren, and the affective quality of these relationships evidenced greater distance and disengagement. Although a similar pattern characterized biological fathers within intact households, so that to some

degree these changes reflected developmental aspects of parenting adolescents, stepfathers were almost twice as likely to use this pattern. Thus, increasing disengagement seemed to be a particularly apt description for many of the stepfather–stepchild relationships.

Santrock and coworkers (1982) reported that the most negative parent–child relationships involved stepdaughters in relation to stepfathers. Clingempeel and colleagues (1984), however, reported that in a sample of 9 to 12 year olds relationships with stepdaughters were more problematic than relationships with stepsons regardless of the gender of the stepparent.

Stepfathers with their own biological children in residence assume a more active role in parenting (Ganong & Coleman, 1994), perhaps because of a greater sense of responsibility for these offspring (Palisi, Orleans, Caddell, & Korn, 1991). Moreover, these experienced stepfathers may use a more successful strategy of gradual engagement with the custodial parent's residential children. Evidence from two studies by Hetherington (1993; Hetherington et al., 1982) indicate that stepfathers able to generate the most acceptance in stepchildren had focused on first developing warm, involved, and communicative parent–child relationships. These successful stepfathers had also initially served in a supportive capacity toward the custodial mother's disciplinarian role.

The type of parenting style stepparents adopt has long-term implications. An authoritative parenting style is characterized by affection and involvement, along with establishing and consistently enforcing household rules, and effective monitoring of children's behaviors. Two years after the remarriage, stepfathers who had been able to adopt a more authoritative parenting style had stepchildren who evidenced better outcomes, particularly for boys (Hetherington, 1987). This finding has also been supported by Santrock, Warshak, Lindbergh, and Meadows (1982), and is consistent with strategies often recommended in the clinical literature (Papernow, 1993; Visher & Visher, 1988). Similarly, Anderson, Lindner, and Bennion (1992) found that authoritative parenting consistently related to better adjustment in children regardless of family type. The beneficial effects of authoritative parenting have been noted extensively elsewhere (Steinberg, 1990) and, in fact, show consistent benefits across a wide range of subgroups (Steinberg, Mounts, Lamborn, & Dornbusch, 1991). Thus, stepfathers who were able to establish close, supportive relationships, and later to develop an appropriate authoritative role, rather than increasing disengagement, had stepchildren who evidenced better adjustment.

Before extending a specific recommendation to stepfathers, though, we must be cautious about the direction of effects. Relationships in stepfamilies do not exist in a vacuum, and children are active contributors to the nature of the relationship. Children, particularly adolescents, often give only limited acceptance to stepparents (Hetherington, et al., 1982; Stanley Hagan et al., 1992). This limited acceptance is evidenced by higher levels of negativity toward stepfathers, relative to counterparts with biological fathers (Stanley Hagan et al., 1992). Importantly, in one longitudinal study, the extent to which stepfathers followed the pattern of increasing disengagement was predicted by the earlier behavior of their stepchildren (Anderson et al., 1992). Maccoby (1992) concluded from these results:

> We see vividly in the remarried families that the ability of a parent to function effectively in the parental role with children who have reached adolescence depends on the readiness of the adolescent to take up the reciprocal role—the role of a younger person who accepts authority and trusts the older person to be supportive of the adolescent's interests. (p. 236)

Thus, disengagement on the part of residential stepfathers and custodial mothers may be a form of surrender—giving up parental efforts to monitor and control children because of previous ineffectiveness. This lack of acceptance for parental authority may in part be traced to the legacy of an earlier divorce process. Stanley Hagan and colleagues (1992) found that children in divorced families were less willing than intact counterparts to accept maternal authority, even though mothers were using an authoritative parenting style and were generally warm and supportive. Unfortunately, children's behavior within these single-parent households failed to improve over time. Perhaps effects of witnessing the noncustodial father's anger and contempt toward the mother subsequently undermined maternal authority within the divorced household; maternal authority may continue to be undermined even within a stepfamily setting if conflict between households continues.

Children's relationships with stepmothers. A number of studies find that in contrast to stepfathers, stepmothers have more problematic relationships with residential children (Brand et al., 1988; Clingempeel & Segal, 1986; Hobart, 1987; Kurdek & Fine, 1993; Zill, 1988). In particular, stepmother–stepdaughter relationships appear more problematic (Brand et al., 1988). Some of this negativity may derive from girls displaying more negative and less positive behavior to stepmothers rather than as a consequence of the stepmothers' behavior (Clingempeel et al., 1984). There is evidence, though, that these relationships improve over time (Clingempeel & Segal, 1986).

Greater stress in stepmother families may stem from more frequent contact between children and their biological mothers, regardless of where offspring reside (Clingempeel & Segal, 1986; Furstenberg & Nord, 1985). Noncustodial mothers are generally more involved with their children than noncustodial fathers (Cherlin, 1992; Hetherington, 1993), so more disruption may occur in stepmother households as appropriate rules and level of involvement are negotiated among more sets of parents. Hobart (1987) finds that this differential level of involvement between noncustodial mothers and fathers also reflects greater loyalty on the part of children toward their biological mothers, regardless of living arrangements.

Children's relationships with nonresidential parents. Bray and Depner (1993) found that nonresidential parents continue to play a role in family life after a custodial parent's remarriage. Over time, though, declines in involvement are noted, with less frequent contact, shorter visits, and fewer child support payments resulting (Buehler & Ryan, 1994).

A relevant concern is whether continued involvement helps children adjust to stepfamily arrangements. Bray and Berger (1990) found positive effects of continued involvement, dependent on the child's gender and time of assessment subsequent to the remarriage, with improvements noted for boys at 6 months, and girls at 2.5 years. Hetherington (1989) found that the nature of the postmarital relationship also influences adjustment; continued involvement with the noncustodial father was associated with improved adjustment only when the postmarital relationship was relatively nonconflictual, with low levels of negativity and hostility.

Marital Relationships

Relationship quality among remarriers is comparable to levels noted for first marriages (Anderson & White, 1986; Pink & Wampler, 1985). Bray (1988), however, reveals important differences. Newly remarried couples demonstrate more coercion, along with less expressed positivity and poorer communication skills than longer married, nondivorced couples. These patterns may arise over time, given that some note an initial honeymoon period involving higher levels of relationship satisfaction and less negative interchanges (Deal, Stanley Hagan & Anderson, 1992; Hetherington, 1988).

Remarriers also report less success with conflict resolution, although overall frequencies of perceived conflict were indistinguishable from first marrieds (Larson & Allgood, 1987). The content of these conflicts does distinguish groups, with nondivorced dyads more likely to report problems arising from household tasks, as compared to remarried couples experiencing trouble with children (Hobart, 1990, 1991). Moreover, simply the presence of children elevates risk for eventual marital dissolution within remarried dyads (Ganong & Coleman, 1989). Some authors suggest, therefore, that stepfathers can work to ensure positive marital functioning through improving their relationships with the spouses' children (Hetherington, 1989; Hobart, 1987). In addition to strengthening the marital dyad, this strategy is also thought to prevent negative reactions in children (Brand & Clingempeel, 1987). Although some authors note that the presence of a positive remarried relationship can generate negative reactions in children (Brand et al., 1988; Bray, 1987, 1988; Hetherington, 1988, 1989), others find that negativity within marriages correlates with observed measures of negativity by children toward mothers and residential stepfathers (Anderson et al., 1992). A study by Hanson, McLanahan, and Thomson (1996), though, suggests that differences in levels of marital conflict between stepfamily and intact households does not by itself account for differences in children's adjustment.

Sibling Relationships

In contrast to data on parent–child relationships, few studies have included assessments of sibling relationships. The available evidence indicates that these relationships are more accurately characterized by rivalry, disengagement, and hostility, than by positive, mutually supportive behaviors (Anderson & Rice, 1992; Hetherington, 1988, 1989; White & Reidman, 1992). When supportive behaviors do arise, girls are more likely than boys to extend offers (Hetherington, 1988; Wallerstein et al., 1988). Even when boys offer support, sisters, more often than brothers, are the targets of these gestures (Anderson & Rice, 1992). Thus, female siblings initiate and receive more support than male counterparts.

In a longitudinal study (Anderson et al., 1992), the presence of negative sibling relationships predicted later levels of externalizing behavior in children—the only significant longitudinal predictor of children's adjustment in remarried families (Anderson et al., 1992). Though generally overlooked, the sibling relationship holds great potential as a target for treatment interventions with stepfamilies.

Interestingly, the arrival of "mutual" children (i.e., offspring born from the current remarriage (Ganong & Coleman, 1988, 1994) generates a mixed response from family members. Not surprisingly, the new parents generally perceive more benefits (Ganong & Coleman, 1988). Effects to existing residential children are less clear, with some evidence that the arrival of a half-sibling negatively affects stepmother–stepchild relationships (Santrock & Sitterle, 1987). Others find no such relationship, however (Ganong & Coleman, 1988). These conflicting findings need to be resolved through studies that address structural relationship characteristics (e.g., gender combinations, age distributions).

More recent analyses (Anderson, 1998) support the findings that although conflict and rivalry are ubiquitous features of sibling relationships in all family types, higher levels of support are noted among full biological siblings in intact families, rather than among biological or half-siblings in remarried families. Interestingly, though, the least negative relationships were found in stepfamilies between unrelated siblings. These stepsiblings were more likely to characterize their relationships as friendly and amicable, with less hostility, but often more distance as compared to other sibling arrangements. One explanation for this difference is that competition arises less often within these families, given that each sibling has access to a residential biological parent for attention and affection. An animal model provides an interesting alternative explanation for these findings: Littermates who experienced stress together were subsequently more aggressive toward one another than when exposed to unfamiliar animals (Berkowitz, 1983). Thus, unrelated stepsiblings may be less reactive to each other because of having been spared a shared history of exposure to the conflictual process of their respective parent's divorces. Note too that although the Anderson (1998) sample comprised long-term stepfamily arrangements, similar results have emerged for more recently formed families (Ganong & Coleman, 1994; White & Reidman, 1992).

From these limited studies, sibling relationship quality has emerged as a key predictor of long-term adjustment to remarriage, with less support and more negativity found among biologically related siblings in remarried families, as compared to intact sibling counterparts. More recent analysis, though, indicates that among *unrelated* siblings in stepfamilies, friendly relationships were more common (26–30%) than in intact families (17–25%). Unrelated stepsiblings, though, were also most frequently characterized as detached or indifferent—between 43 and 50 percent of stepsibling relationships. Perhaps these distant stepsiblings have formed workable "satellite" parent–child subsystems within the larger household (Ihinger-Tallman, 1987). Given the intriguing findings thus far, sibling relationships clearly warrant further study toward a better understanding of family process in remarried families.

Relationships with Grandparents and Quasi-Kin

As noted earlier, the presence of grandparents increases the structural complexity of stepfamilies; these relatives are considered quasi-kin in relation to their child's former spouse (Bohannon, 1970). At postdivorce, the role grandparents assume in relation to grandchildren largely depends on whether their own child has custody (Johnson, 1988), with maternal grandparents having an advantage, given current arrangements that favor mothers. Thus, maternal grandparents generally demonstrate consistency in contact with grandchildren following their daughter's divorce, and even after her eventual remarriage (Clingempeel, Colyar, Brand, & Hetherington, 1992). Cherlin and Furstenberg (1986) report similar findings, noting also that financial assistance from grandparents decreases after their child's remarriage.

Following a parental remarriage, children potentially gain a new set of grandparents from the stepparent's family. Cherlin and Furstenberg (1986) report that older children were less likely to regard these stepgrandparents with the same level of importance as biologically related grandparents. Yet others find that younger children demonstrate a desire for involvement with stepgrandparents (Sanders & Trygstad, 1989). Desires for contact may, therefore, demonstrate a developmental aspect that favors involvement between younger children and grandparents. Another source of influence may be whether opportunities for contact with biologically related grandparents and grandchildren are possible.

Summary of Family Relationships

Longitudinal studies of stepfamily formation indicate that relationships become more conflictual and tense following a parental remarriage. Over time, these relationships typically stabilize, although stepfathers and children entering early adolescence continue to experience difficulties. General consensus holds that successful integration of stepfathers depends on whether they can slowly engage with children in a friendly manner, while providing initial support to the custodial mother's disciplinarian role. A common pathway for stepfathers, though, is one of increasing disengagment, rather than adopting an authoritative role. It is important to remember that children influence the process by which a stepfather or other adult can successfully assume a parenting role. The legacy of the prior divorce process, along with any continuing animosity between former spouses, also influences how stepparent–stepchild relationships develop. Moreover, other family relationships, such as those between (step)siblings, strongly influence children's eventual adjustment to remarriage, findings that underscore this area as a potentially important source of support. Relationships between children and nonresidential relatives (e.g., noncustodial parents, [step]grandparents) have been largely overlooked, but likely influence how stepfamilies negotiate the transition to remarriage.

CLINICAL IMPLICATIONS

As mentioned earlier, measures of central tendency such as group averages indicate that children in stepfamilies typically fare worse than intact counterparts, particularly on conduct–behavioral problems and psychological adjustment. Amato (1994) points out that measures of dispersion show substantial overlap in distributions, revealing a different picture of stepfamily functioning: a sizable proportion of these families produce offspring who outperform the average adjustment scores of intact counterparts. Unfortunately, clinical literature largely reflects a central tendency perspective, perhaps because therapists are more likely to encounter poorly functioning over well-functioning remarried families. This central tendency perspective is evident in several clinical ideas, including the idea that stepfamilies inherently involve negative experiences, the notion of optimal pathways to remarriage, and the belief that legal remarriage brings about new adaptations.

Stepfamilies, for example, are viewed as having been born of grief, separation, and loss (Visher & Visher, 1978; 1988) because the earlier marital breakup removed opportunities, dreams, relationships, and experiences (Ganong & Coleman, 1994). Such a view casts stepfamilies in a largely negative light, also dictating that adaptation to the new family situation depends upon having achieved adequate mourning of prior family situations (Coale Lewis, 1985; Sager et al., 1983; Visher & Visher, 1982, 1988, 1991). Similarly, a self-help program for stepfamilies outlines "dealing with losses and changes" as the first task they must resolve (Burt, 1989). Papernow (1984, 1987) elaborates on this idea, proposing that efforts to ease the pain of prior losses lead members to adopt unrealistic expectations, fantasies, and wishes. Martin and Martin (1992) even provide a timeline for the mourning process (1 to 5 years after the divorce), along with specific stages as outlined by Kubler-Ross (1969): denial, depression, anger, bargaining, and acceptance.

Fortunately for stepfamilies, this clinical lore is largely unsupported by empirical data. Although it is true that children experience more adjustment problems immediately after the marital dissolution, evidence suggests that such problems predate the alleged period of mourning, arising during the duration of the distressed marriage, long before the divorce occurs (Block, Block, & Gjerde, 1986; Chase-Lansdale, Cherlin, & Kiernan, 1995), and thus most likely is a consequence of marital conflict (Amato & Keith, 1991; Emery, 1982). Moreover, many children acknowledge that parental divorce brings forth positive events, such as reduced exposure to marital conflict (Felner, Terre, & Robinson, 1988; Sandler, Wolchik, Braver, & Fogas, 1991). Existing evidence does indicate that child maladjustment may persist after the divorce, not because of unresolved loss per se, but due to negative postmarital conflict, disruptions in parenting, and changes in financial status (Amato & Keith, 1991; Hetherington, 1988, 1993; Hetherington et al., 1985). Many adjustment problems return to baseline within 2 years of the divorce, because the residential parent resumes an effective parenting role (Hetherington, 1987, 1989, 1993; Hetherington & Jodl, 1994).

Another clinical idea concerns issues of timing, that is, when to introduce potential partners and children. Clinicians often warn prospective remarriage partners against introducing children to partners except during later stages of the courtship process (e.g., Walker & Messinger, 1979). Retrospective accounts do indicate that stepfathers assume an increasingly active role in the activities of the child as the relationship progresses toward remarriage (Montgomery et al., 1992), although little is known about the context of this involvement. Many relationships between future stepparents and children arise without a delayed or formal beginning. Because Montgomery and colleagues (1992) only investigated situations resulting in remarriage, little is known about dating relationships that end prematurely or how such relationships affect children's adjustment. Some eventual remarriers may break up and reconcile several times, while other custodial parents may date several partners seriously before remarriage. Thus, it seems that many varied routes lead to remarriage. No empirically based answer yet exists that outlines a preferable or optimal pathway to enhance children's adjustment. Interestingly, the sole study on this topic would suggest little effects for the strategy chosen (Montgomery et al., 1992).

Another clinical idea concerns the belief that stepfamilies face challenges upon the actual event of the remarriage. These challenges arise because these families come with a "fully formed" structure (Ganong & Coleman (1994), but lack interaction patterns or a shared group identity (Ahrons & Perlmutter, 1982; Goldner, 1982; Pill, 1990). Further, until family rules and rituals emerge, stepfamilies are thought to feel somewhat artificial or unnatural (Imber-Black & Roberts, 1993; Whiteside, 1988). Stepfamilies may well face challenges around formational issues, but a shared identity, family rules, and even rituals would seem likely to emerge before the actual legal decree during day-to-day contact between potential stepparents and stepchildren. McGoldrick and Carter (1989) acknowledge the importance of this preremarriage period for stepfamily formation, but set up the accomplishment of specific prerequisite attitudes and developmental issues that must be resolved within a specific sequence of stages. Given a lack of data about normative processes within successful stepfamilies (Ihinger-Tallman & Pasley, 1994), specification of stages would seem premature. Moreover, existing data suggest that a common sequence of developmental patterns within stepfamilies is unlikely. Long-term adjustment seems to have less to do with timing of events or particular sequences of stages than the nature of

the relationships that develop within these newly forming families.

Perhaps more important than the search for a single preferable pathway is the actual time spent in preparing for remarriage. Ganong and Coleman (1994) report little active preparation on the part of remarried persons, such as seeking counseling, support, or education. Some (Sager et al., 1983; Visher & Visher, 1988) view the potential problems confronting stepfamilies as preventable through education. To date, we are unaware of any formal evaluations of educational intervention programs for remarriage preparation, though this would seem to be a fruitful avenue for prevention efforts.

SUMMARY AND CONCLUSIONS

In conclusion, we have tried to communicate strongly the idea that stepfamilies are not inherently negative and that there are large individual differences in how children react to their parent's remarriage and in the relationships that develop within these families. There is little evidence regarding optimal pathways for successful development and adaptation and, in our view, any such recommendations would be premature. We can, however, identify some points of commonality across research on stepfamilies.

Mean levels of children's psychosocial adjustment are lower for children in stepfamilies compared to intact families. Although the magnitude of effects across all studies is not yet known, the differences are clearly consistent and large enough to warrant further investigation into the processes that give rise to these differences. That having been said, the majority of children in stepfamilies still function in the normal range of adaptation, and many may benefit from the special strengths and resources that stepfamilies can provide.

Relationships in stepfamilies form long before the event of remarriage. Just as in divorce, remarriage is a process and not an event. Decisions are made and relationships begin well in advance of any formal ceremony. To date, we know little about the series of transformations taking place prior to remarriage that may help set the stage for later relationships.

Stepfamilies develop in a broader social context. Most research has focused on how relationships between stepparents and their stepchildren develop after remarriage, which is obviously a central feature of the child's environment. Yet these relationships are influenced by a broader network of relationships, of which we know precious little. Other relationships exist within the residential household itself, such as sibling relationships, which could be a fruitful focus for future research. Relationships existing outside the residential household, such as noncustodial relationships, and relationships with grandparents and quasi-kin, play important roles in the lives of children in stepfamilies.

Much work remains to be done with respect to understanding stepfamilies. In our view, a critical need for informing theory is to identify discrete microsocial processes that occur within *potential* remarried arrangements and how, over time, such processes give rise to successful or unsuccessful relationships within stepfamilies. Microsocial information has utility for interventions with this population given that most clinicians working with stepfamilies have a family systems perspective (Ganong & Coleman, 1994), which focuses on changing problematic interactions. Thus, for our theories and interventions to be based firmly on reality, we need to identify the ways in which relative strangers unite to become satisfying families.

REFERENCES

Ahrons, C. R., & Perlmutter, M. S. (1982). The relationship between former spouses: A fundamental subsystem in the remarriage family. In L. Messinger (Ed.), *Therapy with remarried families* (pp. 31–46). Rockville, MD: Aspen Systems.

Amato, P. R. (1994). The implications of research findings on children in stepfamilies. In A. Booth & J. Dunn (Eds.), *Stepfamilies: Who benefits? Who does not?* (pp. 81–87). Hillsdale, NJ: Erlbaum.

Amato, P. R. & Keith, B. (1991). Parental divorce and the well-being of children: A meta-analysis. *Psychological Bulletin, 110,* 26–46.

Anderson, E. R. (1998). *Sibling, half-sibling, and step-sibling relationships in remarried families.* Manuscript submitted for publication.

Anderson, E. R., Greene, S. M., Nelson, K., & Wolchik, S. (1998). *Children's mental health in stepfamilies: A meta-analysis.* Manuscript submitted for publication.

Anderson, E. R., Hetherington, E. M., & Clingempeel, W. G. (1989). Transformations in family relations at puberty: Effects of family context. *Journal of Early Adolescence, 9,* 310–334.

Anderson, E. R., Lindner, M. S., & Bennion, L. D. (1992). The effect of family relationships on adolescent development during family reorganization. *Monographs of the Society for Research in Child Development, 57,* (#2–3, Serial No. 227).

Anderson, E. R., & Rice, A. M. (1992). Sibling relationships during remarriage. *Monographs of the Society for Research in Child Development, 57,* (#2–3, Serial No. 227).

Anderson, J. Z., & White, G. D. (1986). Dysfunctional intact families and stepfamilies. *Family Process, 25,* 407–422.

Berkowitz, L. (1983). Aversively stimulated aggression: Some parallels and differences in research with animals and humans. *American Psychologist, 38,* 1135–1144.

Block, J. H., Block, J., & Gjerde, P. F. (1986). The personality of children prior to divorce: A prospective study. *Child Development, 57,* 827–840.

Bohannon, P. (1970). Divorce chains, households of remarriage, and multiple divorcers. In P. Bohannon (Ed.), *Divorce and after: An analysis of the emotional and social problems of divorce* (pp. 127–139) New York: Doubleday.

Bowerman, C., & Irish, D. (1962). Some relationships of stepchildren to their parents. *Marriage and Family Living, 24,* 113–121.

Brand, E., & Clingempeel, W. G. (1987). Interdependencies of marital and stepparent–stepchild relationships and children's psychological adjustment: Research findings and clinical implications. *Family Relations, 36,* 140–145.

Brand, E., Clingempeel, W. G., & Bowen-Woodward, K. (1988). Family relationships and children's psychological adjustment in stepmother and stepfather families. In E. M. Hetherington & J. D. Arasteh (Eds.), *Impact of divorce, single parenting, and stepparenting* (pp. 299–324). Hillsdale, NJ: Erlbaum.

Bray, J. H. (1987, August). *Becoming a stepfamily.* Symposium presented at the meeting of the American Psychological Association, New York.

Bray, J. (1988). Children's development during early remarriage. In M. Hetherington & J. Arastech (Eds.), *Impact of divorce, single parenting, and stepparenting on children* (pp. 279–298). Hillsdale, NJ: Erlbaum.

Bray, J. H., & Berger, S. H. (1990). Non-custodial father and paternal grandparent relationships in stepfamilies. *Family Relations, 39,* 414–419.

Bray, J. H., & Berger, S. H. (1993). Developmental issues in Stepfamilies Research Project: Family relationships and parent–child interactions. *Journal of Family Psychology, 7,* 1–6.

Bray, J. H., Berger, S. H., Silverblatt, A. H., & Hollier, A. (1987). Family process and organization during early remarriage: A preliminary analysis. In J. P. Vincent (Ed.), *Advances in family intervention, assessment, and theory* (pp. 253–279). Greenwich, CT: JAI Press.

Bray, J., & Depner, C. (1993). Perspectives on nonresidential parenting. In C. Depner & J. Bray (Eds.), *Nonresidential parenting: New vistas in family living* (pp. 3–12). Newbury Park, CA: Sage.

Buehler, C., & Ryan, C. (1994). Former-spouse relations and noncustodial father involvement during marital and family transitions: A closer look at remarriage following divorce. In K. Pasley & M. Ihinger-Tallman (Eds.), *Stepparenting: Issues in theory, research, and practice* (pp. 127–150). Westport, CT: Greenwood Press.

Bumpass, L. (1984). Children and marital disruption: A replication and update. *Demography, 21,* 71–82.

Bumpass, L., & Sweet, J. A. (1989). Children's experience in single-parent families: Implications of cohabitation and marital transitions. *Family Planning Perspectives, 6,* 256–260.

Burt, M. (Ed.). (1989). *Stepfamilies stepping ahead.* Lincoln, NE: Stepfamily Association of America.

Capaldi, D. M., & Patterson, G. R. (1991). Relation of parental transitions to boys' adjustment problems: I. A linear hypothesis. II. Mothers at risk for transitions and unskilled parenting. *Developmental Psychology, 27,* 489–504.

Chase-Lansdale, P. L., Cherlin, A. J., & Kiernan, K. E. (1995). The long-term effects of parental divorce on the mental health of young adults: A developmental perspective. *Child Development, 66,* 1614–1634.

Cherlin, A. J. (1978). Remarriage as an incomplete institution. *American Journal of Sociology, 84,* 634–650.

Cherlin, A. J. (1992). *Marriage, divorce, remarriage.* Cambridge, MA: Harvard University Press.

Cherlin, A. J., & Furstenberg, F. F., Jr. (1986). *The new American grandparent.* New York: Basic Books.

Cherlin, A. J., Furstenberg, F. F., Jr., Chase-Lansdale, P. L., Kiernan, K. E., Robins, P. K., Morrison, D. R., Teitler, J. O. (1991). Longitudinal studies of the effects of divorce on children in Great Britain and the United States. *Science, 252,* 1386–1389.

Cherlin, A. J., & McCarthy, J. (1985). Remarried couple households: Data from the June 1980 current population survey. *Journal of Marriage and the Family, 47,* 23–30.

Clingempeel, G. (1981). Quasi-kin relationships and marital quality. *Journal of Personality and Social Psychology, 41,* 890–901.

Clingempeel, G., & Brand, E. (1985). Quasi-kin relationships, structural complexity, and marital quality in stepfamilies: A replication, extension, and clinical impressions. *Family Relations, 34,* 401–409.

Clingempeel, W. G., Brand, E., & Ievoli, R. (1984). Stepparent–stepchild relationships in stepmother and stepfather families: A multimethod study. *Family Relations, 33,* 465–473.

Clingempeel, W. G., Brand, E., & Segal, S. (1987). A multilevel-multivariable-developmental perspective for future research on stepfamilies. In K. Pasley & M. Ihinger-Tallman (Eds.), *Remarriage and stepparenting: Current research and theory* (pp. 65–93). New York: Guilford Press.

Clingempeel, W. G., Colyar, J., Brand, E., & Hetherington, E. M. (1992). Children's relationships with maternal grandparents: A longitudinal study of family structure and pubertal status effects. *Child Development, 63,* 1404–1422.

Clingempeel, W. G., Ievoli, R., & Brand, E. (1984). Structural complexity and the quality of stepfather–stepchild relationships. *Family Process, 23,* 547–560.

Clingempeel, G., & Segal, S. (1986). Stepparent–stepchild relationships and the psychological adjustment of children in stepmother and stepfather families. *Child Development, 57,* 474–488.

Coale Lewis, H. C. (1985). Family therapy with stepfamilies. *Journal of Strategic and Systemic Therapies, 4,* 13–23.

Coleman, M., & Ganong, L. (1990). Remarriage and stepfamily research in the 80's: New interest in an old family form. *Journal of Marriage and the Family, 52,* 925–940.

Dahl, B. B., McCubbin, H. L., & Lester, G. R. (1976). War induced father absence: Comparing the adjustment of children in reunited, non-reunited, and reconstituted families. *International Journal of Sociology of the Family, 6,* 99–108.

Dawson, D. A. (1991). Family structure and children's health and well-being: Data from the 1988 National Health Interview Survey on Child Health. *Journal of Marriage and the Family, 53,* 573–589.

Deal, J. E., Stanley Hagan, M., & Anderson, E. R. (1992). The marital relationship in remarried families. *Monographs of the Society for Research in Child Development, 57,* (#2–3, Serial No. 227).

Dornbush, S., Carlsmith, J. M., Bushwall, S. J., Ritter, P. L., Leiderman, H., Hastorf, A. H., & Gross, R. T. (1985). Single parents, extended households, and the control of adolescents. *Child Development, 56,* 326–341.

Emery, R. E. (1982). Interparental conflict and the children of discord and divorce. *Psychological Bulletin, 92,* 310–330.

Felner, R. D., Terre, L., & Rowlinson, R. T. (1988). A life transition framework for understanding marital dissolution and family reorganization. In S. A. Wolchik & P. Karoly (Eds.), *Children of divorce: Empirical perspectives on adjustment* (pp. 35–66). New York: Gardner.

Fine, M. A., & Kurdek, L. A. (1992). The adjustment of adolescents in stepfather and stepmother families. *Journal of Marriage and the Family, 54,* 725–736.

Fine, M. A., Kurdek, L. A., & Henningen, L. (1992). Perceived self-competence, stepfamily myths, and (step)parent role ambiguity in adolescents from stepfather and stepmother families. *Journal of Family Psychology, 6,* 69–76.

Flewelling, R. L., & Bauman, K. E. (1990). Family structure as a predictor of initial substance use and sexual intercourse in early adolescence. *Journal of Marriage and the Family, 52,* 171–181.

Forgatch, M. S., Patterson, G. R., & Ray, J. A. (1996). Divorce and boys' adjustment problems: Two paths with a single model. In E. M. Hetherington & E. A. Blechman (Eds.), *Stress, coping, and resiliency in children and the family* (pp. 67–105). Hillsdale, NJ: Erlbaum.

Furstenberg, F. F., Jr. (1987). The new extended family: The experience of parents and children after remarriage. In K. Pasley & M. Ihinger-Tallman (Eds.), *Remarriage and stepparenting: Current research and theory* (pp. 42–61). New York: Guilford Press.

Furstenberg, F. F., Jr. (1988). Child care after divorce and remarriage. In E. M. Hetherington & J. Arasteh (Eds.), *Impact of divorce, single parenting, and stepparenting on children* (pp. 245–262). Hillsdale, NJ: Erlbaum.

Furstenberg, F. F., Jr., & Nord, C. W., (1985). Parenting apart: Patterns of child rearing after marital disruption. *Journal of Marriage and the Family, 47,* 893–904.

Ganong, L. H., & Coleman, M. (1984). The effects of remarriage on children: A review of the empirical literature. *Family Relations, 33,* 389–406.

Ganong, L., & Coleman, M. (1988). Do mutual children cement bonds in stepfamilies? *Journal of Marriage and the Family, 50,* 687–698.

Ganong, L. H., & Coleman, M. (1989). Preparing for remarriage: Anticipating the issue, seeking solutions. *Family Relations, 38,* 28–33.

Ganong, L. H., & Coleman, M. (1993). A meta-analytic comparison of the self-esteem and behavior problems of stepchildren to children in other family structures. *Journal of Divorce and Remarriage, 19,* 143–163.

Ganong, L. H., & Coleman, M. (1994). *Remarried family relationships.* Thousand Oaks: Sage.

Glick, P. (1980). Remarriage: Some recent changes and variations. *Journal of Family Issues, 1,* 455–478.

Glick, P. (1984). Marriage, divorce, and living arrangements: Prospective changes. *Journal of Family Issues, 5,* 7–26.

Glick, P. (1989). Remarried families, stepfamilies, and stepchildren: A brief demographic analysis. *Family Relations, 38,* 24–27.

Glick, P. C., & Lin, S. (1986). Recent changes in divorce and remarriage. *Journal of Marriage and the Family, 48,* 737–747.

Goldner, V. (1982). Remarriage family: Structure, system, future. In J. C. Hansen & L. Messinger (Eds.), *Therapy with remarried families* (pp. 187–206). Rockville, MD: Aspen.

Goldscheider, F. K., & Goldscheider, C. (1989). Family structure and conflict: Nest-leaving expectations of young adults and their parents. *Journal of Marriage and the Family, 51,* 87–97.

Hanson, T. L., McLanahan, S. S., & Thomson, E. (1996). Double jeopardy: Parental conflict and stepfamily outcomes for children. *Journal of Marriage and the Family, 58,* 141–154.

Herrera, H., & Anderson, E. R. (1989, March). Maternal perceptions of children's responses to divorce and remarriage. Presented at the meetings of the Southeastern Psychological Association, Washington, DC.

Hetherington, E. M. (1987). Family relations six years after divorce. In K. Pasley & M. Ihinger-Tallman (Eds.), *Remarriages and stepparenting today: Current research and theory* (pp. 185–205). New York: Guilford Press.

Hetherington, E. M. (1988). Parents, children and siblings six years after divorce. In R. Hinde & J. Stevenson-Hinde (Eds.), *Relationships within families* (pp. 311–331). Cambridge, England: Cambridge University Press.

Hetherington, E. M. (1989). Coping with family transitions: Winners, losers, and survivors. *Child Development, 60,* 1–14.

Hetherington, E. M. (1993). An overview of the Virginia Longitudinal Study of Divorce and Remarriage: A focus on early adolescence. *Journal of Family Psychology, 7,* 39–56.

Hetherington, E. M., & Anderson, E. R. (1987). The effects of divorce and remarriage on early adolescents and their families. In M. D. Levine & E. R. McAnarney (Eds.), *Early adolescent transitions* (pp. 49–67). Lexington, MA: Heath.

Hetherington, E. M., Camara, K. A., & Featherman, D. L. (1983). Achievement and intellectual functioning of children in one-parent households. In J. Spence (Eds.), *Achievement and achievement motives: Psychological and sociological approaches.* San Francisco: W. H. Freeman.

Hetherington, M., Cox, M., & Cox, R. (1982). Effects of divorce on parents and children. In M. Lamb (Ed.), *Nontraditional families* (pp. 233–287). Hillsdale, NJ: Erlbaum.

Hetherington, M., Cox, M., & Cox, R. (1985). Long-term effects of divorce and remarriage on the adjustment of children. *Journal of the American Academy of Child Psychiatry, 24,* 518–530.

Hetherington, E. M., & Hagan, M. S. (1986). Divorced fathers: Stress, coping, and adjustment. In M. Lamb (Ed.), *Nontraditional families* (pp. 233–288). Hillsdale, NJ: Erlbaum.

Hetherington, E. M., & Jodl, K. M. (1994). Stepfamilies as settings for child development. In A. Booth & J. Dunn (Eds.), *Stepfamilies: Who benefits? Who does not?* (pp. 55–79). Hillsdale, NJ: Erlbaum.

Hetherington, E. M., Stanley Hagan, M., & Anderson, E. R. (1989). Marital transitions: A child's perspective. *American Psychologist, 44,* 303–312.

Hill, J., Holmbeck, G., Marlow, L., Green, T., & Lynch, M. (1985a). Menarcheal status and parent–child relations in families of seventh grade girls. *Journal of Youth and Adolescence, 14,* 301–316.

Hill, J., Holmbeck, G., Marlow, L., Green, T., & Lynch, M. (1985b). Pubertal status and parent–child relations in families of seventh grade boys. *Journal of Early Adolescence, 5,* 31–44.

Hobart, C. (1987). Parent–child relations in remarried families. *Journal of Family Issues, 8,* 259–277.

Hobart, C. (1990). Relationships between the formerly married. *Journal of Divorce and Remarriage, 14,* 1–23.

Hobart, C. (1991). Conflict in remarriages. *Journal of Divorce and Remarriage, 15,* 69–86.

Ihinger-Tallman, M. (1987). Sibling and stepsibling bonding in stepfamilies. In K. Pasley & M. Ihinger-Tallman (Eds.), *Remarriage and stepparenting today: Current research and theory* (pp. 164–182). New York: Guilford Press.

Ihinger-Tallman, M., & Pasley, K. (1994). Building bridges: Reflections on theory, research, and practice. In K. Pasley & M. Ihinger-Tallman (Eds.), *Stepparenting: Issues in theory, research, and practice* (pp. 239–250). Westport, CT: Greenwood Press.

Imber-Black, E., & Roberts, J. (1993). *Rituals for our times.* New York: Harper Perennial.

Johnson, C. L. (1988). *Ex familia: Grandparents, parents and children adjust to divorce.* New Brunswick, NJ: Rutgers University Press.

Kellam, S. G., Ensminger, M. E., & Turner, R. J. (1977). Family structure and the mental health of children. *Archives of General Psychiatry, 34,* 1012–1022.

Kinnaird, K. L., & Gerrard, M. (1986). Premarital sexual behavior and attitudes toward marriage and divorce among young women as a function of their mothers' marital status. *Journal of Marriage and the Family, 48,* 757–765.

Kubler-Ross, E. (1969). *On death and dying.* New York: Macmillan.

Kurdek, L., & Fine, M. (1993). The relation between family structure and young adolescents' appraisals of family climate and parenting behavior. *Journal of Family Issues, 14,* 279–290.

Kurdek, L. A., Fine, M. A., & Sinclair, R. J. (1994). The relation between parenting transitions and adjustment in young adolescents: A multisample investigation. *Journal of Early Adolescence, 14,* 412–432.

Larson, J. H., & Allgood, S. M. (1987). A comparison of intimacy in first-married and remarried couples. *Journal of Family Issues, 8,* 319–331.

Lindner, M. S., Stanley Hagan, M., & Brown, J. C. (1992). The adjustment of children in nondivorced, divorced single-mother, and remarried families. *Monographs of the Society for Research in Child Development, 57,* (#2–3, Serial No. 227).

Maccoby, E. E. (1992). Family structure and children's adjustment: Is quality of parenting the major mediator? *Monographs of the Society for Research in Child Development, 57,* (#2–3, Serial No. 227).

MacDonald, W. L., & DeMaris, A. (1995). Remarriage, stepchildren, and marital conflict: Challenges to the incomplete institutionalization hypothesis. *Journal of Marriage and the Family, 57,* 387–398.

Martin, D., & Martin, M. (1992). *Stepfamilies in therapy: Understanding systems, assessment, and intervention.* San Francisco: Jossey-Bass.

McGoldrick, M., & Carter, E. A. (1989). Forming a remarried family. In E. A. Carter & M. McGoldrick (Eds.), *The family cycle: A framework for family therapy* (pp. 399–429). New York: Gardner.

Miller, K. S. (1989). *Family composition and its effect on the behavior of children*. Unpublished doctoral dissertation, Emory University, Atlanta, GA.

Montgomery, M. J., Anderson, E. R., Hetherington, E. M., & Clingempeel, W. G. (1992). Patterns of courtship for remarriage: Implications for child adjustment and parent–child relationships. *Journal of Marriage and the Family, 54,* 686–698.

Needle, R. H., Su, S. S., & Doherty, W. J. (1990). Divorce, remarriage, and adolescent substance use: A prospective longitudinal study. *Journal of Marriage and the Family, 52,* 157–169.

Palisi, B. J., Orleans, M., Caddell, D., & Korn, B. (1991). Adjustment to step-fatherhood: The effects of marital history and relations with children. *Journal of Divorce and Remarriage, 14,* 89–106.

Papernow, P. L. (1984). The stepfamily cycle: An experimental model of stepfamily development. *Family Relations, 33,* 355–363.

Papernow, P. L. (1987). Thickening the "middle ground": Dilemmas and vulnerabilities of remarried couples. *Psychotherapy, 24,* 630–639.

Papernow, P. L. (1993). *Becoming a stepfamily: Patterns of development in remarried families.* New York: Gardner.

Pasley, K., Dollahite, D., & Ihinger-Tallman, M. (1993). Bridging the gap: Clinical applications of research findings on the spouse and stepparent roles in remarriage. *Family Relations, 42,* 315–322.

Pasley, K., & Ihinger-Tallman, M. (1982). Stress in remarried families. *Family Perspective, 16,* 181–190.

Peterson, J., & Zill, N.(1986). Marital disruption, parent–child relationships, and behavioral problems in children. *Journal of Marriage and the Family, 48,* 295–340.

Pill, C. J. (1990). Stepfamilies: Redefining the family. *Family Relations, 39,* 186–193.

Pink, J., & Wampler, K. (1985). Problem areas in stepfamilies: Cohesion, adaptability and the stepparent-adolescent relationship. *Family Relations, 34,* 327–335.

Rodgers, R. H., & Conrad, L. M. (1986). Courtship for remarriage: Influences on family reorganization after divorce. *Journal of Marriage and the Family, 48,* 767–775.

Sager, C. J., Brown, H. S., Crohn, H., Engel, T., Rodstein, E., & Walker, E. (1983). *Treating the remarried family.* New York: Brunner/Mazel.

Sanders, G. F., & Trygstad, D. W. (1989). Stepgrandparents and grandparents: The view from young adults. *Family Relations, 38,* 71–75.

Sandler, I., Wolchik, S. A., Braver, S., & Fogas, B. (1991). Stability and quality of life events and psychological symptomatology in children of divorce. *American Journal of Community Psychology, 19,* 501–520.

Santrock, J. W. (1972). Relation of type and onset of father's absence to cognitive development. *Child Development, 53,* 472–480.

Santrock, J. W., & Sitterle, K. A. (1987). Parent–child relationships in stepmother families. In K. Pasley & M. Ihinger-Tallman (Eds.), *Remarriage and stepparenting today: Current theory and research* (pp. 273–299). New York: Guilford Press.

Santrock, J. M., Warshak, R., Lindbergh, C., & Meadows, L. (1982). Children's and parent's observed social behavior in stepfather families. *Child Development, 53,* 472–480.

Stanley Hagan, M., Hollier, E. A., O'Connor, T. G., & Eisenberg, M. (1992). Parent–child relationships in nondivorced, divorced single-mother, and remarried families. *Monographs of the Society for Research in Child Development, 57,* (#2–3, Serial No. 227).

Steinberg, L. (1987). Single parents, stepparents, and the susceptibility of adolescents to antisocial peer pressure. *Child Development, 58,* 269–275.

Steinberg, L. (1990). Autonomy, conflict, and harmony in the family relationship. In S. S. Feldman and G. R. Elliott (Eds.), *At the threshold: The developing adolescent* (pp. 255–276). Cambridge, MA: Harvard University Press.

Steinberg, L., Mounts, N. S., Lamborn, S. D., & Dornbusch, S. M. (1991). Authoritative parenting and adolescent adjustment across varied ecological niches. *Journal of Research on Adolescence, 1,* 19–36.

Visher, E. B., & Visher, J. (1978). Common problems of stepparents and their spouses. *American Journal of Orthopsychiatry, 48,* 252–262.

Visher, E. B., & Visher, J. S. (1982). Children in stepfamilies. *Psychiatric Annals, 12,* 832–841.

Visher, E. B., & Visher, J. S. (1988). *Old loyalties, new ties: Therapeutic strategies with stepfamilies.* New York: Brunner/Mazel.

Visher, J. S. & Visher, E. B. (1991). Therapy with stepfamily couples. *Psychiatric Annals, 21,* 462–465.

Walker, K. N., & Messinger, L. (1979). Remarriage after divorce: Dissolution and reconstitution of family boundaries. *Family Process, 18,* 185–192.

Wallerstein, J. S., Corbin, S. B., & Lewis, J. M. (1988). Children of divorce: A ten-year study. In E. M. Hetherington & J. D. Arasteh (Eds.), *Impact of divorce, single-parenting, and stepparenting on children* (pp. 198–214). Hillsdale, NJ: Erlbaum.

Wallerstein, J. S., & Kelly, J. B. (1980). *Surviving the breakup: How children and parents cope with divorce.* New York: Basic Books.

Weiss, R. S. (1979). Growing up a little faster: The experience of growing up in a single-parent household. *Journal of Social Issues, 35,* 97–111.

White, L. K., & Reidmann, A. C. (1992). When the Brady Bunch grows up: Relations between fullsiblings and stepsiblings in adulthood. *Journal of Marriage and the Family, 54,* 197–208.

Whiteside, M. F. (1988). Creation of family identity through ritual performance in early remarriage. In E. Imber-Black, J. Roberts, & R. Whiting (Eds.), *Rituals in families and family therapy* (pp. 276–304). New York: Norton.

Wiser, A. W., & Burch, T. K. (1989). The family environment and leaving the parental home. *Journal of Marriage and the Family, 51,* 605–613.

Zill, N. (1988). Behavior, achievement, and health problems among children in stepfamilies: Findings from a national survey of child health (pp. 324–368). In E. M. Hetherington & J. D. Arastech (Eds.), *Impact of divorce, single parenting, and stepparenting on children.* Hillsdale, NJ: Erlbaum.

CHAPTER 22

CHILDREN OF ADOPTIVE FAMILIES

Gordon E. Finley

Today we are experiencing a multitude of family forms and reproductive technologies not even envisioned a few decades ago. Let us begin, therefore, by considering the meaning of family and parenthood in the context of adoptive parenthood. At the core of adoptive parenthood is the issue of biological bonds versus psychological bonds. Reciprocally, it is the issue of the adoptee's biological dispositions (genetic and fantasized) versus the adoptee's socialized dispositions (adoptive home experience) in determining outcome.

In our culture, it is noteworthy that much ado is made about *raising someone else's biological child*. However, no ado is made about *marrying someone else's biological child*. Indeed, the law requires it!

What then *is* the family, biology or psychology? Why do we value psychological bonds in marriage but biological bonds in childrearing? What *is* important in socialization, the biological parent or the psychological parent? What makes for good parenting, biological children or cherished children?

And, can the study of the adoptive family shed light on other family forms, such as stepfamilies and blended families?

As this chapter was being drafted, the case of Susan Smith—who strapped her two young boys into their car seats and drove them into a lake to drown—went to court. This brings to mind the earlier case of Pauline Zile who initially abandoned her daughter to the care of grandparents, later reclaimed custody through the courts (even though her circumstances were such that no judge would have granted either adoption or foster care to an equivalently situated nonblood adult), and stood by as she watched her husband (the girl's stepfather) kill her daughter. Both mothers made tearful and highly publicized pleas for the return of their already murdered biological children on national television.

Clearly, as demonstrated by these two cases alone, biology is no guarantee of good parenting. Perhaps, then, it is time for society and the courts to define "the best interests of the child" in psychological rather than biological terms. Perhaps too it is time for the twin stigmata of infertility and adoption to become destigmatized and to recede from public and private consciousness. Were these "perhaps" to come to pass, perhaps we would be in a better position to determine whether children of adoptive families are in any way

I am grateful to Yuan-yu Chiang, Laura Ferrer, Wendy Roth, Wendy Silverman, and Rita Soza for comments on earlier drafts of this chapter.

substantially different from children of a multitude of other family forms such as intact/biological, divorced, widowed, never-married, single, step, blended, teen, deferred, gay, lesbian, dual-career, military, abusive, HIV-positive, and so on.

All things considered, and as family forms go, children of adoptive families may not be so bad off. To keep things in perspective, children of any family form, under a microscope, are bound to show flaws (Melina, 1994).

CHAPTER FRAMEWORK

The chapter is divided into three sections. The first section critically evaluates the widely published epidemiological view that adoptees have elevated rates of psychopathology and contrasts it with the traditional view that adoption *is* a successful intervention into the lives of abandoned children. The second section reviews the clinical literature to see if adoptees manifest different behavior problems than "non-adoptees" in clinical settings and explores possible explanations including genetic dispositions. The third and longest section provides a detailed discussion of the adoptive family life cycle focusing on developmental challenges unique to members of the adoption triangle (birthparents, adoptive parents, and adoptees) and interventions designed to meet these challenges.

IS ADOPTION INHERENTLY PATHOGENIC?

Many publications on adoption cite the epidemiological view that adoptees have elevated rates of psychopathology (e.g., Brodzinsky, 1993). However, the data truly required to support this view do not exist. Further, the extant data supporting the epidemiological view have methodological shortcomings that erode its empirical foundation. The present critique consists of five major points and a related issue of comparison groups.

The essence of the epidemiological view rests on evidence of disproportional representation of adoptees among individuals referred to various mental health settings compared to the proportion of adoptees in the general population. The problems with this argument are as follows.

First, the true incidence of any of the several different types of adoption in the United States population is not currently known because no comprehensive national adoption data have been collected since 1975 (Stolley, 1993). Unfortunately, estimates of adoptee prevalence based on less than comprehensive national data may be subject to error.

Second, there are also no comprehensive national data on the true incidence of adoptees referred to all mental health settings. The existing data have been derived from limited samples, frequently from one setting, with unknown sampling biases, and yielding substantially different estimates of adoptee prevalence from one setting to another (e.g., 2.5 to 33.3% in one study by Kirk, Jonassohn, & Fish, 1966).

For example, consider a critique by one of the field's leading figures, H. David Kirk, of the work of another leading figure, "Schechter's claim that adopted children are 100 times more liable to require psychiatric attention than their participation in the general child population would suggest was not only based on observations of a small group of children seen in private practice by one psychiatrist, but was furthermore based on an erroneous interpretation of a published adoption rate" (Kirk et al., 1966, p. 291).

A sampling concern arises if one asks whether Schechter was known then, as he is known now, as a clinical expert on adoption—the kind of expert clinician professionals and adoptive parents would seek out if they believed that their adoptee required treatment. The concern is that Schechter's reputation and specialization in adoption would, in and of itself, have elevated adoptee rates in his practice in the same way that cardiologists have elevated rates of patients with heart problems. This concern also may extend to reports of elevated adoptee referral rates in inpatient treatment facilities. Of the universe of inpatient treatment facilities, are the ones selected for adoption studies randomly selected, or are they selected because one or more persons on staff have an interest in adoption which, in and of itself, might elevate adoptee rates?

A third problem is that the estimates used in epidemiological comparisons sometimes are derived from different cohorts of birthparents, adoptive parents, and adoptees. For example, in Brodzinsky's 1993 review, the estimate of adoptees in the general population (2%) came from a 1985 Society for Research in Child Development Convention Paper reporting on a national health survey (Zill, 1985) (other estimates in the literature range from 1 to 4%); the estimate of adoptee outpatient referrals (5%) came from a 1973 chapter that reviewed studies of adopted children referred for psychiatric treatment from 1942 to 1966 (Mech, 1973); and the estimate for adoptees in inpatient psychiatric settings (10–12%) came from one review and two articles published in 1987 and 1988 (cited in Brodzinsky, 1993, p. 154).

Importantly, the characteristics of birthparents relinquishing, adoptees placed, and adults adopting have changed substantially over the time frame of these estimates. For example, in 1942 there were no crack-addicted or AIDS-infected birthparents and most likely more infants of "nice family" birthmothers selected for placement (with the balance selected for orphanages). Likewise, few special needs, older, black, or international children were adopted and more white infants from "good homes" were placed and there were few older, single, gay, lesbian, black, or lower-income adoptive parents and more white, middle and upper class adoptive parents. The question arises: Is it appropriate to compare estimates from different adoption cohorts when it is known that there have been substantial changes in the characteristics of these different cohorts? Further, has the decline in the availability of infants for adoption (supply) and the increase in the number of adults seeking to adopt (demand)—along with changes in attitudes towards special needs, transracial, and international adoptions—influenced selection criteria and risk rates?

Fourth, as consciousness has been raised regarding methodological problems with existing adoption studies (see Brodzinsky, 1993, Finley, 1998, and Wierzbicki, 1978, 1993 for a detailed discussion of additional methodological issues) concern has been increasing regarding conclusions that can be drawn from these studies. One problem involves the possible attributional bias that may be introduced by not being blind to adoptive status. Specifically, behavior problems may be attributed to adoptive status when, in fact, they are due to other causes (Melina, 1994). In support of possible attributional bias, Wierzbicki's (1993, p. 451) meta-analytic study found that: "the largest differences between adoptees and non-adoptees occurred with the most global and subjective measurements."

Fifth, and currently receiving much attention, is recent evidence (Warren, 1992) that adoptees are much more likely to be referred to mental health settings than other children, even controlling for the extent of problems. Warren offers several possible explanations for this including that: Adoptive families are prone to see the adoptee as being at risk for problems and thus requiring treatment; adoptee problems are perceived as a threat to the integrity of the adoptive family; and adoptive families may be prone to initiate referrals due to their higher socioeconomic status or their adoption experience with social service agencies. Similar issues have been raised earlier by Kirk and colleagues (1966), Grotevant and McRoy (1990), and Wierzbicki (1978). Of both methodological and clinical importance is the reality that mental health referrals are not blind to adoptive status. Thus, the widespread publication of possibly incorrect and elevated epidemiological estimates of adoptee psychopathology could, in and of itself, be a "cause" for referral (Warren, 1992).

A final methodological issue related to the epidemiological view is that of appropriate comparison groups (Finley, 1998). In trying to reach reasonable conclusions about psychopathological risk and to avoid "double messages" in the adoption literature, one must ask, Who should adoptees be compared to and how should we integrate the comparisons?

The problem is illustrated below with quotations from two recent reviews.

> As a means of insuring the physical and emotional well-being of children, adoption has proved to be an unqualified success. Adopted children fare significantly better than children reared in institutional environments or in foster care...they show better long-term adjustment than children living with biological parents who are ambivalent about rearing them, or in fact, do not want them... (Brodzinsky, Lang, & Smith, 1995, p. 209)

> Although most adoptees are well within the normal range of functioning, as a group they are more vulnerable to various emotional, behavioral, and academic problems than their nonadopted peers living in intact homes with their biological parents (Brodzinsky, 1993, p. 153).

To eliminate double messages, the "unqualified success" of the 1995 review must be qualified by the "vulnerability" of the 1993 review. More importantly, however, by combining comparison groups from these two quotations alone, we can begin to develop a rank-ordering of how adoptees stack up against relevant comparison groups. In this example, adoptees as a group are not as well off as biological children from intact families but are better off than children selected for and reared in institutions and foster care or reared by biological parents who may not want them. Such an inclusive–comparative approach not only reduces the risk of readers of different reviews coming away from the literature with different messages, but also helps to place adoptees in their rightful comparative position.

The question remains, however, with whom *should* adoptees be compared? Should abandoned children selected for adoption be compared to abandoned children selected for institutional or foster care? Should adoptees be compared to the children of families similar to the adoptive parents or children of families similar to the birthparents? Or, should adoptees be compared to children of the many family forms listed in the introduction?—intact/biological, divorced, widowed, never-married, single, step, blended, teen, deferred, gay, lesbian, dual-career, military, abusive, HIV-positive, and so on.

To improve the current situation, it appears desirable to design research that (1) targets children of specific family forms for comparison to answer theoretical questions (e.g., Brodzinsky, 1990); (2) uses multiple comparison groups that, over studies, will give us a clearer picture of how adoptees stack up against children of different family forms; (3) subdivides adoptive families into relevant categories such as intact, divorced, single, transracial, international, and so forth and also subdivides adoptees by genetic background, prenatal history, age of placement, pre-placement experience, special needs status, and so forth; and (4) omits as a comparison group the heterogeneous category of non-adoptive families.

Although commonly used in the adoption literature, the category of non-adoptive families is not helpful because, while the specification "non-adoptive" tells us what the comparison families are *not,* it does not tell us what they *are.* As discussed also in Chapters 9, 13, 20, and 21 of this volume, revolutionary changes in family structures over the past few decades have rendered the non-adoptive category too heterogeneous to be an interpretable comparison group. The model non-adoptive, intact/biological, breadwinner/homemaker, two- to three-child family in a suburban home with a white picket fence, station wagon, and dog Spot, is long gone.

In summary, and three decades after Kirk and colleagues' (1966) original critique, the epidemiological view continues to present more problems than solutions and, if incorrect, may be harmful to adoptees and their families. The related issue of appropriate comparison groups and their integration continues to require consideration.

In contrast to the downbeat epidemiological message critiqued above, this section will close on an upbeat message by summarizing a second tradition of evaluating adoptee outcome, empirical estimates of adoption success. Although this line of research is based on subjective judgments, it does provide a second opinion on adoptee outcome. In this tradition, adoptive family life and adoptees are rated on various scales by either: (1) adoptive parents (e.g., the overall adoptive experience was extremely satisfying, more satisfying than dissatisfying, about half and half, more dissatisfying than satisfying, or extremely dissatisfying) (Kadushin, 1967); or (2) professionals judging the adoption to be successful (if the adoptee was rated at or above cutoffs such as capable, getting along satisfactorily, good adjustment, successful, good to excellent, or self-supporting) (Mech, 1973).

Spanning the time frame from 1967 to 1995—and even though the adoptees were evaluated by different criteria, with different cutoffs, and at different ages—the reviewed success rates remain robustly consistent: 78 to 86 percent (Kadushin, 1967); 75 percent (Mech, 1973); 84 percent (Kadushin, 1980); 70 percent (Hoopes, 1990); and 75 to 80 percent (DeAngelis, 1995). Because these success rates refer to judgments made only on adoptees, what is needed are comparison success rate judgments made on children of other family forms. However, and as interventions into the lives of abandoned children go, a 70 to 86 percent success rate only can be described as remarkable.

IS THERE AN ADOPTED CHILD SYNDROME?

Five recent points of entry into the clinical literature can be found in reviews by Brodzinsky (1987, 1993), Brodzinsky and Schechter (1990), Schulman and Behrman (1993), and Wierzbicki (1993). The questions for this portion of the chapter are, Do adoptees in clinical settings have a shared pattern of presenting symptoms (e.g., the adopted child syndrome, Kirschner & Nagle, 1988) which is different from the symptoms of other group(s) in the same clinical setting, and, if so, how might this behavior pattern be explained?

Reviews have generally agreed that there are higher levels of externalizing problems, such as acting-out and academic/hyperactivity disorders, among adoptees when compared to heterogeneous groups of non-adoptees in the same clinical populations. For example, Wierzbicki (1993), reporting on a meta-analysis of adoptee clinical studies, noted significantly higher levels of externalizing disorders and academic problems among adoptees as compared to non-adoptees. And Brodzinsky and colleagues (1995) list the following externalizing behaviors as ones commonly reported for adoptees at referral: Increased aggression; oppositional behaviors; defiant behaviors; lying; stealing; running away; substance abuse; antisocial tendencies; learning disabilities; and attention-deficit hyperactivity disorder (ADHD).

Although there is a general consensus on the presenting symptoms in the clinic, *there is disagreement on whether these symptoms represent deep-seated psychiatric pathology or simply the adoptee's way of rising to the challenges inherent in adoptive family life.*

There are at least five possible explanations for the above noted pattern of presenting symptoms discussed below, and all of them may be contributing influences. In addition, and as Brodzinsky (1990), Cadoret (1990), and Finley (1998) emphasize, the role of individual differences in the adoptive parents' parenting skills, mental health, and/or psychopathology also is critical in determining whether or not these symptoms become manifested.

First, Brodzinsky and his colleagues argue that the behavior problems listed above are not pathological but rather represent a normal and highly adaptive grieving process involving the loss of the biological parents (Brodzinsky, 1990). These adjustment problems are viewed as a normal part of adoptive development and reflect neither adoptive parent failure nor inherent adoptee psychopathology. Brodzinsky and his colleagues (Brodzinsky et al., 1995) recommend maintaining open communication, supporting the adoptee's curiosity about his or her origins, painting a positive picture of the birthparents, and helping the child work through the grief associated with the loss of the biological parents.

Second, another nonpathological explanation has been suggested by Rosenberg (1992). She points out that adoptees frequently have "an intense need to test the permanency of the relationship" (Rosenberg, 1992, p. 76) once the adoptee truly understands relinquishment and the absence of bloodlines to the adoptive parents. This testing frequently involves engaging in obnoxious or provocative behaviors that the adoptee knows are beyond the limits of tolerance of the adoptive parents. She also suggests that adoptive parents must recognize that they likely are going to be tested more frequently and more intensely than biological parents. She recommends that adoptive parents set firm limits and choose battles wisely.

Third, perceived parental acceptance–rejection is at the heart of Rohner's (1986) phenomenological theory. Rohner argues that what determines socialization outcome is not the actual behavior of parents, but rather the child's *perception* of the parents' behavior. Given the reality of abandonment, it requires little imagination for the adoptee to construe relinquishment as rejection, and rejection as due to the personal characteristics of the adoptee. In the phenomenological view, the "true" reasons for relinquishment and the "true" characteristics of the birthparents are unimportant. What *is* important is the adoptee's perception of the reasons for relinquishment and the adoptee's perception of the characteristics of the birthparents. What is potentially helpful about Rohner's phenomenological approach for the study of adoption is the emphasis it puts on looking at adoption from the adoptee's point of view as well as Rohner's empirical work on the outcomes of perceived parental rejection.

Using both cross-cultural and within-cultural studies, Rohner finds that the following personality dispositions characterize children who perceive their parents to be rejecting: Emotionally unresponsive; hostile and aggressive; negative self-esteem; negative self-adequacy; negative world view; and emotionally unstable. What is interesting, is the similarity between Rohner's findings for perceived parental rejection (in the present context, perceived birthparental rejection) and the externalizing behaviors of clinic referred adoptees noted above.

Fourth, the notion of rejection also is found in the psychodynamic literature: "Added to these basic feelings of being unconnected and different are the feelings of being unwanted and of being unwanted because of 'badness' inside oneself. The theme of being unwanted leads inevitably to thoughts of not belonging and perhaps eventually to thoughts of not wanting to belong." (Anthony, 1990, p. vii).

Another psychodynamic perspective by Small (1987) (cited in Winkler, Brown, van Keppel, & Blanchard, 1988, p. 85) emphasizes loss as well as rejection: "Adoptive families are structured out of loss…For the child, adoption always means a loss of relationship with emotionally significant objects and a symbolic loss of roots, a sense of genetic identity, and a sense of connectedness. Becoming disconnected from one's ancestry is perhaps the loneliest experience known." Many adoptees experience a lifelong fear of abandonment and rejection along with feelings of being different, of not belonging, and of being powerless over what has happened in their lives.

The fifth explanation is the current version of the "bad seed" theory, Behavior Genetics. Following Cadoret (1990), our approach will be to use knowledge derived by behavioral geneticists from the adoption paradigm to shed light on adoptee outcome. (A discussion of genetic issues in counseling adoptive families can be found in Roth & Finley [1998] and Stewart [1990]). In seeking genetic explanations for adoptee outcome, the most revealing statement in Cadoret's review (1990, p. 34) is, "In the author's own work with four different adoption agencies over the past 15 years, the commonest psychopathologic condition found among biologic parents giving up children for adoption has been antisocial behavior or antisocial personality." Because a disposition to antisocial personality clearly is heritable (Cadoret, 1990; Gottesman & Goldsmith, 1994; Roth & Finley, 1998) and because the characteristics listed by Gottesman and Goldsmith for antisocial behavior (substance abuse, impulse control problems, adjustment disorders, conduct disorder, oppositional defiant disorder, and delinquency) match the "externalizing" problems commonly cited for adoptees, we *may* have a gene-to-behavior pathway explanation. In this context, Cadoret asks, "In how many cases of adoptees who come to clinics are biologic parents antisocial, depressed, and so on?" (Cadoret, 1990, p. 40).

The above discussion oversimplifies the complexities of a possible gene-to-behavior pathway by failing to consider gene-on-gene, prenatal, and postnatal interactions that may accentuate or attenuate the expression of genetic dispositions (Roth & Finley, 1998). Cadoret (1990) particularly emphasizes that conditions in the adoptive home interact with genetic dispositions to accentuate or attenuate the expression of psychopathology.

Brodzinsky (1993) characterized adoptees as mostly falling within the normal range of functioning—but with adoptees as a group having higher levels of emotional, behavioral, and academic problems than children of intact, biological families. This characterization—plus the behavior genetic perspective discussed above—suggests a new way of looking at behavior problems in adoptees. Essentially, the new perspective asks whether adoptees can be divided into two major classes: (1) adoptees free of genetic dispositions to psychopathology and placed with "normal" adoptive parents; and (2) adoptees with genetic dispositions to psychopathology placed with pathogenic adoptive parents who accentuate these dispositions. If so, are the adoptees free of genetic dispositions to psychopathology *and* with "normal" adoptive parents the ones "mostly falling within the normal range of functioning"? And, are the adoptees with genetic dispositions to psychopathogy *and* pathogenic adoptive families, the adoptees with "higher levels of emotional, behavioral, and academic problems"? The two remaining logically possible categories would be experiencing cross-pressures and thus presumably would yield mixed or intermediate results.

While speculative, this perspective may have important practical implications. If true, and were birthparents screened for antisocial personality (Cadoret, 1990) and were their offspring either not placed for adoption or placed with prospective adoptive parents well able to deal with this personality (Cadoret, 1990), then the expression of antisocial behaviors in adoptees might well be sharply reduced.

To maximize positive adoptee outcomes, adoption professionals must gather information on the genetic and prenatal background of prospective adoptees, use this information to select appropriate adoptive parents for individual adoptees, and share this information with the prospective adoptive parents (Finley, 1998). Matching adoptees and adoptive parents on the basis of psychological characteristics may well turn out to be more fruitful than many of the matching criteria used in the past.

THE ADOPTIVE FAMILY LIFE CYCLE: DEVELOPMENTAL AND CLINICAL IMPLICATIONS

The adoptive family life cycle *is* different from other family life cycles. This section will focus on these differences and on challenges that are both inherent to and unique to adoptive family life and development. The contributions of birthparents, adoptive parents, and the adoptee at seven stages of the adoptive family life cycle will be considered. Acknowledged at the outset is the reality that birthparents, adoptive parents, and adoptees are not homogeneous groups. Indeed, the inherent heterogeneity of these groups makes firm conclusions difficult (Finley, 1998). Also acknowledged at the outset is the author's view that adoptive family life is not inherently pathogenic, but that pathology may be found in some adoptive families, as it is in some of all family forms.

The developmental focus will be narrow. It will be limited to the emotional life of the traditionally healthy, white, infant adopted prior to 6 months of age by infertile, white, middle or upper class parents in a closed adoption. Major adoption sub-topics such as special needs adoption (McKenzie, 1993; Rosenthal, 1993), international adoption (Bartholet, 1993), transracial adoption (Silverman, 1993), and open adoption (Baran & Pannor, 1993; Berry, 1993) have been reviewed elsewhere and will not be covered here.

An expanded family systems theory approach will be followed throughout. The core notion is that all members of the adoption triangle are permanently present, if not physi-cally, in the hearts, minds, and fantasies of all members of the adoptive triad.

Stage I: Pre-Adoption

For the infertile couple, the pre-adoption stage is an emotional seesaw of anticipation and disappointment (Winkler et al., 1988). Infertility is a major stressor which, in adulthood, may reactivate and challenge previously resolved adolescent issues such as sexuality, reproduction, independence, and identity.

Jette (1990) provides a sensitive and empathic discussion of the multiple and emotionally depleting challenges that must be met during the pre-adoption stage. Essentially, couples must grapple with two sets of options spawned by infertility: medical and adoptive. Should the medical (and the fantasized biological child) be abandoned, the choice then becomes to adopt or to join the involuntarily childless. Traumas of loss and grief are experienced and the standard recommendation is that they are best resolved quickly if the couple is to move forward either with adoption or with childlessness.

As risks exist in infertility treatment, so too do they exist in seeking to adopt. Increasingly, concern is being expressed regarding the prenatal environment of unwanted fetuses, the major source of adoptees. Potential birthmothers likely are under substantial stress, experiencing intensely conflictual decision making, and perhaps lacking both adequate nutrition and prenatal medical care (Brodzinsky, 1993; Hajal & Rosenberg, 1991; Winkler et al., 1988). Both drug and alcohol and sexually-transmitted disease screens are mandatory for birthparents as is a detailed genetic history focusing on the extended families of both the birthmother and birthfather.

Importantly, adoption—like infertility treatment—is not guaranteed. In independent adoptions, Jette (1990) estimates that from one-third to one-half of birthmothers fail to relinquish even after receiving financial support and contractually agreeing to do so. She insightfully describes this emotional and financial loss as an "adoptive miscarriage." For the couple who were unsuccessful with infertility treatment, this is yet another burden of loss and grief. In light of the stresses of infertility and adoption seeking, and the probable emotional state of the prospective adoptive parents, both Jette (1990) and Cadoret (1990) caution prospective adoptive parents to be thorough and thoughtful in selecting an adoptee. They recommend thoroughly examining information on the background of a prospective adoptee (birthparents and their relatives) and on the pregnancy to minimize both genetic risk and prenatal biological risk. Although this is an extraordinarily difficult task for desperate prospective adoptive parents, they must weight heavily the possible long-term consequences of their decision (Finley, 1998).

Therapeutically, the issues are the continued resolution of grief over the losses of infertility, possible adoptive miscarriage, and the fantasized biological child. Work to be done involves the development of a sense of entitlement to their adopted child and the sense that they *are* the real parents of the adoptee. Self-help support groups can be particularly helpful in sharing feelings with others with similar experiences.

Stage 2: Pari-Adoption

The time surrounding adoption is an anxious one for prospective adoptive parents as they worry about two pivotal decisions over which they have no control. The absence of control over critical portions of one's life is a central theme for both the adoptive parent (infertility/uncertain adoption) and the adoptee (who abandoned me?/why?). The burden of control rests primarily with the birthparents and secondarily with the intermediary and the court (Schaffer & Kral, 1988). Prospective adoptive parents experience a wide range of feelings towards the birthparents at this time including envy and gratitude, but mostly fear and anxiety.

The first pivotal decision involves the birthparents' (often birthmother's) willingness to sign the final consent forms. For birthmothers, this is the last opportunity to carry through or reverse a conflicted decision involving the abandonment of her baby at his or her most vulnerable moment, the moment of birth (A. Brodzinsky, 1990; Winkler et al., 1988). As reported extensively in the media, the rights and responsibilities of birthfathers, who may or may not have been involved in the adoption placement process, and who may or may not have supported the birthmother during pregnancy, now have moved to the courts (Deykin, Patti, & Ryan, 1988). News reports of court decisions supporting birthfathers' claims to have the adoptee returned to them strike further fear into the hearts of adoptive parents and, if they are sufficiently of age, adoptees.

The second set of pivotal decisions made by others involves the probationary period and the final adoption decree. The successful completion of both frees the adoptive parents from most of their fears that the birthparents might reclaim the adoptee and from further scrutiny and judgment of their capacity to parent. Many policy, legal, and procedural issues remain unresolved regarding this pivotal stage in the adoption process (Cole & Donley, 1990). These issues often involve value judgments and require careful consideration by both policy makers and those who carry out public policy.

The transition to parenthood is exhausting for all parents. Commonly cited problems for biological parents include increased fatigue, decreased social relations, increased work and family role conflicts, increased financial strain, decreased sexual relations, a heightened sense of responsibility for another person, and a decline in marital satisfaction (Brodzinsky & Huffman, 1988, p. 270).

As Brodzinsky and Huffman (1988) note, however, there are several additional complications or "role handicaps" that adoptive parents must deal with in addition to those faced by biological parents. Five are elaborated on here: (1) resolving individual and couple emotions involved in mourning the loss of the fantasized biological child; (2) the uncompromising uncertainty of whether or when the adoptee will arrive; (3) the inherently judgmental and intrusive evaluation process to determine their fitness as potential parents; (4) the social stigma and perhaps internalized personal stigma of announced infertility and having to settle for the "second best" alternative of raising someone else's biological child; and (5) a shortage of role models for guidance and support. In addition, because there is no preprogrammed 9-month timetable, when it finally does become clear that the adoptee will, in fact, arrive, there often is an intense flurry of activity. Adoptive parents often find themselves in the dead of night frantically buying or borrowing the basic elements of neonatal care, and perhaps some basic caretaking advice and assistance as well.

Clinicians can help adoptive parents as they work through feelings surrounding pari-adoption and provide perspective and balance. Adoption support groups are especially important because those who have gone through the experience can provide support, encouragement, practical advice, and, most importantly, example.

Stage 3: Infancy and Toddlerhood

Images of and emotions toward birthparents and infertility fade as adoptive parents experience the long-sought joy and fulfillment of their many years of travail—their adopted child. Perhaps the most critical transition for the adoptive parents is relinquishing their fantasized biological child and coming to see themselves as they really are, the eminently entitled and very "real" psychological parents of their adoptee (Hajal & Rosenberg, 1991; Miall, 1987).

The first affective developmental milestones are the bonding of the adoptive parents to the adoptee and the attachment of the adoptee to the adoptive parents. Absence of bonding (believed rare) likely would represent adoptive parent psychopathology (and thus screening failure) or marked violations of expectations for the adoptee in domains such as health, drug addiction, temperament, or physical appearance (Hajal & Rosenberg, 1991). The very limited data available indicate that adoptees attach themselves to their adoptive mothers much the same as biological infants attach themselves to their biological mothers (Singer, Brodzinsky, Ramsay, Steir, & Waters, 1985). No data on adoptee attachment to adoptive fathers were found.

In reviewing the literature on the early stages of adoptive family life, Brodzinsky and Huffman (1988) report that the affective quality of adoptive parenting is equal to or superior to that of biological parenting. Although counterintuitive, given the extra stressors involved in the transition to adoptive parenthood discussed earlier, they believe that four protective factors account for the higher affective quality of early adoptive parenting: (1) the older age of adoptive parents; (2) the longer marriages of adoptive parents; (3) the greater emotional fulfillment in adoptive parents after intense and often lengthy emotional deprivation; and (4) the development of better coping patterns. Indeed, in non-adoptive families, there is some evidence that older parents (fathers in their thirties and mothers in their forties) are perceived more favorably by their children than parents in their twenties (Finley, Janovetz, & Rogers, 1990, 1991) and that older fathers (late twenties and thirties) report greater joy and satisfaction in fathering and have more child-centered child-rearing attitudes than younger fathers (early twenties) (Finley, Stephenson, Williams, & Janovetz, 1993). The parental ages reported above are calculated as the parent's age at the birth of the child while the children's ratings were done when the children were late adolescents.

Markers of psychopathology linked to adoptive status generally are not seen at this stage, and clinical intervention typically is not required (Brodzinsky, 1987). Adoption support groups become a delight as adoptive parents share their experiences with other adoptive parents and serve as role models of adoption success and a source of advice for prospective adoptive parents.

Stage 4: Preschool

The critical issue at this stage of the adoptive family life cycle is "telling" the child that she or he is adopted. Although telling at this stage is commonly recommended, telling, in and of itself, can be viewed as a substantial contributor to the behavior problems attributable to adoptive status. The only alternative to telling, however, is not telling, and this is widely regarded as far more risky. It is more risky because of the probable consequences for the adoptee's feeling of trust and confidence in his or her adoptive parents and the parent–adoptee relationship should the adoptee learn of his

or her adoptive status from other sources and/or under adverse circumstances.

Adoption professionals generally recommend telling the child that they are adopted in a warm and loving context and when things are going well with the family. A primary task of the adoptive parent is to create an atmosphere in which adoption can be discussed freely throughout the life cycle. Most recommend telling as soon as the child can label themselves as adopted and by using some variant of the "chosen child" story (Rosenberg, 1992).

The key issue for the adoptee is the intellectual comprehension and emotional realization that the adoptive parents who have cared for, loved, nurtured, and "chose" him or her are not the biological parents who conceived him or her. This, in turn introduces the reality of abandonment, possible perceptions of birthparent rejection, and perhaps a lifelong preoccupation with the "why" of abandonment.

A seminal contribution to the adoption literature is the work of Brodzinsky and his colleagues on the adoptee's social–cognitive developmental *understanding* of the *meaning* of adoption. Their research has made it clear that the child's understanding of adoption follows a developmental timetable. Briefly, most 4 to 5 year olds do not understand the meaning of adoption and often fuse birth and adoption concepts. However, by age 6 most children understand the difference between entering a family through birth versus entering a family through adoption, and it is this differential understanding that—psychologically—makes all the difference (Brodzinsky, Schechter, & Brodzinsky, 1986).

Preschool adoptees generally accept the warm, glowing embrace of adoptive family life and the chosen child story told to them. In the chosen child story, adoptive parents emphasize the positives of how they longed for a child and were fortunate to be able to choose the adoptee to love and cherish. Adoptive parents generally underplay or omit issues of relinquishment and loss. Because the adoptee's social–cognitive developmental level does not permit them to distinguish between entering a family through birth versus adoption, adoptees at this stage often assume that all children are adopted. The processes of conception and birth are little or not understood. In one adoptive family, for example, when the oldest adoptee was 3½ they picked up the second adoptee at an airport. For a long period thereafter, whenever the family passed an airport, the oldest would point to the airport and talk about how that is where babies come from. Presumably she or he had in mind a giant silver stork!

As Brodinsky's work has made clear, birthparents are far from the consciousness of adoptees at this stage of the adoptive family life cycle. However, the telling process definitely returns the birthparents to the hearts and minds of the adoptive parents. Although there are a multitude of feelings and thoughts flooding the adoptive parents, certainly among them are the reminders of infertility, the fantasized biological child, and fears that the birthparents will change their minds and seek to retrieve the adoptee. This fear is elevated by media accounts of legal proceedings where adoptees have been returned to birthparents. Above all, however, adoptive parents are concerned with how their adoptee is going to respond to the telling. Most adoptive parents experience anxiety, discomfort, and concern about what to say and how to say it.

In our culture, it is easy to understand why an adoptive parent might wish to postpone, avoid, or minimize the "required" telling. It is difficult to imagine adoptive parents delighting and experiencing joy in the process of telling. In large part, one suspects, this is because the telling process inherently creates a psychological, and a later-to-be-realized biological gulf between the adoptive parents and the adoptee where none existed prior to the telling. How do you tell a child you love that, biologically, they are not yours, that they came from some other mommy's tummy? And, what other mommy?

A comforting thought to parents is that if they begin the telling process early enough, the adoptee's limited social–cognitive developmental understanding will compensate for a less than perfect performance on the part of the adoptive parents. In addition, if parents follow the "standard" advice, they will have an opportunity to correct any early awkwardness with continuing discussions of adoption as the adoptee's social–cognitive level matures. Further comfort may be derived from the fact that, like infancy and toddlerhood, there tend to be no major signs of adoption-induced behavior problems in the preschool stage. Adoption-linked clinical interventions typically are not required at this stage.

Stage 5: School-Age Child

Brodzinsky (1987) and his colleagues made an important contribution to the research literature when they found that the timing of the emergence of behavior problems in adoptees was linked to social–cognitive developmental stages. It is only as the adoptee enters Piaget's concrete operational stage that she or he comprehends the difference between entering a family through adoption versus entering a family through birth. It is the self-realization of this distinction that causes the adoptee—for the first time in his or her life—to intellectually comprehend and affectively experience the existence of a second set of parents—those who gave birth to him or her—and consequently, the reality of abandonment, loss, and the probability of perceived birthparent rejection.

Unfortunately, as suggested by Rosenberg (1992), this comprehension introduces the darker side of the telling pro-

cess. She notes that the first autobiographical information adoptees receive about themselves is that they are a mistake, unplanned, unable to be cared for, perhaps unwanted, or perhaps loved but given away for the adoptee's best interest in a better life. No matter what the explanation given for relinquishment, the adoptee is left to construe a story involving the assignment of goodness or badness and fault or blame for relinquishment. Above all, having been relinquished by their birthparents, will they also be relinquished by their adoptive parents? Permanency is often a preoccupation for adoptees that may show up in many guises, including perfectionism. Given that the above realizations come at this cognitive developmental stage, it is perhaps not surprising that externalizing behaviors also appear at this time.

Additional consequences of this self-realization for the adoptee include a greater curiosity about their origins (the characteristics of their birthparents and the circumstances of their relinquishment), an intense interest in the "why" of their abandonment, and concern for the security of their adoption and their adoptive family (Brodzinsky et al., 1995). The task of assimilating and accommodating both birth and adoptive families at both the intellectual and emotional levels is indeed a daunting one for a 6 to 12 year old. The most detailed presentation of these developmental changes combining both Piagetian and Eriksonian perspectives can be found in Brodzinsky (1987).

A major task of the adoptive parents at this stage is to help their adoptee to go through the process of "adaptive grieving" for the lost birthparents either on their own, with support groups, or with clinical intervention (Winkler et al., 1988). Oftentimes the adoptee seeks specific information regarding his or her birthparents and the circumstances of the relinquishment, information the adoptive parents may or may not have and may or may not wish to share.

Because this is the first stage in which adoption-linked behavior problems may emerge, adoptive parents and clinicians must determine whether the problems are related to adoption or to some other event (Melina, 1994) *and* whether the behavior represents an adjustment reaction or a full-blown psychiatric disorder. This task is difficult because the adoption experience may be intertwined with other pathogenic factors (LeVine & Sallee, 1990). For example, attention-deficit hyperactivity disorder (ADHD) is known to have a strong genetic–biochemical component. The question might be to treat the adoptee as a typical ADHD case, or to examine whether the challenges of adoptive family life have accentuated or attenuated the disorder, or whether adoption challenges led to the development of symptoms frequently associated with ADHD such as concentration or attentional difficulties in the absence of underlying ADHD. The same question arises for externalizing or antisocial conduct, which also is known to have a genetic component in some individuals (Roth & Finley, 1998). An excellent handbook that discusses clinical issues for all members of the adoption triangle and that may assist in attributing etiology is that of Winkler and colleagues (1988). Another psychodynamic source is LeVine and Sallee (1990).

Stage 6: Adolescence

The central issue of adolescence is identity formation. Unfortunately, existing research does not clearly indicate whether identity formation is more difficult for adoptees (as commonly believed) than for appropriate comparison samples of biological adolescents (Hoopes, 1990). Hoopes notes that all three logically possible outcomes are possible: (1) the adopted adolescent can achieve a regular mature identity; (2) they may master the task better than adolescents of other family forms because they have to work harder at it; or (3) the stresses of the adoptive family may lead to crisis and difficulty. Whether or not the search for identity also involves a search for the birthparents (Hoopes, 1990; Schechter & Bertocci, 1990), it is difficult to imagine an adoptee giving no thought to birthparents at this stage (Schaffer & Kral, 1988). Additional hurdles for the adoptee in search of an identity include a lack of physical resemblance to the adoptive parents, two families (birth and adoptive) to individuate from, and the role of the fantasies about the absent and unknown birthparents that inevitably will arise (Kirschner & Nagel, 1988).

The adolescent adoptee's fantasies about his or her birthparents may have a more powerful impact on him or her during adolescence than at any other stage of the adoptive family life cycle (Hajal & Rosenberg, 1991). The power of such fantasies to dominate behavior in the adolescent adoptee is dramatically illustrated in the following four abbreviated case studies. As will be seen, "living down" to, and identifying with, a degraded image of one's birthparents can have quite negative consequences that are inconsistent with the lifestyle and values of the adoptive parents. The four case studies are quoted below.

> An 11-year-old girl, Janet, who had enjoyed a loving and close relationship with her adoptive parents, became reclusive and irritable as her breast development began...she confessed her fears that her body was becoming like her birthmother's. She was afraid that with her emerging sexuality, she was on her way to becoming a 'slut' like (her) mother had been. She was losing her sense of herself as the good, decent kid (Hajal & Rosenberg, 1991, p. 83).

> Sarah, an 18-year-old adoptee, believed that her birth parents were still married, living a poor life in a small apartment, constantly arguing and in turmoil because they had given her away. She fantasized that her birthmother was a

"hooker," and identified with the fantasized mother through her own promiscuity (Kirschner & Nagel, 1988, p. 306).

> Jody's response was that she was more comfortable with people of the *same class* as she imagined her birthmother to be from. Disadvantage had more meaning for her than the material and cultural advantages of her adoptive family. At age 16, Jody married a young man from one of these families, a family with many relatives and in which there were a number of out-of-wedlock pregnancies (Schechter & Bertocci, 1990, p. 84).

And there is the rescue fantasy:

> Bobbie responded to one projective test item with the following story: A child gets in trouble with the law. His "real" parents read about the crime in the newspaper and come to rescue him. They fight legal battles and raise money to free him from jail (Kirschner & Nagel, 1988, p. 306).

For adoptive parents, the budding sexuality and reproductive capacity of their adolescent may remind them of their own infertility, and it may heighten fantasized or real sexual relations because the biologically based incest taboo is absent. Worrisomely, concern may arise about whether the adolescent will identify with the infertile but presumably responsible and nurturing adoptive parents or the demonstrably fertile but perhaps abandoning, rejecting, or irresponsible birthparents.

Importantly, Rosenberg (1992) suggests that the solution for adoptive families is to view the permanence of their relationship as based on their shared life experiences rather than on blood ties. Family emotional and psychological connections can remain permanent in the absence of blood ties. The task for adoptive parents is to manage these difficult behaviors through appropriate limit setting and guidance along with providing an environment in which adoption and birthparent issues may be openly explored, including a possible search. The adoptive parent must remain available to the adoptee and perhaps bond with the adoptee through their shared experience of loss (Winkler et al., 1988).

An important task for adoptive parents and clinicians is to "normalize" the developmental challenges facing all members of the adoption triangle (Rosenberg, 1992). Key to this approach is the recognition that it is normal and natural for all adoptive families to deal with these challenges. The goal of normalization is to lessen the feelings of abnormality and detoxify the struggles. For Winkler and colleagues (1988), the central focus of therapeutic work is helping all parties to understand and accept the fact that the adoptive family is structured out of loss. In their view, denying the difference between adoptive families and biological families is the major cause of dysfunction in the adoptive family. It also is possible that a factor contributing to denial is not knowing how to handle or not feeling comfortable with the differences between adoptive and biological families on the part of the adoptive parents.

Stage 7: Adulthood

The endpoint at which one judges adoption as success or failure is adult functioning. It is the author's view that one should rely on concrete, objective, real-life indices in adulthood because so much of the evaluation of differences between adoptees and children of other family forms in childhood and adolescence is based on psychological instruments or subjective judgments. Indices might include common indicators of adult well-being or malfunctioning such as education (amount, quality, and grades), marital history (including divorce and remarriage), parenting quality (as judged by children), physical health, mental health (including inpatient and outpatient treatment or commitment), alcohol or drug abuse, contact with the criminal justice system (arrests, convictions, and incarceration), occupational history (unemployment, job changes, job status, and work achievement), financial history (income and assets), military service, welfare status, contact with social service agencies, and so on.

The logic of evaluating outcome in adulthood is twofold: (1) if adoptive status is inherently pathogenic, then the longer one spends in this status, the greater the psychopathology that ought to emerge; or (2) it is possible that one would find less psychopathology among adoptees in adulthood if their struggles in childhood and adolescence have strengthened them beyond the emotional well-being of most adults.

What then does the empirical literature suggest? Two recent reviews indicate discordant results and claim too few studies to reach a definitive conclusion (Brodzinsky, 1993; Wierzbicki, 1993). One review, however, concludes that adult adoptees are as well off as non-adoptees and better off than child and adolescent adoptees (Schaffer & Kral, 1988). Further, a recent study by Feigelman (1997) suggests that although adoptees have more problems during adolescence, by adulthood they are similar to adults from intact biological families and better off than adults from stepfamilies and single parent families in terms of drug, alcohol, and cocaine abuse, clinical depression, educational attainment, employment, earnings, and assets.

Clearly, the adoption literature could benefit from additional research on adult adoptees and research focusing on real-life outcomes. The literature also could benefit from a more thorough consideration of the advantages and disadvantages of adoption as well as the strengths and weaknesses of adoption *in comparison to* other family forms.

Such an inclusive–comparative approach will provide a more integrated perspective on adoption by "decentering" our perhaps somewhat microscopic focus on adoption and looking at adoptees in relation to the multitude of family forms found in the world today.

With recent increases both in the number and types of adoptions, as well as increases in adoption research, progress is in the making.

SUMMARY AND CONCLUSIONS

This chapter has reviewed portions of the adoption literature and has (1) concluded that the epidemiological view that adoptees have elevated rates of psychopathology cannot be supported due to methodological shortcomings in existing studies and the absence of comprehensive national data; (2) concluded that adoption *is* a successful intervention into the lives of abandoned children; (3) concluded that—in clinical settings—adoptees tend to present more externalizing and academic/hyperactivity problems than non-adoptees and noted possible etiological factors including genetic dispositions; and, (4) provided a detailed discussion of the adoptive family life cycle focusing on developmental challenges unique to members of the adoption triangle (birthparents, adoptive parents, and adoptees) as well as interventions to help meet these challenges.

REFERENCES

Anthony, E. J. (1990). Foreword. In D. M. Brodzinsky & M. D. Schechter (Eds.), *The psychology of adoption* (pp. vii–viii). New York: Oxford University Press.

Baran, A., & Pannor, R. (1993). Perspectives on open adoption. *The Future of Children, 3*(1), 119–124.

Bartholet, E. (1993). International adoption: Current status and future prospects. *The Future of Children, 3*(1), 89–103.

Berry, M. (1993). Risks and benefits of open adoption. *The Future of Children, 3*(1), 125–138.

Brodzinsky, A. B. (1990). Surrendering an infant for adoption: The birthmother's experience. In D. M. Brodzinsky & M. D. Shechter (Eds.), *The psychology of adoption* (pp. 295–315). New York: Oxford University Press.

Brodzinsky, D. M. (1987). Adjustment to adoption: A psychosocial perspective. *Clinical Psychology Review, 7*, 25–47.

Brodzinsky, D. M. (1990). A stress and coping model of adoption adjustment. In D. M. Brodzinsky & M. D. Schechter (Eds.), *The psychology of adoption* (pp. 3–24). New York: Oxford University Press.

Brodzinsky, D. M. (1993). Long-term outcomes in adoption. *The Future of Children, 3*(1), 153–166.

Brodzinsky, D. M., & Huffman, L. (1988). Transition to adoptive parenthood. In R. Palkovitz & M. B. Sussman (Eds.), *Transitions to parenthood* (pp. 267–286). New York: Haworth Press.

Brodzinsky, D. M., Lang, R., & Smith, D. (1995). Parenting adopted children. In M. H. Bornstein (Ed.) *Handbook of parenting: Vol. 3. Status and social conditions of parenting* (pp. 209–232). Mahwah, NJ: Erlbaum.

Brodzinsky, D. M., & Schechter, M. D. (Eds.) (1990). *The psychology of adoption*. New York: Oxford University Press.

Brodzinsky, D. M., Schechter, D., & Brodzinsky, A. B. (1986). Children's knowledge of adoption: Developmental changes and implications for adjustment. In R. Ashmore & D. M. Brodzinsky (Eds.), *Thinking about the family: Views of parents and children* (pp. 205–232). Hillsdale, NJ: Erlbaum.

Cadoret, R. J. (1990). Biologic perspectives of adoptee adjustment. In D. M. Brodzinsky & M. D. Schechter (Eds.), *The psychology of adoption* (pp. 25–41). New York: Oxford University Press.

Cole, E. S., & Donley, K. S. (1990). History, values, and placement policy issues in adoption. In D. M. Brodzinsky & M. D. Schechter (Eds.), *The psychology of adoption* (pp. 273–294). New York: Oxford University Press.

DeAngelis, T. (1995, January). Adoptees, new families fare well, studies show. *APA Monitor,* p. 36.

Deykin, E. Y., Patti, P., & Ryan, J. (1988). Fathers of adopted children: A study of the impact of child surrender on birthfathers. *American Journal of Orthopsychiatry, 58,* 240–248.

Feigelman, W. (1997). Adopted adults: Comparisons with persons raised in conventional families. In H. E. Gross and M. B. Sussman (Eds.), *Families and adoption* (pp. 199–223). New York: Haworth Press.

Finley, G. E. (1998). On individual difference, choice, selection, and complexity in adoption research. *Adoption Quarterly, 1*(4), pp. 83–91.

Finley, G. E., Janovetz, V. A., & Rogers, B. (1990). *University students' perceptions of parental acceptance–rejection as a function of parental age.* Poster presented at the Conference on Human Development, Richmond, VA.

Finley, G. E., Janovetz, V. A., & Rogers, B. (1991). *Parental age and parenting quality as perceived by late adolescents.* Poster presented at the 99th annual convention of the American Psychological Association, San Francisco.

Finley, G. E., Stephenson, D., Williams, S., & Janovetz, V. (1993). *Father's age and the paternal feelings and attitudes of firsttime fathers.* Poster presented at the Society for Research in Child Development Convention, New Orleans.

Gottesman, I. I., & Goldsmith, H. H. (1994). Developmental psychopathology of antisocial behavior: Inserting genes into ontogenesis and epigenesis. In C. A. Nelson (Ed.), *Threats to optimal development: Integrating biological, psychological, and social risk factors* (pp. 69–104). Hillsdale, NJ: Erlbaum.

Grotevant, H. D., & McRoy, R. (1990). Adopted adolescents in residential treatment: The role of the family. In D. M. Brodzinsky & M. D. Schechter (Eds.), *The psychology of adoption* (pp. 167–186). New York: Oxford University Press.

Hajal, F., & Rosenberg, E. B. (1991). The family life cycle in adoptive families. *American Journal of Orthopsychiatry, 61,* 78–85.

Hoopes, J. L. (1990). Adoption and identity formation. In D. M. Brodzinsky & M. D. Schechter (Eds.), *The psychology of adoption* (pp. 144–166). New York: Oxford University Press.

Jette, S. H. (1990). The adoption alternative. In M. Seibel (Ed.), *Infertility: A comprehensive text* (pp. 563–570). Norwalk, CT: Appleton & Lange.

Kadushin, A. (1967). A follow-up study of children adopted when older: Criteria of success. *American Journal of Orthopsychiatry, 37,* 530–539.

Kadushin, A. (1980). *Child welfare services* (3rd ed.). New York: Macmillan.

Kirk, H. D., Jonassohn, K., & Fish, A. D. (1966). Are adopted children especially vulnerable to stress? *Archives of General Psychiatry, 14,* 291–298.

Kirschner, D., & Nagel, L. (1988). Antisocial behavior in adoptees: Patterns and dynamics. *Child and Adolescent Social Work, 5,* 300–314.

LeVine, E. S., & Sallee, A. L. (1990). Critical phases among adoptees and their families: Implications for therapy. *Child and Adolescent Social Work, 7,* 217–232.

McKenzie, J. K. (1993). Adoption of children with special needs. *The Future of Children, 3*(1), 62–76.

Mech, E. V. (1973). Adoption: A policy perspective. In B. M. Caldwell & H. N. Ricciuti (Eds.), *Review of child development research* (Vol. 3). Chicago: University of Chicago Press.

Melina, L. R. (1994). Adoption in perspective: When is an issue adoption-related? *Adopted Child, 13*(12), 1–4.

Miall, C. E. (1987). The stigma of adoptive parent status: Perceptions of community attitudes toward adoption and the experience of informal social sanctioning. *Family Relations, 36,* 34–39.

Rohner, R. P. (1986). *The warmth dimension: Foundations of parental acceptance–rejection theory.* Beverly Hills CA: Sage.

Rosenberg, E. B. (1992). *The adoption life cycle: The children and their families through the years.* New York: Free Press.

Rosenthal, J. A. (1993). Outcomes of adoption of children with special needs. *The Future of Children, 3*(1), 77–88.

Roth, W. E., & Finley, G. E. (1998). Adoption and antisocial personality: Genetic and environmental factors associated with antisocial outcomes. *Child & Adolescent Social Work Journal, 15*(2), 133–149.

Schaffer, J., & Kral, R. (1988). Adoptive families. In C. S. Chilman, E. W. Nunnally, & F. M. Cox (Eds.), *Variant family forms* (pp. 165–184). Beverly Hills CA: Sage.

Schechter, M. D., & Bertocci, D. (1990). The meaning of the search. In D. M. Brodzinsky & M. D. Schechter (Eds.), *The psychology of adoption* (pp. 62–92). New York: Oxford University Press.

Schulman, I., & Behrman, R. E. (Eds.) (1993). Adoption. *The Future of Children, 3*(1), 1–182.

Silverman, A. (1993). Outcomes of transracial adoption. *The Future of Children, 3*(1), 104–118.

Singer, L. M., Brodzinsky, D. M., Ramsay, D., Steir, M., & Waters, E. (1985). Mother–infant attachment in adoptive families. *Child Development, 56,* 1543–1551.

Small, J. W. (1987). Working with adoptive families. *Public Welfare,* 41–48.

Stewart, B. J. (1990). Adoption, personality disorder and parental guilt: Implications of genetic research for social work. *Child and Adolescent Social Work, 7,* 233–246.

Stolley, K. (1993). Statistics on adoption in the United States. *The Future of Children, 3*(1), 26–42.

Warren, S. B. (1992). Lower threshold for referral for psychiatric treatment for adopted adolescents. *Journal of the American Academy of Child and Adolescent Psychiatry, 31,* 512–517.

Wierzbicki, M. (1978). *The psychological adjustment of adopted children.* Unpublished manuscript.

Wierzbicki, M. (1993). Psychological adjustment of adoptees: A meta-analysis. *Journal of Clinical Child Psychology, 22,* 447–454.

Winkler, R. C., Brown, D. W., van Keppel, M., & Blanchard, A. (1988). *Clinical practice in adoption.* New York: Pergamon Press.

Zill, N. (1985). *Behavior and learning problems in adopted children: Findings from a U.S. national survey of child health.* Paper presented at the meeting of the Society for Research in Child Development, Toronto.

CHAPTER 23

CHILDREN OF ABUSIVE PARENTS

Sandra T. Azar
Sharon L. Bober

WHAT'S SO BAD ABOUT CHILD ABUSE FOR CHILDREN?

This may seem like a strange question to ask. It, however, is the question that needs to be posed carefully if one is to gain a thorough understanding of the developmental impact of abuse on children's lives and intervene appropriately. Developmental research has told us that child outcome evolves out of the multiple transactions between child characteristics, caregiver adequacy, and environmental factors that occur over time (Sameroff & Chandler, 1975). Breakdown occurs only when some continuous factor is present that results in the child "organizing" his or her world in a manner that is maladaptive. This perspective, therefore, requires examining child abuse from a wider lens than has been typical and considering it in the context of all the domains of children's lives (Azar, 1986; Wolfe, 1987).

From this perspective, abuse and neglect of children can be viewed as a heterogeneous event, not a unitary one. That is, when abuse has an impact upon the course of a child's development, it is typically associated with a series of events, any one of which or all of which might potentially "de-rail" developmental progress temporarily or permanently (Azar,

Barnes, & Twentyman, 1988). Its effect may be temporary, in the sense that it influences functioning at that point in time only, or permanent, in that it negatively influences important capacities and/or inhibits specific relational transactions that form foundations for subsequent development. For example, if early peer transactions are unduly restricted (e.g., due to lack of interpersonal trust or physical handicaps resulting from abuse), the child may be deprived of later transactions important for further social learning (e.g., contact in the playground, social support). In addition, maltreatment does not occur in a vacuum, but in a familial, community, and societal context of other events (e.g., domestic violence, supportive or unsupportive kin network, poverty), all of which may merge to produce outcome (what have been called compensatory and destabilizing factors: Azar & Wolfe, 1989; Cicchetti & Rizley, 1981). Identification of maltreatment may also trigger societal responses that may further influence a child's developmental trajectory (e.g., foster care; testifying in court).

Furthermore, maltreatment itself is not a unitary phenomenon. Outcomes may vary with the type or types of maltreatment present (physical, emotional, sexual or neglectful behavior), frequency and chronicity, the number of perpetrators and their relationship to the child, and when in the child's development it occurs. For example, if the perpetrator is a focal figure in a child's life, it may have a different type of impact upon views of social relationships than if he or she were a stranger.

Finally, and perhaps most importantly, abuse occurs to a specific child who has specific characteristics (e.g., cognitive delays, temperament, handicaps). It may be interpreted by that child in multiple ways (e.g., as evidence of lack of worth, as evidence that relationships are untrustworthy). It is, therefore, important to consider how the child brings meaning to this event and to the interventions that follow (e.g., foster care). Moreover, this meaning may change from one developmental era (e.g., childhood) to another (e.g., as they begin their own parenting).

Given this variability, abuse may leave lesser or greater physical, social, and emotional "scars" with which children must cope, and these "scars" may be more or less visible at different points in their development. For some children, there may be little in the way of observable consequences and for others, functioning may be severely affected. This continuum of responses must be considered carefully in clinical work. Clinicians may be too ready to see abused children as severely troubled. This may cause us to miss their strengths.

To begin our discussion, the multiple aspects of maltreatment in a child's life will be examined, along with the outcomes that may follow from them. Clearly, maltreatment may involve one or more of these aspects and their interactive effects may be difficult to predict. Artificially breaking this experience into separate domains, however, will make our task more manageable and provide a conceptual framework for clinical assessment and intervention. Throughout our discussion implications for treatment will be highlighted.

This chapter will attempt to provide an integrating framework in which to view the impact of maltreatment, both developmentally and clinically. Because the typical focus of clinical intervention is on the parent and family setting, our formulation focuses on the potential for a more general breakdown in the caregiving environment that may be associated with maltreatment (Azar, 1986; Azar, Barnes, & Twentyman, 1988). The more pervasive this breakdown, the more the course of children's development may be influenced. It will also highlight the impact of abuse as being on a continuum from mild distress to trauma, which may result in greater or lesser disturbance in children's core schema regarding the self, others, and the world.

Abuse/Neglect as a Physical Event

The physical consequences from abuse are very real. In 1995, 996 children died as a result of maltreatment, with an estimated 77 percent of these children under the age of three (National Center on Child Abuse and Neglect, 1997). More generally, maltreatment (physical and in some cases, sexual abuse) can produce mild to severe physical consequences to children (e.g., burns, broken limbs, bruises). Some of these have lasting impact, while others heal quickly and fade. Children's functioning may be affected directly (e.g., reduced mobility; impaired neurological functioning) or indirectly (e.g., increased fear of any physical contact). The physical elements of abuse are often forgotten in psychological accounts of the experience and need to be considered therapeutically in terms of their links to the psychological impact (e.g., embarrassment due to disfiguring scars increasing social distance from peers) and in terms of the child's ability to deal with therapeutic intervention itself (e.g., attentional problems; perceptions of threat while alone with a therapist) (Azar, Breton, & Miller, 1998). The types of physical damage done to children vary greatly. Some examples are presented below.

One form of maltreatment found in infants is "shaken baby syndrome" (Caffey, 1972, 1974). It is believed that some parents feel that shaking an infant when they are frustrated with them is "better" than striking them. This act, however, may result in severe damage to the infant's brain and intracranial blood vessels. In some cases, mental retardation, seizures, or blindness may occur. It is now believed that shaking alone may not produce these injuries, rather that some kind of impact must co-occur with it (e.g., shaking a baby and then throwing him or her against the side of a crib; Duhaime et al., 1987).

Unfortunately, given the possibility of little observable physical evidence from shaking and the private nature of abuse, this type of maltreatment may not come to the attention of authorities. Although early intervention agents may not think to discuss "discipline" as a topic with parents of infants, education on the effects of shaking and training in stress management skills may be crucial at this point in children's development.

More commonly maltreatment involves either direct blows to children's bodies or in some cases, burns. A variety of physical traumas can result, including bruises, welts, lacerations, abrasions, and skeletal, head, and internal injuries (Pagelow, 1984). Clinicians need to be especially attentive to potential subtle neuropsychological problems that may affect academic performance and communication. In some cases, abuse causes lasting disabilities, which produce additional stress (e.g., periodic medical care, ongoing rehabilitation, and adjustments to having a disability), that requires further coping.

Although the circumstances surrounding physical abuse have not been shown to vary in any consistently identifiable patterns, there is some evidence that the types of physical abuse vary with the age of the child. For example, young children tend to be exposed to burns (e.g., scalding) and suffer from hemorrhages and bone fractures; younger school-age children tend to be hit with objects (e.g., electrical chords, belts) and suffer erythema and marks; and older school-age children and teenagers tend to be struck with fists or by caregivers' feet (Johnson & Showers, 1985). This suggests that the triggers for maltreatment may vary with development or with the ability of the child to defend himself or herself (Azar & Siegel, 1990). For example, the incessant crying of infants may trigger an attempt to silence them (e.g., suffocation, scalding, shaking); whereas adolescent behavior that may be interpreted as rebellious might trigger other kinds of control attempts (e.g., belittling them, being overly restrictive of their contact with peers) and result in parent–child physical fights (e.g., punching the teen with a fist).

Younger children may be the most vulnerable. Head injury fatalities, for example, appear to decline with age during childhood (below age 15) (Luersson, Klauber, & Marshall, 1988). Overall, although physical outcomes are more frequent in infants and young children, the health and safety needs of older children and teenagers should not be ignored (Azar, 1991a).

The physical consequences of sexual abuse are only beginning to be examined. Clearly, it carries physical risks (e.g., exposure to sexually transmitted disease, vaginal and rectal tears). Recently, other physical effects have been suggested (e.g., hormonal activity and premature puberty; Trickett & Putnam, 1993). Clinically, for the young child, the experience of sexual abuse may also trigger many concerns (e.g., worries about body integrity). A "therapeutic" physical during which these concerns can be addressed by a physician may be helpful (Madansky & Santora, 1989). It is reported clinically that many sexually abused children believe that they are different from other children because of the abuse, and in some cases believe that people can tell they were sexually abused just by looking at them. Group work may be helpful here, where peers, whose feedback may be more powerful than the therapist's, can challenge such perceptions.

Establishing a sense of body integrity is also an important therapeutic goal for children who may feel that they do not have control over what is either done to their bodies or what their bodies can do to others (e.g., perpetrators might emphasize the idea that the child is producing their loss of control or the child may make attributions to the self for the abuse like "I must have done something to make him think I wanted him to abuse me.") (Cohen & Mannarino, 1993; James, 1989). Cognitive restructuring work to challenge beliefs regarding control may be helpful here. Assertiveness training and safety education may also be helpful, but the

therapist must be clear on the level of control a child might have in situations that are threatening and must be careful not to create conflict for the child by creating unrealistic expectations that they can protect themselves (Cohen & Mannarino, 1993). Because the trauma of abuse is very much a physical experience, some clinical reports emphasize that nonverbal techniques be integrated into therapeutic work with sexually abused children, such as music, movement, and body-awareness exercises. Empirical validation for the effectiveness of these techniques has yet to be tested.

Many abused children also experience concurrent undernourishment and poor medical care, which may play a role in the deficits they show. For example, anemia due to poor nutrition may lead to apathy and may account for poor school performance (Martin, 1976). In some cases, a condition called *failure to thrive,* which can have short-term and long-term negative consequences (Oates, Peacock, & Forrest, 1985), may result from neglect by caretakers. Environmental risks may also be present in the homes of maltreating families (e.g., lead paint; poorly stored cleaning solvents). These safety risks coupled with less monitoring may pose greater potential for harm than the abuse itself. Indeed, maltreatment and accidental injuries have common contextual elements (Peterson, 1994). Children being left home alone unsupervised, a form of neglect, has been behind many of the childhood injuries and deaths found in house fires (Dubowitz, 1991).

Although there has been little attention paid to the indirect impact of the physical harm done by abuse, it might be posited that abuse which leaves visible scars or disabilities may be a constant reminder of the experience for the child (and for the perpetrator, if they remain in the child's life) and thus, may have reverberations throughout the child's life. For example, scars from being scalded on the legs may make wearing shorts and other revealing clothing more awkward and possibly threaten self-worth, as well as interfere with social development. This may be an especially potent factor in adolescence when physical appearance becomes more important. Continuing physical handicaps (e.g., brain damage) may make child care stressful and thus expose children to risk of further poor treatment by others (e.g., foster parents, peers) (Ammerman, VanHasselt, & Hersen, 1988). Such scars and disabilities may also make children's caretakers overprotective and this may convey a message of vulnerability or being "damaged," and this may limit experiences in the world. Again, this may have far-reaching developmental consequences. These kinds of concomitant psychological effects will be outlined in further detail later in the chapter.

Even if visible scars are not present, environmental cues may continue to trigger a state of physical distress. For example, a child may continue to sleep in the room where he or she was beaten or go to the playground where molestation occurred. The impact that such *chronic* arousal may have is just beginning to be examined.

In summary, the experience of physical threat and the failure to have basic needs for care and protection met may hamper multiple aspects of development to a greater or lesser extent. Children are forced to channel energy and attention, normally directed towards growth, into protection from abusive parents and concerns about survival. Methods used to cope with abuse may become ingrained in children's coping repertoires that do not serve them well outside the family (e.g., avoidant behavior, dissociation, aggressive behavior, hoarding of food). Indeed, some abused children exhibit an intense vigilance. For those who have been sexually and emotionally abused, evidence of post-traumatic stress symptomatology may also be present.

Finally, attention must be given to the idea that a portion of maltreated children, like all children, may start off life with medical problems, and the difficulties of caring for such children and/or their greater vulnerability may be a precursor to maltreatment or even act as a trigger (Ammerman, VanHasselt, & Hersen, 1988). Thus, this may add a special risk.

Disentangling the interactive impact of these direct and indirect factors is difficult clinically, if not impossible, but remaining cognizant of them may enrich clinical decision making (e.g., regarding the structure and content of treatment). For example, because fears of being alone with adults may hamper individual therapy, group work or peer-based interventions have been suggested as more beneficial (Aber & Allen, 1987; Fantuzzo, et al., 1988). Training children in new coping strategies and sensitizing adult caregivers to the "historical" origins of what might appear to be strange behaviors (e.g., hoarding of food, dissociation) may be useful in reducing their negative reactions and/or their inadvertently responding in such a way as to maintain them. Also, addressing a broader array of targets with parents (e.g., home safety, nutrition, etc.; Drotar, Wilson, & Sturm, 1989; Lutzker & Rice, 1984; Sarber, Halasz, Messmer, Brickett, & Lutzker, 1983; Tertinger, Greene, & Lutzker, 1984; Tymchuk, Yokota, & Rahbar, 1990) may reduce risk as much as reducing parental aggression. Finally, each developmental era brings with it certain high-"risk" parenting tasks, as well as stage-salient child issues that require specific skills to negotiate successfully. These areas may be targeted for intervention to reduce conflict and frustration within the family (e.g., in adolescence, the need for increased tolerance of moves toward autonomy) (Azar & Siegel, 1990). Conflict resolution training with parents and adolescents, for example, may reduce the potential for physical fights and ultimately, the potential for physical harm to teenagers (Schellenback & Guerney, 1987).

Abuse/Neglect as a Social Context

Abuse occurs to children and adolescents within a specific family setting, peer and school group, and community. Thus, no two incidents may present exactly the same challenge to their victim. Children's familial, socioeconomic, historical, geographical, and cultural background give a unique character to each such event. Consideration of these factors is crucial clinically. Despite such variability, however, abuse and neglect have been associated with specific social contexts and sociological variables that bear discussion.

Ever since child maltreatment was identified as a societal problem, poverty has been a constant correlate.[1] There are two ways in which this association is relevant to abused children's outcomes. The first focuses on the production of stress on the family (e.g., lack of physical resources like medical care, good nutrition) and the social context in which families must live (e.g., high-crime neighborhoods, unsafe housing). These stressors, independently or coupled with abuse, may produce negative outcomes. Abuse may have different impact on a child in a neighborhood of high crime and violence or in a family where a parent is also the object of violence than in more benign contexts. For example, Hennessy, Rabideau, Cicchetti, and Cummings (1994) found that abused and nonabused children differed in their reaction to interadult anger, with the former experiencing higher levels of fear. Thus, experiencing domestic violence, in addition to the personal experience of victimization, may increase vulnerability.

Because not all parents exposed to poverty abuse their children, a second explanation of the links among abuse, poverty, and negative child outcomes must be entertained, namely, that there are other factors that are producing this relationship. For example, social–cognitive problems in parents, such as poor problem solving, may lead to both economic difficulties (e.g., trouble keeping jobs) and higher levels of interpersonal frustration (e.g., inability to resolve conflicts with partners, as well as children) and poor child care (Azar, 1986; 1997). As will be seen later, we posit that these factors are at the core of what produces both an abusive environment and the poor outcomes seen in abused children. Such mediating factors may be more amenable to treatment.

In line with the latter explanation, specific types of interaction characterize maltreating families. As might be expected, higher levels of negative transactions have been found in such families (Bousha & Twentyman, 1984; Burgess & Conger, 1978). However, it should be pointed out that it is lower levels of overall interactions, as well as positive interactions, in particular, between parent and child that have most consistently differentiated abusive households (Lorber, Felton, & Reid, 1984; Reid, 1985). Both amounts of interaction and positive interactions have been strongly tied to children's positive social, cognitive, and emotional outcomes. Interactions in abusive families have also shown a discordant pattern. Abusive parents have been observed to be less able to modify their behavior in response to cues from their infants and children and to make inappropriate demands on them (Crittenden, 1982; Trickett & Kuczynski, 1986). They appear to be more indiscriminant in the attention they provide (Wahler & Dumas, 1986); to spend less time in close proximity to their infants (Dietrich, Starr, & Kaplan, 1980); to be less stimulating auditorily and tactilely to their infants (Dietrich, Starr, & Kaplan, 1980); and to be less sensitive and responsive to their children's distress cues and lower in the socioemotionally growth-fostering behavior that they provide their children (Bee, Disbrow, Johnson-Crowley, & Barnard, 1981). Thus, while the more abusive types of negative patterns of behavior may come more easily to mind in considering such families, it may be these *other patterns* that may be most detrimental to children's development.

We again suggest that at the root of these interactional problems are a set of parenting skills deficits that drive problems both within the family and outside of it. These deficits make such parents less than adequate role models for positive social interactions and poor providers of the stimulation necessary for cognitive development and the consistency needed for children's emotional stability. These include a narrow repertoire of parenting responses and poor impulse control, as well as deficits in social skills and in ability to cope with stress (Azar & Twentyman, 1986). Each of these skills has been effectively addressed in abusive parents with behavioral and cognitive–behavioral therapeutic strategies (see review by Azar, 1989).

Most relevant to our discussion, however, is a set of social–cognitive problems. Abusers appear to have scripts for relationships with others and in particular, with children, that are inappropriate and marked by a negative tone. Physically abusive and neglectful parents have been shown to have rigid and unrealistic standards for acceptable child behavior that children are likely to violate (e.g., a 2-year old can be expected to comfort you when you are sad and crying) (Azar, Robinson, Hekimian, & Twentyman, 1984; Azar & Rohrbeck, 1986). Similar cognitive distortions have been suggested among sexual offenders (Abel et al., 1989; Stermac & Segal, 1989).

These basic foundational beliefs about children and their role in relation to parents may lead to another cognitive problem found among maltreaters, a negative attributional bias toward children. That is, physically abusive parents in some studies have shown a tendency to over-ascribe negative intent to child behavior (Bradley & Peters, 1991; Larrance & Twentyman, 1983). Clearer is evidence that

maltreaters view their children more negatively than nonmaltreating parents (Mash, Johnston, & Kovitz, 1983; Reid, Kavanaugh, & Baldwin, 1987). Parents at risk for physical abuse appear to view child transgressions as being more grave in some domains (personal and conventional transgressions) than nonabusive parents and show less variability in their disciplinary techniques across transgressions with a predominance of coercive ones (Barnes & Azar, 1990; Chilamkurti & Milner, 1993; Trickett & Kuczynski, 1986). They also have poor interpersonal problem solving.

Such poor problem solving, distortions in interpretations of child behavior, and coercive responses would limit experiences that would foster social–cognitive learning in children. For example, parents who have such high unrealistic expectations have been shown to use explanation less often in disciplinary situations with preschoolers (Barnes & Azar, 1990). Such explanations are important for mastery of social rules and the development of perspective-taking and empathy. Behavioral and cognitive–behavioral treatment approaches to reducing negative family transactions and increasing positive and developmentally facilitating ones have shown much promise with abusive parents. To date, these have been directed toward families with preschoolers and early school-age children (Azar, 1989; Wolfe, Sandler, & Kaufman, 1981). Some small-scale efforts have also been applied with parents of infants (Lutzker, Lutzker, Braunling-McMorrow, & Eddleman, 1987) and teenagers (Schellenbach & Guerney, 1987) as well.

Disturbances in other parts of the family system have also been linked with maltreatment. Marital discord and disruptions have been common in such families. Wife battering also often co-occurs with child abuse in families (McKibben, DeVos, & Newberger, 1989; Stark & Flitcraft, 1988; Straus & Gelles, 1990). Although boys and girls appear equally affected by domestic violence in some studies (Jouriles & LeCompte, 1991), more frequent and severe levels of husband's marital aggression have been shown to covary with higher levels of both parents' aggression towards boys.

We are just beginning to understand how such couple interactions may impact upon children's development. There appears to be a relationship between marital discord, interspousal aggression, and increased internalized and externalized behavioral problems in children (Jouriles, Murphy, & O'Leary, 1989; Rosenbaum & O'Leary, 1981; Wolfe, Jaffe, Wilson, & Zak, 1985), although this relationship has not been found in all studies. A number of possible causal mechanisms have been posited including the children's being exposed to modeling of aggressive solutions to conflict, maternal unavailability (as women struggle with the emotional and physical consequences of their victimization), and the effect of multiple disruptions in residence/school and separations that such violence produces (Jaffe, Hurly, & Wolfe, 1990).

Preschool children appear particularly vulnerable to the negative impact of witnessing violence (Hughes, 1988; Hughes & Barad, 1983). This may be due to stage-salient issues characteristic of this age group (e.g., emergence of empathy and prosocial behavior) that may be affected by exposure to negative models (Cicchetti, 1989). It must be emphasized, however, that not all children are affected. In one study, for example, 50 percent of children exposed to domestic violence did not show problems at a clinical level (Jouriles, Murphy, & O'Leary, 1989).

Even if domestic violence is not present, other stressors on parents may impact on abused children's outcomes. For example, in sexual abuse, the responses of nonperpetrator parents (typically mothers) have been seen as crucial to dealing with the experience. Indeed, interventions aimed at improving their coping have begun to be developed (Deblinger, McLeer, & Henry, 1990).

Abuse may affect other parts of the family, depriving children of potential buffers against the stress of abuse. The sibling relationship has been discussed as an important potential buffer in situations of family conflict (Kempton, Armistead, Wierson, & Forehand, 1991; Kurdek, 1989). Although even siblings in normal families show high levels of aggression toward each other (Pagelow, 1989), sibling cohesion and mutual caregiving may deteriorate under extreme stress and aggression may increase. This may be especially true in situations in which parents are not monitoring children or are tolerant of the aggression.

Sometimes in families in which sexual abuse to children has occurred, relationships between young siblings can also become sexualized. Although clinical interventions may clearly convey the unacceptable nature of sexual behavior between siblings, it is crucial for clinicians to keep in mind that siblings who share extremely traumatic pasts often develop an intense relationship that practically served a survival function.

Great efforts may need to occur to reduce the amount of psychological loss suffered when abused siblings are taken out of an abusive context and separated from each other. Similarly, interventions to strengthen other aspects of the sibling relationships may also be useful. These relationships may also be a tremendous resource in therapeutic work with abused children and adolescents, as siblings often share a common experience base (e.g., sexual abuse often occurs to more than one child in a family). Finally, in some abusive families, older children may be parentified, and thus therapeutic work must address their tremendous sense of responsibility to siblings, in some cases at the expense of their own

needs. They may carry this overdetermined sense of responsibility into new relationships as they develop.

Overall, abusive family environments are ones that may provide a less secure base for both parents' and children's forays out into the world. The weakened bonds within the family may also reflect disturbances with extended family and the larger networks within which the family is embedded (e.g., schools, neighborhoods, workplace, communities). Abusive parents have been shown to be more socially isolated, to have disturbed friendship patterns, and to have more negative relationships with extended family members (National Research Council, 1993; Newberger, Hampton, Marx, & White, 1986; Salzinger, Kaplan, & Artemyeff, 1983).

Such contacts provide instrumental help that can be an important buffer against stress, and their absence may be detrimental to the overall health of the family environment. Parents' social networks are also valuable sources of information needed to support children's outcomes (e.g., providing feedback about parenting responses, referrals for doctors, schools, etc.). Parental modeling of social skills and providing children with peer contact (e.g., visiting friends who have children) have also been seen as crucial to children's own social development.

There is evidence of high mobility among abusive families, and abused children appear to show poorer school attendance (Eckenrode, Laird, & Doris, 1993; Salzinger, Kaplan, Pelcovitz, Samit, & Krieger, 1984). Thus, abused children may have an unstable connection with the neighborhood and school, both of which are critical contexts in children's development. Peer contact, for instance, is a prominent source of support and provides a backdrop against which many skills are mastered (e.g., negotiation skills, learning prosocial behavior). Beginning efforts at working on social skills with abused children have shown promise (Fantuzzo et al., 1988). Therapeutic day care centers that have a goal of promoting positive peer contact have also been developed (Ayoub, 1991). To date, most of this work has been done with preschoolers.

In summary, the abusive family seems disconnected from the influence and support of larger social networks that might act as resources and provide feedback vital to maintaining adaptive functioning in both parents and children. At the close of this section and in the next, a picture of abused children emerges in which their experiences and ultimate style of functioning may mirror that of a boat that rarely docks for rest and relaxation and is less able to stock up on provisions. The dockings with the land are marked by inconsistency, a failure to pick up adequate resources, and potential for brawls. As visitors, the child may not be given the skills needed to operate well with the natives on shore and are likely to be rejected. As will be seen in the next section, they may not choose to stay on any specific shore long enough to make friends because their expectations may be of chaos, loss, and potential harm.

Abuse/Neglect as Psychological Events

Researchers and theorists continue to wrestle with the thorny issue of defining what abuse means from a psychological perspective (McGee & Wolfe, 1991). They vary from positing that psychological maltreatment is the center of all forms of abuse to identifying psychological abuse as an event altogether distinct from other events such as physical or sexual abuse.

Throughout our discussion, we have seen abuse as an event or events that can have damaging impact upon children's ability to organize and develop adaptively in the context of a broad range of functioning (e.g., socially, cognitively). Thus, although abuse may be physical, it does not necessarily need to include physical and/or sexual contact in order to have significant psychological impact. Moreover, what is abusive may vary, depending on the child's social, cognitive, and emotional development. For example, name-calling to an infant may have little or no consequence compared to the effect it may have on an older child who has the requisite cognitive skills to interpret the meaning of this experience and may be in the midst of identity development. In contrast, a lack of physical contact for an infant may have a quite severe impact compared to the effect upon an adolescent, who may no longer be as dependent upon such contact to ensure a sense of emotional and social security.

Finally, development is an ongoing process whereby later growth is dependent upon earlier foundations (i.e., cognitive processes and behavioral repertoires are shaped over time and move toward more sophisticated and complex forms of functioning). Abuse in one developmental period, therefore, may have ongoing consequences that extend beyond the particular point at which it happened. "Internal working models" or schemas of how the self, the world, and relationships work continue to develop throughout children's lives. New information and experiences are incorporated and elaborate these schemas. If all goes well, the child moves toward increasing perceptions of mastery, greater capacities to regulate affect and behavior, and greater skill in the environment. If the early frameworks are tainted, however, new information may fail to be incorporated or may be incorporated in a distorted fashion, such that optimal development is thwarted.

Thus, in order to understand whether abuse has had a negative psychological impact and to intervene effectively,

clinicians need to be able to understand how a child perceives and makes meaning of what may viewed as a potentially traumatic experience (James, 1989). Again, this individual experience of processing and interpretation in part rests upon a child's social, cognitive, and emotional development. For example, the young toddler who may feel hurt, scared, and confused may not experience the sense of shame and humiliation that can be central to an older child. Also, as previously noted, the difference between an uncomfortable experience and a traumatic one may depend upon numerous other factors, such as temperament, preexisting perceptions of competence, and history of previous trauma, which in combination, yield varying degrees of resilience and vulnerability to a particular event (Pynoos, 1993). However, even though every child's circumstances are to some degree unique, experiences that produce perceptions of rejection, fear, isolation, helplessness, exploitation, and humiliation have been commonly cited as central to psychological abuse (Brassard, Germain, & Hart, 1991; McGee & Wolfe, 1991). Clinically, it is noted that these experiences are manifest in various types and levels of impaired social functioning, such as extreme social inhibition, agitation, aggression, and lack of social skills. Including social skills work that focuses on replacing dysfunctional thoughts regarding social relationships and interactions and on decreasing inappropriate social behaviors may be useful therapeutically.

As noted earlier, the abusive parent's negative bias toward their children colors their transactions with them and taints the feedback they provide children about their performance in the world. Furthermore, in many abusive homes, one does not see that constant taking of joy in children's developmental accomplishments typically seen in most families. For example, in parenting groups, the concept of praise is difficult for many abusive parents to master and therapists need to model the pride taken in children learning to walk, talk, and other basic developmental accomplishments (Azar, 1989).

In addition, because of their egocentric thinking, young children may attribute their thoughts, actions, and feelings as being the precursor to an abusive incident. In some cases the perpetrator may reinforce this perspective. For example, in sexual abuse, children are often threatened by the perpetrator and told they are bad and will "get in trouble if they tell anyone" what has occurred. Such an experience may foster a feeling of shame and powerlessness in children, which may lead the child to progressively alienate himself or herself from relationships. This may occur even though this perception of the others' judgments may be completely distorted. Therapeutically, it is paramount to focus on empowerment. The clinician can make significant efforts to provide opportunities for the child in which he or she can express choices, act effectively, and experience a sense of mastery in the therapeutic setting and elsewhere. This work may be difficult in that it is often the case that such children may continue to be placed in situations in which they have little control (e.g., foster care, courtroom).

Along with experiences that contribute to a negative view of the self, another primary element of psychological maltreatment are experiences that produce a loss of trust in others and the world. Maltreated children may experience recurrent episodes of inconsistent caregiving, that is, care which at times may be adequate and, at other times, may be completely inadequate, leading to overwhelming feelings of anxiety and frustration. Such children may build a working model of caregiving that reflects this highly conflictual experience. In this sense, the child may learn that he or she cannot rely on any kind of social or emotional grounding to be firm and constant, but rather, he or she may ultimately reach the conclusion that socioemotional relationships are tenuous at best. The notion of trust, that is, the sense that one may rely on certain "givens" in the environment, may be violated on a number of levels. The child that is well-fed and properly clothed, yet sexually abused, may clearly feel a violation of trust regarding power, boundaries, and control. As well, the child who may have food one day and goes hungry the next, also may lose his or her sense of trust in the world as a place that can reliably fulfill the most basic, yet critical, of needs. It has been argued that the therapeutic environment may be crucial in providing an emotionally corrective experience in which consistency of care is unshakable. The notion of establishing appropriate boundaries, both emotional and physical, between the child and the therapist is itself an important learning experience. One of the most fundamental goals of therapy is to help reestablish the child's sense of trust in an adult who is supportive and does not transgress physical, emotional, or psychological boundaries.

In general, the psychological experience of abuse, although undoubtedly broad, may also be thought about in the context of loss. Although the "what" may vary widely, the sense of loss more generally seems to be a pervasive characteristic of abuse experiences. Children may lose their sense of hope that their situation can ever change, a sense of trust in the social world around them, and a sense of power or autonomy that is critical in the development of healthy functioning. In some cases, when internal models of the social world are built upon experiences characterized by such immense loss, a child may not be able to refer to a time in their experience when their situation was different from their current one. If they do experience a period of stability, it may seem so unfamiliar to them, that they may act out in order to reproduce the more familiar environment of rejection and negative reactions with which they are accustomed.

Although clinically, some children may be able to describe verbally their experience, other children, particularly very young ones, are often unable to organize, articulate, and express their experience in language for various reasons, including age, developmental level, and severity of trauma. Clinicians may need to pay attention to how children express themselves through non-verbal or symbolic activities such as play. In particular, play activity that is marked by extreme aggressivity or passivity, inappropriate oversexualized behavior, and self-destructive or dissociative behavior may all be consistent with a child's experience of traumatic or abusive experiences.

Abuse/Neglect as a Legal Event

The reporting of abuse sets in motion a set of legal events of lesser or greater impact. At the very least, the family becomes identified by a social service agency and other adults enter the child's world. In the extreme, children are permanently removed from their parents' custody and in a minority of cases, the perpetrator, who may be a parent, is incarcerated. Each level of legal intervention may impact upon children's outcomes in both positive and negative ways.

The mandate of protective service agencies is to keep families intact, protect the child, and provide help to families. For many parents, therefore, being reported may be experienced on some level as a relief from what may be a crisis situation. Ideally, services such as therapy, parent education, day care, and medical care are provided to increase family resources, decrease stress level, and place the family on the road to better functioning.

Despite potential positive family outcomes and safety for the child, the possibility of causing harm has received some discussion in the literature. Concerns include the iatrogenic impact of labeling (e.g., increasing resistance to intervention), failures of the system to provide real interventions to families once they are identified, and subjecting already traumatized children to further trauma (e.g., placement in foster care). Some evidence exists supporting such concerns. For example, Schene (1991) noted that despite an increase of 55 percent in abuse reporting between 1980 and 1985, there was only a 2 percent increase in resources at federal, state, and local levels combined (U.S. House of Representatives Select Committee, 1987). More recent surveys have suggested a dearth of services in most states (Berkowitz & Sedlak, 1993).

Clearly, a child with a suspicious injury is provided with safety by removal to emergency foster care until further investigation can take place. Court action to prosecute offending adults also has protection of children as a goal. Such actions, however, may be viewed differently by a child who has just encountered one frightening situation (the abuse itself), only to be placed in another (being kept from his or her parents and being sent to live with strangers). Therapists need to keep in mind the child's perspective on these "helping" actions.

Being interviewed about sexual abuse perpetrated by a parental figure or testifying against this parent in court may raise issues of loyalty and add to children's distress. Indeed, recanting does occur (estimates of recanting range from 3 to 27% of cases; Bruck, Ceci, & Hembrooke, 1998). We know little about the impact of such interviewing and testifying in court, although both negative and positive outcomes have been discussed (Berliner & Barbieri, 1984; DeFrancis, 1969; Katz & Mazure, 1979; Parker, 1982). For example, it has been suggested that testifying may produce a sense of self-efficacy and psychological closure (Pynoos & Eth, 1984). Empirical support for either contention, however, is still limited. One study by Gibbens and Prince (1963) found that child victims involved in court proceedings experienced greater trauma than those who were not. Unfortunately, it was the more severe cases that were seen in court and thus, it is difficult to reach a firm conclusion based on their findings. Goodman, Taub, Jones, and England (1992) also found more disturbance in children who had testified than in matched controls, but only after seven months (controls had improved, whereas those who had testified did not). Factors associated with poorer outcome include: the number of times testifying, severity of abuse, the level of maternal support, history of violence in the home, and level of fear during the testimony (Goodman et al., 1992; Sas, 1997). Thus, not all children are affected equally.

If a parental figure is incarcerated, new stress may be placed on the child. The child must then deal with the stigma and potential economic consequences of this event (Gabel, 1992).

Foster care placement is intended as temporary to protect children from harm and to provide them with a stable and therapeutic environment. The therapeutic benefit of foster placement, however, has been under scrutiny (Arvanian, 1975; Geiser, 1973; Mass & Engler, 1959). Indeed, in recent national reports, the quality (e.g., basic care issues) and availability of qualified foster families have been questioned (The U.S. Advisory Board on Child Abuse and Neglect, 1993). One study, for example, indicated that the medical care of foster children is significantly neglected (Schor, 1982). Placements may be overly lengthy and some children may make multiple moves before being permanently placed (Fanshel & Shinn, 1978; Knitzer & Allen, 1978; Wald, 1976). This may be considered an additional stress. Further, it has been assumed that during placement, the parent would receive treatment, an assumption that has been questioned (Williams, 1983).

Research on the impact of such placements is limited and much of it is flawed methodologically. Some work suggests that those children who showed poor adjustment as adults (e.g., incarceration) after foster care are ones who showed more symptoms before placement (Widom, 1991), and other studies suggest long-term negative outcomes (e.g., higher levels of homelessness as adults; Mangine, Royse, Wieche, & Nietzel, 1990). Comparing the psychosocial development of foster children to home-reared children, both in poverty and nonpoverty, McIntyre, Lounsbury, Bernton, and Steel (1988) found that although foster children share many of the same patterns of development with other home-reared children in poverty circumstances, a specific pattern of psychosocial issues unique to foster children also emerges. In particular, foster children are more likely to make external attributions, relying on an external explanation of events rather than seeing themselves as being able to influence the course of events. McIntyre (1991) also showed that consistent with an emphasis on external agents, these children are more oriented towards impulsiveness and towards an exploitation of others in order to gratify their impulses. Finally, in peer relationship development, McIntyre, Lounsbury, Bernton, and Steel (1988) also found that foster children were more disliked and rejected than home reared children.

Some suggestion has been made that outcomes may vary with the age at which children have been placed, although again the data are limited. Rutter (1989) cites data from the British National Survey (Wadsworth, 1985), which found that women who experienced family disruptions in the preschool years were more likely than those from nondisrupted families to have been divorced or separated by the age of 26 and those experiencing disruption during middle or later childhood were intermediate in these outcomes. Another study found that children who entered placement at older ages showed more developmental problems when assessed within the first 3 months of placement (Horwitz, Simms, & Farrington, 1994). The authors argued that two explanations of their findings are possible. First, such children may have had longer to develop an attachment to their parents and thus experience more distress at separation. Second, it may be that they have been exposed to a negative home environment for longer and thus display more problems. Nonetheless, these children placed at older ages were more likely to remain in foster care. More study of the effect of age of placement is needed to inform clinical practice in this area.

In clinical practice, one must consider the child's experience of foster care. Referring back to the metaphor used earlier, the abused child may be seen as a boat seeking a safe haven, which ostensibly foster care is designed to be. Because the specific caretaking history of each child may vary, so may their hopes and expectations or fears that may become attached to a foster care family. Moreover, although numerous checks and balances have been established by supervising social service agencies in order to ensure a minimum standard of care, foster families, like all families, vary in strengths and weaknesses (emotional, financial, and social resources). Many factors may affect the child's experience (e.g., whether the foster family is of the same race; the types of other children present in the home, such as the mix of foster and biological children; co-placement of siblings; whether visitation with biological parents takes place in the foster home). The issues discussed in the previous sections all may be activated differently within a foster care context and are worthy of consideration (e.g., neighborhood of the family, foster parents' skills).

Many times, the families chosen to provide substitute care are members of the child's own extended family, whose homes, aside from the abuse itself, may not be significantly different in quality from the original family setting. Extended family members, however, may provide some continuity for the child and help in the reunification process. Indeed, in their review, Price and Brew (1998) note that children placed with relatives have better social outcomes. In some cases, children may experience multiple losses with foster care (and later adoption), such as when siblings are not placed together, or when the foster family undergoes stressors such as divorce or death.

Despite these concerns, it needs to be emphasized that foster families may be a tremendous resource both for the child and his or her parents. For example, foster parents may develop a positive relationship with the biological parents and provide useful modeling of caregiving skills and other kinds of advice. In addition, if the child requires additional foster care after being returned to their parents, foster families can provide continuity by having the child return to their home.

The child's level of adjustment and behavioral difficulties may affect the stability of a placement and the foster family's reaction to him or her. Abused children and adolescents have many disturbances that interfere with their social relationships (e.g., heightened aggressiveness, distrust of others). For example, for a portion of the very severely abused children, multiple placements (e.g., foster care, psychiatric hospitalizations) are common due to very aggressive and disturbed behavior (e.g., urinating on the floor, biting and kicking others). Such children appear intolerant of close relationships in a family setting. How such changes in placement are construed by these already highly traumatized children has not received much attention.

Although not discussed in the literature, foster placement may also indirectly affect the family when reunification occurs. One abusive mother who successfully underwent treatment and had her children returned, spoke sadly of her children crying for their foster parent and taunting her with the fact that the foster parent would be able to buy them things she could not. Such economic discrepancies may be similar to ones experienced by children of divorce and may lead to similar anger, confusion, and upset on both the parents' and child's parts.

In some cases, children are permanently removed from parental custody through a legal process of termination of parental rights (Azar & Benjet, 1994). Based on one of the few studies done in this area, Jellinek and colleagues (1992) found that both chronic neglect and parental drug abuse are common factors in such cases. Termination involves a lengthy legal process. In one study, the average time from first foster placement to being freed for adoption was 3.5 years (Sedlak, 1991). Children may thus live in a legal limbo, perhaps continuing to have contact with parents intermittently and living with foster or pre-adoptive parents. The impact of this experience has not been studied.

In summary, although concerns have been raised in this section on the potential stress that the legal system produces, it must be emphasized that the failure to identify maltreatment when it has occurred may have even greater repercussions. Clearly, early intervention with families who are at risk for abuse has been shown to be helpful (Olds, Henderson, Chamberlin, & Tatelbaum, 1986). Thus, identification that occurs early, before maltreatment becomes chronic, may be most useful. In clinical work, the meaning and repercussions of transactions with the legal and social service systems, however, are important to keep in mind and may need to be a focus of intervention for some children.

Abuse/Neglect as an Historical Event

Abuse has long been thought to have a historical context. That is, an intergenerational cycle of maltreatment has been posited. Recent reviews of the literature in this area, however, suggest that while occurring differentially within families, it is far from a surety across generations. Little prospective work has occurred. Reviews suggest that approximately 25 to 35 percent of maltreated women go on to abuse their own offspring (Kaufman & Zigler, 1987), which is far from what is popularly perceived as the inevitability of the repetition of violence. What may be more probable is the transmission across generations of a set of subtle parenting responses, skill deficits, and transactional scripts or themes that may in some cases lead to mild disturbances in parenting and, in others, maltreatment (Azar, 1991a; Zeanah & Zeanah, 1989). We would argue that it is these more subtle elements that warrant study. Whether or not these disturbances erupt into abuse, a parent having such a trauma history may enact maladaptive response patterns that reverberate across generations, as has been discussed in the literature on children of Vietnam veterans and Holocaust survivors (Freyberg, 1980; Harkness, 1991; Sigal & Weinfeld, 1989;). It is these subtle relational outcomes in abuse that need to be kept in mind clinically. In intervening with abused children and adolescents, we may be short circuiting a process of transmission by altering relational skills. Interventions aimed at the parenting readiness of adolescents who have abuse histories may need greater attention (Azar, 1991a).

A Clinical Framework for Considering Abuse and Its Impact on Children

Throughout this chapter we have argued for a view of child maltreatment that encompasses not only the consequences of the physical act itself, but the myriad environmental factors associated with it that combined may derail children's and adolescents' developmental progress. On the surface, this view is not dissimilar from ones that have been presented in the literature on child development, at-risk parenting, and child abuse more generally (e.g., social ecological perspectives, Belsky [1980], Belsky & Vondra [1989]; behavioral theory, Patterson [1980], Wolfe [1987]; organizational perspectives, Cicchetti & Rizley [1981], Sameroff & Chandler [1975], Werner [1948]; attachment formulations, Cicchetti [1989], Crittenden & Ainsworth [1989]). However, in departing from these views slightly, we place greater emphasis on the child as an active constructor of reality and on the idea that abuse that disturbs development is part of a context of a more general breakdown in caregiver behavior and environmental stress. We also place greater emphasis on *the locus of causality beginning in parental disturbances.* This emphasis does not see maltreatment as being separate and distinct from all the other aspects of parenting a child receives and the myriad other environmental forces that are operating upon them. That is, these factors operate *as a whole* to produce outcome and from the child's perspective are seen *as a whole.* Indeed, physical abuse may be overshadowed in its influence by other negative aspects of the parent-driven caregiving environment (e.g., a nonperpetrator parent who is unavailable emotionally; the effects of lack of adequate levels of food and supervision; multiple negative foster care placements in which caregivers again fail the child), or in some cases, by other more positive elements (e.g., a nonperpetrator parent's skills; cohesive sibling group; positive foster parents).

Clinicians typically work with family members or the child and their foster or adoptive parents. Thus, while the larger contextual factors discussed earlier (poverty, violent neighborhoods) are relevant and might be dealt with in some limited ways (e.g., interventions with social workers, advocacy efforts), ultimately, a more clinically useful framework is one that addresses the more malleable components of the "abuse" experience that have been described above. In addition, such a framework aimed at caregiving change might focus on the members of the system with the most power to produce such changes—namely the parents or parent figures in the child's life. It would only focus on the child alone if no caregiver is available, or she or he refuses treatment, or the child's needs exceed those of even the best of caregivers (e.g., when children are placed in residential care). Finally, when abuse occurs in infancy, it is more likely that abused infants will be removed from parents, often permanently if the abuse is severe. Thus, the most common consumer of treatment services tends to be families with preschool or older children. Therefore, a clinically useful framework is one that focuses on these older children who in some, but not all, cases have already been exposed to a disturbed caregiver environment for some period of time.[2] Based on these requirements, the comprehensive models posited above, while providing a broader framework in which to view development, are too global to be clinically useful. They either do not allow for a prioritizing of factors from one ecological level versus another, and thus provide little guidance as to where to target intervention, or they focus too much on disturbances in one developmental era (e.g., attachment in infancy) to the exclusion of other periods in which abuse may take place, providing a deterministic picture with little hope of change, or focus exclusively on the occurrence of aggressive parental behavior, ignoring the absence of positive and more nurturant behavior (Azar, 1991b).

The framework that has been woven into our discussion thus far and that will be outlined in more detail here, has its roots in a social cognitive theory. It is a model designed to explain both the etiology of abuse and the developmental disturbances observed among affected children across childhood and adolescence (Azar, 1986, 1989). That is, it is a model that emphasizes malleable variables that may mediate both the occurrence of maltreatment and the other factors that lead to disturbances in children. This model will be briefly described. Less research is available on sexual abuse and the family environments in which it occurs, and thus, this extension of the model to this form of maltreatment is speculative at this point in time.

The model suggests that child maltreatment is one of many possible signs of a family environment that has broken down in its capacity to provide an optimal socialization environment for a child (the term *environment* includes both the parental care received and the transactions that occur both within the family and with the larger outside environment that contribute directly and indirectly to children's outcomes). Thus, intrafamilial child abuse is part of a cluster of responses at one end of a continuum of parenting, one end of which results in optimal outcome in children and at the other end are ones that lead to heightened risk. While models of parenting generally have emphasized its affective quality, this social cognitive model focuses more heavily on the crucial role of cognitive processes in guiding parenting. That is, socialization requires a "thinking" parent, not just an affective one. Socialization is highly dependent upon complex and sophisticated parental *schemas regarding role relationships* and perception of the social cues that children and others provide. It also requires *a set of sensitive and flexible cognitive processes* for interpreting children's behavior (e.g., attributional style, problem solving, decision-making skills) and a broad repertoire of responses, especially to problematic situations.

These cognitive schemas and processes are seen as guiding parents' moment-by-moment interpretations of the causes of children's behavior, the valence of these interpretations (positive or negative), and whether the behavior warrants a response or not. These same cognitive processes also guide the parents' contacts with other family members and the outside world (e.g., their partner, employer, the child's teacher, potential friends) and may determine myriad contextual influences that in turn impact upon parenting quality further (e.g., stress level, social support). If these processes are disturbed, then both childrearing and the other aspects of a child's environment will be affected. These processes may thus facilitate the occurrence of adaptive or maladaptive responses (i.e., ones that do or do not foster development, such as anger regulation with one's children and one's partner), as well as a social context that does or does not promote development (e.g., ones that are rich or devoid of economic, social, and emotional resources).

In this view, the appropriateness of responses are seen as being dependent upon the sensitivity and accuracy (or at the very least the adaptiveness) of the interpretations made about others. By adaptive, we mean responses that facilitate continued contact with others, produce success in transactions with them and the environment, and maintain as much as possible a positive mood state. For example, it is adaptive for parents (and foster parents) to see strengths in children both from an egocentric perspective (e.g., "I have produced a good child") and from the perspective of a growing child (e.g., "my caregiver thinks positively of me, so I must be o.k."). This tendency may even at times result in positive distortions (e.g., when a child runs across the street after being told not to, a parent might say "Isn't he strong willed!" or "She's so independent" versus "He's such a brat" or "She's always trying to make me look stupid!"). Positive interpretations keep parents calm and allow them to problem solve and increase the probability they will respond in the

most adaptive manner, keeping children's short-term and long-term socialization needs in focus.

Such interpretive processes are important in the parenting of young children. Parents' selectively attending to and responding to children's actions are believed to be crucial in guiding them toward more sophisticated means of responding, as well as laying the foundation for children's own schemas about how the world, relationships, and the self operate. Across childhood, we all develop cognitive sets or schemas regarding basic social roles (e.g., the self, parent, child) and scripts that define how people in these roles behave and relate to others (e.g., mothers attempt to put their children's needs ahead of their own; it is not young children's job to care for parents) and of how the world works generally. The sources of these schemas include societal norms, subcultural beliefs, and personal experiences within one's own families. Thus, while a good deal of overlap occurs, we each have somewhat unique role schemas and world views.

We also develop more specialized schemas regarding the meaning of the responses we make and those of individuals we encounter on a regular basis in our lives (e.g., our own mother, our children, friends) and of the self-in-relation to others (e.g., people in my family try not to hurt me; people are generally friendly to me). These schemas or scripts make social interaction with strangers and with those we encounter often more "automatic" and less "effortful." These schemas also guide our judgments about ourselves as we react to the feedback we receive from others and the environment. Finally, these schemas also come to shape our processing of the information that we encounter in interpersonal situations (i.e., they may lead to selective attention to some pieces of information—that which is consistent with the schema and ignoring or giving less attention to other information—that which is inconsistent). The sum of such processing colors our perspective on our lives generally (e.g., if our schemas about relationships and the self are predictable, the world too is perceived as a safe place in which what happens is predictable).

It has been argued in this chapter that abusive parents show disturbances in cognitive areas that result in disruptions in their capacity to appropriately interpret, problem solve, and respond to their children's behavior (Azar, 1986, 1989), and this in turn alters the schemas that children develop. The abusive parent has developed maladaptive schema regarding how children operate in the world, how children should treat them, and children's role in relation to parents. (There is also some evidence that their schemas more generally may be distorted about others and the world [Miller & Azar, 1996].) Fundamental is the lack of or a reversal of the typical hierarchical relationship between parent and child, with the parent providing and the child being provided for (e.g., what early writers in this area called role reversal) and seeing children as having the capacities of another adult (e.g., perspective-taking, self-care, provision of help and affection to the parents). Physically abusive parents, for example, evidence unrealistic expectations regarding both the social cognitive and physical care capacities of children (e.g., believing a 3 year old can comfort them when they are upset or that a 4 year old can pick out the right clothing for the weather or that a teenager can help patch up their marital problems; Azar & Rohrbeck, 1986; Azar, Robinson, Hekimian, & Twentyman, 1984). There is some evidence that such cognitive distortions may also occur in sexual offenders as well (e.g., seeing the child as a source of sexual pleasure; arguing the offender is "educating them"; or that they "wanted it"; Abel et al., 1989; Stermac & Segal, 1989).

Such unrealistic expectancies are constantly violated by children. This may be especially apparent in the early years, when child care needs are high, but still may be present in adolescence. Because of other cognitive disturbances observed in such parents (e.g., poor interpersonal problem solving) and their limited repertoire of social and parenting skills, difficulties that ensue cannot be easily resolved by such parents and parenting becomes an aversive task in which the parent feels incompetent and after repeated failures, begins to perceive a lack of self-efficacy in their role. When further evidence of social incompetence occurs (e.g., marital problems, life issues) triggered by similar cognitive disturbances expressed both within and outside the family, stress increases further. Ultimately, the parent, in a self-protective stance, blames the child for his or her difficulties, labeling them as "the problem" (i.e., he or she develops a negative attributional bias toward the child). As the parents' processing capacities become overwhelmed, they may also inappropriately seek comfort from the child when these other events occur. As discussed in the last section, it is also possible that such individuals come into the role of parenting with a tendency toward such a negative schema regarding children which is activated under stress. This negative bias, coupled with a more restricted repertoire of parenting responses, leads them either to avoid contact with the child or when contact is necessary, to react with negative verbal and physical control behaviors. These coercive responses and lack of positive ones begin to dominate the interactions and combined with the experiencing of the child as purposefully noncomplying and not living up to the standards of other parents' children, the process of parenting becomes even less rewarding.

These cognitive problems detract from children's developmental potential in other ways. These parents are less able to operate within what has been termed children's *zone of proximal development* (Rogoff & Wertsch, 1984) (i.e.,

they show less of an ability to respond to children within their developmental reach so as to produce mastery experiences and to pull children to higher levels of functioning). Because of their disturbed interpretations of child behavior (i.e., misjudgments as to what children actually can do) and negative bias, they do not provide children with the kind of "scaffolding" and positive support required to allow children to gain mastery over tasks. They provide the child with inadequate levels of cognitive stimulation and with feedback about the self that is negatively toned, and from the child's perspective, the parent behaves in an inconsistent and dyssynchronous manner. They are asked to engage in tasks above their capacities and then, may be berated for their failures. As noted earlier, this kind of negatively based transactional style may pervade the interactions within the family and between the family and the outside world, providing distorted modeling for the child. Children may also incorporate negatively based schemas regarding relationships and maladaptive skills as to how to operate within them. For example, abusive parents believe children *should* know what they are thinking and feeling. Incorporating such beliefs that others can "read your mind" has been shown to be related to relationship problems (Eidelson & Epstein, 1982). Placement in foster care or testifying against a parental figure in court may further contribute to children's stress by further requiring them to perform (and cope) at a level beyond their capacities. In addition, foster parents may have preconceived ideas regarding what an "abused" child is like and, as discussed earlier, may contribute to the child seeing themselves as somehow "damaged". They also may react negatively to the abused child's maladaptive attempts to cope (e.g., hoarding of food; aggression when physical contact occurs), further marginalizing the child. Similarly, as will be seen in the next section, as the child ventures out into the world, he or she will be less equipped to keep up with the expectations of teachers and peers. This will contribute further to a lowered sense of mastery, doing further damage to the self and making it difficult for the child to utilize aspects of these other relational environments that could act in a compensatory role. It will also keep the child "unbalanced" in their interactions with others and the world, reinforcing the idea that relationships are not to be trusted and the world is unpredictable.

As can be seen in the discussion above, the caregiving that abused children receive and the feedback they get from the environment may lead to schemas about the self, others, and the world that have maladaptive elements. The more developmental periods within which the factors described above exist, the more disturbed the feedback and the more disturbed will be children's construction of the self, others, and the world. Abuse that occurs early and is chronic may cause the very foundation of basic schemas to become distorted. For example, such children will have less opportunity to be exposed to a world in which they see themselves as well cared for, others as trustworthy and meeting their needs, and the world as being a place where good things are likely to happen. In the extreme, their schemas will be laced with elements of emotional pain, a sense of helplessness and lack of control, the threat of physical harm, and fears regarding survival, giving rise to what may be labeled as posttraumatic stress symptomatology.

Specific Outcomes Observed in Abused Children and Adolescents

Consistent with the multidimensional perspective taken in our discussion thus far, we suggest that the occurrence of maltreatment and its associated factors has the potential to make a clear and defining impact on cognitive, social, and affective development. It must be emphasized again, however, that not all children will show the same level of impact. For example, one study of the social functioning of abused children, while indicating on average that they showed problems with peers, also found that approximately 13 percent of the 87 physically abused children studied were judged as popular among peers (Salzinger, Feldman, Hammer, & Rosario, 1993). Similarly, in a recent review by Kendall-Tackett, Finkelhor, and Williams (1993) of studies of outcomes in sexually abused children, 21 to 49 percent of the children studied did not evidence symptoms. Our discussion will, therefore, provide areas worthy of exploration in assessing such children and suggest potential targets for intervention, rather than indicate definitive areas of disturbance.

Some of the most salient effects upon which clinicians might focus include *difficulties in the ability to form and maintain stable relationships, impairment in affective and behavioral self-regulation,* and *cognitive and intellectual deficits.* Interestingly, these disturbances parallel in many ways those seen in the abusive and neglectful parent and are ones that may also result from the kinds of stressors observed to characterize the abusive family's environment (e.g., domestic violence, poverty). Furthermore, research on the impact of abuse continues to provide evidence that the outcomes that create disturbances in functioning are inherently linked together. For example, looking at physically abused children in the classroom context, Salzinger and her colleagues (Salzinger, Feldman, Hammer, & Rosario, 1993) have found that such children are at risk for poor peer relationships, lower social status, and peer rejection. This combination of stressors frequently makes perceptions of competence and self-esteem issues important to address in

therapy. At the same time, the children in the study by Salzinger and colleagues also displayed evidence of cognitive distortions. For example, when asked to indicate who their friends were, they tended to include children who did not even like them. This suggests that abused children's cognitive appraisals of social situations might need to be addressed before social skills training can be effective, as they may master new skills, but not be as accurate in where these need to be applied. Along with supporting the critical link between impairments in social and cognitive functioning, this finding also underlines the position that abuse may come to shape core schemas or models of relationships (e.g., distorted ideas regarding what constitutes a friendship and how one interacts with friends). In general, therefore, although we artificially focus on one "piece" at a time, it is important to remember that in terms of children's experience, various domains of functioning are inherently tied together. Because maltreatment impacts the development of a variety of skills, the focus of treatment must also be on the interactive effects of the outcomes, including decreasing deficits and increasing resiliency and compensatory factors.

In light of this, it is notable that until recently, the impact of abuse has been viewed in two ways in the literature. First, it has been examined in terms of its specific effects upon children's outcomes. For example, researchers have pointed to the emergence of self (Cicchetti, 1989); language ability (Gerstein et al., 1986); and capacity for peer relationships (Mueller & Silverman, 1989), as areas that are directly affected by abuse. More recently, it has come to be viewed as one of a constellation of events that might produce distress or trauma to children, suggesting that symptoms observed are not specific to this one experience, but are more characteristic of all trauma (Deblinger et al., 1990; Ribbe, Lipovsky, & Freedy, 1992). Writers arguing for this latter view have pointed to the similarities in outcomes between traumatized children and abused ones.

In our opinion, the two views are not incompatible, and we believe they can be incorporated into our social cognitive view of abuse. That is, for the abused child, there can be specific or more pervasive failures in their socialization environment. The family is viewed as the context in which the initial frameworks for social, emotional, and cognitive development are formed (e.g., perceptions of the trustworthiness of relationships, stimulation of language skills), and when this environment lacks richness or is characterized by unpredictable and disturbed transactions, in the absence of compensatory factors, the context of development may become maladaptive and socialization will be affected (Azar, 1986, 1989). As noted earlier, developing a trusting relationship with the therapist and the words for thoughts and feelings are often a necessary starting point for treatment. In the extreme, as these disturbances become more pervasive, the child's coping becomes overwhelmed and we can see a derailment of adaptive development and psychopathology, including post-traumatic stress symptomatology.

Overall, we have argued that abused children and adolescents lack the consistent and synchronous caregiving required for more adaptive development (e.g., they are interacted with less, receive high levels of negative feedback, and low levels of nurturant and positive contact), and because of their parents' cognitive distortions, the parenting they receive is a mismatch with their developmental capacities, resulting in demands being made upon them that are not within their developmental reach. At times, the parents' expectancies may be so distorted that their interpretations may have nothing to do with what the child is doing. That is, the parent is responding to developmentally normal child behavior with interpretations of negative intent on the child's part and responding accordingly (e.g., with rejecting or punishing behavior). For example, we have already noted that there is evidence of a lack of responsive and discriminant caregiving in abusive parents of infants. Such caregiving in turn has been linked to the attachment problems that have been observed in maltreated infants (Carlson et al., 1989; Egeland & Sroufe, 1981; Gordan & Jameson, 1979). A particular form, "insecure disorganized/disoriented" attachment has been observed (Main, Kaplan, & Cassidy, 1985), in which abused toddlers, in laboratory studies, respond to parental separations with extreme avoidance and marked distress and appear "dazed" or affectless, confused, and/or show signs of depression. Interestingly, parents of such children in studies of parenting more generally have been described as having a significant degree of trauma in their own personal histories (Main et al., 1985), suggesting the intergenerational transmission of disorganized relational patterns described above. Also, consistent with our discussion above, such children are described as not having a secure base from which to explore relationships, a secure base that is typically rooted in the predictability and consistency of a child's environment. Children learn the rules of how to relate to others from such environments and, without consistency, relationships are perplexing to them and they will be unsuccessful.

This relational problem is echoed in the many other *social disturbances* found in abused children and adolescents. In infancy, toddlerhood, and the preschool years, abused children have been shown to have deficits in interpersonal responsiveness (Bee, Disbrow, Johnson-Crowley, & Barnard, 1981; Crittendon, 1985; George & Main, 1980). This lack of responsiveness has been suggested to create stress for caregivers (Azar & Twentyman, 1986; Gaensbauer & Sands, 1979; Hay & Hall, 1981). Impairment in abused children has also been found in their capacity for empathy in interpersonal relationships, a disturbance that has also been found among children who show self-regulation problems (e.g., disruptive children and delinquents); (Chandler, 1973; Azar, Gentile, Orton, & Talbot, 1986). For example, Main and George (1985) have shown that when maltreated preschoolers were confronted with peers that were upset, they demonstrated less empathic responses than did controls, in some cases even responding with impulsive aggression. Howes and Espinosa (1985) found that physically abused preschoolers evidenced decreased ability to initiate interactions with peers, fewer displays of positive affect with playmates, and deficits in the capacity for complex play. Examining 8- to 12-year-old physically abused children, Salzinger, Feldman, Hammer, and Rosario (1993) found them to have lower peer status, to have more insular social networks, and to be rated by peers as more aggressive and less cooperative. In the family setting, abused children of all ages show high levels of negative transactions (e.g., yelling, screaming, name calling, physical aggression; Bousha & Twentyman, 1984; Burgess & Conger, 1978). Adolescents, while less studied, have also shown similar disturbances in social skills (Azar & Wientzen, 1993).

Affective regulation is another area of difficulty for the abused child. One explanation is that in dysfunctional, stressful households, children develop maladaptive coping mechanisms for self-preservation. These learned responses to the family can become the "mode of operation" for coping with the world outside the home as well. These behavioral difficulties can also be contextualized as a response to and/or modeling of the poor interpersonal skills and violence of their parents. That is, they have not learned methods of cognitively regulating their affect (e.g., problem-solving skills) and are given the message that aggressive conflict resolution is appropriate. Indeed, Haskett (1990) has found abused children to have poorer interpersonal problem-solving skills and Barahal, Waterman, and Martin (1981) found poorer ability to take the perspective of others. Other emotional difficulties have also been found. Camras, Ribordy, Spaccarelli, and Stefan (1986) found abused preschoolers to have deficits in affective expressive and recognition skills. Learned maladaptive coping responses along with these deficits may account for the unusual, negative reactions abused children have to the distress of peers that were described above. Effective treatment might include role-playing to learn problem solving and perspective-taking skills. Finally, disturbances in affective regulation may be seen as at the heart of post-traumatic stress symptomatology.

The *emotional effects* of abuse may be substantial, resulting in lower self-esteem and adversely affecting the development of healthy conceptions of self (Barahal, Waterman, & Martin, 1981; Sirles, Walsma, Lytle-Barnaby,

& Lender, 1988; Steward et al., 1986; Terr, 1991). As noted throughout our chapter, abuse may disrupt the child's ability to trust others and to respond to positive attention and love. When the level of unpredictability and negative nature of the environment overwhelm a child's coping capacities, trauma may occur. Trauma may lead to the onset of post-traumatic stress disorder symptoms, including "flashbacks" of the traumatic event, repetitive behavior, trauma-specific fears, changed attitudes about people, life and the future (e.g., depression), sleep problems, exaggerated startle responses, developmental regressions (e.g., clinging behavior), panic, irritability, and hypervigilance (Terr, 1991). Recent evidence suggests, however, that post-traumatic stress disorder (PTSD) symptoms may be more characteristic of children who have experienced emotional and sexual abuse than physical abuse or neglect (Famularo, Fenton, & Kinscherff, 1993).

With some exceptions (Pynoos, 1993), most discussions of PTSD with children, however, have occurred around discrete stressors (e.g., disasters, crimes), not the chronic physical threat that may occur in some abusive homes. One might argue that the occurrence of extreme and chronic abuse leaves children with a very distorted set of schemas regarding how relationships work and because they have only limited behavioral capacities to protect themselves, they may only be left with cognitive methods to control their exposure to negative experiences (e.g., dissociation). This may be most marked in sexual and emotional abuse. As noted earlier, it is, therefore, essential that that the relationship between the child and the therapist be very predictable for abused youth.

Along with problems in affective regulation, *behavioral regulation problems* have also been observed. These include overly compliant and passive behaviors, extremely aggressive, demanding, and rageful behaviors, and inappropriately adult and responsible behavior or extremely dependent behavior (Fantuzzo, 1990). Children may become overly compliant as an attempt to avoid confrontation with parents who could be abusive. On the other hand, aggressive behaviors may be caused by the repeated frustrations of not having basic needs met and parental inconsistency. Indeed, abused children have been found to have poor frustration tolerance (Green, 1978; Kent, 1976).

Reviews in this area indicate that behavioral outcomes in childhood include increased amounts of aggression, provocative behavior, noncompliance, and conduct problems (Azar, Barnes & Twentyman, 1988; Widom, 1989). In adolescence, greater risk for problems such as delinquency, running away, and truancy are also found (Azar & Siegel, 1990; Lewis & Schaeffer, 1981). One might postulate that seeing abuse as chronic and as being random, indiscriminate, and uncontrollable, children, as noted earlier, may learn they have little control over their environment. At the same time, a distorted perspective may have developed regarding places where they can exert control (e.g., by acting out). Therapeutic efforts may help such children better discriminate those situations for which they have control and those for which they do not.

The disorganized aspects of the abusive home and the lack of cognitive stimulation of abused children may also result in *cognitive and language delays and poor academic performance*. Abused children evidence cognitive delays and disturbances, such as greater distractibility and limited problem-solving ability, and have difficulties in school (Haskett, 1990; Hoffman-Plotkin & Twentyman, 1984; Smith, 1975; Trickett, McBride-Chang, & Putnam, 1994). In a study of 420 maltreated children in grades K through 12, Eckenrode, Laird, and Doris (1993), for example, found that they performed significantly below peer norms on standardized tests, had lower grades, and had more discipline referrals and suspensions than nonmaltreated children. Although this study found fewer disturbances for sexually abused children, a more recent study with a significantly larger sample of such children did find such disturbances (Trickett, McBride-Chang, & Putnam, 1994). Again, the poor academic performance found may be multiply determined (e.g., resulting from head injuries, inconsistent school attendance, poor nutrition, lack of cognitive stimulation, decreased self-efficacy, etc.). For any given child, each of these potential causal domains needs to be explored and addressed in psychotherapy, as well as in educational planning.

Before ending our discussion, the topic of the potential of biases in over-ascribing symptoms to abused children and adolescents must be addressed. As noted early in this section and throughout the chapter, we have argued that clinicians must be careful not to make an automatic assumption of "damage" due to abuse. There is some evidence that such biases do exist. Some biases may favor the need for treatment for one type of abuse over another. For example, the sexually abused child is more likely to be referred for treatment than the physically abused one (Vitulano, Lewis, Doran, Nordhaus, & Adnopoz, 1986). While the former group may have more extreme and visible PTSD symptoms, we may have preconceived ideas that abuse of a sexual nature will do more damage and that the physically abused child merely needs to be removed to safety to resolve his or her difficulties. The physically abused child's need for psychological intervention may be overlooked. On the other hand, when studies have found no evidence of disturbances in abused samples, these results have been questioned. It has been argued that disturbances may unfold across development and that this may explain the lack of findings

(Kendall-Tackett, Williams, & Finkelhor, 1993). Farber and Egeland (1987), based on their longitudinal work with abused infants, for example, present some evidence that such children may in fact show different patterns of disturbance over time. Indeed, as a group, they appeared to have a deteriorating picture. Yet not all children showed problems. Factors that appeared to be linked to positive outcomes were ones that related to the early development of competency. That is, children who showed early competency (a good foundation) did better. Although their data set is limited, it also appeared that maternal early responsiveness and having emotional and other supports also factored into better outcome. These researchers nicely point out that distinctions among adaptation, competence, and emotional health must be made in considering outcome in abused children. It may be that abused children adapt to the oddities of their particular socialization environment (e.g., multiple moves, living with threats of harm), and that this adaptation may in some cases lead to coping mechanisms that do or do not serve the child well throughout development.

In addition, some children may have or will develop competencies once they are able to adapt to environments other than the one in which they are raised. Despite evidencing a capacity to adapt and to perform competently, however, there may still be subtle disturbances in their emotional health that may be long-standing. For example, they may appear to survive multiple foster care placements, but may still harbor a fundamental distrust of relationships and a weakened sense of self that despite external evidence of success leaves them struggling more than would be necessary. In this sense, it may be important not to assume a complete absence of disturbance. It is an understanding of this last area that is most crucial in doing interventions with children and adolescents who have encountered abuse. To date, we have mostly examined such children's competencies and adaptation, but it is this last area, emotional health, that warrants further study. That is, it is crucial that clinicians be sensitive to the fact that a child's initial behavioral presentation may or may not reflect an alternative internal picture that may be characterized by more or less disturbance than was first thought or perceived.

SUMMARY AND CONCLUSIONS

In conclusion, we have argued that clinicians, in approaching abused children, must take a broader perspective than has been discussed previously. There will be a tendency for professionals to see abuse itself as the "causal" agent in selecting the treatment focus. This narrow focus can be distracting and may restrict the areas in which the child is seen as needing help. Clearly, for many children, this will be the focal

event around which disturbance is organized. However, for many children, their disturbances are multidetermined and clinicians may have to hold in abeyance their desire to work with the abuse issue and address the multiple other events that have led the child into their care. In doing so, they may be better able to return the child to the developmental path from which they may have strayed. Work may thus be directed at the child's making sense of his or her experience and altering aspects of his or her caregiving environment, by either helping parents to respond in more developmentally appropriate, as well as less coercive, ways, or helping foster or adoptive parents to understand the full spectrum of issues the maltreated child or adolescent has encountered and aid them also in not focusing solely on the abuse experience.

NOTES

1. It must be noted that most research has been done with "identified" cases and there may be systematic error in who is "identified." For example, while almost 2 million reports of child abuse and neglect were made in 1995, only about 30 percent of these were substantiated (NCCAN, 1997). A portion of those that are not may involve situations that may nonetheless pose some risk. Also, detection biases have been identified (e.g., underreporting of middle class and nonminority families). In addition, younger children appear to be identified more than teenagers. Thus, what is known regarding the context of abuse may not be comprehensive.

2. While not discussed much, abuse can begin at any point in children's development.

REFERENCES

Abel, G. G., Gore, D. K., Holland, C. L., Camp, N., Becker, J. V., & Rathner, J. (1989). The measurement of the cognitive distortions of child molesters. *Annals of Sex Research, 2,* 135–152.

Aber, J. L., & Allen, J. P. (1987). The effects of maltreatment on young children's socioemotional development. *Developmental Psychology, 23,* 406–414.

Ammerman, R. T., Van Hasselt, V. B., & Hersen, M. (1988). Maltreatment of handicapped children: A critical review. *Journal of Family Violence, 3,* 53–72.

Arvarian, A. L. (1975). Dynamics of separation and placement. In N. B. Ebeling & D. A. Hill (Eds.). *Child abuse: Intervention and treatment* (pp. 45–62). Acton, MA: Publishing Science Group.

Ayoub, C. (1991). Physical violence and preschoolers: The use of therapeutic day care in the treatment of physically abused children and children from violent families. *The Advisor, 4,* 1–18.

Azar, S. T. (1986). A framework for understanding child maltreatment: An integration of cognitive behavioral and development perspectives. *Canadian Journal of Behavioral Science, 18,* 340–355.

Azar, S. T. (1989). Training parents of abused children. In C. E. Shaefer & J. M. Briesmeister (Eds.), *Handbook of parent training* (pp. 414–441). New York: Wiley.

Azar, S. T. (1991a, April). *Concern about the physical abuse of adolescents: A case of neglect.* Paper presented at the annual meeting of the Eastern Psychological Association, New York.

Azar, S. T. (1991b). Models of physical child abuse: A metatheoretical analysis. *Criminal Justice and Behavior: Special Issue on Physical Child Abuse, 18,* 30–46.

Azar, S. T. (1997). A cognitive behavioral approach to understanding and treating parents who physically abuse their children. In D. Wolf & R. McMahon (Eds.), *Child abuse: New directions in prevention and treatment across the life span* (pp. 78–100). New York: Sage.

Azar, S. T., Barnes, K. T., & Twentyman, C. T. (1988). Developmental outcomes in physically abused children: Consequences of parental abuse or the effects of a more general breakdown in caregiving behaviors? *The Behavior Therapist, 11,* 27–32.

Azar, S. T., & Benjet, C. L. (1994). A cognitive perspective on ethnicity, race, and termination of parental rights. *Law and Human Behavior, 18,* 249–268.

Azar, S. T., Breton, S. J., & Miller, L. P. (1998). Cognitive behavioral group work and physical child abuse: Intervention and prevention. In K. C. Stoiber & Kratochwill, T. (Eds.). *Group intervention in the school and the community* (pp. 376–400). Boston: Allyn and Bacon.

Azar, S. T., Gentile, C., Orton, H., & Talbot, N. (1986, August). *Metamanagement deficits and self control: Cognitive skills, self efficacy, and peer status among disruptive and non-disruptive adolescents.* Paper presented at the annual convention of the American Psychological Association, Washington, DC.

Azar, S. T., Robinson, D. R., Hekimian, E., & Twentyman, C. T. (1984). Unrealistic expectations and problems solving ability in maltreating and comparison mothers. *Journal of Consulting and Clinical Psychology, 52,* 687–691.

Azar, S. T., & Rohrbeck, C. A. (1986). Child abuse and unrealistic expectations: Further validation of the Parent Opinion Questionnaire. *Journal of Consulting and Clinical Psychology, 54,* 867–868.

Azar, S. T., & Siegel, B. (1990). Behavioral treatment of child abuse: A developmental perspective. *Behavior Modification, 14,* 279–300.

Azar, S. T., & Twentyman, C. T. (1986). Cognitive-behavioral perspectives on the assessment and treatment of child abuse. In P. C. Kendall (Ed.), *Advances in cognitive-behavioral research and therapy* (Vol. 5, pp. 237–267). New York: Academic Press.

Azar, S. T., & Wientzen, J. (1993, March). *Abuse, social skills, and social support in adolescent runaways.* Poster presented at the biannual meeting of the Society for Research in Child Development, New Orleans.

Azar, S. T., & Wolfe, D. (1989). Child abuse and neglect. In F. J. Mash & R. A. Barkley (Eds.), *Treatment of childhood disorders* (pp. 451–489). New York: Guilford Press.

Barahal, R. M., Waterman, J., & Martin, H. P. (1981). The social cognitive development of abused children. *Journal of Consulting and Clinical Psychology, 49,* 508–516.

Barnes, K. T., & Azar, S. T. (1990, August). *Maternal expectations and attributions in discipline situations: A test of a cognitive model of parenting.* Poster presented at the annual meeting of the American Psychological Association, Boston.

Bee, H. L., Disbrow, M. A., Johnson-Crowley, N., & Barnard, K. (1981, April). *Parent–child interactions during teaching in abusing and non-abusing families.* Paper presented at the biannual convention of the Society for Research in Child Development, Boston.

Belsky, J. (1980). Child maltreatment. An ecological integration. *American Psychologist, 35,* 320–335.

Belsky, J., & Vondra, J. (1989). Lessons from child abuse: The determinants of parenting. In D. Cicchetti & V. Carlson (Eds.), *Child maltreatment* (pp. 153–202). New York: Cambridge University Press.

Berkowitz, S. & Sedlak, A. J. (1993). *Study of high risk: Child abuse and neglect groups. State survey report.* Washington, DC: National Center on Child Abuse and Neglect.

Berliner, L., & Barbieri, M. K. (1984). The testimony of the child victim of sexual assault. *Journal of Social Issues, 40,* 125–137.

Bousha, D., & Twentyman, C. T. (1984). Abusing, neglectful and comparison mother-child interactional style. *Journal of Abnormal Psychology, 93,* 106–114.

Bradley, E. J., & Peters, R. (1991). Physically abusive and nonabusive mothers' perceptions of parenting and child behavior. *American Journal of Orthopsychiatry, 61,* 455–460.

Brassard, M. R., Germain, R., & Hart, S. N. (1991). *Psychological maltreatment of children and youth.* New York: Pergamon Press.

Bruck, M., Ceci, S. J., & Hembrooke, H. (1998). Reliability and credibility of young children's reports. *American Psychologist, 53,* 136–151.

Burgess, R. L., & Conger, R. D. (1978). Family interaction in abusive, neglectful and normal families. *Child Development, 49,* 1163–1173.

Caffey, J. (1972). On the theory and practice of shaking infants: *American Journal of Diseases of Children, 124,* 161–169.

Caffey, J. (1974). The whiplash shaken infant syndrome. *Pediatrics, 54,* 396–403.

Camras, L. A., Ribordy, S., Spaccarelli, S., & Stefani, R. (1986, August). *Emotion recognition and production by abused children and mothers.* Paper presented at the meeting of the American Psychological Association, Washington, DC.

Carlson, V. Cicchetti, D., Barnett, D., & Braunwald, K. G. (1989). Find order in disorganization: Lessons from research on maltreated infants' attachments to their caregivers. In D. Cicchetti & V. Carlson (Eds.), *Child maltreatment.* (pp. 494–528). New York: Cambridge University Press.

Chandler, M. (1973). Egocentrism and antisocial behavior: The assessment and training of social perspective taking skills. *Developmental Psychology, 9,* 326–332.

Chilamkurti, C., & Milner, J. S. (1993). Perceptions and evaluations of child transgressions and disciplinary techniques in high- and low-risk mothers and their children. *Child Development, 64,* 1801–1814.

Cicchetti, D. (1989). How research on child maltreatment has informed the study of child development: Perspectives from developmental psychopathology. In D. Cicchetti & V. Carlson (Eds.), *Child maltreatment* (pp. 377–431). Cambridge, England: Cambridge University Press.

Cicchetti, D., & Rizley, R. (1981). Developmental perspectives on the etiology, intergenerational transmission, and sequelae of child maltreatment. *New Directions for Child Development, 11,* 31–56.

Cohen, J. A., & Mannarino, A. P. (1993). Sexual abuse. In R. T. Ammerman, C. G. Last, & M. Hersen (Eds.), *Handbook of prescriptive treatments for children and adolescents* (pp. 347–366). Boston: Allyn and Bacon.

Crittenden, P. M. (1982). Abusing, neglecting, problematic, and adequate dyads: Differentiating by patterns of interaction. *Merrill-Palmer Quarterly, 27,* 201–218.

Crittenden, P. M. (1985). Maltreated infants: Vulnerability and resilience. *Journal of Child Psychology and Psychiatry, 26,* 85–96.

Crittenden, P. M., & Ainsworth, M. D. S. (1989). Child maltreatment and attachment theory. In D. Cicchetti & V. Carlson (Eds.), *Child maltreatment* (pp. 432–463). Cambridge, England: Cambridge University Press.

Deblinger, E., McLeer, S. V., & Henry, D. (1990). Cognitive behavioral treatment for sexually abused children suffering from post traumatic stress: Preliminary findings. *Journal of the American Academy of Child and Adolescent Psychiatry, 29,* 747–752.

DeFrancis, V. (1969). *Protecting the child victim of sex crimes committed by adults: Final report.* Denver, CO: American Humane Association.

Dietrich, K. N., Starr, R. II, & Kaplan, M. G. (1980). Maternal stimulation and care of abused infants. In T. M. Field (Ed.), *High risk infants and children* (pp. 25–41). New York: Academic Press.

Drotar, D., Wilson, F., & Sturm, L. (1989). Parent intervention in failure-to-thrive. In E. Schaefer & J. M. Briesmeister (Eds.), *Handbook of parent training* (pp. 364–391). New York: Wiley.

Dubowitz, H. (1991). The impact of child maltreatment on health. In R. H. Starr & D. A. Wolfe (Eds.), *The effects of child abuse and neglect* (pp. 278–294). New York: Guilford Press.

Duhaime, A. C., Gennarelli, T. A., Thibault, L. E., Bruce, D. A., Margulies, S. S., & Wiser, R. (1987). The shaken baby syndrome. *Journal of Neurosurgery, 66,* 409–415.

Eckenrode, J., Laird, M., & Doris, J. (1993). School performance and disciplinary problems among abused and neglected children. *Developmental Psychology, 29,* 53–62.

Egeland, B., & Sroufe, A. (1981). Developmental sequelae of maltreatment in infancy. *New directions of child development: Developmental perspectives on child maltreatment* (pp. 77–92). San Francisco: Jossey-Bass.

Eidelson, R. J. & Epstein, N. (1982). Cognition and relationship maladjustment: Development of a measure of dysfunctional relationship beliefs. *Journal of Consulting and Clinical Psychology, 50,* 715–720.

Famularo, R., Fenton, T., & Kinscherff, R. (1993). Child maltreatment and the development of posttraumatic stress disorder. *American Journal of Diseases of Children, 147,* 755–760.

Fanshel, D., & Shinn, E. B. (1978). *Children in foster care: A longitudinal investigation.* New York: Columbia University Press.

Fantuzzo, J. (1990). Behavioral treatment of the victim of child abuse and neglect. *Behavior Modification, 14,* 316–339.

Fantuzzo, J. W., Jurecic, L., Stovall, A., Hightower, A. D., Goins, C., & Schachtel, D. (1988). Effects of adult and peer social initiations on the social behavior of withdrawn, maltreated preschool children. *Journal of Consulting and Clinical Psychology, 56,* 34–39.

Farber, E. A, & Egeland, B. (1987). Invulnerability among abused and neglected children. In E. J. Anthony & B. J. Cohler (Eds.), *The invulnerable child* (pp. 253–288). New York: Guilford Press.

Freyberg, J. T. (1980). Difficulties in separation-individuation as experienced by offspring of Nazi Holocaust survivors. *American Journal of Orthopsychiatry, 50,* 87–95.

Gabel, S. (1992). Children of incarcerated and criminal parents: Adjustment, behavior, and prognosis. *Bulletin of the Academy of Psychiatry & the Law, 20,* 33–45.

Gaensbauer, T. J., & Sands, K. (1979). Distorted effective communication in abused/neglected infants and their potential impact on caretakers. *Journal of the Academy of Child Psychiatry, 18*(1), 236–250.

Geiser, R. L. (1973). *The illusion of caring: Children in foster care.* Boston: Beacon Press.

George, C., & Main, M. (1980). Social interactions of young abused children: Approach, avoidance and aggression. *Child Development. 50,* 306–318.

Gersten, M., Coster, W., Schneider-Rosen, K., Carlson, V., & Cicchetti, D. (1986). The socio-emotional bases of communicative functioning. In M. E. Lamb, A. L. Lamb, and B. Rogoff (Eds.), *Advances in developmental psychology* (Vol. 4). Hillsdale, NJ: Erlbaum.

Gibbons, T. C., & Prince, J. (1963). *Child victims of sex offenses.* London: The Institute for the Study and Treatment of Delinquency.

Goodman, G. S., Taub, E. P., Jones, D. P., & England, P. (1992). Testifying in criminal court: Emotional effects on child sexual assault victims. *Monographs of the Society for Research in Child Development* (Vol. 57). New York: Society for Research in Child Development.

Gordon, F., & Jameson, J. (1979). Infant–mother attachment in patients with nonorganic failure to thrive syndrome. *Journal of the American Academy of Child Psychiatry, 18,* 251–259.

Green, A. H. (1978). Psychopathology of abused children. *Journal of Child Psychiatry, 17*(1), 92–103.

Harkness, L. (1991). The affect of combat-related PTSD on children. *Clinical Newsletter, National Center for Post-Traumatic Stress Disorder, 2,* 12–14.

Haskett, M. E. (1990). Social problem-solving skills of young physically abused children. *Child Psychiatry and Human Development, 21*(2), 109–118.

Hay, T. F., & Hall, D. K. (1981, April). *Behavioral, psychological, and developmental differences between abusive and control mother-child dyads.* Paper presented at the biannual convention of the Society for Research in Child Development. Boston.

Hennessy, K., Rabideau, G., Cicchetti, D., & Cummings, E. M. (1994). Responses of physically abused and nonabused children to different forms of interadult anger. *Child Development, 65,* 815–828.

Hoffman-Plotkin, D., & Twentyman, C. T. (1984). A multimodal assessment of behavioral and cognitive deficits in abused and neglected preschoolers. *Child Development, 55,* 794–802.

Howes, C., & Espinosa, M. (1985). The consequences of child abuse for the formation of relationships with peers. *Child Abuse and Neglect, 9,* 397–404.

Hughes, H. M. (1988). Psychological and behavioral correlates of family violence in child witnesses and victims. *American Journal of Orthopsychiatry, 58.* 77–90.

Hughes, H. M., & Barad, S. J. (1983). Psychological functioning of children in a battered women's shelter: A model preventative program. *Family Relations, 31,* 495–502.

Hurwitz, S. M., Simms, M. D., & Farrington, R. (1994). Impact of developmental problems on young children's exits from foster care. *Developmental and Behavioral Pediatrics, 15,* 105–110.

Jaffe, P. G., Hurly, D. J., & Wolfe, D. (1990). Children's observations of violence: I. Critical issues in child development and intervention planning. *Canadian Journal of Psychiatry, 35,* 466–470.

James, B. (1989). *Treating traumatized children.* Lexington, MA: Lexington Books.

Jellinek, M. S., Murphy, J. M., Poitrast, F., Quinn, D., Bishop, S. J., & Goshko, M. (1992). Serious child mistreatment in Massachusetts: The course of 206 children through the courts. *Child Abuse & Neglect, 16,* 179-185.

Johnson, C. F., & Showers, J. C. (1985). Injury variables in child abuse. *Child Abuse and Neglect, 9,* 207–215.

Jouriles, E. N., & Lecompte, S. H. (1991). Husband's aggression toward wives and mothers' and fathers' aggression toward children: Moderating effects of child gender. *Journal of Consulting and Clinical Psychology, 59,* 190–192.

Jouriles, E. N., Murphy, T., & O'Leary, K. D. (1989). Interspousal aggression, marital discord, and child problems. *Journal of Consulting and Clinical Psychology, 57,* 453–455.

Katz, S., & Mazur, M. A. (1979). *Understanding the rape victim: A synthesis of research findings.* New York: Wiley.

Kaufman, J., & Zigler, E. (1987). Do abused children become abusive parents? *American Journal of Orthopsychiatry, 57,* 186–192.

Kempton, T., Armistead, L., Wierson, M., & Forehand, R. (1991). Presence of a sibling as a potential buffer following parental divorce: An examination of young adolescents. *Journal of Clinical Child Psychology, 20,* 434–438.

Kendall-Tackett, K. A., William, L. M., & Finkelhor, D. (1993). Impact of sexual abuse on children: A review and synthesis of recent empirical studies. *Psychological Bulletin, 113,* 164–180.

Kent, I. T. (1976). A follow-up study of abused children. *Journal of Pediatric Psychology,* (1), 25–31.

Knitzer, J., & Allen, M. J. (1978). *Children without homes.* Washington, DC: Children's Defense Fund.

Kurdek, L. (1989). Siblings' reactions to parental divorce. *Journal of Divorce, 12,* 203–219.

Larrance, D. T., & Twentyman, C. T. (1983). Maternal attributions in child abuse. *Journal of Abnormal Psychology, 92,* 449–457.

Lewis, M., & Schaeffer, S. (1981). Peer behavior and mother–infant interaction in maltreated children. In M. Lewis & L. A. Rosenblum (Eds.), *The uncommon child* (pp. 193–223). New York: Plenum Press.

Lorber, R., Felton, D. K., & Reid, J. B. (1984). A social learning approach to the reduction of coercive processes in child abusive families: A molecular analysis. *Advances in Behavior Research and Therapy, 6,* 29–45.

Luerssen, T. G., Klauber, M. R., & Marshall, L. F. (1988). Outcome from head injury related to patient's age. *Journal of Neurosurgery, 68,* 409–416.

Lutzker, J. R., & Rice, J. M. (1984). Project 12-Ways: Treating child abuse and neglect from an ecobehavioral perspective. In R. F. Dangel & R. A. Polster (Eds.), *Parent training: Foundations of research and practice* (pp. 260–293). New York: Guilford Press.

Lutzker, S. Z., Lutzker, J. R., Braunling-McMorrow, D., & Eddleman, J. (1987). Prompting to increase mother–baby stimulation with single mothers. *Journal of Child and Adolescent Psychotherapy, 4,* 3–12.

Madansky, D., & Santora, D. (1989, November). *Pediatrician–therapist cooperation in the treatment of sexually abused children.* Paper presented at the National Child Abuse and Neglect Conference, Philadelphia.

Main, M., & George, C. (1985). Response of abused and disadvantaged toddlers to distress in agemates: A study in the day care setting. *Developmental Psychology, 21,* 407–412.

Main, M., Kaplan, N., & Cassidy, J. (1985). Security in infancy, childhood, and adulthood: A move to the level of representation. In I. Bretherton & E. Waters (Eds.), Growing points in attachment theory and research. *Monographs of the Society for Research in Child Development, 50* (1–2, Serial No. 209, pp. 66–106). New York: Society for Research in Child Development.

Mangine, S., Royse, D., Wieche, V., & Nietzel, M. (1990). Homelessness among adults raised as foster children. *Psychological Reports, 67,* 739–745.

Martin, H. P. (1976). *The abused child: A multidisciplinary approach to developmental issues and treatment.* Cambridge, MA: Ballinger.

Mash, E. J., Johnston, C., & Koviiz, K. (1983). A comparison of the mother-child interactions of physically abused and non-abused children during play and task situations. *Journal of Clinical Child Psychology, 12,* 337–346.

Mass, H. S., & Engler, R. (1959). *Children in need of parents.* New York: Columbia University Press.

McGee, R. A., & Wolfe, D. A. (1991). Psychological maltreatment: Toward an operational definition. *Developmental and psychopathology* (pp. 3–18). New York: Cambridge University Press.

McIntyre, A., Lounsbury, K., Bernton, D., & Steel, H. (1988). Psychosocial characteristics of foster children. *Journal of Applied Developmental Psychology, 9,* 125–137.

McIntyre, A. (1991). Attribution of control and ego development: Marker variables for a model of foster care risk. *Journal of Applied Developmental, 12,* 413–428.

McKibben, L., DeVos, E., & Newberger, E. H. (1989). Victimization of mothers of abused children: A controlled study. *Pediatrics, 84,* 531–535.

Miller L. R., & Azar, S. T. (1996). The pervasiveness of maladaptive attributions in mothers at-risk for child abuse. *Family Violence and Sexual Abuse Bulletin, 12,* 31–37.

Mueller, E., & Silverman, N. (1989). Peer relations in maltreated children. In D. Cicchetti & V. Carlson (Eds.), *Child maltreatment* (pp. 529–578). New York: Cambridge University Press.

National Center on Child Abuse and Neglect (1997). *Child mal-treatment 1995. Reports from the states to the National Center on Child Abuse and Neglect.* Washington, DC: U.S. Department of Health and Human Services.

National Research Council (1993). *Understanding child abuse and neglect.* Washington, DC: National Academy Press.

Newberger, E. H., Hampton, R. L., Marx, T. J., & White, K. M. (1986). Child abuse and pediatric social illness. *American Journal of Orthopsychiatry, 56,* 589–601.

Oates, R. K., Peacock, A., & Forrest, D. (1985). Long-term effects of nonorganic failure to thrive. *Pediatrics, 75,* 36–40.

Olds, D. L., Henderson, C. R., Chamberlin, R., & Tatelbaum, R. (1986). Preventing child abuse and neglect: A randomized trial of nurse home visitation. *Pediatrics, 78,* 65–78.

Pagelow, M. D. (1984). *Family violence.* New York: Praeger Scientific.

Pagelow, M. D. (1989). The incidence and prevalence of criminal abuse of other family members. In I. Ohlin & M. Tonry (Eds.), *Family violence* (pp. 263–314) Chicago: University of Chicago Press.

Parker, J. (1982). The rights of child witnesses: Is the court a protector or perpetrator? *New England Law Review, 17,* 643–717.

Patterson, G. R. (1980). Mothers: The unacknowledged victims. *Monographs of the Society for Research in Child Development, 45* (5, Serial No. 186).

Peterson, L. (1994) Child injury and abuse–neglect: Common etiologies, challenges, and courses toward prevention. *Current Directions in Psychological Science, 3,* 116–120.

Price, J. M., & Brew, V. (1998). Peer relationships of foster children: Development and mental health service implications. *Journal of Applied Developmental Psychology, 19,* 199–218.

Pynoos, R. S. (1994). Traumatic stress and developmental psychopathology in children and adolescents. In R. S. Pynoos (Ed.), *Post traumatic stress disorder: A clinical review* (pp. 65–98). Lutherville, MD: Sidran Press.

Pynoos, R. S., & Eth, S. (1984). The child as witness to homicide. *Journal of Social Issues, 40,* 87–108.

Reid, J. B. (1985). Behavioral approaches to intervention and assessment of child abusive families. In P. H. Bornstein & A. E. Kazdin (Eds.), *Handbook of clinical behavior therapy with children* (pp. 772–802). Homewood, IL: Dorsey.

Reid, J. B., Kavanaugh, K., & Baldwin, D. V. (1987). Abusive parents' preceptions of child problem behavior: An example of parental bias. *Journal of Abnormal Psychology, 15,* 457–466.

Ribbe, D., Lipovsky, J., & Freedy, J. (1992). Posttraumatic stress disorder. In A. R. Eisen & C. E. Schaeffer (Eds.), *Critical handbook of anxiety disorders in children and adolescents.* Northvale, NJ: Jason Aronson.

Rogoff, B., & Wertsch, J. V. (1984). *Children's learning in the "zone of proximal development."* San Francisco, CA: Jossey-Bass.

Rosenbaum, A., & O'Leary, K. D. (1981). Children: The unintended victims of marital violence. *American Journal of Orthopsychiatry, 51,* 692–699.

Rutter, M. (1993) Intergenerational continuities and discontinuities in serious parenting difficulties. In D. Cicchetti & V. Carlson (Eds.), *Child maltreatment* (pp. 317–348). Cambridge, England: Cambridge University Press.

Salzinger, S., Feldman, R., Hammer, M., & Rosario, M. (1993). The effects of physical abuse on children's social relationships. *Child Development, 64,* 169–187.

Salzinger, S., Kaplan, S., & Artemyeff, C. (1983). Mothers' personal social networks and child maltreatment. *Journal of Abnormal Psychology, 92,* 68–76.

Salzinger, S., Kaplan, S., Pelcovitz, D., Samit, C., & Krieger, R. (1984). Parent and teacher assessment of children's behavior in child maltreating families. *Journal of the American Academy of Child Psychiatry, 23,* 458–464.

Sameroff, A. J., & Chandler, M. J. (1975). Reproductive risk and the continuum of caretaking casualty. In D. Horowitz, M. Herthington, S. Scarr, S. Salapatak, & G. Siegel (Eds.), *Review of child development research* (Vol. 4, pp. 187–243). Chicago: University of Chicago Press.

Sarber, R. E., Halasz, M. M., Messmer, M. C., Brickett, A. D., & Lutzker, J. R. (1983). Teaching menu planning and grocery shopping skills to a mentally retarded mother. *Mental Retardation, 21,* 101–106.

Sas, L. (1997). Sexually abused children as witnesses: Progress and pitfalls. In D. A. Wolfe, R. J. McMahon, & R. D. Peters (Eds.), *Child abuse: New directions in prevention and treatment across the lifespan* (pp. 248–267). Thousand Oaks, CA: Sage.

Schacht, A. J., Kerlinsky, D., & Carlson, C. (1990). Group therapy with sexually abused boys: Leadership, projective identification, and countertransference issues. *International Journal of Group Psychotherapy, 40,* 401–417.

Schellenbach, C. J., & Guerney, I. F., (1987). Identification of adolescent abuse and future intervention. *Journal of Adolescence, 10,* 1–12.

Schene, P. A. (19). Intervention in child abuse and neglect. In J. C. Westman (Ed.), *Who speaks for the children?* (pp. 205–220). Sarasota, FL: Professional Resources Exchange.

Schor, E. L. (1982). The foster care system and health status of foster children. *Pediatrics, 69,* 521–528.

Sedlak, A. J. (1991). *Study of adoption assistance: Impact and outcomes. Phase II report.* Washington, DC: Administration for Children, Youth, and Families, U.S. Department of Health and Human Services.

Sigal, J. J., & Weinfeld, M. (1989). *Trauma and rebirth.* New York: Praeger.

Sirles, E. A., Walsma, J., Lytle-Barnaby, R., & Lender, C. L. (1988). Group therapy techniques for work with child sexual abuse victims. *Social Work with Groups, 11*(3), 67–78.

Smith, S. M. (1975). *The battered child syndrome.* London: Butterworth.

Stark, E., & Flitcraft, A. H. (1988). Women and children at-risk: A feminist perspective on child abuse. *International Journal of Health Services, 18,* 97–118.

Stermac, L. E., & Segal, Z. V. (1989). Adult sexual contact with children: An examination of cognitive factors. *Behavior Therapy, 20,* 573–584.

Steward, M. S., Farquhar, L. C., Dicharry, D. C., Glick, D. R., & Martin, P. W. (1986). Group therapy: A treatment of choice for young victims of child abuse. *International Journal of Group Psychotherapy, 36,* 261–277.

Straus, M. A., & Gelles, R. J. (1990). *Physical violence in American families*. New Brunswick, NJ: Transaction.

Terr, L. (1991). Childhood traumas: An outline and overview. *American Journal of Psychiatry, 148,* 10–20.

Tertinger, D. A., Greene, B. F., & Lutzker, J. R. (1984). Home safety: Development and validation of one component of an ecobehavioral treatment program for abused and neglected children. *Journal of Applied Behavior Analysis, 17,* 150–174.

The U.S. Advisory Board on Child Abuse and Neglect (1993). *The continuing child protection emergency: A challenge to the nation.* Washington, DC: Administration of Children, Youth and Families, U.S. Department of Health and Human Services.

Trickett, P. K., & Kuczynski, L. (1986). Children's misbehaviors and parental discipline strategies in abusive and nonabusive families. *Developmental Psychology, 22,* 115–123.

Trickett, P. K., McBride-Chang, C., & Putnam, F. W. (1994). The classroom performance and behavior of sexually abused females. *Development and Psychopathology, 6,* 183–194.

Trickett, P. K., & Putnam, F. W. (1993). Impact of child sexual abuse on females. Toward a developmental psychobiological integration. *Psychological Science, 4,* 81–87.

Tymchuk, A. J., Yokota, A., & Rahbar, B. (1990). Decision-making abilities of mothers with mental retardation. *Research in Developmental Disabilities, 11,* 97–109.

U.S. House of Representatives Select Committee on Children, Youth, and Families (1987). *Victims of official neglect.* Washington, DC: U.S. Congress.

Vitulano, L. A., Lewis, M., Doran, L. D., Nordhaus, B., & Adnopoz, J. (1986). Treatment recommendation, implementation, and follow-up in child abuse. *American Journal of Orthopsychiatry, 56.* 478–480.

Wald, M. S. (1976). Legal policies affecting children: A lawyer's request for aid. *Child Development, 47,* 1–5.

Wahler, R. G., & Dumas, J. E. (1986). Maintenance factors in coercive mother-child interactions: The compliance and predictability hypotheses. *Journal of Applied Behavior Analysis, 19,* 13–22.

Werner, H. (1948). *Comparative psychology of mental development.* New York: International Universities Press.

Widom, C. S. (1989). Does violence beget violence? A critical examination of the literature. *Psychological Bulletin, 106,* 3–28.

Widom, C. S. (1991). Role of placement experience in mediating the criminal consequences of early childhood victimization. *American Journal of Orthopsychiatry, 61,* 195–209.

Williams, G. (1983). The urgency of authentic prevention. *Journal of Clinical Child Psychology, 12,* 312–319.

Wolfe, D. A. (1987). *Child abuse: Implications for child development and psychopathology.* Newbury Park, CA: Sage.

Wolfe, D. A., Jaffe, P., Wilson, S. K., & Zak, L. (1985). Children of battered women: The relation of child behavior to family violence and maternal stress. *Journal of Consulting and Clinical Psychology, 53,* 657–665.

Wolfe, D. A., Sandler, J., & Kaufman, K. (1981). A competency-based parent training program for abusive parents. *Journal of Consulting and Clinical Psychology, 49,* 633–640.

Zeanah, C. J., & Zeanah, P. D. (1989). Intergenerational transmission of maltreatment: Insights from attachment theory and research. *Psychiatry, 52,* 177–196.

CHAPTER 24

CHILDREN OF ALCOHOLICS

Michael Windle
Jonathan G. Tubman

The adage that alcoholism runs in families is commonplace, having been passed on via folk knowledge for centuries. Systematic, empirical research over the past 20 to 25 years on the genetic and/or environmental transmission of alcoholism within families has generally yielded findings that are congruent with the age-old adage, suggesting that alcoholism does indeed run in families. Nevertheless, there remains considerable controversy in the research literature over the presumed causes of alcoholism within the family, as well as the strength of specific factors or constellations of factors (e.g., Sher, 1991; Windle & Searles, 1990). It has been estimated that children of alcoholics (COAs) are from four to nine times as likely to develop an alcohol disorder in adulthood as children who are non-COAs (e.g., Russell, 1990). However, while this increased risk for alcoholism among COAs is of substantive significance, it should not be sensationalized to suggest that an alcohol disorder is (deterministically) inevitable among COAs; in fact, the majority of COAs never develop alcohol disorders and often manifest life course patterns that resemble those of non-COAs (including some who appear to be functioning extraordinarily well, others who have difficulties in interpersonal spheres, and still others who manifest psychiatric disorders, criminal behaviors, or indicators of maladjustment or deviance).

It is the *heterogeneity of outcomes* among COAs that we believe suggests the value of integrating a life-span developmental psychopathology perspective with existing COA research to provide a roadmap of potentially fruitful avenues and expressways for future inquiry. That is, the existing literatures from multiple disciplinary orientations (each with their own set of methods and entrenched biases) are in agreement that a family history of alcoholism is a risk factor for a subsequent alcohol disorder among COAs, but also that many COAs will not develop such a disorder. These findings have stimulated investigators to study not only specific factors that increase risk for the expression of an alcohol disorder, but also to study specific protective factors that may distinguish COAs who do not develop this disorder. Furthermore, it is generally recognized that prospective, longitudinal research designs are required to understand the complex unfolding of interindividual differences and intraindividual change trajectories across the life span to accommodate such heterogeneous outcomes. It is proposed in this chapter that a conceptualization that emphasizes dynamic, person–environment relations and that emphasizes the timing, duration, sequence, and co-occurrence of events (e.g., onset of alcohol use, physical or sexual abuse) and behaviors (aggression, family/peer relations) across time, will facilitate the study of diverse outcomes and multiple pathways associated with a COA, high-risk status. Such a conceptualization is also beneficial for preventive intervention research by identifying which factors are important when, and how. Given that a constellation of attributes (e.g., temperament, cognitive functioning, family relations) have been identified as potentially significant to COA risk, some factors may be of differential importance at different times in the life span (e.g., during childhood, middle adolescence) or for some children and adolescents versus others.

As noted previously, research on COAs has been an interdisciplinary and multidisciplinary endeavor. This has been a strength in that there have been scientific contributions by scholars from different disciplines, ranging from molecular genetics to cultural anthropology. However, variation in metatheoretical and disciplinary orientation has also yielded the integration of findings across studies a challenging proposition. In this chapter, we attempt to provide at least some coverage to the various disciplines that have contributed to the rapidly expanding literature on COAs, although more coverage is allocated to research from the behavioral than biological sciences due to the perceived audience of this book. We have also restricted our focus to the infancy through adolescence phases of the life span and have, therefore, not (extensively) included literature pertinent to adult children of alcoholics (ACOAs) or to adult treatment samples. However, when appropriate, we have provided references to the interested reader who desires to study these particular areas in more detail. The chapter is divided into eight sections. First, a summary of epidemiological studies of COAs and associated methodological issues are presented. Second, a dynamic diathesis-stress model of developmental psychopathology for COAs is provided; this model is used to organize and integrate literature presented in the chapter. Third, research on biological risk factors, including studies of electrocortical arousal and neurochemical markers, is presented. The fourth and fifth sections provide study findings on temperament–personality and cognitive–intellectual factors, respectively. The sixth section describes research on family and extra-familial (e.g., peer) relations among COAs, and the seventh section focuses on existing COA prevention programs. The last section provides a succinct summary of the chapter findings and proposes future research directions for COA studies that is guided by a developmental psychopathology conceptualization and encourages a greater exchange of information among developmental and clinical researchers and practitioners.

EPIDEMIOLOGICAL FINDINGS ON COAS

Eigen and Rowden (1995) proposed a "best single estimate" of the number of COAs in the United States under age 18

years at 17.5 million in 1988 (with an estimated range from 15 to 19.9 million contingent on given assumptions). These children were identified as the offspring of parents who met clinical criteria for an alcohol disorder at any time in their lifetime. Eigen and Rowden provided two additional useful estimates based on subsamples of these COAs. First, they estimated that the number of COAs who actually lived with an alcoholic parent during his or her parent's period of expressing an alcohol disorder was approximately 14 million (i.e., this excluded those COAs who were not directly exposed to the parental alcoholism due, for example, to birth subsequent to the expression of the alcohol disorder). Second, they estimated that the number of COAs who currently (within the last year) lived with an alcoholic parent was approximately 11 million.

The breakdowns by subsample reported by Eigen and Rowden (1995) highlight one source of heterogeneity among COAs that is highly relevant for etiologic theories and preventive interventions. That is, the level of direct exposure to parental alcoholism and associated adverse consequences is variable across COAs, with some having direct and perhaps highly intense aversive experiences (e.g., sexual abuse) associated with parental alcoholism, whereas others may have had limited or no direct exposure. The exposure element is significant for etiologic theories that posit that social learning (e.g., parental role modeling of alcohol use and drinking to cope with stressful events) is a salient feature associated with increased risk for alcohol disorders among offspring. For example, Moos and Billings (1982) reported that COAs whose parents were in recovery viewed their families similar to a control group as being trusting, affectionate, and cohesive. Similarly, Beardslee and Vaillant (1986) reported that degree of exposure to parental alcoholism among COAs was associated in subsequent years with a range of adverse outcomes for offspring, including alcoholism, time in jail, sociopathy, and premature death. Thus, heterogeneity in outcome among COAs may be influenced by differential exposure to distal and proximal parental alcoholism variables.

Further sources of heterogeneity in definition and probable adult outcome among COAs have been extensively reviewed by Russell (1990). Russell accurately noted that estimates of the prevalence of alcohol disorders, and thus of the number of COAs, is greatly influenced by the definition of alcoholism adopted, the diagnostic instrument used, and the representativeness of the sample employed. For example, many of the early estimates of COA risk were based on treatment samples, which may be highly biased (e.g., Berkson, 1946). The use of the *family study method,* which involves direct interviews of all first-degree relatives (e.g., parents, siblings, and offspring) regarding their own alcohol disorder history, versus the *family history method,* which typically involves the direct interview of a single family member regarding their own and other first-degree relatives' alcohol disorder history, have produced different prevalence estimates (e.g., Thompson, Orvaschel, Prusoff, & Kidd, 1982). Recent evidence from alcohol typology research (e.g., Cloninger, Bohman, & Sigvardsson, 1981; Zucker, 1987) has suggested that there are multiple alcohol disorders and that genetic (i.e., COA) risk is not constant across all subtypes. Russell concluded on the basis of such subtype heterogeneity that COA risk for an adult alcohol disorder ranges from a little over 1.0 to over 9.0. Hence, it appears that although COAs are at risk for the development of alcohol disorders in adulthood, much remains to be known about the specific pathways and trajectories that account for the heterogeneity in outcome that has been observed.

DYNAMIC DIATHESIS-STRESS MODEL OF DEVELOPMENTAL PSYCHOPATHOLOGY: AN APPLICATION TO COAS

A host of life span, ecological, and developmental psychopathology perspectives have emerged over the past 20 to 25 years to account more adequately for the dynamic, multiple level influences that appear to characterize human functioning (e.g., Bronfenbrenner, 1977; Lerner; 1978; Sroufe & Rutter, 1984). The conceptual model provided in Figure 24.1 is consistent with these broad perspectives in that it recognizes that the confluence of factors at different levels of analysis (e.g., biogenetic, psychological, sociocultural) is important for understanding complex human behaviors, and that the study of human development necessitates the investigation of the cross-temporal dynamic relations among these variables to optimally describe and explain phenomena of interest. In addition, the conceptual model in Figure 24.1 attempts to incorporate working models in psychiatry and psychopathology that have been rooted in a diathesis-stress approach that has viewed the interrelations between vulnerable, person characteristics (e.g., personality traits, coping styles) and stressful life encounters as salient in describing differential thresholds for the manifestation of behavior pathology. In the model proposed in this chapter, the diathesis-stress model is expanded in two highly significant ways. First, both the diathesis and the stress components are viewed as multidimensional, thus necessitating the consideration of more complex kinds of additive and synergistic relations for the interrelations among variables from both domains (e.g., Haynes, 1992). Second, both diathesis and stress components are conceptualized within a larger matrix of environmental and contextual influences, and developmentally oriented, temporal features of evolving person–environment relations are em-

phasized. In this chapter, we use this more general dynamic diathesis-stress model to organize information for the COA child–adolescent literature, although the more general model is restricted neither to COAs nor to alcoholics; of course, some of the specific exemplars identified for given categories would need to be tailored to the relevant literature. For instance, rumination and hopelessness may be more appropriate exemplars for cognitive factors, rather than alcohol expectancies, if the focus was on affective disorders.

In subsequent sections data relevant to some of the specific boxes in Figure 24.1 are provided. The larger picture provided by Figure 24.1 illustrates a general flow of the multivariate (often bidirectional) influences that contribute both to risk for health compromising behaviors among COAs and to an appreciation of the variable patterns of influence that may contribute to heterogeneous outcomes. The model posits that risk for difficulties among COAs may (but do not necessarily) begin prenatally, with possible assaults on the fetus and the developing central nervous system via maternal alcohol consumption. The investigation of fetal alcohol syndrome (FAS) and fetal alcohol effects (FAEs) has indicated both short- and long-term effects on the offspring of heavier alcohol-consuming women during pregnancy across multiple domains of functioning (e.g., neuropsychological and intellectual deficits, externalizing behavior problems), as well as across the various portions of the life span that have been studied. For example, in Streissguth's ongoing prospective, longitudinal study, prenatal alcohol exposure has been associated with lower performance on cognitive functioning indices (e.g., IQ scores, learning problems, attention and short-term memory tasks) at ages 4, 7, and 14 years (e.g., Streissguth, Barr, & Sampson, 1990; Streissguth, Bookstein, Sampson, & Barr, 1995). Similarly, Nanson and Hiscock (1990) reported a range of attentional deficits among a sample of children with high exposure to maternal alcohol use during pregnancy, and Coles and her colleagues (e.g., Brown, Coles, Smith, Platzman, Silverstein, Erickson, & Falek, 1991; Coles, Brown, Smith, Platzman, Erickson, & Falek, 1991) reported cognitive and behavioral problems among a school-age sample of children exposed to alcohol prenatally.

The full range, or spectrum, of effects associated with FAS and FAEs include growth deficits, mental retardation, behavioral and emotional problems, and morphological abnormalities. Much of the existing prospective research on fetal alcohol influences on offspring is relatively recent, with some mixed findings for the longer term effects (beyond infancy). Nevertheless, there is a general convergence in suggesting a dose-response relationship between prenatal alcohol exposure and offspring functioning for at least a certain portion of the life span (e.g., infancy through early childhood) and for certain domains of functioning. Much of

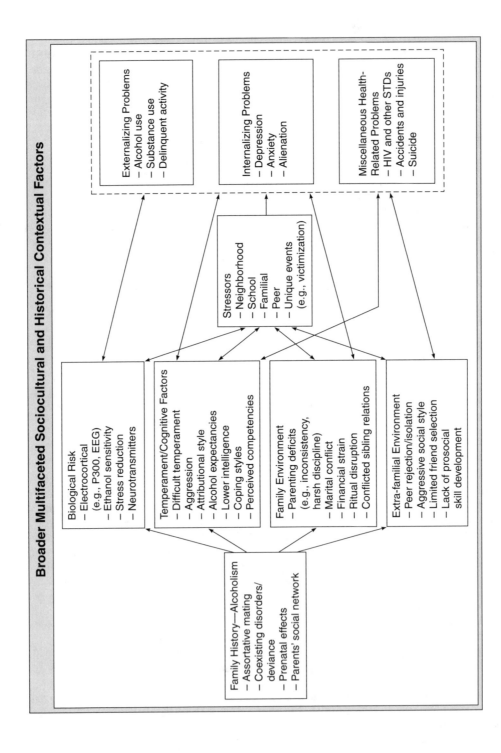

FIGURE 24.1 Dynamic diathesis-stress model of development psychopathology: An application to children of alcoholics (COAs)

this research has adopted a teratogenic perspective to investigate these dose-response relationships, and this strategy has provided fruitful results. However, to accommodate the heterogeneity in individual developmental trajectories and outcomes associated with FAEs and FAS, the teratogenic model may be complemented by a more encompassing developmental model such as the one proposed in Figure 24.1. From this perspective, the distal and proximal links between prenatal alcohol exposure and differential health outcomes across the life span may be more clearly delineated via mediated and moderated effects.

In addition to potential adverse prenatal influences via maternal alcohol consumption, COAs may also be at heightened risk due to (assortative) mating characteristics of their parents and the potential for increased levels of comorbidity (i.e., co-occurring alcohol and psychiatric disorders) among parents. Assortative mating by daughters of alcoholics has been reported, as has the tendency for alcoholic women to marry alcoholic men (e.g., Hall, Hesselbrock, & Stabenau, 1983a, 1983b; Hill & Hruska, 1992). Such selective mating practices may produce a double jeopardy situation for the offspring of such pairings. First, the offspring may inherit a genetic predisposition toward alcoholism by the combination lineages of both the paternal and maternal sides of the family. Second, the rearing environments of children raised with two alcoholic parents may be more highly compromised, with higher levels of unpredictability, lower levels of parental monitoring, and higher levels of child maltreatment. McKenna and Pickens (1983) compared children with two alcoholic parents, one alcoholic parent, and no alcoholic parents on several characteristics related to offspring alcohol-related behaviors. Children with two alcoholic parents reported the earliest age of alcohol intoxication, more behavioral problems preceding alcohol treatment, and a shorter duration between first intoxication and initial alcoholism treatment than did the other two groups. Parenthetically, children with one alcoholic parent also consistently differed from children in the no alcoholic parent group on the measures of alcohol-related behaviors.

In addition to assortative mating specific to alcoholism, it has been recognized that nonrandom, partner pairings may occur between (1) alcoholics and partners with psychiatric disorders (e.g., major depression), and (2) alcoholics with coexisting disorders or a criminogenic lifestyle, and a "like" partner. In the larger field of alcohol studies, the role of coexisting psychopathology and alcoholic subtypes has emerged as a focal topic, with distinct profiles proposed for etiologic factors, time course of the disorder, treatment matching, and prognosis (e.g., Babor, Hoffmann, Del Boca, Hesselbrock, Meyer, Dolinsky, & Rounsaville, 1992; Zucker,

Ellis, & Fitzgerald, 1994). The impact of such differential parental pairings on offspring development has not been systematically studied, although some studies have begun to investigate the influence of certain alcoholic subtypes (e.g., antisocial alcoholics) on multiple features of child development (e.g., Zucker & Fitzgerald, 1986).

The influences of alcoholic parents' social network on offspring development is another area that has been underresearched, although there are some existing findings that suggest that this domain of influences should not be overlooked. Miller, Downs, Gondoli, and Keil (1987) reported that sexual abuse among the offspring of alcoholics was more likely to have been perpetuated by "friends" of the family rather than by fathers or other male figures in the household. Social-learning perspectives would also suggest that the exposure of children to a larger number of alcoholic role models (i.e., parents and parents' friends, other relatives) may foster given expectancies and social norms for drinking and drinking-related behaviors and may undermine the development of more constructive coping strategies and perceptions of competency in multiple domains. Furthermore, the undermining of perceived competencies in multiple domains (e.g., social, cognitive, physical), the lack of the development of appropriate prosocial skills, and the observational learning of perhaps less-than-optimal friendship patterns may yield COAs susceptible to dysfunction in intrafamilial and extrafamilial interpersonal situations. The extrafamilial environment box in Figure 24.1 illustrates some potential adverse consequences that may be causally linked to genetic and familial–environmental factors for COAs. Note that such outcomes are not unique to COAs, but rather reflect common, pernicious family influences that are often initiated early in development and are perpetuated over time via negative regulatory cycles (e.g., Dishion, French, & Patterson, 1995). Additionally, in many instances in which such negative regulatory cycles are initiated, diversified, and strengthened across time, the probability that the influence of family members or community supports disrupting such functioning in the manner of a protective factor decreases.

In summary, there are a variety of potential genetic and environmental risk factors associated with COA status. Such genetic and stress-inducing environmental risk factors may function in additive or synergistic ways to impact child development. Further, it is highly probable that there are gene–environment relationships (e.g., gene–environment interactions and correlations) across the course of development that account for the increased risk for alcohol disorders among COAs. We now turn toward some specific domains that have been implicated in risk expression among COAs.

BIOLOGICAL RISK FACTORS

Research with adult alcoholics has indicated significant differences in measures of electrocortical arousal, including differences in electroencephagrahic (EEG) and P300 responses (a positive event–related potential response wave that occurs approximately 300 msec after stimulus presentation) (for review, see Tarter, Laird, & Moss, 1990). The psychological significance of some of these electrocortical responses (e.g., P300) has been associated with features of information processing, including the allocation of attentional resources and the maintenance of working memory (e.g., Polich, 1993). Initial studies in this domain often utilized alcoholics in treatment and observed, for example, reduced amplitude P300 responses (e.g., Porjesz & Begleiter, 1987). However, these initial findings were viewed with some uncertainty because it was unclear if the reduced P300 responses existed prior to chronic alcohol use, and thus were a consequence of habitual inebriation, or if such differences existed prior to the onset of alcoholic drinking patterns.

The P300 response is known to be highly heritable, and because alcoholism also was noted to run in families, studies of children of alcoholics were initiated to investigate the possible role of reduced P300 amplitude and other measures of electrocortical arousal in COAs *prior to* the onset of drinking. Begleiter, Porjesz, Bihari, and Kissin (1984) recruited boys aged 6–10 years (without prior drinking experiences) and reported that COAs did indeed differ significantly from non-COAs with regard to a reduced P300 response in a visual task paradigm. These findings have been replicated in several other studies (e.g., Hill, Steinhauer, Park, & Zubin, 1990; Hill & Steinhauer, 1993; Whipple, Parker, & Noble, 1988) and converge in suggesting a decreased amplitude for the P300 response for COAs that generalizes across visual and auditory sensory modalities. Parenthetically, Hill and her colleagues used a multigenerational definition (i.e., both parental and grandparental alcoholism) to form high-risk groups, thus increasing the genetic (and possibly environmental–risk) loading for the expression of alcohol disorders.

Other research on electrocortical responses have indicated that COAs and non-COAs differ on spontaneous EEG activity. Resting or spontaneous EEG wavelength responses reflect ongoing, fluctuating, electrical activity in the brain without reference to a discrete stimulus presentation or cognitive task (as used in an event related potential [ERP] paradigm). Gabrielli, Mednick, Volavka, Pollock, Schulsinger, and Itil (1982) reported that 11- to 13-year-old COA boys, but not girls, had significantly higher percentages of fast EEG activity than non-COAs. However, this finding has not been replicated and most of the electrocortical research among COAs has focused on the P300 response because of its identification with later stage cognitive processing, that is, working memory and attentional resource allocation. Other evoked potential paradigms that have focused on brain stem electrical activity or on earlier onset response parameters have not yielded significant differences among COAs and non-COAs (e.g., Neville & Schmidt, 1985).

Although a large number of studies in the adult alcohol literature have focused on biochemical state and trait markers (for one review, see Chan, 1990), a limited number of studies have focused on such markers for COAs. In addition, few studies of individual differences in neurotransmitters have been conducted despite Cloninger's (1987) personality conceptualization that suggests that given biologically based traits (rooted in lower or higher levels of neurotransmitter concentrations) predispose one toward higher risk for an alcohol disorder. Gabel, Stadler, Bjorn, Shindledecker, and Bowden (1995) studied boys in a residential center for disruptive youth (mean age = 12.3 years) and focused on levels of monamine oxidase (MAO) and homovanillic acid (HVA) in a two (substance abusing father—yes or no) by two (boys with conduct disorder—yes or no) research design. MAO is a versatile and important mitochondrial enzyme involved in the catabolism (breakdown) of catecholamines (dopamine and epinephrine) and serotonin, and HVA is a major peripheral metabolite of dopamine. Prior research (e.g., Devor, Cloninger, Hoffman, & Tabakoff, 1993) has suggested that lower MAO activity levels are associated with an early onset, antisocial type of alcoholism.

The findings of Gabel and colleagues (1995) suggested that boys (with or without conduct disorder) of substance-abusing fathers differed significantly in MAO levels from boys without substance-abusing fathers, although no significant differences were indicated for levels of HVA. These researchers interpreted their findings to suggest that sons of substance-abusing fathers were at increased (genetic) risk of dopaminergic dysregulation, thus yielding them vulnerable to impulsive and undersocialized behaviors and to substance abuse. However, the sample of the study by Gabel and colleagues was small (total $N = 65$) and nonrepresentative, and findings regarding associations between various biochemical markers and psychiatric disorders among children have been inconsistent (e.g., Rogeness, Hernandez, Macedo, & Mitchell, 1982). Nevertheless, the research conducted by Gabel and colleagues suggests a future research direction pertinent to the identification of early onset biochemical variables that may predispose children of substance abusers to risk for the subsequent development of dysfunctional behaviors. The systematic mapping of how such biochemical markers influence variables at other levels of analysis (e.g., temperamental and coping variables), which in turn influence psychosocial variables and behavioral interactions, and ultimately substance abuse, remain objectives to strive toward in future research.

In summary, the existing research on biological risk factors among COAs has been limited and precludes definitive statements about the causal status of any of the indices investigated. However, a number of studies have supported the significance of a decreased P300 response among COAs, and to the extent that this marker is associated with decreased functioning in working memory and attentional resource allocation, it could be significant. That is, working memory and attentional processes are valuable functions in key contexts in society (e.g., school, work settings), and deficits in these domains may contribute to higher distractibility and impulsivity, and to the establishment of perpetuating negative cycles that are maintained across the life span. For example, children with poor attentional control may not perform well in school and may then associate with deviant peers who are also not performing well in school. Such deviant peer groups engage in higher levels of delinquent activity and early onset substance use, and social labeling (as deviant) may follow. Thus, an elementary deficit in attentional processes may, across time, contribute to suboptimal life course trajectories. Future research that incorporates multilevel assessment strategies and prospective, longitudinal research designs are required to examine such dynamic relations.

TEMPERAMENT AND PERSONALITY FACTORS

Early theories of alcoholism posited that a singular, "alcoholic personality" formed the etiologic basis for the expression of this disorder. Although few (if any) current alcohol researchers would subscribe to the notion of a singular alcoholic personality, features of temperament and personality continue to be incorporated in many existing theories of alcohol disorders (e.g., Cloninger, 1987; Tarter, 1988). Windle (1990) conducted an extensive review of differences in personality and temperament among COAs and non-COAs. Perhaps the most consistently significant difference was indicated for a dimension of behavioral undercontrol, characterized by features of impulsivity, antisocial behavior, and distractibility. A few studies (e.g., Kern, Hassett, & Collipp, 1981; Prewett, Spence, & Chaknis, 1981) conducted with children also suggested that COAs reported a more external locus of control orientation than their non-COA counterparts. However, there were few consistent significant differences among COAs and non-COAs for a number of other personality dimensions (e.g., neuroticism, self-esteem).

Tarter and his colleagues (e.g., Tarter, 1988; Tarter, Alterman, & Edwards, 1985) adopted a difficult temperament conceptualization, framed within a multifactorial model of

genetic and environmental transmission, to account for interrelations among substance-abusing parents (including alcoholics), difficult temperament, and offspring risk for substance abuse disorder. Briefly, Tarter and colleagues proposed that substance-abusing fathers with difficult temperaments transmit features of their difficult temperament to their offspring (as a component of multifactorial liability) which, in turn, increases the offspring's risk for substance abuse disorder. The behavioral expressions associated with a difficult temperament include heightened activity and hyperactivity in infancy and childhood, aggression and conduct problems in childhood and adolescence, and alcoholism or substance abuse in adulthood with coexisting antisocial behavior. In addition, the family environment of children of substance abusers may be highly conflicted due to the similarity of difficult temperaments among fathers and their offspring. Rutter (1987), for example, reported that within the family context, children with difficult temperaments were more likely than their siblings to be the target of parental hostility and criticism. Blackson, Tarter, Loeber, Ammerman, and Windle (1996) also reported that the difficult temperaments of substance abusing fathers and their sons (aged 10–12 years) contributed to the sons' earlier disengagement from the family and the earlier engagement in deviant peer networks. This movement toward engagement in a deviant peer network has been associated with conduct problems, school difficulties, and early onset of substance use (e.g., Dishion et al., 1995). Thus, genetically influenced temperament traits influenced psychosocial processes (e.g., hostile father-son exchanges) that may have precipitated a movement away from the family and toward a risky, deviant peer context.

The findings of Jansen, Fitzgerald, Ham, and Zucker (1995) also supported an association between COA status and a difficult temperament profile with a sample of 3- to 5-year-old boys. The boys from the COA and control samples in this study were rated on the Child Behavior Checklist (McConaughy & Achenbach, 1988). Those boys who were rated (by parents) within the clinical range for total behavior problems were also rated as having the most difficult temperament (i.e., high activity levels, short attention span, high reactivity, and biological arrhythmicity). Furthermore, these boys scoring in the clinical range for total behavior problems were more likely than controls to have parents with alcohol-related problems, high levels of antisocial behavior, and low levels of income and education.

The findings of Jansen and colleagues (1995) dovetail well with those of Tarter and colleagues (e.g., Blackson et al., 1996; Tarter, 1988) in suggesting a potentially prominent role for temperament (and specifically, difficult temperament) in increasing risk for pathways to developmental psychopathological outcomes (e.g., substance abuse, antisocial behavior). These findings were also consistent with other non-COA studies that have reported concurrent and prospective relations in childhood and adolescence between difficult temperament and substance use and other problem behaviors (e.g., Maziade et al., 1985; Tubman & Windle, 1995; Windle, 1991). Wills, DuHamel, and Vaccaro (1995) have suggested that specific features of temperament, such as activity level and mood quality, may be influential in predicting substance use onset among children and early adolescents via associations with coping behaviors, self-control mechanisms, and friend substance use.

Research on the impact of temperament on substance use initiation, continuation, and abuse (or termination) among COAs and the offspring of other substance abusing parents is in the nascent stages of development. The initial findings (e.g., Blackson et al., 1996; Jansen et al., 1995) are promising, but more refined studies need to be conducted prior to any more definitive conclusions. However, multivariate, life span, dynamic conceptualizations that embed temperament within other contexts (e.g., family, peers, school) and that seek to identify influences via direct and indirect pathways, may yield findings that are more useful than a reliance on a monolithic, "alcoholic personality" conceptualization. The study of temperament on evolving developmental processes may provide a valuable landscape for understanding individual trajectories toward, and away from, adverse outcomes (e.g., internalizing, externalizing, and other health-related problems).

COGNITIVE AND INTELLECTUAL FACTORS

Investigation into the early formation of knowledge structures about alcohol have indicated that preschool children can identify alcoholic beverages and have already developed certain concepts and schemas about drinking behaviors (e.g., Gaines, Brooks, Maisto, Dietrich, & Shagena, 1988; Noll, Zucker, & Greenberg, 1990; for review, see Lang & Stritzke, 1993). For example, Noll and coworkers (1990) investigated preschoolers' ability to provide accurate associations to alcoholic beverage odors. Interestingly, an olfactory identification task was used in this research to facilitate the evaluation of more proximal experiences to the child (i.e., the smell of alcohol) that would be independent of media exposure (e.g., television, radio). That is, verbal identification of visual stimuli (e.g., pictures of alcoholic beverages) may have resulted from media exposure, whereas identification via smell presumably required a more immediate experience (exposure) of the substance to the child. The preschool children were requested to identify different substances (e.g., apple juice, coffee, perfume, beer, cigarettes) subsequent to clos-

ing their eyes and inhaling odors from jars that contained the various substances. The findings of the study indicated that 79 percent of the preschoolers successfully identified at least one alcoholic beverage odor, and furthermore, that the identification of alcoholic beverages was associated with heavier parental drinking practices.

In a separate investigation, Zucker, Kincaid, Fitzgerald, and Bingham (1995) studied differences in alcohol schema development among 139 male COA and 82 male non-COA preschool children. The Appropriate Beverage Task (Penrose, 1978) was used to assess the preschool children's understanding of the normative use structure for alcoholic beverage consumption. This task consisted of ten drawings of adults and/or children in various contexts, with each character in each drawing drinking an unidentified beverage. Children were requested to specify the beverage that each person in each drawing was drinking, and alcohol beverage attribution scores were derived for several indices (e.g., the number of alcoholic beverages identified, gender, and age of those perceived to be drinking alcohol). The findings indicated that COAs were more likely than non-COAs to identify at least one alcoholic beverage, to correctly identify a larger number of alcoholic beverages, and to tend to attribute heavier alcohol use to male versus female adults. Zucker and colleagues concluded that their findings were supportive of detectable levels of alcohol schema formation in early childhood that was heightened among COAs and that may pose risk for subsequent earlier onset of higher levels of alcohol involvement.

A number of other studies have been conducted that focus on the acquisition and elaboration of knowledge structures pertinent to alcohol use and drinking behaviors across childhood, although they have not specifically studied differences between COAs and non-COAs. Gaines and colleagues (1988) studied children in grades three, six, and eight for their understanding of adult drinking and their knowledge of rules of drinking. A somewhat complex picture emerged from this cross-sectional study, as there were age differences in some areas (e.g., knowledge of where people typically drink was not known by third graders but was known by sixth and eighth graders; recognition that different concentrations of alcohol were contained in different beverages such as beer, wine, and hard liquor occurred only among eighth graders), and no age-related differences in others (e.g., knowledge of legal drinking age). However, similar to other studies (e.g., Noll et al., 1990), parental drinking practices (in this instance, frequency of drinking) was significantly associated with children's intentions to drink, thus suggesting potential parental role modeling influences on the early development of cognitive schemas about drinking behavior.

Miller, Smith, and Goldman (1990) investigated age differences in the development of alcohol-related expectancies for children in grades one through five. Alcohol expectancies are defined as beliefs about the anticipated positive and/or negative consequences of imbibing alcohol (e.g., that alcohol use increases cognitive and motor performance). Alcohol expectancies have been associated cross-sectionally and longitudinally with alcohol consumption and treatment outcome variables (e.g., length of stay, staff ratings of long-term prognosis) among both adolescents and adults. Therefore, a focus on the early origins and developmental elaborations of alcohol expectancies may prove useful in identifying early risk for subsequent alcohol problems (for review, see Smith & Goldman, 1994). Miller and coworkers reported a trend toward increasingly positive alcohol expectancies across the grade levels, with a precipitous increase among the third and fourth grade cohorts. These cohorts were more likely to report that they believed that alcohol would facilitate a range of behaviors (e.g., social behaviors). However, these elementary school children manifested much less cognitive differentiation with regard to specific alcohol expectancies than has been reported with adults (i.e., they had more global, undifferentiated expectancies than adults).

Brown, Creamer, and Stetson (1987) used a sample of adolescent alcohol abusers in treatment and compared them on alcohol expectancies with a sample of demographically comparable nonabusing peers. The adolescent treatment sample had higher levels of alcohol expectancies; hence, they expected more reinforcement from using alcohol than the nonabusing peers. In addition, adolescents with an alcohol-abusing parent had higher alcohol expectancies for improved cognitive and motor performance subsequent to alcohol use than adolescents without an alcohol-abusing parent. Christiansen, Smith, Roehling, and Goldman (1989) used a two-wave longitudinal design (with a 1-year interval) with early adolescents and found that alcohol expectancy scores prospectively predicted alcohol onset, alcohol consumption, and problem drinking.

A number of studies have also concentrated on possible differences among COAs and non-COAs with regard to intellectual functioning and school performance. Werner's longitudinal study (1986) with the children from Kauai indicated that intellectual deficits at age 2 years (identified by a pediatrician) were predictive of subsequent and ongoing poor scholastic performance (e.g., low standardized aptitude and achievement test scores) and serious behavior problems among COAs by age 18 years. Ervin, Little, Streissguth, and Beck (1984) reported that COAs scored, on average, approximately 7 points lower than non-COAs on standardized intelligence tests (e.g., WISC-R, WAIS). Bennett, Wolin, and Reiss (1988a) also reported that COAs scored significantly

lower than non-COAs with regard to the WISC-R full-scale score, and the Reading and Arithmetic subscale scores of the Peabody Achievement Test. Using an adoptee design, in which COAs were raised by nonalcoholic parents (thus removing the alcoholic biological parent from the rearing environment), Knop, Teasdale, Schulsinger, and Goodwin (1985) nevertheless identified deficits in academic achievement, verbal information processing, and planning and abstracting abilities among COAs. Whipple, Parker, and Noble (1988) reported lower performance IQ scores on the WISC-R, including lower scores on digit span memory, verbal learning and memory, perceptual closure, and visuspatial organization among COAs (with a strong genetic loading of an alcoholic father plus at least an additional second-degree relative with alcoholism) relative to non-COAs. Finally, several studies have reported higher rates of discipline problems in school (e.g., Rimmer, 1982), higher rates of dropping out of school and receiving counseling (e.g., Miller & Jang, 1977), and higher rates of repeating a grade and receiving referrals to a school psychologist (e.g., Schulsinger, Knop, Goodwin, Teasdale, & Mikkelsen, 1986) among COAs than non-COAs.

Although these studies on school performance and intellectual functioning converge in suggesting substantial difficulties in academic contexts for COAs, several caveats need to be noted. First, not all of the studies conducted have indicated statistically significant differences between COAs and non-COAs. For instance, Johnson and Rolf (1988) did not find significant differences for COAs and non-COAs on standardized measures of intellectual functioning (e.g., WISC-R, WAIS) or on an achievement test (WRAT) for a sample of children 6 to 18 years of age. Second, in many instances (e.g., Bennett et al., 1988a) significant group differences between COAs and non-COAs were indicated, but the large majority of COAs were functioning within the normal range. Third, the source(s) of such group differences between COAs and non-COAs remains unknown. That is, because COAs and non-COAs differ on measures of intellectual functioning and academic achievement does not necessarily imply a reduced "intellectual potential" or the inheritance of an impaired or deficient central nervous system. Such differences may arise from a variety of sources within the home (e.g., disruptive parenting, child maltreatment), constitutionally based characteristics (e.g., temperament), and the operation of dynamic, multifactorial genetic–environmental relations, some of which are illustrated in Figure 24.1.

In summary, the acquisition and elaboration of knowledge structures pertinent to concept formation for alcohol use have been demonstrated for children as young as preschoolers and are increasingly differentiated across the course of childhood and adolescence. Both the identification of alcoholic beverages and higher levels of knowledge about the normative rules associated with drinking are elevated in children of heavier drinking parents and COAs. Alcohol expectancies also appear to manifest a developmental trend with regard to the valence of alcohol use; prior to third and fourth grade, beliefs about alcohol use are generally negative and intentions to drink are low (e.g., Casswell, Gilmore, Silva, & Brasch, 1988; Miller et al., 1990). However, around the third and fourth grade level, expectancies regarding alcohol use become much more positive and more positive expectancies are associated with higher levels of parental drinking. Although developmental research regarding alcohol-related knowledge structures and schemas is in its nascent stages, the preliminary findings of the early identification of alcohol beverages and alcohol concept formation by preschoolers suggest that this may be a salient domain of inquiry in subsequent risk-behavior studies. To the extent that such early formative beliefs contribute to increased risk for early onset and persistent drinking among children and adolescents, preventive interventions may focus on the modification of beliefs that may subsequently prove harmful. The causal factors associated with intellectual deficits and poor academic performance among COAs also need to be targeted in future research to provide optimal interventions in educational settings and to foster constructive problem-solving skills and healthy development.

FAMILIAL ENVIRONMENTAL FACTORS

Researchers attempting to identify risks associated with parental alcoholism for the expression of alcohol disorders or other adverse outcomes among COAs have long recognized that specific intraindividual and social–contextual factors are inextricably linked for this high-risk population. Children and adolescents in families containing an alcoholic are embedded in a developmental context that dynamically interacts with child characteristics to influence a wide range of adaptive and nonadaptive outcomes. To understand the role of family level variables as mediators or moderators of risks associated with a positive family history of alcoholism, investigators from multiple disciplines have long documented group differences between "alcoholic" and comparison families. The existing surveys of these studies distill a set of risk factors that may be incorporated into a dynamic stress-diathesis model to account for a portion of the heterogeneity of outcomes among COAs and the potential for multiple pathways to alcohol disorders in this population (see for example, Burk & Sher, 1988; Seilhamer & Jacob, 1990; Sher 1991; West & Prinz, 1987).

Current research employing developmental models of psychopathology emphasizing nongenetic influences upon children and adolescents suggests both direct and indirect paths of influence between parental psychopathology and the expression of internalizing and externalizing symptoms by offspring (Dodge, 1990; Richters & Weintraub, 1990; Rutter, 1990a). Among COAs, direct paths of influence between parental psychopathology and children's risk of alcohol disorders in adulthood may include such a stressful distal influence as the personal experience of violence and victimization within the family. Some COA studies suggest that children's experience of physical abuse may be more prevalent in families with an alcoholic parent (e.g., Havey & Dodd, 1992; Lund & Landesman-Dwyer, 1979) while many others do not (Orme & Rimmer, 1981), and this entire body of studies may confound socioeconomic status and parental alcoholism (West & Prinz, 1987). Yet, data collected from adolescents in treatment for substance abuse indicate that a consistent predictor of comorbid depressive disorders among these adolescents is childhood physical and sexual abuse (Deykin, Buka, & Zeena, 1992), although there is not clear evidence of higher rates of sexual abuse among COAs compared to non-COAS. However, a family environment in which a parent is actively abusing alcohol may constitute a significant proximal stressor that increases risk for internalizing and externalizing symptoms among children (Moos & Moos, 1984; Rubio-Stipec, Bird, Canino, Bravo, & Alegria, 1991).

A second direct pathway between parental alcoholism and higher risk for alcohol abuse among COAs involves children's observation of parental drinking patterns and parental socialization of drinking behaviors. The parental socialization of children's drinking behavior may occur via the dual processes of imitation and social reinforcement (Barnes, 1990). Evidence for this direct path of influence between parental alcohol disorders and higher risk for maladaptive outcomes among children include positive associations between the alcohol use patterns of parents and children (Barnes, Farrell, & Cairns, 1986; Brook, Whiteman, & Gordon, 1983) and the early internalization of alcohol-related definitions and behavioral norms by COAs (Zucker & Fitzgerald, 1991). The use of alcohol to cope with psychological distress related to negative life events or family disruption may be learned by COAs both by exposure to parental attitudes toward and actual use of alcohol (Cooper, Russell, & George, 1988).

Indirect paths between parental alcohol disorders and increased risk for expression of internalizing and externalizing symptoms in COAs often involve family-level variables that are influenced by the alcohol use of one or both parents. Family-level variables thought to increase risk for maladaptive outcomes among COAs include marital conflict and dissatisfaction, disrupted family environments, and ineffective or inefficient parenting practices (Seilhammer & Jacob,

1990; Sher, 1991; West & Prinz, 1987). Deficits in these domains of family functioning may influence the expression of internalizing and externalizing problems among COAs by constituting a class of significant stressors for the child or adolescent or via maladaptive person–environment interactions or negative regulatory cycles. Therefore, parental alcohol use may influence the expression of internalizing and externalizing symptoms in children and adolescents through a number of indirect paths that will be detailed further in the following discussion.

Although the quality of marital and parent–child relationships are likely to be quite heterogeneous across the families of alcoholics, it is generally accepted in the research literature that living conditions in these families are more stressful than in "normal" comparison families, thereby increasing risk for the expression of externalizing and internalizing symptoms in children. For example, the families of actively drinking alcoholics have higher levels of marital and parent–child conflict (Filstead, McElfresh, & Anderson, 1981; Reich, Earls, & Powell, 1988), lower levels of marital satisfaction (Leonard, 1990), and higher levels of family disruption with regard to negative life events including unemployment (Rubio-Stipec et al., 1991), disrupted family rituals (Bennett, Wolin & Reiss, 1988b), and a generally compromised family environment (Havey & Dodd, 1992; Moos & Billings, 1982). In addition, deficits in parenting practices that may be more prevalent in families containing an active alcoholic include harsh, inconsistent discipline (Reich et al., 1988), emotional unavailability or parental indifference (e.g., due to alcohol use or parental depression) (Robinson, 1989), and compromised ability to provide guidance or monitoring for children (Chassin, Pillow, Curran, Molina, & Barrera, 1993). Furthermore, deficits in parent–child, marital, spousal, or family functioning may exist simultaneously and additively (or interactively) influence internalizing and externalizing problems in co-resident children (Tubman, 1993a, b). Therefore, a number of stressful conditions may exist within families containing an alcoholic that may moderate or mediate risk for internalizing or externalizing symptoms among children, influencing the heterogeneity of outcomes observed among COAs (Clair & Genest, 1987; Seilhamer & Jacob, 1990; Sher, 1991).

The characteristics of families with an alcoholic member that operate as stressful distal and proximal influences on children's development may also initiate or maintain negative person–environment interactions that increase risk for the expression of internalizing and externalizing symptoms among children. For example, lack of "fit" between parent and child characteristics or the lack of predictability of parental demands for child behavior may increase the expres-

sion of internalizing symptoms among COAs (Whipple & Nobel, 1991). Emotional unavailability or indifference on the part of depressed, preoccupied, or actively drinking parents is associated with lower self-esteem and emotional and behavioral problems among children and adolescents and conflict in parent–child relationships (Downey & Coyne, 1990). Parenting styles (e.g., authoritarian parenting) in families containing alcoholics may be incompatible with adolescents' developmental needs to renegotiate autonomy and identity statuses and may increase risk for parent–child conflict, peer orientation, or alternatively, lower social competence or psychological adjustment (Krauthamer, 1979; Lamborn, Mounts, Steinberg, & Dornbusch, 1991). Sher (1991) has proposed that parenting behavior (i.e., control and monitoring): (1) mediates relationships between family history of alcoholism and child's temperament and personality and (2) moderates relationships between either temperament and personality or school failure and peer influence. An empirical test of a related model found that mechanisms involving (a) child stress and negative affect and (b) parental monitoring predicted adolescent substance use equally well for both COAs and non-COAs (Molina, Chassin, & Curran, 1994).

Parental alcohol abuse may also initiate and maintain patterns of negative parent–child interaction or negative regulatory cycles within families. Family interaction studies in laboratory and naturalistic settings have demonstrated the negative effect of alcohol consumption by alcoholics upon family processes such as decision making in marital dyads via increases in the expression of negative affect, an effect that may be exacerbated by alcoholism subtype (i.e., steady vs. episodic) (Jacob & Krahn, 1988; Jacob & Leonard, 1988). This effect has not consistently generalized to parent–child relationships using a similar experimental paradigm (Jacob, Krahn, & Leonard, 1991). Yet time series analyses of sons' satisfaction with their father–child relationships have indicated a causal relationship between fathers' daily alcohol consumption and sons' satisfaction that was not associated with either drinking location or the pattern of drinking (Seilhamer, Jacob, & Dunn, 1993). Equal proportions of sons reported positive and negative perceptions of fathers' drinking, suggesting that in some families, drinking served a short-term adaptive function, while in other families paternal drinking had a disruptive impact on dyadic processes of parenting and communication. Other dynamic, self-reinforcing transactions between parents and children may exist in these families, particularly if they are distressed by ongoing parental drinking (e.g., between maternal depression and boys' problem behavior) (Patterson, 1986). Therefore, patterns of drinking may be perpetuated in families of alcoholics through parallel processes of family interaction with widely varying influences on parent–child and marital relationships.

EXTRAFAMILIAL ENVIRONMENTAL FACTORS

Negative person–environment interactions that increase risk for the expression of internalizing and externalizing symptoms among COAs may also occur at intersections between these children and the broader social contexts in which they live, including their peer groups, their schools, and their communities. Individual characteristics and biological risk factors among COAs and the stressors associated with the family environments in which they live may interact with the demands and opportunities posed by peer and school contexts to increase the potential range of outcomes among COAs (Sher, 1991). These larger social contexts may function to ameliorate or exacerbate the expression of internalizing and externalizing symptoms in this at-risk population. The following discussion describes some of the potential pathways to the expression of externalizing and internalizing symptoms among COAs influenced by children's and adolescents' interactions within larger social contexts.

One developmental pathway of increased risk for the expression of externalizing symptoms among COAs, in particular male COAs, involves long-term transactions among children's attentional deficits, high activity levels, temperamental difficulty, and ineffective parenting practices to influence the development and generalization of maladaptive styles of social interaction from family settings to peer groups and school settings (Blackson et al., 1996; Fitzgerald et al., 1993; Windle, 1990). Rearing a child with one or more of these characteristics would require patience, consistency, and coping skills from predominantly female caregivers in family environments characterized by disruption, marital conflict, or marital dissatisfaction, placing extraordinary demands on women who are often challenged to meet their own needs for emotional support (Fischer, 1990). Therefore, children with these characteristics may contribute significantly to their mother's psychological distress by serving as an additional source of unremitting stress. Mismatches between maternal depression, frustration, or emotional unavailability and children's demands may contribute to the onset, maintenance, and escalation of coercive exchanges between mother and child with significant impact on the psychological well-being of both mother and child (Barkley, Fischer, Edelbrock, & Smallish, 1991; Vuchinich, Bank, & Patterson, 1992). In addition, parent–child conflict and the observation of marital conflict may influence how COAs interpret and respond to conflict in peer contexts, directly influencing the development of social competence (Grych & Fincham, 1990).

School-age children who witness marital violence or who participate in coercive exchanges with parents may be more likely to make attributions of hostile intent to others in ambiguous social situations or to overreact in situations of interpersonal conflict (Cummings & Cummings, 1988). This is a potent mechanism by which interactional styles established within the home may generalize to relationships in wider social contexts (Dodge & Frame, 1982). In processes of friend selection, children with an aggressive social style who respond with hostility to peers in ambiguous situations, would tend to be rejected as potential friends (Parkhurst & Asher, 1992). These children would thereby be excluded from the potentially remediating influence of interaction with more socially skilled peers (Reid, 1993). Aggressive children, regardless of family history of alcoholism, are more likely to become either increasingly isolated or segregated into deviant peer networks whereby maladaptive behavior patterns are likely to be mirrored and reinforced (Blackson et al., 1996; Coie, Terry, Lenox, Lochman, & Hymel, 1995; Patterson, 1992). More severe forms of delinquent or antisocial behavior may be socialized by older members of these peer networks, and include truancy, substance abuse, physical violence, and criminal activity. This escalation of delinquent behavior in the context of deviant peer groups would initiate and maintain processes detrimental to the accomplishment of key developmental tasks of adolescence and young adulthood including school failure, lower occupational attainment, and social redefinition with negative identity statuses, all with long-term negative consequences (Patterson, 1992; Loeber et al., 1993).

Parallel person–context interactions may contribute to increased risk for internalizing disorders among COAs (e.g., Reich, Earls, Frankel, & Shayka, 1993; Rolf, Johnson, Israel, Baldwin, & Chandra, 1988; Rubio-Stipec et al., 1991), although these pathways remain poorly studied among COAs in contrast to pathways leading to externalizing problems. The formulation of Rubin and colleagues provides a model of how inhibited behavioral style among preschool and school-age children may undergo developmental transformations resulting in internalizing problems in late childhood and adolescence (Rubin & Mills, 1991; Rubin, Stewart, & Coplan, 1995). Briefly, infants who are highly reactive to novel stimuli are thought to develop insecure attachments to their parents and subsequently, an avoidant or withdrawing style of social interaction. These socially inhibited children are less likely to explore their physical or social environments or to engage in routine social interaction, thereby delaying acquisition of developmentally appropriate skills and cognitions related to social competence. Parents and teachers may attempt to correct the child's social withdrawal pattern with controlling and overinvolved strategies that these children find aversive, resulting in continued social withdrawal. The confluence of social competence deficits, "social wariness," negative self-concept, and social withdrawal in childhood is related to poor quality peer relationships, namely, peer neglect, and is predictive of loneliness and more severe internalizing problems in adolescence (Asher, Parkhurst, Hymel & Williams, 1990; Rubin & Mills, 1991).

The model proposed by Rubin and colleagues may generalize to families that contain one or more alcoholics (Rubin & Mills, 1991; Rubin et al., 1995). Inconsistent or exaggerated behavior related to alcohol abuse may be aversive stimuli to highly reactive children. Children's withdrawal from such stressful stimulation in combination with punitive, insensitive, or nonresponsive parental reactions to that withdrawal may reduce the likelihood of secure attachments developing between parents and children. This particular combination of children's temperamental characteristics and coercive or directive parenting techniques, in the context of a family environment that is stressful and unpredictable, may form the template for later social relationships. That is, this combination of individual, relational, and contextual characteristics among preschool COAs may be predictive of inhibited responses to new social relationships upon the transition from the home to primary school settings. While inhibited responses to ambiguous or conflict situations may be adaptive in conflicted families (Grych & Fincham, 1990), this pattern of response to similar situations in peer settings may be evaluated negatively by peers.

In turn, negative peer evaluations may be predictive of unpopularity and peer rejection, effectively depriving COAs of opportunities to practice age-appropriate social skills or to develop social competence and positive self-perceptions (Boivin, Hymel, & Bukowski, 1995; Vasey, 1993). Intrusiveness or overdirective corrective actions on the part of teachers or parents are likely to maintain rather than resolve this pattern of social withdrawal (Rubin & Mills, 1991; Vasey, 1993). Continuity of social inhibition or withdrawal and correlated self-conceptions in peer contexts are predictive of subsequent loneliness and internalizing problems that may be precursors to patterns of alcohol abuse related to negative affect in adolescence and adulthood (Sher, 1991; Zucker, 1987).

The two preceding scenarios represent pessimistic examples of how interactions among variables measured at the levels of the individual, the family, and larger social contexts may increase risk for the expression of internalizing and externalizing problems among COAs. It is likely, however, that a significant proportion of the heterogeneity of outcomes in internalizing and externalizing symptoms among COAs is due to the remediating effects of interaction

with peers or adults in school, neighborhood, or community settings. Rutter (1989, 1990b) used the term *protective process* to describe turning points in developmental trajectories from risk to adaptation and emphasized the critical roles of positive school experiences and supportive others outside the family in facilitating developmental transitions toward positive outcomes. The ability of teachers, adult mentors, and peers to act as external support systems to COAs and other at-risk populations is related to their participation in protective processes including reducing the impact of stressful family environments, interrupting chains of negative life transitions, enhancing individual attributes such as self-esteem and self-efficacy, and providing previously unavailable opportunities (Rutter, 1987). The significance of extrafamilial protective mechanisms are increasingly supported by findings from long-term longitudinal studies (e.g., Werner, 1992). The value of a resilience enhancement orientation to the prevention of adverse outcomes among COAs will be considered again later in this chapter.

COMMON AND UNIQUE INFLUENCES UPON PSYCHOPATHOLOGY AMONG COAS

The wide range of adaptive and maladaptive outcomes reported by child and adolescent COAs suggests that these outcomes are determined by multiple influences, some of which are individual vulnerability characteristics or environmental influences unique to COAs. Other individual-level and contextual influences upon the heterogeneity of outcomes among COAs are experienced by a broader range of high-risk populations. We will briefly describe the potential influence of both common and unique precursors upon the expression of internalizing and externalizing problems among COAs. In addition, we will consider to what extent factors increasing risk for maladaptive outcomes are unique to COAs or generalizable to a broader range of high-risk populations.

Common Influences on COAs

Many of the stressful familial and extrafamilial conditions associated with COA status are commonly experienced by other high-risk groups of children and adolescents. For example, higher levels of parent–child or marital conflict or marital dissatisfaction, deficient parenting practices, and family disruption are also reported by families experiencing high levels of environmental stress or by families containing mothers or fathers reporting psychiatric disorders such as depressive disorder or antisocial personality disorder (Downey & Coyne, 1990; Hare, Forth, & Strachan, 1992; Shaw & Bell, 1993; Webster-Stratton, 1990). The role of negative regulatory cycles between parents and child in the development, maintenance, and escalation of oppositional–antisocial or inhibited–avoidant interaction styles is not limited to families containing alcoholics but generalizes to a range of families in which parent and child characteristics or demands are poorly matched (Miller, Cowan, Cowan, Hetherington, & Clingempeel, 1993; Patterson, 1992; Rubin & Mills, 1991). Similarly, processes of peer rejection, neglect, or acceptance are likely to be influenced by factors that are not specific to COAs but that generalize to broader groups of children who experience distressed or violent family relationships, including cognitive and attributional deficits and related aggressive social interactions (Grych & Fincham, 1990; Vuchinich et al., 1992).

The influence of individual and interactional factors common to stressful family and peer contexts upon outcomes among COAs is indicated by the variety of outcomes unrelated to alcohol use for which COAs are at high risk. In addition, descriptive profiles of the maladaptive outcomes for which COAs are at high-risk mirror profiles of outcomes for populations of children and adolescents experiencing other stressful life circumstances such as extreme domestic violence (e.g., Jaffe, Wolfe, & Wilson, 1990). Therefore, the potential for confounds among parental alcoholism, socioeconomic status, parental psychiatric symptoms, and family interaction patterns is a salient concern when conducting research with COA samples (West & Prinz, 1987). Without the use of prospective, longitudinal designs to describe interindividual differences in intraindividual change patterns, the relative influences of these and other individual and contextual factors among COAs are not easily disentangled (Sher, 1991). Similarly, comorbidity of internalizing and externalizing problems among COAs raises research issues regarding the origins of the comorbidity: shared risk factors, overlapping risk factors, or one symptom pattern increasing risk for a second distinct symptom pattern (Caron & Rutter, 1991). Effective treatment or prevention approaches with COAs must address the influence of alcohol-specific factors and more general vulnerability factors in the development and maintenance of internalizing and externalizing problems.

Unique (Alcohol-Specific) Influences on COAs

Whereas a number of adverse family influences may be common to children from a variety of high-risk circumstances (e.g., families with parental depression or schizophrenia, poverty), COAs in some alcoholic families may be at heightened susceptibility to dysfunction due to the disinhibitory nature of heavy alcohol consumption. Such an alcohol-influenced disinhibitory effect on parental behavior may contribute to more unpredictable parenting, including periodic reduced monitoring, lower nurturance, and aggressive–hostile expressions toward offspring. Furthermore, for some alcoholics, there is a spillover of problems into other domains of life such as the marital context (e.g., increased marital conflict, physical abuse of wife or children) or work context (e.g., loss of job) that impact adversely on children and their development. Likewise, the high rates of psychiatric comorbidity associated with alcoholics (e.g., Kessler et al., 1994) and patterns of assortative mating for psychological disturbance may contribute to multiple deficits in the rearing environments of COAs, especially if both parents manifest disturbed behavioral patterns.

Perhaps even more potent, unique alcohol-specific factors exist for COAs that moderate biogenetic influences more so than environmental influences. That is, considerable research on COAs has indicated a heightened susceptibility to alcoholism via biogenetic mechanisms (e.g., Begleiter & Kissin, 1995; Sher, 1991; Windle & Searles, 1990). Some of the biological markers for alcoholism that have been identified, such as the reduced amplitude P300 electrocortical response, are not unique to alcoholism but have also been identified as biological markers for other disorders (e.g., schizophrenia). Similarly, lower MAO levels have been associated with major depressive disorder as well as with alcoholism. However, support for two alcohol reactivity mechanisms that may be unique to COAs has been identified. First, converging findings from several laboratories have suggested that alcohol use among COAs may reduce (or dampen) cardiovascular reactivity in response to stress (e.g., Finn & Pihl, 1987; Sher & Levenson, 1982). For example, COAs received greater negative reinforcement (i.e., a greater reduction in heart rate response) from alcohol use under stressful conditions (e.g., unavoidable shock) than non-COAs. The higher levels of reinforcement by alcohol consumption under stressful conditions is proposed to increase susceptibility to alcohol disorders via (habitual) learning mechanisms in which alcohol use is positively associated with reduced feelings of stressfulness.

A second proposed biological mechanism suggests that COAs have reduced judgmental capacities (or innate insensitivities) about the impact of levels of alcohol consumption on behaviors. Schuckit (1980; 1985) has reported a series of studies indicating that COAs report lower levels of subjective feelings of intoxication after drinking than non-COAs. Similarly, on behavioral measures of static ataxia (body sway), COAs appear less affected by the alcohol consumption because they are more steady than non-COAs. Note that these findings are based on controlled experimental conditions (with various alcohol dose levels) with young adult, non-alcoholic COAs and non-COAs, with a matched group design. These findings of Schuckit suggest that the lower intensity response to alcohol consumption by COAs may pose susceptibility to alcohol disorders for two reasons. First, reduced subjective recognition of the impact of consuming alcohol may lead to increased drinking to achieve a desired (euphoric) effect; persistently high drinking levels may contribute to the full-blown expression of an alcohol disorder and to medical complications (alcoholic liver cirrhosis). Second, a failure to appropriately calibrate the impact of the amount of alcohol consumed may contribute to an overestimation of individual capacities to perform tasks (e.g., safely driving a vehicle, performing well at work, interacting competently with others such as family members or co-workers) and may result in a host of adverse social consequences.

Research and clinical implications of common and unique (i.e., alcohol-specific) biogenetic and environmental influences on COAs is in its early stages. Such research may be facilitated by prospective research designs that include other high-risk families (e.g., children of depressed parents) as well as COAs and a standard control group (e.g., see Jacob & Krahn, 1988).

PREVENTION AND INTERVENTION APPROACHES WITH COAS

A number of primary prevention strategies have been developed or refined to prevent substance abuse among children and adolescents in school settings. The goals of these prevention programs include delaying the onset of substance use, preventing the escalation of normative, exploratory patterns of licit substance use to problematic levels, and the prevention of illicit substance use. The most successful of these programs include psychoeducation training components that focus on the enhancement of psychosocial skills that are negatively related to the onset and escalation of substance use (e.g., in the domains of drug resistance, assertiveness, coping, decision making, interpersonal competence, self-esteem, and self-efficacy) (Botvin, Baker, Dusenbury, Tortu, & Botvin, 1990; Johnson et al., 1990). The prevention of substance abuse problems via psychosocial skills training or community mobilization efforts may be used with COAs and non-COAs alike, and these programs may be useful components of a larger system of health promotion. This uniform approach to substance abuse prevention, however, does not necessarily address the multiplicity and heterogeneity of vulnerability factors and stressors experienced by COAs that are manifest in proximal mechanisms exacerbating risk for internalizing and externalizing problems.

To minimize the impact of the heterogeneous constellations of vulnerability factors and stressors experienced by COAs, prevention programs have been constructed specifi-

cally to meet the needs of this high-risk population. Prototypical programming efforts are short-term, school-based, and commonly include components designed to reduce the impact of stressors experienced by COAs (e.g., lack of information, social isolation) while enhancing coping skills and social competencies that may be deficient in this population (Ayers, Short, Gensheimer, Roosa, & Sandler, 1988; Emshoff, 1989). The goals of these programs are not to change the environments in which COAs live but to augment individual-level protective factors (e.g., refusal and assertiveness skills, self-esteem, and self-efficacy), thereby reducing risk for adverse outcomes including substance use (Johnson & Rolf, 1990). In addition, the interventions are typically conducted in small peer group settings to increase peer support and social competence and to harness the potentially remediating effects of extrafamilial social relationships. This approach to prevention with COAs has produced positive results, particularly in the enhancement of social support, social competence, peer relationships, and feelings of control and self-efficacy and the reduction of feelings of loneliness (Emshoff, 1989).

For COAs with existing internalizing and externalizing problems, more intensive individual or group counseling strategies may be beneficial. Therapeutic strategies useful in assisting young COAs to identify and express alcohol-related feelings include play therapy, psychodrama, bibliotherapy, artwork or other creative activities, and the use of film or other media (Robinson, 1989). Adolescent COAs, experiencing a range of vulnerability factors in conjunction with interpersonal and environmental stressors in the context of broader developmental transitions, have more complex psychosocial issues to articulate and negotiate. Therapeutic issues addressed in individual and group counseling settings may include emphases on developmentally appropriate topics such as individuation, autonomy, identity, denial, guilt, and rationalization (Bogdaniak & Piercy, 1987). In this manner, individual or group counseling allows child or adolescent COAs to identify and articulate feelings in a supportive and encouraging setting, a prerequisite to effective psychoeducational efforts to remediate individual-level vulnerability factors. In addition, treatment for child and adolescent COAs may be incorporated into marital and family interventions targeting adult alcoholics and their spouses as part of larger efforts to change behaviors and relationships and to maintain sobriety (O'Farrell, 1993).

Intervention and prevention efforts with COAs require attention to several feasibility issues. First, significant barriers exist to the identification of child and adolescent COAs including denial on the part of caregivers, lack of training or hesitation on the part of teachers and service providers, and

COAs' unwillingness to seek assistance (McElligatt, 1986). Recruitment procedures may lose substantial proportions of potential participants when parental consent is requested, thereby failing to adequately sample the target population, or alternatively, raising ethical concerns if passive consent procedures are used (Michaels, Roosa, & Gensheimer, 1992). Second, sample recruitment through referrals by teachers and school counselors may have the undesired effect of provoking negative stereotyping by peers and service providers. Burk and Sher (1990) demonstrated that the process of identifying and labeling COAs in school settings is associated with stigmatizing attributions by other people in those settings, which in turn may function as potential influences upon processes of peer rejection and peer neglect. Third, many practical barriers exist to the implementation of school-based prevention programs including obtaining access to school settings, gaining the trust of school staff, and gaining acceptance of the curriculum, the recruitment procedures, and the assessment procedures (Gensheimer, Ayers, & Roosa, 1993). Therefore, in choosing methods of service provision to child and adolescent COAs, mental health professionals must weigh the potential benefits and the numerous practical obstacles to broad-based secondary prevention efforts with options of more limited scope such as treatment following physician or teacher referral.

Preventative interventions with COAs are likely to grow in popularity with continuing efforts to slow the growth of health care costs. The recent focus in COA research on resilience, vulnerability, and protection has encouraged the description of differences between COAs and non-COAs at the individual, family, and larger social levels of analysis, generating potential targets for intervention or prevention efforts (Johnson & Rolf, 1990). The identification of vulnerability and protective factors for adverse outcomes among COAs, however, provides limited information regarding underlying mechanisms leading to positive or negative outcomes (Rutter, 1987). To better account for individual differences in outcomes among COAs, key "turning points" in developmental trajectories need to be described in relation to normative developmental transitions and nonnormative life events. Protective or vulnerability processes may be linked to key decisions or transitions (e.g., parental divorce, leaving home for college), or to new social relationships (e.g., shifts in peer group membership, acquiring a mentor) that redirect a COA onto a different life pathway (Rutter, 1990b). Within a heterogeneous population like COAs there are likely to be multiple pathways to any positive or negative outcome, making the search for unique vulnerability and protective factors of dubious value (Cicchetti, 1990). An alternative focus, one on the "forks in the road" (i.e., personal experiences related to

resilience), may be more useful in the planning and implementation of effective and efficient intervention and prevention strategies with COAs.

SUMMARY AND CONCLUSIONS

One of the greatest challenges in future studies of COAs is to adequately describe and explain the wide heterogeneity of the outcomes reported in this population. Continued progress in extending COA studies from simple descriptions of differences between COAs and non-COAs to explanations of variations in short-term and long-term outcomes among COAs will require greater integration of efforts between clinicians and developmentalists serving this at-risk population. The dynamic, diathesis-stress model (see Figure 24.1) used as an organizational and heuristic tool in this chapter provides a conceptual lens for the investigation of individual differences and patterns of intraindividual change observed by researchers as well as clinical practitioners in their daily practice. However, what factors are important for which COAs, when and how, remains to be systematically studied by researchers and clinicians, as does the efficacy of alternative prevention and treatment programs. Bidirectional, or two-way, communication between researchers and clinical practitioners would greatly enhance the potential benefits to the constituent populations of COAs being served. Advances in the design and implementation of treatment and prevention strategies for internalizing and externalizing problems among COAs are likely to proceed at a faster pace via an integration of clinical and developmental approaches.

One endeavor that clinicians and developmentalists may jointly pursue is improving the assessment and diagnosis of clinical disorders and subsyndromal problem behaviors among COAs (e.g., Reich et al., 1993). Perhaps only a minority of COAs need additional therapeutic treatment beyond the primary interventions about alcohol and other substance misuse typically provided in school settings. Community-based studies are only now beginning to adequately describe the proportions of COAs who, under specific stressful conditions, may be expected to present particular disorders or problem behaviors. This subset of COAs may need intensive and extensive interventions, including peer group or individual counseling. In addition, although developmentalists utilizing quantitative methods may identify individual, contextual, and relational risk factors for disorders among COAs at particular developmental periods, insights from skilled clinicians are useful for translating findings regarding risk factors into descriptions of underlying mechanisms of risk, vulnerability, and protection as they operate in the lives of individual COAs (Rutter, 1990b).

Future progress in COA research will involve conducting longitudinal studies of high-risk children to describe robust underlying processes leading to the onset and maintenance of internalizing and externalizing disorders and problems in this population (Loeber & Farrington, 1994; Rutter, 1994). Knowledge of clinical disorders and subclinical problems among COAs is likely to be enhanced through the mapping of multiple pathways to and from specific disorders and problems (i.e., the developmental concept of equifinality) and better descriptions of the confluence of conditions (individual, contextual, and relational) that increase or decrease the probability that disorders and problems will be expressed (i.e., the developmental concept of multifinality) (Cicchetti, 1993; Rutter, 1993). Longitudinal comparisons among COAs and other samples of children experiencing stressful living conditions (e.g., parental psychopathology, family violence) using multiple control group designs (including psychiatric control groups) will allow developmental and clinical researchers to further distinguish unique precursors to disorders expressed by COAs from those precursors common to a wider range of stressful environments. The delineation of common and unique precursors to disorders among COAs will have significant implications for the structuring of treatment or prevention efforts for this population, providing additional opportunities for the integration of clinical and developmental approaches to the study of COAs.

Increased emphasis on mapping the underlying processes leading to internalizing and externalizing disorders among COAs should promote the development of significantly more effective and efficient interventions as well as better matching between the needs of individual COAs and available treatment modalities (Cicchetti & Toth, 1992). Systematic evaluation of appropriate treatments using clinical trials designs and the widespread use of valid and reliable diagnostic instruments to assess disorders among COAs are integral to progress in this domain and require the expertise of both developmentalists and clinicians. Identification of alcohol-specific precursors of psychopathology among COAs and their distinction from precursors common to a wider range of persons and stressful environments should provide a fuller understanding of the vulnerabilities to disorders that are overrepresented among COAs. Similarly, the identification of individual, contextual, or relational variables that are associated with lowered probabilities of onset and maintenance of particular disorders among COAs is a prerequisite to mapping underlying protective processes contributing to the heterogeneity of outcomes among COAs. The efforts of developmental and clinical researchers to delineate these conjoint underlying processes of vulnerability and protection and outcomes associated with their

interplay are essential to the treatment or prevention of disorders among COAs.

REFERENCES

Asher, S. R., Parkhurst, J. F., Hymel, S., & Williams, G. A. (1990). Peer rejection and loneliness in childhood. In S. R. Asher & J. D. Coie (Eds.), *Peer rejection in childhood* (pp. 253–273). New York: Cambridge University Press.

Ayers, T. S., Short, J. L., Gensheimer, L. K., Roosa, M. W., & Sandler, I. N. (1988). *The Stress Management and Alcohol Awareness Program: A preventative intervention for children of problem drinking parents.* Program for Prevention Research, Arizona State University, Tempe, AZ.

Babor, T. F., Hoffmann, M., Del Boca, F. K., Hesselbrock, V., Meyer, R. E., Dolinsky, Z. S., & Rounsaville, B. (1992). Types of alcoholics: I. Evidence for an empirically derived typology based on indicators of vulnerability and severity. *Archives of General Psychiatry, 49,* 599–608.

Barkley, R. A., Fischer, M., Edelbrock, C., & Smallish, L. (1991). The adolescent outcome of hyperactive children diagnosed by research criteria: III. Mother–child interactions, family conflicts, and maternal psychopathology. *Journal of Child Psychology and Psychiatry and Allied Disciplines, 32,* 233–255.

Barnes, G. M. (1990). Impact of the family on adolescent drinking patterns. In R. L. Collins, K. E. Leonard, & J. S. Searles (Eds.), *Alcohol and the family: Research and clinical perspectives* (pp. 137–161). New York: Guilford Press.

Barnes, G. M., Farrell, M. P., & Cairns, A. L. (1986). Parental socialization factors and adolescent drinking behaviors. *Journal of Marriage and the Family, 48,* 27–36.

Beardslee, W. R., Son, L., & Vaillant, G. E. (1986). Exposure to parental alcoholism during childhood and outcome in adulthood: A prospective longitudinal study. *British Journal of Psychiatry, 149,* 584–591.

Begleiter, H., & Kissin, B. (Eds.). (1995). *The genetics of alcoholism.* New York: Oxford University Press.

Begleiter, H., Porjesz, B., Bihari, B., & Kissin, B. (1984). Event-related brain potentials in boys at risk for alcoholism. *Science, 225,* 1493–1496.

Bennett, L. A., Wolin, S. J., & Reiss, D. (1988a). Cognitive, behavioral and emotional problems among school-age children of alcoholic parents. *American Journal of Psychiatry, 145,* 185–190.

Bennett, L. A., Wolin, S. J., & Reiss, D. (1988b). Deliberate family process: A strategy for protecting children of alcoholics. *British Journal of Addiction, 83,* 821–829.

Berkson, J. (1946). Limitations of the application of fourfold table analyses to hospital data. *Biometrics, 2,* 47–53.

Blackson, T. C., Tarter, R. E., Loeber, R., Ammerman, R. T., & Windle, M. (1996). The influence of paternal substance abuse and difficult temperament in fathers and sons on sons' disengagement from family to deviant peers. *Journal of Youth and Adolescence, 25,* 389–411.

Bogdaniak, R. C., & Piercy, F. P. (1987). Therapeutic issues of adolescent children of alcoholics (AdCA) groups. *International Journal of Group Psychotherapy, 37,* 569–588.

Boivin, M., Hymel, S., & Bukowski, W. M. (1995). The roles of social withdrawal, peer rejection, and victimization by peers in predicting loneliness and depressed mood in childhood. *Development and Psychopathology, 7,* 765–785.

Botvin, G. J., Baker, E., Dusenbury, L., Tortu, S., & Botvin, E. M. (1990). Preventing adolescent drug abuse through a multimodal cognitive–behavioral approach: Results of a 3-year study. *Journal of Consulting and Clinical Psychology, 58,* 437–446.

Bronfenbrenner, U. (1977). Toward an experimental ecology of human development. *American Psychologist, 32,* 513–531.

Brook, J. S., Whiteman, M., & Gordon, A. S. (1983). Stages of drug use in adolescence: Personality, peer, and family correlates. *Developmental Psychology, 19,* 269–277.

Brown, R. T., Coles, C. D., Smith, I. E., Platzman, K. A., Silverstein, J., Erickson, S., & Falek, A. (1991). Effects of prenatal alcohol exposure at school age: II. Attention and behavior. *Neurotoxicology and Teratology, 13,* 369–376.

Brown, S. A., Creamer, V. A., & Stetson, B. A. (1987). Adolescent alcohol expectancies in relation to personal and parental drinking patterns. *Journal of Abnormal Psychology, 2,* 117–121.

Burk, J. P., & Sher, K. J. (1988). The "forgotten children" revisited: Neglected areas of COA research. *Clinical Psychology Review, 8,* 285–302.

Burk, J. P., & Sher, K. J. (1990). Labeling the child of an alcoholic: Negative stereotyping by mental health professionals and peers. *Journal of Studies on Alcohol, 51,* 156–163.

Caron, C., & Rutter, M. (1991). Comorbidity in child psychopathology: Concepts, issues and research strategies. *Journal of Child Psychology and Psychiatry, 32,* 1063–1080.

Casswell, S., Gilmore, L. L., Silva, P., & Brasch, P. (1988). What children know about alcohol and how they know it. *British Journal of Addiction, 83,* 223–227.

Chan, A. W. K. (1990). Biochemical markers for alcoholism. In M. Windle & J. S. Searles (Eds.), *Children of alcoholics: Critical perspectives* (pp 39–72). New York: Guilford Press.

Chassin, L., Pillow, D. R., Curran, P. J., Molina, B. S. G., & Barrera, M., Jr. (1993). Relation of parent alcoholism to early adolescent substance use: A test of three mediating mechanisms. *Journal of Abnormal Psychology, 102,* 3–19.

Christiansen, B. A., Smith, G. T., Roehling, P. V., & Goldman, M. S. (1989). Using alcohol expectancies to predict adolescent drinking behavior after one year. *Journal of Consulting and Clinical Psychology, 57,* 93–99.

Cicchetti, D. (1990). A historical perspective on the discipline of developmental psychopathology. In J. Rolf, A. S. Masten, D. Cicchetti, K. H. Nuechterlein, & S. Weintraub (Eds.), *Risk and protective factors in the development of psychopathology* (pp. 2–28). New York: Cambridge University Press.

Cicchetti, D. (1993). Developmental psychopathology: Reactions, reflections, projections. *Developmental Review, 13,* 471–502.

Cicchetti, D., & Toth, S. (1992). The role of developmental theory in prevention and intervention. *Development and Psychopathology, 4,* 489–493.

Clair, D., & Genest, M. (1987). Variables associated with the adjustment of offspring of alcoholic fathers. *Journal of Studies on Alcohol, 48,* 345–355.

Cloninger, C. R. (1987). Neurogenetic adaptive mechanisms in alcoholism. *Science, 236,* 410–416.

Cloninger, C. R., Bohman, M., & Sigvardsson, S. (1981). Inheritance of alcohol abuse: Cross fostering analysis of adopted men. *Archives of General Psychiatry, 38,* 861–868.

Coie, J., Terry, R., Lenox, K., Lochman, J., & Hyman, C. (1995). Childhood peer rejection and aggression as predictors of stable patterns of adolescent disorder. *Development and Psychopathology, 7,* 697–713.

Coles, C. D., Brown, R. T., Smith, I. E., Platzman, K. A., Erickson, S., & Falek, A. (1991). Effects of prenatal alcohol exposure at school age: I. Physical and cognitive development. *Neurotoxicology and Teratology, 13,* 357–367.

Cooper, M. L., Russell, M., George, W. H. (1988). Coping, expectancies, and alcohol abuse: A test of social learning formulations. *Journal of Abnormal Psychology, 97,* 218–230.

Cummings, E. M., & Cummings, J. L. (1988). A process-oriented approach to children's coping with adults' angry behavior. *Developmental Review, 8,* 296–321.

Devor, E. J., Cloninger, R., Hoffman, P. L., & Tabakoff, B. (1993). Association of monoamine (MAO) activity with alcoholism and alcoholic subtypes. *American Journal of Medical Genetics, 48,* 209–213.

Deykin, E. Y., Buka, S. L., & Zeena, T. H. (1992). Depressive illness among chemically dependent adolescents. *American Journal of Psychiatry, 149,* 1341–1347.

Dishion, T. J., French, D.C., & Patterson, G. R. (1995). The development and ecology of antisocial behavior. In D. Cicchetti & D. J. Cohen (Eds.), *Developmental Psychopathology: Vol. 2. Risk, disorder and adaptation* (pp. 421–471). New York: Wiley.

Dodge, K. A. (1990). Developmental psychopathology in children of depressed mothers. *Developmental Psychology, 26,* 3–6.

Dodge, K. A., & Frame, C. L. (1982). Social cognitive biases and deficits in aggressive boys. *Child Development, 53,* 620–635.

Downey, G., & Coyne, J. C. (1990). Children of depressed parents: An integrative review. *Psychological Bulletin, 108,* 50–76.

Eigen, L. D., & Rowden, D. (1995). A methodology and current estimate of the number of children of alcoholics in the United States. In H. Adger, C. Black, S. Brown, L. D. Eigen, D. W. Rowden, J. L. Johnson, J. Moe, E. R. Morehouse, S. Wolin, & S. Wolin (Eds.), *Children of alcoholics: Selected readings* (pp. 78–97). Rockville, MD: National Association for Children of Alcoholics.

Emshoff, J. G. (1989). A preventative intervention with children of alcoholics. *Prevention in Human Services, 7,* 225–253.

Ervin, C. S., Little, R. E., Streissguth, A. P., & Beck, D. E. (1984). Alcoholic fathering and its relation to child's intellectual development: A pilot investigation. *Alcoholism: Clinical and Experimental Research, 8,* 362–365.

Filstead, W. J., McElfresh, O., & Anderson, C. (1981). Comparing the family environments of alcoholic and "normal" families. *Journal of Alcohol and Drug Education, 26,* 24–31.

Finn, P. R., & Pihl, R. O. (1987). Men at high risk for alcoholism: The effect of alcohol on cardiovascular response to unavoidable shock. *Journal of Abnormal Psychology, 96,* 230–236.

Fischer, M. (1990). Parenting stress and the child with attention deficit hyperactivity disorder. *Journal of Clinical Child Psychology, 19,* 337–346.

Fitzgerald, H. E., Sullivan, L. A., Ham, H. P., Zucker, R. A., Bruckel, S., Schneider, A. M., & Noll, R. B. (1993). Predictors of behavior problems in three-year-old sons of alcoholics: Early evidence for the onset of risk. *Child Development, 64,* 110–123.

Gabel, S., Stadler, J., Bjorn, J., Shindledecker, R., & Bowden, C. L. (1995). Homovanillic acid and monoamine oxidase in sons of substance-abusing fathers: Relationship to conduct disorder. *Journal of Studies on Alcohol, 56,* 135–139.

Gabrielli, W. F., Mednick, S. A., Volavka, J., Pollock, V. E., Schulsinger, F., & Itil, T. M. (1982). Electroencephalograms in children of alcoholic fathers. *Psychophysiology, 19,* 404–407.

Gaines, L. S., Brooks, P. H., Maisto, S., Dietrich, M., & Shagena, M. (1988). The development of children's knowledge of alcohol and the role of drinking. *Journal of Applied Developmental Psychology, 9,* 441–457.

Gensheimer, L. K., Ayers, T. S., & Roosa, M. W. (1993). School-based preventative interventions for at-risk populations: Practical and ethical issues. *Evaluation and Program Planning, 16,* 159–167.

Grych, J. H., & Fincham, F. D. (1990). Marital conflict and children's adjustment: A cognitive contextual framework. *Psychological Bulletin, 108,* 267–290.

Hall, R. L., Hesselbrock, V. M., & Stabenau, J. R. (1983a). Familial distribution of alcohol use: II. Assortative mating of alcoholic probands. *Behavior Genetics, 13,* 373–382.

Hall, R. L., Hesselbrock, V. M., & Stabenau, J. R. (1983b). Familial distribution of alcohol use: I. Assortative mating in the parents of alcoholics. *Behavior Genetics, 13,* 361–372.

Hare, R. D., Forth, A. E., & Strachan, K. E. (1992). Psychopathy and crime across the life span. In R. D. Peters, R. J. McMahon, & V. L. Quinsey (Eds.), *Aggression and violence throughout the life span* (pp. 285–300). Newbury Park, CA: Sage.

Havey, J. M., & Dodd, D. K. (1992). Environmental and personality differences between children of alcoholics and their peers. *Journal of Drug Education, 22,* 215–222.

Haynes, S. N. (1992). *Models of causality in psychopathology: Toward dynamic, synthetic, and nonlinear causal models of behavior disorders.* New York: Macmillan.

Hill, S. Y., & Hruska, D. R. (1992). Childhood psychopathology in families with multigenerational alcoholism. *Journal of the American Academy of Child and Adolescent Psychiatry, 31,* 1024–1030.

Hill, S. Y., & Steinhauer, S. R. (1993). Assessment of prepubertal and postpubertal boys and girls at risk for developing alcoholism with P300 from a visual discrimination task. *Journal of Studies on Alcohol, 54,* 350–358.

Hill, S. Y., Steinhauer, S. R., Park, J., & Zubin, J. (1990). Event-related potential characteristics in children of alcoholics from high density families. *Alcoholism: Clinical and Experimental Research, 14,* 6–16.

Jacob, T., & Krahn, G. L. (1988). Marital interaction of alcoholic couples: Comparison with depressed and nondistressed couples. *Journal of Consulting and Clinical Psychology, 56,* 73–79.

Jacob, T., Krahn, G. L., & Leonard, K. E. (1991). Parent–child interactions in families with alcoholic fathers. *Journal of Consulting and Clinical Psychology, 59,* 176–181.

Jacob, T., & Leonard, K. E. (1988). Alcoholic-spouse interaction as a function of alcoholism subtype and alcohol consumption. *Journal of Abnormal Psychology, 97,* 231–237.

Jaffe, P. G., Wolfe, D. A., & Wilson, S. K. (1990). *Children of battered women.* Newbury Park, CA: Sage.

Jansen, R. E., Fitzgerald, H. E., Ham, H. P., & Zucker, R. A. (1995). Pathways into risk: Temperament and behavior problems in three- to five-year-old sons of alcoholics. *Alcoholism: Clinical and Experimental Research, 19,* 501–509.

Johnson, C. A., Pentz, M. A., Weber, M. D., Dwyer, J. H., Baer, N., MacKinnon, D. P., Hansen, W. B., & Flay, B. R. (1990). Relative effectiveness of comprehensive community programming for drug abuse prevention with high-risk and low-risk adolescents. *Journal of Consulting and Clinical Psychology, 58,* 447–456.

Johnson, J. L., & Rolf, J. E. (1988). Cognitive functioning in children from alcoholic and nonalcoholic families. *British Journal of Addiction, 83,* 849–857.

Johnson, J. L., & Rolf, J. E. (1990). When children change: Research perspectives on children of alcoholics. In R. L. Collins, K. E. Leonard, & J. S. Searles (Eds.), *Alcohol and the family: Research and clinical perspectives* (pp. 162–193). New York: Guilford Press.

Kern, J. C., Hassett, C. A., & Collipp, P. J. (1981). Children of alcoholics: Locus of control, mental age, and zinc level. *Journal of Psychiatric Treatment and Evaluation, 3,* 169–173.

Kessler, R. C., McGonagle, K. A., Zhao, S., Nelson, C. B., Hughes, M., Eshleman, S., Wittchen, H. U., & Kendler, K. S. (1994). Lifetime and 12-month prevalence of DSM-III-R psychiatric disorders in the United States: Results from the National Comorbidity Study. *Archives of General Psychiatry, 51,* 8–19.

Knop, J., Teasdale, T. W., & Schulsinger, F., & Goodwin, D. W. (1985). Prospective study of young men at risk for alcoholism: School behavior and achievement. *Journal of Studies on Alcohol, 46,* 273–278.

Krauthamer, C. (1979). Maternal attitudes of alcoholic and nonalcoholic upper middle class women. *International Journal of the Addictions, 14,* 639–644.

Lamborn, S. D., Mounts, N. S., Steinberg, L., & Dornbusch, S. M. (1991). Patterns of competence and adjustment among adolescents from authoritative, authoritarian, indulgent, and neglectful families. *Child Development, 62,* 1049–1065.

Lang, A. R., & Stritzke, W. G. K. (1993). Children and alcohol. In M. Galanter (Ed.), *Recent developments in alcoholism: II. Ten years of progress* (pp. 73–85). New York: Plenum Press.

Leonard, K. E. (1990). Marital functioning among episodic and steady alcoholics. In R. L. Collins, K. E. Leonard, & J. S. Searles (Eds.), *Alcohol and the family: Research and clinical perspectives* (pp. 220–243). New York: Guilford Press.

Lerner, R. M. (1978). Nature, nurture, and dynamic interactionism. *Human Development, 21,* 1–20.

Loeber, R., & Farrington, D. P. (1994). Problems and solutions in longitudinal and experimental treatment studies of child psychopathology and delinquency. *Journal of Consulting and Clinical Psychology, 62,* 887–900.

Loeber, R., Wung, P., Keenan, K., Giroux, B., Stouthamer-Loeber, M., van Kammen, W. B., & Maughan, B. (1993). Developmental pathways in disruptive child behavior. *Development and Psychopathology, 5,* 103–133.

Lund, C. A., & Landesman-Dwyer, S. (1979). Pre-delinquent and disturbed adolescents. The role of paternal alcoholism. In M. Galanter (Ed.), *Currents in alcoholism: Vol. 5. Biomedical issues and clinical effects of alcoholism* (pp. 339–348). New York: Grune & Stratton.

Maziade, M., Capéraà, P., Laplante, B., Boudreault, M., Thivierge, J., Côté, R. & Boutin, P. (1985). Value of difficult temperament among 7-year-olds in the general population for predicting psychiatric diagnosis at age 12. *American Journal of Psychiatry, 142,* 943–946.

McConaughy, S. H., & Achenbach, T. M. (1988). *Practical guide for the Child Behavior Checklist and related methods.* Burlington: Department of Psychiatry, University of Vermont.

McElligatt, K. (1986). Identifying and treating children of alcoholic parents. *Social Work in Education, 9,* 55–70.

McKenna, T., & Pickens, R. (1983). Personality characteristics of alcoholic children of alcoholics. *Journal of Studies on Alcohol, 44,* 688–700.

Michaels, M. L., Roosa, M. W., & Gensheimer, L. K. (1992). Family characteristics of children who self-select into a prevention program for children of alcoholics. *American Journal of Community Psychology, 20,* 663–672.

Miller, B. A., Downs, W. R., Gondoli, D. M., & Keil, A. (1987). The role of childhood sexual abuse in the development of alcoholism in women. *Violence and Victims, 2,* 157–172.

Miller, D., & Jang, M. (1977). Children of alcoholics: A 20-year longitudinal study. *Social Work Research Abstracts, 13,* 23–29.

Miller, N. B., Cowan, P. A., Cowan, C. P., Hetherington, E. M., & Clingempeel, W. G. (1993). Externalizing in preschoolers and early adolescents: A cross-study replication of a family model. *Developmental Psychology, 29,* 3–18.

Miller, P. M., Smith, G. T., & Goldman, M. S. (1990). Emergence of alcohol expectancies in childhood: A possible critical period. *Journal of Studies on Alcohol, 51,* 343–349.

Molina, B. S. G., Chassin, L., & Curran, P. J. (1994). A comparison of mechanisms underlying substance use for early adolescent children of alcoholics and controls. *Journal of Studies on Alcohol, 55,* 269–275.

Moos, R. H., & Billings, A. G. (1982). Children of alcoholics during the recovery process: Alcoholic and matched control families. *Addictive Behaviors, 7,* 155–163.

Moos, R. H., & Moos, B. S. (1984). The process of recovery from alcoholism: III. Comparing functioning in families of alcoholics and matched control families. *Journal of Studies on Alcohol, 45,* 111–118.

Nanson, J. L., & Hiscock, M. (1990). Attention deficits in children exposed to alcohol prenatally. *Alcoholism: Clinical and Experimental Research, 14,* 656–661.

Neville, H. J., & Schmidt, A. L. (1985). Event-related potentials in subjects at risk for alcoholism. In N. C. Chang & H. H. Chao (Eds.), *Early identification of alcohol abuse* (pp. 228–239). Rockville, MD: NIAAA Monograph 17.

Noll, R. B., Zucker, R. A., & Greenberg, G. S. (1990). Identification of alcohol by smell among preschoolers: Evidence for early socialization about drugs occurring in the home. *Child Development, 61,* 1520–1527.

O'Farrell, T. J. (Ed.). (1993). *Treating alcohol problems: Marital and family interventions.* New York: Guilford Press.

Orme, T. C., & Rimmer, J. (1981). Alcoholism and child abuse: A review. *Journal of Studies on Alcohol, 42,* 273–287.

Parkhurst, J. T., & Asher, S. R. (1992). Peer rejection in middle school: Subgroup differences in behavior, loneliness, and interpersonal concerns. *Developmental Psychology, 28,* 231–241.

Patterson, G. R. (1986). Performance models for antisocial boys. *American Psychologist, 41,* 432–444.

Patterson, G. R. (1992). Developmental changes in antisocial behavior. In R. D. Peters, R. J. McMahon, & V. L. Quinsey (Eds.), *Aggression and violence throughout the life span* (pp. 52–82). Newbury Park, CA: Sage.

Penrose, G. B. (1978). *Perceptions of five and six year old children concerning cultured drinking norms.* Unpublished doctoral dissertation. University of California, Berkeley.

Polich, J. (1993). P300 in clinical applications: Meaning, method, and measurement. In E. Niedermeyer & F. Lopes da Silva (Eds.), *Electroencephalography: Basic principles, clinical applications, and related fields* (3rd. ed., pp. 1005–1018). Baltimore, MD: William & Wilkins.

Porjesz, B., & Begleiter, H. (1987). Evoked brain potentials and alcoholism. In O. A. Parsons, N. Butters, & P. E. Nathan (Eds.), *Neuropsychology of alcoholism: Implications for diagnosis and treatment* (pp. 45–63). New York: Guilford Press.

Prewett, M. J., Spence, R., & Chaknis, M. (1981). Attribution of causality by children with alcoholic parents. *The International Journal of the Addictions, 16,* 367–370.

Reich, W., Earls, F., Frankel, O., & Shayka, J. J. (1993). Psychopathology in children of alcoholics. *Journal of the American Academy of Child and Adolescent Psychiatry, 32,* 995–1002.

Reich, W., Earls, F., & Powell, J. (1988). A comparison of the home and social environments of children of alcoholic and nonalcoholic parents. *British Journal of Addiction, 83,* 831–839.

Reid, J. B. (1993). Prevention of conduct disorder before and after school entry: Relating interventions to developmental findings. *Development and Psychopathology, 5,* 243–262.

Richters, J., & Weintraub, S. (1990). Beyond diathesis: Toward an understanding of high-risk environments. In J. Rolf, A. S. Masten, D. Cicchetti, K. H. Nuechterlein, & S. Weintraub (Eds.), *Risk and protective factors in the development of psychopathology* (pp. 67–96). New York: Cambridge University Press.

Rimmer, J. (1982). The children of alcoholics: An exploratory study. *Children and Youth Services Review, 4,* 365–373.

Robinson, B. E. (1989). *Working with children of alcoholics: The practitioner's handbook.* Lexington, MA: Lexington Books.

Rogeness, G. A., Hernandez, J. M., Macedo, C. A., & Mitchell, E. L. (1982). Biochemical differences in children with conduct disorder socialized and undersocialized. *American Journal of Psychiatry, 139,* 307–311.

Rolf, J. E., Johnson, J. L., Israel, E., Baldwin J., & Chandra, A. (1988). Depressive affect in school-aged children of alcoholics. *British Journal of Addiction, 83,* 841–848.

Rubin, K. H., & Mills, R. S. L. (1991). Conceptualizing developmental pathways to internalizing disorders in childhood. *Canadian Journal of Behavioral Science, 23,* 300–317.

Rubin, K. H., Stewart, S. L., Coplan, R. J. (1995). Social withdrawal in childhood: Conceptual and empirical perspectives. In T. H. Ollendick & R. J. Prinz (Eds.), *Advances in clinical child psychology* (Vol. 17, pp. 157–196). New York: Plenum Press.

Rubio-Stipec, M., Bird, H., Canino, G., Bravo, M., & Alegria, M. (1991). Children of alcoholic parents in the community. *Journal of Studies on Alcohol, 52,* 78–88.

Russell, M. (1990). Prevalence of alcoholism among children of alcoholics. In M. Windle, & J. S. Searles (Eds.), *Children of alcoholics: Critical perspectives* (pp. 9–38). New York: Guilford Press.

Rutter, M. (1987). Psychosocial resilience and protective mechanisms. *American Journal of Orthopsychiatry, 57,* 316–331.

Rutter, M. (1989). Pathways from childhood to adult life. *Journal of Child Psychology and Psychiatry and Allied Disciplines, 30,* 23–51.

Rutter, M. (1990a). Commentary: Some focus and process considerations regarding effects of parental depression on children. *Developmental Psychology, 26,* 60–67.

Rutter, M. (1990b). Psychosocial resilience and protective mechanisms. In J. Rolf, A. S. Masten, D. Cicchetti, K. H. Nuechterlein, & S. Weintraub (Eds.), *Risk and protective factors in the development of psychopathology* (pp. 181–214). New York: Cambridge University Press.

Rutter, M. (1993). Developmental psychopathology as a research perspective. In D. Magnusson & P. J. M. Casaer (Eds.), *Longitudinal research on individual development: Present status and future perspectives* (pp. 127–152). New York: Cambridge University Press.

Rutter, M. (1994). Beyond longitudinal data: Causes, consequences, changes, and continuity. *Journal of Consulting and Clinical Psychology, 62,* 928–940.

Schuckit, M. A. (1980). Self-rating of alcohol intoxication by young men with and without family histories of alcoholism. *Journal of Studies on Alcohol, 41,* 242–249.

Schuckit, M. A. (1985). Ethanol induced changes in body sway in men at high alcoholism risk. *Archives of General Psychiatry, 42,* 375–379.

Schulsinger, F., Knop, J., Goodwin, D. W., Teasdale, T. W., & Mikkelsen, U. (1986). A prospective study of young men at high risk for alcoholism: Social and psychological characteristics. *Archives of General Psychiatry, 43,* 755–760.

Seilhamer, R. A., & Jacob, T. (1990). Family factors and adjustment of children of alcoholics. In M. Windle & J. S. Searles (Eds.), *Children of Alcoholic: Critical Perspectives* (pp. 168–186). New York: Guilford Press.

Seilhamer, R. A., Jacob, T., & Dunn, N.J. (1993). The impact of alcohol consumption on parent–child relationships in families of alcoholics. *Journal of Studies on Alcohol, 54,* 189–198.

Shaw, D. S., & Bell, R. Q., (1993). Developmental theories of parental contributors to antisocial behavior. *Journal of Abnormal Child Psychology, 21,* 493–518.

Sher, K. J. (1991). *Children of alcoholics: A critical appraisal of theory and research.* Chicago: University of Chicago Press.

Sher, K. J., & Levenson, R. W. (1982). Risk for alcoholism and individual differences in the stress-response-dampening effect of alcohol. *Journal of Abnormal Psychology, 91,* 350–367.

Smith, G. T., & Goldman, M. S. (1994). Alcohol expectancy theory and the identification of high-risk adolescents. *Journal of Research on Adolescence, 4,* 229–248.

Sroufe, L. A., & Rutter, M. (1984). The domain of developmental psychopathology. *Child Development, 55,* 17–29.

Streissguth, A. P., Barr, H. M., & Sampson, P. D. (1990). Moderate prenatal alcohol exposure: Effects on child IQ and learning problems at age 7 years. Alcoholism: *Clinical and Experimental Research, 14,* 662–669.

Streissguth, A. P., Bookstein, F. L., Sampson, P. D., & Barr, H. M. (1995). Attention: Prenatal alcohol and continuities of vigilance and attentional problems from 4 through 14 years. *Development and Psychopathology, 7,* 419–446.

Tarter, R. E. (1988). Are there inherited behavioral traits that predispose to substance abuse? *Journal of Consulting and Clinical Psychology, 56,* 189–196.

Tarter, R. E., Alterman, A. L., & Edwards, K. L. (1985). Vulnerability to alcoholism in men: A behavior–genetic perspective. *Journal of Studies on Alcohol, 46,* 329–356.

Tarter, R. E., Laird, S. B., & Moss, H. B. (1990). Neuropsychological and neurophysiological characteristics of children of alcoholics. In M. Windle & J. S. Searles (Eds.), *Children of alcoholics: Critical perspectives* (pp. 73–98). New York: Guilford Press.

Thompson, W. D., Orvaschel, H., Prusoff, B. A., & Kidd, K. K. (1982). An evaluation of the family history method for ascertaining psychiatric disorders. *Archives of General Psychiatry, 39,* 53–58.

Tubman, J. G. (1993a). Family risk factors, parental alcohol use, and problem behaviors among school-age children. *Family Relations, 42,* 81–86.

Tubman, J. G. (1993b). A pilot study of school-age children of men with moderate to severe alcohol dependence: Maternal distress and child outcomes. *Journal of Child Psychology and Psychiatry and Allied Disciplines, 34,* 729–741.

Tubman, J. G., & Windle, M. (1995). Continuity of difficult temperament in adolescence: Relations with depression, life events, family support, and substance use across a one year period. *Journal of Youth and Adolescence, 24,* 133–153.

Vasey, M. W. (1993). Development and cognition in childhood anxiety: The example of worry. In T. H. Ollendick & R. J. Prinz (Eds.), *Advances in clinical child psychology* (Vol. 15, pp. 1–39). New York: Plenum Press.

Vuchinich, S., Bank, L., & Patterson, G. R. (1992). Parenting, peers, and the stability of antisocial behavior in preadolescent boys. *Developmental Psychology, 28,* 510–521.

Webster-Stratton, C. (1990). Stress: A potential disruptor of parent perceptions and family interactions. *Journal of Clinical Child Psychology, 19,* 302–312.

Werner, E. E. (1986). Resilient offspring of alcoholics: A longitudinal study from birth to age 18. *Journal of Studies on Alcohol, 47,* 34–40.

Werner, E. E. (1992). The children of Kauai: Resiliency and recovery in adolescence and young adulthood. *Journal of Adolescent Health, 13,* 262–268.

West, M. O., & Prinz, R. J. (1987). Parental alcoholism and childhood psychopathology. *Psychological Bulletin, 102,* 204–218.

Whipple, S. C., & Noble, E. P. (1991). Personality characteristics of alcoholic fathers and their sons. *Journal of Studies on Alcohol, 52,* 331–337.

Whipple, S. C., Parker, E. S., & Noble, E. P. (1988). An atypical neurocognitive profile in alcoholic fathers and their sons. *Journal of Studies on Alcohol, 49,* 240–244.

Wills, T. A., DuHamel, K., & Vaccaro, D. (1995). Activity and mood temperament as predictors of adolescent substance use: Test of a self-regulation mediational model. *Journal of Personality and Social Psychology, 68,* 901–916.

Windle, M. (1990). Temperament and personality attributes of children of alcoholics. In M. Windle & J. S. Searles (Eds.), *Children of alcoholics: Critical perspectives* (pp. 73–98). New York: Guilford Press.

Windle, M. (1991). The difficult temperament in adolescence: Associations with substance use, family support, and problem behaviors. *Journal of Clinical Psychology, 47,* 310–315.

Windle, M., & Searles, J. S. (Eds.). (1990). *Children of alcoholics: Critical perspectives.* New York: Guilford Press.

Zucker, R. A. (1987). The four alcoholisms: A developmental account of the etiologic process. In P. C. Rivers (Ed.), *Nebraska symposium on motivation, 1986: Vol. 34. Alcohol and addictive behaviors* (pp. 27–84). Lincoln: University of Nebraska Press.

Zucker, R. A., Ellis, D. A., & Fitzgerald, H. E. (1994). Developmental evidence for at least two alcoholisms: I. Biopsychosocial variation among pathways into symptomatic difficulty. In T. F. Babor, V. M. Hesselbrock, R. E. Meyer, & W. Shoemaker (Eds.), *Types of alcoholics: Evidence from clinical, experimental, and genetic research. Annals of the New York Academy of Sciences* (Vol. 708, pp. 134–146). New York: New York Academy of Sciences.

Zucker, R. A., & Fitzgerald, H. E. (1986). *Risk and coping in children of alcoholics.* Grant application: National Institute of Alcohol Abuse & Alcoholism R01-AA07065.

Zucker, R. A., & Fitzgerald, H. E. (1991). Early developmental factors and risk for alcohol problems. *Alcohol Health and Research World, 15,* 18–24.

Zucker, R. A., Kincaid, S. B., Fitzgerald, H. E., & Bingham, C. R. (1995). Alcohol schema acquisition in preschoolers: Differences between children of alcoholics and children of nonalcoholics. *Alcoholism: Clinical and Experimental Research, 19,* 1–7.

CHAPTER 25

CHILDREN OF PARENTS WITH DEPRESSION

Ian H. Gotlib
Sherryl H. Goodman

Of all the psychiatric disorders, depression is by far the most common. Each year, more than 100 million people worldwide develop clinically recognizable depression. During the course of a lifetime, it is estimated that between 8 and 20 percent of the population will experience at least one clinically significant episode of depression (Kessler et al., 1994); approximately twice as many women than men will be affected (Frank, Carpenter, & Kupfer, 1988). Moreover, for a significant proportion of these individuals, the depressive episode will result in death by suicide or other causes (e.g., Murphy, Monson, Olivier, Sobol, & Leighton, 1988). Depression is also a recurrent disorder: over 80 percent of depressed patients have more than one depressive episode (Belsher & Costello, 1988). Over 50 percent relapse within 2 years of recovery (e.g., Keller & Shapiro, 1981); individuals with three or more previous episodes of depression may have a relapse rate as high as 40 percent within only 12 to 15 weeks after recovery (Keller, Shapiro, Lavori, & Wolfe, 1982). Finally, depressive episodes are essentially self-limiting, with approximately 70 percent of individuals recovering within 40 weeks after the onset of the episode (Keller et al., 1982; Lewinsohn & Gotlib, 1995).

The term *depression* has a number of meanings, covering a wide range of emotional states that range in severity from normal, everyday moods of sadness, to psychotic episodes with increased risk of suicide. Everyone has at some time felt "sad" or "blue"; clinically significant depression is differentiated from these more common emotions by the increased severity, pervasiveness, and persistence of the alteration in day-to-day functioning. The current diagnostic system in North America, the Diagnostic and Statistical Manual of Mental Disorders (DSM-IV; American Psychiatric Association, 1994), divides depression, or Mood Disorders, into Depressive Disorders and Bipolar Disorders. Whereas a diagnosis of Bipolar Disorder requires the presence of one or more Manic or Hypomanic Episodes, a diagnosis of Depressive Disorder requires one or more periods of clinically significant depression without a history of either Manic or Hypomanic Episodes. Because of the absence of manic episodes, Depressive Disorders are often referred to as *unipolar depression*.

DSM-IV further divides Depressive Disorder into Major Depression and Dysthymia. For a diagnosis of Major Depression, the occurrence of one or more Major Depressive Episodes must be established. In a Major Depressive Episode, the individual exhibits, over at least a 2-week period, depressed mood (can be irritable mood in children or adolescents) or a loss of interest or pleasure in almost all daily activities, as well as a number of other symptoms of depression, such as weight loss or gain, loss of appetite, sleep disturbance, psychomotor agitation or retardation, fatigue, feelings of guilt or worthlessness, and concentration difficulties. In contrast, a diagnosis of Dysthymia requires a more chronic but less intense disturbance of mood. For this diagnosis to be made, the individual must have exhibited some symptoms of depression for most of a 2-year period (1 year for children and adolescents).

The purpose of this chapter is to explore the implications of this highly prevalent disorder as it occurs in parents, particularly mothers, for its potential to disrupt the course of normal development in their children, through genetic and/or environmental mechanisms. We begin by exploring the emergence of interest in this field of study. We then review the findings on the psychosocial and emotional–behavioral development of children of depressed parents and on the proposed mechanisms for these outcomes. Given the developmental focus of this volume, we attempt in this discussion to highlight findings that have particular bearing on issues concerning developmental considerations in the study of the offspring of depressed parents. Unfortunately, as we will discuss in greater detail later in this chapter, investigators in this field have paid relatively little attention to developmental factors in this area of study. Nevertheless, we have attempted to organize this review and discussion around the ages of the children assessed in these investigations, and throughout the chapter we emphasize the need for a developmental perspective in this field of study. Where appropriate, we also discuss clinical implications of the research we review, focusing specifically on issues of prevention and treatment. Finally, we review issues that obstruct progress in the field, highlight unanswered questions, and offer suggestions for the direction and design of future studies.

HISTORICAL CONTEXT

It has been almost three decades since Mednick and Schulsinger (1968) introduced the high-risk method for the study of psychopathology. The high-risk method refers to the identification of a population out of which a large portion eventually will develop the disorder of interest. Researchers then follow the at-risk sample over time and identify variables that at earlier points in time distinguished between individuals who went on to develop the disorder and those who remained disorder-free. Those distinguishing variables are conceptualized as either incipient forms of the disorder (Mednick & Schulsinger, 1968) or as factors that predispose individuals to the disorder (Garmezy, 1971). Factors that predispose to the disorder may be the "defect," or "vulnerability," in a diathesis-stress model (Rosenthal, 1970). The

goal of research with the high-risk method is to identify variables that would allow the prediction, early identification, and, ultimately, the prevention of disordered development.

Probably because Mednick and Schulsinger's (1968) interests were in schizophrenia and, specifically, in genetic risk for schizophrenia, many researchers followed suit and relied on genetic theories for the etiology of the disorder, both to determine their sample selection procedures (i.e., offspring of schizophrenic parents), and to select the variables that might reveal the actual vulnerability or predisposing factor (e.g., psychophysiological, cognitive, motor, or perceptual deficits). Several longitudinal studies were conducted, most beginning with school-aged children and measuring a variety of predictor variables (see Goodman, 1992, for a review; see Watt, Anthony, Wynne, & Rolf, 1984, for reports from each of the major projects).

Other investigators moved beyond an exclusively genetic focus for identifying risk factors, relying either on alternative etiologic models or on models that took into account both genetic and environmental variables. Increasingly, individual and relationship variables were included in tests of the mechanisms through which a parent's pathology might interfere with the child's healthy development. Additionally, investigators began to use different strategies for identifying high-risk groups and for selecting control groups.

With the increased recognition of the importance of environmental variables, even researchers whose primary interest was in schizophrenia began to include offspring of depressed parents as a "low-risk" comparison group (Wynne, 1984). Research was designed to ask whether the findings on children with schizophrenic parents were specific to schizophrenia or were due to general factors associated with being reared by a parent with psychopathology. Moreover, the outcome of interest was broadened beyond the goal of identifying those offspring who would become schizophrenic to include questions such as who would develop behavior problems, who would show relationship difficulties, and who would exhibit other early signs of psychopathology. Consequently, the time frame often shifted from the prior emphasis on late adolescence and early adulthood (the time period in which schizophrenia is most likely to emerge) to increasingly younger ages. Indeed, even infancy and early childhood were studied in efforts to identify aspects of the disturbed mother's relationship with the child that could precipitate early problems in development.

An important finding that emerged in this literature was that offspring of depressed parents were significantly worse off than were children of well parents. Typically, children of depressed parents scored between the offspring of schizophrenic parents and the well controls, although on some measures they were found to score at least as poorly as children of schizophrenic parents (e.g., Sameroff, Barocas, & Seifer, 1984; Weintraub & Neale, 1984). Coincidentally, this conclusion emerged just as other researchers were finding that depression may develop at a considerably younger age than was traditionally thought (Cantwell, 1983), raising interest in studying depression at its earliest onset. These depression researchers, like the schizophrenia researchers before them, recognized the value of the high-risk method (i.e., identifying children with depressed parents, among whom a large proportion would be expected to develop depression themselves). Interest was fueled further by recognition of the implications of findings from epidemiologic studies indicating that depression rates among adults are high, that more women than men are diagnosed with depression, and that women who are raising children and who are not employed outside the home are particularly vulnerable to depression (e.g., Gotlib, Whiffen, Mount, Milne, & Cordy, 1989). Undeniably, a significant number of children are born to, and raised by, at least one depressed parent. Thus emerged the interest over the past decade in the development of children whose parents experience depression.

CHILDREN OF DEPRESSED PARENTS: OUTCOME STUDIES

Given these historical developments, it was not surprising that evidence emerging from the studies on children of depressed parents revealed that the children are at risk for a variety of psychological and social difficulties (Goodman, 1992; Gotlib & Lee, 1990). However, this general conclusion fails to take into account the importance of recognizing that children differ from one another at different periods of development with respect to their behavioral, affective, and cognitive functioning (e.g., Digdon & Gotlib, 1985). Therefore, it is likely that the relation between maternal depression and child adjustment is also different at various stages of child development. In this context, the symptoms of maternal depression may have a differential impact on developmental tasks the child faces in cognitive, affective, social, and physiological domains at different ages. Consequently, we have organized the studies in this section according to the ages of the children assessed in the investigations. We begin with studies that have examined infants and preschool age children of depressed parents, and then turn to studies of the functioning of school-age and adolescent children of depressed parents. We will focus in this section on investigations that have explicitly examined the psychological, social, or cognitive functioning of the *children* of depressed parents. In a later section of this chapter we will examine the results of studies that have assessed the behaviors of depressed *parents* with respect to their children.

Infants and Preschool Age Children of Depressed Parents

A number of theorists have argued that the impact of parental depression, and particularly maternal depression, should be particularly pronounced during the early years of the child's life, the period often considered to be the most critical in a child's development. In part, this impact is anticipated because mothers are likely to be the primary caregivers of young children. Thus, a depressed mother will have more extensive contact with her infant than with older children. The infant, similarly, will likely have less contact with (nondepressed) others than would school-age children and adolescents, who may benefit from supportive peer and other adult relationships. In addition, early mother–infant relationships form a foundation for children's self-perceptions and perceptions of the self in relation to others. Indeed, it is likely that from mother–infant interactions infants form prototypes that shape their expectations concerning other interpersonal relationships. It is also likely that maternal depression interferes with younger children's mastery of developmentally salient tasks. Thus, from a clinical perspective, alleviation of maternal symptoms may not be sufficient to remedy the child's difficulties over the longer term if the child has already formulated maladaptive perceptions and/or has fallen behind in other developmental tasks. Therefore, as we discuss in greater detail later in this chapter, it is important to examine the association between parental depression and the adjustment of infants and young children in a longitudinal design. In the following section, we describe the findings of studies examining the impact of parental depression on infants' functioning.

The results of a growing number of investigations indicate that parental depression, particularly depression in mothers, is associated with problematic functioning in infants and toddlers. Early studies in this area examined the impact of elevated depressive symptoms (as opposed to a clinical psychiatric diagnosis of depression) in mothers on their infants. For example, Field and her colleagues (e.g., Field, 1984; Field et al., 1985, 1988, 1990) found that infants of women with elevated depression scores were rated as more drowsy or fussy and as less relaxed or content than were infants of nondepressed women. Findings from other studies suggest that the infants of dysphoric mothers may be temperamentally difficult. Cutrona and Troutman (1986) and Whiffen (1988) both found depressive symptomatology to be correlated with maternal reports of infant crying and unsoothability.

A number of investigations have now examined the functioning of infants and toddlers of mothers with diagnosed clinically significant depression. One of the earliest longitudinal studies of the adjustment of the infants of depressed women was conducted in England by Ghodsian, Zayicek, and Wolkind (1984). Diagnosed depressed mothers were asked to rate their children at age 14 months, 27 months, and 42 months. Although at 14 months there were no differences between the ratings of depressed and nondepressed women, at both 27 and 42 months depressed women rated their children as having a greater number of behavior problems than did nondepressed mothers.

One of the important indicators of infant adjustment is attachment behavior, which is assumed both to reflect the quality of the mother–child relationship (see Ainsworth, Blehar, Waters, & Wall, 1978) and to provide an important link to the child's later interpersonal competence. Indeed, it is possible that the increased risk of affective disorders among offspring of depressed mothers has its roots in insecure attachment of the infant. Using the Strange Situation developed by Ainsworth (Ainsworth & Wittig, 1969; Ainsworth et al., 1978), Radke-Yarrow, Cummings, Kuczynski, and Chapman (1985) evaluated attachment status among 2- to 3-year-old children whose mothers had a previous diagnosis of bipolar, unipolar-major, or unipolar-minor affective disorder. The authors reported that the rates of insecure attachment were highest among the children of the bipolar and unipolar-major mothers.

Other reports from the same research group describe the interactions of depressed mothers with their children, beginning at the age of 2. The earliest reports focused on the 2-year-old children of 23 mothers who met Research Diagnostic Criteria for lifetime unipolar depression, but who had not been hospitalized during the child's lifetime (Zahn-Waxler, Cummings, Iannotti, & Radke-Yarrow, 1984). Observations of these children suggested two general tendencies that distinguished the children of depressed mothers from those of nondepressed controls. First, the children of depressed mothers were more maladaptively empathic, such that their own activity was disrupted when distress was experienced by other people. Second, the children of depressed mothers showed greater emotional containment by being more likely to suppress the expression of affect. Of particular interest were the findings that these children were more likely than were the control children to attempt to appease a frustrating adult, but were less likely to become physically aggressive across a variety of situations. Zahn-Waxler and colleagues hypothesized that children of depressed mothers are overly sensitive to their mothers' negative affect, while being unable to seek or accept comfort for their own emotional distress. It is likely that children of depressed mothers have learned to suppress aspects of their own emotional experience because the expression of certain affects (such as aggression) has not been accepted by their mothers. Similarly, the greater empathy of the children of depressed mothers reported in this study

may be due to the reinforcement they have received from their mothers for their displays of concern.

As part of a large-scale, longitudinal study of depression during pregnancy and the postpartum period (Gotlib et al., 1989; Gotlib, Whiffen, Wallace, & Mount, 1991), we had an opportunity to assess and follow a sample of infants of women who were diagnosed with clinically significant depression during the postpartum period. In the first report from this project, Whiffen and Gotlib (1989) assessed the effects of a diagnosable episode of depression during the postpartum period on infants' cognitive and socioemotional development. At 9 to 10 weeks postpartum, the depressed mothers reported more difficulties with infant care and perceived their infants as more bothersome than did the nondepressed mothers. Observers' ratings of the infants' behavior provided convergent validity for the mothers' perceptions: the infants of the depressed mothers were rated as more tense and less happy and as showing less tolerance for the test procedures, that is, as deteriorating more quickly under the stress of testing. Perhaps most importantly, the infants of the depressed mothers obtained lower scores on the Bayley Scales of Infant Development, particularly on the Mental, or Cognitive, Development subscale—an effect that was independent of maternal level of education.

In a second report from this project, Carro, Grant, Gotlib, and Compas (1993) examined maternal and paternal characteristics at 1 month postpartum as risk and protective factors for children's internalizing and externalizing problems at 2 to 3 years of age. These investigators found that fathers' depressive symptoms at 1 month postpartum predicted children's internalizing and externalizing problem behaviors at 2 to 3 years of age, and the interaction of the fathers' and mothers' depressive symptoms predicted childrens' subsequent internalizing problems. Contrary to expectation, no evidence was found for the protective effects of marital satisfaction or social support or for low levels of depressive symptoms in a spouse. It appears, therefore, that examination of the effects of fathers' depressive symptoms on child functioning is a promising area for further study.

In a final study conducted when the children were 3 years of age (Gotlib, 1994), mothers were assigned to one of two groups: women who had been diagnosed as clinically depressed during the postpartum period, and those who had not been depressed during pregnancy or the postpartum period. It is important to note that none of the women was currently diagnosed as depressed. The McCarthy Scales of Children's Abilities (McCarthy, 1972) were administered to the child while the mother watched from an adjoining room through a one-way mirror. Analyses indicated that compared with children of the control mothers, children of the previously depressed mothers obtained significantly lower scores on four of the six McCarthy subscales and a marginally lower score on another subscale. Specifically, children of the depressed mothers obtained significantly lower scores on the verbal, perceptual-performance, general cognitive, and memory subscales, and a marginally lower score on the quantitative subscale than did children of the control mothers. In addition, the previously depressed mothers also rated their children on the Child Behavior Checklist (CBCL) as more aggressive and destructive. Thus, at 3 years of age, children of mothers who had been diagnosed with an episode of depression in the postpartum period continued to demonstrate significantly lower functioning on the McCarthy Scales of Children's Abilities and to be rated as exhibiting more externalizing problem behaviors than did children whose mothers were not depressed during that period.

It is clear from these studies, therefore, that infants and toddlers of depressed mothers exhibit a range of behavioral, emotional, and cognitive difficulties. Despite this growing awareness of the apparent adverse effects of maternal depression on the psychological functioning of young children, there have been no systematic efforts to examine the impact of programs designed to prevent the occurrence of depression during pregnancy and the postpartum period, or to treat depression that has already occurred in young mothers. In particular, we do not know whether the adverse effects of maternal depression on infants and toddlers can be prevented or reversed with treatment focusing on symptom reduction, or whether these effects are due to more stable underlying personality characteristics of women who are prone to experiencing episodes of depression, characteristics that may remain relatively unchanged by current approaches to the treatment of depression (see Barnett & Gotlib, 1988, and Gotlib & Hammen, 1992, for reviews of this literature). It will be important for future research to address these issues more explicitly.

School-Age Children and Adolescents of Depressed Parents

In several early investigations of school-age children of depressed parents, researchers interviewed depressed mothers about the functioning of their children. Billings and Moos (1983), for example, conducted a large-scale study of the relation between parental unipolar depression and child adjustment. Depressed parents and matched nondepressed community control parents completed a battery of questionnaires on various aspects of their daily lives, family functioning, and their children's adjustment. Billings and Moos found that the depressed parents reported a greater number of physical and psychological problems in their children than did the nondepressed controls. In a 1-year follow-up,

Billings and Moos (1986) compared the children of remitted and nonremitted depressed parents with children of their nondepressed controls. Interestingly, despite the abatement of their own depressive symptoms, parents in the remitted group continued to report more dysfunction in their children than did the control parents. As expected, the nonremitted depressed group reported the highest incidence of dysfunction in their children.

In a similar study, Weissman and colleagues (1984) interviewed a large sample of mildly and severely depressed parents and normal community controls about their children's adjustment. According to the parents' reports, 34 percent of the children of the depressed parents had psychiatric symptoms or had received psychological treatment, compared with only 16 percent of the children of the controls. Furthermore, 24 percent of the children of the depressed parents were diagnosable by DSM-III criteria, compared with only 8 percent of the control children, and 25 percent of the depressives' children had received treatment for emotional problems, compared with 9 percent of the controls. Differences between the two groups of children were also noted for the use of psychotropic medication and the incidence of problems in school (e.g., school failures, repeating a grade). Finally, Weissman and colleagues found that children with both parents depressed were at greater risk for a diagnosis of a psychiatric disorder than were children with one depressed parent. On the basis of these findings, Weissman and coworkers concluded that children of depressed parents are at increased risk for psychological symptoms, treatment for emotional problems, school problems, suicidal behavior, and multiple psychiatric diagnoses (see also Warner, Weissman, Fendrich, Wickramaratne, & Moreau, 1992).

The results of these studies indicate that school-age children of depressed parents function more poorly than children of nondepressed parents. Although provocative, it is important to bear in mind that these data are based on parental reports rather than on direct observations of the children. Depressed parents' reports may be biased by a tendency to see both their parenting and their children's behavior in a negative light (e.g., Brewin, Andrews, & Gotlib, 1993; Gotlib, Gilboa, & Sommerfeld, in press; Webster-Stratton & Hammond, 1988). Compounding this problem is an issue raised by data reported by Yarrow, Campbell, and Burton (1970) indicating that normal (i.e., nondepressed) subjects recall parenting events to be more *positive* after even a short time span than they did while the event was occurring. Although there are data suggesting that depressed women's perceptions of their children can be accurate (e.g., Conrad & Hammen, 1989; Goodman, Adamson, Riniti, & Cole, 1994), it is critical that the functioning of school-age children of depressed parents be assessed directly.

A number of investigations have examined more directly the psychosocial functioning of older children of depressed mothers. In general, the results of these investigations indicate that children of depressed parents demonstrate poorer functioning than do children of nondepressed parents. For example, Welner, Welner, McCrary, and Leonard (1977) compared children of depressed parents with offspring of nondepressed controls. Both mothers and children were seen in interviews covering such areas as physical problems, academic performance, conduct problems, and other symptoms of psychopathology. Welner and coworkers reported that the children of the depressed parents had more depressed mood, death wishes, frequent fighting, unexplained headaches, loss of interest in usual activities, hypochondriacal concerns, crying for no apparent reason, and more disturbed classroom behavior. In fact, the eight children in the study who were diagnosed as depressed by Welner's criteria (five or more depressive symptoms) all had at least one depressed parent.

Orvaschel, Walsh-Ellis, and Ye (1988) examined the prevalence of psychological problems in the school-age children of parents with recurrent major depression and in children of parents with no history of depression. Relying on both maternal and child responses to the Schedule for Affective Disorders and Schizophrenia for School-Age Children—Epidemiologic Version (K-SADS-E; Orvaschel, Puig-Antich, Chambers, Tabrizi, & Johnson, 1982), these investigators found that 41 percent of the children with affectively disordered parents met criteria for at least one episode of diagnosable psychiatric disturbance at some time in their lives, whereas the rate for children of nondepressed parents was only 15 percent.

Goodman and colleagues (1994) reported the rates of mood disorder in the 8- to 10-year-old children of mothers with a history of at least one episode of unipolar-major depression during the child's lifetime, compared to children with well parents. Children's diagnoses were determined with the K-SADS-E, combining reports from both the mother and the child. Goodman and colleagues found that 20 percent of the depressed mothers had a child who met criteria for current or past major depression or dysthymia, compared with only 5 percent of the well mothers.

Hirsch, Moos, and Reischl (1985) directly examined a group of adolescent children of unipolar depressed parents and compared them to both a community group and to a group of adolescent offspring of arthritic patients. Hirsch and colleagues found that although the children of depressed parents reported more symptoms than the normal group, there were no significant differences between the children of the depressed and the arthritic patients. How-

ever, these authors failed to provide information concerning the psychological adjustment of the arthritic parents. Given the high incidence of reactive depression in rheumatoid arthritis patients (Anderson, Bradley, Young, McDaniel, & Wise, 1985), it is possible that the lack of differences between the children of depressed and arthritic parents was attributable to undiagnosed depression in the arthritic parents rather than to the effects of general disability.

Beardslee, Schultz, and Selman (1987) also assessed the adjustment of adolescent offspring of affectively disordered and normal parents. These investigators assessed parental and adolescent reports on the Diagnostic Interview for Children and Adolescents. Beardslee and colleagues reported that 38 percent of the adolescents in the high-risk group received a diagnosis of past or current affective disorder, whereas only 2 percent of the adolescents in the low-risk group received such diagnoses. In another report from the same project, Kaplan, Beardslee, and Keller (1987) found that the 7- to 19-year-old children of affectively disordered parents demonstrated cognitive impairment in the form of subtest variability on the WISC-R.

Given the consistent findings of the adverse effects of parental depression on children's functioning, a number of investigators have now begun to examine the specificity of child adjustment difficulties to depression. Hammen, Gordon, Burge, Jaenicke, and Hiroto (1987) assessed children of four groups of mothers: mothers suffering from recurrent unipolar depression, mothers with a bipolar affective disorder, chronically medically ill mothers, and nondisordered mothers. Hammen and coworkers found that children of both unipolar depressed and bipolar depressed mothers had high rates of psychiatric diagnoses, compared to children of nondisordered mothers. Although children of mothers who were medical patients had moderate rates of psychiatric diagnosis, these were lower than the rates found in children of affectively disordered parents. These researchers noted that several of the mothers who were medical patients had experienced depressive or other reactions to life circumstances. Consequently, it is unclear whether the rates of diagnosis in children of such mothers were attributable to the effects of maternal disability or to concomitant maternal psychological distress.

In another study, Turner, Beidel, and Costello (1987) examined the young offspring of patients with anxiety disorders, dysthymic disorder, as well as those of community controls. They found a greater number of internalizing problems in the children of psychiatric parents than in children of community parents, but the greatest impairment was in the children of anxiety disordered parents. However, in this study, the anxiety disorder group was composed of parents with agoraphobic and obsessive-compulsive disorders, which likely reflect the severe end of the anxiety disorder spectrum; in contrast, the dysthymic group consisted of parents whose disturbance represents a less severe type of affective disorder. In light of other findings indicating that the severity of parental psychopathology is related to child adjustment (e.g., Harder, Kokes, Fisher, & Strauss, 1980; Keller et al., 1986), it is possible that in both studies the severity of impairment in children was related to the severity of parental impairment rather than to parental diagnostic status. However, because Turner and colleagues did not provide severity ratings for parents, an assessment of this hypothesis is precluded. In future research, it will be important to compare parents with different diagnoses who are equated in terms of the severity of their psychopathology.

Finally, in a recent investigation in our own laboratory (Lee & Gotlib, 1989a, 1989b, 1991a), we examined the psychological adjustment of four groups of school-age children: children of depressed psychiatric patient mothers, children of nondepressed psychiatric patient mothers, children of nondepressed medical patient mothers, and children of community-residing non-patient mothers. Child functioning was assessed both by a clinical interview with the child and by maternal ratings. Children were interviewed using the Child Assessment Schedule (CAS; Hodges, Kline, Stern, Cytryn, & McKnew, 1982), a semistructured protocol designed for the clinical assessment of children 7 years and older. The CAS assesses fears and anxieties, worries and concerns, self-image, mood disturbance, physical complaints, and conduct problems. All mothers also completed the CBCL, on which they describe their child's behavior problems over the previous 6 months.

The results of this study revealed that the children of depressed mothers had more severe psychiatric symptoms on the CAS and poorer overall adjustment on the Global Assessment Scale for Children than did the children of nondepressed mothers. Using the mean ratings on the CAS presented by Hodges, McKnew, Cytryn, Stern, and Kline (1982), the children of the depressed mothers functioned at a level comparable to a group of behaviorally disordered outpatient children. The children of depressed mothers were also rated by their mothers as having a greater number of both internalizing and externalizing problems than were the children of the nondepressed control mothers; indeed, two-thirds of the children of the depressed mothers were placed in the clinical range on the CBCL (greater than the 90th percentile), an incidence three times greater than that observed in the nondepressed controls. Interestingly, the children of depressed mothers typically did not differ from the children of nondepressed psychiatric patient mothers, suggesting

that the effects of maternal depression on child dysfunction may be nonspecific.

In a 10-month follow-up assessment conducted on this sample of children, Lee and Gotlib (1991a) reported that despite a significant reduction in the mothers' depressive symptomatology, the formerly depressed women continued to describe their children as having a higher number of internalizing and externalizing problems than did the nondepressed controls. Finally, interviewer ratings on the CAS indicated that children of both the depressed and the nondepressed psychiatric patient mothers were rated as having a greater number of mood symptoms and somatic complaints than were children of the community mothers. Thus, children of both depressed and nondepressed mothers demonstrated problematic adjustment, even when their mothers were no longer overtly symptomatic, indicating that there may be a substantial lag between alleviation of maternal symptomatology and improvement in child functioning. These findings not only corroborate Billings and Moos' (1986) observations that remitted depressed parents continue to report adjustment difficulties in their children, but further, replicate these results with ratings by clinicians.

Another way that researchers have examined the specificity of child adjustment difficulties to depression is to examine the roles of psychopathology in the father and marital conflict, two common correlates of maternal depression. In this context, Goodman, Brogan, Lynch, and Fielding (1993) studied a sample of 5- to 10-year-old children whose mothers had experienced at least one episode of unipolar-major depression during the child's lifetime. The depressed mothers varied on whether or not the child's father also had a psychiatric disorder. The mothers and fathers of the control children in this study had no psychiatric disorders. Both groups varied on the parents' marital status. Fathers' psychiatric status and parents' marital status were examined, along with mother's depression status, as part of a multiple risk factor model. Goodman and colleagues found support for the multiple risk factor model, in that fathers' psychiatric status and parents' marital status explained much of the variance in children's social and emotional competence. For children whose mothers had a history of depression, having a father with a history of psychiatric disorder and, to a lesser extent, having divorced parents, contributed significantly to the likelihood of the children having lower social and emotional competence. In contrast, mothers' depression in the absence of fathers' disturbance (i.e., depressed mothers with well spouses) had little association with adverse child outcome. Thus, the effects of maternal depression must take into account the additional and interacting effects of paternal disorder, and both must be interpreted within the context of whether the children have also experienced parental divorce.

In sum, maternal depression has been associated with increased rates of behavior problems, social–emotional maladjustment, and deficits in cognitive–intellectual functioning in infancy through adolescence. At each age period, effects were found in age-appropriate developmental tasks and in cognitive, affective, and social functioning. Moreover, longitudinal investigations revealed that the parent's recovery from the depressive episode during which the child was assessed was not associated with the child's improved functioning, regardless of the developmental period during which the parent's episode of depression occurred. This finding is particularly important in light of the absence of studies examining the effects of treatment of maternal depression on children's functioning. Indeed, this pattern of findings suggests that *prevention* of depression is far more important than *treatment* of depression in terms of the emotional health of the offspring of depressed mothers. Further, comparisons between children with depressed parents and children whose parents have either chronic medical conditions or other psychiatric disorders suggest that the outcome to the children may not be specific to depression in the parents. Nevertheless, further study is needed to clarify whether it is the parent's level of functioning or the presence of high levels of depressive symptoms in the nondepressed controls that may account for the nonspecificity. Finally, studies that have also included variables such as psychopathology of the father, marital conflict, and other stressors suggest that these add important information in helping to understand the association between maternal depression and adverse child outcomes. Clearly, therefore, these variables should also be considered in programs designed to reduce the adverse impact of maternal depression on children's functioning (e.g., Gotlib & Beach, 1995; Gotlib & Colby, 1987).

MECHANISMS OF TRANSMISSION

Genetics

It is widely accepted that genetic transmission of some as yet unknown biological defect plays a role in increasing the risk for the kinds of problems that we have just reviewed in children of depressed parents (Tsuang & Faraone, 1990). Twin studies show a higher concordance rate for depression (unipolar and bipolar) for monozygotic (MZ) twins (ranging from 33 to 93%) than for dizygotic (DZ) twins (ranging from 0 to 24%). Similar support comes from adoption studies.

Genetics researchers interpret relevant findings as supporting a multifactorial inheritance model in which there is shared transmission of vulnerability to unipolar, bipolar,

and schizoaffective disorder. Biological abnormality likely plays a greater role in bipolar disorder than it does in unipolar depression. Overall, first degree relatives of individuals with unipolar depression have a 20 to 25 percent risk for developing depression themselves, compared to a general population risk of 7 percent for unipolar disorder and 0.5 percent for bipolar disorder. Thus, either not all relatives inherit the biological defect or the inheritance is a biological vulnerability that is not expressed in all individuals.

In this genetic context, psychosocial factors become important for several reasons. First, psychosocial processes may serve as the stress in a diathesis-stress etiologic model in which the diathesis is genetic. Second, regardless of the etiologic model, psychosocial processes most likely are important determinants of the extent and nature of the influence of the parent's depression on the child's development. Third, not all individuals who become depressed have depressed relatives, and it is likely that psychosocial factors play an even more central etiologic role in these cases.

Impairment of Parental Functioning in Depressed Women

Among psychosocial factors, parenting behavior has most often been studied as a mechanism for the transmission of psychopathology. Indeed, the disturbed relationship between a depressed mother and her child may be one key means by which a vulnerability to depression in adulthood is transmitted (e.g., Goodman, 1992; Lee & Gotlib, 1991b). A poor parent–child relationship may moderate genetic risk for disorder (Carlson & Strober, 1983). Support for the importance of parent–child relationships also comes from retrospective data: Several studies have found that currently depressed adults report having experienced difficult early family environments and problems in their relationships with their parents (e.g., Gotlib, Mount, Cordy, & Whiffen, 1988; Parker, 1981) and, further, that early adverse experiences predict the onset of depression in adulthood (e.g., Gotlib & Hammen, 1992; Gotlib, Whiffen, Wallace, & Mount, 1991). Moreover, some of the common correlates of depression (e.g., the depressed parent's cognitive bias, marital conflict, and high levels of stress in the family) may play a role in children's adverse outcomes through interfering with effective parental functioning.

Indirect Reports of Depressed Parent Functioning

Until relatively recently, the only information available on the parenting behavior of depressed women was based on the parents' self-reports. For example, interviews with depressed women painted a vivid picture of how mothers' depression can interfere with their provision of adequate parenting to their children (Weissman & Paykel, 1974). Depressed women reported feeling helpless and hostile towards their children and described being only moderately involved in their children's daily lives. Even following recovery from an episode of depression, these women reported persistent interpersonal dysfunction in their relationships with children and family members.

Although Weissman and Paykel (1974) found disturbance in parenting at all stages of development, it was most marked in infancy and adolescence. Mothers of infants reported feeling hostile, immobilized, helpless, and overwhelmed, paralleling a behavioral pattern of being overindulgent and overprotective. Mothers of adolescents described angry outbursts alternating with withdrawal, a tendency to either over control or under control their adolescents, and an inability to set limits, negotiate conflicts, or show an active interest in their teens' daily life.

Finally, in Billings and Moos's (1983, 1986) study of the relation between parental unipolar depression and child adjustment, depressed parents described their families as less cohesive, less expressive, and higher in conflict than did the nondepressed parents. These results suggests that it may not be depressive symptomatology per se through which depressed parents adversely affect their children. Thus, even relying exclusively on depressed parents' self-reports, a picture emerges of inadequate parental functioning. Depressed mothers view their own parenting negatively and have negative views of their children.

Observations of Depressed Mothers and Their Children

More recently, specific information about the quality of parent–child interactions has been generated from observations of the behaviors of depressed parents, or of parents with elevated depression scale scores, compared to nondepressed controls, in interaction with children ranging in age from infancy through adolescence.

As we noted earlier, the major developmental task of infancy is the formation of a bond between mother and baby (Ainsworth et al., 1978). The foundations for this bond are laid early in the infant's life, when mother and infant spend time becoming familiar with one another through mutual gazing, vocalization, and touch. Consequently, many investigators have examined the relationship between mother and infant as they interact soon after birth. Livingood, Daen, and Smith (1983), for example, examined a group of symptomatic (Beck Depression Inventory scores of greater than 9) and nonsymptomatic mothers with respect to the level and quality of stimulation they provided for their newborn infants during an in-hospital feeding session. The symptomatic mothers were found to shift their positions more frequently during

feeding, interrupting the smooth flow of their rocking movements, and to gaze less often at their infants, which may interfere with the development of a strong attachment bond.

Consistent with Livingood and colleagues' (1983) findings, Field and her colleagues (e.g., Field, 1984; Field et al., 1985, 1988, 1990) observed lower levels of involvement with their infants in mothers who were symptomatically depressed. Compared with nonsymptomatic women, symptomatic mothers were rated by observers during interactions with their babies as more depressed and anxious, less active and playful, and less contingently responsive to their infants' behavior. In a similar study, Bettes (1988) found that symptomatic mothers took longer to respond to their infants' vocalizations and failed to modify their own speech after this had occurred. In contrast, nonsymptomatic mothers were quicker to respond, and uttered shorter phrases after their infants had vocalized. Similarly, Fleming, Ruble, Flett, and Shaul (1988) found that, compared to nondepressed mothers, women with postpartum depression showed less reciprocal vocalization and affectionate contact with their infants.

Considered collectively, these studies demonstrate that with young infants, the interactions of depressed mothers are characterized by withdrawal and a lack of engagement with, and responsiveness to, their infants. The results of other studies suggest that some depressed mothers may, in fact, be explicitly negative in interactions with their infants. Compared with nondepressed mothers, depressed mothers have been observed to display covert hostility and flattened affect (Lyons-Ruth, Zoll, Connell, & Grunebaum, 1986), angry and intrusive behaviors (Cohn, Matias, Tronick, Connell, & Lyons-Ruth, 1986; Field et al., 1990), and more negativity toward their infants (especially boys) (Cohn, Campbell, Matias, & Hopkins, 1990). In the latter study, the infants themselves were more negative in the interactions. Are babies affected by the depressed mothers' behavior and affect? Studies of simulated depression indicated that infants of nondepressed mothers react with protest (Cohn & Tronick, 1983; Field, 1984). Field and colleagues (1990) observed that the infants of depressed mothers "matched" their mothers' state particularly when she was negative and less so when she was positive toward them.

Radke-Yarrow and her colleagues provided a wealth of information based on observations of unipolar and bipolar depressed mothers of toddler-age children compared to nondepressed controls. The unipolar depressed mothers were observed to spend significantly more time in a negative mood when interacting with their children, compared to both bipolar depressed and nondepressed mothers (Radke-Yarrow et al., 1985; Radke-Yarrow & Nottleman, 1989). The children and their mothers with affective disorders spoke less to each other than did nondepressed control mothers and children (Breznitz & Sherman, 1987). The depressed mothers also responded more slowly to the children's speech. In "control" episodes, in which the mothers attempted to influence children's behaviors, women with affective disorders were less successful than were normal mothers in resolving these conflict situations, commonly avoiding confrontation when the child resisted (Kochanska, Kuczynski, Radke-Yarrow, & Welch, 1987).

In a sample of disadvantaged black women, Goodman and Brumley (1990) compared depressed, schizophrenic, and normal mothers interacting with their young children. The depressed mothers were not as impaired as the schizophrenic mothers, but compared to normal women they were significantly less responsive and involved with their children and used less structure and discipline. Children's IQ and aspects of their social behavior were related to maternal responsiveness, positive affect, and interest. Mills, Puckering, Pound, and Cox (1985) observed depressed community non-patient women to be less responsive and reciprocal in their interactions with their 2- to 3-year old toddlers than were nondepressed women. The children with the greatest levels of behavior problems had mothers with the lowest proportions of reciprocated interactions.

Whiffen and Gotlib (1991) observed interactions between postpartum depressed and nondepressed mothers and their infants at 2 and 7 months of age. A discriminant function analysis of the mothers' and infants' behaviors indicated that at 2 months, maternal depression was associated both with the mother looking less at the infant and with the infant looking more at the mother and smiling less. The discriminant function accurately classified 72 percent of the depressed dyads. At 7 months, the depressed dyads were distinguished by lower levels of maternal involvement with the infant across a number of behavioral dimensions, and by the infant vocalizing and crying more; this function correctly classified 83 percent of the depressed dyads. These findings are consistent with those of analog studies in suggesting that postpartum depression is associated with comparatively low levels of maternal involvement with the infant.

Moving into the preschool-age group, researchers have observed mothers with higher levels of depression to interact more negatively with their preschoolers, including disapproval and shouting (Panaccione & Wahler, 1986). Webster-Stratton and Hammond (1988) found that these mothers of 3- to 8-year-old clinic-referred children made more critical statements directed toward their children than did nondepressed mothers.

Affectively charged negative statements were also characteristic of depressed mothers of 8- to 10-year old children (Goodman et al., 1994). Using a modified Expressed Emotion coding system, mothers with a history of depressive episodes,

compared to well mothers, were found to significantly more often describe their child using negative characterizations, indicating maternal disapproval, dislike, and/or rejection. Moreover, rates of childhood disorder were highest among children of those depressed mothers who expressed affectively charged negative attitudes, relative both to depressed mothers who did not express these attitudes and to well mothers.

Hops and colleagues (1987) collected extensive observation data in the homes of maritally distressed or nondistressed depressed or nondepressed women, carefully coding interaction sequences of exchanges between the women, their husbands, and children. Depressed mothers displayed higher rates of dysphoric affect and lower rates of happy affect than did nondepressed mothers. Moreover, Hops and colleagues interpreted their results as suggesting that the mothers' sadness served to suppress aggressive affect by other family members and the latter behavior suppressed mothers' dysphoric affect. Although functional in the short run, the patterns were seen as mutually aversive interchanges with maladaptive long-term consequences.

Finally, the most extensive analysis of direct interactions of depressed mothers and their school-age children has been reported by Hammen and her colleagues, who conducted systematic observations of a conflict discussion task involving unipolar depressed women and their children, as well as similar pairs from bipolar, medically ill, and normal families. Gordon and colleagues (1989) found the unipolar depressed women to be the most negative and critical, the least positive and confirming, and to have the most difficulty sustaining the task focus compared to all three other groups. Moreover, the negativity of the mother–child interaction predicted the children's diagnosis of depression, school behavior, and academic performance at a 6-month follow-up assessment (Burge & Hammen, 1991; Hammen, Burge, & Stansbury, 1990).

Results of causal modeling analyses revealed a more reciprocal picture in which characteristics of both the mother and child influenced their interactions with each other (Hammen et al., 1990). Moreover, Conrad and Hammen (1989) found that mothers with more than one child interacted more negatively with the child who actually had behavior problems than with their other children whose behaviors were "normal." This finding underscores the likelihood that depressed mothers are not invariably dysfunctional in their parenting roles. Rather, while they may have problems with their difficult children, they appear to interact relatively positively with their well-functioning children. Finally, Hammen, Burge, and Adrian (1991) noted a significant association in the timing of symptoms between mothers and children over a longitudinal course. The symptoms of the mothers and children apparently affected the other person. All of these findings are consistent with a reciprocal model of the depressed mother–child relationship in which each person affects the other.

Another contribution of the Hammen studies has been to examine the predictors of maternal interaction quality. Burge and Hammen (1991), for example, demonstrated that whereas chronic stress was uniquely related to the affective quality of the interaction, depressed mood was especially related to task productivity. Thus, women who are stressed due to chronic aversive conditions may be relatively more critical and impatient with their children. On the other hand, women whose mood is depressed seem to be unable or unwilling to stay focused on resolving a conflict.

Caveat: The Nature of Nurture

In interpreting the findings on impairment of parental functioning in depressed women, many researchers have limited themselves to environmental constructs. Thus, poor parenting is conceptualized as evidence of a negative environmental influence on children's development. Yet, it has become increasingly clear over the past decade that genetic factors contribute to a variety of measures that typically are conceptualized as environmental. Indeed, the "nature of nurture" has been the subject of two recent books (Plomin, 1994; Wachs, 1992). Using human quantitative genetic methods such as family, adoption, and twin studies, researchers have demonstrated that genetic factors contribute to both self-reported (Plomin, Reiss, Hetherington, & Howe, 1994; Rowe, 1983) and observed "environmental measures" (Braungart, 1994; O'Connor, Hetherington, Reiss, & Plomin, 1995). In these studies, adopted identical (MZ) twins were found to be more similar to each other than were adopted fraternal (DZ) twins in several aspects of their family environments, even though both types of twins had been reared in different families. In fact, almost one-quarter of the variance in perceived or observed family environment could be accounted for by genetic differences among the children (O'Connor et al., 1995; Plomin et al., 1994).

Overall, these findings provide support for a major role of nongenetic environmental influences of maternal depression on child functioning. Nevertheless, a clear implication of these studies is that unless parenting and other family environment measures, and their associations with adverse outcome, are studied in a genetic design, their effects cannot be presumed to be purely environmental.

ISSUES IN THE STUDY OF CHILDREN WITH DEPRESSED PARENTS

Despite the wealth of research on children with depressed parents that has accumulated in the last two decades, con-

clusions that can be drawn are limited by several unresolved issues. In this section, we will discuss some of these issues and offer suggestions for future research.

Specificity of Outcomes to Children with Depressed Parents

There are several reasons to suspect that the child outcomes *associated* with parental depression may not be *specific* to depression. First, many of the studies of the effects of maternal depression did not include as control groups either parents with another psychiatric disorder or parents with no disorder but with high levels of stress or marital problems. Given high rates of comorbidity among disorders (e.g., Gotlib & Cane, 1989), as well as high correlations between depression and stress (e.g., Rutter & Quinton, 1984), it should not be surprising that similar problems are found in the children of schizophrenic, depressed, and other-psychiatrically disturbed parents, as well as in children exposed to parents' marital distress or divorce and general social disadvantage (Gotlib & Avison, 1993).

Second, as we reviewed earlier, a small number of studies have examined the specificity to parental depression of problematic child functioning. Interestingly, the results of these investigations suggest that child dysfunction is not associated specifically with parental unipolar depression. Hammen and colleagues (1987), Turner and coworkers (1987), and Lee and Gotlib (1989a, 1989b), for example, all found child difficulties to be associated not only with maternal unipolar depression, but with bipolar depression, anxiety disorder, and general maternal psychopathology as well. Moreover, as we also noted earlier, there is a large literature demonstrating that offspring of schizophrenic parents are also characterized by cognitive and emotional disturbance. It appears, therefore, that there is little specificity of child dysfunction to unipolar depression, at least as these constructs have been assessed in research to date. As we outline in greater detail below, it may be more profitable for researchers in this area to move away from examining the effects of discrete diagnostic categories in parents and to begin assessing aspects of psychopathology that may be common to a number of specific psychiatric disorders.

In this context, studies have not been designed to test the importance of symptom dimensions and level of impairment that may cut across psychiatric disorders and that may be differentially associated with child outcomes. With regard to symptoms, there is a clear need to give further attention to dimensional, as opposed to typological or categorical, aspects of the parents' psychiatric disorders in order to describe the symptom cluster for individuals, namely, the extent to which an abnormal behavior such as anhedonia may characterize both individuals with schizophrenia and individuals with depression (Cudeck, Mednick, Schulsinger, & Schulsinger, 1984).

With regard to impairment, few researchers have attended to levels of adaptive functioning in the parents, that is, the extent to which the parents are effectively managing family and work responsibilities, are involved in a social network, and so forth. (Goodman, Sewell, Cooley, & Leavitt, 1993; Gotlib & Lee, 1989). More socially impaired parents: (1) may be the most disturbed (higher genetic loading for the disorder); (2) may be more often separated from their children due to hospitalizations; (3) may provide less adequate models for healthy social functioning for their children; and (4) may neglect to provide adequately for the needs of the children.

Perhaps most intriguing is the fact that a number of researchers have found a striking similarity in the emotional unavailability or unresponsiveness of parents who exhibit any of several forms of psychopathology (e.g, depression, anxiety, alcoholism, schizophrenia), of parents experiencing marital distress, and of parents experiencing general social disadvantage (e.g., Gotlib & Avison, 1993; Lee & Gotlib, 1991). Moreover, parental emotional unavailability has been strongly implicated in adverse outcomes for children (Maccoby, 1980). Emotional unavailability and unresponsiveness have been conceptualized as ranging from dysfunctional attachment in mother–infant relationships (Ainsworth et al., 1978) to inadequate parental monitoring of school-age and older children (Loeber & Stouthamer-Loeber, 1986). Thus, it is possible that the association between diverse high-risk family situations (those with depressed, alcoholic, or schizophrenic parents, marital conflict, high stress, and poverty) and the commonality of outcomes (children's development of psychiatric disorders, not only depression, but also conduct and other disorders and other adjustment problems) might be mediated by parental emotional unavailability.

Without sufficient studies with these controls, we caution against any assumption at the present time that there are factors specific to having a depressed parent that produce child problems. Several alternative explanations have been proposed and further study is needed.

Individual Differences within a Group of Depressed Parents: Symptom Clusters, Severity, Chronicity, and Treatment History

Nearly all of the studies reviewed in this chapter can be criticized for sample selection biases with regard to their depressed parent group. Whereas some simply did not adequately describe their sample selection procedures, others did not control for potentially relevant variables. What are the ways that depressed parents may vary that could confound the findings?

First, we have little understanding of the importance of the relative predominance of vegetative symptoms (sleep, energy, and eating disorders), as opposed to cognitive (low self-esteem, low self-confidence, guilt, pessimism) or mood symptoms (depressed, irritable, loss of interest or pleasure), and how they may be differentially associated with child outcome. For example, different symptom clusters may reflect higher genetic loading and may be associated with differences in quality of parenting.

Second, severity, chronicity, and treatment history vary tremendously within a group of depressed adults. Yet much of the research that we have reviewed in this chapter examined subjects who were patients in university hospitals and other treatment settings. There is a pressing need to study the child problems associated with the less severely depressed and first-episode parents who are more likely to be found at outpatient clinics and other primary care settings as well as in untreated community samples.

A related challenge to researchers concerns the episodic nature of depression. Researchers need to clearly describe their depressed sample with respect to whether subjects are currently in episode. An understanding of the interepisodic level of functioning will also prove to be useful.

Finally, more careful control and/or selection on characteristics of the depression are needed. In the absence of such research, we must be cautious about generalizing from the findings discussed in this chapter. Moreover, we expect that studies designed to explore these individual difference dimensions will help to clarify the finding that children of depressed parents exhibit not only elevated rates of depression, but also high levels of conduct disorder and multiple psychiatric diagnoses. Greater attention to differences within a group of depressed parents may help to identify patterns that are differentially associated with, for example, internalizing as opposed to externalizing disorders in the children.

Moderators of the Association between Parental Depression and Child Outcome

Few of the studies reviewed here question whether there are variables that may strengthen or diminish the association between parental depression and child outcome. Among the variables that would likely be important to consider are characteristics of the child, such as age, gender, temperament, intelligence, and social–cognitive skill level, and characteristics of the family such as race, socioeconomic status, and the presence and mental health of the spouse.

In this context, the age of the child as a possible moderator of the association between parental depression and child outcome warrants further discussion. As we noted earlier, there has been a surprising lack of attention to developmental considerations in this area of study. Researchers have tended to study children of depressed parents either in one developmental period or in such a broad range of children's ages that two or more distinct developmental stages were included. Both strategies fail to address developmental issues (Goodman, 1992). It is unlikely that conclusions drawn from studies of children in one developmental stage can be generalized to another (Goodman et al., 1993a). Moreover, knowledge of the underlying developmental processes in risk for psychopathology is critical in the study of the etiology of depression occurring in childhood (Cicchetti & Schneider-Rosen, 1986; Digdon & Gotlib, 1985), in gaining a better understanding of the development of any disorder or problem in social–emotional development and in the design of preventive interventions (Goodman, 1984). Indeed, at present we cannot even state with certainty whether children are more protected from adverse outcomes if they are older at the time of first exposure to the mother's depression.

Among other possible moderators, there is some evidence to suggest that children with depressed mothers may be somewhat protected against adverse outcome if they have higher IQ (Radke-Yarrow & Sherman, 1990; Rutter, 1979), better social–cognitive skills (Beardslee, Schultz, & Selman, 1987; Downey & Walker, 1989), easier temperament (Bates, Maslin, & Frankel, 1985; Cutrona & Troutman, 1986), a psychiatrically well father (Carro et al., 1993; Goodman et al., 1993a), an intact parental marriage (Goodman et al., 1993a), if they are not in poverty or of minority status (Belle, 1982; Lyons-Ruth, Zoll, Connell, & Grunebaum, 1986), and if they are female, although that may vary by age of child (Cummings, Lanott, & Zahn-Waxler, 1985). However, few of these studies involved direct tests of hypothesized moderators and few of the findings have been replicated. Finally, from a somewhat different perspective, as we have noted throughout this chapter, it is also now imperative that investigators begin to examine the impact on children's functioning of programs designed to prevent or treat maternal depression.

Reliability of Depressed Parents' Self-Reports

Not only is there great variability in the samples of these studies, but there is also considerable variability in their methods, and this further contributes to the tentativeness of these summaries. One recurring methodological issue concerns the comparability of interview and self-reports of parents and children. Specifically, the reliability of depressed parents' reports on their children has been questioned. For example, Kashani, Orvaschel, Burk, and Reid (1985) found that depressed parents underreport depression in their children, but overreport oppositional and attentional problems. However, we should note that the trend in the study of child psychopathology is toward greater reliance on structured interviews with children as well as in obtaining teacher reports and conducting observations of the children. In the interest of comparison and comparability of findings, researchers examining the children of depressed parents would do well to include these approaches in their studies.

SUMMARY AND CONCLUSIONS

We believe that we are currently at the point of diminishing returns with respect to simple demonstrations that the offspring of depressed or psychiatric parents have high rates of disorder and exhibit other difficulties in their psychosocial functioning. It is now time that we focus our efforts on elucidating the *mechanisms* or *processes* underlying the relation between maternal psychiatric disturbance and child dysfunction (e.g., Goodman, 1992; Goodman & Gotlib, in press; Gotlib & Lee, 1991b) as well as the temporal relation between these two constructs. In this context, there are a number of promising directions for study.

First, several investigators have found that individuals experiencing unipolar depression are characterized by a heightened state of self-focused attention (e.g., Ingram, Lumry, Cruet, & Seiber, 1987; Pyszczynski & Greenberg, 1987). These may be individuals whose symptom pattern reflects a predominance of cognitive, as opposed to vegetative or mood, symptoms. One obvious effect of an increased self-focus in depressed parents would be a relative lack of awareness and responsivity of the parents to the emotional needs of their children. Prolonged parental self-focus, therefore, and the consequent unavailability of the parent, may be one mechanism through which difficulties in children's adjustment are established (cf. Gotlib & Avison, 1993; Lee & Gotlib, 1991b).

Second, as we noted earlier, recent direct observations of families with depressed parents suggest that depressive symptoms may be functional in reducing aversive exchanges among family members (e.g., Hops et al., 1987; Kochanska et al., 1987). If this is in fact the case, children's mastery of appropriate conflict-resolution and affect-regulation skills would be disrupted, leading to problems in adjustment.

Therefore, future research might profitably focus on these mastery issues in the offspring of depressed parents.

Third, given both these possibilities, it will be important in future studies to examine the effects on the children's functioning of various forms of treatment for depression in the mothers. To date, there are no studies that have examined the effects of preventions or interventions for depression on the behavior and functioning of the patients' children. It is clear, however, that if treatment affects the processes that may mediate the relation between maternal depression and child maladjustment, intervention for depression should have positive effects on the children, although this almost certainly will be a function of the developmental stage of the children and the frequency and duration of the mothers' depressive episodes.

Fourth, as we also noted earlier, the results of several investigations suggest that a common pathway from the exposure of the children to a wide range of parental and marital problems (e.g., parents' depression, parents' personality disorder, marital discord, economic distress) to child outcome involves the association of each of these types of problems with inadequate parenting. However, inadequate parenting can take more than one form. It will be important for future studies to identify the specific aspects of parental depression and its correlates that are differentially associated with neglectful parenting (unresponsive, uninvolved, inadequate monitoring) and aversive parenting (overcontrolling, aggressive, or abusive behavior).

Fifth, children's risk might best be conceptualized within the context of a stress-diathesis model. That is, being the offspring of a depressed parent may put children at biological risk for depression and other disorders, as we have reviewed. That predisposition to the development of psychopathology, however, may manifest itself only in the face of major stressors. This is a particularly cogent argument given the mounting evidence that parental depression is associated with multiple precipitating, concomitant, and consequential stressors, including poverty, job loss, and economic stress (Belle, 1982) and marital discord, conflict, and divorce (Biglan et al., 1985; Gotlib & Whiffen, 1989; Gotlib & Hooley, 1988; Ruscher & Gotlib, 1988). Moreover, it is increasingly understood that stressors tend to co-occur, and that the risk to children of exposure to multiple stressors increases in a multiplicative rather than in an additive manner (Rutter & Quinton, 1977; Sameroff, 1987).

Finally, we strongly suspect that the future of this area of investigation lies in elucidation of the different pathways that may link parental depression and specific child outcomes. As suggested by Quinton and Rutter (1985), despite the seemingly similar risks to children of parents who differ in psychiatric disorder, not all forms of parental disturbance

necessarily give rise to psychiatric risks for children in the same way. Thus, while it remains for future studies to examine more explicitly the viability of alternative explanations in accounting for the significant association of maternal psychiatric disorder and child dysfunction, we must remain cognizant of the possibility that there may be more than one path linking parent depression and child dysfunction.

REFERENCES

Ainsworth, M. D. S., Blehar, M. C., Waters, E., & Wall, S. (1978). *Patterns of attachment: A psychological study of the strange situation.* Hillsdale, N.J.: Erlbaum.

Ainsworth, M. D. S., & Wittig, B. A. (1969). Attachment and exploratory behavior of one-year-olds in a strange situation. In B. M. Foss (Ed.), *Determinants of infant behavior* (Vol. 4, pp. 111–136). London: Methuen.

American Psychiatric Association. (1994). *Diagnostic and statistical manual of mental disorders* (4th ed.). Washington, DC: Author.

Anderson, K. O., Bradley, L. A., Young, L. D., McDaniel, L. K., & Wise, C. M. (1985). Rheumatoid arthritis: Review of psychological factors related to etiology, effects, and treatment. *Psychological Bulletin, 98,* 358–387.

Barnett, P. A., & Gotlib, I. H. (1988). Psychosocial functioning and depression: Distinguishing among antecedents, concomitants, and consequences. *Psychological Bulletin, 104,* 97–126.

Bates, J. E., Maslin, C. A., & Frankel, K. A. (1985). Attachment security, mother-child interaction, and temperament as predictors of behavior problem ratings at age three years. *Monographs of the Society for Research in Child Development, 50* (No. 1–2), 167–193.

Beardslee, W. R., Schultz, L. H., & Selman, R. L. (1987). Level of social-cognitive development, adaptive functioning, and DSM-III diagnoses in adolescent offspring of parents with affective disorders: Implications for the development of the capacity for mutuality. *Developmental Psychology, 23,* 807–815.

Belle, D. (Ed.) (1982). *Lives in stress.* Beverly Hills: Sage.

Belsher, G., & Costello, C. G. (1988). Relapse after recovery from unipolar depression: A critical review. *Psychological Bulletin, 104,* 84–96.

Bettes, B. A. (1988). Maternal depression and motherese: Temporal and intonational features. *Child Development, 59,* 1089–1096.

Biglan, A., Hops, H., Sherman, L., Friedman, L. S., Arthur, J., & Osteen, V. (1985). Problem-solving interactions of depressed women and their husbands. *Behavior Therapy, 16,* 431–451.

Billings, A. G. & Moos, R. (1983). Comparison of children of depressed and nondepressed parents: A social environmental perspective. *Journal of Abnormal Child Psychology, 11,* 483–486.

Billings, A. G., & Moos, R. H. (1986). Children of parents with unipolar depression: A controlled one year follow-up. *Journal of Abnormal Child Psychology, 14,* 149–166.

Braungart, J. M. (1994). Genetic influence on "environmental" measures. In J. C. DeFries, R. Plomin, & D. W. Fulker (Eds.), *Nature and Nurture during Middle Childhood.* Cambridge, MA: Blackwell.

Brewin, C. R., Andrews, B., & Gotlib, I. H. (1993). Psychopathology and early experience: A reappraisal of retrospective reports. *Psychological Bulletin, 113,* 82–98.

Breznitz, Z., & Sherman, T. (1987). Speech patterning of natural discourse of well and depressed mothers and their young children. *Child Development, 58,* 395–400.

Burge, D., & Hammen, C. (1991). Maternal communication: Predictors of outcome at follow-up in a sample of children at high and low risk for depression. *Journal of Abnormal Psychology, 100,* 174–180.

Cantwell, D. P. (1983). Depression in childhood: Clinical picture and diagnostic criteria. In D. P. Cantwell & G. A. Carlson (Eds.), *Affective disorders in childhood and adolescence: An update* (pp. 3–18). New York: Spectrum.

Carlson, G. A., & Strober, M. (1983). Affective disorders in adolescence. In D. P. Cantwell & G. A. Carlson (Eds.), *Affective disorders in childhood and adolescence: An update* (pp. 85–96). New York: Spectrum.

Carro, M. G., Grant, K. E., Gotlib, I. H., & Compas, B. E. (1993). Postpartum depression and child development: An investigation of mothers and fathers as sources of risk and resilience. *Development and Psychopathology, 5,* 567–579.

Cicchetti, D., & Schneider-Rosen, K. (1986). An organizational approach to childhood depression. In M. Rutter, C. E. Izard, & P. E. Read (Eds.), *Depression in young people* (pp. 71–134). New York: Guilford Press.

Cohn, J. F., Campbell, S. B., Matias, R., & Hopkins, J. (1990). Face-to-face interactions of postpartum depressed and nondepressed mother–infant pairs at 2 months. *Developmental Psychology, 23,* 583–592.

Cohn, J. F., Matias, R., Tronick, E., Connell, D., & Lyons-Ruth, K. (1986). Face-to-face interactions of depressed mothers and their infants. In E. Tronick & T. Field (Eds.), *Maternal depression and infant disturbance.* (New Directions for Child Development, No. 34, pp. 31–46). San Francisco: Jossey-Bass.

Cohn, J. F., & Tronick, E. Z. (1983). Three-month-old infants' reaction to simulated maternal depression. *Child Development, 54,* 185–193.

Conrad, M., & Hammen, C. (1989). Role of maternal depression in perceptions of child maladjustment. *Journal of Consulting and Clinical Psychology, 57,* 663–667.

Cudeck, R., Mednick, S. A., Schulsinger, F., & Schulsinger, H. (1984). A multidimensional approach to the identification of schizophrenia. In N. F. Watt, E. J. Anthony, L. C. Wynne, & J. E. Rolf (Eds.), *Children at risk for schizophrenia: A longitudinal perspective* (pp. 43–70). Cambridge, England: Cambridge University Press.

Cummings, E. M., Lanott, R. J., & Zahn-Waxler, C. (1985). Influence of conflict between adults on the emotions and aggression of young children. *Developmental Psychology, 21,* 495–507.

Cutrona, C. E., & Troutman, B. R. (1986). Social support, infant temperament, and parenting self-efficacy: A mediational model of postpartum depression. *Child Development, 57,* 1507–1518.

Digdon, N., & Gotlib, I. H. (1985). Developmental considerations in the study of childhood depression. *Developmental Review, 5,* 162–199.

Downey, G., & Walker, E. (1989). Social cognition and adjustment in children at risk for psychopathology. *Developmental Psychology, 25,* 835–845.

Field, T. M. (1984). Early interactions between infants and their postpartum depressed mothers. *Infant Behavior and Development, 7,* 517–522.

Field, T., Healy, B., Goldstein, S., & Guthertz, M. (1990). Behavior-state matching and synchrony in mother–infant interactions of nondepressed versus depressed dyads. *Developmental Psychology, 26,* 7–14.

Field, T., Healy, B., Goldstein, S., Perry, S., Bendell, D., Schanberg, S., Zimmerman, E. A., & Kuhn, C. (1988). Infants of depressed mothers show "depressed" behavior even with nondepressed adults. *Child Development, 59,* 1569–1579.

Field, T., Sandberg, D., Garcia, R., Vega-Lahr, N., Goldstein, S., & Guy, L. (1985). Pregnancy problems, postpartum depression and early mother–infant interactions. *Developmental Psychology, 21,* 1152–1156.

Fleming, A., Ruble, D., Flett, G., & Shaul, D. (1988). Postpartum adjustment in first-time mothers: Relations between mood, maternal attitudes, and mother–infant interactions. *Developmental Psychology, 24,* 71–81.

Frank, E., Carpenter, L. L., & Kupfer, D. J. (1988). Sex differences in recurrent depression: Are there any that are significant? *American Journal of Psychiatry, 145,* 41–45.

Garmezy, N. (1971). Vulnerability research and the issue of primary prevention. *American Journal of Orthopsychiatry, 41,* 101–116.

Ghodsian, M., Zayicek, E., & Wolkind, S. (1984). A longitudinal study of maternal depression and child behavior problems. *Journal of Child Psychology and Psychiatry, 25,* 91–109.

Goodman, S. H. (1984). Children of disturbed parents: The interface between research and intervention. *American Journal of Community Psychology, 12,* 663–687.

Goodman, S. H. (1992). Understanding the effects of depressed mothers on their children. In E. F. Walker, R. H. Dworkin, & B. A. Cornblatt (1992). *Progress in experimental personality and psychopathology research* (pp. 47–109). New York: Springer.

Goodman, S. H., Adamson, L. B., Riniti, J., & Cole, S. (1994). Mothers' expressed attitudes: Associations with maternal depression and children's self-esteem and psychopathology. *Journal of the American Academy of Child and Adolescent Psychiatry, 33,* 1265–1274.

Goodman, S. H., Brogan, D., Lynch, M. E., & Fielding, B. (1993a). Social and emotional competence in children of depressed mothers. *Child Development, 64,* 516–531,

Goodman, S. H., & Brumley, H. E. (1990). Schizophrenic and depressed mothers: Relational deficits in parenting. *Developmental Psychology, 26,* 31–39.

Goodman, S. H., & Gotlib, J. H. (in press). Risk for psychopathology in the children of depressed mothers: A developmental model for understanding mechanisms of transmission. *Psychological Review.*

Goodman, S. H., Sewell, D. R., Cooley, E. L., & Leavitt, N. (1993b). Assessing levels of adaptive functioning: The Role Functioning Scale. *Community Mental Health Journal, 29,* 119–131.

Gordon, D., Burge, D., Hammen, C., Adrian, C., Jaenicke, C., & Hiroto, D. (1989). Observations of interactions of depressed women with their children. *American Journal of Psychiatry, 146,* 50–55.

Gotlib, I. H. (1994). The effects of maternal depression on infant behavior and development: A longitudinal perspective. In W. R. Avison (Chair), *Family stress and children's mental health.* Symposium presented at the Fifth International Conference on Social Stress Research, Honolulu, HI.

Gotlib, I. H., & Avison, W. R. (1993). Children at risk for psychopathology. In C. G. Costello (Ed.), *Basic issues in psychopathology* (pp. 271–319). New York: Guilford Press.

Gotlib, I. H., & Beach, S. R.H. (1995). A marital/family discord model of depression: Implications for therapeutic intervention. In N. S. Jacobson & A. S. Gurman (Eds.), *Clinical handbook of couple therapy* (pp. 411–436). New York: Guilford Press.

Gotlib, I. H., & Cane, D. B. (1989). Self-report assessment of depression and anxiety. In P. C. Kendall & D. Watson (Eds.), *Anxiety and depression: Distinctive and overlapping features* (pp. 131–169). Orlando, FL: Academic Press.

Gotlib, I. H., Gilboa, E., & Somerfeld, B. K. (in press). Cognitive functioning in depression: Nature and origins. In R. J. Davidson (Ed.), *Wisconsin Symposium on Emotion (Vol. 1).* New York: Oxford University Press.

Gotlib, I. H., & Hammen, C. L. (1992). *Psychological aspects of depression: Toward a cognitive–interpersonal integration.* Chichester: Wiley.

Gotlib, I. H., & Hooley, J. M. (1988). Depression and marital distress: Current status and future directions. In S. Duck (Ed.), *Handbook of personal relationships* (pp. 543–570). Chichester: Wiley.

Gotlib, I. H., & Lee, C. M. (1989). The social functioning of depressed patients: A longitudinal assessment. *Journal of Social and Clinical Psychology, 8,* 223–237.

Gotlib, I. H., & Lee, C. M. (1991). Children of depressed mothers: A review and directions for future research. In C. D. McCann & N. S. Endler (Eds.), *Depression: New directions in theory, research, and practice* (pp. 187–208). Toronto: Wall & Thompson.

Gotlib, I. H., Mount, J. H., Cordy, N. I., & Whiffen, V. E. (1988). Depressed mood and perceptions of early parenting: A longitudinal investigation. *British Journal of Psychiatry, 152,* 24–27.

Gotlib, I. H., & Whiffen, V. E. (1989). Depression and marital functioning: An examination of specificity and gender differences. *Journal of Abnormal Psychology, 98,* 23–30.

Gotlib, I. H., Whiffen, V. E., Mount, J. H., Milne, K., & Cordy, N. I. (1989). Prevalence rates and demographic characteristics associated with depression in pregnancy and the postpartum. *Journal of Consulting and Clinical Psychology, 57,* 269–274.

Gotlib, I. H., Whiffen, V. E., Wallace, P. M., & Mount, J. H. (1991). A prospective investigation of postpartum depression: Factors involved in onset and recovery. *Journal of Abnormal Psychology, 100,* 122–132.

Hammen, C., Burge, D., & Adrian, C. (1991). Timing of mother and child depression in a longitudinal study of children at risk. *Journal of Consulting and Clinical Psychology, 59,* 341–345.

Hammen, C., Burge, D., & Stansbury, K. (1990). Relationship of mother and child variables to child outcomes in a high risk sample: A causal modeling analysis. *Developmental Psychology, 26,* 24–30.

Hammen, C., Gordon, D., Burge, D., Adrian, C., Jaenicke, C., & Hiroto, D. (1987). Maternal affective disorders, illness, and stress: Risk for children's psychopathology. *American Journal of Psychiatry, 144,* 736–741.

Harder, D. W., Kokes, R. F., Fisher, L., & Strauss, J. (1980). Child competence and psychiatric risk: IV. Relationships of parent diagnostic classifications and parent psychopathology severity to child functioning. *Journal of Nervous and Mental Diseases, 168,* 343–347.

Hirsch, B. J., Moos, R. H., & Reischl, T. M. (1985). Psychosocial adjustment of adolescent children of a depressed, arthritic, or normal parent. *Journal of Abnormal Psychology, 94,* 154–164.

Hodges, K. K., McKnew, D., Cytryn, L. Stern, L., & Kline, J. (1982). The Child Assessment Schedule (CAS) Diagnostic Interview: A report on reliability and validity. *Journal of the American Academy of Child Psychiatry, 21,* 468–473.

Hops, H., Biglan, A., Sherman, L., Arthur, J., Friedman, L., & Osteen, V. (1987). Home observations of family interactions of depressed women. *Journal of Consulting and Clinical Psychology, 55,* 341–346.

Ingram, R. E., Lumry, A., Cruet, D., & Seiber, W. (1987). Attentional processes in depressive disorders. *Cognitive Therapy and Research, 11,* 351–360.

Kaplan, B. J., Beardslee, W. R., & Keller, M. B. (1987). Intellectual competence in children of depressed parents. *Journal of Clinical Child Psychology, 16,* 158–163.

Kashani, J. H., Orvaschel, H., Burk, J. P., & Reid, J. C. (1985). Depressed children of depressed parents. *Canadian Journal of Psychiatry, 30,* 265–268.

Keller, M. B., Beardslee, W. R., Dorer, D. J., Lavori, P. W., Samuelson, H., & Klerman, G. R. (1986). Impact of severity and chronicity of parental affective illness on adaptive functioning and psychopathology in children. *Archives of General Psychiatry, 43,* 930–937.

Keller, M. B., & Shapiro, R. W. (1981). Major depressive disorder: Initial results from a one-year prospective naturalistic follow-up study. *Journal of Nervous and Mental Disease, 169,* 761–768.

Keller, M. B., Shapiro, R. W., Lavori, P. W., & Wolfe, N. (1982). Recovery in major depressive disorder: Analysis with the life table and regression models. *Archives of General Psychiatry, 39,* 905–910.

Kessler, R. C., McGonagle, K. A., Zhao, S., Nelson, C. B., Hughes, M., Eshleman, S., Wittchen, H-U., & Kendler, K. S. (1994). Lifetime and 12-month prevalence of DSM-III-R psychiatric disorders in the United States. *Archives of General Psychiatry, 51,* 8–19.

Kochanska, G., Kucynski, L., Radke-Yarrow, M., & Welsh, J. D. (1987). Resolutions of conflict episodes between well and affectively ill mothers and their young children. *Journal of Abnormal Child Psychology, 15,* 441–456.

Lee, C. M., & Gotlib, I. H. (1989a). Clinical status and emotional adjustment of children of depressed mothers. *American Journal of Psychiatry, 146,* 478–483.

Lee, C. M., & Gotlib, I. H. (1989b). Maternal depression and child adjustment: A longitudinal analysis. *Journal of Abnormal Psychology, 98,* 78–85.

Lee, C. M., & Gotlib, I. H. (1991a). Adjustment of children of depressed mothers: A ten-month follow-up. *Journal of Abnormal Psychology, 100,* 473–477.

Lee, C. M., & Gotlib, I. H. (1991b). Family disruption, parental availability, and child adjustment: An integrative review. In R. J. Prinz (Ed.), *Advances in the behavioral assessment of children and families* (Vol. 5, pp. 166–199). London: Jessica Kingsley.

Lewinsohn, P. M., & Gotlib, I. H. (1995). Behavioral theory and treatment of depression. In E. E. Beckham & W. R. Leber (Eds.), *Handbook of depression: Treatment, assessment, and research* (2nd ed., pp. 352–375). New York: Guilford Press.

Livingood, A. B., Daen, P., & Smith, B. D. (1983). The depressed mother as a source of stimulation for her infant. *Journal of Clinical Psychology, 39,* 369–375.

Loeber, R., & Stouthamer-Loeber, M. (1986). Family factors as correlates and predictors of delinquency. In M. Tonry & N. Morris (Eds.), *Crime and justice: An annual review of research* (Vol. 7, pp. 29–149). Chicago: University of Chicago Press.

Lyons-Ruth, K., Zoll, D., Connell, D., & Grunebaum, H. U. (1986). The depressed mother and her one-year-old infant: Environmental context, mother–infant interaction and attachment, and infant development. In E. Tronick & T. Field (Eds.), *Maternal depression and infant disturbance: New directions in child development* (pp. 61–82). San Francisco: Jossey-Bass.

Maccoby, E. E. (1980). *Social development.* New York: Harcourt Brace Jovanovich.

McCarthy, D. (1972). *McCarthy Scales of Children's Abilities.* New York: The Psychological Corporation.

Mednick, S. A., & Schulsinger, F. (1968). Some premorbid characteristics related to breakdown in children with schizophrenic mothers. In D. Rosenthal & S. S. Kety (Eds.), *The transmission of schizophrenia* (pp. 267–291). Oxford: Pergamon Press.

Mills, M., Puckering, C., Pound, A., & Cox, A. (1985). What is it about depressed mothers that influences their children's functioning? In J. E. Stevenson (Ed.), *Recent research in developmental psychopathology* (pp. 11–17). Oxford: Pergamon Press.

Murphy, J. M., Monson, R. R., Olivier, D. C., Sobol, A. M., & Leighton, A. H. (1988). Affective disorders and mortality. *Archives of General Psychiatry, 44,* 473–480.

O'Connor, T. G., Hetherington, E. M., Reiss, D., & Plomin, R. (1995). A twin-sibling study of observed parent-adolescent interactions. *Child Development, 66,* 812–829.

Orvaschel, H., Puig-Antich, J., Chambers, W. J., Tabrizi, M. A., & Johnson, R. (1982). Retrospective assessment of child psychopathology with the K-SADS-E. *Journal of the American Academy of Child Psychiatry, 4,* 392–397.

Orvaschel. H., Walsh-Allis, G., & Ye, W. (1988). Psychopathology in children of parents with recurrent depression. *Journal of Abnormal Child Psychology, 16,* 17–28.

Panaccione, V. F., & Wahler, R. G. (1986). Child behavior, maternal depression, and social coercion as factors in the quality of child care. *Journal of Abnormal Child Psychology, 14,* 263–278.

Parker, G. (1981). Parental reports of depressives: An investigation of several explanations. *Journal of Affective Disorders, 3,* 131–140.

Plomin, R. (1994). *Genetics and experience: The interplay between nature and nurture.* Thousand Oaks, CA: Sage.

Plomin, R., McClearn, G. E., Pedersen, N. L., Nesselroade, J. R., & Bergeman, C. S. (1988). Genetic influence on childhood family environment perceived retrospectively from the last half of the life span. *Developmental Psychology, 24,* 738–745.

Plomin, R., Reiss, D., Hetherington, E. M., & Howe, G. (1994). Nature and nurture: Genetic contributions to measures of the family environment. *Developmental Psychology, 30,* 32–43.

Pyszczynski, T., & Greenberg, J. (1987). Self-regulatory perseveration and the depressive self-focusing style: A self-awareness theory of reactive depression. *Psychological Bulletin, 102,* 122–138.

Quinton, D., & Rutter, M. (1985). Family pathology and child psychiatric disorder: A four-year prospective study. In A. R. Nicol (Ed.), *Longitudinal studies in child psychology and psychiatry* (pp. 91–134). Chichester: Wiley.

Radke-Yarrow, M., Cummings, E. M., Kuczynski, L., & Chapman, M. (1985). Patterns of attachment in two- and three-year-olds in normal families and families with parental depression. *Child Development, 56,* 884–893.

Radke-Yarrow, M., & Nottleman, E. D. (1989, April). *Affective development in children of well and depressed mothers.* Paper presented at Society for Research in Child Development, Kansas City, MO.

Radke-Yarrow, M. & Sherman, T. (1990). Hard growing: Children who survive. In J. Rolf, A. Masten, D. Cicchetti, K. Nuechterlein, & S. Weintraub (Eds.), *Risk and protective factors in the development of psychopathology.* Cambridge, England: Cambridge University Press.

Rosenthal, D. (1970). *Genetic theory and abnormal behavior.* New York: McGraw-Hill.

Rowe, D. C. (1983). A biometrical analysis of perceptions of family environment: A study of twin and singleton sibling kinships. *Child Development, 54,* 416–423.

Ruscher, S. M., & Gotlib, I. H. (1988). Marital interaction patterns of couples with and without a depressed partner. *Behavior Therapy, 19,* 455–470.

Rutter, M. (1979). Protective factors in children's responses to stress and disadvantage. In M. W. Kent & J. E. Rolf (Eds.), *Primary prevention of psychopathology: Vol. 3: Social competence in children* (pp. 49–74). Hanover, NH: University Press of New England.

Rutter, M., & Quinton, D. (1977). Psychiatric disorder: Ecological factors and concepts of causation. In H. McGurk (Ed.), *Ecological factors in human development.* Amsterdam, The Netherlands: North-Holland.

Rutter, M., & Quinton, D. (1984). Parental psychiatric disorder: Effects on children. *Psychological Medicine, 14,* 853–880.

Sameroff, A. J. (1987). Transactional risk factors and prevention. In J. A. Steinberg and M. M. Silverman (Eds.), *Preventing mental disorders: A research perspective.* Rockville, MD: Department of Health and Human Services.

Sameroff, A. J., Barocas, R., & Seifer, R. (1984). The early development of children born to mentally ill women (pp. 482–514). In N. R. Watt, E. J. Anthony, L. C. Wynne, & J. E. Rolf (Eds.), *Children at risk for schizophrenia: A longitudinal perspective.* Cambridge, England: Cambridge University Press.

Tsuang, M. T. & Faraone, S. V. (1990). *The genetics of mood disorders.* Baltimore: Johns Hopkins University Press.

Turner, S. M., Beidel, D. C., & Costello, A. (1987). Psychopathology in the offspring of anxiety disorder patients. *Journal of Consulting and Clinical Psychology, 55,* 229–235.

Wachs, T. D. (1992). *The nature of nurture.* Newbury Park, CA: Sage.

Warner, V., Weissman, M. M., Fendrich, M., Wickramaratne, P., & Moreau, D. (1992). The course of major depression in the offspring of depressed parents: Incidence, recurrence, and recovery. *Archives of General Psychiatry, 49,* 795–801.

Watt, N. R., Anthony, E. J., Wynne, L. C., & Rolf, J. E. (Eds.). (1984). *Children at risk for schizophrenia: A longitudinal perspective.* Cambridge, England: Cambridge University Press.

Webster-Stratton, C., & Hammond, M. (1988). Maternal depression and its relationship to life stress, perceptions of child behavior problems, parenting behaviors, and child conduct problems. *Journal of Abnormal Child Psychology, 16,* 299–315.

Weintraub, S., & Neale, J. M. (1984). The Stony Brook High-Risk Project. In N. R. Watt, E. J. Anthony, L. C. Wynne, & J. E. Rolf (Eds.), *Children at risk for schizophrenia: A longitudinal perspective* (pp. 243–263). Cambridge, England: Cambridge University Press.

Weissman, M. M., & Paykel, E. S. (1974). *The depressed woman: A study of social relationships.* Chicago: University of Chicago Press.

Weissman, M. M., Prusoff, B. A., Gammon, G. D., Merikangas, K. R., Leckman, J. F., & Kidd, K. K. (1984). Psychopathology in the children (ages 6–18) of depressed and normal parents. *Journal of the American Academy of Child Psychiatry, 23,* 78–84.

Welner, Z., Welner, A., McCrary, M., & Leonard, M. A. (1977). Psychopathology in children of inpatients with depression: A controlled study. *Journal of Nervous and Mental Disease, 164,* 408–413.

Werner, E. E. (1989). High-risk children in young adulthood: A longitudinal study from birth to 32 years. *American Journal of Orthopsychiatry, 59,* 72–81.

Whiffen, V. E. (1988). Vulnerability to postpartum depression: A prospective multivariate study. *Journal of Abnormal Psychology, 97,* 467–474.

Whiffen, V. E., & Gotlib, I. H. (1989). Infants of postpartum depressed mothers: Temperament and cognitive status. *Journal of Abnormal Psychology, 98,* 274–279.

Whiffen, V. E., & Gotlib, I. H. (1991). *Assessing the effects of postpartum depression on infant cognitive and socio emotional development.* Presented at the Annual Meeting of the Canadian Psychological Association, Calgary.

Wynne, L. C. (1984). The University of Rochester Child and Family Study: Overview of Research Plan (pp. 335–347). In N. R. Watt, E. J. Anthony, L. C. Wynne, & J. E. Rolf (Eds.), *Children at risk for schizophrenia: A longitudinal perspective.* Cambridge, England: Cambridge University Press.

Yarrow, M. R., Campbell, J. D., & Burton, R. V. (1970). Recollections of childhood: A study of the retrospective method. *Monographs of The Society for Research on Child Development, 35,* (No. 5).

Zahn-Waxler, C., Cummings, E. M., Iannotti, R. J., & Radke-Yarrow, M. (1984). Young children of depressed parents: A population at risk for affective problems. In D. Cicchetti (Ed.), *Childhood depression* (New Directions for Child Development, No. 26, pp. 81–105). San Francisco: Jossey-Bass.

CHAPTER 26

CHILDREN OF PARENTS WITH MEDICAL ILLNESS

Jack W. Finney
Kathryn M. Miller

The family context has increasingly been recognized as a crucial determinant of children's physical health and psychological development (Drotar, 1994; Finney & Bonner, 1992). Physical illness represents one aspect of the family context that may impact children. Illness, especially chronic illness, imposes many burdens and challenges on the patient and the family and has the potential to disrupt individual as well as family functioning. Although there is an abundance of literature documenting the impact of child illness on the family and the impact of illness on the adult patient and his or her spouse, the impact of parental health on children remains a neglected area in family-centered research (Drotar, 1994).

THE NATURE OF THE IMPACT

Although the nature of the impact of parental illness on children has not been fully described in the extant literature, it has been suggested that behavioral and adjustment problems may emerge as children attempt to integrate parental illness into their everyday life. For example, particular fears could arise or be exacerbated in children through exposure to parental illness, including fear of abandonment triggered by acute symptoms or hospitalizations, fear of parental disabil-

ity or death, and fear that the disease will happen to them (Kornblum & Anderson, 1985). It is also possible that children may experience concerns that they are somehow responsible for their parent's illness and/or well-being (Christ et al., 1993; Glass, 1985; Kornblum & Anderson, 1985).

For example, Christ and colleagues (1993) gathered and analyzed data from a comprehensive pre-death assessment conducted with children as part of their participation in a psychoeducational intervention for children confronting parental death from cancer. Pre-death assessment interviews were conducted with eighty-seven children between the ages of 7 and 11 whose parents were in the terminal stage of cancer. Among the common fears and concerns revealed through the interviews included fears of the symptoms (e.g., vomiting, bleeding, hair and weight loss), which often resulted in somatic reactions from the child, fears of death, a sense of guilt and responsibility for their parent's illness, and concerns about the vulnerability of the well parent. Misconceptions regarding the illness and its treatment were also common. Behavioral distress was often manifested as sleep disorders, somatic complaints, difficulty concentrating and completing assignments at school, increased conflict with parents and siblings, and conflict or withdrawal from peers and adults.

In addition to describing the nature of children's reactions to parental illness, it is important to evaluate whether these children differ significantly from children with healthy parents. Siegel and coworkers (1992), for example, evaluated the psychosocial adjustment of sixty-two children, ages 7 to 16, with a terminally ill parent (advanced cancer) as compared to children in a community sample. Both self-report and parent-based reports revealed poorer adjustment among children with a terminally ill parent when compared with control children. Specifically, children with a terminally ill parent reported greater levels of depressive and anxious symptoms and lower levels of self-esteem than did control children. Ill parents also reported significantly higher behavior problems in their children for both internalizing and externalizing problems and significantly lower social and school competence. Moreover, not only did they score significantly different than control children on these measures, but a higher proportion of children with a terminally ill parent also scored in the clinical range for depression, behavior problems, and social and school competence. Whereas the present findings provide some evidence that children exposed to parental illness differ from control children, it is important to recognize that children in this study were dealing with a terminal illness in a parent. It is unclear whether all types of parental chronic illness would result in similar outcomes. Thus, although these findings need further validation, they suggest that children's emotional well-being during serious parental illness warrants increased professional and familial attention (Siegel et al., 1992).

In another study that assessed multiple areas of family functioning among families with a mother with chronic pain, diabetes, or no illness, objective data were collected regarding the impact of parental chronic pain on children ages 7 to 13 (Dura & Beck, 1988). No significant differences were revealed among groups in terms of children's level of social skills, behavior problems, school absenteeism, maternal health rating, and illness complaints during the 2 weeks prior to the study. However, the authors reported a trend for children from families with a mother with chronic pain to have lower social skills and higher behavior problem ratings, lower rated health, greater school absenteeism, and greater illness complaints than children from no-illness families. Children of mothers with diabetes consistently fell between these two groups. In addition, children from families with a mother with chronic pain also reported significantly more depressive symptoms than children from no-illness families. Again children of diabetic mothers scored between the chronic pain and no-illness families, with no significant difference from either. Significant differences were also not found for self-reported state or trait anxiety among the three groups. The authors conclude that generally speaking it seems that children of mothers with no illness appear physically healthier and better adjusted than children of mothers with diabetes, who, in turn, appear healthier and better adjusted than children of mothers with chronic pain.

In addition to the deleterious outcomes that may arise as a result of parental illness, the potential for positive outcomes also exists. For example, children may develop a more sophisticated range of coping skills as a result of dealing with their parent's illness. Thus, research aimed at understanding the effects of parental illness on children is warranted both by the clinical relevance of parental health problems for children as well as the conceptualization of parental illness as a family experience, of which children are an integral part. The need for research in this area is further highlighted by the substantial number of children exposed to parental illness (Drotar, 1994) and the potential for parents to downplay the psychological impact of parental illness on their child (Kornblum & Anderson, 1985; Niebuhr, Hughes, & Pollard, 1994).

DEVELOPMENTAL FACTORS

As is the case with children's responses to other life stressors, there is likely to be wide individual variation in the psychological impact of parental illness on children (Drotar, 1994). Consideration of developmental factors appears crucial for understanding the impact of parental illness on children's health. Children may experience very different effects of their parents' illness due to developmental differences in areas such as cognitive capacity, developmental tasks, coping skills, and roles in the family (Drotar, 1994).

An obvious developmental variable involves differences in cognitive skills that may influence children's understanding of their parent's condition and may determine the precise impact of the illness. Glass (1985) noted that the primitive and magical thinking of young children may make it difficult for them to understand the abstract concepts associated with changes brought about by parental illness, possibly resulting in bewilderment and insecurity. The limited cognitive capacity of young children with a parent with cancer has been suggested to result in the children confusing the consequences of treatment (e.g., weight loss, nausea, hair loss) with the symptoms of the disease. As a result, the child may believe that the parent is getting sicker (Christ et al., 1993). In contrast, the older child whose thinking is more rational and conceptually sophisticated may identify with the parent and his her concerns, and thereby the child may have similar feelings of loneliness, helplessness, apprehension, anger, and perhaps guilt (Glass, 1985).

In their studies of families whose mother had nonmetastatic breast disease, Lewis, Ellison, and Woods (1985) found that children's perceptions of the mother's illness were, in fact, consistent with their presumed stage of cognitive and psychosocial development. Specifically, they found that the responses of 7- to 10-year old children were characterized by a concern for the maintenance of the family unit and uncertainty about the future and by the emotions of fear, loneliness, and anger. As also suggested by Glass (1985), the authors hypothesized that the concept of cancer may have been more difficult for them to understand given the concrete, operationalized nature of their thinking. Consistent with the developmental task of becoming more involved outside the family (e.g., school, peers) that confronts older school-age children, 10- to 13-year old children's responses to parental illness emphasized the degree of disruption or change their mother's illness had caused for them, particularly with regard to how it took time away from their own interests and activities. Finally, during the developmental period characterized by autonomy and separation from parents, responses of adolescent children, ages 14 to 19 years, revealed a conflict between their attempts to become more independent and the need for them to be available functionally (e.g., assuming additional household responsibilities) and emotionally (e.g., providing support for the ill and well parent) at home. At the same time, adolescents were also able to identify positive aspects of the illness.

Similar trends in age-related reactions were observed in children who were participating in an intervention program for children whose parent had terminal cancer (Christ et al., 1993). Young children were more concerned about changes in day-to-day functioning whereas older children were more concerned with longer range issues such as new responsibilities and the limitations these responsibilities might place on their own functioning. These apparently developmentally related themes also emerged in the context of a psychoeducational group intervention for children with a parent diagnosed with cancer (Taylor-Brown, Acheson, & Farber, 1993). The concerns of children younger than 10 focused on the ill parent's actual physical experience, their own sad feelings for the ill parent, and the impact of the parent's illness on the family. Children aged 10 to 12, however, emphasized how the event of cancer affected them personally. As found previously, the adolescents reported conflict between emancipation and having to assume extra responsibilities at home.

Developmental differences in the form of cognitive skills may influence children's response to parental illness, and the tasks associated with different developmental levels may also determine the impact of parental illness on children. Lewis and colleagues (1985) note that families with an ill parent are confronted with the task of integrating two aspects of their lives: the life associated with the illness and its contingencies and the "normal," natural life of the family.

They further note that this process presents a particular challenge for children whose developmental tasks may conflict with the demands associated with parental illness. For example, one of the goals for adolescent children is to develop increasing levels of independence and their own identity apart from their parents. Adolescents with an ill parent, however, face this task at a time when their parent's illness dictates increased interdependence among family members.

Compas and colleagues (1994) compared levels of distress among male and female preadolescent, adolescent, and young adult children whose mothers or fathers had cancer. The findings revealed that psychological distress reported among children was influenced by their gender and age and whether it was their mother or father who was ill. Anxiety and depression were higher for adolescents and young adults than for children while stress response symptoms were higher for children than for adolescents and young adults. While the observed difference in child outcomes may be a function of developmental differences in response to serious parental illness, it may also reflect a response bias among young children to minimize or deny the significance of their parent's disease. Not only did children's responses vary as a function of age, but the response of adolescents and young adults also appeared to vary as a function of the interaction of the sex of the ill parent and the sex of the child. Stress response symptoms were greatest for daughters whose mothers were ill and sons whose fathers were ill, with the strongest effect found for adolescent girls whose mothers were ill. Similarly, the highest levels of anxiety and depression were also reported by adolescent girls whose mothers were ill. Such results suggest that adolescent females may be a highly vulnerable group (Compas et al., 1994). Overall, although children's scores on the anxiety and depression measures were not sufficient for diagnosis, there is evidence that the impact of cancer on children is meaningful and may necessitate intervention in the form of short-term support services (Compas et al., 1994). Moreover, while children's responses were evaluated in terms of their clinical significance, an obvious limitation of this study is that it lacked a comparison group so it is unclear whether the mean response of children with a parent with cancer differed from families in which there was no parental illness present.

Overall, the above findings strongly suggest that attempts to understand and assist children with an ill parent must be developmentally driven with recognition that the psychosocial developmental stage of the child is likely to influence the child's response and ability to cope with this stressor. Most researchers acknowledge the importance of considering developmental influences on children's reaction to parental illness. However, given the overall paucity of research in this area, knowledge of developmental differences related to the impact of parental illness on children remains limited. Future research should be directed towards describing differences in children's reactions to parental illness when illness onset varies across children's developmental level. Longitudinal research is also needed to determine the continued impact of parental illness across children's development.

In addition to recognizing developmental influences, a particular challenge confronting researchers in this area is the notion that a particular parental illness can result in a variety of child outcomes (e.g., social functioning, anxiety, school performance, behavior problems) and can influence any one outcome through multiple pathways (Drotar, 1994). Not only should research identify the child outcomes associated with parental illness, but also the underlying processes through which parental illness exerts its influence and leads to health or disorder in children need identification. A dynamic developmental systems framework with its emphasis on equifinality and multifinality may be most useful for conceptualizing research questions (Sameroff, 1995).

PATHWAYS OF INFLUENCE

Researchers and clinicians who are concerned with the influence of parental illness on children's health and mental health must identify the pathways through which parental illness exerts its influence. A number of pathways of influence can be posited for any one illness, all of which have enticing, but limited support in the extant literature. These include social learning–modeling influences, changes in the parent–child relationship, and shifts in family functioning. Each of these pathways directs attention to possible influences that might mediate the effects of parental illness.

Social Learning and Modeling

A parsimonious social-learning theory explanation might predict that children's reactions to parental illness mirror those of the ill parent or the healthy parent (Stein & Newcomb, 1994). According to this perspective, it might be expected that parental illness would result in greater somatic complaints in their children. Several studies have provided evidence in support of this perspective.

For example, Dura and Beck (1988) found that 7- to 13-year-old children of parents who suffer chronic pain were more somatically focused than controls. Similarly, Mikail and von Baeyer (1990) reported a greater somatic focus in 9- to 17-year-old children of chronic headache sufferers than that found in control children. Another study documented greater levels of somatic symptoms in a group of adolescents with physically ill parents as compared to controls

(Morgan, Sanford, & Johnson, 1992). In each case, it is important to point out that the cross-sectional nature of the studies does not permit causal relationships between parent and child symptoms to be identified, and thus the results should be interpreted with considerable caution. Moreover, given that these studies evaluated children whose parents either suffered from pain-oriented symptoms (Dura & Beck, 1988; Mikail & von Baeyer, 1990) or self-reported physical illness (Morgan et al., 1992), the apparent relationship between parental illness and increased somatic concerns in children awaits further validation among samples of children whose parents have diagnosable illnesses.

Stein and Newcomb (1994) investigated the impact of a range of maternal health related constructs (physical symptomatology, health services utilization, subjective health status, depressed mood, medical–psychological complaints, and marital adjustment) on children's internalizing and externalizing behavior problems in a community sample. Their results both supported and refuted a social-learning mode of impact. Specifically, a syndrome consisting of psychosomatic complaints and anxiety in children was found to be strongly related to seizure symptoms (e.g., dizziness, fainting) in the mother. In addition, psychosomatic complaints in children were predicted by greater levels of major health problems in the mother. Thus, psychosomatic complaints in children may arise through imitative processes as a result of this increased exposure to parents with physical symptoms; similar findings have been reported in studies of learned illness behavior in children and adults (Walker & Zeman, 1992; Whitehead, Busch, Heller, & Costa, 1986). However, the results also revealed that greater physical symptomatology in the mother, reflecting a heightened concern with symptoms and illness, predicted a broad range of problem behaviors in children rather than an isolated somatic focus or a set of specific symptoms. Mother's health status and health care use has been associated with a range of children's behavioral and emotional problems (Riley et al., 1993); clarification of the processes that account for these relationships is needed. As these results suggest, it is likely that the impact of parental illness occurs through more than one pathway.

Changes in the Parent–Child Relationship

The functional effects of parental health problems on caretaking and the quality of the parent–child relationship is another proposed pathway through which parental illness may impact children (Drotar, 1994; Kornblum & Anderson, 1985; Thurman, Whaley, & Weinraub, 1985). It may be difficult for the ill parent, especially in the case of a primary caretaker, to fulfill child-rearing responsibilities due to increases in self-care associated with the illness or separations due to hospitalization.

Nelson and Allen (1994) conducted an analog study that evaluated children's anticipation of anxiety in response to maternal hospitalization for surgery or childbirth in comparison to a separation unrelated to hospitalization. It was found that children identified anticipated maternal separation for surgery as most anxiety-provoking whereas separation for childbirth and an out-of-town trip were rated as being lower, but also anxiety-provoking. The authors suggest that children's fears about surgical procedures, lack of knowledge about medical procedures, and/or newly developed cognitive abilities to understand the irreversibility and permanence of death may have contributed to the elevated anxiety levels related to separation due to surgery. A major limitation of this study is that it is not clear whether a true relationship exists between children's anticipated anxiety and their actual, observed anxiety during separation. However, it does suggest that the impact of maternal separation due to illness may be more anxiety-provoking than maternal separation in general. The study also does not address the impact of illness-related separations on the actual parent–child relationship, nor does it elucidate the processes involved.

In addition to the practical consequences of the illness (e.g., parent–child separation), parenting practices may also be altered by parental recognition of the health consequences associated with their illness. For example, parents may experience psychological concerns regarding the implications of their illness (including a shortened life span) with regard to their ability to fulfill their parental role. In a descriptive report of the impact of parental diabetes on children, Kornblum and Anderson (1985) noted that some parents reported a tendency to spoil their child while others reported that they pushed their children to become independent due to the uncertainty of how long they would be around. Although parents may report changes in their parenting practices, it is not evident that these changes necessarily lead to differential outcomes in their children. While intriguing, these findings await empirical validation.

One variable that remains to be studied and may compensate for the deleterious effects of any negative consequences to the child's relationship with the ill parent is the relationship with the healthy parent (Drotar, 1994). Further considerations of family factors (e.g., single-parent families, families of varying socioeconomic status, families with varying sociocultural values and practices) must also be investigated to better understand the influence of parent–child relationships. The notion that children may be impacted by parental illness through changes in the parental relationship or parenting practices is intuitively appealing, but this too awaits empirical demonstration.

Family Functioning

Based on the notion that illness is a family experience, many researchers have commented on the potential for parental illness to create stress within the family system and to disrupt family life and routines (e.g., Glass, 1985; Stein & Newcomb, 1994). For example, illness may impair the parent's ability to fulfill household roles and responsibilities and may thus require reallocation of roles to preserve family stability (Northouse, Cracchiolo-Caraway, & Appel, 1991; Vess, Moreland, Schwebel, & Kraut, 1988). It is through such disruptions to the family system that parental illness may have its most direct and negative effects on children's psychosocial health and development (Stein & Newcomb, 1994). Thus, when evaluating the effect of parental illness on children, the impact of family functioning on children needs to be considered as well (Lewis et al., 1985; Lewis, Hammond, & Woods, 1993).

There is some evidence that children with an ill parent may perceive their family environment differently than children with healthy parents. Peters and Esses (1985) measured the perceptions of family environment in thirty-three adolescents who had a parent with multiple sclerosis (MS). In comparison to the responses of children from control families, children with a parent with MS rated their family higher on the conflict subscale, and lower on the cohesion, intellectual orientation, moral–religious emphasis, and organization subscales of the Family Environment Scale. Although such findings lend support to the notion that children of MS patients perceive their family environment differently than children from non-MS families, what is not clear from the present study is whether these differences are associated with family dysfunction and/or differences in child outcomes or are specific to MS families.

Another study, which examined the coping strategies of families experiencing parental illness, suggested that alterations in family life do, in fact, accompany parental illness. Stetz, Lewis, and Primomo (1986) interviewed 125 families to examine coping strategies used by families across three diagnostic categories of illness in the mother: nonmetastatic breast cancer, diabetes, and fibrocystic breast disease. Based on families' responses to a semistructured interview, no significant differences among the three groups with regard to types of management strategies were identified. Thus, it appears that the presence of different types of illness in the mother does not influence the specific strategies used by families to manage their day-to-day problems. Representing

38 percent of all types of strategies reported by families, the most frequently endorsed strategy by all groups was "alterations in household management," which "reflects behavior on the part of the family to alter its internal structure and relationship rules in order to manage the challenge or problem" (p. 521). Thus, there is some evidence that parental illness is associated with changes in family functioning, but again it is not evident from the study by Stetz and colleagues. (1986) whether such coping strategies positively impact the adjustment of the family or the child. It may be that families who do not implement these changes in management practices, or who experience difficulty in doing so, function in ways that contribute adversely to a negative impact on children's psychological functioning.

In yet another study, Vess and colleagues (1988) examined fifty-four families who were coping with cancer to determine if certain factors facilitated their ability to deal with this role disruption. It was found that families who had more open communication and greater flexibility in allocating roles were more effective for managing the role changes associated with parental illness. Moreover, the fact that successful role reallocation was also a function of the developmental level of children points to the need to consider developmental factors in the case of parental illness. Specifically, it was found that families with younger children seemed to have greater difficulty in reallocating roles than families with older children. The authors commented that older children were more likely to be equipped cognitively and physically to assist with such household responsibilities than younger children who were unable to assume primary family roles (Vess et al., 1988).

Further, Moguilner, Bauman, and De-Nour (1988) provide limited but important evidence that better adjusted families result in more positive outcomes among children who are exposed to parental illness. In this case, twenty-five children ranging in age from 8 to 17 years whose parents were on chronic hemodialysis were assessed using a clinical interview, the Tennessee Children's Self-Concept Scale, and three cards from the Thematic Apperception Test (TAT) that assessed the child's emotional adjustment. Parental adjustment was also evaluated using the Psychosocial Adjustment to Physical Illness Scale (PAIS; Derogatis, 1986) and the Beck Depression Inventory (BDI). Based on the combined scores of parents on the PAIS and BDI, families were separated into three groups (well adjusted, moderately adjusted, and maladjusted). Significantly higher levels of adjustment were found among children in well-adjusted families compared to children in maladjusted families. Children from moderately adjusted families, however, presented a more complex picture. They were found to fall between the other two groups and near the norms with regard to self-concept,

but were almost identical to the maladjusted group on the TAT. Specifically, Moguilner aand coworkers hypothesized that these children may have been using denial and suppression, resulting in a near normal self-concept, while evidencing problems on the projective measure. Although these results provide some evidence that child adjustment is related to how well the family adjusts, it should be recognized that family adjustment in this study actually represented a combination of the parents' adjustment scores. Thus, it may be more accurate to state that child adjustment in this study was related to parental adjustment rather than family adjustment per se. In addition, the relationship between parental adjustment and child adjustment was found to be very strong for young children (up to 12), but less so for older children (13 and up), so that age, as an estimate of developmental level, may modify the relationship between parental and child adjustment. Overall, given the positive relationships between the adjustment of the ill parent and his/her spouse and between parent and child, the authors advocate that chronic hemodialysis should be considered a "family affair" which, in turn, dictates a family approach to interventions (Moguilner et al., 1988).

Summary

In summary, our understanding of how, to what extent, and through what mechanisms parental illness affects child outcomes, is severely limited. Although researchers have begun to address these issues, a systematic approach to research in this area has yet to be undertaken. For example, the practice of using different measures to assess similar outcomes makes it difficult to draw meaningful conclusions across studies. Furthermore, findings from studies of a variety of parental illnesses are not yet available, let alone well integrated. Although differential outcomes among children exposed to different illnesses have been reported (e.g., Dura & Beck, 1988), the current state of the literature does not permit tests of the influence of specific parental health problems on children and whether this influence generalizes across different parental illnesses. In addition, as is the case with most family-centered research, the mother is generally relied on for information regarding the child and the family (Drotar, 1994; Finney & Bonner, 1992), which may result in limited if not biased information. Future research should attempt to incorporate a variety of sources to assess child outcomes (e.g., teacher, peer, child self-report), a broader view of the family, and a more integrative psychosocial model to elucidate factors that influence children's health and development (Bonner & Finney, 1996). For example, the majority of research investigating the impact of parental illness on children yields little information concerning the impact of *paternal* illness on children. Obviously, this should become a target for systematic and comprehensive future research. Although available evidence suggests that children exposed to parental illness may be at risk for negative outcomes, further research also needs to be directed towards evaluating the "normality" of children's responses to this experience, as it is equally important, albeit difficult, to examine normal as well as pathological reactions to parental illness (Christ et al., 1993).

PARENTAL DEPRESSION VERSUS PARENTAL MEDICAL ILLNESS

In an attempt to clarify the relationship between parental illness and children's adjustment difficulties, several researchers have compared the adjustment of children of parents with a physical illness to children of parents with a psychological disorder (e.g., depression). Researchers have intended for such comparisons to provide information as to whether children's difficulties are unique to parental illness or are common to all children whose parents have a disability, including a psychological one. For example, Hirsch, Moos, and Reischl (1985) examined the influence of parental arthritis on adolescents between the ages of 12 and 18. The results revealed that adolescents with a parent with arthritis reported lower self-esteem and less involvement in school activities than normal controls. However, children of parents with arthritis did not differ significantly from children with depressed parents on either of these measures. There were no significant differences between groups in terms of school grades, school life satisfaction, or family social climate. In addition, both negative and positive life events were found to be related to more symptomatology among the arthritic and the depressed group, but not the normal group. Although the three groups did not differ in terms of family social climate, within-group comparisons revealed that a positive family social climate was related to better adjustment among all three groups. Specifically, for adolescents with a parent with arthritis, a more cohesive and expressive family with less conflict was related to decreased symptomatology whereas a similar family climate was related to higher self-esteem in the other two groups. Is the illness stressful for the child or does the illness negatively influence the parent (interferes with their usual level of parental functioning), who, in turn, influences the child's adjustment? Inasmuch as the arthritic group did not significantly differ from the depressed group on symptomatology, self-esteem, or school and family adjustment, it appears that the primary risk factor for children with a parent with a disability is disability in general as opposed to deleterious consequences associated with a particular disability (e.g., psychological vs. physical) (Hirsch et al., 1985). For example, it is possible that the relative differences among the

arthritic and depressive groups in Hirsch and colleagues' (1985) study were due to the fact that the arthritic mothers may have been experiencing depressive symptomatology; however, depressive symptomatology was not assessed in this study. It is important to note that the psychological status of the arthritic parents was not assessed, and therefore it is possible that the lack of differences between the children was attributable to the presence of depression in the parents with arthritis rather than the effects of physical disability per se (Lee & Gotlib, 1989).

A similar study was conducted in which children of parents with arthritis were compared to children of parents who were depressed (Lee & Gotlib, 1989). According to parent-rated scores on the Child Behavior Checklist, no child of a mother with arthritis was rated as functioning in the clinical range while two-thirds of the children of mothers with depression were rated in the clinical range. It is possible that such a finding is a function of a maternal negative response set associated with depression. Given that maternal reports of child behavior have been found to be influenced by the mothers' own psychological functioning, it is possible that the depressed mothers rated their children more negatively as a result of their own state. However, consistent with the maternal ratings, clinicians' blind ratings of these children on the Child Assessment Schedule revealed a greater number of symptoms and poorer overall adjustment in the children of mothers with depression as well as mothers with other psychiatric disorders. In contrast, children of mothers with arthritis did not differ significantly from children in the control group in terms of their scores on the Child Assessment Schedule and did not differ from children of community mothers in terms of their scores on the Global Assessment Scale for Children. Thus, the present results seem to suggest that the psychosocial functioning of children whose parents had arthritis is comparable to that of their "normal" peers (children who were community control subjects). Moreover, these findings suggest that children's difficulties, in fact, may be related to psychological disturbance (Lee & Gotlib, 1989), in that children of both depressed and nondepressed psychiatric patients demonstrated greater difficulties than did the children of medical patients and women without disabilities obtained from community samples. The absence of statistically significant differences in the adjustment of children of medical patients and the children of women in the community contradict the previous findings of Hirsch and colleagues (1985). Lee and Gotlib (1989) hypothesized several reasons to explain this discrepancy, including age differences between the two samples (i.e., adolescence vs. elementary/middle school age) and failure to assess for psychological adjustment in the arthritic group in Hirsch and colleagues' (1985) sample.

Parental medical illnesses and psychological disturbances may share some influences on children's development and may be associated with distinctive outcomes. Only continued research will fully explicate the similarities and differences of children's reactions to parental health and mental health problems.

HIV/AIDS: AN EXEMPLAR PARENTAL ILLNESS

One illness that is affecting a growing number of parents and their children is acquired immunodeficiency syndrome (AIDS). Current epidemiological estimates suggest that women of childbearing age and heterosexuals constitute two of the growing groups of adults infected with HIV (Barth, 1993). Thus, the impact of parental AIDS poses an increasing risk for an increasing number of children. As with other types of parental illness, research concerning families affected by AIDS has emphasized the adult members of an infected patient's family or the parents of an infected child rather than the child of an infected parent (Niebuhr et al., 1994). Thus, as is the case with parental illness in general, little research has been conducted on the impact of HIV infection on the children of infected parents (Niebuhr et al., 1994).

A particular concern associated with the increasing rate of HIV infection among women of childbearing age is the risk of children contracting the disease from the mother. With vertical transmission as the primary route of infection in children, it is estimated that up to 30 percent of children born to infected mothers will become HIV-infected (Barth, 1993). Thus, in the case of parental AIDS, there is a physical–medical risk associated with parental illness. In addition to the health problems confronting these children, most children with HIV disease experience neurological effects, cognitive deficits, loss of previously achieved milestones, and/or developmental delays (Spiegel & Mayer, 1991).

Children, both infected and noninfected, of infected mothers and fathers also constitute a growing number of "AIDS orphans" who are survivors of a parent who has died from HIV infection (Barth, 1993; Sherwen & Boland, 1994). Given that AIDS is the leading cause of mortality among young adults, those who are likely candidates for having young children (Niebuhr et al., 1994), many young children will lose their parents at a young age (Black, Nair, & Harrington, 1994). Michaels and Levine (1992) estimate that approximately 80,000 children and adolescents will be orphaned by the year 2000 as a result of the AIDS epidemic. Nicholas and Abrams (1992) also point out that many children are also effectively orphaned prior to their parents' death.

With injection drug use and sexual transmission fueling the spread of AIDS among heterosexuals, births to infected mothers will result in more HIV-infected infants (National Commission on AIDS, 1993). Women of childbearing age represent almost 10 percent of the reported AIDS cases and constitute one of the fastest growing groups of newly infected adults (Barth, 1993). With this increase in women as well as heterosexuals with HIV/AIDS, there is an increase in the number of parents with HIV/AIDS (Niebuhr et al., 1994).

Besides medical and developmental difficulties that arise as a result of children being infected with HIV/AIDS, the impact of parental illness has the potential to impact these children in other ways as well. Effective parenting can be impaired because of the illness-related effects of HIV or because of separations and hospitalizations or emotional consequences such as depression, anxiety, mood fluctuations, fear, and secrecy. These potential consequences not only exist for children infected by their parents but also children who are not infected. Parent–child bonding presents an interesting and unique issue when both the mother and child are AIDS-affected (Cohen, 1994). Many of the children infected with HIV have mothers who are themselves disabled by AIDS and thus may not be able to provide continuing care for their children (Kazak, 1989). Many children with AIDS are exposed to drugs prenatally and their mothers, who may also be abusing drugs, may have dysfunctional parenting skills (Zuckerman, 1993).

HIV-infected families often decry the lack of both emotional and tangible support that results from the isolation they experience because they cannot divulge their children's diagnosis for fear of discrimination and stigma. They may need assistance in communicating with significant others who could help reduce their isolation and provide assistance obtaining services, such as respite care, transportation, treatment, and financial assistance for which they may be eligible (Barth, 1993).

The combination of parenthood and HIV infection raises complex issues related to family functioning and children's mental health, including communication between parent and child about the parent's diagnosis, the child's emotional needs related to the parent's illness, the parent's and family's needs related to helping the child, and the parent's fear of discrimination against the child (Niebuhr et al., 1994). Niebuhr and colleagues (1994) found that nearly one-third of the HIV-infected patients at a university clinic were parents and that women comprised two-fifths of the parent sample. Only half of the parents reported that their children (4 years) knew about their diagnosis. Unfortunately, Niebuhr and colleagues (1994) offered no information with regard to children's emotional reaction to knowing about their parent's illness. Moreover, two-thirds of the parents reported they believed their children did not need to talk to someone about their parent's health, and nearly half of the parents reported that they did not need help dealing with their children concerning issues related to AIDS. This finding is complicated by the fact that these children are already at high risk for lack of access to mental health care as a result of barriers associated with low socioeconomic status and family functioning. As a result, the mental health needs of AIDS patients as well as of children are underserved in this country (Niebuhr et al., 1994). In addition, families with HIV/AIDS may be reluctant to seek help as result of stigma associated with the disease and may not be comfortable seeking support from their social support network because of the same stigma. Niebuhr and colleagues (1994) raised the question of whether we know enough about the emotional needs of children with an HIV-infected parent to develop interventions targeting the same. Given that the percentage of HIV/AIDS patients who are also parents is high, the emotional needs of parents and their children are likely to become an increasingly important issue.

Although true for any research investigating the impact of parental illness on children, the difficulty of isolating the effects of any single parental health risk factor is particularly salient for children exposed to parental (primarily maternal) HIV infection. This relationship is generally confounded by maternal drug addiction, family instability, and economic disadvantage (Drotar, 1994). Complex models that account for multiple influences on children's outcomes, as well as consideration of the transactional nature of the child, parent, and family influences, will be needed to address the multiple problems and interventions for this population (Cicchetti & Cohen, 1995).

INTERVENTIONS FOR CHILDREN AND FAMILIES

The literature on the impact of parental illness on children is limited, and there are even fewer empirical studies of interventions aimed at ameliorating the effects of parental health on children as well as on families. Limited and methodologically flawed research is characteristic of all areas of family-based interventions to improve children's health (Finney & Bonner, 1992). Additional research on the nature of the impact of parental illness on children and families would be useful for identifying appropriate targets for such interventions. There does, however, appear to be agreement that any intervention in this area should be developmentally sensitive and family-focused.

Parents should receive guidance on how to deal effectively with children's concerns, questions, and possible adjustment problems (Northouse et al., 1991), and these interventions should be appropriate for the child's developmental level (Northouse et al., 1991). Services need to be directed to the entire family, not just the ill parent (Lewis et al., 1985; Northouse et al., 1991). Siegel and coworkers (1992) suggest that family-focused intervention programs that include assessment and treatment of child and parent distress related to the illness, preparation for the death of the parent, enhancement of resources for bereavement, and ongoing family care and support, may be necessary to promote healthy development among both mothers and children and to prevent subsequent child psychopathology.

Parents could benefit from assistance in helping their children understand their illness and in adapting their explanations to the child's developmental level (Kornblum & Anderson, 1985). It is especially difficult for the parent to handle his or her own emotional upheaval after the diagnosis of a chronic illness, especially when the parent is also heavily involved in the care of young children. Quite obviously, these parents could benefit from access to counseling or a peer support network at the time of diagnosis (Kornblum & Anderson, 1985). In terms of intervention, it is also important to learn what the needs of the non-ill family members are, because their adaptation to the illness exerts a powerful influence on the ill parent's adaptation and health. Lewis and colleagues (1985) suggested that psychosocial interventions can be derived by identifying changes in children's patterns of behavior following parental illness. It is essential that the identification of children's reactions to parental illness be viewed in the context of normative development; population-based studies will be necessary to distinguish psychosocial adjustment difficulties that are related to adjustment to parental illness from those difficulties that are associated with normative development.

SUMMARY AND CONCLUSIONS

Parental illness can influence children's health and psychological development. Outcomes can be varied for a particular parental illness and similar for different, distinctive parental illnesses. A number of pathways of influence can be identified leading to the varied child outcomes, including social-learning influences, changes in the parent–child relationship, and disruption of usual family functioning. Outcomes have been linked somewhat to children's developmental stages, but developmental research is extremely rare. Similar limits are apparent for the few interventions that have been evaluated to mediate the influence of parental illness. With the growing incidence of parental illness and an awareness of its potential influence, identification of risk, vulnerability, and protective factors associated with differential child outcomes is needed to guide the development of interventions to promote optimal child development and to maximize individual and family adaptation to parental illness.

REFERENCES

Barth, R. P. (1993). Rationale and conceptual framework. In R. P. Barth, J. Pietrzak, & M. Ramler (Eds.), *Families living with drugs and HIV: Intervention and treatment strategies* (pp. 3–17). New York: Guilford Press.

Bonner, M. J., & Finney, J. W. (1996). A psychosocial model of children's health status. In T. H. Ollendick & R. J. Prinz (Eds.), *Advances in clinical child psychology, (Vol. 18,* pp. 231–282). New York: Plenum Press.

Christ, G. H., Siegel, K., Freund, B., Langosch, D., Henderson, S., Sperber, D., & Weinstein, L. (1993). Impact of parental terminal cancer on latency-age children. *American Journal of Orthopsychiatry, 63,* 417–425.

Cicchetti, D., & Cohen, D. J. (1995). Perspectives on developmental psychopathology. In D. Cicchetti & D. J. Cohen (Eds.), *Developmental psychopathology: Vol. 1. Theory and methods* (pp. 3–20). New York: Wiley.

Compas, B. E., Worsham, N. L., Epping-Jordan, J. E., Grant, K. E., Mireault, G., Howell, D. C., & Malcarne, V. L. (1994). When mom or dad has cancer: Markers of psychological distress in cancer patients, spouses, and children. *Health Psychology, 13,* 507–515.

Derogatis, L. R. (1976). *Scoring and procedures manual for PAIS.* Baltimore, MD: Clinical Psychosomatic Research.

Drotar, D. (1994). Impact of parental health problems on children: Concepts, methods, and unanswered questions. *Journal of Pediatric Psychology, 19,* 525–536.

Dura, J. R., & Beck, S. J. (1988). A comparison of family functioning when mothers have chronic pain. *Pain, 35,* 79–89.

Finney, J. W., & Bonner, M. J. (1992). The influence of behavioral family intervention on the health of chronically ill children. *Behaviour Change, 9,* 157–170.

Glass, D. D. (1985). Onset of disability in a parent: Impact on child and family. In S. K. Thurman (Ed.), *Children of handicapped parents: Research and clinical perspectives* (pp. 145–154). Orlando, FL: Academic Press.

Hirsch, B. J., Moos, R. H., & Reischl, T. M. (1985). Psychosocial adjustment of adolescent children of a depressed, arthritic, or normal parent. *Journal of Abnormal Psychology, 94,* 154–164.

Kornblum, H., & Anderson, B. J. (1985). Parents with insulin-dependent diabetes: Impact on child and family development. In S. K. Thurman (Ed.), *Children of handicapped parents: Research and clinical perspectives* (pp. 97–109). Orlando, FL: Academic Press.

Lewis, F. M., Ellison, E. S., & Woods, N. F. (1985). The impact of breast cancer on the family. *Seminars in Oncology Nursing, 1,* 206–213.

Lewis, F. M., Hammond, M. A., & Woods, N. F. (1993). The family's functioning with newly diagnosed breast cancer in the mother: The development of an explanatory model. *Journal of Behavioral Medicine, 16,* 351–370.

Mikail, S. F., & von Baeyer, C. L. (1990). Pain, somatic focus, and emotional adjustment in children of chronic headache sufferers and controls. *Social Science and Medicine, 31,* 51–59.

Moguilner, M. E., Bauman, A., & De-Nour, A. K. (1988). The adjustment of children and parents to chronic hemodialysis. *Psychosomatics, 29,* 289–294.

Morgan, J., Sanford, M., & Johnson, C. (1992). The impact of a physically ill parent on adolescents: Cross-sectional findings from a clinic population. *Canadian Journal of Psychiatry, 37,* 423–427.

Nelson, C. C., & Allen, J. (1994). Effects of maternal hospitalization in early childhood: Anticipated anxiety associated with an analog separation for childbirth and surgery. *Journal of Pediatric Psychology, 19,* 629–642.

Nicholas, S. W., & Abrams, E. J. (1992). The "silent" legacy of AIDS: Children who survive their parents and siblings. *Journal of the American Medical Association, 268,* 3478–3479.

Niebuhr, V. N., Hughes, J. R., & Pollard, R. B. (1994). Parents with human immunodeficiency virus infection: Perceptions of their children's emotional needs. *Pediatrics, 93,* 421–426.

Northouse, L. L., Cracchiolo-Caraway, A., & Appel, C. P. (1991). Psychologic consequences of breast cancer on partner and family. *Seminars in Oncology Nursing, 7,* 216–223.

Peters, L. C., & Esses, L. M. (1985). Family environment as perceived by children with a chronically ill parent. *Journal of Chronic Diseases, 38,* 301–308.

Riley, A. W., Finney, J. W., Mellits, E. D., Starfield, B., Kidwell, S., Quaskey, S., Cataldo, M. F., Filipp, L., & Shematek, J. P. (1993). Determinants of children's health care use: An investigation of psychosocial factors. *Medical Care, 31,* 767–783.

Sameroff, A. J. (1995). General systems theories and developmental psychopathology. In D. Cicchetti & D. J. Cohen (Eds.), *Developmental psychopathology: Vol. 1. Theory and methods* (pp. 659–695). New York: Wiley.

Siegel, K., Mesagno, F. P., Karus, D., Christ, G., Banks, K., & Moynihan, R. (1992). Psychosocial adjustment of children with a terminally ill parent. *Journal of the American Academy of Child and Adolescent Psychiatry, 31,* 327–333.

Stein, J. A., & Newcomb, M. D. (1994). Children's internalizing and externalizing behaviors and maternal health problems. *Journal of Pediatric Psychology, 19,* 571–594.

Stetz, K. M., Lewis, F. M., & Primomo, J. (1986). Family coping strategies and chronic illness in the mother. *Family Relations, 35,* 515–522.

Taylor-Brown, J., Acheson, A., & Farber, J. M. (1993). Kids Can Cope: A group intervention for children whose parents have cancer. *Journal of Psychosocial Oncology, 11,* 41–53.

Thurman, S. K., Whaley, A., & Wienraub, M. A. (1985). Studying families with handicapped parents: A rationale. In S. K. Thurman (Ed.), *Children of handicapped parents: Research and clinical perspectives* (pp. 1–9). Orlando, FL: Academic Press.

Vess, J. D., Moreland, J. R., Schwebel, A. I., & Kraut, E. (1988). Psychosocial needs of cancer patients: Learning from patients and spouses. *Journal of Psychosocial Oncology, 6,* 31–51.

Walker, L. S., & Zeman, J. L. (1992). Parental response to child illness behavior. *Journal of Pediatric Psychology, 17,* 49–71.

Whitehead, W. E., Busch, C. M., Heller, B. R., & Costa, P. T. (1986). Social learning influences on menstrual symptoms and illness behavior. *Health Psychology, 5,* 13–23.

PART 6

EVALUATIVE AND ETHICAL AND LEGAL ISSUES

In this, the final section of the volume, two main issues that pertain to developmentally sensitive child evaluation treatment research—process and outcome—are discussed in two separate chapters. In the first chapter, an overview of psychotherapy process research is presented. The chapter proposes a model to be used for designing research programs to test clinically relevant, developmentally driven process questions. In the second chapter, the ways in which outcome research can be made maximally developmental are discussed. This includes a discussion about the types of variables that need to be assessed to conduct developmentally driven outcome research and the implications of certain principles of developmental psychology (e.g., heterotypic continuity) in conducting this type of research.

The last chapter discusses ethical and legal issues involved in clinical work with children, presented within a developmental perspective. Three major ethical and legal challenges are examined in the chapter: (1) protecting chil-

dren's intrinsic value as persons through appropriate informed consent procedures, (2) balancing children's rights to privacy and self-governance with the obligation to protect their welfare and the welfare of others through appropriate confidentiality procedures, and (3) protecting children's rights to adequate diagnoses and effective treatment through the use of developmentally and culturally valid assessment and treatment techniques. The chapter also presents a framework of "best practices" to assist mental health professionals' ethical decision making in their work with children.

In sum, the final set of chapters in this book shows us once again the critical ways that development can inform what we do as clinicians and researchers with respect to evaluating psychotherapy (process and outcome) and with respect to handling thorny ethical and legal issues. In addition, the chapters provide stimulating and innovative material that should serve to improve clinical research and practice with children and adolescents and their families.

CHAPTER 27

DEVELOPMENTAL PROCESS RESEARCH

Myrna L. Friedlander

Consider Alix, a 14-year-old girl of Peruvian heritage who was adopted shortly after birth by a well-to-do, white, professional couple. With a stable, nurturing family and all the advantages of a middle class lifestyle, Alix fared exceedingly well until ninth grade. Now, however, her parents are bewildered. Over the past few months Alix's grades have dropped precipitously. She isolates herself from the family, shows little interest in friends or extracurricular activities, and is particularly hostile with her mother.

Alix's many assets suggest she will do well in psychotherapy. She is bright, talented, and personable, and her parents are loving and supportive. Although a diagnosis of depression seems obvious, and any number of treatment approaches are viable, the therapist's first goal is to understand the precipitants of Alix's depression.

After some initial hesitancy, Alix willingly describes her recent difficulties. Having been ignored socially since entering high school, she no longer sees the point in trying to do anything well. Over the next few sessions, Alix slowly reveals that cruel teasing by classmates about her dark skin has triggered intense feelings about her self-image—indeed, her very identity—and about racial discrimination, her adoption by a white couple, and her Peruvian heritage. Many of these issues affect and are affected by Alix's awak-

ening sexuality. Recent discussions in her health class about sexual behavior, unwanted pregnancy, birth control, and abortion have led to other thoughts and feelings about her birth mother, and these she does not want to share with her parents.

Consider another child, Beth, a bright, friendly girl whose parents seek therapy because of her underachievement at school, temper tantrums at home, and low self-esteem. Like Alix, Beth was adopted at birth by a middle class, white couple. And, like Alix, Beth is of Peruvian heritage.

Exploration of Beth's problems suggests that her depression began, like Alix's, with teasing by peers about her physical features. Adoption issues have surfaced for Beth, too, in this first brush with discrimination. But for her, the confusing feelings about her identity have to do with attachment and loss. Beth is 8 years old.

These children, both bright and personable, are being raised in similar families and similar communities. Not only are their diagnoses similar, but the psychosocial stressors precipitating their depressive reactions are similar, as are the adoption-related feelings—confusion, anger, sadness, shame—that were triggered by peer rejection. For purposes of discussion, let us consider these two fictional clients, Alix and Beth, as one child at different ages.

There are, of course, other differences. The behavioral manifestations of depression are likely to be different, with Beth showing fewer vegetative symptoms. More important, however, are differences in the underlying conflicts. Alix, for example, has thoughts and feelings about her body image that Beth has not yet experienced. Alix has an understanding of racial discrimination and social injustice that Beth is just becoming aware of. Alix's understanding of her immigrant status in the United States is greater than Beth's, and Alix is more aware of political, social, and economic differences between her native country and the United States. As an adolescent, Alix's search for identity is likely to be more intense than Beth's. Beth is dealing not with issues of biculturalism but with conflicts about attachment, belonging, and loss. Although both girls feel anger toward their birth parents, Beth's issues have more to do with abandonment while Alix's have to do with her struggle to understand sexuality and parenting.

Differences in the two girls' difficulties reflect not only developmental changes in an adoptee's search for self (Brodzinsky, Schecter, & Henig, 1993) but also differences in their levels of cognitive and ego development. These are differences that their therapists need to consider, along with important differences in psychosocial development. Because for 14-year-old Alix social rejection is more salient than it is for 8-year-old Beth, more time may need to be spent helping her cope with peer group problems. Being sensitive to the adolescent's need for separateness, the therapist may opt not to challenge Alix's reluctance to share her feelings with her parents. On the other hand, it may be wise for the therapist to guide Beth's parents to help her sort through her feelings of anger and grief. While caring may be the most important element in the therapy for Beth, for Alix the salient factor may be the autonomy she feels with her therapist.

In other words, because of differences in depressive symptoms, in social–cognitive development, and in the psychosocial tasks of middle childhood versus adolescence, psychotherapy with these two clients should be quite different—despite their similar demographic backgrounds, diagnoses, precipitants, and underlying issues. And whereas the desired outcomes of treatment are identical—reduced depression and anxiety, improved self-esteem, academic performance, social skills, and relations with parents, working through feelings about adoption—the therapeutic processes will differ, not only the content but also the nature and development of the therapeutic relationship, the strategies and interventions used by the therapist, and the degree of client involvement.

Unfortunately, the available research offers little guidance to clinicians charting a course for work with children like Beth and Alix. Although the outcome evidence suggests that many childhood disorders can indeed be treated successfully (e.g., Casey & Berman, 1985; Kazdin, 1993), there are no studies on the process of therapy with depressed children. Indeed, there is very little empirical literature on the unfolding process of psychotherapy with *any* children or adolescents. This state of affairs is in stark contrast to the process literature on therapy with adults, with studies numbering in the thousands.

As Kazdin (1993) pointed out, it is not a recognition of the need for clinical research with children that has been lacking. Researchers are as aware as policy makers of the staggering numbers of children and adolescents who suffer from psychological disorders which, if untreated, may continue into adulthood. Rather, the lack of attention to children by therapy researchers reflects the lag in theorizing that is essential for designing and evaluating appropriate treatment programs for youth. Since the 1980s, however, groundbreaking work in developmental psychopathology (e.g., Lewis & Miller, 1990) has provided child and adolescent researchers with some important assessment and diagnostic tools for creating and implementing developmentally based treatment programs (Kazdin, 1993).

Evaluations of treatment outcomes are, however, limited in the absence of information about process variables that facilitate client change. Developmentally sensitive process research, the subject of this chapter, refers to the identification of differences in the process of effective treatment with children and adolescents at different developmental levels. The term *process* refers not to treatment approaches per se, nor to treatment components, nor to moderators of outcome like frequency of sessions or parental involvement, but rather to the overt and covert in-session behaviors of clients and therapists and to the unfolding sequences of interaction between them (Hill & Corbett, 1993).

Three interrelated assumptions underlie the present argument for the need to conduct process research that is sensitive to development. The first is that the child's level of development interacts with the psychological problem or disorder being treated (e.g., Holmbeck & Updegrove, 1995; Kazdin, 1993). Several studies support this notion. With respect to diagnosis, there are differences between antisocial youth who develop symptoms in childhood and those whose symptoms first appear in adolescence (Patterson, DeBaryshe, & Ramsey, 1989). With respect to treatment response, Miller, Barrett, Hampe, and Noble (1972) reported that younger children with phobias fared better than their older counterparts, both with desensitization and with individual psychotherapy.

The second assumption is that many therapeutic interventions have as their goal furthering the child's development (e.g., Heinecke & Strassman, 1975). Although reduction of symptoms is as important in child therapy as it is in adult treatment, developmental issues are arguably more important in working with youth. With respect to language, for example, a recent review of child therapy concluded that (1) language improves more often in individual than in group therapy, (2) treatment length is predictive of improvement, (3) treatments that emphasize spontaneous verbal activity may be most effective, and (4) language proficiency may be most improved with children whose problems are not behavioral (Russell, Greenwald, & Shirk, 1991). Indeed, designing interventions to enhance development requires not only a consideration of the child's age but also an assessment of the developmental nature of the child's presenting problem or disorder (Heinecke & Strassman, 1975). A problem that originates during a developmental transition should be treated differently from a problem that reflects a developmental standstill or a more pervasive developmental regression (Heinecke & Strassman, 1975).

The third assumption is that to be effective therapeutic interventions must be targeted to the individual child's level of ego, cognitive, and psychosocial development (e.g., Holmbeck & Updegrove, 1995). With respect to ego development, Hartmann and colleagues (1968), for example, reported that various ego functions, for example, control of aggressive impulses, were predictive of treatment outcome among adolescents in an inpatient setting. With respect to cognitive development, a recent meta-analysis concluded that "children entering treatment with more advanced levels of cognitive functioning benefit more from [cognitive–behavioral treatment] than do children with less advanced levels" (Durlak, Fuhrman, & Lampman, 1991, p. 210). With respect to psychosocial development, treatment that is not sensitive to age differences in the quality and importance of interpersonal relations (i.e., parents, peers) is likely to be ineffective (Kazdin, 1993).

In this chapter, an overview of psychotherapy process research is presented, followed by a model for designing research programs to test clinically relevant, developmentally driven process questions. The chapter concludes with a discussion of some promising avenues for future study.

OVERVIEW OF PROCESS RESEARCH

In Kiesler's (1973) groundbreaking work, process research was defined globally as research based on behavioral data from the therapy interview. Kiesler's criticism of the lack of attention paid by process researchers to outcome data set the stage for a more narrow definition of process, one that linked it with change over time. In the past 10 to 15 years, process researchers have moved away from merely describing what occurs in therapy toward delineating how change occurs within

and across sessions and how cumulative changes over time are related to ultimate client improvement. This emphasis on "change process research" (Greenberg, 1986, p. 4) was fed by the growing need for accountability in the field and by important technological advances like video recordings, computers, and one-way mirrors (Greenberg & Pinsof, 1986).

The interest in therapy effectiveness by process researchers was paralleled by a growing interest on the part of outcome researchers, disillusioned with the repeated finding of no differences in comparative studies, to consider the specific and nonspecific features of therapy in order to identify what, precisely, "works" (Greenberg & Pinsof, 1986). The result has been a blurring of the traditional process–outcome distinction. In other words, behaviors occurring within a session can be viewed as mini outcomes, and behaviors occurring outside the therapy hour can be viewed as important therapeutic processes (Greenberg & Pinsof, 1986).

A more recent development has been the acceptance of qualitative approaches for studying psychotherapeutic processes. Rather than assessing numeric differences in traditional confirmatory investigations, qualitative researchers use linguistic data to identify important subjective phenomena from an inductive, discovery-oriented perspective. Authors recommending qualitative approaches have argued that what is salient for clinicians is the identification of qualities, aspects, or variations in therapeutic experiences, phenomena that do not lend themselves easily to quantitative measurements or traditional data analysis (e.g., Hoshmand, 1989; Stiles, 1993).

Levels of Therapeutic Process

One useful way to organize and understand process data was suggested by Greenberg (1986). In this schema, there are four hierarchically ordered levels of the therapeutic process: content, speech act, episode, and relationship.

At the most basic level is *content,* that is, the substance of what is discussed in a therapy interview. In the cases of Alix and Beth, for example, there are likely to be large content differences with respect to presenting concerns as well as in adoption-related issues. Therapeutic conversations with Alix are likely to focus on peer relationships, ethnic identity, racial discrimination, concerns with intimacy and sexuality, body image, autonomy from parents, and so forth; the therapy with Beth is likely to include discussions about anger, loss, attachment, and the meaning of adoption.

At present, few process studies with adult clients are being conducted at the content level, and few observational coding systems are currently being developed to take into account content variables. Early process researchers, by contrast, were particularly interested in content. Early coding systems include Hall's (1966) scheme for categorizing dream content, Gottschalk, Winget, Gleser, and Springer's (1966) system for coding psychodynamic themes, and Dollard and Auld's (1959) system for categorizing clients' dynamic motive states.

The present assumption seems to be that differences between client communications at the content level are less meaningful than differences at higher levels of the hierarchy (Greenberg, 1986). This may not be true for describing and understanding therapy with children, however. Indeed, it may be particularly useful for clinicians to know what kinds of material can be discussed with youth at different levels of cognitive and ego functioning. One way to study these content differences would be to use qualitative methods like interviewing or qualitative analyses of transcripts or case notes.

At the next process level—*speech act*—verbal, nonverbal, and paralinguistic cues are observed. Speech acts—requests, instructions, questions, and so forth—have less to do with what is communicated and more to do with how speakers communicate. In the treatments of Beth and Alix, differences are likely to be observed in both the therapist's and the client's speech acts. The predominant therapist response modes (Friedlander, 1982; Hill, 1986; Stiles, 1979) with Beth, for example, might be encouragement and reassurance, questioning, providing information, and guidance, while with Alix the therapist might be more likely to use interpretations, reflections, and self-disclosure. On a measure of discourse activity (e.g., Friedlander, 1984), we might observe Alix to contribute significantly more to the dialogue than Beth.

At this level of the process, client behaviors can either be overt—for example, speech disfluency (Mahl, 1963), nonverbal cues (Hill, Siegelman, Gronsky, Sturniolo, & Fretz, 1981), level of emotional experiencing (Klein, Mathieu, Gendlin, & Kiesler, 1986), vocal quality (Rice & Kerr, 1986)—or covert, for example, reactions like "feel misunderstood" (Hill, Helms, Spiegel, & Tichenor, 1988). Likewise, therapist behaviors can either be covert, for example, the intentions to clarify, to promote feelings, to challenge, to focus (Hill & O'Grady, 1985), or overt, for example, verbal response modes (Friedlander, 1982; Hill, 1986; Stiles, 1979).

In the literature, the majority of process studies to date have relied on analyses of speech acts. While some coding systems are relevant only for client or therapist behaviors, for example, client experiencing or therapist response modes, others can be applied to the speech of either participant. These include nonverbal cues (Hill et al., 1981), discourse activity (Friedlander, 1984), speech disfluency (Mahl, 1963), and interpersonal behavior (Benjamin, 1986; Friedlander & Heatherington, 1989).

Increasingly, process researchers have been using these kinds of coding systems to identify salient client–therapist

sequences. The assumption is that sequences of behavior offer a clinically richer description of the therapeutic process than therapist or client speech acts considered in isolation. Sequences can be identified using instruments that measure interpersonal complementarity, for example, with Benjamin and colleagues' (1986) Structural Analysis of Social Behavior and Strong and colleagues' (1988) Interpersonal Communication Rating System, or relational control (e.g., Friedlander & Heatherington, 1989; Friedlander & Phillips, 1984; Tracey & Ray, 1984).

The third level of the process hierarchy, *episode,* is currently receiving attention among process researchers because it allows for a fuller appreciation of therapeutic context than any of the three other levels. An episode, or therapeutic "event," refers to the following (Greenberg, 1984):

> an island of behavior distinguishable from the surrounding behaviors in the ongoing psychotherapeutic process. To the client the event has the quality of a whole and its completion is experienced as a closure of some interaction with the therapist. For the therapist the event represents a therapeutic activity that comes to some closure in the hour. The event is like a short incident in a novel or a drama. (pp. 137–138)

This unit of analysis has particular meaning for therapists, because analyses of key events in therapy can provide a detailed understanding of the complex and unfolding behaviors of therapists and clients as they work on a specific therapeutic task. Unlike the traditional analyses of content and speech acts in which random sampling of behaviors occurs within and across sessions, analyses of episodes do not presume that the therapeutic process is static or uniform, even within a single case. Rather, the observation of a given speech act—therapist interpretation, let's say—has importance in the context of a particular kind of therapeutic episode, such as repairing a rupture in the therapeutic alliance (Safran, Crocker, McMain, & Murray, 1990).

One of the earliest events-based studies of the therapeutic process was Rice and Saperia's (1984) work on problematic reactions. A problematic reaction refers to "a point at which the client recognizes that his or her own reaction to a particular situation is problematic in some way" (Rice & Saperia, 1984, p. 33). In this study, theorizing and data collection were carried out in an iterative manner, with each informing the other and resulting in a conceptual model of how clients progress, in the session, from an initial description of a problematic reaction (the "marker") to a greater understanding of its idiosyncratic meaning for themselves (the "resolution").

In the cases of Alix and Beth, problematic reaction episodes might unfold differently. The marker might be identical—both children describing an angry encounter with their mothers during which they realized that their reactions were excessive or inappropriate. The in-session resolutions are likely to vary, however. Whereas Alix might come to a complex understanding of her reaction as related to adoption and separation-individuation issues, Beth may simply come to understand that she reacted angrily because she was hurt. Not only might these resolutions differ, but also the client and therapist behavioral sequences might differ. Alix should be more able to examine her cognitive constructions (Friedlander & Heatherington, 1998) than Beth, for example, and Alix's therapist should rely more on questions, reflections, and interpretations. Beth's therapist, on the other hand, may best help her by encouraging her to express her thoughts and feelings.

The highest and most inclusive level of the process hierarchy is the *therapeutic relationship.* In Greenberg's (1986) schema, the assumption is that knowledge of content, speech acts, and key therapeutic episodes is most relevant when we have information about the quality of the relationship between therapist and client. Take an event marked by Alix's anger toward her therapist, for example. The successful resolution of an anger episode is likely to proceed differently in a relationship that has been rocky from the start than in one in which the client is feeling safe and supported.

Studying relationship variables can be meaningful even in the absence of content and speech act data. Early researchers interested in the therapeutic relationship observed the strength of therapist-offered facilitative conditions using Truax and Carkhuff's (1967) rating scales for accurate empathy and respect or Barrett-Lennard's (1962) self-report measures of therapist empathy, positive regard, and genuineness. More recently, attention has been paid to the *therapeutic alliance,* defined as a strong emotional bond that accompanies a mutual agreement between client and therapist on the goals and tasks of therapy (Bordin, 1979). Considerable evidence has accumulated showing that (adult) clients' ratings of the alliance early in treatment—that is, between the third and fifth sessions—are predictive of treatment outcome (Horvath & Symonds, 1986). Furthermore, this relationship has been observed across theoretical approaches (Horvath & Symonds, 1986). Adult measures of the therapeutic alliance include client and therapist self-report instruments (e.g., Horvath & Greenberg, 1986; Marmar, Horowitz, Weiss, & Marziali, 1986) as well as observer rating scales (e.g., Alexander & Luborsky, 1986). Recently, Shirk (1992) developed a self-report instrument of the alliance for child psychotherapy, with parallel versions for client and therapist.

In the cases of Beth and Alix, differences in relationship variables may be predicted based on their developmental levels. Whereas, for Beth, the most important facilitative condition may be the therapist's empathy for her, for Alix it may be unconditional regard and genuineness. With respect to the therapeutic alliance, treatment outcome might be best predicted from Beth's perception of the emotional bond with her therapist, while in Alix's case it might well be the perception of mutuality in negotiating the goals and tasks of therapy.

In the next section, a summary of the developmentally relevant process literature with children and adolescents is presented. This discussion sets the stage for the introduction of a model to design clinically meaningful, developmental process research.

Process Research with Children: Developmental Implications

In 1995, a computer and manual search of the published literature resulted in the location of fewer than twenty investigations of individual psychotherapy with children, spanning half the century. Although no studies have compared the behaviors of children at different developmental levels, support for the notion that chronological age affects the therapeutic process was found in the earliest literature.

Three investigations conducted in the 1940s and 1950s had as their aim the development of observational coding systems to describe behaviors in play therapy. In the earliest study, Landisberg and Snyder (1946) applied Snyder's (1945) coding system for adults to the behaviors of four preschoolers in play therapy. A dissertation by Finke (cited in Mook, 1982b) represented the first attempt to create a coding system specifically for children in nondirective play therapy. Lebo (1955) used Finke's coding system to identify differences in play with children at different ages. Sampling three sessions with each of twenty children, age 4 to 12 years, Lebo concluded that maturation affected the children's behaviors. Older children, for example, tested the limits less frequently, were less disclosing, and less likely to invite the therapist to play. Older children also tended to be more assertive.

In 1972 Wright, Truax, and Mitchell questioned the appropriateness of using instruments with children that had been developed for studying psychotherapy with adults. Applying Truax and Carkhuff's (1967) measures for estimating accurate empathy, nonpossessive warmth, and genuineness to videotaped segments of thirty-two child–therapist dyads, Wright and colleagues found adequate but weaker reliability correlations than those typically reported with adults. The authors attributed this difference to the large nonverbal component in therapeutic interactions with children.

A decade later, Mook (1982b) also found that client-centered paradigms could reliably be used in process research with children. In her factor analytic comparison of the verbal behaviors of two girls, age 8 and 12, Mook (1982a) found similarities as well as differences. Both clients spoke most frequently (and affirmatively) about others and about events unrelated to their problems and, secondarily, about their problems and themselves. Whereas both children questioned the therapist and asked for advice and information, this pattern was more pronounced for the younger client. The latter also used a simpler pattern of verbal responses, expressed herself more through play, and focused more on the present. The older child, by contrast, used a more complex pattern of responses and was overall more direct and people-oriented. She was also more likely to focus on the past. Interestingly, the rate of self-exploration was low for both children, particularly the younger one. Whereas the younger child increased her levels of self-exploration over time, these levels "fluctuated in a striking manner across sessions" for the older child (Mook, 1982a, p. 268). Other changes suggested a gradual but steady increase over time in "understanding" and "action" responses for the 8 year old. Wide variability was observed in these responses for the 12 year old, however, with "a fast initial progress, which was temporarily lost but regained by the fourth recorded session" (Mook, 1982a, p. 273).

In 1985 Braswell and colleagues developed a thirteen-category coding system for child and therapist behaviors relevant to cognitive–behavioral treatment, and this system was used to predict client improvement in a randomized trial for children with self-control difficulties. Results showed that client behavior reflecting active involvement in treatment was predictive of teacher-rated gains in classroom behavior, improvement as well as maintenance. Although none of the active involvement categories was related to age, younger children (and their therapists) exhibited significantly more off-task behaviors.

Results of these studies provide limited support for the notion that variability in children's verbal responses may have something to do with development. The sequencing or patterning of client behaviors in interaction with those of the therapist have not, however, been illuminated in any of these studies, and in only one investigation (Braswell et al., 1985) have process variables been linked with treatment outcomes. Conclusions are further limited by the absence of contextual information on the therapeutic tasks being addressed in the sessions. It would be important to know, for example, whether the variability observed in the early treatment of Mook's (1982a) 12-year-old client had to do with her testing the relationship with the therapist, a therapeutic event that is more probable for a child of her age than for an 8 year old. In other words, development is important not only for understanding the psychosocial issues of the client but also for assessing the unfolding processes in the therapy itself.

DESIGNING PROCESS RESEARCH: A GENERIC MODEL

Many books and articles describe numerous approaches to the design and evaluation of clinical research (e.g., Kazdin, 1992). Selecting from among the array of methodologies can be bewildering, however. Each approach has distinct advantages and disadvantages, but none is clearly superior. Discovery-oriented case studies, for example, can provide clinically rich descriptions of a single psychotherapy treatment but have limited external validity. Field experiments can provide some information about links between therapeutic processes and client outcomes but tend to ignore the contextual information that is most meaningful to the practitioner.

A better strategy is to allow the question to guide subsequent methodological decisions. As Elliott (1994) argued, "rigor in psychotherapy research" involves "selecting important questions and methods appropriate to them, and then following principles of good practice specific to the research genre defined by those questions and methods" (p. 1).

In the model that follows, research goals and theoretical or clinical questions provide direction for the researcher's subsequent choices of empirical paradigm, method of inquiry, sample, and behavior (see Figure 27.1). Although the model is a generic one, the examples illustrating each step in the model reflect developmentally informed research questions.

As seen in Figure 27.1, the first step in the model involves specifying the research goal as either to explain, describe, or understand. At the second step of the model, the research question is specified. Theory-driven questions have as their aim to explain (in a causal sense) or describe phenomena, whereas discovery-oriented questions seek to describe and/or understand. These differences reflect the positivist versus the phenomenological perspectives on scientific inquiry (Bogdan & Biklan, 1992).

Research that is theory-driven is deductive and can be based on formal theory, conceptual models, logic, or the results of past research. Developmental theories could prompt any number of research questions about the treatments of children like Alix and Beth. From psychosocial development theories, we might predict that Alix will be more actively involved in selecting topics for discussion than Beth (cf. Lebo, 1955) or that Beth will be more responsive to therapy if she is first engaged in some kind of play with the therapist. From a cognitive development perspective, we might predict that better outcomes will be achieved for Alix when she negotiates the goals and tasks of therapy with the therapist, whereas this aspect of the alliance will be less salient for Beth. Based on models of developmental psychopathology (Lewis &

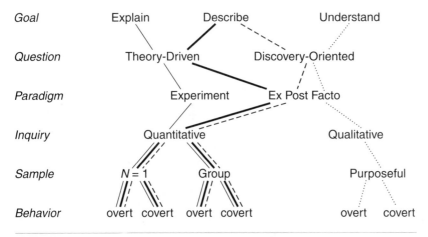

FIGURE 27.1 Generic model for designing process research

Miller, 1990) and the identity development of adoptees (Brodzinsky et al., 1993), we might predict that Alix's depression would be reflected in figurative language (Mc-Mullen, 1985) about shame, guilt, and loss of control while Beth's difficulties would be reflected in metaphors about anger and loss.

Research that is discovery-oriented, on the other hand, is inductive. It has as its aim the identification of patterns or regularities in the data that can guide future theorizing. From a discovery-oriented perspective, research questions are posed in an open-ended fashion. This approach is likely to yield clinically rich information, particularly given the paucity of available findings to guide theory-driven questions about psychotherapy with children.

Most of the early studies in the literature were discovery-oriented and focused on the speech acts of clients. Discovery-oriented investigations can also be used to identify therapist behaviors. As an example, one could identify the patterns of verbal response modes used by experienced therapists in the successful treatments of children at different developmental levels. We might find that with children like Beth the more effective therapist relies exclusively on questioning, encouragement, and providing information, whereas with adolescents like Alix the successful therapist's repertoire is more varied, including more interpretation and confrontation. Discovery-oriented studies could also be used to identify sequences of therapist and client behaviors in important, or key, events that occur with regularity. Because anger is an important component of depression, we might study the unfolding dynamics in anger events, that is, episodes that are marked by the child expressing anger directly at the therapist. Comparing anger events with Beth and Alix might yield important clinical in-

formation that reflects the successful therapist's sensitivity to children's developmental differences.

It should be noted that no discovery-oriented research is purely discovery-oriented (Hill, 1990). Rather, there must be some conceptual underpinning to guide the sampling method and selection of instruments. Although we may have no specific theoretical model from which to predict differences in the successful resolution of anger events for Beth and Alix, implicit in the choice of this event for study is the assumption that children at different ages experience interpersonal anger differently.

At the third step of the model, once the research question is specified, the empirical paradigm is identified. As shown in Figure 27.1, studies that seek to explain, in a causal sense, are experimental, but those that seek to describe or understand require, by definition, an ex post facto design.

Therapy experiments can be laboratory analogues or randomized quasi-experiments (Cook & Campbell, 1979). Analogue research is particularly useful for testing theoretical propositions about the therapy process, in which the external validity is not deemed as important as the internal validity. Based on theory, for example, we might predict that younger children, like Beth, would view a directive therapist more favorably than would older children, who would respond favorably to less direction. A two-by-two experiment could be conducted in which groups of younger and older children view a 15-minute videotaped vignette of an initial therapy session with a directive or a nondirective therapist. Participants' ratings on the Barrett-Lennard Relationship Inventory (Barrett-Lennard, 1962, 1986) or on the Counselor Rating Form (LaCrosse & Barak, 1975) could be used to test the interaction effect. Significant differences on the empathy, attractiveness, and trustworthiness subscales of these instruments by participant age and by therapist behavior would support the interaction hypothesis.

This hypothetical study has the advantage of providing the identical stimulus for children at two age levels. The same therapist would be used in both vignettes, which are piloted to ensure realism as well as the integrity of the manipulation—therapist directiveness versus nondirectiveness. Significant results would be, however, tempered by limits to the study's generalizability. Not only does a videotape stimulus represent a single therapist and a single presenting problem, but the participants are not actual clients, may not have emotional difficulties, and do not interact with a therapist. Therefore, inferences need to be made cautiously.

Quasi-experiments, on the other hand, can be viewed as analog studies with relatively better external validity. Volunteers are sought who are experiencing a particular, well-defined problem or disorder, and random assignment to therapists maximizes internal validity. Quasi-experiments can either be conducted in the laboratory or in a field setting. Events-based studies can also be conducted as quasi-experiments. Volunteers with a particular concern, for example, a problematic reaction (Rice & Saperia, 1984), can be solicited to participate in an experiment involving one or more sessions. The therapeutic interventions could be varied to assess their relative effectiveness in resolving the client's presenting concern.

When the researcher specifies the number of interpretations to be made by the therapist in a given session, the study is experimental. When, on the other hand, the therapist is free to conduct the therapy in any way she or he deems best, the study is ex post facto, or descriptive. As shown in Figure 27.1, ex post facto research can be used to answer either theory-driven or discovery-oriented questions, but the latter can only be studied with ex post facto paradigms.

Whereas process variables can be manipulated in an experiment in which the dependent variable is client outcome, ex post facto process research need not be conducted in the absence of outcome data. Indeed, some indication of therapeutic effectiveness is desirable in order to evaluate the importance of the process variables that are observed in a discovery-oriented investigation. This methodology lends itself well to traditional process–outcome studies to test hypotheses like, "Better outcomes with depressed adolescents will be observed with more frequent therapist interpretations." A discovery-oriented example, suggested by the cases of Beth and Alix, might be, "How do therapists work most effectively with depressed children in middle childhood versus adolescence?" A variety of coding systems could be used to observe the content and speech acts of therapists and clients; self-report instruments could be used to evaluate each session, to estimate the strength of the therapeutic alliance, and

to rate the clients' perceptions of therapist-offered conditions; and pre and post measures could be obtained to assess changes in depressive symptoms over time.

At the fourth step of the model, the method of inquiry is specified. Whereas experiments are limited to quantitative methods, ex post facto paradigms can use either quantitative or qualitative methods (and analyses). Ex post facto studies whose aim is to describe typically require quantitative methods, but when the goal is to understand a phenomenon, a qualitative method is necessary. The two inquiry methods can, of course, be used in a single study whose aim is both to describe and understand.

In quantitative research, differences within and between individuals are quantifiable. Process instruments can be self-report measures (client, therapist, significant other), observational coding systems (of verbal or nonverbal behavior), or clinical ratings of sessions by trained observers. Each genre provides numeric data by which comparisons are made. In theory-driven paradigms, the comparisons are used to test hypotheses (e.g., "Adolescents' ratings of the goals and task components of the therapeutic alliance will be more predictive of outcome than will the ratings of younger children"), whereas in discovery-oriented studies comparisons are made to elucidate relations between phenomena (e.g., "Do older and younger children differ in the frequency of initiating topics for discussion?").

In the traditional process study, the frequency of a given behavior, for example, topic initiation, is used to predict a proximal (e.g., session evaluation) or distal (e.g., client improvement) outcome. Because of the growing recognition that aggregated behaviors do not elucidate clinically meaningful phenomena (Greenberg & Pinsof, 1986), process researchers are increasingly relying on other kinds of quantitative analyses, such as sequential analysis (Friedlander & Phillips, 1984), chronographic analysis (Czogalik & Russell, 1994), and multidimensional scaling (Friedlander et al., 1987). In a sequential analysis, for example, temporal relationships are observed. That is, each behavior is both an antecedent and a consequent, reflecting the mutual influence process that characterizes psychotherapy.

In qualitative research, by contrast, the methods reflect subjective, phenomenological experiences, and the data are linguistic. Although there are numerous qualitative methods, including ethnomethodology, symbolic interaction, grounded theory and analytic induction, they share a core concern with developing "meaning" (Bogdan & Biklan, 1992). Qualitative data can be transcripts of psychotherapy sessions (Friedlander, Heatherington, Johnson, & Skowron, 1994; Russell et al., 1993; Stiles, Meshot, Anderson, & Sloan, 1992), interviews with clients or therapists, clinical observers' evaluations of a case, or therapists' case notes.

Analyses involve extensive coding of the linguistic data with the aim of generating themes that "illuminate the inner dynamics of situations" (Bogdan & Biklan, p. 32).

Qualitative methods, which are particularly useful for understanding little known phenomena, can be worthwhile for initiating a program of research on a developmental question. One might interview children like Alix and Beth, for example, to discover how children at different stages of psychosocial development work through adoption-related grief in therapy. One might conduct a Comprehensive Process Analysis (Elliott, 1993) on episodes or sessions that depressed children have identified, immediately after the session, as particularly helpful. Such an investigation might provide an understanding of how children at the concrete versus the formal operational level experience the treatment process differently.

In the next step of the model, a decision is required about the appropriate sample. In quantitative research, studies can either be $N = 1$ or group, depending on whether the focus is idiographic or nomothetic. An idiographic approach is particularly valuable for studying rare cases. In qualitative research, by contrast, purposeful sampling is used. Purposeful sampling refers to selecting participants specifically because the researcher believes that their data, in particular, will expand the developing model (Bogdan & Biklan, 1992). To conduct a qualitative study with clients like Beth and Alix, we might deliberately seek children at different ages with similar adoption histories and life circumstances.

In the process literature, most $N = 1$ studies are ex post facto in nature because of the difficulty involved in manipulating process variables in an experimental (e.g., *ABAB*) or multiple baseline design. This is not to say that such experiments cannot be conducted. One could, for example, vary the therapist's use of adoption-related interpretations for their effects on Alix's vocal quality (Rice & Kerr, 1986), level of experiencing (Klein et al., 1986), and session evaluations (Stiles & Snow, 1984).

Case studies could also be used to elucidate the therapeutic processes that help children move through important developmental transition periods. One such investigation might involve an intensive analysis of the successful therapy of a young child who refuses to attend school. Another might involve studying the successful therapy of a maltreated child with an attachment disorder.

Theory-driven, ex post facto case studies can be designed to elucidate the specific change mechanisms that may account for successful treatment. In recent years, psychodynamic researchers have developed several structured methods for formulating a conceptual model that is tailored to a specific client (e.g., Curtis, Silberschatz, Weiss, Sampson, & Rosenberg, 1988; Luborsky & Crits-Christoph,

1990). Once the case formulation is completed by a panel of clinicians, interview data are analyzed to determine whether the treatment unfolded as predicted by the model. Although the various case-formulation methodologies emphasize different aspects of psychodynamic treatment, they all use trained clinical observers to identify important relationship conflicts that are discussed repeatedly in the therapy sessions (Luborsky et al., 1993). Modifications over time in the quality, frequency, or intensity of the client's conflict provide empirical support for the theorized mechanism of change.

Because the goal of psychodynamic treatment with children is to further their psychosocial development, an interesting case study might involve observing a theoretically predicted change, over the course of treatment, in a child's in-session narratives. We might hypothesize, for example, that Alix avoids intimate relationships because of unresolved feelings about her birth history. The Core Conflictual Relationship Theme method (Luborsky & Crits-Christoph, 1990) could be used to assess qualitative differences in the stories she presents in therapy about her relations with peers and important family members.

As shown in Figure 27.1, the final step in the model involves a decision about sampling overt or covert behaviors. Overt behaviors could be analyzed—quantitatively or qualitatively—from transcripts of psychotherapy sessions, whereas covert behaviors could be obtained through client or therapist interviews, self-report instruments, or videotape-assisted recall procedures (e.g., Elliott, 1986; Hill & O'Grady, 1985). The most comprehensive approach would, of course, be to combine overt and covert data in a single investigation.

SUMMARY AND CONCLUSIONS

Of course, no one investigation can provide definitive answers to the kinds of research questions posed in the above illustrations. However, a clinically meaningful program of research that is prompted by a developmental question can be designed by following the steps in the model described above.

One stumbling block, however, may be finding an appropriate measure. Researchers in the child therapy field have long decried the lack of instruments—self-report measures, clinical rating scales, and observational coding systems—for analyzing in-session change. Consequently, recent efforts have been geared toward developing measures and methodologies that are appropriate for child psychotherapy. Smith-Acuna, Durlak, and Kaspar (1991), for example, adapted a well known self-report instrument for adults (Orlinsky & Howard, 1975) and found that different dimensions of child and therapist emotion and behavior were internally consistent and related to session goals. Shirk and Saiz (1992) designed the Therapeutic Alliance Scales for Children based on a developmental, social–cognitive model of the alliance. Estrada (1995) and colleagues at Loyola University of Chicago developed a process rating scale for therapy with children. Several investigators have been studying children's stories, or "narratives," as a means for understanding effective therapeutic interventions (Brandell, 1986; Mook, 1991; Russell et al., 1993).

None of these measures, however, was designed to take development into account. To devise such an instrument, one would need to include items that either assess developmental gains or that reflect behaviors at different developmental levels. An observer rating scale could be devised, for example, in which specific technical errors on the part of the therapist are assessed. One such error might be expecting a child at the concrete operational level to engage in metacognition. Another error might be discouraging constructive autonomous behavior on the part of an adolescent.

With the appropriate instruments, research is needed to identify therapeutic processes that facilitate—or fail to facilitate—a child's development (e.g., Heinecke & Strassman, 1975) as well as to compare and contrast the in-session behaviors of children at different developmental levels who are successfully helped in psychotherapy (e.g., Durlak et al., 1991). Development can be defined in terms of cognitive skills, psychosocial tasks, ego functions, language proficiency, or psychopathology. Simply equating chronological age with development can be misleading.

Given the paucity of theory and available research evidence on developmental issues in therapy, one might well begin with a discovery-oriented investigation whose aim is to describe and understand differences in the effective treatments of children at different developmental levels. Development could be defined cognitively, psychosocially, or with respect to the course of the disorder of interest. The initial study might combine (1) a quantitative, descriptive analysis of content, speech acts, and relationship variables in successful child therapy cases with (2) a qualitative analysis of interviews or therapeutic episodes identified as memorable or meaningful by the clients. Inferences from this study could inform subsequent theory-driven research—laboratory analogs, case studies, or field experiments.

This chapter has focused uniquely on development as the client attribute of interest for child therapy researchers. Many other individual difference variables could, of course, provide a worthwhile focus for process researchers. These include motivation, attachment style, and openness to experience, among others—variables that affect and are, themselves, affected by development. Indeed, there are enough important,

unanswered questions about effective psychotherapy with children to keep all of us busy for years to come.

REFERENCES

Alexander, L. B., & Luborsky, L. (1986). The Penn Helping Alliance Scales. In L. S. Greenberg & W. M. Pinsof (Eds.), *The psychotherapeutic process: A research handbook.* (pp. 325–366). New York: Guilford Press.

Barrett-Lennard, G. T. (1962). Dimensions of therapist response as causal factors in therapeutic change. *Psychological Monographs, 76* (43, Whole No. 562).

Barrett-Lennard, G. T. (1986). The Relationship Inventory now: Issues and advances in theory, method, and use. In L. Greenberg & W. Pinsof (Eds.), *The psychotherapeutic process: A research handbook* (pp. 439–476). New York: Guilford Press.

Benjamin, L. S., Foster, S. W., Roberto, L. G., & Estroff, S. E. (1986). Breaking the family code: Analysis of videotapes of family interactions by Structural Analysis of Family Behavior (SASB). In L. Greenberg & W. Pinsof (Eds.), *The psychotherapeutic process: A research handbook* (pp. 391–438). New York: Guilford Press.

Bogdan, R. C., & Biklen, S. K. (1992). *Qualitative research for education* (2nd ed.). Needham Heights, MA: Allyn and Bacon.

Bordin, E. S. (1979). The generalizability of the psychoanalytic concept of the working alliance. *Psychotherapy: Theory, Research, and Practice, 16,* 252–260.

Brandell, J. R. (1986). Using children's autogenic stories to assess therapeutic progress. *Journal of Child and Adolescent Psychotherapy, 3,* 285–292.

Braswell, L., Kendall, P., Braith, J., Carey, M., & Vye, C. (1985). Involvement in cognitive–behavioral therapy with children: Process and its relationship to outcome. *Cognitive Therapy and Research, 9,* 611–630.

Brodzinsky, D. M., Schecter, M. D., & Henig, R. M. (1993). *Being adopted—The lifelong search for self.* New York: Doubleday.

Carkhuff, R. R. (1969). *Helping and human relations* (Vol. 2). New York: Holt, Rinehart, & Winston.

Casey, R. J., & Berman, J. S. (1985). The outcome of psychotherapy with children. *Psychological Bulletin, 98,* 388–400.

Cook, T. D., & Campbell, D. T. (1979). *Quasi-experimentation: Design and analysis issues for field settings.* Boston: Houghton Mifflin.

Curtis, J., Silberschatz, G., Weiss, J., Sampson, H., & Rosenberg, S. (1988). Developing reliable psychodynamic case formulations: An illustration of the plan diagnosis method. *Psychotherapy, 25,* 256–265.

Czogalik, D., & Russell, R. L. (1994). Therapist structure of participation: An application of P-technique and chronographic analysis. *Psychotherapy, 31,* 75–94.

Dollard, J., & Auld, F. Jr. (1959). *Scoring human motives: A manual.* New Haven: Yale University Press.

Durlak, J. A., Fuhrman, T., & Lampman, C. (1991). Effectiveness of cognitive–behavior therapy for maladapting children: A meta-analysis. *Psychological Bulletin, 110,* 204–214.

Elliott, R. (1984). A discovery-oriented approach to significant events in psychotherapy: Interpersonal process recall and comprehensive process analysis. In L. Rice & L. Greenberg (Eds.), *Patterns of change* (pp. 249–286). New York: Guilford Press.

Elliott, R. (1986). Interpersonal Process Recall (IPR) as a psychotherapy process research method. In L. Greenberg & W. Pinsof (Eds.), *The psychotherapeutic process: A research handbook.* (pp. 503–527). New York: Guilford Press.

Elliott, R. (1989). Comprehensive process analysis: Understanding the change process in significant therapy events. In M. Packer & R. B. Addison (Eds.), *Entering the circle: Hermeneutic investigation in psychology* (pp. 165–184). Albany: State University of New York Press.

Elliott, R. (1994, June). *Rigor in psychotherapy research: Questions in search of appropriate methodologies.* Paper presented at the meeting of the Society for Psychotherapy Research, York, England.

Estrada, A. (1995, June). The training of child psychotherapists. In R. Russell (Chair), *Child psychotherapy research: Developments and implications for research and training.* Symposium conducted at the annual conference of the Society for Psychotherapy Research, Vancouver, Canada.

Friedlander, M. L. (1982). Counseling discourse as a speech event: Revision and extension of the Hill Counselor Verbal Response Category System. *Journal of Counseling Psychology, 29,* 425–529.

Friedlander, M. L. (1984). Psychotherapy talk as social control. *Psychotherapy, 21,* 335–341.

Friedlander, M. L., Ellis, M. V., Raymond, L., Siegel, S., & Milford, D. (1987). Convergence and divergence in the process of interviewing families. *Psychotherapy, 24,* 570–583.

Friedlander, M. L., & Heatherington, L. (1989). Analyzing relational control in family therapy interviews. *Journal of Counseling Psychology, 36,* 139–148.

Friedlander, M. L., & Heatherington, L. (1998). Assessing clients' constructions of their problems in family therapy discourse. *Journal of Marital and Family Therapy, 24,* 289–303.

Friedlander, M. L., Heatherington, L., Johnson, B., & Skowron, E. A. (1994). "Sustaining engagement": A change event in family therapy. *Journal of Counseling Psychology, 41,* 438–448.

Friedlander, M. L., & Phillips, S. D. (1984). Stochastic process analysis of interactive discourse in early counseling interviews. *Journal of Counseling Psychology, 31,* 139–148.

Gottschalk, L. A., Winget, C. M., Gleser, G. C., & Springer, K. J. (1966). The measurement of emotional changes during a psychiatric interview: A working model toward quantifying the psychoanalytic concept of affect. In L. A. Gottschalk & A. H. Auerbach (Eds.), *Methods of research in psychotherapy.* (pp. 93–126). New York: Appleton-Century-Crofts.

Greenberg, L. S. (1984). Task analysis: The general approach. In L. N. Rice & L. S. Greenberg (Eds.), *Patterns of change* (pp. 124–148). New York: Guilford Press.

Greenberg, L. S. (1986). Change process research. *Journal of Consulting and Clinical Psychology, 54,* 4–9.

Greenberg, L. S., & Pinsof, W. M. (1986). Process research: Current trends and future perspectives. In L. S. Greenberg & W. M. Pinsof (Eds.), *The psychotherapeutic process: A research handbook* (pp. 3–20). New York: Guilford Press.

Hall, C. S., & Van de Castle, R. L. (1966). *The content analysis of dreams.* New York: Appleton-Century-Crofts.

Hartmann, E., Glasser, B., Greenblatt, M., Solomon, M., & Levinson, D. J. (1968). *Adolescents in a mental hospital.* New York: Grune & Stratton.

Heinecke, C. M., & Strassman, L. H. (1975). Toward more effective research on child psychotherapy. *American Academy of Child Psychiatry, 14,* 561–588.

Hill, C. E. (1986). An overview of the Hill Counselor and Client Verbal Response Modes Category Systems. In L. Greenberg & W. Pinsof (Eds.), *The psychotherapeutic process: A research handbook* (pp. 131–160). New York: Guilford Press.

Hill, C. E. (1991). Almost everything you ever wanted to know about how to do process research on counseling and psychotherapy but didn't know who to ask. In C. E. Watkins & L. J. Schneider (Eds.), *Research in counseling* (pp. 85–118). Hillsdale, NJ: Erlbaum.

Hill, C. E., & Corbett, M. M. (1993). A perspective on the history of process and outcome research in counseling psychology. *Journal of Counseling Psychology, 40,* 3–24.

Hill, C. E., Helms, J. E., Spiegel, S. B., & Tichenor, V. (1988). Development of a system for categorizing client reactions to therapist interventions. *Journal of Counseling Psychology, 35,* 27–36.

Hill, C. E., & O'Grady, K. E. (1985). List of therapist intentions illustrated in a case study and with therapists of varying theoretical orientations. *Journal of Counseling Psychology, 32,* 3–22.

Hill, C. E., Siegelman, L., Gronsky, B., Sturniolo, F., & Fretz, B. R. (1981). Nonverbal communication and counseling outcome. *Journal of Counseling Psychology, 28,* 203–212.

Holmbeck, G. H., & Updegrove, A. L. (1995). Clinical-developmental interface: Implications of developmental research for adolescent psychotherapy. *Psychotherapy, 32,* 16–33.

Horvath, A. O., & Greenberg, L. S. (1986). Development of the Working Alliance Inventory. In L. S. Greenberg & W. M. Pinsof (Eds.), *The psychotherapeutic process: A research handbook* (pp. 529–556). New York: Guilford Press.

Horvath, A. O., & Symonds, B. D. (1991). Relation between working alliance and outcome in psychotherapy: A meta-analysis. *Journal of Counseling Psychology, 38,* 139–149.

Hoshmand, L. T. (1989). Alternate research paradigms: A review and teaching proposal. *The Counseling Psychologist, 17,* 3–79.

Kazdin, A. E. (1992). *Methodological issues and strategies in clinical research.* Washington, DC: American Psychological Association.

Kazdin, A. E. (1993). Psychotherapy for children and adolescents: Current progress and future research directions. *American Psychologist, 48,* 644–657.

Kiesler, D. J. (1973). *The process of psychotherapy: Empirical foundations and systems of analysis.* Chicago: Aldine.

Klein, M. H., Mathieu, P. L., Gendlin, E. T., & Kiesler, D. J. (1986). The Experiencing Scale. In L. S. Greenberg & W. M. Pinsof (Eds.), *The psychotherapeutic process: A research handbook* (pp. 21–72). New York: Guilford Press.

LaCrosse, M. B., & Barak, A. (1976). Differential perceptions of counselor behavior. *Journal of Counseling Psychology, 23,* 170–172.

Landisberg, S., & Snyder, W. U. (1946). Nondirective play therapy. *Journal of Clinical Psychology, 2,* 203–214.

Lebo, D. (1955). Quantification of the nondirective play therapy process. *Journal of Genetic Psychology, 86,* 375–378.

Lewis, M., & Miller, S. M. (Eds). (1990). *Handbook of developmental psychopathology.* New York: Plenum Press.

Luborsky, L., Barber, J., Binder, J., Curtis, J., Dahl, H., Horowitz, M., Perry, J., Schacht, T., Silberschatz, G., & Teller, V. (1993). Transference-based measures: A new class based on psychotherapy sessions. In N. Miller, L. Luborsky, J. Barber, & J. Docherty (Eds.), *Psychodynamic treatment research: A handbook for clinical practice.* (pp. 326–341). New York: Basic Books.

Luborsky, L., & Crits-Christoph, P. (1990). *Understanding transference: The CCRT method.* New York: Basic Books.

Mahl, G. F. (1963). The lexical and linguistic levels in the expression of the emotions. In P. H. Knapp (Ed.), *Expression of the emotion in man* (pp. 77–105). New York: International University Press.

Marmar, C. R., Horowitz, M. J., Weiss, D. S., & Marziali, E. (1986). The development of the Therapeutic Alliance Rating System. In L. S. Greenberg & W. M. Pinsof (Eds.), *The psychotherapeutic process: A research handbook.* (pp. 367–390). New York: Guilford Press.

McMullen, L. M. (1985). Methods for studying the use of novel figurative language in psychotherapy. *Psychotherapy, 22,* 610–619.

Miller, L. C., Barrett, C. L., Hampe, E., & Noble, H. (1972). Comparison of reciprocal inhibition, psychotherapy, and waiting list control for phobic children. *Journal of Abnormal Psychology, 79,* 269–279.

Mook, B. (1982a). Analyses of client variables in a series of psychotherapy sessions with two child clients. *Journal of Clinical Psychology, 38,* 263–274.

Mook, B. (1982b). Analysis of therapist variables in a series of psychotherapy sessions with two child clients. *Journal of Clinical Psychology, 38,* 63–76.

Mook, B. (1991). The significance of hermeneutics to child psychotherapy. *Journal of Psychiatry and Neuroscience, 16,* 182–187.

Orlinsky D., & Howard, K. (1975). *Varieties of psychotherapeutic experience: Multivariate analyses of patients' and therapists' reports.* New York: Teachers College.

Patterson, G. R., De Baryshe, B. D., & Ramsey, E. (1989). A developmental perspective on antisocial behavior. *American Psychologist, 44,* 329–335.

Rice, L. N., & Kerr, G. P. (1986). Measures of client and therapist vocal quality. In L. S. Greenberg & W. M. Pinsof (Eds.), *The psychotherapeutic process: A research handbook* (pp. 73–105). New York: Guilford Press.

Rice, L., & Saperia, E. (1984). Task analysis of the resolution of problematic reactions. In L. Rice & L. S. Greenberg (Eds.), *Patterns of change* (pp. 29–66). New York: Guilford Press.

Russell, R. L., Greenwald, S., & Shirk, S. R. (1991). Language change in child psychotherapy: A meta-analytic review. *Journal of Consulting and Clinical Psychology, 59,* 916–919.

Russell, R. L., & Trull, T. J. (1986). Sequential analyses of language variables in psychotherapy process research. *Journal of Consulting and Clinical Psychology, 54,* 16–21.

Russell, R. L., Van den Broek, P., Adams, S., & Rosenberger, K. (1993). Analyzing narratives in psychotherapy: A formal framework and empirical analyses. *Journal of Narrative and Life History, 3,* 337–360.

Safran, J. D., Crocker, P., McMain, S., & Murray, P. (1990). Therapeutic alliance rupture as a therapy event for empirical investigation. *Psychotherapy, 27,* 154–165.

Shaffer, D. (1984). Notes on psychotherapy research among children and adolescents. *Journal of the American Academy of Child Psychiatry, 23,* 552–561.

Shirk, S. R., & Saiz, C. C. (1992). Clinical, empirical, and developmental perspectives on the therapeutic relationship in child psychotherapy. *Development and Psychopathology, 4,* 713–728.

Siegel, C. L. F. (1972). Changes in play therapy behaviors over time as a function of differing levels of therapist-offered conditions. *Journal of Clinical Psychology, 28,* 235–236.

Smith-Acuna, S., Durlak, J. A., & Caspar, C. J. (1991). Development of child psychotherapy process measures. *Journal of Clinical Child Psychology, 20,* 126–131.

Snyder, W. V. (1945). Investigation of non-directive psychotherapy. *Journal of Genetic Psychology, 33,* 193–223.

Stiles, W. B. (1979). Verbal response modes and psychotherapeutic technique. *Psychiatry, 42,* 49–62.

Stiles, W. B., Meshot, C. M., Anderson, T. M., & Sloan, W. W., Jr. (1992). Assimilation of problematic experiences: The case of John Jones. *Psychotherapy Research, 2,* 81–101.

Stiles, W. B., & Snow, J. S. (1984). Counseling session impact as viewed by novice counselors and their clients. *British Journal of Clinical Psychology, 31,* 3–12.

Strong, S. R., Hills, H. J., Kilmartin, C. T., DeVries, H., Lanier, K., Nelson, B. N., Strickland, D., & Meyer, C. W. (1988). The dynamic relations among interpersonal behaviors: A test of complementarity and anticomplementarity. *Journal of Personality and Social Psychology, 54,* 798–810.

Tracey, T. J., & Ray, P. B. (1984). Stages of successful time-limited counseling: An interactional examination. *Journal of Counseling Psychology, 31,* 13–27.

Truax, C. B., & Carkhuff, R. R. (1967). *Toward effective counseling and psychotherapy.* Chicago: Aldine.

Wright, L., Truax, C. R., & Mitchell, K. M. (1972). Reliability of process ratings of psychotherapy with children. *Journal of Clinical Psychology, 28,* 232–234.

CHAPTER 28

DEVELOPMENTAL OUTCOME RESEARCH

John R. Weisz
Vanessa Robin Weersing

Many of the treatments for children and adolescents that are currently represented in psychotherapy outcome research are adevelopmental in important respects. Many are based in part on models of psychopathology originally developed for adults, and a number of the treatment procedures are largely modifications or junior versions of treatment programs originally designed for adults. Despite heavy overlap in their populations of interest, and despite their common emphasis on the study of *change,* the fields of child clinical and developmental psychology have remained surprisingly separate, insular enterprises, and most child treatments show surprisingly little evidence of the influence of empirical findings from developmental psychology (see also Furman, 1980).

Although most of the child and adolescent treatments that have been tested empirically do show beneficial effects (see Weisz & Weiss, 1993), it is likely that treatment effects can be improved, and one approach to generating such improvement may be to link the study of child and adolescent treatment to the study of child and adolescent development. In principle, treatment benefit should be enhanced to the extent that treatments are adjusted to fit the developmental characteristics of the treated individuals. In practice, though, we know little about whether this proposition is actually true, because the issue is so rarely addressed in research. To test the proposition may require that we link both treatment development and outcome assessment to developmental considerations in a much more comprehensive way than has generally been done in the past. In the present chapter, we discuss ways that this might be done.

Outcome research can guide the development and refinement of treatment procedures by providing feedback on the level of treatment benefit generated by various interventions with various groups. Of course, outcome research can be—and often is—done in ways that largely ignore developmental issues, even when children and adolescents are being treated, and in these cases outcome research does little to inform the creation or refinement of developmentally sensitive interventions. Alternatively, outcome research can be structured in ways that attend closely to developmental issues, helping to stimulate cross-pollination between clinical and developmental research and generating the information needed to guide treatment refinement along developmental lines. This latter approach might be called *developmental outcome research,* as distinguished from simply *child and adolescent outcome research.* In this chapter, we discuss themes and questions relevant to developmental outcome research. We begin by noting some of the boundary conditions that make outcome assessment different for children and adolescents than for adults. We then offer an overview of the technology and substantive findings of outcome research with young people, with an emphasis on the use of meta-analysis. Next we discuss the kinds of variables that researchers would need to assess if outcome research and meta-analysis were to be made maximally developmental. And finally, we discuss several general principles of developmental psychology and their implications for developmental outcome research. For simplicity of presentation, we refer to children and adolescents collectively as "children," except where we intend to emphasize a distinction between the two age groups.

DEVELOPMENTALLY SIGNIFICANT BOUNDARY CONDITIONS FOR OUTCOME ASSESSMENT: THE WHODUNIT OF OUTCOME RESEARCH WITH CHILDREN VERSUS ADULTS

One way to think about the relation between outcome research and development is to note some of the circumstances that tend to make outcome assessment different for psychotherapy with children than for psychotherapy with adults. If we think of tracking outcomes as something like solving a mystery, it is perhaps not too fanciful to construe some of these differences in terms of the who, what, when, where, and why of assessment, in other words, the whodunit of outcome research.

Who? Constituencies, Informants, and Effective Agents of Treatment

The "Who?" of outcome research involves at least three questions. First, for whose benefit are we assessing outcomes, meaning, which constituencies have a stake in the outcome of treatment. In most adult outcome research, although people in the family and workplace may be affected, clients themselves are the constituency of major interest; frequently the client is self-referred, and sometime no one else even knows that the adult has sought treatment. In child research, by contrast, the stakeholders may include the treated child, that child's family members (especially the parents, who typically refer the child), teachers and others in the child's school, and perhaps peers with whom the child's interactions may have been problematic. As with adult clients, there are other potential stakeholders outside the child client's immediate circle: the therapist, perhaps clinic administrators, and the payor who funds the treatment (e.g., an insurance carrier). A key distinction, though, is that, unlike adults, children rarely seek treatment, and children fre-

quently do not think their problems are as serious as their parents believe. To illustrate this point, Figure 28.1 shows ratings from clinic-referred children and their parents, taken near the time of outpatient clinic intake, in a longitudinal study of child mental health care that we are conducting in California clinics. The ratings were made in response to the questions, "How serious are your problems?" and "How important is it for you to get help for your problems?" The disparity between parents' and children's investment in treatment prompted Howard (1995) to suggest that in child psychotherapy a distinction should be drawn between the "patient" (i.e., the child) and the "client" (i.e., the parent, and perhaps school staff, who sought treatment for the child).

A second focus of the "Who?" question concerns informants. Who will provide outcome information, and accordingly, by whose standards will change in the child be judged? The answer is likely to be more complicated for children than for adults, in part because of the multiple constituencies noted above, and in part because the individuals being treated in child therapy may be less able than adult clients to report accurately on their behavior and their internal states. It also seems undeniable that child psychopathology is best construed as a combination of actual child behavior and the lens through which that behavior is viewed and interpreted by people in the child's world (see Weisz, McCarty, Eastman, Suwanlert, & Chaiyasit, 1997). The same behavior may be acceptable when viewed by some people in some contexts (e.g., parents at home), but not when viewed by other people in other contexts (e.g., teachers in the classroom). Thus, to properly assess outcomes for children, we may need to tap multiple informants—parents, teachers, the treated children themselves, possibly peers, and—where possible—trained observers and diagnostic interviewers. Using observers and interviewers who are uninformed as to whether a child was treated or not may be particularly valuable, given the obvious dilemma that those who have the best opportunity to observe the child for long periods of time (e.g., parents and teachers) are also likely to know whether the child has received treatment. Finally, we must recognize that in some situations (e.g., abusive families, serious parental psychopathology) some of those in critical relationships with the child cannot be relied upon to give trustworthy outcome information.

A third form of the "Who?" question concerns the proximal agent who will carry out the treatment procedures. Unlike adult psychotherapy, the treatment of children often involves a transfer of skills from therapist to parents or teachers, who then carry out intervention procedures in the settings in which children spend most of their time. For some target problems, such as aggression and delinquency,

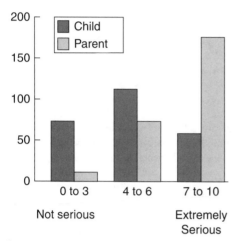

"How serious are your problems?"[1]

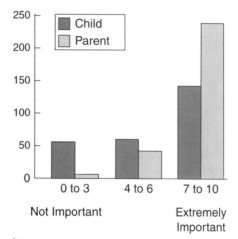

"How important is it for you to get over your problems soon?"[2]

[1]Question appropriately rephrased when posed to parent.

[2]Question appropriately rephrased when posed to parent.

FIGURE 28.1 Responses of clinic-referred children and their parents to two questions (answered near the time of clinic intake): (1) "How serious are your ["your child's" for parent form] problems?" and (2) "How important is it for you to get help for your ["your child's"] problems?" Scale for both questions was 0 to 10

the training of parents or teachers is predicated on the view that skill deficits by these adults have contributed to the child's problem behavior (see, e.g., Patterson, 1982, 1984, 1989). In other cases, no such assumption is made, but adult allies are called upon because their ongoing presence in the child's environment permits them to make the intervention procedures a regular part of the child's daily routine. Examples include the contingency contracting used by parents in Silverman's anxiety treatment program (see, e.g., Silverman, Ginsburg, & Kurtines, 1995; Silverman & Kurtines, 1996) to facilitate children's exposure to feared objects or situations, and the extensive behavioral training provided to parents in Lovaas's treatment program for autistic children (see, e.g., Lovaas, 1987; McEachin, Smith, & Lovaas, 1993) to facilitate continued skill building through a structured regimen of operant procedures at home.

What? Which Outcomes to Measure

Given the diverse constituencies noted above, especially careful thought must be given to the kinds of information needed for fair outcome assessment. Different stakeholders will orient toward different dimensions of outcome. For the treated child, outcomes such as personal well-being, or development of usable skills (social and other) may be para-

mount; and for children receiving treatment under duress, termination (as soon as possible) may be both the objective, and the outcome of greatest interest. For parents, relief of the immediate presenting problems may be most important, together with improved interactions with their child in the family context. For teachers, such outcomes as academic performance and social behavior (toward teacher and peers) in the school setting will be of special interest. By contrast, for the therapist, such outcomes as change in diagnostic status and child accomplishments that fit the therapy model (e.g., achievement of insight, change from depressogenic to realistic self-talk, change scores on various questionnaires) may be of primary interest; of course, such outcomes might be considered arcane by the child, family, and teachers, whose concerns are practical and functional.

In our work reviewing and integrating child and adolescent outcome research (e.g., Weisz & Weiss, 1993; Weisz, Weiss, et al., 1995), we have been struck by the heavy reliance on measures of theoretical interest to outcome researchers and therapists and the very limited emphasis on measures of practical importance to the child, family, and teachers. Particularly notable is the rarity with which referral concerns specific to individual children and their families are ever even noted, much less included in outcome assessment. In this respect, the "What?" of published outcome research with children may be faulted for being somewhat psychocentric and insufficiently developmental, at least in the sense that it is relatively insensitive to the outcomes of greatest interest to the child, family, and school.

Where? What Settings to Sample

Children live their lives in several settings, some quite different from those frequented by adults; each setting has its own implicit expectations for what children should be and how they should behave. Moreover, children have considerably less freedom to select their settings than do adults. Accordingly, it is important for outcome researchers to assess children's post-treatment behavior in multiple contexts, reflecting the variety of setting-specific expectations applied to the youngsters. Minimally, home, school, and less structured peer interaction situations may all need to be sampled to understand the full impact of an intervention program; and for many children, problems that are situation-specific (e.g., fear of darkness) dictate other settings in which outcomes must be gauged. Treatment researchers who take this multiple setting notion seriously may discover that their intervention produces benefits in some settings but not in others. In some cases, situation-specific treatment benefit may fit the child's and family's needs well. As an example, a high level of physical activity may be seen as a problem at school but not at home, in which case a treatment that reduces activity level at school but not at home might be considered quite successful. In other cases, a finding of situation-specific change may indicate that treatment failed to generalize as needed and thus may guide further refinement of the intervention. In such cases, limited intervention effects in a particular setting may highlight the need for additional treatment sessions, new exercises within existing sessions, or homework assignments focused on applying the core lessons of the treatment to that particular setting.

When? Timing of Assessments

Although people at all ages are developing, the rapid pace and radical transformations accompanying development from infancy through adolescence are unparalleled at other points in the life span. Assessment with young people thus means tracking a moving target. For example, bedwetting shows a highly predictable developmental curve, and the prevalence of various childhood fears changes markedly over time (see, e.g., King, Hamilton, & Ollendick, 1988; Ollendick, King, & Frary, 1989). Such developmental flux may argue for rather frequent assessments of child functioning during treatment, and it certainly argues for follow-up assessments to determine whether effects hold up beyond the termination of treatment, over and above the changes associated with development alone.

Current practice of outcome assessment is not strong in these respects. In the pool of outcome studies we have reviewed (see Weisz, Weiss, et al., 1987; Weisz, Weiss, et al., 1995), we find very little in the way of assessments between pre-therapy and post-therapy, and only about a third of published studies report any follow-up assessment beyond immediate post-treatment. For the minority of studies that have included follow-up, the mean lag between the end of treatment and the follow-up assessment is about 6 months. The news from these assessments is good, with no significant decline in treatment benefit over the follow-up period. However, it seems likely that effects of many treatments will eventually fade, and 6-month follow-up periods may not be sufficient to detect such fading. Learning when the benefits of particular treatments do tend to fade could help treatment developers plan for booster sessions and other means of enhancing durability of treatment effects in rapidly developing youngsters.

Why? Reasons for Outcome Assessment

Even the reasons for doing outcome research may be somewhat different for children than for adults. In treating children we are, in a sense, "chasing the normal developmental curve." As Shirk, in this volume, puts it, the goal of treatment is to "return children to healthy developmental pathways" (p. 68). As implied in our earlier "When?" section, few child problems are static across developmental periods within the same individual, and for many child problems the prevalence of various problems and syndromes in the general population shifts with changes in developmental level (see e.g., Achenbach & Edelbrock, 1981). Thus, we need relatively brief measurement intervals within individuals, and we need age-normed outcome measures that tell us where individuals stand relative to age- and gender-matched youth in the general population. Such measures permit us to go beyond merely knowing whether treatment groups are doing better than control groups, to knowing whether treated youngsters are moving toward the elusive "normal range" on various dimensions of functioning.

Another significant reason for doing outcome research with children is to understand how well we are doing at minimizing the cumulative developmental cost of child problems. Significant behavioral or emotional problems in childhood can be particularly devastating because they can interfere with the acquisition of diverse social, academic, and other skills needed for successful adaptation during the remainder of the life span. To know how well we are doing at minimizing such effects, we will need to include measures of social development and academic progress in our batteries of outcome measures. Child outcome research, to date, has a weak record with regard to such potentially important measures of real-world functioning.

THE CURRENT STATE OF THE ART: FROM OUTCOME STUDIES TO META-ANALYSES

Having considered ways that the constraints and boundary conditions of outcome assessments are different for children than for adults, we turn now to features of outcome research that are quite similar across the age range. Most of these features are related to the basic technology of outcome assessment. We cover this ground because any effort to make outcome research more developmental will need to build on current technology. Thus, to set the stage for a developmental discussion, we will briefly characterize the state of the art, and the substantive findings, of child outcome research.

Experimental Evidence on Child Psychotherapy Effects

Our knowledge about treatment effects comes primarily from outcome studies in which measures of behavioral and psychological functioning are used to compare a treatment group of children who have received a particular treatment with a control group of children who did not receive the treatment. In addition to testing the significance of group differences post-treatment, investigators may also compute an *effect size* (ES) statistic, an index of the magnitude and direction of treatment effects. For typical outcome studies, the ES is the post-treatment mean for the treated group on an outcome measure minus the corresponding mean for the control group, divided by the standard deviation of the outcome measure. Figure 28.2 provides a guide to interpreting ES values; note that the range of possible ES values is much broader than that shown in the figure. As the figure shows, ES values may be positive, indicating treatment benefit, or negative, indicating a detrimental treatment effect. Each ES corresponds to a percentile standing of the average treated child on the outcome measure(s) if that child were placed in the control group after treatment; for example, an ES of 0.50 would indicate that the average treated child scored better after treatment than 69 percent of the control group. Finally, note that Cohen (1992) has suggested that an ES of 0.20 indicates a "small" effect, 0.50 a "medium" effect, and 0.80 a "large" effect.

Experimental findings on child and adolescent psychotherapy effects tend to be summarized in the form of meta-

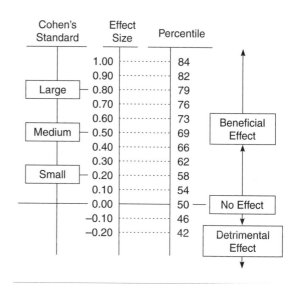

FIGURE 28.2 An aid to interpreting effect size (ES) statistics. Each ES value can be thought of as reflecting a corresponding percentile value (i.e., the percentile standing of the average treated child, after treatment, averaging across outcome measures, relative to the untreated group).

Source: Weisz, J. R., Donenberg, G. R., Han, S. S., & Weiss, B. (1995). Bridging the gap between laboratory and clinic in child and adolescent psychotherapy. *Journal of Consulting and Clinical Psychology, 63,* 688–701. Copyright 1995 by the American Psychological Association. Reprinted by permission.

analytic reviews (see Mann, 1990; Smith, Glass, & Miller, 1980; see also critiques of meta-analysis, e.g., by Wilson, 1985). In most psychotherapy meta-analyses, ES is the unit of analysis. Typically, a single mean ES is computed for each study (or each treatment group) in the collection to be reviewed by averaging across the various outcome measures. This makes it possible to compute an overall mean ES for the entire collection of studies and to compare mean ES for studies differing in potentially important ways—for example, type of therapy employed, target problem being treated, and importantly, age or gender of the children involved.

Findings of the Broad-Based Meta-Analyses of Child Psychotherapy Research

We know of four broad-based child therapy meta-analyses, that is, meta-analyses in which a variety of treated problems and types of intervention were included. Together, these four meta-analyses encompass more than 300 individual treatment outcome studies. Casey and Berman (1985) surveyed outcome studies published between 1952 and 1983 and focused on children age 12 and younger. Mean effect size (ES) was 0.71 for the studies that included treatment–control comparisons; the average treated child scored better after treatment than 76 percent of control group children, averaging across outcome measures. Weisz, Weiss, Alicke, and Klotz (1987) reviewed outcome studies published between 1952 and 1983 that included children age 4 to 18. The mean ES was 0.79; after treatment, the average treated child was at the 79th percentile of control group peers. Kazdin, Bass, Ayers, and Rodgers (1990) surveyed studies published between 1970 and 1988, which included youngsters age 4 to 18. For studies that compared treatment groups and *no-treatment control groups,* the mean ES was 0.88, indicating that the average treated child was better off after treatment than 81 percent of the no-treatment youngsters. For studies in the Kazdin et al. collection that involved treatment groups versus *active control groups,* the mean ES was 0.77, indicating that after treatment the average treated child was functioning better than 78 percent of the control group. Finally, a recent meta-analysis by Weisz, Weiss, Han, Granger, and Morton (1995) included studies published between 1967 and 1993 and involved children age 2 to 18. Mean ES was 0.71, indicating that after treatment the average treated child was functioning better than 76 percent of control group children. [For more detailed descriptions of the procedures and findings of the various meta-analyses, see Weisz & Weiss, 1993.]

The evidence from these four broad-based meta-analyses shows rather consistent positive treatment effects; ES values ranged from 0.71 to 0.84 (estimated overall mean for Kazdin et al., 1990), near Cohen's (1988) threshold of 0.80 for a "large" effect. Figure 28.3 summarizes findings from the four child meta-analyses and compares them to findings from two often-cited meta-analyses—Smith and Glass's (1977) analysis of predominantly adult psychotherapy outcome studies, and Shapiro and Shapiro's (1982) analysis of exclusively adult psychotherapy outcome studies. The figure shows that mean effects found in child meta-analyses fall roughly within the range of the mean effects found in these two adult meta-analyses.

Beyond overall mean effect size values, meta-analyses may also generate estimates of the impact of various factors of interest on treatment outcome (see, e.g., Weisz, Donenberg, Han, & Weiss, 1995). Such comparative estimates need to be carried out and interpreted with caution because of the confounding among factors that is common in meta-analyses. Some of the confounding can be addressed via statistical control and testing of interaction effects (see, e.g., Weisz et al., 1987, 1995); but in general, it is best to carry out such tests for primarily heuristic purposes and to view the findings as hypothesis-generating rather than hypothesis-testing. With these caveats in mind, let us consider a few illustrative findings. In our two meta-analyses (Weisz et al., 1987, 1995)

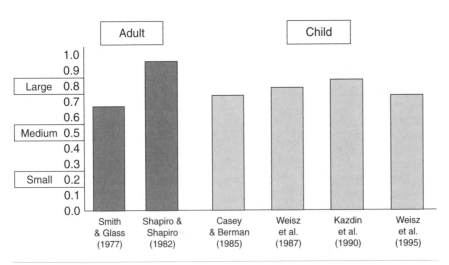

FIGURE 28.3 Mean effect sizes found in the predominantly adult meta-analysis by Smith and Glass (1977), in the exclusively adult meta-analysis by Shapiro and Shapiro (1982), and in four broad-based meta-analyses of psychotherapy outcome studies with children and adolescents

Source: Weisz, J. R., Donenberg, G. R., Han, S. S., & Weiss, B. (1995). Bridging the gap between laboratory and clinic in child and adolescent psychotherapy. *Journal of Consulting and Clinical Psychology, 63,* 688–701. Copyright 1995 by the American Psychological Association. Reprinted by permission.

studies involving behavioral treatments generated larger effects than studies using nonbehavior treatments (The Casey-Berman [1985] meta-analyses showed that same effect, at $p = 0.06$; Kazdin et al. [1990] did not make this comparison). By contrast, with minor exceptions (see Casey & Berman, 1985, pp. 392–393), meta-analyses have not found treatment outcomes to differ reliably as a function of type of problem being treated; ES values have been similar for internalizing and externalizing problems. The relation between age and treatment outcome has been variable across meta-analyses. However, the meta-analysis of the most recent collection of studies (Weisz et al., 1995) found mean ES to be larger for adolescents than for children. That main effect was qualified by the age × gender interaction shown in Figure 28.4; mean ES for samples of predominantly or exclusively adolescent girls was twice as large as mean ES for adolescent boys and for children of both genders. Perhaps the treatments used in this particular collection of studies was an especially good fit to the characteristics and needs of adolescent girls, but other interpretations are possible.

Group comparisons of this sort, using effect size as hard currency, might well become a useful tool in the hands of developmentally oriented outcome researchers. However, for meta-analytic data to be maximally useful in this way, the raw material that goes into the system needs to include variables of real developmental significance. Most child outcome studies include relatively few variables of this sort. In what follows, we offer several examples of the kinds of variables that might be useful developmentally, with a brief discussion of why these developmental variables may be related to outcome.

DEVELOPMENTAL FACTORS AND THEIR IMPLICATIONS FOR OUTCOME RESEARCH

In this section we consider some specific developmental factors to which outcome researchers might attend in assessing treatment effects. We tend to agree with Shirk (this volume) that

> we should not expect uniform outcomes for treatments delivered to children who vary widely in their social, cognitive, and emotional capacities. Instead, it is likely that developmental differences will moderate the effectiveness of many child treatments. (pp. 60–61)

An important task for the developmental outcome researcher, then, will be identifying those factors that do moderate treatment effects and using the moderating effects thus identified to modify treatments and enhance their impact with children of different developmental characteristics. Identifying candidate moderators of treatment outcome may help us move toward an agenda for developmental outcome research, one that could ultimately support the creation and refinement of developmentally sensitive treatments. Some of the relevant factors are simply developmental characteristics of the youth involved in the research, and perhaps the most obvious of these is age.

Age

For a variety of reasons (several suggested in the remainder of this chapter), age may be a moderator of outcome with many treatments. As our report on age effects in the meta-analyses might suggest, most published outcome research does report mean age of the children sampled, with the range or SD frequently added, as well. On the other hand, one sees almost no articles in which the potential moderating effect of age is directly assessed. Thus, we miss an important opportunity for first steps toward developmental outcome research. As noted above, three meta-analyses have assessed age effects; but note that these assessments are not the most precise possible, in part because they involve examining relations between *mean* age of the sample and mean ES, with

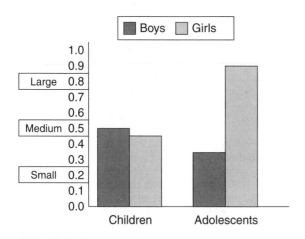

FIGURE 28.4   Mean effect size for samples of predominantly male and female children (11 years of age and younger) and adolescents (12 years of age and older)

Source: Weisz, J. R., Weiss, B., Han, S. S., Granger, D. A., & Morton, T. (1995). Effects of psychotherapy with children and adolescents revisited: A meta-analysis of treatment outcome studies. *Psychological Bulletin, 117,* 450–468. Copyright 1995 by the American Psychological Association. Reprinted by permission.

an entire study as the unit of analysis. And, as noted, these meta-analyses have not generated a consistent picture of the relation between age and outcome; it may be that the global meta-analytic approach is not the best strategy for addressing the impact of the age variable.

An important limitation of the global meta-analytic approach may be that age effects differ depending on type of therapy. The fact that each meta-analytic collection of studies has a particular array of therapies—differing from the array in each other meta-analysis—may explain why each meta-analysis generates its own distinctive picture of the relation between outcome and age. One example of how we might move beyond this limitation is found in Durlak, Fuhrman, and Lampman's (1991) meta-analysis of sixty-four treatment outcome studies involving cognitive–behavioral therapy (CBT). Durlak and colleagues hypothesized that effect sizes would be larger with adolescents than with preadolescent children; the reasoning was that adolescents are more likely to be functioning at a formal operational level and thus to be ready to learn the cognitive skills involved in CBT, particularly the use of cognitive strategies to guide behavior. The hypothesis was supported. Durlak and colleagues found a mean effect size of 0.92 for adolescents (ages 11–13), but only 0.55 for ages 7 to 11 and only 0.57 for ages 5 to 7. This unusual and important meta-analysis certainly deserves replication with forms of treatment other than CBT.

So analyses of age as a moderator of effects may make important contributions, and we regret that most researchers in individual outcome studies have failed to assess the potential moderating effect of even this, the simplest of developmental variables to measure. However, we must also note an important limitation of the age variable: It is, at best, an imperfect summary marker for multiple and diverse developmental factors—cognitive, social, and contextual—each of which deserves attention in its own right. Accordingly, we turn our attention now to a discussion of some of these more specific factors.

Cognitions about the Therapy Process and Its Purpose

In most therapy with adults, it is fair to assume that the individuals being treated understand the concept of psychotherapy and its purpose. Young children, by contrast, may have little grasp of the nature or purpose of therapy, and the concepts children at various developmental levels apply to the process are apt to be partly a function of their cognitive developmental level. There is room for a great deal of basic inquiry into how children construe psychotherapy, and outcome research could eventually profit from such inquiry. It seems likely that the ways children understand the process

will influence their response to it, and thus ways of construing and thinking about therapy might moderate treatment outcome. At present, we know too little about how to assess the relevant cognitions to even investigate their potential moderating role in outcome research.

Ability to "Decenter" and View Self from the Perspective of Others

Piaget (e.g., 1929, 1962) wrote a good deal about development of "decentration," the ability to detach from one's own point of view and perceive objects or events from an alternate perspective. Although the initial work on this theme dealt with visual perception, the notion of decentration was eventually extended to social contexts to encompass the ability to take the cognitive perspective of others on activities, events, and even oneself. In this more recent incarnation, the notion of cognitive decentration, or perspective-taking, is potentially relevant to treatment outcomes. For example, limited ability to decenter may set limits on the impact of treatments that involve considering other people's perspectives on events, self, and so forth. Such treatments certainly include cognitive–behavioral and psychodynamic interventions, both of which frequently involve efforts to help children see events, conditions, and even themselves from the perspective of others. To understand the success or failure of such techniques, it might well be useful to have some assessment of children's perspective-taking ability. Of course, it would also be useful to disaggregate assessment in such a way that we could determine whether those aspects of treatment that require perspective-taking were actually successful, independently of the overall behavioral changes that are more commonly assessed in outcome research; such disaggregation of assessment—akin to "manipulation checks" in experiments—is surprisingly rare in child outcome research.

Language Ability

Another dimension of cognitive development to which treatment outcomes may be related is language ability. Developmental variations in children's ability to encode and decode language may set limits on the success of therapies that rely heavily on language. Low-level encoding skills may limit children's ability to let the therapist know their thoughts and feelings and thus limit the therapist's ability to plan intervention that is well-tailored to the child's inner state. As a simple example, both cognitive behavioral and psychodynamic treatments for anxiety may require that the young client describe his or her anxious state in terms of physiological arousal (e.g., "I feel tense, my heart pounds, and I have a knot in my stomach") and psychological state (e.g., "Feels like everyone is staring at me; I'm afraid if I make a mistake, they'll think I'm stupid, and I'll feel humiliated."). Children whose encoding facility is too limited to permit such descriptions may not be able to help their therapist understand their anxious states well enough to target interventions with precision.

Limited ability to decode comments by the therapist may limit how helpful those comments actually are. Prescriptive, manual-driven therapies that are language-rich and rigidly scripted may not provide sufficient flexibility for therapists to adjust the language to the young client's capacities. And, of course, lack of assessment of language skills may hamper our ability to detect language-related reasons for variations in the outcomes of such therapies.

Finally, considerable developmental theory and research, dating at least to the work of Piaget (1923/1955) and Vygotsky (1934/1962), points to developmental differences in the ability to use "private speech" or "inner speech" to guide or inhibit behavior (see also Kohlberg, Yaeger, & Hjertholm, 1968; Zivin, 1979). Piaget and Vygotsky offered rather different predictions about the shape of the developmental trend over time, and subsequent evidence has been equivocal and complexly linked to the specific type of inner speech involved (see, e.g., Meichenbaum & Goodman, 1979). However, it does seem clear that developmental differences in the use of language to guide behavior might well lead to differences in children's responsiveness to therapies in which language is used to promote self control. An obvious example is CBT, in which children are taught to use "self-talk" to make themselves less impulsive, less anxious, less depressed, less aggressive, more prosocial, and/or more skilled at entering social groups. Use of such procedures assumes a well-developed connection between language and action, and this assumption may not be equally valid for all children, across developmental levels.

In some therapies, language skill, and the capacity to use language to guide behavior, are made targets of treatment as a step toward reducing problem behavior. In assessing the outcome of these therapies it would clearly be important to assess changes in language and in language-behavior coordination in addition to assessing changes in the problem behavior; such assessment could help clarify the degree to which language-related change played a mediating role. A meta-analysis by Russell, Greenwald, and Shirk (1991) suggests that some kinds of language facility can indeed be modified via psychotherapy. These authors reviewed twenty-six treatment-control comparisons in eighteen child therapy outcome studies that included at least one language measure; they found that therapy had a significant positive effect on language proficiency, particularly when the treatment was individually (vs. group) administered. Thus, the evidence suggests that it may be worthwhile to target certain kinds of language functioning for change during treatment. However, whether language change will be associated with desired behavioral changes is an empirical question, one that can only be addressed if researchers assess both language and behavioral outcomes.

Comprehension of Concepts or "Lessons" of the Treatment Program

Closely related to language ability is another phenomenon that seems likely to vary with developmental level: comprehension of the conceptual content and the central principles of a therapy program. Many therapies for young people are, to some extent, educational programs. For example, some treatment programs for depression are aimed at teaching young people the basic components of depression, plus strategies for alleviating depressed mood; and some programs for anxiety try to teach children the building blocks of anxiety (e.g., fear, physiological arousal, habitual avoidance, relief that rewards the avoidance), plus specific techniques for promoting exposure to the feared situation. Are there developmental differences in children's acquisition of these skills and might such differences influence treatment outcome? Intuitively, the answer to both questions would seem to be yes. But in fact, so little evidence has been collected to address these questions that we simply cannot provide an empirically respectable answer. Here is one area in which developmental outcome research is sorely needed.

At a minimum, it seems that therapy outcome researchers might try to identify the primary concepts they expect children to learn during their treatment program and then assess the degree to which treated children do acquire those concepts as a function of child developmental characteristics (even chronological age or mental age). At a higher level of sophistication, it seems possible that therapy researchers of a developmental bent might design and refine their treatment programs in light of the extensive empirical literature on the development of various concepts (e.g., causality, justice, emotion, morality). The researchers' expectations about which concepts fall within the treated youngsters' capacities could then be tested empirically by focusing assessment on concept acquisition as well as on behavioral outcome.

Abstract Reasoning

Certain kinds of abstract thinking, including forms of hypothetico–deductive reasoning, are thought by many developmentalists to emerge with the advent of formal operations, typically in adolescence. Yet many treatment programs for preadolescent children appear to involve considerable abstract reasoning. Consider, for example, social skills training programs in which children are taught to imagine hypothetical stressful social situations, imagine various ways that they might respond, imagine ways that others in the situation might respond to their response, and imagine various possible outcomes of the successive interactions that might ensue. This sort of chess-like, hypothetical reasoning may be possible for preadolescents, but developmental literature at least makes the question worthy of investigation. Consider also, the kind of movement from concrete instances to abstract categories required by many cognitively oriented therapies. For instance, some therapies for depression involve efforts to teach young clients to recognize instances of depressogenic cognitive errors, such as *overgeneralization* and *catastrophizing.* Outcome research could be used to guide treatment developers in the use of such procedures by providing information on the extent to which clients at various developmental levels do, indeed, learn the skills involved. If it should be found, say, that elementary school–age children have difficulty learning to use complex hypothetical reasoning, or to detect their own use of such abstract processes as overgeneralization, this might set the stage for development of more efficient ways to promote desired change in this age group.

Cognition–Behavior Connections

Developmental outcome research may also be used to examine one of the basic tenets of cognitive–behavioral intervention: The notion that cognitive changes will lead to behavior changes. This may not be a safe assumption for youth at all ages. In the meta-analysis of cognitive–behavioral treatment outcome studies by Durlak and colleagues (1991), cited above, the authors found that changes in cognitive processes and changes in behavior were essentially uncorrelated ($r = -.22$, *ns*). This suggests that we have a good deal to learn about the processes by which therapeutic change takes place among young people. The finding reminds us that positive effects of treatment based on a particular model do not necessarily validate the model.

This fact seems especially important in the child treatment domain, given the great extent to which treatments have been downloaded from the adult psychotherapy literature. So, another element of developmental outcome research should be the search for true mediators of therapeutic change among treated children at different developmental levels. As a step in this direction, investigators might disaggregate their treatment programs into component concepts and skills, as we suggested above, but then assess not only the degree to which those concepts and skills are acquired

but also the degree to which acquisition of each predicts the behavioral and affective outcomes toward which the treatment is directed. The findings of Durlak and colleagues (1991) suggest that researchers who follow such an approach may be in for some surprises.

CORE DEVELOPMENTAL PRINCIPLES AND THEIR IMPLICATIONS FOR OUTCOME ASSESSMENT

Finally, we turn from dimensions along which development can be tracked to some general principles that characterize ontogenesis. Each of these principles has potentially significant implications for developmental outcome research. And some of those implications bring us full circle, back to issues originally previewed in the "Whodunit" section of this chapter.

1. *Heterotypic Continuity*

Kagan (1969) suggested that the behaviors indicative of some human traits may show changes, across development, in their phenotypic manifestation. Such *heterotypic continuity* (see Hinshaw, 1994) is both intriguing and problematic for developmental outcome assessment. Consider aggression, as an example. Appropriate measures of the phenotypic display might include pushing and taking toys away from peers in preschool, starting fights in elementary school, and verbal harassment or even the use of a gun in adolescence. Thus, treatment programs for aggression that are designed to work with a broad age range might need to be assessed via quite different outcome measures for different age groups. This, in turn, would make comparison of outcomes across developmental periods a significant challenge, to put it mildly.

2. *Developmental Changes in "Measurability"*

A related problem, one that has complicated the work of longitudinal researchers for decades, is that developmental change creates changes in what it is possible to measure. For the developmentally oriented outcome researcher, this means that the array of possible treatment outcomes that can actually be assessed is dictated to some extent by the developmental capacities of the children involved. For example, because very young children may lack both the insight and the language needed to report on their internal state, changes in internal state may simply not be accessible to outcome researchers until middle childhood or beyond. Moreover, even in middle childhood, child self-reports may not be very reliable for certain kinds of symptom reports and diagnostic interviews (see, e.g., Edelbrock, Costello, Dulcan, Kalas, & Conover, 1985). This linkage between child maturity and the kinds of information outcome researchers can access complicates the process for those who want to compare outcomes across developmental levels. For those who want to make such comparisons, outcome assessment may need to include "common denominator" measures that are workable across the developmental range of interest (e.g., observational measures, parent-report questionnaires), and other measures of specific interest to the in-. vestigators but of limited developmental range may need to be omitted. Even with this common denominator approach, investigators may still face an interpretive problem; the same measure may have a different meaning when applied to children at very different developmental levels.

3. *Equifinality*

Another general principle of development, *equifinality*, holds that different developmental pathways may lead to the same eventual outcome. For psychopathology, an interesting application of this notion is Loeber's (1988, 1990) research showing distinct developmental pathways to adolescent substance abuse—one involving late-onset exclusive substance use with little externalizing behavior, another involving overt aggressive behavior, and a third involving covert antisocial behavior. The problem of equifinality poses a problem for developmental outcome research, making it difficult for us to know which of several possible behaviors we can measure today may actually predict the outcomes we hope to influence in the future. In many cases, evidently, behavior that appears worrisome will antedate serious dysfunction in some youth and healthy long-term adjustment in others.

4. *Werner's Orthogenetic Principle and Piaget's "Organization"*

The early developmental theorist Heinz Werner (1957) proposed what he called the *orthogenetic principle,* the notion that "wherever development occurs it proceeds from a state of relative globality and lack of differentiation to a state of increasing differentiation, articulation, and hierarchic integration" (p. 126). One interpretation of this viewpoint is that the developing individual is continually assimilating new skills and information and fitting them into an increasingly well-integrated system. An implication of this principle for intervention researchers is that skills and information taught as part of a treatment program may be gradually integrated into the developing child's cognitive system, but not necessarily within the time frame of the typical child outcome study. If we take this notion seriously, we might find in it another reason for longer-term outcome assessment. Earlier we wrote of the need to extend outcome assessment so as to detect fading of treatment effects. Werner's reasoning reminds us that longer-term follow-up might also permit us to detect slow-blooming improvements in functioning, as the

child's developing system makes ever-better use of the lessons of therapy.

Werner's orthogenetic principle overlaps to some degree with Piaget's (1970) notion of *organization,* the process by which the developing system integrates cognitive building blocks into a working structure. In Piaget's view (and this was supported by experimental evidence), even memories of past experience can be reorganized to integrate that experience with newly developed cognitive structures. If such ongoing reorganization were to operate after the experience of therapy, producing delayed benefits or "sleeper" effects, detecting such effects could well require longer-term follow-up than has been typical of child therapy outcome research to date.

5. *Context-Boundedness of Development*

Perhaps the most challenging developmental principle to accommodate in outcome research is this—Development is not a solitary pursuit in a sterile environment but rather an ongoing transaction within a complex, multifaceted physical and social tapestry. Numerous theorists and researchers (e.g., Bronfenbrenner, 1979; Masten, Best, & Garmezy, 1991; Shirk, this volume) have emphasized the context-boundedness of development and discussed implications for adaptation and dysfunction. It seems clear that the psychosocial ecosystems within which individuals develop may enhance or undermine mental health. It is also clear that there are marked developmental differences in people's capacity to select their contexts; for young children, the luck of the draw may be critical. All this means that contextual factors may moderate treatment outcome, and perhaps differentially so with development, with some social environments facilitating treatment gains and other environments having undermining effects. And, of course, the child's relationship with the social environment (e.g., other family members, peers) may be a target of treatment. This is likely to complicate developmental outcome assessment, particularly for those who seek to understand factors that account for variations in treatment effect. The ecological perspective leads beyond mere assessment of child characteristics and on to assessment of potentiating and inhibiting forces in the social systems within which the child is growing up.

SUMMARY AND CONCLUSIONS

In this chapter we have offered several perspectives on what "developmental outcome research" might be. We highlighted significant boundary conditions that make the "Whodunit" of outcome assessment rather different for children than for adults. We characterized the current state of the art of outcome assessment with children, and we summarized substantive findings to date on the effects of child psychotherapy. Then we noted several dimensions along which development occurs, each of which may need to be considered by developmentally oriented outcome researchers. And finally, we discussed five general principles of human development, each of which has significant implications for developmental outcome research. Much of what we have suggested here goes well beyond current practice in outcome research, and we would not underestimate the difficulty of some of the changes proposed. However, we do believe that the relative insularity of developmental psychology and child and adolescent clinical psychology has had unfortunate consequences. One such consequence is that treatment outcome research with young people has not yet become truly developmental. This, in turn, has meant that the feedback function of outcome research has not prompted refinements that make treatments more developmentally sensitive. Our hope for the future is that the rich body of work generated by developmental theorists and researchers can be used to refine both treatment development and outcome assessment, sharpening the goodness-of-fit between children and the interventions used to help them.

REFERENCES

Achenbach, T. M., & Edelbrock, C. (1981). Behavioral problems and competencies reported by parents of normal and disturbed children aged four to sixteen. *Monographs of the Society for Research in Child Development, 46* (Serial No. 188).

Bronfenbrenner, U. (1979). *The ecology of human development.* Cambridge, MA: Harvard University Press.

Casey, R. J., & Berman, J. S. (1985). The outcome of psychotherapy with children. *Psychological Bulletin, 98,* 388–400.

Cohen, J. (1992). A power primer. *Psychological Bulletin, 112,* 155–159.

Durlak, J. A., Fuhrman, T., & Lampman, C. (1991). Effectiveness of cognitive-behavior therapy for maladapting children: A meta-analysis. *Psychological Bulletin, 110,* 204–214.

Edelbrock, C., Costello, A. J., Dulcan, M. K., Kalas, R., & Conover, N. C. (1985). Age differences in the reliability of the psychiatric interview of the child. *Child Development, 56,* 265–275.

Furman, W. (1980). Promoting social development. In B. Lahey & A. E. Kazdin (Eds.), *Advances in clinical child psychology* (Vol. 3, pp. 1–40). New York: Plenum Press.

Hinshaw, S. P. (1994). Conduct disorder in childhood: Conceptualization, diagnosis, comorbidity, and risk status for antisocial functioning in adulthood. In D. C. Fowles, P. Sutker, & S. H. Goodman (Eds.), *Progress in experimental personality and psychopathology research* (pp. 3–44). New York: Springer.

Howard, K. (1995). *Discussant's comments.* Annual meeting of the Society for Psychotherapy Research. Vancouver, British Columbia.

Kagan, J. (1969). The three faces of continuity in human development. In D. A. Goslin (Ed.), *Handbook of socialization theory and research* (pp. 983–1002). Chicago: Rand McNally.

Kazdin, A. E., Bass, D., Ayers, W. A., & Rodgers, A. (1990). Empirical and clinical focus of child and adolescent psychotherapy research. *Journal of Consulting and Clinical Psychology, 58,* 729–740.

King, N.J., Hamilton, D. I., & Ollendick, T. H. (1988). *Children's phobias: A behavioural perspective.* New York: Wiley.

Kohlberg, L., Yaeger, J., & Hjertholm, E. (1968). The development of private speech: Four studies and a review of theories. *Child Development, 39,* 691–736.

Loeber, R. (1988). Natural histories of conduct problems, delinquency, and associated substance use: Evidence for developmental progressions. In B. B. Lahey & A. E. Kazdin (Eds.), *Advances in clinical child psychology* (pp. 73–124). New York: Plenum Press.

Loeber, R. (1990). Development and risk factors of juvenile antisocial behavior and delinquency. *Clinical Psychology Review, 10,* 1–41.

Lovaas, O. I. (1987). Behavioral treatment and normal educational and intellectual functioning in young autistic children. *Journal of Consulting and Clinical Psychology, 55,* 3–9.

Masten, A. S., Best, K., & Garmezy, N. (1991). Resilience and development: Contributions from the study of children who overcome adversity. *Development and Psychopathology, 2,* 425–444.

Mann, C. (1990). Meta-analysis in the breech. *Science, 249,* 476–480.

McEachin, J. J., Smith, T., & Lovaas, O. I. (1993). Long-term outcome for children with autism who received early intensive behavioral treatment. *American Journal of Mental Retardation, 97,* 359–372.

Meichenbaum, D., & Goodman, S. (1979). Clinical use of private speech and critical questions about its study in natural settings. In G. Zivin (Ed.), *The development of self-regulation through private speech* (pp. 325–360). New York: Wiley.

Ollendick, T. H., King, N.J., & Frary, R. B. (1989). Fears in children and adolescents: Reliability and generalizability across gender, age, and nationality. *Behaviour Research and Therapy, 27,* 19–26.

Patterson, G. R. (1982). *A social learning approach: Vol. 3. Coercive family process.* Eugene, OR: Castalia.

Patterson, G. R., DeBaryshe, B. D., & Ramsey, E. (1989). A developmental perspective on antisocial behavior. *American Psychologist, 44,* 329–335.

Patterson, G. R., & Stouthamer-Loeber, M. (1984). The correlation of family management practices and delinquency. *Child Development, 55,* 1299–1307.

Piaget, J. (1929). *The child's conception of the world.* Totowa, NJ: Littlefield, Adams.

Piaget, J. (1955). *The language and thought of the child.* New York: Meridian. [Originally published, 1923]

Piaget, J. (1962). *Play, dreams, and imitation.* New York: Norton.

Piaget, J. (1970). Piaget's theory. In P. H. Mussen (Ed.), *Carmichael's manual of child psychology* (Vol. 1, pp. 703–732). New York: Wiley.

Russell, R. L., Greenwald, S., & Shirk, S. R. (1991). Language change in child psychotherapy: A meta-analytic review. *Journal of Consulting and Clinical Psychology, 59,* 916–919.

Shapiro, D. A., & Shapiro, D. (1982). Meta-analysis of comparative therapy outcome studies: A replication and refinement. *Psychological Bulletin, 92,* 581–604.

Silverman, W. K., Ginsburg, G. S., & Kurtines, W. M. (1995). Clinical issues in the treatment of children with anxiety and phobic disorders. *Cognitive and Behavioral Practice, 2,* 95–119.

Silverman, W. K., & Kurtines, W. M. (1996). A transfer of control approach to treating internalizing disorders in youth: The evolution of a psychosocial intervention. In E. D. Hibbs & P. Jensen (Eds.), *Psychosocial treatment research for child and adolescent disorders.* Washington, D.C.: American Psychological Association.

Smith, M. L., & Glass, G. V. (1977). Meta-analysis of psychotherapy outcome studies. *American Psychologist, 32,* 752–760.

Smith, M. L., Glass, G. V., & Miller, T. L. (1980). *Benefits of psychotherapy.* Baltimore: Johns Hopkins University Press.

Vygotsky, L. (1962). *Thought and language.* Cambridge, MA: MIT Press. [Originally published, 1934]

Weisz, J. R. (in progress). *Studying clinic-based child mental health care.* Ongoing research project, University of California at Los Angeles.

Weisz, J. R., Donenberg, G. R., Han, S. S., & Weiss, B. (1995). Bridging the gap between laboratory and clinic in child and adolescent psychotherapy. *Journal of Consulting and Clinical Psychology, 63,* 688–701.

Weisz, J. R., McCarty, C. A., Eastman, K. L., Chaiyasit, W., & Suwanlert, S. (1997). Developmental psychopathology and culture: Ten Lessons from Thailand. In S. S. Luthar, J. Burack, D. Cicchetti, & J. R. Weisz (Eds.), *Developmental psychopathology: Perspectives on adjustment, risk, and disorder.* New York: Cambridge University Press.

Weisz, J. R., & Weiss, B. (1993). *Effects of psychotherapy with children and adolescents.* Newbury Park, CA: Sage.

Weisz, J. R., Weiss, B., Alicke, M. D., & Klotz, M. L. (1987). Effectiveness of psychotherapy with children and adolescents: A meta-analysis for clinicians. *Journal of Consulting and Clinical Psychology, 55,* 542–549.

Weisz, J. R., Weiss, B., Han, S. S., Granger, D. A., & Morton, T. (1995). Effects of psychotherapy with children and adolescents revisited: A meta-analysis of treatment outcome studies. *Psychological Bulletin, 117,* 450–468.

Werner, H. (1957). The concept of development from a comparative and organismic point of view. In D. Harris (Ed.), *The concept of development* (pp. 125–148). Minneapolis: University of Minnesota Press.

Wilson, G. T. (1985). Limitations of meta-analysis in the evaluation of the effects of psychological therapy. *Clinical Psychology Review, 5,* 35–47.

Zivin, G. (Ed.) (1979). *The development of self-regulation through private speech.* New York: Wiley.

CHAPTER 29

ETHICAL AND LEGAL ISSUES

Celia B. Fisher
Michi Hatashita-Wong
Lori Isman Greene

Mental health professionals working with children and youth face special ethical challenges because children's changing cognitive and emotional characteristics, their limited social power, and relative lack of legal status make them especially vulnerable to treatment risk. When working with children and adolescents, practitioners must constantly balance their professional obligation to promote client welfare with their responsibility to protect client autonomy and human dignity. The younger the child the more limited his or her ability to understand the nature of psychotherapy and the right to receive or reject treatment, the more ambiguous his or her standing as a "person" before the law, and the more likely others have the power and responsibility to determine what type of psychological treatment he or she will receive. As a consequence, in many instances the ethical safeguards typically employed in the clinical treatment of adults provide inadequate guidelines for work with children.

Consistent with recent attempts to take a developmental contextual approach to the prevention, assessment, and treat-ment of childhood disorders (Cole, 1990; Edelbrock, 1994; Fisher et al., 1993; Fisher & Lerner, 1994; Kendall, Lerner, & Craighead, 1984; Lerner, 1995; Rebok et al, 1991), ethical practices in the psychological treatment of children and youth must be based on an understanding of maturational milestones, life transitions, and psychosocial factors and guided by an understanding of the plasticity and reciprocity of the child's relationships with his or her environment. This chapter examines three major ethical and legal challenges facing those who provide psychological services to children and adolescents: (1) protecting children's intrinsic value as persons through appropriate informed consent procedures; (2) balancing children's right to privacy and self-governance with the obligation to protect their welfare and the welfare of others through appropriate confidentiality procedures; and (3) protecting children's right to adequate diagnoses and effective treatment through the use of developmentally and culturally valid assessment and treatment techniques. Drawing upon both practical and empirical work on child development and ethical practice we also present a broad framework of "best practices" for each of these ethical challenges in the hopes that these suggestions will contribute to the ethical decision making of mental health professionals.

The authors wish to thank Dr. Kathleen Doyle and Mr. Jeffrey Stillman for their generous guidance in the writing of this chapter.

CHILDREN'S COMPETENCE TO CONSENT TO PSYCHOLOGICAL TREATMENT

Informed consent to treatment is seen by many as the major means of protecting an individual's right to self governance and respecting his or her dignity, worth, and intrinsic value as a person. As of 1992, the Ethics Code of the American Psychological Association requires psychologists to obtain appropriate informed consent to therapy and discuss with clients, in a language that is reasonably understandable, related issues such as the nature and anticipated course of therapy and limits of confidentiality (APA, 1992, Standards 4.01 and 4.02; Fisher & Younggren, 1997). Based upon limitations posed by their legal status, cognitive and emotional maturity, and social power, consent procedures for psychotherapy with children and adolescents require special considerations to ensure that the client's participation is informed (provided with all information that might influence willingness to participate), rational (that the client has the cognitive and emotional ability to understand the information), and voluntary (that consent is uncoerced) (Fisher, 1993; Fisher, Hoagwood, & Jensen, 1996; Freedman, 1975).

Competency to consent to treatment is a legal status and under the law is not based on a single determination, but on three factors: age, mental capacity, and the legal decision at hand (Harvey, 1995). Under current legal standards children and most adolescents are not considered competent to consent (Melton, Koocher, & Saks, 1983; Schaefer & Call, 1994) based on the assumption that in most situations their cognitive immaturity would impair their ability to understand the reason for and nature of treatment. Empirical studies support this conclusion for children under 14 years of age, suggesting that limitations in their ability to understand the future consequences of treatment, to read and comprehend "rights" vocabulary, and to make inferences about others' motives and feelings compromise their ability to weigh the risks and benefits of psychotherapy and to make fully informed consent decisions (Ambuel & Rappaport, 1992; Belter & Grisso, 1984; Grisso, 1981; Grisso & Vierling, 1978; Kaser-Boyd, Adelman, Taylor, & Nelson, 1985; Lewis, Lewis, & Ifekwunique, 1978; Thompson et al., 1990; Tymchuck, 1992; Weithorn & Campbell, 1982).

In addition, for treatment to be truly "consensual" children must understand the voluntary nature of consent, that is, that they are free to elect to engage in the activities described (Fisher, 1993). However, even when children have the cognitive skills to understand their rights in treatment, the ability to assert these rights is often a function of their social ecology (Melton, Koocher, & Saks, 1983). Children do not have experience exercising their rights independent

of adult authority and as a consequence, young children may see rights as entitlements permitted by adults (Melton, 1980; Thompson et al., 1990). For example, in a study examining 10- to 17-year-old psychiatric inpatients' understanding of written consent material, Morton and Green (1991) found that the younger patients often misread a statement of patients' rights (e.g., the right to refuse restraints) as a rule allowing institutions to perform the action. Moreover, young children's views of adults as legitimate and powerful authorities with superior qualities (Damon, 1977) make them vulnerable to coercive manipulation and more likely to respond in the therapeutic setting in ways that may be inconsistent with their own wishes, desires, and beliefs (see Thompson et al., 1990).

WHO HAS THE RIGHT TO PROVIDE INFORMED CONSENT FOR CHILDREN?

In recognition of children's cognitive and social vulnerabilities, federal and state laws as well as professional ethical standards require that parents or legal guardians provide informed consent for their treatment. As family structure has become more diversified in the United States, psychologists need to be alert to their legal responsibility to confirm that the parent or adult who is providing informed consent for the child does, in fact, have legal custody of that child (Fisher, Hoagwood, & Jensen, 1996; Schaefer & Call, 1994). For example, except in emergency situations, noncustodial parents (e.g., in the case of divorce) or grandparents cannot provide legal consent for assessment or treatment. Similarly, in many instances foster parents may not have legal authority to give informed consent for psychological treatment. In these cases consent often needs to be obtained from child protection agencies, usually in coordination with the biological parents. In the case of a child whose parents' custodial rights have been revoked by the state (i.e., as a consequence of child abuse, neglect, or parental incompetence), the psychologist should consult with legal officials and caseworkers involved with the particular child to attain information as to how to acquire appropriate consent to treatment. Additionally, the process of attaining informed consent may vary by treatments and disciplines in an inpatient setting, and a psychologist should not assume that consent for admission to a hospital or other medical facility meets ethical guidelines governing consent for psychotherapy.

Consent and planning, used as a facilitative tool of the treatment itself can be instrumental in the formation of trust in the therapist and commitment to the therapy (Jensen, Josephson, & Frey, 1989). Consequently, although noncustodial or foster parents may not have the legal authority to provide consent, when working with children in which these family members participate in protecting the child's well-being, psychologists should involve these adults in the treatment consent process (DeKraai & Sales, 1991; Fisher et al., 1996).

Exceptions to Parental Consent

Requiring parental consent assumes that the child comes from a reasonably secure and loving family setting and that parental judgments will be in the best interest of the child (Gaylin, 1982). However, social challenges facing today's youth raise questions concerning the rights of minors to provide consent to treatment without the knowledge or permission of their legal guardians. In recent years, the legal model defining the rights of adolescents to independently consent to medical interventions provides a framework under which guardian consent for psychological treatment might be waived. For example, all states currently allow minors to waive parental consent for medical treatment for venereal disease, and states specify ages (usually 15 or 16) at which teenagers can consent to abortions, HIV testing, and alcohol and drug abuse treatments without parental involvement (Ambuel & Rappaport, 1992; Holder, 1981; North, 1990; Schwartz, 1989). In these instances it seems both reasonable and ethical to grant youth the autonomy to make decisions regarding psychological treatments associated with these medical decisions. Furthermore, some states provide that children (as young as 12 years in California) can consent to treatment if the child is thought by the therapist to have been abused or if the therapist deems that without treatment the child will be of harm to himself or herself or others.

Outside of emergency or medically relevant treatment contexts, each jurisdiction has statutes outlining the conditions of "emancipation" (i.e. adolescent parenthood, independent living and financial arrangements, enlistment in the military) that can be used as guides for ethical decisions about the rights of minors to give autonomous consent for treatment (DeKraai & Sales, 1991). Moreover, many states recognize certain adolescents as "mature minors" who, though not emancipated legally, are considered to have the capacity to understand the information and rights provided in informed consent forms and who are close to their state's age of legal adult status (Capron, 1982). Almost half of the jurisdictions within the United States have statutes allowing minors to consent to outpatient mental health counseling and treatment, although some of these statutes include caveats such as limitations on the number of visits that can occur without parental consent (English, 1990). In general, it is advisable that mental health professionals become familiar with their own states' statutes, doctrines, and case law regarding exceptions to parental informed consent.

The Right to Refuse Treatment

There are no legal or professional guidelines specifically outlining under what outpatient or inpatient conditions a child's wish to refuse treatment supersedes consent to treatment granted by parents or legal guardians. Primarily, the courts have ruled and the American Psychological Association assumes (APA, 1992, Standard 4.02c) that the mental health professional is unbiased and will consider the minor's preferences and best interests keeping in mind both the child's developmental level and presenting problem.

Children rarely refer themselves to treatment, and seeking help is often a function of how disturbed adults are by the child's behavior. Parental concerns over aggressiveness, withdrawal, or expressions of poor self-esteem, and teacher's concern over disruptive behavior or academic underachievement are common reasons for referral (Tuma, 1990). Recent research suggests that clinical referral rates vary with parental cultural values and attitudes toward gender and dysfunctional behaviors (Weisz & Weiss, 1991). Moreover, parental concerns often coincide with developmental transitional periods; for example, both toddlerhood and early adolescence are developmental periods marked by increases in exploratory and autonomous behaviors, limit testing, and emotional outbursts that often elicit parental concerns about compliance behaviors and disciplinary problems (Brazelton, 1974; Campbell & Cluss, 1982; Fisher & Johnson, 1990). In such circumstances the psychologist should apply stringent safeguards to ensure that the behaviors that are the focus of the referral are indeed dysfunctional and not just difficulties that are evidence of transient adjustment problems characteristic of normal child and adolescent development (Edelbrock, 1994; Kazdin, 1993).

When considering how to respond to a minor client's reluctance to enter therapy, the practitioner must also take special care to protect the child from coercive elements in the power structure of the family and to consider the child's needs separately from the family (Margolin, 1982). In so doing, the therapist must recognize that the status of children and most adolescents in treatment is complicated by their emotional, instrumental, and material dependency on the adults who hold primary responsibility for deciding when and if help is sought (Campbell, 1989; Weisz & Wiess, 1991). The practitioner must be alert to social or professional biases that exclusively target the child's behavior as the problem to be addressed, when in fact maladaptive responding of adults or living conditions such as poverty or community violence may be significant factors causing these behaviors (Coie & Jacobs, 1993; Kazdin, 1993).

In some situations, child characteristics that prompt negative reactions on the part of parents, teachers, or peers and which disrupt opportunities for learning and social development may in themselves be considered risk factors for mental health and social problems in later life (Costello, 1989; Patterson, 1982). In these situations, children or adolescents may not be able to adequately consider the future consequences of psychological problems that are left untreated. The psychologist may urge the child to attend several sessions to have the opportunity to explore what the treatment has to offer. Ethically, the presence of maladaptive behavior alone may not be enough to warrant the decision to initiate treatment (Reekers, 1983). The sensitive clinician assumes the responsibility to ascertain child attitudes toward mental health services, how these perceptions may impact upon the efficacy of treatment, and whether the possible repercussions of treatment coercion outweigh treatment benefits.

Best Practices for Obtaining Informed Consent for Children and Adolescents to Participate in Psychotherapy

• When a child below the age of 18 requests treatment, the psychologist should determine whether the reason for the treatment or the minor client's legal status entitles the client to make autonomous consent decisions regarding psychotherapy.
• When an adult requests that a child be seen for psychotherapy, the psychologist should determine which adult(s) has the legal responsibility for consenting to the child's treatment.
• When possible, all family members or legal guardians responsible for the care and welfare of the minor client should be included in consent procedures.
• In situations in which the child expresses the desire not to receive treatment, the psychologist should balance the child's right to be free from coercion with the child's best interest.
• Irrespective of the child's legal status to consent, as early as feasible the psychologist should discuss with the minor client the specific risks and benefits of psychotherapy, the nature and course of the treatment, as well as the scope and limits of confidentiality in language that matches the client's developmental level.
• Informed consent to psychotherapy should be viewed as a continuing process in the therapeutic relationship and should be reintroduced and revised to meet the minor client's changing developmental status, needs, and capabilities.

PRIVACY, PRIVILEGE, AND CONFIDENTIALITY

Privacy, client privilege, and confidentiality are often considered among the most important aspects of the therapeutic relationship. The duty not to reveal to others information derived during the course of psychotherapy enhances client trust in the therapeutic alliance and protects an individual's right to determine with whom he or she will share personal thoughts and feelings. However, from both a legal and moral perspective this duty is not absolute, especially when maintaining confidentiality jeopardizes a client's welfare or violates the rights of others. While psychologists are always ethically obligated to evaluate the context within which confidential information should or should not be disclosed, these judgments are more complicated in child psychotherapy as a consequence of limitations in children's legal rights and ability to make autonomous decisions concerning their own welfare. Rigidity in ethical decision making occurs when a practitioner establishes a policy under which he or she will share with other concerned adults only that information they are compelled by law to disclose or which dictates that parents should have access to all information disclosed in therapy irrespective of the minor client's developmental level or treatment status. Such rigidity fails to take into account either the importance of parents as a context for the promotion of healthy developmental processes or the importance of promoting child dignity and autonomy, respectively.

Privacy

Privacy refers to the right of an individual to make decisions about how much of their physical person, thoughts, feelings, and personal information will be shared with others (Canter, Bennett, Jones & Nagy, 1994; Koocher & Keith-Spiegel, 1990). Despite Fourth Amendment and other constitutional limitations on invasion of privacy, Supreme Court decisions regarding medical records suggest that psychotherapeutic interactions may not be held as constitutionally private (Smith-Bell & Winslade, 1994). As a consequence, in the psychotherapeutic context, protection of an individual's right to privacy reflects moral values associated with human dignity and freedom through self-determination. By its very nature, psychotherapy in its exploration of personal thoughts and feelings runs the risk of invading individual privacy. To protect clients, psychologists need to be alert to therapeutic techniques and specific client characteristics that may jeopardize these protections.

Special privacy issues arise in mental health services for children and youth, because the cognitive capacities and experience of minor clients may hinder their ability to understand their privacy rights. For example, younger children's perception of adults as powerful and legitimate authorities with superior qualities (Damon, 1977) may make them less resistant to responding to questions they feel are personally invasive. As Melton (1983) points out, children's understanding of their own privacy interests are in part a product of how they are treated. Preschool children, for example, may rarely experience physical privacy in toileting and grooming behaviors and may not possess the reflective cognitive processes necessary to understand that adults are not aware of what they are thinking. Unlike adults, children may not believe they have the right to refrain from answering questions about thoughts or behaviors they consider private (e.g., angry thoughts about a parent, masturbation) or they may not have the social skills to refuse such inquiries. Moreover, privacy concerns move from an initial focus on physical and possessional privacy to psychological and informational privacy as children mature (Thompson et al., 1990). As a consequence with age, adolescent privacy can be a marker of self-esteem and identity, making adolescents more psychologically vulnerable to privacy intrusions (Thompson et al., 1990). Thus, at the outset of psychotherapy, psychologists need to explain these rights to minor clients, be sensitive to intervention techniques that may violate the child's sense of personal integrity, and integrate into their therapeutic techniques ongoing means of teaching minor clients how to recognize and exert their privacy rights during psychotherapy.

Privilege

While privacy is typically associated with a client's right to limit what type of information she or he will share within the therapeutic context, *privilege* is a legal term that protects the client from having a therapist disclose this shared information with others without the client's permission. Privilege is granted by state or common law, belongs to the client, and is reserved for situations in which a therapist–patient relationship has been established and in which disclosures are made with the expectation that they will remain confidential (Koocher & Keith-Speigel, 1990; Liss, 1994; Smith-Bell & Winslade, 1994). However, not all states extend privilege to the psychologist–client relationship and in those states that do the nature of privilege for children is often unclear. In some states, for example, communications between school counselors and student clients are offered some form of legal protection (Sheeley & Herlihy, 1987). In most instances, the child's legal guardian is afforded the right to uphold or waive the divulgence of the minor's privileged information. However, in some cases in which a judge decides there is a conflict of interest between parent

and child, judges may appoint a guardian *ad litem* to make this decision in the best interest of the child (Capron, 1982).

Ethical decisions associated with protecting a minor client's right to privacy with respect to privilege thus differs from those related to confidentiality issues (discussed in the next section) because with respect to the former, the decision to disclose information revealed during the course of therapy rests with neither the minor client nor the psychologist. Informing children of the legal limitations on whether information will be publicly disclosed is not sufficient protection because minors, especially younger children, may not have the cognitive skills nor experiential history to envision what type of information might be potentially damaging or the ability to monitor their comments to avoid such damage. This means that practitioners need to be especially vigilant in ensuring that what is discussed in therapy and what is included in client records is only that information that is directly relevant to diagnosis and treatment and that this information is written in ways that avoid misinterpretation by others. For example, if a 7-year-old girl reports to a psychologist that she "hates" her father because he scolded her for not completing her homework assignment, the psychologist should recognize that if included in a chart note that is later subpoenaed, this comment might have disproportional import in a custody dispute.

Confidentiality

Whereas privilege is a legal standard, confidentiality is a professional standard that requires that a psychologist not disclose information revealed in therapy except for specific circumstances agreed to by the client, mandated by law, necessary to provide adequate services, or required to protect the client or others from harm (APA, 1992, Standard 5). The duty to maintain confidentiality has both a moral and practical basis in that it protects a person's right to privacy and self-determination and increases therapeutic efficacy through enhancement of trust in the therapeutic alliance. In psychological treatment for children the moral and practical benefits of confidentiality are complicated by the absence of clear legal and professional parameters outlining parental access to information. For example, state laws vary in the extent to which minors are entitled to confidentiality of information revealed during psychotherapy and in the extent of parental access to mental health records (DeKraai & Sales, 1991; Schaefer & Call, 1994). In cases in which the therapist and minor client believe that parental access to records may be detrimental to the client, there may be legal recourse to protect the records. In some states a psychologist may seek exemption from the Record Access Law of the state's Public Health Law, which ordinarily permits parents and legal guardians access to children's records. On the other hand, in some states client consent must be obtained in cases in which a practitioner working with a legally emancipated minor wishes to discuss the case with parents (De-Kraai & Sales, 1991).

Within such legal parameters, confidentiality is at the professional discretion of the psychologist, who can determine what is in the best therapeutic interests of the child. Professional decisions on what information to share with parents must take into account the level at which the child conceptualizes interpersonal relationships, the client's presenting problems, the nature of therapy and therapeutic goals, and situational variables including parental abilities, expectations, and social and institutional supports. For example, young children's physical and emotional dependence on significant adults, lack of control over the dissemination of information in their everyday lives, and egocentric perspective of social relationships (Selman, 1980; Thompson et al., 1990) suggest that they would have difficulty understanding the concept of patient–therapist confidentiality and that maintenance of strict confidentiality procedures might hinder rather than facilitate positive growth by failing to reflect the actual contexts in which children grow and develop. On the other hand, older youths' participation in social organizations in which their parents play little or no part, adolescents' efforts to establish a distinct social identity, enhanced perspective-taking skills, and the ability to take a self-reflective perspective on one's own thoughts and feelings (Fisher & Johnson, 1990; Youniss & Smoller, 1985), suggest that clients at this developmental level would have little difficulty understanding the nature of confidentiality and that clearly articulated guidelines regarding what will and will not be shared with parents might facilitate personal autonomy and psychological growth.

Sharing Information with Parents

Clinical child psychologists often become aware of client behaviors hidden from parents that place the child at some physical or psychological risk, but not in immediate or severe danger. Low-risk sexual activity, alcohol and drug usage, gang involvement, truancy, and petty theft are but some of the "secret" activities that require ethical decisions regarding the limits of minor client–therapist confidentiality. In such situations, therapists must weigh the costs and benefits of sharing information with parents. For example, revealing the presence of problematic behaviors can lead to physical protections for the child through increased parental monitoring of the client's after-school activities and promote psychological growth through therapist-directed family discussions about the underlying reasons for current

behaviors. Alternatively, sharing such information with parents may place the child at greater risk if parental reactions can be predicted to be physically violent. Other client behaviors to which the therapist may become privy have legal implications. For example, states vary with respect to the age at which adolescents have the right to consent to having abortions or other medical procedures without the knowledge of their parents (English et al., 1994). In states in which parental consent is required, a therapist can be helpful in bringing the parent into such decision making; whereas support for the minor client's seeking of such medical attention in the absence of parental consent might be seen as encouraging or even abetting illegal activities. Practical issues, such as the parent withdrawing the child from therapy for lack of access to information and the child's misuse of confidentiality as a weapon in their conflict with parents pose additional problems that need to be considered when therapists weigh the costs and benefits of particular confidentiality frameworks (Taylor & Adelman, 1989).

Psychologists must also consider how entering into a secrecy pact with a minor client regarding risky behaviors can adversely impact the therapeutic alliance. While some may argue that maintaining confidentiality under such circumstances enhances client trust, practitioners must be wary when assuming that minor clients expect and desire confidentiality when they reveal during therapy that they are engaging in high-risk behaviors. Two recent studies (Fisher, Higgins, Rau, Kuther, & Belanger, 1996; O'Sullivan & Fisher, 1997) found that middle and high school students view the maintenance of confidentiality *un*favorably in situations in which teenaged research participants disclose to a psychologist that they have been victimized or are engaging in behaviors that the adolescents themselves perceive as serious problems. This raises the disconcerting possibility that in some clinical situations in which a teenaged client reveals information about high-risk behavior, a therapist's failure to share this information with parents may unintentionally send a message that the behavior is not problematic, that parents cannot be trusted to act in their child's best interests, or that knowledgeable adults cannot be depended upon to help children in need.

Disclosing sensitive information about low-income and ethnic minority clients. When deciding whether to share information with parents or legal guardians, therapists must also be sensitive to the possibility of over or underestimating high-risk behaviors of clients from low-income and minority populations. At present there is little empirical information concerning developmental correlates and consequences of high-risk behaviors for either middle class or disenfranchised ethnic minority children and youth (Fisher, Jackson, &

Villarruel, 1997). Consequently, when working with youth from these populations child clinicians must rise above social stereotypes to identify for each particular client the extent to which certain behaviors (e.g., gang membership) are serving a protective or dangerous context for development.

On the one hand, practitioners need to move beyond cultural myths that an urban youth's engagement in sexual practices or in delinquency merely reflect adherence to inner city cultural values in light of recent empirical work suggesting that young African American and Latino females often seek sexual intimacy and early parenthood as a maladaptive solution to depression arising from low levels of self-esteem (Chase-Lansdale & Brooks-Gunn, 1994) and that some ethnic minority male adolescents turn to delinquency when racism and disadvantage give rise to alienation and a crisis of societal meaninglessness (McLeod, 1987; Singleton, 1989; Taylor, 1991). Practitioners working with children from distressed urban environments need to also be familiar with literature suggesting that coping with chronic danger can force adoption of behaviors that are adaptive in the face of immediate threat, but that are dysfunctional and possibly pathological in noncrisis situations (Garbarino, Kostelny, & Dubrow, 1991).

Practitioners must also avoid the risk of misapplying "duty to protect" guidelines to ethnic minority youth. Following the California Supreme Court decision *Tarasoff v. Regents* (1976), a number of states have held that psychologists have certain obligations to disclose to third parties that a client may present a serious threat of danger to them. Although research indicates a low degree of psychotherapeutic certitude in predicting violence (Wettstein, 1984), and psychometric assessment has little predictive validity for imminent violence (Monohan, 1981), in many states the legal standard is one of "reasonable foreseeability" (whether a prudent psychotherapist would have predicted violence on the part of the client) not certainty (Truscott, Evans, & Mansell, 1995). In the absence of valid instruments to assess individual risk, professional judgments concerning predictions of violence often rely upon statistical probabilities that may be biased against minority youth. For example, in a recent article on guidelines for decision making on client proneness to violence, practitioners were encouraged to take into consideration the fact that violent behavior is most often perpetrated by non-white males in their late teens, with histories of substance abuse, low education, and unstable residential and employment history (Truscott et al., 1995). Although it was not the intention of the authors, some practitioners can misinterpret these statistics as a rationale for using client race and gender as factors in decisions to disclose confidential information revealed by an adolescent during therapy.

Reporting Child Abuse

An important limitation on confidentiality is state-mandated reporting of suspected child abuse initiated in 1974 under the Child Abuse Prevention and Treatment Act. Since that time, courts have upheld that the general rights of children to be protected from abuse and neglect outweigh legal bounds of confidentiality and that the requirement to report child abuse supersedes therapist–client privilege (Liss, 1994; Schaefer & Call, 1994). Despite state child abuse reporting laws, some psychologists believe that filing a report of suspected child abuse conflicts with the therapeutic and ethical demands of confidentiality (DeKraai & Sales, 1991; Pope & Bajt, 1988; Smith-Bell & Winslade, 1994). Some professional resistance to child abuse reporting is most likely a reaction to those state mandates that demand reports of "suspected" child abuse, wherein "suspected" is so vaguely defined that it requires practitioners to make official reports under circumstances in which they may not believe there is any evidence of abuse. For others, however, this rigid adherence to principles of confidentiality often reflects empirically unfounded beliefs that therapy itself will stop abusive behaviors and that abuse reporting automatically compromises clinical efficacy (Watson & Levine, 1989). Some child clinicians also fail to consider how strict allegiance to principles of confidentiality may in and of itself compromise therapeutic goals by unintentionally communicating to the child client that abusive parental behaviors are implicitly condoned or that other adults are unable or unwilling to prevent continued abuse. Practitioners must also be sensitive to their own subjective and emotional responses to suspicions of abusive situations and not have their professional judgment blinded to indicators that abuse may not have occurred (Bennett, Bryant, VandenBos, & Greenwood, 1990; Fisher, 1995).

Given the lack of consistency in reporting laws across states, how can psychologists ensure that their response to indications of child abuse are in compliance with ethical and legal guidelines? First, the therapist must find out what age group meets the legal definition of "minor" in his or her state (Smith-Bell & Winslade, 1994). While most states consider children under the age of 18 minors, in some jurisdictions 16 years is the cutoff for reporting. Moreover, many states extend the legal age limit to 21 for individuals with mental or physical disabilities. Second, clinicians must consider what types of abusive situations come under their state's reporting laws. Some states require reporting of suspected abuse regardless of the relationship of the perpetrator to the victim, while other states mandate reporting only when the abuse is perpetrated by someone who is responsible for the care of the child. The types of abuse included under mandated reporting vary as well (DeKraai & Sales, 1991); some statutes specifically refer to sexual abuse as well as physical abuse and neglect, while others do not specifically cite sexual abuse, but refer to "psychic injury" that may arise from molestation. Third, psychologists need to be familiar with the temporal parameters of particular reporting laws. For example, some states require practitioners to contact local authorities within 24 hours of their coming in contact with information that would give them reasonable cause to suspect child abuse and to follow-up telephone reporting with a written report. Additionally, states vary with respect to whether their specific reporting mandate is restricted to suspicion or knowledge of current abuse or extends to past abusive incidents. Fourth, mental health service providers need to be aware of legal and professional penalties (e.g., revocation of state licensure, malpractice liability, sanctions by the American Psychological Association) associated with failure to comply with reporting statutes and whether the breach of confidentiality associated with a mandated report is protected from litigation (Bennett et al., 1990; DeKraai & Sales, 1991; Smith-Bell & Winslade, 1994). In this regard, psychologists should always document in their records incidents that might lead one to suspect abuse and why they did or did not act upon those suspicions (Bennett et al., 1990).

Although state laws and professional guidelines (APA, 1991, Standard 5.05a) agree that mandated abuse reporting is an important means of protecting children's welfare, it is often quite traumatic for a child when such a report is made. As detailed below, clear, honest communication with minor clients and their families about the limits of confidentiality and involvement of the client in disclosure decisions is always good practice and may decrease the trauma associated with a report if such a situation arises (Taylor and Adelman, 1989). One important source of client protection is for psychologists to be familiar with the procedures in their community for children and adolescents to make such reports, as well as the procedures for abusive parents to report their own actions. For example, in a situation in which a child tells the psychologist that he or she has been sexually fondled by a parent, unless therapeutically contraindicated or potentially harmful to the client, in addition to fulfilling his or her duty to report the abuse to the authorities, a psychologist who is knowledgeable about local child protection agency procedures can advise parents on steps they can take to decrease the likelihood of permanent separation or severe criminal charges.

Disclosure of Confidential Information Concerning HIV/AIDS

The growing numbers of children and adolescents who test positive for human immunodeficiency virus (HIV) or who have acquired immunodeficiency syndrome (AIDS), highlight the importance of addressing ethical and legal responsibilities to protect HIV/AIDS patients' rights to privacy and confidentiality, to provide adequate services, and to protect clients from harming themselves or others (Bowler, Sheon, D'Angelo, & Vermund, 1992; Boyd-Franklin, Staloff, & Brody, 1995; Centers for Disease Control, 1992; Rotheram-Borus & Gwadz, 1993). Therapists working with children and adolescents with or at risk for HIV/AIDS are faced with an ever-changing literature, vague professional guidelines, varying state regulations on confidentiality, insufficient policies and funding for health-related services, psychological reactions of family and society, and the discomfort of health providers themselves (Boyd-Franklin et al., 1995; English, 1990; North, 1990). Ethical and treatment issues are further complicated by the fact that HIV/AIDS is often a multigenerational family disease. Children may have contracted the HIV virus prenatally, through sharing of needles with family members, or through incest. As such, treatment of children with HIV/AIDS requires multisystem coordinated care to help clients navigate social service systems, to assist children mourning an AIDS-related death in the parental generation, and to help minor clients and their families cope with the complicated emotional reactions to the disease.

Disclosing a client's HIV/AIDS status can lead to social stigma, discrimination, isolation, and even the right to attend school (Cooke, 1990, Eisenberg, 1986). Moreover, in some jurisdictions there may be strict state mandates against revealing the HIV/AIDS status of individuals in psychological treatment. In states in which there is no absolute protection of HIV status information, psychologists should inform clients at the beginning of treatment of the possibility that such information could be disclosed irrespective of the psychologist's attempts to keep it confidential. Particularly with minor clients, psychologists need to be extra vigilant in anticipating potential risks associated with information in their progress and process notes and in taking steps to protect their minor clients from invasions of privacy and breaches of confidence. Some have argued that in states in which minors can receive treatment for sexually transmitted diseases independent of parental consent, the therapist should discuss reasons for and ways to inform parents of the clients HIV/AIDS status, but realize that the final decision rests with the client (Ginsburg, 1991).

The issue of disclosure is further complicated by the fact that in some states the "duty to protect" (*Tarasoff*, 1976) may be applied to situations in which an adolescent patient discloses he or she is infected with HIV and is having unprotected sexual relations (Schaefer & Call, 1994). This raises many as yet unanswered ethical questions: How can the psychologist meet the legal and ethical obligations implied by *Tarasoff* (1976), while maintaining the ethical responsibility to minimize intrusions on patient privacy? Should the clinician interrupt the natural flow of the therapy to investigate the type of relations (i.e. kissing, intercourse) in which the patient is engaged to assess the likelihood of transmission? If transmission of HIV is a possibility but not an intent of the patient, does the *Tarasoff* (1976) case even apply? Would it be sufficient for the psychologist to initially discuss the use of contraceptive protection from HIV transmission with an HIV positive adolescent client and only report the patient's status if it is clear he or she does not use such protection? To whom should such information be reported? Case law is beginning to answer some of these questions on HIV and the continued unfolding of ethically relevant issues will take place in the courts over time.

Best practices for "duty to protect" decisions regarding HIV/AIDS. Currently, psychologists are encouraged and advised to be familiar with statutes and cases in their state that set precedence for reporting the risk of exposure to HIV and to consider and discuss with clients their legal and ethical obligations. Drawing upon recommendations from the American Psychological Association (1991) and Boyd-Franklin and colleagues (1995), we provide the following guidelines for deciding whether or not a minor client's HIV/AIDS status poses a *Tarasoff*-type risk.

- The therapist has an established professional relationship with the minor client.
- The therapist knows the client is HIV/AIDS-infected.
- The therapist knows that the client is engaging in unsafe behavior (having unprotected sexual intercourse, sharing IV needles) on a regular basis.
- The therapist knows the identity of the third party placed at risk by the client's behavior.
- The therapist has reason to believe that the third party does not suspect the risk.
- The therapist works with the client to help him or her terminate behaviors that place others at risk.
- The client intends to continue such behavior even after such counseling.
- The client has refused, is unreliable, or unwilling to notify the third party.
- HIV transmission will be the likely result of the continued behavior.
- The therapist is familiar with state laws regulating and/or requiring disclosure of client HIV/AIDS status.

In following these guidelines, therapists should maintain careful documentation of the information they have gathered

and the steps they have taken to intervene (Bennett et al., 1990). If the therapeutic context meets the criteria outlined above, even in states that do not require a "duty to protect," practitioners may decide they have an ethical obligation to protect third parties. In some cases, disclosures to parents may ensure sufficient safeguards against the client's continued engagement in behaviors that endanger others. In other cases, the therapist may be required by law or feel ethically obligated to ensure that the third party is directly warned. Under either of these circumstances, child clinicians may wish to follow the general disclosure guidelines suggested below.

Best Practices for Promoting Client Welfare and Autonomy When Disclosing Confidential Information

Protecting the welfare and autonomy of minor clients requires that decisions to disclose confidential information are accompanied by ethical procedures that empower children to independently pursue their best interests (Taylor & Adelman, 1989). Viewing disclosures within the context of ongoing therapeutic goals to promote the development of autonomous functioning reframes confidentiality dilemmas to work in the child's best interest (Battle, Kriesberg, O'Mahoney, & Chitwood, 1989; Taylor & Adelman, 1989). We offer the following guidelines as a means of buffering the potential negative effects of breaches in confidentiality through honest communication with child clients and their families and encouragement of client participation in disclosure decisions.

- As a first step we suggest that following an initial assessment of the child's developmental level, family context, and therapeutic needs, the therapist should utilize his or her empirical and professional knowledge to identify the types of information and circumstances under which it would be appropriate to maintain or disclose confidential information to parents or legal guardians.
- As a second step, the scope and limitations of confidentiality should then be explicitly described to both parents and the minor client, giving specific examples where possible. Specificity is important because it avoids misperceptions that may later result in the parent(s) or client feeling that they have been betrayed by a therapist's decision to withhold or share information. For example, therapists, parents, and minor clients may hold different assumptions about which types of behaviors (e.g., protected sexual activity, use of alcohol or marijuana) jeopardize patient welfare or the welfare of others and thus require disclosures. Discussing specific examples of the scope of confidentiality not only

helps to avoid problems of misperception that might arise in the future, but allows the therapist to learn more about client and family sociomoral values and attitudes toward privacy and provides a means to establish good communication patterns among the therapist, client, and parents that can enhance the efficacy of treatment.

• When, during the course of therapy, the client reveals information that the psychologist believes needs to be shared with others, he or she should explore with the client the costs and benefits of divulging such information. This therapeutic approach to disclosures should focus less on how to avoid breaking confidentiality and more on how to enhance client motivational readiness for sharing information (Kaser-Boyd et al., 1985; Taylor & Adelman, 1989). The purpose of this discussion is not to "convince" the child about the appropriateness of disclosing, but to facilitate comprehension within the context of the ongoing therapeutic goal to increase client autonomous functioning (Taylor & Adelman, 1989). During this phase, the psychologist should remind the child that the current need to share the specific information is consistent with the types of issues that were raised during discussion of confidentiality at the beginning of therapy. Although the child may not agree with the therapist's decision and may feel hurt or angry, discussing the rationale for disclosure and the therapist's prior statements can minimize feelings of betrayal and distrust and enable the child to see that even under difficult circumstances the therapist maintains a standard of professional values designed to protect the client's welfare.

• The fourth step in the process is to discuss with the child how to proceed so that negative consequences of disclosure are minimized and the child feels in control of both the information shared and the procedures taken to share it (Taylor & Adelman, 1989). While ideally, this involves helping the child communicate the information directly, in some circumstances this may not be possible (e.g., when child abuse must be reported to authorities). This final step also requires that the psychologist be prepared to help parents deal with the information either through therapeutic strategies or by referring them to an appropriate agency or other institutional resources. For example, if the information to be shared entails a minor client's extensive use of drugs, the psychologist should be prepared to help the family understand and work with the client on the psychological problems underlying the behavior and in finding community services that can help ameliorate drug dependencies.

• Finally, the psychologist should follow-up on actions taken by parents or community agencies (e.g., in the case of child abuse reporting) and help the client or family members to benefit from these services or to consider additional courses of action if services are inadequate.

VALIDITY OF ASSESSMENT AND TREATMENT PROCEDURES

Critical evaluation of the validity and reliability of assessment and treatment procedures is a cornerstone of ethical practice in psychology (APA, 1992, Principle 2; Fisher, 1995; Fisher & Younggren, 1997). The diversity of client characteristics and needs that all practitioners encounter means that psychologists must be able to recognize limits to the certainty with which diagnosis or predictions can be made about individuals as well as identify situations in which particular assessments or treatments may not be applicable (APA, 1992, Standard 2.04). Psychologists working with children can avoid misuse of assessment and treatment techniques through adequate training in normative and atypical developmental processes across diverse populations and through sensitivity to the fact that psychological techniques may not have the same relationship to or impact on psychopathology in different populations.

Developmental Validity

Psychologists treating children and youth face certain ethical challenges involving the validity of diagnosis and treatment that do not arise in work with adults. These ethical challenges revolve around the unique temporal and contextual factors influencing normative and pathological pathways in the developing child. At present, scientific efforts to determine the nature of psychological disorders of childhood and interventions that can prevent or remediate these disorders have simply not paralleled the amount of research and work that has been done with adults (Jensen, Hoagwood, & Fisher, 1996; Kazdin, 1993; McCord, 1990). Consequently, misapplication of methods and unethical practice may occur if the clinician assumes that diagnostic categories established for adults generalize directly to children. Moreover, because current diagnostic categories for developmental psychopathology have been developed to focus on broad categories of symptomatology and disorder, severe and rare childhood disorders may be missed altogether (Edelbrock, 1994).

Because the stability of problematic behaviors of childhood vary from adulthood, diagnostic labeling might prove to be problematic if longitudinal evidence does not support the assumption that early symptom identification is an indication of later dysfunction. For example, although data based on group means indicate that early problems such as aggression, hyperactivity, disruptive behaviors, and peer rejection are statistically associated with the emergence of later disorders, the clinical relevance and predictability of prognosis of such behaviors for individuals depends on age of onset, chronicity of the behavior, and contribution of other life events and environmental stressors such as marital distress, normative transitional periods, and academic problems (Baum, 1989; Campbell, 1989). Moreover, some disorders in early childhood, such as social withdrawal, isolation and symptoms of anxiety, show less stability and less predictive value than externalizing behaviors (Campbell, 1989; see Daleiden, Vasey, & Brown, this volume). Failure to take into account stressors associated with normative developmental transitions also presents ethical challenges. Assessments based exclusively on models of developmental psychopathology, and the erroneous assumption that problem behaviors in childhood are indicative of a linear course toward maladaption and disorder, may lead a clinician to misdiagnose transient behaviors that reflect normative developmental reactions as evidence of pervasive psychological disorder, resulting in unnecessary intervention and potential stigmatization.

Ethical problems can also arise when practitioners apply diagnostic categories or utilize specific treatment modalities without considering how the nature of psychopathology may change as a function of the client's maturational level (Coie et al, 1993; Kendall, Lerner, & Craighead, 1984). For example, depressive disorders in childhood and adolescence may differ both with respect to gender distribution and patterns of anxious and aggressive symptoms and from indicators that are reported for adults (Kazdin, 1990; Murray, 1970). A clinician who does not consider the temporal course of specific developmental disorders may fail to anticipate dysfunctional behaviors that may emerge at later points in the child's development. For example, research tracing the relationship between childhood dysthymia, depression, and adolescent suicide (Elliot, Huizinga, & Menard, 1989; Kovacs et al., 1984) suggests that psychotherapy with children at risk for affective disorders should include preventive steps, such as periodic observations and reevaluations following the completion of an intervention, to detect and address later indications of major depression that may arise.

Empirical evidence suggests that a fuller, more comprehensive picture of child maladaptation is not achieved unless attention to the broader social context is included (Coie & Jacobs, 1993). Valid assessment and treatment of psychological disorders of childhood, such as school phobia and attention-deficit hyperactivity disorder (ADHD) need to be contextualized within the child's interactions with family, school, and peers (Glenwick & Altman, 1992). Failure to consider the evolving bidirectional interplay between the child and his or her environment (Fisher, 1993) can lead to potentially iatrogenic treatments that erroneously focus on either child or familial characteristics as singular causes of maladaptation. Recognition of psychological development as a product of the relationship of the developing individual

to his or her changing world leads to the validation of diagnoses through multiple measures and multiple informants. In this regard, clinicians should be alert to the fact that reports from different informants (e.g., parents and teachers) are not likely to show high correlations with respect to any one particular child's functioning and may reflect valid differences in behavioral patterns due to differences in environmental demands (Achenbach & Edelbrock, 1989; Glenwick & Altman, 1992). To proceed without taking into account such discrepancies may result in unnecessary services or ineffective treatment.

Cultural Validity

When considering the special needs of children and adolescents, attention to the appropriate delivery of mental heath services is compounded not only by developmental issues, but by the complex diversity that arises from the amalgam of cultural and ethnic communities within the United States. Valid application of therapeutic techniques to ethnic minority children and youth requires professional sensitivity to both the cultural and political circumstances of clients' lives (Comas-Dias, 1992; Reekers, 1983; Sue & Sue, 1991). As trained professionals, clinical child psychologists are not likely to act in grossly prejudicial ways. However, the paucity of research on ethnic minority development, and the scientific focus on developmental deficits when such research is conducted, provides child clinicians with an inadequate empirical base for understanding cultural influences on and treatment implications for normative development and developmental disorders (Fisher & Brennan, 1992; Fisher, Jackson, & Villarruel, 1997; Graham, 1992; Kazdin, Bass, Ayers, & Rogers, 1990). Moreover, current training models produce students who are less than practiced at recognizing when silent stereotypes and subtle distortions limit understanding of what it means to suffer persistent stressors associated with discrimination and minority status. In an attempt to be culturally sensitive, clinicians are challenged to take culture into account while simultaneously avoiding the ethical pitfalls of assuming that sociopolitical and racial discrimination are sufficient and acceptable explanations for psychopathological symptoms (Korchin, 1980).

In general, clinical practice predicated on the assumption that current psychological tools and services are equally applicable and effective across diverse populations increases the danger of ineffective, potentially harmful treatments (Laosa, 1990). Ethical practice with ethnic minority youth involves recognizing when members of the client's cultural group have not been sufficiently represented in test standardization or treatment efficacy studies to ensure valid application of these techniques. Thus, appropriate consideration of population generalizability entails ascertaining whether application of conventional tools to the assessment and diagnosis of linguistically or culturally diverse populations is inappropriate, ineffective, inconsequential, or even harmful (Laosa, 1990). However, the degree of confidence one can place in delivering culturally sensitive and objective assessments is affected by the lack of agreement on whether separate norms are indeed needed and the relative absence of uniform diagnostic criteria and culturally validated measurements (Malgady, Rogler, & Costantino, 1987).

In selection of appropriate measurements, language differences pose significant barriers and potential bias. The clinician is required to provide test administration in the language level that is not only appropriate to the child's developmental level but that also considers the child's degree of language fluency and cultural differences (Reekers, 1983). Child clinicians also need to be familiar with research on developmental correlates of different language patterns. For example, the effectiveness of communication in therapy can be enhanced when the clinician recognizes that "Black English" can be either a positive form of symbolism and artistic expression (Gibbs, 1990) or a potential sign of decreased verbal competency in both academic and therapeutic settings (Mancini, 1980). Psychologists should also be aware of research indicating that the common practice of selecting the most readily accessible and available interpreter, such as a family member or bystander unfamiliar with psychiatric terminology, leads to interpreter distortion including selective underestimation of severity of emotional problems (Malgady et al., 1987; Marcos, 1980).

Cultural Bias

Bias in psychological assessment exists when conventional psychiatric nosology and measurements are applied as if existing classification of disorders represents natural distinctions or disease-like entities with universal characteristics and symptomatology (Kirmayer, 1991). The implications of "category fallacy," that is, diagnosis according to guidelines set by a culture other than the patient's, become prominent if assumptions of generalizability go unchecked (Rogler, 1989). An example of possible forced categorization commonly mentioned in the literature is the tendency of clinicians to assume that Asian Americans somaticize depression, distress, and other psychological disturbances (Kinzie, Fredrechson, Rath, Fleck, & Karls, 1984; Kleinman, 1977; Tanaka-Mastumi & Marsella, 1976).

Ethical risks also occur when the independence and free agency that is valued within the majority culture is assumed to be an indicator of healthy psychological development, in direct contradiction to the client's and his or her family's cultural valuing of community, nation, and family roles as primary and self as secondary (Landrine & Klonoff, 1994). When clinicians disregard culture: (1) Interdependence might be erroneously interpreted as an inability to identify self as separate from others and misconstrued as symptoms of compartmentalization, paranoia, or borderline features; (2) the compelling influence of duty and filial obligation might be mislabeled as over-dependency; and (3) genuine reactions of anxiety and panic to failing roles may be misdiagnosed as depression or failure to achieve autonomy (Landrine & Klonoff, 1994).

Misdiagnosis can also result when clinicians erroneously interpret expression of symptoms that are valued or expected within the child's specific cultural context as indicative of pathology (Kirmayer, 1991; Rogler, 1989). For example, the pervasiveness of the culturally instilled concept of respect in Mexican American and Korean children that characteristically manifests itself in politeness and deference to adults and authority figures is often misinterpreted as withdrawal symptoms or mild depression (Trakina, 1983; Ryu & Vann, 1992). Societal biases, if not checked by the clinician, can also lead to missed diagnoses. For example, negative racial stereotypes can misdirect the clinician to evaluate an African American adolescent who is suffering from feelings of depression and helplessness as obstructive, uncooperative, and unwilling to communicate (Gibbs, 1990). "Positive" prejudices such as the "model minority" stereotype can lead clinicians to neglect the social and mental health problems of Asian American adolescents even in the face of data indicating rapid increases in suicide rate in Chinese American youth during the last decade (Liu, Yu, Chang, & Fernandez, 1990).

Psychologists striving to implement culturally sensitive practices must also be wary of panethnic classifications, such as "Hispanic," "Asian," or "African American," which divert clinical attention away from individual client characteristics and cultural backgrounds (i.e., Puerto Rican or Mexican; Korean or Chinese; Carribean or African). Panethnic constructs can have the objective effect of "MINORitizing" actual social class and national origin differences as well as obscure socioeconomic and sociodemographic subgroup differences within the larger classifications (Comas-Dias, 1992; Giminéz, 1989; Laosa, 1990; Rogler, Malgady, Costantino, & Blumenthal, 1987). For example, well-intentioned therapists attempting to understand all clients from Spanish-speaking families in terms of "Hispanic" family patterns, will fail to consider the unique immigration and cultural histories that distinguish children with Cuban, Puerto Rican, Colombian, and Mexican heritages (Fisher, Jackson, & Villarruel, 1997; see Malgady & Costantino, this volume).

CONSIDERATION OF THE CHILD'S CULTURAL IDENTITY

Psychologists must consider the meaning of race and ethnicity within the client's construction of self (Fisher et al., 1997) Understanding the centrality (degree of immersion in a cultural group) and salience (degree of personal identification with a cultural group) of culture in a child's self-concept and self-esteem is required for clinical sensitivity to acculturative processes in the child's life. Acculturation is defined as the extent and process through which ethnic minorities participate in the cultural traditions, values, beliefs, assumptions, and practices of the dominant society, remain immersed in their own cultures, or participate in traditions of their own and of the dominant culture, in other words, the degree to which one can be considered to be bicultural (Fisher et al., 1997; Phinney, 1990)). Whether voluntary or forced, aspects of the acculturation process can impact development in the domains of language use, cognitive style, and personality and identity development (Berry, 1980). Issues of cultural identity are especially pertinent during adolescence, because the need for appropriate identity models may produce family conflict due to differences in attitudes, beliefs, and definitions of legitimate behaviors (Gibbs, 1990; Liu et al., 1990; Phinney, 1990; Ryu & Vann, 1990).

However, practitioners need to avoid stereotypic assumptions that low levels of acculturation indicate poor psychological adjustment. On the contrary, recent developmental research suggests that "acculturative stress" may arise when children and adolescents attempting the transition into a new culture, experience difficulties in the areas of language, perceived discrimination, and communication problems with their parents (Gill, Vegas, & Dimas, 1994; Szapocznik & Kurtines, 1993). Moreover, research suggests that maintenance of traditional cultural values and a bicultural orientation often buffer adolescents against high-risk behaviors such as delinquency and early sexual activity because they are more likely to accept family control (Buriel, Calzada, & Vasquez, 1982; Busch-Rossnagel & Zayas, 1990; Slonim-Nevo, 1992; Sommers, Fagan, & Baskin, 1993). Clinicians must be vigilant to avoid interpretation of biculturalism as manifestation of primitive defenses, namely, splitting. Such pathologizing of acculturative reactions is less productive and less therapeutically facilitating than viewing culturally valued behavior in specific settings as an adaptive developmental process (Chin, 1994).

Determination of acculturative level, within group or ethnic subgroup differences, and range of acculturation levels among individual family members, also lend clarity to assessment and treatment (Sue & Morishima, 1982; Sue & Sue, 1991). For example, what is labeled as problematic school behaviors may be due to the discontinuity between home and school when cultural values regarding appropriate child behavior within each environment do not correspond. Degree of acculturation, if accurately ascertained, can also be used to identify individuals who are appropriate for conventional assessment and treatment methods and those who need culturally specific interventions (Laosa, 1990). Psychologists should also not ignore or over-pathologize the extent to which experiences with ethnic discrimination and subsequent feelings of racial distrust can contribute to personal devaluation and alienation in adolescence (Berry, 1980a, 1980b; Terrell & Terrell, 1981; Thompson et al., 1990).

Best Practices for Developmentally and Culturally Valid Assessment and Treatment

• Mental health practitioners should not assume that diagnostic categories and treatments established for either adults or nonminority populations generalize to children or ethnic minority clients and their families, respectively.
• Therapists working with children and adolescents should become familiar with the empirical literature on normative developmental transitions to avoid misdiagnosis, unnecessary intervention, or iatrogenic treatments.
• Clinicians should also be familiar with the course of developmental disorders and qualitative changes in their symptomology so that they can recommend periodic reevaluations where indicated.
• Clinicians should be conservative in their use of potentially stigmatizing diagnostic labels for child behaviors that longitudinal research indicate are not related to later dysfunction.
• Developmental diagnosticians need to rely on multiple measures and multiple informants to look beyond individual child variables to ascertain the interrelationships among the client's presenting problem and his or her familial, school, and cultural contexts.
• Clinical child psychologists should not dismiss or overpathologize reactions of ethnic minority youth to experiences with and perceptions of racial prejudice and discrimination.
• When working with ethnic minority children and youth, psychologists should vigilantly monitor their own social biases and attend to the cultural dimensions of their client's life without applying panethnic stereotypes.

SUMMARY AND CONCLUSIONS

Responsible practice requires sensitivity to children's treatment vulnerabilities peppered with respect for their maturing abilities to understand and contribute to decisions that impact upon their psychological well-being. Knowledge about normative developmental processes, cultural influences, and the developmental course of disorders of childhood and adolescence will enhance the practitioner's ability to make sound ethical judgments. Responsible practice also entails ethical decision-making that takes into account state laws and community services that can assist the clinician in protecting both the welfare and rights of minor clients.

REFERENCES

Achenbach, T. M., & Edelbrock, C. (1989). Diagnostic, taxonomic, and assessment issues. In T. H. Ollendick and M. Hersen (Eds.), *Handbook of child psychopathology* (2nd ed., pp. 53–73). New York: Plenum Press.

Ambuel, B., & Rappaport, J. (1992). Developmental trends in adolescents' psychological and legal competence to consent to abortion. *Law and Human Behavior, 16,* 129–154.

American Psychological Association (1991). *Legal liability related to confidentiality and the prevention of HIV transmission.* Washington, DC: APA Council of Representatives.

American Psychological Association (1992). Ethical principles of psychologists and code of conduct. *American Psychologist, 47,* 1597–1611.

Battle, C. U., Kriesberg, R. V., O'Mahoney, K., & Chitwood, D. L. (1989). Ethical and developmental considerations in caring for hospitalized adolescents. *Journal of Adolescent Health Care, 10,* 479–489.

Baum, C. G. (1989). Conduct disorders. In T. H. Ollendick & M. Hersen (Eds.), *Handbook of child psychopathology,* pp. 171–196. New York: Plenum Press.

Bennett, B. R., Bryant, B. K., VandenBos, G. R., & Greenwood, A. (1990). *Professional liability and risk management.* Washington, DC: American Psychological Association.

Berry, J. W. (1980a). Acculturation as varieties of adaptation. In A. M. Padilla (Ed.), *Acculturation: Theories, models, and some new findings* (pp. 45–56).

Berry, J. W. (1980b). Acculturative stress: The role of ecology, culture, and differentiation. *Journal of Cross-Cultural Psychology, 5,* 382–406. Boulder, CO: Westview Press.

Bowler, S., Sheon, A. R., D'Angelo, L. J., & Vermund, S. H. (1992). HIV and AIDS among adolescents in the United States: Increasing risk in the 1990's. *Journal of Adolescence, 15,* 345–371.

Boyd-Franklin, N., Staloff, H., & Brady, P. M. (1995).Professional, ethical and moral issues. In N. Boyd-Franklin, G. L. Steiner, & M. G. Boland (Eds). *Children, families, and HIV/AIDS: Psychosocial and therapeutic issues* (pp. 256–269). New York: Guilford Press.

Brazelton, T. B. (1974). *Toddlers and parents.* New York: Delta.

Buriel, R., Calzada, S., & Vasquez, R. (1982). The relationship of traditional Mexican-American culture to adjustment and delinquency among three generations of Mexican-American male adolescents. *Hispanic Journal of Behavioral Sciences, 4,* 41–55.

Busch-Rossnagel, N., & Zayas, L. (1991). Hispanic adolescents. In R. Lerner, A. Peterson, & Brooks-Gunn (Eds.), *Encyclopedia of Adolescents.* New York: Garland.

Campbell, S. B. (1989). Developmental perspectives. In T. H. Ollendick & M. Hersen (Eds.), *Handbook of child psychopathology* (2nd ed., pp. 5–28). New York: Plenum Press.

Campbell, S. B., & Cluss, P. (1982). Peer relations in young children with behavior problems. In K. H. Rubin & H. S. Ross (Eds.), *Peer relationships and social skills in childhood* (pp. 323–351). New York: Springer-Verlag.

Capron, A. M. (1982a). The authority of others to decide about biomedical interventions with incompetents. In W. Gaylin & R. Macklin (Eds.), *Who speaks for the child: The problems of proxy consent,* (pp. 115–152). New York: Plenum Press.

Capron, A. M. (1982b). The competence of children as self-deciders in biomedical interventions. In W. Gaylin & R. Macklin (Eds.), *Who speaks for the child: The problems of proxy consent* (pp. 57–114). New York: Plenum Press.

Centers for Disease Control (1992, April). *HIV/AIDS surveillance report.* Atlanta, GA: Author.

Chase-Lansdale, P. L., & Brooks-Gunn, J. (1994). Correlates of adolescent pregnancy and parenthood. In C. B. Fisher & R. M. Lerner (Eds.), *Applied developmental psychology* (pp. 207–236). New York: McGraw-Hill.

Chin, J. L. (1994). Psychodynamic approaches. In L. Comas-Dias and B. Greene (Eds.), *Women of color: Integrating ethnic and gender identities in psychotherapy* (pp. 194–222). New York: Guilford Press.

Coie, J. D., & Jacobs, M. R. (1993). The role of social context in the prevention of conduct disorder. *Development and Psychopathology, 5,* 263–275.

Cole, M. (1992). Culture in development. In M. H. Bornstein & M. E. Lamb (Eds.), *Developmental psychology: An advanced textbook* (3rd ed., pp. 731–789). Hillsdale, NJ: Erlbaum.

Comas-Dias, L. (1992). The future of psychotherapy with ethnic minorities. *Psychotherapy, 29,* 88–94.

Cooke, M. (1990). Ethical issues related to AIDS. In P. T. Cohen, M. Sande, & P. A. Volberding (Eds.), *The AIDS knowledge base* (pp. 1214.1–1213.8). Waltham, MA: Medical Publishing Group.

Costello, E. J. (1989). Developments in child psychiatric epidemiology. *Journal of the American Academy of Child and Adolescent Psychiatry, 28,* 836–841.

DeKraai, M. B., & Sales, B. D. (1991). Liability in child therapy and research. *Journal of Consulting and Clinical Psychology, 59,* 853–860.

Edelbrock, C. (1994). Assessment of child psychopathology. In C. B. Fisher & R. M. Lerner (Eds.), *Applied developmental psychology* (pp. 294–314). New York: McGraw-Hill.

Eisenberg, L. (1986). The genesis of fear: AIDS and the public response to science. *Law, Medicine, & Health Care, 14,* 243–249.

Elliot, D. S., Huizinga, D., & Menard, S. (1989). *Multiple-problem youth: Delinquency, substance use, and mental health problems.* New York: Springer-Verlag.

English, A. (1990). Treating adolescents: Legal and ethical considerations. *Medical Clinics of North America, 74,* 1097–1112.

English, A., Matthews, M., Extavour, K., Palamountain, C., & Yang, J. (1994). *State Minor Consent Statutes: A Summary.* San Francisco: National Center for the Law.

Fisher, C. B. (1993). Integrating science and ethics in research with high-risk children and youth. *Social Policy Report, 7,* 1–27.

Fisher, C. B. (1995). American Psychological Association's (1992) ethics code and the validation of child abuse in day-care settings. *Psychology, Public Policy, and Law, 1,* 461–478.

Fisher, C. B., & Brennan, M. (1992). Applications and ethics in developmental psychology. In R. M. Lerner & M. Perlmutter (Eds.), *Life-span development and behavior* (Vol. 11, pp. 189–219). Hillsdale, NJ: Erlbaum.

Fisher, C. B., Higgins, A., Rau, J. M. B., Kuther, T., & Belanger, S. (1996). Referring and reporting research participants at risk: Views from urban adolescents. *Child Development, 67,* 2086–2099.

Fisher, C. B., Hoagwood, K., & Jensen, P. (1996). Casebook on Ethical issues in research with children and adolescents with mental disorders. In K. Hoagwood, P. Jensen, & C. B. Fisher (Eds.) *Ethical issues in research with children and adolescents with mental disorders* (pp. 135–238). Hillsdale, NJ: Erlbaum.

Fisher, C. B., Jackson, J. F., & Villarruel, F. A. (1997). The study of ethnic minority children and youth in the United States. In R. M. Lerner (Ed.), *Theoretical models of human development:* Vol. 1. *Handbook of Child Psychology* (5th ed.) (pp. 1145–1207). Editor in Chief: William Damon. New York: Wiley.

Fisher, C. B., & Johnson, L. B. (1990). Getting mad at mom and dad: Children's changing views of family conflict. *International Journal of Behavioral Development, 13,* 31–48.

Fisher, C. B., & Lerner, R. M. (Eds.). (1994). *Applied developmental psychology.* New York: McGraw-Hill

Fisher, C. B. & Murray, J. P. (1996). Applied developmental science comes of age. In C. B. Fisher, J. P. Murray, & I. E. Sigel (Eds.). *Applied developmental science: Graduate training for diverse disciplines and educational settings* (pp. 1–22). Norwood, NJ: Ablex.

Fisher, C. B., & Younggren, J. (1997). The value and utility of the APA Ethics Code. *Professional Psychology: Research and Practice, 28, 582–592.*

Garbarino, J., Kostélny, K., & Dubrow, N. (1991). What children can tell us about living in danger. *American Psychologist, 46,* 376–383.

Gaylin, W. (1982). Who speaks for the child? In W. Gaylin & R. Macklin (Eds.), *Who speaks for the child: The problems of proxy consent* (pp. 3–26). New York: Plenum Press.

Gibbs, J. T. (1990). Mental health issues of Black adolescents: Implications for policy and practice. In A. R. Stiffman and L. E. Davis (Eds.), *Ethnic issues in adolescent mental health* (pp. 21–52). Newbury Park, CA: Sage.

Gill, A. G., Vegas, W. A., & Dimas, J. M. (1994). Acculturative stress and personal adjustment among Hispanic adolescent boys. *Journal of Community Psychology, 22,* 43–54.

Gimenéz, M. E. (1989). Latino/Hispanic—who needs a name? The case against a standardized terminology. *International Journal of Health Services, 19,* 557–571.

Ginsburg, H. M. (1991). Legal issues in the medical care of HIV infected children. In P. Pizzo & C. Wilfert (Eds), *Pediatric AIDS: The challenge of HIV infection in infants, children, and adolescents* (pp. 756–764). Baltimore: Williams & Wilkins.

Glenwick, D. S., & Altman, N. E. (1992). Children and parents with psychological disorders. In M. E. Prociadano & C. B. Fisher (Eds.), *Contemporary families: A handbook for school professionals* (pp. 252–271). New York: Teachers College.

Graham, S. (1992). "Most of the subjects were white and middle class." Trends in published research on African Americans in selected APA journals; 1970–1989. *American Psychologist, 5,* 629–639.

Grisso, T. (1981). *Juveniles' waiver of rights: Legal and psychological competence.* New York: Plenum Press.

Grisso, T., & Vierling, L. (1978). Minors' consent to treatment: A developmental perspective. *Professional Psychology, 9,* 412–427.

Harvey, D. C. (1995). HIV/AIDS and public policy: Recent developments. In N. Boyd-Franklin, G. L. Steiner, & M. G. Boland (Eds), *Children, families, and HIV/AIDS: Psychosocial and therapeutic issues* (pp. 256–269). New York: Guilford Press.

Jensen, P. S., Hoagwood, K., & Fisher, C. B. (1996). Bridging science and ethical perspectives: Towards synthesis. *Ethical issues in research with children and adolescents with mental disorders* (pp. 287–298). Hillsdale, NJ: Erlbaum.

Jensen, P. S., Josephson, A. M., & Frey, J. (1989). Informed consent as a framework for treatment: Ethical and therapeutic considerations. *American Journal of Psychotherapy, 43,* 378–386.

Kaser-Boyd, N., Adelman, H. S., & Taylor, L. (1985). Minor's ability to identify risks and benefits of therapy. *Professional Psychology: Research and Practice, 16,* 411–417.

Kazdin, A. E. (1993). Adolescent mental health: Prevention and treatment programs. *American Psychologist, 48,* 127–141.

Kazdin, A. E., Bass, D., Ayers, W. A., & Rogers, A. (1990). Empirical and clinical focus of child and adolescent psychotherapy research. *Journal of Consulting and Clinical Psychology, 58,* 720–740.

Kendall, P. C., Lerner, R. M., & Craighead, W. E. (1984). Human development and intervention in childhood psychopathology. *Child Development, 55,* 71–82.

Kinzie, J. D., Fredrechson, R. H., Rath, B., Fleck, J., & Karls, W. (1984). Posttraumatic stress disorder among survivors of Cambodian concentration camps. *American Journal of Psychiatry, 141,* 645–650.

Kirmayer, L. J. (1991). The place of culture in psychiatric nosology: Taijin Kyofusho and DSM-III-R. *Journal of Nervous and Mental Disease, 179,* 19–28.

Kleinman, A. (1977). Depression, somatization and the "new cross-cultural psychiatry." *Social Science Medicine, 11,* 3–10.

Koocher, G. P., & Keith-Spiegel, P. C. (1990). *Children, ethics and the law: Professional issues and cases.* Lincoln: University of Nebraska Press.

Kovacs, M., Feinberg, T. L., Crouse-Novak, M., Paulauskas, S. L., Pollock, M., & Finkelstein, R. (1994). Depressive disorders in childhood: II. A longitudinal study of the risk for a subsequent major depression. *Archives of General Psychiatry, 41,* 634–649.

Laosa, L. M. (1990). Population generalizability, cultural sensitivity, and ethical dilemmas. In C. B. Fisher & W. W. Tryon (Eds.),

Emerging ethical issues in an emerging field. Ethics in applied developmental psychology (pp. 227–252). Norwood, NJ: Ablex.

Lerner, R. M. (1995). *America's youth in crises: Challenges and options for programs and policies.* Thousand Oaks, CA: Sage.

Liss, M. B. (1994). Child abuse: Is there a mandate for researchers to report? *Ethics and Behavior, 4,* 133–146.

Liu, W. T., Yu, E. S., Chang, C.-F., & Fernandez, M. (1990). In A. R. Stiffman & L. E. Davis (Eds.), *Ethnic issues in adolescent mental health* (pp. 92–112). Newbury Park, CA: Sage.

Malgady, R. G., Rogler, L. H., & Costantino, G. (1987). Ethnocultural and linguistic bias in mental health evaluation of Hispanics. *American Psychologist, 42,* 228–234.

Mancini, J. K. (1980). *Strategic styles: Coping in the inner city.* Hanover, NH: University Press of New England.

Marcos, L. (1980). The psychiatric evaluation and psychotherapy of the Hispanic bilingual patient. *Hispanic Research Center Research Bulletin, 3,* 1–7.

Margolin, G. (1982). Ethical and legal considerations in marital and family therapy. *American Psychologist, 37,* 788–801.

McCord, J. (1990). Problem behaviors. In S. S. Feldman & G. R. Elliot (Eds.), *At the threshold: The developing adolescent* (pp. 414–430). Cambridge, MA: Harvard University.

McLeod, J. (1987). *Ain't no makin it: Level of aspirations in a low-income neighborhood.* Boulder, CO: Westview Press.

Monohan, J. (1981). *Predicting violent behavior: An assessment of clinical techniques.* Beverly Hills, CA: Sage.

Morton, K. L., & Green, V. (1991). Comprehension of terminology related to treatment and patients' rights by impatient children and adolescents. *Journal of Clinical Child Psychology, 20,* 292–399.

Murray, P. A. (1970). The clinical picture of depression in school children. *Journal of the Irish Medical Association, 63,* 53–56.

North, R. L. (1990). Legal authority for HIV testing of adolescents. *Journal of Adolescent Health Care, 11,* 176–187.

O'Sullivan, C., & Fisher, C. B. (1997). The effect of confidentiality and reporting procedures on parent–child agreement to participate in adolescent risk research. *Applied Developmental Science, 1,* 185–197.

Patterson, G. R. (1982). *Coercive family process.* Eugene, OR: Castalia.

Pope, K. S., & Bajt, T. R. (1988). When laws and values conflict: A dilemma for psychologists. *American Psychologist, 43,* 828–829.

Rebok, G. W., Kellam, S. G., Dolan, L. J., Werthamer-Larsson, L., Edwards, E. J., Mayer, L. S., & Brown, C. H. (1991). The Johns Hopkins Prevention Center on early risk behaviors: Process issues and problem areas in prevention research. *Community Psychologist, 24,* 26–27.

Reekers, G. A. (1983). Ethical issues in child behavioral assessment. In T. H. Ollendick & M. Hersen (Eds.), *Child behavioral assessment* (pp. 244–262). Elmsford, NY: Pergamon.

Rogler, L. H. (1989). The meaning of culturally sensitive research in mental health. *American Journal of Psychiatry, 146,* 296–303.

Rotheram-Borus, M. J., & Gwadz, M. (1993). Sexuality among youth at high risk. *Sexual and Gender Identity Disorders, Child and Adolescent Psychiatric Clinics of North America, 2,* 415–430.

Ryu, J. P., & Vann, B. H. (1992). Korean families in America. In M. E. Prociadano & C. B. Fisher (Eds.), *Contemporary families: A handbook for school professionals* (pp. 117–134). New York: Teachers College.

Schaefer, A. B., & Call, J. A. (1994). Legal and ethical issues. In R. A. Olson, L. L. Mullins, J. B. Gillman, & J. M. Chaney, (Eds.), *The sourcebook of pediatric psychology* (pp. 405–413). Boston: Allyn and Bacon.

Schwartz, I. M. (1989). Hospitalization of adolescents for psychiatric and substance abuse treatment: Legal and ethical issues. *Journal of Adolescent Health Care, 10,* 473–478.

Selman, R. L. (1990). *The growth of interpersonal understanding: Developmental and clinical analyses.* New York: Academic Press.

Sheeley, V. L., & Herlihy, B. (1987). Privileged communication in school counseling: Status update. *School Counselor, 34,* 268–272.

Singleton, E. G. (1989). Substance use and black youth: Implications of cultural and ethnic differences in adolescent alcohol, cigarette, and illicit drug use. In R. L. Jones (Ed.), *Black adolescents* (pp. 385–402). Berkeley, CA: Cobb & Henry.

Slonim-Nevo, V. (1992). First premarital intercourse among Mexican American and Anglo American adolescent women: Interpreting ethnic differences. *Journal of Adolescent Research, 7,* 332–351.

Smith-Bell, M., & Winslade, W. J. (1994). Privacy, confidentiality, and privilege in psychotherapeutic relationships. *American Journal of Orthopsychiatry, 64,* 180–193.

Sommers, I., Fagan, J., & Baskin, D. (1993). Sociocultural influences on the explanation of delinquency for Puerto Rican youths. *Hispanic Journal of Behavioral Sciences, 15,* 36–62.

Sue, D., & Sue, D. W. (1991). *Multicultural issues in counseling: New approaches to diversity.* Alexandria, VA: American Association for Counseling and Development.

Sue, S. N. & Morishima, J. K. (1982). *The mental health of Asian-Americans.* San Francisco: Jossey-Bass.

Szapocznik, J., & Kurtines, W. M. (1993). Family, psychology, and cultural diversity: Opportunities for theory, research, and application. *American Psychologist, 48,* 400–407.

Tanaka-Matsumi, J., & Marsella, A. J. (1976). Cross cultural variations in the phenomenological experience of depression: I. Word association studies. *Journal of Cross-Cultural Psychology, 7,* 379–396.

Tarasoff v. Regents of the University of California, 551 P.2d 334 (Cal. 1976).

Taylor, L., & Adelman, H. S. (1989). Reframing the confidentiality dilemma to work in children's best interests. *Professional Psychology Research and Practice, 20,* 79–83.

Taylor, R. L. (1991). Poverty and adolescent black males: The subculture of disengagement. In P. Edelman & J. Ladner (Eds.), *Adolescence and poverty: Challenge for the 1990's* (pp. 139–162). Washington, DC: Center for National Policy Press.

Terrell, F., & Terrell, S. (1981). An inventory to measure cultural mistrust among blacks. *Western Journal of Black Studies, 5,* 180–185.

Thompson, C., Neville, N., Weathers, P., Poston, C., & Atkinson, D. (1990). Cultural mistrust and racism reaction among African-

American students. *Journal of College Student Development, 31,* 162–168.

Trakina, F. J. (1983). Clinical issues and techniques in working with Hispanic children and their families. In G. J. Powell (Ed.), *The psychosocial development of minority group children* (pp. 307–343). New York: Brunner/Mazel.

Truscott, D., Evans, J., & Mansell, S. (1995). Outpatient psychotherapy with dangerous clients: A model for clinical decision making. *Professional Psychology: Research and Practice, 26,* 484–490.

Tuma, J. M. (1990). Traditional therapies with children. In T. H. Ollendick & M. Hersen (Eds.), *Handbook of child psychopathology* (pp. 419–437). New York: Plenum Press.

Watson, H., & Levine, M. (1989). Psychotherapy and mandated reporting of child abuse. *American Journal of Orthopsychiatry, 59,* 246–256.

Weisz, J. R., & Weiss, B. (1991). Studying the "referability" of child clinical problems. *Journal of Consulting and Clinical Psychology, 59,* 266–273.

Weithorn, L. A., & Campbell, S. B. (1982). The competency of children and adolescents to make informed treatment decisions. *Child Development, 53,* 1589–1598.

Wettstein, R. M. (1984). The prediction of violent behavior and the duty to protect third parties. *Behavioral Sciences & the Law, 2,* 291–317.

Youniss, J., & Smollar, J. (1985). *Adolescent relations with mothers, fathers, and friends.* Chicago: University of Chicago Press.

NAME INDEX

Page numbers for references are in italic.

Abe, T., 308, *317*
Abel, E.L., 218, *227*
Abel, G.G., 375, 383, *387*
Aber, J.L., 61, 374, *387*
Abidin, R.R., 1, *24*, 47, 53, *58*
Abikoff, H., 288, 289, *290, 292, 294*
Ablon, S., 287, *294*
Abramovitch, R., 144, *153*
Abrams, E.J., 440, *442*
Abrams, L.A., 127, 130, *135*
Abrams, S., 84, *86*
Abwender, D.A., 189, *198, 278*
Achenbach, T.M., 3, 12, *24*, 35–40, *42, 43*, 47, 49, 53, *58*, 67, *71*, 103, *104*, 117, *121, 261, 275, 279, 280, 281, 290*, 322, *338*, 399, *412*, 460, *468*, 480, *483*
Acheson, A., 435, *442*
Ackerman, B.P., 90, 99, 100, *105*
Ackerman, P.T., 89, *105*
Acosta, F., 233, *237*
Adair, R., 83, *85*
Adams, A., 310, 313, *315*
Adams, G.R., 128, *134*
Adams, L., 79, *85*
Adams, P.F., 218, *227*
Adams, R.M., 232, *237*
Adams, S., 452, 454, *456*
Adamson, L.B., 419, 420, 424, *429*
Addy, C., 232, *237*
Adelman, H.S., 471, 475, 477, 478, 479, *484, 485*
Adelson, J., 131, *134*
Adler, R.J., 283, *293*
Adnopoz, J., 386, *392*
Adrian, C., 420, 424, 425, *429, 430*
Afflek, G., 221, *227*
Agli, S., *24*
Aguinis, H., 199, *210*
Aguinis, M., 199, *210*
Ahrons, C.R., 353, *354*
Aicardi, J., 308, *316*
Ainsworth, M.D.S., 12, 17, *24*, 94, *104*, 109, *121*, 311, *315*, 381, *389*, 418, 423, 426, *428*
Albano, A.M., 263, 264, *275*
Alegria, M., 281, *291*, 402, 404, *413*
Alessandri, S.M., 285, *290*
Alexander, J.F., 287, 288, *290, 291*
Alexander, L.B., 449, *454*
Alicke, M.D., 460, 462, *469*
Allen, A.J., 287, *291*
Allen, J., 437, *442*
Allen, J.P., 374, *387*

Allen, L., 89, *106*
Allen, M.J., 379, *390*
Allgood, S.M., 350, *356*
Allison, P.D., 323, 324, 325, *338*
Allred, E.N., 218, *229*
Alpern, L., 334, *340*
Alter, M., 300, *304*
Alterman, A.L., 399, *413*
Altman, I., 4, 17, *24*
Altman, N.E., 480, *484*
Alvarez, R., 233, *237*
Amato, P.R., 322, 323, 324, 325, 332, *338*, 343, 344, 351, *354*
Ambrosini, P.J., 52, *58*
Ambuel, B., 471, 472, *483*
Ammerman, R.T., 373, 374, *387*, 399, 400, 404, *409*
Anastopoulos, A.D., 287–288, *290, 291*
Anders, T.F., 82, *85, 87*, 101, 102, 103, *104*
Anderson, B.J., 433, 434, 436, 437, 441, *442*
Anderson, C., 403, *410*
Anderson, C.A., 281, 282, *292*
Anderson, E.R., 20, 322, *339*, 343, 344, 345, 347–351, 353, *354, 355*, *356, 357*
Anderson, J.C., 232, *237*, 264, *275*, 282, *290*
Anderson, J.Z., 350, *354*
Anderson, K.E., 148, *152*
Anderson, K.O., 420, *428*
Anderson, T.M., 452, *456*
Andersson, L., 311, *317*
Andreoletti, C., 21, *25*
Andrews, B., 419, *429*
Andrews, D.W., 288, *291*
Andrews, J.A., 264, 271, *277*
Angold, A., 110, *122*, 262, 263, 264, 265, 269, 270, *275, 276*, 289, *290*
Anthill, J.K., 246, *255*
Anthony, E.J., *24*, 358, 362, 416, *432*
Antonak, R.F., *304*
Antonucci, T.C., 133, *135*
Apolloni, T., 176, *193*
Apospori, E., 232, *238*
Appathurai, C., 248, 252, 253, *257*
Appel, C.P., 437, 441, *442*
Applebaum, M.I., 296, *305*
Applegate, B., 280, 281, 284, *292, 293*
Appleton, P., 84, *86*
Aptekar, L., 17, *24*

Apter, D., 9, *24*
Arbuthnot, J., 23, *24*
Archer, R.P., 48, 53, *58*
Arend, R., 270, *277*
Arieti, S., 18
Armistead, L., 376, *390*
Armstrong, P.M., *303*
Armstrong, S., 161, *169*
Arndt, S.V., 287, *291*
Arnold, L.E., 288, 289, *294*
Arrega-Mayer, C., 161, *168*
Artemyeff, C., 376, *391*
Arthur, J., 126, *134*, 424, 427, *428, 430*
Arvarian, A.L., 379, *387*
Asher, S.R., 96, *106*, 117, 119, *123, 124*, 142, *152, 155*, 165, *167, 169*, 171, 175, 178–183, 185, 187, 189, *193, 197*, 404, 405, *409, 412*
Astone, N.M., 213, 214, *228*
Atkinson, D., 471, 474, 475, 482, *485*
Attili, G., 143, *152*
Atwell, C.W., 83, *86*
AuClaire, P., 223, *227, 229*
Auld, F., Jr., 448, *454*
Avison, W.R., 425, 426, 427, *430*
Axelrod, S., 301, *303*
Ayers, T.S., 407, 408, *409, 411*
Ayers, W.A., 62, 462, 463, *468*, 480, *484*
Ayllon, T., 301, *303*
Ayoub, C., 91, *105*, 376, *387*
Azar, S.T., 10, *24*, 221, *227*, 371–375, 377, 380–386, *387, 388, 390*
Azrin, N., 301, *303*

Babigian, H., 165, *167, 171, 194*
Babor, T.F., 397, *409*
Bachman, J.G., 129, *135*, 206, *211*
Bachorowski, J., 159, *168*
Baer, N., 407, *411*
Bailey, J.M., 242, 244, 245, *255*
Bajt, T.R., 476, *485*
Baker, A.H., *24n*, *29*
Baker, E., 407, *410*
Baker, L., 262, 275, 295, *304*
Baker, R.W., 18, *24*
Baldwin, D.V., 375, *391*
Baldwin, J., 404, *413*
Baldwin, J.M., 108, 117, *122*
Baldwin, M.J., 143, *152*
Bale, P., 163, *167*

Balla, D.A., 11, *28*, 47, 51, 52, *59*, 296, *306*
Baltes, M.M., 132, *134*
Baltes, P., 132, *134*, 142, *153*
Bandura, A., 63, *71*, 109, *122*, 161–165, *167*
Bane, M.J., 215, 216, *227*
Bank, L., 64, *72*, 148, 149, 150, *153, 155*, 181, *198*, 404, 405, *413*
Banken, J.A., 310, *316*
Banks, K., 434, 441, *442*
Banyard, V., 321, *340*
Barad, S.J., 376, *390*
Barahal, R.M., 385, *388*
Barak, A., 451, *455*
Baran, A., 358, *363*
Barber, J., 453, *456*
Barbieri, M.K., 379, *388*
Barbour, J., 83, *86*
Barclay, J.R., 171, *193*
Bardenstein, K., 323, *340*
Barkley, R.A., 103, *104*, 159, *167*, 281–289, *290, 291, 292, 294*, 404, *409*
Barlow, D.H., 261, 263, 264, 266, 267, 275, *277*
Barnard, K., 375, 385, *388*
Barnes, G.M., 402, *409*
Barnes, J., 161, *168*
Barnes, K.T., 371, 372, 375, 386, *388*
Barnett, D., 94, *105*, 385, *388*
Barnett, P.A., 419, *428*
Barocas, R., 219, *229*, 417, *431*
Baron-Cohen, S., 311, *315*
Barr, H.M., 218, *230*, 395, *413*
Barr, R.G., 78, 79, 80, *85, 86*
Barrera, M., Jr., 403, *410*
Barrett, C.L., 446, *456*
Barrett, P.M., 268, 271, 272, *275, 276*
Barrett-Lennard, G.T., 449, 451, *454*
Barrickman, L.L., 287, *291*
Barten, S.S., *24, 24n*
Barth, J., 21, *24*, 143, *153*
Barth, R.P., 440, *442*
Bartholet, E., 358, *363*
Barton, C., 288, *291*
Barton, M., 94, 102, 103, *107*
Barton, M.I., 19, *24*
Baskin, D., 482, *485*
Bass, D., 62, 172, *195*, 207, 210, *211*, 288, *293*, 462, 463, *468*, 480, *484*
Bates, J., 93, 96, *105*
Bates, J.E., 54, *58*, 143, *154*, 220, 221, *227*, 427, *428*

487

SUBJECT INDEX